WRISTON

Also by Phillip L. Zweig

Belly-Up: The Collapse of the Penn Square Bank

WRISTON

*Walter Wriston,
Citibank, and the
Rise and Fall of
American Financial
Supremacy*

BY PHILLIP L. ZWEIG

CROWN PUBLISHERS, INC.   NEW YORK

Published by Crown Publishers, Inc., 201 East 50th Street, New York,
New York 10022. Member of the Crown Publishing Group.

Random House, Inc. New York, Toronto, London, Sydney, Auckland

CROWN is a trademark of Crown Publishers, Inc.

Manufactured in the United States of America

Design by June Bennett-Tantillo

Library of Congress Cataloging-in-Publication Data
Zweig, Phillip L.
Wriston: Walter Wriston, Citibank, and the rise and fall of American financial
supremacy / Phillip Zweig.
1. Wriston, Walter B.   2. Bankers—United States—Biography.
3. Citibank (New York, N.Y.)—History.   I. Title.
HG2463.W75Z93 1995
332.1′092—dc20
[B]   94-37343 CIP

ISBN 0-517-58423-9

10 9 8 7 6 5 4 3 2 1

First Edition

*To Josie, whose love, dedication, and
intellect helped make this book possible*

WRISTON

PROLOGUE

*I*n early September 1991, Walter Bigelow Wriston, the tall, trim former chairman of Citicorp, stepped into an elevator in the vast atrium of New York's Citicorp Center to return to his fourth-floor office from a meeting nearby. A few of the fresh-faced young Citibankers in the elevator knew him slightly, having joined the huge company just before he retired in 1984. The others knew him only from hearing older colleagues speak wistfully of the "Wriston era." Almost in unison, they snapped soldierlike to attention and said reverently, "Hello, Mr. Wriston."

Wriston smiled faintly, but his eyes were downcast. He had spent the morning in a directors' meeting at bankrupt Pan Am, where he had participated in the wrenching discussion on the sale of the Washington–New York–Boston shuttle and most of the trans-Atlantic routes to Delta Airlines, the latest phase in the dismantling of the once proud pioneer of global aviation.

"Hello, boys," he said, trying hard to be cheerful. "Just got back from Pan Am. It's so sad to see a great company go down the tube." As Wriston breezed out of the elevator, the bankers stared at one other, each certain that the other was thinking the same gloomy thought: Wriston was clearly referring to the airline, but his comment could also apply to the banking company he had run for more than seventeen years before turning it over to a cocky, impish technocrat named John Shepard Reed, once considered the boy wonder of American banking.

In those seventeen years, Wriston had built Citicorp into the world's mightiest banking power and established for himself an unchallenged reputation as the world's most influential banker. Along with J. P. Morgan and Bank of America founder A. P. Giannini, he ranked as one of the three most important bankers of the twentieth century. During his regime, Citicorp flexed more financial muscle around the globe than most countries. By force of intellect, acerbic wit, and hobnail boots, he transformed Citicorp from a genteel utility, where golf scores counted for more than IQ, into a tough, arrogant corporate meritocracy that dragged the rest of the industry out of the era of quill pen banking. Using Citicorp as an assault weapon for promulgat-

1

ing free market principles, he blew away many of the archaic rules that prohibited banks from operating across state lines, from competing with Wall Street investment banking houses, and from paying small savers the same market rates of interest earned by wealthy investors. By betting on youth and brains and by pouring hundreds of millions of dollars into automated teller machines and other advanced technology, he revolutionized the way Americans managed their money—and built a money machine for Citicorp in the process.

Yet for all the praise Wriston and Citicorp received for their managerial acumen, Citicorp was constantly in a state of turmoil and chaos. Reflecting Wriston's own combative personality, Citibankers spent much of their time fighting one another, rather than other institutions, for business—in one instance, at least, in the parking lot of a corporate client. Though Wriston constantly spoke of the need for financial and management controls, they were often abysmal, and eventually broke down completely. Citicorp held itself out to corporate America as a shrewd adviser on mergers and acquisitions, but its own efforts to build the company by buying other companies often ended disastrously.

Most significantly, Wriston was blindsided by his hardheaded views that countries don't go bankrupt and that banks don't need capital. Armed with those convictions, he led the world banking system into Third World lending, ill-prepared, as it turned out, for the decade-long quagmire that was to come.

Wriston regarded the choice of a successor as the single most important decision any chief executive officer can make. To make that choice, Wriston orchestrated one of the longest and most publicized succession dramas in American business history, and his eventual selection of Reed was lauded at the time as a stroke of genius.

But now, in 1991, his beloved bank was in deep trouble. The wisdom of picking John Reed as his heir was being challenged by regulators, the media, and employees. While the fifty-two-year-old Reed was struggling to rid the bank of the burden of billions in Third World debt that he had inherited— "Walt's loans," he often wisecracked to colleagues—Reed's own top managers had made billions in bum loans to high-rolling real estate promoters, Australian wheeler-dealers, and leveraged buyout artists. The solvency of the nation's largest banking institution was being questioned publicly in the *New York Times* and by leaders of Congress. Thousands of employees were being sacked to slash expenses. Morale was at an all-time low. If that wasn't enough, chairman Reed, a married man with four children, was humiliated by gossipy news stories and bawdy jokes about his affair with a young married stewardess on the corporate jet. Rumors were flying up and down Park Avenue that Reed himself would soon be canned and that possible replacements included everyone from Wriston's onetime nemesis, former Federal Reserve chairman Paul Volcker, to Wriston himself. "Don't hang by your thumbs waiting for that one," Wriston said with characteristic wit.

There are many criteria for judging the performance of the leader of a giant public company. The easiest criterion to quantify, and to many the most important, is how much wealth he created for shareholders. But the head of a global bank is responsible to a multitude of constituencies, including depositors, individual and corporate customers, employees, local communities, and society at large. His performance is the sum total of how well he has served them all. Eight years after Wriston left office, the jury had finally come in on every measure, including the one he himself regarded as the most critical: how well he provided for the survival of his institution.

Wriston was not one to agonize over a decision, and certainly not after the fact. But never, since the sudden death of his forty-six-year-old first wife a quarter century earlier, had he felt such pain and disappointment. The institution he had nurtured to the pinnacle of power and prestige was now a crippled giant. And there was little that even Walter Bigelow Wriston could do to fix it.

In fact, the institution Wriston had created was so complex that few, if any, American bankers could comprehend it.

To bring Citicorp back from the brink in the face of endless criticism, John Reed drew on the capacity for pain he had tapped into as chief of the once troubled consumer business. As the board mulled over the possibility of replacing him, Reed hacked away at the bank's troubled loan portfolio, its overweight bureaucracy, and the ruthless corporate culture he had helped create. By 1993 Citicorp was on the mend, and Reed had begun to regain the confidence of Wall Street and the man who had appointed him.

Citicorp had essentially lost a decade. But along the way, Reed and his institution had also lost much of their hubris. Because of that, there was finally reason to believe that their near-fatal mistakes would not soon be repeated.

1

THE EARLY YEARS

*W*alter Wriston was born on August 3, 1919, without a silver spoon in his mouth but with a leather-bound copy of Adam Smith's *Wealth of Nations,* the bible of free enterprise, near his cradle.

In the years following World War I, the material wealth of Henry Merritt Wriston, then a $1,200-a-year history professor at Wesleyan University in Middletown, Connecticut, and his wife, Ruth, was modest indeed. But the intellectual capital that this brilliant, imperious educator and his quiet, reserved wife imparted to their only son, Walter, almost from day one, more than compensated for the lack of ready cash.

For Walter, Henry Wriston was a larger-than-life father figure, the shoes to be filled, and the footsteps to be followed. He was his son's B.A., his M.B.A., and his Ph.D. Henry would, by his own success in education, inspire his son to become a world leader in banking.

It seems fitting that Henry Wriston, who grew up to be a staunch defender of American values, was born on July 4, 1889, in a clapboard cabin in Laramie, Wyoming, where his parents had moved after meeting and marrying in Colorado.

Both Henry Lincoln Wriston and Jennie Atcheson Wriston had wound up in Colorado in a roundabout way. Jennie's father had earned a comfortable living in the mid-1800s as a marine woodcarver. But he had an abiding curiosity about the frontier that lay far to the west of their tidy home in Astoria, Queens, just across the East River from Manhattan. In 1868, his wanderlust prevailed. He and his wife packed up Jennie and her four siblings and left New York by train for the three-day journey to Pleasant Hill, Missouri. In her privately published memoirs, *A Pioneer's Odyssey,* Jennie later wrote of their arrival in Reconstruction era Missouri, where, as New Yorkers, they met with resentment from locals sympathetic to the Confederate cause. They had expected to be transported from Missouri to their eighty-acre farm in a carriage drawn by a team of horses. Instead, the carriage was hitched to a mule team, prompting Jennie's father to complain that his family "was not in the habit of appearing in public behind jackasses." Like the spirit of rugged individualism that brought the Atchesons to the wilderness, this disdain for any association with jackasses, real or figurative, was a trait that would be passed down through every generation of the Wriston family.

Mr. Atcheson's demand for a horse-drawn carriage was accommodated, but after five years in Missouri, during which they endured bouts of malaria, the family embarked on yet another westward journey. This one, by wagon train, lasted six months. It took the family on a perilous trek through Kansas, along the Republican River in Nebraska, the land of the Sioux, Arapahoe, and Cheyenne, and on to a small settlement near Denver. En route, the Atchesons met up with legendary army scout William F. "Buffalo Bill" Cody, and in one tense encounter with the Indians, a warrior on a pinto pony tried to exchange some blankets and ponies for Jennie, whom he dubbed "the little squaw."

Jennie later spent the winter months teaching in the Denver schools, and the summer commuting seven miles each day on horseback between the family ranch and a rural school, packing a pistol to protect herself from bandits and bobcats. Jennie was one in a long line of Wriston women who were liberated long before the feminist movement began, though some of her talents were never fully developed because of the mores of the era. "She was a talented person, a beautiful singer with an operatic-quality voice, but nice girls didn't sing in the opera in those days," said her grandson Walter years later. "The women in my life were all people with minds of their own."

Henry Lincoln Wriston journeyed to Colorado via an equally circuitous route. Originally from West Virginia, he attended Ohio Wesleyan for two years and, after a brief stay in Texas, traveled to Denver where he completed a bachelor's degree at the university there. While attending college, he preached part-time in nearby Castle Rock, where he met his future wife, Jennie Atcheson. Their first son, George, arrived in 1887, followed two years later by Henry Merritt, who was born shortly after the family moved to Laramie, where Henry Lincoln served as minister of the First Methodist Episcopal Church.

Frugality and asceticism were Wriston watchwords. The Reverend Henry Lincoln Wriston eschewed alcohol and later refused to go to the movies on Sunday. He carried a small black book in which he scrupulously recorded every expenditure, including three cents for a newspaper, and every evening tallied up all his disbursements. Family legend has it that Jennie once found a five-dollar bill on the street and rushed home to carefully wash and iron it. It was probably the first time anyone in the Wriston clan ever heard anything about laundering money.

Shortly after Henry Merritt's birth, his father succumbed to the same craving for an eastern education that he had once felt for the western frontier. The family moved to Boston, where he enrolled at Boston University and became a pastor at a church on Cape Cod.

In the summer of 1903, after having lived and preached in several small Massachusetts towns, Henry Lincoln finally put down more permanent roots in Springfield. That fall, young Henry entered Classical High School, where he displayed an aptitude for Latin, English, and history. For a superior student with a Methodist upbringing, Connecticut's Wesleyan University was a logical destination.

Now a beanpole-thin six-footer, Henry Merritt "Wris" Wriston pursued his interest in history and English literature, served as class publicity agent, played on the basketball team, and became editor-in-chief of the *Wesleyan Argus.* Though he was raised and educated in New England, he greatly admired his mother's pioneer spirit and rugged individualism. So it was no surprise that he readily embraced the teachings of Adam Smith and Herbert Spencer, the English philosopher who coined the term "survival of the fittest."

Henry Wriston was later described by his Wesleyan associates as a fellow of boundless drive, energy, and intelligence. Although he did not always ingratiate himself with other undergraduates, who chafed at his caustic sense of humor, he was generally admired as a gifted student and leader.

Wriston earned a bachelor's degree in English and a master's in history in four years at Wesleyan, graduating Phi Beta Kappa and collecting most of the other honors the college could bestow. Having developed a deep interest in government and international affairs, he wrote his master's thesis on the constitutional history of democracy in the United States. In 1911, Henry moved on to Harvard to study for a doctorate in diplomatic history, a stressful experience that reinforced his belief in the nurturing value of the small liberal arts college.

On June 6, 1914, immediately after completing his Harvard course work, Henry married Ruth Colton Bigelow, his high school sweetheart. The daughter of William Dwight Bigelow, an employee of the Springfield Fire & Marine Insurance Company, and Idelle Colton Bigelow, Ruth had graduated from Vassar in 1911 with a degree in chemistry and physics, an auspicious accomplishment for a young woman of that era. After graduation, she had returned to Springfield to teach physics.

In the summer of 1914 the newlyweds left Cambridge for Middletown, Connecticut, where Henry embarked on a career in academia that could only be described as meteoric. His freshman history class was packed with students thirsting for history enlivened by Wriston witticisms and vignettes, said former student and colleague Ted Cloak. He was a "beautiful lecturer," said Cloak, recalling that in his talk on the history of New England Wriston quipped, "You know about New England. It's where they paint the rocks green to get the cows out to pasture." Henry Wriston was also a campus activist whose interests extended beyond the classroom; he relished stirring up the pot through controversial speeches, letters to editors, and participation in political activities, including presidential campaigns. Despite his Churchillian eloquence, the prospect of addressing a large audience put him through agonies of stage fright.

The couple's first child, Barbara, born in 1917, was followed by Walter in 1919, the year Henry was promoted to full professor. In 1920, Henry—known to his friends as Hank—displayed a talent for fund-raising that would stand him in good stead later on, when he became a college president.

The origin of Walter's interest in foreign affairs can be traced to a foundation grant that enabled his father, in 1920, to spend a year at the U.S. State Department while completing his Harvard dissertation. In Washington, where Henry had access to the highest levels of the State Department, he observed the formulation of American foreign policy firsthand. It was a heady experience for the young educator. He found life in the inner sanctum intoxicating. Although he kept his ambitions to himself, Henry apparently dropped enough hints so that his faculty colleagues later speculated that he dreamed of becoming secretary of state. He was never appointed to that post, but he wound up having more influence on American foreign policy than many of the men who did hold that office. His doctoral dissertation, *Executive Agents in American Foreign Relations,* was published as a book in 1929 and was for years the State Department's final word on the subject.

Henry had become a globalist, a believer in an interdependent world, who marveled at the technologies that transcended borders and bonded nations together. In a 1924 speech he observed that "the cable and the wireless have been shrinking the effective size of the world beyond the dreams of our fathers. In place of the three months it took Washington to communicate with Gouverneur Morris, we apparently get news in less than no time, for by reason of the difference in time, the resignation of a French premier at noon was reported by the Department of State at ten o'clock in the morning. It was bulletined by the newspapers before another thirty minutes had passed."

In late 1924, Henry Wriston's dream of becoming a college president was about to be fulfilled. With the death of the Methodist minister who for thirty years had served as president of Lawrence College, a small coeducational school in Appleton, Wisconsin, Dr. Wriston was placed on the short list to succeed him, and on July 3, 1925, one day before his thirty-sixth birthday, he was elected president of the seventy-eight-year-old institution, becoming America's youngest college head. Lawrence and Wesleyan were close spiritually if not geographically. Both had been founded by Methodists, and Lawrence regarded Wesleyan as a sort of sister school, albeit one with somewhat more intellectual cachet.

It is hard to imagine a better place to nurture an American capitalist than at Hank Wriston's knee in the parlor of the president's residence, a stately Victorian home overlooking the Fox River on the edge of the Lawrence campus. Walter Wriston's belief in rugged individualism and patriotism and his views on the proper role of government in people's lives were shaped there by his father, a self-described "discontented Republican." The world immediately beyond the Wriston dining table would certainly reinforce those views.

Populated by descendants of German, Scandinavian, and Scottish settlers, the Fox River valley was in the 1920s and 1930s a pristine, tranquil paradise in the north woods that locals still refer to as Happy Valley. Wisconsin was, and still is, a state with clashing political crosscurrents. It was a stronghold of the kind of progressive Republicanism personified by Wisconsin governor and senator Robert La Follette, the reformer and political guiding light of the state for the first quarter of the twentieth century. Yet the Appleton of the early 1900s was in other respects no social pacesetter. For years the town is said to have posted a policeman at the railway station to make sure blacks traveling up from the South did not even think about disembarking.

The Republican party itself was founded at Ripon, Wisconsin, and despite Appleton's intellectual tradition, the ultra-right-wing John Birch Society apparently considered the city sufficiently hospitable to its views that in 1989 it moved its national headquarters there. Extreme right-wing sentiments in the forties and fifties were virulent enough to permit the political rise of the state's most notorious son, Senator Joseph McCarthy. But when McCarthy embarked on his reign of terror, Henry Wriston emerged as one of his earliest and most persistent critics.

Thanks largely to the presence of Lawrence College, Appleton was the intellectual heartbeat of eastern Wisconsin and a bastion of enlightenment and open-mindedness. Appletonians considered themselves culturally superior to their counterparts in Oshkosh and Green Bay, where the unscholarly influence of the Packers football team held sway. Music and the arts flourished in Appleton. That was due in part to generous support from local paper companies such as Kimberly-Clark and to the efforts of the Wristons. During the Depression, the college's respected Conservatory of Music fell on hard times, but Henry Wriston rejected the urgings of many trustees to shut it down. While Henry was a music lover, Ruth Wriston enjoyed watercolor painting and interior decorating. Appalled at the Spartan appearance of dormitory rooms, Mrs. Wriston arranged for students to rent high-quality reproductions of original works, mostly by Chicago area artists who exhibited at Lawrence, for a nominal sum with an option to buy.

Appleton nurtured literary talent, notably that of Pulitzer Prize–winning novelist Edna Ferber, whose works, including *So Big, Show Boat,* and *Cimarron,* glorified America and American values. Later, another graduate of Appleton High, Walter Wriston, would continue in that tradition. The city was also home to famed magician and escape artist Harry Houdini, who was born in Appleton shortly after his parents immigrated to this country from Hungary. The Houdini influence apparently rubbed off on Wriston. As a youth, Walter studied magic and entertained friends by pulling quarters from his ear. Years later he would emerge as a kind of Harry Houdini of the marketplace as he fought to unshackle American business from burdensome government legislation and regulation.

Although Hank Wriston was the first president of Lawrence College who was not a Methodist minister, he attacked the job with a missionary's zeal. When Henry Wriston first set foot on the Lawrence College campus, it was, said current president Richard Warch, an "inhospitable environment dominated by vocationalism." Within a few years, Wriston fired the figurehead Methodist board of advisers, scrapped business and other vocational courses, and set out to build for the school a reputation as a leading midwestern nondenominational liberal arts college.

In Henry Wriston's view, vocational courses had no place in a liberal arts education. But Henry was a pragmatist. In his 1926 commencement address, he told the graduating seniors, and perhaps six-year-old Walter as well, that they "must have some grasp upon the principles of finance. It was a poor merchant, half a century ago, who did not own his own business. It was an unusual manufacturer who did not attend to his own financing. I once knew a businessman," he went on, "who boasted that he had never borrowed a dollar. Needless to say, he retired from business long since. . . . The habit of thrift, and the conservation of assets, shrewd buying and selling, no longer suffices. It is essential today that everybody should understand the fundamental principles of the management of capital, the essentials of banking, and at least the elements of investment." Though he had no business experience himself, Henry Wriston ran Lawrence College with a sharp pencil. He learned at least enough about university balance sheets to be able to determine whether his business managers were competent, and didn't hesitate to fire them if he determined otherwise. In his memoir, *Academic Procession,* he told of a parent who wanted to pay his daughter's tuition on an installment plan but balked at paying interest. Wriston asked him if his own business involved any installment selling and, if so, whether he charged his customers extra for the privilege. The answer to both questions was yes. "When I inquired what the difference was in the two situations," Wriston wrote, "his answer was classic: one was business, the other education."

Even Henry's parents, Henry Lincoln and Jennie Wriston, had an instinct for business. In the early years of the twentieth century, there was no life insurance for ministers, because, as Walter Wriston remarked later, the prevailing view was that "God would take care of widows." When Walter's grandparents were in their seventies, they helped establish a life insurance company to serve ministers, which was later acquired by a major insurer.

To the Lawrence College community, Henry Wriston was a godlike figure. He was bold and decisive in dealing with everything from faculty hiring to student discipline. "There was a feeling that Hank was always right," recalled Ted Cloak. "He was a sharp thinker, a hard thinker. He brought a breath of scholarly influence and organization."

In hiring faculty members, "I simply haunted the graduate schools looking for the kind of people I wanted," Henry Wriston said later in an interview. He looked for three key qualities in a prospective professor: great teacher, great scholar, great personal force.

"He told me a couple of things I never forgot," son Walter said later. "One was, the smarter the people you hire the more trouble you'll have with them. You hire a lot of dumb people, you won't have problems, and you won't get anywhere, either." Both loathed yes-men. In *Academic Procession,* Hank Wriston wrote, "I never had any of those about me, nor wanted any; the office is already too isolated; yes-men remove it further from vital contacts."

While Henry Wriston believed in careful planning, he was also an opportunist. He regarded plans as guidelines for handling only routine matters.

"When something unusual supervenes," he later wrote, "seize the opportunity and let the plan stay on ice for a while."

Henry Wriston was also a master at intelligence gathering. His ever-present bowl of jelly beans, said Walter Wriston, apparently induced faculty and students to volunteer equally juicy nuggets of campus gossip. "He always seemed to know what was going on on campus," Wriston said. "People accused him of having a spy system. I asked him how [he knew] what [was] going on, and he used to say, 'People will tell you absolutely anything if you'll listen.' "

When Wriston arrived at Lawrence there was no mandatory retirement age, and some professors continued teaching into their eighties. He forced the retirement of tenured professors he considered incompetent or too old, lowered the status of football to the point where locals snickered that Lawrence had become a girls' school, and sparked a revolt among faculty members over what they considered his high-handed methods. Said Lawrence professor of history emeritus Charles Breunig, "He could walk into a room and within ten minutes he would have the room totally divided for or against him."

Henry Wriston was universally respected, but he was not universally loved. He and Ruth erected a wall between themselves and their friends. They guarded their privacy jealously, to the extent that this was possible in the Lawrence fishbowl, and they revealed few details of their personal lives. "That's true of the whole family," said their daughter, Barbara Wriston, later. "You develop that habit if you appear in public a lot. People who reveal a lot of intimate details don't have much else to reveal." Though stingy with intimate details about himself, he was generous when it came to digging into his own pocket to help hard-pressed students.

Henry Wriston thrived on intellectual combat and controversy, another characteristic he passed on to his son. "I was urged, again and again, not to become 'controversial' by taking public positions with which there would be disagreement in 'influential quarters,' " Henry Wriston later wrote. "It was not advice that appealed to either my temperament or my judgment." As a public figure, a university president "should make clear that his views are not necessarily those of his faculty colleagues or the trustees," Wriston went on. "Once he has made those points explicit he should speak his mind, if he has one. It should be done on most matters with persuasive good temper; but there are occasions when indignation and even wrath are not only appropriate but necessary."

One such occasion followed Henry Wriston's decision to end the tradition of giving students the day off after Thanksgiving. When Wriston entered the chapel to attend a service, then compulsory for all students, he was greeted by a loud chorus of stamping feet. Wriston immediately summoned the head of the student council and demanded, "Are you the president of this college or am I?"

The student was shaking in his shoes. "You are," he replied.

"Then you'll have that foot stamping stopped," Wriston commanded in his booming authoritative voice.

At Lawrence, Henry further honed the sharp needle of wit and sarcasm, which he aimed at "whoever needed it," as his daughter put it later. "He could be fierce if he thought it was necessary." Needling each other, keeping each other on their toes, was a kind of family hallmark.

Though he might have angered others, Henry rarely lost his temper. "When I became a president, I knew well what not to do. Never move in a hurry, much less upon impulse. Never get angry. If possible, use such temperate language as to give no occasion to the other man to blow his top." It was advice that son Walter would take to heart.

Although Henry Wriston was not a minister, no one forgot that he was the son of one. Smoking, drinking, and movies on Sunday were forbidden on the Wriston campus, as they were in the Wriston household. Henry Wriston didn't permit liquor in his home until the early 1950s, and even then served it with hesitation. He insisted on compulsory chapel for students, though he obviously didn't take religion as seriously as his father did, and he often wrote his own speeches while listening to Sunday sermons in church. Though the Wristons, including Walter and Barbara, participated in church activities, formal religion did not play a critical role in Walter's life. The religion that really mattered was unerring self-reliance and the notion that everyone was responsible for his own life.

Despite his sometimes austere and stubborn demeanor—"he didn't slap the Rotarians on the back, superficialities didn't interest him," said a colleague—the elder Wriston was nonetheless a jovial, even emotional man who enjoyed a hearty laugh, followed the New York Yankees with a passion, and cried at the movies.

For all of Henry Wriston's rigor, he gave Walter plenty of freedom to experiment and to control his own personal domain. Professor Cloak recalls arriving at Lawrence for a job interview in 1927 and staying overnight at the president's house. Mrs. Wriston matter-of-factly told him he could "go anywhere you want except Skippy's room. It's a mess." Cloak couldn't resist finding out whether it was really as bad as Ruth Wriston had described it. Indeed, it was. Young Walter lived amid utter chaos and clutter. "It was a shambles," Cloak said, adding that Walter "seemed to be interested in a lot of things. He was more than an ordinary kid."

Distinguished Americans from all walks of life, from statesmen to churchmen, visited the Lawrence campus and spent the night at the Wriston residence, bombarding Walter and Barbara with new ideas. But from Hank Wriston, they also acquired an irreverence toward people in positions of authority. After the guests departed, the Wristons typically sat around the dinner table laughing uproariously as Walter and Barbara took turns imitating or otherwise poking fun at their just departed guests. Before most youngsters had ever even seen a senator, cabinet member, or eminent scholar up close, Walter Wriston learned that they, like everyone else, put on their pants one leg at a time.

As a hard-nosed, disciplined scholar, Henry Wriston imparted to his offspring a jaundiced eye. Imbued with such skepticism, Walter Wriston was not easily awed. The only person who came close was his father.

Of his mother Walter Wriston would later concede to his sister that "I didn't know her that well." Ruth Wriston was a slight and, later, sickly woman, but one with backbone and compassion. When Cloak, as a Wesleyan undergraduate, was seriously ill with typhoid, Mrs. Wriston visited him regularly in the hospital. She was also a brilliant, no-nonsense woman with a clear sense of right and wrong, correct and incorrect. Ruth supplied the balance, the steady hand, that offset Henry's sharp mood swings and emotional theatrics, such as when he arrived home after delivering a lecture, threw himself on the sofa, and declared it was "the worst lecture I've ever given."

"Dad used to get up and down," recalled Wriston later. "He'd say, 'I'll never have another idea in my life,' and all this baloney. She bought absolutely zero of that. . . . She'd just laugh at him and say he'd have fifteen more the next day." While Henry Wriston presented a tough exterior to his constituency at Lawrence College and later at Brown, the intellectual and emotional stresses incurred in battling faculty, trustees, alumni, and students revealed themselves when Henry retreated to the presidential residence. "You go through hard times at a university," Walter said. "She was a strong supporter of the notion that the sun will rise tomorrow morning, which was useful to him." She was also "a great leveler" who kept Henry Wriston's considerable ego in check, said Walter.

Ruth Wriston imparted to Walter and Barbara a sense of the power of the individual to shape events. As a child growing up during the Depression, Walter Wriston shared the widespread pessimism about the future of humankind. "What can one person do?" he asked his mother.

She replied, "You're only one, but you *are* one."

"She was not one to say, 'Let's throw in the towel,' " Wriston said later.

From his mother, Wriston also received early training on such social niceties as how and when to leave a reception. As the teenage son of a college president, one of his duties was to scoop ice cream at freshman receptions. He would sit in the parlor as his mother seethed over the students' ignorance as to when to call it an evening. "The night used to drag on," Wriston said later, "with the kids sitting in the living room. It used to drive her mad."

"These kids don't know how to go," she lamented. "You've got to learn how to get out of a place. It's very simple," she explained. "You go up to your hostess, put out your hand, shake her hand and say, 'Thank you very much. I had a wonderful time.' Then you leave." It was advice that stood Wriston in good stead when he left Appleton for Wesleyan and went on to begin his business career in New York.

For a life and career where personal discretion was part of the job description, there could have been no better preparation than growing up on the Lawrence campus, where altercations between the college president and his son would have been welcome grist for the campus gossip mill.

One family friend remembers Walter Wriston as a somewhat sluggish youth who needed encouragement from his father to pick up his pace. "Henry Wriston was big and imposing," said Appleton native John Reeve, and would yell *"Mach Schnell"* at young Walter in trying to get him to move faster. Wriston apparently picked up the pace, earning the nickname "Skippy" for his habit of alternately walking, running, and skipping through the streets of Appleton.

The Wristons were among the privileged residents of Appleton, and Walter and Barbara were sheltered from the pain and hardship that others of their generation experienced growing up in the Oklahoma dust bowl or on the streets of New York. Walter typically was sent away to camp for the summer, and in 1935, after his sophomore year in high school, the family sailed for Europe, a trip financed with money Ruth and Henry had received as a wedding present twenty years earlier.

In Appleton generally, and in the Wriston household in particular, thrift was a virtue. When Walter and Barbara received their first allowance of fifteen cents a week on entering the first grade, they were told that five cents was for Sunday school, five cents was to be placed in a bank account, and five cents was "to raise Cain with or save up," according to Barbara Wriston. But the Wriston family rarely talked about money, and certainly never made any show of affluence. While Walter and Barbara learned how to manage money at an early age, they never aspired to make lots of it. In the Wriston household, the only currency that counted was ideas and ideals.

While the Wristons were well off by any standard, the contrast between them and other Appletonians of that period was by no means glaring. The Depression did not bypass Happy Valley, but it did not devastate it, either. Thanks to the college and the paper mills, most of which continued to operate, unemployment remained relatively low, as longtime residents recall. "Nobody was poverty-stricken, and nobody was extremely wealthy. Nobody was showing off money. It just wasn't done," said Barbara Wriston.

Indeed, Appleton in the thirties was an unlikely time and place to produce a banker whose name would become nearly synonymous with "credit." "It was not a credit-card society," said one native. "It's a long way from Appleton High to Third World debt."

But it was an appropriate setting to produce a banker who would become an unbending proponent of laissez-faire capitalism. Henry despised President Franklin D. Roosevelt's New Deal, regarding it as an ill-conceived attempt to create a planned economy. It was a "flawed concept," he said, for at least three reasons: it attempted "to foresee the future and control it . . . it envisages society as a machine . . . and it destroys freedom." Throughout the Roosevelt era, Henry fought "administrative and legislative injustice" that favored labor while crippling business. At every opportunity, he railed against a centralized, bureaucratized economy, tapping his wealth of historical anecdotes to make the point. Controls, he said, wouldn't work any better in the United States than they did in eighteenth-century France, when "armies of bureaucrats" sought to codify everything from the size of handkerchiefs to the design of fishing boats.

Henry Wriston had an opinion about, and an interest in, every issue, from morals to monetary policy. He was a tight-money man who was aware of the evils of inflation even when there was none. He decried government hostility to business, but called on businessmen to be business statesmen. Henry Wriston believed that "the railroad financier [Cornelius Vanderbilt] who many years ago said 'The public be damned' wrote an important chapter in the history of human stupidity." And he might have been imparting advice to his son when he said that business statesmanship had three goals: "Its first duty is to develop operating techniques with a view to economy and efficiency. The second function is constantly to develop new products through research and innovation. The third obligation is to cultivate human relationships along lines calculated to bring the highest morale, the most initiative, and the greatest amount of resourcefulness."

To his boyhood friends, Walter Wriston seemed alternately outgoing and introverted, cheerful and serious. His diverse interests ranged from scouting and puppetry to chemistry and mechanics. He spent some of his happiest days hiking with his Boy Scout troop and his dog, Black Robin, along the Fox River to Lake Winnebago. At the age of fifteen, Wriston became an Eagle Scout, making him, for a fleeting moment, the youngest boy in the nation to achieve that rank. Henry Wriston encouraged his students, and his son, to learn to work with their hands as well as their minds, to become craftsmen in both the literal and the figurative sense. With several high school friends, Wriston created a puppet theater with papier-mâché marionettes; they concocted the stories, and Ruth Wriston sewed the costumes. Henry got Walter interested in mechanics, woodworking, and photography, and the two developed their pictures in a basement darkroom. One of the differences in their personalities manifested itself as they collaborated on woodworking projects. "He had much more patience than I had," Wriston confessed later. "He spent an hour sanding. I would get on with it."

As a teenager, Wriston was constantly experimenting and tinkering. On one occasion, while his parents were hosting a faculty luncheon, Wriston nearly suffocated the guests with a smoke bomb he manufactured with his chemistry set in the basement. Though usually tolerant of experimentation that bordered on mischief-making, this time Hank Wriston was "not amused," as Barbara Wriston recalled.

Wriston clearly had a sense of who he was at an early age. He was the son of the man who was arguably Appleton's leading citizen and almost certainly its smartest. "The Wristons were better than most of us," said Betty Brown Ducklow, a lifelong resident of Appleton and a contemporary of Walter's. "It was difficult for him to be a normal little boy."

That was evident to the librarian at the Appleton public library, who recalled to a friend that Walter, as a junior high student, once appeared at the library for no apparent reason. When the librarian asked him if he had found a book he liked, Walter replied haughtily, "I never read anything from your library. I use the Lawrence library. My father's the president there."

Former classmates remember that Walter was usually buttoned up, literally and figuratively. In contrast to his classmates, who often appeared disheveled even in school pictures, Walter always showed up with his shirttails tucked in, his sleeves down, and his shirt buttoned up to the collar.

There was, however, a more devilish side. Betty Ducklow sat next to him in the clarinet section of the junior high school band, and she remembers her stringy classmate as "funny, charming, lots of fun." Music was not his forte, however. He took up the clarinet only after abandoning the cello, and the clarinet soon met the same fate. For a time, Wriston attended Friday evening dance classes. He was clumsy, but he kept his classmates in stitches by waltzing with a coat hanger.

Life with Henry was not always easy for Walter, according to his contemporaries. One family friend remarked that "Walter Wriston was not the easiest kid to bring up, but Henry Wriston wasn't the easiest father to be brought up by." As the son of a college president, Walter was under heavy pressure to excel scholastically. On one occasion, when Wriston received a poor grade in high school, Henry admonished him, saying, "It's very hard for me to make public speeches about improving the educational system if you're getting a C or a D in something." Wriston quickly got the message that it would be "appropriate if I spent a little more time on books and a little less time playing soccer."

Home life for a college president's child was highly cerebral. While his peers spent a mere six hours a day in the classroom, Wriston in effect spent most of his waking hours either in school or in the intellectual atmosphere of his parents' house, where dozens of books competed for space with the evening meal on the dining room table. "He was a teacher," Wriston said later of his father. "He was always dredging up examples of this, that, and the other thing. Mother was a teacher. We all argued with him all the time. Everybody argued with everybody. It was sort of a Socratic method of teaching."

Henry Wriston regaled his children with tall tales of American history's most colorful characters. Favorites were Daniel Boone and Hawaii's Queen Liliuokalani.

Walter used to read the short biographies of successful people in *Who's Who,* seeking some common thread or a key ingredient in a person's success. He concluded that there was none. "I was struck by the fact that there was no pattern," he said later. "They started from all parts of America and from overseas," he said later. "They attended all kinds of schools, from P.S. 2 in small towns to famous prep schools."

At Appleton High, Wriston participated in the German and math clubs, took pictures for the school yearbook, worked in the library, played on the tennis team, acted in the senior play, competed in the oratorical contest with a speech called "Peace," and managed the debate team. In his senior year, he was chosen to "marry" a popular girl in a mock wedding—foreshadowing, perhaps, Wriston's real-life early marriage. Years later, Rose Heinritz, whose daughter Lucille dated Wriston in his senior year, quoted her daughter as saying, "Every girl should have as a first love a gentleman like Walter Wriston." And for teachers, having the children of the president of Lawrence in their classrooms was something of a status symbol.

In 1936, when Walter was a senior in high school, his father became president of Brown University in Providence, Rhode Island, replacing an ailing Baptist minister who had headed the school since 1929. Dr. Clarence Barbour's regime had been a mediocre one. Brown lacked a national reputation and was considered the stodgy black sheep of the Ivy League. Under Henry Wriston, the first Brown president in years who was neither a minister nor a Baptist, that would soon change. Brown would become Lawrence redux.

Walter rebelled at the idea of leaving Appleton to complete his senior year of high school in a strange place. Barbara had already left the nest for Ohio's Oberlin College, so Walter moved into the home of an Appleton teacher and was placed under the watchful eye of Ed West, a family friend. West's approach toward handling young Walter was laissez-faire. "If I didn't get in from the school dance until five in the morning, he'd make some remark," said Wriston. For all intents and purposes Wriston was physically out of his father's reach, but it would be decades before he moved out of his father's shadow.

Given Henry's Wesleyan legacy, no one was surprised when Walter was accepted there. But for Appletonians, it was still big news. In a community that prided itself on its Methodist College and its Methodist roots, going east to "Connecticut Wesleyan" was a major accomplishment. He could, of course, have gone to Lawrence or Brown, but opted not to attend a college where his father held a position of influence. He was afraid that if he excelled, people would gossip that "the old man gave me the grades. And if I did poorly, he'd be embarrassed," Wriston said later. Though Wriston shared his father's keen interest in foreign affairs, he contemplated majoring in chemistry, his mother's subject, and perhaps becoming a chemist. He knew he didn't want to return to Appleton, and he would not become a college professor, because he didn't want to be seen as riding on his father's coattails, but Wriston did not overly concern himself with his future career. "We were brought up to get a good liberal arts education," said Barbara later. "My father was dead set against people who try to get a kid in the sixth grade to decide what he wanted to do."

Wriston and his sister left Appleton having been assured by their parents that the world was their oyster and that they could be whatever they chose to be. But despite his accomplishments at Appleton High, Wriston wasn't seen by all his contemporaries as someone who would wind up running the nation's largest bank. Says Betty Ducklow, "When I saw [his picture] later in *Time* magazine, all I could think of was this kid who danced with a coat hanger."

Years later Wriston often referred in speeches to his Wisconsin roots, but he rarely returned to Appleton. Though he was fascinated with history, he considered it pointless to dwell on his own. "I had a great time," he reflected later. "But tomorrow's another day."

For Wriston, the son of the president of an Ivy League university and legendary Wesleyan teacher, arriving on the Wesleyan campus in the fall of 1937 was not exactly like coming in from a farm in Iowa, as his classmate and fraternity brother Jack Faison put it later. He had, of course, been born in Middletown, Connecticut, and spent the first six years of his life there. A number of Hank Wriston's colleagues from his own undergraduate days still taught at Wesleyan, so Walter Wriston's appearance on campus did not go unnoticed.

In some ways, however, he seemed like any other unpolished and insecure college freshman. Like his father, Wriston had developed an eye twitch that would last a lifetime, and he sometimes spoke with his hand over his mouth, a disconcerting habit that made his comments difficult to understand and suggested that he was embarrassed by what he was saying. But Wriston began his college years with a well-developed value system and with strong views on everything from personal conduct to political and economic theory.

Early on, Wriston's interest in chemistry flagged. Freshman lab, it turned out, conflicted with basketball practice, and he opted for the latter. With his six-foot-four-inch frame, Wriston should have been a natural. But he proved to be slow and awkward in his stint on the basketball team, and spent much of the time on the bench. So he chose to forgo chemistry and basketball in favor of history and foreign affairs, and for those subjects Wriston had come to the right place. The Wesleyan of the late 1930s was no mere ivory tower. The faculty included some of the nation's leading thinkers in political science and foreign affairs, and there were political practitioners as well as professors. One prominent example was President McConaughy, who in November 1938 became lieutenant governor of Connecticut.

Walter's college career was essentially a rerun of his father's, except that the son joined a different fraternity and didn't do as well scholastically. As a freshman, he joined the prestigious Eclectic Society of Phi Nu Theta, an independent fraternity that was the first Wesleyan house willing to accept students of all races and religions.

Wriston achieved distinction in his sophomore year, when he won, by unanimous acclaim, the school's coveted Parker Prize for public speaking. The inspiration for Wriston's talk was a university professor's conclusion, based on a poll, that the youth of the era had a defeatist attitude. In rebutting the professor's findings, Wriston declared, "It seems to me that in Professor Zachary's exhaustive survey, she has merely succeeded in unearthing some fundamental truths about part of the youth of any age."

Wriston's campus years were marked by rigor and discipline. While the youthful Wriston enjoyed the company of the funny and the fun-loving, he did so on his own terms. Jack Faison, the self-described court jester of the class of 1941, recalls that Wriston often skipped off-campus excursions, explaining that he had to study. "When we were all jumping into Johnny Wing's car for a sweep through Harlem, he'd say he had a paper due at the end of the week," Faison said.

Despite Wriston's studiousness, he and the happy-go-lucky John Wing (a.k.a. "Wacky Wing") were roommates and the best of friends, a relationship that others—like his future brother-in-law Richard Brengle, who matriculated when Wriston was a senior—found difficult to understand. Most of Wriston's friends throughout his life were highbrows, but his inner circle invariably included some affable, devil-may-care fellow whom others regarded as an intellectual featherweight.

With war clouds gathering over Europe, Wriston's college years were dominated by soul-searching over the proper role for the United States in the inevitable conflict. In March 1939, five months before Hitler's panzer divisions rolled over Poland, Wesleyan debated the U.S. role in a discussion of foreign policy that included prominent isolationists of the era such as Senator Gerald P. Nye, a North Dakota Republican. Wriston led the campus forces favoring intervention.

But it was an August 1939 visit to Europe, just before the start of his junior year, that confirmed forever Walter Wriston's view of the dangers of government regulation taken to its ultimate and terrible conclusion. Walter's father was a great believer in showing his children the world, and the family made two trips to Europe during Walter's summer vacations in high school and college. During that summer of 1939, Henry Wriston, as chairman of the American Coordinating Committee for International Studies, chaired the U.S. delegation to the American Exchange Conference in Bergen, Norway, and Walter served as his father's assistant. The family traveled the Continent by train, visiting, as Wriston put it later, "every cathedral known to man." Huddled in their compartment, they whiled away the hours reading a single paperback book, which they shared by ripping out the pages and passing them from one member of the family to another, starting with Barbara, the fastest reader, then on to Hank, Walter, and Ruth. "It was a weird way to do it," said Wriston, "but it was economical."

In mid-August 1939, just weeks before the Germans invaded Poland, the Wristons found themselves standing outside the Frankfurt railway station watching in horror as waves of Nazi Youth units goose-stepped by, waving swastika banners and singing "Deutschland über Alles," the Third Reich's national anthem. "I saw what happens with total regulation of people's lives, which starts with economic regulation and leaps over into politics and abolition of free speech." That experience, more than any other, made Walter "chary of anyone who wants to tell you how to run your life." By September 1, the day of the invasion, the Wristons had made their way back to Bergen to prepare for the voyage home on the *Bergensfjord.* Early on, Wriston drew a rigid line between the legitimate province of government and the zone where it had no right to tread. He conceded that the government had a role in regulating business activities affecting human health and safety—the design and location of railroad signals, for example, and rules barring the manufacture of drugs that "would cause a mind to atrophy"—but he believed that government intrusion beyond those limits should be viewed with suspicion.

A small clutch of high-powered professors reinforced the principles that

Wriston had first been exposed to at his father's knee. No one made a more profound impression on Walter than did Sigmund "Siggie" Neumann, a professor of political science. Neumann, a German Jew, had been one of the youngest full professors at the Reich Politik until he was kicked out by the Nazis. He came to the United States under the sponsorship of the Emergency Committee in Aid of Displaced Scholars, and found his way to Wesleyan through the efforts of CBS correspondent Edward R. Murrow.

Not surprisingly, Neumann had a keen personal and academic interest in dictatorships and wrote a benchmark work called *The Permanent Revolution,* in which he attempted to explain that form of government. If, after growing up with Henry and witnessing war preparations firsthand in Germany, Wriston needed further intellectual support for what would become a lifelong disdain for any form of centralized power, he could have found it in Neumann's teachings. A practitioner of the Socratic method, Neumann was a magnet for Wesleyan's intelligentsia, and Wriston and other students and their weekend house-party dates frequently sat cross-legged on the floor of the professor's living room until two in the morning "arguing about the world," as Wriston put it later. Neumann would hold forth on the monumental problems that would arise after the war. Someone, Wriston recalled, said that it would be virtually impossible to solve the problems of the postwar world Neumann described. "I never told you it was going to be easy," he replied. From Sigmund Neumann, Wriston learned that "intellectual property" was far more valuable than any other commodity. Speaking of his life in Hitler's Germany, Neumann said, "I had absolutely nothing. I didn't have a dollar, but they couldn't take away what was in my head."

Neumann once told Wriston's class, "It is just possible that one of you guys might do something useful someday." Wriston yearned to be that someone.

Another profound influence was Professor Elmer E. "Shaggy Schatts" Schattschneider, a brilliant lecturer, writer, and intellectual provocateur. This dedicated, good-humored teacher, who was later elected president of the American Political Science Association, appealed to Wriston's appreciation of the unconventional. A faculty profile later cited him for advocating "the necessity of breaking down departmental barriers and modernizing the traditional lecture–reading assignment–examination pattern of teaching." Schattschneider was not content simply to teach his students about public life; he wanted "to do something about it," as a later profile put it.

Neumann and Schattschneider were the leading faculty intellects at the time, said scholar-in-residence David Potts. "They were Young Turks," he said, whose arrival on the campus represented an injection of new intellectual blood into a staid conservative institution. "They espoused the life of the mind in a way students weren't accustomed to," Potts said.

Walter Wriston was not a brilliant student, but he was, as one classmate put it, "the man who made things happen." By his junior year, he was a campus force to be reckoned with. He was an editor of the college newspaper and a member of the board of Wesleyan's radio station. He also worked as a stringer for the *Hartford Courant,* selling the newspaper an occasional photograph and earning ten cents an inch for a sports column. And he was a member of the Mystical Seven, an elite senior society of campus leaders who had the right to wear a purple beanie for the duration of their senior year. "He wore the purple hat a great deal," said Brengle later.

At Wesleyan, Wriston got more than an education; he also found a wife. In his junior year he might not have known exactly where he was going, but he knew whom he wanted to accompany him. At a mixer with New London's all-women Connecticut College, Barbara "Bobby" Brengle, a sophomore and the belle of the ball, stood out in the crowd for her good looks and infectious personality. Wriston crossed the dance floor, extended his hand to her, and said, "Hi. I'm Walt Wriston. Will you marry me?" He didn't get his answer immediately, but it wasn't long in coming.

Henry Wriston was as decisive in affairs of the heart as he was in academic matters. As soon as he met his son's sweetheart, he commanded, "Walter, marry that girl!" Indeed, both the Wristons and the Brengles were thrilled by the match between Walter and Barbara—a marriage made at Wesleyan in more ways than one: both their fathers had graduated from Wesleyan, where they had opposed each other on the debating team.

Barbara, the daughter of George S. Brengle, a leading New York admiralty lawyer, grew up in the fashionable Westchester County suburb of Scarsdale and was educated at private schools. She attended the Baptist Church, sang in the high school glee club, served as captain of the hockey team, and was a devoted reader of the *Reader's Digest, The Ladies' Home Journal,* and *Life.* A talented aspiring commercial artist, Bobby illustrated campus publications with clever cartoons depicting the social and family life of the American upper class. One such cartoon shows a young woman trying on an expensive dress in a clothing salon while her boyfriend, who faintly resembles the youthful Walter Wriston, is fast asleep on a chair with a copy of *Foreign Affairs* tucked under his arm. In addition to her outgoing personality, she had an uncanny ability to remember names, an attribute that would prove invaluable to her future husband in his business career. More important, Bobby was exuberant and fun-loving, in contrast to her serious and sarcastic companion. Wriston would later tell close friends that "Bobby taught me how to live."

In the second semester of his junior year, Walter Wriston was elected editor-in-chief of the *Argus,* the campus newspaper, following once again in the footsteps of his illustrious father. In his first editorial, Walter made it clear that he intended to expand the paper's breadth to include news and commentary on important developments in the world at large.

As editor of the *Argus,* Wriston demonstrated his activist tendencies and brought to the paper a more controversial tone. He ran a series of editorials about the college's archaic charter that ultimately led to the drafting of a new one, and he infuriated the faculty with his Candid Course Review, a series that rated the effectiveness of courses and faculty. In one editorial, he lambasted an unpopular course that attempted to teach the history of the world from 1500 to the present day in one semester. That course was later eliminated. Years later a faculty widow would recall bitterly the searing criticism her husband suffered at the hands of Walter Wriston and his Candid Course Review.

The paper's editorials during Wriston's stewardship attacked communism and fascism and condemned the hypocrisy of U.S. Communist and fascist leaders for using the right of free speech to attack the American system of government while throwing hecklers out of their rallies. "Freedom of speech is a two-edged sword," declared one editorial. "Communists wield it against the government of the United States, but they forget that this same weapon stands ready to defend any individual who wishes to poke fun at Communist activities. Humor is the one thing that Communists cannot stand."

The big story early in Wriston's final year at Wesleyan was the visit of Republican presidential candidate Wendell Willkie to central Connecticut during the 1940 election campaign. Just before a planned stop in Middletown by Willkie on October 9, Wriston was elected president of the Willkie for President Club, and he and his fellow *Argus* reporters spent the day trying to snare an exclusive interview with the candidate. When Willkie arrived in Middletown, he was four hours behind schedule and was unable to make a planned address to the citizenry because of a 9:00 P.M. radio broadcast in New Haven. Wriston and his fellow reporters chased him from Middletown south to New Haven, scurrying along the tracks in the railroad yards trying to buttonhole him. Wesleyan's president, who accompanied Willkie on his Connecticut tour, got the *Argus* reporters through the gates to Willkie's private car, where the candidate was said to be eating dinner. But when they arrived, they were told that he was sleeping, and they had to settle for a press release instead of an interview. In a letter addressed to Wriston, Willkie later apologized for his inability to meet with them personally. "The big news," said Wriston later, "was that he was traveling with a mistress."

That fall, both Henry and Walter hopped aboard the Wendell Willkie bandwagon. Henry challenged Franklin Delano Roosevelt's candidacy for a third term based on what he saw as the dangers of a leader remaining in office for such a long period, rather than on the basis of his dissatisfaction with Roosevelt's leadership. Meanwhile, back in Middletown, Walter was attacking Roosevelt in the *Argus*.

The specter of war altered the course of Walter Wriston's life. He had briefly considered a career in journalism, but he abandoned his plan to apply to the Columbia Journalism School, in part because of his atrocious spelling. In his senior year at Wesleyan, he had applied and been accepted to Yale Law School. That plan changed, however, as a result of a phone call in early 1941 from his father. Henry Wriston had given a speech to undergraduates at Brown, telling them that America would be at war within a year and that they would have to fight. "I've got to tell my son the same thing," he told Walter.

"You'll never finish law school." That same morning, Wriston notified Yale that he wouldn't be coming and got on the phone to Tufts University's Fletcher School of Law and Diplomacy, which was well on its way to becoming the unofficial prep school for American diplomats. At Fletcher, where his father was on the board of counselors, he could earn a master's degree in less than a year.

No graduating class in American history could have received their degrees with more mixed feelings than the class of 1941. "This June," the editors of the 1941 Wesleyan yearbook, the *Olla Podrida,* wrote, "as the one hundred sixty–odd seniors descend the steps of the Terrace they will face a more dubious future than any class for the past few decades."

By his senior year, Wriston had nearly equaled his father's undergraduate accomplishments, in some respects outshining his famous father in every way but one: according to the *Wesleyan Bulletin,* he didn't make the honor roll (B average or better) until his senior year. His passion was American diplomatic history, and he received his degree with distinction largely because of an honors thesis entitled "The Embargo As an Instrument of American Foreign Policy." Unlike his father, however, he left Middletown without a Phi Beta Kappa key.

After being accepted at Fletcher, Wriston was informed that he needed to be able to speak a foreign language. His high school German didn't cut it for the master's program, so he enrolled in the summer session at Middlebury's École Française and drove to Vermont for an interview. The dean began interrogating him in French. Wriston stared at him and said, "I'm sorry, sir, but I don't have any idea in the world what you are talking about," as he later recalled to a reporter.

"You are supposed to speak French when you come here," the dean replied.

"I'm here because I don't speak it," Wriston snapped back.

"Well, you have more courage than brains, so you might as well stay."

At Middlebury, students were not permitted to eat if they didn't speak French, Wriston recalled. "By the end of the day," he said later, "I was able not to starve to death in a French restaurant."

Wriston's career as a campus radical ended abruptly with his arrival on the Medford, Massachusetts, campus of the Fletcher School. In the months leading up to the attack on Pearl Harbor, the mood on the nation's campuses became dead serious. With America's entry into the war, there was little time for campus activism and frivolity. The students' thoughts had turned to the conflict and the role they would play in it.

Having grown up in a household where prominent figures were regular dinner guests, Wriston was never inclined to bow and scrape to people in authority. He had also learned something about the exercise of influence and how a single phone call, sometimes to his father, could move mountains. One

such instance occurred during Wriston's year at Fletcher, a school adminis-
tered jointly by Harvard and Tufts, and whose library was owned by an organization called the World Affairs Foundation.

Wriston had learned that one of the school's top officials was leaving
and apparently taking at least part of the school's library with him. Wriston
phoned his father in Providence, reporting to him that "This is kind of weird.
I don't understand this, but it looks like they're taking the library out."

The elder Wriston phoned one of his highly placed friends at Harvard
and the movement of books out of the library was brought to a halt almost
instantly.

In his later banking career, Wriston had few opportunities to apply directly the knowledge of international law and diplomatic history he had acquired at Fletcher. But in conducting the foreign policy of the Citibank, he
would frequently draw on his vast "Fletcher network" of former classmates
and alumni.

Dr. Wriston's prediction about the inevitability of America's involvement in the war came true early on the morning of December 7, 1941, just
before he went on a nationally broadcast NBC radio program to argue, in a
debate with former Illinois congressman-at-large T. V. Smith, for rapid and
substantial cuts in federal nondefense spending.

"He was right," Wriston said later of his father's prophecy. "I never
went to graduation." Instead, Wriston left Fletcher immediately after his last
exam in May 1942 to serve as a junior foreign service officer with the State
Department in Washington, and received his diploma in the mail.

By that time, with its ranks decimated by the departure of seasoned diplomats for military service, the State Department was a heady place for
young foreign service officers like Wriston, who arrived there almost exactly
two decades after his father. At twenty-three, he found himself routinely
drafting orders for the ambassador to the Court of St. James and other emis-
saries and presenting them to Secretary of State Cordell Hull for his signature. Having taken a special interest in international law, Wriston was
assigned to a unit responsible for, among other things, the exchange of inter-
nees with the Japanese. In that assignment, Wriston demonstrated his uncanny knack for grabbing opportunity. Throughout his career, he seized the
moment first and worried about how he was going to perform later.

On one occasion, when a cable was received in the spring of 1942 that
the Japanese had seized a Dutch hospital ship, the *Op Ten Noort,* a senior
State Department official asked Wriston if he knew anything about the treaty
on these vessels. "Sure," Wriston replied confidently, even though he knew
absolutely nothing about such a treaty. That evening he returned home with
a briefcase full of papers on international law, and by four in the morning, he
could cite chapter and verse on the hospital ship agreement.

When he arrived at the office, he drafted a message to the Japanese government protesting the seizure and was told to dispatch a messenger to deliver it to the White House for President Roosevelt's signature. "You're
looking at the messenger," Wriston quickly replied. He had never visited the

White House, and eagerly seized the chance to deliver this vital document personally to the command post of the free world, perhaps to the president himself. On arriving at 1600 Pennsylvania Avenue, he was directed to the situation room. The door opened, revealing President Roosevelt in his wheelchair, and Wriston presented the document to a White House aide. Later, Wriston was waiting on the dock when former prisoners whose release he had helped secure limped or were carried down the gangway.

Having been charged at his tender age with such weighty responsibilities, Wriston had no difficulty picturing himself one day sitting in the elegant office then occupied by Cordell Hull. More than anything else in the world, Walter Wriston, like his father, wanted to be secretary of state of the United States. He never got there, of course, but he applied in his own career a conclusion that he drew from his brief stint at State: that the greatest secretaries of state were those who did not waver from the basic principles on which the country was founded. He admired Hull as one of the greatest and most underrated secretaries for his role in helping to lay the intellectual foundation for free and reciprocal trade. "He didn't make the [Hawley-Smoot Tariff Act] mistake that plunged the world into the Depression," said Wriston, referring to the 1930 legislation that raised U.S. tariffs so steeply that it sparked retaliatory measures by other countries and caused world trade to plunge. "That was an extraordinary achievement. [Hull] lectured the Japanese and one thing or another, but his vision of a trading society that was open or relatively open was remarkable." Wriston later came to know, on a first-name basis, most of the secretaries of state who followed Hull, and he regarded Dean Acheson and his own close friend George Shultz as two of the greatest modern-day secretaries.

Then, as now, a career foreign service officer could realistically aspire only to the number two slot, never the top job, and Wriston knew he might toil at Foggy Bottom for twenty-five years and wind up as "ambassador to Gabon," as he said later. "Then where are you? You're at the end of somebody's buzzer. And the guy that buzzes you might be like I was, twenty-three years old. That went through my head often."

On October 24, 1942, Wriston married Bobby Brengle, to the delight of both families. While Bobby's parents were overjoyed with their new son-in-law, Mrs. Brengle yearned for some sign of affection from him. "I wish he would loosen up a little bit," she confided to family members, eventually resigning herself to life without a lot of hugs and kisses from Walter. "He's New England," she would say. In contrast to his father, who took every opportunity to compliment the women in his life on their appearance and their clothes, Wriston did not expend much charm on his mother-in-law.

In the early years of their marriage, he was often withdrawn and moody. Said his daughter, Cassy, "My mother used to say they were married for five years before he said anything at breakfast."

Wriston could have secured an exemption to remain in the State Department through the war, but he knew that the United States had obtained the release of as many American civilians from Japan as it would until the end of the war, and he began to contemplate his options for military service.

In the process, he learned that family connections had their limits. While in Washington, he received a call from Colonel Edward Buxton, deputy head of the OSS, the predecessor to the CIA. Buxton, a native of Rhode Island and a friend of Hank Wriston, asked Walter if he would consider volunteering for a hazardous mission that called for someone who could speak French. Buxton planned to secure for him a commission as a lieutenant in the navy, and then Wriston would be sent to operate undercover with the American expeditionary forces in North Africa. But in late 1942, while waiting for the navy commission to materialize, Wriston was drafted into the army. He reported for duty in February 1943 as Private Walter B. Wriston.

Henry Wriston apparently had no influence with the army top brass, and son Walter would have to suffer through most of his thirty-eight-month military career as an enlisted man. That was tough to take for someone who had just spent nearly a year drafting top-secret cables for the secretary of state. After basic training, Wriston did a stint with the medical corps learning how to treat battle injuries. Then he was assigned to the Coast Artillery to serve in what he later termed the "New York archipelago"—Staten Island, Sandy Hook, and the islands in and around New York Harbor.

Throughout the war, Wriston was frustrated by his lowly status as an enlisted man, according to one relative. He applied for the army air force officers' training, but while passing through Grand Central station one day en route to his assignment, he was stopped by two military policemen. They informed him that on that very day the army air force administrative school had been closed to all but air force personnel. When Wriston reported the story to the captain of his unit, the officer asked him what he knew about the signal corps.

Wriston replied that he knew all about codes and ciphers. That was something of an exaggeration, of course, but it got him into the signal corps school at Fort Monmouth. Wriston had always been fascinated with electrical and mechanical devices and was handy with the tools used to repair them. In 1945, as the war was nearing its conclusion, he was finally commissioned as a second lieutenant. Bobby moved in with her parents and taught kindergarten, and Wriston shipped out to the Philippine island of Cebu, where he was placed in charge of a lonely signal corps outpost. Sitting under a sign saying "The Sun Never Sets on our Shortwave Sets," Wriston operated the SIGABA machine, the military's most secret encoding device, an assignment that would mark the beginning of a lifelong fascination with information technology.

One of Wriston's buddies was a wizard on the "bug," the device used to transmit coded messages. Like Wriston, he was a passionate Benny Goodman fan who tapped his foot to the music on the shortwave while sending and receiving coded messages. One day, however, the music stopped abruptly;

Wriston received the one message that would stick in his mind forever. In early 1946, six months after the war in the Pacific had ended, a fellow corpsman handed him a Red Cross cable. Thinking it was intended for another soldier, Wriston promised to deliver it. "It's for you," the corpsman said solemnly. He read the cable, which informed him that his mother was dying of cancer and he had been granted emergency leave to return home to Providence.

2

THE STIFF-COLLAR BOYS

*T*he stoical Ruth Wriston had not wanted anyone to know just how sick she really was. But Henry Wriston knew, and asked a U.S. senator from Rhode Island to move heaven, earth, and the U.S. Army to bring his son back to his mother's bedside.

When Walter arrived in Providence in March 1946 and saw the condition his mother was in, he knew his ten-day leave would not be enough. He journeyed to Fort Dix, New Jersey, to try to get the leave extended. After requesting and being denied a discharge, he started to leave the base in a driving rainstorm and was forced to take shelter in another building. By sheer chance he had wound up at the right place. A sergeant asked him if he had come to be discharged. "I sure have," Wriston replied gleefully. The sergeant steered him to the appropriate line, and four hours later Wriston was once again a civilian. Several weeks later, on May 12, 1946, his mother died.

Adding to his sorrow was the discovery that many friends and fraternity brothers had been killed during the war, four of them in Stateside flight training exercises. Shortly after he returned home, he received a call from classmate Jack Faison, inviting him to their fifth reunion. "If you don't come now you'll miss a chance to see as many of your old friends as you'll ever see again," Faison told him—a remark he would regret for years.

"I've lost most of my old friends already," Wriston replied sadly. Years would pass before he could bring himself to revisit his alma mater, despite the pleas of classmates.

Wriston had originally planned to pick up where he'd left off at the State Department, but with his mother on her deathbed and Bobby in the middle of a school term, he had no interest in heading back to Washington right away. Unwilling to accept handouts or even loans from his family, he wanted to earn some money in the few months remaining before the end of the school year.

One of his mother's physicians suggested that he consider a career in banking, a notion that had never crossed Walter's mind. The doctor arranged for him to meet the chairman of one of Providence's leading banks, who offered him a job starting at $2,000 a year. Though relatives would later describe the twenty-six-year-old Wriston as "quiet and shy," he was anything but timid when it came to salary negotiations. He rejected the offer as wholly inadequate. "But it's an honor to work for the Rhode Island Hospital Trust," the banker replied, clearly shocked at his answer. "It's an honor to eat, too," Wriston retorted. Wriston had other reasons for not accepting a job in Providence. He had lived in the long shadow of his father for most of his life. His accomplishments so far were his alone, but Dad had always been there to pull strings when the need arose, and he did not want to begin his career in yet another place where he would be labeled the son of Henry Wriston. He decided to work elsewhere so that "if I fell on my face it wouldn't be so embarrassing," he later told a reporter.

Having begun to mull over the idea of working for a bank, at least temporarily, Wriston asked his father which was the best one in New York. The answer was National City, and it happened that Hank Wriston had a friend there, too: the executive committee chairman, Randolph Burgess, a Brown alumnus and former senior official of the Federal Reserve Bank of New York.

Within weeks after he assumed the presidency of Brown back in 1937, Henry Wriston had written to Burgess offering to present an honorary degree to him at the June commencement, according to university archives. Burgess, of course, accepted. Wriston would later tell reporters that he ambled into the bank off the street "stone-cold dead with nothing going for me," but that was an exaggeration. He may have walked in off the street, but he did so with a recommendation from one of the top university educators in the United States and a senior member of the eastern establishment. In 1946, National City paid recent college graduates $2,800 a year. A job seeker with a master's in any subject was a rare animal, however, and Wriston floored the interviewers by demanding a premium salary because of his advanced degree. They had never even heard of the Fletcher School of Law and Diplomacy. Nonetheless, Wriston managed to land the job and wring out of them an additional $200 a year.

Walter and Bobby set up housekeeping in a tiny one-room apartment on Manhattan's Upper East Side, just a few blocks from the apartment of Bobby's parents. On June 29, 1946, Walter reported for his first day on the job, leaving behind the world of the Brown president's residence at 55 Power Street, Providence, for the National City Bank at 55 Wall Street in lower Manhattan. "I didn't have any set of goals and perspectives," Wriston recalled later. "I came in looking for a job so I could eat. If I were to sit up at night making a list of everything dull, banking would come out on top." It was, he said, "the last thing in the world I wanted to do." So he made a pact with the bank that if his first assignment, as a junior inspector in the comptroller's division, proved to be as boring as he expected it to be, he'd quit within a year.

When Wriston first mounted the steps of the bank's headquarters, a multicolumned Greek-style structure that was once the U.S. Custom House, the American banking system was, and arguably still is, the most regulated of the nation's industries. The government dictated nearly every aspect of a banker's life, from the kinds of activities he could engage in and where he could engage in them to what he could pay on deposits. That was due in no small way to National City's questionable practices in earlier years. Indeed, Henry Wriston might have regarded National City as the best bank in New York, but others would have disputed that assessment.

Wriston joined National City in the 134th year of a mostly proud but also tumultuous and scandal-ridden past that is interwoven with the financial and economic history of the United States itself. Chartered in 1812, the original City Bank, as it was then named, was the de facto successor to the Bank of the United States, America's controversial first attempt at central banking. When Congress voted not to renew the bank's charter, a group of New York merchants stepped into the credit void created by that decision. The group's leader, Samuel Osgood, was a Revolutionary army colonel who went on to become a senior treasury official and the nation's first postmaster general. Along with Aaron Burr, he also founded the Bank of the Manhattan Company, which would over the generations, as it became Chase Manhattan, challenge City Bank and its descendants for the leadership of American banking.

In its first quarter century, City Bank was run as a kind of private piggybank for its merchant directors, whose fortunes were subject to the vagaries of a developing economy and a primitive and unregulated financial system. Their personal or business reversals often led to severe losses for the bank. The panic of 1837 was a turning point in American economic history and in the future of the City Bank. With skimpier reserves than other New York institutions, City Bank was saved from collapse only through the intervention of some of New York's leading merchants, including John Jacob Astor—then the richest man in America—and his business associate, Moses Taylor, a prosperous and highly respected sugar trader. Taylor's formula for success in banking, as in trading, was "Personal control, silence, and ready cash," and for the next forty-five years City Bank's success followed Taylor's. In 1856, Taylor became president of the City Bank, and a year later he took a key step toward expanding his own fortune along with the bank's when yet another financial panic presented him with a chance to buy a stake in the Delaware, Lackawanna & Western Railroad. Within seven years, the value of his railroad shares had surged fiftyfold and he had gained control of the line. Taylor and the City Bank played a pivotal role in the expansion and consolidation of American railroads, which enhanced New York's role in the nation's rail network and, in turn, its importance as the center of commerce and finance.

Since the earliest days of the Republic, populist agrarian interests who opposed concentrated banking power had been at war with monied urban interests who favored it. Until 1863 the populists clearly held sway. The federal government exercised virtually no central control over banks or money, and states chartered banks as they saw fit—a seriously flawed system that allowed state banks to print their own, often worthless, notes, leaving the economy vulnerable to frequent panics.

In part to address these problems, Congress passed the National Currency Act of 1863 and the National Bank Act of 1864. Among other things, the first act created a uniform national currency, and the second established the Office of the Comptroller of the Currency to charter national banks and to issue a uniform national currency. Ultimately this package of legislation drove out of circulation all bank notes other than those issued by national banks. It also inaugurated a dual banking system, unlike any other in the world, of national and state-chartered institutions and ushered in the golden age of the big New York banks. In 1865, City Bank received the U.S. government's charter number 29 and renamed itself the National City Bank, though it would be known informally by its original name. (Several years after Wriston became chairman, it was officially renamed Citibank.)

Unfortunately, the creation of a national banking system did not put an end to financial panics. For National City, the crises that plagued the nation over the next two decades were tailor-made opportunities. As weaker competitors fell by the wayside, Citibank grew in strength and prestige. When Taylor died in 1882, leaving a personal fortune estimated at $45 million, National City was one of the strongest financial institutions in New York.

Taylor was succeeded as president by his top aide and son-in-law, Percy Pyne, who lacked the drive, leadership, and business savvy of his patron. In nine years under Pyne, the bank lost much of its earlier momentum, and things did not change for the better until he suffered a stroke in 1891. During his tenure, however, two men appeared who would change the bank's direction dramatically.

In 1884, James Stillman, a prominent investor, joined the board and brought to the big table some of the top men in American business, including William Rockefeller, the finance man of family-controlled Standard Oil. After Pyne's resignation in November 1891, Rockefeller and Stillman took charge of National City, and Stillman assumed the presidency.

James Stillman had big ideas. With Rockefeller and Standard Oil behind it, there would be no stopping National City. Stillman and Rockefeller continued Moses Taylor's policy of maintaining huge cash reserves. Like Taylor, Stillman believed in the importance of "personal control, silence, and ready cash."

Stillman used silence to expose the flaws in the countless business propositions brought to his office. A colleague later wrote that Stillman would "keep silent while such a man talked. The man would finish his talk and Mr. Stillman would remain completely silent." The weaknesses of any proposal were "revealed under the test of embarrassed repetition." Stillman and Rockefeller also believed in keeping everything in the family: two of Stillman's daughters married Rockefeller's sons.

Timing was on Stillman's side. In 1893 yet another severe panic struck fear into the hearts of depositors, again to the benefit of National City. Thanks also to Standard Oil's huge deposits, the bank's deposits grew in just two years from $12 million to $31 million. But the panic had other consequences that would enhance the power of the bank and the men who controlled it. It triggered the collapse of the railroads, enabling Stillman, Rockefeller, railroad man Edward Henry Harriman, and financier Jacob Schiff to step in and gradually gain control over the Union Pacific.

Where once control of the railroads had rested with thousands of small stock- and bondholders, it would now shift into the hands of only two small Wall Street cliques that would become known as the "money trusts." One clique consisted of Stillman, Rockefeller, Union Pacific, Standard Oil, and the Wall Street firm of Kuhn, Loeb & Company. The other clique included J. P. Morgan, James Hill, and George F. Baker, head of the First National Bank. It was inevitable that the Stillman-Rockefeller group and the Morgan-Hill forces would one day steam down the track on a collision course.

Both the City Bank group and the Morgan group, which dominated the Great Northern Railway and the Northern Pacific, coveted the Chicago, Burlington & Quincy Railroad. Control over the Burlington would extend the reach of either line into the western states. When Morgan ally James Hill attempted to absorb the Burlington into their empire, the National City Bank group made their move. In May 1901 they snapped up $115 million of Northern Pacific stock, triggering one of the worst market panics of all time. Thousands of unsuspecting small investors were wiped out.

" 'Twasn't the money we were after," Stillman is reported to have said. " 'Twas the power. We were all playing for power. It was a great game."

The Northern Pacific battle gave further impetus to the use—indeed the misuse—by Wall Street moneymen of the trust as a vehicle for acquisition and consolidation. Though national banks were required to keep 25 percent of their deposits in cash, New York State law permitted banks to establish affiliated trust companies that weren't saddled with such restrictions. While the trust companies were originally set up to oversee the affairs of wealthy clients, they in fact provided banking barons Morgan and Stillman with a convenient device for gaining an even tighter stranglehold over American business and finance.

Meanwhile, Stillman moved to bolster National City's position as a worldwide institution. Almost from the day it opened for business, National City had played a role in overseas banking, financing exports and imports and buying and selling foreign exchange on behalf of customers. Although it wasn't the first bank in the United States, or even in New York State, to establish a foreign exchange operation, it did in 1897 become the first American bank to consolidate all of its overseas activities into a formal foreign department. By 1902 National City could claim that it was able to disburse "any sum of money . . . in any city in the world within twenty-four hours."

Under Stillman, National City became a major depository for holding and redistributing U.S. Treasury funds. On the advice of Lyman Gage, secretary of the Treasury in the McKinley administration, Stillman aggressively built up the bank's capital position to ensure that the bank would always be able to serve in that capacity.

Through Gage, Stillman met and recruited a young Treasury aide named Frank Vanderlip, whom Gage brought with him from Chicago when he was appointed to the cabinet. Vanderlip had handled the Treasury Department's bank relationships and had earned Stillman's admiration through his successful management of a $200 million Spanish-American War bond issue. In style and temperament, the two men were polar opposites. Stillman eschewed the public spotlight and was reluctant to actively solicit business; he was so secretive he used code names in referring to William Rockefeller (Tumacar), Harriman (Zoosperm), and other members of his inner circle. In contrast, Vanderlip had a promoter's instincts.

Vanderlip, a former financial reporter, blew into National City like a gust of fresh air. From day one, he began tapping his Treasury department banking contacts to drum up new "correspondent" accounts with other banks around the country. In his first year he solicited 365 new accounts. He applied his newspaper training, and his bent for full disclosure, to his job, causing considerable uneasiness for Mr. Stillman, who "avoided reporters like lepers," according to Vanderlip. "A great deal of my success at the City Bank was due to the fact that I was, in addition to being a banker, a publicist," said Vanderlip, who wrote articles and started up bank publications that became widely quoted in the financial press. But, he added, "To be a publicist you have to have something to say."

Vanderlip maintained his ties to Washington. He was one of only two men in the country whom President Theodore Roosevelt asked to edit his speeches; the other was Secretary of State Elihu Root. Vanderlip, said one Citibanker later, "broke the white-shoe tradition."

Vanderlip was apparently one of the few men able to earn the full confidence of James Stillman, who seemed to sense that his own sons were not up to the task of succeeding him at National City and who soon recognized Vanderlip as the best available substitute.

In 1906, after five years at National City Bank, Vanderlip took the historic plunge into international banking, leading the bank, as he put it, "into an adventure with some of its funds that was an entirely new thing in American banking." It was a deal that in the short run, at least, worked to perfection and appeared immensely profitable. Two decades later, Vanderlip would conclude that it was all a terrible mistake.

The bank's overseas experiment began in Latin America with its involvement in financing the construction of a $27 million railroad line from La Paz, Bolivia, south to the Chilean port of Antofagasta, where it would link up with a British-owned Chilean line. Under the deal, National City would take $15 million in first mortgage bonds, and the Bolivian government $12 million in second mortgage bonds. Around the time the Bolivian deal was being concluded, Stillman informed Vanderlip over dinner that he would succeed him as president two years later.

Meanwhile, the stock market was growing dangerously frothy with speculative stock issues. Prices plunged in early 1907, and European bankers, who had lent money to the United States to help bring in the crops, backed away from that traditional role. In an early internal debate that would recur frequently over the rest of the century, Vanderlip and Stillman clashed over the appropriate level of reserves for National City. Vanderlip argued that excessive reserves were hampering profitability, but Stillman stuck to Taylor's policy of holding on to large reserves of ready cash. In early 1907, Stillman emphasized to Vanderlip the necessity of remaining "ridiculously strong and liquid." Luckily for National City, Stillman prevailed.

The trigger for the Panic of 1907, one of the most severe in American financial history, was a late October run on New York's Knickerbocker Bank. Only the intervention of J. P. Morgan and James Stillman saved the day. Putting aside their differences, the two men and their monied colleagues propped up their peers and calmed the waters, in effect serving as a kind of central bank. In 1908, National City reinforced its image as a financial pillar of strength when it moved into its new Wall Street headquarters. Stillman had bought the old Custom House, and hired a leading architectural firm to remodel it to look like the Pantheon.

The panic solidified the business and personal ties between Morgan, Stillman, and Baker. In fact, Morgan, who had owned a sizable stake in the National City Bank even before the panic, boosted his ownership afterward. And Stillman, Vanderlip wrote later, suggested to George Baker of the First National Bank that they combine their two institutions, but Baker responded that he was busy enough with domestic banking and didn't have the time to immerse himself in foreign banking.

The case against the money trust was further reinforced in the wake of the Panic of 1907, when instead of battling over the chance to underwrite new domestic and international issues, the banking barons congenially divided up the pie. But the panic had a much more profound effect than simply cementing the friendship among the moneymen. More than any previous event, the 1907 bust convinced Washington and the bankers, including Vanderlip, of the need for a radical overhaul of the financial system that would include a central bank to hold reserves for emergencies. The government could no longer count on the big New York banks to serve as a quasi-central bank and bail the country out of every crisis. Vanderlip, who in January 1909 assumed the $50,000 a year post as National City president, later became a key player in the drive to create a central bank.

Soon after the panic Congress passed temporary legislation that provided for the issuance of emergency currency during crises. It also set up a National Monetary Commission to develop a proposal for banking reform. The Senate's resident banking expert, Senator Nelson Aldrich of Rhode Island, who happened to be John D. Rockefeller's father-in-law, was appointed to head the panel. He promptly tapped his Wall Street friends, including Vanderlip, to advise him.

After making a banking tour of Europe, Senator Aldrich became convinced of the need for a central bank and a more flexible currency. In a historic November 1910 meeting on Jekyll Island, Georgia, which was disguised as a duck-hunting expedition, Vanderlip and other top financiers drew up a plan for a central bank. Vanderlip wrote the final version, which called for a National Reserve Association overseeing fifteen regional banking centers run by private institutions. The Aldrich plan contained one item especially dear to Vanderlip's heart: authority for national banks to establish overseas branches.

Vanderlip and Stillman, meanwhile, continued to expand the horizons of National City. They felt that President William Howard Taft would look more kindly on their efforts to broaden their activities than had trust-busting Theodore Roosevelt. In 1911, on the eve of the bank's one hundredth anniversary, they set up the National City Company to get the enterprise into new businesses, including investment banking. James Stillman had his own vision of a central bank as a chain of banks with National City Company at the center. To that end, National City acquired shares of a number of out-of-state institutions. Although National City Company was first established with the idea of holding various investments that the bank couldn't make, National City Company later became an underwriting operation as well.

That idea didn't sit well with the solicitor general of the United States, Frederick W. Lehmann. In a scathing November 1911 report on the new venture, he wrote that the link between the bank and its affiliate was illegal. National City Company, he wrote, "had made investments in the shares of sixteen banks and trust companies and approximately $3.2 million in other companies of different character. The National City Company may expand its power to the full control of all the banks into which it has made entrance. Nor need it stop with these. As it grows by what it feeds upon, it may expand into a great central bank with branches in every sector of the country. It is in its incipient stage a holding company of banks, with added power to hold whatever else it may find to be to its advantage." According to one account, Stillman met with President Taft at the White House to urge him to keep the government's hands off the new affiliate. More than two decades would pass, and incalculable damage would be done, before Lehmann's report would see the light of day.

In the spring of 1911, to drum up public support for the Aldrich plan, its backers set up the National Citizens' League for the Promotion of a Sound Banking System. But the Aldrich plan died in 1912 without even making it to the floor of Congress for a vote. That happened largely because of President Taft's insistence on "government supervision and ultimate control," as he stated in a message to Congress, as well as Aldrich's image as a stooge for Wall Street interests. With the Aldrich plan dead, interest in banking reform shifted to the Democrats, especially Representative Carter Glass of Virginia, the senior member of the House Banking Committee. Meanwhile, the House Committee on Banking and Currency under chairman Arsène P. Pujo was preparing to investigate the influence of the money trust, including the newly formed National City Company, over American finance and commerce. Pujo had sought to take control over banking reform as well, but in the end that assignment was handed to Glass.

Among other things, the Pujo hearings revealed the breadth and scope of the control exerted by Morgan, First National Bank, and National City Bank via their network of banks and brokerage firms. Through 341 director-ships on 112 companies, they controlled some $22 billion in resources. In their testimony, these so-called masters of capital acknowledged that perhaps they did exert a bit too much financial clout. Morgan, for one, conceded that when he combined the Great Northern and the Northern Pacific railroads into the Northern Securities Company, he wiped out the competition be-tween them. And Baker acknowledged that concentration of credit "has gone about far enough." Stillman by now was living in Europe in semiretirement and thereby escaped having to appear at the hearings.

While the Pujo hearings generated public outrage over the practices of the money trust, the investigation essentially died in 1912, when Pujo ran for the Senate, and Glass, who didn't care for the probe to begin with, as-sumed the chairmanship of the banking committee.

Ironically, however, public anger over the revelations that came out of the hearings actually furthered the cause of banking reform, which the money trust had wanted all along. With the demise of the Pujo investigation, atten-tion focused once again on creating an apparatus to prevent future financial crises. There was little debate on the need for such a mechanism; the contro-versy swirled around the shape it should take.

Immediately after his election as president in 1912, Woodrow Wilson immersed himself in the details of legislation being proposed by Representa-tive Glass. The bill that emerged out of these discussions contained the basic elements of the Aldrich Plan but called for a central bank under public rather than banker control. Although Vanderlip endorsed most of the provisions of the Glass bill, he took issue with a number of the details. He wanted greater centralization than the Glass measure proposed, and he objected strenuously to the plan to issue paper currency not backed by gold. Vanderlip fought the bill to the bitter end. In a famous November 10, 1913, debate at the New York Economic Club, the two men discussed the legislation before 1,100 fi-nanciers.

Vanderlip took issue with those who accused him and other top bank-ers of pushing for a plan that would benefit the monied interests. "I stand charged with the offense of being the president of the largest bank in the United States," he said. "Who are the officers of that bank? Let me tell you that with a single exception they are men whose boyhood started in poverty. I myself wore the blue overalls of a farm hand and a machine shop operator."

Finally, on December 23, 1913, President Wilson signed the Federal Reserve Act, which established a central Federal Reserve Board and twelve regional reserve banks. It also provided that national banks would have to be members of the Federal Reserve System whereas state banks could elect not to be. But in the end this legislation did virtually nothing to limit the power of the money trust. Wisely, the Pujo panel had recommended a ban on dummy securities affiliates, but that never materialized. The Clayton Anti-Trust Act of 1914 attempted to deal with some abuses, such as interlocking directorates, but the tangible results of the investigation were meager indeed. To keep the peace with the new Wilson administration, the financiers dissolved some of their corporate ties—at least officially. If the monied interests were tainted by the Pujo probe, the smell did not last long. Led by Morgan, the moneymen reestablished themselves in the nation's good graces by helping to finance the Allied cause in World War I. At the end of the war, National City, J. P. Morgan, and the First National Bank remained the masters of capital.

Vanderlip was one of the leading internationalists of his day, and about the time Henry Wriston was lecturing Wesleyan undergraduates on America's growing global role, Vanderlip was putting his economic theories into practice. More than anyone, he was responsible for the early vision of National City as an international banking power. He dreamed of the day when the bank would "have a well ordered branch in every important center in the world outside the United States."

For the future of National City, one of the most significant provisions of the Federal Reserve Act was the one—said to have been included as a concession to Vanderlip—allowing national banks to open branches overseas. Until then only state-chartered banks and trust companies could operate foreign branches, and they had done so in a limited way as early as 1895. But until 1914 and the onset of World War I, there was little economic need for overseas expansion. International trade and American investment abroad were relatively limited, and the United States was still a net importer rather than an exporter of capital. The Federal Reserve Act, subsequent changes in New York State banking law mirroring it, and the Edge Act of 1914, which permitted U.S. banks to set up foreign banking corporations in this country, combined to improve the climate for overseas expansion. Except in Canada, which barred branches of foreign institutions, American banks generally would be welcomed with open arms. Led by National City, U.S. banks wasted no time in taking advantage of the new freedom.

On November 10, 1914, National City opened a branch in Buenos Aires, becoming the first nationally chartered institution to set up a branch on foreign soil. Other expansion moves followed in rapid succession. On October 29, 1915, National City Bank acquired a controlling interest in the International Banking Corporation, which operated sixteen branches in England, Panama, and Asia. Vanderlip had coveted the network for years. Formed in 1901 after receiving a charter from the Connecticut legislature, the IBC and its contingent of quirky English and Scottish traders were empowered to operate almost any business outside Connecticut. They did everything from financing a railroad in China to serving as fiscal agent for the United States for the Panama Canal.

Thus, in one fell swoop, National City became the preeminent international bank. Its overseas representation rose to twenty-two branches, which performed such bread-and-butter transactions as trade finance, foreign exchange trading, local branch banking, and correspondent banking. In 1918, National City Bank acquired the remainder of IBC, but National City Bank did not integrate the IBC into its operations until 1927. With the money trust still a high-profile issue, no one wanted the spotlight to focus on the IBC, as it already had on National City.

The most serious constraint on City Bank's overseas expansion was the lack of competent bankers to man the foreign outposts. Though Vanderlip raided the foreign staffs of other banks, he couldn't find nearly enough qualified men to meet his voracious appetite for new territory. He realized that "we evidently have got to grow men rather than hire them." Accordingly, in 1915, National City became the first New York bank to set up a college hiring program and training class—a West Point, Vanderlip said, for "financier cadets" recruited from top U.S. colleges. Operating out of a Brooklyn brownstone, the inaugural class consisted of fifteen college graduates who received a salary of $50 a month but paid for bed and board out of their own pockets.

One of Vanderlip's dreams was to build a branch network in Russia, a goal encouraged by the Wilson administration. Alas, in a classic case of bad business timing, National City opened its first Russian branch in Petrograd in January 1917, just two months before the onset of the Russian revolution. The following December, about a month after the Bolsheviks seized power, Vanderlip's dream turned into his worst nightmare: the new Communist rulers seized the bank's branches, giving National City its first bitter taste of nationalization. It was to be one of the bank's shortest stays in a foreign country. "It was a rude introduction to the problem of sovereign risk," wrote Citibank's official historians, Thomas F. Huertas and Harold van B. Cleveland.

James Stillman, now an absentee chairman, was furious when he heard the news of the Bolshevik coup and, that same day, reasserted direct control of National City. Summoning Vanderlip back from Washington, where he was on loan to the government, Stillman let him know that his days were numbered. Wrote author Clarence Barron, "Kerensky fell, and so did Vanderlip."

On March 15, 1918, shortly after telling his son James "Jamie" Stillman never to "accept the presidency of the bank," Stillman died—and was succeeded as chairman by Jamie. His other dying wish was not fulfilled either. He had wanted his coffin to be placed in the rotunda of 55 Wall Street "with the mourners grouped about and the Metropolitan orchestra playing softly." The family rejected that idea in favor of a simple ceremony at the old Saint Bartholomew's Church, which in 1918 still stood on Madison Avenue.

Predictably, Jamie was not up to the job. On June 3, 1919, when Vanderlip was forced to resign from the presidency, Jamie gave up the chairmanship for the lesser post. For almost two years the post of chairman remained vacant. In his nearly thirty years at the helm, Stillman had built National City into the largest commercial bank in the United States, and had amassed a personal fortune then estimated at $200 million. Had he lived another year he would have presided over the first bank in the Western Hemisphere to reach $1 billion in assets.

In 1919, National City Bank opened more new branches—thirty-three of them, including twenty-two in Cuba—than it had in any year since its foreign crusade began. By then the pitfalls of expanding too fast with too few trained people became evident.

The worst debacle in National City's first half century of foreign lending resulted from its ill-fated tie to Cuba. War-related shortages of sugar sent prices skyrocketing. National City, which seemed to be in the right place at the right time, poured money into the booming sugar industry. Allowing no margin for error, it lent on the basis of highly inflated prices not only for sugar in the warehouse but also for future crops and farmland. By the time sugar prices crashed, National City had nearly one-fifth of all the loans to the Cuban banking system. The now sour sugar loans threatened to wipe out the total capital of the bank. James Stillman had been proven right. Son Jamie lacked both the temperament and the ability to run the biggest banking empire in the Western world. It is questionable whether things might have been different if Jamie had devoted his full attention to bank business. But his highly publicized matrimonial difficulties certainly didn't help matters—although they may have established a Citibank tradition!

While Jamie Stillman's wife, Fifi, explored the Canadian wilderness with an Indian guide, Stillman, using an alias, kept a mistress named Flo and their illegitimate son at a spacious apartment on Manhattan's Upper East Side. Though Fifi was apparently unaware at the time of her husband's second family, she decided that the marriage wasn't working and consulted a lawyer about a divorce. Stillman also sued for a divorce, charging that Fifi had a son by the Indian guide. An industrious reporter revealed the existence of Jamie's other family, which Fifi now suspected but could not prove. Despite the vast legal resources Stillman brought to the case, he lost his suit and Fifi's baby boy was confirmed as his son. With that decision and the screaming headlines that accompanied it, Jamie became a pariah among his Wall Street friends. After years of litigation, he and Fifi were finally divorced in 1931.

Beset by bad loans and a scandalous private life, James Stillman resigned as president on May 3, 1921. One Eric P. Swenson was appointed chairman, and the charismatic Charles Mitchell, who had been hired in 1916 to run the National City Company, was named president.

Mitchell was dashing, fast on his feet, a salesman and promoter extraordinaire. He had, Vanderlip once said, "an astonishing capacity to create energy." For all his skill at salesmanship, however, Mitchell was not a man of the masses. James Stillman's grandson, James Stillman Rockefeller, once said that Mitchell "considered himself a big shot and acted like a big shot." He used a private elevator at 55 Wall Street and allowed no one else to ride in it with him.

Mitchell demonstrated extraordinary creativity in bailing out the Cuban loans, however. More than a decade later, congressional hearings revealed that National City Company had created a shell entity, the General Sugar Company, and floated a $25 million stock issue to purchase the bum sugar loans from the bank. Then National City Company immediately wrote down its investment to $1. Sitting on the witness stand, Mitchell told investigators that "I hardly think there was any necessity" to inform investors on how the funds were to be used. National City later packaged up and sold other bond issues for other Cuban sugar companies of questionable financial standing.

In the midst of that crisis, National City came close to shutting down its foreign branches, as other foreign banks in Cuba wound up doing. Throughout the twenties and into the thirties, foreign exchange trading would provide the foundation for whatever success the foreign department enjoyed. In the twenties, the principal function of the foreign exchange department was to accommodate customers. Very few banks took currency positions. The dominant players were German and Swiss banks, and the major currency was pounds sterling.

There was at least one bright spot in that otherwise dreary year: in 1921, National City planted the seed for the "retail" business that would one day provide the bulk of its income. At the suggestion of muckraking New York newspaperman Roger Steffan, the bank established a "compound interest department" to handle savings accounts of as little as one dollar, becoming the first big U.S. commercial bank to offer interest-paying savings accounts. Depositors were paid interest on balances of five dollars or more. Several years later the bank began promoting passbook savings at its overseas branches.

Loan-sharking was rampant at the time, and New York State asked the banks to combat usury by making personal loans. In 1928, National City became the first and only bank to heed the call. It hired Steffan, who had written a series on the evils of loan-sharking, to head up a unit to make unsecured personal loans to individuals. Within a year, about two hundred other banks had established similar units. First as a newspaperman, then as a banker, Steffan was credited with breaking New York's loan-shark system. He believed in the basic willingness of small borrowers to repay their debt, and he operated successfully on instinct. "If I go into the Lexington Avenue subway and lend money to the first ten people I meet, eight will pay it back, the ninth I'll dun, and the tenth I'll write off," he used to say. By the 1930s, according to Citibank documents, Steffan supervised half of the personal loan business in New York City. National City later became the first bank in the New York area to offer consumer checking accounts without requiring a minimum balance. In 1928 the bank came out with yet another concept aimed at Main Street. It was called the mutual fund. But its days would be numbered.

The National City Company proved to be the bank's downfall. Though National City Bank was not alone among banks in operating a securities affiliate, it parted ways with the old elite Wall Street of J. P. Morgan by focusing on the small saver and investor. A sales force of two thousand brokers peddled often shaky securities to individuals, including National City Bank depositors, becoming the world's largest and most aggressive marketer of stocks and bonds. Brokers were highly motivated by the promise of fat bonuses and prizes, which were frequently announced in sales offices as "flashes." National City Company securities salesmen worked out of bank branches, where tellers signaled them whenever customers made large deposits. The salesmen would then buttonhole them and persuade them to use their savings to buy securities, extremely risky ones, as it turned out. National City Company was also the primary pusher and trader of National City Bank's own shares. Salesmen received commissions for selling the bank's stock, which reached $550 a share before the stock market crash of October 1929.

Insider dealings and conflicts of interest of all kinds were rampant at National City Company. Perhaps the worst instance involved dealings with Swedish "match king" Ivar Kreuger, who fraudulently perpetrated the myth that he was one of the world's richest men. The National City Company was one of the underwriters of some $100 million in Kreuger's bonds, while the bank was one of five creditors on millions more in loans. Percy Rockefeller, the elder Stillman's son-in-law, served as a director of both the National City Bank and Kreuger's International Match Company, which in fact was nothing more than a holding company for some ninety dummy entities. But by early 1932 it was becoming clear that the Kreuger interests were a massive international shell game. On March 12, 1932, as the real financial condition of the company leaked out, Kreuger shot himself to death in his Paris apartment. The company filed for bankruptcy, and Kreuger was revealed to have been a criminal rather than the financial genius he claimed to be.

After Cuba, one might have expected National City to take a cautious attitude toward Latin America, but that was not to be.

During the 1920s the National City Company led or participated in syndicates that underwrote approximately $750 million in mostly government-backed or -sponsored bonds for the nations of Latin America, principally Chile, Brazil, Peru, and Argentina. Germany was another big underwriting customer, representing from 1921 to 1929 about one-third of the affiliate's foreign activities. Investigators later revealed that National City Company helped underwrite $90 million in bonds for Peru, despite the finding by its own analysts that the country was grievously "careless in the fulfillment of its contractual obligations." A "gratuity" of $450,000 was made to the son of the president of Peru. The bonds defaulted in 1931, and by 1933 they were virtually worthless. National City, though well aware of the perils, also underwrote other issues. Among the deals that cratered was Vanderlip's pioneering Bolivian railroad bond issue. Although all the Bolivians with whom Vanderlip dealt, he wrote later, "inspired confidence" and the deal was done without "a dollar of graft," he later regretted the transactions, confessing that they were an "improper" activity for a bank. While bondholders received their interest, the Bolivian government defaulted on the principal. But National City apparently escaped unharmed.

By the late 1920s, some people were worried about the speculative fever that had gripped the market. One who wasn't, or at least didn't appear to be, was Charlie Mitchell. He was, after all, a speculator without peer. In his role as a director of the Federal Reserve Bank of New York, he assured officials that all the concern was unwarranted. In March of 1929, however, money began to tighten, and in a curtain-raiser for the main event, stocks tumbled.

On April 2, 1929, Mitchell succeeded Swenson as chairman of the bank. That same month, National City announced plans to merge with the Farmers' Loan and Trust Company [which was renamed City Bank Farmers Trust Company], a move that would provide Charlie Mitchell with yet another outlet for his Latin bonds. There were no Chinese walls, or walls of any kind, at Mitchell's National City. At least one branch housed not only the banking offices but also the offices of National City Company *and* the trust department.

Over the next several months, Mitchell helped keep the lid on the stock market with rosy public reassurances.

In mid-October, as the final countdown began for the crash of 1929, Mitchell declared that "the industrial condition of the United States is absolutely sound." On October 22, the day after prices took a nosedive, Mitchell told reporters that "the decline had gone too far." As the panic gathered momentum on "black Thursday," Mitchell and other top bankers huddled at the Broad Street headquarters of J. P. Morgan & Co., and Mitchell characterized the difficulty as "purely technical." Finally, on Tuesday, October 29, 1929, Mitchell, the man most associated with the era of excess and speculation, would have to eat his words.

Mitchell had yearned to combine National City Bank with the Corn Exchange Bank to preserve National City's status as the world's largest bank. He had virtually completed the deal, which was premised on a grossly inflated price of at least $450 per share. When the stock market bubble burst, National City's shares collapsed, and so did the merger.

For all of National City's problems and misdeeds, one writer of the era still referred to it as the "greatest bank in the Western Hemisphere." By 1930 National City's empire consisted of ninety-four overseas offices, about 40 percent of the total number of foreign offices operated by U.S. banks and trust companies. Mitchell created an overseas division that year, folding all but two International Banking Corporation branches into the new unit.

Nonetheless, National City lost its status as the world's largest bank that same year when Chase National combined with the Rockefeller-controlled Equitable Trust Company. With that transaction, Chase instantly was dubbed "the Rockefeller bank." John D. Rockefeller Jr. became the largest shareholder, and brother-in-law Winthrop Aldrich assumed the presidency under chairman Albert Wiggin.

The global house of cards continued to crumble with the turn of the decade. The Hawley-Smoot tariff legislation imposed severe levies on foreign imports, and one country after another responded in kind until world trade was virtually paralyzed. National City was stuck with $20 million in near-worthless Chilean paper when Germany triggered Chile's default with a crippling 120 percent tariff on nitrate imports.

Although National City had fueled the pre-crash frenzy, it suffered less than other banks in the wake of it. At least it survived, though barely. City Bank's problems weren't limited to foreign bonds, con artists, or corporate securities. There was what Wriston would later call "good old American real estate." National City eagerly participated in the real estate boom of the 1920s. One of its most visible—but ultimately not viable—properties was New York's Hippodrome, since 1905 a Midtown landmark and showplace for circuses, sports events, vaudeville acts, and other entertainment extravaganzas. Financed by John W. "Bet-a-Million" Gates, "the Hip" had cost $4 million to build. After acquiring it for $6 million in 1929, the new owners defaulted on their mortgage, forcing City Bank Farmers Trust Company to foreclose on it in 1932. It was demolished in 1939.

Although National City managed to stay afloat during the bank runs of the early 1930s, many of the bank's customers were burned when the Latin securities plummeted in value and National City stock sank to $20 a share. One of the biggest losers was Charlie Mitchell himself. Later, a congressional committee determined that half of the approximately $50 billion in stocks floated during the twenties were "undesirable or worthless."

In 1932 the Senate Banking Committee opened an investigation into the abuses that had helped trigger the Great Depression. But the investigation got nowhere until after the election of President Franklin Roosevelt, and the appointment of a determined Sicilian-born lawyer named Ferdinand Pecora to head the probe.

When public hearings got under way in February 1933, Charlie Mitchell, appropriately enough, was subpoenaed to be the first witness. Though Mitchell had handed over stacks of documents to Pecora, he took the stand confident that the investigators would be unable to pin anything on him. He was wrong. For openers, Pecora forced Mitchell to admit that in the late twenties he had sold stock at a loss to his wife to avoid paying income taxes on compensation that amounted to $25,000 in salary plus bonuses of more than $1 million per year. Each day, Pecora wrung out of Mitchell new, headline-making admissions of insider abuse, including details of the transactions that had bailed National City out of its Cuban problems. In Pecora, Pujo finally got his revenge. During the hearings, that prophetic solicitor general's report on securities affiliates, written twenty-two years earlier, finally became public.

Equally damning was the testimony of one National City customer, Edgar Brown of Pottsville, Pennsylvania, who recounted how a National City Company salesman had advised him that his investments in government bonds were "all wrong." The National City Bank and its affiliate had persuaded him not only to invest at least $100,000 of his own money with them but also to borrow and invest thousands more in what Pecora later described as "a bewildering array of Viennese, German, Greek, Peruvian, Chilean, Rhenish, Hungarian, and Irish government obligations" as well as U.S. corporate bonds. Adding insult to injury, National City had denied him a loan after the securities became worthless.

On February 27, 1933, just days after first taking the witness stand, Mitchell was forced to quit in disgrace. He was replaced by James Perkins, president of the City Bank Farmers Trust Company, who fully supported the separation of commercial and investment banking. A week after Mitchell's departure, Perkins dissolved the marriage between the National City Bank and the National City Company.

In some respects, Chase National was even greedier in those days than National City. In the days leading up to the crash, Mitchell had actually increased his National City holdings. In contrast, Chase chairman Albert Wiggin, called the "most popular banker on Wall Street," shorted Chase stock in the same period, so that he profited as the shares plunged. Compared with Wiggin, who retired in December 1932, Mitchell "looms up as an heroic and laudable figure," Pecora later wrote. Mitchell was indicted for tax evasion, but prosecutors were unable to make the charge stick. He spent the rest of his working life as chairman of the Wall Street firm of Blyth & Co., repaying his debts and back taxes and trying to redeem his reputation.

Even as Mitchell was testifying before the Senate Banking Committee, the banking system continued to crumble. Lines of frantic depositors seeking to withdraw their money stretched for blocks outside the nation's banks. On March 4, a week after Mitchell resigned, President Franklin Roosevelt was inaugurated, and two days later he declared a bank holiday, shutting down the nation's banking system for four days. On March 11, Roosevelt announced a timetable under which various categories of banks would be licensed to reopen. Many, however, closed their doors forever.

Charlie Mitchell turned out to be just the opening act in a drama that would play out for an entire year. Compared with Mitchell, J. P. Morgan Jr. got off easy at the hearings. He came across as a relatively cautious and prudent banker, but his appearance before Pecora and Company would be remembered as a symbol of the scandal for reasons unrelated to his own business activities. During his testimony, a public relations man wormed his way through the packed hearing room and set a circus midget down on the financier's lap. "I've got a grandson bigger than you," Morgan said paternally. "But I'm older," the midget responded. Realizing he'd been snookered, Morgan slid the midget off his knees as the flashbulbs exploded around him. For future generations of City Bankers, the midget on Morgan's knee would become a metaphor for the whole sordid episode.

In June, with the hearings still in progress, Congress passed the Banking Act of 1933, extending federal oversight of banking to all commercial banks for the first time. In large part because of the high-rolling activities of National City's securities affiliate, the legislation strictly separated commercial and investment banking. Under the portion of the bill known as the

Glass-Steagall Act, commercial bankers and investment bankers who had not already done so now had to give up either their deposit business or their underwriting business. J. P. Morgan, for one, split into Morgan Stanley & Co., the investment banking firm, and J. P. Morgan & Co., a private commercial bank.

With the establishment of the Federal Deposit Insurance Corporation and deposit insurance, the government spread a vast safety net under the industry, beginning its transformation from a carnival into a sedate public utility. The act also prohibited Fed member banks from paying interest on checking deposits and empowered the Fed to place ceilings on the rate of interest that member banks could pay on time and savings deposits. Two years later Congress extended those rules to cover institutions that were not Fed members. The goal of these restrictions was not to punish banks but to enable them to weather the Depression by keeping their interest payments low. The punishment would come later.

A barrage of other legislation followed. The Securities Act of 1933, also known as the Truth-in-Securities bill, called for disclosure of vital information on new debt and equity offerings. With the passage of the Securities Exchange Act of 1934, which extended the disclosure requirements to existing issues, the curtain finally fell on the Pecora hearings, and on one of the most dramatic and far-reaching episodes in American financial history.

Overnight, the role of National City and its fellow commercial banks in the nation's business and economic life was drastically diminished. In 1933 the National City Bank was forced to write down a massive portion of its capital and to crawl to the newly created Reconstruction Finance Corporation for an emergency loan. With the black cloud of the crash of 1929 and the Pecora hearings hovering over them, National City and American banking would go into a deep sleep, from which they would not awake for decades.

It was now up to Perkins to begin to repair the damage Charlie Mitchell had inflicted. Appropriately enough, Perkins's temperament was quite the opposite of Mitchell's. A low-key, informal man, Perkins "looked like and acted like a New England farmer," as one colleague put it later. Ironically, Perkins had had a hand in hiring Mitchell to run the National City Company back in 1916. But according to another future chairman named George Stevens Moore, Perkins said in a memo that Mitchell was too much of a salesman and should under no circumstances be allowed to be the boss.

With loan demand virtually nil, National City would become largely a repository for government securities. Well into the forties, bank officers would spend most of their time collecting slow loans rather than making new ones.

Fortunately, Mitchell had resisted the temptation back in 1921 to dissolve the overseas operations. When Perkins took over, he also made the pivotal decision to hold on to the overseas operations. During the Depression, National City was able to maintain its dividend only because of some $7 million in profits—about 40 percent of the gross earnings of the overseas network—generated by its Chinese branches, mostly from silver trading and speculation. Even after the Japanese invaded Manchuria in 1931, the bank's Chinese branches continued to operate, albeit at a reduced level. In the late 1930s, when Japan invaded the rest of China, the noose began to tighten.

Just before the outbreak of World War II, National City operated one hundred offices around the world. But by 1942 the war had forced National City to shut down most of its offices in Asia, including all of the Chinese branches, and all of its European branches except for the one in London.

By the time Wriston arrived at National City in 1946, the phrase "banking business" was an oxymoron. The Depression-era legislation had reinstilled public confidence in the banking system, but at a steep price. With its guts kicked out of it, the humbled American banking system lacked any inclination toward risk-taking or innovation. Heavy government regulation coupled with low and relatively stable interest rates made for an industry that could be mastered by nearly anyone who could add, subtract, multiply, and divide, as Wriston put it later. "Banking was a kind of a nice club," he said. "You had your inventories under control because the government told you how much you could pay on deposits."

Bankers of the day operated according to what was only half-jokingly referred to as the "three-six-three rule: borrow at three, lend to the Federal Reserve at six, and get to the golf course at three." The National City Bank of the mid-1940s was less a bank than a bond portfolio. Of its total $5.59 billion in assets, National City held $2.93 billion in U.S. government obligations and just $1.24 billion in loans. Although it might have been patriotic to help finance the nation's war debt, it certainly required little or no banking skill. Bank profits in the forties were not large, but they were virtually guaranteed. In fact, the measure of prestige was the size of the balance sheet rather than earnings, which were reported just once a year.

The debacles of the previous quarter century could not help but instill caution in the minds of lenders in general and in the minds of those at National City in particular. They had spent years collecting troubled loans and had seen their institution nearly destroyed by wild and woolly underwriting practices. Bank loans were mostly short term (under one year) and self-liquidating, and they were used to finance trade, inventory, and receivables. Term loans—loans of more than one year to finance things like factories and acquisitions—had been used in the thirties and forties, but until well into the fifties they were viewed with skepticism by risk-averse bankers who still carried the scars of the Depression.

Lending policy at Citibank reflected the experience of the 1930s. No loan could be made without the signatures of three officers. If a loan request exceeded a certain level, it might require the approval of a more senior officer and a review by the credit policy committee. Federal banking law allowed the bank to lend a single customer an amount equal to 10 percent of its capital, but a request for any amount over 5 percent triggered intense scrutiny at the highest management levels at the bank. In the wake of the real estate debacle, the bank imposed tough controls on real estate lending. Before National City could make a short-term construction loan, financing from a long-term lender, such as an insurance company, had to be firmly in place.

Federal and state banking laws sharply restricted where banks could operate. Concerned that banks like National City and Bank of America would try to expand across the country, Congress in 1927 passed the McFadden Act, which blocked them from establishing banking offices (taking deposits and making loans) outside their home state unless they were expressly permitted to do so by state law.

Historically, banking laws evolved differently from state to state; the most visible differences are seen in the rules governing a bank's ability to open branches within the state. In fact, when Wriston came on board, New York State banking laws confined New York City–based banks like National City to the five boroughs. In an interview years later, Wriston summed up the history of U.S. banking in a few sentences: "The country was settled with the wagon train. Every time the train stopped, four guys got off, built a city and started a bank. That's why you've got fourteen thousand banks in this country, the only country in the world without nationwide banking."

And of course banks wouldn't dare to even *think* about underwriting corporate securities.

In the quarter century that followed World War II, the world financial system itself would operate under a similarly rigid set of rules and guidelines based on the supremacy of the United States and of the dollar in the global economy. In 1944, with an Allied victory on the horizon, the financial leaders of the free world met at Bretton Woods, New Hampshire, to shape the postwar financial order. There they created the International Monetary Fund, which would extend short-term credit to member states to remedy balance-of-payments difficulties, and the World Bank, which would make long-term loans for projects such as roads, power plants, and agriculture in the developing world. Under the Bretton Woods system, currencies would be pegged to the U.S. dollar at fixed rates.

The conservatism of the New York City commercial banks was also reflected in their personnel practices. They were a bastion of white Anglo-Saxon Protestant males. Jews and Catholics were virtually unknown. College-educated women could not hope for employment other than as secretaries or clerks. And blacks worked only as porters. The bluest of the blue blood institutions was the First National Bank, the bank of J. P. Morgan crony George Baker. National City was not much more egalitarian. "First National was a New England Protestant bank and National City was an American Protestant bank," said management guru Peter Drucker. The standing joke in New York banking circles at the time was "What's the difference between First National and National City?" Answer: "At First National you come from Boston." A bank officer's personal behavior was a matter of institutional interest in the 1940s. Divorce, for example, was grounds for termination.

Perhaps for good reason, postwar National City Bank maintained a low public profile, even in its advertising, which was aimed at creating an image of strength and security rather than at promoting or selling any particular service. After all, it was sales and promotion that got the bank into trouble in the first place.

In one sense, Wriston arrived at National City at the perfect moment. In 1946 bankers were either very young or very old. Thousands of banks had failed during the Depression, putting tens of thousands of bankers out of work. Banks that managed to stay afloat did little or no hiring and tried to avoid firing employees because their prospects for employment elsewhere were virtually nonexistent. Any bright person with a choice between accepting a job at an industrial firm or at a bank invariably chose the former. By 1946, that policy had left banks with an oversupply of older officers.

The leadership of National City Bank when Wriston reported for work was as odd a mix of personalities as one could find in American banking. National City prided itself on its home-grown management, in contrast to other banks, which often pirated top talent from their competitors. City was now headed by Gordon Rentschler, the scion of an Ohio sugar equipment manufacturing family, who had helped rescue the bank from the disastrous Cuban sugar loans of the 1920s. Two years later Rentschler died suddenly and was succeeded by National City president William Gage "Iron Duke" Brady Jr., a rough-hewn, abrasive Brooklynite who parted his slicked-down hair in the middle like a pool player and spoke with the accent of his native borough. To his credit, Brady dispensed discipline without fear or favor. According to Peter Grace, chairman of the W. R. Grace Company and for many years a National City Bank director, Brady, an officer of an elite country club in the Hamptons, censured the late Henry Ford II for getting drunk and scrawling graffiti with a lipstick on club property. Ford Motor later rejected Grace's attempts to win the automaker's account for National City.

Waiting in the wings were Howard Sheperd, an enormously popular traditional banker, and taciturn James Stillman Rockefeller, the grandson of James Stillman and William G. Rockefeller. On July 7, 1924, after he'd graduated Phi Beta Kappa from Yale, a photograph of the sinewy young Rockefeller graced the cover of *Time* magazine as captain of the Yale crew team, which was setting off to France to capture an Olympic title for the United States. After his victorious return, Rockefeller spent six years at the stuffy Wall Street banking firm of Brown Brothers Harriman before joining National City in 1930. (At Brown Brothers, a top officer had told him he had no future as a banker.)

In 1946 Chase National was, and for the next twenty-five years it would remain, New York's premier banking institution, so much so that Wriston's acquaintances frequently asked him why he hooked up with a "second-class outfit." Founded in 1877, Chase National was the nation's largest commercial bank, with $6.10 billion in assets at the end of 1945. Close behind were Bank of America and National City. Chase's rank was due largely to its key wartime role in the U.S. Treasury's war loan program, which had boosted deposits by $1.25 billion by the end of 1945. By early 1947, however, those funds had shrunk to about 10 percent of that level, leaving Chase in third place behind Bank of America and National City.

Although National City and Manufacturers Trust could claim more branches, personal loans, and savings deposits, Chase enjoyed a national reputation and unsurpassed prestige. For as long as anyone could remember, a line graph had hung in the Citibank boardroom showing deposits at National City, Chase, and the other New York banks going back to 1860. The graph reflected, at least in part, the rivalry between the two sides of the Rockefeller clan that dominated the two banks.

Banking was an industry, and National City an institution, just waiting for the arrival of Walter Wriston. Almost from his first day on the job, he and the status quo were on a collision course.

Wriston's assignment as a junior inspector at the still humble and ultra-cautious National City Bank was an improbable one, given his education, work history, and intelligence. The most prestigious slots were traineeships in the domestic division, which catered to America's largest corporations. They were usually offered to Harvard, Yale, and Williams men with low golf handicaps and fathers whose companies kept large deposits with the bank. The domestic division, Wriston said later, was clearly "the place to be." According to one Wriston contemporary, he was not considered "pretty enough" for the rarefied world of corporate banking. In fact, Wriston said later that he was one of only two college graduates in the entire comptroller's division— the other was comptroller Rowland Hughes.

Wriston's assignment to the less than glamorous unit had something to do with the fact that Hughes was yet another member of National City's Brown University mafia. A bear of a man who wore a patch over his right eye, he headed the department later known as auditing, which was responsible for keeping the bank honest, solvent, and reasonably efficient. Though it lacked the visibility of the credit departments, there was no better place for Wriston to learn how money moved in a big bank, and there was no better man to show him the ropes than Hughes, whom Wriston would come to regard as one of banking's "greatest geniuses." Known for his serious, calm demeanor, Hughes, nearly fifty in 1946, had joined National City in 1917 after graduating from Brown and had spent ten years working for the bank in the Far East before joining the comptroller's unit. As comptroller, he earned a national reputation as a tax and budget expert, and in 1954 he was appointed U.S. budget director by President Eisenhower. If Wriston felt any disappointment that the comptroller's office was not the "in" place, he could take comfort in two facts: that Hughes was considered among the best in his business; and that Stillman Rockefeller himself had been assigned to the division when he joined the National City Bank, probably because he was incapable of carrying on a conversation with a customer.

With the hiring of Wriston and the other trainees of 1946 and with the return of war veterans to their old jobs, the National City Bank would begin to be shaken out of its old ways.

Having risked their lives on the battlefields of Europe and Asia, the returning GIs had little patience with the silly bureaucratic conventions perpetuated by those who had stayed behind. Wriston himself was once slapped with a written reprimand for reading the *Wall Street Journal* at his desk. On another occasion, when he reported to work wearing a button-down shirt, he was ordered to go home and replace it with a stiff detachable collar. Men were required to wear black shoes at all times. The hero of this group of no-nonsense young veterans, Wriston recalls, was an independently wealthy man who refused to bow to Iron Duke Brady's sartorial tastes. "You're wearing a bow tie," the mustachioed bank president said, cornering the young trainee in a corridor. "You know I don't like bow ties."

"I guess that's why I'm wearing one and you're not," the young banker shot back.

Lewis B. "Buzz" Cuyler, a Princeton-educated army air force veteran in his mid-forties who had joined Citibank before the war, hobbled into the bank after V-J day with a cast on his broken leg, an injury received in a parachute landing. Brady greeted Cuyler warmly on his return. But Cuyler had a blunt message for the boss, one that in Wriston's view would largely shape the way the bank hired and rewarded its people from that day forward.

"Welcome back, Buzz, nice to have you back," Brady is said to have told Cuyler.

"I don't know if I'm coming back," Cuyler replied icily.

"Why not?" Brady asked.

"If you want me to come back, you have to give me the authority to hire people and pay them the same money General Motors and Du Pont pay."

"That's ridiculous. It's an honor to work for the Citibank."

"It may be an honor, but it's a tough world out there. Good-bye."

To Brady's credit, Wriston said later, he beckoned Cuyler back and met his demands. Cuyler's astute hiring as personnel manager enabled Citibank to more than hold its own in the competition for young talent, at least for another thirty years. Cuyler, Wriston said, "didn't know federal funds from the south end of the post office." He was a warm, avuncular man who was driven by a desire to hire bright people. Wriston later told the *New Yorker* that Cuyler "persuaded people on campuses that banks weren't a place to go to die." "We had these terrible classes," Wriston recalled, "where people would get up and say, 'You know, boys, you can never pay back Citibank for what Citibank will do for you.' " Seated with Wriston in the classroom were the first soldier to storm across Germany's Remagen Bridge, a P-38 fighter pilot, and a sailor who had spent twenty-four hours in shark-infested waters after his aircraft carrier sank beneath him. Such sermons didn't go over well, Wriston recalled, and no one sympathized more than Cuyler, who was regarded as the mother superior of the class.

Cuyler, said Wriston, changed the policy so as to allow men who had led companies or battalions to be spared "a little of the old soft soap and concentrate a little more on training and opportunity." In the real world of postwar corporate America, says Wriston, "that took a lot of courage." Almost from the day he landed at 55 Wall Street, Wriston challenged the status quo and questioned the rules, customs, and conventions of forties-era banking. His first immediate boss was thirty-one-year-old Charles Siebert, an inspector in the comptroller's department who had joined National City Bank as a clerk in 1931, right out of high school. In his fifteen years with the bank, he had risen to the point where he was in charge of inspecting safe deposit boxes in the bank's branch system, making sure, among other things, that rental payments had been collected and that every box was accounted for. Siebert wondered why an alumnus of Wesleyan and Fletcher had wound up in banking, much less in his department.

On Wriston's first day on the job, Siebert and his new assistant set out to inspect the boxes at a branch in lower Manhattan, an assignment that did not square with Wriston's idea of banking. During the audit, the safe deposit manager sent out for ice cream for himself and his visitors, prompting Wriston to question whether they would be guilty of a conflict of interest if they ate it. They ate it.

For nearly two years, Wriston spent most of his time auditing branches, a boring and exhausting two-day exercise that called for reconciling, or "proving," a branch's demand deposit accounts, stuffing the statements and canceled checks into envelopes, licking the stamps and seeing to it that the statements were mailed. But it allowed Wriston to see the guts of the bank from the inside. He audited every department at 55 Wall Street and personally took responsibility for closing the bank's books. He also got a firsthand look at all of the bank's bum loans, among the worst of which were the real estate loans made in the heyday of the twenties. But Wriston also learned that yesterday's disaster could become tomorrow's recovery.

One of his duties was to compile a comptroller's report, a task that called for Wriston and his colleagues to work through the night in a room at Brooklyn's Saint George Hotel. Wriston would later recall returning to Manhattan by subway at three o'clock one snowy morning to drop off the report at Hughes's apartment. He discovered that warmth and hospitality were not Hughes's strong points. When Wriston rang the doorbell, a hand reached out, grabbed the report, and shut the door in his face without even inviting Wriston in to warm up.

Three months after he started, he received a call from an assistant secretary of state inviting him to return to Washington. Despite his misgivings about his bank job, he replied that he had promised to stay at National City for a year. The State Department official promised to check in with him in another nine months. Wriston was frustrated and impatient with the inefficiencies of the bank back offices of the 1940s, said his longtime friend Stephen Eyre, who worked as an inspector in the international division. "When Walter would ask, 'Why is something done this way?' the answer frequently was 'Because it's always been done that way.' That was like waving a red flag before a bull," Eyre said later.

"New ideas were not well received," said Wriston with characteristic understatement. During one audit, he told Siebert about a new machine that was being used at the Wall Street headquarters to stuff and stamp envelopes automatically. In what was perhaps his first attempt to apply state-of-the-art technology to back office operations, Wriston proposed to his boss that they carry the canceled checks to the main office for processing. That, he figured, "would save the bank a lot of money and a lot of dumb work," but that suggestion resulted in his being taken to the woodshed by Hughes himself. Wriston reminded the comptroller that messengers routinely transported unpaid checks through the streets to the New York Clearing House, adding that carrying paid checks is far less risky. During this discussion, it occurred to the young and impatient Walter Wriston that he was, in a sense, crossing the Rubicon in taking on the bank's veteran bean counter. "I must have been out of my mind," he said later. To Wriston's surprise and delight, however, the comptroller relented, albeit reluctantly, in the face of the irrefutable logic of Wriston's argument. "And that, says Wriston, is how we stopped this nonsense of stuffing statements in branches all night."

Wriston questioned everything. He pushed doggedly for whatever he believed to be a good idea, and if he had a flaw, said Siebert later, it was lack of political finesse. While Wriston was accepted and respected for his aggressiveness and innovativeness, his brusque and often chilly manner and social awkwardness did not win him any popularity contests. He did not mind stepping on the toes of veteran supervisors who had done things their way since the early 1900s. "He was not the placid type who would accept everything," said Siebert later.

"At that time, people were operating by outlines," Siebert said. "Wriston didn't operate by outlines." He believed that fools had made the rules and only fools followed them. Siebert rated his new charge exceptional on every measure of performance but one: in his relationships with other employees, he rated Wriston "high, but not tops." Siebert said later, "I thought Walter would be part of senior management."

The world of a branch inspector in the 1940s was a far cry from the intellectual ferment Wriston had known as a youth sitting at the family dinner table in Appleton. When he wanted ferment, intellectual *and* emotional, Wriston needed only to visit his father at Brown University. On May 15, 1947, just over a year after his mother's death, the parents of Marguerite Woodworth, dean of women at Oberlin College, announced their daughter's engagement to Henry Merritt Wriston, whom she had met while serving as dean of women at Lawrence. The wedding would take place in late June. Peggy Woodworth's credentials were nearly as impressive as Henry's. A graduate of Syracuse University, she studied at Columbia, Oxford, and the Sorbonne. Walter, however, was not impressed. He was outraged. He berated his father for his insensitivity in remarrying before the soil over his mother's grave had even settled.

His anger apparently did not stop him from spending the long commencement weekend in Providence with his father and sister, however. That Monday, June 16, 1947, General George Marshall, who had served as U.S. Army chief of staff during the war and was now secretary of state, was scheduled to receive an honorary degree, one of only three that he had accepted out of more than two dozen he had been offered that year. While Henry Wriston was delighted to have snared Marshall, he undoubtedly would have wished that Marshall had chosen Brown, instead of Harvard, to deliver his historic June 5 speech proposing massive aid to rebuild war-ravaged Europe—soon to be known as the Marshall Plan. After picking up an honorary degree from Amherst, General Marshall arrived in Providence to spend Sunday evening with Dr. Wriston, Walter, and Barbara at the president's residence.

Barbara was a bit nervous about what to say and how to act around the great man. But Dr. Wriston assured her, "Either he'll be as easy as an old shoe or it doesn't matter." He turned out to be an old shoe. For dessert that evening, Barbara served gobs of coffee ice cream, Dr. Wriston's favorite and, it turned out, the general's favorite as well; Marshall remarked to other guests that Barbara must have done much research on his culinary preferences. The next morning, hours before the commencement ceremony, the general could hardly keep his eyes open. It turned out he had stayed up late into the night reading *A Pioneer's Odyssey,* by Walter's grandmother, Jennie Wriston.

About two weeks later, Walter, despite his objections to his father's marriage plans, served as best man at a quiet family wedding ceremony performed by the Reverend Henry Lincoln Wriston at his home in Hingham, Massachusetts. Henry Wriston's decision to remarry so soon after his first wife's death toppled him from the lofty pedestal on which he had stood in his son's eyes and soured their relationship for quite some time.

Bobby was the force for understanding and reconciliation. Only at her urging did Wriston finally accept his stepmother as the new Mrs. Henry Wriston. "Bobby's attitude to Peggy was hugging and accepting," said Richard Brengle.

"I was wrong," Wriston admitted later. "The only saving grace is that I recovered from that stupidity with relative rapidity. Children somehow think that when one parent goes, the other should live a life of celibacy to please them. It's 100 percent wrong, and 100 percent human." Almost exactly twenty years later he would find himself in the same position as his father.

Back in New York, Wriston and Bobby struggled to make ends meet on his meager bank salary, a struggle made even more difficult with the birth on December 8, 1947, of Catherine "Cassy" Wriston. During Bobby's pregnancy, Wriston was working out of a branch across the street from his apartment, and the couple communicated with each other through the window. Bobby went into labor while sitting on the windowsill, and notified her husband with frantic hand motions that it was time to head for the hospital. Despite the financial strain, the birth of a daughter was a welcome and joyous event for the Wristons, coming as it did after several miscarriages.

Early on, Siebert said, Wriston voiced disappointment at what he regarded as the slow progress of his career, the lack of opportunity to further his education as a banker, and the difficulty of supporting a family on sixty dollars a week. Things were so tight that when the Wristons brought Cassy home from the hospital, they used a freestanding bureau drawer as a cradle until they could afford to buy a crib.

Wriston's sole indulgence during this period was custom-made suits, more the result of his gangly physique than of his taste for fine clothes. Chided by a close friend for buying hand-tailored suits, Wriston replied, "When you're [built like] an orangutang you've got to."

Walter's first significant career move occurred some eighteen months after he joined the bank. His advancement to senior inspector required him to satisfactorily complete a branch audit that proved to be a treasure trove of examples of how a branch should not be run. In his audit, Wriston uncovered sloppy procedures in the management and protection of the cash, findings that pointed to serious errors by the branch's chief clerk. The clerk accused Wriston and Siebert of fabricating the exceptions. He was later forced into early retirement, but not without a fight. Bank guards had to remove him bodily from his desk.

Small triumphs notwithstanding, after some two years of counting cash and stuffing envelopes, Wriston concluded that he was the only member of the class of 1946 who had not climbed to the first rung of the officer ladder, a hierarchy modeled closely after the military chain of command. "I was still looking at the secret code [designation] of the branch I was going to audit tomorrow morning," recalled Wriston.

Those early years at National City were frustrating for Walter Wriston. He was not inclined to unburden himself to family, friends, or colleagues, but it was clear to all that his lack of visible progress gnawed at him. "What does one have to do to get a promotion around here?" Wriston asked his associates. Promotions weren't easy to come by in the years immediately after the war. In those days it was not unusual to work for thirty years before becoming an assistant cashier, the first step in the officer's career ladder. In later years, appointment to a vice presidency would be rendered nearly meaningless by title inflation, and vice presidencies would be handed out with the same abandon as degrees at a mail-order diploma mill, but in Wriston's early years they were hard to win.

According to friends, family, and colleagues, Wriston's failure to get promoted stemmed from a certain social awkwardness and personal insecurity. He was, said a friend, aloof, reserved, and even a bit frightened. "He has a difficult time being easy with people, putting his arm around someone," his friend Barrett Emmerts said. Nor was he one to boast about his achievements.

In the hail-fellow-well-met atmosphere of mid-twentieth-century banking, when being a good banker called for a respectable golf handicap, Wriston was the odd man out—a terrible golfer who lacked the ability to schmooze. What Wriston lacked as a golfer, however, he made up for as a poker player. Siebert, Wriston, and other inspectors would occasionally gather at Wriston's apartment for an evening of card playing accompanied by jazz and big band music from Wriston's extensive record collection.

Fortunately, National City required that employees be interviewed once a year as part of a performance review, so Wriston met with a personnel officer for the review. When the officer asked him how he thought he was faring, Wriston said, "I'm doing poorly." The personnel man asked him why he thought he was doing poorly and Wriston replied that he had not yet been made an officer. The conversation was supposed to be confidential, but when Wriston returned to his desk the phone was ringing. It was Rowland Hughes demanding to know why Wriston was unhappy. "That sure tells me how confidential those talks in personnel are," Wriston fumed.

"Never mind that. You're doing a fine job. Why didn't you come to talk to me?"

"You never asked," Wriston replied.

Wriston later unburdened himself to personnel chief Buzz Cuyler, the man who saved Wriston for the National City Bank and the American banking industry. After explaining that his job had become unbearably repetitive and that the training program wasn't challenging enough, Wriston offered Cuyler his resignation. Cuyler asked him what he would like to do. Wriston said he wanted to immerse himself in the guts of banking: credit. "That's what a bank is all about," he said.

Cuyler immediately told president Howard Sheperd that he had a trainee who was capable of moving faster. He asked for authorization to set up his own program for trainees who were on the fast track.

In contrast to Brady, Howard "Shep" Sheperd, who later succeeded Brady as chairman, was a warm, personable man, whom Wriston would later credit with restoring to the bank the luster it had lost in the 1930s. He was, said Wriston, an "Indiana Hoosier who was the only chairman who could have won a popular election." Sheperd was admired as well for his tough, commonsense approach to lending money. His guiding principle was that "You can't do good business with bad people and you can't get hurt with good people," Wriston recounted later. "That's all there is to know." Referring to the troubles Citicorp got into in the eighties, Wriston added, "Some guys have forgotten that lately."

But Sheperd was skeptical of Cuyler's plan. He wanted the bank's policy committee to approve the trainees first. Sheperd asked Cuyler for the name of the trainee, suggesting that he meet with him personally. Cuyler begged off. "If we had a committee and if trainees felt they could only get places if somehow they got in touch with the chairman, I would lose all my clout," he said. Cuyler got the authority to set up a special program for Wriston and one other promising recruit. Sheperd, meanwhile, continued to press Cuyler for the name of this superstar, but Cuyler held his ground. "Someday you'll find out," he said.

In 1948, Wriston was placed under the protective wing of the bank's top credit officer, De Witt "Art" Forward, a man who lacked the common touch but was one of the most respected credit men in the United States. Under his tutelage, Wriston embarked on the study of what bankers call the three C's of credit: character, capacity, and collateral.

Wriston was assigned to a unit of the bank that received requests for credit from account officers. An account officer, for example, might call the credit unit for a ninety-day note for General Motors, and Wriston or one of his colleagues would write out a note, to be signed by GM, declaring that it promised to pay back the amount lent plus interest at the end of ninety days. But much of the work of the department was not so simple as that. Some requests called for credit analysts to conduct a comprehensive review of a company's financial condition and its ability to repay the loan. One of Wriston's duties was to analyze these financial statements.

The training given to would-be lenders such as Wriston included a course that covered most of the major lending debacles experienced by the bank in its modern history. It contained an example of nearly every way that a borrower could stiff his banker, and Wriston committed all of them to memory. The story of Match King Ivar Kreuger, for instance, made Wriston aware of the hazards of lending to holding companies. "I learned that all of the subsidiaries of a holding company had to close their books on the same day or they'd pass the marble under the hat," said Wriston later. He learned another valuable lesson from the tale of McKesson & Robbins, a big bankrupt wholesaler. "They had a big loan secured by a warehouse receipt," said Wriston. But then "somebody went to Canada and learned they had no warehouse."

In that class, said Wriston, "the names of the lending officers were changed to protect the innocent." But on occasion, a lender taking the course would break into a cold sweat as he realized that one of the case studies "looks just like the one we put on [the books] yesterday." In one such instance, Wriston and his colleagues were reviewing a loan National City had just extended in which it took a building on Manhattan's Upper East Side as collateral. One colleague said, "I live in that neighborhood and there isn't any such building." Said Wriston later, "We went there and sure enough, there was no building." The Hippodrome was demolished in 1939, but it was still standing on the moribund loan list. By studying how properties like these wound up on the books, Wriston acquired a healthy skepticism of real estate loans. The course in flimflams, said Wriston later, "was a wonderful concept. Obviously they haven't been teaching that lately."

While working on the credit side of the National City Bank, Wriston experienced the first of several chilly receptions he would receive as he moved up in the hierarchy. For some reason, the manager of the department that analyzed the creditworthiness of branch customers virtually slammed the door in Wriston's face, so he moved on to the unit that investigated the statements made by customers in order to get loans.

The investigations unit is a banking institution's detective bureau. A credit investigator, at least back in the days when money was not shoveled out the door for the asking, was a kind of financial sleuth who scrupulously checked references, queried accountants, and visited a customer's place of business. Wriston's boss in credit investigations was a man who "could find out anything about anybody in the world," said Wriston later. Despite his law degree and his uncanny ability to ferret out information about credit seekers, the man was stuck in place because of one fatal flaw: his unattractive appearance. But no one taught the future chairman of Citibank more about how to spot the dogs. In his stint as a credit investigator, Wriston traveled throughout the five boroughs of New York City applying the lessons of his credit training, "asking people about people," he said, and "asking whether the oil was in the tanks."

Nowhere in the bank was that skill more necessary than at Wriston's next stop, the fur district branch at Fifth Avenue and Twenty-eighth Street, in New York's garment district. That branch provided a baptism by fire for bankers. Many of its customers were marginal operators who needed to trim every possible corner just to stay afloat. "If you survive the fur district, you'll survive anywhere," a branch officer told Wriston. Wriston managed to survive. Before long, he was essentially running the branch's credit department. In that capacity, he had to serve a stint on the platform approving checks, making on-the-spot decisions about customers' creditworthiness. At the time, National City had a strong disincentive for officers to cash bad checks: the loss was taken out of their salary. Customers showed up at the branch with every kind of bizarre explanation and identification—one voluptuous high-fashion model offered her leather-bound portfolio of photographs. There Wriston became an expert at detecting flimflam—and cashed his first and only rubber check. "A guy came in with a chauffeur's license," Wriston recalled, "which even in those days had his picture on it," and presented a check purportedly drawn on a Greenwich Village bank. The check seemed legitimate and even included a phone number for the bank branch. Wriston called the number, asked if the customer had adequate funds, and was told he did, but "It bounced like an India rubber ball," Wriston said later. Wriston was stunned. He attempted to explain to his boss that the customer had "good identification."

"Son," his supervisor explained. "There is no good identification." The would-be customer had printed up his own checks, which he cashed with the help of an accomplice who answered the phone and swore that the money was in the account.

In 1949, about a year after Wriston had his heart-to-heart talk with Buzz Cuyler, he received a phone call at his desk at the Twenty-eighth Street branch from George S. Moore, a vice president in the bank's national division. Moore was unhappy with the shortage of good men joining the bank and had instructed the personnel chief to send him the file on every college graduate hired since the war's end. One of the files that had landed on his desk was Wriston's, and it included a statement by the comptroller that he was the brightest guy who had ever worked in the department. When Moore berated the personnel man for failing to alert him sooner, he replied sheepishly that he had promised the comptroller he would keep Wriston's performance a secret so that Moore wouldn't pluck him out of the department. "You look like a pretty smart guy, so you're coming to work for me tomorrow morning," Moore said to Wriston. So Walter reported once again to 55 Wall Street, where he was assigned to the bank's domestic credit division as an official assistant.

Born in 1905 in Hannibal, Missouri, Moore was the son of a claims inspector for the Burlington railroad. As a boy, he showed a remarkable bent for hard work and wheeling and dealing, earning his way by doing everything from selling honey and the *Saturday Evening Post* to working on a road crew. After attending Washington University in Saint Louis for a year, he transferred to Yale as a freshman on a Yale Club of Saint Louis scholarship, taking his zest for business with him. He helped put himself through school arranging tours of Europe and booking Broadway shows for fellow Yalies. He wrote for the *Yale Daily News* and earned $7,000, he claimed, cranking out thousands of words a day as a stringer for newspapers and wire services. In his senior year he cofounded *Yale Scientific Magazine.* Though he was a C student, he was voted most likely to succeed.

In his final year Moore was steered away from journalism and into banking by a banker who journeyed to Yale in search of the two seniors who had earned the most money as undergraduates. And so, upon graduation in 1927, Moore joined the Farmers' Loan and Trust Company, which merged with National City in April 1929.

Moore was on City Bank's fast track almost from day one. A man of boundless energy with a mind like an electronic calculator, Moore had a photographic memory for names and a seemingly natural inclination for leadership and deal-making. After the merger with the trust company, National City unearthed some bum loans in a Florida bank owned jointly by Farmers and Hanover Bank. James Perkins, then president of the City Bank Farmers Trust, sent Moore to Florida to clean up the mess. Later on, shortly after Perkins was named chairman, he appointed Moore as his assistant, giving him the chance to immerse himself in every facet of the bank's operations. Of Perkins, Moore would say that "hardly a day goes by that I don't refer to some bit of wisdom he gave me. Next to my mother, he influenced my life more than anybody." Moore later wrote that Perkins taught him that the "way to manage was not to give orders but to lead people." With Perkins as his mentor, Moore rose rapidly at National City, becoming a vice president in 1939 at the age of thirty-three, when bank vice presidents could still be counted on a few hands.

One of Perkins's few flaws, Moore once recalled, was that "he wasn't as tough as Moore" in dealing with weak employees. In contrast to Perkins, Moore himself claimed to have no problem firing an incompetent subordinate. "You have to be 10 percent s.o.b. to be a banker. Perkins didn't have one percent in him," said Moore later.

On a blind date, in 1938, Moore met Beatriz Bermejillo y Braniff, the daughter of the marquis de Mohernando, protocol chief for King Alfonso XIII of Spain, and the two were later married. There was little doubt that Moore was among the brainiest men ever to set foot in the National City Bank, but in the world of New York banking, it didn't hurt for this poor son of a Missouri railroad inspector to have found a rich wife.

George Moore was a driven man. He was "a cheerleader, inspirational kind of guy, lightning in a bottle," as a former City Banker put it. Wriston would later say that Moore "always regarded five hours of sleep as excessive." Certainly one of the principal driving forces behind him was an obsession with beating the Chase bank in every measure of success. Though other banks appeared on the boardroom chart, none of them really mattered to Moore except the Chase. Declines in National City's deposits relative to Chase turned Moore into a wild man. Wriston quickly caught the dump-on-Chase disease. Every time he saw brother-in-law Richard Brengle, who worked at National City's archrival, he asked him how things were going at the "pawnshop."

In the late thirties and throughout the forties, Moore also became a proponent of term loans, a radical departure from the ninety-day self-liquidating loans that had long been the bread and butter of banking. Term lending had gotten a boost in the Depression, when the market for public corporate issues dried up and the Federal Reserve pumped reserves into the banking system. After World War II, the practice grew dramatically.

Banks for years had been extending de facto term loans in the form of short-term loans made with the understanding that they would later be rolled over (renewed). During the Depression, however, both borrowers and lenders suffered severe losses when lenders panicked and refused to renew these short-term loans. Throughout the 1940s and into the 1950s, term lending remained a controversial issue—as controversial, perhaps, as junk bond financing became in the 1980s. According to one former senior officer, National City Bank officers in London in the late 1940s were "horrified" when New York forced the London branch to extend term loans denominated in sterling.

As time went by, the term loan grew in importance as a contributor to the bank's bottom line. Said George C. Scott, a future chief credit officer of the bank, who was often confused with the actor of the same name, "If banks were going to be the servant of corporations they had to make term loans."

In the late 1940s, Moore got what he called another "lucky break" when he was designated by then chairman William Gage Brady to chair a committee to examine the bank's operations from top to bottom and to formulate recommendations for improvement.

One of the bank's shortcomings was that it lacked divisional profit and loss statements. "Every division had their own little numbers they kept in a desk," said Moore later, which "added up to twice the earnings of the bank."

Divisions such as foreign exchange claimed to be making money, but none of them wanted to contribute any of those so-called earnings to corporate overhead to cover the cost of an economics department or even an annual stockholders meeting. In fact, said Moore, the overseas division questioned why the bank needed a shareholders meeting in the first place. Moore was later appointed head of the bank's domestic division because, as he put it, "They said, 'Moore's been recommending these things, so let him try it.' "

The phone call Walter Wriston received from George Moore marked the beginning of an often tumultuous relationship between the two men. It did not take Moore long to conclude that Wriston was one of the few people in the bank—besides himself, of course—who seemed to possess all the attributes he regarded as essential for top management. Moore would later agree that a banker's character should be contradictory; he must, said Moore, be a salesman who can say no. Difficult as it may be to find good salesmen and good analysts, Moore used to say that it is even tougher to find the good salesman who is also a good analyst. That man is worth ten times what either of the others is worth alone. And the man who can sell, analyze, and run a business is worth forty times the salary of the mere salesman or analyst.

Having realized that in Wriston he had discovered that rare mix of skills, Moore would see to it that Wriston succeeded him in every position he achieved at the National City Bank. "He was my boy," said Moore years later. "I raised him."

As a New York–based official assistant in the unit responsible for serving midwestern companies, Wriston was involved in corporate banking in ten states. There, his boss was a veteran banker named Robert Hoguet, a graduate of Harvard and the Harvard Business School who had joined National City in 1935 after a couple of years rehabilitating failed banks for the newly created Reconstruction Finance Corporation.

Hoguet quickly went to bat for more money for Wriston, claiming, "You're paying him nothing at all," and Moore agreed to raise his salary. Hoguet soon realized Wriston had great potential and went to Moore again a month later. Moore, he said, "looked at me as if I were nuts" but gave in once again. In the several months Wriston was in Hoguet's unit, Hoguet managed to secure three raises for him. "Wriston," he said, "was able to see the fundamental problem and didn't waste time."

Wriston had other allies who felt that his talents weren't adequately appreciated. Thomas Creamer, a former assistant to the president of MIT who was well acquainted with the Wriston lineage, told vice chairman Art Forward that if Wriston wasn't moved along more quickly, the bank would almost certainly lose him. Perhaps as a result, in 1950, Wriston moved on to a unit that handled commercial accounts based in Canada and New York. It was there that he finally got his promotion to assistant cashier.

One of Wriston's superiors at the time was a young assistant vice president named Tom Wilcox, a gregarious, charismatic man who earned the nickname "Atomic Tommy" because of his energetic, gung-ho disposition.

Wilcox had grown up in a family of modest means in Queens, New York, joined the bank before completing high school, earned his diploma in night school, and was sent to Princeton by the bank. Because of his ability to memorize large amounts of confidential information, Wilcox was selected by the State Department to be a diplomatic courier. Later, after serving in the navy in World War II, he rejoined National City. Wilcox and his pals thrived on the entertainment side of banking, the golf outings, ball games, and theater parties, and having a sharp analyst like Walter Wriston around to do the grunt work of the unit allowed him and his friends more time for such activities. "The work was all dumped on Wriston," said a former colleague. "They were merciless."

Wriston literally worked himself sick. He was often so stressed and exhausted from twelve-hour workdays that when he arrived home, he vomited and collapsed in bed to await the next day. In a gesture that Wriston would never forget, Wriston's boss, Robert MacFadden, lectured Wilcox and his colleagues sternly, ordering them to do more of the work themselves. "You've got a hell of a bright fellow here. You're not being fair," he told them. Wilcox, said a contemporary, saw Wriston as a future threat early on, but he would never admit that Wriston was a better man than he was.

The transfer to the Canadian district proved to be well worth the stress and suffering, however, if only because it provided an introduction to a short, stocky Greek shipowner who would dramatically alter the course and velocity of Wriston's career. His name was Aristotle Socrates Onassis.

3

PLANES, TRAINS, SHIPS, AND AUTOMOBILES

*B*y 1950, when Wriston was assigned to the Canadian district, Aristotle Onassis had been a customer of the National City Bank for more than twenty years, since his early days as an entrepreneur in Argentina. Onassis had fled to Buenos Aires in September 1923 when political turmoil engulfed his hometown of Smyrna, on the west coast of Turkey, after World War I. In Argentina, Onassis took his first plunge into business by pledging his wealthy father's bills of lading as security and borrowing $20,000 from National City's Buenos Aires branch to manufacture mild cigarettes that he thought would appeal to women.

It was almost inevitable that Onassis, as a Greek living in a thriving port city, would eventually be attracted to the shipping business. Rejecting the advice of friends, Onassis in 1931 salvaged and repaired a shipwrecked freighter, which sank in a storm not long after he refloated her. Undeterred, he shortly thereafter bought six small mothballed Canadian-built freighters for $20,000 each, two-thirds of the asking price. But for Greek shippers, it was tankers, not cargo ships, that had sex appeal. In 1938, Onassis christened his first tanker, the *Ariston,* and ordered two more even before the first one slid down the shipway. With the outbreak of war in Europe, two of his three tankers were immobilized in neutral Sweden, and one was commandeered by the Norwegian government. So Onassis had no choice but to devote his attention to his cargo fleet in Argentina.

Throughout the war, National City Bank lent substantial amounts of money to Onassis but kept him on a tight leash: his loans were secured with U.S. Treasury bills with a 10 percent cushion. Despite his growing fortune, borrowers still needed banks more than banks needed borrowers, and Onassis was forced to pace the vast ornate lobby of 55 Wall Street, hat in hand, while waiting to see Howard Sheperd, the man they called "the Pope."

Sheperd occupied the catbird seat, off to one side of the lobby, where he was surrounded by three junior officers seated at desks on either side of his. "Ari used to stand there and wait until Shep was free, and say 'I want to borrow a million dollars,' or some wild number," Wriston recalled. National

City could earn a decent return on risk-free government instruments and didn't need Onassis as much as he needed City.

At one point, Sheperd, concerned that Treasury bill prices would fall after the end of the war, as they had after World War I, informed Onassis that the 10 percent margin was too thin. Onassis stormed out of the bank in a huff. Half an hour later he was back, peering at Sheperd from behind one of the massive marble columns. Sheperd beckoned him to his desk and smoothed his ruffled feathers.

When the war ended, Onassis wasted no time in expanding his fleet, an effort that would be greatly facilitated by the passage of the Ship Sales Act of 1946, through which large numbers of tankers and cargo ships built during the war were put up for sale. Many more foreigners than Americans lined up to avail themselves of this once-in-a-lifetime maritime garage sale, among them Onassis and Stavros Niarchos, his brother-in-law and archrival in love and commerce.

Armed with contracts to transport coal to Europe and South America on sixteen war surplus Liberty ships, Onassis approached National City for a loan to buy the vessels. Having done business with Onassis for more than two decades, National City agreed, albeit reluctantly, to put up half the purchase price. Onassis thus became the first Greek to acquire ships with U.S. bank financing.

The real money, however, was in tankers, not dry cargo vessels. Trade was now flowing freely, but the war had decimated the tanker fleets of the major oil companies. With the world economy beginning to recover from the war, there was more oil to be moved than there were tankers and tankermen to move it. Onassis knew that the oil companies would gladly pay someone else, and pay him well, to haul their oil for them. Prior to World War II the oil companies had owned more than 60 percent of the world's tanker tonnage, while the independents had held the remainder. By 1957 that situation would exactly reverse itself. Onassis had his eye on the T-2 tankers. With a capacity of about 16,600 deadweight tons, the 523-foot-long T-2 was the workhorse of the oil trade, the seagoing equivalent of the DC-3. They were being sold at the fire sale price of just $1.5 million each. Trouble was, the 1946 Ship Sales Act reserved them exclusively for American citizens. But Onassis, like Wriston later, would stretch interpretations of the law in order to get business. With the blessing of the U.S. Maritime Administration, Onassis set up the United States Petroleum Carriers, a Delaware company whose majority stockholders were American citizens, and proceeded to snap up every T-2 he could lay his hands on. He even went so far as to make sure that his wife was in the United States when their children were born so that he would be able to, in effect, register the ships in their names and claim that the ships were owned by U.S. citizens.

Onassis had nature as well as clever lawyers on his side. Thanks to the frigid winter of 1947, the demand for fuel oil soared, and tanker rates along with it. By this time Onassis was "coining money," as one former City Banker put it later.

Onassis liked to do things on a big scale. There was no reason, he thought, why tankers couldn't be larger than 16,600 deadweight tons. On the strength of his proven success as an operator he was able to commission the construction of a tanker nearly twice as big: the 28,500-ton *Olympic Games.* Launched in the spring of 1948, it was to be the first of an entirely new class of supertankers. It would become a toy by later standards.

Financing was the only obstacle standing in the way of his stamping out these ships at an assembly-line pace. Onassis was a firm believer in using other people's money, so he asked Sheperd to lend him money to build his tankers based not on the market value of the tanker but on the cash flow that would be generated by chartering them to the major oil companies. Howard Sheperd admired Onassis's skill as a ship operator, and his unblemished record for repaying his loans, but at that time the National City Bank had hardly begun to get back into the lending business. During the late 1940s the bank had been dominated by conservative gray-haired lenders who had suffered through a depression and a war and for whom any deviation from tried and tested lending was heresy. Many of them felt that financing the likes of Onassis without the full protection of government securities was an unacceptable financial risk. Sheperd himself winced at the thought of making loans for terms of five or ten years. The only institutions that lent that kind of money were insurance companies. National City suggested that Onassis pay a visit to Walter Saunders and Harry Hagerty at the Metropolitan Life Insurance Company, a proud, conservative old-line insurer with headquarters in a landmark building on Madison Square.

Met Life was flush with funds to make long-term loans, but had no interest in short-term lending because the yields were too low. New York State insurance regulations limited insurance companies in how much of their assets they could invest overseas, but Onassis and his lawyers had a simple solution to that problem. He would pledge the charter of a U.S.-based company and borrow the money through a Delaware corporation, which in turn would lend it to a U.S. subsidiary. Under this arrangement, Met Life was delighted to commit $40 million in long-term money so that Ari could build his tankers. The Met, said Wriston later, "went gung-ho, flat out on ship loans."

Onassis still needed short-term money, however, so Walter Wriston was tapped to deal with him. He told Wriston that he had obtained a bareboat charter from Texaco and would pledge the charter to finance the construction of the ship that would transport the oil. The chairman of Texaco himself had attested to Onassis's honesty and competence as an operator.

Though it was not obvious to either man at the time, the proposal that Onassis brought to Wriston would not only launch scores of ships and generate enormous wealth for Onassis, but would also focus attention on Wriston as future top management material.

Tanker hulls had always been and would always be one of the world's most volatile assets. In the early 1950s, for example, a T-2 was worth less than $1 million, but in 1957, at the height of the Suez crisis, its value soared to $4 million and then, a year later, plummeted to $600,000. Nonetheless, Wriston trekked to the apartment of his father-in-law, George Brengle, several nights a week to learn from a top admiralty lawyer about the intricacies of bareboat and time charters, contracts of affreightment, and other maritime technicalities.

The method of financing using a charter as collateral was probably less controversial than the kinds of ships Onassis and his Greek competitors would now be able to build. Shortly after Onassis began dealing with Wriston, George Moore and Stillman Rockefeller received calls from the head of Bethlehem Steel, then the Tiffany's of the shipbuilding business. According to Hans Angermueller, a shipping lawyer with Shearman & Sterling, Citibank's principal law firm, who would later become vice chairman of the bank, the steel company spokesman told the bankers, "You've got a crazy man there who's going to finance a supertanker [to carry Texaco oil] that's going to break apart at the seams." Bethlehem Steel refused to get involved at all in the design of Onassis's early supertankers. Ari, said Wriston, had to find his own architect to design the ships. Nevertheless, Brengle finally conceded that the Texas bareboat charter was money in the bank. Texaco would pay the money to City, which would then deduct interest and principal and put the remainder in the shipowner's account. As a sort of window dressing, a senior bank officer insisted on Onassis's personal guarantee. But that, said Wriston later, "was sort of ridiculous."

Wriston worked with Onassis to perfect the details of a financing concept that was revolutionary at the time and would soon be used to underwrite other big-ticket items such as airplanes, railroad cars, trucks, and even high-rise office buildings. For apparently the first time, a lender relied on the cash-generating ability of a piece of property; in the past, a borrower had received a mortgage for the property based on its cost or appraised value. But such an approach often bore little relationship to the cash such an asset could generate and consequently constrained a borrower's ability to grow. Using this new method, Onassis could own his ship free and clear in seven years rather than at end of the ship's normal twenty-year life. Onassis thanked Wriston by presenting him with a large-scale rudderless model of the tanker *Olympic Games,* which Wriston displayed prominently in his office throughout his career at the bank.

With every passing year, the definition of a supertanker expanded, along with the sums of money National City and Metropolitan Life would lend to Onassis to build them. Thanks to quantum leaps in technology that strengthened steel manyfold, Onassis was by the mid-1960s able to launch yet another generation of 210,000-ton VLCCs—very large crude carriers—ships so big that the old *Olympic Games* could almost have been carried on their decks as a lifeboat.

With National City's short-term money and the Met's long-term loans, the two institutions, taken together, became the world's largest single source of ship financing. Soon, Stavros Niarchos and other Greek shipowners would find their way to Wriston, Saunders, and Hagerty, and other banks and insurance companies would seek a piece of the action. Prior to World War II the total volume of ship loans outstanding by all U.S. financial institutions was estimated at perhaps $100 million. By 1950, however, it had risen to about $250 million and, by the end of 1956, thanks in large part to National City, it had quintupled to $1.25 billion. At that point, Metropolitan Life held more than $500 million, National City $400 million, and Chase about $150 million.

Initially, recalled Thomas Lincoln, a Shearman & Sterling lawyer who later became Onassis's chief counsel, individual charters supported the construction of individual ships. Then groups of charters secured groups of ships. The lawyers then invented a collateral trust mortgage that combined the ships in a collateral pool which secured notes and bonds. This instrument enabled ten-year bonds to be issued on seven-year charters; staggering the charters enabled the debt to be easily serviced, even though the bonds were of longer duration than the charters. Moreover, these instruments eliminated the horrendous paperwork and legal time that would have been expended in issuing a mortgage for and keeping track of each individual ship. The idea was to make sure that the life of the charters essentially matched the life of the loans.

As a result of these early transactions, Wriston became the resident expert on ship financing, and National City the largest ship-financing bank in the world. The launching of a new Onassis tanker was always a cause for celebration. Early on, a number of the tankers were built by Bethlehem Steel, which obviously became comfortable with supertankers, at its Sparrow Point yard in Quincy, Massachusetts. Wriston recalls that Bethlehem's president customarily chartered a train to bring people up for the launching of a ship. "Fueled almost entirely with Scotch," Wriston recalled later, "they were blowouts like you couldn't believe."

All of this was made possible by the discovery by the likes of Onassis and Niarchos of flags of convenience. Although some of the ships were built in the United States, the vast majority were constructed overseas at less than half the cost of U.S. construction and were registered in countries like Liberia and Panama where the shipowners paid virtually no taxes on the charter income. So while Wriston was a key player in the ascendancy of the Greek shippers, he likewise contributed, perhaps unwittingly, to the demise of the American flag tanker fleet.

"You wouldn't have to be a brilliant person to make money in a business where you never paid taxes," said Joseph Doyle, a Shearman & Sterling lawyer who worked with Wriston on these transactions.

In their operating practices, the Greek shipowners were in many ways unconventional and unsophisticated, but the prominent ones were always good for their word, and for the money, and their family-owned operations eschewed formal management and business practices. Said Anne Meschino, a statistician in National City's shipping department in the 1950s and later the head of the New York shipping unit, "You could never get an audited statement out of a Greek." Yet they were, she said, color-blind and gender-blind. "It didn't faze them at all that I was a woman who had a Jew and a black working for me."

Ship financing, said Met Life financial analyst George Jenkins, "was very safe." Referring to the dual sources of repayment—the charter income and the value of the ship—he said, "You got a belt and suspenders to hold your pants up." The risks of ship lending, to the extent there were any, didn't faze Wriston. After all, taking risks on people and ideas ran in the Wriston family. If Walter Wriston didn't inherit that predisposition from his father, Dr. Henry Wriston certainly exposed him to it. But even though the risks and the losses proved to be minimal, ship lending required care and diligence. One lawyer recalled that Wriston, unlike most lenders, was not content to wash his hands of a deal once he'd turned it over to the lawyers for closing. "Watch which hat the pea is under," Wriston would warn. Attorney Joseph Doyle said later, "He wasn't there but he didn't want anyone to think he wasn't concerned."

However cool and self-assured Wriston would appear in his later career, as a young ship financier he was anything but. "He was a nervous young fellow," recalls Henry Harfield, a Shearman & Sterling lawyer who assisted Wriston in the legalities of letters of credit issued to guarantee the construction of the ships Wriston financed. On at least one occasion, there was serious doubt whether a backup letter of credit issued by a Japanese bank would get paid. Like expectant fathers in a maternity ward, Wriston and Harfield sat anxiously at the lawyer's desk waiting for the business day to begin in Japan. Wriston had sent irate cables to Japan that reflected, in Harfield's view, the enmity Wriston felt for the nation he had fought in World War II. "You lost one war. Stop. Do you want to start another one? Stop," the cable read. There was only one thing the two men could do while waiting for the sun to rise over Tokyo. Harfield pulled a bottle of bourbon from his bottom drawer and invited Wriston to take a couple of slugs to calm himself down. Although few people ever saw Wriston drink hard liquor, Harfield's bourbon had the intended effect, and the deal ultimately worked out.

The dealings between National City and Met Life weren't always harmonious, either. In one major Niarchos transaction, Wriston prepared exhaustive documentation and then issued a letter of credit to a shipyard in order to induce it to build a ship for Onassis's rival. Met Life had guaranteed the letter of credit to City Bank and had agreed to "take out," or replace, the construction financing of the ship. As things turned out, however, the letter of credit had to be called, National City was forced to pay, and Met Life was obligated to reimburse the bank. But when Wriston phoned the Met, he was told, "We don't think we'll pay out." Wriston was furious. He sprinted to the subway for the trip to Met headquarters, where he demanded that the insurer cut a check for $5 million on the spot.

Walter Saunders, the Met's ship financier, was virtually a one-man show, and at that time he was junketing, presumably with his shipowner clients, in Monte Carlo. The Met refused to write a check without his approval, and Wriston refused to leave Met Life without the money. "That's not the way a letter of credit works," he fumed. "We're an insurance company. We don't understand letters of credit," was a Met official's lame excuse. Wriston did not hesitate to call Saunders in the middle of the night in Monte Carlo, and he approved the payment. Wriston stuck the check in the headband of his hat and walked home, assuring his wife when he arrived that his job was safe—something that had not been a foregone conclusion earlier in the day.

Few business relationships would have more impact on the lives of the respective parties than that between Wriston and Onassis. Wriston became very fond of Onassis, whom he considered shrewd, imaginative, and very persuasive. And for pure fun and excitement, nothing—not even deliberating economic policy in the Oval Office with a succession of U.S. presidents—ever rivaled his early years working with the Greek shipper. Close as the relationship became, however, Wriston didn't give Onassis all that he wanted. "Onassis always wanted to borrow 110 percent of everything," former National City Bank chief credit officer George C. Scott said later. Wriston didn't turn Onassis down per se on a single request, but he sometimes insisted on terms that forced Onassis to turn him down. According to Scott, Wriston would agree to put up the bulk of the financing if Onassis gave him a lien on his gold holdings. That, of course, was unacceptable to the shipowner. Whatever his reputation as a womanizer and bon vivant, Onassis kept his word and paid his debts, secured or unsecured. "I never knew him to tell anything that wasn't true," Wriston said later.

National City had never been let down, and by the mid-fifties the bank didn't hesitate to extend to Onassis and other Greek shippers huge lines of credit to buy their ships without demanding that they assign a charter to the bank. They only had to agree not to pledge the ship for credit anywhere else.

Some of the loans, however, were put to controversial uses. Special industries division chief Robert Hoguet would later recall lending Onassis the money to buy a fleet of "fishing boats"—actually whaling ships—held by a dummy corporation, to harvest the waters off Peru. One morning, Hoguet picked up the morning paper and read that Peru had confiscated Onassis's fleet. When Hoguet arrived at his office, he found Onassis standing in the doorway. He then sat down at Hoguet's desk to write the check to pay off the loan.

Despite their professional friendship, however, socially Wriston and Onassis moved in different worlds. Wriston cultivated many narrowly focused friendships, whereas Onassis entertained many segments of world society. Nonetheless, in at least one instance, they came face to face through an apparent lapse in protocol and planning. After Onassis finished fitting out the yacht *Christina,* Wriston and Bobby were occasional guests when the sumptuous vessel tied up at a Hudson River pier. Bar stools upholstered with the soft white skin of the scrotum of an adult whale and footrests made of whale teeth were not exactly their style, but they always looked forward to their visits with Ari on the *Christina.* On one occasion, however, Wriston and Bobby appeared for dinner and realized immediately that something was amiss. Prince Rainier and Princess Grace were there, Wriston recalled, but the "rest of the folks were wild characters—the beautiful people from Cannes, Nice, and Monaco. I don't think I knew two of them." Onassis, who entertained different crowds on different nights, seemed to sense that something had gone wrong. Late that evening he came by and told the Wristons sheepishly, "Gee, I invited you guys on the wrong night."

In 1952, as a reward for his success with ship loans, Wriston was promoted to assistant vice president. At about this time, he moved from Stuyvesant Town, where he had lived since 1949, across the street to the slightly more upscale Peter Cooper Village. But even as he was showered with raises and promotions, Wriston clung to his tightfisted ways. Walter, Bobby, and Cassy, now five, personally hauled all their belongings across the street using Cassy's baby carriage as a moving van.

Among the other tenants of Peter Cooper Village and Stuyvesant Town were a number of struggling young actors who would later become household names: John Forsythe, James Whitmore, Tony Randall, and Karl Malden, who lived with his wife and children a few floors below the Wristons. While Wriston was doing shipping deals with Onassis, Malden was starring on Broadway in Eugene O'Neill's *Desire Under the Elms.* The two families became especially close. Malden once asked Wriston to figure out a way to smooth the cash flow of hard-pressed actors, a request that taxed the ability of even the most imaginative financier. Said Malden, "I had the feeling he was very inhibited. He was a very self-conscious kind of person." He added, "I think he is a very private man, really. He holds a lot in, and everybody knows a little bit of Walt but no one knows all of Walt."

At the end of 1952, with the retirement of chairman Brady, the top managers at National City all moved up a notch—Howard Sheperd to the chairmanship, Stillman Rockefeller to the presidency, and George Moore to the executive vice presidency in charge of the domestic division. The board was then faced with two critical problems: giving proper recognition to Art Forward's prodigious ability to make and collect loans, and finding a way to compensate for Stillman Rockefeller's reluctance or inability to carry on a conversation with a customer. Hoguet recalled that "Someone would say, 'I've got the chairman of Allis-Chalmers here.' And Rockefeller would reply, 'I don't have time for him.' "

To solve the first problem—recognizing Art Forward—the board created for him the post of chief credit officer, where he would reign as a kind of King Solomon over loan policy, serving as judge and jury in disputes over credit. To address the second problem—Rockefeller's silence—National City in 1953 appointed as vice chairman Richard Perkins, the engaging son of former chairman James Perkins, who had been working for Smith Barney as an investment banker. In 1951, eleven years after his father's death, he moved to City Bank Farmers Trust Company as executive vice president to help build its lackluster pension and trust business, and a year later became president. Though he had no training as a commercial banker, Perkins moved in the upper circles of American business and became a kind of roving ambassador for National City Bank. Despite his upper-crust origins, Perkins, like his father, was a down-to-earth, unpretentious man. "They needed someone who could talk to people, so they got Perkins," said Wriston later. Rockefeller apparently wasn't pleased, but George Moore was downright furious that someone whom he regarded as less capable than himself would be brought in from the outside and placed over him. Moore later said that he tried to pacify himself with the words of one of his superiors, who told him, "If you're going to jump off the pier every time a great organization doesn't do [things] exactly the way you want, you'll drown someday."

Wriston admired Stillman Rockefeller for his administrative skills and credit judgment, but he had misgivings about other traits. He viewed Rockefeller as an insensitive man whose management decisions reflected his personal prejudices against minorities. "He's a funny guy, this Rockefeller," Wriston once remarked to a colleague. He then told of how Rockefeller had lowered the flag on the grounds of the family's Greenwich, Connecticut, estate to half-mast during the wedding reception for one of his daughters because he didn't care for her new husband.

On one occasion, at a dinner for domestic division officers at the University Club in Manhattan, Rockefeller horrified his colleagues by denigrating a well-regarded officer, a man with a huge family, who a week or so earlier had collapsed and died at his desk. Mocking the deceased man, Rockefeller put his hand in his vest, let his head droop against the wall, and proclaimed, "I have no use for anyone who pulls their cork before the end of the race," Wriston remembered.

One of the classical debates in American banking pits industry specialists against territorial calling officers. George Moore had always envied the industry expertise at rival First National Bank of Chicago, and proposed that certain key industries, including transportation, oil and gas, and public utilities, be pulled out of geographic districts and placed together in a special industries division. The advantages of such an arrangement at National City were compelling. Just as Onassis was handled by the Canadian district, the Scandinavian Airline System was served by the same officer at a Midtown branch who handled the Christmas Club and passbook savings accounts of hundreds of small depositors.

Although the Greek shippers encouraged National City to set up a specialized department, the near loss of SAS as a customer was the final blow to the old order. SAS was seeking to finance a new generation of airplanes, and it was clear that the man on the platform at one Midtown branch was not up to the task. "The manager of the branch was a nice fellow but didn't have the slightest idea about available seat miles," Wriston recalled. SAS put it to National City bluntly. "This guy's a nice guy. We have lunch at '21,' " the SAS executive said. "But do you want our business?"

The change from geographic districts to a special division was the first major restructuring in the bank's postwar history. It also "tore the organization apart," Wriston said. In later years Wriston himself would preside over many more restructurings that would have an even more drastic effect.

The districting issue was thrashed out in a heated meeting in 1953, presided over by president Stillman Rockefeller, at the University Club. At that time, all the key players could fit into one small room. "There was very great resistance to that [the reorganization] by everybody," Wriston said. Two typical comments: "Chicago is my area" and "What do you *mean* Ed White's going to call on Chicago Light and Power and Wriston is going to call on Santa Fe Railroad?" The branches also lost big accounts. The move toward specialization and away from geography would once again pit Wriston against Tom Wilcox, a branch officer who had been, and would continue to be, his nemesis.

Specialization was the route National City had to take, but the way the news was put out was a lesson in how not to handle a major reorganization. "Word filtered down one Christmas Eve that something was afoot," Wriston said later. "But little effort was made to notify all the personnel involved."

The special industries group was inaugurated on January 1, 1954, and Wriston transferred from the Canadian district into a new transportation unit that was part of it. His marching orders were essentially to finance anything that flew, floated, or rolled—in short, anything that moved. For all of its organizational disarray, the National City Bank was still arguably the leading financier of ships, planes, cars, and railroads in the United States. It had provided more than money. As head of the bank's Middle Western district, George Moore, for example, had played a major role in the move by Greyhound Bus Lines to integrate its many, and often ill-managed, regional operations into a national carrier.

City Bank had long-standing dealings, some of them not so savory, with U.S. airlines and aircraft manufacturers dating back to the days when Charlie Mitchell et al. routinely traded on their shares using insider information. Even after the old United Aircraft & Transport was forced to split up, National City retained ties to each of the pieces: Boeing, United Airlines, and United Aircraft. Chairman Howard Sheperd, for example, was a United Aircraft director, National City was their primary bank, and Shearman & Sterling their principal lawyers. Now, with the creation of the transportation unit, however, National City would be the undisputed leader in transportation financing.

Shortly after the unit was organized, Wriston was once again butting heads with Wilcox. When Wriston called on the Boeing Company in Seattle he was taken aback by the greeting he received from the company's treasurer: "You're the technician Tom Wilcox said was going to come around to see me." Wriston replied, "I don't know if I'm a technician, but I'm the one responsible for your account."

"Some of the geographic guys—Tom was one of them—didn't ever want to admit that they weren't all things to all people," Wriston said later.

Wriston, still an assistant vice president, did not appear on the masthead as the unit's chief. That honor was bestowed on a vice president named Nicholas Vancil, a courtly fuddy-duddy who had acquired a virtually encylopedic knowledge of anything and everything related to railroads, but the choice turned out to be a poor one. No one knew railroads like Vancil, but railroads were *all* that Vancil knew. At one time, nearly every mile of railroad track in America was financed with a special bond issue, and Vancil knew all of them by heart. But in his long career with National City, Vancil had never before occupied a line position, and he was paralyzed by his new duties. Suddenly he was called upon not merely to make a recommendation but to make a decision. On the first major deal, Vancil demanded that everyone in the small department sign the loan tickets before he did. "It was extraordinary," said Wriston. "He had this fear of responsibility. From day one, Vancil was either unwilling to take a position, unavailable, or sick." He was not a credit man, and this notion of financing ships on the basis of cash flow was alien to him. If deals were to get done, they had to be shunted through senior credit officer Sterling Bunnell, a Yale classmate of Stillman Rockefeller's and scion of one of the founding partners of National City's law firm, Shearman & Sterling.

According to former colleagues, Wriston was a man in a hurry, and Vancil was an obstacle to be circumvented. And Vancil, former bank officers said, was not pleased by Wriston's now rapid advancement. "There were some raw patches left on people's skin by Walter Wriston's elbows," said Henry B.R. Brown, who worked directly for Wriston in the transportation department. Shortly after the transportation department completed its first deal, Vancil suffered a severe heart attack, and Wriston was placed in charge of the department on a temporary basis. When Vancil returned to work, his superiors decided to make Wriston's appointment more or less permanent. While the episode gave Wriston his first real shot at management, it also drove home for all time the business and human consequences of putting the wrong man into the wrong job. "Within a year," said Citibanker Al Ambs, "it became obvious Vancil couldn't run the department. When Wriston became head of transportation, everybody welcomed it."

While its significance might not have been apparent at the time, another Wriston deal would represent yet another chink in the armor of stiff-collar banking. United Parcel Service, founded by nineteen-year-old James Casey in 1907 as a message delivery service and then a contract delivery service for department stores, was now at a turning point in its history. In 1953, the employee-owned company made a pivotal decision to go head to head with the U.S. Post Office and recast itself as a national package delivery operation, aiming to deliver all sorts of packages, large and small, for private citizens and businesses, between any two addresses in the United States. Incredibly, the law then prohibited UPS from delivering its parcels across state lines, in much the same way that banking law blocked banks from delivering their services across state lines. The company's solution was to establish, over three decades of struggling against government red tape, a holding company with subsidiaries in each state where it obtained authority to do business. UPS also decided to resume its air service, which it had abandoned in 1931 because of weak demand. No lovers of rules that constrain the operation of free markets, Wriston and National City—which had been UPS's bank since 1930—saw in the delivery service a kindred spirit.

Wriston teamed up with Harold Oberkotter, a UPS vice president who had worked his way up from his first job as a bicycle messenger, to arrange term loan financing when many banks still were not lending on that basis.

National City had relished its role as the sole banker for UPS and its chairman, James Casey. But the loan UPS now needed to take on the post office was simply too big for the bank to handle alone. To take it all would be a violation of the basic rules of diversification. So Citibank, in a watershed move, broke down and invited other banks into the deal. Syndication, Wriston said, was "the first step in the breakdown of strictly geographic markets." The prohibition against interstate banking was not yet in jeopardy, but a small, almost invisible incursion had been made.

Another important transportation account was Hertz Rent-A-Car. Aided by its presence in Europe, National City Bank and Wriston facilitated Hertz's expansion into western Europe by financing the acquisition of auto fleets. At a luncheon for the company's president, someone asked him to review Hertz's performance. In Europe, he said, one market that was thriving was London. The reason, recalled former transportation lender Henry B. R. Brown, was that Hertz cars had become the preferred place of business for London prostitutes, who rented the most expensive cars, drove them only a few miles, and used them only in the evening, so they could be rented twice in the same day. According to the Hertz president, there was only one problem. "What is that?" Wriston inquired. "We can't use our slogan ['Let Hertz put you in the driver's seat'] over there."

One thing Wriston was not, according to George Moore, was a new-business getter of the old school: the fact that he did not drink or play golf eliminated the two principal devices for stroking new clients. On top of that, Moore said, Wriston was not inclined to flatter anyone, including potential customers. "He was too frank, too honest." But, Moore added, "He picked the guys" who would charm customers. Referring to himself in the third person, Moore asserted that Wriston "never liked to be with little people, dumb people. He didn't have the patience Moore has with that." In some respects, Wriston was more like the taciturn Stillman Rockefeller than he was like his gregarious mentor, George Moore. Anne Meschino, the transportation department stat-

istician, recalled that some colleagues were irritated at Wriston's habit of failing to greet people when he walked past them in the corridors. Like his father,
Wriston possessed a sense of humor that was not universally appreciated. "I
never thought he meant to be sarcastic," she said. "I thought he meant to be
funny."

Wriston, though no supersalesman, admired those who were. Floyd
Blair, a Beau Brummel whose trademark was his homburg hat, was an incredible salesman. "He could walk into any place in the world and come out
with the business," said Wriston. "The brass of the man blew my mind."
Blair's worldwide circle of friends supposedly included Mahatma Gandhi
and even a pope. As the story goes, Blair visited the Vatican and told the
reigning pontiff, "Your Holiness, there's one thing I want to get straight. I'm
a Unitarian and I won't kiss your ring. 'The guys with him almost died,' "
Wriston recalled later, adding that Blair and the pope wound up becoming
fast friends. One of Blair's most significant contributions to Wriston's transportation department was persuading the nation's railroads to bring their
business back to National City even though the bank had virtually cut off
credit to the financially troubled railroads during the 1930s.

At a black tie banquet in Philadelphia for officers and directors of the
Atlantic Coast Line Railroad, Blair, the only nonsmoker at the dinner,
quickly got his guests' attention by informing them that "we don't smoke
here." Gesturing toward a railroad official, Blair went on to say that "my
friend tells me here that the Atlantic Coast Line is reopening its account with
the Citibank." The official was stunned; he had never said anything of the
sort. Nonetheless, thanks to Blair, the Atlantic Coast Line returned to the
National City fold, according to Wriston.

George Moore's style was something else altogether. Although Wriston
admired Moore as a cheerleader, he had serious doubts about his modus operandi as a bank calling officer. Moore's idea of a day's work was to visit at
least a dozen clients or prospective clients. To Wriston and others, it did not
seem to matter to Moore whether anything of substance was discussed or accomplished, only that a call was made. On team calls to corporate customers,
Wriston and his colleagues would inform Moore at four-thirty that they intended to quit for the day. He'd say, "No no no no no. We can make another
four calls. Another four calls." And Wriston and his colleagues would reply,
"No, we're going home."

Much as Wriston admired Moore, and despite his gratitude toward his
mentor for plucking him out of the Twenty-eighth Street branch, Wriston
found Moore a volatile and unpredictable superior who threatened to fire
him with disconcerting regularity. On one such occasion, Wriston was working on a complex deal involving numerous Panama companies and more than
a dozen charters, and he produced a memo on the transaction that he regarded as a masterpiece. When he presented it for approval, however, Moore
responded almost hysterically, calling Wriston an idiot and ordering him out
of his office. When he arrived home that evening, Wriston informed his wife
of Moore's latest outburst and said that he intended to quit his job. He was

scheduled to host a group of visiting Canadian bankers at a forum the following morning, and when he arrived, he found Moore holding court with the
Canadians and motioning for him to join them. "Come over here, come over
here, come over here," ordered Moore, repeating his instruction three times,
as he habitually did. "I want you to meet the future senior lending officer of
the Citibank," Moore proudly told the Canadians.

"That's not what you said yesterday," Wriston replied.

"Whad I say? Whad I say, whad I say?" Moore asked.

"You called me an idiot."

"I wouldn't talk to you if I didn't think I could teach you something,"
Moore said.

When the meeting ended, Moore told Wriston of his own sometimes
unhappy relationship with a former boss named William Lambie, a senior
lending officer who had retired in 1948.

In a rare admission that he occasionally made some bad loans, Moore
said that he often got stuck with the credit file of a customer whose bankruptcy had been reported in the morning paper, whereas other bankers
picked up the rumor at the Links Club the day before and called the loan.
When Moore brought Lambie a loan proposal, the elder banker invariably
told him "four things that were wrong with it" and then asked, "You got it?
You got it?" Later, when Moore was promoted to senior vice president, the
retired Mr. Lambie cabled him with the short message: "You got it." That,
Wriston said, was George Moore's oblique way of explaining to him that,
although he was an idiot, "he wouldn't waste his time talking to me if he
didn't think I was worth something."

Within the tight-knit Wriston family circle, Moore was referred to with
some disdain as Tigger, the bouncing tiger in *Winnie-the-Pooh,* because of his
tendency to hop madly from one activity to another, often leaving confusion
in his wake. Moore was always gracious and friendly toward Bobby and
Cassy, but not always toward Wriston himself. Wriston's feelings for Moore
would always be in conflict. He was grateful for Moore's support and admired his energy and raw intelligence. But he had misgivings about Moore's
erratic temperament and his inability to listen and to focus on a single issue at
a time.

No one was more responsible for Wriston's early survival and subsequent success than Bobby Wriston. She was warm and cozy and an inveterate
optimist, which was what Wriston needed when he returned home depressed
after being told by Moore that he would be fired. "That's okay," Bobby responded consolingly.

The stress took a different form, however, when Wriston emerged from
the doghouse into the boardroom. According to relatives, he, like his father,
would often become physically ill in anticipation of making a presentation to
top management or directors. But as he climbed the management ladder and
realized that people respected his opinion, he gradually shed his early awkwardness and insecurities, his friend Barrett Emmerts said later.

Bobby was responsible for bringing her husband out of his shell and cheerleading him through his career at National City. If Wriston himself was consumed by ambition, it was certainly not apparent to anyone. "Bobby gave him ambition," said her brother, Richard Brengle. While Wriston himself never boasted to anyone of his business successes, Bobby regularly reported them to family and friends.

Bobby Wriston had as much to do with the way Wriston dressed in his later career as the Iron Duke did when he first started. As a young banker, Wriston was quiet, reserved, even awkward. He dressed with the reckless abandon of a small-town college professor, wearing suits with the stripes going one way and shirts with the stripes going the other. His trousers had all the shape of pajama bottoms. Only at his wife's urging did he finally begin dressing for success. "She polished him up," said their daughter Cassy. Later, Wriston's wife was responsible for adding a touch of flamboyance to her innately shy, reserved spouse by sewing silk linings decorated with red foxes into his suit jackets. After all, said Cassy later, "He was a foxy fellow."

By the mid-fifties the Liberty ships and other surplus vessels were becoming old and obsolete. In 1954 there was a groundswell of sentiment for guaranteeing as much as 100 percent of loans for the construction of ships built in the United States by U.S. citizens and operated under the U.S. flag. In something of a departure from his views on the proper role of government, Wriston, then still a lowly assistant vice president, appeared on Capitol Hill with the leaders of the American shipping industry to testify in favor of a bill that would do just that. Though Wriston almost invariably opposed federal subsidies and guarantees, he believed that an exception had to be made when national defense was concerned. "The fact was that you couldn't finance an American flagship because of wages and operating costs," he said later. Added former transportation lender Al Ambs, "The U.S. shipbuilding industry couldn't compete with the Europeans. The shipbuilders were run by the AFL-CIO. We were in the cold war at the time."

The subsequent approval by Congress of more liberal guarantees opened the floodgates of ship financing. National City and other banks generally encouraged the entry of insurance companies into the field. With tighter money conditions in the middle to late 1950s, having more willing long-term lenders enabled the banks to lend more short-term money so that more deals could be made.

Walter Saunders made a fortune for Metropolitan Life in ship lending, and his success prompted an employment offer from Stavros Niarchos that in any era would have been impossible to refuse: $1 million a year after taxes. Saunders had become a one-man show, however, and his departure left a huge void at the Met. In the game of one-upmanship between Onassis and Niarchos, Niarchos scored a major coup when he obtained Saunders's exclusive services. That triumph ranked at least a distant second to the acquisition of a highly desirable wife or mistress. So it was not long before Wriston heard from Onassis with a similar proposition. "I'm sure that's what gave Ari the idea," Wriston said later.

Wriston turned the offer down flat. "Bobby was unenthusiastic," he said later. Onassis's proposal had "an air of unreality. The idea of $1 million was hard to visualize," said Wriston. "It just didn't seem like the thing to do." And so Saunders moved to Monte Carlo while Wriston remained in Peter Cooper Village.

Wriston's decision had nothing to do with the hot water the Greek shippers now found themselves in as a result of their earlier purchase of surplus U.S. ships. Onassis and Niarchos were indicted for allegedly acquiring the ships through fraudulent means. But the shippers reached settlements with the government and the charges were dropped. In 1958, however, Onassis found himself standing in front of a congressional committee to explain his activities. Ever the negotiator, the five-foot, five-inch Onassis told Wriston he remained standing while testifying to be "on the same level of these fellows sitting up on the throne."

Moore, too, received a tempting offer, he said, from Kuhn Loeb. The investment bankers offered him a senior partnership with a $1 million annual salary, after taxes, "sort of to be the front guy," but he claimed he told the firm that he "liked Citibank and wasn't going to leave."

According to former Citibank director J. Peter Grace, chairman of W. R. Grace & Company, Henry Hagerty, financial vice president of Metropolitan Life, was in hot pursuit of Wriston as well. Grace and Hagerty were at 55 Wall Street one day, waiting for an elevator to take them to a directors' meeting when Wriston breezed past them and bounded up the stairs. "That's the smartest guy in the whole institution," Hagerty said. "I'm trying to hire him." Hagerty soon was on the phone to Wriston pleading with him to train Saunders's replacement at Met Life, a young financial analyst named George Jenkins. "George cross-examined me as if I was stealing the goddamned Metropolitan Life," Wriston recalled. Years later, Jenkins would wind up as chairman of the Metropolitan Life, and a member of the Citicorp board of directors. And Wriston and Jenkins would later kid each other that the shipping departments of their two companies were the road to the chairmanship.

When National City formed its transportation unit, it had only a few trucking company accounts. To remedy that, Wriston and his colleagues undertook a search for the ten top trucking companies in the United States. The name that kept popping up on Wriston's radar screen was McLean Trucking of Winston-Salem, North Carolina, one of the largest and most profitable truckers in the United States. Its principal shareholder, Malcom McLean, had started the company with one truck in 1934 at the age of twenty-one, and by the mid-1950s he had amassed a net worth of $25 million. On Wriston's first trip to Winston-Salem, he found out why. In a business whose leaders were not known for their resounding intellect, Wriston discovered in the idea-a-minute Malcom McLean something of a soul mate, a man with an unabiding curiosity about how the world really works.

When Wriston noticed that the sides of McLean's trailers were corrugated, not smooth, he thought he had found an opportunity to clue McLean in on the laws of nature. "It seems you'd save gas if the sides were smooth, so you'd have less wind resistance," Wriston offered.

McLean, however, had already thought the matter through. "You're right," he replied, "except that I had a study made of the prevailing winds on the McLean routes that showed we pick up maybe a mile a gallon when we're pulling heavy freight with a following wind."

"That," Wriston said later, "led me to think this is a very remarkable guy."

What catapulted McLean into the ranks of the titans of American industry was his recognition that he was really in the transportation business, not the trucking business. Back then the vast majority of American businessmen defined their businesses in terms of their traditional products or services. The rigid, fifties-era regulatory apparatus certainly encouraged that view. The government neatly segregated the various modes of transportation from one another, forbidding trucking and shipping companies and railroads, for example, to meddle in each other's business.

"What changed the world," said Wriston years later, "is that McLean saw the ship as just another piece of highway to transport goods on." From there it was an easy jump to the notion of installing racks on T-2 tankers and loading trailers on them for the run between New York and Houston. Earlier McLean had approached a top railroad executive with a proposal to transport containers on flatbed rail cars in piggyback fashion. The railroad man rejected that suggestion out of hand, saying that he didn't want to do anything that would help truckers, his archcompetitors. If not "piggybacks," then why not "fishybacks"? McLean asked himself. By this time Wriston had his own small staff of underlings who did the number crunching. "There was always some flunky who did the work," said Henry Brown, the transportation lender. "Walt said, 'Here, Brown, see if it'll check out.' I did the analysis and concluded that it would."

Wriston would learn from McLean that regulatory roadblocks were merely temporary obstacles around which a detour could usually be found. The vehicle, so to speak, for McLean's move out of the trucking business and into the transportation business was the Waterman Steamship Corporation and its subsidiary, the Pan Atlantic Steamship Corporation, whose ships transported cargo up and down the Atlantic coast and through the Gulf of Mexico. Waterman, based in Mobile, Alabama, was so conservative it had no debt, and its cash holdings actually exceeded the $20 million market value of its stock. McLean discovered the company while leafing through the *Moody's Guide,* and learned from Waterman officials that it probably could be acquired for about $42 million, or $48 a share. With McLean wielding his trademark gold pen in a series of late-night meetings at New York's old Essex House, Wriston and McLean devised a deal that would cause some of Wriston's gray-haired colleagues to blanch with trepidation. National City would lend the entire $42 million, an amount approaching the bank's legal lending limit. Although the buyers, in theory, would put up $7 million in preferred stock, they would not actually have to invest any of their personal funds. Upon closing, the buyers would declare a cash dividend repaying $25 million of the bank loan.

The deal was a watershed in several respects. For one, it called for no out-of-pocket investment on the part of the buyers, foreshadowing the multibillion-dollar leveraged buyouts that would come into vogue in the eighties. This unprecedented use of leverage "didn't bother Wriston," McLean recalled later. But in a move that would represent a turning point for the investment banking business, Wriston demanded that White Weld, the underwriters of the preferred stock offering, commit themselves to buying any unsold shares. For years, the custom had been for investment banks simply to agree to handle an underwriting on a "best efforts" basis.

The Waterman Steamship deal was the RJR Nabisco of its day, and Wriston was the genius behind it. It was moving forward and had been approved in principle when McLean got a phone call at his New York hotel from Wriston. "You'd better get here. Things are blowing apart," Wriston told McLean, who hailed a cab and headed for 55 Wall Street. When McLean arrived, Wriston said that his superiors had decided not to go through with the transaction. They had, among other things, concluded that trucking and shipping did not mix. Wriston told McLean if he wanted to get the deal done, he would have to persuade C. Sterling Bunnell, vice president in charge of national banking, and veteran banker Robert Hoguet, who apparently had had second thoughts. Wriston declined to accompany McLean to meet with them.

"It's too risky," Bunnell and Hoguet told McLean.

"What about Wriston? He's done all this work on it," McLean said.

"He's just a trainee," one of the old school bankers replied.

"He may just be a trainee, but he's going to be the boss of both of you pretty soon," McLean fired back. "That seemed to get things back on track," McLean said years later. "They said, 'Maybe we'll take another look.'"

Still other hurdles arose along the way. Waterman itself resisted McLean's initial offer. Meanwhile, a second company, backed by another National City Bank lending unit, entered the bidding for Waterman. This conflict would represent the first time, but by no means the last, that the bank found itself on both sides of competing offers. This situation raised a question that went right to the heart of the bank's role as a financial intermediary: is the bank a source of funds for all creditworthy borrowers, or does it owe an allegiance to a single relationship? Out of this transaction emerged Wriston's "common carrier" theory of lending, which held that the bank should lend to any creditworthy customer. This view would shape Citibank's relationships with its many corporate and correspondent banking customers. But it would also force competitors to choose between the common carrier approach and traditional relationship banking.

The common carrier theory would become one of the banking principles Wriston would steer his ship by until the day he retired. That National
City was backing the rival bid did not bother McLean. "I never had the feeling," he said later, "that I was the only child of Citibank. I don't let anything
I can't control bother me." But for other customers the common carrier approach was a source of constant abrasion.

National City Bank subsequently applied the common carrier theory to
all of its business and banking dealings. Citibank account officers outraged
correspondent bank clients by frequently offering to sell money directly to
their local customers. Consequently, the bank would over the years all but
relinquish to competitors Manufacturers Hanover and Chase Manhattan the
less aggressive role of banker's banker. As Wriston colleague Henry Brown
put it, "I was taught at Citibank to go out and sell money."

McLean's plan, and Wriston's participation in it, also found detractors
among the upper echelons of America's then powerful shipping community,
in particular the redoubtable James Farrell, head of Farrell Lines and a close
friend and customer of Wriston's. The two men met regularly for lunch at the
India House, a favorite Manhattan haunt of shipping executives. As Wriston
recalls, Farrell "came over and saw my boss [chairman Howard Sheperd] and
said, 'Walt's a nice guy and has learned a lot about the shipping business. I
hate to see him make this terrible mistake. Cargo is supposed to go on a ship
with a winch, and this guy's going to put trucks on ships and he's going to
fail.' "

"This is the finest guy in the shipping business saying this, and you'd
better listen to him," Sheperd urged Wriston.

"Well, Shep," Wriston replied. "I respect Farrell. He's the admiral. The
guy is a wonderful man, but I still think this will work."

If those obstacles weren't enough, the deal was also being blocked by
shareholder suits, which charged that the $75,000 fee paid by McLean to
Waterman to give up its Interstate Commerce Commission certificate, a
prerequisite to completing the transaction, was inadequate. In January
1955, McLean acquired control of Pan Atlantic and then moved to acquire
Waterman.

With so much opposition to the deal, lots of things had to happen, and
happen on cue, for Wriston and McLean to pull it off. It was something like a
chemical formula in which the ingredients had to be brought together in the
right quantities, at the right time, under the right temperature, for the desired
reaction to take place. "We couldn't take any chances that something might
blow up," McLean said later. "We had to have the resignation of the Waterman directors and the election of the new board simultaneously to make sure
the thing worked." At that instant National City would fund the loan, and
the $25 million cash dividend would be issued to pay down the loan. As Wris-
ton and McLean and the lawyers gathered at the boardroom of a Mobile,
Alabama, bank, it suddenly dawned on them that the Waterman board
didn't have a quorum. One of the Shearman & Sterling lawyers bolted from
the boardroom, headed for the elevator, and rushed out onto the sidewalk.

Buttonholing the first passerby, the lawyer asked him if he'd like to earn a quick fifty dollars. Within minutes, the befuddled man was elected a director of what was then one of the nation's great steamship companies. One minute later he was asked for his resignation, and the new board immediately declared the dividend. "To this day," McLean said later, "nobody knows who he was."

Through it all, said McLean, Wriston demanded top dollar for the bank for his efforts. "I never saw an ounce of personal egotism with him. The success of the bank was number one."

Although Wriston was well acquainted with Stillman Rockefeller, he experienced the real power of the Rockefeller name when he attempted to return to New York after completing the shipping deal. Eastern was then the only airline flying out of Mobile, and seats on the small propeller-driven aircraft of the day weren't always easy to come by. Fortunately for Wriston, the lawyers had to remain behind to dot the *i*'s and cross the *t*'s for several days after the business of the bankers was completed, and one of those lawyers happened to be Shearman & Sterling's William Rockefeller. He, of course, had no trouble getting a ticket, which he passed on to Wriston. After that, said Wriston, it was "Yes, Mr. Rockefeller, no, Mr. Rockefeller, won't you sit here, Mr. Rockefeller?"

Even after the first T-2 tanker converted into a truck container ship left Newark for Houston in April 1956, the new venture and the loans used to finance it did not work out entirely as planned. The deal came close to financial ruin on many occasions, and there would be a battle with the regulators. In late 1956, the Interstate Commerce Commission sought to force McLean to divest itself of Waterman, on the grounds that he had acquired control of the two companies without obtaining ICC approval. But even the protesting ICC examiner was forced to admit that "Malcom McLean is pioneering in the integration of sea-land transportation and in the application of the latest technological developments," adding that he was a "man of vision, determination and considerable executive talent."

The relationship with McLean was important to Wriston in another critical way. The numbers don't tell the whole story about any company, and the best information about a company's reputation and prospects often comes from competitors. Since few knew the trucking business better than McLean, Wriston relied heavily on him for advice on whom to lend to and whom to avoid.

If the Onassis, Niarchos, and McLean loans represented the decline of traditional ninety-day bank financing and the coming of age of the term loan, the loans that enabled U.S. airlines to acquire the first Boeing 707s weren't far behind.

By this time bankers knew that ninety-day credits simply couldn't be used to finance tankers, and five-year term loans were here to stay. The idea of lending for ten years was something else altogether, but with the advent of the jet age, that barrier also began to fall. As head of the transportation unit, Wriston recalls Moore walking up to his desk and saying excitedly that A. M.

"Andy" de Voursney, the treasurer of United Air Lines, was flying in to meet with them. "They bought a thing called a jet, a 707," Moore said. "They can't pay for the thing in five years."

When de Voursney arrived, Wriston asked him just how long it would take United to pay off a loan for the $5 million aircraft. The answer was seven to ten years. Soon the National City Bank was participating in huge syndicated credits, notably with Chase and Bank of America, to finance the purchase by foreign and U.S. airlines of the first generation of jet aircraft from Douglas and Boeing. Ultimately, most of the loans made by National City's transportation department were term loans based on cash-flow projections. As this notion took hold in the shipping, aircraft, and petroleum industries, it quickly spread to other sectors as well. In lending to a major New York real estate developer for the construction of a Manhattan skyscraper, National City applied the same basic idea: it assembled in advance commitments for long-term leases against which the bank made its construction loan.

In the mid-1950s, as the airline industry moved into the jet age and the shipping industry moved into the era of the supertanker, banking itself was beginning to build up a head of steam. Howard Sheperd, Stillman Rockefeller, and George Moore were stunned when Chase, in early January 1955, agreed to merge with the Bank of the Manhattan Company, propelling it ahead of National City in total assets and making it second only to Bank of America. In the process, Chase abandoned its national bank charter in favor of the state charter held by the Bank of the Manhattan Company.

Sheperd et al. wasted no time in responding. The obvious merger candidate was the old First National Bank, an institution one tenth the size of National City. The ties between City Bank and the First National Bank dated back more than half a century to the money trust, when James Stillman had tried to persuade George Baker to join forces with him. Their successors, including Sheperd, had maintained those ties. By the 1950s, First National Bank was still a top-quality corporate lending institution—the "bluest of the blue chips," as one former City Banker put it—but in other respects it was a mere shell of its once powerful self, a banking anachronism. No one there would have dreamed of soliciting customers. In fact, First National demanded that prospective customers supply an introduction before it would deign to do business with them. As early as 1946, the minimum deposit was $25,000, and as a result the bank had nothing but large deposits.

Nor did FNB have anything resembling an international network. Much later, Wriston said, "First National was Tiffany's when the world was going to Wal-Mart," said Wriston. "It was an endangered species." The banker's bank was dying a slow death. But National City coveted the First's close ties to leading U.S. corporations. When the deal was concluded on March 31, 1955, the new institution was renamed First National City Bank. The merger combined under one roof some of America's biggest companies, but First National City was still too small to cut Chase Manhattan's lead by more than half.

By the mid-1950s, First National City had already started to put its post-Mitchell conservatism behind it and to get back into the business of lending money. It had come a long way since 1946, when the U.S. government securities exceeded loans by more than two and a half times. In 1951 loans overtook government obligations for the first time since the Depression. By 1956, loans exceeded government securities by 2.3 to one and made up almost half of the bank's assets. To some, that meant the bank was "fully loaned." In another key respect, banking was becoming more complex. As interest rates edged up, corporate treasurers were beginning to wake up to the possibilities for making use of their interest-free checking account balances instead of leaving them in banks. And serious competition for the deposits of small savers was starting to be felt from mutual savings banks and savings and loan institutions.

Moore, as the bank's most vociferous advocate of term lending, and Wriston, as one of the bank's leading big-ticket term lenders, played no small role in leading First National City out of the world of stiff-collar banking. Somehow Wriston managed to spend more than six years making loans to transportation companies with barely a bum loan to his discredit. "There was," he conceded later, "one loan that was hard to get back." According to Hoguet, Wriston rose quickly without causing much evident resentment among his peers. "He was clearly head and shoulders above the people with whom he worked," Hoguet said.

So as Howard Sheperd and Stillman Rockefeller turned their attention to another anachronism—the overseas division—they looked to two men for leadership: George Moore and his protégé, Walter Wriston.

4

BANKING ON THE MOON

The merger of Chase and Bank of the Manhattan Company had caught Howard Sheperd and Stillman Rockefeller off guard and forced them to play catch-up ball. That scenario would not often be repeated, certainly not in the international arena. From now on First National City would rarely be surprised by Chase. Several developments had alerted Sheperd and Rockefeller to the need to rejuvenate their overseas division, which had remained stagnant since the end of the war. By the mid-1950s, international trade and U.S. investment abroad were reawakening after a deep sleep. The billions of dollars in Marshall Plan aid that the United States had poured into war-devastated Europe had begun to have its intended effect. The work of repairing the war damage was virtually complete, and Europeans were beginning to savor a newfound prosperity.

Despite earlier disappointments, U.S. investors, with Washington's encouragement, were now looking seriously at investment opportunities on the Continent. A Chase study of that era identified two key reasons for this: Europe's population, now 170 million, was growing at twice the pace of that of the rest of the world, and production of goods and services had doubled to $40 billion since the thirties. Moreover, the birth of the commercial jet age promised to launch a new era of European tourism.

In Latin America, one of the driving forces behind expansion was the growth of the import substitution movement, where the Latin countries demanded that U.S. companies set up local assembly plants so that they wouldn't have to import the finished product.

By 1955, Rockefeller and Sheperd had become increasingly troubled by the overseas division's meager contribution to First National City Bank's profits since the end of the war, particularly in light of the resurgence of foreign trade and investment. In numbers of overseas offices and affiliates, the National City overseas empire had dwindled from eighty-three in 1930 to sixty-three in 1940 and sixty-one in 1955. Most of its business was in the underdeveloped world, sandwiched between 15 degrees north and 15 degrees south latitude. Recognizing the need for new blood, Stillman Rockefeller summoned George Moore into his office for a private meeting.

"Who's your best man?" Rockefeller asked.

Moore's response was uncharacteristically terse: "Wriston, no doubt," he said.

"Can you persuade him to go into the foreign department?" Rockefeller inquired. "We've got to put some people in there behind Shaw." Leo Shaw was the curmudgeonly former foreign exchange trader who had run the division with an iron hand from 55 Wall Street since 1946.

Despite his fascination with international affairs, Wriston reacted coolly to the prospect of this new assignment, equating it with being handed a one-way ticket to Siberia. This was a heady and exciting time to be running the transportation lending business of a major American bank. With the flick of a pen, Wriston, now thirty-six, was launching supertankers and fleets of Boeing 707 jets. In just a few months, Malcom McLean's *Ideal X,* a converted T-2 tanker stacked with trailers, would sail from Newark to Houston to inaugurate the era of containerization. Robert Hoguet, head of the special industries division, was equally distressed at the prospect of losing his top producer.

But no one was more unhappy than Leo Shaw—in spite of, or perhaps because of, Wriston's growing reputation at First National City. As legend had it, Shaw was the man who had spirited National City's gold out of Russia in trucks when the bank's branches were taken over during the Bolshevik Revolution. It was said that his views on overseas expansion were forever shaped by that experience. A solidly built man with cold, steely blue eyes, Shaw was a fearsome figure seated behind his huge desk.

Though Shaw was a shrewd banker and foreign exchange trader, he ran the overseas division like a medieval fiefdom. Shaw hired few young people and handed out promotions stingily. As a result, most of the overseas officer staff were now in their fifties, but Shaw had made no provision for succession, and had made little attempt to build teams of managers in key departments. "All he thought about was a sixteenth [of a percentage point] here and a thirty-second there," said a former senior officer, referring to the spreads then earned from trading currencies.

All power in the foreign division emanated from Shaw's desk. He maintained a little book with a page for every city where the bank did business. The mere mention of any First National City Bank location—Havana, Rio, London—would prompt Shaw to turn to the pertinent page in his ledger and announce whether that branch was in the black or in the red. He centralized decision-making to the point of absurdity and managed his staff with as much sensitivity as Attila the Hun. A country head couldn't hire a maid to clean a toilet in Bombay or award a raise to a clerk in London without the approval of the New York–based district vice president. Although the bank's overseas network, as measured by pins on the map, was the largest of any American financial institution, the cumulative earnings of the foreign division since its inception amounted to zero, according to Moore. It had made money during World War I, lost it all afterward in Cuba, made it back in the twenties, and lost it again after the crash. By 1956 it was apparently making money, but barely.

One perennial problem faced by the division was getting profits out of countries where it did business. At one time or another, all or most of them imposed exchange controls that blocked or restricted the dollar earnings that could be sent to New York. First National bankers found ingenious ways around these restrictions, including swapping local currency for dollars with other American companies. In inflation-wracked Argentina, City Bank at one point even converted its local currency profits to Scotch whisky to maintain the value of its earnings until it could remit them in dollars to New York.

Since its inception, the overseas business of National City had been relatively simple. The bank made its money largely from facilitating international trade, earning commissions on import-export financing, letters of credit, and foreign exchange transactions. In Europe a substantial amount of the business involved transfer payments associated with Marshall Plan aid. Much of the business was conducted through correspondent banks. Direct lending per se was still limited primarily to conservative short-term self-liquidating transactions, in contrast to the infinitely more interesting long-term cash-flow deals Wriston had concocted for Onassis and his brethren. The overseas division was at least a decade behind its domestic counterpart.

It would take some gentle coaxing from chairman Howard Sheperd, and the offer of a "repurchase agreement" from George Moore, to entice Wriston to leave the fast-track world of jets and tankers for the clubby white-suit and Panama-hat subculture of international banking, where his first assignment would be to supervise from Stateside the bank's London operations.

Wriston's first meeting with Shaw was not a pleasant one. In that icy encounter, Shaw was seated at his baronial desk, complete with his omnipresent bottle of Poland Spring water. "You've got to be born into this business, and I'm sorry you're here," Shaw told Wriston without even inviting him to sit down. "You're too old to learn anything. I didn't want you, so here we are. Good-bye."

It was "not a very outstanding beginning," says Wriston. "Thank you very much," he said sarcastically as he turned on his heel and left. His next stop was a visit to Charles Sheehan, a kind but frail man with a glass eye who then ran the European district, at least what there was of it, out of New York. Upset by Shaw's rudeness, Wriston asked Sheehan if he wanted him to return to the transportation unit. "I had a lot of fun there," Wriston said bitterly. "No," Sheehan replied, "I asked for you." Over the next year, while Wriston remained in the overseas division, Shaw went to great lengths to make his life miserable, and he had help doing it. Other overseas veterans also resented the intrusion of a domestic division officer into their private club. Wriston "was about as popular as a skunk at a tea party," said one former top officer. "People who had spent their entire lives in international said, 'What is this upstart coming into this area for?' "

The overseas division that Wriston joined in the mid-1950s could only be described as antediluvian. Things had gotten so bad that Sheperd and Rockefeller seriously contemplated folding the division altogether. With plenty to do in the United States, and with the economies of western Europe still recovering from World War II, the overseas division had been virtually ignored by the bank's management and remained a sleepy backwater of American capitalism. The Communist peril was on the minds of all Americans, and the board of the First National City Bank was no exception. Understandably, National City thought twice about reopening in areas that didn't fall under U.S. military protection.

The accounting systems then used by the American banking industry were generally useless in pinpointing how or where an institution *really* made its money. Latin America was the cornerstone of the empire, despite the difficulties in remitting profits. Japan and the Philippines were the hot spots in Asia, thanks to profitable branches at U.S. military bases. Europe, which Wriston would soon supervise from his rolltop desk at 55 Wall Street, was a dog.

With the outbreak of World War II, the bank had shut down all of its European branches except the one in London. Now, in the mid-1950s, it operated branches only in London and Paris, and both locations were money losers. One London branch was nothing more than a convenient place for tourists to cash traveler's checks. In other European countries, National City hadn't bothered to reopen at all. According to Wriston, someone had sold the bank's Brussels operations to Belgian banking interests under the mistaken notion that National City couldn't reopen there until five years after a peace treaty was signed. Surrender agreements were dictated by the Allies to the Germans, but no peace treaty was ever signed after the cessation of hostilities in Europe. From that experience, Citibank learned to hold on to its branches at all costs, because it was far easier to close a branch than to get a government's permission to reopen one. Wriston commented later, "When I joined the international group we had two branches: the London branch, which was losing money, and the Paris branch, which was losing money, but elegantly."

Another problem was the dismal work ethic in the overseas ranks. Wriston confidant Stephen Eyre later recalled a comment made by the manager in West Germany that typified the European attitude. "I only want one account," the manager is said to have remarked. "That's an expense account." Another contemporary claimed that this same officer was happy as long as he had an ample supply of "good German Rhine wine."

In Latin America, First National City had at least one branch in nearly every country of any economic consequence. If there was an establishment American bank in South America, National City was it. Lacking strong and dependable local banks, Latin businessmen and American companies relied heavily on First National City to finance and expedite trade. Unlike Europe and Asia, of course, Latin America had suffered no war damage, and the bank's business in raw materials–producing countries like Argentina and Brazil actually flourished during the war. In addition to Puerto Rico, three Latin countries—Cuba, Brazil, and Argentina—accounted for the bulk of the bank deposits of the entire overseas division.

Other U.S. banks, including Chase Manhattan and First National Bank of Boston, had branch operations in Latin America, but none was as large as that of National City Bank. A few British banks, including the Bank of London and South America, now Lloyds Bank, were also active there.

Cuba had brought National City to its knees in the early twenties, but the bank's eleven-branch system there prospered under the oppressive Fulgencio Batista y Zaldívar regime. Once again First National City was *the* bank for the sugar interests and the principal U.S. depository for the many American companies that operated in Cuba during the heyday of the fifties.

Although Brazil performed better during the war than after it, City Bank business actually grew slightly in the postwar years, from five branches in 1947 to seven in 1955. According to Nick Clute, who served there during that period, First National City and the Brazilian government avoided publicizing the size of the bank's operation. "We never advertised that. We didn't want [the Brazilians] to think we were getting too big," he said. At a time when interest rates in the United States were well below 6 percent, they were 12 percent in Brazil, enabling First National City to earn a decent profit. Taxes were low, and double taxation was nonexistent, according to Clute. During this period the Brazilian government permitted the bank to remit its profits to the States. At other times, however, the government of Brazil imposed exchange controls blocking such remittances. With large amounts of currency tied up in the country, Brazil became a training ground for young international bankers, because they could be paid in cruzeiros, which could not be converted to dollars and remitted anyway.

As for Argentina, National City early in the 1900s followed its meat-packing customers, such as Swift and Armour, to the cone of South America. The bank's experience in Argentina was a tumultuous one, and its fortunes rose and fell with every change of leadership in that erratic, perpetually ill-managed country. When Juan Perón grabbed power in 1946, he in effect nationalized the bank's deposits, placing them under control of the central bank. The Perón regime exerted tight control over every facet of the bank's business, including the kinds of loans that could be made. Bank employees were unionized and couldn't be dismissed after a brief trial period unless they were caught stealing. A quarter of the National City staff was preoccupied with paperwork related to the government's banking regulations, which changed daily. Worse still, the Perón regime, by taking control of agricultural markets for meat, grain, and other products, robbed farmers of the incentive to produce. Under Perón, one Argentina hand recalled, the big meatpackers left because of rampant featherbedding permitted by the regime. By the time Juan Perón was overthrown in 1955, the country's wealth was drained, and the citizenry had become accustomed to a socialistic system that had all but eliminated individual initiative. "They basically said you don't have to work anymore," said one former top officer in Argentina. This pervasive national psychology would set the stage for the debt crisis of three decades later.

During the Perón regime, Argentine importers had to pay cash for all their merchandise. Only after his fall was the country redeemed in the eyes of its bankers. The free use of bank deposits was restored, and in early 1956, First National City and Chase lent Argentina $15 million in short-term credits to finance imports. In 1957, according to James Farley, then a top officer in Argentina, First National City was able to wire $1 million in profits to New York headquarters.

The nationalization by Egypt of the Suez Canal in 1956 touched off an oil boom in Venezuela, which caught National City unprepared, and its Venezuelan operation ossified. The Far Eastern operation was decimated by the war and its aftermath. Consequently, the bank's postwar strategy in Asia was unaggressive, and the operations there were best described as threadbare. After being thrown out of China, and with the Korean War fresh in mind, First National City was less than eager to expand in those two countries. Continental Asia did not look upon foreign banks with great affection, and City Bank returned the feeling in kind. The bank was so chary of Continental Asia, in fact, that nearly all of its business there was done on a fully cash-collateralized basis.

After the war, National City, along with several other U.S. banks, had resurrected its branches in the Philippines and opened branches in Japan to serve American service personnel. It was making money in both countries because of the huge amount of U.S. military and financial aid flowing in there. A strong sentimental attachment between National City and the Philippines reflected the close historical ties between the Philippines and the United States. After the Japanese shut down the bank's Filipino branch on December 29, 1941, all members of its staff, including the manager, were imprisoned in the decrepit Santo Tomas Internment Camp. They obtained food by tossing hand-scrawled chits to Filipinos over a fence promising to repay them after the United States had won the war. According to Wriston, all of the chits were duly redeemed. When National City reopened in the Philippines in 1945, it was the only foreign bank that repaid its depositors, according to Wriston. It also extended loans for construction and trade.

Though National City did actually reopen in China after the war, its return there was short-lived. With the 1950 expropriation by the Communists of the Shanghai branch, the bank's business on the mainland came to a close. When the Communists broke into a bank-owned staff residence in Shanghai, one Asia hand, Ray Kathe, had to roll himself up in an Oriental carpet to protect himself from ricocheting bullets. On taking over the branches, the Chinese demanded that National City return all deposits at the exchange rate that was in effect at the time they were made. Because of inflation, that would have been disastrous, and National City left the country with that issue unresolved. Consequently, the Red Chinese government refused to let three employees leave the country, and the bank was forced to ransom two of them for $500,000. National City continued to pay the salary of one Chinese national who remained there, but the matter wasn't settled until the 1970s, when détente was achieved between the United States and the People's Republic of China. Meanwhile, however, National City held on to its branches in Hong Kong.

The bank remained in India during the war. But afterward, under government pressure, the operation dwindled to a shell of its former self. At one point, the bank even considered pulling up stakes.

First National City's only toehold in black Africa was Liberia's Bank of Monrovia. In 1955 it earned the dubious distinction of being the only U.S. bank on the African continent when Firestone Tire & Rubber Company, an important client that virtually ran the country's finances, threatened to yank its account unless National City relieved it of the burden of running Liberia's banking system.

Liberia was plagued with defalcations, theft, and corruption. Besides serving as the de facto central bank, First National City in Monrovia unwittingly served as the bank for the diamond-smuggling trade between Sierra Leone and Liberia. Liberia was a hardship post without peer. It rained much of the year, natives practiced voodoo, murders were commonplace, and staff shared their homes with poisonous snakes. Its sole attraction was tax exemptions that enabled employees to save much of what they earned. "There was an unwritten understanding," said one former officer, "that if you put in time in crappy places, hellholes, they'd try to balance it out and get you to someplace good. But they didn't have very many good places in the old overseas division."

Liberia was a prime example of a profligate Third World country. At one point, First National City lent $1 million to Liberia's president, William Tubman, to build an executive mansion. The tab eventually reached $22 million, leaving countless angry and unpaid suppliers around the globe. After persuading Tubman to bring in the International Monetary Fund to fix the economy, National City eventually got its money back. Besides the constant demands for credit, another drawback of the Monrovia operation was Tubman's insistence that the bank host gala dinners for him at the Waldorf whenever he visited New York.

For all his shortcomings, Leo Shaw was responsible for at least one initiative that would serve the bank well for the rest of the century: opening up the Middle East. On a trip there in the mid-1950s he concluded that the region, with its vast oil resources, held enormous promise for the bank. In 1955 he opened branches in Cairo, Beirut, and, most important, Jidda, Saudi Arabia. Cairo and Beirut would never amount to much, but Jidda would represent the foundation for years of profits that would be the envy of every other international bank. Shaw knew a good thing when he saw one, Wriston conceded later.

On his visit to Egypt to cut the ribbon for the new branch, Shaw added to his personal legend. In Cairo's marketplace, he engaged in some hard bargaining with a merchant for a silver dagger. After Shaw had beaten the guy down for an hour and a half, Wriston said, "the merchant was just beginning to smile at the thought that he had a deal. Then Leo would say, 'That's for two, isn't it?' " On that same trip, Shaw and his colleagues rented camels for the ride from the Sphinx to the Great Pyramid. At the end of such treks, visitors customarily give the camel driver a small gratuity, and as Shaw and his party were nearing the pyramid, the driver asked him, "Do you have a present for me?" Shaw reached down and extended his hand to the driver, saying, "I shake your hand and I give you my friendship. It's the biggest gift a man can give."

Although Shaw was a shrewd banker and trader, he lacked the attribute Wriston most respected in a businessman. Says Wriston, "He didn't build anything." In contrast, Wriston once told a colleague, "It's fun to build something from scratch. That's how I get my jollies. It's fun to see people you bet on do well." To be sure, Shaw was a character with few equals in the ranks of National City. But the overseas division of that era resembled the French Foreign Legion in that it was populated by hundreds of oddballs who had been lured by the romance of international banking.

The traditional oversees banker, said one former National City officer, was a "peculiar" person, "almost like the Scottish second or third son who wasn't going to inherit the family farm." From the vantage point of National City's domestic officers, the members of the bank's foreign legion were cigar-smoking kooks who drifted in from the field every few years or so wearing white suits. Although the legionnaires were regarded as the messenger boys for the U.S. corporate bankers, their perceived lifestyle was viewed with some envy. Visitors from the head office would typically be met by a limousine, taken to the local British club for lunch on the lawn, and catered to at the country head's home by a retinue of servants. "The New York guys would say, 'You guys live like fucking kings,' " recalled one former Asia hand. In reality, however, the perks varied dramatically from post to post. The accommodations ranged from luxurious in the Philippines to Spartan in Indonesia to snake-infested in Liberia.

Though lending and spending decisions were made in New York, overseas staff, particularly before the advent of the commercial jet, were very much their own bosses. "If left on your own," said former Argentina hand James Farley, "you could become an alcoholic recluse." Or, he said, "you could be a big fish in a little pool." Foreign inspectors were vagabonds who crisscrossed the world using any and all available means of transport, from ocean liners to the Trans-Siberian Railroad.

There was a side to life overseas, however, that the casual visitor typically never witnessed. In many of the countries where National City operated in the first half of the twentieth century, the climate was oppressively hot, air and water were contaminated, medical facilities were substandard, and civil disorder was not uncommon. Officers who were dispatched abroad to open branches, to the extent there were branch openings at all, had to operate simply, often without the benefit of telephones or telexes. Carrying a general ledger under his arm, the officer "hired a hall, found some staff, and posted the ledger," said Wriston. If the foreign operations generated little profit, they at least supplied wags in New York with a steady stream of tales of foreign intrigue, military coups, daredevil escapes from unfriendly regimes, and exotic sexual encounters. "People cheated on their wives, took up with local mistresses, and got into every conceivable mess you could think of," claims one former overseas hand. It was not unusual for officers overseas to have concubines.

Through the 1950s, a prospective overseas recruit signed on for a three-year hitch at $2,500 a year with a two-month furlough at the end of that period. If he quit before meeting that commitment, he received a bill for his $250 clothing allowance. Prospective recruits were single men who had to sign a waiver promising not to get married for at least three years, because the bank wanted to avoid the expense of flying the family home if the wife couldn't tolerate the living conditions. In colonial days, an overseas banker had to remain with the bank for five years and earn $3,000 annually before the bank gave him permission to get married. The first married officer wasn't hired in the overseas division until after World War II. If he passed muster, a new employee received nine months' home leave at half pay to find a wife. The couple also had to get Leo Shaw's blessing before they could return to an overseas post. But as an officer moved up in the organization, having a wife was considered a useful business-getting tool.

Many overseas officers left the United States as young men, married local women, and remained in their posts for their entire careers, rarely returning to the States. According to one veteran, recruits were dispatched to overseas posts according to a pecking order based on their educational background: Harvard, Yale, and Princeton men were sent to Europe, Williams graduates to Tokyo, and lesser lights to the Caribbean or other remote corners of the bank's empire. Richard Valelly, who joined National City in 1947, asked to be posted in London. "I was told that was only for influential people. I went to the Caribbean, which was the most a boy from Missouri could hope for." The evaluation procedure for overseas prospects included a visit to the bar at the Downtown Athletic Club to see if they could handle their liquor.

Leo Shaw treated Wriston as persona non grata, keeping him out of the loop and not giving him any work. Senior officials of European corporations and top European monetary officials, including the governor of the Bank of England, would show up in New York for lunch, and Wriston would not find out about it until later. George Moore soon realized that his young protégé was being frozen out. On one occasion, Moore attended a luncheon for the president of International Harvester to discuss the company's British credit line, and found that Wriston was conspicuously absent. When Moore asked about the omission he found that Shaw "didn't have a good reason" for not having invited him, he said years later.

Not long after Wriston moved into the European district, the head of that unit, Charles Sheehan, asked Wriston to assume his responsibilities and retired because of declining health. Over Shaw's objections, Wriston in 1956 was appointed head of the district, which included Africa, the Middle East, Australia, and New Zealand as well as Europe. Wriston soon embarked on a grand tour of Europe to size up his staff, hire new personnel, seek sites for new branches, challenge the legal myths that had blocked the reopening of European branches, and in general let people know things were going to change. Said Wriston, "The biggest barrier in Europe was the [attitude of National City's] people in Europe. They had no interest in reactivating the business in Europe." In London, for example, Wriston placed a ship loan in the branch over the objections of a longtime branch manager, edging that branch into the black for perhaps the first time since it had opened for business in 1902. Wriston's energetic development of a European presence would launch his career as the leading international banker of his generation and would eventually give National City the most extensive network of any American bank in Europe. Ironically, however, Europe would continue to be a thorn in the bank's side until well beyond Wriston's own tenure as chairman. Despite its vast infrastructure of branches and staff—First National City later became the only bank in the world with a branch in every Common Market country—for a variety of reasons it never achieved the status of a major banking power on the Continent or in the United Kingdom.

Shortly after joining the overseas division, Wriston took his first trip to the Middle East and discovered that Shaw's three new branches in that area had not made First National City a household name. Prospective customers examined Wriston's business card, and asked, "What's Citibank?" For them, Wriston said, "It was a brand-new experience."

On his return to New York, he showed himself to have changed little from the days at Appleton High when he danced with a coat hanger. For all his seriousness, Wriston was always open to any silliness, highbrow or otherwise. That Halloween, Wriston and his friend Karl Malden, dressed up as King Farouk—Egypt's deposed playboy ruler—in Arab robes and headgear, with cigars and sunglasses, and went trick-or-treating in Peter Cooper Village with their daughters. And Wriston was a devoted fan of the Lone Ranger and Tonto, faithfully watching the TV program every Saturday morning with daughter Cassy.

Wriston was not one to forget those who had befriended him along the way, and after taking over the European division, he began to repay his debts. One of the beneficiaries was Robert MacFadden, who had taken Wilcox to task several years before for unloading all of his work on Wriston. Now Wriston plucked MacFadden out of the special industries department and appointed him head of London's Berkeley Square branch, one of the division's cushiest assignments. While serving in London, MacFadden lived in the grand manner expected of someone in his position. According to former National City officers, he appeared to spend as much time in a dinner jacket as in a business suit, entertaining regularly in the bank's elegant Berkeley Square apartment, where a liveried butler took guest cards as visitors arrived at the door. At a time when other officials were required to fly back and forth between New York and London, MacFadden and his wife made the round trip on the *Queen Elizabeth*.

Wriston, according to several former colleagues, first grabbed the attention of the bank's directors for a presentation on overseas compensation he made to the board as head of the European division. At the time, National City Bank had a system of designating officers by color—gold, blue, green, or red—according to their potential in the organization, gold being reserved for officers with potential for top management. They were rated according to four categories of proficiency: credit judgment, administration, new business, and operating experience.

Former executive committee chairman Richard Perkins recalls that Wriston was not yet a gold, but after hearing his presentation to the board, Perkins turned to chairman Howard Sheperd and said, "There's a guy with some potential. We sort of marked him down then as someone to look at." George Moore later said he had Wriston pegged as the future CEO from the moment he asked him to join the foreign division. "There was no one of his stature," Moore said later. "He was obviously destined to be CEO. He was better than Moore. We didn't have to draw pictures for each other. We had a team deal."

When Wriston joined the overseas division, he didn't abandon his transportation clients. Instead, he used his new role to extend the transportation department's reach into Europe. Also, among other transactions, Wriston helped finance the new jet fleets of major European airlines such as KLM and SAS. Some of the loans to the overseas carriers, however, touched a sensitive nerve in high places. The British Overseas Airline Corporation, known today as British Airways, was on cloud nine, as it were, when First National City agreed to bankroll its 707 fleet. But borrowing from Americans, it turned out, struck some high-placed Britons as a sign of weakness, an insult to British pride. Tails between their legs, the airline's finance officers asked City Bank to make the loan to Barclays Bank, which would then relend the money to them.

The loans to the European airlines were early examples of what would become known as cross-border loans—loans denominated in dollars to companies whose principal source of revenue is a foreign currency. To make them, First National City had to secure permission from the head of the central bank of the country or from the finance minister, because the loans would have to be repaid by converting local currency to dollars. Then, recalled transportation lender Al Ambs, the loans would have to be defended within the bank, which the officers would do by pointing out that the central bank had approved the deal.

In one such deal, First National City in 1956 helped underwrite Onassis's purchase of Olympic Airways from the Greek government, according to Ambs. "Olympic was Onassis's plaything," said former shipping lender Anne Meschino.

———

In August 1955, a few months before Walter Wriston was assigned to the European district, Henry Merritt Wriston retired from Brown and moved to New York to head the American Assembly, a public issues think tank affiliated with Columbia University.

Sadly, Dr. Wriston's retirement coincided almost to the day with the death of his own father, Henry Lincoln Wriston, at the age of ninety-four.

Dr. Wriston's move to an apartment at 12 Beekman Place in Manhattan marked the renewal of a relationship between father and son that had been interrupted for nearly twenty years by school, war, and career, and also by Walter's desire to escape the indomitable, and sometimes oppressive, judgments of his father. Henry, of course, had strong opinions on everything from cars to clothes. In the mid-1950s, when Walter bought a red convertible, Henry railed, "You'll freeze in winter, fry in summer, and if you roll over you're dead." He even tried to discourage his granddaughter from wearing ribbons in her hair. "You've got snakes in your hair!" he growled.

During the uncertain formative years of Walter's business career, he had avoided his illustrious father. Although Hank Wriston maintained a summer home on Cape Cod, Walter's daughter, Cassy, later recalled that she didn't visit her grandfather there until the early 1960s. Part of the reason may have been the cool reception Walter received from his father one time after driving seven hours to visit him on the Cape. When he arrived, Hank was glued to a TV public affairs program and didn't bother to get up to greet him. It was a hurtful incident, and one Walter never forgot.

As soon as he could afford it, Walter bought his own weekend retreat, a modest Cape Cod–style farmhouse overlooking a tree-shaded pond in Sherman, Connecticut. Wriston didn't believe in taking work home with him, and Sherman would become his refuge from the stress of the working week at 55 Wall.

"You couldn't be around my grandfather and not [want to] set off on your own," said Cassy. "When my father became successful, he could be comfortable with him." With Hank Wriston out of the Brown presidency and Walter on his way to one, the balance of family power had finally begun to tilt in Walter's favor. Though Walter Wriston was an aloof man who maintained a certain personal distance from everyone except members of his immediate family, he would now rediscover in his father an invaluable ally and confidant, one of a handful with whom he could converse freely and openly. "If you're the big cheese it's very handy to have somebody in whom you can confide and talk something over who is not personally involved and who will keep his trap shut," said Walter's sister, Barbara. "I think our father played that role."

Wriston's father also had some ideas on personnel and management that apparently rubbed off on the son. In 1954, shortly before he retired as president of Brown, the elder Wriston was appointed by Secretary of State John Foster Dulles to head a panel to study State Department personnel practices. At that time, morale at Foggy Bottom was rock bottom. The department was staffed by a relatively small elite corps of foreign services officers who manned the embassies and missions around the world, and a much larger corps of Washington-based civil servants, including specialists and administrators. Traditionally, the primary requirements for an FSO were a degree from Harvard or Yale and "knowing when to wear white gloves," as Barbara Wriston puts it.

Like Henry Wriston himself, the recommendations of the Wriston Commission were highly controversial, and once implemented, their impact was far-reaching. Mincing no words, the committee concluded that the foreign service "stands in need of repair" and suffered from weak leadership and unfair personnel practices. To infuse new blood into the service, the commission called for boosts in pay and allowances and recommended a scholarship and training program, resembling that of West Point and Annapolis, that would attract top college graduates. In addition, the Wriston report recommended the merger, within a two-year period, of foreign service and civil service personnel by enabling civil servants to move laterally into the foreign service. In mid-1954, shortly after receiving the report, Secretary Dulles adopted nearly all of Wriston's recommendations.

Foreign service officers fumed at the idea of allowing civil service employees to enter their elite ranks without even taking an exam, and hundreds quit as they saw their opportunities for advancement dwindle. But Wristonization was generally deemed a success. By 1957 the foreign service had tripled to more than 3,600 slots. Some fifteen years later most of the top overseas career positions were occupied by foreign service officers who had gotten in through the side door.

Wriston later claimed that he never even read his father's report, but he must have heard about it when he ran into his former Fletcher classmates at the U.S. missions in Europe. Foreign service officers who would have been content to spend all of their time in Washington took out their wrath on the son of the man responsible for their reassignments. One FSO newly assigned to Finland complained to Wriston, "Jeez, I got Wristonized. I thought I was going to spend the rest of my life in Washington, and here I am in Helsinki." Wriston replied, "Don't look at me. I was fat, dumb, and happy lending to railroads last week, and here *I* am in Helsinki. It happened to me too."

Whatever Wriston's doubts about his father's influence on his own management style, it is clear that the two men held similar views on hiring, motivating, and managing people.

As Wriston's responsibility broadened, he remembered what his father had told him about the willingness of people to spill their guts to an interested listener. Plying subordinates with jelly beans as his father did was not Walter Wriston's style. In the late afternoon, Wriston would walk the sixth floor, sit down in his subordinates' guest chairs, put his feet up on their desks, and puff on his cigar. "He'd sit there with his feet up on your desk and chew the fat," said a former overseas hand. Said Wriston, "If you go out and walk around the floor talking with bookkeepers, if you create a climate where people know you care what they're saying they'll tell you a lot. That's really your database on operations." Over the next thirty years, Wriston would make his fair share of mistakes, but failing to listen to workers in the trenches would be the least of them.

Both Henry and Walter Wriston were fascinated with the gathering and dissemination of information. Early in his banking career, Wriston concluded that information about money was more important to the business than money itself. Much of the edge that First National City was able to offer customers around the world was based on its being able to tap into a wellspring of data about industry trends and trends in local economies.

Hank Wriston's memoir, *Academic Procession,* could well have been a memo to his son for running City Bank. Turnover, for example, bothered neither Henry nor Walter. "The search for first class teachers and scholars for college instruction is likely to have a corollary: there will be considerable turnover," Henry Wriston had written. To some, First National City under Wriston's leadership became a veritable revolving door of Ivy League M.B.A.'s. Some would join and stay for the long haul; many others would find the bank a valuable training ground but an unsuitable permanent home.

Similarly, both men believed that rotating people reinvigorated organizations. In later years, Walter Wriston would be roundly criticized by some colleagues as well as customers for constantly moving officers from job to job. Managers, like money, were supposed to be fungible. But for Hank and Walter, the status quo was a condition to be avoided; it was both boring and debilitating.

Wriston always came away from his visits to 12 Beekman Place intellectually renewed. "You could tell when he came back from seeing his father," said one colleague. "He'd come back with all kinds of ideas." And if he needed a model for sheer courage, he couldn't have found a better one than Henry Merritt Wriston. At the height of Senator Joseph McCarthy's frightening anti-Communist crusade, Henry Wriston, then president of Brown, was unflinching in his attacks on the demagogue in Washington, in stark contrast to many of his colleagues. His fellow academics would complain that McCarthy's activities had a chilling effect on their public statements, but as Wriston commented later, "it turned out after McCarthy died that they didn't have anything to say anyway." Wriston also attacked political corruption in Providence, and received death threats as a result.

Life with Henry was not all cerebral, of course. In a lifetime of fighting battles on college campuses and at the State Department, he had never lost his wry wit. Said Cassy, "He was not averse to putting bells around his neck at Christmas and playing reindeer."

Bobby Wriston relished the duties she acquired when her husband got his new assignment. When First National City hired an overseas employee, it got two for the price of one; the other was his wife, who received no salary but spent most of her waking hours serving First National City. Overseas employees were known by the kind of wives they had, and whether their wives were considered helpful in their service to Mother Bank. But for Wriston, in his new role as head of the European district, a "good wife" was imperative. Showing his new subordinates and their families that he really cared about them did not come easy. Wriston came across to some as icy and aloof, and he knew it. At Brown, Henry Wriston had had an aide, who, among other duties, followed in his wake to patch up the wounds inflicted by his sharp tongue. Similarly, Bobby took some of the harsh edge off her husband's personality and some of the sting out of his pungent remarks. "She provided the softening," said Walter's friend Barrett Emmerts. Said Cassy, "People got to know him better through her." In one rare instance where he let his hair down with colleagues, Wriston acknowledged that Bobby was the "transmission point"—the link between him and thousands of overseas employees. In the managerially unsophisticated and relatively small overseas network of the 1950s and early 1960s, Bobby helped preserve a strong sense of family. A woman of boundless energy and goodwill, she took a personal interest in other people's problems, ensuring that an employee's sick child was admitted to the right Paris hospital or arranging for polio vaccine to be dispatched to Asia, Africa, or Latin America. She maintained a voluminous index-card file to help her keep track of children's birthdays and other pertinent data on overseas staff. There were places, said overseas banker Richard Valelly, where you couldn't get diapers for babies. "They [the Wristons] would see that you got them."

"She was a loved person," said Wriston. When bank officers arrived in New York for meetings, Bobby served lunch, cramming as many people into their apartment as possible. But what some overseas staff wives appreciated most about her was that she didn't criticize their performance as hostesses or check for dust on their windowsills. "Some would take notes right in front of you," said Nancy Valelly. "She went down easy." Bobby wouldn't have cared about dust, but with her prodigious memory she wouldn't have needed a notepad to remember it, either. She also served as one of her husband's antennae, gathering intelligence on the problems of overseas staff. "Bobby made Walter's career easier for him," said Barrett Emmerts. "She was a supersaleswoman. She facilitated his progress, and the money started coming in."

Money seemed to matter less to Wriston than to Bobby. Both avoided pretentious people and chafed at the phoniness of the New York society scene. Money certainly wasn't the driving force in her life, but she enjoyed buying her husband monogrammed shirts at Manhattan's Custom Shop and receiving from him gifts of jewelry that he had helped design. "I love capitalism," Bobby used to say. "She taught him [Wriston] life could be enjoyable," Cassy said later. "There was nothing Spartan about my mother."

In addition to the boom in global trade and investment, the move toward import substitution in Latin America, and the 1956 Suez crisis, there were other compelling reasons for lighting a fire under the overseas division. The Chase Manhattan and First National City mergers notwithstanding, all signs pointed to less freedom to expand domestically for American banks.

In 1956, Congress passed the Bank Holding Company Act, which restricted interstate banking by bank holding companies and reinforced the separation between industry and commerce. It also gave to the Federal Reserve the power to regulate the activities of holding companies. The new legislation arose out of the moves by several institutions in the early 1950s to form so-called multibank holding companies to expand outside their home states. However, the holding company legislation did make one exception that twelve years later would give rise to another legislative battle. Recognizing that many small-town banks in states such as Minnesota operated various non-bank businesses under a holding company umbrella, it allowed the formation of single-bank holding companies for such purposes.

Not long after the bill was signed, First National City launched the first test of the new act in a bid to expand into neighboring Westchester County. New York State law then divided the state into banking districts, prohibiting the New York City banks from opening branches outside the five boroughs, even though many of their customers resided in the bedroom communities of adjoining Westchester and Nassau counties. The city banks were forced to look on helplessly as their customers left New York for the suburbs after World War II. In effect, the status quo protected banks in those suburban counties from outside competition.

Stillman Rockefeller asked Henry Harfield, a Shearman & Sterling banking lawyer, to figure out a way to overcome what Harfield wryly called the "unsound barrier" and get First National City into Westchester. The angle they developed was to set up a holding company and merge County Trust, a bank in the Westchester City of White Plains, into it.

The move was promptly condemned by banking authorities, suburban banks, and New York governor Averell Harriman as a threat to bank competition. After holding hearings on the plan, the Federal Reserve Board, in July 1958, rejected the application as anticompetitive.

Nonetheless, the episode proved that First National City could win by losing. It helped force a legislative review of New York State's banking laws, which two years later were changed to allow New York City banks to enter adjoining counties. In that effort, First National City was joined by John J. McCloy, chairman of Chase Manhattan.

The Fed clearly didn't want National City to even think about acquiring a bank outside its home turf, or merging with one in its home territory that would threaten local competitors. The Comptroller of the Currency, while more benign than the Fed in its view of bank expansion, was nonetheless mired in minutiae. According to former Comptroller James Smith, his predecessor in the 1950s insisted on reviewing personally each proposed branch site of every bank his agency supervised.

No voice was louder than that of George Moore in condemning the barriers to expansion in Westchester as absurd and outrageous. Around this time, however, the Bank of America's so-called Edge Act office in New York began to expand at a breakneck pace. (This legislation allowed U.S. banks to set up out-of-state offices to conduct international business.) For all of George Moore's attacks on the "unsound barrier" and the unfair limitations on First National City's expansion, it was a far different matter when Moore's ox was being gored. "George would say, 'People can't come here and get into our backyard,'" said a source familiar with the episode. " 'The government's got to do something.' " Moore's call for deregulation was based on his desire to accumulate territory for National City, of course, not on any deeply held philosophical belief in free and open competition for everyone.

Although Wriston, as a vice president in the overseas division, was not directly affected by the newly legislated restrictions on domestic expansion, the inherent flaws of geographic restrictions on bank expansion were driven home to him in a very personal way shortly after the passage of the Bank Holding Company Act of 1956. On September 7, 1956, his father, now sixty-seven, suffered a severe heart attack while summering at his country home in Massachusetts, whose commercial banking laws then did not allow banks to operate branches more than 15 miles beyond their home base. Wriston's local doctor was unable to diagnose his condition accurately because the local bank had refused to lend him the money to buy a lateral X-ray machine. So Henry Wriston had to be transported to a Providence hospital.

Some years later, however, when Henry suffered another heart attack, the same doctor did have a lateral X-ray machine, and when Walter Wriston met with him this time he was grinning. When asked why, the doctor said, "They now have branch banking." In other words, the banking laws had since been liberalized to allow banks to expand and therefore lend more money to a single customer.

The doctor apparently did have plenty of old-time medicine on hand. After that first heart attack, he prescribed a thimbleful of sherry. Wriston's sister, Barbara, was horrified at the conservative dosage. "My God," she said, "he's waited sixty-seven years for a drink. Give him a good one."

Not long after Henry's brush with death, Walter was on his way to Idlewild Airport to catch a plane for Beirut when he felt an excruciating pain in his chest. The driver turned around and drove him to a hospital, where X rays revealed a large tumor on the lung. Wriston figured, as he put it later, that he "had had a pretty good run," but in an era of less than generous employee benefits, he was concerned about how his young family would support themselves if he died. Organized religion had not played a major role in Wriston's later life, but as Karl Malden recalls, his Bible was by his bedside in his hospital room. The tumor proved to be benign. Shortly thereafter, Bobby herself went under the knife for the identical operation.

While Wriston was recuperating, his subordinates streamed into his Peter Cooper Village apartment seeking his approval for things like salary increases for porters at the Paris branch. Wriston, furious that they would bother him with such trivial matters, ordered them out of his apartment.

Ever since his army days, Wriston had been a pack-a-day Lucky Strike smoker. He had quit some time before his illness, but until then he was uncertain whether smoking was "good or bad for you," as he put it later. As he climbed the ladder at the bank, the evidence on the hazards of smoking piled up. Eventually, when there was no longer any doubt that the habit was unhealthy, it became for Wriston a litmus test of a colleague's intelligence and his qualifications for a senior post. By the time Wriston made it to the top, underlings understood that smoking in Wriston's presence was a surefire way to derail their careers.

A little over a year after Wriston landed in the overseas division, the frustration Sheperd and Rockefeller felt about the effectiveness of the bank's operations abroad finally reached the boiling point. They ordered Moore to get on an airplane, visit the bank's branches around the world, and tell them what was wrong. On his return, Moore reported that morale was "zero" and that the bank's overseas employees were just looking forward to retirement. After giving Moore's report and recommendations their seal of approval, Rockefeller and Sheperd informed him one morning in March 1957 that he would take charge of overseas that afternoon. Leo Shaw was then demoted from executive vice president to senior vice president of that division. Before being sent by the bank on a slow boat around the world, ostensibly to make a final inspection of the foreign branches, Shaw made no attempt to conceal his belief that Moore would destroy the division. In his parting shots at his successor, he said that morale overseas "is going to be shot."

Wriston recalled that a worried George Moore ran to his desk saying, "Leo says this. Is that true? Is that true? Is that true?"

"George, I've got news for you, they're [overseas staff] dancing in the streets," Wriston replied. "They hate his [Shaw's] guts." Veteran international banker Frank Mitchell, with only a few years to go before retirement, was designated Moore's second-in-command. Though Wriston was officially responsible only for the European district, he would in fact become Moore's right-hand man in the push to plant the bank's flag on foreign shores. Moore left little doubt that Wriston's star was firmly hitched to his. He told colleagues, "As I move up, one fellow I'm going to pull with me is Walt Wriston. He's got the makings of a great leader." From then on, Wriston succeeded Moore in every job he had.

With these changes at the top, George Moore launched what was possibly the most aggressive overseas expansion of American capitalism in U.S. business history. A decade after George Marshall announced his plan for rebuilding Europe, George Moore would launch his own version of the Marshall Plan. In his frequent globe-hopping following his appointment, he made it clear, as former Citibanker Rick Wheeler put it later, that "we're no longer going to be a sleepy bank."

First National City's mission, as Moore and Wriston defined it, was to perform every useful legal banking service anywhere in the world where it could do so at a profit. This was an unprecedented leap of faith by this modern-day Marco Polo called Citibank, but the strategy was simple. It consisted of three overlapping phases that Moore and Wriston compared to a three-stage rocket. The first phase consisted of planting the First National City logo, preferably a branch, along the major trade routes of the world, in every major commercial center and port. The second stage, said Wriston later, called for pushing deeper into countries by setting up "satellite or mini-branches" to solicit local currency deposits. And the third stage, he said, "was to export retail services and know-how from New York," including financial services related to banking.

Wriston and Moore's unscientific, seat-of-the-pants strategy did not involve reams of demographic studies and market analysis. Underlying the plans for expansion, said Wriston, was the expectation that "world trade was going to explode." Both had to face the fact that the bank's board was still far from certain that overseas expansion was a good thing, but Moore pushed ahead anyway. Adding branches in existing territory and breaking into new territory were only one part of the effort. Another key part of it was simply letting staff know that things were going to change, and for the better.

Led by General Electric in the early fifties, decentralization was now the rage in industrial America. But that principle had not begun to be applied in banking institutions. Under the Moore-Wriston plan, responsibility would be decentralized by raising lending authority. Term loans, by now accepted in domestic transactions, would be made overseas in local currencies. Employees would be better paid, and a massive effort to inject new blood would be undertaken.

It was probably not a complete coincidence that George Moore replaced Leo Shaw just days before the signing, on March 25, 1957, of what would become known as the Treaty of Rome. This historic pact, a benchmark event on the road to the economic and political integration of Europe, established the European Common Market to facilitate the free movement of goods and services among France, West Germany, Italy, Belgium, the Netherlands, and Luxembourg. It also set up a European atomic energy federation to develop peaceful uses of nuclear energy. The implications of this pact for an international bank like First National City were enormous. Wriston kept some of his troops busy writing papers on the treaty and the prospects for the European Economic Community. In fact, he concluded in amazement that "Americans were the only ones who read the treaty. The Deutsche Bank didn't have branches. None of the other banks were in the other guy's backyard."

In his conversations with European commercial and central bankers, Wriston didn't hesitate to express his free market–oriented views on the unification movement, at least those aspects of it related to banking and finance. The Europeans' view at the time of how currency and trade moved was a "rigid" one, he said. He had no use for people who set up complex bureaucratic organizations to perform functions that the free market could perform naturally. One such bureaucracy was the European Payments Union, an agency created to settle payments between member nations. He told the financial authorities in his trips to Europe, "You ought to dismantle the whole thing," informing them that the "greatest two-way trade in the world is handled by seven traders in Montreal and New York." Said Wriston later, "The bureaucracy just couldn't believe that. [But] they did in fact dismantle it and no one remembers it at this point."

Wriston and Moore would wind up spending the next decade seeking cracks in the door to Europe. In Paris they established a free counseling service for clients seeking to understand and do business in the new Common Market, and they frequently called on local monetary officials to try to persuade them to allow them to compete with local banks.

Ambitious as Moore's European plan was, however, the bank's greatest growth for the next several years, as measured by pins on the map, occurred mostly in Latin America, where the overseas business was already concentrated. It was always easier for the bank to expand in a country where it was already represented, than to gain licenses where it was not. Full-blown expansion in Europe would not begin until the early 1960s, and with a couple of notable exceptions, significant expansion in Asia would have to wait until the late 1960s.

Said Asia hand Ray Kathe, "George was really the fellow who wanted to put pins on the map. George had a philosophy that anytime the door opened, we should walk into a country, because it was so hard to expand. In the earlier days, we knew that if we got into a country we could make out well. It was just axiomatic: if we got in, we could do it."

It would take more than enthusiasm to return the overseas empire to its pre-crash heights. Some formidable obstacles would have to be overcome. First and foremost was the ingrained laziness of men who had grown up in the division since the IBC days. Then there was the difficulty in finding brainpower that could be dispatched overseas to build the business. Moreover, First National City faced tough regulatory barriers in trying to establish itself for the first time, or after a long absence, in foreign countries. Local bankers and finance ministers did not welcome First National City with open arms. In many respects, the bank's ability to expand was as limited overseas as it was in the United States. One reason was that New York banking laws blocked foreign banks from opening branches in the state, so foreign governments responded in kind by raising legal barriers to First National City's attempt to move onto their turf.

Where the presence of a major international bank like First National City was imperative to facilitate trade, the bank was admitted, typically on a limited basis. This was acceptable, since the idea was to get a toehold in every major commercial center by any possible means and on any possible basis. While the ideal solution was to establish a branch that could offer unlimited banking services to anyone and everyone, more often Wriston and Moore had to be content with setting up a representative office, purchasing a small finance company or affiliate, or acquiring some other entity with limited powers in the hope that eventually those powers would be broadened.

Overnight, George Moore became the General Patton of American banking. But Moore was a general whose troops were reluctant to fight, or were wedded to the fighting methods of the past. The biggest obstacle Moore faced, he said later, was "turning around people who were stodgy and negative." From the outset, the old guard overseas resisted nearly every move of the Moore-Wriston team, citing decades-old notions about how a U.S. bank in a foreign market should and should not operate. Old-time officers refused to call on local companies, for example, for fear of disrupting their own cordial relationships with correspondent banks.

In 1957, other U.S. banks, including Bank of America, First National Bank of Boston, and Continental Illinois, also operated overseas, but in general their networks were smaller and they were reluctant to expand as aggressively as First National City.

George Moore knew he had little more than two years before Howard Sheperd would be retiring. And he was determined to show Sheperd and the board that he was the only possible choice to succeed Stillman Rockefeller as president. Over the next ten years Moore would rarely listen to the voices of restraint, and he would later regret the few instances in which he did heed them. "We could have gone into Guatemala," he said, but at the urging of subordinates "we turned it down and the Bank of America went in, and we couldn't get in for another twenty years. The boys turned down Thailand, and BofA went in and made a million dollars in their second year. We couldn't get in there for [many] years."

One of Moore's first moves was to bring all the field hands home from their posts for the first of many gatherings of officers from around the world. These conferences became a National City overseas tradition and a forum for announcements of major changes in personnel and organization. The first one, however, turned into a massive group therapy session for long-suffering overseas hands. They streamed into the Westchester Country Club, refusing to believe that anyone in New York really cared about their problems, and for several days they sat around stiff and tight-lipped. Eventually they got so tired, Wriston recalled, that they began to pour out grievances that had gone unheeded for decades. They griped, for example, about New York's false perception of their lifestyles, including the myths about twenty-five-cent steaks. Some claimed that they lacked basic amenities like refrigerators. Many couldn't afford to own even a stripped-down Ford, which then cost $25,000 in many countries. That first meeting in Westchester, said Argentina hand James Farley, "was a turning point in the rejuvenation of overseas."

"We felt the élan very quickly," said Richard Valelly, who was an officer in Venezuela when the drive to build the overseas division began. Moore quickly implemented a 25 percent increase in salaries and allowances, bringing overseas compensation up to the level offered to domestic officers and employees and enabling many overseas hands to buy cars for the first time. "Our economic life was improved greatly by George Moore," said Valelly. "Our status began to improve. George turned the world around for us."

In his effort to find imaginative, energetic people to staff the overseas branches, Moore called Robert Feagles, a thirty-seven-year-old mechanical engineering graduate who had served as a communications officer in Asia during the war and later attended the Thunderbird School of International

Management. After training in Puerto Rico, where he set up a personnel office, Feagles returned to New York to work in National City Bank's branch system.

Moore had read Feagles's master's thesis on the personal attributes associated with success and longevity in the overseas division. Having quit overseas himself for the domestic side of the bank, Feagles was leery when Moore asked him to return. "Just two years. Just two years. Give me just two years," Moore implored. Feagles agreed, and became a key player in the revitalization of the division. Moore's marching orders to his new overseas personnel chief were simple: scour the country for the best and the brightest, hire as many as the bank could cram through its system, and pay them whatever it took to compete with Ford, GM, and U.S. Steel.

Moore found the players he needed for his new team after searching throughout the world—in merchant banks, at J. P. Morgan, and in the top business schools. He knew he couldn't waste time hiring mediocre people and putting them through the traditional slow-track training system, so he made a revolutionary bet on intelligence. "Bright people don't make mistakes that are too big to handle," Moore said excitedly. "Hire the best."

Except for their insistence on high IQs, Wriston and Moore were egalitarians. Wriston loathed privilege seekers and anyone who thought family wealth would be the passport to success at the bank. "He didn't like people [who were to] the manner born," said former personnel chief James Griffin. "He didn't like anyone from a three-car-garage family." Moore liked to describe himself as the son of a railroad worker, and Wriston referred to himself as the "son of a poor itinerant schoolteacher." Few of those who rose to the top at First National City under Wriston came from privileged backgrounds, and no one who did advertised it, at least in front of him. Wriston preferred to surround himself with colleagues and customers, like McLean and Onassis, who were entrepreneurs and self-made men.

In the 1950s the top graduates of America's best business schools seemed uninterested in a career in banking, and Moore and Wriston realized they would have to call on the Harvard Business School and Professor Charles Williams, then one of the nation's leading banking academicians. So Moore, in a passionate pitch, begged Harvard business students to consider First National City. Only half jokingly he told them that in this age of Sputnik, Citibank would one day open branches on the moon. The initial reception at Harvard was not warm. Disappointed when only a handful of students even bothered to sign up for interviews, Moore turned for advice to Williams's research assistant, Donald Howard, a Clark Kent look-alike who had financed his Harvard education with money he'd won playing bridge in the navy. Moore wound up hiring Howard, and Wriston dispatched him to London to work his way through the various units of the branch and to write up reports on bilateral trade agreements between European countries.

Meanwhile, Williams became a sort of campus recruiter for Citibank, making sure, he said later, that Wriston and Moore "got a special look" at the best prospects. As a result, First National City soon became the largest single employer of newly minted Harvard M.B.A.'s. One of Moore's dreams was to set up his own "university" and in-house M.B.A. program. He came close, thanks to Williams, who created "mini-M.B.A. programs" for overseas staff who'd been brought back to New York for "retreading," as one former overseas officer put it. Besides serving as Citibank's headhunter and visiting lecturer, Williams made at least one other far-reaching contribution to the bank's management culture. He was convinced, recalled a former student who went on to become a top bank officer, that the problem with American banks was that they were too full of people who were "functional specialists." In Williams's view, banks, like industrial companies, needed managers and managerial discipline. He believed that as a banker rose through the ranks he should stop lending money and concentrate on being a manager. Wriston would be among the first top American bankers to apply that lesson.

Both Moore and Wriston believed in warehousing smart people. Recognizing that their major constraint was brainpower, they hired people without having the slightest idea what they would do with them. Wriston, like Moore before him, would tell prospective overseas staff, "We'll hire you. We don't know where you're going to work, but there will be a job for you." Moore assured them that if they joined First National City, they would in eighteen months be running their own operations. In many instances, the recruits created their own niches. Nor did Moore or Wriston care whether they knew anything about banking. When one top officer complained that there were too many people in the training program, Moore snapped back, echoing a philosophy that many say started with chairman Howard Sheperd: "You're wrong. You've never got too many guys in this bank. They'll . . . leave when you've got too many." Over the next fifteen years, National City, according to Moore, hired some two hundred M.B.A.'s a year and combed the world for regional specialists. The hiring of the new trainees created a thirty-year age gap in the division, so that by 1960 the staff members were either approaching sixty or under thirty.

In the Shaw era, ten years might have passed before a new hire became an assistant branch manager, providing he smiled, kept his hands out of the till, and arrived at work on time. Now trainees were achieving that status in eighteen months, and running new overseas branches in two years. Recruiter Robert Feagles used a simple three-point scale for rating a trainee's performance and potential. "We were ruthless," said Feagles later. "It was up or out. We said, 'We're giving you the career opportunity of a lifetime,' and we crammed them into the organization."

Moore would later claim to be "more of a people person" than his protégé. His style in dealing with subordinates was certainly different from Wriston's. "Moore had a good feel for people," said Argentina banker James Farley, but "Walt had a knack for making people feel good about themselves." While Moore was a cheerleader and pep-talker without peer, he did not take the time to look after his subordinates' basic needs the way Wriston and Bobby did. "Walt took a lot of personal time to meet the [employee's] wife and family and talk to him about his career. There was never a senior guy who came back from abroad who didn't spend personal time with Walt and his wife."

As George Moore's legions of young bankers, all of them men, fanned out around the world prospecting for new territory, the pressure mounted on the support staff, including service assistants and credit analysts. Their job was to review financial statements, write letters to clients, and carry out other vital but unglamorous behind-the-scenes tasks. For years these duties had typically been performed by what one former Citibanker called the "has-beens and never-would-be's," men who had flopped as lending officers or had trouble interacting with corporate clients. Moore concluded that the bank couldn't afford to waste high-priced talent on such lowly tasks. It occurred to him to expand his recruitment campaign to include women from top eastern women's colleges to fill those positions. Moore, however, felt that women were unsuitable for the loftier jobs because all they really wanted to do was get married. It would be left to Wriston to take the next step in advancing the cause of women.

Though it was clear to Moore that he would have to offer top business prospects competitive base salaries to lure them to banking, he was disinclined to correct the vast differences in the cost of living caused by local exchange rate fluctuations—a demoralizing problem. To remedy this, Feagles proposed a compensation plan calling for employees performing the same job anywhere in the world to receive essentially the same after-tax base salary, plus a 15 percent tax-free bonus, adjusted for hardship and cost-of-living adjustments. In Feagles's view, Moore didn't want to bring such an expensive and revolutionary proposal to his boss until he got the top prize, so that plan, too, would have to await Walter Wriston.

Half-century-old practices went by the board with the arrival of Moore and Wriston. Moore knew from gut instinct, and Wriston from his eight months at State, that people who remained in the same place too long forgot who the client was. With Donald Howard, the Clark Kent double Moore had hired away from Harvard, Wriston began a practice of sending overseas staff recruits abroad for relatively short stints in different countries, rather than to a single country for an entire career. That principle, said one former banker, enabled Wriston and Moore to begin replacing the powerful postwar country barons with fresh blood. Many of these men had "gone native," as one ex-Citibanker put it. In many instances, they owned shares of local businesses and were often able to avoid paying U.S. taxes.

By and large, First National City's resident country heads were Americans. It would be years before the bank's leadership abroad was truly made up of natives of every country in which it did business. But to further promote upward mobility, Wriston and Moore also stipulated that no foreign national could head the bank's operations in his homeland until he had achieved that status in another country. That would enable new hires in a particular country to feel they had a shot at the top job even if they weren't born there.

With Moore's arrival in the overseas division, the granting of local-currency term loans also became an acceptable practice. Said Valelly, "It was breaking new territory to make a five-year term loan. Until then we only did self-liquidating loans." But according to George C. Scott, who would later rise to chief credit officer of the bank, the overseas division was making de facto term loans without calling them "term loans" and without the controls. In an internal interview, Scott explained that "advances were never completely liquidated and went on from year to year," he said. Later, he said, "We abandoned this policy and made term loans."

In the 1950s, however, dollar loans to foreign countries were generally limited to short-term loans for currency stabilization, in conjunction with International Monetary Fund and U.S. Treasury programs. In 1957, for example, First National City joined with eight other U.S. banks in extending a $27 million revolving credit to the central bank of Argentina. Among the other recipients of such programs were Chile and France. Gradually, the barriers to cross-currency lending, like term lending before it, would fall by the wayside.

Besides pushing for new people and new branches, Moore quickly moved to modernize the old operations. He began to discard archaic methods such as the hand posting of accounts and replace them with computers and other automated equipment. Wriston and Moore dispatched one trusted Brazil hand to spruce up the physical appearance of the branches around the world, remodeling old branches and building or leasing new ones.

As the overseas division was put on a more businesslike footing, some of the romance and adventure began to leave it. But most overseas hands were glad to make the trade-off.

———————

In trying to stake out new territory, First National City took whatever it could get. Said former personnel chief Feagles, "We were just running through the world, à la smorgasbord, picking up everything we could lay our hands on." In 1958, the bank gained entry into Paraguay, then led by dictator General Alfredo Stroessner. It was not exactly a thriving center of world commerce, but before long First National City was a major force in the nation's economy, holding half of its deposits.

Sometimes the reception the bank was given overseas was outright hostile. In 1958, First National City received what it thought was an invitation to visit the Union of South Africa to discuss opening branches there for the first time, so Richard Perkins headed for Johannesburg. Through his longtime blue-chip business contacts, Perkins knew Charles Engelhard, whose Engelhard Industries was one of the most prominent American companies in South Africa. Other key customers, including Otis Elevator and Caterpillar Tractor, also operated there. American companies naturally wanted an American bank to handle their transactions. The timing of Perkins's visit couldn't have been worse. In early 1957, Vice President Richard Nixon had made a three-week grand tour of Africa, scrupulously avoiding racially segregated South Africa. Also, at the United Nations, the United States had recently supported a resolution condemning apartheid. On Perkins's first evening in Johannesburg, Charles Engelhard threw a dinner party for him attended by top South African business, banking, and government officials. After giving a brief talk about the bank's objectives in the country, Perkins was the target of insults from the other guests, including top cabinet officials and South African bankers.

"The head of Barclays Bank got up and said they ought to throw me out of the country," Perkins recalled. The next day Perkins reminded the prime minister that it was his office that had extended the invitation in the first place.

"Do you want us or not?" Perkins asked indignantly.

"What do you want?" the prime minister replied.

"Five branches," Perkins said.

"You got them," the prime minister said.

In 1958, First National City (South Africa) opened for business, and less than a year later it opened its first branch in Cape Town.

Wriston traveled to South Africa with Perkins on at least one of his trips, but there, as in many other countries, Perkins took the lead. Wriston liked Perkins and regarded him as down-to-earth despite his silver-spoon upbringing. "Perkins was good as an ambassador," he said. "He always moved at a high level and knew all the right people."

By December 1958, when Wriston was appointed a senior vice president, he had begun to realize that he could wind up in the top job. The subject first came up about this time over the dining room table when Bobby said, "I think you have a shot at that." In a "gee whiz" sort of way, Wriston replied, "I think I might." Until then, Wriston said later, the thought of being CEO had "never entered my mind." Walter Wriston himself wasn't particularly ambitious. He would just as soon have worked in a hardware store, said his daughter Cassy. "I came into the business by accident and stayed by inertia," Wriston later admitted. "There was no master plan."

While many of the younger overseers welcomed the growth, opportunities, and excitement that the exuberant Moore brought to the division, some of them came to dread his whirlwind junkets around the world. Moore would leave the local staff exhausted and wondering how they could possibly implement the many plans and ventures Uncle George had laid on them during his visits. Typically, Moore would bark his orders to a young officer, who would later seek the branch manager's guidance in carrying them out. Many managers simply told their subordinates to forget everything George had told them. That sometimes included Moore's choices of new branch sites. On one visit to Caracas, Venezuela, Moore summoned a helicopter to take him to the airport for the flight home. Hovering high above the city, Moore pointed excitedly to places where he thought new branches should be opened.

And while Moore considered himself a "people person" with a unique ability to spot talent, others found his methods for doing so somewhat questionable. Arriving at Japan's Osaka Airport, Moore was once greeted by a young officer who escorted him into the city. On the way, Moore asked him for the name of a river and the bridge that spanned it. The junior officer replied that it was in fact a drainage ditch. "It's a river, a river, a river!" Moore exclaimed. Moore later reported to the trainee's boss that this particular trainee didn't know the territory.

Leo Shaw's claim that Moore didn't know anything about the international business was in part correct. In the late 1950s the U.S. balance-of-payments deficit was becoming a worrisome issue for government officials and bankers alike. Wriston would recall later that Moore ran up to him, asking, "What is this balance of payments?" But because he was married to a Spanish woman who spent much of her time in Mexico, Moore wasn't exactly oblivious to events outside the world of domestic banking. He told friends, as one senior Citibank officer recalls, that "marrying a foreigner opened up the world to him." But his appointment as head of overseas certainly extended his horizon even further.

In the Wriston family, *Foreign Affairs,* the quarterly magazine of the Council of Foreign Relations, was as familiar as *Time* and *Newsweek,* but when Wriston escorted Moore to his first council reception, Moore's reaction was like that of a Little Leaguer visiting the Yankee dugout for the first time. He scanned the gathering excitedly, asking, "Who are all these people? Who are all these people? Who are all these people?" As Wriston discreetly told him the names of some of the guests, Moore seemed to realize in a flash that banking and business were not the only games in town. "My God," he exclaimed, "I've been shaking hands with the wrong people for twenty years. Twenty years, the wrong people!"

Ironically, when Wriston was nominated for membership in the Council on Foreign Relations several years earlier, the head of the nominating committee was a young Chase banker named David Rockefeller. According to Robert Hoguet, Rockefeller reacted to the nomination with some surprise. "You mean Henry Wriston has a son?" he asked.

Nor had First National City ever bothered to dispatch a delegation to the annual meeting of the International Monetary Fund and the World Bank, the preeminent event of the year in the world of international finance. Although the annual meetings of the IMF, with their nonstop caviar, had been de rigueur for the world's finance ministers, central bankers, and commercial bankers since 1946, it wasn't until October 1958 that Moore finally journeyed to New Delhi, India, for his first meeting.

He arrived not a moment too soon. In late 1958 the United States was running up the largest balance-of-payments deficit since World War II, and New York banks, including First National City, could barely find enough deposits to meet loan demand. First National also lacked the intellectual horsepower to deal with this problem.

On the first leg of the return trip, Moore stopped in Ceylon, and, to his dismay, was met in Colombo with no fanfare whatsoever. He soon discovered the reason why: all of the attention was being showered on a tall, patrician official of the Federal Reserve Bank named John Exter, whose advice to the government earlier in the decade had helped bail it out of a severe financial crisis. Moore thought to himself, "I'd better hire this guy. He's more important than I am." When he returned home, Moore did hire Exter as a vice president, in part to handle relationships with the world's central banks.

Shortly after Exter joined the bank, then president Stillman Rockefeller said to him, "Tell me what we're doing wrong." To the casual observer, it might have appeared that there was nothing wrong at that moment. With a hefty percentage of the nation's banking assets, the big New York banks were at the pinnacle of their financial power, New York City was the unchallenged financial center of the free world, and First National City was considered the toughest and smartest, if not yet the largest, of the New York banks. But despite their banks' size, prestige, and financial strength, the leaders of the New York banking community were terribly worried.

In 1959 the United States economy and the New York City banks were at a watershed. In each year of the past decade except 1957, the United States had posted a balance-of-payments deficit. Massive U.S. aid to Europe, business investment overseas, and grants and loans had all caused more money to flow out of the country than flowed into it. By 1958 the situation had become alarming. Because dollars were convertible into gold at the fixed rate of $35 an ounce, foreigners readily swapped their dollars, causing a massive outflow of U.S. gold reserves. Meanwhile, as the U.S. economy expanded, interest rates rose, exceeding the rates banks could pay on time and savings accounts under the Fed's Regulation Q. The Fed had last raised the ceilings by one half of one percentage point on January 1, 1957, to 3 percent for savings deposits and time deposits of six months or month, 2½ percent for time deposits between ninety days and six months, and just 1 percent on deposits under ninety days. By comparison, rates in August 1959 on three-month and six-month Treasuries were 3.15 percent and 3.69 percent, respectively. Money, particularly foreign time deposits, was flowing out of the New York banks like water through a sieve. From 1959 to 1960, New York City commercial banks lost almost $1 billion in deposits.

Demand deposits, or checking accounts, then the lifeblood of banking, had not grown for the New York Clearing House banks as a group for about ten years and, in real terms, may have actually declined. For its part, First National City's deposits grew from $4.78 billion at year end 1949 to $7.23 billion at year end 1959, but nearly a third of that was due to National City's merger with the First National Bank. With the economic growth that followed the end of the 1957–1958 recession, the New York banks were no longer able to keep pace with the loan demand of American industry, though not for a lack of trying. "The message was that if we continued the way we were going, we would die," said Wriston later.

One reason for the decline in demand deposits was that corporate treasurers were increasingly investing their so-called idle cash into interest-bearing instruments rather than keeping it in banks. For years, bankers had required that corporations maintain with them compensating balances, usually checking account deposits, amounting to as much as 20 percent of their outstanding loans. In return, companies received services such as wire transfers and checking accounts. Throughout the 1950s, corporate America virtually self-funded its own loans with compensating balances. But by 1959 corporations held more than $20 billion in short-term government obligations.

To make matters worse, New York City banks still couldn't reach beyond the five boroughs for deposits. In early 1959, the New York State legislature rejected a bill that would have allowed branching into neighboring counties.

Squeezed for funds, First National City, Chase, and others became more and more solicitous of their so-called retail customers, devising a variety of innovations to attract consumer deposits in the five boroughs. In 1959, the bank became the first New York bank to offer individual borrowers a revolving line of credit tied to their checking accounts. And, as usual, in retail banking, Chase was nipping at First National City's heels. In December 1956, when the Fed permitted commercial banks to raise their rate on savings deposits by one half of 1 percent to 3 percent, Chase moved quickly, while National City stalled for a year. As a result, Chase's savings deposits surged from $174 million in 1955 to about $500 million by the end of 1958. In 1959, Chase achieved something of a milestone in the history of American consumer finance when it became the first bank to pay interest on savings deposits from the day of deposit to the day of withdrawal, so long as the customer kept a minimum balance through the end of the quarter.

Ultimately, although Regulation Q would undermine New York's role as a world financial center, it would, in the long run, create opportunities for First National City. The shift of foreign time deposits out of United States banks would give rise to the Euromarkets and the Eurodollar and to the emergence of First National City as a global banking power.

The Eurodollar is not currency per se, but rather a dollar entry on the books of a financial institution outside the United States that is backed up by an actual dollar on deposit in the United States. Nothing is ever bought with a Eurodollar except another currency; it is used only as an accounting device for the transfer of financial resources around the globe. There are many accounts of the origin of the Euromarket; some have even suggested that it originated in 1914, when National City opened its first branch overseas, in Buenos Aires, and accepted a dollar deposit. Don Howard, who trained in London in the late fifties, would later contend that it began in London in 1958. Citibank in London had heard that another U.S. bank there had accepted a dollar deposit and paid interest on it, and sent Howard on a mission to determine what the fuss was all about. "It took me a while to find out what was going on," Howard recalled. "But once I got ahold of the people doing the transaction, it was clear it was a very simple concept." Howard wrote up a report on the transaction, and thereby became, for the rest of his career at Citibank, the resident Eurodollar expert.

In the public's mind, the Eurodollar would forever appear an arcane and mysterious concept. But for Wriston and Moore, the emergence of the Euromarkets—which, unlike U.S. financial markets, were subject to few if any government regulations—would both justify and accelerate their plans for international expansion. Indeed, First National City's bold push overseas would itself contribute to the rise of the Euromarkets as the principal arena for global finance. The immediate problem, however, was the domestic funding squeeze. The solution was a revolutionary instrument called the negotiable certificate of deposit. Like many successful innovations, this one had several fathers. Wriston, Exter, and a junior officer named Lawrence Heath would all claim that the idea began with them. Wherever it originated, there is no question that all three men, and perhaps others as well, contributed to it.

"You didn't have to be too smart to know you had to do something to survive. We were hemmed in in this country, and the stagnation in New York led to the invention of the CD," said Wriston. He later recalled that the notion occurred to him as a result of a visit in the late 1950s by one of the Greek shippers he had served as a young officer. "I want to put some money in your bank," the shipper said, but "I don't want my name on it because frankly I don't trust your Internal Revenue Service. Is there any way I can put my money in your bank and not have my name on your records?" Wriston told a Shearman & Sterling lawyer that his customer wanted a receipt for his deposit in the form of a bearer instrument. After being informed that it was legal, the bank issued a million-dollar negotiable CD for the shipping magnate.

John Exter would later recall that he began to zero in on the funding problem right after Stillman Rockefeller asked him what the bank was doing wrong. He quickly focused in on the fact that the New York banks continued to insist on "free" compensating balances while banks outside New York were accepting interest-bearing nonnegotiable time deposits. It was no wonder that New York banks were losing deposits. But the banks were worried that if they began to pay interest on time deposits, corporations would simply replace all of their interest-free demand deposits with interest-bearing instruments, driving up interest costs. According to George Moore, bankers like chairman Howard Sheperd were beginning to realize that the bank would "have to begin paying for its inventory." In a September 1959 memo that began simply, "We need deposits," Exter outlined his proposal for the creation of a bearer "time certificate of deposit" that would be issued to corporations and foreign banks and traded in the secondary markets. Exter also believed that the instrument would force the Fed to eliminate Regulation Q, the principal source of the problem.

In the eighteen months before the final version was introduced in early 1961, Wriston became its leading advocate within the bank. It would be the first of many high-stakes gambles in which he would put his institution and his own career on the line. The notion of innovation in banking had long been a contradiction. That was finally about to change.

By the end of the 1950s, Wriston's and Moore's box score was not all that impressive. Wriston had opened a new branch in London and, with considerable help from Richard Perkins, had added South Africa to the bank's empire. First National City had also opened two branches each in Brazil and Argentina, and one more in Uruguay and in Singapore. Malaya and Paraguay had also been added to the fold.

More important were the changes they had made in the bank's overseas culture. They had recruited scores of eager, hard-charging new people, and they had rekindled the fire in the bellies of some of the older officers. And for that accomplishment, they would soon receive their rewards.

5

CHANGING OF THE GUARD

*I*f anyone could read the Citibank tea leaves, it was Ray Kathe, the gregarious Asia hand who had barely escaped with his life when the Communists seized the bank's Chinese branches. In the fall of 1959, Kathe was First National City's man in Hong Kong. He and his colleagues thought it was a bit odd that Wriston, the New York–based head of the European district, should be traipsing around the Orient with his wife, since the bank had its own district head for Asia. One evening, during a party at Kathe's home, Wriston received an overseas phone call that cleared up the mystery.

At this time, the overseas division was still not contributing to bank earnings in a meaningful way. Indeed, with the fuzzy, archaic accounting methods of the era, no one would have known where it was really making money, or whether it was at all. But in less than three years Moore and Wriston had succeeded in kicking up lots of dust in the once staid operation. Bright young faces were now at work around the world, shiny new facades were being constructed on stodgy-looking gray buildings, and state-of-the-art computer equipment was being installed to improve productivity. All told, the division now consisted of over seventy-eight branches in twenty-seven countries and over six thousand employees.

In the midst of these developments Howard Sheperd retired, and Stillman Rockefeller, now fifty-seven, became chairman. Moore was named president, and Wriston, as he learned over the phone in Hong Kong, was chosen to succeed Moore as head of the overseas division. Less than a year later, in June 1960, Wriston was appointed an executive vice president. In other words, it all worked out just as the ambitious George Moore had planned it. Moore's election as president of FNCB later would be followed by the ascendancy of Walter Wriston into the limelight as a rising star of American business. The third member of the top management troika, Richard Perkins, who had desperately wanted to follow in his father's footsteps as chairman, now became head of the executive committee, but he was treated by both Rockefeller and Moore as if he simply didn't exist for the rest of his career. Both Rockefeller and Moore despised Perkins—Rockefeller because Perkins

115

was brought in to compensate for his personality quirks, and Moore because Perkins had earlier been placed over him in the pecking order. For all of his warm, human qualities, he would never become an insider.

The succession, which took effect on November 1, 1959, wasn't accomplished without some ferocious boardroom infighting and politicking. It was something of a Citibank tradition that the top man was always stuck with senior colleagues not of his own choosing. This time around, the lineup was one of the most bizarre combinations of personalities ever assembled in the top ranks of American banking. By choosing Rockefeller and Moore, First National City wound up with "a chairman who didn't talk and a president who wouldn't listen," as Frederick Donner, then chairman of General Motors, would say. Wriston later claimed that "Stillman was perfectly capable of taking a customer to lunch and saying absolutely nothing the entire time."

The top management team, in other words, was a veritable matrix of bitterness, rancor, and resentment. Though Wriston's relationship with Moore was almost always cordial, Rockefeller and Moore were a corporate odd couple. Both Wriston and the cautious and conservative Mr. Rockefeller regarded Moore as a brilliant, even inspirational leader and supersalesman, but also as a loose cannon who operated by the seat of his pants with little or no planning and forethought. To the bank's amateur sociologists, the relationship between Moore and Rockefeller was a uniquely American class struggle. As the theory went, it was Rockefeller *versus* Moore, the son of a midwestern railroad worker, graduate of Yale, Rockefeller's own alma mater, the bastion of the eastern elite. In turn, Wriston and Moore were frustrated with Rockefeller because of his unwillingness to move as fast as they might have liked. "They were allies against Stillman," said one source. For Wriston, Rockefeller was a man to be circumvented and Moore was a man to be controlled.

According to former executives, chairman Howard Sheperd had backed Perkins for the presidency while Rockefeller, despite his reservations, had supported Moore. Another faction had supported Howard Laeri, considered one of the premier lenders in the United States. The struggle was ultimately resolved with Moore's election to the presidency and Perkins's ascendancy to chairman of the executive committee, traditionally the number two job. In the heat of the battle, chief credit officer Art Forward reportedly asked Moore if he would be upset if he wasn't elected president. Moore replied sullenly that he would work under any conditions, adding that he had outlived all the bosses who weren't as smart as he was. Forward is said to have told Sheperd that not being president didn't matter to Moore. "I've spent three days fighting with Sheperd over this, and you say it doesn't make any difference to you," Rockefeller told Moore, who, of course, wanted the job so badly he could have screamed. Later, Rockefeller asked the board to amend the bylaws to make the president second-in-command in the absence of the chairman—relegating Perkins to a largely figurehead role. As for Laeri, who became an executive vice president in charge of the bank's National Division, he was so devastated at not being considered for the presidency that he spent a year recovering while colleagues ran his division. Moore, meanwhile, ran over Laeri like a four-minute miler with steel spikes. With Moore's appointment, the message flashed through the empire that anyone who aspired to the top job had better get his ticket punched in the overseas division first. For his part, Wriston would later tell colleagues that he was "too dumb" to comprehend the swirl of corporate politics going on around him.

Wriston and Moore regarded Rockefeller as a no-nonsense, decisive, and hard-nosed banker and administrator, but one whose personality and personal prejudices often interfered with his judgment. He was introverted, measured, sarcastic, "not a fellow you had a drink with after work," as one Citibanker put it later. "Diplomacy," said one top executive, "was not his forte. He breaks eggs with a hammer."

While Stillman Rockefeller rarely, if ever, openly expressed disapproval of any Wriston initiative, Wriston clearly was not enamored of Rockefeller's management style and personnel policies. In fact, the two men clashed fiercely on personnel issues. They waged a three-year battle, for example, over Rockefeller's refusal to grant a raise to one officer because he once wore a dirty shirt to work. "I don't care if he had on a dirty shirt," Wriston insisted. "He's a hell of a good banker." Every December, Rockefeller, like a modern-day Scrooge, sat at his desk crossing out the names of people he didn't like who had been recommended for raises or bonuses.

Rockefeller saw his mission as making sure Catholics didn't get the upper hand in the bank. "We didn't have the minorities problem," Rockefeller said in an internal interview, "but we had to be very careful not to let too many Catholics get in one branch or one department, because if so they would exclude everybody else." He added that "you had to keep things in balance." In contrast to George Moore, who was enamored of Latinos in general and Mexicans in particular, Rockefeller had little use for them. "His view of other cultures was not always charitable," said Wriston later. Perhaps more commendable was his determination to knock "politics in the head whenever it cropped up."

Rockefeller presided over First National City until his retirement in 1967, relying all the while on the philosophy of his illustrious maternal grandfather, James Stillman: "personal control, silence, and ready cash." Rockefeller didn't simply play his cards close to his vest; he never revealed them at all—to colleagues, customers, or even directors. According to Wriston, Rockefeller told board members that he had, on his own, purchased some land on Long Island, but refused to tell them where it was or how much he had paid. "You guys talk too much," he told them. To Rockefeller, the financial press, which was relatively unaggressive during his reign, was the lowest form of life, and he was vehemently opposed to the bank's seeking a high media profile. Occasionally, however, the press got its revenge. On a trip to Montevideo, Uruguay, Rockefeller, along with his prominent nose, got off the plane and was greeted by a clutch of reporters. He refused to talk, but a photographer snapped an unflattering profile shot that was published with the caption, *"El tiene nariz grande para su negocio"* (He has a big nose for business).

Rockefeller liked to prowl the corridors of 55 Wall Street like a New England prep school headmaster, poking his head unexpectedly into subordinates' offices to keep abreast of events and leaving terse, critical notes for occupants of messy desks. It became such a chore for young officers to store their papers in drawers every evening and to sort them out the next morning that they devised a system they called "overnight float." At the end of each day, they stuffed their papers into bags and attached to them self-addressed pink routing slips. Every evening, before Rockefeller made his rounds, female pages in black and white dresses collected the bags, stored them overnight, and returned them the next morning.

Out of earshot, Rockefeller was often at the receiving end of Wriston's well-honed needle. "Stillman's greatest tragedy," Wriston used to say, "was that he wasn't born in a log cabin." Others, however, detected a more tender side in the chairman. "He appears to have a heart of ice, but he is really a warm guy," claimed former corporate secretary Paul Kolterjahn. Retired Citibanker Rick Wheeler recalls that on one occasion when a lender in the special industries group lost a substantial sum of money on a loan, Rockefeller did not dress the man down. Instead, he asked the beleaguered loan officer, "What are we going to learn from this?"

Rockefeller also possessed a dour wit and a playful, whimsical streak. The wife of one senior officer would later recall meeting him for the first time at a dinner party at a new two-level branch at Park Avenue and Fifty-seventh Street. While officers and employees were dining on the upper floor, the woman's husband was escorting her on a tour of the vault on the lower level, which had been left open for the occasion. As they strolled through the huge stainless-steel chamber into the lobby, Rockefeller scrambled down the up escalator, and slid to a halt just in front of them on the newly waxed marble floor. After the officer introduced his bemused wife, she asked him if he was now going to run up the down escalator as well. "Sure am," he said wryly.

"I don't think I've ever had dinner in a bank before," she said, struggling to make small talk with her husband's boss.

"Not likely to again either," he said.

For all his wealth, Rockefeller was in many ways as austere as Wriston. Each morning he drove himself to the Greenwich railroad station in an old Ford and rode the club car to Grand Central. As the story goes, he installed a pool on his estate with great reluctance, concerned that it would appear ostentatious.

One of Stillman Rockefeller's major initiatives during his years as president was his battle in the mid to late 1950s to persuade his colleagues, including then chairman Howard Sheperd, to move the bank's headquarters uptown, from Wall Street to a new building to be constructed on Park Avenue. Moore, for one, opposed the move on the grounds that it would hurt the bank's image among Wall Streeters. Wriston recalled that Moore went so far as to assemble binders of statistics intended to prove that the move would be a disaster. The debate went on for months. "We had terrible arguments," said Perkins. Moore was outvoted, but after the die was cast, Moore, ever the team player and political animal, fully supported the decision and discarded his reams of data.

But the move to 399 Park Avenue in 1961 did turn out to have its drawbacks. For one thing, the bank lost twenty-five minutes of precious check-clearing time because it took that much longer for the checks to travel from the new headquarters to the New York Clearing House in the financial district, where each day the New York banks swap billions of dollars' worth of checks. Thousands of checks that missed the clearing deadline were left over at the end of the day, causing the bank to lose one day's use of the funds. Consequently, the bank was later forced to build yet another glass-and-aluminum tower on Wall Street to serve as an operations center.

The new uptown headquarters building was one example of the fact the real estate deals Citibank negotiated on its own behalf over the years proved shrewder than those done by some of its lenders for customers. Perkins had been inspecting footings with engineers under the tracks beneath a plot of land near Grand Central Station when a call came from the bank's real estate department advising him that a plot on Park and Fifty-third had become available. Originally owned by wealthy fur trader John Jacob Astor, the land had been excavated on speculation by his descendant, Vincent Astor, who had run out of money before he could begin construction. By taking over the site, First National saved $10 million, and Astor avoided the expense of filling in the hole. The building ultimately cost $40 million.

But Rockefeller lost the next round, according to one former bank executive. Stillman wanted eighteenth-century-style furniture for the building, while other senior executives insisted on sixties modern. Like a society matron redecorating the manor house, Rockefeller fussed over virtually every detail of the construction of his new tower, an austere glass-and-aluminum edifice that was conspicuous for its selfish lack of public space. According to former officers, battles raged in the boardroom over whether the bathroom tiles should be green or blue.

As his contribution to the decor, Moore commissioned a Spanish artist to sculpt a bronze relief for the lobby. For years this massive relief of a fisherman with a paddle was Citibank's white elephant. Moore wasn't identified by name in the work, but he is said to have been the model, or at least the inspiration, for a wiry fisherman stripped to the waist and flexing his muscles. No one ever knew exactly what was spent on it, because various expenses associated with it were charged to different departments, including the security unit for the guards responsible for its protection. It was entirely unsuitable for the location, because part of it was blocked by pillars, and viewers couldn't step back far enough to see it from end to end.

From his fifteenth-floor perch at 399 Park, Rockefeller could now indulge his passion for firemen and fire engines. Whenever he heard sirens, he would grab his binoculars and follow the trucks as they barreled down Park Avenue.

Later, when asked how many people worked at his new building, Rockefeller echoed Calvin Coolidge when he replied: "About half."

George Moore, at this time, seemed to be distracted by difficulties of a personal nature. About the time he was elected president, he entered New York Hospital for an operation to remove stones from both kidneys. For weeks thereafter, his Spanish-American wife, Beatriz, remained in Mexico City, where she spent much of her time. To Citibankers, she was something of a mythical figure; many had heard stories about her, but few had actually seen her. Moore was hurt and angry at her apparent lack of concern for his health. As soon as he was well enough to walk, he flew to Puerto Rico to recuperate at a resort hotel. On the beach, he met Charon Crosson, the blond, blue-eyed daughter of a political writer for the New York *Daily News,* a woman thirty-two years younger than Moore. For the next eight years, while trying to obtain a divorce, he made no secret of his affection for Charon Crosson, whom he was finally able to marry in 1968. Recalled Perkins, "He got into an awful jam there. He was occupied with this situation much of the time." Beatriz did not take this well.

Nor was Beatriz pleased with their son George Junior's choice of a wife, a young blond model. In the middle of the engagement party, Beatriz stormed through the crowd into the bedroom of the Moores' house, slamming the door behind her. Wriston asked Moore what the problem was. "Her son is marrying a gringo," Moore replied.

As president, and later as chairman, Moore was constantly harassed at the office by crank calls and a practical joker. Citibankers had their suspicions about who might be responsible, but these were never proven. Ambulance crews showed up at Wriston's fifteenth-floor office looking for "the body," and on at least one occasion, an automobile dealer called to inform Moore that "the Rolls Royce he'd ordered was now ready." Worse still, Moore received several death threats, prompting him to install a bulletproof glass barrier outside his office.

Despite his Methodist roots and Boy Scout demeanor, Wriston was no more perturbed by Moore's marital difficulties than he was by Onassis's well-publicized romantic entanglements. Another former colleague called Moore "90 percent genius and 10 percent pure fool."

The selection of new senior management in 1959, of course, set the stage for the race to succeed Moore in 1967, when Rockefeller was due to retire. Until then, besides having to cope with Rockefeller and Moore, two men with vastly different personalities and leadership styles, neither of which he particularly admired, Wriston had to deal with a rival who seemed to go out of his way to undermine him.

It was now obvious that Wriston and Tommy Wilcox, an executive vice president and head of the metropolitan division, were the two leading candidates for Moore's job. The only other possible contender was Laeri, considered the most able banker, but he would be nearing retirement in 1967.

Rockefeller did not discourage speculation that Wriston and Wilcox were the two principal contenders, and even took steps to give each horse an opportunity to perform at top speed in the homestretch. To many, Wriston was the front-runner from the moment he was appointed overseas chief. "He was so far intellectually superior to all these other guys," said former corporate secretary Carl Desch later. Wilcox was regarded as too flamboyant. He preened, he strutted, he boasted. He was, said one former officer, "the only man in the bank who could strut when he was sitting down." Said Perkins later, "Wilcox had a big-shot complex. If I gave a lunch for the president of a company, he'd try to take the lunch over. He was his own worst enemy."

Though Wriston did not express any ambition openly, Bobby wasn't so shy. "My husband's going to be the president of Citibank, and I'm going to see that he gets there," she told friends. In addition to Bobby, Wriston had another not-so-secret weapon in his father. In 1958, at about the time the bank began planning for the move uptown to 399 Park, Wriston moved his family into a two-bedroom apartment in the same East Side town house where his father now lived. That made it even more convenient for his father—wordsmith, orator, and editor without peer—to evaluate Walter's speeches. Soon after Walter's appointment as overseas chief, he found himself in demand on the business speaker's circuit and wasted no time in using his new prominence to advance his views on the proper role of the government in the economy. As Henry Wriston got older, his mind remained agile, but his official duties wound down, and editing Walter's speeches filled a major void in his life. "He'd call me up and say, 'It's a terrible piece of work,'" Walter said later. "He was helpful to me in the sense that I was trying to move opinion in the direction of freedom."

In principle, Wriston was a fiscal conservative. In a May 1960 talk to the Bankers' Association of Foreign Trade, he said, "The usefulness of the dollar as a reserve currency rests upon the distributive judgment around the world that the government which controls that currency will act decisively to protect its integrity," adding that "reserves tend to flow toward nations which discipline their creation of money and away from those which do not." But fiscal discipline would soon give way to an era of easy money. While Wriston would rail about easy money in his speeches, he and his institution would soon contribute significantly to it, and benefit greatly from it.

Despite Stillman Rockefeller's conservatism, the high-growth strategy that Wriston and Moore were now pursuing did not happen without his agreement, or at least his acquiescence. Rockefeller had his quirks and personal biases, but few bankers possessed sounder judgment about strategy, credit, and character. "He was the kind of fellow who went out of his way to appear to be negative about almost everything, yet a large number of things happened while he was chairman," said former executive committee chairman Ed Palmer in an internal interview. "He used to chuckle and shrug his shoulders and then say, 'Go ahead and do it.' " But, Robert Hoguet asserted later, "Stillman didn't move the bank fast enough for Moore and Wriston. And time has shown him to have been right." Rockefeller "was of the old school at a time when the school was changing," said Wriston later, conceding that "he did a lot for the bank. He did it in a way that was totally different from Uncle George."

No one—least of all Wriston—operated like George Moore. While the two men were usually in harmony on strategy and objectives, they were light-years apart on style. Moore was a bundle of frenetic energy who needed airplanes and telephones the way a drug addict needs a fix. He was forever generating ideas and doing deals in airplanes, elevators, and swimming pools and leaving the details to Wriston and others. He had clearly provided the spark to ignite the revitalization of the overseas division, but he was often undisciplined and uncontrollable in his approach to that task. George, Wriston would say later, "was the worst administrative officer in the world, bar none."

Like "Uncle George," Wriston was determined to build a meritocracy in the overseas division. But Wriston did it with more discipline and planning than his colorful predecessor. Wriston operated, said Ray Kathe, according to "the Harvard Business School way of doing things." He ran the overseas division, and later Citibank itself, according to a set of ironclad principles. Citibank was to be a kind of corporate microcosm of American democracy, where risk-taking and entrepreneurship would thrive. In that democracy, competition, chaos, and tension would often be rampant as well.

Said former Citibanker Hamilton Meserve, Wriston moved the bank "from being a fiduciary to being entrepreneurial. He evolved the idea that if you couldn't make money entrepreneurially, you weren't worth your salt." Accordingly, there was a tolerance for honest error that was equaled by few other American companies at the time. As ex-Citibanker John Rudy put it later, "There was a willingness to accept mistakes as a cost of doing business."

In assuming responsibility for the overseas division, Wriston was determined to make it a growth operation. "Once you create an organization," he said later, "it does one of two things: it expands or dies. It doesn't stay static." But in 1959 Wriston still faced huge obstacles to growth. There were, of course, federal and state legislative and regulatory restrictions. Internally, First National City was a risk-averse institution with a staff that was content to maintain the status quo. Said Richard Valelly, "The focus was more on negatives than positives. People got ahead by not making mistakes." Most foreign governments, encouraged by their banks, were protectionistic and resisted penetration from banking institutions beyond their borders. Wriston despised the financial barriers imposed by national boundaries. Besides wanting to build a global banking organization, he saw the bank and his legions of M.B.A.s as warriors in the fight against protectionism and other forms of economic nationalism. To him, multinationals like Citibank "were the future of the world," said ex-Citibanker Ham Meserve.

Wriston's "breakout concept" called for his troops to rattle the cages of the central banks and finance ministries of the world. They were to penetrate every opening, squirm through every loophole, and dance around every barrier standing in the way of the bank's efforts to establish a beachhead on their soil. Wriston referred to it as "prudent pioneering." One early controversy surrounded the question as to whether Citibank should expand through new branches or through acquisitions. Citibank preferred the branch route, but it frequently wound up, often to its dismay, buying other people's mistakes. And there was no more enthusiastic purchaser than George Moore himself.

Unlike Moore, Wriston did not feel compelled to tour the world and stand on every receiving line to promote the business of National City. Like Chase's David Rockefeller, Moore frequently traveled abroad with an entourage of young aides, and thrived on meeting and greeting the elite everywhere he went. Said Nancy Valelly, "Moore loved bagmen. There were always young smart guys who went around with him. It was part of the show." While posted in Colombia, the Valellys hosted several parties for Moore during his visit there. "They were so good he came back again. He loved standing in reception lines. Walt knew it was a put-on. He never struck me as a person who wanted to be with the beautiful people. That seemed banal to him."

Wriston's appointment as head of the overseas division coincided with the impending retirement, in the early to mid-1960s, of many of the old-line overseas veterans who had joined the bank in the 1920s and 1930s, providing him with a new opportunity to reinvigorate the bank with new blood.

First National City was quickly becoming the hot destination for bright young college or business school graduates seeking overseas adventure, opportunity, and responsibility. Wriston insisted on sizing up each of them personally. Said former banker Hamilton Meserve, "Wriston was not just our leader. He was a god." And he added: "We felt we were part of an incredible experiment. Wriston was a guy who breathed excitement, ideas." In the United States, a newly minted young banker might deal directly with an assistant treasurer of Xerox, but in Wriston's overseas division, a twenty-seven-year-old graduate of the Harvard Business School might sit at the big table with the finance minister of Japan.

In Wriston's view, there was no more important managerial function than choosing the right person for the right job. "The personnel business," he used to say, "was the only game in town." He probably learned that truism at his father's knee, but it was reinforced by others, like his longtime friend, management expert Peter Drucker. Drucker, Wriston recalled later, once told him that "one intelligent and visible personnel decision is worth a hundred memorandums." In a later speech, Wriston added that "finding, training, and motivating the right men and women is the only way to achieve our goals. All organizational structures are designed to be run by average people. If this were not so, all organizations would break down because most of us are average. If you have outstanding people, as we do, any organization will run at 150 percent of rated capacity, which is about the right speed to achieve our goals."

At a time when civil rights activists were struggling to extend to black Americans and other minorities the basic human rights that had long been enjoyed by white Americans, Wriston was fighting his own battle to persuade his superiors that talent has "no passport, gender, color, or anything else," Wriston said later. At National City and elsewhere, blacks had to wait longer to achieve real opportunity for equal employment and promotion than they did for the elimination to barriers to voting and education. Wriston clearly had his hands full in overcoming the ingrained prejudice in banking to the employment and promotion of Jews, Catholics, and women.

George Moore had recognized that women would be useful as the workhorses of the back office, but it was Wriston who enabled them to compete head to head with men. To his colleagues, Wriston always seemed more comfortable with women than with men, and more at ease with young people than with old people. In the 1960s, major U.S. corporations actually conducted seminars on the "problem" of women in business. Wriston, said Drucker, saw women "as a resource, not a problem." Some American businessmen at the time gave lip service to the notion of women as managers, but Wriston, the professor said, was the first to "see and understand that women belong in management." Of all of the specific contributions that Wriston would later make to American banking and business—overseas expansion, technological innovation, regulatory decontrol—Drucker asserts that the most important was his contribution to the emergence of women in the corporate workplace.

Even at Citibank, however, the expectations for advancement for women were so low that *Citibank* magazine bragged in 1967 that in the ten-year period beginning in 1957 more than fifty women had achieved officer status, an average of just five a year. And even for Wriston, getting a woman promoted to officer required some ingenuity. By 1963 only a handful of women in the bank's history had ever made it to assistant cashier, the first officer grade. That year Wriston succeeded in getting a woman banker, Zelda Wakeman, a cum laude graduate of Mount Holyoke and a Fletcher School classmate who had worked for First National City for twenty years, elevated to that rank. In his first failed attempt to get her through the board of directors, Wriston had made the mistake of disclosing her full name. She made it on the second try—because Wriston revealed only her last name and first and middle initials.

The principal opponent of advancement for women was clearly the chairman, Stillman Rockefeller. "Stillman felt fairly strongly that that wasn't their role in the world," said Wriston later. But Moore also acknowledged that he was skeptical about the potential of women as account officers and managers. Wriston's views on women in management didn't always trickle down to the troops. Even with a high-level advocate, the women Wriston hired in the early 1960s faced some old and nearly impenetrable barriers, which they didn't begin to overcome in a major way until after Wriston became chairman in 1970. One former Citibank officer said that the prevailing view in the 1960s was that women joined the bank to get married. "When I hired the first women in early 1964," he said bluntly, "I hired them for big tits and to jolly customers."

One young woman, who joined the bank in 1964 fresh out of the Fletcher School, recalls that in those days women were barred from overseas service and were told to sign only their initials on correspondence because the bank didn't want clients to know that their accounts were being handled by women. Even the thirty-ninth-floor officers' dining room in the new Park Avenue headquarters was for men only, and groups that included a woman were shunted to private rooms. At an employee gathering, the Fletcher graduate boldly asked Wriston why women weren't allowed in the dining room, said one young women. "He became visibly upset. He fixed that right away."

It would take even longer for First National City to get comfortable with the idea of sending women, particularly single women, to overseas posts. When they were finally deemed capable of handling foreign assignments, First National City faced a whole new kind of problem—"We had to spend time finding jobs for their husbands," remembered one former officer. Yet for all of Wriston's efforts to promote women, very few rose to the higher levels of the bank.

Wriston's rise to overseas chief eventually marked the end of other archaic customs and taboos of the colonial era, and often the change was accomplished without so much as a memo being written or a policy manual amended. There was, for example, an unwritten ban on bank officers marrying Asians, particularly Japanese. One officer who had served in prewar China married a Chinese woman he'd met in a Japanese prison camp, a union the bank later deemed acceptable because the Chinese had sided with the Allies during the war. But until Wriston gave his blessing in the early sixties to what was believed to be the first postwar betrothal of a bank officer and a Japanese woman, men contemplating such a move were pressured to leave the bank, according to former Citibanker Ham Meserve. Meserve recalls that Wriston quietly broke that rule when he wrote a letter to one Asia hand in the early 1960s assuring him that if he pursued his marriage plans he wouldn't lose his job.

The first black overseas trainee was hired in the mid-sixties, recalled a former personnel officer. When blacks were hired, however, personnel officers in New York had to twist the arms of managers in the field to take them, and many of the best eventually quit. On a trip to Monrovia, George Moore got a taste of black discontent within the ranks. At a party at the First National City compound, one employee, slightly inebriated, stood up and lambasted Moore to his face about the bank's shoddy treatment of black employees. According to Cedric Grant, an officer in Monrovia, Moore simply brushed the incident off.

As Wriston sought to purge the overseas division of ancient business and personnel practices, he sometimes stumbled onto other financial fossils from a bygone era. When he took over the division, he learned, for example, that Chile, which then had branches in Santiago and Valparaiso, suffered under a huge deficit. Wondering how this could be possible, since the bank had only two branches in the country, Wriston dispatched auditors to sift through the records. They discovered that decades earlier, deposed chairman Charlie Mitchell had stuck the Chilean branch with one of his defunct bond issues, and the losses were still being amortized at the branches' expense.

With the transition, Wriston could now implement another major change in the compensation plan for overseas hands, a move intended to boost the appeal of serving overseas and to increase the mobility of the overseas staff. Wriston wanted to be able to move his staff around the world on short notice whenever and wherever they were needed, without their having to worry about whether transferring from London to India or Hong Kong would have harmful tax and cost-of-living consequences. In early 1961, Wriston instructed overseas personnel chief Robert Feagles to implement the plan, saying, "Okay, I'm ready."

By now hundreds of smart young bankers were competing for the attention of Moore and Wriston by dreaming up new ways to expand the bank's operations and make money. "Walt loved the contention. He loved to sit and watch them fighting among themselves, floating new ideas up to him every day," said Feagles. With this constant influx of talent from the nation's best schools, Wriston himself didn't have to think up all the new ideas. Instead, he would occupy himself with deciding which ones to implement and which to discard.

Whatever Moore's shortcomings, he clearly broke the ice for Walter Wriston, just as Vanderlip had broken it for him. Said former comptroller and Wriston confidant Stephen Eyre, "It was easier for Wriston to pick up from where Moore left off."

Others would later express a more cynical view. "George was a wild man, but Walter Wriston never did anything but sail the ships George Moore launched," said one former Citibanker. "George was incredible to deal with. He was a bully, he was mad. But he was the one with the vision."

After Wriston became overseas chief, his marching orders, issued only partly in jest, from Moore were to be "aggressive enough to scare David but not aggressive enough to scare him." The David referred to was, of course, Chase Manhattan vice chairman David Rockefeller, Stillman's cousin. In 1960, David Rockefeller was the Goliath of American banking. He was the man to beat.

But the top management relationships that were shaping up at David Rockefeller's bank were perhaps even more rancorous than those at City Bank. And at Chase, the dissension would prove far more destructive. On October 21, 1960, Chase announced that George Champion, a gruff and blunt-spoken native of Normal, Illinois, and Rockefeller of New York, Maine, Pocantico Hills, and Venezuela would become co-CEOs effective at year end, succeeding the retiring chairman John J. McCloy. The hostility between Rockefeller and Champion, combined with long-standing institutional hang-ups, would enable Citibank, a decade later, to steal from Chase the un-official title of world's premier banking institution.

Like First National City, Chase was led by a commoner and an aristo-crat. The crusty, card-playing George Champion was the quintessential domestic banker, who had cut his teeth during the Depression helping to bail out banks in which Chase held a financial interest. David Rockefeller had joined Chase in April 1946, a couple of months before Wriston arrived at National City. Rockefeller had graduated from Harvard, studied at the London School of Economics, and earned a doctorate in economics at the University of Chicago in 1941. Champion regarded David Rockefeller as a rich kid who had attained his position because his name happened to be Rockefeller.

Perhaps more significant, the two top men held vastly different visions of the kind of institution Chase Manhattan was and should become. Whereas David wished to see Chase evolve into a truly international bank serving American and local customers around the world, Champion viewed Chase mainly as a domestic institution whose sole mission overseas was to serve U.S. corporations doing business there. Wriston, of course, believed that "you can't survive as a domestic bank unless you're a major international bank," according to former assistant secretary of state Robert Hormats.

"He [Champion] and I didn't see eye to eye on how the bank should develop, which may be one reason it didn't develop in that direction as fast as I would have liked," David Rockefeller acknowledged later. Pointing out that he and Champion were equals for eight years before he finally assumed the reins alone, Rockefeller said of those years, "That was a very critical pe-riod when Citibank was moving aggressively and effectively. I think we would have had a greater chance to move effectively if we'd had clearer objectives than we did in the 1960s." It may be too strong to say that Champion bullied David, but in the view of one Chase banker, he certainly "leaned on him."

To be sure, Citibank for more than half a century had emphasized doing business overseas through a so-called bricks-and-mortar branch system, while Chase preferred to operate overseas—and in the United States, for that mat-ter—through correspondent banks. Although Citibank also had an overseas correspondent network, albeit a much weaker one, it was not a prisoner of these or any other institutional relationships to the degree that Chase was. For years, Chase regarded branches and correspondent relationships as mutually exclusive. Open up branches, the argument at Chase went, as it had at Citi, and you'll destroy all those close and profitable relationships with other banks. "When we finally decided to go ahead anyway and have branches, we soon discovered that that need not be the case," David Rockefeller said later. "In many cases we had just as good correspondent relationships afterward as we did before. It was a false concept, but it held us back for a long time." On the other hand, Rockefeller said, "loyalty to relationships is something I think is important. It was an important factor in the strength of Chase."

Even if David Rockefeller had prevailed in his vision of international operations, the Citibank philosophy, dating back to the twenties, had given it a huge head start. Nor did Chase have First National City's staying power; it was clearly a gun-shy competitor. Concerned about the long-term political status of Hong Kong and possible ripples from the Korean War, Chase closed its branch in the British crown colony, while Citibank kept its branch open. In another key business—traveler's checks—Chase was also held captive by its long-standing ties to the American Express Company. At one time, Chase actually owned American Express and was the company's clearing bank. As a result, Chase, unlike Citibank, never issued its own traveler's checks. Chase, said a former officer, "was encumbered by baggage, relationships, correspondents, and American Express."

David Rockefeller wasn't quite as obsessed with Citibank as George Moore was with Chase, but he was concerned. "I'm not sure we had a chart on the wall," Rockefeller said later. "But we were equally conscious of what was going on." This wavering approach to doing business would characterize Chase's approach in every aspect of its business, from technological innovation to its dealings with bank regulators.

Wriston and Rockefeller differed in another key respect. David Rockefeller seemed to thrive on frequent highly publicized overseas trips, where he would typically meet with a head of state and clinch some deal for Chase. Wriston, on the other hand, was a delegator who preferred to let his officers in the field develop the business. And while Rockefeller met with prime ministers and kings, Wriston and his colleagues dealt with central bankers and finance ministers. Prime ministers "come and go," said former Citibanker Ray Kathe. "Central bankers and the finance minister will always be more the key."

"We operated at a much lower political profile than they did," Wriston reflected later. "David is a unique world figure," who "built good relationships with many different countries." The problem with having a friend at court, Wriston said, is that when there's a revolution, "then you're a friend to a bum, or worse."

Oddly enough, Citibankers were often invited to the frequent Rockefeller receptions in foreign countries, where they ate Chase's caviar, drank Chase's booze, mingled with Chase's customers—and generated business for themselves. For all the hoopla, the Rockefeller trips didn't appear to Citibankers to create as much business for Chase as one might expect. Said retired Citibanker Rick Wheeler, "David would come through trailing clouds of glory, with emperors and kings going to meet him. But there was no link between this and Chase's ability to follow through." Added another ex-Citibanker, John Rudy, "David could go to see the head of Fiat. But if we were providing the value, they'd buy David lunch and give us their business." Whenever the subject of David's globe-trotting came up in conversation, George Moore would say, "We'll let David talk to the kings, the kings, the kings. [But] we'll get the business, the business, the business."

After four years under Moore and Wriston, the overseas division was neither
a money machine nor a paragon of managerial excellence and efficiency, but
compared with other financial institutions in the Third World, and even in
much of the industrialized world, Citibank was the state of the art. When and
where Citibank did make money overseas, its secret was often the gross inefficiency and turmoil in those markets, and the corruption, waste, and ineptitude of the local banks that operated in them. Third World borrowers were
panting for capital, and would flock to any institution that could supply them
with it. For every foreign office First National City managed to establish,
however, many native oxen would be gored. Evidence of the inefficiencies of
Third World financial markets could be seen in the spreads—often a whopping ten percentage points—between the rates banks paid for deposits and
the rates they charged for loans. The reasons for this were numerous and varied. In India, for example, as many as nine percentage points resulted from
overhead created by corruption, nepotism, and payroll padding at local
banks, according to former Citibanker Hamilton Meserve, who served as an
officer there in the early 1970s. National City, in contrast, needed just one or
two percentage points to turn a profit. "You could drop anyone with a liberal
arts education into that country and make money," he said.

In India and elsewhere, central bank officials, many of whom had been
trained in the United States, welcomed First National City and other Western banks as agents of change. They recognized that the fat and corruption
built into the spread represented a terrible drag on their country's economic
growth. To permit Citibank to operate and expand, however, they often had
to do battle with local bankers and finance ministers who, unlike central
bankers, were frequently under intense political pressure. But there was no
way, of course, that a country like India was going to allow First National
City to take advantage of its more efficient operating practices to completely
undercut the local banks. Consequently, in making loans in local currencies
to local businesses, National City was forced to charge the going rate. It paid
eight percentage points or so in taxes to the Indian authorities and remitted
one or two points to the United States, receiving a U.S. tax credit for taxes
paid over and above the prevailing 48 percent corporate rate. In effect, by
subsidizing the fat that was built into Third World banking systems, the U.S.
taxpayer funded a kind of phantom foreign aid program.

In India the inefficiency of the banking system was rooted in the country's chronic unemployment. A job as a bank teller was like gold, Meserve
recalled. Being a bank manager was like owning an employment agency on
the side. An ordinary teller ultimately supported a vast extended family, and
a manager who contemplated firing one knew he would be taking "food off
the table for thirty people," Meserve said. The result was that it sometimes
took nearly an hour for a customer to cash a check at a local bank, because
that check had to make its way through five tellers, each of whom would sign
and inspect it, and count and recount the cash.

According to Meserve, one of the major threats to job security for Indian bank employees was the introduction in the late fifties by National Cash

Register of a machine that electronically posted transactions, including deposits and withdrawals, to the bank's ledger. By eliminating hand posting, a single machine could put as many as thirty people out of work. Although the central banks felt the local banks should use the machine, denouncing the devices became a rallying cry for bank employee unions.

Besides introducing the latest equipment to local banking, the new international bankers were constantly developing new financial instruments and marketing gimmicks to expand their business, and traipsing into finance ministries and central bank offices seeking permission to offer them. Meserve recalled that he visited the central bank so often with proposals for new instruments that one top official typically greeted him by saying, "Oh, my God, what have you got for us today?"

"There was always a pact with the governor of the central bank to let us push just so far, and when he said back off, we'd back off," said Meserve. In India, First National City introduced a form of cash-flow lending that enabled businesses to get instant cash for sales made on credit to their customers. The bank in turn would receive cash for the receipts from the central bank—provoking the ire of the local banks. The monetary authorities "loved it [cash flow lending] because it was shaking up the local market," recalled Meserve. But as soon as local banks started complaining that [First National City] was stepping on their toes, the minister of finance told the bank to "cool it."

"India was never-never land," said Meserve. "We were always walking on eggs."

The quid pro quo for central bank protection was for First National to bring local bankers and monetary officials to New York for training, a practice that would have a vast yet immeasurable impact on local banking industries. By training an entire generation of foreign bankers in American methods, Citibank helped create its own competition. But Wriston, who was convinced that there was nothing more dangerous than a dumb competitor, reasoned that the bank would benefit in the long run. Thus Citibank became an agent for social as well as financial change. In the 1960s and 1970s, women bank employees, even tellers, were still a rarity in many countries and were totally unknown in some. In the early seventies, First National City became the first employer in Saudi Arabia to employ women, much to the horror of religious leaders, and even hired a Saudi princess. Of her Meserve said, "She was utterly incompetent with numbers, but we found something for her to do."

Foreign governments typically looked the other way as Citibank figured out clever gimmicks to get around local tax and foreign-exchange rules. "If you could figure out a way to get around the exchange regulations of certain countries, and [if] other people did it, it wasn't that great a sin," said Meserve. In India, for example, a Citibank official who earned a $40,000 annual salary paid in India would be taxed at a rate well over 90 percent. So the bank would pay the officer $10,000 in India, to be taxed at a still high but much lower rate, and $30,000 in New York subject to less draconian U.S. tax rules. It was understood that as long as you didn't "go to extremes," said Meserve, such practices would be condoned in order to keep the foreign banks open.

Paying bribes, of course, was a mortal sin, and yet even that ironclad rule had to be bent now and then. If, for example, a payoff wasn't made to the appropriate official, shipments of personal items for overseas employees would somehow disappear in transit from the United States. To avoid having to pay a bribe directly to such officials, the bank hired customs forwarders, who presented a bill for "services rendered."

On the surface, the banking rules of many of the countries where Citibank did business were prohibitively restrictive. But there was a tacit understanding that if the bank's presence helped modernize the country's financial markets, accommodations would be made. Later, for example, when First National City opened in Taiwan, pressure from local banks forced the central bank to limit the volume of deposits it could solicit from the public. But the central bank compensated for this by lending to Citibank at a rate that allowed it to make money. "They wanted us there but didn't want us to destabilize the market," said Meserve. Because National City had operated in Nationalist China before World War II, it was viewed by government officials as an "old and trusted friend," he said.

One device the bank used to muscle its way into new markets was its longtime expertise in foreign exchange trading. Forex trading became known, in the bank's jargon, as a "wedge product." As the world economy began to pick up after World War II, intermediaries were needed to facilitate sales and purchases of currency. Companies doing business in more than one country needed access to adequate supplies of foreign exchange. No one was more ready and willing to fill this financial void than Wriston and Citibank. By the late 1950s, countries that had been used to quoting prices in dollars began to quote in their own currencies. "Somebody had to be willing to take the foreign exchange risk themselves," said Edwin Reichers, Citibank's top forex trader. At a time when rates were fixed and world financial markets were still relatively stable, foreign exchange trading was not wildly profitable as a stand-alone activity, but by gaining a position as the leading market maker in major currencies, forex trading forced buyers and sellers into business relationships with Citibank, making it a natural source for trade financing and other types of credit and services.

Citibank, in fact, played a pivotal role in developing local foreign exchange markets. In the early 1960s, according to Reichers, Japan's foreign exchange market was rudimentary at best. Trade was limited to dollar-yen transactions, and most of those were quoted in dollars. So Wriston dispatched Reichers to Japan to expand that market to include the six major currencies. After he returned to New York, Reichers sent the Tokyo branch quotes in dollars on every currency on the evening of each business day, and the next morning received Tokyo's reply. For nine months Reichers enjoyed a stranglehold on the business while other banks struggled to figure out how the operation worked. The creation of a forward foreign exchange market in

Japan enabled local companies trading with other countries to reduce their foreign exchange risk by quoting prices in dollars and locking in those quotes for months into the future. The advent of more sophisticated foreign exchange trading in Japan not only brought Japanese companies and American companies in Japan to Citibank's door but also stimulated more trade between Japan and its major trading partners, including the United States.

In the Philippines before 1962, the peso was pegged at two to the dollar. In January 1962, according to Reichers, Wriston got wind of a possible move by the central bank to float the peso and ordered him to get on a plane for Manila to prepare for that possibility. A day or so after his arrival, monetary officials called bankers for a meeting to make the floating peso official. The market could no longer support the artificial two-to-one ratio. With Reichers in Manila, Citibank was in a position to dominate peso trading in the new floating rate arrangement. "I opened the market at four to one, and we floated the peso," Reichers recalled later. "I was the only guy who made a market." For a while, he said, "Citibank was doing all of the exchange business."

Under the Bretton Woods fixed exchange rate system, making money in the forex business wasn't easy. Traders operated on a spread of one-half of one percent on either side of par. "If you could earn a million dollars a year, that was a lot," said Reichers later. There was little money to be made on commercial business alone. The money was earned by taking positions, or putting the bank's money at risk. Banks had taken large and highly risky currency positions in the twenties, but that stopped abruptly with the wave of bank failures in the early thirties and didn't pick up again until after the war. According to Reichers, Wriston was far more amenable to position-taking than Moore had been. "I could contact Walt and argue my point on a position; I could take one. If I had to go to Moore, it would be more difficult to explain to him. I'd have to write a memo."

For Citibank, unlike Chase, getting the business meant being there. Replanting the flag in Europe, where Wriston most wanted to be, required overcoming certain obstacles. One of the biggest ones was right in Wriston's own backyard, in Albany, New York. Until the seventies, First National City never had anything resembling an organized strategy for dealing with lawmakers in either Washington or Albany. Stillman Rockefeller was proud of the fact that he had never shaken hands with a U.S. congressman—and probably not even with a state representative. "He was cynical in that he had no use for the political process, and he would say so. He was very proud to say, 'I never met my congressman and I don't want to meet him,'" said Wriston later. George Moore, however, was more pragmatic.

In his efforts to achieve passage of the New York State Omnibus Banking Bill, which would allow the New York City banks to expand into suburban Westchester and Nassau counties, George Moore displayed his considerable talent for glad-handing and persuasion. One of the most vocal opponents of big bank expansion was seventy-one-year-old Emmanuel Celler, a U.S. congressman from Brooklyn, who was influential in banking legislation at both the state and federal levels. During this period, Moore had been recruited by the financially troubled Metropolitan Opera to serve as a board member and treasurer and untangle the company's books. He discovered that Celler was a longtime opera buff and Met subscriber who regularly attended Saturday evening performances. The two men soon struck up a warm friendship.

That may have had something to do with the fact that the New York State Legislature, after defeating a similar bill a year earlier, enacted in March 1960 the Omnibus Banking Law, effective on July 1, that allowed banks to operate holding companies statewide and permitted New York City banks to cross into neighboring counties. The passage of this bill was the biggest breakthrough for the banks in years. Under the new law, banks would be able to acquire institutions in other banking districts with the approval of three-fifths of the members of the state banking board.

First National City was also a major force behind the drive by the New York Clearing House to amend New York State banking law to permit foreign banks to open for business in New York. In April 1960, Governor Nelson Rockefeller, David's brother, signed the new foreign banking measure into law. Until this law was enacted, reciprocity had been the order of the day between the United States and other countries, but now those barriers would begin to tumble in rapid succession.

The new branching law didn't sit well with banks like the Franklin National, based in Long Island's Nassau County, whose chairman, Arthur Roth, had battled Citibank ever since it attempted to expand into Westchester. Shortly after the new law took effect, Roth sued to have it declared invalid—a move that Wriston would never forget.

In the early 1960s, the Danbury, Connecticut, radio station, which Wriston picked up on his farm in nearby Sherman, seemed to deliver the news in reverse order of importance. The truly significant events of the day invariably were read after the announcer had run through a litany of minor traffic accidents, robberies, and upcoming church suppers. And so it was early on a Saturday morning, September 17, 1960, when Wriston was relaxing at home. After offering the local news, the announcer mentioned offhandedly that the government of Fidel Castro had nationalized the branches of three American banks: First National City Bank, Chase Manhattan, and the First National Bank of Boston. Wriston bolted from his armchair and headed for the phone. "I guess that means we're going to New York," Bobby said.

For years, First National City had been the leading foreign bank in Cuba; it was the bank's biggest foreign operation and one of its most lucrative. As a leading financier of sugar and tobacco production and export under the Batista regime, Citibank was a linchpin in the economy, and its personnel had enjoyed the good life on the island nation. Now the good life was coming to an abrupt end.

The news did not come as a complete shock to Wriston. Thanks to the intuition of Juan Sanchez, the ex-professor who was the bank's man in Havana, Wriston and the bank had been preparing for trouble for some time. Born in Spain in 1909, Juan "Johnny" Sanchez had emigrated to New Brunswick, New Jersey, when he was eleven. While working as an office manager at a Sears store in 1930, he struck up a friendship with a local banker who recruited him to work for him. Later, while working at the bank, he taught accounting and credit management at Rutgers University. In 1947, Sanchez was snapped up by National City, where he "worked like he was born on the steps of 55 Wall Street," as Wriston put it later. Two weeks after reporting for work, Sanchez was shipped off to a branch in Colombia, arriving there in time to witness the 1948 "Bogotá revolution." One of the participants in that uprising was Fidel Castro, who then represented the revolutionary party of the University of Havana. Castro had teamed up with another revolutionary, Ernesto "Che" Guevara, in 1956, and Sanchez knew then that this partnership did not augur well for Cuba or Citibank.

In early 1958, Sanchez was dispatched to Havana to run Citibank's eleven-branch Cuban network, and he watched with concern as Castro's guerrilla activities intensified. Finally, on December 31, 1958, Batista fled Cuba, and Castro seized power. After shutting down the banks, Castro allowed them to reopen a week later under rigid foreign exchange controls. Shortly thereafter, he began making other demands on foreign banks and corporations, ordering them, for example, to supply the names of people who had done business with the Batista regime. In addition, he transferred all of Cuba's reserves in U.S. banks and the Federal Reserve Bank of New York to the Canadian central bank. Cuban employees of Citibank were conscripted into a militia that roamed the halls at will.

At that time, Castro was still basking in the warmth of American goodwill. But Sanchez had heard enough of his long-winded speeches to know the climate in Cuba would soon be inhospitable to American business, and he began slowly and discreetly to wind down First National City's operations. By discouraging new deposits and declining to roll over existing ones, he shrank the balance sheet at every opportunity. Meanwhile, the revolutionary government confiscated farms and factories but not banks. Castro, Sanchez figured, was leaving the banks for last.

At the head office in New York, some bank officials remained hopeful that Castro wouldn't severely disrupt the bank's operations, but Sanchez was under no such illusions. Not long after the January 1, 1959, revolution, he flew to New York to meet with his superiors, bringing along some reading material that he knew would interest them. Titled *Political, Economic and Social Thought of Fidel Castro,* the treatise was Castro's answer to *Mein Kampf;* it was an English-language tract that drew on Castro's speeches and writings to spell out his plans for ruling the country. "Johnny said, 'You ought to read this,' " Wriston recalled, "and I went home and stayed up most of the night reading it." In a section on economic policy objectives, the treatise cited Castro's plans to "nationalize," or "socialize," existing businesses in order to "give a growing participation in national wealth to the Cuban businessmen and the State."

Wriston and Sanchez regarded the Castro treatise as a virtual engraved invitation to Citibank to leave the country, one that both corroborated the wisdom of the efforts already under way and accelerated that process. "We had to get out without arousing noise, making trouble, or attracting attention, and I think we did a pretty good job," Wriston said. By the end of 1959, as Sanchez recalled, the Castro regime began to make its goals even more clear. Around Thanksgiving, Guevara, the newly appointed president of Cuba's central bank, met with local bankers, telling them that it was "only a matter of time before Cuba eliminated Wall Street interests, the State Department, and you American banks." There was a moment of humor in that otherwise grim session when Guevara told how he'd gotten his new job. Two weeks earlier, at a cabinet meeting, Guevara said, Castro had announced that he was seeking the "best economist in the country" to replace the outgoing central bank chief. Guevara had immediately raised his hand. "Okay, Che, you have it," Castro had said, looking a bit puzzled. When the meeting was over, he took Guevara aside. "Che, who said you were an economist?" he asked. "Oh, no!" Guevara replied. "I thought you said, 'the best *Communist* in the country.' " Despite Guevara's lack of financial training, he actually turned out to be a tough, astute central bank head, Sanchez said. Nevertheless, American employees of First National City quietly exited Cuba with little more than the clothes on their backs, and by June 1960 only five American staffers remained in the country.

The final act in the Cuban drama began on the evening of September 17, 1960, when Sanchez received a call at home from one of his managers. He informed Sanchez that the revolutionary militia had arrived and was demanding the keys to the main branch and access to the vault. By this time Sanchez was the only non-Cuban employee still holding down the fort for National City Bank.

"I knew then that Uncle John had died," said Sanchez later, using the bank's code phrase for the takeover of the branches. He and the bank had in effect been placed under arrest. Shortly thereafter, the calls started coming in from the other branches. Throughout the night, Sanchez was on the phone with his superiors in New York, alerting them to the death of "Uncle John." Wriston immediately and repeatedly ordered Sanchez out of Cuba, but despite the potentially life-threatening situation, he insisted on remaining until he could wind up the bank's affairs there. "I will leave when I'm ready," Sanchez replied defiantly.

By the evening of Saturday, September 17, some thirty employees had drifted into New York headquarters. Their first task was to ensure the safety of the Cuban employees, who had remained in Havana. The second was to limit the loss of assets. Tapping the experience of veterans of the earlier seizure of the Chinese branches, they moved to cut the losses. As soon as Castro seized the branches, National City's bookkeepers and lawyers swung into action, having decided, as Wriston put it later, to "take everything we can find and argue about it later." They quickly attached cash and bonds collateralizing Cuban loans and offset the loans, the bank's capital, and the value of its Cuban property against the liquid assets.

Back in Havana, the tension was mounting. Sanchez supervised the destruction of traveler's checks and documents, burning some and flushing the shredded remains of others down the toilets. Sanchez would later admit to one crime against the Cuban state: clogging Havana's sewer system. While he and the few remaining employees were burning bags of traveler's checks, he was surprised by a clutch of screaming, gun-toting militia made up of the bank's own employees, who demanded that he hand over the checks. They accused Sanchez of destroying national property. "We shivered and shook," said Sanchez later. The militia returned the checks only after Sanchez convinced them that they were worthless and outdated. Over that emotionally wrenching weekend, Sanchez and the remaining loyalists "sang and cried and drank a lot of rum," he said.

As the day of reckoning approached, Sanchez canceled the test words that authorized correspondent banks to transfer funds, instructing them to ignore any such order. He also revoked the powers of bank officers. When Sanchez entered the main branch early on September 19, the revolutionary anthem was blaring over the radio throughout the building. Forty-five minutes later, a representative of the central bank presented a teary-eyed Juan Sanchez with papers, signed by Guevara, authorizing the takeover of the branch network. Like a customer executing a routine banking transaction at a teller window, Sanchez insisted on being given a receipt. Craftily, he had arranged for the bank's Cuban lawyers to wait in a café across the street to solve whatever legal problems arose from this encounter—and sure enough, the central bank representative said he was not authorized to provide a receipt.

"Couldn't we just draw up a little piece of paper saying I'm here, you're here, and you're handing me certain documents, and I accept the documents?" Sanchez asked. As soon as the official agreed, Sanchez whistled to the lawyers, and in a flash they appeared with the papers. They were Sanchez's only evidence of the transaction and the only papers he would carry out of Cuba. While they ultimately had no legal significance, Sanchez was pleased that he was the only foreign bank representative who got a receipt. "The others had left Saturday and Sunday with nothing," he said.

With his receipt, four dollars in cash, and a suitcase containing only a change of underwear and an extra pair of shoes, Sanchez grabbed a cab for Havana Airport. Eschewing the Cuban airline for Pan Am, Sanchez, the last American banker out of Cuba, fled to Miami, where he picked up two hundred dollars in cash from a local bank and flew to New York, where his colleagues were deeply worried about his safety.

"What are you so shook up about?" Sanchez asked Wriston when he arrived.

Wriston reminded him that the Chinese had captured the bank's manager years before and National City had had to ransom him with a letter of credit. "I wasn't about to do that a second time," he told Sanchez.

First National City, Wriston said later, decided to hire any of its former employees who got out of Cuba, which many did in open boats. "Exxon went the other way," Wriston said. "They wouldn't hire anybody [its former personnel]." Citibank even helped the central bank official who had given Sanchez the receipt. A few months after the takeover, he showed up in New York and phoned Sanchez, begging for a job. Citibank later estimated that the bank lost about $45 million as a result of the nationalization—$35 million in dollar-denominated term loans to Cuban customers, and $10 million in capital, property, and equipment in Cuba and in unremitted earnings for 1959 and 1960. When Sanchez had first arrived in Cuba, First National City's operation had about $600 million in assets. During his tenure, he managed to whittle that down to $500 million, he asserted later.

In the midst of the Cuban crisis, Wriston found the secretary who would accompany him through the bank for the next twenty-five years, and then some. A petite, feisty woman who had joined the National City Bank just before Pearl Harbor, Gerry Stover was as gruff as her boss was sarcastic. Asked why he had hired such a crusty woman, Wriston once said, "She got more work done than anyone in the whole place"—one reason Wriston employed just one secretary while many of his subordinates had two. "She hated the young officers," said a former Citibanker, and referred to them as "those young snips." Walter and Gerry fought like an imperfectly matched married couple, but, Wriston quipped, "she only threatens to quit four times a day."

With the drama in Havana beginning to wind down, the action shifted to the courts and the legal hairsplitting that would go on for more than two decades. Among the Cuban assets First National City had seized in the United States was $12.4 million in securities that Guevara had posted as collateral for a loan to the Banco Nacional de Cuba. National City immediately used the collateral to pay $10 million outstanding on a loan to the central bank, and retained the remaining $2.3 million to offset its losses on the seizure. In a remarkable display of legal chutzpah, the central bank filed suit against the bank, contending that the central bank and the government of Cuba were two separate entities and demanding the return of the excess collateral. Nonsense, Citibank retorted, as the case made its way to the U.S. Supreme Court. The Cuban case reminded Shearman & Sterling lawyer Henry Harfield of a similar deception cited in the Book of Genesis, in which Jacob attempts to trick his blind father and displace his brother Esau. "The voice is the voice of Jacob but the hand is the hand of Esau," Harfield said.

"You can't argue that before the Supreme Court," Wriston said. But Harfield did exactly that, and ultimately won the case. On that momentous occasion years later, Wriston phoned Harfield to congratulate him—for two reasons: "One, it is a great victory," he said, "and second, we've now been able to recover half of what you've charged in legal fees." In the end, said Wriston, "We never lost any money on the deal [the Cuban nationalization]." And since there was plenty of Cuba-related legal business to go around, George Moore threw some of it to Emmanuel Celler's New York law firm.

While the Cuban episode added a page of helpful hints to the procedure manual on how to beat a retreat from a totalitarian regime, Wriston and First National City apparently failed to totally absorb another object lesson. The penalties of that failure would not become evident for more than twenty years.

One of the American properties that Castro nationalized was a nickel slurry plant owned by the Moa Bay Mining Company, a subsidiary of the Freeport Sulphur Company. The plant had been built with a syndicated loan in which Citibank had an approximately $25 million share—the largest single chunk of the $35 million in dollar-denominated loans that went down the tube after the company was expropriated. In effect, Castro got the plant and the revenue it produced for free. Freeport, meanwhile, got a tax loss that it did not share with its banks, prompting First National City to threaten a lawsuit. The bank eventually recovered some of its losses when it was awarded an interest in Freeport's Louisiana facility, but for years it refused to do business with the company or its successors. Freeport was one of the few corporate borrowers in recent bank history to renege on its obligations. Ironically, the Freeport Sulphur Company was originally organized by two retired Citibank chiefs, Frank Vanderlip and E. P. Swenson.

As the bank's president and then chairman, George Moore, through contacts with the Central Intelligence Agency, followed Cuba's attempts to make use of Freeport's Cuban plant. According to documents in the bank's archives, the CIA reported to him on the plant's condition and the amount of nickel slurry it was shipping. Former vice chairman Hans Angermueller, who worked on the case as an attorney with Shearman & Sterling, reflected later that the episode was a "lesson in sovereign risk." To Wriston, however, the lesson of Cuba was a simple and positive one: "We learned to exit a country going down the drain with minimal damage."

Several months after the Cuban revolution, another crisis erupted, this time in Egypt, but First National City's exit was somewhat less dramatic. When Wriston was notified that the United Arab Republic intended to nationalize the bank's branches, he immediately hopped a plane to Cairo to negotiate with the minister of finance, who proved to be a less than savvy deal-maker. The branches were written off, but the bank was eventually compensated at an acceptable rate. "We walked away from that train wreck without any loss," Wriston said, except for the lost time value of the money.

The nationalizations in Cuba and Egypt did little if anything to slow down First National City's global expansion. Wriston considered these incidents mere examples of the "actuarial base" principle in action—a term he liked to use for "spreading the risk." When one part of the empire was down and out, the rest, as the theory went, would churn out profits.

Thanks in large part to the recent changes in state banking law, the bank announced in mid-October 1960 that its Frankfurt representative office would be upgraded to branch status. The West German authorities had, of course, approved the move, but German bankers growled. At a "welcoming" dinner for George Moore in Frankfurt, Dresdner Bank's chief voiced his displeasure over the Yankee incursion. But Deutsche Bank rallied to Moore's defense. Shaking his finger at the banker from Dresdner, the Deutsche Bank chairman told him, "The competition will do you good," Moore recalled.

Meanwhile, Citibank was disappointed to learn that County Trust, its would-be Westchester bride that never was, had agreed to merge with New York's Bankers Trust using a holding company. But National City's disappointment was short-lived. On October 28, on land that was once a potato field in Plainview, Long Island, National City became the first New York commercial bank to open a suburban branch under the new Omnibus banking law, celebrating the event by throwing a party in a circus tent for prospective customers. Soon, Citibank and Chase began to file applications fast and furiously in their push into the suburbs. Several months later, Franklin National Bank chairman Arthur Roth won a brief victory when a New York Supreme Court justice declared the new legislation invalid on technical grounds, agreeing with Roth's contention that it had not been passed properly in the legislature. But Roth's celebration would be brief. A few days later the same bipartisan coalition that had passed the law in the first place fixed the technical flaws, and the bill was signed by Governor Nelson Rockefeller on March 17, 1960.

With the move to the suburbs the race for the consumer dollar was on— and so was the Wriston-Wilcox race to succeed George Moore as president of the bank. In 1961, Tommy Wilcox plunged in a big way into mortgage lending, a business traditionally dominated by thrift institutions. For all his conservatism, no one could accuse Stillman Rockefeller of being a short-term thinker. The investment in domestic branch growth didn't pay off for years, and overseas expansion, as Vanderlip and Mitchell discovered years before, was far from a sure bet as well.

6

PINS ON THE MAP

*F*ive months after Wriston was elected executive vice president of First National City, John F. Kennedy, two years his senior, was elected president of the United States. Wriston would no more have voted for, or even have claimed association with, a Democrat than he would have embraced a Communist. But while Wriston and Kennedy were miles apart in their views on the proper role of government, they were bound together by several common goals. They shared, of course, a desire to attract the best and the brightest into their respective professions— government and banking. Even more significantly, both men believed in growth. Kennedy breezed into office promising to get the economy, and the country, moving again, a pledge that called for expansionary fiscal and monetary policies. Likewise, Wriston was determined to turn Citibank into a fast-growth operation. Their efforts would turn out to be mutually reinforcing.

Kennedy, Wriston said later, was a "tremendous leader, who did for the country what Ronald Reagan did: he restored its spirit. He was young, fresh, a pick-me-up for the country in an outstanding way."

Coincidentally, just weeks after Kennedy was inaugurated, First National City announced the introduction of the negotiable certificate of deposit, the financial instrument designed to rescue it from the funding squeeze that had hampered its growth for the past three years. For the first time since the government got into the business of regulating bank interest rates, banks would be able to bid for large slugs of money in the marketplace against other financial institutions.

The U.S. economy was now on the threshold of an unprecedented nine-year period of prosperity and growth, and the negotiable CD would in no small measure help fuel that expansion by pumping funds into the banking system. In turn, the monetary expansion encouraged by John F. Kennedy and then Lyndon B. Johnson would feed the rising economic tide that lifted all ships, especially the First National City Bank of New York and Walter B. Wriston. Internationally, the United States was at the peak of its economic prestige. America was the world's preeminent trading nation, and the U.S. dollar was its reserve currency. It was not unreasonable to expect that U.S.

banks, led by National City, would spearhead the expansion of American multinationals around the world, just as the British banks had done in the nineteenth century. "It was a heady culture," said former Citibanker Ham Meserve. "We were the number one international bank in the number one country in the world."

On his role in the creation of the CD, Wriston would later tell a reporter, "I had something to do with the CD, but it was an invention of Citibank. Somehow you put all these things into the Waring blender and out comes a unified idea. A lot of people worked on it." While several later claimed credit for the concept, one thing is clear: Wriston was its principal promoter within the bank, and the individual most responsible for persuading top officers to adopt it.

Along the way, the effort met with at least one false start. In August 1960 the bank offered CDs, with little fanfare, to foreign bank customers. For the instrument to take off, however, Citibank would have to create a secondary market for it to trade in. At the time, that meant the Discount Corporation, a government securities dealer whose chairman, Herbert N. Repp, was one of the most respected names on Wall Street. Wriston stopped by John Exter's desk and asked him to accompany him to a meeting with Repp.

Herbert Repp was excited about the CD, Exter recalled, but he did exact one condition—Citibank would have to lend the Discount Corporation $10 million unsecured. Making uncollateralized loans to brokers was generally prohibited at Citibank, but Wriston was able to persuade his superiors that this was one rule that was made to be broken.

Repp asked Wriston how big he thought the market would be. Exter was taken aback at Wriston's response, not because his estimate was too large but because he considered it much too small. "I could see this going to two to three billion dollars," Wriston replied expansively. Having held some lofty positions himself before joining National City, Exter was not shy about venturing opinions when it came to economics, even if it meant contradicting his boss. He felt that Wriston hadn't begun to appreciate the potential of the new device. "Walt, it'll go much higher than that," Exter said with a hint of exasperation. "It will go into the tens of billions."

With the secondary market in place, Citibank in February 1961 finally announced that it would offer large-denomination certificates of deposit to investors, a story that made the front page of the *New York Times.* For a $100,000 instrument, the rate was to be 1.25 to 1.75 percentage points higher than the rate on passbook savings. Like the shot fired on Lexington Green that unleashed the American Revolution, the introduction of the negotiable CD was a shot heard around the world. While it may not have been apparent to its creators at the time, this new instrument would spark a revolution in banking and finance whose effects would be felt for decades.

Wriston's response to Repp's question about the potential of the CD market turned out to be correct, but only for the first year's volume. By 1967 outstanding CDs of large commercial banks reached $18.5 billion, surpassing the volume of outstanding commercial paper, a form of short-term corporate debt. Although the other major banks quickly followed suit, privately the initial reaction at many was less than enthusiastic. Morgan, Wriston said later, was "unhappy" because of limitations on state-chartered banks in offering the instrument, which were later overcome. "We never did ask the Federal Reserve," Wriston said. "If we had, we'd still be in the process of going through the board." But the Fed didn't attempt to block the plan, in effect giving the instrument its blessing. The question also arose as to whether it was a deposit or a security; at the time, federal banking law prohibited banks from underwriting securities. Citibank argued that it was merely a receipt for a deposit. That debate was settled when someone died and left a negotiable CD in his estate; the judge ruled that it was a deposit, not a security.

As the negotiable CD gained momentum in the marketplace, bankers fretted that a rise in rates above Reg Q ceilings would cause depositors, particularly foreigners, to dump their CDs, forcing banks to liquidate their portfolios of longer-term assets. The negotiable CD would eventually cause its share of trouble, but not the kind bankers originally expected. "A lot of banks were worrying about cannibalism, about companies taking free deposits and shifting them to time deposits," said Ken MacWilliams, a New York investment banker. Wriston and Citibank were saying, in effect, 'If we don't do it somebody else will.' "

Taking negotiable time deposits gave banks more stomach to make term loans than they had before, according to MacWilliams. That, he said, made them more competitive with insurance companies, which then had a lock on the long-term lending market. For Wriston, the success of the negotiable CD was a vindication of sorts for the long view. "He could have sat there and looked good in the short term," observed MacWilliams. "But he knew that if you didn't do something, someone would come in and nail you."

Before the negotiable CD was introduced, Wriston and his colleagues had felt that institutions with extensive branch networks and retail as well as wholesale businesses would survive and prosper, while purely "wholesale" banks like Morgan would wither and die. Then, in 1961, newly merged Morgan Guaranty contemplated setting up a statewide holding company—Morgan New York State—that would have allowed it to operate retail branches throughout the state. But when the Comptroller of the Currency balked at the plan, Morgan abandoned it in favor of its traditional strong suit—corporate banking. "The negotiable CD," Wriston used to claim, "saved the Morgan bank." For years it was also the savior of the Chicago banks, which were denied the ability to branch by Illinois state law. "It sure helped," Lewis Preston, former chairman and CEO of J. P. Morgan & Company, acknowledged later, adding that the company's expansion would have taken an altogether different shape without it. "We might have been worried about interstate banking," Preston said, if Wriston hadn't invented the negotiable CD.

The CD heralded a new era of growth for big money-center banks, enabling them not only to meet the financing demands of a booming economy but also to create demand by purchasing and selling money. It would change the banking business irrevocably from one that depended on consumer deposits and compensating balances to make short-term self-liquidating loans for business inventory, to one that bought money at will in the market-place to fund term loans for plant construction and equipment. It also represented the opening salvo in a war that Citibank, as an advocate of free markets, would wage against the Federal Reserve and Regulation Q. Said John R. Price, government relations director at New York's Chemical Bank, "Citibank, with hobnail boots, forced the move toward market determination of interest rates."

Equally important, the negotiable CD gave rise to an entire new industry within an industry: liability management. For years, bankers had focused their attention on the asset side of their balance sheet, where items like loans, bonds, and cash are posted. Historically, banks had had little control over the liability side, since interest rates were largely determined by the government. From now on, however, a banker's profits would depend not only on what he charged for loans but also on what he paid for funds. Success and even survival in banking would no longer be automatic.

The negotiable CD also transformed First National City from a big regional bank to one that exported its surplus "inventory" throughout the United States and around the world. That would spell the beginning of the end of old traditional loyalties, relationships, and obligations. Purchased money carried no baggage. Said Harvard professor emeritus Charles Williams, "It gave them a degree of freedom from having to lend to their depositors and depend on their depositors. It gave them mobility. You could buy in one market and lend to another." Appearing on the financial scene just months after the passage of the New York State Omnibus Banking Law and the move to the suburbs, the negotiable CD also demonstrated that changing the law was not the only way banks could tailor the world to their liking. These events marked the transformation of banking from a public utility to a business, and of bankers from staid men with green eyeshades to gunslinging entrepreneurs.

For that reason, the CD was to some an ominous development. To conservative market watcher Dr. Henry Kaufman, it was the beginning of "spread banking," which allowed big banks "to defy the position of central banking." In fact, as Kaufman noted in a 1976 speech, the rate of growth in bank credit, which had "rarely exceeded" nominal growth in gross national product in the 1950s, began to surpass the rate of growth of nominal GNP on a regular basis in the 1960s.

Nearly two decades later, *American Banker* argued that the U.S. banking system would be smaller than it was if the negotiable CD had not been invented. The CD, it asserted, was "the product of banking's and the nation's 'overconfident' period—one in which serious recessions came to be viewed as obsolete." The absence of a recession in the period from 1961 to 1969 "obviously encouraged the spread of liability management."

Ironically, National City's John Exter, an outspoken advocate of the gold standard and a tight-money policy, later harbored mixed feelings about his role in the invention of the CD. He saw it less as a force for economic growth than as an engine of inflation and an instrument of economic destruction, and he viewed himself as a kind of devil's accomplice. He felt that aggressive bank lending coupled with the Fed's policy of monetary expansion would spell disaster for the world's economic system. In Exter's view, the expansion of the economy was aided by a Federal Reserve chairman named William McChesney Martin who, in the early sixties, was too anxious to be on good terms with the new president. "Little did I know," Exter contended years later, "that Kennedy would wrap Martin around his little finger and get him to begin a monetary expansion that has gone on to this day, [taken] us off the gold standard, and brought us to the brink of the worst economic disaster of all time." Exter realized, of course, that his views made Wriston "uncomfortable." Wriston believed in budgetary discipline, but not at the expense of economic growth, whereas Exter became Citibank's resident prophet of doom and gloom. Putting his money where his mouth was, he bought gold at $35 an ounce for the next decade, and his pessimistic outlook made him a wealthy man. It also made him a pariah at National City and led to his eventual departure. Exter, said Wriston later, "got hung up on the gold crap" to the point where "it became kind of a joke."

While the international banking community was applauding First National City's new device for attracting deposits, the Kennedy administration was taking notice of the bank's success in attracting people for overseas assignments. Shortly after John F. Kennedy took office, Wriston received a phone call from an administration aide summoning him to a White House meeting with the president and other top business and labor officials. For the next quarter century, whenever a White House staffer was asked to round up the usual suspects for any presidential gathering on financial matters, Wriston would find himself snared in the dragnet and paraded into the Roosevelt Room to advise the president. Wriston clearly relished his presidential encounters but characteristically made light of them. "They say, 'Let's call the Ute Indian chief and twenty-two Seminoles and bring them in.'"

At an auspicious June 30, 1961, luncheon, Kennedy lamented the poor quality of personnel who were working for the U.S. government in its foreign affairs agencies and asked Wriston and the other business and labor leaders to help him find better people for these jobs. According to Kennedy administration archives, George Moore himself was on the short list for assistant secretary of state for Latin American affairs, with the notation that he had a "South American wife."

Wriston wanted to help. But he told the president bluntly that top executives were reluctant to serve in government because of the difficulties they would have to face when they tried to return to their old jobs, particularly the grilling they would be forced to endure on potential conflicts of interest. In fact, Wriston asserted, the government should try to recruit people who *did* have a conflict of interest, because they were the only ones capable of accomplishing anything. Kennedy, according to Wriston, replied that he had never thought about that, adding optimistically that the problem could be corrected by creating a new "category of officers."

In Wriston's view, another deterrent to public service by capable people was the blind trust. That, he quipped later, "is not a legal instrument but a description of the financial acuity of the trustee." More than three decades later, nothing had changed.

One program President Kennedy had in mind when he called Wriston to Washington in June 1961 was his effort to spur economic development in Latin America. On that issue, Wriston and Kennedy shared a close community of interest but differed on how to solve the problem. Wriston, of course, had just lost eleven branches to Fidel Castro, and eight months later, on April 17, 1961, Kennedy had suffered the first major embarrassment of his young administration with the failure of the Bay of Pigs invasion. Both Kennedy and Wriston stood to lose in a major way from the spread of communism from Cuba to the rest of Latin America, and they would gain directly from the economic revitalization of the region.

The centerpiece of Kennedy's foreign aid program and policy toward Latin America was his much heralded Alliance for Progress, which had been chartered at Punta del Este, Uruguay, on August 16, about six weeks after the White House meeting. The goal was to spur a net annual inflow of private investment into Latin America of about $300 million. In May 1961, Congress had appropriated about $600 million for economic and social development projects in countries that in September 1960 had adopted the Act of Bogotá. Two-thirds of the funds were designated for loans, on generous terms, for such projects as land settlement, housing, and sanitation.

To Wriston and other top American businessmen familiar with Latin America, however, the Alliance for Progress was seriously flawed in at least one crucial respect: it emphasized government-to-government grants and giveaways and did little or nothing to create a free market environment in Latin America that would foster private investment. The upshot was that the Kennedy administration established a Commerce Committee for the Alliance for Progress (COMAP), housed in the Commerce Department and chaired by J. Peter Grace, president of W. R. Grace & Company and a Citibank director. On April 17, 1962, Secretary of Commerce Luther Hodges invited Wriston, Chase co-CEO David Rockefeller, and other top businessmen to become members of the committee. By the end of the year, the strong-willed Peter Grace had produced a voluminous report, crammed with statistics which bluntly asserted that investing in Latin America was an opportunity a prudent businessman could easily pass up. The Grace report concluded that the amount of aid earmarked for Latin America was grossly inadequate and recommended tax incentives to spur direct business investment. On the basis of the study, President Kennedy in early April 1963 proposed an investment guarantee and tax incentive program to give U.S. companies a 30 percent tax credit on their Latin American investments.

Wriston, Rockefeller, and Emilio G. Collado, vice president and director of Standard Oil of New Jersey, broke with the committee, issuing a minority opinion in early 1963 emphasizing the need to allow free markets to work their magic. The minority memo was leaked to the *New York Times,* which reported that Wriston, Rockefeller, and Collado had "disowned" the Grace report. Hard as the three men tried to disclaim the *New York Times* account and minimize their differences, the fact remained that the two factions saw the problem and the solution very differently.

Grace was furious. He concluded that the impetus for the split came from Standard Oil, which, he said later, did not stand to benefit from the proposals he had advanced to change U.S. tax laws to spur Latin American investment. Grace was convinced that Collado had used Standard Oil's financial clout to pressure Wriston and Rockefeller to support its position. "He had several million in those institutions [Citibank and Chase]," Grace said later of Collado. "He just used his muscle." Grace, of course, had known Wriston casually since the mid-1950s, but COMAP was his first opportunity to deal with him at length. "It was not a friendly introduction to Walter Wriston," he said.

Wriston urged Kennedy to state publicly that rapid economic growth in Latin America would best be achieved through private capital, not through the nationalization of local industries.

His colleague George Moore was highly enthusiastic about the potential of Latin America. His marriage to Beatriz had given him great affection for Mexico, if not for Beatriz, and he was eager to jump into nearly any venture and support any cause that was somehow linked to Latin America in general and to Mexico in particular. But Moore's activities in Latin America disturbed Stillman Rockefeller, according to former associates. He felt that Moore's business judgment was clouded by his marriage to a Spanish woman and by his love for everything Latin. Whenever Moore traveled south of the border, Rockefeller's concerns intensified. He would inquire anxiously of Latin hand Juan Sanchez, "What do you think George is up to in Mexico?" Eventually, Rockefeller actually forbade Moore to have anything to do with Mexico whatsoever. In an internal interview, Wriston said that Rockefeller "hated Latin Americans. . . . He just did everything he could to make George unhappy. Constantly."

With all the ballyhoo over the Alliance for Progress, dozens of committees, commissions, and panels, public and private, were created to find ways to foster economic development in Latin America. Moore would recall in his memoirs that such committees proliferated to such an extent that in 1962 the Latins sought his help in persuading the administration to coordinate all these efforts. Weeks before Kennedy was assassinated, David Rockefeller and George Moore traveled to Washington to appeal to the president for coordination among the agencies dealing with Latin policy. In the end, perhaps the most accurate assessment of the Alliance was made by veteran Latin hand Victor Prall. "I don't think it amounted to a hoot in hell," he said.

When Kennedy took office, a number of mergers of big national banks were in the works that had received the blessing of the incumbent Comptroller of the Currency Ray Gidney. Another big merger of two state-chartered banks—the Hanover Bank and the Manufacturers Trust Company—had been announced in January 1961, just days before Kennedy was inaugurated. Gidney was an avid believer in the benefits of bank mergers, an attitude that did not sit well with the U.S. attorney general, Robert F. Kennedy, who complained to his brother about Gidney's permissiveness. As a result, on September 21, 1961, President Kennedy announced that he was replacing Gidney with James Saxon, a hard-driving, table-pounding lawyer for the First National Bank of Chicago.

Even Wriston himself could not have appointed a Comptroller of the Currency more sympathetic to big banks in general and to First National City in particular. Working closely with George Moore and other pro-deregulation bankers, Saxon blew into the banking industry with hurricane force and unleashed a storm of initiatives that enabled big banks to expand into new financial services. Immediately after being sworn in, he made it clear in interviews that he took issue with government regulations, including Regulation Q, that impeded the growth of the commercial banking industry.

Saxon was bright, articulate, charming, and impeccably dressed. As a Treasury attaché in the Philippines, he had escaped with the Filipino government's gold reserves just after the Japanese attack and had placed them with the Treasury Department for safekeeping until the end of the war. After leaving the Treasury Department in 1952, he had spent three years with the American Bankers Association and then joined the First National Bank of Chicago in 1956. Saxon's effectiveness, however, was hampered by his volatile temper. He "was a very difficult man" who was "too emotional," too inclined to "fly off the handle" at the slightest provocation, recalled Carter Golembe, a leading Washington bank consultant. Saxon, *Fortune* wrote, "made 10,000 enemies overnight."

Citibank was stunned and chagrined by one of Saxon's first decisions, but the disappointment was short-lived. Indeed, Saxon's decision proved to be a blessing in disguise. Citibank at that time was eager to break into Westchester County. Right after losing County Trust to Bankers Trust, Citibank struck an agreement with the National Bank of Westchester to acquire its twenty-six offices and $216 million in deposits, a deal that would give it instant representation in that wealthy suburban county. But the price was steep. The 1960 Omnibus Banking Law had given rise to what Wriston called "Westchester prices": any New York bank seeking to get into the county had to pay 150 percent of book value. Said Wriston later, "That also meant that you didn't live long enough to earn back the premium."

On December 19, 1961, about a month after he took office, Saxon rejected Citibank's deal on the grounds that it "would cause an unreasonable distortion and dislocation in the present and future banking structure of Westchester County not consistent with the public interest." That gave rise to a new banking buzzword: "de novo," meaning "from scratch." With the acquisition door closed, Citibank had no choice but to set up branches de novo, as it was doing overseas. Citibank later discovered that it could branch out into Westchester for a mere 20 percent of the cost of acquiring an established bank. By branching rather than buying, the bank saved a cool $50 million.

Even as he was preparing to reject the Citibank deal, Saxon, like his predecessor, was already tangling with the attorney general on antitrust issues. President Kennedy seemed to be amused by the animosity between his brother and his comptroller. In a photo session at the White House, a grinning John F. Kennedy is said to have put his arm around Saxon and told him, "I hear you're having some trouble with my little brother. Keep at it."

Saxon's natural inclination was to say yes to banks. Shortly after his appointment, he established a panel of bankers, including his friend George Moore, to review the bank regulatory structure, with a view toward rewriting the National Bank Act. There was little doubt about the outcome. The recommendations were revolutionary. Among other things, the panel recommended stripping the Federal Reserve of its regulatory authority over banks and bank holding companies and awarding it to the comptroller, leaving the Fed with monetary policy alone. The panel also proposed reducing reserve requirements for demand deposits, eliminating them entirely for time and savings deposits, and abolishing interest rate ceilings. Moreover, it called for expanding lending authority and liberalizing rules on real estate loans. Under the proposals, foreign banks in the United States would be subject to the same regulations as U.S. banks. To the extent that he could change the rules without changing the law, Saxon incorporated the panel's recommendations into his *Comptroller's Manual for National Banks.*

One especially contentious move was Saxon's ruling that banks could set up operating subsidiaries to use as vehicles for new activities. That forced the Fed to apply the same rules both to national banks and to state-chartered banks that were members of the Fed. Said lawyer Westbrook Murphy, "The Fed was appalled," and the Fed and the Comptroller's office took to calling each other names in public. Saxon's rulings enabled his client institutions to dramatically expand their business activities. In 1963, for example, he decided that direct lease financing was a legitimate activity for national banks. This opened up a whole new arena for nationally chartered banks, particularly large ones like First National City. Not only did it give them yet another service to sell but it provided them with a device to minimize their corporate income taxes as well. Using this new power, Citibank would itself become a major player in the leasing of everything from office equipment to jet aircraft.

Encouraged by James Saxon, Citibank in 1963 bent the brokerage industry out of shape when it announced that it planned to offer a "collective" investment account to its trust customers. When the Securities and Exchange

Commission immediately claimed jurisdiction over such activities, Saxon re-torted that the SEC had no authority over banks. Since the late 1950s, Citi-bank had been trying to find a loophole that would enable it to get around the Glass-Steagall Act and into the mutual fund business.

When Saxon became comptroller, he appointed Shearman & Sterling lawyer Henry Harfield, who had been looking for a way into the mutual fund business, to his trust advisory board. Stumbling through a maze of arcane securities and banking rules and regulations, Harfield and his fellow lawyers found a rule that they believed would exempt the fund from the Investment Company Act of 1940. They figured that since the bank was advising and investing for the account of a trust customer, not underwriting and distribut-ing a fund to the public at large, the rule would not violate securities laws. This initiative was the beginning of a long, tortuous saga that would reach its climax in the Supreme Court.

Saxon liberalized the rules to such an extent that many state banks switched charters to take advantage of the comptroller's more benevolent policies. In his legislative initiatives, Saxon proved to be years ahead of his time. Among the most controversial was his proposal to liberalize branching opportunities for national banks by sweeping away state laws that limited them. This did not sit well with Charls Walker, executive director of the American Bankers Association, the principal banking trade group. Walker was in the unenviable position of having to juggle two often conflicting con-stituencies: a small group of large, mostly nationally chartered institutions that paid the bills, and thousands of small, mostly state-chartered banks that wielded the political clout and lived in fear of competition from their big-city brethren.

The liberalism that began with James Saxon precipitated major schisms between the comptroller's office and the Federal Reserve and the Federal De-posit Insurance Corporation. For two years, according to former senior dep-uty Comptroller Paul Homan, the chief administrator of national banks refused to talk with the chairman of the Federal Reserve, who had primary responsibility for the safety and soundness of the nation's financial system. According to Robert Bloom, who would later serve as Acting Comptroller of the Currency, Saxon also refused to attend meetings of the FDIC, where he was an ex-officio member. The banking agencies were always rivals, but never was that rivalry more contentious than during Saxon's tenure.

For his part, Wriston parted ways with Saxon on the notion of merging all of the bank regulatory agencies into a single agency. He favored competi-tion among regulators just as he did among banks. "Every industry that's been regulated by one federal regulator has gone bankrupt over time," Wris-ton said later. "The number one example, of course, is the railroads."

Wriston certainly shared Saxon's disdain for the Fed, though, particu-larly when it put on its bank-regulator hat. In the early 1960s the Fed's regulatory responsibility for national banks extended only to their interna-tional activities. In Citibank's drive to plant a branch in every trading center in the world, the Fed was often as much of an obstacle as were the host country authorities. About the time Citibank applied to the Fed to open a branch at the Hilton Hotel in Panama City, it also asked Indian banking authorities for permission to establish one in New Delhi. In a surprising twist, India okayed the New Delhi branch before the Fed signed off on the one in Panama. Wriston's subsequent discussion with the Fed illustrated the Fed's view of banks as institutions that needed government protection. "Being the wise guy that I am," Wriston said, "I called the Fed and said, 'Congratulations. You are now the slowest bureaucracy in the world. Up until this time, that was an honor held by the Indians. What's the problem?' "

"Well, the Chase Bank has a branch across the street [from the Panama Hilton]."

"I know," Wriston replied.

"But it's not making any money."

"I'm delighted," Wriston shot back.

"Do you think we should approve yours before [the Chase branch gets] in the black?" the bureaucrat asked.

"Yeah, I think you should," Wriston replied sarcastically.

Though Wriston took a keen interest in Saxon's domestic initiatives, his top priority was extending Citibank's reach overseas, particularly in Europe. Wriston and Moore traveled frequently to Europe, trying to cajole local monetary officials into awarding Citibank licenses or powers of one kind or another. For all their effort, the European operation had expanded little since Wriston took charge in 1956. The goal of establishing a branch in every Common Market country had remained an elusive one. Now that New York State was allowing foreign banks to set up shop, however, the door to Europe began to open as well. Still, the reception from European regulators and bankers was rarely warm, and Europe would always be a problem child in the Citi empire. Said John Fogarty, a former Citibank officer in Paris, "The Europeans believed Americans were going to scoop them up. They had an expertise in elegant refusal."

Nearly everywhere Citibank planted the flag, it was restricted by local banking authorities in the way it could operate and the services it could offer. Using their old-boy ties with corporate customers and political influence with banking regulators, the indigenous banks went out of their way to make sure that this upstart did not gain the upper hand.

Nowhere was that attitude more obvious than in Paris. For all its apparent glamour, France was always one of the stodgiest, most difficult markets in which to do business. It was clearly not one of Wriston's favorite places. He referred to the country sarcastically as "La Belle France" because of the obstacles, including harsh exchange restrictions, that it threw in the path of American banks trying to operate there. In Europe and elsewhere, Citibank's only hope for turning a buck, a franc, a yen, or a mark was to play on its ties to U.S. multinationals, its strength as an international institution, the inefficiencies of the local banks and banking system, and its knack for technological and financial innovation.

Wriston's strategy for invading Europe consisted of breaking down the door with foreign exchange trading, then supplying loans, letters of credit and transfer, and other noncredit services to institutional customers and prospects. One tactic was to lead American companies into Europe, walk them through the maze of regulation, and then, as former Citibanker John Rudy put it, "claim a chunk of their business in Europe." In the case of American companies such as Eastman Kodak, which were already well established in Europe by the 1960s, getting in the door of the company was often tougher than getting a toehold in a European firm.

When Citibank opened a new branch in Europe, the quickest way to show a profit was through foreign currency trading. Indeed, Wriston identified currency trading as a business in its own right rather than a lowly back office function that simply supported sexier activities like corporate lending. With each new branch opening, a foreign exchange team would typically lead the frontal assault on the new market by cranking up a trading operation almost from day one. That would be followed by a push to sell local corporations and U.S. clients on loans and other wholesale banking services. Only then would the branch attempt to diversify into other lines of business, such as retail banking and consumer finance. Important as the foreign exchange business was, however, it would also represent the source of many of Citibank's future problems.

In Europe in the 1960s, the term loan was a banking novelty, just as it had been twenty years earlier in the United States. "We'd take something from the States and try to mold it [so that] it could be used in the United Kingdom or France," said John Rudy. As the relatively efficient new kid on the block, one of Citibank's advantages was that it could be the low-cost producer compared with the establishment banks. Another, Rudy said, was that the indigenous banks (the European banks) were disdainful of clients. They "weren't used to competing with each other."

In August 1962, six years after he took charge of the European district, Wriston achieved a major breakthrough when First National City finally opened a branch in Brussels, where it had sold out years earlier on its lawyers' bad advice. A month later, Wriston cut the ribbon for a new branch in Milan. Having had a branch in Italy before the war, the bank was able to get back in before other American banks, and for a while it had the country to itself. In Italy the bank brought another device to bear on entrenched bank-corporate relationships: its expertise in transferring money, which was useful in countries like Italy, which had no particular incentive to move their customers' funds quickly and efficiently.

One of the first Italian customers it called on was Fiat, with whom it had done business in Latin America and which, like many similar companies, was at the mercy of the Italian bank cartels. Citibank eventually got a toe in the door with the automaker by demonstrating that it could bring dollars into Fiat's account and convert them to lire faster than the Italian banks could. Moreover, First National City was willing to assume credit risks that the establishment banks had no stomach for. While the local banks continued to stick to short-term loans, or at best loans based on asset values, Citibank offered borrowers term loans based on cash flow, just as Wriston had done with Onassis and McLean. The Milan branch's marketing gestures—free coffee for customers and up-to-the-minute bulletins on the progress of bicycle races and other athletic events—earned Citibank the nickname "La Banca Sexy" and the admiration of Italians accustomed to banking practices little changed since the days of the Medici.

In the postwar period, Citibank's principal American competition had been Chase Manhattan and Morgan Guaranty. But as American companies began opening plants and offices in Europe, domestic banks expanded, and other foreign banks followed Citibank's lead. As Wriston himself quipped at the time, "Europe is a pretty girl everyone has just discovered at the dance."

Several weeks after flying to Milan to celebrate Citibank's return to Italy, Wriston was once again on a plane to Latin America. He was meeting with overseas staff in Santiago, Chile, when President Kennedy disclosed, on October 21, 1962, the presence of Soviet intercontinental ballistic missiles in Cuba, and announced that the United States was preparing for a showdown with the Soviet Union to get them removed. Citibank immediately went onto a wartime footing. Wriston telexed his colleagues in New York, ordering them to duplicate the bank's records and move them into a vault buried deep in an upstate New York mountain where they would, in theory, be safe from all but a direct nuclear strike. The order turned out to be unnecessary, however. Back in New York, the bank had already microfilmed the records and shipped them to the vault, and at Citibank locations around the world managers were taking similar measures. Bank officials pulled out the contingency plan for management succession in the event New York received a direct hit. In six countries around the world, Citibank had placed a list of people designated to assume control of the bank if New York was wiped out. Meanwhile, in Chile, the American ambassador called Wriston and advised him to secure the vault and send everyone home.

During the missile crisis, John McCloy, the retired chairman of Chase Manhattan and one of Kennedy's advisers, represented a positive example of a high-level business executive having free access to the policymaking inner circle without being accused in the press of a conflict of interest. "Today," Wriston said later, "the *Washington Post* would say the chairman of Chase had branches in Cuba. There's no way he could have given good advice. That's a lot of bull."

In the six years or so since George Moore and Wriston had taken charge of the overseas division, their first goal—the initial stage of Moore's "three-stage rocket"—had been to grab territory, to put a branch or office at nearly every crossroads on the globe where money changed hands or business was conducted, and then to expand on that traditional banking business.

By 1963 the first stage of that rocket was solidly on course, and the second and third stages had already been ignited. The second stage—penetrating deeper into local markets—was exemplified by the bank's efforts to establish branches in secondary cities away from the capitals and principal ports. Citibank's top priority was to build a network to collect domestic deposits everywhere it went. In some out-of-the-way locations, mostly in Latin America, Citibank opened mini-branches, which were often started with as little as $20,000 in capital. These were Wriston's "Robert Hall, low overhead deposit catchers," a reference to the mass-market clothing retailer.

The buzz phrase for the third stage was "congenerics"—business units engaged in activities related to banking, such as merchant banking, leasing, and consumer finance. If Wriston's troops couldn't obtain licenses for full-fledged branches that could take deposits and make loans, they attempted to do end runs by acquiring or establishing congeneric companies, forming congeneric joint ventures, or getting special licenses to conduct non-bank activities. Another technique Citibank used to its advantage was the practice of obtaining special licenses that gave it powers not held by other banks. That way, said former overseas officer James Tozer, "You didn't get treated as one of the masses." Then, he said, "You could make a special license into something that works for you."

Wriston was a firm believer in what he called the "actuarial base"— Wristonese for the commonsense notion that one should spread his risk and not put all his eggs in one basket. Wriston believed that Citibank, properly diversified, would be unstoppable.

In its drive to break into a new business or a new country, Citibank was open to any and all proposals for forms of ownership. In 1963, for example, it bought a 17 percent stake in the British merchant banking house of M. Samuel—an effort which provided an early indication that joint ventures were not Citibank's cup of tea. After the deal was consummated, M. Samuel's staff, while training in New York, spent most of their time rifling through Citibank credit files in search of *American* business prospects, according to Tozer. About five years later, Citibank dissolved the relationship.

In the short term at least, some of these congenerics turned out to be financial boondoggles that drained talent from more conventional ventures, but to some extent they did stake a claim in virgin land. While the tents that Citibank pitched on foreign soil often collapsed through fraud, mismanagement, or economic downturns, their successor institutions were sometimes more profitable and enduring.

In March 1963, Citibank announced that in July it planned to open its first Swiss branch in Geneva without expecting to make loads of money. The Swiss, however, were considered the world's preeminent bankers, and a franchise in Zurich or Geneva was the ultimate 1960s status symbol. Citibank was so awed—even scared—at the prospect of operating in Switzerland that it considered assigning a vice chairman to head the operation there. To Citibank, it was as if the manager of a McDonald's outlet had, through some bizarre accident, wound up as the head chef at Maxim's of Paris. In the end, said a former officer, Switzerland "wasn't as awesome as we thought."

At any rate, after spending nearly a year trying to win Swiss approval, Citibank became the first foreign bank in Switzerland, thereby breaking the Swiss monopoly on banking in that country. The move into Geneva, however, created consternation among some Citibankers with vested interests and among U.S. regulatory authorities. Citibank's old-timers, for example, once again protested that the move would destroy decades-old correspondent banking relationships. Although the "Swiss cried a lot," Wriston recalled, the major obstacles were legal and regulatory problems, and the popular but skewed perception that Switzerland was only a haven in which tax evaders and other miscreants could deposit their ill-gotten gains. Citibank wanted to avoid being associated with that image, especially in the eyes of the U.S. government, so it agreed not to accept accounts of U.S. nationals in its Swiss branch. The regulatory problem was resolved when the Federal Reserve agreed to permit the branch to be examined by a Swiss auditing firm, which would submit its results to the Fed. And then, as things turned out, most of the early business in Switzerland was of the plain vanilla variety: lending to holding companies and commodities brokers.

A front-page article in the *New York Times* reported that other New York banks had expressed interest in picking up correspondent deposits that the Swiss banks had traditionally left with Citibank. According to Moore, Chase's David Rockefeller thought that Citibank would lose all of its correspondent business and claimed that his bank would not follow in Citibank's footsteps. But, Moore said later, "An hour after *we* did it, *he* did it."

In the end, Citibank concluded that the title of the man dispatched to head up Switzerland was less important than the personal qualities of the man himself. Instead of sending a vice chairman, Wriston dispatched Ellis Bradford, a popular, congenial banker known for his ability to get along with everyone and anyone, a man not likely to ruffle Swiss feathers. Geneva was no hardship post, but it did have its annoyances. On the second day of operation, the new management received a list of rules, including one that required that the hedges on the bank's lot be maintained at a certain height. "Opening a branch," said one overseas hand, "is like being the father of a baby."

Wriston's new babies in Europe and his growing public acclaim could not have pleased his in-house rival, Tommy Wilcox. According to some insiders, Stillman Rockefeller showed his preference for a successor in early 1962 when General Electric announced that it had selected Wriston as a director. As the story goes, General Electric chairman Ralph J. Cordiner had first approached Rockefeller himself, but Stillman had protested that he was nearing retirement age, and that GE should choose a younger man. Cordiner is said to have asked Rockefeller who his successor would be, and Rockefeller replied unequivocally, "Wriston."

"GE wanted the number one man," said former Citibanker Tom Creamer. After all, GE had always been considered one of the most desirable directorships. Most of the major automobile companies supplied their directors with a new car of their choice every year, but GE dispatched a huge van filled with appliances—stoves, refrigerators, and dishwashers—to the home of every new director. "They equip your house with everything they make, whenever you want it," said one former Citibank official familiar with the company.

By 1963 the flowers had started to come in for Wriston from the financial press and from his alma mater. On November 24 of that year, the *New York Times* wrote that "If Walter Wriston becomes president of First National City Bank one day, as some bankers predict, the event probably will do irreparable damage to the stereotype of the banker as a stuffed shirt with a lemon-flavored personality." In June, between overseas trips, Wriston had stopped in Medford, Massachusetts, to pick up an honorary doctor of laws degree from the Fletcher School, which cited him as a "distinguished son of a distinguished father."

Wriston may not have achieved his Fletcher School ambition to become secretary of state, but by now he was running the banking equivalent of the U.S. foreign service. Being head of the overseas division clearly gave him a leg up on his peers in the business community. To Wriston, First National City was a vast reservoir of information on world events. He regarded his branch managers around the world as far more reliable news sources than the *New York Times.* In fact, Wriston considered the paper's foreign coverage seriously distorted, particularly its articles on Latin America. Whenever he wanted to know what was really happening in any country, he phoned the branch manager there. In January 1964, for example, Panama erupted in anti-American riots, and several Citibank branches sustained minor damage. Wriston recognized that the *New York Times* stories on the riots were 180 degrees away from the truth, and told the editors so at an editorial luncheon. "I told them what was really going on in Panama. They asked, 'How do you know?' " Wriston told them, "I'm talking to the guys down there every day." The editors, Wriston claimed later, verified his account, and transferred one reporter, whom Wriston regarded as a leftist, out of the country.

Opening up a new country was rarely a hassle-free project, but Switzerland was a piece of cake compared with Canada. In the years since George Moore had taken charge of the overseas division, the Citibank juggernaut had expanded around the globe, but had been unable to gain a foothold in Canada, then the healthiest and most stable economy in the world after the United States itself. Given the country's increasing sensitivity about its domination by U.S. interests, there was no way an American bank would be allowed to acquire a Canadian institution, and only one bank in the whole country—the Mercantile—was foreign-owned. A subsidiary of the Rotterdamsche Bank of the Netherlands, the Mercantile had been chartered in 1953 to finance foreign trade.

At a tennis match in the fall of 1962, Wriston heard from a Canadian banker friend that the Mercantile might be for sale. He lunged at the opportunity, hopping a plane to Amsterdam, where he was presented with terms he regarded as clearly "ridiculous." Discouraged, he flew home, only to receive a cable from the Dutch bankers indicating that they were now willing to talk.

Stillman Rockefeller's response to their new overture was predictable: "Another wild-goose chase." But Wriston returned right away to Amsterdam, where he received another lesson in negotiation from the hard-nosed Dutch bankers. Expecting to deal one on one with the chairman, he walked into an office and found himself face to face with the entire board. After repeatedly throwing Wriston out of the room, they asked him, "What can you do in writing?"

"Where's the typewriter?" Wriston asked. He then adjourned to a back room, where he pecked out the terms. Then he fired off a cable to Rockefeller that read, "This goose is not wild."

While the Dutch bankers lived up to their reputation as difficult negotiators, subsequent events showed that their reputation as savvy lenders was not well founded. Their bank, as it turned out, was virtually insolvent. Their loans proved to be under water, reducing to about $1 million the price the Americans eventually paid for Mercantile, which, with $90.6 million in assets, was a piggybank by most standards. It was by far the smallest of the Canadian banks, only half the size of the next-largest institution. Nonetheless, Wriston had to compete against a half dozen other suitors.

The real test for Wriston and Rockefeller, however, occurred not in Amsterdam but in Ottawa, where a furor erupted over who said what to whom in two meetings between Citibank officials and Canadian financial authorities during the summer of 1963 when Citibank first officially notified the Canadians of their acquisition plans. Then, after the purchase agreement was signed, Citibank informed the Canadians that it wished to arrange a meeting between the minister of finance, Walter Gordon, and Stillman Rockefeller. An intimate friend of the new prime minister, Lester Pearson, Gordon was a virulent nationalist, particularly on economic matters, who bitterly resented U.S. domination of Canadian business. He would become Citibank's archenemy. The meeting between Gordon and Rockefeller was scheduled for July 18, 1963, a fateful day in the financial history of both Citibank and the United States.

———

Although John Kennedy shared Wriston's views on the need for economic growth and the free flow of people between business and government, the two men were clearly poles apart when it came to the free flow of capital around the world. Kennedy was seeking to stimulate economic growth and investment in the United States, and he apparently believed that one way to do that was to discourage investment elsewhere. Wriston was pushing to expand First National City Bank around the globe, and he believed that free movement of capital would ultimately benefit the United States as well as the bank.

On July 18, 1963, Kennedy proposed a balance-of-payments program that included a temporary 15 percent tax on purchases by Americans of foreign securities and a tax on loans made by American banks to foreign borrowers. This tax, known as the interest equalization tax, was intended to curtail the current surge in offerings of foreign securities in the United States. And of course nothing would incite Wriston more than a move to suppress the free movement of goods and services.

On that same day, Shearman & Sterling attorney Hans Angermueller stopped by Wriston's office shortly after the news of the Kennedy proposal had flashed across the wire. "Wriston was livid," Angermueller recalled. "Who is this upstart president interfering with the free flow of capital?" he seethed. Declaring that "you can't dam capital," Wriston damned "politicians in general and one Irish politician in particular."

Enacted by Congress on September 2, 1964, the interest equalization tax was retroactive to July 19, 1963, was set to expire on December 31, 1965, and applied initially only to foreign securities. In the short term, the legislation clearly had its intended result: reducing the purchase of securities and, thereby, the U.S. balance-of-payments deficit. The deficit once again began to edge upward toward the end of 1964 and into 1965, but the interest equalization tax would be remembered more for its destructive long-term impact than for its seemingly beneficial short-term effects. This was the first in a series of moves to discourage the export of U.S. capital, but it would not be the last.

Walter Gordon, the Canadian finance minister, learned of the American plans to impose the interest equalization tax from Rockefeller during their Ottawa meeting on July 18. He was just as angry over the proposal as Wriston was, though for different reasons. The tax enraged Gordon because it directly threatened Canada's $1 billion annual sale of bond issues on Wall Street. Canada later successfully negotiated with the Kennedy administration for an exemption, but having to grovel to Washington was a humiliating experience for Canadians. And U.S. efforts to redress the balance-of-payments problems remained a thorn in Canada's side.

Gordon later contended that at that same July 18 meeting, he warned Rockefeller against going ahead with the acquisition of Mercantile before Canada's Bank Act was revised. If Citibank did so, it would be proceeding at its own risk. A month later, however, Citibank obtained Federal Reserve approval, and on September 30, it acquired 50 percent of Mercantile. By April 1965 First National City owned the entire institution. Because it was buying an existing bank—and a foreign one at that—and not chartering a new one, the Canadians could not block the deal. They would, however, view the transaction as one in which Citibank cleverly used a loophole to gain a foothold on their soil. If Wriston and his colleagues gave a moment's thought to the possibility of a Canadian protest, those worries were nullified by the fact that this was a transaction between two foreign interests.

Ironically, Citibank saved the Canadians and the Dutch from the embarrassment of having to bail out a failing bank. The Canadians clearly had

had no problem with tiny Mercantile Bank being owned by the Dutch, but the American ownership became the symbol of American imperialism. Like a match thrown on a gasoline-soaked haystack, the deal kindled an outburst of Canadian economic nationalism and anti-U.S. sentiment unmatched in recent history. In the mid-1960s the United States clearly dominated the Canadian economy. U.S. interests controlled approximately 60 percent of Canada's manufacturing activity and 90 percent of the oil and gas industry. Banking was one industry sector not controlled by Americans, and the Canadians saw the Mercantile acquisition as the first step in that direction. "Wriston," claimed former Argentina-based Citibanker James Farley, "bought Mercantile on the back of an envelope and told the Canadians about it after the fact." As a result of Canadian opposition to Citibank's ownership of Mercantile, Chase Manhattan, in 1963, abandoned plans to buy a stake in Toronto Dominion, a major Canadian bank.

All of this would reinforce for Wriston the folly of government interference in economic and financial markets and would soon demonstrate once again the principle that Wriston referred to as the "unintended secondary consequences of primary events." In this instance, however, the unintended consequence could hardly be called secondary. Although the existence of a Eurodollar market had been recognized since the late 1950s, few events caused it to explode more than the interest equalization tax. And by the early 1970s the Euromarket was to become the principal vehicle for another development that was to have equally momentous consequences for Wriston, Citibank, the banking system, and the world economy: the coming of age of the syndicated cross-border loan. The Euromarket got its start through market distortions caused by what Wriston described as "extreme regulation on two sides of the Atlantic."

In the Eurodollar market, the physical dollars themselves would never actually leave the United States. Instead, they would become liabilities on the books of financial institutions located outside the country and therefore not subject to American bank regulation, though U.S. bank regulators would later look for ways to regulate the very market they themselves had inadvertently created. As credit conditions in the United States tightened in the mid-1960s, borrowers turned increasingly to London for Eurodollar loans for domestic purposes.

Perhaps more than any other single event, the establishment of the interest equalization tax kicked off a brain drain of financial talent from Wall Street to London that in Wriston's view set the United States back at least ten years in global financial competitiveness. "It was," said Wriston, "a denial of the global market." In effect, business that would otherwise have been done in the United States moved to London, which became the center of an unregulated market where U.S. banks would be able to accept Eurodollar deposits free of the Fed's requirements and the Regulation Q ceilings. In that environment, banks would be able to pay more for deposits and charge less for loans. Moreover, since they were free of the constraints of the Glass-Steagall Act, banks could underwrite securities issues and perform other securities-related activities that were strictly off limits to banks operating in the United States. In that respect, the emergence of the Euromarket would have something of a silver lining for U.S. banks. It became a kind of training ground that would prepare American bankers for the day when they were no longer subject to the dictates of Glass-Steagall on their home turf.

Cracks were now beginning to appear in the postwar Bretton Woods system of fixed exchange rates pegged to the dollar. As European economies began to recover, and as the balance of payments began to shift in their favor, the Bretton Woods system was becoming less and less tenable. Attempts to control these flows, in the Kennedy and Johnson administrations, weakened the position of the United States as the preeminent financial center. By and large, said Nobel economist Milton Friedman, the banking industry in general was strongly opposed to discarding Bretton Woods in favor of floating rates. Wriston, he claimed, "was the only major figure in banking who saw the problems coming and was willing to take a public stand." But, as it turned out, the very distortions and imbalances that the government was aiding and abetting by imposing controls would accelerate the expansion of the Euromarket, and create enormous opportunities for Citibank.

The world of global Eurofinance got its first look at the future in the early 1960s when Shell Oil called Citibank headquarters to say it wanted to buy a company in Italy and needed a $100 million term loan immediately. In a matter of days, Wriston and several colleagues put together the first Euro-syndicated loan, taking $55 million for Citibank and allocating $30 million to Manufacturers Hanover and $15 million to Irving Trust. Besides being the first Eurosyndication, the seven-year term loan would prove to be significant for still another reason: it alerted Citibank to the need for a system to protect itself against interest rate volatility. Because movements in interest rates had been few and relatively inconsequential, Citibank based the rate for each six-month period on the average cost of funds over the *previous* six months, plus one quarter of one percent. For years, that single $55 million, representing 10 percent of the assets of the London office, would be a major contributor to London's profitability. But in 1966 when rates surged, the flaws in that arrangement became obvious, and Shell wound up getting the better end of the deal.

Wriston's last official service to the Kennedy administration began within minutes after the first announcement, early in the afternoon of Friday, November 22, 1963, that Kennedy had been shot in Dallas. After being summoned to the fortresslike headquarters of the Federal Reserve Bank of New York in lower Manhattan, Wriston and other top bankers were ordered to buy dollars around the world. While the world sat frozen in front of television screens, there were banking details to be dealt with. Few senior bankers of that era had risen to the top by way of the back office, however, and as a result, they knew virtually nothing about the workings of payments systems and bank vault time locks.

Within hours, governors of some states had proclaimed a day of mourning for the slain president, a decision that called for the closing of banking institutions. As the emotional and financial tidal wave surged around the world, pressure was building, particularly in Europe, for a similar decision from New York. After combing the state by phone in search of Nelson Rockefeller, Wriston finally called the governor's brother David at the family's Pocantico Hills estate. "This thing is getting out of hand," Wriston said, advising him that Citibank had huge volumes of letters of credit expiring that evening. With half the nation's banks closed, it was unclear how Citibank was going to pay on them. Then there was the problem of the time locks that would open the next morning and trigger alarms from Brooklyn to Buffalo if adequate preparations weren't made for resetting them. "Can't you get your brother?" Wriston asked David.

"He's right here," David replied.

After talking with Wriston, Governor Rockefeller issued a proclamation for a day of mourning, and preparations were launched for closing the state's banks on Monday.

Incredibly, a British bank later cabled Citibank demanding an extra day's interest on its deposits, asserting that the day of mourning was not technically a bank holiday. Wriston fired back an angry telex demanding an extra day's interest for Saint Swithin's day in return. The Brits got the point and dropped the matter.

At the very moment Wriston was getting his marching orders from the Fed, representatives of Citibank and other major New York banks were convened a few blocks away at the New York Stock Exchange in a frantic effort to salvage the brokerage firm of Ira Haupt & Company—and their reputations. What became known as the salad oil scandal reminded Wriston and Citibank of their vulnerability to determined and sophisticated con artists. About ten U.S. and British banks, including Citibank, had together lent more than $37 million to Haupt, secured by warehouse receipts posted by New Jersey's Allied Crude Vegetable Oil Refining Corporation. Anthony (Tino) De Angelis, the short, heavyset head of Allied, had managed to persuade dozens of banks and securities firms to lend him some $175 million with the pledge of salad oil supposedly stored at a huge depot in Bayonne, New Jersey, subleased by an American Express subsidiary.

When Allied folded, bankers discovered that the oil had never existed and their loans were now nearly worthless. In turn, Allied's failure triggered the fall of the house of Ira Haupt & Company. Although Citibank had thrown De Angelis out of the bank for writing bad checks, it apparently believed that it was safe with Ira Haupt as a buffer and the receipts for the oil as security.

For Citibank, things turned out somewhat better than expected. A year later, Stillman Rockefeller told shareholders that the bank expected to collect about $1.7 million of its $3.8 million in loans, $500,000 more than it had anticipated. But the episode reinforced, albeit briefly, one of the basic tenets of credit analysis. Said Lawrence Glenn, former chief credit officer, "You've got to see if the tank is full. We were not dealing with Mr. De Angelis, but we got caught up anyway. We learned not to get caught in a secondary way."

Equally important in Wriston's grooming was his familiarity with Citibank's so-called front office loans. Former chairman Howard Sheperd used to remind his colleagues that in the old days of the National City Bank all the bum loans were made in the front office. Since the 1930s, Citibank chief executives had generally recognized the hazards of making loans to buddies at the Links Club bar. Prospective borrowers who entered the bank through the front office were routinely turned over to the appropriate loan officer for an independent credit analysis. Deviations from that policy by president George Moore in the 1960s reconfirmed for Wriston just how wise it was and led to additional measures to strengthen it. One high-profile episode began in 1961 when master builder Robert Moses asked Moore to head the finance committee for the 1964–1965 New York World's Fair, an invitation Moore readily accepted. Moore pledged to open a branch at the fair and assembled a group of ten banks to purchase $10 million in debentures, all of which was ultimately written off. But then, in late 1964, amid accusations that Moses was falsifying attendance records and cooking the books for the fair's first season, Moore and his fellow bankers insisted that Moses open the records to an outside auditor. In January 1965, after Moses balked at Moore's demands for audited financial information, Moore resigned from the finance committee along with most of the other members. Moses responded to the charges by accusing Moore of pressuring the fair to make a $750,000 loan to the Better Living Center, a financially troubled exhibit to which Citibank had lent $6 million. The auditor's review revealed massive irregularities.

With Kennedy's death, the Alliance for Progress lost its driving force. Its detractors had claimed that the program was flawed from the outset, relying as it did on government-to-government assistance. The policies of the recipient nations didn't help either. As historian and Kennedy adviser Arthur Schlesinger pointed out in *A Thousand Days: John F. Kennedy in the White House,* the alliance was hampered by "the stipulations and rigidities in the [American foreign] aid legislation" and by the fact that the "Latins themselves were often slow to produce good projects and effective development programs."

When it came to aiding Latin America, one failed program begot other equally unsuccessful programs. One of the latter was the Atlantic Community Development Group for Latin America, known as ADELA. It began in 1964 with a call from New York senator Jacob Javits to his close friend George Moore. Given Javits's liberal instincts and Moore's relative conservatism, the camaraderie between the two men seemed to some a bit odd, but "They were two very smart guys who came up the hard way," Wriston said later. "George was forever talking to him." During that 1964 phone call, Javits proposed to Moore that they set up a private enterprise version of the Alliance for Progress, and Moore, always quick to embrace new concepts, agreed. The program was to be part development bank and part venture capital fund, with participation equally divided among big American, European, and Asian companies. From the outset, Rockefeller and Wriston viewed the venture as just another one of Moore's harebrained schemes. "George was very gung-ho about ADELA," Wriston said later, but others, including Wriston himself, had to "try to pick up the pieces later."

Citibank's investments in ADELA were placed under a corporation set up in 1961 known as the First National City Overseas Investment Corporation, or FINOIC, which was formed to take advantage of the banks' power, under the Edge Act, to make equity investments overseas. Among Citibankers, this corporation was variously known as the "special effects" or "funny money" department. FINOIC became a kind of dumping ground for untraditional investments and untraditional people. But like so many other creations that produced little payback, FINOIC marked a refinement in the evolution of investment banking at Citibank in that it gave the bank an opportunity to analyze venture capital equity investments.

ADELA became a major nuisance, however, and was kicked around like a deflated financial football from one overseas unit to another. ADELA eventually fizzled out of existence.

In point of fact, Wriston would ultimately generate more investment in Latin America than all of the other economic development programs combined. More than anyone, he was responsible for leading the world's banking industry into the era of cross-border lending to Latin America. At about the time Kennedy was kicking off his Alliance for Progress, Wriston was planting the first seeds for cross-border lending by hiring a top International Monetary Fund official named Gesualdo A. "Al" Costanzo.

Wriston and Costanzo had met in 1960 in Argentina, when the soft-spoken, self-effacing Costanzo was serving as a deputy director of the IMF for Latin America. After rejecting Wriston's initial overtures, Costanzo finally succumbed in 1961 to the persistence of George Moore, who phoned Costanzo for lunch every time he visited Washington. His first assignment was to take charge of Citibank's relationships with central banks and governments, to become Citibank's ambassador to the world. From being a bag carrier and speechwriter for Moore, who on occasion awakened him in the middle of the night to revise one of his speeches, Costanzo went on to become the most influential voice in Citibank's policy toward Latin America. In 1964, he was promoted to senior vice president in charge of Latin America.

Costanzo had been brought in to use his balance-of-payments expertise to evaluate the capacity of foreign countries to earn dollars and repay dollar loans, and thus determine the proper level of dollar loan exposure that Citibank should maintain in the countries where it was doing business. With a few exceptions, cross-border lending had been taboo since the days of Charlie Mitchell. With Costanzo's arrival, that taboo would undergo a reappraisal.

Few men were more like-minded than Wriston and Costanzo. They were from the same generation, moved to Washington at the same time, and almost wound up in the same apartment building. They had received a similar education, and both of them got married and went into the service at the same time. "It [the War] made us idealists," said Costanzo later. While both became economic conservatives, they shared a liberal, open-minded attitude toward giving heavy responsibility to young people. "The greatest thing he [Wriston] did was create an environment where people could come in and participate from day one," said Costanzo later. "There was great enthusiasm and esprit de corps." Costanzo was typical of the well-educated men from ordinary origins with whom Wriston liked to surround himself.

The son of an Alabama coal miner, Costanzo was an unpretentious man who ate corn bread and black-eyed peas and spent his leisure hours gardening and listening to country music. After high school, he hopped a freight train for Birmingham, where he put himself through Birmingham-Southern College, graduating Phi Beta Kappa in 1937. He won scholarships to the University of Virginia, where he earned a doctorate in economics in 1941. Growing up poor in the Depression, Costanzo felt that he could make no greater contribution than to rejuvenate sick economies, and by the time he graduated, he was a staunch proponent of Keynesian economics. In 1942, the same year Wriston arrived in Washington for his stint at the State Department, Costanzo went to work for the Commerce Department. During the war he served as a Japanese language specialist with the Office of Naval Intelligence.

In 1948, Costanzo was sent to Europe as an assistant Treasury representative to help supervise the distribution of Marshall Plan funds, and often worked through the night calculating balance-of-payments estimates for Spain, Turkey, and other aid recipients. Having risen quickly from modest beginnings into the rarefied world of international finance, Costanzo might have been expected to feel optimistic about his own future. But his experience as a young U.S. representative on the Greek Currency Board in the early 1950s also inculcated in him an unshakable optimism about the possibility of quickly improving the world's most troubled economies by implementing the right policies.

After the war, Britain had assumed financial responsibility for Greece and had injected about 40 million pounds as a reserve to try to stabilize the Greek economy. When Costanzo arrived there, the central bank easily succumbed to government pressures to print money, which drove up prices and prompted people to buy gold. By establishing and adhering to monthly goals for currency in circulation, the Currency Board became the vehicle for budget discipline, and inflation was soon brought under control. Costanzo's role in administering fiscal discipline didn't win him many friends, though. Opponents of the program put a price on his head. In Greece, Costanzo was assisted by George "Jack" Clark, whom Costanzo hired in 1964 to work with him at Citibank. Together, Costanzo and Clark succeeded in quickly turning the Greek economy around. According to Clark, it "went from a $200 million deficit to a $200 million surplus almost overnight."

Later, as a top IMF official in Latin America, Costanzo was largely responsible for transforming "the Fund" from an ineffective institution that had sought to change deficient economic policies with generalizations that smacked of motherhood and apple pie to one that relied on tough austerity measures based on quantifiable performance.

Belying his gentle southern manner, Costanzo earned for the IMF a reputation as an enforcer of draconian policies. In pushing these programs, Costanzo dealt directly with Latin heads of state, most of whom were military dictators. Costanzo negotiated tough agreements with Paraguay, Bolivia, Ecuador, Peru, and post-Perón Argentina. "If I could, I would always go for the drastic solution," Costanzo said later. "I'd cut off the dog's tail in one shot rather than a little bit at a time. . . . To be effective you've got to do that. Otherwise you're just throwing money down a rat hole." Costanzo's optimistic view of the prospects of developing countries was driven by the conviction that when things get bad enough, politicians will invariably be forced to take tough, unpleasant measures, and the country's economy will once again be set straight. With the appropriate economic policies, a country could bounce back from despair in much the same way as a chronically unemployed steelworker who suddenly lands a job. Referring to the Latin economies generally, Costanzo used to say, "Throw it all open and it'll be bad, but it'll be over in six months."

By lending money to build, say, an airport in a foreign country, American commercial banks were really lending dollars to the government of that country against its future foreign exchange export earnings. By accepting the loan, the government was effectively committing itself to provide the semigovernmental airport entity with enough foreign exchange to repay it. But to the traditionalists, the proper function of an international bank was to use dollars to finance trade. These were short-term credits, often guaranteed by an agency such as the Export-Import Bank, that were generally repaid in less than a year. The risk of loss was next to nil. Nations and enterprises knew that defaulting on trade credits was economic suicide. No one epitomized this view more than credit policy chief Sterling Bunnell, a classmate of Stillman Rockefeller's.

Exceptions were few and far between. Robert Hoguet, Wriston's former boss, recalls that Citibank was once approached by Sears Roebuck chairman General R. E. Wood about financing some of the retailer's receivables in its emerging Mexico City market. Even though the spread between U.S. and Mexican rates was about six percentage points at the time, Citibank refused to make the loans unless they were fully guaranteed by the U.S. parent.

In the late 1950s and early 1960s, according to former Citibankers, a few cracks began appearing in that old barricade. For example, Japan was beginning to emerge as an economic power to be reckoned with and was intent on gaining respectability in world capital markets. Just as an individual with a poor or nonexistent credit history might establish creditworthiness by borrowing and repaying fully collateralized loans he doesn't really need, Japan borrowed dollars backed 125 percent by its gold reserves. On that risk-free basis, cross-border lending to Japan was particularly appealing. In addition, Citibank had made small cross-border loans—collaterized with gold bullion in the vault of the New York Fed and rarely for more than $50 million—to other countries to help them overcome temporary foreign exchange shortages.

Yet despite its extreme caution, Citibank occasionally got burned. In the Cuban affair, for instance, it learned something about the political risks inherent in lending to the foreign subsidiaries of American companies.

Wriston himself later described the move to cross-border lending as a point on a continuum rather than a watershed. It began, he said, with the early term loans that he and George Moore had made to the likes of United Airlines. Recognizing that supertankers, containerships, and Boeing 707s couldn't be underwritten with ninety-day self-liquidating loans, Citibank financed the aircraft with term loans. "Form follows function," Wriston said. "And I suspect international lending followed the same deal." Similarly, he said, "you can't build a coffee mill with ninety-day money. It would turn into two-year, five-year money. I don't believe a cross-border loan is any different from a domestic loan." What *was* different about this form of lending was that ultimate repayment would depend entirely on the foreign central bank's ability to generate dollars rather than on the borrower's ability to generate cash. "That's why Al [Costanzo] was brought in—to set up the mechanism to monitor that," Wriston said.

George "Jack" Clark, Costanzo's former colleague in Greece, later said that Wriston was the first commercial banker in history to realize that lending in dollars required sophisticated balance-of-payments analysis of the kind the International Monetary Fund had been doing for years, and to act on that recognition by hiring IMF officials like Costanzo. "Wriston was the only commercial banker in the world who thought in these terms," said Clark. "He knew you could make a perfectly good loan—the cash flow [and] collateral could be there—then the loan matures and you go to the central bank and, whoops, there are no dollars." Costanzo and Clark taught courses at the bank on the workings of the IMF and the international payment system, increasing the comfort of international officers in cross-currency lending and improving their understanding of the "right" amount of exposure. Although Citibank first recognized the notion of transfer risk in the early 1960s, more than a decade would pass before the bank had an opportunity to put it into practice.

In early 1964, when a new branch opened for business in Amsterdam, Wriston achieved his long-standing goal of establishing a branch of First National City Bank in every significant Common Market country. Shortly thereafter, Greece was brought into the fold, thanks to a Citibank officer who had cultivated a following among some of the leading merchants and shippers of Athens.

With that benchmark achieved, it was time for Citibank's officers to turn their attention to the relatively threadbare Far East operations. Although Asia remitted more earnings to New York in the mid-1960s than any other district, it had grown rather more slowly than other areas since Moore and Wriston took over. Citibank remained chary of Asia and vice versa. One reason was that Asian countries had recovered more slowly than those of Europe from the ravages of World War II. Moreover, until the early 1970s, many governments in the region were "inhospitable to foreign banks," said Asia hand Rick Wheeler. As a result, "we really didn't push aggressively in expanding in Asia."

Citibank officers in Asia were more comfortable doing business through correspondent banks than through branches. To the extent that the bank was lending directly, loans were for the most part fully secured. In the 1960s, said Wheeler, the only "real lending"—based on balance sheets and income statements—in Asia was being done in the Philippines. The legionnaires who were holding down Citibank's fort in the Far East felt like a neglected lot and regarded themselves as the stepchildren of the overseas family. New York, they believed, was incapable of understanding how to do business in the Far East. Wriston's colleagues felt that he was not at ease in a society where he couldn't sit down with a businessman and seal a deal on the spot with a handshake. He had a "skepticism about things not done in a totally straightforward fashion," said Citibanker Rick Roesch, and Wriston referred to any arcane transaction as a "Chinese accounting system."

There was, however, at least one advantage to working at such a vast geographical and psychic distance from New York: because managers in Asia were awake when their superiors in New York were asleep, they couldn't always phone headquarters for approval of their every move. As a result, they tended to be somewhat more entrepreneurial, or so they felt, than their counterparts elsewhere. Said Rick Wheeler, "Our perception was that Wriston didn't like Asia, but that was totally incongruent with the fact that he'd let us do anything." Despite the insularity of the Far East group, he added, "at the end of each year a huge wad of money was handed to the bank."

The postwar rebirth of Citibank in Asia began in 1962 with the opening of a branch in Kowloon, a peninsula of Hong Kong. Hong Kong was always something of a paradox for Citibank. On the one hand, it was as close as any market got to the Adam Smith–Walter Wriston ideal of a free and unfettered economy: bank exams were lax, regulation was minimal, and exchange controls were nonexistent. On the other hand, there were, according to one former officer, more defalcations in Hong Kong than in the rest of the bank put together. As former branch manager Ray Kathe recalled, "Every morning when I went down the hill to my desk . . . I was scared silly that some great blowup would take place, some credit blowup, some defalcation, or that somebody would defraud us in some way." Another former officer explained that despite all vigilance by management, "we got taken to the cleaners by Chinese officers and the marketplace." One reason, he said, was that Citibank never managed to win the loyalty of the Chinese staff. Notwithstanding such difficulties, Wriston's trip to the Philippines in September 1964—his first since becoming head of the overseas division—was a signal to Asia hands that the Far East was about to become a vital part of the empire.

Citibank exerted more financial influence over the Philippines than it did over most other countries in its worldwide orbit; eventually a third of the heads of the Filipino banks were Citibank alumni.

Unlike Moore, who loved to be greeted with fanfare and driven into foreign capitals with motorcycle escorts, Wriston was decidedly low key.

Though senior officers overseas were spared the ordeal of arranging motorcades for Wriston, they clearly understood that they were expected to arrange tennis matches for him with suitable doubles partners, and they handled these arrangements as if their careers depended on it. Rick Wheeler, then the Philippines country head, thought he had been given a prized assignment in the summer of 1964 when he was designated to host a Saturday tennis match for his boss. But then, one by one, all of Wheeler's regular tennis buddies and other members of Manila's elite tennis set declined his invitation. Wheeler's and Wriston's tennis partners, as it turned out, were two barefoot ball boys from the Polo Club. "I could have walked off the court thinking my career was over because I didn't have two important people he could play with," Wheeler recalled years later, but to his relief, "it wasn't important to Walter that we didn't have the president of Shell Oil."

Wriston was less pleased with the informality of certain other arrangements, however, including the preparations for an inspection tour of the branch at Clark Air Force Base, north of Manila. Citibank, of course, had a long history of supplying banking services to U.S. military personnel around the world. The banking franchises on military bases were awarded on a bid basis, and Wriston wanted to inspect the facilities personally to make sure the customers were getting good service. At six o'clock one morning, Wriston and two colleagues showed up at Manila Airport and were directed to the twin-engine Cessna that would fly them to the base. Shortly thereafter, their Filipino pilot arrived, and with Wriston in the co-pilot's seat and the other officers behind him, stunned his passengers by announcing, "I've never flown one of these before." After taking off, the pilot turned to Wriston and asked him where he wanted to go.

"Clark Air Force Base," replied Wriston, who was accustomed to seasoned pilots who filed flight plans beforehand. Incredibly, the pilot didn't have flying directions for Clark. Wriston suggested that he fly the "iron compass"—the railroad line that runs roughly north from Manila. The pilot did so, but as they approached Clark Air Force Base, a voice from the control tower crackled repeatedly over the radio: "You will not land. You will not land." The passengers and pilot quickly realized why: some forty days earlier, Congress had passed the Gulf of Tonkin Resolution, escalating dramatically the U.S. involvement in the Vietnam War, and military transports were taking off and landing at a rate of one every few minutes.

Wriston grabbed the microphone and announced, "Sir, I work for the

Citibank. We operate your banks. I have a date with your commanding general. Request permission to land." After a few tense moments, permission was granted.

Japan was neither as friendly as the Philippines nor as free as Hong Kong. Owing to Citibank's long-standing presence in Japan, it enjoyed some privileges and preferences not accorded to other foreign banks. It was also the largest foreign bank in Japan, but that wasn't saying much. In 1965, according to Rick Wheeler, the total foreign bank share of Japan's banking assets was less than 1 percent. Citibank and other American banks made money by extending dollar loans backed by Japanese banks, but a "bamboo curtain" restricted their participation in some activities and blocked it entirely in others. Furthermore, Citibank's efforts to strengthen its ties to Japan were often rebuffed by the finance ministry, which galled Wriston no end.

One of the bank's goals in Japan was to find the key to the tightly locked doors of Japanese companies. To do business with them, an American bank had to be introduced by a Japanese bank, Wheeler recalled. In an attempt to stop Citibank from developing its nascent consumer banking business, Japanese financial authorities asked Citibank officials to sign an agreement pledging to stay out of consumer banking. Citibank refused to sign. Later on, Citibank even helped Japanese banks get set up in New York, hoping that the Japanese would relax the hurdles to U.S. participation in their economy.

Wriston's frequent railing about Japan's discriminatory rules against foreigners led many of his colleagues to conclude that he still hated the Japanese and loathed having to visit the country, a sentiment Wriston denied. That notion, he said, "became almost a cult. It was totally untrue. I've been to Japan I don't know how many times." Nonetheless, he clearly was not pleased with the way the Japanese government stacked the deck against American business there. Thus, when faced with the task of flying 11,000 miles to a country that was not a major contributor to the bank's earnings, Wriston figured, "maybe I should go to some [other] country where we've got a better shot." But he continued to encourage his staff in Japan to "tangle" with the authorities to get a larger share of the market, according to Wheeler, who was transferred to Japan from the Philippines in 1965. Wheeler felt that Wriston was acutely aware of how the Japanese government was "rigging the game." But back then Japan was only a small cloud on Citibank's horizon.

In Japan, as in the rest of Asia, a clash of cultures occurred not just between the Eastern and Western style of doing business, but between Citibank's overseas veterans and the brash new recruits. While this conflict had been apparent to one degree or another in every country since 1957, when George Moore and Wriston began their drive to hire Ivy League M.B.A.'s, it reached a crescendo in Japan in 1966. That year Japan received a larger than usual complement of top business school trainees who, among other things, chafed at being assigned to housing that was discernibly inferior to that of the country's more senior officers. But the last straw, Citibanker Rick Roesch recalled, came when the wife of a senior officer, on a visit to the home of a junior officer, took a liking to a chest of drawers and some other pieces of furniture and requisitioned them for her own home. At that point the trainees threatened to quit, prompting Wriston and Moore to make an unscheduled trip to Japan to calm the waters—and make some changes in the management.

At the end of one joint visit to Japan by Wriston and Moore, someone suggested to Moore that he take in the *ofuro*—the baths. Moore turned to his protégé. "Wriston, we're going to the baths," he said. "Wriston looked pale" as he was escorted to the baths, said former banker Ham Meserve later. When the masseuses appeared, Wriston became "absolutely paranoid" about being placed in a compromising situation. Meanwhile, Moore was chattering excitedly, saying "Show me, show me, show me." To Citibank officers, it appeared that Moore and Wriston were forever engaged in a game of baiting each other. Moore, as always, seemed to relish tweaking Wriston for his prudishness.

If Wriston had seemed neglectful of Asia before his 1964 trip, he certainly focused on it when he returned. In a 1964 speech to the National Association of Manufacturers, he pointed up the lack of understanding in the West of Asian cultures: "Our lives have been shaped by the ideas of Western culture," he said. "Our educational curriculum is designed to teach us about the Battle of Waterloo, but usually omits even the result of the Battle of the Talas River. The wisdom of Aristotle we are taught to take seriously, but the sayings of Confucius we make into jokes."

He encouraged the industrialists not to fear the markets of the Far East but to learn to understand the territory. In Italy and Great Britain, he pointed out, 40 percent and 20 percent of the gross national product, respectively, came from government-owned industries, whereas in Hong Kong, Japan, Thailand, and Pakistan private interests predominated. Of those four countries, Thailand was the only one where Citibank didn't have an affiliate or a branch by the mid-1960s. It was a bastion of free enterprise, and Citibank desperately wanted in. On a trip to Asia as Wriston's emissary, Richard Perkins stopped in Bangkok to meet with General Praphas Charusathien, then deputy premier and head of the secret police. Perkins and Praphas immediately hit it off, and the general hosted a dinner for the visiting banker. Perkins and his wife sat on either side of the general at the dinner, where they were entertained by some of the nation's most beautiful dancers. After toasting President Johnson, the general turned to Perkins and asked, "Do you like the dancing girls?"

"Yeah," Perkins replied.

"Which one do you like best?"

Perkins could sense trouble coming. "The one in white," he replied nervously.

"Fine. I'll make arrangements for you to be with her after dinner."

Perkins broke into a cold sweat. "My wife's right here," he whispered anxiously to the general.

"That's no problem. I'll send her back home with a military escort," the general said. Perkins managed to wriggle out of the predicament—and the general was ultimately deposed. But the trip was for naught: Citibank turned down the local banks' demands for payoffs and didn't gain a foothold in Thailand until several years later.

In early 1965 the bank celebrated a major coup when it landed its first branch in Taiwan, and the first for a U.S. commercial bank. Taiwan, said Rick Wheeler, wanted foreign banks to come in as finance companies and investment banks but not necessarily as deposit-taking branches. In Taiwan, and elsewhere, the quid pro quo for being allowed in was that the bank would train its local bankers and monetary officials in American techniques. By doing so, however, First National City virtually created its own competition. In some places, including Taiwan, that helped drive profit margins to such narrow levels that Citibank had to begin looking elsewhere for business opportunities.

If there was ever an example of an acquisition made solely to gain territory, the Banque Internationale pour L'Afrique Occidentale was it. In April 1965, Citibank's International Banking Corporation bought a 40 percent interest in the sleepy French-owned bank, which served as a kind of central bank for many countries in colonial west Africa. On the face of it, Citibank got thirty-nine offices in fifteen countries, including three in France. But it also inherited some more of the oddballs it had long been trying to get rid of. Said Citibanker Cedric Grant, "The loans were dicey. The Frenchmen took two- to three-month vacations. They had white tellers because they didn't trust blacks." Even where the bank did practically no business, the local managers lived in huge apartments. "It was like the French Foreign Legion," said Grant.

Later, Citibank realized that the Banque Internationale was a lost cause and unloaded its interest. Indeed, Africa would always be a trouble spot for Wriston and his successors. In the mid-1960s when the civil rights movement in the United States was in full flower, protest groups began to take note of the activities of Citibank and Chase in South Africa, and for the next twenty-five years, anti-apartheid protesters were unwelcome guests at Citibank's annual meetings.

By 1965, Wriston's overseas division could boast of 177 offices in 58 countries. In the nearly ten years since Wriston had joined the division, it had evolved from a banking backwater to one of the most desirable destinations for bankers on the fast track. "People who had never dreamed of working abroad [now] felt that more opportunities were there," said former Citibanker John Rudy. Though Citibank still ranked behind Chase and Bank of America in size, it was achieving widespread acclaim as the toughest and smartest bank in New York, if not the country. It began the year with a two-for-one stock split and ended by posting record net operating earnings of nearly $94 million. In a glowing profile in its September 1965 issue, *Fortune* called Citibank "the bank with the boardinghouse reach."

By now Wriston's views on global finance were being solicited at the highest levels. To be sure, he had some strong opinions on the program of economic controls instigated by Kennedy and perpetuated by Johnson. The tax on foreign securities purchases had caused foreigners to increase their reliance on bank loans. So Johnson imposed still more controls. In February 1965 he called on U.S. banks and financial institutions to voluntarily restrict their foreign loans, slapped a tax on foreign bank loans over one year, and asked U.S. corporations to restrain their direct investment overseas. Wriston was not happy about the balance-of-payments deficit, but he knew that this was not the cure for it. In the short term it appeared to reduce the deficit, but the long-term effect was to increase foreign borrowing in the Euromarket.

In testimony before a U.S. Senate subcommittee probing the connection between the balance-of-payments deficit and national security, Wriston reminded the senators that "before attacking the root cause, nations sometimes go down the dark road of exchange control despite the fact that exchange control has a perfect record of failure in curing balance-of-payments deficits anywhere in the world." Controls, he said, "breed more controls because it is impossible to write down the permutations and combinations of a free economy."

The failed British experience with controls was an object lesson for the United States, he said. He told of a luncheon he'd had with a friend from Beirut and an official of the Bank of England, in which the Lebanese asked the British central banker how many people were administering the controls. The man from the Bank of England said there were forty. "Well," said the man from Beirut, "there are two million Lebanese thinking up ways around them."

Wriston was troubled over the dollar's deterioration against other currencies, and warned the senators that allowing the dollar to erode through "extraordinarily large doses of credit expansion" could exacerbate the balance-of-payments deficit. "A bad currency," he said, "which is often the mirror image of a balance-of-payments deficit, is capable over a period of time of reducing a great power to a nation without influence in the world." Wriston's prescription was a "moderate taking in of sail" by the Fed in its monetary policy. He would prove to be a prophet, but one who didn't always act on his own prophecies.

But despite the gushing copy about Wriston and Citibank in the financial press, the bank had some severe managerial shortcomings. Wriston and Moore had a plan for growth and expansion, but they had no strategy for managing, planning, and controlling. Even in Wriston's overseas division, managers of new branches still operated largely by gut instinct. Though earnings reached a record, operating expenses were rising at a much more rapid clip than operating income. Interest costs were skyrocketing, thanks to higher interest rates as well as to Wriston's negotiable CD. About one-third of the bank's interest-bearing deposits were now made up of these jumbo certificates. Pressure was mounting to take an ax to spiraling costs.

Citibank's first attempt to bring "modern" management techniques to bear on this problem was an unmitigated disaster that brought the bank as close as it would ever come to union rule. In the 1960s time and motion studies and efficiency experts were in vogue. Recognizing correctly that the bank was seriously overstaffed, George Moore fell for the pitch of a leading consulting firm. Promising to slash operating expenses by 30 percent, the Alexander Proudfoot Company marched into 399 Park Avenue like the gestapo. The bank's senior executives were nervous about bringing in consultants from the outside. "We knew what the problem was," said a former top officer, but "we didn't know how to tackle it."

Standing over secretaries with stopwatches, the consultants dictated how many letters they should be churning out each day. "They move into every department and shoot every fifth guy," Wriston recalled. Instead of working through a bank supervisor, the stopwatch brigade summarily dismissed clerks and other low-level personnel, telling them, "Don't come back. We'll clean out your desks for you." As Wriston recalls, "George would have charts and Magic Markers and say, 'Isn't it wonderful that we got all of this?' "

At first the clerical staff felt that Wriston couldn't possibly have been responsible for hiring Proudfoot. According to one former officer, "The clerks said, if only Mr. Wriston knew about this, it would be done right." Word of the turmoil in the back offices of Citibank quickly reached union organizers, and before long they were handing out union cards to Citibank staff. Faced with a revolt provoked by one consultant, Citibank reacted by hiring yet *another* consultant to advise it on how to keep the union out. As Wriston recalled, this consultant showed up for a midnight appointment at Wriston's apartment accompanied by "a pneumatic blond with a greyhound on a leash." Wriston and his colleagues cringed when he pulled out his bag of tricks. "Look," this consultant said to Wriston, "you must be a pretty smart guy or you wouldn't have the job you've got, but I live in the gutter and that is where the fight is. . . . What you want is a picture of the [union] organizer being led away in handcuffs." That picture, Wriston recalled, was obtained and distributed to all staff.

The very thought of unionization turned Citibank's top managers and board members ashen. Speaking from his own bitter experience, one captain of industry declared to his fellow directors that "you cannot exert too much energy or pay too high a price to keep the unions out." Personnel chief Robert Feagles was put in charge of doing just that. A war room was set up for public relations men and labor lawyers. Meanwhile the unions distributed handbills as employees entered and left the building. And, in a subplot, the battle pitted a reasonably legitimate union against a notorious labor agitator. At one point Feagles learned through a friend, labor writer Victor Reisel, that the union was trying to enlist the help of AFL-CIO chief George Meany in bringing Citibank down by yanking union deposits.

Despite the protests, Moore declined to fire the Proudfoot consultants, hiding them instead in a back room. But two days after Moore left on a trip to Latin America, demonstrations heated up again. Organizers demanded to know if Proudfoot had really left. The answer, of course, was no. Wriston, Tom Wilcox, and oil and gas chief William Spencer didn't always agree on where the bank was going or how it should get there, but on the issue of Proudfoot there was a clear consensus. The consultants were tearing apart the fabric of the bank. They had to go. And so, in a rare display of unity, Wriston, Wilcox, and Spencer marched into Stillman Rockefeller's office and urged him to bring the nightmare to an end. Separately, Feagles also told Rockefeller that he didn't think the unions could be contained with Proudfoot around.

Stillman, his thumbs hooked around his red suspenders, ordered Feagles to arrange a meeting with the consultants for the next morning. The firm's top managers flew in and tried to dazzle Rockefeller with a presentation crammed with charts and graphs, but Rockefeller sat poker-faced throughout it. For all his faults, no one ever accused Stillman Rockefeller of indecisiveness. After listening impassively to the presentation, he spoke: "A great doctor, but the patient died. We'll have to ask you to leave." When the consultants started to protest, Stillman Rockefeller rose silently, turned on his heel, and strode out of the room. Citibank was spared union rule.

Moore later claimed that Rockefeller panicked. "It was ridiculous. We didn't have any threat," he told Wriston.

"The day Stillman panics," Wriston replied, "I don't want to be on this earth."

Later, Feagles asked Rockefeller if he should notify Moore of the decision to get rid of Proudfoot. Rockefeller growled, "He went away. Let him find out when he gets back," Feagles later recalled. According to Moore, Rockefeller did notify him in South America. In the opinion of former officers, the Proudfoot episode reinforced Rockefeller's growing disenchantment with Moore.

Even as Citibank was ridding itself of Proudfoot, trouble was brewing elsewhere in the empire, this time over foreign exchange trading. By the mid-1960s, Citibank was trading in fifty currencies and executing upward of five hundred transactions a day worth about $50 million. Forex trading was Citibank's passport to new countries and eventually a mainstay of Citibank's profits. Traders were under the gun to support the bottom line while the branch tried to develop other business.

The downside of forex trading first reared its costly head in Milan. In 1963, Citibank appointed Carlo Bordoni manager of the Milan operation. Regarded as a genius in this arcane business, Bordoni reputedly could juggle five currencies in his head simultaneously and, according to Wriston, had an IQ that was off the chart. Thanks to forex, the Milan branch, which Wriston had opened in 1962, was in the black from the start. But Citibank later discovered that Bordoni, by overtrading and falsifying the rates of exchange on the monthly profit-and-loss statement, had quickly begun to report profits on the order of $1 million when in fact they were losses.

In December 1964, on a jetliner bound for Paris, Wriston was catching up on his reading, which included a treatise on foreign exchange trading written by Bordoni. In it, Bordoni offered a piece of advice that jolted Wriston: "Never tell your branch manager what you're doing." That was all Wriston needed to know about his crackerjack forex trader. Soon after landing at Orly Airport, Wriston phoned Paris branch manager Paul Austin and ordered him to fire Bordoni. Austin was incredulous and asked why his boss wanted to sack the brilliant trader who was making piles of money for the bank, including $1 million in a recent reporting period alone. "He said he made a million for us," Wriston told his man in Paris, "but when someone won't tell his branch manager what he's doing, we're in trouble." According to Wriston, the Milan branch took the books apart and found that the $1 million in profits was fictitious. "The bank had to write it off."

Although Bordoni had traded beyond his authority, he apparently did not gain personally from his dealings. Later, after running his own trading firm for a while, he hooked up with Italian financier Michele Sindona. But this was not to be the last Wriston would hear of Bordoni, Sindona, and trouble in the world of foreign exchange trading.

For First National City Bank, Milan and Bordoni were merely a warm-up for Brussels, which would be the first major obstacle—at least in the eyes of his colleagues—in Wriston's race to the top. In Belgium another foreign exchange trader was playing roulette with pounds sterling, a currency in which Citibank traded heavily. In late 1964, owing to a dramatically widening balance-of-payments deficit, Britain was on the verge of a currency crisis that threatened to provoke a devaluation of the pound. By this time, European traders knew something was out of whack in Brussels because of the inordinate amount of trading being done there.

Just as a good bridge player has a gut feel for his opponents' cards, a savvy forex trader acquires a strong hunch about the positions of fellow traders. That was why one of the currency traders in the bank's newly opened Geneva branch told his boss sometime in 1965 that the Brussels branch, which then enjoyed a reputation as the bank's best-managed European operation, must have a loss position. Foreign exchange trading was a mystery to most branch managers, who were generally incapable of determining the gaps in their traders' positions, but the Swiss manager dutifully reported his trader's concern to his Brussels counterpart, who reported that there was no problem. Some time later a team of Citibank auditors descended on the branch in *Switzerland* and dissected the entire operation. When asked by the manager when they planned to visit Brussels, they said they weren't going there because that branch was so well managed.

In the Citibank overseas division of the early 1960s, a good manager was not necessarily one who made a lot of money for the bank. The Brussels branch manager had a reputation as a gracious host, had been decorated by the Belgian government for services to the country, wrote good memos, and was a "real gentleman," said one of his colleagues. Moreover, unlike some branch managers, he did not cause trouble for the top brass in New York.

Wriston's first indication of trouble in Brussels came from a close friend named Paul Jeanty, a partner in the British firm of Samuel Montague & Company, then one of the world's largest gold dealers. Like the trader in Geneva, Jeanty was concerned about Citibank's forex operation. He told Wriston that his firm, Montague, had a $100 million contract coming due the following week with the Belgian branch. "I almost dropped my teeth," Wriston said, "because that was ten times the contract a branch that size could possibly have."

That evening, the officers of Citibank's overseas unit gathered for a meeting at the Westchester Country Club. But the last thing on Wriston's mind was schmoozing with colleagues. Uppermost on his mind was to get a reading on the Brussels situation from Edwin Reichers, who had begun his Citibank career as a page in 1923 and eventually earned a reputation as the world's best forex trader. At any instant he could quote the buy-and-sell rates on any of fifty currencies and juggle several transactions. Wriston grabbed him on the terrace of the country club and told him about his conversation with Jeanty. Reichers, in turn, informed Wriston of a call he had received that afternoon from his London trader, reporting that Brussels seemed to need more and more balances to meet its payments and that the trader there seemed to be avoiding him. Reichers said he had also received a call from a trader at First National Bank of Boston [now Bank of Boston], who told him about $250 million in foreign exchange contracts that Citibank Brussels had established with Bank of Boston's London branch. Though Reichers was unaware of any relationship between the two banks, he tried hard to hide his anxiety.

After comparing notes with Reichers, Wriston told him, "Get your tail to Brussels." Reichers caught the first Pan Am flight to London the next morning, and the morning after that was in the Brussels branch. The inspectors had just visited the branch and found nothing alarming. Reichers reviewed the contracts and phoned his boss at one o'clock the next morning to report that there were a lot of large positions, but they were properly offset. "We don't have a financial problem," Reichers told him.

"Thank God," Wriston replied, adding that this would not be a good time for unpleasant surprises. Citibank was then in the throes of completing through First Boston [the New York investment banking firm] the first offering of subordinated debt ever issued by a bank. While Citibank was working on its convertible debenture deal, Chase was also rushing to issue its own offering, using First Boston as its lead underwriter. The thought of sharing underwriters with Chase was anathema to Stillman Rockefeller. "Citibank only or out!" he reportedly fumed.

On a Friday evening, as Reichers was preparing to leave Brussels for Amsterdam, he stopped to say good-bye to the Belgian trader, and during the conversation asked him about a certain transaction. The trader's answer didn't make any sense. Instantly Reichers abandoned his plans to leave and instead proceeded to take the trader's position apart and value it himself. The next morning, with the trader out of the loop, Reichers and a clutch of branch personnel closed out the branch's positions as if they were getting out of the business altogether. At day's end everyone compared notes. Reichers was stunned by the results. They had all come within $20,000 of each other—on a loss of $8 million. He dreaded having to phone Wriston with the news.

The timing couldn't have been worse. Citibank was then trying to sell the debt issue, and Stillman Rockefeller was less than two years away from naming his successor. "It was a great load on my mind," Wriston acknowledged later. It was particularly scary, he said, to learn that there was someone in the world who could fool Reichers.

When the bad news reached New York, George Moore exclaimed hysterically, "Close all the branches in Europe! Close 'em all. Terrible, terrible, terrible. Close 'em all. Fire everybody, fire everybody, fire everybody. Close 'em all. Close 'em all. Close 'em all!" In his rage, Moore beat up on his protégé. "If you can't run the overseas division, we'll get someone who can!"

"We couldn't get him to be quiet long enough to explain what the problem was," Wriston said. "He doesn't know to this day what it was."

"The Brussels incident was tough on Walt," Costanzo recalled. "When the chips are down you can't have a better friend than George, but when something like that happened, George was all over the lot. He made life pretty miserable for Walt."

But Wriston would later play down his concern about the possible impact of the Brussels episode on his career: "I never really thought about my career—almost never. I was a day-to-day fellow who got a lot of lucky breaks along the way."

The control systems that were in place at the time had been designed for the forex trading world of the past. There were limits and controls on long positions and short positions, but not on the gaps between them that would have revealed what the trader was doing. In effect, since the fall of 1964, the trader had been betting the Belgian branch on his belief that the Bank of England would lower its discount rate to relieve the pressure that had been building on the pound through 1965, that sterling would rise in value against other currencies, and that he would be a hero.

The Brussels trader had been buying long, for delivery six months down the road, while selling sterling short for one month away. Because he had bought 10 million pounds long and sold 10 million short, his positions were always square and therefore raised no eyebrows. Spot and forward positions were matched, as were obligations to buy and to sell in the forward market. But as he continued to double up on his long position, he kept rolling up short-term losses by continuing to borrow Eurodollars to fund his spot market contracts as they came due—all of this in the hope that sterling would eventually rally. It was learned that Brussels branch manager Arthur Worthington had ordered the trader to cut his positions, but the forex trader had ignored his instructions. Ultimately the gap between his long and short positions grew to just over 500 million pounds. That meant that the branch needed to swap 50 million pounds every day just to meet its contractual obligations. Reichers later said, "The problem was that he was short near and long far," adding, "He was so desperate in his need for sterling that he'd pay almost any price to get it."

When Citibank went public with the loss in mid-June 1965, it did so in an almost offhand manner, prompting calls for more financial disclosure by banks. Shocked by the news, bankers scratched their heads at how so much money could be lost in one office, or in one currency. Initially, Wriston disclosed only that the loss had been incurred by an overseas office that had engaged in "foreign exchange transactions in excess of authorized limits."

Although the trader apparently did not profit personally from his activities, he did conceal them. And for that he was fired and his professional career was nearly destroyed. Branch manager Arthur Worthington was demoted and his salary cut. "Walt didn't fire [many] guys who got into trouble" or "the guys who got him in trouble," John Reed recalls. As a result of the incident, Citibank was forced to issue a second prospectus on its debt issue fessing up to the problems in Brussels. After he was dismissed, the trader told colleagues that if he had just been left alone for a few more days he would have recovered the loss, and he wasn't far off. If Citibank had held on to its position for another few months, it would have actually made money in Brussels.

But the significance of Brussels went far beyond the $8 million loss. Bankers, especially Americans, had been naive in their understanding of foreign exchange, in part because for so long they had operated in a relatively stable economic climate. Brussels signaled that what had been a relatively simple business—one that was primarily concerned with buying and selling foreign exchange for corporate customers—had evolved into a complex and treacherous enterprise. Indeed, banking itself had entered a new and riskier era. It was the wake-up call to the perils of international trading and expansion.

In the wake of the debacle, the bank's gossip mill was working overtime, speculating that the Brussels incident would derail Wriston's career. Since he had figured out what happened, Wriston was expected to explain the incident to a jittery board of directors not accustomed to that kind of bad news. He had to find a way to package the story for executives accustomed to nuts and bolts, not spots and forwards.

What may have saved Wriston was a presentation on the incident to the board put together by the garrulous, backslapping Argentina hand named James Farley. Farley, who had joined Citibank in 1950, was a master corporate politician with common sense and an uncanny ability to think on his feet. In trying to figure out exactly what had happened and how to explain it, Wriston and Farley had worked forty hours without sleep. Farley stole the show by comparing the episode to a flock of birds perched on telephone wires. In an animated show-and-tell session, he compared a long position to a bird that popped up and a short position to one that fell down.

After the dust settled, Wriston took Farley's birds on a European road show to explain the problem to Citibank personnel there. He then assembled a task force of traders and accountants to set up a system of controls to guard against a repetition of the incident. While in London, Wriston was summoned to the Bank of England by its governor to explain what happened. "What do you mean, sir, by being this short of sterling?" the governor demanded. "It's an attack on the honor of England."

"Sir," Wriston replied, "there is only one person in the world who could buy my long position today, and I am sitting in his office."

"But I understand that you're short sterling."

"That's good," Wriston replied. "When I leave your office and go to a pub, I'll continue to create that impression. If the world ever knew how long we were, we could never get out [of Citibank's position]."

In the wake of this and other scattered foreign exchange losses around the globe, some Citibankers urged that decision-making on foreign exchange positions be centralized in New York. In a momentous decision that perhaps more than any other enabled Citibank to avoid future foreign exchange disasters, Wriston responded with an emphatic no. He did not want one, or even a few, top traders making a global institutional bet on foreign exchange rates. By allowing hundreds of traders around the world to make their own mistakes independently, he knew that at any given time some would be right and others would be wrong—but no one would have the power to bet, and possibly lose, the entire institution.

The Brussels incident had made Wriston extremely uneasy about foreign exchange trading, former colleagues said, but Wriston saw it as the cheapest insurance premium that Citibank ever paid. As a result of the controls developed by the bank task force, Citibank was spared the more costly foreign exchange debacles later suffered by several of its competitors, even as its daily foreign exchange trading activity surged from $50 million to $50 billion in the twenty-five years that followed the incident.

Besides giving rise to tighter controls, the Brussels affair reinforced the bond between Walter Wriston and James Farley. By helping Wriston through the most troublesome episode of his career, he guaranteed his own future at Citibank. Farley was a graduate of Georgetown University's School of Foreign Service, where he had roomed briefly with the son of James Aloysius Farley, FDR's postmaster general, and he shared Wriston's fascination with foreign affairs, but Wriston did not value him for his shining intellect. Though not a close relative of the postmaster general, Farley was a close friend. "He used to send people to the bank—bricklayers, plumbers—looking for jobs, saying 'go see my relative Jim Farley,' " Farley the banker said later. Indeed, the contrast between Farley, a product of the old school of international banking, and the new breed of whiz kids arriving from Harvard, Johns Hopkins, and other top schools could not have been sharper. Farley was unable to carry on a conversation without using a generous supply of four-letter words and telling one raunchy story after another. Over the next two decades, Farley would be one of a handful of close associates to whom Wriston would turn for help in solving delicate problems. Perhaps most important, Wriston could let his hair down with Farley. "He was one of the few who would tell him what he didn't want to hear," said James Griffin, who later became personnel chief.

For his exploits as a young bachelor in Argentina, Farley had become something of a legend in the Citibank overseas network and in Buenos Aires business and social circles. On one occasion, he and Latin hand Victor Prall were disparaging a local businessman and his foulmouthed wife while being chauffeured to a cocktail party in Buenos Aires. When they arrived, the driver said he knew the businessman and intended to tell him about their comments. Farley handed the driver a calling card belonging to the local manager of the Bank of Boston. "Can I give you my card?" he asked.

Another Citibanker who filled a role similar to that of Farley was Carl Desch, a German-speaking veteran of the branch system. Like Wriston, Desch had been saved from obscurity by personnel chief Buzz Cuyler and later went on to write the branch system operating manual. With Wriston's election as president and the subsequent decentralization of Citibank, Farley and Desch would become his informal management information system, his eyes and ears. "He [Desch] and Jimmy knew what was going on because people trusted them," said Wriston later. For instance, people told them there was a supervisor who was anti-black, and suddenly the problem would get taken care of without any memos, said Wriston. Referring to Desch, Wriston said that "he'd just love to come in and say, 'There's no way you can do that.' And I always listened to him because he was right," adding, "You need somebody around who keeps coming in and telling you you're out of your mind."

If there were those on the Citibank board who believed that Brussels would derail Wriston, they did not include William "Mil" Batten, chairman of J. C. Penney and a director since 1962. Having observed Wriston in board meetings, Batten was convinced he would be running the bank when Rockefeller retired, and he wanted to recruit Wriston as a director of Penney before he became the obvious choice of still more big companies. In 1965, Batten approached Stillman Rockefeller and George Moore, but they dismissed his request with the explanation that Wriston was too busy. "I'm not coming to you with my hat in hand," Batten persisted, stressing that Wriston's membership on the Penney board would be as useful to the bank as it would be to the retailer. "You think you're in the banking business. You're in the financial services business. We're all in the merchandising business," Batten told Rockefeller and Moore. A week later Moore and Rockefeller relented, and in May 1965 Wriston succeeded former chairman Howard Sheperd as a J. C. Penney director.

In Wriston, Batten would find a staunch ally as he sought to move Penney from a company that peddled bib overalls for cash to blue-collar workers to a fashion-conscious retailer that sold sport coats on credit. Like Citibank, the J. C. Penney of the 1950s had operated on a commonsense philosophy: "If it ain't broke, don't fix it." But Batten, like Wriston, believed that speed and convenience would soon be top priorities for the American consumer. At the time, though, "If people wanted soft goods in small and medium markets and would pay cash J. C. Penney was competitive," said Batten. "Otherwise we would have to send them to competitors."

Batten was convinced that catalog sales were essential for Penney's competitiveness in the new age. He viewed the catalog as a way of turning a small store into a bigger one. But the Penney board was not prepared for the years of losses the catalog effort would inflict on the company. Store managers saw the catalog as a competitor, and supporters of the initiative among Penney top management could be counted on one hand. Of all the board members, Wriston was his most vociferous backer. Without that support, says Batten, the effort might have been abandoned. "If we'd cut and run, it would have been one of the most serious mistakes we could have made," said Batten later. "J. C. Penney would be devastated today if it wasn't for the catalog business." Curiously, Wriston would find himself in Batten's shoes just a few years later when he sought to convince skeptics that Citi would eventually be rewarded for persistence after years of losses in the consumer banking business.

If Wriston was worried about the fallout from Brussels, it did not stop him from going through with his plans to plunk down $64,000 for a seven-room apartment at fashionable 870 United Nations Plaza, adjoining the UN and overlooking the East River. When the Wristons prepared to move in 1965, they found that their new home included a maid's room. While they employed a cook who helped out several nights a week with the entertaining, they shared an obsession with privacy that ruled out a live-in housekeeper. On discovering the maid's room, "we laughed and said, 'What are we going to do with that?' " Cassy Wriston recalled. Wriston would call 870 UN Plaza home for the rest of his life. Sadly, Bobby Wriston would get to enjoy it for less than a year.

7

THE ROCKET SCIENTISTS

*I*t was the age of Robert McNamara and his Defense Department whiz kids, of think tanks, management information systems, and long-term planning. Although George Moore shot from the hip and managed by the seat of the pants, he intuitively knew that Citibank needed more of this new science of management and less improvisation. Citibank, as *Fortune* concluded, may have been the leader in the art of banking, but in the art of management it was still operating in the Middle Ages. It had never focused on how and where it made its money and which customers were profitable. At the end of each year, Citibank learned that it took in more interest on loans than it paid for deposits and lost on bad loans, but much of what happened in between remained a mystery. In the 1960s, a bank's status was still measured in deposits and assets rather than in earnings, and Citibank was not alone in lacking profit objectives and rigorous cost analyses. Even though big mainframe computers had made their banking debut, Citibank's bookkeeping systems were still mostly manual. And the computers the bank did own were spewing forth lots of data, but little useful information.

"There was total chaos," Wriston admitted later. "It was unbelievable." Wriston summed up the state of affairs when he said, "We were a historical society. Every Christmas we'd get together and say, 'That was a good year,' or 'That was a bad year.' We were professionals with other people's money, amateurs with our own."

The company that Citibank, and much of the rest of corporate America, looked to as a managerial role model was General Electric. GE was clearly the company that Wriston admired the most. He felt a special bond with a long succession of GE chairmen, and to a large degree his later style and management practices mimicked those at General Electric. "GE," said former corporate secretary Carl Desch, "was always the precursor of what we did."

Every business organization needs a budgeting system before it can even think about long-term planning. The dawn of modern management at Citibank began in 1962 with the arrival from GE of Robert V. Owen, who was mandated to force Citibank's budgeting procedures out of the financial stone age. To his credit, Moore was responsible for this initiative, according to Charles Kelly, a wiry, pug-nosed former marine who was Owen's effective successor. "I can't make all the decisions of the banking business in my office anymore," Kelly recalled Moore admitting. Kelly, who claimed credit for preparing the first consolidated budget for Citibank with a pencil and a spreadsheet, said the early budgets were actually revenue-expense forecasts of limited usefulness. Each department, he explained, prepared an expense budget; the economics department made an income forecast; and the expense budget was consolidated and matched off against the economics department's projections.

As for long-term planning, Stillman Rockefeller regarded that as a useless activity, according to former Citibankers. Even Wriston, a believer in the power of serendipity, recognized the limitations of long-term planning and referred to it as "incipient fascism." Moore's first baby steps into long-term planning were awkward at best. To spearhead the effort, he hired Sherman Adams, a pontificating academic theoretician, who infuriated Wriston with his memos informing Moore that he planned to work at home on a particular day. Early on, much of what passed for planning consisted of Moore and Adams feeding Comptroller of the Currency James Saxon ideas on how to liberalize the banking system.

There were a number of forces pressing Citibank to take charge of its future. First and foremost was the fact that earnings in recent years were growing at a paltry average annual rate of less than 7 percent. In those days the "big thrill," said Charles Kelly, was to finish at the top of the bank asset rankings compiled by the *American Banker,* the trade daily. "You could be careless and sloppy and [still] make money," he said, though obviously not enough money to satisfy Wriston and Moore. "Walt and George saw what was happening to the industry and said, 'We've got to get ahead of it.' "

The bank's first serious efforts at planning began when a small planning and merger and acquisition unit was started within Wriston's overseas division that developed a budget and a plan for the division. The unit later enlarged its mission to include the entire bank.

Jack Heilshorn, the planning unit's head, latched on to the idea of establishing an earnings objective for the bank, something that was unheard of in the 1960s. The move away from the obsession with size occurred when Heilshorn asked a colleague in the money management division what level of earnings growth the bank would need to attract enough capital to enable it to expand. To become a darling of Wall Street, the money manager said, Citibank's stock price to earnings ratio should be 20. That, in turn, implied annual earnings growth of 15 percent, about twice the current rate. But Sherman Adams said: "No way."

Indeed, Citibank discovered that in some cases profitability could be boosted significantly simply by overcoming internal resistance to old ways of doing things. For example, Moore chastised trust department chief Robert Hoguet for not meeting the earnings target. Hoguet didn't think it could be done. Moore suggested raising fees, and Hoguet replied that that wasn't possible because they were largely set by New York State law; the fees hadn't been raised in years. Citibank then petitioned and received an increase from the state legislature, and lost just one account out of three hundred while reaching the 15 percent target, according to Moore.

Wriston later said, "If your company is growing at five to six percent a year, and you're number three in the country, you have to create something very simple that everybody can get their mind around . . . very clear goals that were easily understood and that everybody could sign on to." For the moment, however, he put off a decision on establishing the target, according to former colleagues. To make that possible, Citibank would have to have a better idea of how and where it made its money and it would also have to expand its notion of what business it was in and where it was going. Both of those efforts got a shot in the arm with the arrival of a cocky young engineer named John Shepard Reed and a rocket scientist named Thomas O. Paine.

Everyone in the American academic community knew that Wriston and Moore wanted the first crack at the best graduates of the nation's best colleges and business schools. Heilshorn recalls pursuing three top Harvard M.B.A. candidates. None of them had contemplated working for a bank, but Heilshorn felt that an audience with Wriston would change their minds. "They'd be flying at 20,000 feet when they walked in," said Heilshorn, and "at 100,000 feet when they walked out." Nonetheless, they felt they should interview with some other banks, including Chase. But what they got at Chase was a lunch appointment with the personnel director, who at the last minute sent word through his secretary that something more important had come up and foisted the three M.B.A. candidates off on some other trainees. As a result, all three chose Citibank. At Citibank, said Heilshorn, "the head of personnel would never say, 'I have a more important lunch.' He wouldn't have lasted."

One recruit who would dramatically shape the future of Citibank and American banking came to Wriston's attention in a phone call from a professor in Boston. The caller told Wriston that a remarkable guy named John Reed was running a consulting service out of the Massachusetts Institute of Technology and that if Wriston had any brains, he'd hire him. Slim and boyish with close-cropped hair, Reed had attended Pennsylvania's Washington and Jefferson College and MIT on a 3-2 program where he spent three years at the former and two at the latter, winding up with a bachelor's degree in American literature and metallurgy and a master's degree in management. After a hitch with the Army Corps of Engineers in Korea, Reed had worked briefly for Goodyear Tire and Rubber. There was some initial resistance to Reed because of his unconventional education. However, he had grown up in Argentina, where his father was a plant manager for Armour & Company, an old and valued Citibank customer. "Reed's entrance was easier because the

South American people knew his father," Al Costanzo said later, adding that Reed was hired with the idea of sending him back to Argentina. One Citibanker who knew him well was James Farley, Wriston's aide-de-camp, then in charge of planning and coordination for the overseas division. As a youth, Reed had even caddied for Farley, who had issued him his first set of traveler's checks and escorted him on a tour of Citibank's main branch in Buenos Aires.

Wriston phoned Reed, invited him to New York, and "gave him my pitch," and Reed promised to think about the invitation. But in the meantime, the Brahmin First National Bank of Boston, where Reed had worked weekends on management information projects while at MIT, offered him the job of assistant to the chairman. Wriston said, "John being John, just as square as a box, he said he'd had this wonderful offer," but Wriston told Reed, "Come to see me anyway."

In their next meeting, Wriston said, "I sold as hard as I could." In rapid-fire succession, he mixed every metaphor in the book to try to entice Reed to New York. "Would you rather be the first man in an Iberian village or the second man in Rome?" Wriston asked. "It would be great to be with the First of Boston, but you ought to play with the Yankees."

Reed decided to sign with the Yankees, but he had his own agenda, one that did not include any desire to be a banker, at least not in the traditional sense. So Reed wasn't subjected to the indignity of credit training. Years later, after Reed himself followed Wriston into the top job, critics would cite this as perhaps his foremost handicap. In fact, Wriston may have been thinking of Reed when he boasted later to a reporter that Citibank hired people who had little idea of how to make a loan and get it back—a boast that would come back to haunt him.

Reed proved to be as smart as he was cracked up to be. Accordingly, because it was Citibank's practice to place the sharpest of the new recruits in the overseas planning department, Reed went there first. It gave the bank an opportunity to look closely at him, and it gave him a chance to gain a broad view of overseas operations. Among other things, the planning department was charged with evaluating overseas investments for First National City Overseas Investment Corporation (FINOIC), acquisitions and branch locations, and other new business activities, which Wriston would then present to the board for approval. When Reed told his mother that he would report to Farley, however, Mrs. Reed was aghast. Recalling vividly Farley's reputation in Argentine social circles as a bon vivant, she advised her son to reconsider working for Citibank.

On his first day at the bank, Reed walked into Wriston's fifteenth-floor office and asked him what he was supposed to do. Wriston informed Reed that the overseas division had no accounting system "worth a damn," no management information system, and no chart of accounts. Farley recalls that Wriston and Reed "used to spend a lot of time talking about the lack of information to run the bank independent of the accounting system, and not to have to wait for the accountants to add up everything. There was the feeling that that was the number one priority for us. That and the back office and technology."

Citibank was still a novice in automation, computerization, and technology. When Byron Stinson, a computer specialist, arrived at Citibank in the mid-1960s, he found that the bank was still using "stone age" systems and methods. "My God!" he exclaimed. "We're still using calculators cranked by hand."

For bankers in the sixties, the computer was arcane and mysterious. The IBM mainframe computer had given rise to an entirely new cultlike race of mutant humans known as programmers and analysts, who spoke a strange language, carried pens in plastic pocket-protectors, and thrived on the power that their unique knowledge gave them over ordinary mortals. "The banks were having a tough time coping with the computer," said Tom Paine, the rocket scientist and former consultant to Citibank. "The information revolution at the time was full of magic and sorcerers. It was a closed technology, and if you weren't a computer programmer you couldn't hope to fathom it." Paine remembers when computer departments would ask top management yearly for increases of 20 to 40 percent in computer-related expenses, and the bankers had no idea whatsoever whether these requests were reasonable or absurd. Bankers, Paine said, fell victim to almost every snake oil computer salesman who got in the door and waxed enthusiastic about the incredible power computers had to solve every problem. All of them would begin by pointing to a terminal and saying, "Imagine, if you will . . ."

"There were too many presentations about 'Imagine, if you will,' " said Paine, "and not enough where you flipped on the computer and it did it." Then, once the equipment was on-line, the in-house computer people dumped reams of printouts, mostly error-filled gobbledygook, on senior officers' desks, telling them that this is what they needed in order to manage effectively.

The overseas bookkeeping system—it was too primitive to be called an accounting system—presented a special set of problems. Because of exchange restrictions in many of the countries where Citibank operated, only about a third of local earnings were actually remitted to New York. Managers in New York judged a country's profitability almost entirely by the volume of remitted earnings, which indicated nothing about the economics of the business or about what accounts and business activities were profitable. So Wriston assigned Reed to develop a management reporting system for the division.

Though Reed reported to Farley, it was Reed who was "doing all the innovation and thinking," as Costanzo recalled. Farley would take the train home at four to play an early-evening round of golf, but would typically leave his desk in a mess so that colleagues would think he was still around. One of Reed's tasks, as he explained later, was to clean up the desk around the time Farley should have left. The Brussels episode notwithstanding, Farley was not known for putting in long hours. Said a former colleague, "His idea of taking work home with him is to leave the office with *Time* magazine under his arm."

Wriston, of course, knew very well what was going on. On one occasion, he walked by Reed's office and remarked wryly, "You haven't cleaned up Jim's desk yet." But Farley's early departures gave Reed the opportunity to get better acquainted with Wriston, who would select him as Farley's successor.

Though Wriston's working day typically began well before nine o'clock and ended well after five, he made a point of not arriving at the office before nine or leaving later than five. He once told a colleague that he left at five so that the senior vice presidents would leave at five-fifteen and the vice presidents at five-thirty. And Reed, like the hero of *How to Succeed in Business Without Really Trying,* made a habit of dropping by Wriston's office after five with reports and analyses that Farley by all rights should have presented to Wriston.

In Reed's early Citibank career, Farley playfully cut him down to size whenever he made some precocious remark, saying, "Give me my five-iron, kid," a not so subtle reminder that in another time and place Farley had been the boss. Indeed, Farley realized he had a prodigy on his hands when Reed began to spend as much time in Wriston's office as he did, but he denied later that he was bothered by all the attention Reed received. "I felt quite comfortable having him go in and talk about areas I didn't know about," Farley recalled.

While Reed described his family as an average American household— "my parents were very happy with each other," he said—his upbringing was anything but ordinary. Like Wriston's, Reed's roots were in the Midwest and New England, which, Reed came to think, partly explained his early feeling of kinship with his mentor. "I'm plain vanilla," Reed said. "I'm a basic midwestern guy in many ways." His father, Calvin "Big Cal" Reed, and his mother, Virginia, were high school sweethearts in Toledo, Ohio. The Reeds were not a family that identified with New York, Paris, and London.

Trained as an engineer at MIT, "Big Cal" Reed traveled to Argentina to work in the meatpacking plants in 1926, but returned to Chicago in 1935. Four years later Reed was born, and in 1944 the family, including his older brother, "Little Cal," moved to Argentina.

Reed's mother, though "not as bright" as her husband, Reed said later, was "warmer and more textured." In contrast, Cal Reed Sr. was a serious, disciplined, and formal man. "It would not have been hard to call him sir," Reed said , "but I called him Dad." Like Hank Wriston, Big Cal Reed played a most important role in shaping the mind of his son. Big Cal was the quintessential loyal, diligent company man who maintained rigid Calvinistic distinctions between his business life and his family life. As a youngster growing up in Buenos Aires, John and his brother walked to the train station each morning because his father refused to drop them off, even in the worst weather. He felt it was wrong for them to ride in a company car when they didn't work for the company. "He'd drive right by the train station," Reed said, "and we'd walk in the rain."

As in the Wriston household, the evening meal was an occasion for serious conversation, and Big Cal never missed a dinner at home during Reed's entire childhood. Over dinner, Reed's father challenged him with practical cost accounting problems, such as how to figure out how much each piece of a steer would be worth after the steer was butchered. Big Cal, said Reed, was a "big thinker and a big reader," who didn't have much use for childhood frivolities. Try as he might, Reed could never persuade his father to attend his baseball games; Cal told his son bluntly that he'd rather stay home and read a good book. Reed acknowledged that on first glance one might conclude that he had a "horrible father." On the other hand, that "taught me a lot about the relative importance of reading a good book versus playing baseball."

For all the discipline that Reed was subjected to at home, elsewhere he was a mischievous, rambunctious youngster whose behavior was somewhat bizarre and whose grades were mediocre. In the mistaken belief he would be less of a cutup in a private school setting, his family sent him to the exclusive Saint Andrew's School in Buenos Aires, where he was once forced to drop his pants in front of the class for a paddling. But even that did not take the spunk out of young John.

The discipline and values of the Reed household contrasted sharply with the chaos and permissiveness that reigned in Perón's Argentina. That clash of cultures, Reed reflected later, enabled him to figure out earlier than most who he was. "Those of us who have been raised in foreign cultures probably are forced as individuals to deal with the real world earlier in life," he said, because "you have discontinuities in value systems . . . to deal with." Just before Reed began the fifth grade, the family moved to Brazil, where his antics continued. Reed nearly sent one teacher into cardiac arrest by pretending to swallow a fistful of sewing needles. That year he received five F's and a D. "The topic was whether little John would be allowed to go to sixth grade," Reed recalled later. "My parents thought yes, the teacher no." His parents ultimately prevailed.

Though the family lived in South America, they still called Chicago home. On vacations, they would sail into the port of New Orleans and ride the overnight train to Chicago, where John Reed would head for Comiskey Park to watch the White Sox. By the time he was ready to graduate from the equivalent of high school, he had done well enough to qualify for the MIT 3-2 program. He chose to spend the first three years of the program at Washington and Jefferson, an obscure Pennsylvania liberal arts college, because it was not a traditional East Coast school.

After John graduated from college, Calvin Reed seemed acutely aware of his impending mortality, and approached death in the same clinical manner that he approached life. Stricken with cancer, Big Cal charted his vital signs and statistics on a graph and told his son he would die when his weight reached a certain point. In 1962, while Reed was serving with the army in Korea, Big Cal died in Argentina, almost to the day he predicted he would.

In light of Reed's parentage and strict private school upbringing, it is not surprising that his attitude toward Wriston was deferential at first. Though he addressed Wriston as "sir" until Wriston told him to quit, he privately referred to him somewhat jocularly as Walter Bigelow. "It took me a long time to think of Walter as Walt," Reed said. Years later he would describe himself as a "mere piece of genetic material left over from Walter Wriston."

Like his father, Reed—at least initially—maintained a wall between his work and his family. Whenever his wife, Sally, his college sweetheart, met him after work in New York, she was under standing instructions to wait for him across Park Avenue rather than in the lobby of 399 Park. That was, Reed said, because of his notion that "wives don't come to the office."

In Reed's early interaction with Wriston, he was impressed with Wriston's insistence on reading everything he signed word for word. In analyzing transactions, Wriston invariably used a T-account, a simple chart showing debits and credits, to figure out where the money was going. "You couldn't wing something by him," said Reed. "He wasn't going to be embarrassed into thinking he had to pretend to understand something when he didn't." But what struck Reed most about Wriston was his unflinching trust in the smart young crowd he had gathered around him. "He really had a faith that there was a next generation around that would solve all the problems."

Despite Wriston's often steely, intimidating demeanor, Reed observed another, softer side that emerged when one of his associates got into trouble. Like a boxer in a championship match, Wriston could be merciless with colleagues or subordinates as long as he knew they could absorb his jabs without suffering permanent injury. But as soon as anyone started to falter, Wriston would become supportive. "If you ever were in trouble, if you had a sick wife, kids in trouble in school, if you embarrassed yourself, Walt was there," said Reed. During his stint as a trainee, Reed witnessed several fellow officers "seriously botch" major presentations. One officer, while giving a talk to the board, tensed up to the point where he couldn't speak, nearly fainted, and had to be helped from the boardroom. Wriston told the mortified officer that the same thing had happened to him in his own early years at Citibank. "He'd put his arm around you and pick you up off the ground," said Reed.

Later, when Reed embarked on his first assignment, he found that the Citibank officers in Chile, Argentina, and Brazil needed to be held to rigorous management standards that required much more than monthly accounting statements. Each branch filed a form that showed its balances, foreign exchange positions, and profit and loss. The P&L statements were seriously misleading, however, because, among other things, they didn't give the various branches credit for generating interest-free deposits, nor did they charge the branches for things like overdrafts. As a result, nobody knew whether the branch was making or losing money.

Building a system to determine who was making the money demanded a "transfer pricing" mechanism to indicate how units or branches that were net lenders of money should be compensated for their funds. Such systems, in which the cost of capital is charged to business units—or profit centers, as they would soon be labeled—were old hat at leading-edge companies like GE.

Among other innovations, Reed installed a system that called for a branch to pay for money it was borrowing from the Citibank pool, and that allocated the bank's capital against the loans made by branches and other lending units. This move received little or no attention outside Citibank at the time, but it launched a quiet revolution in the way American banks conducted their business from that day forward. It was a watershed in the bank's move away from relying solely on accounting as a means of managing the business, and toward using management information. The MPR, or management profit report, soon became the foundation for managing Citibank. With the beginnings of a management information system, Wriston and his colleagues could set goals and objectives. Reed, said Costanzo, "developed the kind of language where you could compare Chile and Brazil on the same basis, not apples and oranges, and translate results into profitability in terms of return on capital. He made something real out of budgeting." Before Reed designed and implemented the MPR system, profits and losses had never added up, or else they amounted to far more than the bank's bottom line. In contrast, MPR was a "closed" accounting system which ensured that two plus two equaled four. Citibanker George Davis observed that "people began to worry about what their costs were and how much they were making."

Reed's ideas and abrasive manner were not well received by the old guard, however. As the MPR system was put into place throughout the bank, some bankers who had once been regarded as big moneymakers were revealed to be poor bottom-line performers. In one early session on the new system that included Wriston and Reed, "most of the guys around the table began to pee all over it," recalled one former top officer. But Wriston laid down the law: "The new system is here to stay." Reed had little tolerance for mistakes and incompetence, however, and did not go out of his way to build relationships with old line officers, who referred to him among themselves as "that little shit." Wriston was inundated with complaints about Reed and the slide-rule types who worked with him. The bank's comptroller, for example, fumed that Reed was meddling in an area that was "none of his damn business," Costanzo recalled. "They began to make waves from the day they walked in," he said.

Along with the profit center, Reed would also introduce to the company, and to American banking, a heretofore unknown disease called profit centeritis. In 1966 the overseas planning unit prepared a five-year budget forecast and plan that identified areas for expansion, the amount of additional capital required, and the number of people needed to launch the operations. This effort evolved into a corporate planning department that, in 1967, prepared the bank's first one-year, five-year, and ten-year plans. Although this project was taken for granted a decade later, it was a major managerial breakthrough in the mid-1960s. John Reed recalled that when he joined Citibank it "had no language for management, no framework within which to motivate behavior and performance. He [Wriston] laid the groundwork with profit center earnings and budgeting, measuring of performance, to begin to develop this."

Within two years after arriving at the bank, Reed was boasting to colleagues: "I'm going to be chairman. If I'm not going to be chairman, I'll leave. And if I leave, I'd like to run the U.S. Post Office." According to a former colleague, Reed "was very eager, very aggressive when he was put into planning." Another colleague was not so generous: "He was arrogant and immature." To many, Reed was "the brat" who carried a slide rule in his belt and read a book on higher math while waiting on the coffee line. But despite the criticisms, it was soon clear to most of Reed's associates that his ambitions were well founded. "People had a lot of respect for Reed because he could go into a meeting and Wriston would say, 'Hi, John,' while others were hoping Wriston would remember their name and face," said former Citibanker Byron Stinson.

Intertwined with Citibank's drive to understand how it made its money and the move to transfer pricing was the need to devise a way to put a price tag on its funds. At any point in time, a bank's deposits consist of a mix of funds, including checking deposits, certificates of deposit, debt, and federal funds, and other instruments of varying rates and maturities. Many lenders, in the days of cheap interest-free demand deposits, assumed in making their loans that this money was "free." For years, Citibank and other American banks figured that the value of any chunk of this money was an average of these rates, weighted, of course, according to the amount of money of a given yield and maturity. That was fine as long as rates remained low and stable and bank portfolios consisted largely of so-called core deposits, such as corporate compensating balances. But with the escalation of the war in Vietnam and the dramatic acceleration of government spending for President Johnson's Great Society programs, inflation and interest rates surged.

By 1966 it was clear that John Exter, co-inventor of the CD and Citibank's Chicken Little, was right—at least to a point. He had warned the bank in the early sixties that the stimulative monetary policies of Fed chairman William McChesney Martin would fan inflation and interest rates. In the first serious burst of inflation in the postwar era, short-term rates rose above long-term rates. The world had not yet ended, as Exter had predicted. But, said John Heimann, later a Comptroller of the Currency, "That [the rise in short-term rates] had to tell you the world had changed." A few years later a newly appointed Fed chairman named Arthur Burns would refer in a speech to the "fateful policies of 1965," saying that "one of the serious economic blunders of recent years was the failure to alter the course of fiscal and monetary policies when early warnings of inflation began to flash" late in 1964 and in 1965. In this era of more expensive money, corporate treasurers became stingier with their balances and demanded more and better services in return for them. Understanding what money really cost and where the bank made its money would become critical in the tug-of-war between corporate treasurers and their bankers.

But, thanks to Wriston's negotiable CD, more and more funds on deposit in American banks were now being purchased in the open market. In meetings of Citibank's brain trust, it occurred to the likes of Reed and budget manager Charles Kelly that a bank's inventory should be priced in the same manner that industrial companies had long priced theirs: last in, first out—a method that became known as marginal pricing. In other words, the real cost of money was to be the price the bank paid for the last slug it bought in the open market.

This recognition would irrevocably alter Citibank's lending decisions, and its analyses of acquisition targets, prospective businesses, and the profitability of its business units and customers. But while Citibank was gradually beginning to comprehend the economics of banking, its ability to benefit from that understanding would be limited as long as the marketplace in which money was bought and sold did not operate freely. That was evident in July 1966, when the Fed reacted to surging interest rates by slapping a Reg Q ceiling over the rates big banks could pay on jumbo CDs. The result was a severe credit crunch in the United States and accelerated movement of dollars to the Euromarkets. In effect, the dawn of intelligent banking collided head-on with the old-time regulation.

"As we recognized through marginal cost evaluation of products and our businesses that we knew the economics," said Kelly, "we then ran into the realization that this was what we should do, but conditions in the market didn't always allow us to do it." For nearly two more decades, the economics of the American financial services industry would remain distorted by legislative and regulatory constraints on the cost and flow of money. No one would be more influential in finally ridding the system of those constraints than Walter B. Wriston.

Like the law, which is shaped largely by case precedent, the world of banking and finance is often shaped by precedent-setting transactions. One precedent was the $100 million Eurodollar syndication that Wriston, Don Howard, then an officer in London, and their colleagues had put together for Shell Oil a few years earlier. Perhaps more than any other deal, this one drove home to Wriston the hazards of pricing loans based on the historical average cost of funds. When the transaction was being assembled, there had been very little movement up or down in interest rates for years. So it seemed logical to agree to set the rate for each six-month period on the basis of an average of the cost of funds for the previous six months, plus a quarter of a point for the rent and profit. That was fine so long as rates remained stable or declined. But when rates rose, the deal turned sour. Because Citibank's $55 million stake in the seven-year term loan represented 10 percent of the assets of the London branch, where the loan was booked, earnings there plummeted with every uptick in rates. "You quickly learned that you have to price in anticipation instead of retroactively, particularly in an environment of moving rates," Don Howard said later. Howard Laeri, who became a vice chairman in 1965, might have been thinking of the Shell loan when he told *Forbes* later that "many loans are being made that barely break even."

Almost overnight, average cost of funds became an anachronistic concept ill-suited for a volatile age. Henceforth loans would either have to be priced so as to reflect the cost of funds at the margin or would have to be matched off against a slug of fixed rate deposits that would mature no sooner than the loan itself. Despite its boldness in many initiatives, Citibank for some while remained cautious in the way it funded its loans. It generally ran what bankers call a "matched book," where for every loan of a certain maturity there is a deposit of equal length. The profit comes from the difference in the yields between the two. As time went on, Citibank would learn that the real money—and the real risk—comes from "gapping," which means, essentially, borrowing a little shorter and lending a little longer.

It would take years for the simple truth about marginal pricing to become self-evident at the vast majority of American banking institutions. Many would weaken or even fail in the meantime. But Wriston quickly embraced the idea that money was money and that its value was what someone would have to pay for it in the marketplace. With that realization, a new buzzword crept into bankers' lingo—"fungibility"—but that concept was too abstract for some traditional bankers. Said former senior officer Mike Callen, "Only professors at Princeton thought about [fungibility]."

The advent of marginal costing embarrassed some Citibank heavies. In the early 1960s, metropolitan branch chief Tom Wilcox, now a contender for the presidency of the bank, invested excess savings deposits paying a mere 3.5 percent heavily into thirty-year fixed rate mortgages yielding 5 percent. As market rates rose above that level, Wilcox's mortgages were under water according to marginal pricing. At one of Kelly's presentations on the subject, Wilcox openly displayed his irritation. "Charlie, what are you showing that [losses on mortgage loans] for?" he demanded. "That's crazy."

There was yet another piece of the profitability puzzle. Just as Citibank didn't know which of its businesses made money, it also had little idea which of its customers were profitable. In the case of Shell Oil, for example, Citibank knew it wasn't making money on that huge syndicated loan, but it had little idea whether Shell or any other company was earning its keep on a national or worldwide basis. Nobody knew. Bankers tended to think that if a company deposited some money in the bank, the bank must be making money. But when Citibank began to examine each of its corporate accounts more closely, it often got a rude shock. The classic example of Citibank getting the short end of the stick involved certain of its correspondent banks, notably the Bank of Montreal. Bankers call it "playing the float." Citibank discovered to its dismay that the big Canadian bank that it called a friend had made a practice of depositing checks in its Citibank account and selling the money in the federal funds market before the checks cleared. "You'd hear these guys saying they had a hundred million dollars on deposit with us. The fact is, they didn't," said former Citibanker Ed Hoffman. "It's a phony balance." Citibank lacked the information it needed to determine that the Bank of Montreal was drawing the money out faster than its deposits could be collected. Admitted Wriston, "We were not paying attention to collected balances."

Recognizing it had a problem, Citibank formed a committee made up of some of its top officers to create a computerized account profitability system. To establish the committee's credibility at the outset, they studied ten corporate accounts. About half were unprofitable, according to former chief credit officer Henry Mueller. Citibank spent years trying to perfect this system. The whole idea, Wriston joked later, was to know whether "General Motors was stealing you blind in Venezuela."

For Citibank, the Euromarkets of the 1960s provided a vision of an open, competitive, and volatile market of the future, where money was bought and sold and traded like pork bellies. Unlike their counterparts in the United States, who continued to live in a fantasy world in which demand deposits were regarded as "free" money, the new players in the Euromarkets knew that every slug of funds had a price. "The experience in the Eurodollar market really taught us a lot about cost of funds," said Don Howard, because in the United States so much of the bank's loan pricing was influenced by demand deposits and savings accounts that didn't go up or down: one was supposedly free, and the other didn't change. "We learned in the relatively volatile Euromarket what was going to happen to us when the domestic market changed," he said.

Bad monetary policy and bad regulation was a potent combination. With real-world rates above Regulation Q ceilings, banks were hard-pressed to fund their commitments in the United States. Meanwhile, the interest equalization tax continued to drive funds offshore. The world financial system was becoming something like a leaking dike with the United States trying to plug it up.

In London, Citibank was ready and waiting. Piggybacking on Wriston's negotiable certificate of deposit, Citibank announced on June 23, 1966, that three days later it would offer the first Eurodollar certificate of deposit. The so-called London dollar CDs were issued in multiples of $1,000 for a minimum of $25,000 for 30 to 360 days. The idea was to circumvent the Johnson administration's controls by attracting dollars from non-Americans and lending them back to American customers in Europe to finance international trade. They were not subject to U.S. taxes, reserve requirements, or other U.S. regulations.

In 1966, thanks in part to the London dollar CD, borrowings by the overseas branches of U.S. banks surged in the Eurodollar market. Then, right on the heels of the London dollar CD, Citibank introduced other Euromarket innovations, including a three-year certificate and a sterling certificate of deposit. Soon after that, in the late 1960s, Citibank in London developed the first multicurrency loan agreement, which gave corporate treasurers flexibility in borrowing in different currencies. Although they would have to repay in the same currency they borrowed in, the agreement simplified the process of borrowing in different currencies.

Along with the money, financial innovation to a large extent shifted to London and Europe, generating what one former Citibanker described as a "real élan" in those operations.

"The Euromarket," said Wriston later, "broke open the mobility of capital like the world had never seen. And it turned out we had the catchments all over the world to capitalize on it."

In February 1967 the Johnson administration, apparently realizing it was playing a losing game, announced that dollar loans made by overseas branches of U.S. banks would be excluded from the interest equalization tax.

Just as Wriston knew he couldn't achieve 15 percent earnings growth using the operating assumptions of a bygone era, he was convinced it wouldn't happen as long as Citibank stuck to banking alone. Among other things, higher interest expenses were pressuring banks to find new ways to make money. To be sure, scrappy Comptroller of the Currency Jim Saxon had already awakened Citibank and others to the idea that there was more to life than just making loans. Egged on by Saxon, Citibank was pushing the boundaries of banking on several fronts. In nearly every instance, however, Citibank would ultimately lose its battle in the courtroom.

After three years of legal wrangling and securities industry opposition, Citibank in June 1966 offered a commingled mutual fund to customers who could invest at least $10,000. In offering the fund, the bank succeeded in obtaining from the Securities Exchange Commission exemptions from the Investment Company Act of 1940, which generally prohibited bank-sponsored funds but gave the SEC authority to make certain exceptions. Charging that the agency had no right to supervise such funds, the Investment Company Institute sued the Comptroller of the Currency, and the National Association of Securities Dealers asked the U.S. Court of Appeals to overturn the SEC exemptions. In the view of sources familiar with the effort, the plan was doomed to failure because of a flawed legal strategy that also killed bank-sponsored mutual funds for years to come, and the thrill of momentarily circumventing Glass-Steagall was short-lived.

At about this time, the banks got a taste of what they would later face from a curmudgeonly Texan named Wright Patman, chairman of the House Banking Committee. Known as the "Last Populist," Patman was the gadfly of the banking industry and regulatory establishment almost from the day he was elected to Congress in 1929. He so hated banks that in the late 1930s he launched a long and unsuccessful campaign to eliminate the tax-exempt status of the newly completed Federal Reserve Board headquarters, contending that it was really owned not by the federal government but by twelve reserve banks that were in turn controlled by commercial banks.

Patman saw himself as a kind of congressional Robin Hood whose mission in life was to use the American banking and financial system to shift the nation's wealth from the few to the many. In the process, he contributed in no small way to the distortion of capital flows, causing banking institutions to make uneconomic choices and contributing to the weakening of the American banking system. He would be Citibank's nemesis for a decade as it attempted to break into new businesses. He vigorously opposed the bank's effort to offer the commingled fund and, at about this time, issued a "study" calling into question the bank's management of trust assets.

In 1965 Citibank made its first attempt to get into the travel and entertainment card business, which ultimately met a fate similar to that of the commingled fund, though for different reasons. When hotel magnate Barron Hilton, a close friend of Tom Wilcox, offered Citibank a stake in Carte Blanche, the hotel chain's credit card, Citibank was prepared to deal. Though it was the third-largest credit card, Carte Blanche had never really caught on and was only sporadically profitable for Hilton. Nonetheless, Citibank agreed to pay $12 million for half of the operation, and Wilcox was named chairman of Carte Blanche Corporation. "Wilcox sold us on buying Carte Blanche," said former corporate secretary Paul Kolterjahn. "Hilton was astute enough to know Carte Blanche was not known outside of California. It was a sad day for us when we got it."

When the Justice Department challenged the bank's acquisition of Carte Blanche on the grounds that it was anti-competitive, Saxon rushed to Citibank's defense. He pointed out that the Justice Department didn't question American Express's purchase of Uni-Serve, another credit-card company. In January 1966 Justice granted Citibank a stay of execution, agreeing to allow the bank to acquire Carte Blanche pending the court action.

In those days, the Department of Justice was public enemy number one for banks bent on expansion through merger or diversification. But Citibank, having accomplished a benchmark merger in 1955 with the combination of First National and National City, was content to sit out the merger wave of the 1960s that ultimately saw the combination of Manufacturers Trust and Hanover, and to watch on the sidelines as the government's case against this and other big bank marriages wound their way through Congress and the Supreme Court. As part of the compromise that led to the Bank Merger Act of 1966, a provision was included that permitted the banking agencies, including the Comptroller of the Currency, to intervene against the Justice Department on behalf of their client banks.

Not surprisingly, Comptroller Saxon's office was deluged with applications from state-chartered banks seeking to switch charters to take advantage of expanded powers and more lenient supervisory exams. One of these banks was Chase Manhattan, which among other things wanted to engage in direct leasing. House banking committee chairman Wright Patman was so riled by Saxon's moves that in March 1965 he submitted a bill to abolish the Office of Comptroller of the Currency. He didn't succeed, of course, but the days of James Saxon and the golden age of bank reform were clearly numbered.

For some time, Citibank's planners had been trying to peer into the future for fresh ideas about the kind of business Citibank should be ten or fifteen years hence. The planners, however, were unable to divorce themselves from internal politics. Acutely aware of the horse race shaping up for the presidency of the bank, they hedged their bets in discussing Wilcox's or Wriston's operations, heaping praise upon both of them. "They had to say kind words about Wilcox's domestic branches and Wriston's international activities, so the net result," according to one source, was that Moore wasn't getting the objective "outsider's" viewpoint he'd been hoping for. And so, for a bright and independent look into Citibank's future, Wriston and Moore in 1965 once again plugged into their good friends at the General Electric Company.

Through the GE board connection, Moore and Wriston became acquainted with the Technical Military Planning Operation (TEMPO), GE's in-house think tank. The GE subsidiary also sold its advice to other corporations on the theory that it could better serve GE if it was forced to remain relevant enough to command a fee from others. Wriston loved think tanks, but TEMPO, largely defense-oriented, had been floundering. Overshadowed by the Santa Monica–based Rand Corporation, it had operated in the red until the arrival in October 1963 of Thomas O. Paine, a tall, professorial Brown alumnus with a doctorate in physical metallurgy from Stanford. Among his other distinctions, Paine was a direct descendant of Thomas Paine, the Revolutionary-era pamphleteer. Paine, then forty-one, was charged with either making TEMPO profitable or shutting it down. Appropriately, when he was introduced to the TEMPO staff at a southern California movie theater, a minor earthquake struck. And Paine quickly began to shake up TEMPO by setting up shop near a beach in Santa Barbara, a site that enabled him to steal talent away from Rand. "They had all the kooks in Santa Monica, and we figured they'd all want to move to Santa Barbara. We picked a few of their leading lights. They called their friends and said, 'It's great up here.' "

TEMPO had never studied banking or financial services—and Moore and Wriston regarded that as a plus. Paine agreed: "Our very strength was our innocence." Citibank's marching orders to TEMPO were to look a quarter century ahead and tell the bank how it should take advantage of future trends—a kind of long-term planning that was nonexistent in American banking at that time. Moore specifically instructed them not to worry about banking. Said Dale J. Hekhuis, the project leader, "George Moore kept saying, 'We know all about banking. Don't concern yourself with that. We want an independent viewpoint on key world trends.' " But despite the friendly corporate connection that had led Citibank to TEMPO, the early relationship with the GE whiz kids was less than harmonious. After several false starts, Paine took charge of the project. Paine, said Citibank planner Jack Heilshorn, was a "brilliant but pragmatic technocrat" who said "these guys [from Citibank] want to be able to *do* something."

Out of the conversations between Wriston, Moore, Heilshorn, and Paine came the epochal recognition that Citibank should not view itself merely as a bank but as a global, technology-based financial services company. Citibank at that moment, Paine said, was a DIB—a differential interest bank. TEMPO staff members believed there was little future in the DIB and used the term scornfully. The new opportunities, TEMPO concluded, lay in developing the "capital appreciation and services" bank. Capital growth could be achieved, TEMPO said, by taking equity positions overseas, as Citibank had already been doing through its Edge Act units, and through so-called leasing residuals—the equity remaining at the end of the lease of equipment such as aircraft. As George Moore recalled, "They [TEMPO] said, 'You don't want to be a bank anymore. You want to be a global financial institution. You want to perform every financial service anywhere in the world [that] you can do at a profit, and that you can do legally.' "

The future, the whiz kids concluded, was in things like advanced computers and satellite communications. Technology, Paine said, would soon make it possible for Citibank to deliver global financial services profitably. At a meeting between TEMPO and the Citibankers, one uninhibited young TEMPO staff member caused Paine to cringe when he told Moore and Wriston bluntly: "The future of your bank is not going to be ensured by chasing housewives down Queens Boulevard." Still, TEMPO identified the retail market as the funds source of the future. "These notions may have been in people's minds, but they were crystallized" by TEMPO, Heilshorn said.

Paine, who was subsequently appointed administrator of NASA just before the first manned lunar landing, informed Wriston that Citibank was in the "high-tech information business." Several years earlier, General Electric had pioneered magnetic ink character recognition on checks and, as a result of further research on the payments system, had concluded that electronic payment systems would lead to a checkless society. TEMPO informed the bank that it should be thinking about swapping information instead of paper in clearing payments. Said Hekhuis, "It got us looking at electronic handling of payments, ATMs, and the notion of integrated financial communications networks."

TEMPO's ideas about high-tech banking squared with Wriston's own long-standing love affair with machines and electronic wizardry, an interest shared by his father. Walter Wriston never did anything by hand that could be done by machine. His friend Barrett Emmerts recalls that when he gave Wriston and his wife potted daffodils or lilies as an anniversary present, he'd haul his massive backhoe out of the barn to plant them, even if the job could be accomplished in less time with a spade. "It was a case of technological overkill," Emmerts said later. And Henry Wriston, who by now wore a pacemaker, always yearned to have a new one installed whenever a new model came on the market. Citibank, too, was receptive to the latest banking technology, such as interoffice teleconferencing systems and branch "ready teller" machines to collect deposits, which enabled it to shorten teller lines. Paine concluded that technology was the passport for the bank out of the highly regulated and restricted world in which it operated. The banking laws applied to the "technological environment of the past," Paine said. By developing tomorrow's technology today, the bank could create a new game for which the rules had not yet been laid down. "You should use technology," Paine advised, "to actually do something that by the time the regulators wake up to the fact, it's too late. . . . We encouraged them to think in these terms and to move quickly to do bold things."

One way that goal might be accomplished, TEMPO suggested, was with the credit card. "We had the feeling that they'd be able to do things with credit cards that they couldn't do with checks and loans and other stuff," Paine said later. TEMPO also advised Citibank to develop special banking expertise in computers, transportation, and energy, which it had concluded were the growth industries of the future. TEMPO predicted, for example, that computer sales would grow by about 20 percent annually through 1975. "Therefore," said Moore, "we should go in with both feet." Most prophetically, TEMPO advised Citibank that its future lay in providing capital and financial services to the capital-poor developing world. First National City Bank "is in an excellent position to initiate and capitalize upon such opportunities," TEMPO wrote in its final report.

Once Wriston and Moore began to see themselves less as being in the banking business and more as being in the money business, a long list of new possibilities dawned on them. One of them was the insurance business, and in one TEMPO meeting someone suggested that the bank buy the Chubb Corporation, the Tiffany's of the insurance industry. Drawing on its own background and interest in aerospace, TEMPO also reinforced Citibank's interest in buying aircraft and leasing them to airlines. There would be, Paine said, a gold mine in the residuals—the value of the aircraft remaining at the end of the lease. "We said the same thing about containers." Citibank, of course, had been financing aircraft for years with term loans. As with the ship loans, the banks took the early maturities and gave the longer maturities to insurance companies.

After the passage in the early sixties of a 7 percent investment tax credit, Citibank pioneered an entirely new industry called the tax lease. Like many other innovations, this one began with a call from a customer who had a problem. United Airlines, which was seeking to buy six DC-8 jets, told Citibank that it couldn't use the tax credits from the new program. Led by its transportation lender, Fred Bradley, who would emerge as the dean of American aerospace lenders, the bank figured that if it bought the planes from the manufacturers and took an accelerated depreciation and investment tax credit, it could lease the planes to United at a lower rate than the market could offer the airline. With that discovery and a favorable IRS tax opinion, an entirely new industry was born. Taking the concept a step further, Citibank soon figured that it could make even more money if it put up only 15 percent itself and borrowed the rest from insurance companies, which would not share in the tax benefits, a maneuver that later became known as the leveraged lease. In the mid-1960s, Citibank served as the agent bank on a benchmark $1.2 billion deal to finance the first Boeing 747s, a transaction that was not without risk. At first, Fred Bradley recalled, the engines didn't work, and the planes didn't fly. Then, in 1970, Citibank and Manufacturers Hanover teamed up to buy five Boeing 747s each and lease them back to Pan American for sixteen years. The transaction made Citibank the world's largest single owner of the new aircraft. After that, there would be no end to the applications of tax-oriented leasing. In later years, the technique was even used to lease satellites.

TEMPO also brought to Citibank some nonstarters, including the notion that the gold standard would someday be replaced by the nuclear power standard and the kilowatt-hour standard, and that Citibank should be ready to capitalize on this development. Also, because of widespread concern about nuclear weapons proliferation, TEMPO was certain that someone would have to keep track of every ounce of uranium 235, and that Citibank should own and store the fuel and rent it out to utilities. In doing so, claimed TEMPO, Citibank would have the "currency of the future." That idea, of course, never saw the light of day.

Citibank's first ten-year plan, completed in 1967, drew heavily from the TEMPO study—notably its emphasis on satellite communications and leasing, and its prediction that world trade would double in the next ten years. Even under its most conservative leadership, Citibank and its predecessor institutions had shown a willingness to try something new. Thanks largely to TEMPO, Citibank was about to become America's experimental bank.

TEMPO had reinforced Citibank's recognition that it was more than just a bank. In the United States real progress in the push for congeneric, or bank-related, activities would have to await congressional action in 1970. Internationally, however, Citibank was just getting warmed up.

Overseas, expansion through traditional branch banking was showing signs of slowing, and Wriston wanted to "maintain the growth of overseas in the total company," John Reed said later. Simply collecting deposits and making loans wouldn't be enough. Beginning with that modest 1963 foray into consumer finance in Panama, the term "congeneric" almost overnight appeared on the lips of Citibankers around the world, from the freshest recruit from Harvard Business School to the movers and shakers on the fifteenth floor. For them, finding or managing a congeneric would become the way to catch the eye of Wriston or Moore. And for Moore—the most zealous booster of congeneric acquisitions and joint ventures—such deals would represent another way to show up archrival David Rockefeller at Chase.

To the erratic, brilliant, ubiquitous George Moore, everyone—passengers on airplanes, the man in the next seat at the opera, a guy in a swimsuit on a sundeck—was a prospective source of congenerics. But there was a price to be paid for the helter-skelter, devil-may-care global expansion of the late 1960s and early 1970s. Businesses were acquired, joint ventures initiated, and branches opened at a breakneck pace, and young, green hires assigned to run them with little thought given to their managerial or moral qualifications.

Some congenerics, notably a finance company in Belgium, were bought without even a pretense of audits or due diligence. Citibankers bought up everything from a leasing company in South Africa to an insurance company in Libya—in that case, coping with Libyan rules against foreign ownership by finding a Libyan national who owned an insurance company license.

But while George Moore was the spark that ignited the overseas expansion, he also left in his wake a series of conflagrations that his successor would be obliged to contain. Some of them were easily extinguishable; others would smolder for years. One such deal that would loom large in Citibank history was the 1966 acquisition, for $3.5 million, of a 50 percent interest in Waltons Credit Corporation, the sales finance affiliate of a big Australian department store chain. That debacle became known to Citibank wags as the "swimming pool deal."

Citibank had always had a fascination for Australia; it was seen as a kind of extension of the American frontier. Australia, said a former Citibank officer, is "a big place, and everybody fell in love with the big idea, like Texas." And Citibank was not alone. Many other foreign banks became intoxicated with the Aussie frontier spirit. But few countries were more xenophobic than Australia. In 1965 the Aussies allowed Citibank to open a representative office in Sydney, but the powers of such offices were limited. Unsatisfied with a mere rep office and blocked from buying a bank, Citibank saw that the only other way to get a foot in the door was through a finance company. But for an American company to operate a company that didn't fulfill the definition of a bank, it had to have an Australian partner on a fifty-fifty basis.

It was this deal, as the story goes, that was struck at poolside in Australia, where George Moore first encountered John R. Walton, a self-made Australian retailer who had begun his career as a cash register salesman. He bootstrapped a small retail operation to the point where it was one of the largest retail chains in the country, specializing in big-ticket items such as large appliances and furniture. And Moore, of course, admired self-made entrepreneurs.

Waltons, said one former Citibanker, was a "tad above Woolworth's." The chain employed traveling salesmen who, as Wriston put it, "would call on Mrs. McGillicuddy in Sydney," remark to her over coffee how "that refrigerator of yours looks a little beat up. How about buying a new one?" and then offer to finance it through the Waltons finance unit. The sales force's methods of monitoring receivables were not very scientific; they learned of changes in a customer's financial condition through the neighborhood gossip mill. It was, as Wriston put it later, "an incredibly high-cost operation."

Waltons would represent the granddaddy of the congeneric acquisition binge. It was one of the bank's first significant joint ventures, one of the first consumer finance operations outside the United States, and one of its most disastrous acquisitions. Later, Waltons confirmed for Citibank the folly of engaging in joint ventures overseas. That enterprise "was far from smooth," said Wriston. "But we were always a long-term player."

Some weeks after Moore stumbled into Walton, the action shifted to New York, where Walton had come to meet with New York bankers, including David Rockefeller, looking for investors to help prop up his foundering finance company. As the story goes, George Moore learned that Walton was in town only because he mistakenly called Moore at Citibank instead of William H. Moore, chairman of Bankers Trust Company. The day after that phone call, Moore returned to the bank in an excited state. Wriston recalls that Moore walked into his office and said "ought to buy, ought to buy, ought to buy a finance company!"

"Well, we'll see if we can [buy] Waltons," Wriston said. He then phoned the hotel and told Walton, "You met Mr. Moore, and Mr. Moore would like you to come to lunch today." Walton, it turned out, was waiting for a phone call from Chase co-CEO David Rockefeller, but the call never came, so Walton agreed to have lunch with Wriston and Moore to discuss the acquisition. (It turned out that David Rockefeller had indeed called and left a message for Walton, but the hotel desk clerk had misplaced it.) Over lunch, Moore haggled with Walton over the finance company. According to one former officer involved in the transaction, Walton told Citibank that he would guarantee a high return on the bank's investment and take responsibility for the bad debts. Moore was so excited he refused to allow Walton to leave 399 Park until the deal was done. Announced in June 1966, the joint venture was renamed City Bank–Waltons Credit Corporation. Citibank had dreamed that this would be a base from which to create an organization that would finance receivables not just for Waltons, but also for many other stores.

Even Stillman Rockefeller apparently was pleased. On a buck slip attached to one of the Waltons documents, Rockefeller wrote, "At last, an investment in a white man's country," according to the recollection of former vice chairman Tom Theobald, as recorded in bank archives. And Moore, as soon as the transaction was completed, dumped it in Wriston's lap. When one officer arrived at Wriston's office to help out with the transaction, Wriston said in disgust, in a reference to Moore, "The crank upstairs wants you up there."

In looking for someone to run the new joint venture, senior vice president George C. Scott ran his finger down a Citibank personnel directory and stopped at the name of Theobald, a tall, lanky, twenty-eight-year-old assistant vice president and graduate of the Harvard Business School. At the time, Tom Theobald called on domestic companies in Illinois and Wisconsin, but he had indicated his interest in an overseas assignment when one arose.

When Theobald returned from a Midwest business trip, he was summoned into Moore's office, where he had never set foot before. He was asked whether he had just bought a new house or a new car, and whether his wife was pregnant. The answer to the first two questions was no, but Theobald's wife was expecting a child. "Well, that's two out of three," Wriston said. "How would you like to go to Australia?"

Theobald's colleagues cautioned him that his career would likely fall off a cliff if he accepted the assignment. And, in fact, because of certain legal concerns that surrounded the acquisition of a foreign subsidiary, Theobald would have to resign from the bank. To say that he would be totally on his own in Australia was an understatement, but despite all this, a few days later, Theobald took off for a three-week inspection tour of Australia.

Almost from the moment he arrived there, he understood why the others in the bank wanted to keep their distance from George's folly. City Bank–Waltons was a faltering organization whose creditors were cutting back on its borrowings and whose life expectancy could be measured in weeks. At one point, a respected Citibank senior vice president visited Australia to study the market and concluded there was no way Citibank could ever make money there.

It turned out that the operation had some built-in flaws that a little due diligence might have uncovered. Salesmen did not simply sell and collect; they were also authorized to rewrite the financing contract to alter the terms to the customer. Citibank found itself in the awkward predicament of having signed an ironclad contract to fund Waltons receivables without having any idea from the outset just how bad those receivables were.

The entire Australian episode did not exactly cause Theobald to respect Moore as a prudent risk-taker. Theobald said later that the thing that saved [Moore] was that he picked guys like Wriston who had their feet on the ground.

"No one," said Theobald later, "had been able to tell me what the long-term objective of Citibank and Waltons was." Nonetheless, City Bank–Waltons soon began diversifying into auto leasing, equipment financing, factoring, and real estate lending. By the early seventies both Waltons and another related Australian acquisition would fall victim to the excesses of Australian real estate lending.

"Anytime you go into a strange market and acquire a company in a different culture, you have nothing but trouble," Wriston said later. "On the other hand, if you have the guts to stay, you're in there when the clouds lift. International banking is not a sometime deal. It's a long-term deal."

In 1967, the congeneric movement marked another milestone with the acquisition, in the United Kingdom, of Laurentide Finance, which operated a chain of "money shops." This was the first instance in which Citibank acquired a majority interest in a congeneric and the first acquisition overseas in which the bank enjoyed majority control. Reed brought a somewhat more scientific approach to the task of finding new companies to buy overseas. He combed through IMF statistics analyzing country funds flows and deposit data in an effort to determine what kinds of acquisitions might offer the best growth and profit prospects.

Notwithstanding GE's myriad contributions to Citibank, the bank's relationship with the big conglomerate was not painless for Wriston, Moore, and other senior officers. Among the first to be suckered into the notorious

Home-Stake oil swindle were some of General Electric's leading lights, including Fred J. Borch, its future chairman. He was followed by Moore, and a long list of other notables, including Senator Jacob Javits, singer Liza Minnelli, comedian Buddy Hackett, and Walter Wriston, who controlled billions of other people's money but couldn't be bothered managing his own.

According to David McClintick's *Stealing from the Rich,* the Home-Stake–GE connection was made in 1958, when Home-Stake chief R. S. Trippet met a prominent New York tax and estate attorney whose practice included the GE officials. To maintain the swindle, it was essential that particularly influential investors like Borch and the GE crowd remain totally satisfied, so their returns were typically higher than those of lesser lights. In 1964, two years after Wriston joined the GE board, George Moore kicked in $56,400 and Wriston invested $18,800. They were soon joined by William Spencer, the otherwise savvy head of Citibank's oil and gas department. By 1966, Moore had invested $312,000, but was starting to harbor suspicions about the company, and in the early 1970s, Moore and Wriston began to leave Home-Stake "through the back door." Using the method pioneered by fellow GE investors years earlier, they donated their shares to their favorite charities. According to McClintick, Moore gave his shares to Lincoln Center, the Spanish Institute, the Metropolitan Opera, and New York Hospital and Wriston contributed one unit to the Fletcher School. Wriston might have been thinking about Home-Stake when he later admitted to a reporter, "I don't have any personal investment philosophy. I'm like the shoemaker whose kids are barefoot."

"They were all involved in that and trying to figure out how to get the hell out by making contributions of ownership," said a former top Citibank officer. "But the tax guy said, 'No way.' "

Home-Stake, and the widespread publicity that the scam later received, clearly struck a blow to Wriston's pride. He would later boast that he got out early, pointing to a new and larger weekend home in Sherman as evidence that he didn't really lose any money on the deal.

———

On Friday, June 17, 1966, Moore and Wriston were in Santa Barbara chastising the TEMPO technocrats for their worthless first draft and ordering them back to the drawing board. Wriston had decided to remain overnight in California, while Moore opted to fly back to New York that evening on the red-eye. When Moore arrived at his East Side apartment early the next morning, he received some shocking news: Bobby Wriston was dead of an apparent heart attack. She had been planning a luncheon for some Citibank wives and was found by a maid who had arrived at the apartment to help with the serving. Meanwhile, daughter Cassy was at a debutante party in Saint Louis. Moore called Wriston in California, but told him only that his wife was very sick. When Wriston's plane touched down at La Guardia, Moore, Emmerts, and the family doctor were on hand to greet him, and Emmerts delivered the bad news. Wriston was ashen, and for the first and only time in Emmerts's memory, the tough, controlled Walter Wriston was in tears. On the trip into Manhattan, he glanced at his watch, noted the time, and said, "This is the end of the world for me." Bobby's death represented perhaps the first time the inner Wriston was laid bare, even to his closest friends.

After visiting his wife's body at the mortuary, the three men headed back on foot to Wriston's UN Plaza apartment. While still several blocks away, Wriston, consumed by grief, asked to return home by himself. He spent the next ten hours alone, playing and replaying the songs that he and Bobby had loved to listen to together. For weeks after the funeral, he remained in seclusion, grieving. "I wasn't worth the powder to blow me to hell," Wriston said later.

Tough as Bobby's death was for Wriston, it was devastating for Cassy, who worshiped her mother and modeled herself after her. Wriston was ill-equipped to deal with the emotional demands of a daughter in distress. Instead of responding to her by "hugging and embracing, he dealt with it with logic," said one friend. Wriston was not inclined to reveal his deficiencies or his emotional bare spots to anyone. Groping for a way to reach out to Cassy, he asked a confidant, "What am I doing wrong with this kid? What am I doing wrong?" Said a close friend later, "He is kind and thoughtful, but it is all through his prism."

Bobby's untimely death was also a blow to Citibank families around the world, and officers and employees from each country where Citibank operated chipped in to send a delegate to the funeral. She was immensely popular, having committed to memory the names of virtually all overseas employees, their children, and their children's birthdays. "Bobby went down easy," said Nancy Valelly. "She had something to do with making gold glitter more."

Among the shoulders that Wriston leaned on in his time of need were those of his friends Carl Desch, Jim Farley, and Aristotle Onassis, all of whom took turns looking after Cassy. Onassis showered her with postcards from far-flung ports of call, and on his visits to New York, he and his current love, opera star Maria Callas, took her to lunch at the posh "21." At the time, Cassy attended Manhattan's Finch College, which required students to sign in and out at night and indicate where they would be going and with whom. Cassy reveled in signing the register, "Ari Onassis and Maria Callas—'21.'" All of this, of course, prompted considerable snickering by cynics who were convinced that the wily Mr. Onassis was taking advantage of Wriston's bereavement to further ingratiate himself with the man who would soon be the nation's most influential banker. But Wriston said later, "I don't really think that was true. He was a friend of ours, [and] he could not have been nicer to us."

The two men were close enough, apparently, for Onassis to offer his services as a matchmaker. Among the eligible women Onassis sought to pair off with Wriston was, surprisingly enough, Jacqueline Kennedy, whom Onassis himself would marry in late 1968. According to Cassy, Onassis had suggested that the two meet over dinner, but Wriston, who loathed dating, turned the offer down flat. Meanwhile, the Citibank rumor mill was working overtime. Later, Cassy got a job writing for a medical newspaper in Manhattan, and she and her father frequently walked to work together. For years, Wriston had worked so hard to separate his personal life from his business life that few of his business acquaintances even knew he had a daughter. On one occasion, someone reported to him that the talk was that he was "running around with an eighteen-year-old girl."

On the outside, Wriston remained controlled and stoical, but he was deeply troubled by his loss. When he returned to work, he seemed to some to be almost clinically depressed. Stillman Rockefeller told a colleague, "If Walt can't get hold of himself, our plans for him aren't going to work out."

Wriston's friends and colleagues considered Bobby's premature death a turning point for him. The softer side of Wriston that had emerged in the early years seemed to fade. Without Bobby's moderating influence, he seemed to take on a harder edge. His wit, always acerbic, became ever more pointed. "It went beyond the needle," said one former Citibanker. "It included putting people down who couldn't come back at him because they worked for him." On a few occasions, Wriston revealed to colleagues how important Bobby had been to him as head of overseas. "Bobby was a transmission point to the younger people. When she died I felt that loss," he told colleagues. Bobby was more socially attuned than her husband, and her antennae were more sensitive to the personal problems of overseas personnel. Wriston would acknowledge to associates that he had learned a lot from his wife. "Wriston was cold, and he knew it," said a former colleague.

Her death occurred at a time of major change in American banking that Wriston himself was helping to bring about. The passing of this vivacious, gentle woman coincided with the end of the era of soft and gentle banking. Wriston's colleagues differed on whether Wriston's tougher and more caustic demeanor reflected his bitterness over his loss, the pressures imposed by his growing responsibility, or a combination of the two. In less than a year, Wriston would stand at center stage in the American banking world. But his wife was tragically denied the opportunity to share the spotlight that she had helped to brighten.

Wriston did of course get hold of himself. One reason was his chance encounter with the young woman who would soon become the second Mrs. Walter B. Wriston.

On the day Bobby died, Wriston's meeting with TEMPO was interrupted by a phone call notifying him that the California banking authorities intended to revoke a long-standing but dormant license Citibank owned to operate an Edge Act office in San Francisco. These operations allowed banks to conduct international transactions, such as foreign exchange and letters of credit, outside their home states. The office had been kept alive for future use with

$100,000 in capital, and California was now telling Wriston to use it or lose it. Wriston and Moore pondered the arcane legal question as to whether a bank could operate two Edge Act offices. The lawyers later informed them that there didn't appear to be any reason why they couldn't, but no one had ever done it before. Banks, including Citibank, still worried about the consequences of acting precipitously in the regulatory arena, but within a few short years, Citibank would act first and ask questions later. The upshot of this discussion was that Citibank, with the encouragement of Stillman Rockefeller, opened an unprecedented second Edge Act office in 1967, the first one by a New York bank outside of New York since World War II. The opposition, in fact, came not from the lawyers or regulators but from within their own ranks, in the person of Wriston's rival, Tom Wilcox. "Tommy marshaled a lot of facts and said we'd lose every account in California," Wriston recalled. Citibank later opened other Edge Act offices in Los Angeles, Miami, Houston, and Chicago. "Tommy fought it till the end of the day. [But] Stillman or George overruled him and we opened it up, and suddenly it changed the world," Wriston said later. As the first domestic branch outside of New York, the modest San Francisco office represented the first step on the road to interstate banking, at least for Citibank and others that weren't grandfathered under old banking rules that allowed some banks to operate in more than one state.

While Tom Theobald was Down Under trying to clean up George Moore's swimming pool deal, Stillman Rockefeller was headed for a showdown with the Canadian parliament over the long-simmering Mercantile affair. In the three and a half years since Citibank bought half of the tiny bank from the Dutch, the acquisition had become a cause célèbre in Canadian-American economic relations. At the crux of the dispute were the assurances that Citibank contended it received from Canada's financial authorities that it would encounter no government opposition to the transaction. Central bank governor Louis Rasminsky "was against it, and how and to what extent he told us he was against it is in the fuzzy area," remarked Stillman Rockefeller in an unpublished interview.

In July 1966, Mitchell Sharp, who had replaced Walter Gordon as finance minister, submitted to Canada's parliament his recommendations for revising the Bank Act. These changes would require Citibank, by December 31, 1967, either to sell its stake down to 25 percent, to restrict its assets to twenty times its capital, or about $200 million, or to pay a $500-a-day penalty.

A month later, New York senator Jacob Javits, Moore's close friend and tennis partner, responded by introducing a bill in the U.S. Senate that would have awarded the Comptroller of the Currency the power to regulate activities of foreign banks in the United States, in effect providing for reciprocity in the treatment of foreign banks. At the time, there was no overall regulation of foreign institutions; the rules varied from state to state. Shortly thereafter, a friendly New York congressman introduced a similar measure in the House and wrote to President Johnson soliciting his support, and in December 1966, the U.S. State Department lodged a formal protest with Canada over their proposed legislation.

In Canada, the Mercantile transaction was page one news. A cartoon in the January 19, 1967, edition of the *Vancouver Sun* depicted two Canadian businessmen sitting in a men's club, one reading a headline stating, "Our Curb on U.S. Bank Brings U.S. Retaliation Threat," and remarking to the other, "You know how they escalate . . . Next thing you know, it's the Marines and B-52's." Canadian banks, which enjoyed wide freedom to compete in U.S. markets, were divided on the Mercantile issue. Some fiercely opposed the entry of Citibank onto their turf; others acknowledged that the competition would rouse them from their lethargy. One Canadian banker, G. Arnold Hart, chairman and president of the Bank of Montreal, rallied to Citibank's defense, calling the measures "discriminatory." Still others, according to Stillman Rockefeller, told Citibank one thing and did another. In fact, as Wriston recalled later, Canadian bankers, including one close friend of his, enjoyed ribbing Wriston and other American bankers about their competitive advantages in the U.S. The reason for that edge was very simple: Canadian banks were able to book dollar deposits in New York and lend them out at a fatter profit than U.S. banks because they were not subject to Federal Reserve Board reserve requirements.

In a rare public appearance, the dour, taciturn Stillman Rockefeller journeyed to Ottawa to testify on the acquisition. Before Rockefeller testified, he confidently told his Shearman & Sterling lawyer, "We don't need any lawyers. We'll just sit quietly." But this time Rockefeller was forced to be more talkative than usual. He insisted that Citibank had agreed to buy Mercantile weeks before the meetings with the Canadian finance officials and that he had informed then finance minister Gordon of the plans "as a matter of ordinary courtesy." Rockefeller complained that the retroactive legislation was "discriminatory." His presentation, marked by a series of public relations gaffes, did not exactly charm the Canadian legislators into submission. Describing himself as a "bank clerk," he referred to former finance minister Gordon as an "accountant"—a remark that was taken as an insult by Canadians. The performance was quintessential Rockefeller.

During the hearings it became apparent that Citi had actually played fast and loose with the facts. It turned out that in 1963 Citibank's Robert MacFadden had written a memo indicating his plan to "clear" the acquisition with Gordon. That memo actually lent credence to the Canadian position. Later, however, MacFadden composed a second memo based on the July 18, 1963, meeting between Rockefeller and Gordon that represented the bank's official position. Incredibly, at one point a Citibank lawyer accidentally displayed the first memo. "Oops. Wrong memo," he said when he discovered his blunder.

Rockefeller and MacFadden were berated and humiliated. "They were treated shabbily," said a former top Citibank officer. "It was the coldest reception we ever got from people we thought were friends." The appearance at the hearing of Stillman Rockefeller—a symbol of American capitalism—made headlines throughout Canada. It "appealed to the yellow dog press up there," Wriston said later. "They just blew everything out of [proportion]." Wriston would later acknowledge that he had underestimated the ferocity of anti-American sentiment in Canada and was unaware that they would become so impassioned over the sale of a "piggybank" by one foreigner to another. He was also appalled at how little real help Citibank received from the U.S. State Department. "We raised hell and said, 'Look at the agency banks here and what they're doing to us,' " he said. "The American ambassador moused around on the thing and lodged a protest," said Wriston. "It's a sad fact of life that the Department of State is not a great deal of help to American business abroad."

When the Canadian parliament passed the amended Bank Act in March, Citibank was faced with two unacceptable choices: don't grow, or cut your ownership down to 25 percent. Nothing was more repugnant to Wriston and Citibank than having limits placed on growth, so they chose the latter.

In the opinion of one former Citibank international officer, "Stillman antagonized everybody and left Wriston to fix it."

"Gentleman Jim" Farley was not enamored of staff jobs, such as the one he had held in the overseas planning department since he returned home from Argentina in 1964. Ever the politician, he asked Wriston in 1967 to give him the dirtiest job at Citibank. That, of course, was Mercantile. "If I do a good job, you owe me one," Farley told Wriston. Apart from the furor over who told what to whom, Mercantile was a money-losing operation. Farley was not a business builder, but he knew fat, waste, and inefficiency when he saw it, and he began to bring Mercantile into the black. He cut the high-priced U.S. staff and, because the bank wasn't big enough to lend to large companies, zeroed in on the middle market, export financing, and money market business. Farley would later claim that by the time he left, the bank had gone from losing more than a $500,000 a year to earning $1.5 million.

Whatever the merits of Citibank's version of the Mercantile story, Wriston and his colleagues, if not Stillman Rockefeller, learned one key lesson from the affair. "You're a guest in the country," said Farley. "Rather than fight them, you have to deal with the situation differently. We were a little bit arrogant in dealing with Parliament. It did teach me personally that there was a nicer way of doing business. I spent a lot more time with ministers of finance before I told them what I thought of them," he said later.

Even though Citibank agreed in 1971 to sell down to 25 percent, by 1980 the deal did have a bright side. The Mercantile stock contained provisions that enabled Citibank to profit handsomely when the shares were sold. And while Citibank was selling down Mercantile, it was also building a so-called nonbank bank, which would later be converted into a full-fledged bank when the Canadian laws loosened up. Eventually, the marketplace exposed what Wriston termed the "unsustainable" position of the Canadian government, and Citibank Canada became a profitable part of the Citibank empire. "It [the Mercantile affair] motivated us to go out and build a parallel operation," Wriston said later. "They hit you in one place and it motivates you to go someplace else."

"Sometimes," he said, "you win by losing."

Former Citibankers said that the Mercantile affair left Wriston and his colleagues bitter toward their neighbors to the north, a sentiment Wriston would later deny. But his friend and colleague Stephen Eyre said that "Walt never had a warm feeling for Canada, [and] there is still a feeling that Canada is not a friendly place."

8

THE NEW ORDER

*T*o hear the silent, cynical Stillman Rockefeller tell it, there was little in the way of CEO material in the senior ranks of the First National City Bank. According to Carl Desch, who would become Wriston's eyes and ears in the corridors of Citibank, Rockefeller used to say that "Laeri was lazy, Perkins was stupid, Moore was erratic, and Wilcox talked too much."

That left only Wriston. But to most observers in 1967 the race for the presidency of Citibank appeared to come down to Wriston and Thomas Wilcox, the personable but stubborn chief of Citibank's branch operations. As the hour approached for Stillman to anoint his successor, Wriston, in the view of at least one top overseas hand, seemed to turn exceedingly cautious. Rick Wheeler, then a senior officer in Asia, recalled the bank's "apocalyptic" response to a $33,000 write-off in Singapore just before the succession decision was to be made. The guilty officer was told that a recurrence would spell the end of his career. "It was illustrative of how tight things were," Wheeler recalled. "I had the sense that Walt was keeping people on a short leash. The real takeoff in the bank [did not occur] until . . . Stillman was out of there."

Using the scorecards of the day, both Wriston and Wilcox had much to show for their time on the job. Both had greatly expanded their operations. For every branch Wriston established in a place like Pakistan, Wilcox opened one in the greater New York area. In a telltale sign that Wriston might be the front-runner, the cover of the 1966 annual report, issued in early 1967, displayed the flags of all the countries where the bank was now represented. If the decision about a successor had been made on the basis of pure charm, Wilcox would have won hands down. "He was one of the most charismatic people ever to work in the bank," said former corporate secretary Paul Kolterjahn. But as a manager, Wilcox was also a one-man show. Tom Creamer, who worked for Wilcox in the branches, once complained to him about his managerial style. "You make every decision," he said defiantly. "You never consult with us. We work *for* you but not *with* you." Wilcox didn't miss a beat. "Tom, you're absolutely right," he replied, "but I like it the way it is."

Wilcox was even difficult on the golf course, because he couldn't stand to lose. And some of his judgment calls were nothing short of bizarre. One Sunday a top branch operations official got a call reporting that there was a naked cleaning man prancing around inside one of the Long Island branches. Before the branch security personnel arrived on the scene, someone had taken a picture of the man through the front window and sold it to a newspaper. Wilcox was furious and blamed his deputy for the incident.

Rockefeller had made the rounds to directors seeking their support for his personal choice of a successor, but the decision itself was a well-kept secret, with no leaks to the press, and only the board and a handful of top-ranking insiders were privy to it. But there was never any doubt in the minds of those in the know that the nod would go to Wriston. "Wilcox was a superb marketer of the bank, business—and Wilcox," said Jack Heilshorn later. "People tried to pretend there was a choice," said Moore later. "There wasn't any."

Wilcox didn't disguise the fact that he wanted the job with a passion. In trying to prepare himself for broader responsibility, he ventured onto Wriston's turf, making a tour of Asia in an attempt to learn the international banking business. Then, according to one Wriston confidant, Wilcox returned from his trip abroad "knocking the hell out of the overseas branches," criticizing their appearance and operations.

Said one former top Citibank officer, "Wilcox and Wriston were knifing each other all the time. Wilcox thought he had it in the bag until the end." Wriston would later contend that the tension between himself and Wilcox was exaggerated, but to those watching from ringside, it couldn't have been more real. Wilcox considered himself an intimate friend of Stillman Rockefeller, and right up until he received the bad news had apparently banked on that relationship carrying the day. But as it turned out, "the personal equation was important to Wilcox, but not to Rockefeller or Wriston," according to Robert Hoguet.

Nick Clute, a former senior officer, recalled encountering Moore, Wriston, and Wilcox in a corridor when Moore informed Wilcox of the decision in early June 1967. He heard Moore say, "Now, don't get mad, Tommy, but we decided Walt is going to get it." Clute remembered that "Tommy was fuming." Rockefeller then summoned Wilcox to the boardroom and reportedly said, "Well, Tommy, you lost the race. You get the consolation prize. We're going to make you vice chairman." On July 1, 1967, Wriston, now forty-seven, succeeded Moore as president, and Moore became chairman. The only real surprise—and it was a major one—was Stillman Rockefeller's decision to amend the bank bylaws to enable him to designate the president, rather than the chairman, as chief executive officer. While George Moore used to say, "Walter frightens me," Moore apparently frightened Stillman Rockefeller even more. The day before the board meeting, Rockefeller called Moore into his office and told him, "George, we're making you chairman but not CEO."

Moore replied, "I take that as a vote of lack of confidence in me."

"That's right," Rockefeller reportedly replied.

Said Perkins later, "George was mad as hell that he wasn't CEO. He was ready to kill Rockefeller."

The change in the bylaws reversed the roles of the president and chairman. In effect, Moore was to be the nominal leader of the bank, but with little authority over bank policy. Henceforth, the president instead of the chairman would preside at meetings of the policy committee and would be responsible for the "formation and execution of policy." A press release sought to disguise the true nature of the move, indicating that no one would be designated chief executive officer. It said the chairman would have "general executive authority," while the president would take on "maximum possible responsibilities." One consequence of Moore's appointment as chairman was that he relinquished direct responsibility for corporate lending.

Rockefeller never publicized the reasons for his decision, but there was little doubt among insiders that he felt uncomfortable with Moore's impulsiveness. Rockefeller may have been remembering the World's Fair loans, the Proudfoot incident, and Moore's tendency to make commitments first and ask questions later, not to mention the fact that Moore was living openly with a woman half his age while seeking a divorce from his wife. After the announcement, Rockefeller reportedly told the board, in his characteristic deadpan manner, "The king is dead, long live the king. Now let's get down to work." The upshot, Rockefeller added, was that he lost two good friends— Moore, for a period, and Wilcox. Wriston, he said, has also "been cooler to me. I can't explain it."

Rockefeller looked for certain traits in a chief executive, he said later: "The way their minds work, ability to analyze facts, to make decisions rather than shilly-shally. To be able to pick people is the most important." A former top Citibank official and friend of Rockefeller's speculated on the reasons for his decision: "George had the misfortune of talking too much. On a personal basis it was the eternal chatter. On a more fundamental basis [Rockefeller] thought Moore would take the bank and grow it too fast. Little did he know what Mr. Wriston's ideas were."

Others in Wriston's shoes might have felt elated. But Wriston felt an ache in the pit of his stomach. With Bobby gone and George clamoring for a divorce, the two men had become closer than ever. Wriston talked about his dilemma with his father, who advised him that there wasn't much he could say or do about it. Wriston assured Moore that he would never disclose to anyone that Moore was not indeed the CEO. "You're Uncle George to everyone in this bank, and we're going to be a team," Wriston told Moore. Wriston let it be known that he didn't approve of the change in the bylaws, and ordered Moore listed first in all documents. According to G. A. Costanzo, who succeeded Wriston as head of the overseas division, Wriston "always treated George as the chairman." While it was clear to most who was really running the bank after July 1, 1967, only a small inner circle knew that Moore was not chief executive officer. In later years, Moore would say, "Wriston was a better man than [I was]. I just got there ahead of him. He's always treated me with more respect than I deserve."

Wriston's triumph was bittersweet for other reasons. He assumed the presidency just after the first anniversary of Bobby's death. He confided to Cassy that Bobby was the real reason he became president. Adding to Wriston's already heavy burden was Stillman Rockefeller, who earlier had pushed the board to change the bylaws to require that directors retire at the age of sixty-five. Now, however, when Rockefeller himself was about to step down, he decided that he wanted to remain on the board for another three years. Making the rounds among the outside directors, he told them of his concern about Wriston's inexperience and Moore's erratic behavior, and said he wanted to stay on "to keep George and Walter from fighting." Said another top official, "Stillman recognized that he would have to control Moore and that his successor would have to do the same." After that, Rockefeller seemed to go out of his way to "make George feel bad," Wriston said later in an interview. Furthermore, in designating Wriston, Rockefeller apparently felt he had earned the right to look over Wriston's shoulder and advise him on how to run the bank. Even on Wriston's first full day on the job, according to former director Peter Grace, Rockefeller sauntered into Wriston's office and mumbled, "Hi, Walt, what's new?"

There is probably no busier day in a CEO's life than the day after his appointment, as he fields congratulatory phone calls, gives interviews, and tries to get organized. There is little time for idle chatter. Gritting his teeth, Wriston glanced at his watch. "It's eight minutes after ten," was his steely reply.

Wriston would have none of Rockefeller's interference. "He gave me the job, and that was damn nice of him," said Wriston later. "It was also very brave, given my age." Wriston would later confess in a talk to colleagues that "I can promise you that at the time we got our jobs, we were not qualified to do them in the judgment of the people who made the decision." But after Rockefeller retired as chairman, no one, most of all Wriston, sought or listened to his advice, which appeared to irk him tremendously. Although some felt Wriston resented Rockefeller for putting him in the awkward position of having to pretend that George Moore was his boss, Wriston was most annoyed by Rockefeller's efforts to be a shadow chairman and by his incessant offers of unsolicited advice.

One of the bits of wisdom Rockefeller attempted to pass on to Wriston was his advice on how to manage the bank's car pool. To Rockefeller, control over the bank's cars was an essential tool for rewarding and punishing employees, and he insisted on approving personally every request for a car. So when Wriston took over, Rockefeller stopped by to advise him how to "run the cars." Rockefeller was unprepared for Wriston's unfriendly answer: "I've got terrible news for you, Stillman. I won't go near the cars. I'm going to put that in the cashier's department and have a dispatcher run it. I don't operate that way."

To Wriston, ex-chairmen were about as useful as yesterday's newspaper. According to acquaintances of both men, he never sent Rockefeller a birthday or Christmas card and found it difficult even to say hello, much less consult with him on matters of any consequence. This hurt Rockefeller deeply, according to his friends. "Wriston did everything but put a sign in the officers' dining room saying 'No former chairmen allowed,' " said a former officer.

After his appointment, Wriston summed up his climb to the top with self-deprecating wit: "My mother had the baby in the right year," he told a reporter. "I am a victim of the lack of foresight of our forebears. Nobody wanted to work for banks in the 1930s. . . . Those of us who came to work for banks in the 1940s found a vacuum in our age group."

For decades, Tommy Wilcox remained bitter about losing the top spot. "I was there thirty-seven years," he said later. "Citibank was my home." And the end of the seven-year horse race didn't calm things between Wriston and Wilcox. Wilcox remarked to another senior officer at the time, "There seems to be a lot of tension around here. I wonder what's causing it."

The other officer replied, "What about you?"

No responsibilities of any substance were given to Wilcox, and in 1971 he resigned from the bank. "The only person I've heard Walter put down was Wilcox," said a Wriston confidant. "He didn't care for Tommy at all." When Wilcox finally left the bank, it was a cause for cheering in the Wriston clan.

After Wriston became president, hordes of people whom he had known only slightly came out of the woodwork seeking to be part of his circle of friends and acquaintances. He liked to tell his friends that before he was elected president he was "kicked out of Quaker Hill," a village near Sherman whose residents had included such notables as Lowell Thomas, Norman Vincent Peale, and Thomas E. Dewey. The community association had rejected Wriston's plans for a new country home because the house was too small.

On his first day as president, Wriston relegated another age-old tradition to the past. To the shock of some of the tradition-bound old-timers, and to the delight of the new recruits, Wriston arrived at work wearing a striped shirt. By day's end, white shirts were out and striped shirts were in. But most of the changes that took place after July 1, 1967, were more of substance than of style. If there was ever any question about whether the chief executive officer was the chief management officer or the chief lending officer, that was settled for all time with the appointment of Wriston. Perhaps more than any other banker of his era, he understood that his role was not to sign off on the biggest loans but to manage the institution. He also took a more scientific approach to management. For example, credit inspection had for years been a very general function conducted as part of an overall operations review of the bank. But under Wriston, said Al Costanzo, this was separated and conducted by auditors specially trained in scrutinizing loans and other credit instruments. Moreover, said Costanzo, the sanctity of the personal lending limit became institutionalized. That meant, he said, that no one, including a banker's boss, could order him to put his initials on a loan. Moreover, as president and later as chairman, Wriston almost always declined to participate in loan negotiations. Although Citibank under Wriston had a policy whereby unresolved disputes between the chief credit officer and a division head were bucked up to the president or chairman, in no more than two instances did that occur.

During the three years following his appointment, Wriston was the inside man, running Citibank on a day-to-day basis, while his mentor George Moore was Mr. Outside, representing the bank to the external world. Wriston saw as his primary task ensuring the long-term survival of an institution operating in an industry whose growth prospects were severely limited. Wriston had cogitated for months over the notion of setting a 15 percent annual earnings growth target, but embraced the idea wholeheartedly only after he got the number two job, according to Jack Heilshorn, who recalled hearing his new boss say, "Net, net. Why the hell not?" Suddenly Citibank was no longer measuring its progress, as reflected in the bank's annual reports, according to how many branches were added, or how big Citibank was, compared with Chase. "Walt said that didn't matter," Heilshorn asserted. "What mattered was making money for stockholders."

Setting the earnings target and the broad mission of the bank was one thing. Getting there was quite another. That goal would have to be accomplished through diversification, both in the locations where the bank operated and in the services that it offered. Wriston would have to put into place a management team not constrained by the Depression-era mind-set. And Wriston would have to reorganize Citibank into a truly market-driven organization. He would later say that he made a "conscious decision" when he became president to "stay home and get the place organized against markets." When he took over, there were no businesses per se. Except for the special industries division, the bank was still organized geographically into districts and regions. Wriston had always favored specialization over geography and had locked horns with Wilcox over this issue for years. He would also have to find a way to enable Citibank to engage in activities that went beyond traditional lending and deposit-taking. To accomplish that, he would in effect have to redesign the American financial services system, which then reflected industry interests more than consumer needs. Wriston looked north to Canada as the prime example of how to expand and diversify geographically. "The first rule of banking is disperse your risk, yet the laws of your country tell you not to," he said. To date, Citibank's efforts to diversify had been spotty and almost always frustrated by government intervention. And sometimes Citibank proved to be its own worst enemy, as in the Mercantile affair.

Just months before Wriston took office, Citibank and other like-minded institutions lost their biggest booster in the bank regulatory establishment. Comptroller of the Currency James Saxon had virtually been chased out of Washington for his bombastic, litigious approach to liberalizing banking rules. Nearly everything he attempted was challenged by lawsuits, most of which were ultimately decided against him. Saxon's successor,

William B. Camp, was not nearly as vociferous in his efforts to liberalize banking. After Saxon left, officials of the agency would say, "Saxon made the fire. Now Camp is cooking over it."

With Saxon out of the picture, banks had to shift to their fallback position and make use of a device called the one-bank holding company. "The formation of the one-bank holding company was a direct consequence of the collapse of the Saxon initiatives," said Carter Golembe, a leading Washington bank consultant. One-bank holding companies were nothing new, but the vast majority of them were small-town miniconglomerates that included everything from the local hardware store to the insurance agency.

In 1956, when Congress moved to regulate bank holding companies, it had purposely exempted the one-bank variety. Specifically, under the Bank Holding Company Act of 1956, a bank holding company was defined as one that owned 25 percent or more of the voting shares of two or more banks. That provision excluded about 117 companies that owned just one bank, a group that included such diverse entities as the United Mine Workers, Montgomery Ward, and even Hershey Foods. The sponsors of that benchmark legislation apparently did not foresee that the children—the banks—would circumvent the law by giving birth to their parents—the holding companies. Anticipating the controversy that was to come, the Fed in 1966 tried unsuccessfully to eliminate the one-bank holding company loophole.

To bankers trying to break out of the industry's legal strongbox, the one-bank holding company seemed like the key, and the opportunities seemed unlimited. In theory at least, banks could now own anything from auto manufacturers to pizza parlors. Ironically, one of the pressures pushing Citibank in this direction was its increased dependence on purchased money in the form of Wriston's own negotiable CD, which drove up the cost of funds for banks and intensified the competition in the bread-and-butter business of banking. Bankers also saw an opportunity in the holding company to set up businesses that would produce fees rather than interest income. Fee income is better than interest income. To earn interest income, unlike fee income, banks have to pay a tax to the Fed known as reserve requirements on deposits.

In early 1967, Citibank lawyers delivered a memo itemizing all the wonderful new activities that a holding company could perform. According to chairman George Moore, they figured that the added expense of the new structure could be paid for just by shifting the traveler's check business out of the bank and into the holding company, eliminating the 18 percent reserve requirement on outstanding traveler's checks. Because the Fed viewed traveler's checks as demand deposits, Citibank operated at a serious competitive disadvantage against American Express, the nation's leading issuer. Bankers were relatively late in discovering this loophole. Many had believed that Saxon would win their battle for new powers and non-bank activities for them, while others were more interested in expanding through mergers with other banks, according to Rodgin Cohen, a top New York bank attorney.

With a holding company, banks could finally achieve some semblance of equality with non-bank financial firms. Wriston was appalled, for example, that a finance company could buy a bank while Citibank couldn't purchase a finance company. He frequently cited the recent acquisition by CIT, the big finance company, of Long Island's Meadow Brook National Bank.

The crux of the matter was that when Wriston assumed the presidency of Citibank, there was really no definition of the "business of banking," a phrase that first appeared in the American legal lexicon in 1838. No one—not the Fed, the states, the Congress, or the Comptroller—had ever really spelled out precisely what a bank was and what it should do. "The business of banking," Wriston told *Fortune* at the time, was no better defined in the late 1960s than it was when "the first banker sat cross-legged on the banks of the Euphrates." He now took it upon himself to define the term, not only for Citibank but also for the rest of the American banking industry. For the remainder of his banking career, Wriston would fight the battle to define that business in Congress, in state legislative chambers, in regulators' conference rooms, in the nation's highest courts, and in the media. This appetite for combat would be the hallmark of his leadership at Citibank.

Wriston generally favored the separation of commercial and investment banking as dictated by Glass-Steagall. But a bank, he believed, needed to be able to sell mutual funds in order to compete with non-bank retail financial services companies. In the court battle to win the right to peddle mutual funds, the federal court in the District of Columbia ruled against Comptroller of the Currency William Camp in the suit brought by a securities industry group, and Citibank soon ceased accepting new accounts.

Citibank was not named in the lawsuit, but after losing the first round, Comptroller Camp informed Citi that the Comptroller's office would not continue to fight the bank's battle without its financial support. Wriston rarely shied away from a court fight. He took a keen interest in legal matters, read attorney's briefs with intense interest, considered himself the "world's greatest amateur lawyer," said a colleague, and "got right down to the guts of the law as it applied to the edges he was pushing on." Within a week, according to then counsel Westbrook Murphy, Citibank's lawyers showed up with a motion to appeal. To press its case in the U.S. Court of Appeals, Citibank hired the august Archibald Cox, who challenged the decision on the grounds that it applied only to the Comptroller. Wriston was skeptical. "That's like kissing through a blanket," he reportedly told one of Cox's partners. Nonetheless, as a testimony to his awesome legal skills, Cox succeeded in persuading the appeals court to reverse the lower court ruling, and in November 1969 Citibank once again began accepting applications. But the thrill of victory would be brief. The next stop was the Supreme Court of the United States.

George Moore had been the first Citibank top executive, and perhaps the first in American banking, to "inventory" people. Both he and Walter Wriston believed in building bench strength, and felt that even if they hired twice as

many people as they needed, those who quit would remain friends and customers of Citibank. To Wriston, the contents of his fifteenth-floor "corporate
property room" were far more valuable than all the cash in the bank's vaults.
On display on a board in the locked room were the names and photographs
of hundreds of Citibank's hottest prospects. For the next seventeen years,
while Wriston was in command, he and his lieutenants would spend thousands of hours there, shuffling the names and faces on the board in an effort
to pick the right man or woman for the right job. Colleagues would often find
him in this room, leaning back in his chair and gazing in silent contemplation
at the faces on the board. In 1967, just three of those 350 stars were women.
By the late seventies, many more would be. Less than a year after Wriston
became president, Citibank appointed its first woman branch manager and
its first black woman officer, moves that would have been almost unthinkable
a couple of years earlier. Still, by the late sixties the highest-ranking black in
the bank was an assistant vice president. Wriston was determined to remedy
that as well.

Everyone agreed that there was something cold and crass about the
term "corporate property." Wriston admitted that "it was a terrible term, yet
all of us sitting around couldn't think of a better one." The idea, which Wriston credited to personnel chief Robert Feagles, arose out of the recognition
that with the bank and its contingent of trainees growing so rapidly, some
mechanism had to be devised to make sure that the most promising officers
didn't get lost in the shuffle. Wriston knew that managers a few layers down
in the corporate pecking order often hid their best and brightest from view
out of fear of losing them, just as his own superiors had attempted to hide
him twenty years earlier when he was a junior inspector in the comptroller's
division. As an additional check on that managerial tendency, Wriston used
to evaluate his top managers in part on the number of people from their areas
they could produce for the board. So, every quarter, Wriston, Moore, and
their senior colleagues would meet in the room to discuss the progress of
the people on the board, what slots were open, and who was available to
fill them.

IQ was a religion in Wriston's Citibank, and brash young M.B.A.'s
competed for time with Wriston to show how smart they were. But at least
some of the young bankers-to-be were shocked to learn that Wriston, an avid
Beatles fan, enjoyed talking about popular culture more than interest rates.
At one cocktail party for some of the bank's hottest prospects, Wriston didn't
want to talk about banking, recalled former Citibanker Byron Stinson. He
wanted to talk about Jefferson Airplane, the rock band. "I had never heard of
Jefferson Airplane," Stinson admitted, "and was surprised that he knew who
they were." When Stinson revealed to Wriston his ignorance of the group, "I
got the feeling that I had dropped in his esteem."

These social gatherings were another opportunity for Wriston to keep
his finger on the pulse of the bank and pick up rumblings of problems in its
vast reaches. Perhaps more than any Citibank CEO before him, Wriston
maintained his ties with colleagues he had long since passed by on the road to

stardom. Having served in the State Department and the Army Signal Corps, Wriston was acutely aware of the need for timely and accurate intelligence. From his father he had also learned that the head of an organization could learn a lot simply by listening.

While it might not have been apparent at the time, Citibank's appointment of Al Costanzo as head of the overseas division was in many ways as significant as the election of Wriston himself. But for all Wriston's efforts, the overseas division was still a relatively small contributor to total profits when he passed the baton to Costanzo. In 1966, the division generated only about $18 million in remitted earnings, or just 17 percent of net operating earnings. Moreover, the division still retained remnants of the colonial culture when Costanzo took over. District vice presidents continued to rule over their regions like feudal lords over medieval fiefdoms. In 1967 the highest loan limit was $500,000 in Buenos Aires, and $300,000 elsewhere. Country heads had to obtain head-office approval for amounts over those ceilings. That was a quantum leap over the situation Wriston found back in 1956, but not enough for Citibank to become a serious player in corporate lending in Brazil or anywhere else.

Determined to jolt the overseas division out of that mind-set, Costanzo ordered his managers around the world to conduct studies of local markets and funds flows so as to identify new opportunities, a move that gave even more authority to local officers. Though Wriston had helped women achieve gains in the overseas division and had launched a program to bring more foreign nationals into the officer ranks, there were still only two classes of overseas employees: Americans and local staff. According to Costanzo, an American employee could join Citibank in Argentina and earn as much as a local employee who had worked there for fifteen years. Eliminating such inequities among overseas staff was one of Costanzo's top priorities.

Wriston delegated to Costanzo the task of shaking hands with kings and princes and, perhaps most important, central bankers and finance ministers. According to Costanzo, Wriston was never especially fond of overseas travel: "He did it, but I don't think he was the kind of guy who enjoyed going to Saudi and sitting on the floor of a tent and eating camel and goat [meat] with his hands."

With the energetic assistance of the worldly-wise Costanzo, Wriston would lead Citibank, and the entire international banking community, slowly but surely into the perilous world of cross-border lending. Just as U.S. bankers in the 1950s gradually grew comfortable with the practice of lending money to domestic enterprises for more than a year, those same bankers now would begin to cross another major risk hurdle by making term loans in dollars to foreign governments and enterprises. Indeed, all of the components of cross-border lending were now falling into place. The appointment of Costanzo and the election of Wriston coincided with the surge in the prospects of a number of Third World nations, notably in Latin America, whose so-called economic miracle was gaining widespread notice in the United States. The macroeconomic indicators of nations like Brazil were apparently moving in the right direction, and fat returns could be made on loans to these countries. There seemed to be no good reason to deny these countries what would become a principal financing mechanism for development.

Writing in an internal Citibank publication, Costanzo waxed enthusiastic about the economic progress made by many of the Latin nations over the previous seven years and their prospects for future growth. In 1960, he observed, "we were still debating whether inflation was a fact of life for developing countries and whether growth was possible without inflation. This is a dead issue today. Growth with stability is now the declared policy of all Latin American governments." In economic terms, Latin America "has done far better in the sixties than we had any right to expect at the beginning of the period." Though economic growth in Argentina, Brazil, and Uruguay during the 1960s had been disappointing, he pointed out that "promising changes are under way in those countries." He projected that the Latin American market would surge from the $100 billion level in 1967 to $250 or $300 billion by the end of the century." Latin America, he wrote, "has to produce people who know how to govern." And today, he observed, "Argentina is on the threshold of achieving its full potential." Unfortunately, Argentina would remain on that threshold for years to come.

Many bankers viewed cross-border lending as a natural by-product of the surge in world trade and commerce in the 1960s, and the internationalization of banking and foreign exchange markets and capital flows that accompanied that surge. The erosion of U.S. balance of payments helped produce a dramatic expansion of the Euromarkets, and the coming of age of the offshore funding center and syndicated floating Eurodollar loans, such as those Citibank had made to Shell and IBM. By the early 1970s, Eurodollar loans would become the primary instrument for international lending.

Costanzo was confident that by maintaining personal contacts with the monetary officials of client countries he could determine when economic policies were taking a troublesome turn, and perhaps even influence their direction. "We'd back away from countries when we didn't like the policies," he said later. His confidence in the future of countries like Brazil was also strongly influenced by his experience with them in the mid-1950s, when the ministries of finance and the central banks had virtually no trained economic policymakers. "In 1955," Costanzo said later, Brazil "wouldn't have had anyone domestically to tell them what to do. It would have had to hire outside experts."

Coincidentally, Sterling Bunnell, Citibank's chief credit officer and one of its most vociferous opponents of cross-border lending, had retired just months before the appointments of Wriston and Costanzo. Bunnell had been responsible for extricating Citibank from the bad loans made to Germany's Weimar Republic, according to Wriston. Former officers recalled that at his 1966 retirement dinner Bunnell warned against abandoning the traditional mission of international banking. At that same dinner Bunnell said, "I want to leave one message behind: do not lend money to governments abroad and depart at all from the tradition of sticking to trade. If you do that, it's going to come home to roost." Said Robert Hoguet, former head of the bank's special industries division, "If Bunnell had been running the bank, we would not have been lending cross border." Bunnell's retirement marked the end of an era in other respects as well. In 1966, Citibank's charge-offs on bum loans amounted to a mere $12.4 million on a loan portfolio of $8.8 billion. Bunnell recalled vividly the Citibank experience in the 1930s when Peru and Chile and other Latin countries defaulted on bonds underwritten by the National City Company. History, like statistics, can be used selectively to prove a point, and Wriston believed the experience of the United States as an undeveloped country was the more relevant historical analogy. During the nineteenth century, this country defaulted massively on its debts to the Europeans. But without British and European capital, he said, the United States would never have grown into the world's premier economic power.

Although Moore would later contend that Wriston "broke Moore's rules" in lending heavily cross border to Third World countries, Wriston contended that no one was more enthusiastic than Moore about lending to Latin nations, especially Mexico. "George Moore wanted to fund the Mexican government," Wriston claimed later. "He was very close to Mexico, a great fan of Mexico." It was George Moore, Wriston said, who backed the first term loan to Mexico in the late 1960s, adding that Moore seemed to forget about that later. According to Jack Clark, who succeeded Costanzo as head of Latin America, that was a $50 million loan to Pemex, the Mexican state-owned oil company. The Bank of America, which had a close relationship to the government of Mexico, had already lent Pemex $100 million, Clark explained. The loan was made at Clark's urging. There was no rule—even one against cross-border lending—that couldn't be broken to gain a leg up on a rival. Whatever the role played by Bank of America in prompting Citibank to lend to Pemex, there was little doubt in the minds of most international financiers of Wriston's influence on the rest of the industry.

In fact, cross-border lending picked up slowly. According to internal Citibank documents, cross-border exposure by the late 1960s was no more than $10 million in the Philippines and perhaps $6 million in India, and it was considered a major stretch to even consider lending $100 million to Japan. In 1967, Citibank, in recognition of the improved outlook for Argentina, led a consortium of eleven top American banks in making a $100 million standby credit to that country to support its efforts at stabilization and economic reform. In another sign of its faith in Brazil, Citi and several other banks established Investbanco to provide medium- and long-term financing to private Brazilian borrowers. By all accounts, Costanzo had a profound influence on Wriston's view of Third World dollar lending. Said former Citibanker Robert Meyjes, "Walter had unbridled faith in Al Costanzo. There's no question Al influenced Walt enormously."

Wriston pushed to diversify Citibank and redefine the business of banking, but there were few opportunities to do so, and he had to fight for nearly every change. One exception occurred in late 1967, almost like a surprise Christmas gift for a risk-loving CEO.

That year, populist House Banking Committee chairman Wright Patman was seeking to close the door, at least halfway, on the opportunity for banks to make venture capital investments through wholly owned small business investment companies. Wriston and Moore were determined not to be left out in the cold. Like their move to set up the San Francisco Edge Act office, their decision to seek an SBIC license and establish a venture capital unit was a case of avoiding the loss of a power before they knew exactly how the power would be used. "I think Citi wanted to get in because Patman wanted to keep them out," said Russ Carson, a young Citibanker who later became head of the venture capital unit. "That fit the philosophy of Walter Wriston." In December 1967, just days before the maximum bank ownership was to be cut from 100 percent to 50 percent, Citibank obtained its license. It would prove to be one of the most profitable moves Citibank ever made. Ironically, twenty years later, Wriston's successor would be forced to dip into the unrealized profits earned by the venture capital unit to dress up an income statement suffering from losses caused by excessive cross-border and real estate loans.

Like so many other fledgling businesses at Citibank, venture capital began modestly, with $5 million in capital, a secretary, and two professionals—Russ Carson and Phil Smith, the group's first head. Citibank was not the first bank to start up a venture capital unit; First Chicago, Chase, and Bank of America were also in the business. But a quarter century later, about $2 billion of the estimated $30 billion in America's venture capital pool, according to Carson, was being managed by former Citibank venture capital specialists. And the unit would play a pivotal role in some of the nation's legendary postwar start-ups, including Cray Research, Datapoint, James River, Federal Express, and Genentech, itself later headed by an alumnus of the unit. The venture capital group found prospects by beating the bushes and receiving referrals from the commercial lending units. Like a bitch in heat, they attracted would-be entrepreneurs from miles around. One of the wackier proposals—and one that was politely declined—was a plan to recycle pig manure using a chemical process that would purportedly enable the pig to eat the recycled product. When the venture capital unit was folded into the First National City Overseas Investment Corporation, set up in 1961 to take equity kickers on overseas loans, it inherited a Costa Rican shrimp farming operation that was left high and dry when the shrimp harvest failed. One officer spent a year trying to sell the operation's shrimp boats, and Citibank ultimately recovered most of its original investment, according to Carson. Citibank's first serious problem resulted from backing the launch of *Psychol-*

ogy Today magazine, which went from being one of the hottest items in the
Citibank portfolio to the brink of bankruptcy. Citibank lost nearly $400,000
on that investment. "We thought we had a winner on our hands," Carson
recalled.

Fearing that Citibank wouldn't continue to capitalize the investment
group, Phil Smith placed the original $5 million in twenty-four investments in
the first year. "I think a lot of people in corporate banking thought it was
crazy," said Carson, who was appointed head of the unit by the time he was
thirty. But venture capital did get another $5 million and by 1969 had in-
vested in twenty-five companies. "In the first couple of years we really didn't
know what we were doing. None of us had any training, and virtually all of us
were M.B.A.'s just out of school. We backed a number of guys who didn't
have any track record." According to Carson, the unit didn't write off an
investment until the early 1970s.

Wriston's involvement in the venture capital unit was largely philosophical. In fact, the unit's godfather was William Spencer, a rugged Coloradan who for years had headed the bank's prestigious oil and gas department.
Citibank Venture Capital, said Citibanker William Comfort, was "the catalyst for the venture capital business in the United States."

It was not easy for Walter Wriston to be a widower and the heir to the throne
at Citibank at the same time. After Bobby's death, Wriston was "worth
something less than nothing, a basket case" as he admitted years later. All the
emotional control instilled in the son by the father was relinquished with the
sudden loss of his ebullient wife and companion. Within a year, however,
Wriston faced up to the task of settling the inevitable paperwork occasioned
by her death. But for the rising star of Citibank, the burden of such tasks was
lightened by proximity to the august law firm of Shearman & Sterling.

The relationship between Shearman & Sterling and Citibank dated
back to the days of James Stillman. Frank Vanderlip, in his memoirs, described Stillman and John Sterling, the firm's co-founder, as "Siamese twins"
who talked to each other constantly. Both men were eccentrics in their own
way. For his part, Sterling was so afraid of dying that he barricaded the doors
and windows of his home with steel bars and refused to go on fishing expeditions with his business associates, choosing to do his angling from a bridge
while his friends headed out to sea. Over the years, the head of the law firm
and the chairman of the bank were so close that it was often unclear whether
the bank ran Shearman & Sterling or vice versa. As the story goes, the meeting to fire Charlie Mitchell took place not at 55 Wall Street but at the home of
a Shearman & Sterling partner. Tight as the relationship was, the two had
apparently never been bound in marriage, at least at the top levels. Soon,
however, Wriston's twenty-eight-year-old in-house lawyer would take up residence at 870 UN Plaza as the new Mrs. Walter B. Wriston.

Wriston was never one to stew over a decision. The first time around, he had proposed virtually on the spot. This time, he thought about it for five weeks, according to his daughter, Cassy.

Tom Ford was the Shearman & Sterling lawyer who handled wills and estate matters for important clients. Once, when Ford and Wriston met to iron out some details on the will, "in walked this pretty girl," whom Ford introduced as Kathy Dineen. "My light went on" for two reasons, Wriston said. For one, her father, Robert Dineen, as it turned out, was chairman of the Northwestern Mutual Life Insurance Company, whom Wriston had taught how to make ship loans during his days in the transportation department. "He made millions of dollars with that information and never opened an account with us. It used to burn me up. I'd spend hours with this guy, and they had their account with Morgan," notwithstanding the fact that Wriston's father, Henry, was a trustee of the insurance company. It also dawned on Wriston that this was the very same woman who used to pick up Henry when her father traveled to New York for meetings of Northwestern's general agents. "So Dad would come over to our house for dinner and say, 'I met this terrific girl. She's got a five handicap, was at the top of her class in law school, she's pretty, and blah, blah, blah.' We got tired of hearing about this." And so when Kathy Dineen arrived that morning, Wriston knew exactly who she was even though he had never met her. "Being the character I am, I began to make snide remarks about the Northwestern Mutual Life Insurance Company." Dineen's face flushed as she grew more and more angry; Ford kicked her under the table while muttering, "This is a client," out of the corner of his mouth.

"You know, I spent the best years of my life teaching those turkeys how to make ship loans," Wriston told her. "They made millions of dollars, and they never opened an account [with us]. It's got to be the cheapest outfit in the history of the world." He said later that he knew she was "boiling mad."

Dineen later phoned her father and told him, "I met this turkey Wriston," and then recounted the story about the ship loans. "You know, he's right," her father replied. "That's what we did."

Wriston's initial anger, released after fifteen years, soon turned to affection. For a forty-eight-year-old man brought up to value privacy and discretion, the experience of dating—and dating a woman twenty years younger than he—was awkward. The couple taxed their imagination to avoid the known and likely haunts of business associates and casual acquaintances. On their first date in public, on New Year's Day 1968, they went to the Café Renaissance, a West Side watering hole featuring flamenco guitarists, a place they felt would surely be off the bankers' and lawyers' beaten bath. They were barely seated when Cedric Grant, manager of Citibank's Jidda branch, strolled in with his wife. From Wriston's shocked expression, Grant quickly concluded that this was not something to be discussed over the water cooler in the corridors of Citibank. Grant's lips were sealed.

Grant's appearance at the café was only the first of two shocks Wriston received that New Year's Day. The second was President Lyndon Johnson's announcement that he was escalating his war against the mounting balance-of-payments deficit by attempting to control international capital flows. Restrictions on financing the overseas investments of U.S. corporations that previously were voluntary would now be mandatory, giving the Eurodollar markets yet another boost by driving U.S. banks to London to book loans for such purposes. Moreover, overseas subsidiaries of U.S. companies would have to repatriate earnings over certain levels. Among other things, Johnson asked Americans to put off for two years all nonessential travel outside the Western Hemisphere. The accelerating growth of the Euromarkets—itself the engine that would be largely responsible for propelling Citibank's global expansion—continued to be driven by what Wriston regarded as bad policy. Paradoxically, U.S. banks enjoyed an edge over their British counterparts because they paid less for their dollar deposits. But little by little, U.S. policy was chipping away at New York's position as the world's money center.

In a widely publicized speech in Milan later that month, Wriston attacked Johnson's policies, saying, "Foreign exchange controls in peacetime never have operated effectively, and man being what he is, they never will." At a time when some were hailing the multinational corporation as an engine of global economic development, Wriston observed that some of the same people were "at work privately deploring foreign capital in their particular industry or in their particular country." Yet another example, he said, was the tendency to "build nontariff barriers to trade as rapidly as we destroy the tariff barriers." The United States, he urged, needed to bring its balance of payments under control, "but markets and world economies would adjust far better if the United States achieves this goal through monetary and fiscal policies instead of proliferation of controls. . . . History teaches that the means employed do in effect shape the ends," Wriston concluded, "and it is almost impossible to have a good result achieved through bad means." Wriston and Citibank used every means at their disposal to condemn the controls, including editorializing on the subject in its annual reports, but their pleas apparently fell on deaf ears. After plummeting from their 1966 highs, interest rates began to shoot up again in mid-1967 and through 1968. By late May, gold had soared to a record $42.60 an ounce. Troubled by the inflationary spiral, Wriston had reluctantly testified in favor of a tax increase in September 1967 before the House Ways and Means Committee, but by June 1968, with no tax bill in sight, he gave up hope that even that would have much impact. "Rates are going up," he told *Newsweek* in May, "and will probably go higher. The tax boost might stop the rise, but I can't see rates dropping even if we get it."

In the modern history of world banking and finance, no conclave was more epochal than the 1944 Bretton Woods conference, where the world's economic leaders designed the postwar financial system. Twenty-four years after that meeting, Wriston and Citibank's senior advisers, including those who would form his top management team, gathered in February 1968 on Paradise Island in the Bahamas to chart the course for Citibank for the next seventeen years. Unlike the earlier meeting in Bretton Woods, the gathering on Paradise Island received no publicity and never amounted to so much as a footnote in world economic history. Nonetheless, the decisions taken there would not only create the nation's most powerful banking organization but would alter forever the American banking industry.

The meeting occurred at a turning point in American banking. The TEMPO study had confirmed the feeling that consumers were going to grow in importance as a source of deposits and that one important way to capture them was with the credit card. At the time, earnings from consumer banking represented only a small fraction of the total, and according to Costanzo, "we felt 20 percent was about where we would try to get to." In the space of a few days on Paradise Island, Citibank's top management moved to create a one-bank holding company, decided to abolish the decades-old organization based on geography into one focused on customers and markets, assigned top priority to cleaning up the antiquated back office, and agreed that consumers would have to be milked to supply a greater portion of the bank's earnings. Said planner Jack Heilshorn, "Wriston wanted to change the earnings momentum. He wanted to leave a big shadow, which he did. A lot of people got caught up in the excitement."

To outsiders, Citibank's business initiatives appeared to be the result of careful planning and calculation. But according to Wriston, a believer in the power of serendipity, some of the boldest moves happened entirely by chance. At Paradise Island, Wriston recalled, "we sat around for two days debating whether we should form a holding company." Costanzo and Wriston were all for it; Laeri, the traditional banker, was neutral to mildly opposed. Tommy Wilcox was dead set against it, probably for no other reason than because Wriston was for it. Wilcox "didn't see the big picture," said George Moore later.

The debate was even. But Moore, dressed in Bermuda shorts, was deep in thought. Wriston figured that his colleague was probably contemplating his pending divorce and upcoming remarriage. Then the phone rang. It was Onassis on the line. His yacht, the *Christina,* was anchored in the harbor, and he was calling to invite the Citibank executives aboard for dinner. "Everyone thought what fun that would be," Wriston said later. Moore was fascinated by Onassis. Since he had relinquished lending responsibility, his friendship with Onassis deepened, and he had spent some of his most pleasant days with Ari and Charon on Skorpios, the shipowner's private island. The invitation from Onassis quickly lit a fire under Moore. "We're going to the yacht!" he said excitedly. As Wriston recalled, Moore said, "What's the issue we're talking about? The holding company? Got to have one, got to have one!" In Wriston's view, the phone call from Onassis jolted Moore into participation in the debate and broke the deadlock in favor of the pro–holding company faction.

That decision, Wriston said later, "was made by a narrow margin." Indeed, one-bank holding companies had many detractors inside and outside the bank. In the two-year debate over the proper role for holding companies, Wriston rarely, if ever, conceded that the structure was flawed in any way, but he did admit to colleagues that the critics had "many valid points." He later told a meeting of Citibank officers that "we went the holding company route because it was the only way out of the geographic box in which we found ourselves, not because we admire the structure." When Citibank tried to offer travel or data processing services or commingled funds, rivals sued Citi and its regulators, Wriston explained later to a Senate panel. Such challenges were usually avoided by using a holding company subsidiary, he said.

Although Citibank wasn't the first to set up a holding company, its aggressive use of the entity prompted other institutions to follow suit, vastly expanding the geographic and legal boundaries of American banking. Many regard that day on Paradise Island as one of the most important in U.S. banking history. "It was absolutely epochal," said William Spencer. Indeed, with the one-bank holding company, bankers thought they had caught the brass ring and that their stodgy institutions would be turned overnight into one-stop financial supermarkets. As it turned out, however, their euphoria wouldn't last long.

According to former corporate secretary Carl Desch, the Citibankers quickly wound up the meeting and proceeded to the *Christina,* where they were greeted by Onassis, whose guest on that cruise was Maria Callas. The yacht was filled with French beauties, there were seven glasses for different kinds of wine, and "eighty-two guys in starched white uniforms," Desch recalled.

That night, on board the *Christina,* Wriston let Onassis in on his secret plans to marry Kathy Dineen. It was, after all, the marrying season. George Moore would marry Charon Crosson in the fall, and on October 20, 1968, Onassis would marry not Maria Callas but Jacqueline Kennedy, who joined Ari on the *Christina* in May. As part of the Onassis-Kennedy nuptial pact, Onassis gave Jackie $3 million in nontaxable municipal bonds in 1968 when rates were about 4½ percent. Rates continued to move higher, and a year later Onassis and trust department chief Robert Hoguet spread them out on the floor of Hoguet's office to price them. Onassis was a shipper, not a bondman. He had given his new wife munis instead of taxables to avoid a joint tax return. But by now the value of the wedding package had plummeted 20 percent. "I should have given her a tanker instead," Onassis sighed.

Onassis wasn't the only one who took a bath on government securities in the late 1960s. U.S. banks, including Citibank, traditionally had invested heavily in long-term Treasury and municipal securities. In an era of stable interest rates, these were seen as safe and secure investments that could be sold without loss when loan demand rose. But John Exter, Citibank's Chicken Little, had seen the inflationary pressure building for years and pleaded with Moore and Citibank's short-term interest rate committee to dump the government obligations. By 1966, Exter's worst fears had materialized. Over the next four years, the bank lost more than $33 million on securities transactions, nearly twice what it lost in loans in the same period. George Moore would later confess to colleagues that one of the bank's biggest mistakes was "tuning out" Exter.

Around this time, Wriston had bought a new candy-red Corvette, a car as supercharged as its owner's bank. Sometime later, during a period of credit expansion, Exter spotted Wriston with his pride and joy and said that he was still driving a five-year-old Buick. Wriston suggested that he buy himself a new car. "They'll be much cheaper next year," said Exter. "Why is that?" Wriston inquired. "When the great depression comes, because of this horrible expansion of credit, it will make 1933 look like a picnic," said Exter. "I'll be able to get a car for nothing."

There was other business to be attended to on Paradise Island. One of the thorniest problems facing Wriston and Citibank was surging operating expenses and the Stone Age systems Citibank had for running the bank's back office. The problem had been building for years, but it was now exacerbated by the mountain of paperwork generated by Wall Street's bull market. Citibank was struggling to process three million transactions a day using the methods of the 1920s. Unanswered correspondence and customer inquiries were piling up to the ceiling. There was a growing recognition that drastic action needed to be taken. That awareness was certainly raised to a higher level when, as the story goes, the back office lost a check for $20 million that was later found in a trash basket. Wriston observed later, "We were running wide open and out of control."

Everyone agreed that Citibank's grandiose plan to dominate world banking couldn't proceed until the back office monster was wrestled to the ground. The man Wriston was eyeing for that assignment was William Ira Spencer. The well-respected cigar-smoking oil and gas chief had, in 1965, been placed in charge of the special industries division. In that role, Spencer had sat at the top of the bank's social pecking order. In the status hierarchy, the special industries group was followed by overseas and the *Fortune* 500. From there it was a big drop to branch banking and a free fall to operations, and Spencer was a customer man who had never even set foot in operations. But Wriston felt he had the grit needed for the job.

Knowing that Spencer would not jump for joy over the new assignment, Wriston waited for the right moment to broach the delicate subject. The decision in Nassau to focus on operating costs also represented another banking industry watershed. Operating costs had always been viewed passively by banks. That, of course, was possible before inflation began to rear its ugly head. Some seven years later, Wriston would cite Nassau as the turning point in the shift from "passive administration to active management of the cost base. We have moved from basically a zero information base to an increasingly sophisticated financial and management accounting system."

Wriston thought he'd found the right moment when he and Spencer were strolling along a beach on Paradise Island. When Wriston raised the subject Spencer became furious. But he was well aware of the consequences of turning down a request from the man who would be his boss for the next fourteen years. He knew that if he declined he could give up any hope of advancement and, indeed, should be prepared to find a new job.

"I thought he'd give me a right hook," Wriston recalled later. "He picked up a rock and threw it, and as far as I know that rock is still in the air." Spencer would say later that he "cried for two weeks" before accepting the assignment to the department that he later called the "greased pig." Nonetheless, Spencer took over the operating group in November 1968. Shortly thereafter, while walking with Spencer on Manhattan's East Side, Wriston first hinted to him, in an offhand manner, that Spencer would be his choice for the presidency of the bank when Moore retired.

Spencer, then fifty, was typical of the self-made men from ordinary roots with whom Wriston preferred to surround himself. Powerfully built with a viselike handshake, Spencer was a man's man who had grown up on a Colorado cattle ranch. After graduating from Colorado College, he had traveled to New York for the first time at the behest of three spinster teachers who asked him to escort them to the 1939 World's Fair. A college administrator suggested that three weeks with these women might get "a little dull" and had offered to write letters recommending him for Wall Street jobs. "I went to Trinity Church and looked down Wall Street and something clicked," said Spencer later. After twelve years at Chemical Bank, he had quit when a memo was circulated stripping his vacationing boss of much of his authority. "I decided if they would do that to a senior vice president, this was no place for me," Spencer said later. A workaholic with a chronic back problem, he kept in shape by climbing fifteen flights of stairs backwards. Spencer was also an insomniac who arrived for work at 6:00 A.M., more than three hours before Wriston.

More at home hunting big game in Alaska or Africa than on the fifteenth floor of 399 Park, Spencer filled his office at Citibank with the mounted heads of antelope, deer, even a rare African bongo, objects that overflowed from the trophy room at his home in Westchester's Sleepy Hollow, where, as Wriston put it, "there's an old lion looking down at you from the balcony, and greater erdu or lesser erdu and a wily whatever all around." Two massive elephant tusks sat at either end of his leather sofa, and a bronzed leopard skull decorated the coffee table. On his wall was mounted the big game hunter's grand slam: the heads of four species of North American mountain sheep. Spencer's secretary once told the bank's employee newspaper that "the hardest part of this job is remembering the names of the animals."

The rocket scientists from TEMPO, among others, had driven home to Citibank the importance of the consumer and the credit card, something that would soon force modernization of bank operations. But that effort suffered a setback shortly after Wriston and his colleagues returned home from Paradise Island. On very flimsy anti-trust grounds, the Department of Justice had been fighting Citibank's purchase of Carte Blanche, the travel and entertainment card, for years. Citibank finally caved in under government pressure and, in April 1968, sold its one-half interest in Carte Blanche for a respectable profit to the Avco Corporation, which was trying to build a financial services business.

To Citibank, Carte Blanche was a prime example of the need for a holding company. Citibank, Moore observed, couldn't even lend the Carte Blanche Corporation money to fund its operations. Wriston had always claimed that the fact that the credit card had not been invented by a bank demonstrated the banking industry's tendency to fall asleep at the switch. Citibank's own early efforts to produce a viable credit card were marked by failure as well. Just as the holding company debate got back on track serendipitously, so did Citibank's effort to create a profitable credit card.

In August 1967, Citibank introduced a piece of plastic known as the Everything card. This was Citibank's answer to the BankAmericard (the predecessor of Visa), invented by Bank of America, and Master Charge, which was set up as an alternative to the BankAmericard. Though Citibank was the first New York bank to offer its customers a general-purpose card, it failed dismally in its attempts to sell the card to other banks. The Everything card was a dud, but Citibank in the late 1960s couldn't figure out why. The end of Everything occurred quite by accident, as a result of a conversation Wriston had with a banker friend late one night when he was in Cincinnati on business. The other banker explained that he had just returned from California, where he had tried unsuccessfully to use the Everything card to pay for gas at a service station. The attendant said he had never heard of the card. The banker observed that a guy pumping gas won't recognize more than one or two cards, and if there's any trouble he'll tell you they're junk. "All of these cards are going to be taken at the point of sale by people who are not Rhodes scholars," the banker said, adding that if Citibank hoped to make it in the credit card business it would have to join Master Charge or Bank-Americard. The basic problem was that the Everything Card lacked national-brand recognition; it was a local card aimed at New York–area residents and merchants.

Wriston found the logic tough to dispute. "I went home and said [to my colleagues], 'This fellow makes so much sense I can't believe it. What's the story?' " Wriston's men told him that even though Manufacturers Hanover Trust had joined Master Charge, the credit card's charter required them to take anyone, even Citibank. But Manny Hanny's John McGillicuddy was furious and lectured Wriston that his bank had the exclusive right to be New York's Master Charge bank. So Wriston calmly picked up the phone and called his friend Richard Cooley, the West Coast banker who had helped found Master Charge. "Hey, Cooley," Wriston said. "Good news. Citibank's going to join Master Charge."

"We kidded around for a while," Wriston recalled. "They [the card company] were kind of between a rock and a hard place. Legally they couldn't stop us," Wriston said. In November 1968, "we flipped into Master Charge because of a fellow in Cincinnati who was smarter than we were."

Portending the debt-ridden society of the 1980s, Wriston later proclaimed to *Business Week,* "Our job is to help people spend money, not to save it."

Kathy Dineen was having a tough time keeping her big secret from colleagues at Shearman & Sterling, where associates labored seventy hours a week on legal briefs. When her weekend attendance started to slip, Kathy was taken to task by her boss, Tom Ford. The awkwardness wouldn't last long, however. On March 14, 1968, Walter Wriston and Kathy Dineen were married. "I feel like I've always known him," Kathy Wriston would reflect in later years.

Irving Shapiro, a lawyer who later become chairman of Du Pont and a Citibank director, remarked that "any banker who marries his lawyer can't be all bad." And the standing joke in New York legal circles was that Shearman & Sterling had become a "full service law firm." Wriston had managed to keep his wedding plans a secret from even his closest business associates. Kathy's brother, Robert Dineen, also a Shearman & Sterling lawyer, was aware she was dating Wriston, but even he learned of the marriage plans less than two weeks before the wedding, while he was in Algeria on business. The overseas call came not from his sister but from the senior Shearman & Sterling partner. Dineen replied that he wouldn't be able to attend the wedding. "You *have* to come home," his boss ordered. "They are our *clients.*"

The wedding and reception were strictly private, limited to members of the immediate family. Even Wriston intimate Carl Desch found out about the marriage quite by accident. He happened to be having dinner at the Sky Club, atop the Pan Am building, when the wedding party arrived after the reception. "When [Wriston] doesn't want to tell you something, he won't tell you," said a friend. "Nobody knew he was going to get married, and nobody knew it was Kathy," the friend added.

Coming less than two years after Bobby's death, Wriston's remarriage stood in ironic parallel to his father's second marriage twenty years earlier. And as Walter prepared to do the same, he remembered that Bobby herself had encouraged him to go easy on his father and embrace his stepmother as a member of the family. Cassy Wriston reacted better to her father's plans to remarry than Wriston himself had to his father's remarriage. Cassy said later that her father sat her down and "asked me how I felt about it. I told him, 'I think it's wonderful—go right ahead.'"

When Wriston decided to remarry, he wrote letters explaining his decision to members of the Brengle family, including his brother-in-law, Richard. "He didn't have to do that," said Brengle later. The Brengle family would continue to endure tragedy after tragedy over the next two years. In 1970, two years after Mrs. Brengle's death, Bobby's father and sister Jackie also died. Within an hour after hearing of Jackie Brengle's death, Cassy Wriston was on her uncle's doorstep, Bible in hand. For the new Mrs. Wriston, Bobby would be a tough act to follow.

Later, Kathy Wriston said wryly that Walter married her to finally get the Northwestern Mutual account. And Walter kidded her that she had really married his father. To be sure, the affection that the elder Wriston felt for his new daughter-in-law was returned in kind, although she almost always called him Dr. Wriston. "I always worshiped [Walter's] father," Kathy Wriston said later. "He had this twinkle in his eye. He'd always said to me, 'Call often.' " Her own father, Robert, shared her awe of Henry Wriston. Mr. Dineen had risen to the top ranks of American insurance executives without a college education and always felt he had missed out on something. So he passed the time at Sunday mass reading Henry Wriston's books and speeches.

Shortly after the Wristons were married, J. P. Morgan & Company, where Kathy Wriston had worked during summer vacations from law school and where her father's Northwestern Mutual Life did its banking, asked her to take her checking and savings accounts elsewhere. At that time, the chairman of the venerable Morgan Bank was John Meyer, known to fellow bankers as John "Morgan" Meyer to distinguish him from the Meyer at the Mellon Bank, who, appropriately, was nicknamed John "Mellon" Meyer. John "Morgan" Meyer was as serious as his institution, and when he and Wriston met for lunch shortly after Kathy Wriston received the letter from Morgan, Wriston tweaked his competitor about the incident. "Gee, you threw my bride out of your bank," Wriston chided. Appalled by the news, Meyer bolted from his table and phoned the bank, eventually locating the officer who was responsible. Meyer made a practice of jotting notes over the weekend on small pieces of white paper that he would distribute to various bank officers on Monday morning. "They [Morgan bankers] would say it would snow on Monday morning," Wriston recalled. "These notes would fall all over the Morgan Bank." On this occasion, one note inquired sternly, "Why did you throw Kathy Wriston's account out of the bank?" As it turned out, the purpose had not been to punish a customer for marrying the de facto head of a competing institution. "It was," said Wriston, "a perfectly logical thing for them to do. It was a lousy account with very little money in it." The action, Wriston said, had resulted from a routine decision to get rid of the money-losing accounts. Indeed, Morgan was always ahead of the pack in knowing which accounts were profitable and which were not.

An alumna of Smith, the University of Michigan Law School, and graduate schools in Switzerland, Kathy Wriston was the newest addition to a long line of self-assured Wriston women. Like Wriston's mother and sister, she had been groomed to assume a place in the world on an equal footing with men. And like Hank Wriston, her own father was a strong, somewhat authoritarian figure, who insisted that she attend an eastern "girls' " college and all but ordered her to go to law school at a time when women were barred from her law school's dining room. Equally important, he taught her to play golf better than most men. All that discipline would be essential for the role she would now play. In a real sense, Walter Wriston wanted not just a wife but a mother figure who would tend to the needs of an extended family of thousands of Citibankers around the globe. "We always tried to make it a sense of family," she said, referring to the institution that she came to call "Mother Bank." For thousands of Citibank wives overseas, Kathy Wriston, much like Bobby, would become the link to New York and civilization. The problems faced by women overseas ran the gamut from those in Saudi Arabia who couldn't work because of local customs and couldn't leave their homes because of the heat, to those in Paris and London who were constantly called upon to entertain visiting bank officers and customers. "Walter always expected Bobby and me to look after the bankers' wives. So I always felt I was working for the bank," she said later.

The transition from preparing legal briefs to arranging flowers for luncheons went relatively smoothly for the new Mrs. Wriston, and she approached the task with lawyerlike efficiency. She created files on catering establishments, cross-referenced to the names of the guests, what they were served, and who attended with whom. Like her husband, Kathy Wriston was conscious of the need to plan for succession. "I set it up so that someone— even another Mrs. Wriston—could take over if something happened to me," she said later. Because 870 UN Plaza had been furnished and decorated with entertaining in mind, Kathy thought of a tree farm the couple later bought in Sherman, Connecticut, not New York, as her real home, something that Walter found appalling. Part of the problem, according to sources close to Wriston clan, was that Wriston insisted on keeping their apartment much the same as it was when Bobby was alive, removing little except her clothes.

Travel—tens of thousands of miles of it each year—was part of the job description of the chief executive officer's wife, and Kathy Wriston had no problem with the travel part. It was the eating part that proved difficult. Her allergic reaction to all but the blandest of food proved especially troublesome at state dinners for easily offended foreign potentates. Citibank's reach by then included, or would soon include, some points on the globe, such as Indonesia, Thailand, and India, where the spiciest and most exotic foods were served. The strategy for getting Kathy Wriston through such ordeals was well orchestrated in advance. She would typically sit opposite her husband, and as she pointed to the various dishes with her knife or fork, Wriston would nod yes or no as unobtrusively as possible. If a dish was off limits, she would cut it up and push it around her plate to give her hosts the impression she had sampled some. One of the closest calls occurred on a visit to Kuwait during which Kathy became ill just before a dinner with top government officials that included huge portions of succulent lamb. She arranged with the wife of Citibank's country head to swap plates secretly so that the other woman could eat both portions and Kathy could tell her hosts convincingly how delicious the meal was.

The marriage was also a godsend for Wriston's personal finances. Wriston the banker was still a babe on Wall Street, so Kathy would see to it that there were no more Home-Stake deals. As Henry Wriston often said, "If Walter's wife didn't take care of his own business, he'd be in the poorhouse."

To some, the contrast between Bobby and Kathy was as stark as that between the genial, laid-back banking era now fading into history and the hotly competitive, dog-eat-dog era that lay ahead. Kathy Wriston was a new wife for a new age, and for some Citibankers, who had become accustomed to Bobby's easy demeanor, the change was a difficult one. "Kathy was more polished," said the wife of one country head, "and was much less interested in how many kids you had. Kathy reflected women's lib as we know it today." But liberated or not, Kathy Wriston immediately picked up where her predecessor had left off in the service of "Mother Bank." Wriston viewed as one of his primary duties the care and feeding of his "corporate property," and to that end, especially during the summer months, the Wristons played host at 870 UN Plaza to as many as fifty members of that elite group of future managers, sometimes as often as three times a week. "That was an important part of building morale in the organization," Wriston said later, and contributed to what he called a "strong sense of Citibank feeling. People felt they were having fun." And, Wriston would add acerbically, some seven years after he had turned over the reins to his successor, "people still talk about it. One of the reasons is there hasn't been anybody around for the last four or five years to do that."

At those affairs, Citibankers would talk with Kathy Wriston, assuming that she knew everything her husband knew about what was going on in the empire. They were sometimes shocked to find that she learned more about what was going on at the bank from visitors than from her husband. While the Wristons' private life and business life in many respects were virtually inseparable, they rarely spent their private time together discussing the bank. Wriston would occasionally consult his wife on legal matters and ask for her advice on who might make a good board member, but discussion of bank business was otherwise off limits. Kathy Wriston would later insist that her husband's practice of keeping his own counsel extended even to his wife, "on things he didn't think I should know," she said. Later, as Kathy became a sought-after corporate director, she and Wriston built a kind of wall between his companies and hers. "He doesn't talk about his companies, and I don't talk about mine," she insisted later.

Walter and Kathy would remain childless. While Kathy would have liked to have children, according to family members, Walter apparently felt that at forty-eight he was too old. He didn't even like to leave his grown daughter to travel overseas for six weeks at a time, and felt such a routine would take an excessive toll on young children.

By May of 1968, it was time for the board to put its official seal on the ambitious plans laid out earlier by Wriston and Moore. The occasion was the board's first "offshore" meeting at the Dorado Beach Hotel in Puerto Rico. Stillman Rockefeller had felt such outings were wasteful and unnecessary, and the idea of packing up the directors and their wives and flying them to a tropical island never got off the ground until Rockefeller was relegated to the status of a mere director. Catering to more than twenty demanding board members, each with his own ego and idiosyncrasies, presented the planners of these meetings with monumental logistics and protocol problems. One director required a hard board for his bed—but only for half of it, because his wife couldn't sleep on it. Another couldn't sleep in the same room with his wife because they both snored. Harry Gray, the chairman of United Technologies, was so safety conscious that he demanded that his security guard have a room next to his. It is not surprising, then, that things did not get off to an auspicious start in Puerto Rico. When the wife of one director was met at the airport by a hotel station wagon, she objected to the presence of another woman seeking a ride to the hotel and hit the other woman across the face with her pocketbook. As a result of the altercation, a hotel manager woke up a Citibank official at three o'clock in the morning to inform him angrily there would be no more service for Citibank. According to a former Citibanker, the bank had to "buy off" the woman to persuade her to drop assault charges against the director's wife.

In addition to the discussions that were to take place behind closed doors, Wriston was scheduled to deliver a speech to a San Juan business group. Late that afternoon, Wriston and Moore were stuck in a rush-hour traffic jam on the way back to the hotel from downtown San Juan.

"What are you going to talk about tonight, talk about tonight, talk about tonight?" Moore demanded. Wriston told him what he had in mind, a topic that clearly didn't meet with Moore's approval. "That's no good, no good, no good. What you need is to give the speech you gave in Chicago last week."

"George," Wriston replied, "I've been working on this. It's a whole new deal."

"Got to have it, got to have it, got to have it."

But there were no copies of the Chicago speech in Puerto Rico, and Wriston reminded Moore that he was to speak at 7:00 P.M., just three hours later. "We're sitting here," Wriston said, "and haven't moved a millimeter in an hour."

"Got to do it, got to do it, got to do it," Moore insisted. He bolted out of the car and headed up the road alongside the line of traffic. Wriston felt awkward about sitting in the limousine while his chairman was sprinting down the highway, and so he set out in hot pursuit of Moore. Moore shortly reached the entrance to the Bacardi Rum distillery, where he approached a soldier at the gatehouse and told him, "I'm the chairman of Citibank and I'm a personal friend of the chairman of Bacardi. I want to use the telephone."

"The soldier looked at him like he was from the moon," Wriston recalled. "George then spoke to him in what he firmly believed was Spanish but which at that point bore very little relationship to Spanish. That poor guard. He didn't know who George was, or even who the chairman of Bacardi was, and couldn't care less." Finally the two of them managed to make the guard understand that they wanted to use the phone. They called New York and instructed someone to transmit Wriston's Chicago speech by telex to the Citibank branch where the dinner was to be held.

That evening, recalled Wriston, "I'm sitting there with two or three hundred people, having drinks [and] watching the telex machine spitting out this stuff. We had a bunch of guys cut the speech up and paste it with rubber cement on ledger cards." As things turned out, the mayor of San Juan spoke for hours, so Wriston didn't reach the podium until about 10:30 P.M. He told his boss it was too late to give the speech. "No," Moore insisted, "you've got to make a speech, make a speech, make a speech."

"There will be a lot of white tablecloths out there," Wriston said. In the minutes before he was to go on, he sat on the sidelines tossing out ledger cards, and slashing his hour-long talk to just five minutes. Later, Citibank's branch manager in Puerto Rico remarked to a colleague that he thought he had seen the chairman of Citibank running down the highway followed by the president, but knew such a thing couldn't possibly have happened.

In July 1968, First National City finally announced plans to give birth to its parent, the First National City Corporation, which it said would allow "greater flexibility" and geographic expansion. In an article in *American Banker,* banking consultant Carter Golembe declared that the possibilities for expansion into other businesses, including even manufacturing, were "virtually unlimited." *Business Week* noted the significance of the move when it wrote, "Commercial banks, long the butt of jokes as the Stepin Fetchits of the business world, looked strangely exciting this week as they began to try out the role of the freewheeling conglomerate." *The New Yorker* later wrote that some called the day of the Citibank announcement "the most important day in American banking history." By the end of 1968, over fifty banks had established bank holding companies.

In connection with the move, the bank put aside some seven million shares of authorized but unissued common stock, then valued at more than $500 million, for acquisitions by the new entity. Citibank's legal model, packaged up by Shearman & Sterling, would also be sought after as the template for other banks. The white-shoe law firm had obtained from the IRS and the SEC rulings and "no action" letters, which were not subject to disclosure at that time. Wriston refused to disclose the documents to competitors, raising some hackles. "They [Citibank] wanted a good jump on this and let the other guys figure out how to do it," said one legal expert familiar with the filing. "I know absolutely that we influenced most of the banks in the country," said former Citibank planner Jack Heilshorn. "When we formed the holding company, I don't know how many bankers called and said, 'We're going to form one too.' " Before the creation of the holding company, First National City shares were thinly traded over the counter. Now, after many years' absence, the bank would once again be represented on the Big Board as the First National City Corporation. That move, they hoped, would boost demand for the shares and would also increase that all-important price-earnings ratio.

The Comptroller of the Currency would still have to approve the new entity, but that approval was a foregone conclusion. What was far from certain was how Citibank would be able to use the new entity. The national debate on the business of banking now shifted into high gear. The one-bank holding company movement became the catalyst for defining what a bank is and what it should do. Indeed, the decision to form the holding company would turn out to be the easy part. For the next two and a half years, until the enactment of the 1970 Amendments to the Bank Holding Company Act, the issue would be hotly debated in the halls of Congress and whenever two or more bankers were found in one place.

Soon, as Wriston complained later, the word "loophole" would be emblazoned in the headlines of the nation's press. Opponents of one-bank holding companies raised the specter of a vast expansion of banking power in the United States and the emergence of U.S.-style *zaibatsu,* the banking-industrial megaconglomerates that dominate Japan's economy. Bankers and legislators were worried about tie-ins—that banks would lend on more favorable terms to companies that were customers of affiliates and that when funds were tight, the banks would give preference to the affiliates' customers. Critics feared that the holding company device would allow banks to climb the walls that had for years so neatly separated insurance, brokerage, and other financial services businesses and bring about a return to the high-rolling 1920s. Skeptics also questioned how the bank would be protected if the holding company failed, and whether the bank would be called upon to bail out a troubled holding company affiliate. In the long run, these would prove to be the least troublesome problems in the age of go-go banking that was to come.

The debate quickly crystallized into a big bank versus small bank issue, just as it had more than half a century earlier over plans for the creation of a U.S. central bank. Before long, congressman Wright Patman would appear on the scene with guns blazing, condemning the one-bank holding company as an end run around federal regulation that was designed to benefit big eastern bankers, and calling for new legislation to rein them in. One-bank holding companies, Patman said, were a move toward "a cartelized economy."

Wriston had no interest in operating steel mills or retail stores, but some bankers, such as First Pennsylvania Bank's John Bunting, supplied opponents like Patman with ammunition by declaring publicly that the one-bank holding company would allow banks to own automobile dealerships if they wanted to. That was the kind of rash statement that Wriston had come to expect of his colleague in Philadelphia. At a time in American life when it had become fashionable to talk about putting students on college boards of trustees, Bunting placed a college student on his own board. "He was a trendy fellow," Wriston said later. "I used to argue with him. He said, 'Do you really think I'm doing something crazy?' I asked him, 'What can a sophomore in college contribute to your problem?' To be avant-garde, he put minorities, college students, teenage women on the board. He was the first one out of the box on that. We used to kid around. He wished to be perceived [as being] in advance of the social mores of the time. He was very smart, but he got his institution into a lot of trouble." Some, in fact, believed that Bunting's comments, including what seemed to be the flip comment about the automobile business, actually brought Patman and other opponents of bank diversification down on the banks. At any rate, little more than ten years later, Wriston was called upon to help bail out Bunting's bank.

In October, the Office of the Comptroller of the Currency, a champion of bank diversification, blessed the Citibank move. But the battle lines were already being drawn in the showdown over what should and should not be a permissible bank activity. The bank holding company debate sharply divided the membership of the American Bankers Association, the nation's largest bank trade organization. The Comptroller of the Currency, which supported the big banks' expansionist aims, was at odds with the Fed, which regulated the smaller, state-chartered banks. In trying to mollify big bank and small bank members, the ABA's leaders managed to please no one. "Small banks," said Wriston, "were trying to protect their monopoly. Large banks were trying to diversify."

ABA executive director Charls Walker, an admirer of the Federal Reserve and a close friend of Fed chairman William McChesney Martin, was outraged by the bank holding company trend and actually referred to the companies as *zaibatsu*. He feared that the banking industry of the United States, like that of Japan, would be transformed into a handful of all-powerful conglomerates, and he saw the preservation of the independent banking system as his mission. Walker sympathized with the small banks and wanted to fashion a compromise with the Fed on bank holding companies. But institutions like Citibank that had already gone the one-bank holding company route were not interested in compromising with Martin. And they were convinced that the ABA no longer represented their interests.

Things came to a head, recalls D.C. banking consultant Carter Golembe, at the American Bankers Association's annual convention in Chicago in late September 1968. There, George Moore brashly convened a meeting of representatives of twenty-two big banks to create the Association of Corporate Owners of One-Bank Holding Companies, and named as its executive director a genteel southerner named Jack Yingling, Citibank's Washington lobbyist. A former legislative assistant to Senator J. William Fulbright, Yingling was described by one Washington insider as "the classiest lobbyist in Washington." The move by Moore was the banking world's equivalent of a palace coup. Said Walker later, "The one-bank holding company movement scared the bejesus out of me, but to George it was the greatest thing since sliced bread."

Top officials of the Fed used the occasion to warn of dire ramifications. Fed vice chairman J. L. Robertson, reminding bankers of the consequences of the "permissiveness" that prevailed in the 1920s, cautioned that the one-bank holding company movement was a "repetition of serious errors." Comptroller of the Currency William B. Camp dismissed the idea of subjecting bank holding companies to Fed regulation. "What I should like to emphasize is that the hard-won new spirit of initiative in banking may not be self-generative," he told the bankers. "Bankers must assert their determination to hold the gains that have been achieved and continue the enlargement of their activities as new opportunities appear."

As ABA president, Citibank's Howard Laeri was in a predicament. The small banks were suspicious enough of the large-bank domination of the ABA. But they were even more wary of Citibank because of its push to expand through the holding company. Laeri's advocacy of more powers and fewer regulations made him a hero to the large banks and a pariah to small ones.

Citibank clearly rubbed ABA executive director Charls Walker the wrong way, and vice versa. According to Yingling, Wriston resented Walker's harsh attitude toward former comptroller James Saxon and his role in getting Saxon replaced. ("I did my best," Walker acknowledged later.) Walker chafed at the big New York bank's arrogance and frequently made snide remarks about it.

Comptroller Camp's approval of the holding company was a welcome wedding gift for George Moore. On Wednesday, October 9, 1968, after an eight-year relationship, Moore married Charon Crosson in a civil ceremony at the Westport home of his Connecticut attorney. In an unusual wedding announcement in the *New York Times* on October 11, Moore's daughter-in-law revealed that she and her husband had not been informed in advance of the wedding date, nor had they attended the wedding, and that she had not yet even met her father-in-law's bride. "We knew they were getting married," she told the *Times,* "but didn't know when." Marriage license in hand, the couple took off for a honeymoon in southern Spain, where Moore had built a home.

In November 1968, in the thick of the debate over one-bank holding companies, Richard Milhous Nixon defeated Hubert Humphrey and was elected president. Shortly thereafter, Wriston got a call from John Mitchell, Nixon's old friend and campaign adviser, asking if he could drop by Wriston's office. Wriston, who had held his new job for just over a year, had never met the jowly John Mitchell, who took a seat on a sofa in his office and proceeded to offer him the job of secretary of the Treasury. Wriston didn't commit himself, but subsequently called bank director Mil Batten, chairman of J. C. Penney and head of Citibank's personnel committee. Wriston felt at once a fascination with and a suspicion of Washington, and thought at the time that he might not get another shot at the cabinet post. Yet he had misgivings about leaving the job he had held for "just a few minutes—it wasn't right," he explained later.

What really made all the difference to Wriston, and perhaps altered the course of financial history, was that he had been asked not by the president-elect himself but by his proxy. Wriston had always felt that if the president asked him to do something, he was obliged as an American to do it. He later said that if Nixon himself had phoned, "I probably would have [accepted the offer]. But the president didn't offer. He sent an emissary. That makes a big difference. If an emissary comes, maybe they're hanging you out to dry. That's normal in Washington. Maybe the fellow is really acting for the president, but on the other hand if the president of the United States really wants you to do something, he'll pick up the phone and say, 'I'm asking you to do this.' It's not a simple place down there."

During his entire banking career Wriston never disclosed the invitation to anyone except his wife and a handful of Citibank insiders. If he had learned anything from his father, it was discretion. Hank Wriston had been offered more university presidencies than he could remember and had counseled his son that "the worst thing you can do is talk about it, because it doesn't do you any good and it hurts the other fellow. You tell your bride and that's it." That, Wriston said later, "is the principle I've always operated by." Kathy Wriston knew that her husband "didn't like politics-politics. He's probably not interested in politics as an independent subject. He's not someone who bends on principle. He would have been unhappy [as Treasury secretary]. He thinks he's right."

According to one published account, Chase's David Rockefeller was also approached and turned down the job for similar reasons. With Wriston and Rockefeller out of the running, Maurice Stans emerged as front-runner for Treasury. That prospect was anathema to ABA executive director Walker. "After Wriston turned it down, the main thing was to stop Stans," said Walker later. So Walker, for one, threw his support behind Continental Illinois chairman David Kennedy. Ironically, Moore acted as the go-between for Nixon in approaching Kennedy. On Thanksgiving Day, 1968, Moore phoned Kennedy at his daughter's home in California and told him he was the president-elect's choice, and Nixon later called him to offer the job. So Kennedy, rather than Wriston, took the heat from Wright Patman in the confirmation hearings. Congressman Patman, Kennedy recalled later, threatened to impeach him and at every hearing "lectured me for forty-five minutes on my integrity."

Though Wriston lacked political savvy himself, he enjoyed his trips to Washington and his dealings with the high and the mighty. In the opinion of former associates, he seemed to thrive on the public acclaim and media attention that went along with business stardom. Wriston found himself on the guest list for frequent White House dinners in the Nixon administration, and he enjoyed regaling his policy committee at its regular Thursday meetings with snippets of his conversations with Washington power brokers. His name and face were becoming familiar to everyone who followed American business. But when his picture appeared on the cover of *Business Week* in November 1968, at least one reader did a double take. Wriston bore such a striking resemblance to New York Yankee slugger Joe DiMaggio that the reader wrote to the magazine insisting that the man on the cover was not Wriston but the Yankee Clipper, who must now be working for Citibank.

Late in 1968, as the Nixon administration was preparing to enter the White House, was a tumultuous time not only in American history but also in world financial history. Thanks in part to the cost of financing the Vietnam War, inflation was accelerating. Meanwhile, rapid economic growth and improved European balance of trade continued to take a heavy toll on the U.S. balance of payments and the dollar, which was still convertible into gold. The result was a severe drain on U.S. gold reserves, as anxious holders of dollars exchanged greenbacks for gold. The source of the problem, in Wriston's view, was the multitude of controls on the movement of capital and goods between the United States and foreign countries. U.S. banks and multinational corporations still labored under the interest equalization tax, which limited the flow of capital abroad. And foreign governments, while lowering tariffs, were erecting other, more clever, protectionist barriers, including border taxes and import quotas, to U.S. goods.

In a November speech before the National Foreign Trade Convention that was clearly aimed at the incoming administration, Wriston rebuked the protectionists and the advocates of economic controls, whom he believed were cut from much the same cloth as the dictators who had sought to enslave the world thirty years earlier. "The men who distrust freedom never sleep," Wriston declared. "They are always looking for an opportunity to control your life and mine and to do it with the best of intentions. Usually we are told that controls are for our own good in a complicated and uncertain world. The origin of this idea in modern times was the dictator Mussolini, who said, 'We were the first to assert that the more complicated the forms assumed by civilization, the more restricted the freedom of the individual must become.'" Wriston would be proved correct when he predicted that the price of gold, then fixed at $35 per ounce, might have to be abandoned if keeping it required the world to return to "the morass of exchange controls."

9

MATRIX WARS

*C*entralization, Wriston once told a friend, is a fascist state. That was true, he believed, in corporate society as well as in society at large. Although decentralization was a novelty to bankers in the mid-1960s, it had already been widely embraced by industry leaders like GE. While the reorganization and the creation of the holding company were not directly linked except in time, it was clear that the expanded activities envisioned for the new growth-oriented holding company couldn't be carried out effectively under the old organization. In other words, if Wriston's growth plans materialized, Citibank would simply be too big to be centrally managed from the fifteenth floor of 399 Park Avenue.

Centralized authority was also a turnoff to the highly talented personnel Wriston was trying to attract and incompatible with the entrepreneurial spirit he sought to engender. No single individual could possibly call all the shots, and call them correctly, for every business and market in which Citibank was now operating around the world, especially in foreign exchange trading. At one time, chief traders had issued categorical dictums to their underlings to be long or short sterling. "We decided that was wrong," explained Wriston later. "Everybody took his own position, within limits." Wriston had also assimilated the lesson of Sewell Avery, the autocratic chairman of Montgomery Ward & Company, who had presided over the demise of the retailer in the years following World War II. "He sat there on that huge pile of cash waiting for the end of the world," Wriston said later, while "Sears and J. C. Penney ate his lunch. If he had listened to the guys in the stores, they would have told him that people were buying like crazy to make up for the shortages created during the war. [But] he didn't listen to the market."

Unlike most other major American banks, which operated according to groupthink, Citibank under Wriston functioned as a collection of individuals. Indeed, Citibank under Wriston would become a microcosm of democracy, with all, or very nearly all, the permissiveness of society generally. "In an open society, no one has all the answers. Ideas from everywhere will be listened to, although management is a tough jury," said Wriston in a talk to officers some years later. "Very bright people often see a dozen different alternative ways to handle any given problem," he told them. "The history of the world and the history of Citibank demonstrate conclusively that when decision-making is centralized, trouble eventually follows." Wriston, said former officers, pooh-poohed the hokey tribal rituals that other large companies used to indoctrinate their officers with the corporate line. At J. C. Penney, for example, where Wriston himself was a director, those who reached job levels covered by the retailer's incentive compensation scheme were called upon to recite the James Cash Penney credo at a formal induction ceremony. "That's Painted Post, that's Hicksville," Wriston snorted, according to one former officer. Wriston's belief in corporate democracy was also reflected in other ways, some of them symbolic. Each day he invariably walked from his apartment to the office, where he presided over Citibank from a large round table rather than from behind a desk.

There was a time and a place for centralization, and a time and a place for decentralization. A centralized Citibank was the right strategy for defending the bank against bad times. But for a bank to take full advantage of economic prosperity, an offensive strategy founded on decentralization seemed to be the only way to go.

The troubles that led to the reorganization were long-simmering ones. Although some moves had been made to break up the old geographic organization, those were the exception rather than the rule. A decade earlier, Citibank, like other major banks, had shifted the most important corporate accounts out of its 55 Wall Street headquarters and into the branches. As a result, a major branch that housed big corporate accounts, like the one at Fifth Avenue and Fifty-first Street, was quite a big operation. Had it been an independent bank, it would have been one of the largest banks in the United States. That transfer had been done largely to pacify branch czar Tommy Wilcox. But by the late sixties there was no longer any need to please Atomic Tommy.

Although Citibank had organized industry units, including transportation and oil and gas, in the early 1950s, there were still glaring exceptions to the general rule that, for example, oil companies should be handled by energy specialists. The manager of the Citibank branch in New York's Mobil Oil building was still responsible not only for the giant oil company but also for customers with $187 in their passbook savings accounts. Despite the irrefutable logic that would seem to dictate that a Seven Sisters oil company should be served by an oil and gas expert, the special industries department had repeatedly lost its battles with Wilcox over who should handle oil companies. These big companies regarded branch managers as little more than clerks and insisted on dealing with the high-powered bankers at 399 Park. In at least one instance, Citibank is said to have lost a major corporate account after a teller refused to cash the personal check of a CEO brought to a branch by his secretary.

Wriston knew that this arrangement could not continue. "But to convince anybody of that, what you do in the real world is to hire a consultant," said Wriston. "That adds verisimilitude to what you were going to do all along." The decision really boiled down to which consultant to hire, and for that advice Wriston turned to Peter Drucker, the counselor to corporate America. A close friend of Wriston's, Drucker was a ubiquitous presence, physically and spiritually, in the corridors of 399 Park. But Drucker's impression was that "Walt very often paid [little] attention to my opinion. Very rarely did he do anything because I suggested it. Which, by the way, is something I appreciate. There's nothing more dangerous than a client who does what you tell him to do. You want a client who listens, thinks things through, and makes his own decision." Indeed, Drucker's most significant contribution would be to serve as Wriston's intellectual sparring partner and father confessor.

One piece of Drucker's advice that Wriston *did* listen to, however, was his recommendation on how to reorganize the bank, and whom he should hire to do the job. When Wriston said, "I know I can't get you, so who do I get?" Drucker mentioned the name of a man at the New York–based consulting firm of McKinsey & Company and then laid out for Wriston the precise scenario he should follow to get the right McKinsey man for the job. "You will call McKinsey and be told he can't do your job because he's too busy," counseled Drucker. "At which point you'll say, 'Thank you very much, I guess I'll go to Booz Allen,' and hang up. Then they'll call and say he's available."

And that's exactly what happened. Wriston told McKinsey's Richard Neuschel that he wanted to "completely reorganize this thing so that we're faced off against the marketplace and get generally into the twentieth century." Neuschel warned Wriston that such a drastic move would lead to full-scale internecine warfare. "You don't have enough guts to do that," Neuschel said bluntly.

"I don't know whether that's a sales pitch that you hand out, or you don't know us, or what the story is, but we'll let it go over our shoulder," Wriston replied with undisguised annoyance.

Internal warfare certainly did break out, but it was tempered by the decision to implement the McKinsey plan—known in business school jargon as "decentralization by market segment"—with a steering committee of top bankers. Wriston astutely recognized that such a controversial plan would not be an easy sell if it was presented as the McKinsey plan or even the planning department plan. The judge and jury over how accounts would be split up would be Howard Laeri, Citibank's own banker's banker, a highly respected and popular figure whose decisions were to be final. Fresh from his stint as president of the American Bankers Association, he was the obvious choice to preside over the overhaul. "The reason the reorganization went so well when it could have gone so badly was due to the towering job Howard did in resolving these issues," said Wriston later. "It was an agonizing time."

It was a foregone conclusion that with Wilcox relegated to a figurehead role, the branch men would finally lose their battle to hang on to the big, glamorous, and profitable corporate accounts. After the fifteen-month study, Wriston announced in late 1968 that Citibank would be reorganized into six

market-oriented divisions. Three new divisions were carved out of the old organization: a corporate, or wholesale, division for all large national companies; a commercial division for mid-sized firms; and a retail division that
included individual depositors and mom-and-pop businesses. The other three
units—operating group, overseas, and trust, which was renamed investment
management and took aim at wealthy individuals—remained essentially un-
touched. "The days when a branch manager can properly supervise the accounts of major corporations, local merchants, and personal loan accounts
are gone forever," Wriston said in a prepared statement.

The massive shift of personnel and accounts began on Christmas Eve
1968 and continued through New Year's Day. A few made it to the most
sought-after wholesale unit; some, as a compromise, wound up in the commercial division. But most remained—stripped of their big balances, their
lofty titles, their pride, and their status—in the largely emasculated branches.

While Wriston equated centralization with fascism, the decentralization that
McKinsey wrought left Citibank in turmoil. "We only bought the first book
in the set on how to reorganize," said one former officer. "We didn't buy the
second on how to manage a decentralized organization." The overhaul did
more than simply reshuffle names and boxes on an organizational chart. It
eliminated what was left of the genial banking culture and replaced it with a
new, youthful, profit-oriented psychology that demanded an entirely new approach to management.

Having taken a sledgehammer to the old geographic structure, Wriston
now confronted the classic problem faced by large, complex organizations
that must coordinate a variety of people, skills, products, and functions to
meet a customer need or solve a problem in many geographic locations. The
experts call it matrix management.

The "matrix" organization dovetailed perfectly—perhaps too perfectly—with the new profit center concept introduced by young John Reed.
Each new customer-oriented business unit was to be a profit center run by a
manager responsible for executing a profit plan that would produce earnings
growth of 15 percent a year. The task now was to manage the monster that
John Reed and McKinsey had created. Ultimately, Wriston had little choice
but to embrace profit centers and decentralization if he was to create a diversified, fast-growing global financial services company.

But in solving one problem, Wriston created an entirely new set of
problems. Where once he had waged war against sloth and indifference, he
now had to fight the "matrix wars" with troops afflicted with a highly contagious disease called profit centeritis.

The shift in employee loyalty from the institution as a whole to the
profit-and-loss statement was almost instantaneous. In one not unusual example, the Beirut branch responsible for a deutsche mark deposit in Germany shifted the funds to the Deutsche Bank to gain an extra eighth of a

percentage point that would be reported as income on the branches' profit-and-loss report, thereby depriving Citibank of the use of the funds.

Similarly, in Japan, a Citibank subsidiary placed a newspaper ad for a secretary and wound up hiring the secretary of an officer at another Citibank unit—at a higher salary than she'd been earning in her first job.

Officers at the new Citibank lived and died by the profit-and-loss statement. "If you want me to have loyalty to something else, you've got to figure that out," one officer said at the time. Employees no longer said they worked for Citibank. When asked who they did work for, they almost always gave their bosses' names. Moreover, said a former senior officer, employees who earlier would have been inclined to blow the whistle on dishonest or incompetent bosses now thought twice.

The reorganization marked the beginning of the end of the era of the old-time relationship banker and gave rise to a corporate culture in which officers were branded either as transactors or administrator-managers.

As the managerial cult took hold, Citibank placed a higher premium on management skills than on traditional banking skills. The best manager was now more valued than the best banker. Said former comptroller Stephen Eyre, "It became known in the bank that if you weren't a manager you weren't successful. Good account officers wanted to be managers." This was in sharp contrast with the practice at Morgan, where top account officers were encouraged to remain in that role. Eventually Citibank attempted to remedy this with the creation of the so-called senior corporate banker, a title that attempted to elevate top bankers to the same status as top managers.

Overnight, people were handed full business responsibility who had never had it before. Before McKinsey, only the CEO and the country heads had total responsibility for an entire operation; all others, even high-level officers, were essentially functional specialists. The only officers truly prepared to run the new business units were country heads. Because they had experience in overseeing all aspects of a large operation, including marketing and planning, they wound up playing a major role in the McKinseyized institution. Wriston himself acknowledged the problem shortly after the reorganization in a talk to correspondent bankers that was appropriately titled, "Those were the days." The "new supervisors," he said, "will of necessity have to be account managers concerned not only with the transactions but answering the question of where are we going and why are we going there. We found a dearth of real supervisors. A lot of the department heads were put into place through the power of survival, and not because they understood work flow, how to handle absenteeism, standard hours or standard costs, or even the basic leadership role." In the overhaul, planners failed to recognize the need to train people to act as business managers rather than transactors and lenders.

Pushing lending authority and business responsibility down to lower levels and diversifying into new financially related enterprises placed an even greater premium on youth and brains. Battlefield responsibility was awarded to hundreds of smart people in their twenties and thirties. Wriston had always favored the young over the old, the energetic over the flaccid and the content. "There was a generational changing of the guard," said William Heron, who was hired in 1969 after graduating from Yale and the Wharton School, serving in the Marine Corps Reserve, and working briefly for the consulting firm of Cresap, McCormick. Anyone older than forty-five, Heron said, was "yesterday's newspaper. There was a lot of trauma, turmoil, and anxiety on the part of people who had signed on after World War II or before."

One of the veterans was Richard Valelly, who had joined the bank after the war. "You had all these kids coming in not much older than your own son, taking your place," he said, adding that in the era of the one-bank holding company the horizons of older officers "were not wide enough." Earlier, someone who worked hard could hope to rise to branch manager by the time he was in his late forties, and perhaps aspire to run a country. But the new breed was not content to run on such a slow track.

Former Citibanker Ed Harshfield remarked that "everyone running a country was a junior Walter Wriston." In an annual report, Citibank boasted that more than two thirds of its non-officer staff were under forty years of age and that almost three quarters of the officers were between thirty-one and fifty-five.

The new managerial cult embraced the notion that managers were interchangeable and could be moved around from place to place and from job to job. Out of his dealings with Malcom McLean, Wriston had concluded that banks were "common carriers" of money. When he took charge of the overseas division in 1959, Wriston had in effect extended that theory to people as well, shifting officers frequently from country to country. With the arrival of McKinsey & Company, that theory was taken one step further. There was no reason, Wriston believed, that a successful manager of corporate banking in France couldn't run a consumer branch operation in New York. And so managers were moved around with reckless abandon, and top prospects with their eyes on senior management scrambled to get their tickets punched in the right locations. "The McKinsey matrix wars were very emotional, and burned a lot of people out," said former overseas personnel chief Jim Griffin. The glory boys were those who got promoted and moved from place to place.

There were, of course, some serious drawbacks to the rapid turnover and reshuffling. For all of Wriston's emphasis on long-term goals, somehow that view didn't always filter down to the hundreds of profit center managers. Managers were naturally tempted to put their stamp on any operation to which they were assigned, even if that meant undoing what had already been implemented by their predecessors. By manipulating the numbers, a profit center manager could show a streak of improved earnings long enough to earn himself a promotion to another area of the bank. "Citibank was like an ongoing leveraged buyout," said former officer Peter Greenough. "Everybody who got responsibility tried to strip assets and overturn what the previous guy did" to make a good showing. "It was like a drunk staggering down a darkened alley bouncing off a light post." And by the time the underlying weaknesses of the changes revealed themselves, the new officer would be long gone, and the problems he'd caused in the unit would be blamed on his successor. This process became known among Citibankers as the art of FUMU—"Fuck up, move up."

To some, the McKinsey reorganization and the rapid growth that followed dehumanized Citibank and spelled the end of the era of genteel bankers who, as one veteran banker put it, "got their kicks from building the bank." Before the changes that Wriston wrought, employees felt an assurance, implied if not written, that if they performed well, they would not have to worry about their next job. McKinsey signaled the beginning of the "me" generation of Citibankers. "You could see quickly that all of a sudden people were starting to think, 'What's this going to do for me?'," the banker said.

In the view of Citibank planner Jack Heilshorn, a decade passed before the management style and culture fostered by the McKinsey reorganization was absorbed into the organization. Others have said that Citibank never adapted to it; certainly many old line employees felt threatened.

In general, McKinseyization facilitated growth and market penetration, but certain business segments—those that depended on long-term personal relationships between bankers and customers—became casualties. Particularly hard hit were the middle market business in the United States and the corporate business in Europe. Citibank became less effective in serving so-called mid-sized companies that fell between the mom-and-pop shops and the *Fortune* 1000 companies. In New York, Chemical Bank and Manufacturers Hanover Trust, which merged in 1992, eventually dominated this business, one of the most profitable markets in American banking for those institutions that know how to cater to it. But this business was not compatible with Wriston's fast-track meritocracy of Ivy League M.B.A.'s, where lingering too long on one rung of the ladder was not healthy for one's career. Moreover, Citibank's strength was technology-based high-volume processing operations, which the middle market was not. "Citi is good if you're off the rack," said one former officer. "But the minute something's wrong and the customer needs special advice, it's not." Besides, he said, "it's costly to put a middle market guy opposite the customer." Others said that the commercial division simply never attracted the brightest officers and that some who should have remained in the branches filling out signature cards managed to maneuver their way into the commercial unit.

In Europe, the rapid succession of managers and strategies that followed the McKinsey reorganization over the next two decades left the bank's corporate business there in shambles. During this period, income from foreign exchange trading, where Citibank was the leader, masked the inability of the rest of the business to make money. Said Stephen Eyre, "Customers got tired of seeing new faces all the time."

Wriston later conceded that the profit center had its drawbacks, but he defended the theory. Profit centers, he said in a talk to bank officers, "carry the message of earnings per share with great clarity to the account officers.

But we learned painfully that like any wonder drug, the profit center concept has undesirable side effects." Account managers, he went on, "can grow so profit center–minded that they look at their own profits to the detriment of those of the institution or even to the detriment of their own customers. This does not invalidate the profit center concept; it only means that it has to be used, like anything else, with a strong mixture of common sense and some caution."

Consultant Peter Drucker has suggested that matrix management was probably invented by Napoleon in the nineteenth century and perfected by NASA in the Apollo program in the 1960s. In the corporate world, GE, which typically assigned five functional managers to one general manager, was the classic model of a matrix organization. Comparing matrix management to trying to play basketball, tennis, and soccer on the same court with the same people at the same time, Drucker said that "people have to be constantly alert to what others are trying to do" at the far end of the court. "Matrix management is brilliant but incredibly hard to do. Maybe you have to have it, but don't kid yourself, you're not going to enjoy it." One thing that must be avoided, Drucker warned, is imposing "your own organizational concept on the customer."

Refereeing the matrix wars would be perhaps the single biggest management challenge that Wriston would face for the next fourteen years, and perhaps the biggest one faced by his successor as well. "It is the classic dilemma of moving an organization from a domestic bank with foreign branches to a global organization," said Wriston later. "The dilemma is that you have product expertise, whether typewriters or lightbulbs or leveraged buyouts, and you have a foreign culture. The argument was that the fellow in France had to know where the Crazy Horse saloon was [and] how to get tickets to the Follies . . . but you couldn't have the same fellow who did all that be the world's expert on ship loans."

In the real world, said Wriston, "you can't train enough people to play all the instruments in the orchestra. You have to devise a management system so that when you need the clarinet player, he's there. But you can't have a clarinet player in a hundred countries, so you devise a matrix." This was a problem, Wriston pointed out, faced by every large organization seeking to expand the products it offered and the territory it served. When, for example, IBM sold only computers, and sold them only in the United States, it didn't need a matrix. But as it introduced new product lines and sold them overseas, it too had suffered through matrix management. And now it was Citibank's turn. "That type of organization is the most difficult in the world. It depends just about 100 percent on goodwill. You can write all the memos you want. But if Spencer in the oil department doesn't have a good relationship with whoever is running England, and [if] British Petroleum has a real problem in financing reserves, it won't work," Wriston said.

Not surprisingly, Tommy Wilcox was said to have considered McKinseyization a total failure. Others, including Edward Palmer, who would soon be named executive committee chairman of Citibank, felt that something was certainly lost with the demise of the geographic organization. Now no single individual in the United States had a complete picture of how Citibank was performing in a particular part of the country. That information could be gleaned only by talking to a dozen or so account officers, each of whom was responsible for a particular customer segment.

One of the stickiest problems in constructing the matrix is creating an accounting system to allocate the credit and the rewards. While that would be the most critical issue for many Citibankers, Drucker regarded it as the least important. "The first issue is who does anything," he said. In matrix management, the great danger is that nine out of ten things fall between the cracks. Nobody's responsible. Who gets credit is the last issue. You can eliminate that. But who does what is very difficult."

When he took charge of the overseas division in 1959, Wriston had dealt with a relatively simple version of this problem. Upon arriving in Europe, he had discovered that branches such as Paris and London had little incentive to sell First National City Bank traveler's checks. Because all the profits flowed to New York, the business there was a money loser. Branch managers would naturally engage in banking activities for which the results showed up on their own profit-and-loss statements. Later, Wriston and his colleagues split off the marketing of traveler's checks from the branches and double-counted traveler's check profits so that both the branch and the traveler's checks unit got equal credit.

The advent of a separate global marketing organization for traveler's checks was the first chink in the armor of the all-powerful country head, known in Cititalk as the SENOF. "The SENOF," said former Citibanker Jim Tozer, "was the lord of many. Neither a bird shall sing nor a flower grow without his written permission." But now for the first time, the SENOF did not control every Citibank employee who operated in his country, or every business activity that was conducted there. Indeed, the manager placed in charge of the the traveler's check business was not easily controllable. He was a rough-and-tumble individualist who admonished staff members who crossed him by saying, "You do that again and I'll reach up your asshole and grab your tongue."

In the wake of the McKinsey reorganization, the first effort to manage the matrix—to somehow serve a variety of customers in different locations with a multitude of "products"—was the creation in 1968 of a company to sell leasing services in the United States, and a year later another one to sell these services around the world. Former Comptroller of the Currency James Saxon had prompted his banks to set up leasing operations back in 1963. Wriston later told *New York* magazine that the bank's entry into leasing began with the discovery that three out of five officers leased cars, "so we started a leasing company." He said this flippantly, but there was more forethought to it than that.

Plugging the leasing company into the Citibank organization was akin to arranging a blind date between a Brooklyn cabdriver and a Park Avenue debutante. In contrast to the elitist corporate bankers, the leasing specialists were fire-breathing salesmen who were judged not on their golf scores but on the volume of leasing transactions they could generate. A lease was a product—like hair spray or deodorant—and their marching orders were to sell it.

Fifteen years earlier, the notion that Citibank was a common carrier of money had driven the first nail into the coffin of old-time relationship banking. Now Wriston would hammer in another nail. Said leasing company chief Ed Harshfield, "We didn't understand that that's what we were doing. We thought we were augmenting relationship banking." And at the same time he ever so quietly opened another crack in the door to nationwide banking.

As the leasing group expanded around the country, setting up regional offices in five major U.S. cities and hiring experienced personnel, they were ordered not to rent space in buildings already occupied by other Citibank units, such as the Edge Act office in San Francisco. Although Citibank's presence outside New York was limited mainly to Edge Act offices, Wriston and others were concerned about Citibank becoming a lightning rod for opponents of bank expansion across state lines. Most of the bank's units were in high-rent districts anyway, and the lease salesmen were more interested in fat paychecks than in spacious offices. "Bankers didn't know how to close deals, to turn over the rocks till they find a deal, dog it till they got it done," Harshfield said. For him, success was the "kill ratio"—done deals, business on the books. In contrast, bankers tended to cultivate relationships and then wait for customers to call them.

The leasing group underwrote everything from IBM 360 mainframe computers and private jets to nuclear power plants. Among the world-scale projects financed by Citibank and the leasing company was the 800-mile trans-Alaska pipeline, which runs from the Prudhoe Bay field to the south coast port of Valdez. Citibank was the principal lender to the consortium of eight oil companies that built the pipeline, and the leasing units owned much of the equipment and many of the work camps deployed in the huge project.

One early proposal came from publisher Malcolm Forbes in a transaction that reinforced Wriston's policy of not making front office loans. Forbes had wanted to lease a jet, ultimately named the *Capitalist Tool,* from the leasing company, and stopped in Harshfield's office to discuss the deal. Forbes boasted that he was a good friend of Bill Spencer. But Spencer later warned, "He's on my Christmas card list, but beyond that you're on your own." He then reminded Harshfield that "we don't make front office loans in this bank."

Just how unprepared the Citibank culture was for lease salesmen was seen when one of them got into a traffic accident while driving one of the unit's many company cars. Although Harshfield had thought he was following proper bank procedure by sending lists of his employees and their cars to the bank's insurance department, he soon discovered that these messages had been falling into a bureaucratic black hole. Shortly after Harshfield called the insurance department to report the accident, he received a phone call from corporate secretary and Wriston confidant Carl Desch, who said, "I understand one of your guys got into an accident in Chicago."

"Yes, sir," Harshfield replied.

"You don't understand," Desch said. "There are only five bank cars. We don't have a fleet of cars."

Harshfield said he had been writing memos for more than a year reporting the car assignments.

Desch was astounded to learn that the bank had acquired a national fleet of cars without his knowledge. "We don't give bank officers cars," he told Harshfield.

"These aren't bank officers," Harshfield emphasized. "These are leasing officers." He said later that this incident "caused a big uproar. Nobody knew what to do. We were breaking down the rules."

That, however, was a minor flap compared with the battle going on between the lessors and the bank account officers. Although the lessors were theoretically supposed to contact a Citibank account officer before approaching a prospective customer, that apparently rarely happened. The turf war between the line bankers and the newcomers ultimately reached Wriston's office, and Harshfield was called on the carpet. In a scene that would be repeated frequently over the next fourteen years, Wriston "just kind of laughed," Harshfield recalled. Wriston told the bankers, "If you guys are in there two times and the other banks are in there once, we got two shots and the other banks only got one. You're going to have to live with it." This was a variation on the General Motors principle, which both Wriston and Moore believed should work for Citibank. "Chevrolet competes with Oldsmobile," Moore used to say, "but that gives General Motors twice as much opportunity to sell a car."

Wriston, said Harshfield, "never objected to the kinds of things we were doing as long as we didn't embarrass the bank. He didn't care whether we talked to the treasurer of General Motors. He thought that was a great thing." But amid the flap over turf, over who "owned" the customer and who had the right to serve that customer, one issue that was never settled was whether the customer was better off with Citibank competing against Citibank. Citibank, in fact, became the most aggressive competitor Citibank ever had.

Some of the drawbacks of decentralization and matrix management were apparent immediately. Others wouldn't manifest themselves for years. While Wriston may have had no choice but to create a decentralized matrix organization, Citibank would suffer, to a greater or lesser degree, from all of the ailments that commonly afflict such organizations: anarchy, power struggles and internal competition, profit centeritis, and the red tape and massive overhead that go hand in hand with the creation of more layers of bureaucracy to manage the matrix.

While the newly decentralized organization gave rise to a level of entrepreneurship unprecedented in American banking, the freedom that it afforded proved too much for some managers to handle. Over the next several years, bombshells exploded in such areas as computer leasing, real estate, and the bank's effort to penetrate upstate New York.

Decentralizing tax planning was like setting a time bomb. By giving local managers around the world responsibility for minimizing their own taxes, Citibank set the stage for the closest thing to a scandal that would ever taint Wriston's career. Decentralization and matrix management also proved to be expensive, for a variety of reasons. Decentralization became such a religion that Citibank purposely declined to take advantage of its immense buying power by centralizing the purchase of goods and services. Every profit center manager was responsible for his own purchasing—from paper clips to sophisticated telecommunications systems. Over the years, the need for additional layers of management and accountants, budget specialists, planners, and other staff personnel to control and coordinate caused overhead to skyrocket.

For the moment, however, the holding company and the McKinsey reorganization were the springboards for growth that would propel Citibank into the top spot in American and global banking.

While reorganizing his domestic forces, Wriston sidestepped, at least for the moment, the sensitive issue of how to realign his overseas empire to serve the bank's most important clients: multinational corporations like IBM and Exxon. As major U.S. companies began to break out of their cocoons in the 1950s and 1960s and expand overseas, Citibank found itself ill-prepared to meet their needs with equal fervor in Chicago and Caracas, in Boston and Buenos Aires. As late as the mid-1960s, Citibank was still sufficiently uncompartmentalized for an account officer in, say, the European district to cable his counterpart in Rio seeking assistance for a multinational customer there. By the end of the decade, however, it was becoming apparent to all but the die-hard traditionalists that it was inappropriate for the customer's man in Paris to be handling the local business of Du Pont as if that were Citibank's only relationship with the global chemical giant. As George Moore said, "They found they couldn't have twenty-one guys saying yes and no to IBM worldwide." Because Citibank wasn't viewing multinational companies as a total relationship, it had no idea whether any single customer was profitable to the bank as a whole. And as a result, country heads treated the local units of multinationals solely on the basis of how much those operations contributed to their own profit center earnings.

To be sure, every large multinational company selling different products in different countries had the same problem, including Exxon and IBM. Trouble was, as Wriston knew well, solving the problem of how best to serve the multinationals and transforming Citibank into a truly global organization would represent another frontal assault on the country head, or SENOF. That process had begun when Citibank organized the traveler's check business on a worldwide basis.

Nowhere was the problem more apparent than in the way SENOFs, particularly in developing countries, made decisions on how to allocate often scarce local currency among their multinational clients, which typically couldn't get enough currency to transact business and invest in projects such as factories. Part of the problem was that money markets were relatively undeveloped and foreign banks, such as Citibank, were limited by local regulation in their ability to expand their deposit-taking facilities. As Third World economies boomed, more currency was needed to fuel economic growth. Because of the large spreads that could be earned by lending in foreign currencies to smaller local companies, the SENOF naturally preferred to lend to those companies rather than to IBM and Du Pont, even though the multinationals were more important to Citibank in the global scheme of things.

The problem of allocating credit for a transaction was even more complex in the overseas arena than it was domestically. A loan, for example, could originate in Brazil, be booked in Nassau, and the account managed in New York. Ed Palmer, then an executive vice president, would later contend that Wriston himself, in his early days as head of the overseas division, was deaf to the problems of serving multinationals. But when Palmer told Wriston, "We've got a hell of a problem. It's your problem," Wriston replied, "Well, we have lots of people. We have people who are experts all over, in every place." The debate went on, but ended inconclusively.

Neither the U.S. corporate bankers nor Costanzo's SENOFs wanted to let go of their respective pieces of the multinational pie. The corporate banking group, which picked up the big domestic accounts from the branches, wanted to complete the process by taking over worldwide multinational relationships, but Costanzo would have none of that. It was one thing to emasculate branch officers, already low on the corporate totem pole, by snatching away their prized corporate accounts, but it was quite another to take on the all-powerful SENOFs. Wriston put some of the blame for this development on McKinsey & Company. "The only thing McKinsey did poorly was overseas, because they didn't understand the business," he said later. Four more years would pass before the rest of the empire was ready for matrix management.

Whatever its limitations, the new decentralized structure of Citibank fit very neatly Wriston's laissez-faire style of management. Like his father, Walter believed in picking the best people and then delegating to them as much responsibility as they were able to handle—and in some cases more than they could manage. Tom Theobald, who would later be one of three contenders for Wriston's job, said that in the fifteen years he reported more or less directly to Wriston, Wriston never questioned one of his numbers or told him to stop doing something. "He had an interest in personnel, ideas. There was very little interference, harassment—maybe to the point where I had very little guidance. It was almost as if he didn't have very good ideas about how the business should develop. He was betting on each to do what he thought best." Wriston was, said Theobald, the "least bosslike individual you could imagine in a corporation."

The Citibank assignment, which was McKinsey's first major bank study, propelled the big consulting firm into preeminence as a font of wisdom for the banking industry. McKinsey's modus operandi was to implement a new program at great expense to one bank, then sell the same formula to others. Before the 1970s were over, McKinsey made untold millions in consultant fees by installing the concept at banks throughout the country. It wasn't long before Chase Manhattan, a trend follower like the other big banks, hired McKinsey to do for them what it had done for Citibank. That, of course, did not go over well with Wriston. "Chase did what they always do," he said later. "They wait a few minutes and do what Citi does," adding that "I told McKinsey I thought it [implementing the plan at Chase] was a little bit questionable—at that point it was semi-proprietary. Now it's conventional wisdom." But before long others, like Seattle–First National Bank and Continental Illinois, also became smitten with McKinsey, decentralization, and 15 percent fever. But there McKinsey either omitted the chapter on internal controls or the banks failed to read it. By the early 1980s many of those institutions would be on the sick list, and in a few instances—namely Continental Illinois Bank & Trust and Seattle–First National Bank—their obituaries would show up on the evening news and on the front pages of the nation's newspapers.

On January 2, 1969, the new market-oriented Citibank opened for business. But the battle to make it all work was just beginning. If ever there was a time when Wriston's favorite quotation—"Every good and excellent thing in the world stands moment by moment on the razor-edge of danger and must be fought for," from *The Skin of our Teeth* by Thornton Wilder—seemed to fit, this was it. In the short run at least, a hostile Justice Department, Congress, and tight money would conspire to deny Wriston's bank the fruits of its labors.

As the head of a company that aspired to offer every financial service that it could at a profit anywhere in the world, George Moore couldn't have helped to choose a more unsympathetic man at the U.S. Treasury Department. As then secretary of the Treasury David Kennedy recalls, Moore "wanted to do anything on earth," including manufacturing. "George Moore wanted no restrictions. I thought they should be in the banking business. Charls Walker was with me on it."

After he was appointed by Nixon, Kennedy tapped Walker to serve as his deputy. Walker, meanwhile, had been in touch with his friend Arthur Burns, the gravelly-voiced sixty-four-year-old professor who had been Nixon's economic adviser during the campaign and would soon become counselor to the president. In a late-fall phone call, Walker asked Burns if he had ever heard of the one-bank holding company and then warned him that "it's leading us toward *zaibatsu.* . . . It's something that should be dealt with right away." Burns asked Walker to draft a memo for him on the issue.

On January 20, 1969, the very day that Nixon was inaugurated in Washington, Citibank fired the banking industry's opening salvo in the battle for insurance powers and confirmed Walker's deepest concerns. Wriston and Moore had long yearned for the day when they could really break into the insurance business. Wriston, especially, had long been envious of the freedoms enjoyed by the insurance industry, particularly the exemptions it had secured from anti-trust statutes. Wriston's new father-in-law, as New York state's insurance commissioner in the 1940s, helped push through the legislation that granted those exemptions. Even before plans were made to form the holding company, Wriston and Moore had singled out Chubb Corporation, the big property and casualty insurer, as their first major acquisition target. Overseas, the business of Citibank and Chubb seemed to present endless opportunities for collaboration, and in the United States, there were no apparent conflicts. Though Citibank was in the throes of a long and expensive court battle to enable it to offer mutual funds, Chubb was not in that or any other business that was specifically off-limits to banks.

In its announcement of the proposed $376 million transaction, Moore stated, "The ability to make this kind of deal is precisely the reason for First National City Corp.'s formation. First National City Corporation regards the insurance business as directly within the scope of planned extension into related financial fields." He added that "we consider insurance as entirely complementary to the banking business." It seemed like a perfect fit. Too perfect.

Shortly after Nixon was sworn in, Walker received from Arthur Burns a regurgitation of his own memo instructing him to draft legislation to address the *"zaibatsu* problem." On this issue Kennedy and Walker were agreed; Kennedy later told *Fortune* that unless the government blocked linkages between financial and nonfinancial firms, the United States would be "dominated by some fifty to seventy-five huge centers of economic and financial power, each of which would consist of a corporate conglomerate controlling a large bank or a multibillion dollar bank controlling a large nonfinancial conglomerate." No one was more influential than Walker in getting the new administration focused on a bill to regulate one-bank holding companies.

Opponents of the one-bank holding company movement didn't have to wait long for more ammunition to fight their battle. In early February, Leasco Data Processing Equipment Corporation, headed by investor Saul Steinberg, launched a raid to gain control of New York's Chemical Bank, the first attempted takeover of a big bank in modern financial history. Meanwhile, Walker, in Washington, was pulling strings behind the scenes to stop Steinberg. Walker would say later that "we engineered it through [Senator John J.] Sparkman. He called hearings and got so much publicity that Steinberg had to back off."

The formation of its holding company, and the prospect of legislation to regulate such companies, would present Citibank with its first major opportunity to try to influence Congress on a critical bill that would dramatically affect its business. At that time, large banks in general, and Citibank in particular, had little insight into or influence on the machinations of Congress. Previously, Citibank had neither the occasion nor the inclination for glad-handing, and it suffered from a certain naïveté about the ways of Washington and Capitol Hill. The bank's politicking largely centered around George Moore's personal relationships with fellow opera buffs like Representative Emmanuel Celler, tennis partner Jacob Javits, and sympathetic regulators like Comptroller of the Currency James Saxon. "We didn't develop in my period relations with Washington that we should have, and [the bank] didn't do any of it before my day," said Moore later. Citibank most often dealt with Washington on an ad hoc basis and lacked anything resembling a legislative lobbying program. For years the bank's activities had been driven more by regulatory fiat than by legislative developments, so lobbying was to Citibank almost a dirty word—and Wriston was not known for his political savvy, either. Even Shearman & Sterling, Citibank's otherwise shrewd law firm, had remained aloof from Washington's realities. Said S&S partner Hans Angermueller, who would later become Citibank vice chairman, "It [the law firm] took the law as it found it."

In the mid-1960s, Citibank had set up a small Washington office run by lobbyist Jack Yingling. He had misgivings about the creation of the holding company, but Wriston and Moore didn't consult with him on their decision. "If they had," he said later, "I would have told them of the dangerous political consequences." At one policy committee meeting, Yingling got the executives' attention when he informed them that they needed to begin making political contributions. "Jack," Wriston replied, "if you went around this room and talked to each one of these officers, probably almost all of them would tell you that they would not do it, that they think politics is a dirty business and they don't want any part of it."

It wouldn't be long before Citibank shed its puritanical scruples.

On February 17, 1969, Wright Patman, the nemesis of the big banks, submitted legislation aimed at closing forever the one-bank holding company loophole—in effect killing the parent and leaving the child an orphan. Obviously responding to Citibank's bid for Chubb, the Patman bill named insurance as just one of the activities from which banks would be banned. Though Patman was obsessed with sinister tie-ins, *Fortune* later observed that they were "not as dangerous as they appear" and that the concern over them "ignores the existence of antitrust laws." But for the duration of the legislative battle, Citibank was Patman's whipping boy. Whenever he needed an example of the evils of one-bank holding companies, he cited Citibank.

The original Nixon administration's Senate bill, drafted by Charls Walker, proposed to limit bank holding companies to financially related businesses and bring them under the control of the primary regulator—be it the Comptroller of the Currency or the state banking departments—which would decide what was and was not related. Walker wanted to avoid letting the Fed into the act. But because of the high esteem in which Congress held the Fed, it quickly became clear that keeping the central bank out of the loop would not sell, and the revised bill, introduced in the Senate on March 24, 1969, by Senators Wallace F. Bennett and John J. Sparkman, proposed that a triumvirate of bank regulatory agencies make those decisions. Although the bill proposed to bring one-bank holding companies under the 1956 Bank Holding Company Act, it also sought to liberalize that law somewhat by dropping the requirement that non-bank activities be "closely related to banking," and it would have allowed banks to engage in computer leasing, data processing, insurance, and some securities operations. Moreover, it included a grandfather clause that would have permitted bank holding companies to keep non-bank businesses acquired before June 30, 1968. Although Patman and the small banks viewed the Nixon bill as a sellout to the big banks, it was, to some, oppressive enough to be regarded as Charls Walker's revenge on George Moore. Thus began the long and tumultuous voyage of one of the most significant pieces of bank legislation since the 1930s, one that would redefine the business of banking and set the basic structure of the industry in the United States.

At an offsite conference in early 1969, Wriston gave his staff their instructions: scour the country for congenerics (businesses related to banking) that could be grandfathered; don't buy anything within 300 miles of New York City; acquire relatively small congenerics in different areas of the country, but don't buy more than one of any single type of business in the same region. If the bank bought bushels of relatively small congeneric businesses in the United States and overseas and didn't bet the bank on any single one, most of them, Wriston figured, should pan out in the long run. He was prepared to take losses in the short term for a long-term gain. The ideas and proposals and pilot tests came fast and furious. Wriston was willing to try just about anything; Citibank planners formed a dozen or so subsidiaries under the holding company to accommodate the new activities.

Mortgage banking was another special interest. Wriston's merger and acquisition SWAT team found a relatively small company, Advance Mortgage, in Detroit, that operated in the upper Midwest and seemed to fit the bill. Advance was to be a key device for setting up shop outside New York City. Citibank would then sell Advance customers other bank products. In early 1969, Citibank made its overture to the company, and in March of that year, announced that it would try out an income tax preparation service. A few months later the computerized service would be offered through its New York branches to all customers, so the plan went.

Two months later, in an effort that represented the seed corn of a trend that would take hold in a major way more than a decade later, Citibank announced that it would establish its own sales finance unit, the FNC Credit Corporation, which would allow the bank to convert loans to cash and then use the cash to make still more loans. Under this arrangement, loans would be purchased using the proceeds of holding company commercial paper, enabling the bank to circumvent both reserve requirements on deposits and Regulation Q ceilings. It would be a kind of one-two punch at federal regulation of banking.

Many proposals that were implemented in the excitement following the formation of the holding company later withered on the vine, and some never saw the light of day. One that fell into the latter category, to Wriston's enduring relief, was a device called the real estate investment trust, or REIT. Created by Wall Street in response to recent changes in the federal tax laws that encouraged real estate investment, the REIT appeared to be an attractive device for bank holding companies. In effect, a REIT was an interim construction lender that would borrow from the bank and make construction loans to developers. "Everyone wanted to form a REIT," said one former Citibank officer. But Wriston, ever the Lone Ranger, was not one to ride with the posse. When his planning group broached the idea, he rolled his eyes, according to one member of the team. "I want a novel idea here," the officer quoted Wriston as saying. "Don't just bring me a suit off the rack." But he had deeper objections to the REIT concept, viewing it as a serious conflict of interest.

Though Wriston followed his instincts on the REIT, he ignored them when he agreed to establish, in 1969, a real estate lending unit. He was not fond of real estate developers. "Some members of that profession aren't the most fun people you'll ever work with," he said later with some understatement. Because of his early credit training, he was well aware of the toll the "sharp practices" of real estate operators had taken on Citibank in the first half of the century. But now Citibank was prepared to try anything, even turning into a kind of innkeeper when it acquired a stake in the Ramada chain. Almost everything began to smell "congeneric."

Meanwhile, the Department of Justice's anti-trust squad was once again on Wriston's case. Less than two months after the Chubb announcement, Justice announced that it had sent a formal "investigative letter" to Citibank indicating it had a more than casual interest in the move. If that wasn't subtle enough, anti-trust chief Richard W. McLaren told *American Banker* in an interview of his concern for concentrations of economic power that could result from combinations of banks and insurance companies. Amid all the hints from Washington that the Chubb deal might not fly, First National on March 19, 1969, said it had ended discussions to buy Advance Mortgage just two weeks after it had announced it was considering the acquisition. But a year later it made a tender offer of $30 million in cash for the company.

In early 1969, Wriston and Laeri trekked to Washington in the hope of obtaining the blessing of the attorney general, John Mitchell, and his deputy, Richard G. Kleindienst. In the meeting, the two government lawyers expressed concern over the dangers of tie-in sales. According to Wriston, Kleindienst said, "You would come in with a card in your pocket that a borrower could read. The card in effect would say that if you wanted a loan you would have to insure your factory through Chubb & Son." Wriston tried to convince them that the world was too competitive for a bank to try to force customers to buy its brand of insurance or borrow its money. Finally, despite their differences, Wriston and Laeri left the meeting "feeling pretty good," according to bank archives.

In late April, shareholders of Citibank and Chubb approved the merger, and chairman George Moore announced that there have been "no developments to date which lead us to believe the merger will not be consummated." Nonetheless, in early May, Citibank agreed to postpone the deal until the Justice Department weighed in with its opinion. That came with a thud in mid-June, when Justice threatened Citibank with a temporary restraining order if it moved to complete the deal. The department had demanded all the files on the acquisition, including a memo written by James Tozer on all the synergies that could be realized. In a classic case of Citibank shooting itself in the foot, that memo, said Tozer, became "Exhibit A in the Justice Department's argument opposing the acquisition."

Temperamentally, Wriston and Moore were inclined to slug the Chubb issue out in court. But Citibank board members and Sherman & Sterling's Fred Eaton had a poor opinion of Citi's chances of winning there. This as well as the generally weak internal support for the acquisition caused Citibank to throw in the towel, marking the second time in little over a year that the bank had chucked its merger plans when confronted with the threat of an anti-trust action. Within days the Justice Department called off its suit. But Wriston forever clung to the hope of a marriage between banking and insurance, and that the ceremony would be consummated at Citibank. For the moment, however, Wriston would have to be content with a spot on Chubb's board, to which he was elected in 1970.

In 1974 Wriston gingerly asked Fred Eaton to resign from the board, thereby drastically altering the cozy decades-old relationship between Shearman & Sterling and Citibank. As the Chubb affair had demonstrated, there was, in Wriston's view, a built-in conflict of interest for a partner in a company's law firm to serve on the company's board. To Wriston's relief and surprise, Eaton replied, "You're right." And he advised Wriston never to nominate another lawyer from the firm.

The lesson from the ill-fated merger attempt was that the banking industry would have to "think small" when it came to congenerics, as *American*

Banker put it. The Justice Department was clearly determined to discourage reciprocity between banking and insurance and other financial services that would lead to concentrations of power in financial congenerics. One obvious conclusion was that a bank that serves largely retail customers should aim to link up with a corporate insurer, and vice versa. One of Justice's concerns was reportedly the conflict that they thought could arise out of the fact that Citibank was one of the major lessors of aircraft and Chubb was a major insurer of aircraft. Later, anti-trust chief Richard McLaren made it clear that the division would have sued Citibank if it had not abandoned its merger plans. He added that the "significant market power" of commercial banks alone established reciprocity, among other violations of anti-trust statutes. When it came to insurance, the regulators had Citibank stymied, even offshore. Just a few months after the Justice Department prevailed on the Chubb issue, the Fed turned down Citibank's application to buy a life insurance company in Taiwan on the grounds that it was not "closely related to banking."

Meanwhile Wriston and Moore were getting somewhat better treatment at the hands of British authorities.

Lord Toby Aldington—former member of Parliament, deputy chairman of the Conservative Party, and chairman of the billion-dollar-deposit Grindlays Bank, which operated nearly three hundred branches in India, Pakistan, Sri Lanka, Somalia, Kenya, Jordan, and other remnants of the defunct British Empire—stopped by for lunch with Moore and Wriston. When he said he was on his way to see David Rockefeller about a badly needed capital injection, Moore's response was predictable. Moore perked up at the thought of another acquisition. "Stay right here," he insisted.

Aldington questioned, albeit briefly, whether a joint venture between two direct competitors—Citibank and Grindlays—would make sense, prompting Moore to rattle off a list of corporate customers and markets not shared by the two institutions. "That was another George Moore deal. He met Lord Aldington on an airplane or someplace, and had to buy Grindlays," said Wriston later. Part of the thinking behind the deal, to the extent there was any, was for Grindlays to link up with BIAO, Citibank's subsidiary in Africa, and give Citibank a formidable foothold there—a dubious prize.

Over lunch, Aldington agreed to sell Citibank a piece of Grindlays. Wriston and Moore would have liked a majority stake, but the Bank of England, according to Shearman & Sterling's Henry Harfield, objected to a "Yankee" bank owning a significant interest in a British institution. To circumvent that objection, Citibank acquired a 40 percent interest in the London-based bank for about $47.3 million in stock and subordinated notes and became a partner with Lloyds Bank in a holding company that owned the remaining 60 percent. As a result, Citibank wound up with a 49 percent position. Completed in early April 1969, the transaction expanded the Citibank empire to 578 offices in seventy-eight countries and territories, including 234 branch offices or subsidiaries in fifty countries. The deal made little sense, though not for the reasons that Aldington had cited. In effect, Wriston and Moore had acquired an interest in an institution that culturally was more like the Citibank they were trying to bury than the one they were trying to build. In their frenetic bid to gain territory, they had bought a piece of the past rather than the future.

To celebrate its new affiliation, Citibank scheduled its May board meeting in the United Kingdom, its first overseas board meeting and one that would include a trip by special train from London to Edinburgh. Appropriately, Lord Aldington was named to the board of the First National City Corporation, the first non-American to be so honored. One director who was not caught up in the excitement of the occasion, however, was Stillman Rockefeller. Virtually ignored by Wriston and Moore at the meeting in Scotland, the sullen ex-chairman sat in a corner, complaining to a colleague, "I don't have many friends here anymore."

In the wake of the serendipitous acquisition of Grindlays—one that would serve only to provide a succession of Citibank officers with experience in working out problem loans and unwinding bad deals—Wriston's May 28, 1969, address, delivered in London to top European businessmen and government officials, was right on the mark. Condemning what he called the drift to a "riskless society," Wriston said that "risk cannot be eliminated from the affairs of men." He implored them to "stand up and be counted in the fight to continue to liberalize the movement of capital, labor, goods, and services across international boundaries. He also cautioned against thinking that a riskless existence can be achieved through protectionism, exchange controls, or nationalism.

After the honeymoon with Grindlays ended, the frictions intensified. In addition to personality and cultural clashes, much acrimony resulted from Grindlays' view of Citibank as a bottomless well of capital, according to one source familiar with the relationship. And later, as pressure intensified on Citibank to bolster its own capital, it chafed at the demands from Grindlays.

There was, as always, no controlling George Moore when he had a mind to acquire something. While some referred euphemistically to these transactions as "well-informed intuition," Wriston and others called them George's swimming pool deals. "We just wished he'd let us know before the seller shows up for a check and says, 'I met him in Marseilles two weeks ago,' " said one former Citibank officer. Moore's quest for joint ventures and acquisitions even resulted in a brief meeting in his 399 Park office with the notorious Bernard Cornfeld, the ex–social worker turned mutual fund salesman who later became notorious for a failed Ponzi scheme, Investors Overseas Services Limited, that fleeced unwary investors of millions. Fortunately for Moore, that deal never got beyond the pleasantries stage. "Some guy from Switzerland whom I knew and trusted made an appointment with my secretary to meet Cornfeld," admitted Moore later. "He came into my office for five minutes; he wanted me to do something for him. I had another meeting at the same time, and he went on his way. I knew he was a crook."

Some of Moore's deals, however, showed great "vision and luck," according to former Citibanker Gerard Finneran. In the late 1960s, a friend advised Moore to open a branch in the Channel Islands to take advantage of the low maximum tax rate. Moore instructed Finneran to "go see what's down there," and in 1969 the Channel Islands branch opened with a burst of publicity, none of it especially favorable. Moore, complimenting Finneran on his coup, said, "You got great publicity."

The officer was stunned. "They [the local press] compared the branch opening to the Nazi invasion. They even had the Nazi eagle in the picture," he replied.

"Young man," Moore intoned, "any publicity is good publicity."

But Citibank "made enormous amounts of money" in the Channel Islands, Finneran said, by exploiting its status as a tax haven, and the branch became a mecca for European entertainment and sports personalities seeking relief from the heavy tax burdens in their own home countries.

If Charls Walker was troubled by the thought of *zaibatsu* in the United States, Wriston was equally troubled by the real power of the Japanese variety. Theoretically, the conglomerates had been broken up after World War II, but Wriston knew better. By the late 1960s, Japan was booming, and Citibank's business there and in Asia generally was perking up. According to internal Citibank documents, the Asia Pacific division earned $7.6 million in 1969, took in nearly $12 million in 1970, and expected to make $16 million the next year. The bank's Japanese operations were even outperforming those in London, in part by helping Japanese companies tap into the burgeoning Euromarkets. Nonetheless, the Japanese found imaginative ways to deny American companies and banks the opportunity to do business there. Getting permission to open branches in Japan was like trying to eat broth with a fork.

In the late 1960s, Wriston asked Richard Perkins to travel to Japan to try his gentle diplomacy on the finance minister, but that didn't work. The reason given for the refusal was perhaps the most creative ever offered by a host country. The minister informed Perkins that construction of new high-rise office buildings had been banned, and that since bank branches were generally located on the ground floor of skyscrapers, he had no choice but to reject the application. In April 1969, Wriston flew to Japan on a ten-day expedition sponsored by the Council on Foreign Relations, to tell the Japanese authorities that they weren't playing by the rules, that they had stacked the deck against American business in general and against Citibank in particular. In a speech to startled Japanese business and government leaders, Wriston "told them so to their face," he said later. "They had 1200 violations of the General Agreement on Tariffs and Trade (GATT). The embassy nearly died [from] 1000 cuts."

Led by George Moore, Citibank figured if it couldn't beat the Japanese,

it would have to join them. According to former Citibank officers, the effort
to join them began in the mid-1960s, when Moore struck up a friendship with
Yoshizane Iwasa, chairman of the Fuji Bank, Citibank's principal bank client in Japan, when the two men found themselves stuck at New York's JFK
Airport during a snowstorm. In 1968, Moore and his bride honeymooned in
Asia, and during his visit to Japan, Iwasa took Moore and Charon and several Citibank Asian hands to a geisha house to toast the newlyweds. After a
few drinks, Moore suggested that the two institutions "do something together," as one former Citibanker put it. Iwasa was receptive. "Like what?"
he asked. "Something on a grand scale," Moore is said to have replied. The
finance minister at the time was nearly as restrictive when it came to the
desires of Japanese banks to expand internationally as he was in guarding the
gate against foreign expansion in Japan. "Fuji saw Citibank as its breakout
strategy," said Asia hand Richard Wheeler. Over the next few years, Fuji and
Chairman Iwasa would enter into an assortment of joint ventures, some
profitable, others not, that gave Citibank entrée to the Fuji *zaibatsu.* These
ventures included a merchant bank, a leasing and consulting company, even a
joint venture to lend Japanese consumers yen to buy automobiles.

Citibank plunged into the marriage with Fuji even as it was discovering
that it [Citibank] made a bad partner, and that joint ventures as such never
really panned out. Those that did were typically aimed at doing something
that neither partner could possibly do on its own. "We were sitting there trying to figure out why, if we had a good piece of business, we should put it into
APCO [the Asia Pacific Company, the merchant bank joint venture with
Fuji], when 15 percent of the profits go to Japan," said former Citibanker Jim
Tozer. Still, this collaboration with a Japanese financial institution enabled
Citibank to tap into its local corporate affiliates and help them raise money in
the Euromarkets. According to Wheeler, Citibank also helped open up the
U.S. commercial paper market to Japanese companies.

Controlling operations in Japan and Asia was always something of a
challenge for Citibank. Although officially the Japanese operation was
headed by an American, the real power figure was the number two man, a
highly intelligent and tight-lipped Japanese. He was the Japanese equivalent
of the Chinese comprador, the intermediary between the American and Japanese staff.

Hong Kong, the defalcation capital of the Citi empire, was a perennial
problem. At one point, frequent employee thefts and frauds forced the bank
to administer lie detector tests. Loans were made for speculative stock market, real estate, shipping, and other ventures. Unwittingly, Hong Kong even
made a $2 million loan for a ship to transport contraband to the Philippines,
a transaction that was uncovered when a curious auditor found that the
lender had never even seen the collateral on a loan ostensibly made to buy a
yacht. When the auditor decided to check it out for himself, he found mortar
base plates on the deck of the "yacht."

Korea, where Citibank first opened a branch in 1967, was plagued by
beggars who harassed and mugged the bank's customers as they were leaving

the premises, ripping off their watches and other valuables. Citibank's Korean adviser informed the local branch manager that the "beggar king," who controlled all of the beggars, had complained that Citibank hadn't paid him his dues. Citibank's Ham Meserve responded that Citibank didn't pay bribes. Instead, the bank raised the adviser's fees, and he saw to it that the trouble ceased.

While Citibank was trying to pry open Japan, Ray Kathe, the bank's Mr. Asia, was working to extend the Eurodollar market into Asia. As the Euromarket grew, London naturally emerged as its physical and spiritual center. But there was no reason for excess dollars generated in trade with Asia to wind up in London or other funding centers outside of Asia, other than the concern of local finance authorities about upsetting their own institutions. According to Kathe, a Bank of America official was behind the original effort to persuade Singapore to create an Asian currency market. But, said Kathe, Bank of America was trying to set up its own tight-knit club. The West Coast bank was "trying to hide this thing and keep it with only a few friendly banks that would give them basically U.S. dollars, which they would merely pump into their Eurodollar market people in London." At the urging of Citibank's Singapore manager, Kathe called on Singapore's financial authorities to seek an Asian Eurocurrency license. The finance official wanted to know what Citibank could do for Singapore. "Much more than BofA can," Kathe replied bluntly. On the spot, he promised that if Singapore granted Citibank the authority to accept Asian dollar deposits, then Citibank would promise to lend them in Asia, though not necessarily in Singapore. While that appealed to the Singaporeans, they recoiled at Kathe's insistence that for the market to take off, they would have to give licenses to all creditworthy banks, foreign and local.

Singapore eventually relented and also abolished all reserve requirements and exchange controls. Citibank's Asian branches soon began funneling Asian dollars into the tiny city-state, contributing in no small way to its rise as an Asian financial mecca. On a roll, Kathe shortly thereafter shuttled to Hong Kong, where he warned a friend, a top financial official, that "Singapore is going to run you right off the map." Kathe was trying to persuade him to open up his foreign currency market as well by eliminating its tax on deposit interest. Since Hong Kong placed no restrictions on foreign exchange conversions, the official was afraid that all currency in Hong Kong would be driven to U.S. dollars. Kathe later returned to his base in Tokyo to press the Japanese to follow Singapore's lead. While Fuji Bank's Iwasa was receptive to the idea, other Japanese banks rejected it. Before long, Singapore, which imposed a tax on income from assets, emerged as Asia's liability center, and Hong Kong became the asset center. Singapore ultimately slashed its tax on assets, and Hong Kong removed its tax on deposits. That enabled bankers in both cities to easily gather deposits and make loans, and resulted in their rise as the banking capitals of Asia. By 1974, sixty foreign banks were operating in Singapore, and in three years the Eurodollar market there had tripled to $6 billion.

The year 1969 was a turning point in Asian expansion. Under Costanzo, Citibank's Asian operations grew far more rapidly than they had under Wriston. Citibank established joint ventures or subsidiaries in Malaysia, Singapore, and the Philippines and finally broke into Thailand through a joint venture with the Bangkok Bank of Thailand to finance housing and industrial concerns and to make personal loans and engage in securities dealing. Citibankers even fanned out across the South Pacific, obtaining licenses for joint venture banks and congenerics on idyllic South Seas islands, including Fiji, Tahiti, and Samoa. The idea, said one former Citibanker, was that "tourists were going to come and we'd make money on the local infrastructure in the meantime." But some Citibankers said cynically that the real reason senior overseas officers established operations in places like this was to give them an excuse to take frequent trips there.

Meanwhile, in Washington, House Banking Committee chairman Wright Patman was not content merely to block the big banks' efforts to expand their activities. He also wanted to prevent them from making money in their traditional lines of business while preserving the local monopolies of country banks.

The economic strains created by the Vietnam War and the Johnson-era Great Society programs had begun to show up by the mid-1960s, but it was not until 1969 that they began to reach the breaking point. In December 1968 the Fed slammed on the monetary brakes, raising bank reserve requirements and increasing the discount rate to 6 percent, a level not experienced since the 1920s. While economic growth slowed significantly, inflation continued at a rapid clip, with the consumer price index rising at a rate of one-half of 1 percent a month through most of the year. As a result, interest rates on the open market soared to record heights; by mid-1969 the prime rate had risen to 8.5 percent. But the Fed, in one of the great monetary policy blunders in its history, declined to lift Regulation Q ceilings on time and savings deposits above 4 percent and 6.25 percent, respectively. Not surprisingly, money rushed out of the banks like water over Hoover Dam as depositors put it into instruments yielding 9 percent to 11 percent. During this period, some $6 billion left the money center banks, including $1 billion from Citibank alone. As William Spencer put it later in a speech, "To service our clients, we were forced to borrow Eurodollars, sometimes at rates as high as 13 percent. We were lending this money at 8.5 percent—not a very profitable way to conduct business." But the banks were not buying dear and selling cheap because they wanted to. They had already made loan commitments that they were obligated to fund.

The Fed reacted to the banks' quest for Eurodollars as if they were Public Enemy Number One, forcing up the cost of this form of borrowing by slapping reserve requirements on it. All of this, of course, did nothing to reduce inflationary pressures. In a reference to the McKinsey reorganization,

Wriston said later, "By accident of history, the increased lending authority coincided with the day we ran out of money." Citibank's new ad campaign—"First National City hates to say no"—seemed somewhat ill-timed. In many cases, the bank had no other choice.

Probably more than any other perversion of the bank regulatory and legislative process, the failure to lift Reg Q ceilings, or to abolish Regulation Q altogether, caused banks and thrift institutions to make business decisions over the next two decades that would, in far too many cases, prove fatal.

Market conditions dictated a prime even higher than the 8.5 percent level. But Wright Patman would have none of that. This was a tailor-made opportunity to rub the noses of David Rockefeller, who had earlier in the year become sole CEO of Chase Manhattan, and Walter Wriston in the dirt, and to make some cheap political points in the process. Either the concept that bankers raised the prime in response to market forces escaped Wright Patman, or worse still, he chose to ignore it. Lecturing Rockefeller and Moore from his throne in the House Banking Committee hearing room, Patman charged them and their fellow bankers with raising the prime to boost profits. There was some truth to that. In fact, they were increasing the prime simply to keep their noses above water.

In his testimony before Patman, Moore defended the increases, saying that they were the "result, not the cause of money conditions." He described the Fed's tight money policy as "comparable to putting a car in reverse when it is moving forward at fifty miles an hour." Then Patman took Treasury secretary David Kennedy to task for not jawboning the banks. In a testy exchange, Kennedy said he had not even discussed a "rollback" with the banks.

"Did you discuss it with anybody?" Patman wanted to know.

"No," Kennedy replied.

Patman asked, "Why didn't you?"

"Why should I?" Kennedy snapped.

If it was not clear before, it was certainly evident by 1969 that the prime rate was an anachronism. The prime had come into being during the Great Depression as the rate that banks used in lending to their biggest and best corporate customers. That was a time, of course, when business loan demand was practically nil and banks charged as little as one third of one percent interest. "Although the banks still operating had money to lend, borrowers were as scarce as unadulterated Pinch Bottle Scotch," as Bill Spencer put it later. From 1934 through 1947, the prime never rose above 1.5 percent. That changed for the first time, albeit insignificantly, in December 1947, when it was raised to 1.75 percent. Over the next twelve years, it rose as high as 5 percent, then dropped to 4.5 percent, where it remained until 1965. It then began the first leg of a long roller-coaster ride in which it rose ten times and fell eleven times through June 1971.

By 1969, however, Citibank was not entirely without weapons to fight back. Notwithstanding all the wonderful new activities that the bank now looked forward to performing under the holding company umbrella, it had originally overlooked the one new power that would prove to be among the most important. The one-bank holding company gave First National City Corporation an opportunity to sell commercial paper, a short-term money market instrument. Unlike negotiable CDs and other deposit instruments issued by the bank, holding company commercial paper wasn't subject to Reg Q. By the end of 1969, it had put $324 million in commercial paper on the books. According to sources involved in setting up the new entity, the savings on funding costs covered all the expenses of the holding company. In the holding company prospectus, commercial paper was mentioned only in an offhand way. "I don't think at the time we realized this was the first real dividend to come out of it," said one source. As Wriston later told *Euromoney,* "The CD funded the world for ten years, more or less, and then commercial paper came in for bank holding companies for another ten years."

Citibank also turned the practice of borrowing at the Federal Reserve discount window into an art form. The discount window was originally conceived as a temporary device to help banks through temporary liquidity crunches. Borrowing too much was regarded as a sign of weakness and a stigma to be avoided at all costs. In the late 1960s, however, there was no hard and fast definition of "excessive borrowing." The window opened and closed for a particular bank according to the seat-of-the-pants judgment of the man behind it.

Like a naughty child determined to test the limits of a parent's patience, Citibank's money desk borrowed more money more frequently than any other bank in New York until it received some subtle signal in Fedspeak that it had gone overboard. The reason for all the borrowing was simple. At that time, banks could borrow from the discount window at rates one-half to three-quarters of 1 percent lower than the cost of other kinds of money. The savings went directly to Walter Wriston's bottom line. "They tried to find out . . . if they borrowed three periods in a row, would that be too many. They were always pushing to find the limits that were permissible," said a source close to the Fed.

Much as Patman tried to cast himself as the friend of the consumer, the consumer suffered along with the banks from the pressure the Fed and Congress were putting on banks' ability to earn money the old-fashioned way. Citibank and others started charging fees for services—checking accounts, small government securities trades, and so on—that it had once given away.

On July 23, 1969, in the midst of the furor over interest rates, Patman suffered a setback when a majority of his committee proposed an amended bill that was much milder than expected in its treatment of bank holding companies. But, to be sure, it proposed to close the one-bank loophole, and it assigned to the Fed the power to determine what was "functionally related" to banking. Under heavy pressure from the insurance and securities industry lobbies, it specifically restricted banks from engaging in these businesses. But the committee resisted lobbyist pressure and Patman's demands for a so-called negative laundry list that would keep banks out of other activities, including leasing, travel services, and data processing. And it included a grandfather clause that would have allowed bank holding companies to retain "nonqualifying" subsidiaries bought before February 17, 1969. Ironically, Citibank had acquired nothing that would benefit from the grandfather clause.

Patman was furious at having been outgunned by members of his own committee. "A soaking wet dishrag would have been stronger than that bill," he railed later. Once Patman got his hands on the bill, he mustered his allies and virtually rewrote it on the floor of the House with a series of amendments, producing the toughest possible piece of legislation.

Patman's revised bill did contain the dreaded negative laundry list. One-bank holding companies would be blocked from participating in everything dear to Moore and Wriston, including mutual funds, insurance, travel services, data processing, insurance, and leasing. There was to be no grandfathering. Indeed, the Patman bill would have grandfathered one-bank holding companies all the way back to 1956, treating them just like multibank holding companies. It was the worst possible outcome. That bill, Wriston said later, "would seem to indicate that if there is a banking lobby, it is notably ineffective."

With the passage of the House bill, the prospects for legislation favorable to the big banks appeared poor enough without Citibank provoking Congress into coming down even harder, if that was possible. To avoid becoming a trip wire for Congress, Wriston hired a young lawyer for his planning and acquisition unit to shepherd non-bank acquisitions through the regulatory establishment while the legislation was being fought out. While being interviewed by Wriston for the job, the lawyer, Chris York, a former air force captain and military judge who had run a credit union on his military base, sat awestruck as Wriston engaged in one of his favorite sports: baiting Uncle George.

When Moore, wearing a trench coat and golf hat, stuck his head in Wriston's door just before leaving for the day, Wriston invited him in to meet York and told him mischievously that they had been talking about credit unions. "What do you think about credit unions, George?" Wriston inquired. He knew the answer well. Moore immediately launched into his speech number 420 on the evils of credit unions and how they were part of a Communist conspiracy to drive consumers away from good commercial banks. Clasping his hands behind his head, Wriston leaned back in his chair and smiled wryly. After Moore finished, Wriston said, "This is Captain York, head of the credit union at a Strategic Air Command base. You mean to tell me there's a Communist conspiracy on a SAC base, aided and abetted by Captain York?" (Whether or not Moore really believed that credit unions were a Communist plot may never be known.) Embarrassed, he fumbled about for an explanation. "They were like a couple of old school chums playing games with each other," York said later.

If Wriston felt nothing but disdain for Patman, he was disappointed with his president. On December 24, President Nixon, under pressure to restrain a superheated economy, signed the Credit Control Act of 1969 with "serious reservations and objections." The act was akin to triggering an economic nuclear weapon. It gave the president the power to unleash credit controls—including maximum interest rates, prohibitions on certain kinds of loans, and even minimum down payments—on the economy if he deemed it necessary. Eleven years would pass, however, before a president actually dropped the bomb. In effect, Wriston said later, the Credit Control Act of 1969 "required every borrower and lender to have a license." The "full implementation of this act, of course, would take us well down the road to economic serfdom."

In a February 1970 speech called "Nothing Fails like Success," Wriston summed up the tumultuous events of the previous year by saying, "We bankers were all successful last year. Our success was so great that we failed. We were successful in managing our liabilities under the greatest monetary pressure that the Fed has ever exerted. In restricting the supply of money, the Federal Reserve succeeded in driving up interest rates across the board, including the prime. This successful operation brought the wrath of the politicians down upon the nation's banks, and no amount of explanation that we were at the cutting edge of government policy saved us."

By the turn of the decade, Citibank and Wriston would score yet another success of sorts that he neglected to mention. As long as anyone could remember, Citibank and Chase had battled for the number two spot in American banking, a position that Chase had retained, except for a couple of blips, since its 1955 merger with the Bank of the Manhattan Company. It was rumored that Chase frequently got some deposits from the Rockefeller family oil company to dress up the balance sheet with some extra deposits if it appeared Citibank might gain the edge.

Through the 1960s, Chase dismissed Citibank as a mere upstart, and chairman George Moore as a kind of kook who couldn't be taken seriously, as one former senior Chase officer put it. Then, in early 1969, when ultraconservative George Champion retired and David Rockefeller became sole CEO, he could finally begin to expand aggressively in the United States and overseas. Champion and David Rockefeller had been like a team of horses harnessed together but pointed in opposite directions; Rockefeller was pulling forward while Champion was pulling backward. Champion was opposed to nearly everything David was for. He fought geographic expansion, including international branching, believing that the business could be done better through correspondents. He opposed the creation of a one-bank holding company—"I believe in sticking to your field that you know something about," he said later. Champion contended that it didn't bother him when Citibank edged ahead of Chase in total size. And he was against making cross-border loans. Like Stillman Rockefeller, Champion remained on the board after his retirement, but resigned in 1971. "I quit the directorship because I was unhappy with what David was doing," he explained. "I was unhappy as a director, and David was unhappy having me as a director." Later, Champion would concede only that he was perhaps a little late in embracing Citibank's negotiable CDs and in not offering Chase's own name brand of traveler's checks.

"When David took over, things exploded," said a former Chase international banker, and Chase began opening branches abroad like fast-food hamburger joints. Speaking of Chase and Citibank, he said, "I can't think of a competitive relationship where things so totally flip-flopped because of personalities."

As another former Chase banker recalls, "We didn't know who Walter Wriston was until it was too late. We didn't realize they were beating us until they did." When Citibank overtook Chase, he said, "There was a lot of rationalization. People said, 'We don't want to be like them anyhow.' " Chase officers brushed off the event, figuring that their institution would soon regain its preeminence. The rivalry reminded him of the scene from the 1969 hit movie *Butch Cassidy and the Sundance Kid,* in which the two fugitives watch from their craggy perch overlooking a mountain pass as a persistent sheriff and his posse close in on them, and Butch (Paul Newman) remarks to Sundance (Robert Redford) in exasperation, "Who *are* those guys?"

Confirming that a turning point had been reached in the competition between the two banks, Robert Bennett wrote in *American Banker* that Citibank's "success in outstripping Chase as the nation's second largest bank . . . reflects a year-long trend, and not a year-end statistical aberration." At year end, Citibank's deposits totaled $19.148 billion, $149 million ahead of Chase, the first time since June 1965 that First National had leaped into the number two spot. What made the difference was Citibank's $1.1 billion in additional foreign deposits and its decision to expand overseas by opening branches rather than buying affiliates and subsidiaries, Chase's preferred method. A change in Citibank's accounting practice also helped. In early 1969 it adopted Chase's accounting method, whereby Chase counted outstanding loans in full instead of subtracting reserves for loan losses.

The Bank of America retained the lead in deposits among U.S. banks, but Citibank never really viewed Bank of America as more than a large regional bank anyway. In a few years, its lead would also crumble under the hobnail boots of Walter Wriston. Said Rodgin Cohen, a prominent New York banking attorney, "In 1970 it was not ordained that Citibank would become the dominant bank in the United States." By all rights, he said, Bank of America should have remained the preeminent bank in the country.

Despite their similar roles as heads of the two largest New York banks, no two executives could have been more different in style and temperament than Wriston and Rockefeller. David Rockefeller's hallmark was the well-orchestrated overseas trip, which typically included an audience with the chief of state of the country he was visiting.

While Wriston clearly had access to heads of state, he declined to use that card as a new-business-getting device. "George and I and Billy [William

Spencer] went to see the king too," said Wriston later. "But that wasn't the principal focus of why we were there. Everybody wants a boss that's going to say hello to Margaret Thatcher, which we all did, but David has a big staff of people who promote that image. David is David," Wriston added. "He's a unique, remarkable, and skillful human being who stands on a platform no one else in the world stands on. It would be insane to think you were in competition with that kind of thing. The flip side is [that] we thought we were fairly business-oriented, and the two balance sheets today are somewhat reflective of that."

But Wriston also saw his role much differently than David did. "The function of the chairman," he explained, "is to take your country people into doors they couldn't get into otherwise because of informal caste systems. Once in the door, it's their problem. I could walk in any place in the world, not because my name was Wriston but because I had a card. It wasn't the name at the bottom that counted. It was the name in the middle—Citibank."

Wriston regarded Chase and David as white-shoe bankers; it was clear to colleagues that he didn't hold his rival in the highest regard as a banker. Wriston liked to tell prospective hires that he was "the only chairman of a major New York bank who worked for a living." David Rockefeller's dividends on his Chase stock were reputed to be higher than his salary.

With his spacious apartment at UN Plaza and his tree farm in the country, Wriston's lifestyle was far from austere, but it was no match for Rockefeller's. "I don't live in Pocantico Hills and entertain the Shah of Iran and bring in three hundred people by helicopter for cold duck. David's been nice enough to invite me to some of those things, and they are marvelous." On one occasion, Wriston was at the Rockefeller family estate when a helicopter circled overhead and landed near the playroom. Out of the helicopter stepped Nelson Rockefeller, by that time the vice president of the United States, and his passenger. Turning to Wriston, Nelson said, "You, of course, know King Hussein."

Much would be made in the press of the rivalry between Wriston and Rockefeller in the dozen years before Rockefeller retired. Wriston said it was overblown, attributing it to journalists trying to sell papers. "If I were writing a story about the Giants and the Browns, wouldn't I know that saying the linebackers hate each other would sell more tickets?" he said.

Asked later if he was frustrated at Citibank's pulling ahead of Chase, and if he felt compelled to catch up, Rockefeller said, "I'm a competitive person. Citibank was an obvious rival. Therefore I would have been pleased if things had gone in a different direction." But, he added, "it would be a mistake to feel that was the only driving force we had. We had our own game plan, and beating Citi in assets and earnings was not the only objective. Nevertheless, it was always a measuring post, and therefore to the extent we didn't do as well, it was a disappointment." And he added, "We also felt strongly we had a responsibility that was broader than just bringing the biggest return to shareholders."

In contrast to Chase under Rockefeller, Wriston's Citibank was a boiling pot where conflict at all levels raged openly and where new ideas were constantly being generated and then either discarded or implemented. "Anytime you have a group of highly intelligent people operating on a frontier, you're always going to have conflict," Wriston said later. But while he encouraged the rivalry and, in fact, took devilish delight in watching it in action, Wriston disputed charges that it was destructive to the institution: "Were there personality conflicts? Yes. But at the end of the day, did we have a lot of bright, motivated people leaving? No."

Meetings of Citibank's top-level policy committee more closely resembled a midnight rap session of college students debating abortion than a blue-chip gathering of highly paid bankers. In fact, said one former committee member, "policy committee" was something of a misnomer, for it was less a device for setting policy than a forum for the often rambunctious exchange of information and ideas. Policy matters, he said, were generally decided by Spencer and Wriston before they reached the committee.

This was in marked contrast to Chase's practice, which Wriston learned about through a consultant who thought Rockefeller's bank had a "wonderful" system. As Wriston rolled his eyes, the consultant described in glowing terms a device that enabled Chase officers to propose an idea and then vote on it electronically and anonymously. "I told the policy group about this," Wriston said. "They roared with uncontrollable laughter. Can you imagine a corporation where people are afraid to say they think that's a bum idea? We couldn't even imagine it." In the early 1970s a leading Washington consultant had the rare opportunity to attend top-level planning meetings at Chase and Citibank on the same day. At Citibank, he said, "the first question was 'What can we do?' The last question was 'Can we do it?' " At the Chase meeting, "it was, 'Can we do it, and what *should* we do?' " The joke was that in contemplating any new initiative, Citibank said, "Ready, fire, aim," whereas Chase said, "Ready, aim, aim."

"It's a fair statement that Citibank developed new ideas and implemented them before we did. That's one of their great strengths," Rockefeller acknowledged later.

The momentum was now with Wriston. David Rockefeller's bank would be left in the dust once and for all time. And before long, Wriston would replace Rockefeller as the principal spokesman for the American banking industry. He was, as a *New York* magazine headline later put it, "The Man Who Beat the Rockefeller Bank." But by the time Citibank scored the victory, it would be something of a hollow one.

10

BLEED FOR REED

As the 1960s were coming to a close, Citibank's corporate customers—its basic constituency—were up in arms over the chaos in its back offices. A surge in transactions resulting from a superheated economy and Wall Street's raging late-1960s bull market had caused the paper to pile up faster than the technology and managerial skills of the era could possibly cope with it. According to former officers, things were so bad that Citibank was unable to produce a checking account statement for United Parcel Service, one of its oldest customers, prompting UPS to threaten to pull its checking account from Citibank. Wriston, who always considered himself UPS's account officer, even after he became chairman, reminded the furious UPS chief that his company had "lost a couple of Citibank packages over the years." The UPS account stayed at Citibank. At one point, hundreds of officers and employees were pulled off their regular jobs and loaned to the Wall Street operations center to churn out checks and statements. With the operating group in turmoil, the corporate bankers couldn't even dream about expanding their market share; it was years before Citibank built a system that could easily accommodate new accounts. For a big corporation, however, switching banks is fraught with problems, so there was no mass exodus. But corporate America was fuming mad. To be sure, Citibank was not alone. Every major U.S. bank suffered under a similar burden.

While Wriston and his colleagues were expanding the company's operations around the globe and planning to enter an array of new enterprises, they had failed for years to wrestle the back office beast to the ground. This is the part of the bank that handles the dull but essential paperwork. Bankers refer to it as the "trenches." At Citibank, the back office was a twenty-five-story tinted-glass-and-concrete building overlooking the East River at the foot of Wall Street.

In the late 1960s the back offices of Citicorp employed thousands of clerical personnel who performed the tedious paper-intensive tasks connected with loan transactions, stock and money transfers, check processing, and commercial letters of credit. These operations had for years been run by a bondman named Halsey Cook, described by Wriston as a "wonderful man who didn't have a clue as to how the back office was to be run. A year after he went down there he was still reading the *Bond Buyer* every morning." While Citibank had known for a long time that it had a back office problem, it muddled along by throwing new troops into the fray rather than devising permanent solutions. Cook was eventually succeeded by Nick Clute, a gregarious former Brazil hand who was put in charge in the hope that he would solve the problem with sheer energy and long hours. Clute had an encyclopedic knowledge of the back office and knew how to post every record. He arrived at 4:00 A.M. and "worked all day like a dog," Wriston conceded. Clute kept the lid on the system by force of personality, but transaction volume was just growing too fast for Citi's outmoded systems.

For the previous five years or so, Citi's operating expenses had been rising at a crippling 18 percent a year, and were expected to grow at 15 percent annually for the foreseeable future. As transaction volume rose, the cost of each transaction also increased. Wriston knew that margins were being squeezed so thin that there was no way Citibank could remain competitive, much less achieve 15 percent annual earnings growth. On one particularly awful day he was paged at the airport by an operations manager who reported that a $100 million error had shown up in the checking balances from the branch system.

"How can a clearance clerk fail to balance?" Wriston asked.

"I don't know," the manager replied.

"Why don't you ask him?" Wriston said.

"Well, he's sick today."

"Who's taking his place?"

"We don't have anybody."

By 1968, Wriston knew the bank couldn't go on in this fashion.

Moore's late-1940s study of the bank had recommended the use of more laborsaving devices as a way to save money. For years, banks had employed poorly paid clerks, many of them part-time or aspiring actors like George C. Scott and Fredric March, to sort checks by hand into pigeonholes, debit the customer's account, and return the checks to the branches to be mailed back to the customer. Citibank's experience with automation and technology had been mostly dismal, even comical.

In the late 1950s, as Citibank and other banks began to be overwhelmed by the deluge of checks, ITT built a Rube Goldberg–like prototype device for Citibank that attempted to sort checks mechanically. While the basic concept was ingenious, it took forever to develop, and failed because the engineers were more concerned with the technology than with its purpose. The effort also illustrated another facet of the hubris that would continue to be a hallmark of the bank for years to come. Citibank must have figured that eventually it would be America's only banking institution, because the machine couldn't process non-Citibank checks. Indeed, if this device had any merit to begin with, it was quickly rendered obsolete when the banking industry, led by the American Bankers Association, introduced the MICR, or magnetic ink, system for encoding checks, a system that remains in effect to this day.

Like America's early failed efforts to place a satellite in orbit, this one, literally and figuratively, wound up underwater. After the project team had wasted more than two years trying to implement the system, Stillman Rockefeller lost patience and killed the project. To avoid the expense of shipping this bizarre machinery back to its European builders, it was loaded on a garbage scow and dumped into Brooklyn's Gravesend Bay. The episode was a humiliating blow to ITT and severely damaged the long-standing banking relationship between ITT, Harold Geneen, and Citibank. It also reflected Citibank's go-it-alone philosophy and, particularly, its obsession with developing its own technology. Some time later, Citibank became enamored of an IBM sorter that used a revolving drum to move the checks. When, after much testing, the project team finally demonstrated the machine to Rockefeller, the drum spit the checks out across the room like hundreds of miniature paper carpets. The technicians were speechless. The poker-faced Stillman Rockefeller quickly turned on his heel and left the room.

In the mid-1960s, Tom Paine and TEMPO had convinced Bill Spencer and Wriston of the potential benefits of high-powered computers and technology in banking. That was an eye-opener, particularly in light of the fact that IBM's Thomas Watson, who rode from Greenwich to Grand Central in the club car with George Moore in the 1950s, had told Moore that computers would never have any application to banking.

Several months after that fateful spring 1968 walk with Wriston on the Paradise Island beach, Bill Spencer set foot in the operations division for the first time. "It was a mess," he recalled. "We were $62 million out of balance in the branches the day I went down there." Although Spencer was considered an oil and gas lending officer with few peers, his early efforts in attacking the back office were dismal. "When he got to the operations division he couldn't find his ass with both hands," one colleague said bluntly, adding, however, that the rest of the banking industry wasn't doing much better. "He [Spencer] was thrashing about, putting in one guy after another with nothing to show for a year's effort. With the memory of the employee revolt provoked by Proudfoot back in 1965 still fresh, Wriston knew he couldn't afford to simply throw more consultants at the problem.

Enter brash young John Reed, fresh from success in devising a budgeting and management information system for the overseas division. Reed's pitch to Spencer was irresistible. If he were given the authority, Reed asserted, he could fix the problem by applying the technology and industrial management techniques he had learned at MIT and Goodyear. No one believed him. But faced with his first failure in his Citibank career, Spencer jumped at the suggestion with all the eagerness of a drowning swimmer grabbing a lifeline. The partnership would save face for Spencer and provide Reed with a "rabbi" and father-protector. After a four-hour conversation, Spencer asked Reed to head an internal group to direct the bank's operating departments. In mid-1969, Citibank reorganized its operating group into three areas: systems management under Reed, processing management, and services and premises. There were to be many more reorganizations to come.

Two men couldn't have been more dissimilar. Spencer was the macho big game hunter from Colorado, and Reed the MIT-trained computer wizard who drove a yellow Volkswagen with a flower on the antenna. Despite their differences in age and temperament, Spencer quickly adopted Reed and began grooming him for a top management role.

By April 1970 the operating group was still a mess. But Reed had made enough progress and demonstrated enough potential for Spencer, after he had been made president, to recommend that Reed succeed him as head of the unit. Along with the promotion and a salary of $50,000 a year, Reed was named senior vice president—the youngest person ever to hold that title at Citi. Directors protested that he was too young and immature to occupy a lofty position that carried responsibility for a budget of more than $100 million and some eight thousand employees. "We almost had a revolt among directors. They were horrified," Spencer recalled. "After [I talked] to them for about twenty minutes, explaining to them all that Reed had done, they finally acquiesced," he said. Among other things, directors objected to Reed's personal habits, which included putting his feet, clad in socks that fell below his ankles, on the boardroom table and wearing unpolished shoes that curled up at the toes. Spencer would place Reed's shoes on the table in front of Reed and order him to put them on.

"Son, you have to do a few things," Spencer told Reed. "You've got to polish your shoes." Spencer even bought him a pair of shoe trees. Spencer instructed him to shop at Brooks Brothers and helped him compile a shopping list. Later, when asked in an interview where he bought his clothes, Reed replied, "The uniform shop. Now that I'm a senior officer of a major bank I need a uniform." Spencer also cured Reed of the "I" disease, ordering him to use "we" instead of "I" in discussing his accomplishments. "The guy is so mature and so juvenile. He's a complete charmer. His mind is going at a hundred miles per hour all the time," Spencer remarked with fondness. Reed brought his impressive analytical skills to bear on the mess in the back office, employing, for probably the first time in banking, mathematical models and scientific methodology to analyze the flow of checks and paper and bits and bytes.

That someone so young could have such awesome responsibility came as a big shock to outsiders visiting the operating group for the first time. To old-timers, Reed was a squirt just out of school. On one occasion, a visitor to the back office asked his host, "Who's the kid at his father's desk?"

Before taking the operations assignment, Reed insisted that Wriston and Spencer shelter him from the inevitable stream of account officers seeking fixes to specific paperwork problems. According to one director, "Reed said, 'I can't do it unless you put someone at the door to stop people from coming in every time there's an error and stopping the whole operation to get it cleared up.' " Wriston and Spencer promised to stand at the door if necessary to protect him from such distractions.

Like the earlier efforts, Reed's initial proposals to reinvent back office operations were also off target. Early on, he viewed technology as a kind of magic wand that would quickly eliminate the paperwork morass, and most of his first hires were technology mavens. Reed dreamed of a paperless, checkless electronic society with a cathode ray tube (CRT) terminal in every corporate treasurer's office and automated teller machines in every branch. In 1970 he envisioned technological solutions to banking problems that no one else had begun to think of, and which would be considered state-of-the-art two decades later. Reed believed that technology would solve all of Citi's problems, according to Paul Rudowski, a former operations officer.

Reed realized he would have to turn to managers with industrial experience—men like the Ford Motor Company's Robert White, one of the first of Robert McNamara's protégés to join Citibank. White was a tall, slim, soft-spoken Ford bean counter whose hero was Lee Iacocca, then president of Ford. Over lunch in New York in mid-1970, Reed told the thirty-five-year-old White he didn't know what job he was qualified for, except maybe Reed's own, but he hired White anyway, assuring him that if things didn't pan out he'd have six months to find a new job. Thus White became the vanguard of a minor Ford brain drain. Ford soon became enraged over Reed's recruiting efforts and all but threatened to drop Citibank as one of its lead banks if the raiding continued. Said one former top operations officer, "Reed got lucky when he stumbled into Bob White. White was responsible for Reed's success."

Although he appeared mild-mannered and laid back at first, White soon earned a reputation for ruthlessness and insensitivity that would dog him for his entire Citibank career. Shortly after he arrived, one top manager became ill, and Reed asked White to run his operation on a temporary basis. After two weeks, White asked the sick man's secretary to remove her boss's nameplate from the door and replace it with his own. Horrified by the request, the secretary refused to carry it out, so White replaced the nameplate himself. Word of this incident spread through the building like a forest fire. In less than half an hour, Wriston was on the phone to Reed and Reed to White. White explained his action to Reed, and White prevailed.

It was White who convinced Reed that while technology might solve the back office problem over the longer term, quick and easy technological remedies were not the immediate answer. White also reminded him of two key truisms: first, you can't automate something that you don't understand, that isn't under control, or that doesn't work manually; and second, huge savings could be achieved if workers simply understood their work and the work being done around them.

Bringing Reed around to that realization did not take long. White had been on board as controller of the operating group for only a month when he received a head count report showing a dramatic escalation—by several hundred—in the number of staff. He concluded that the operation was indeed out of control. Reed reviewed the report at poolside at his home in Connecticut and, according to his chief of staff, Paul Rudowski, "had to jump in the pool because he was getting so hot. That's when John said, 'Bob's right. We've got to get control.' "

Reed and White pledged to Wriston and Spencer that they could keep back office expenses flat for the next two years and limit increases to under under 6 percent annually through 1975. By cutting "heads," fat, overtime, and losses from delays in collecting on checks, they could save $70 million before taxes by the middle of the decade. When Reed projected that by 1980 he would be responsible for a goodly share of the bank's profits, the white-shoe bankers turned ashen, according to one observer. In one meeting, Reed told his banker colleagues that he knew some of them "would like to see me fall on my face." According to Rudowski, "John would say the package should look like this. But to get that implemented, you had to do 512 different things. He would never have the vision to make sure those things got done. Bob [White] would. Both skills are necessary." Rudowski added that "John is also more fun."

Along with his big-picture view, Reed brought a tinge of irreverence, even craziness, to the task. "I don't think you can be that bright and have a mind that's just all buttoned down," said Rudowski. For Reed, the conventional wisdom was always something to be challenged. Reed and White, and later other senior colleagues, commuted from Connecticut to Manhattan together by bank car before dawn, giving Reed an hour or so to blow his colleagues' minds with his futuristic ideas. Perhaps inspired by TEMPO, Reed shocked his colleagues one morning by asking, "Wouldn't it be a good idea if we bought RCA?" Asked once how he spent his day, Reed replied that he worked from 5:00 A.M. to 9:00, engaged in corporate politics from 9:00 to 5:00, and went home at 8:00.

Robert White, like Wriston, operated from a set of deeply held principles. While Wriston's actions stemmed from his belief in free market economics, White's were based on his views about the structure and management of organizations. White loathed bigness, and everything he did was aimed at trying to make big things smaller.

To White, channelization was the key to bringing order out of chaos in any factorylike processing operation. Every process, every activity, was a channel. A channel typically was a department of, say, fifteen to fifty people headed by a mid-level manager. One of the new breed of M.B.A.'s would live with the unit, perhaps for months, to document how the manual process worked: how the paper flowed in, what decisions clerks and supervisors made with certain transactions, what reports were generated, and so forth. In many instances they found that there were no procedures. Transactions were performed as they had been for decades. Training was on-the-job, and routines and procedures were passed on by word of mouth from clerk to clerk and from generation to generation, much like oral histories. The M.B.A.'s would try to make each channel's manual activities as efficient as possible, then devise a plan to automate it and reduce the head count. Channelization became a religion. "We did it at Ford and we'll do it at Citibank," White proclaimed.

In the process, however, he would create more chaos than the back office had ever seen.

Out of this process emerged yet another management principle that even the great professor, Peter Drucker, appeared to have overlooked. This was the "pile of shit" theory of management, which held that to eliminate the chaos and backlogs in an operating department, waves of eager young managers should be thrown at the problem, rather than allowing one manager to complete the task. In 1970, Reed and White were faced with a backlog of about 36,000 unanswered customer inquiries. As one former manager described the theory, a manager would walk into a department and find a huge pile of backlogged work, such as unanswered customer inquiries. "He'd . . . say, 'My God, what a pile of shit,' " and work the pile down to two hundred. To keep him from becoming complacent, he'd be reassigned after perhaps six months, and someone new would come in, see the two hundred inquiries, say, "My God what a pile of shit," and whittle the problem down to a pile of twenty. The cycle would then begin anew and continue until the unit ended up with no backlog.

One of the first challenges faced by Reed and White was to make order out of the most fundamental back office function: check processing. When White arrived, this was a vast centralized operation in which mountains of checks—about 1.6 million a day—arrived in bags from Citibank branches and other banks. At the time, these items were electronically encoded by armies of clerks and routed through huge machines that canceled the checks and debited accounts. Besides the manpower and overhead costs that resulted from these inefficiencies, there was yet another cost. For every check that was delayed a day in collection, Citibank lost the use, or "availability" of those funds, or about $4 million a year in earnings.

Check processing would become the first function to be channelized. White and his lieutenants would design the system on paper, and then install it over a weekend in a massive crash overhaul undertaken with a cast of hundreds. Sometimes the ensuing confusion was minor—when, for example, employees couldn't find their desks on a Monday morning. In other instances, like his summer 1971 effort to reorganize the "front end" of check processing, where checks are received and encoded, the result was a back office debacle that reverberated through the banking system and came perilously close to closing the bank. In Citibank lore and legend, it became known as "blowup number one." The blowup of the back end, where checks are filed and redistributed to customers, took place one year later, with different but equally disastrous repercussions. "Both blowups could have closed the bank. You couldn't close the books," said one former top official.

The events leading up to blowup number one began after White had spent the summer trying unsuccessfully to reorganize the front end. He then decided to try to get the job done over a weekend. The old system was operating in a way that was akin to trying to recycle mounds of garbage without separating it into its components. Everyone had been operating the old way for years, and no one bothered to train workers to handle the work the new way. Instead, they were handed trays of checks to process without being told what to do with them and whom to give them to afterward. The discrepancies between the amounts posted by one clerk on a batch of debits, credits, or other documents and the amounts acknowledged by the next worker on the line began mounting from the moment the starting bell rang signaling the implementation of the new system. "All of a sudden the number of them just went off the top," said Rudowski.

This first blowup was transparent to individual and corporate customers, but it wasn't transparent to the Fed. Citibank failed to meet its morning deadlines to swap checks at the New York Clearing House and reportedly fell out of proof with the Federal Reserve Bank by some $5 billion. In the money supply numbers reported to the Fed that week, the entry for Citibank showed simply "n/a," for "not available." Angry senior Fed officials were soon on the phone to Wriston demanding to know what was happening and what he intended to do about it. The episode was so disruptive that some bankers clamored to eject Citibank from the Clearing House.

In the wake of this blowup, operations officer Larry Stoiber was escorting Reed on a tour of the operations center and was so exhausted from working around the clock that he literally bounced from wall to wall. "What is the matter with this guy?" Reed asked. In an act of mercy, Reed sent him home in a cab. Said one former operations officer, "You had to be seen at two in the morning to be considered part of the team." Someone even drew a cartoon showing an employee giving blood with the inscription, "Bleed for Reed," which became the motto of the back office.

During the finger-pointing that followed, Reed backed White, and Wriston backed Reed. Reed's response, the logical one, was always to segregate the problem off to the side, and he set up a special department to do so. "You never read about all the money spent to clean up the mess," said one former operations officer. "It was very close to total chaos. There were brilliant ideas, but implementation was a disaster. They forgot that you had to train people." Typically, White and his SWAT team didn't bother to talk to the people who did the work and therefore didn't recognize the importance of key functional employees. White did seem to recognize his shortcomings in the personnel area, though. He once told one of his secretaries, Maria R. Savarese, that he needed her because "you understand people and I don't," she said later.

A creature of habit, White arrived early at his 111 Wall Street office, which included a private bathroom and kitchen. In the fall and winter he customarily donned a gray cardigan that his staff had given him in the hope that he would not continue to maintain the building's thermostats at the warmest setting. White loved chocolate layer cake, and Maria Savarese obliged him by baking them herself and serving him a breakfast of cake and cranberry juice. At noon she would bring him his tuna fish sandwich, and at three o'clock, when he started getting nervous and fidgety, she would deliver a tray of milk and Lorna Doone cookies.

As chaotic as the back office was when Spencer took it over, nothing matched the turmoil created when Citibank began to convert, in many cases over a weekend, from long-established manual systems into untested, untried automated ones. During that phase, it took the tough marine mentality of Bill Spencer to buffer Reed and White from the artillery fire that was launched at them from the rest of the bank and from the outside world. While Spencer had little or no technical expertise, he did instill in the new group a kind of gung-ho boot-camp mentality. "Bill always said he wanted the place to be like the marines," said White. From the outset, Spencer tended to hire people with military backgrounds, including White himself, an air force veteran. One of White's favorite sayings was "We're going through the wall today. Start marching."

At least one operations manager, a former army officer, virtually lived at 111 Wall. He commuted to New York from Philadelphia before dawn and worked past ten o'clock at night, returning home for one and a half hours' sleep. In Reed's operations group, families were neglected, and divorces and separations were rampant.

Early on, the core group of operations managers, all with military backgrounds, spread a "can do" gospel and the view that no obstacle was insurmountable. Some of the managers, like Rudowski, even talked in military lingo. In the midst of a crash systems conversion, one operations officer recalled, Rudowski met with his staff at 6:00 P.M., and told them, "We'll reconnoiter at midnight." They also created a new jargon all their own. In Cititalk, a "blip" was a mistake, a "rock" a hurdle to be overcome.

Reed's approach to managerial problem-solving was a clinical one. "If there are problems," White said later, "John never has them. Somebody else has them, and he just puts a little box around it. There can be a full-grown cancer in the middle of his organization but it has no effect on John." But Reed himself would say later that he worried more about problems than Wriston did. "He never seemed to spend time on them. He would tell the board how well things were going. I'd tell the board all the problems we were having. I'd never tell them about things that are doing well," he said.

In all the back office operations—check processing, stock and money transfer—Reed and White discovered that workers were attempting to reconcile errors at the same time they were trying to move the existing work. It was like bailing out a sinking ship with one hand while using the other to keep more water from coming in. In the case of money transfer, error investigations were as much as eighteen months old. Reed and White quickly concluded that to keep the current work moving, they would have to separate it from the old work, and pass that to other workers. Part of the cleanup involved a recognition that aiming for 100 percent accuracy was unrealistic, given the volume. "John looked at it as an industrial waste type of issue," said former Citibank lawyer Chris York. Reed "allowed for 99 percent and considered one percent the cost of doing business. Once the work was flowing you could go back and try to reduce the error rate."

Soon after he took over the operating group, Reed furnished his office with a round table that was much larger than Wriston's. In the operating group culture, tables were in, desks were out: desks, unlike tables, allowed people to hide things. From that table, he presided over his new domain like a kind of technological philosopher king, creating a culture that combined MIT with Marine Corps boot camp and with Reed's sometimes zany wisdom.

Another mid-1960s hire who would contribute mightily to the boot-camp mentality was tall, muscular Lawrence Small, a would-be professional flamenco guitarist. Small's primary motive in signing on with the bank was to become a career expatriate, preferably in a Spanish-speaking country. "I was oriented to the exotic side of life and [wanted] to see naked Indians," he said later. His wish was granted almost immediately, and he chose Chile because it was the most distant Spanish-speaking country. There he met and married an American woman who had moved to Chile as a girl with her family. Small would later say that in Chile he aspired only to become head of First National City's Santiago branch and someday earn $10,000 a year, about $4,000 more than his mid-1960s starting salary. Early on in his Citibank career, Small earned a reputation as a smart and hardworking manager who would cheerfully do whatever was asked of him. His tough guy image would not emerge until the back office reorganization began.

Small was a Jewish kid from the Bronx who could have passed for a WASP—a fact that sometimes proved embarrassing for unwitting associates. As a junior officer, he and a trainee once called on the Jewish financial manager of a Brooklyn department store. On the way out, the trainee remarked, "They speak a secret language among themselves."

"You know, I'm one of them and I don't know that [secret language]," Small said. The trainee froze in embarrassment.

Small and White were kindred spirits. The two men often spent their lunch hour in Small's office, where Small gave White guitar lessons. They shared similar styles of management as well. In their bid to make good on their promises to Wriston and Spencer, there was no room for partial success or shades of gray. Reed, White, Small, and company operated according to a "binary," or pass-fail, system of management. There was no room for anything in between. "A corollary to that theory was Small's Rule of Physical Evidence," a colleague recalled. "If you owed him something, he wanted the physical thing." Small would say, "Where is it? Don't tell me it's in the process." Recalled another colleague, "Small would call you up and say, 'You failed today.'"

For his part, White developed a style of communicating his pleasure or displeasure with his subordinates' performance that was unique in the annals of American management. To signal his unhappiness on a memo or report, White embossed it with a rubber stamp resembling the heel of a shoe with the word "FAIL" in large bold letters. On a report he regarded favorably, he simply drew a happy face. "White's motivator was fear," said another colleague. "People were always obstacles in his way."

While Small and White were hard on their own underlings, Wriston was barely fazed by their own much more serious blunders. Wriston had given the operating group—and the rest of the bank, for that matter—carte blanche to manage as they saw fit. He had a tolerance for errors as well as personal quirks and eccentricities that was shocking to many. White, for example, would never allow business obligations to interfere with a casual round of golf, much less a tournament, and even skipped the annual operating group dinner to compete in one.

This leading-edge effort to bring high technology to the back offices attracted wild geniuses to Citibank from miles around. One notable eccentric who found his way to 111 Wall was Lawrence Ray, a brilliant dairy farmer's son with a doctorate in mathematics. When there was a job to be done, there was no stopping Ray, who operated with all the subtlety of his two attack dogs. In the drive to meet deadlines for implementing new systems or conversions, strong men would drop like flies. On one occasion, according to former Citibanker Byron Stinson's humorous account, an exhausted operating group officer told Ray, "I've been here for forty-eight straight hours. I haven't seen my wife for three days. I haven't slept, and I've got to go home."

Ray reached into his jacket pocket, took out his wallet, and pulled out a bill. "Here's fifty dollars," he said to his bleary-eyed subordinate. "Go out and get laid and be back in two hours."

Reed's lieutenants battled constantly over matters of management style and personnel management, including, for example, whether the job could best be done by training the existing staff in the new way of doing things or by replacing all of the people who had become accustomed to the old way. Charles Long, a computer expert and later corporate secretary, preferred to retrain existing employees to perform new jobs. White's "knee-jerk reaction," said Long, was to change the people. "Not squash them. Kill them," he said, adding that "Bob's a very warm fellow. [But] he didn't know how to communicate that."

The clash between Reed's gang of brilliant, eccentric zealots and the old guard was hardly subtle. White stumbled when he tried to turn clerks into technocrats. Having tabulated the cost of messenger services, White mused about the potential for savings by eliminating messengers. He summoned a middle-aged man who had worked as a courier for the bank ever since high school and had risen to become supervisor of twenty messengers. "Put together a profit plan and marketing plan and have it ready by next week," White ordered. "The guy's jaw just dropped," said a former Citibank operations officer.

————

While Reed and White initially clashed on the role technology should play in the short term in cleaning up the back office, they both believed that ultimately technology would drive the American banking industry, particularly consumer banking. Among the recommendations that emerged from the TEMPO study was the need to develop so-called on-line terminals that would enable the bank and its customers to obtain up-to-the-second information on their accounts. On-line technology, TEMPO accurately proclaimed, would dramatically alter the way services are delivered to customers. At the time, the state of the art was so-called batch processing, where paperwork records of various transactions, such as deposits or withdrawals, were collated and processed overnight. But customer inquiries were laborious and at least a day behind.

Equally pressing was the need for a credit-card authorization system that would enable merchants to quickly approve credit card purchases while customers waited at the sales counter. A credit-card society would never emerge if a customer had to wait for a salesclerk to phone an authorization clerk, who in turn had to flip through stacks of computer printouts to approve a thirty-dollar purchase. Reed had also begun to dream of automated teller machines and video display screens installed in corporate treasurers' offices to connect them directly with the bank. He would spearhead the drive for ever-improved technology to facilitate transactions on the spot—known in the jargon as "on-line transaction processing." For the next twenty years, on-line processing systems of increasing levels of sophistication would be among Citibank's top priorities.

Incredibly, no major computer systems manufacturer, including IBM and Digital Equipment Corporation, showed more than mild interest in developing such systems for Citibank exclusively, even though the chairman of IBM's executive committee was on the bank's board. According to Paul Glaser, who would later become Citibank's chief technology officer, IBM told Reed to "come back in a few years." They were not, said Glaser, willing to "go faster than the bulk of the market would take their product." Reed, of course, was not prepared to wait for the rest of the American banking industry to achieve his vision of the bank of the future. He concluded that if he was to make the future happen now, he would have to design his own machines and software.

"It was clear that they would have to reach beyond existing technology and invent some of it themselves," said Lawrence Fouraker, then the dean of the Harvard Business School and a Citibank director. That was fine with Walter Wriston, banking's quintessential Lone Ranger, who almost always supported a go-it-alone approach because he was convinced that Citibankers were different from and smarter than everyone else. Reed also figured that this would pressure traditional manufacturers to step up their own research and development efforts to produce new transaction processing technology. The problem arose not in IBM's failure to develop technology but in Reed's decision, rooted in pride and arrogance, to compete with IBM.

In 1968, Reed set up a subsidiary called Citibank Services, Inc., as his research and development arm. The ease with which he secured funding and approval for the new unit was testimony to Wriston's faith in him and to the spirit of risk-taking that would be the hallmark of the Wriston era. To obtain the $23 million in start-up money for the R&D effort, Reed merely drafted a one-paragraph "major expenditure proposal." Citibank Services was to be an entrepreneurial amalgam of marketing and technical experts located near

MIT (Reed's alma mater) and other top U.S. universities. He wanted to keep the subsidiary at arm's length from New York, believing that its efforts would be undermined by the burgeoning Citibank bureaucracy. He also felt that anyone thrown into the morass at 111 Wall would naturally turn his attention to the mess there rather than to futuristic technology.

The wizards at Citibank Services tinkered with various devices, including automated teller machines and the treasurers' terminal, but the effort faltered almost from the outset, failing to produce even a spark of entrepreneurial creativity, much less any workable systems. While there was lots of testing of various devices, according to Glaser, workers seemed enamored of being a subsidiary of First National City Corporation and spent much of their time squabbling over stock options. Said Rudowski, "It was, by any measure, a pretty big failure."

Reed's predicament took a turn for the better—and the bizarre—when he encountered Milton E. Mohr, who had just taken command of a California-based high-tech brain trust called Scantlin Electronics. Founded in 1957 by John R. "Jack" Scantlin, an eccentric, reclusive electronics genius then in his late twenties, Scantlin Electronics in 1960 introduced the Quotron I machine, the first electronic device that enabled brokers to request a printed quote from a desktop unit. Two years later, he introduced the Quoteboard, a machine that rendered broker chalkboards obsolete. Other Scantlin innovations included electronic paging devices and a computer that enabled law enforcement agencies to produce a single report on a criminal suspect from data fed into it from many different computers around the country. All this earned Scantlin a reputation as perhaps the foremost creator of systems hardware in the United States, if not the world.

Scantlin enjoyed a lifestyle befitting an inventor of technological marvels. In the hills above Los Angeles, an area so steep and rugged it was deemed undevelopable, Scantlin sliced off the top of four peaks and built a huge one-room space-age home in the valley formed by them. Scantlin installed an Olympic-size lap pool, measured to exacting specifications with a laser device, so that part of it was in the master bathroom adjoining the master bedroom. He could literally dive out of his bed into the pool and swim out of his house into his backyard, where a bevy of gorgeous women awaited him, according to visitors. In his office was a large fish tank containing what one former Citibanker called "not very friendly fish," reportedly man-eating Amazonian piranhas.

"Have I got a guy for you," Mohr is said to have exclaimed to Reed in introducing the eccentric Mr. Scantlin. About the time Scantlin met up with Reed, Scantlin Electronics, like Citicorp Systems, was also faltering, but for different reasons. Scantlin was trying to roll out the latest generation of Quotron devices. But he had lost market share to competitors, and was severely constrained by a mountain of debt. Mohr and Reed became convinced that all it would take was money to roll out this device and regain market share.

For all his technical genius, however, Scantlin was not long on management skills. "Jack is an innovator, but after he innovates you've got to get him out because he'll destroy what he innovates," said Glaser. His work habits were erratic at best. He would work tirelessly for months, then suddenly disappear for months at a time. Scantlin and Reed were similar in at least one critical respect, according to Rudowski: they "could design it, but not produce it."

Reed and Mohr hit it off personally, and in 1971 Reed set out to buy Scantlin. Banking laws, however, prevented Citibank from acquiring the manufacturing side of the company. So for a nominal sum—said to be under $10 million—Reed bought the R&D side of Scantlin Electronics, including the patents, and shortly thereafter converted it into Transaction Technology, Inc. From that day forward, TTI would constitute the core of Citibank's R&D effort. Reed continued to be interested in Scantlin's stock-quote machines, and the deal included a lease line to enable Scantlin to manufacture the machines, the Quotron 800, and install them in the offices of a New York brokerage firm. It was the first of several times that Citibank made Scantlin a multimillionaire. When John Reed encountered Scantlin, the faltering Citibank Services was working on a voice answer-back system using analog technology that would, it was hoped, give account information with a computerized voice. Scantlin quickly informed Reed and then Wriston that Citibank was "going the wrong way with the wrong technology at the wrong time. . . . You're going analog in a world that's going to be digital. We don't have the band width . . . to accommodate the analog stuff. What you need is a terminal you put a card in and your balance comes up."

At that time, Scantlin was under orders from Reed to build a credit-card authorization system, which Scantlin had promised to deliver in ninety days. Meanwhile, Citibank was trying to meet a deadline in twenty days for the voice answer-back system to respond to inquiries on checking account balances. According to Rudowski, Scantlin sauntered into Reed's office and informed him he could use the same technology to give him the credit-card and balance account system. Reed, all too aware of Scantlin's tendency to innovate and never produce, said impatiently, "Jack, your job is to do a Visa MasterCard authorization system. I don't want to hear in another thirty days that you're working on check processing, or in ninety days that you're 99 percent done with both." At that time, Reed and his technocrats were most concerned about shortening the wait for credit-card authorizations and cutting credit losses at the point of sale.

But in ninety days, Scantlin had managed to assemble a working prototype of the machine, known as Citicard I, that could do both. To simulate its use, Scantlin jury-rigged the so-called grandfather tapes—electronic records of the previous day's transactions. Rudowski offered his account to test the system. He pulled out his checkbook and calculated the balance. Scantlin dipped the plastic Citicard, and the figure appeared instantly on the screen of the shoebox-sized terminal: it was $35.18. "That's the subtlest way of asking for a pay raise I've ever seen," Spencer commented.

To make this technology work, he built the Scantlin 800 computer.

After extensive testing and simulations in which thousands of cards were dipped simultaneously to make sure the system would not go down (though at times it did), Citibank in late 1973 rolled out the Citicard throughout the branch system, becoming the first American bank to eliminate for its customers the hassle of waiting on line for outdated checking account information.

Equally important, the Citicard would become the technological foundation for the next quantum leap in on-line financial services technology: the establishment of a branch-wide automated teller network. In Reed's view, the future of Citibank, American banking, and John Reed lay in the deployment of the plastic card. "He had the vision that the card could do everything," said one colleague. And Wriston quickly saw that the implications of the technology went far beyond the immediate purpose for which it was intended. "It would be nice," Wriston said, "if someone could walk into a bank in Fargo, North Dakota, and cash a Citibank check."

Operating far beyond the shadow of 399 Park Avenue, Transaction Technology was a corporate subculture unto itself. Even Bob White, who had his own set of eccentricities, was flabbergasted when he first visited TTI. "The vice presidents were all wearing sandals or were barefoot with their feet on their desks and wearing T-shirts and shorts or jeans," said one former White associate. "He was shocked. He said he was going to instill discipline in the place." Reed insisted that his think tank and the eccentric electronics wizards be immune from the usual bureaucratic red tape imposed by his number crunchers. Said Rudowski, Reed's bean counter, "I don't remember him [Reed] telling me 'Don't go near that place,' but he didn't want the controls over that place that he wanted elsewhere."

Scantlin's inventiveness and imagination knew no bounds. Besides creating the Citicard machine, he had developed a cipher device that grabbed the attention of the Defense Department. Wriston was relaxing in the hammock at his country home one day when he received a concerned phone call from a deputy defense secretary, who explained that Scantlin's cipher machine was better than anything at DOD and implored Wriston never to send it overseas.

As much as Reed admired Scantlin's engineering genius, he trembled at the man's unpredictability and cringed at the thought of introducing him to Citibank's policy committee or board of directors.

A year after blowup number one, Citibank thought it was ready to reorganize the back end, where the canceled checks were sorted, filed, and distributed to the people who wrote them. That reorganization was to coincide with the installation of Jack Scantlin's Citicard machines, which would enable tellers and branch personnel to verify customer balances and authorize tellers to cash checks. For months, Scantlin had been promising to install the system but had encountered one delay after another. The automated balance inquiry system had to be installed at the same time to relieve headquarters personnel of the burden of answering inquiries from the branches while they were installing the new system.

Rudowski, the man assigned to that job, was so confident that the

Scantlin terminals would be ready by D day that he ordered his staff to abort plans for a backup system using voice answer-back technology that could have provided balances for the branches if Scantlin didn't come through. But at the appointed hour, the terminals were not in place, according to Rudowski. In September 1972, a year after blowup number one, blowup number two was under way.

Before long, Rudowski recalled, "we were drowning in checks." When the statements were generated, the canceled checks weren't there to go with them. Incomplete statements were mailed out. Checks were sent to the wrong customers, or worse still, lost in the back office black hole. Wriston was furious and embarrassed when a neighbor called him to report that he was missing half of his checks and had received someone else's. Having screwed up this most fundamental banking operation, Wriston's bank appeared to the world to be out of control. And it was.

To some, Wriston's historical perspective, which he acquired from his father, was his major strength. Only with a broad view of history could one tolerate the succession of crises and disasters that would befall the back office, and the financial marketplace, during his leadership at Citibank. "None of the problems we ever had were very big in Walt's historical perspective," said White. "He'd let people like me do my thing. . . . That's why the place was as successful as it was." But in White's view, that perspective was also something of a weakness. "Citicorp itself could go bankrupt and go away and it wouldn't be a big thing," said White.

It would prove to be easier to invent the Citicard machine than to persuade the New York branches, now headed by Wriston confidant Jim Farley, to install them. Farley would later say flippantly that he probably got the job because "I spoke Spanish, had a pretty good suntan, and Farley was a pretty good political name in New York."

The branch system at that time was a tired, stodgy organization that had traditionally been regarded as a supplier of funds to the corporate bankers to make loans to American's major corporations, a view held by Wriston himself. Because consumer deposits were plentiful and virtually free, banks typically made lots of money when rates were high and less when they were low. Its principal consumer activities were taking deposits, in the form of checking accounts, certificates of deposit, and passbook savings, and to a much lesser extent making personal loans. Into the early 1970s, personal and mortgage lending were always separate departments from the deposit-gathering function of the branches, and income from those activities never constituted a major portion of Citibank's revenue.

In reality, the lowly consumer was incidental to the business of branch banking, and marketing was primitive at best. "Our idea of marketing was to give away a toaster and open an account we lost money on," said Wriston. "Our guys were blowing up balloons at state fairs." Under Farley, innovative marketing meant giving away Yankee baseball tickets. Citibank's advertising had changed little from the 1940s and 1950s, when the bank won awards for ads that consisted of paintings of wheat fields, Wriston recalled.

As a manager, Farley operated by gut instinct and by the seat of his pants. He was, said a friend, a man of snap judgments and "quick opinions," not a thoughtful, methodical "process manager." He had done a good job cleaning up the Mercantile Bank in Canada in the late 1960s by consolidating rather than building. "He went right down the line and fired the highest-priced guys," said one former Citibanker. Farley, colleagues say, saw as his mission keeping expenses below the rate of inflation. Many thought that Farley seemed more concerned about controlling expenses than about boosting revenue or winning new customers.

To a large extent, Farley's management style was to react to the most recent phone call from a Citibank executive complaining about customer service in one of the branches. Farley's day would often begin with a phone call from Wriston or Spencer relating the latest horror story of incompetent handling of one of their personal transactions. "Invariably," said former Citibank president Richard Braddock, "Walt would start his day by calling to say he or Kathy had a bad experience in a branch, and 'Why can't this get straightened up?' That would send him [Farley] into a tailspin. When you have the chairman and his wife and the president and his wife doing business with you in a business that's hard to run, well, you're bound to get horror stories." In those days, he said, "Consumer surveys were basically phone calls from executives."

According to Reed, his unrelenting pressure on Farley to use consumer marketing techniques in the branch banking system finally prompted Farley to hire marketing specialists for the first time. The marketer he discovered was Richard Braddock, a General Foods marketing and development manager in charge of products like Shake 'n Bake and Stove Top stuffing. "Braddock was an antibody," said Reed later. Though he was interviewed by Reed, he was hired by Farley to "protect the branch system from Reed." Wriston's style was not to interject himself as a mediator into internecine conflicts. Though he recognized that Farley was old guard, Farley was like an old shoe, and he possessed one quality that Wriston placed on a level with high IQ: loyalty. "I doubt Walt spent more than ten minutes trying to get Jim and John [Reed] to work together," said a former top officer. Braddock was a kind of experiment, and his arrival at Citibank was greeted with quizzical interest. Marketing was something almost mystical and magical; there had never been a major-league consumer-products type at Citibank, and everyone, from Wriston and Spencer on down, was curious as to what this alien discipline could bring to Citibank. Shortly after Braddock arrived, he was invited to a party at Wriston's apartment, where Spencer and Wriston barraged him with questions about this snake-oil business known as marketing.

But Braddock had come to Citibank not to be a full-time marketing manager but to develop his skills as a line manager. He started out as an assistant to Farley, but discovered quickly that he "wasn't good as an assistant, and Jim wasn't good at having an assistant." After indoctrinating Citibank's top management on the wonders of marketing, Braddock was handed a group of branches to manage.

Farley and Braddock teamed up to resist the introduction of the Citicard into the branches, believing that the effort would be too disruptive and that the hefty price tag outweighed all possible benefits. Incredibly, the antipathy to the card on the part of branch employees and officials was so intense that teams of Citicard installers were physically ejected from the branches.

Farley's antipathy toward technology was matched only by Reed's disdain for the traditional system of retail banking based on so-called brick-and-mortar branches. Farley measured his success by the growth in the number of branches, and amassed on a wall a collection of gold-plated ceremonial scissors that he had used to cut the ribbons when he opened new branches. Among Reed and his hi-tech colleagues, Farley's scissors collection was a standing joke.

"Reed's fixation was that branch banking is a loser," said one colleague. "That a secretary would run out and deposit a check on a Friday to cover a check she wrote on a Thursday—that was no way to make money." To drive home the point, Reed took his colleagues on walking tours of the big, ornate Park Avenue branches that Reed disdainfully referred to as "mausoleums." Gesturing toward one of the offices, Reed asked his staff, "What are we going to do about *that?*" To Reed, the answer was twofold: plastic cards and automated teller machines. "He would have a place where the rich could sit around and talk about their problems," said a former operations officer. "But he would have ATMs for the great unwashed."

In October 1973, Citibank announced that it would soon deploy the Citicard, which until then had been used only to verify personal checks, into all of its branches for general use by customers, and that in a year it would switch all of its Master Charge customers to the new card. Wriston described the card as a "significant breakthrough for the consumer in the city of New York and a breakthrough in computer technology." By this time, Citibank had invested more than $30 million in the Citicard.

To Citibank, the Citicard I—the first version of the Citicard—was just what TEMPO ordered. But the introduction of the Citicard I into the branches, allowing customers to dip their cards and determine their balances and other account information, did not prove to be the big draw Wriston and Reed expected. In a speech in early 1974, several months after the Citicard was rolled out, Wriston urged his colleagues not to be disappointed by the less than overwhelming initial public reaction. "At the moment, the terminals are not being used by as many customers as we would wish," Wriston said, "but a change in the habits of the public is not achieved overnight." Still, the Citicard created the technological infrastructure that later generated a dramatic rise in new accounts and deposits.

Reed saw the terminals not just as a convenience for branch and credit-card customers, but also as a spur for increased use of credit-card electronic payments systems. It was a way of using technology to extend the reach of

Citibank beyond geographic boundaries, and of breaking down the legislative and regulatory barriers that generally limited banks' relationships with consumers to the confines of the home states. Reed and Wriston were convinced that such technology would be the catalyst that would enable First National City to become a truly national bank, in a real as well as a nominal sense.

Reed believed that the terminals could be deployed outside the branches—in, say, supermarkets—to capture customers from other banks right at the checkout counter. He believed that a supermarket—or any other merchant, for that matter—would agree to install a machine if only one bank's customers could use it. That proved to be a serious miscalculation. Reed, said the former colleague, "ran up against the logic that people aren't going to be inconvenienced by technology."

Reed, like Wriston, was a Lone Ranger. In no instance was that more evident than in his conviction that Citibank should reinvent the wheel, or the computer, or even the microchip. Reed believed that for the bank to differentiate itself from other banks and compete for consumer business, it had to build its own technology. He had seen how government-owned institutions elsewhere in the world had taken payment-systems functions, such as money transfer, away from private institutions, and he wanted to be sure that in the United States they remained in private hands. He also worried that MasterCard and BankAmericard would grow so big that they would preempt the functions of the institutions they were formed to serve, taking on a life of their own. Reed was determined to prevent this "functional carveout," as he called it. Outsiders saw this as yet another example of Citibank's arrogance.

None of these make-or-buy debates was more heated than the one that took place over which kind of "electronic brain" should be installed in the Citicard and its credit cards. This issue would once again pit Citibank against the rest of the banking world.

Embedded in the blue-and-white plastic Citicard was a state-of-the-art electro-optical core consisting of laser diodes—known among Citibankers as the "magic middle"—containing confidential account data that could be read by the terminal, enabling customers to access their accounts.

Jack Scantlin contended that, unlike the conventional magnetic-stripe technology in use at the time, his technology was tamperproof: anyone who wanted to pull a customer's account without authorization would have to gain access to the magic middle and, in doing so, would destroy the card. To Reed and his colleagues, this appeared to be the brass ring. Citibank would set the standard for the rest of the American banking industry. Because the magic-middle card could be used only in Citibank's machines, the rest of the world would have to pay licensing and vendor's fees to Citibank. The rest of the world, however, had other ideas. The American Bankers Association was pushing the industry to adopt as its standard the magnetic stripe. According to the ABA's criteria, the mag-stripe card could be used by anyone inside or outside the banking industry. In the midst of the bitter debate over this issue, Scantlin concocted a scheme to expose to the world the limitations of the mag-stripe technology. He posted notices at the California Institute of Technology, from which he had graduated in 1950 with a degree in electrical engineering, offering a $5,000 first prize to the student who devised the most effective way to defraud the mag stripe. "You do something like that and all study stops, and everyone goes to work on the contest," said Rudowski, an MIT alumnus. *American Banker* reported that twenty-two students competed and half of them devised ways to trick the mag stripe. "Frankly," Reed said, "we were surprised at the low cost, ease, and cleverness" needed to compromise the other card. One student assembled a unit, small enough to be hidden in a shirtsleeve, that could remove information from the card. Another invented a skimmer that enabled the user to transfer data from one card to another. The contest, which received widespread publicity, threatened to undermine the mag stripe.

The banking industry was furious. Scantlin's competition caused a "bit of a hullabaloo," Rudowski said later with some understatement, but Wriston, Reed, and Spencer chortled with fiendish admiration over Scantlin's cleverness.

Reed opposed any plan that would force Citibank to go public with its technology. He believed that if that happened, Citibank would lose its identity and have nothing to sell.

So Citibank adamantly refused to go along with the demands of MasterCard and Visa for a universal magnetic-stripe technology. "John's philosophy was that we're different and better than everyone else," a view with which Wriston did not disagree. And Wriston was perfectly comfortable having several competing approaches in the marketplace at one time. Although there was little that Chairman Wriston and Chairman Mao agreed on, Wriston did embrace the Mao statement "Let a thousand flowers grow."

Within the industry, proprietary technology was an emotional issue. John Fisher, a former senior vice president at Bank One, also a leader in retail payment systems, said, "Reed was trying to own the technology. But banking is an interrelated industry. He was being a prick."

Reed's preoccupation with proprietary technology was at odds with the recommendations of the rocket scientists from TEMPO. According to Tom Paine, TEMPO told Citibank it "should figure out what's going to wind up as the standard and jump onto that. We always urged them to participate in standards," warning them against buying or making specialized computers designed just for banking. "That can be a trap." General Electric had fallen into the same pitfall, always insisting on non-IBM-compatible equipment. Instead of adopting the standard, brash John Reed would seek to set it. And, like GE, he would learn the hard and expensive way the consequences of going it alone. "Reed pissed away hundreds of millions on Transaction Technology, Inc.," said former Citibanker Frank Partel. "There was nothing IBM couldn't do. It was pure arrogance."

Reed wanted Citibank to make everything, including mainframe computers, then available off the shelf from IBM and others. He felt that by developing his own hardware and software, he could maintain a technological edge in the marketplace. On the other hand, if he bought off-the-shelf equipment, he would have to share his secrets with his competitors and he would be beholden to certain suppliers. "We only used to fight about it day and night," said Charles Long, the computer expert. "Other than that it was calm." Long believed that Citibank should develop its own terminals and network technology, but he strongly disagreed with the idea of making mainframe computers to run the networks. Others supported the development of software but not hardware. Years later Reed would concede that perhaps he went to extremes in his quest for the perfect computer.

Reed's commitment to developing proprietary technology was founded partly on the free market principles Wriston believed in so strongly. In speeches and interviews, Wriston and Reed urged that free market competition prevail in developing payment systems. They also expressed concern about the emergence of technological mini-monopolies that could stifle alternatives. If, for example, a group of banks developed a single switching system for automated tellers that didn't work, consumers would have no alternative but to put up with poor service.

But Wriston was not nearly as inflexible as Reed was when it came to proprietary technology. He conceded that Citibank could lose the war between the mag stripe and the magic middle. "In this rapidly developing picture, if anything is clear, it is probably that one terminal on the merchant's counter is, from his point of view, the optimal number," he said in a talk to colleagues. "If the merchant has to have one terminal for the magnetic stripe and another for the magic middle, and we are the only bank that uses the magic middle, it is clear that we will be in some kind of trouble when we try to go on from where we are." Backing away from the hard-and-fast Citibank line, he suggested to his colleagues that they consider licensing the magic middle to IBM, NCR, and regional banks.

"Currently," he said, "these banks perceive that we are trying to conquer their world, but if we demonstrate that they can use our system, I believe that we could create allies and not enemies." Citibank resisted the move to magnetic-stripe technology for years but finally capitulated to the rest of the industry in 1985, when it distributed a universal-access card that contained both the magic middle and the mag stripe.

Amid the debate over the magic middle, TTI was hard at work on the development of its own automated teller machine that would use the Citicard technology. Citibank was not the first to offer cash machines. That honor was claimed by Chemical Bank, which installed the first cash-dispensing machine on the outside wall of a branch in 1969. But that technology had severe limitations. Scantlin developed a custom-made ATM that would run with 97 percent effectiveness, but that was "not good enough," Bob White said later. For an automated teller network, the machines had to work at a 99 percent level.

To bridge the gap between the design capabilities of Scantlin's device and the business and customer service demands of Citibank, Reed hired Paul Glaser, a Raytheon executive, who "took all of Jack's stuff and made it into an operational system."

The relationship between Scantlin and Citibank eventually broke up, and Scantlin drifted away from the fold. He later returned with ideas for more futuristic back office technology, and Citibank made him a millionaire once again. He was last reported retired, skippering his 140-foot sailing yacht in the South Pacific.

In developing such systems, Citibank became, in effect, the research and development arm of the American banking industry. Though he had limited experience in computers when he arrived at Citibank, White soon rivaled Reed as supreme technocrat. "The clincher," according to one colleague, came when White informed his colleagues that he had just placed an order for electronic robots to deliver the interoffice mail. "Everybody thought he was whacked-out," the officer said. But the robots were delivered and really worked, and they never asked for a raise. A few devices, however, did not always work. To guard against theft at 111 Wall Street, Citibank installed "man-traps" that were supposed to be activated when an authorized employee stuck his index finger in a tube and punched in a pass code. If an unauthorized person tried to enter, a seven-foot-high revolving steel drum would encircle him until he could be apprehended. Trouble was, said former operations officer Jeff Franklin, "you could punch in the code and stick in your finger and someone else could walk through the gate." White's dream was to create a rolling sidewalk with voice-activated computers that would issue instructions at every station. "It was a good idea," said one colleague, "but he wanted to do it in one weekend."

Citibank under Wriston spared no expense in its quest for state-of-the-art hardware and software. At any given moment, said Charles Long, Citibank might have in the pipeline at least five projects that were pushing the boundaries of technology, hoping that one might be successful. Besides some widely heralded multimillion-dollar projects that never saw the light of day, there were dozens of little-known initiatives that were simply scuttled. "If you put twenty programmers on a program, such as traveler's check authorization, and they work six months or ten man-years, and in the end you decide you're not going to have a system, is that a waste?" asked Long. "One of the [principles] that Wriston fostered is that we don't punish failure," said Long.

One of Reed's not-so-secret dreams was to create a checkless society, replacing checks with electronic blips and bytes. But he was realistic enough to understand that while that might be technologically possible, the consumer still demanded the comfort of a canceled check. The next-best thing, however, would be to figure out a way to "digitize," or "kill," the check as soon as it was presented, thus eliminating the need to file, store, and mail it back to the customer. The technology that Reed hoped would make this possible was called image processing. Before Reed finally threw in the towel on that project, ten years and tens of millions of dollars would be spent. The technology, which was being developed in a joint venture with a Dallas computer lab, was similar to that used by spacecraft to send back images of distant planets. In the end, what doomed the project was the researchers' failure to figure out how to compress all the data into a storage file that could be easily accessed whenever a customer demanded to see an actual canceled check.

Citibank's bold experiments in technology soon prompted other less sophisticated banks to try to do the same—at their peril. Said banking consultant Ed Furash, "In the Wriston era, Citi could afford to absorb the cost of failed ideas. Others couldn't afford to, but they copied Citibank products without realizing they were throwaways." Citibank, Furash said, tended to test-market a new product or technology by actually doing it, thereby enticing others to emulate initiatives that Citibank ultimately gave up on.

Despite the failures and the blowups, a mystique quickly developed around anyone associated with these high-profile efforts in back office automation and technology. At back office conventions, other bankers, still mired in Stone Age systems, pointed enviously to Citi's high-tech gurus.

Years later, in an interview, Reed continued to defend his build-versus-buy philosophy. "I'm very comfortable where we came out," he said, but he acknowledged that "you can get carried to extremes" on some projects. His biggest regret was having spent $100 million to build his own mainframes for a futuristic, on-line, real-time consumer banking system. Wriston was "generally supportive" of his R&D efforts, but "he didn't like losses," Reed said. He disclosed in 1991 that since the automation effort began he had spent about $1.75 billion on computer hardware and software, only 10 percent of which he said was "proprietary stuff."

The obsession with proprietary technology, said one former officer, stemmed from the view that IBM was out to sell computers, not to solve Citibank's problems, and that if IBM developed a system for Citibank, it would then hawk it to every other bank. "So how could you have a competitive advantage? That was John's feeling. We spent a lot of money, and wasted a lot on that theory."

At Citibank, Reed was Mr. Technology, and that didn't sit well with some of his colleagues. Besides insisting on overseeing the development of new technology, he wanted to control the use of it within Citibank. Early on, anyone seeking computer time to crank out reports had to go through Reed. And in one instance this led to a showdown in Spencer's office between Don Howard, the chief financial officer, and the computer czar. "You don't know a damn thing, Mr. Howard, about computers," Reed said. "I'm not going to let you screw up the computer center." Howard replied, "Then you're not going to get decent reporting." Reed was Spencer's protégé, but Howard's case was too compelling, and Spencer sided with Howard.

If the front end and back end blowups in check processing were nuclear explosions, then those in tax processing and stock transfer represented the detonation of more conventional weapons.

Among the back offices' recent assignments was the processing of millions of New York City's individual tax returns, a task that called for clerks to remove and sort the returns, transfer the data to computer tape, and deposit the checks in a city account. For eleven months of the year, when only about fifty thousand returns were received each month, the job was slow and simple, requiring perhaps forty workers. Come April, however, the bank felt the full onslaught of 4.3 million returns, for which it was woefully ill-prepared. Wriston soon received an angry call from the city's finance commissioner. "You probably don't know this," he said, "but in a place called 770 Broadway, you got 600,000 tax returns. The checks are sitting in a big pile on the floor. You got a contract signed to process this. You guys aren't doing anything."

Wriston proceeded immediately to the office and was appalled by what he found. Lawrence Small was pulled off another operations assignment and placed in charge of the mop-up.

He and a hastily assembled army of temporary workers toiled eighteen hours a day for forty-five days straight—through bomb scares, building evacuations, one attempted murder, and three assaults—to clean up the mess. By mid-June the problem was fixed, and the bank made money on the contract, Small said later.

Small did have his engaging side, which was apparent in his dealings with difficult customers. In processing the city tax receipts, he discovered that his counterpart in the city bureaucracy, who was constantly berating Citibank, was an amateur gourmet chef. Small succeeded in defusing the bureaucrat's wrath by feeding him a steady flow of recipes.

Check processing, of course, was just one piece of the problem. Stock transfer, the unit responsible for handling stock transactions, including dividend payments to shareholders of companies, was also in shambles. As trading volume soared in the late 1960s, Wall Street was awash in paper. Things got so bad that the New York Stock Exchange had to close one trading day a week to keep up with the volume.

In trying to convert from a manual to a computer system for stock transfer, a programmer had omitted the space where the certificate number belonged. Software writers at the time were an itinerant, uncontrollable lot who rarely stayed on one job for more than six months. While attending an audit committee meeting of the board, Wriston learned to his horror about the cost of a single programming error. Someone interrupted the meeting to inform him that there was a dividend account with $150 million in it. "My God," Wriston said, "what company pays that much in dividends that we're transfer agent for?"

"None," was the reply. "You've got to be kidding? You mean you don't have an account that says General Motors?" Wriston asked.

"No," he said sheepishly.

The funds from every company that paid a dividend had been tossed like garbage into a huge dividend compost pile, with no identification as to whether the money belonged to General Motors or General Electric.

This single software error would cost Citibank at least $100 million in incorrect payments and other expenses. "If you added up all the costs of that, let alone what we paid out to Aunt Minnie who didn't own the stock, it was probably the biggest loss we ever took," Wriston said later. For years Citibank leased an entire floor of an old John Wanamaker department store just to sort out the mess. The losses and the operation intended to correct the problem were virtually invisible to the outside world. But while Wall Street and reporters were preoccupied with loan losses, the biggest losses resulted from software and operating bugs, not from problem loans.

Part of the problem was the New York Stock Exchange and the brokers, who didn't cooperate with the banks. "The president of the exchange took pride in the fact that he had never been to a Clearing House bank," Wriston said later. Meanwhile, in 1969, Wall Street was breaking down under the weight of 20-million-share days. Twenty years later, a 100-million-share day would be described by the blow-dried anchors on the evening news as a day of light trading.

John Lee, then executive director of the New York Clearing House, recalled that the push to clean up the Wall Street paper crisis began about the time Robert Haack, then president of the Stock Exchange, arrived at the Clearing House with an armful of paper, slammed it down on Lee's desk in frustration, and said, "The city's awash in paper. Look at this." Complaints had been pouring in from brokers, transfer agents, and the Securities and Exchange Commission. Something had to give. Industry leaders, including Wriston and the heads of the major banks and brokerages, fretted that if they didn't do something, the "government would step in and nationalize the business," according to Lee.

The upshot was the formation of BASIC, an acronym for the Banking and Securities Industry Committee, jointly financed by bankers and brokers. Early on, brokers and bankers pointed the finger at each other. Several early proposals died in infancy, including a plan to convert stock certificates to IBM cards, and another to use optical scanners to read the certificates. BASIC members overlooked the laws that required the existence of a stock certificate. Finally, BASIC's executive director came up with the idea of safekeeping the physical stock in a vault and using computer printouts to advise all buyers, sellers, and trustees how much they owned. The creation of the Depository Trust Company required changes in legislation and securities and banking regulations. One of the officials who had to be persuaded was the elusive William Casey, chairman of the Securities and Exchange Commission. After many attempts to schedule a meeting for Wriston and other BASIC members with Casey on the proposal, Lee pinned Casey down in a room at a midtown Manhattan hotel. Early one morning, Lee led the group, including David Rockefeller and Wriston, to Casey's room. Casey appeared at the door in his underwear and invited the group in. "He was putting his pants and cuff links on while we were trying to talk with him," said Lee later. "It was the most awkward meeting I ever had in my life. [But] they convinced him he should get on board, and he did."

Although Wriston tended to let his subordinates sweat the details, he was well aware of the need to understand the nitty-gritty, unlike David Rockefeller, who, Wriston said, "tended to come at things more from the, you might say, big picture." After the Depository Trust Company (DTC) was established, the organizers deliberated at length over who would serve on its board. Wriston had emphasized the need for hands-on directors steeped in the nuts and bolts of back office operations. But Rockefeller thought the chairman should be represented, because that would give the board prestige. Wriston shot back, "You want to put your chairman on, that's great. As far as I'm concerned, I want someone who knows the difference between BASIC and FORTRAN and what you do when the books don't balance. That's who we put on."

"Prestige," Wriston said later, "is a stylistic thing that doesn't mean a hell of a lot."

Part and parcel of the Wall Street paperwork and back office check clearing backlog was the logjam caused by the manual system banks were still using to settle up during the business day on checks drawn on each other. That was the function of the New York Clearing House, a 120-year-old institution housed in a monolithic stone building near Wall Street. Under the manual system, banks traded official checks twice a day. With the creation of the Automated Clearing House Interbank Payments System, accomplished in early 1970 with help from Reed and Wriston, as many as seven transactions could be made each day. One result was an increased velocity of money in the U.S. financial system. Solving one problem, however, would set the stage for another. Because the funds moved on one day and settlement took place the next, bank balance sheets expanded due to this so-called float. Four years later the dangers of float—essentially funds left uncleared overnight—would be abundantly clear to world monetary authorities. In fact, the float would come close to bringing down the global financial system.

Meanwhile, neither BASIC nor DTC solved Wriston's own stock transfer problem. Efforts to convert the old manual ledger system to an automated one would blow up many times before the paper and dividends flowed with a modicum of efficiency and accuracy. By the mid-1970s, dividend checks still were sent to the wrong people and in the wrong amounts. According to former operations officers, the ironclad commitments Reed and White had made to achieve certain levels of savings by certain dates—to "make the numbers," in Citispeak—created a culture that forced officers on the line to fudge their numbers, launch systems conversions before they were ready, and even lie about the results. "If you didn't make the numbers you weren't around for a second chance," said former operations manager Jeff Franklin.

Wriston was perhaps the first bank CEO to appreciate the importance of the back office and raise it to a status once accorded only to corporate lenders. He once told banking professor Paul Nadler, "Anybody can put on a vest and lend to Corning Glass. It's the guy who breaks up the knife fights in my computer room who keeps this bank going."

But Wriston's elevation of the boot-camp culture and its disciples to manager-king status had implications that reverberated far beyond the back office. With the ascendancy of John Reed and lieutenants Small and White, Citibank abandoned any pretense of being warm and cuddly. Cost savings, automation, and technology were king, and people were merely "heads" to be lopped off. Old-timers who resisted or couldn't cope with the new technology and methods were especially vulnerable. As one former senior officer put it, "The whole way of thinking about life that John [Reed] represented became more and more Wriston's than the old way." In the drive to cut costs and automate, Reed had created a we-they culture. The new breed of technocrats pitted themselves against the old line back office managers who had grown up in the world of paper and rubber bands and against genteel corporate bankers from uptown headquarters. At one point, even Spencer is said to have told his youthful protégé, "There's a feeling here that there are two banks. Yours and the rest."

In the opinion of his uptown colleagues, one of White's shortcomings was that he never understood the needs of the customers his technology was designed to serve. Nor did Reed's technocrats have any patience with the thousands of often-undereducated minorities who performed many of the low-level clerical tasks at 111 Wall Street. The New York City school system had not prepared many of them well for the workaday world. The clerical workers had also become a convenient excuse, sometimes a valid one, for missing various deadlines. This did not sit well with Wriston. At one meeting, he told the operating group managers that Citibank was a kind of "port of entry" for minorities in New York seeking membership in the middle class. "I don't want to hear that a manager couldn't meet his targets" because of poorly performing minorities, he ordered, according to one manager who was present. Wriston made it clear that "if you had thirty-five blacks who couldn't type, you were going to teach them, and if you couldn't, you were out the door."

Though that showdown was resolved favorably, by 1972 Citibank was nearing another confrontation whose outcome would inflict a major body blow to the old paternalistic banking culture. Ever since anyone could remember, there had been an unwritten, unspoken covenant between Citibank and its staff that workers would not be fired merely because they happened to be superfluous in their department at any point in time. Terminations for reasons other than wrongdoing or incompetence were handled by the personnel department.

It did not take long for word to reach Citibank personnel chief Robert Feagles that Reed had, in effect, junked that policy by planning a round of firings. In a stormy, bitter confrontation, Feagles, the defender of the old policy, phoned Reed, demanding to know if the news of the firings was true. Reed appeared at Feagles's office. "Of course it's so," Reed replied. Feagles told Reed that if the old policy had been changed, nobody had told him about it. Reed responded that it was implicit in the plan for flat expense growth that had been approved by Wriston and Spencer. Feagles was incredulous, demanding to know if Reed had been given authority to fire staff unilaterally. In what Feagles viewed as an insulting lesson in arithmetic, Reed explained that for expenses to remain flat and for staff to receive 6 percent merit increases, 12 percent of the salary expense had to be cut annually.

Reed asked Feagles what he should do with the people if there were no jobs for them, whether he should have the employees sit idly at tables. Reed wasn't advocating throwing everyone out on the street, and Feagles wasn't in favor of keeping all of them until they turned sixty-five. But the two men were miles apart in their philosophy of personnel management, and a showdown was inevitable. Feagles tried to explain that he wasn't arguing with the new policy. He simply wanted to know if the policy had in fact been changed. They asked for a meeting with Wriston and Spencer. Feagles related his understanding of the facts, and Wriston turned to Reed and asked if his account was true. It was. Feagles wondered if Wriston had thought through the human consequences of keeping expense growth flat.

Wriston was in a tough bind. According to Feagles, he was groping for some way out of this terrible predicament. He had worked hard to convey the impression that he as an individual and Citibank as an institution cared for the employees. But he had also committed himself to a 15 percent annual earnings increase, which clearly couldn't be achieved without bringing operations under control.

Feagles was looking for a way to defuse the confrontation. "Look, Walt, if we're going to do this [fire people], that's fine. I'll work with John to do it so as to cause the least harm to the organization and make us least vulnerable to union organization, which is what you're paying me for." In fact, it wasn't long before organizers with the Office and Professional Workers Union were distributing leaflets at 111 Wall.

Reed insisted that if he was to keep his promise to keep expenses flat, the redundant employees would have to go. Finally Wriston spoke. Addressing Reed, according to Feagles, he said, in effect, do it nicely.

Thus the lifetime employment contract went the way of the green eyeshade, the stiff collar, and the hand-cranked calculator. Many of the casualties were low-level clerical workers who had joined the bank after the war and hoped to retire after completing forty or more years of service. One fired worker had started with the bank fifty years earlier as a page. Said White's former secretary, Maria Savarese, "What they've done to people is just appalling. People who worked ten to twelve hours a day seven days a week to get things done got thrown out like Kleenex. They weren't brains or college grads, M.B.A.'s and all that. They were good workers who were there when the going got rough."

Dismissing average workers, Reed and his lieutenants asserted, would allow the better people to stay. And if banking was to become a business, they believed, the lifetime employment contract would have to be scrapped. When the back office workers realized that the purpose of the efficiency measures was to eliminate their jobs, they understandably became reluctant to share their knowledge about their jobs with their new managers, regardless of how friendly and persuasive the managers might be.

Reed, of course, was well aware of his reputation for ruthlessness. But he would later claim that his colleagues had mistaken intellectual rigor and perseverance for lack of compassion. "People thought that because of my style I was somehow very numerically bottom line, cold, and mechanically oriented. I don't think I ever was. I can remember my father saying, 'You're not tough enough for business.' I've never been a particularly tough person." Reed also believed strongly that once a certain course of action, in life or in business, was decided upon, the options for carrying it out would become clear. "I believed totally, as only a young person can, that we had to run the operating group differently. . . . It never crossed my mind that once you came to that belief you just didn't do it. If you persuaded me that I should jump out of a window, the odds are very high that I would. But [first] you've got to persuade me that I should."

Reed's rise to stardom would exact a heavy toll on his family and, ultimately, on his marriage. His admirers saw him as a devoted family man who adored his four children, sent money to his mom in Florida, and helped a brother there start a business. His wife, Sally, was an unpretentious woman who was out of place in the high-tech world. She delighted in simple things— gardens, flowers, her children—prompting one friend to refer to her as "the Earth Mother." For her, the next decade would be especially taxing.

Although no one doubted that Reed achieved real savings, some former colleagues assert that there was also a certain amount of smoke and mirrors. As Reed brought additional back office line operations into his group, he also picked up what the number crunchers called a "historical cost base" from each unit. In many instances, the historical costs actually exceeded revenues. As units were combined, cost reductions could be claimed almost immediately, enabling Reed, with some justification, to take instant credit for the savings. In effect, charged one former associate, Reed created a "phantom expense base" where vast research and development expenditures, such as those for Transaction Technology, Inc., could easily be buried, and where huge cuts could easily be made.

Whatever savings Reed achieved in operational efficiency were largely offset by the inefficiencies of an institution where decentralization was a religion. Reed, of course, had a fetish for proprietary technology, but the problem went far beyond that. Although it purchased bank-wide liability insurance, Citibank most often failed to use its vast buying power to achieve cost savings on the purchase of computers, rental cars, and telephones. Vendors who attempted to offer discount packages to the bank rather than to individual business units scratched their heads in amazement when Citibank declined their bargain-basement propositions. "Vendors don't understand. They throw their hands up in frustration," said Reed aide Charles Long. "We optimize in businesses but not across the corporation." Moreover, the move toward matrix management demanded new, expensive layers of staff people and managers to manage the matrix of product, geography, and function.

For all the upheaval Reed generated throughout the bank, he eventually transformed the back office into the most technologically advanced and efficient one in American banking, and in doing so, he rapidly accelerated the move toward electronic payments systems in the United States. For all the smoke and mirrors, he also produced real savings.

Besides propelling Reed's own career, this experience would create a lasting personal bond between him and those who survived his boot camp. Reed valued most those who had remained loyal to him the longest. He conveyed this often in impromptu history lessons and Maoist metaphors. "If you weren't with Mao on the Long March, you were never going to be anything in running China," Reed told his colleagues, a not-so-subtle reminder that they had to be with him on the Long March at Citibank to be part of his team when he reached the top. People whom Reed hired personally were automatically on board for the march unless they ran afoul of him. Others had to demonstrate their loyalty by spending some time in "purgatory," as one former officer put it. This often took the form of toiling in some undesirable overseas post or proving oneself in an unglamorous back office task. "You had to be made," said a former officer who did not complete the march. "John's need for loyalty and adoration and recognition that he was the resident philosopher king was real high."

11

CRISIS AND CONFRONTATION

*A*t the turn of the decade, Wriston's fiercest competitor was no longer David Rockefeller. He was not even a commercial banker. His principal rival now was pipe-smoking Arthur Burns, the short, stocky Austrian immigrant who was named chairman of the Federal Reserve Board in February 1970. Born Arthur Frank Burnseig in 1904, Burns parted his mop of gray hair right down the middle and, as the *Wall Street Journal* put it, "could pass for a small-town druggist, circa 1910."

Burns was appointed just in time to take the lead in the ongoing debate over the bank holding company legislation pending before Congress. Representative Wright Patman, of course, wanted to define that business by legislative fiat with his so-called negative laundry list. By this time, it was clear that the only way to avoid such a distasteful outcome was for the Fed to be awarded custody of one-bank holding companies and to be given the right to decide what kinds of activities they should engage in. And just two months after his appointment, Burns signaled the go-slow approach that would mark his tenure at the Fed. In a speech to top bankers, he warned them against making large credit commitments, in part because he believed such pledges complicated the Fed's efforts to conduct monetary policy and to fight inflation. But curtailing credit to please the Fed was not Wriston's style, nor was moving slowly. Now and for the rest of Wriston's career Citibank and the Fed would be pitted against each other in a battle over who would control the nation's financial system.

Citibank had a long tradition of viewing itself as a de facto central bank of the United States and challenged the Fed's rules and authority at every opportunity. According to Wriston, the Fed saw Citibank not only as its competitor for the role of central bank of the United States but as its intellectual competitor as well. "I always felt it was important that we figure out who would be the central bank—the Fed, the House of Morgan, or Citibank," a former top Fed official said dryly.

Citibank, Wriston said, disliked "all bureaucracies. The city, the Fed, and Congress like nice quiet stability. Every time they turned around we sent a new application that would require them to do something different. Citi created one new idea after another. That's a real pain when you're a regulator. The Comptroller has always been on the leading edge of assisting the financial system, and the Fed has always said the actions of the Comptroller are illegal or stupid." Bureaucrats like Arthur Burns provoked some of Wriston's most biting sarcasm. "Regulators," he used to say, "sit by while snails go by like rockets."

Until the bank holding company legislation, Citibank's primary regulator had been the Comptroller of the Currency, which traditionally had been sympathetic to the bank's expansionary aims. Citibank had to grovel to the Fed to obtain permission to acquire overseas businesses, and the bank tangled with the Fed over rules, such as Reg Q, that related to interest rates and monetary policy. But it did not generally have to deal with the Fed on matters that directly concerned domestic banking, its principal business. According to former Citibanker Ham Meserve, Wriston told his troops, "Clerks follow the rules. You guys are hired to break the rules." One prominent example was Citibank's liberal use of the Fed discount window to fund itself in 1969, when money was tight.

In contrast to Wriston, most American and foreign bankers tended to regard their central bankers in much the same way that a parish priest might view the pope. "When the Bank of England frowns, the British banks say, 'What is it that displeases you?' " recalled Ed Palmer, who was soon to become chairman of the executive committee. But Wriston, of course, was not inclined to kowtow to Burns or anyone else.

The creation of the one-bank holding company, the passage of legislation that placed these entities under Fed jurisdiction, and Wriston's efforts to stretch the limits of banking intensified the adversarial relationship between the nation's central bank and Citibank, which soon emerged as the Fed's largest and most incorrigible client. Uppermost among the Fed's worries was how to rescue big banks if they got into trouble. And Wriston became the living symbol of the Federal Reserve's conviction that big was bad.

Wriston liked Burns personally and admired his intellect, academic credentials, and ability to turn a phrase. But in their view of markets and economics, the two men had little in common. Burns talked a good line when it came to free markets, but more often than not he readily embraced government-imposed solutions. He had been one of the leading advocates of controls—notably the interest equalization tax—as a way to shrink the balance-of-payments deficit. In his speeches, he advocated moving away from interest rate ceilings on deposits, but his actions helped preserve the regulatory status quo.

Wriston and Burns did share some personal idiosyncrasies, including a penchant for frugality. When Burns became chairman, he ordered that the Federal Reserve Board's fleet of limousines be replaced with Dodge Valiants. At about that time, Wriston decided that Citibank needed a corporate jet, but only because it was able to repossess one from a troubled borrower. As corporate jets go, it was a Spartan affair; the interior wasn't remodeled until the cabin panels began to fall off, according to former Citibank lawyer Chris York.

Wriston and Burns also shared a disdain for House Banking Committee chairman Wright Patman, though for decidedly different reasons. Patman, in turn, was distrustful of the Fed and took Burns to the woodshed every chance he got. Wriston recalls that Burns discovered Patman's weakness and used it to avoid being browbeaten by the demagogic congressman. A shrewd politician in his own right, Burns noticed that Patman frequently brought his wife to hearings, and figured that Patman would be discreet enough not to berate him in front of his own spouse. "So every time [Burns went] to testify, he'd take his wife and she'd sit there with Mrs. Patman," Wriston recalled. "Wright never was rude to Arthur after that."

Once the holding company legislation moved to the Senate, Patman sought to influence the outcome by discrediting Treasury secretary David Kennedy and deputy secretary Charls Walker, the former executive director of the American Bankers Association. He tried to "tar Kennedy and me with the banker's image and undermine our credibility," Walker said later. By this time, however, Burns and the Fed had essentially taken charge of moving the legislation through the Congress. To the Fed, said a former Fed official, Citibank was the institution to be stopped. Its goals for growth, in both size and powers, represented a potential threat to the safety and soundness of the banking system and to the separation of industry and commerce. And the bank holding company legislation was the mechanism for stopping it.

Still, it was evident now that Citibank and others would have to play ball with Burns in order to defeat Patman. "If . . . the Fed [hadn't come] around to a reasonable viewpoint on it, I think we would have been in bad trouble," said lobbyist Jack Yingling. The Fed, he said, started out opposed to new powers, but gradually came around to the idea of granting powers that were "closely related to banking."

In testimony in mid-May 1970, Burns urged the Congress to enact the legislation before the end of the session. Failing to do so, he said, would imply approval of the one-bank exemption. In theory at least, Burns was relatively liberal in his interpetation of what banks should be permitted to do. He felt that the House bill went "too far in protecting insurance agents, travel agents, bookkeepers, mutual funds, and others from competition." He said that the majority of the board favored allowing banking companies to retain nonbank units acquired before June 30, 1968, and he opposed the early Nixon administration proposal to divvy up jurisdiction over bank holding companies among three agencies.

In the thick of the legislative debate, Walker threw a bone to the big banks, which were about to lose powers and privileges they thought they had gained by forming holding companies. To ease the pain, he proposed the creation of a blue-ribbon panel to study the financial services industry and recommend reforms, an idea that was incorporated into the 1970 Economic Report of the President. With the appointment of retired Crown Zellerbach chairman Reed O. Hunt in April 1970, the panel was dubbed the Hunt Commission. Not surprisingly, the senior banker on the panel was not Wriston but the more congenial Ellmore Patterson of J. P. Morgan & Company. As things turned out, however, the panel played virtually no role in shaping the bank holding company legislation.

The White House eventually lost interest in the project, to the point where presidential adviser H. R. (Bob) Haldeman tried to cut off its funding. According to Walker, the panel was saved by director of the Office of Management and Budget George Shultz, and in December 1972 it submitted its final report. That document was a blueprint for the restructuring of the U.S. financial services industry and the granddaddy of many studies to come on the subject. Had its recommendations been followed, they would have increased competition in the financial services industry by leveling the playing field for banks, thrifts, and other providers. And in hindsight, they might have prevented the savings and loan debacle of the 1980s. Among other things, the panel would have eliminated all interest rate ceilings and reserve requirements on savings and time deposits, permitted interstate banking, and enabled thrift institutions to offer credit cards and checking accounts. Significantly, the commission also recommended that banks be allowed to buy thrift institutions. Eight years would pass, however, before any of its recommendations were actually implemented.

To no one's surprise, Wriston on May 1, 1970, moved to the top rung of the Citibank corporate ladder. As chairman, he earned $257,820, just $585 more than he had made as president and CEO the year before.

For the fortunate few who rise to such heights, it is a rite of passage akin to the transition from adolescence to manhood. The new CEO is certainly pleased at having made it to the top, but there are still things he misses about the job he left behind.

As president and CEO, Wriston was more interested in wrapping his arms around Citibank's businesses, particularly those with which he had little previous contact, than in glad-handing. With George Moore making speeches and running board meetings, Wriston "could go have fun with the business," as he put it later. But when Moore retired in 1970, Wriston was no longer permitted the luxury of managing a business on a hands-on basis. "Your dream is that you're going to be able to run your business. The reality is there are pressures from outside that intrude on your time," said Wriston later. "You might have liked the job you left in many respects better than the one you got."

Bill Spencer was elected president. He became Wriston's inside man, responsible for day-to-day administration, blocking and tackling, and the thankless and sometimes dirty chores that fell to the second-in-command. If Wriston was king, Spencer was the prime minister. Wriston, Spencer said later, handled the "big think department; I spent all my time in the internal workings of the place," but "we were in each other's pockets three to four times a day."

Spencer was no intellectual. He was a golden gloves boxing champion from Colorado who broke horses and stalked mountain sheep. He was the practical, commonsense credit man, a counterpoint to his more visionary and often abrasive colleague. Wriston was always more comfortable dealing with concepts, strategy, and ideas and making judgments about people than he was reviewing columns of figures, an activity that now fell to Spencer.

Although Wriston typically declined to immerse himself in petty administrative detail, he took mischievous delight in preempting Spencer's duties when Spencer was traveling, according to associates. Said one colleague, "He put out a memo on some realignment of staff, saying, 'It can't wait for him to get back. Got to do it.' It didn't have to be done at all," the colleague said. "He liked to show Bill he was doing things, like changing unit heads, or implementing some new procedure that had been in the works for six months, and could wait another two weeks." Spencer later remarked that "a dill pickle will always taste like a dill pickle, and that's Walter Wriston."

And of course there were the countless dinners that had to be farmed out among the bank's top managers. Dinners and luncheons with employees, customers, and civic groups were so much a part of his job that Spencer often joked that "I regret that I have but one stomach to give to my bank." If there was a dinner that neither cared to attend, they would typically send Ed Palmer, who became chairman of the executive committee—the number three post—when Richard Perkins retired on July 1, 1970. Like Spencer, Palmer was a Chemical Bank alumnus hired by George Moore. Though originally from Brooklyn, Palmer was a soft-spoken, genial Brown graduate with impeccable social and business credentials. Dubbed "the Silver Fox" because of his silvery crew-cut hair, Palmer filled the void left by the retirement of veteran banker Howard Laeri. Palmer was the quintessential big-time corporate banker and customer man; he was on a first-name basis with the CEO of nearly every major company in America. "Palmer had the biggest Rolodex I've ever seen," said one colleague.

In the gung-ho, boot-camp atmosphere that Citibank would become under Wriston, Palmer exuded a traditional Old World air, smoothing some of the rough edges off an institution that soon became known for taking no prisoners. Among colleagues, Wriston referred to Palmer as "my Morgan white shoe–type banker."

His charm made Palmer Citibank's top customer man. He later supervised the holding company and the bank's increasingly important asset and liability management committee and, in that capacity, spoke for the bank on interest rates and money management. But the three men were virtually interchangeable. Wriston referred to Eddie Palmer, Billy Spencer, and Al Costanzo (head of overseas) as his partners and, in keeping with his belief in corporate democracy, gave them extraordinary leeway to run their operations as they saw fit. "It was not a case of Walter Wriston issuing orders," said a colleague. "Wriston permitted a diffusion of power."

Still, there was less than total harmony among the three top men. Bill Spencer and Ed Palmer were hard-pressed to mask their dislike for each other and spoke to each other only when they had to. When asked how Spencer became president of the bank, Palmer replied on more than one occasion that "every organization needs an office manager." Palmer would later concede that while he respected Spencer as a banker, he "didn't get much juice out of Bill. It would be insincere to say I find him one of the great human beings of the world." He was, said Palmer, a "tough customer." At least part of the ill feeling between the two men was said to stem from what Spencer regarded as Palmer's shoddy treatment of one of his closest friends at the bank. "Wriston and Spencer walked all over Palmer," one officer recalled. While Palmer claimed to be content playing third fiddle, he acknowledged later that "being number three is like being the youngest child in the family. You don't get many new suits." Over time, Wriston and Spencer seemed to develop a genuine affection for each other, but according to colleagues, Spencer appeared on occasion to resent Wriston's getting the flowers for achievements he felt belonged to him. Spencer's wife Kay used to grumble that "Bill does all the work and Walt gets all the credit."

Operating behind the scenes as secretary to the board was Wriston confidant Carl Desch, a short, sprightly lover of things German whom some referred to as Wriston's "valet." Describing his role, Desch used to say that "every organization needs a guy who knows where the toilet paper is." Wriston counted on Desch to handle discreetly the most delicate assignments. Among other duties, he was a shoulder for hundreds of Citibank officers to cry on. He listened to them all—including the men whose wives had served them with divorce papers while they were hospitalized and those who returned to New York from overseas stints with no place to call home; Desch arranged with other banks to grant them mortgages.

Wriston didn't believe ex-chairmen should hang around the store after their terms were up. He had made that clear to Stillman Rockefeller after he became president and to Moore when he became chairman. Even though Moore was now retired, he didn't hesitate to barge into Wriston's office to offer unsolicited advice. But "I couldn't even use the dining room," Moore lamented later. "I couldn't order a chicken sandwich. I had to send out for it. Walt would come up once in a while, maybe."

Moore was not the sort to spend his time cloistered with other retired executives anyway. For him, retirement from Citibank was less the end of one career than the beginning of another. He had begun raising a second family when many men his age were confined to nursing homes. He later humorously boasted that Citibank was the first bank overseas, the first bank to open a branch outside New York City, and the first to offer personal loans, but he was the first bank chairman to father a child the day he retired. At least once a week, he jetted back and forth between Europe and the United States tending to his business interests. He plunged into dozens of new enterprises, becoming, among other things, an adviser to a Spanish bank and honorary chairman of Nashville's Tennessee Valley Bancorp. Moore pushed the Tennessee bank into international lending, a move it would later regret. He was also a financial adviser to Christina Onassis and, later, a trustee for the Onassis American interests. As he looked back at his first career Moore credited Rockefeller and Wriston with being two of the three most important people in his business career. "The guy who influenced me most was James Perkins who trained me, Rockefeller who made me president, and Wriston who made a hero out of me," Moore said later.

Rockefeller himself finally quit the board when he was forced to choose between Citibank and Pan Am. His membership on the boards of both the airline and First National City Corporation, which was then in the travel business, was seen as something of a conflict. But Pan Am gave its directors a lifetime world pass entitling them to free travel, which Rockefeller, former associates say, felt was a better deal.

With Moore's departure, the changes were more of style than of substance. But Wriston was much more disciplined than his mentor—to say the least—and that was clearly reflected in operating practices. Under Wriston, the taboo against front office loans became sacrosanct. In contrast to Moore Wriston rarely got involved with lending decisions. "I didn't have anything to do with that," Wriston said later. "I didn't lend any money." The credit process was controlled by the chief credit officer. If a group executive disagreed with him, Wriston or Spencer would cast the deciding vote. "That didn't happen five times in twenty years."

Loan exposure to various industry sectors was also controlled by the chief credit officer. "Bill and I could have input," Wriston said. Either man could ask lending officers whether the bank was too extended on airline loans, for example. The polite but firm response would be, "When was the last time you made an airline loan?"

"Ten years ago."

"Well, the DC-3 isn't flying anymore."

"The system," said Wriston, regulates exposure, "not the management."

One of the goals of a newly anointed chairman and CEO is to begin replacing retiring members of the board with directors who reflect his temperament and style. For nearly 160 years, Citibank's board had been made up of white male businessmen plus a token Shearman & Sterling lawyer. True to form, Wriston was determined to correct that. Until 1970 few blacks had ever seen the inside of a Park Avenue boardroom. That changed with the appointment of Franklin Thomas, a tall, lean former Columbia University basketball star who headed the Bedford-Stuyvesant Restoration Corporation. When Wriston first encountered Thomas, he concluded that he was "the smartest man he ever met." Among other duties, Thomas soon became the point man on a nasty, contentious issue that would dog Citibank for years: South Africa. Still, in a concession to tradition, Wriston also tapped three plain vanilla captains of industry for his board: Milo

Brisco of Standard Oil (New Jersey), Louis Eilers of Eastman Kodak, and John Hall of the Anaconda Company. And in 1973, the first woman director, Dr. Eleanor H. B. Sheldon, president of the Social Science Research Council, was elected to the board.

Under Wriston, being a Citibank director acquired a cachet among top executives unmatched in corporate America. It was a Who's Who of American business. Yet no one ever forgot who was in charge. "There were no mavericks on the board. He checked them out very carefully before he put them in," said longtime director J. Peter Grace. "If you took him on in an argument in front of forty people, you'd get your head knocked off." Then, a little more than a year later, Wriston's management team became his own with the resignation of Tom Wilcox. Judging from the remarks that each man made about the other when Wilcox left, one would never have imagined that any rivalry ever existed.

In his new role as Citibank's outside man, Wriston's first order of business was to persuade Congress to define the business of banking his way, not Wright Patman's. On May 26, 1970, the big three—A. W. "Tom" Clausen, chairman of BankAmerica Corporation, Wriston, and David Rockefeller, as well as Ernest Arbuckle, chairman of Wells Fargo Bank, appeared before the Senate Banking and Currency Committee to declare that they had no interest in owning automakers or shoe factories.

The bankers hammered away at the committee's charge that the bank holding company movement represented a dangerous trend toward concentration of economic power. For his part, Wriston asserted that the financial clout of the industry and Citibank was actually in decline. The portion of financial assets _outside_ the banking system, Wriston pointed out, had actually grown relative to that of the banking system. From 1956 to 1968, he said, commercial bank assets as a percentage of total assets of financial institutions dropped from 53 to 50. In fact, as Wriston later told a reporter, "the number of zeros in our balance sheet is going up while our percentage of the market declines." He testified that in 1947 the "limit we could lend to one customer was $24 million. That sum then would have financed about 190 DC-3s. Today our lending limit is about $90 million per customer. That sounds big, but it will pay for only four 747s. It is a big world requiring big organizations to finance the trillion-dollar economy around the corner." He added that "legislation that hobbles the service effforts of the commercial banks must hobble the economic growth of the country and the world."

In his Washington appearance, Wriston sought to dispel the senators' concern that holding companies were the "royal road" to _zaibatsu._ That fear, he said, overlooks the fact "that there are no comparable anti-trust laws in Japan, nor [is there] any counterpart of our Justice Department that continually overlooks the state of competition." Wriston enumerated Citibank's long list of attempts to expand or acquire new companies, and the maze of laws and agencies, including the Department of Justice, that blocked the bank's way.

Citibank attempted to bring public as well as congressional opinion to bear upon the debate. In June it released the results of a survey of executives and the general public that purportedly concluded that they wanted "financial supermarkets" where they could obtain a host of financial services in one place. Bankers like Wriston had some heavyweight supporters, including Yale economics professor Henry C. Wallich, who would later become one of the most influential members of the Federal Reserve Board of Governors. Writing in *Fortune,* Wallich declared that the "U.S. has some of the best banks in the world, but it surely has the worst banking system of any major nation." Technology, Wallich wrote, will eventually prevail over regulation, ideology, and political influence. Wallich reiterated Wriston's concern that Patman and his bank holding company bill "could straightjacket banks." That, together with "shrinking or unreliable" funding sources, "could condemn the banks to ultimate irrelevance in the financial framework," Wallich warned. Prophetically, he concluded that "it might point them toward a useful but profitless existence like that of railroads."

Wallich's comparison with railroads was well timed. As he and Wriston were arguing for broader powers for bank holding companies, the largest and most diverse railroad holding company—the Penn Central—was indeed on a collision course with financial disaster. In the spring of 1970, Penn Central's deepening troubles would confirm for Wriston his worst fears about the evils of holding companies. At the same time, however, Penn Central would provide a new cache of small-caliber ammunition for critics of bank holding company expansion. Penn Central ushered in an era of seemingly nonstop financial debacles, and Wriston was destined to participate one way or another in nearly all of them. Indeed, over the next decade and a half, he helped forge a new financial order in part through the pivotal role he frequently played in averting financial calamity.

For Wriston, the troubles of Penn Central would represent a kind of baptism by fire. Even before he officially took over the reins of Citibank, he was thrust into the thick of the largest corporate collapse in American history. At the time, it represented the largest potential loan loss that the American banking industry, and Citibank in particular, had ever faced. Being caught unawares on Penn Central couldn't have been more embarrassing. Although Wriston had been preoccupied with building the overseas division for the last fifteen years, he was also the bank's resident expert on transportation financing. He had prided himself on his intelligence network, but as the long, bone-chilling winter of 1969–1970 gave way to spring, it was clear that this network had not served him well. Moore would later acknowledge that he, too, "made some of the loans."

Late in 1969, Bill Spencer and friends had gathered for their traditional Christmas lunch at "21," the famous former speakeasy. As usual, the group of corporate executives had gone around the room and aired, on an informal and off-the-record basis, their views on the outlook for the economy and their respective industries. On this occasion, one of the friends happened to be Penn Central chief financial officer David C. Bevan. It had been nearly two years since the merger of the Pennsylvania and the New York Central, which a syndicate of banks led by Citibank had helped finance, and Bevan was ebullient. "It is really remarkable," Spencer recalls Bevan saying, "how we went down through the ranks of the two companies, looking at the savings and when we got to annual savings of $100 million we just stopped looking." For 1969, however, the company barely scratched out a profit of $4.4 million.

City Bank, of course, had been instrumental in financing the New York Central and the Pennsylvania Railroad since the nineteenth century. Its role was further enhanced when the merger of the First National Bank and National City brought together two of the nation's premier railroad banks. Penn Central and its predecessor companies had century-old relationships with several hundred mostly small banks, which often took a piece of a Penn Central loan after doing little more than peruse the color photos in the company's annual report.

So it was natural that Citibank would serve as the lead bank in major credits to the leading U.S. railroad company, and perhaps the premier U.S. corporation, of the 1960s. Over the years, the Pennsy and the New York Central had played key roles in the nation's economic growth, and in turn their revenues had grown as the American economy grew.

In the 1960s, however, a number of developments had begun to chip away at the railroads' supremacy in transportation. The federal highway system, the Saint Lawrence Seaway, and other alternative transportation systems drew freight away from the Pennsy and the New York Central, forcing them, on February 1, 1968, into a merger of the two roads and giving birth to an enterprise with about $7 billion in assets. The heady numbers obscured the problems. The real need was less for a merger than for a fundamental restructuring of the Pennsy's entire operation. Its plant was too big and too old. The work force was too big and the work rules too rigid. It could no longer compete against other forms of transport, including trucks and air cargo. In persuading the unions not to fight the deal, chairman Stuart Saunders "gave away the store," said former Citibank transportation lender Al Ambs. Despite Bevan's claims, no economies were ever realized from the merger. Instead, there was utter confusion. The lines were so poorly integrated that entire trains were lost for days.

In the mid-1960s, the Pennsy had initiated a diversification program that drained funds from the railroad instead of contributing cash to it, and that continued after the merger. According to one published account, the cash drain by early 1970 amounted to more than $200 million. The Penn Central was a holding company that embodied all the evils thereof. It was a shell game of paper profits and phony dividends. Bevan was the point man for the banks, and no bean counter in Corporate America was more powerful, or more arrogant. It was, after all, an honor to lend money to this blue-chip aristocratic enterprise.

To finance the merger, Penn Central turned to Citibank. Penn Central obtained its final commitment from the bank in May 1968 for about $100 million. The banks became secured as a result of last-minute wrangling with Penn Central in 1969, when the loan came up for renewal. In its revolving credit agreements, Citibank had always insisted on what bankers call a "material adverse change clause," meaning that they would not have to lend if there was a significant deterioration in the company's condition. This time, however, Bevan balked at the "material adverse change" language, and it appeared that Citibank was prepared to make a rare exception to its long-standing policy. If that happened, the loan would be unsecured with no way out. At the last minute, recalled Citibank's John Ingraham, who was later placed in charge of the Penn Central restructuring, Bevan agreed to give the banks collateral, and in return Citibank dropped its demand for the clause. On April 1, 1969, the Citibank group renewed its loan for $300 million, of which Citibank itself held a $35 million share. Besides that loan, Citibank was agent for a number of other credits, including loans for equipment. Because their loan was secured, the Citibank syndicate of fifty-three banks stood ahead of unsecured creditors waiting on line at the scrap heap later. That security ultimately enabled the banks to recoup their principal and most of their post-bankruptcy interest.

"Bevan must have anticipated that he could not deliver the predictability of the Penn Central cash flows back in 1969, despite the elegant presentations, and that's how the bank got secured at that time. It was a cash-flow loan, but collateral was a final negotiated point," said a source familiar with the loan. Nonetheless, on March 6, 1970, a Citibank officer drafted a memo advising that the bank defer payment of past-due loans to Executive Jet Aviation, another Penn Central unit.

At about this time, a senior Citibank lending officer phoned Ed Palmer asking Palmer to stop by his office. "I want you to hear a story that Pat Bowditch has," he said. Bowditch was a Citibank officer on the Penn Central account.

"What do you mean?" Palmer asked.

"We've decided not to serve as agent in the renewal of the Penn Central line of credit. It's going to cause all hell, and at a minimum Bevan is going to be on your back, so you might as well know about it."

"I just had a luncheon canceled. Let's go to lunch," Palmer said. Over lunch, Bowditch and the other officer told Palmer that Penn Central had not been forthright about its condition. "The figures don't make sense," they said.

Palmer was incredulous. *"This is the Penn Central,"* Palmer said, as a chill went down his spine.

"I tell you, this is what the situation is," one officer said.

While Citibank would ultimately wind up holding the bag on a large hunk of the Penn Central loans, it graciously let Chemical Bank lead the renewal. "This is what kind of began to bring them [Penn Central] down," Palmer recalled. Citibank's failure to renew caused the Wall Street firm of First Boston to get nervous about underwriting a new issue of long-term debt.

The first public indication that something was seriously wrong came on April 22, 1970, when Penn Central reported that it had lost $17.2 million in the first quarter, after a $62.7 million loss in the railroad unit. In the wake of that announcement, chairman Stuart Saunders huddled with secretary of transportation John Volpe to press for federal loan guarantees and a federal takeover of the passenger operations. Those guarantees would be provided under the Defense Department's "V-loan" authority, which allowed it to back loans to companies whose operations were considered vital to national security. The theory was that a solvent Penn Central was essential for the transport of military matériel for the Vietnam War.

Former Secretary of the Treasury David Kennedy would later recall that prior to the bankruptcy he began to sense that the railroad company was not merely in difficulty, but broke. Bevan, he said, told him the company "couldn't raise $100 million for its payroll because the market was too tight," and accused the administration of "not doing our job and letting interest rates go too high." Of Bevan and Saunders, Kennedy said, "They were just ballooning everything. I couldn't tell whether it would cost us $1 billion or $10 million."

In mid-May, Standard & Poor's cut its rating on Pennco bonds. Penn Central's fate was sealed when the underwriters failed to sell its $100 million long-term debt issue, forcing it to announce on May 28, 1970, that the deal would be scrapped. Penn Central was now persona non grata on Wall Street and was forced to draw on its $300 million line of credit to replace maturing commercial paper. It was no longer able to obtain fresh cash. "From there on," said John Ingraham, "it was a fight to the finish."

Despite the negative cash flows, the banks continued to fund on the credit. "If one were to ignore any kind of historic relationship, perhaps the banks might have stopped funding somewhere halfway into the middle of the loan, as opposed to all the way at the end," said one banker.

David Bevan had done a heavy sell of America's small banks, obtaining commitments for their $1 million or $2 million participations in the line of credit. "The banks felt bitter because they'd been bagged. They felt they were making a line of credit available to an old friend who had maintained balances with them," said one Citibanker who worked on the account. The banks were furious with Penn Central, but they were also enraged at Citibank, demanding to know how it could have let this happen and why it had failed to keep them informed of Penn Central's deteriorating condition.

Citibankers were blunt in their disdain for the senior management of Penn Central, notably Bevan. In the midst of Bevan's attempts to get a loan from the Department of Transportation, Citibank's chief credit officer, George C. Scott, let Bevan know unequivocally that his credibility with the bank was shot.

"You don't trust me," Bevan said.

"No, David, I don't," was Scott's brittle reply. Meanwhile, Bevan and other top Penn Central officers were dumping their personal holdings in the company. Wriston phoned Penn Central's directors to let them know in no uncertain terms that he wanted the railroad's management, especially Bevan and Saunders, gone. On June 2, Wriston requested a meeting with Penn Central president Paul A. Gorman and chairman Stuart Saunders for June 5. Bevan was not invited.

Nonetheless, on June 3, Wriston met with Bevan, who asked for Wriston's help in setting up a meeting with Penn Central's bankers. Bevan told Wriston that he was going to ask the bankers to lend millions more.

"There's no way," Wriston replied. "You don't have any assets. You're down the slippery slope.' "

The bankers would pony up new money only if the government would guarantee it under the plan being pushed by transportation secretary John Volpe. If that happened, though, the banks would put up as much as $200 million. The administration desperately wanted to avoid a Penn Central collapse in the middle of its first term in office and just months before congressional elections. To rally the lenders behind the plan, the Fed called a meeting of the banks in the auditorium of the Federal Reserve Bank of New York on a humid afternoon in June. It fell to Wriston, as the de facto spokesman for the industry and chairman of Penn Central's lead bank, to inform his beleaguered colleagues that their loans were frozen, and to spell out the advantages of going along with the government package. This was an unlikely and incongruous role for Wriston. As a believer in the free market system, he was also a believer in the right to fail. He instinctively chafed at the notion of a government bailout, but he did agree that there was a national security argument for maintaining freight service in the Northeast. In this largest test to date of whether a company was too big and important to go belly up, Wriston implored his fellow bankers to join together for the good of the country, according to a former Fed official. But Citibank's prestige was firmly on the line. "He was defending not only the railroads but also the reputation of Citibank for letting this thing get so far out of hand," the Fed official said. "He did it very well."

There were even a few moments of levity in an otherwise somber meeting. As the bank's former corporate lending chief, Reuben Richards, recalled, the delegate from one small bank raised his hand and asked meekly, "Mr. Wriston, we've only been in this credit for two weeks. Can we get any preferential treatment to get out?"

" 'Fraid not," Wriston replied, as the other bankers roared with macabre laughter.

Walter Wriston's pep talk to the panicky bankers would turn out to be a half-time show. The game would never make it to the fourth quarter. On

June 5, 1970, the day after the meeting with the bankers, Wriston met with Gorman and Saunders. The principal item on the agenda was the removal of the management, especially chief financial officer David Bevan. Citibank was weeks away from taking the single largest loss in its history. But in his dealings with Penn Central, Wriston was the one holding the cards. Bevan had to go. Three days later the Penn Central board held a special meeting. Saunders, Bevan, and vice chairman Alfred E. Perlman were informed that their services were no longer required.

The Department of Justice was responsible for advising other agencies of the U.S. government on whether the government had the power to grant the V-loan guarantee. While Wriston kept a fairly low public profile on the federal bailout issue, attorney Joseph Doyle of Shearman & Sterling was quietly advising DOJ's Office of Legal Counsel of the conditions under which such a recommendation could be made. Trouble was, the Defense Department then had to determine that Penn Central was vital for the national defense. Meanwhile, the message the White House received from the Fed was not encouraging. The central bank wrote that the initial guarantees would likely represent only the first step in what would certainly become a bailout that would go on for years. In essence, the Fed said that the guarantees would work if enough money was thrown at the problem.

When Wright Patman read the report and realized how many billions of dollars were at stake, he "raised hell" at the White House and in Congress, as one participant put it later, turning the White House against the guarantee plan. In mid-June, Patman fired off letters to secretary of the navy John Chafee and Deputy Secretary of Defense David Packard, asking them to postpone any guarantees until his committee could probe the Penn Central episode. Although the nation was indeed engaged in an "undeclared" war in Vietnam, it was questionable whether the troubled railroad was vital to the national security. The Defense Department wanted to be sure that legislation providing for more than $750 million in guarantees would pass, so that responsibility for the notes would shift from Defense to the Department of Transportation. In the end, Packard advised against it. In the Oval Office deliberations, David Kennedy reportedly told Nixon he thought the market could absorb a Penn Central failure. Arthur Burns, however, left his office that day fearful that the financial markets would crash.

When Nixon refused to approve the V-loan, it was curtains for Penn Central. At the Federal Reserve Bank of New York's headquarters on Liberty Street, representatives of the banks and the railroad waited anxiously for the word from the White House. The guarantee had been signed but not delivered. Fed vice president Thomas Timlen had to deliver the bad news. "No one could believe it," one participant recalled years later. "They all sat around asking, 'What do we do now?' "

"I better call Wriston," Doyle said.

"I'm glad I don't have to talk to him," Timlen replied.

It was six o'clock on a Friday evening, June 19, 1970, when the phone rang on Wriston's desk. Packard was on the line.

"We're in a tank," Wriston said.

"You're in a tank," Packard wearily confirmed.

Nixon's decision, said Wriston later, "was the correct one." But it was also a painful one for Wriston and Citibank.

Wriston wound up spending the next two days on the phone with Treasury secretary David Kennedy, transportation secretary John Volpe, and other assorted bankers and bureaucrats who thought the world would end that weekend. "I kept saying to Kennedy that all you have to do is call up everybody and say the discount window is open and the world will not stop. Arthur [Burns] kept saying, 'But all the discount windows will be open.'" Wriston informed the new central bank chief that this wasn't true. New York would be open, but not others like Atlanta and Detroit. So the banks would have to be specially informed that the "window" would be open for their borrowing convenience.

On Sunday, in Philadelphia, Penn Central Transportation filed for bankruptcy. It was a watershed in American financial history. Since World War II, no major American company had gone bust, and Citibank had not experienced such a stunning reversal since Cuba expropriated the Moa Bay ore refinery in 1961. The Fed, meanwhile, was terrified that Monday would be calamitous for the financial markets. It was sure that the $40 billion U.S. commercial paper market would nearly evaporate as investors redeemed their paper. In the 1960s, banks and corporations had developed a growing reliance on short-term instruments; the banks had their CDs, and the bank holding companies and corporations, their commercial paper. The credit crunch had exacerbated the problem. When it collapsed, Penn Central had more than $100 million in commercial paper coming due over the next several months.

New York Fed officials had been on the phone all weekend reminding bankers that there was a Santa Claus—the discount window—and that it would be open. At first, there was an eerie calm. Fed officials speculated that all of America's corporate treasurers must have gone on vacation the same week. Then things began to happen as predicted. Discount window borrowing surged, and some banks tried to take advantage of cheap and easy discount window money by blaming the commercial paper market.

Investors began fleeing the commercial paper market like horses stampeding out of a burning stable. Meanwhile, the Reg Q ceiling on jumbo short-term bank CDs—$100,000 or more—limited the rate banks could pay to 6.5 percent, well below the rates on Treasuries and commercial paper. As a result, banks couldn't attract enough funds to meet corporate borrowing needs. The problem occurred because the Fed was more concerned with maintaining a competitive balance between the banking industry and the thrift industry than with allowing the free markets to function. "The issue was how to adjust the ceiling and market rates in an orderly way," said former Fed monetary supply technician Stephen Axilrod. "We wanted to keep an even-handed relationship between banks and thrifts." Fearing a market collapse, the Fed was now forced to open a hole in Regulation Q, allowing banks to pay a market rate on the CDs. The rate on those instruments quickly surged to 8 percent, and the line at the discount window dwindled. Bankers used the occasion to point up the irrationality of Reg Q, and called for dropping it altogether. "That was the beginning of the end," according to Axilrod.

The commercial paper market was devastated. Before Penn Central, commercial paper was not perceived by sophisticated investors as especially risky. The banks' role typically was to supply backup credit lines for commercial paper, so that when a company couldn't roll over its paper those lines would kick in. For companies that had misused commercial paper to fund long-term projects, Penn Central was a shot across the bow. The most vulnerable industrial company was Chrysler. Early in the week, investors began dumping big blocks of Chrysler stock, and soon the panic spread to the automaker's paper. Over the next few days, Chrysler's lead banker, Manufacturers Hanover's John McGillicuddy, slapped together a $410 million package that backstopped Chrysler and averted a default. The deal made McGillicuddy's reputation and helped propel him to the chairmanship of Manny Hanny a decade later.

Penn Central gave Citibank a crash course in Workouts 101. After the bankruptcy filing, the banker who was tapped to pick up the pieces was John Ingraham, a Harvard man who began his career in 1957 as a junior officer in Citibank's transportation department. He learned that he had a new job in a phone call from Palmer. "John," he said, "it's probably an eighteen-month assignment before you get this thing wrapped up, or else it will be an annuity for the rest of your life." The truth, it turned out, lay somewhere in between. For Ingraham, the call from Palmer would be the beginning of a saga that would culminate eight years later with the emergence of Penn Central from bankruptcy. Recalled Ingraham, "Everyone kept saying, 'You'll never get the Penn Central reorganized. It will be nothing more than the Missouri Pacific, a twenty-three-year reorganization' "—a reference to the railroad that entered reorganization in 1933 and didn't emerge until 1956.

Citibank obviously hoped to extricate itself from the mess as quickly as it could with a minimum of damage, but that was wishful thinking. Not until after bankruptcy did investors and creditors realize what a complex and byzantine holding company structure Penn Central was. Money had been diverted in a myriad of directions among the company's holdings. At the outset, Citibank tried to halt payments of dividends from the Pennsylvania Company to the railroad, and to take possession of stock that had been put up to secure $300 million in loans. Pennco's Great Southwest Corporation unit held the crown jewels, which included real estate, hotels, pipelines, and theme parks. Ingraham spent the summer in California struggling with the tangled financial affairs of Great Southwest. By keeping that unit afloat, Citibank hoped to preserve its collateral in the Pennsylvania Company. It was the theme parks that ultimately saved the day. The demise of Penn Central thus led to the establishment of a new institution within the Citibank institution known as the workout department. Ingraham, whose dour expression and dark blue pin-striped suits earned him the nickname "the Embalmer," emerged from the wreckage as the banking industry's top workout man. *Forbes* later dubbed him "Citibank's Saint Jude"—the patron saint of hopeless causes.

In dealing with a bankrupt company, the two basic options are liquidation and reorganization. In some respects, workout men were like venture capitalists, because to maximize a bank's return on a company in reorganization, they often had to put more money in to get more out. Working out bad loans demanded a toughness that surpassed that required in normal credit negotiations. Banks had to jockey for position with layer upon layer of creditors and to fight to secure their claims on the debtor's collateral. Penn Central would come to represent the granddaddy of workouts for a generation of such specialists. For years to come, the same faces would show up at the negotiating table when there was a carcass to carve up. One of those faces almost invariably would be Ingraham's.

Citibank never backed away from a fight, but Wriston's elevation to the chairmanship coincided with the dawn of an era of volatility where only the fittest would survive. The era of the white-shoe banker was definitely over. And no one was more prepared to exchange the white shoes for the boots and gloves of the heavyweight boxer than Wriston. "One always got the sense that the toughest guys at the table would be the Citibank guys," said John Heimann, who later served as Comptroller of the Currency in the Carter administration.

For six months, Ingraham, Shearman & Sterling lawyer Hans Angermueller, and a host of other lawyers and bankers wrangled over the terms of a settlement. In May 1971 creditors announced an agreement in principle in which the bank group, minus a few holdouts, worked out a debt swap whereby they would get $300 million in Pennsylvania Company stock in exchange for the loans and $150 million in new loans for rolling stock. That, too, would soon die under the fall of the judge's gavel.

Coming as it did in the middle of the debate over bank holding companies, Penn Central was cited by some critics as reason enough not to give the banks new powers. Wriston hotly protested this linkage, asserting that "Opponents of bank holding companies would use any stick to beat a dog."

The carcass of Penn Central was still warm when Lockheed Aircraft Company went into cardiac arrest. The big defense contractor had begun to run into trouble in 1969 as a result of cost overruns on the C-5A aircraft. In lending to the company, Lockheed's banks had factored in the terms of its contracts with Rolls Royce, which built the engines for the L-1011 jet transport. But Lockheed had contracted to buy engines from Rolls Royce at a price the

British company couldn't make good on. By 1971, Rolls Royce went bankrupt, propelling Lockheed into a life-threatening financial crisis.

Because of bad blood between Citibank and Lockheed, Citibank did not play an active role in the machinations that led to a federal bailout of the troubled company. Lockheed had picked Bank of America and Bankers Trust as their lead banks, even though Citibank had a larger exposure. When the crunch came, Bank of America and Bankers Trust led the group of a half dozen or so institutions—not including Citibank—to petition the Department of Defense to save their client.

Meanwhile, the British banks took their case to Minister Lord Peter Carrington, the Secretary of State for Defence. According to former Treasury aide James Smith, John Connally, who became secretary of the Treasury in February 1971, and Carrington had become friends when Connally served as navy secretary early in the Kennedy administration. The quid pro quo was that if Britain would rescue Rolls Royce, the U.S. government would do the same for Lockheed. Wriston once again allowed pragmatism to carry the day, as he was prepared to do in the case of Penn Central. Finally, in September 1971, the U.S. Senate, by just one vote, granted Lockheed the guarantees that Penn Central had hoped to get fifteen months earlier. But the bailout had many critics. "The Defense Department panicked. They got sucked in," said one former top government official involved in the transaction. "The banks could have handled it."

Many felt that Lockheed would have survived without government assistance, and might have even done better. But the banks were the real winners—and sinners. In effect, they had persuaded the government to guarantee their loans so they wouldn't have to write them down. Not only did the banks get out with their principal and interest, but they also wound up with fees and equity in Lockheed. According to Brian Freeman, a lawyer who was later appointed to the Lockheed Loan Guarantee Board, the rescue of the aircraft builder was, in effect, a bailout of Rolls Royce and the banks. Though Citibank did not march on Washington, it became a key player in the restructuring that followed. That was due in no small part to the preeminence of Citibanker Fred Bradley in the aircraft lending fraternity. Part of the restructuring was accomplished by forcing Lockheed to scale back its aircraft business, notably the L-1011 program, which was a cash drain financed by the banks.

For more than five years the company operated under the government guarantee loan program. When the guarantees were to expire, most of the banks argued for a renewal and all the fees that went along with it. According to Freeman, who had recommended against an extension, Citibank lender Fred Bradley played a key role in finally weaning Lockheed from the public dole. In Brian Freeman's opinion, the banks' willingness to terminate the guarantee program gave them added credibility with Congress and the government when another major company became a candidate for federal largesse. That company was Chrysler.

The guarantees were repaid, Bradley pointed out, and in fact Lockheed was one of the few instances where the government made money in such a rescue. But when it came to Pan Am, Citibank was more passionate. The airline had played a key role in Citibank's overseas growth, and its pilots had delivered emergency medicines to Citibankers from Monrovia to Montevideo. Wriston regarded Pan Am almost as an extension of America. When the airline began to experience financial difficulty and needed to renew its credit lines, Continental Illinois, for one, declined to participate. "Fred Bradley wouldn't forgive us for that," said a former Continental officer. "He came to see our chairman. He said we were unpatriotic. He was pretty nasty. They [Citibank's officers] were inconsistent there."

Whatever the similarities, real or imagined, between bank and railroad holding companies, they apparently did not matter to the Senate. After the shock of the House holding company bill, banking company chiefs were relieved when the Senate, on September 16, 1970, passed by a vote of 77–1 a version that was much more lenient than Patman's bill, or even the one proposed by the administration. There was no negative laundry list, and the so-called grandfather clause pushed the cutoff date for acquisitions back to June 30, 1968. Under the bill, the Federal Reserve would be the judge and jury of what was related to banking. In effect, the legislation would bar holding companies with just one bank from performing activities that were not "functionally related to banking" and did not produce more public benefits than disadvantages. Walter Wriston could live with that.

He got the good news as he was preparing to fly to Copenhagen for the annual meeting of the International Monetary Fund and World Bank. The international bankers who attended the conference's caviar and crabmeat receptions were less interested in whether Citibank could sell life insurance than in the growing U.S. trade deficit, inflation, and the outlook for the dollar. Indeed, Wriston headed there as a member of President Nixon's newly appointed National Commission on Productivity, a blue-chip labor/management panel Nixon set up to try to stabilize prices. But for his part, Wriston seemed more interested in putting together a competitive foursome for tennis than in listening to speeches on inflation and the balance of payments or mingling at cocktail receptions. At these gatherings, Wriston typically nursed a large glass of ginger ale all evening, and other guests figured he was drinking Scotch. His highs came not from double martinis but from mixed doubles.

For Wriston's tennis-playing colleagues, being invited to play doubles with the boss was both a privilege and an imposition, particularly if they had to make the arrangements. When Wriston suggested mixed doubles to Latin hand George Putnam and his wife, Putnam was faced with the challenge of finding a competent woman player on short notice to play alongside the chairman, having been unable to find a suitable partner from among the conferees. Skipping the formal programs, Putnam visited the nearest tennis club to secure a court and scout around for someone to complete the foursome.

Putnam explained his problem to a locker room attendant, who told him not to worry. "I'll fix you up," he said.

When Wriston asked who the fourth partner would be, Putnam replied, "A mystery guest."

At the appointed time, Wriston, Putnam, and his wife arrived at the club, followed shortly thereafter by the mystery player.

"She was a candidate for Miss Denmark in every department," Putnam recalled wryly. Putnam was then faced with making a snap decision on who should team up with the young woman. "I quickly came to the conclusion that I'd better play with my wife, and Walt should play with Inge," said Putnam. In a fiercely competitive match in which everyone worked up a terrific sweat, she revealed herself to be a first-rate player. She also revealed that she didn't believe in underwear. "Walter never played better in his life," said Putnam.

It was a matter of some debate at Citibank whether good tennis players got ahead faster than nonplayers. But as Putnam put it later, "It didn't hurt." According to another senior Citibanker, "The only thing worse than playing against Walt and winning was playing with him and losing."

Even as Wriston was playing doubles in Copenhagen, the American Bankers Association was mounting an intensive lobbying campaign aimed at eliminating or mitigating the most onerous provisions of the Patman bill in the final legislation. For the most part, they succeeded. After two years in the legislative hopper, the Bank Holding Company Act Amendments of 1970 were passed by Congress and signed into law by President Nixon on December 31. "We got away with a fairly livable, workable piece of legislation," said lobbyist Jack Yingling, adding that Patman had been "thoroughly defeated" on it.

The victory was really measured in what the holding companies avoided losing rather than in what they gained. When the legislation was enacted, the Fed was mulling over about seven proposed functions but had no definitive ideas on what banks should be allowed to do. In fact, essentially all of the activities on the laundry list could already be performed by banks. At the time, Washington insiders observed that the first of the items on the list empowered bank holding companies to make loans. The only thing bank holding companies gained, said veteran Fed watcher Carter Golembe, was the ability to make them across state lines. For example, Citibank was already in the leasing business, in New York and overseas. Now, said veteran Golembe, they were getting the power to "put a leasing company in Alabama. That was quite an innovation." In reality, the battle over the legislation was merely a prelude to a longer battle between the banking industry, led by Citibank, and the Fed over what was "closely related to banking." Citibank's mission was to push the Fed to interpret that phrase broadly rather than narrowly.

Having planted its logo around the world, Citibank now shifted its acquisition thrust from the international to the domestic front. The goal was to replicate in the United States the expansion that had taken place internationally. The strategic planning department scrutinized lists of companies by industry category, looking for anything somehow related to banking and financial services. To disguise the targets, Citibank's planning department used sports code names, including the roster of the 1969 World Champion New York Mets. Catcher Jerry Grote, for example, was the code name for the 1972 acquisition of Nationwide Finance, a consumer finance company.

Actually, Citibank began to test the new act even before Nixon signed it. Less than a week after the bill became law, Citibank revealed that in mid-December it had bought the management consulting firm of Cresap, McCormick & Paget, one of the nation's largest consulting firms. Wriston said in an internal interview that he phoned Fed chairman Arthur Burns and asked him if Citibank was going to be allowed to buy Cresap. According to Wriston, Burns replied that he thought it could. Wriston then went public with his case for management consulting. Addressing charges that bank ownership of a consulting firm constituted a potential conflict, Wriston said in an interview that "The banker has traditionally been an adviser to management even in the days before Christ, and the nature of that advice started out with one rule: that you ought to have a balance sheet." Ultimately the Fed reneged on the informal assurances Burns had given Citibank, ruling that consulting did not qualify as a financial service. The Fed expressed concern about possible conflicts between lending and consulting. "He [Burns] later voted against it and our retention of the thing," said Wriston. The good news was that Citibank had ten years to sell the company, and later sold it back to its own officers.

The ink was barely dry on the new law when Citibank began inundating the Federal Reserve Bank of New York with paperwork on other applications to form a consumer finance company or a mortgage banking business or a leasing business in the United States or elsewhere. The hand-delivered packages of financial data and legal boilerplate poured into the Fed at a rate that sometimes approached one Citibank proposal a day. Citibank incessantly probed the Fed on the size of acquisitions as well as the types of activities it would permit. In doing so, Citibank was in effect the point man for the entire U.S. banking industry, since other banks hadn't even begun to go on the acquisition warpath. At any given time, Citibank's applications were said to represent as many as half of the total.

To insiders, the Fed seemed unprepared for its new role as judge and jury of what bank holding companies should be permitted to do. In mindless bureaucratic fashion, the Fed responded to boilerplate with boilerplate, often turning to Citibank for help in understanding certain technical aspects of the law. Inside the Fed there was a tiny faction that questioned whether it was appropriate to second-guess the business judgment of the regulatee at all. "Someone would ask, 'Do we really want to let Citibank make loans in Salt Lake City?' and the Fed would wind up doing a demographic study on Mormons," said one former functionary. "Regulation had become so picayune where a company had to get permission to do anything. It drives up the cost for everyone." A few Fed officials felt that, because of Citibank's size, no single proposal for acquisition or expansion could possibly damage the bank, and therefore the Fed couldn't justify denying any single application. Indeed, by responding affirmatively to every proposal, with modifications if needed, the Fed would be contributing to Citibank's safety and soundness through diversification. "There was no risk in saying yes to all of them, and no way you could justify saying no to any one of them," said one sympathetic former Fed official. Most didn't see things that way, however, and for years paper piled up on bureaucrats' desks as they pondered such weighty matters as whether Citibank should be permitted to acquire a pisswinkle consumer finance company in Seattle or Saint Louis. Months before Nixon signed the bill, Burns had assured bankers that he planned to expedite all but the toughest applications within ninety days after the Fed formally accepted them. Things didn't quite turn out that way.

With Moore retired, Wriston was determined that acquisitions would be pursued more scientifically than they were when Moore was around. There were to be no more swimming pool or opera deals. He demanded an MEP—a major expenditure proposal—for any acquisitions above a certain threshold. Profit projections and other arguments in favor of the acquisition were to be included in the MEP. It is doubtful, however, that acquisitions made under this approach were any more successful than those made with the Moore method of well-informed intuition. Part of the problem was not so much the manner in which they were acquired, but how Citibank managed them afterward. According to Citibank lawyer Chris York, "They were all profitable when they were acquired."

The Fed's arguments against Citibank engaging in a particular business sometimes had nothing to do with whether that business was related to banking. On one occasion, Chris York traveled to Washington to lobby for permission for Citibank to get into the freight forwarding and customs house brokerage business. The Fed, according to York, said it believed that business was controlled by organized crime. "All the more reason for us to get involved," York replied.

Apart from such exotic incidents, however, one benefit Wriston saw from these small acquisitions was the chance for his troops to mix and mingle with street-smart entrepreneurs who had built these businesses from scratch, before the founders left with their windfalls to enjoy the good life. "By God," he told York, "we need more of that here."

By mid-1973 the Fed had settled on about thirteen permissible activities, ruled out about seven, including management consulting, general life insurance, and real estate syndication, and was still stewing over several others, including whether a bank holding company could own savings and loan institutions, according to David Holland, a Federal Deposit Insurance Corporation analyst. Citibank's biggest disappointment was its inability to break into the insurance underwriting business other than that related to banking transactions, though that was not for lack of trying. For years, ferocious and powerful independent life agents denied Citibank its dream of offering general life insurance.

Wriston would have to learn to live with rejection, not just from the Fed but also from the courts. As Citibank was inundating the Fed with petitions for new powers and lobbying the state legislature for expanded powers in New York, it received news of a major setback at the Supreme Court. In a 6–2 decision, the high court had finally put an end to Citibank's hopes and dreams of being in the mutual fund business by overturning a circuit court of appeals ruling that supported the Comptroller of the Currency's 1962 decision to allow Citibank to underwrite them. The comptroller had expected that over the next ten years the banks might snare $2 billion in mutual fund business.

The appeals court decision was handed up just before Warren Burger left it to become chief justice of the U.S. Supreme Court in June of 1969. So both the comptroller and Citibank figured that with Burger on the high court their chances there were very favorable if, as they expected, the Investment Company Institute petitioned the Supreme Court to review the case. But Burger, having heard the case in the appeals court, disqualified himself. Shearman & Sterling lawyer Henry Harfield said that Justice Potter Stewart "pissed all over it." In the Court's majority opinion, Stewart wrote that underwriting mutual funds involved the same risks and conflicts of interest that had gotten banks into trouble in the 1920s and that were later prohibited by the Glass-Steagall Act. Former Senate Banking Committee staffer Robert Bevan, later a banking industry lobbyist, thinks that Citibank, in registering the commingled funds as securities to begin with, committed the tactical error that deprived banks of the power to underwrite mutual funds to the present day. As a result of that decision, "the court was hard-pressed not to find they were securities," Bevan recalled.

But even as Citibank was churning out applications furiously, some of what was already operating was out of control. Businesses were being added so rapidly that it was becoming increasingly difficult to keep track of them. These incidents would demonstrate the difficulties of managing a decentralized global organization filled with aggressive people.

After spending two years fighting the fire that George Moore had ignited in Australia, Citibanker George Davis returned to the United States in 1970 with no new assignment in sight, but with a growing reputation as an able corporate troubleshooter. In typical Citibank fashion, Davis was placed in "inventory" to await his next mission. After a year managing buildings and staff for John Reed's operating group, Davis was placed in charge of the fledgling Citibank Leasing International, where he was expected to create a coherent business out of a hodgepodge of offices and joint ventures in London, Brazil, Canada, Mexico, the Far East, and other outposts. Davis's first official act was to embark on a round-the-world trip to size up the operations and the people running them. Described by a colleague as a "Scotsman who didn't like anyone doing anything out of whack," Davis was uneasy with what he found in the Far East. A good manager could get a feel for an operation just by walking the factory floor, shaking hands with employees, observing whether the office was clean and how the staff was dressed. Davis, a clean-shaven man with short-cropped hair, was decidedly uncomfortable with the style and appearance of the Tokyo manager, an American he described later as a late-1960s "hippie child" who wore sandals and a beard, despite the antipathy of the Japanese to men with facial hair. The manager's lifestyle was too offbeat for Davis's taste. He had, in Davis's view, gone overboard in going native; visitors to his apartment, which was furnished incongruously with tatami floor mats and a pink piano, were instructed to leave their shoes at the door. "They were a weird group of folks," Davis recalled, but his visit revealed nothing that smacked of wrongdoing.

That changed at two o'clock one morning when Davis, who had just returned to New York, was awakened by a frantic phone call from Tokyo.

"Mr. Davis, this is Tony."

"Who?" asked the annoyed and bleary-eyed executive.

"Don't you remember? I'm a trainee who's going to start with you in a month."

"Sure, Tony, it's good to hear from you," Davis replied facetiously.

Davis bolted from his bed when Tony informed him of the reason for his ill-timed call.

"They're trying to sell the office," Tony said.

Davis was now as wide awake as if he had taken a cold shower. "Tell me more," he insisted. "They're trying to sell the office records to the Continental Bank." When Davis ordered a colleague to fly to Tokyo to investigate the trainee's charges, he learned that the Tokyo-based officer was in Chicago negotiating with a Continental Bank officer to sell the leasing unit's tax opinions, documents that are at the core of the business. Stunned as Davis and his colleagues were by this discovery, they were even more shocked as they dug deeper into the operations of the Tokyo office. Davis had an awful mess to clean up. Said one former Citibanker familiar with the rogue Tokyo operation, "Guys were billing the bank for trips they never took and living high on the hog," adding that "in those days there were no controls." That wasn't the half of it. It also turned out that one activity of the Tokyo office was running dope from Hong Kong to Japan.

With the passage of the amendments to the Bank Holding Company Act, it dawned on Wriston and his colleagues that it no longer mattered whether Citibank or any other bank holding company owned one bank or two. "We were sitting around," Wriston recalled, "and someone said, 'There's no reason why a holding company couldn't own more than one bank,' so we got some lawyers and founded the First National City Bank of Suffolk." Citibank had made its last geographic breakthrough in New York State back in 1960, when it was allowed to open branches in the suburban counties of Nassau and Westchester. It had always craved a presence in Long Island's Suffolk County. "I've never been the founder of a national bank, and it had kind of a nice ring to it. So we founded a national bank out on Long Island," Wriston recalled proudly years later. This was to be the vanguard of an interstate expansion strategy that, it was hoped, would make Citibank the first truly national U.S. financial institution.

In February 1971, Citibank filed an application with the Comptroller of the Currency to charter a new bank in Suffolk. As expected, the independent bankers of Suffolk County went wild, a prelude of things to come in the national arena. The Long Islanders set up a Committee for Sound Banking in a bid to keep out the big banks, or at least severely limit their powers and flexibility. "It was the end of the world. The elephant is coming," Wriston said, adding, "Nobody even thinks about it anymore." If you don't test the limits, he said later, competitors like American Express are "going to eat you alive."

Finally, in June 1971, New York governor Nelson Rockefeller approved legislation permitting New York banks to charter a new subsidiary in each of New York's nine banking districts, and allowing each subsidiary to open a limited number of branches until January 1, 1976, when the districts would be eliminated and the banks could merge and branch freely. This legislation allowed the existing banks to acquire the best branches, leaving the big city banks with sparsely concentrated and uneconomic networks. By the fall, Citibank had overcome all the legal and regulatory hurdles to operating in Suffolk—thanks largely to David Rockefeller's brother, Nelson.

Having been shafted repeatedly by the Justice Department's anti-trust division, Citibank figured this time around that it should think small. The game plan, said a former senior officer, was to buy "entry vehicles"—"piggybanks," as Wriston called them—that couldn't be contested on anti-trust grounds. By the end of 1971, Citibank was bidding aggressively for tiny banks on the outskirts of large upstate cities. "We never really bought anything of substance," said one officer. Citibank paid $1.6 million for the State Bank of Honeoye, just south of Rochester, and $5.5 million for the First Trust and Deposit Company of Oriskany Falls, near Utica. The principal beneficiaries of the strategy were the CEOs of the small banks, who saw Citibank's acquisition binge as a chance to make a killing. In some instances, Citibank was said to have paid seven times book value for these institutions at a time when two times book was considered pricey. When Citibank moved upstate, it quickly discovered, as it would time and time again, that there was no more powerful monopoly than the local banker.

Citibank, said some former officers, deluded itself into thinking that because it had been successful in expanding to Long Island, it must be well known upstate and would be welcomed there as well. Citibank grew too fast in sparsely populated areas and ended up with piles of bum loans to small and mid-sized companies that had been rejected for credit by more knowledgeable local banks. It found itself a kind of Gulliver, hamstrung by bureaucrats on the one hand and by local bankers on the other.

Citibank's efforts to penetrate the commercial market in upstate New York was soon efficiently sabotaged by local banks. As Citibank aggressively chased upstate corporate borrowers, the competition caught on to what Citibank was doing and, as Citibank expansion strategist Jack Heilshorn put it later, "began to give money away. They reacted normally to a new competitor. They said, 'We've got more staying power than they have.' Any number of times we came up with a great, ingenious way to finance a company, only for the company to say, 'You don't have any branches up here. We gave the deal to Lincoln and they priced it one percent less.' " Citibank also shot itself in the foot, as it would do later in Europe and elsewhere, by changing management and strategies with great regularity. It also found out that the problems of acquired banks are almost always worse than they seem to be on initial inspection. To make matters worse, by adopting a risk-averse strategy, Citibank wound up with banks that had no market presence, and in the process it learned that it couldn't make a dent in a market with a mere toehold. One reason was that marketing expenses, such as television advertising, were essentially the same whether a bank had twenty branches or two hundred in a given market.

Upstate bankers asserted that Citibank had blundered by getting rid of the older staff of the acquired banks and moving managers around so often that they could never establish a relationship with customers. George Hamlin, CEO of Canandaigua National Bank and Trust, pointed out that "the Citicorp guy is there for two years, then he's gone. In a big organization a person who has not moved in two years is not going to make it."

———

At the very moment that the powers of American banks were being redefined in the struggle between Citibank and the Fed, America's role as a global economic superpower was also approaching a turning point. U.S. economic supremacy, and with it, the U.S. dollar, was beginning to be challenged by a Europe and Japan intent on flexing their own economic muscle. The global financial crises that were about to erupt would shape Citibank in a dramatic way. And Wriston, operating often behind the scenes, would affect the outcome of these events in a way that was equally profound, though not always apparent.

In 1970, the balance-of-payments deficit reached $9.8 billion, but the United States could still boast a trade surplus. By early 1971, however, Japan and West Germany began to leave the United States in the lurch. With a surge in imports—notably oil, Japanese cars, and televisions—America's trade surplus turned into a deficit, its first since 1888. Inflation, though modest by later standards, was a bothersome 4 percent. Regulation Q also contributed to the problem, causing dollars to leave the United States in search of higher Euromarket yields.

Wriston railed against the developments that were exacerbating America's difficulties. These included the increasing protectionist tendencies of America's European and Japanese trading partners. Citing the surprise of the European and Japanese at the near-passage of protectionist legislation by Congress in 1970, Wriston told a Paris audience in early 1971 that the "European Common Market puts American exports at a disadvantage in various and sundry ways." And he declared that "the double standard used by our friends to criticize current American trade policy is as out of place in this year 1971 as is the double standard in personal conduct."

Regardless of who was to blame, the nation was headed for a show-down over its finances. Union and non-union workers were becoming more strident in their demands for wage hikes, and consumer prices picked up a frightening head of steam. Arthur Burns's tendency to speak out of both sides of his mouth on bank regulatory policy at this critical time was matched, in Wriston's view, only by his habit of speaking of the evils of inflation while doing more than any other top economic policymaker of his era to perpetuate it. One way he did that was by advocating wage-price controls. By early 1971, the drumbeat for wage and price guidelines was getting louder and louder.

In March testimony before the Senate Banking Committee, Burns advocated a "multifaceted incomes policy" to "improve the functioning of our labor and product markets—a policy that the Board believes should include a Wage-Price Board." This board would drum up support for voluntary wage-price curbs. Mandatory controls would be used as a "last resort," he said. Meanwhile, dollars were flowing out of the United States like water over Niagara Falls, and thanks to inflation, the dollar was now greatly over-valued. Traders, speculating that the greenback could not hold its value in the face of the balance-of-payments and trade figures, put heavy speculative pres-sure on the dollar in frantic trading.

Financial leaders began to view realignment of other currencies against the dollar—or devaluation—as inevitable. In May 1971, West Germany al-lowed the mark to float, and shortly thereafter the Dutch unleashed the guil-der. The Swiss and Austrians, meanwhile, revalued their currencies. The United States was unwilling to devalue, however, and the other major indus-trialized nations refused to revalue. Under the circumstances, an interna-tional monetary crisis was a foregone conclusion.

In one respect, the turmoil was good news for Citibank. Until now, for-eign exchange trading had been a relatively slow business, but those days were rapidly coming to a close. Unfortunately, the foreign exchange depart-ment was ill-prepared for the new world. The imminent retirement of chief trader Edwin Reichers couldn't have been more badly timed. He was proba-bly the top foreign exchange trader in the world, but he hadn't built any depth of management in his department. When Reichers left, "there was nothing," Wriston said in an internal interview.

The war of words over money heated up at the annual International Monetary Conference in Munich. One of the premier events of the interna-tional banking scene, the IMC gives the chairmen of the world's top one hundred banking institutions a chance to meet each year in a different city, North American locations alternating with foreign. It is a key forum for the U.S. secretary of the Treasury and the chairman of the Federal Reserve to air their views on the key financial issues of the day and, in a series of elaborate parties and events for the bankers and their wives, to forge friendships that grease the flow of money in a global economy. Kathy Wriston, as usual, accompanied her husband on this trip. Over one of the long picnic tables that had been set up for a luncheon, Wriston greeted Arthur Burns cordially. As Wriston and his youthful wife, who had never met Burns, took their seats, a dour Arthur Burns ignored them completely. "I finally said, 'Arthur, I'd like you to meet my wife, Kathy,' " Wriston recalled.

"Oh, is that right?" he said, apparently relieved, Wriston thought, that the chairman of Citibank had not taken up with "some young floozy."

The man of the hour in Munich, however, was newly appointed secretary of the Treasury John Connally. Through sheer force of personality, Connally quickly made his presence felt as an international financial statesman. "We had dinner in a tent," Wriston recalls, and "he came in with that wonderful wife of his. Nobody in Europe had ever heard of him. He went around and worked the crowd, and he walked away with all of their votes." But Connally would be remembered more for what he said at that conference than for his glad-handing.

Connally figured that the revaluation of the German mark would not do much for the U.S. imbalances, and he wasn't prepared to bite the bullet and devalue the dollar. In a loud and strongly worded speech, Connally took the Europeans to task for their unfair trade practices, notably their barriers against agriculture imports. He chastised them for their alleged failure to assume their fair share of the defense burden. And he declared, "We are not going to devalue. We are not going to change the price of gold." That speech did not go over well. The Europeans did not like to be lectured.

According to Connally, the European bankers attempted to use their American banker contacts to frighten Connally into backing off from his tough position, referring to him in their conversations as a "rough tough cowboy" who shot from the hip. "This got back to me through some of the American banks," Connally said. "They said, 'Well, you know, just be careful. Don't be tough, so we don't lose any clients. But Walter Wriston never said that to me. And I'm sure he [and] others were implored to do it." It was, said Connally, a "war of nerves." His grim view was that when these people have the economic advantage on you, they damn sure want to keep it." Connally met frequently with Wriston and other top bankers, and relied heavily on Citibank for "intelligence" on economic policies and development in the countries where Citi operated.

Not long after the IMC, Wriston's daughter, Cassy, showed up at his apartment at seven o'clock one morning to introduce her husband-to-be to her father and stepmother. Many of the men she dated had fawned all over her father, and she was repulsed by their "salaaming," as she put it later. Her fiancé was Richard Quintal, then a twenty-six-year-old graduate of Yale and University of Virginia's Graduate School of Business who was making $11,000 a year as a junior Bankers Trust officer.

Unlike Hank Wriston, Walter was nonjudgmental, even with his only daughter's intended. Cassy didn't "hear boo" from her father, and asked Kathy if her father had expressed any opinion about Quintal. "He said, 'He's a good-looking blond guy,'" replied Mrs. Wriston. "I know that," huffed Cassy impatiently. She thought that her father was concerned about whether her husband-to-be was capable of supporting her on his meager bank salary, and she assured Wriston that Quintal had some "outside" money. Indeed, his late father had been a lawyer with Mobil Oil and his grandfather a vice president of Chase. That was all Wriston needed to hear. Wriston was death on men of privilege and privilege seekers. Rarely did anyone who behaved like a member of the moneyed class go far at Wriston's Citibank, and he proceeded to lecture his daughter on the deleterious effects of inherited wealth. As Quintal would learn, it was not always easy being the son-in-law of Walter Wriston. "People gave him a hard time," according to Cassy. "'It's not a marriage. It's a merger,' they said."

Being the point man for the banks during the worst postwar corporate crisis did not buy Wriston immunity from other stresses. In the midst of the Penn Central drama, Wriston's secretary, Gerry Stover, buzzed him and uttered six of the most terrifying words in the English language: "Ralph Nader is on the line."

Big companies like Citibank and Du Pont made inviting targets for the investigations Nader was then conducting. The slant of the $15,000 study, which was to be headed by former Justice Department anti-trust attorney David Leinsdorf, son of conductor Erich Leinsdorf, seemed clear from the outset. In his announcement, Nader said he planned to probe the "preferential treatment" Citibank allegedly gave certain customers. Wriston quickly concluded that the Nader team knew nothing about banking in general or Citibank in particular. One of its first requests was to interview an employee Wriston had never heard of. When Wriston asked why, Nader replied, "He determines loan policy."

"No kidding. I'd like to meet him myself," Wriston chuckled. It turned out the subject of Nader's interest was a clerk in the loan department.

Nader had assured Wriston that he would have an opportunity to review and respond to the report before it was made public. On June 20, 1971, Wriston realized the hollowness of that assurance when he got a phone call in the early evening from an Australian reporter. Gerry had already left for the day, so Wriston answered the call himself.

"Am I talking to Mr. Wriston?" the reporter asked, a little surprised to have reached the man himself without secretarial intervention. "I'm doing better now," he said. "I haven't been able to get Mr. Nader on the phone."

"Why do you want to get him on the phone?" Wriston asked.

"He's releasing his report tomorrow. He's given a copy to the press."

Wriston gritted his teeth. "He lied to us about when he was going to release it," Wriston said.

"Look, mate, I don't care," the reporter said. "I'm just telling you we just had a press conference."

Wriston immediately contacted Don Colen, his wily public relations chief, who arranged to have a copy of Nader's report flown to the bank that evening. Well into the early hours, Wriston, Kathy, Colen, and other staff remained at the bank drafting a reply to the report, including a lengthy press release. Kathy Wriston was the first to observe, according to Wriston, that Nader was "on both sides of every issue." At around one in the morning, the Wristons walked to Grand Central Station to pick up a copy of the early edition of the *New York Times,* where they fully expected to see the Nader story splashed all over the front page. Instead of a story on Nader, the story they found, in the financial pages, was based on a leaked copy of Wriston's "state of the bank" speech, in which he bluntly laid out to bank officers some of the key problems facing Citibank. They bought two papers, and stood under a streetlamp reading the leaked story from start to finish.

"This is wild," Wriston said to his wife. "This is what I said in the state of the bank speech."

"How could that be?" Kathy asked.

In his speech, Wriston bemoaned the $28 million in losses on Penn Central—"a mistake in which many shared," his analysis said. Wriston pointed out that Citibank had performed "very poorly on delivery of service and operating errors," warning that "we don't need a computer to realize that unless we get control of our costs, we will be out of business in a measurable period of time." Although Wriston was distressed that a Citibanker had apparently leaked his speech, he was also relieved not to find the Nader story. But Wriston's relief was short-lived. The story did appear on page one of a later edition of the *Times,* the *Wall Street Journal,* and other major papers.

In their report, Nader's Raiders criticized Citicorp for giving poor service to customers, hiring too few women and minorities, and exacerbating the decline of inner-city neighborhoods. The Nader report urged the unionization of clerical staff and called on the Justice Department to probe interest rate setting on loans. It also charged that Citibank was guilty of a conflict of interest in allowing a bank officer to sit on the board of the Metropolitan Transit Authority after lending money to it. To that charge, Wriston replied acerbically, "You're born with a conflict of interest—do you love your father or mother more? These kids are on the kick that if you do two things in this world, you're in conflict. That means there are no honest men in the world, except of course themselves." Among other things, the Raiders accused Citibank of not making enough loans to lower-income people and, in the same breath, charged the bank with forcing loans on small people who didn't know any better, prompting Wriston to ask, "Do I have a third choice?"

New York University professor R. David Corwin, who had conducted a study of bank hiring, quickly rode to Citibank's defense by saying that "Of the banks in New York, First National City has been one of the most progressive."

Citibank's public relations return salvo, published in book form as *Citibank, Nader and the Facts,* sank the Nader report with barely a trace. The report, Wriston stated with satisfaction, was the "slowest selling" of the Nader studies. "Nobody remembers he was in the bank." In a newspaper interview, Wriston said that the Raiders, mostly college and law students, "were very bright and worked like the devil." But he added that they produced an inferior product, showing that Nader was spreading himself too thin. "The result is that Nader is sort of a franchise operation, like fried chicken. . . . He's got the quality control problem that anyone else does. He may be able to read all the reports put out under his imprimatur, but he can't check them." The Raiders did learn one lesson—four of them, according to Wriston, applied for and got jobs at Citi after their tour of duty in Nader's crusade.

"I think we handled the investigation and response pretty well," Wriston observed later.

Responding to Wriston's charges that the report was replete with errors, David Leinsdorf later said, "I'm sure there must have been some mistakes. I don't think there was any flaw in the basic thrust of the report. There may have been some flaws in some of the detail." In the interviews, said Leinsdorf, "they [Citibank officers] were courteous. They were like good smart witnesses." The modus operandi, he said, was for Citibank to make two tapes of meetings, one tape for Citibank and one for the investigators. After his last meeting with Wriston, Leinsdorf claimed that his recording of the interview was blank. Leinsdorf had taken no notes and was convinced this was intentional. "To me it explained the way they played the game. It surprised the hell out of me."

Wriston would acknowledge later that the experience was "a net plus," however. "We got a free audit by a highly biased auditor." For all that Citibank found wrong with it, Wriston conceded that the Nader report pointed up deficiencies that the bank could correct. "Citibank has always been self-critical," he asserted. In fact, Wriston said, Nader pulled much of his information directly out of reports by consultants Citibank had hired to help it improve its services and operations. Nader began the study assuming that, in Wriston's view, "somebody was controlling the world, all this kind of nonsense. They couldn't understand the dispersal of the lending system. He had the idea that somebody sat on top, and said, 'Let's freeze out the Hottentots.' That, of course, was ridiculous." There were some repercussions, however: not long after Nader released his report, the National Organization for Women accused Citibank of discriminating against women in choosing people for senior positions. They yanked their savings from a Citibank branch and picketed with signs saying "Worst National Piggybank, We want 51 percent."

Wriston may have taken issue with Nader's motives and his accuracy, but in December 1971, Citibank finally appointed a woman vice president—Zelda Wakeman, Wriston's Fletcher School classmate. He constantly prodded his top officers for their poor performance in moving women, foreigners, and minorities into top positions. In an internal meeting three years after the Nader report, he lamented the fact that of 163 top jobs, just six were filled by foreign nationals and none by blacks or women. The "principal weakness that we have is that the number of names on the backup list is too small to be credible to me. We have been hiring highly talented men and women for a long time, and yet we are asked to believe that only eight or ten people can succeed the people in this room. I don't believe it." And Wriston added, "Some very brave person took an enormous risk when he gave you and me our jobs, and I can promise you that at the time we got our jobs, we were not qualified to do them in the judgment of the people who made the decision."

Whatever its merits or lack thereof, the Nader report did, in the opinion of some Wriston watchers, seem to contribute to what they called a "hardening" of his personality that had begun with Bobby's death. It was the height of the American involvement in Vietnam, corporate bashing had become something of an American pastime, and "military-industrial complex" had become a favorite media buzz phrase.

Nader ignored some key areas, including investment management and international banking. After putting Wriston and Citibank through the wringer, he had the chutzpah to ask for a second shot. Noting that the first study cost the bank some 10,000 man-hours, Wriston rejected the request, stating that "we don't think we can justify another such unproductive use of bank time and expense to our stockholders."

In 1974, Nader came out with a book titled *Citibank* that included his "findings" on the activities of the investment management unit. Wriston referred to it as "basically a retread" of the 1971 report, saying it was "riddled with errors of fact and interpretation." Later, Nader announced his intention to be a full-time monitor of the consumer practices of financial institutions. But because of the failure of his Citibank report, he had little influence thereafter on the affairs of American financial institutions.

David Leinsdorf acknowledged later that "I think I'm more sympathetic to corporate America than I was twenty years ago." But, he said, "I'm not sure the free market capitalism he [Wriston] advocated for the banking industry has been good for the industry," adding that "the history of banking in the last twenty years [has] proven that the philosophy of Ralph and me has been more correct than the laissez-faire philosophy of the great Walter Wriston."

To seek relief from the Ralph Naders of the world, the Wristons bought a 200-acre farm in Sherman, not far from the weekend home that had been Walter's weekend retreat for about fifteen years. Kathy had wanted a place she could call her own, one that was not filled with reminders of her husband's cherished first wife. The simple, elegant fieldstone farmhouse at Deer Pond Farm was no Pocantico Hills, with its drawing rooms and high, chandeliered ceilings. In fact, the roof had to be raised because Wriston couldn't stand erect on the second floor. The couple turned the spread into a tree farm, complete with its own generator and fuel supply. Their principal indulgence was his-and-hers tractors.

Wriston sometimes invited key aides up to the farm for the day or weekend. On one occasion, Wriston and an aide were sitting on the rear terrace, looking out over a pond in the midst of a vast open field surrounded on either side by woods. Suddenly, a horse ridden by a beautiful young woman galloped out of the woods to the left, stopped to drink from the pond, and then disappeared into the cluster of trees on the right. Wriston's associate was awestruck by this pristine scene, so perfect in every respect that it seemed that Wriston must have staged it to impress his visitor. Wide-eyed, the guest turned to his host and asked, "Where did you get her? From central casting?"

Wriston, quick to appropriate a catchy phrase, adopted "central casting" as one of his stock expressions.

Wriston was never under any illusions that Nader was a friend or soul mate. So the activist's June surprise was disturbing but certainly not shocking. But President Nixon's Sunday, August 15, 1971, announcement that the United States would shut the gold window, slap a 10 percent surcharge on half of the nation's $45 billion in annual imports, and impose a ninety-day freeze on wages and prices was something else altogether. The announcement marked the end of America's global economic supremacy. For Wriston, Republican to the core, hearing that a Republican president had instituted wage and price controls was a personal betrayal. It was the kind of initiative Wriston might have expected from John Kennedy or Lyndon Johnson, not Richard Nixon. At home, Wriston fumed to his wife, "And the Republicans did it!"

In early 1971, it had been no secret that Nixon would try to influence wages and prices. But by June, it seemed that despite the worsening economic situation the president had rejected anything as draconian as wage and price controls. That month, Treasury secretary Connally also firmly declared his opposition to controls.

The first hint that Nixon was yielding came at an August 5 press conference, when he said he would "consider" with an "open mind" the notion of a wage-price board. About ten days later, Nixon convened his top economic advisers, including Fed chairman Arthur Burns and Treasury secretary John Connally, who was summoned back from a Texas vacation. As Connally recalled the meeting, held at Camp David, the advisers argued heatedly about closing the window and imposing an import surcharge. Burns had long opposed such a move and argued violently against it. He felt that the action would precipitate an international monetary crisis and that the Dow would plunge 500 points.

Connally argued in favor of shutting the window, saying that he didn't believe doing so would have that kind of an effect. "We live a lie and everybody knows it," Connally said. The United States couldn't possibly redeem all the outstanding dollars—there were, after all, seven dollars in currency for every dollar in gold. Connally said that if they were so worried about the impact of closing the window and the surcharge, "then let's put wage and price controls on in this country and stabilize this whole economy. We can fight inflation and solve that problem [what to do about the gold window] along with it." Connally could tell that Nixon didn't like the idea, and George Shultz, then director of the Office of Management and Budget, was adamantly opposed to it.

Sometime after the announcement, Nixon met with Wriston and other members of the productivity panel to discuss the implementation of controls. Wriston was not pleased with what he was hearing. During the meeting, he realized that the regulations contained a loophole that permitted salaries to be raised for workers subject to union contracts but not for nonunion workers. This blatantly discriminated against Citibank's people. "There's no way I will sit still for anybody in Citibank being disadvantaged because they don't belong to a union," Wriston fumed. Meanwhile, AT&T chairman John deButts concluded that the rule would have the same impact on Ma Bell. "We pounded the table. We said we would not sit still for it," said Wriston later.

As he crossed Pennsylvania Avenue after the meeting, an official responsible for administering the controls caught up with him. "You've been yelling and screaming about our very first efforts," he whined.

"I have indeed," Wriston replied.

At the end of the impromptu sidewalk meeting, the official said, "You're right. We'll fix it."

"And he did," said Wriston.

In another session Nixon held with Wriston and several other top businessmen to discuss anti-inflation measures, one "captain of industry," Wriston recalled sarcastically, advised Nixon to issue an executive order voiding all collective bargaining agreements.

Wriston's contempt for the idea and its source showed all over his face. "I nearly died," Wriston said.

Nixon set Wriston up for the kill. Turning to him, Nixon asked, "What do you think of that?"

"Let's set aside the First Amendment," Wriston replied angrily. If we're not going to have a government of laws, let's go all the way." He commented later that "the captain of industry was not pleased in the slightest. I was so embarrassed for the business community."

On the day after the guidelines were announced, the Dow Jones industrial average soared by a record 32.93 points, on record volume of 31.72 million shares. By 1972 inflation had fallen by half to 2 percent, and short-term interest rates along with it. To the unsophisticated, it looked as if the guidelines really worked. "None of that fooled Walter Wriston," said William Simon, later secretary of the Treasury. Wriston and Citibank considered Arthur Burns's conduct of monetary policy a key source of inflation, and Wriston undoubtedly had Burns in mind when he said that "inflation doesn't grow on trees. It's made by people, real live people, living in Washington." In early August 1971, the bank took Burns to task for saying one thing about inflation and doing another. After indicating a need to avoid too much expansion in the monetary supply, the Fed permitted the money supply to grow, Citibank said. "The explosion of monetary growth that followed the chairman's statement was deeply upsetting to people who were beginning to believe inflation was slowing down."

Milton Friedman, the father of monetarism and Burns's most prominent pupil, blamed his former mentor for the consequences of wage and price controls. "Burns was my teacher, my friend, but I think he deserves a great deal of blame," he said, adding that wage and price controls were "followed by a rapid increase in the quantity of money. He was the one person in that period who could have made things different."

The Nixon move launched a nearly full-time career for Wriston—bashing controls at every opportunity. "Someone has to point out—and keep pointing out—that every time the tide recedes a little after one of these floods of 'emergency' regulations, there is less sand left on the beach for free people to stand on." He brought a wealth of historical evidence to the task—from ancient Rome, when Diocletian set price limits on 900 commodities and 130 forms of labor, right up to the failed British experience after the war. "Englishmen visiting my office shake their heads in wonder and ask how we [the United States] could embark on this course with British failure still so clearly visible." Wriston explained that "Citibank operates in about ninety countries around the world," and there is no form of controls the bank hasn't seen. "They all have one common denominator. They all fail over the long term. If all they did was fail, controls might be worth a try in the short run. But on the way to failure, controls distort the market, discourage producers, cause shortages, and produce more uncertainty." Wriston could have lived with controls for ninety days, but they would drag on in one form or another until 1974, and the insidious effects would be felt well beyond that. The August 15, 1971, order was followed in two months by another. This one directed a Committee on Interest and Dividends, to be chaired by Arthur Burns, to implement a program of voluntary restrictions on interest rates and dividends. Wriston despised no piece of the wage and price apparatus more than this committee. In effect, it was to become a jawboning device to hold down interest rates—and bank profits.

For doctrinaire advocates of hard money and fixed exchange rates, the closing of the gold window signaled the end of Western civilization. John Exter had long been waging his private war inside and outside the bank for the Fed to stop the printing presses and return to the fiscal discipline of the Eisenhower era. And by late 1971 Exter's gloom-and-doom views had become an embarrassment to the bank and had undermined his usefulness, in the view of colleagues. Shortly after Nixon slammed down the gold window, Exter took early retirement. At his farewell luncheon, Wriston presented Citibank's own Chicken Little with a half-ounce gold money clip. "You could not have given me a more appropriate present," Exter told his hosts. "Because the value of this clip is going to go up, up, up, and the value of the damn paper I put in it is going to go down, down, down," he said, to howls of laughter. He was right.

With the closing of the gold window, it would prove impossible for the world financial system to stick to a system of fixed exchange rates. Citibank was the first and only major U.S. bank to urge a move toward floating rates. Now it was only a matter of months before the world's monetary system recognized the new order of floating currencies. In 1960, Edwin Reichers's foreign exchange department had traded a mere $15 million a day. When the foreign exchange markets reopened a week after the Nixon initiatives, and just a few days before Reichers's retirement after forty-eight years with Citibank, the figure had multiplied tenfold.

Significant economic events such as these had always had a profound effect on the business of all American banks, large and small. But after Citibank expanded into new foreign markets and lines of business, nearly every global political and economic development, from airplane bombings to revolutions, affected the bank's operations. A Pan American 747 that was blown up in Cairo in September 1970 was in fact owned by the bank's leasing company. And a year later, when the leftist government of Salvador Allende Gossens took power in Chile, it announced its intention to expropriate all the foreign banks, including six Citibank branches. After being forewarned that Allende would win the Chilean election, Citibank proceeded to ratchet down its exposure in the country, just as it had done in Cuba twelve years earlier. Wriston often crowed that Citibank had a better intelligence network than the State Department. While not referring specifically to Chile, former Citibank chief lender P. Henry Mueller later said, "The transaction flows would tip you off. We sometimes knew more than our government, because we were there looking out of the window."

Citibank knew from hard experience how tough it was to return to a country after leaving it or being thrown out. Characteristically, it dragged its feet on the sale of the Chilean branches. The job of negotiating the sale fell to Lester Garvin, Citibank's crusty Latin hand. After hammering out an agreement with the central bank, Garvin flew to New York to draft the papers. When he returned, the Chileans denied ever having reached an accord. Garvin refused to renegotiate, prompting Chile to threaten Citibank with stiff fines. When he arrived in New York a second time, Garvin learned that his branch managers had been locked out. The Chileans would soon discover that major international banks do not lack for clout. Garvin put the Chileans on notice that he would cable correspondent banks around the world that Citibank no longer had control of the branches and could not be responsible for any transactions. Threatened with being cut off from the rest of the financial world, the Chileans agreed to give the bank its capital and accumulated profits. And, said Wriston, "When Mr. Allende came in, he did indeed almost destroy the country and its credit."

12

GO-GO BANKING

*W*riston was exasperated. He fumed when Wall Street compared Citibank to other money center banks, and he fretted that it was running in the middle of the pack in that key measure of market valuation, the almighty price-earnings ratio. But to raise it he would have to sustain a high level of earnings growth. One way or the other, Wriston concluded that he had to convince Wall Street that his bank was better than any other American bank—indeed, that his was no mere bank at all. It deserved to be compared not with the best-managed U.S. banks (that, after all, was an oxymoron), but with the most prestigious industrial corporations.

In the fall of 1971, after years of foraging for scraps of information about First National City Corporation, Wall Street's bank analysts felt a little like Cinderella being invited to the ball. That summer they received an unexpected invitation from Wriston to attend, in early October, what would be remembered as the first of the great banking dog and pony shows—the ne plus ultra of dog and pony shows. Wriston had decided to let the genie out of the bottle; 15 percent would be achieved—and maintained.

At the dinner for about one hundred Wall Streeters, Wriston declared that "while our numbers haven't been bad, we have not told our story well. The market for our stock has been a dealer's market, not a broker's market." What he meant was that there was little retail or institutional interest in the shares of First National City Corp.—or in those of any U.S. bank holding company, for that matter. In fact, Wriston said that the 15 percent target was already being met. In overseas operations, he revealed that the target, set three years before, was actually 18 percent, and that this had been surpassed. By this time, the percentage of earnings derived from overseas activities had reached 40 percent of the total. Wriston even revealed one disappointment: that the bank's share of the middle market business was below average. Asked how Citibank had been able to bolster profitability in such difficult times, president William Spencer responded that cost cutting was a major reason. And that was due in no small part to the efforts of Reed and White.

The decision to go public with the 15 percent goal—which implied a 20 percent return on equity—was driven by Wriston's recognition that to raise the capital that would permit further expansion, he would have to convince Wall Street that Citibank's management was capable of delivering a reasonable return on their money. Wriston's goal was to portray Citibank as a unique institution in its depth and breadth of management, diversity of earnings, and international scope. Ironically, Wriston would be aided in achieving his goal by inflation, which, in his view, was exacerbated by the ill-conceived Nixonian wage and price controls that he so vociferously opposed. As inflation rose and the dollar declined in value against other currencies, it would be increasingly difficult, if not impossible, for other institutions to match Citibank's global infrastructure. In the inflation-ridden 1970s that would be like trying to replicate the craftsmanship of Notre Dame Cathedral.

Although few appreciated it at the time, Wriston's bombshell would mark the end of banking as a quasi-public utility. Wriston was telling Wall Street that banking had finally become a business, ushering in the era of loan selling, glass-and-steel skyscrapers, and product marketing. Wriston also ended a long-standing tradition of secrecy, and inaugurated a new era of financial disclosure and collegiality with analysts and investors. Before then disclosure had been mostly voluntary. The bank's comptroller, Bernard Stott, a rigid 1950s-era banker, had been responsible for releasing earnings, and he was as stingy with information as Wriston was with his own money. Citibank's 1970 annual report included the obligatory income statement and balance sheet but told pitifully little about how and where the bank made its money. "Analysts had gotten short shrift," said Thomas Ivanyi, a young planner who was designated chief of Citibank's new investor relations department, the first such unit at a major New York bank.

Wall Street's unquenchable thirst for more information provoked a kind of internecine warfare between Stott and his allies, who felt that the less Wall Street knew, the better, and others, like Ivanyi, who favored full disclosure. "There were some confrontations that always ended up in increased disclosure," said Ivanyi later, adding that Wriston was the leading proponent of divulging more. Analysts were now insisting on knowing, for example, how much Citibank was earning in Brazil or in Europe or from foreign exchange trading—data that Citibank wouldn't have dreamed of revealing just a few years earlier.

First National City Corporation shares quickly became one of the hottest plays on Wall Street. By 1972 the price-earnings ratio of First National City broke through the 20 barrier, and its shares became the most liquid on the New York Stock Exchange. Other New York banking companies benefited as well. When Wriston addressed the analysts, shares of New York banks generally were trading at about 60 percent of the price-earnings ratios of the Standard and Poor's 400. Come 1973, that ratio had nearly doubled to 114 percent. Japanese investors were also tantalized by FNCB's prospects. In the early 1970s, the Ministry of Finance began to allow Japanese investors to buy foreign securities; First National City Corporation shares were the most popular holdings, in part because of frequent road shows to Japan starring top Citibank officials. In what was said to be the largest block purchase ever of U.S. securities by Japanese institutions, several Japanese banks bought 90,000 of the company's common shares for approximately $5 million. The Fed, of course, couldn't resist an opportunity to interfere with Citibank's business wherever it was conducted, and launched an inquiry into whether its links to the Japanese institutions would jeopardize the ability of other American banks to do business with the industrial units of the *zaibatsu.*

Citibank's newfound glamour status also gave it greater entrée to the fixed income markets. In early 1972 it announced a $100 million debt offering, to be used, among other things, for acquisitions, and indicated that it planned to enter the debt market regularly for such funds.

Not everyone at Citibank was enamored of the 15 percent target. Skeptics included director William "Mil" Batten, chairman of J. C. Penney, who told Wriston that the world was too volatile for the bank to control everything that affected profits. Although Wriston may have intended the 15 percent goal to be an average over time, "that's not what was interpreted," Batten said. "I didn't feel the goal should be expressed on an annual basis."

If the McKinsey reorganization of Citibank represented the first nail in the coffin of the old genial culture, the announcement of the 15 percent goal was the final one. Internal competition to achieve profit center goals intensified. As the bank evolved into a vast global organization, it also abandoned its sense of family. After Wriston took over, "Citibank became so profit-minded that it lost the milk of human kindness," said one colleague. William Spencer, for one, apparently recognized the problem, and in one meeting asked the bank's senior officers to write memos on how it could be mitigated. Nearly everyone submitted a long, clinical memo. No one protested, however, when one executive vice president wrote simply, "Do unto others as you would have them do unto you."

John Reed considered the 15 percent goal an "unnatural," unachievable rate, according to former colleagues. Reed's thinking about business was heavily influenced by his understanding of the laws of physics and biology, and he believed that "the natural growth rates you observe in the world are closer to 3 or 4 percent. That doesn't mean one shouldn't do it," he said later. "But you should be cautious."

If there was any uncertainty over the interpretation of the target, the bank's new executive compensation policy certainly clarified it. According to Batten, who was chairman of the board's personnel and compensation committee, employees earned bonuses when Citibank achieved the 15 percent goal. Some years later, Batten proposed to Wriston that the hurdle for bonuses be lowered to 9 percent. Said another former top officer, "It [the 15 percent goal] was a great sin. All compensation was built around that. It caused the bank to do all kinds of crazy things." But Wriston wouldn't hear the naysayers. "My job as manager is to get people to reach a goal 10 percent higher than they think they could reach themselves," he told his colleagues. In the early 1970s, when Wriston instituted the executive incentive plan based on earnings, he summoned a couple of hundred officers into the bank auditorium to tell them they would get a share of the pie. Spencer told the assemblage expansively that "everyone in this room is going to be a millionaire."

"We walked out walking on air," former corporate secretary Paul Kolterjahn said later.

The next deadly sin, according to former insiders, was the introduction in 1977 of employee stock options based on the book value of Citi's shares. That encouraged employees to do whatever it took to inflate the bank's balance sheet, not necessarily the market value of the stock. "It rewarded leadership in a different way than the market evaluated its performance," said one former officer. It was also a disincentive to write down bad assets.

The goal would create severe pressures in the declining national corporate banking market. Facing stiff competition from commercial paper and non-bank banks, and with compensating balances eroding, it was becoming tougher and tougher to make money in this market. "We spent a lot of time figuring out how to do our part," said former corporate banking chief Reuben Richards. Trouble was, he said, "you can't make a Piper Cub go supersonic." And another senior officer said that the pressure to "stretch" caused people to "get pretty schizoid." Citibank's bean counters did everything possible to make the income statement produce the desired result. "In the course of a year if it looked like we needed some money, we tried to hold back advertising or something," executive committee chairman Ed Palmer said later.

While Wriston's relationship with Wall Street became more collegial after that October 1971 dinner, his relationship with the Federal Reserve, and with chairman Burns, became even more strained. The 15 percent target also injected new life into the ancient debate on how much capital a bank—specifically a large money center known as Citibank—should be required to maintain. At the time, there were no specific capital requirements for large banks.

In the public sector, Burns was the most severe critic of Citibank's earnings goal. He frequently told bankers that he felt banks were better off before they became concerned about price-earnings ratios and growth. Wriston, of course, believed that anything that wasn't growing was dying. As chairman of the Committee on Interest and Dividends, Burns was always crusading for lower interest rates, and he occasionally dropped by Wriston's office on Friday afternoons to jawbone him on rates and his earnings objective.

"Walter, you're absolutely wrong to have an earnings target for a bank. It's not seemly, and it's wrong," Burns declared, as Wriston recalled.

"He gave me lecture after lecture on this," said Wriston, "and I always said to him, 'Arthur, you keep telling me that you're right, that banks have to sell more equity, to sell more subordinated debt, and I have terrible news for you. There's a finite number of buyers and an unlimited amount of inventory. I have to go out to the market with General Electric and General Motors and the fact that I say 'But I'm a bank and I'm special' cuts absolutely no ice with widows and orphans in Kansas City. They want to know if I'm going to earn some money and, if so, will I pay a dividend and what's my debt service coverage."

"Well, it's different in the banks," Burns growled.

The perils of the push for profit center earnings by the new managerial elite would soon be evident in Citibank's Investment Management Group, among other businesses. As part of the McKinsey reorganization, Citibank attempted to jazz up the stodgy trust division, changing its name to the IMG. After his stint in Australia, Tom Theobald was summoned into Wriston's office and told that the train was moving and that if he climbed aboard for the long ride, he'd be a winner in the end. With no experience in investment management, Theobald was appointed to run the division, and by 1970 it managed $12 billion in assets, mostly in employee benefit and personal advisory accounts. For a while things went along smoothly. Theobald established a financial counseling service for executives and offered them tax-sheltered investments. Other investments included real estate equities such as shopping centers, land, and commercial offices. In 1972, Citibank boasted of its 1971 performance in managing two funds—an employee benefit fund and a pension fund—saying they outperformed the Dow Jones average in 1971 with rates of return of nearly 23 percent. Later, however, it turned out that some of the properties recommended to investors were located on California's San Andreas Fault. Others were orange groves, gladiola farms, or "swinging singles" apartments whose tenants ran off with the furniture.

With the arrival of the mid-1970s bear market, many of the investments cratered, and Citibank spent gobs of money just trying to fend off lawsuits. Said one former senior officer familiar with the investment management operation, "They were in a fairly shortsighted, short-term results mode. They were trying to hold down expenses and compensation. But with the growth stock phenomenon, all the banks piled into growth stocks, bid them up to new heights, and rode them down together." Wriston freely admitted he didn't understand Wall Street and the investment business. That, of course, was fairly obvious from his ill-conceived dalliance with Home-Stake.

Theobald was the first in a long line of managers who were placed in charge of the investment management business even though they had little or no previous experience in it. "The key to success," said one former Citibank money manager, "is developing a team of highly skilled top professionals in that field and having them work as a team. It requires more than [managing] revenues versus costs." But at Wriston's revamped Citibank, teamwork was rapidly becoming an alien concept.

Meanwhile, inflation was rising at a 4 percent to 6 percent annual clip, and interest rates headed north along with it. Populist Wright Patman saw the big banks as the villains behind the surge in rates and "turned the pressure on the judicial system," Wriston recalled, to find a scapegoat. The Justice Department launched an investigation into rate setting and summoned Wriston and other top bankers to Washington to interrogate them on their alleged back room deliberations. "The political climate when prices are rising is always to find somebody that's doing something that's immoral or illegal or otherwise," Wriston said later.

What derailed the probe, Wriston said, was a presentation by Citibank chief economist Leif Olsen, a former *Wall Street Journal* reporter, to the bureaucrats on how rates are really set in the marketplace, an event that would reinforce the personal bond between Wriston and Olsen. In Citibank's view, the prime had been rendered obsolete by the volatility in market rates that had occurred since 1965. The entire postwar financial system, based as it was on fixed exchange rates and controls, was also rendered obsolete by the same forces that would cause Citibank to lead the way, in October 1971, to abandon the prime.

While other rates, including that of commercial paper, were rising, government jawboning kept the prime artificially low. Corporations naturally switched from commercial paper to prime-based loans, forcing banks to reach into the CD market to fund the additional volume. But Wriston was weary of being accused of "administering" the prime. He, Spencer, and Palmer concluded that they needed to find a formula that would determine the bank's lending rate automatically and without controversy. The upshot was a "floating prime" based on the ninety-day commercial paper rate—a proxy for the incremental cost of money—plus one half of 1 percent.

Although the concept, Wriston said, was "studied to death," the decision on how, when, and where to float the prime occurred serendipitously. On October 20, 1971, three of the four "partners"—Wriston, Spencer, and Palmer—were in San Francisco attending the annual convention of the American Bankers Association. While cooling their heels in the lobby of Nob Hill's elegant Fairmont Hotel waiting for their wives to return from a party, they fretted over the likelihood that Patman and the new Committee on Interest and Dividends would take more potshots at them with the next uptick in the prime.

"When are we going to get off the dime and float this thing?" one of them said. Glancing intermittently at their watches, they were becoming increasingly impatient over their wives' lateness. Spontaneously, they decided to stop wringing their hands over when to act and float the prime then and there. They agreed, however, that Treasury secretary John Connally, who was flying in that afternoon to address the bankers, should be notified first. Palmer offered to intercept him at the airport to brief him on the plan, figuring that if he had some violent objection they could regroup and modify it.

The next day, Wriston would head for the Philippines, and Spencer for Tokyo. "You're holding the birdie," Wriston told Palmer. "If Connally is comfortable, you hold a press conference and float [the prime]." At their airport meeting on that momentous afternoon, Connally warned Palmer that Citibank would likely take a lot of criticism for the move and wished him luck. But Palmer would say later that Connally "didn't know what it was all about." The reaction of the other bankers, Wriston recalled, ranged from cautious endorsement to mockery to outright hostility. Two large banks, including New York's Irving Trust, adopted it instantly. "The political pressure continued, but we had this marvelous thing, where one day in New York we had three [different] prime rates of three major banks, which of course was the object of the exercise," Wriston said. "It destroyed the cartel argument. It's hard to find a cartel with three different prices."

Several months later, Spencer compared the floating base rate in importance to the negotiable CD: "We are hopeful that the fractional and frequent change of rates, as the open market moves, will eventually be accepted as casually, for example, as the weekly change in Treasury bill rates. It may be that in time the word 'prime' will itself become archaic in banking circles and refer only to beef. Hopefully, then, prime ribs will attract more interest than prime rates." But that, of course, would prove to be wishful thinking.

Once Citibank announced its formula, which it later changed, other banks assigned analysts to figure out when Citibank would adjust its prime so they could upstage Citi by announcing their changes first. To the extent that the floating prime tied bank lending rates to the marketplace, this move, like the introduction of the negotiable CD a decade earlier, weakened the Fed's control over bank lending even further. As long as bank lending rates were essentially fixed, profit margins would be pinched when rates rose. That made bankers reluctant to borrow short and lend long. Now, however, the floating prime, on top of the negotiable CD and the holding company, observed economist Henry Kaufman, made them feel more comfortable lending money. Kaufman noted in a 1976 speech that the "substantial removal of the money rate risk served as a strong stimulant to banks to increase bank loans." Although the floating loan rate reduced interest rate risk, Kaufman contended that it increased credit risk. "Their argument," said Kaufman, "is that [they] know how to judge credit risk." Time would demonstrate that their judgment on that score was far from perfect.

While the prime was being floated, Wriston was winging his way to the Philippines. In the view of Citibank's Asia hands, Wriston seemed to ignore Asia. So when the occasion arose for another overseas board trip, Wriston decided to meet the directors in Manila and then escort them on inspection tours of Citibank operations in other Asian nations. In October 1971, the Philippines looked like a nation on the move. A year earlier it had managed to avoid defaulting on its foreign debt. President Ferdinand Marcos looked like a bold, popular leader. Economically, the Philippines was outpacing countries like Thailand, and boasted a respected, capable finance minister in Cesar Virata.

Citibank, according to former top officer Ed Harshfield, was a lender to the Philippines when Marcos came to power in 1965 and was among the first international banks to lend to the new regime. In contrast to Japan, Hong Kong, and Korea, where Citibank's business was small compared to the total economy, Citibank in the Philippines held a sizable chunk of the country's deposits. One special attraction of doing business in the Philippines was that the country permitted Citibank to remit its local currency earnings to the United States. Only two foreign banks, Citibank and Bank of America, conducted a local currency business. When the Philippines needed large foreign currency loans, they turned to Citibank and, to a lesser extent, Bank of America. The local banks did not have the resources to raise large amounts of dollars efficiently and inexpensively. Local banks could extend short-term dollar loans, but only Citibank and the Bank of America could quickly assemble a long-term dollar loan for, say, the Philippine Electric Company. Said one Filipino banker, "Citi was the imprimatur. When Citi gives $2 billion, other banks follow with $500 million," sometimes without regard to sound lending practice.

Citibank's influence over the economic life of the country was also felt, albeit indirectly, in its role as a major dealer in Filipino pesos. In addition to being the major foreign institution in the Philippines, Citibank was responsible for producing a corps of bankers that staffed the indigenous institutions. It maintained its Asia-Pacific training center in the Philippines, where it taught Asians and Africans the latest techniques of financial and credit analysis. At one point, up to one third of the top managers of local banks were former Citibank officers. In a very real sense, Citibank trained the banking elite of the Philippines in modern banking practices and instilled in them a firm belief in free market systems. There was another small fringe benefit in the bank's relationship with the Philippines. The First National City Corporation owned a subsidiary whose principal asset was a private jet. One of the regular renters was the First Lady of the Philippines, Imelda Marcos. "We made good money on that," said a former officer familiar with the arrangement.

The cozy relationship between Citibank and the Philippines mirrored the close ties between the United States and its longtime ally. Because virtually every top official in the Filipino government spoke English and had educational or family ties to the United States, there was an affinity between Citibank and the Philippines that it did not enjoy with many Third World countries. "The problem," said a former top Citibank official, "is that because it's so warm and friendly it's easy to be suckered into the Philippines."

When the Wristons arrived, the Marcoses had just returned from the Shah of Iran's party of the century, an opulent celebration of the 2,500th anniversary of the Persian Empire. The Marcos government pulled out all the stops to impress the Citibank board. Although Citibank had hired a battery of army officers to ensure security for the directors, their arrival in the country was supposed to be low-key. But things didn't turn out that way. When their plane landed at Manila International Airport, they were greeted by a fifteen-man motorcycle escort that led the motorcade of limousines through the city with all the discretion of the Barnum & Bailey circus. Truckloads of soldiers guarded the front and rear of the procession. The Wristons and the directors and their wives were entertained like royalty at Malacanang Palace. A series of special postage stamps was issued commemorating Citibank's seventy years in the country, and special license plates were stamped out for the limousines. The Philippine government was prepared to bestow award after award on Wriston, including its prestigious Order of the Grand Sikatuna, but Wriston scowled at the prospect. "Too much," he told an aide.

Planning these overseas board meetings had turned into a full-time chore, a logistics and protocol nightmare that would challenge a White House advance team. For starters, all of the egos of the directors, and of the companies they headed, had to be taken into account. Because the chairman of Kimberly Clark was on the board, someone had to be sure a box of Kleenex was placed in every room. Years later, when the chairman of PepsiCo was elected a director, no room was complete without a six-pack of Pepsi. W. R. Grace chairman Peter Grace inevitably flew to the meetings in his jet, accompanied by a bevy of secretaries, leaving Citibank planners with the task of booking rooms for the entourage. All the planning didn't prevent a number of directors from coming down with the flu. Concerned that Marcos might want to show off his air-conditioning systems, director George Jenkins of Met Life wore three undershirts under his barong.

The friendship between the Philippines and Citibank, as it turned out, would prove to be more of a minus than a plus. A portent of things to come appeared early in the visit. As the Wristons waited for Marcos in a second-floor study, a rat scurried across the floor into the president's office.

In the Philippines, oddly enough, Wriston launched a public and private campaign against Nixon's wage and price controls that didn't end until the controls were lifted in 1974. "Despite the volume of arguments for more and more controls over the last twenty-five years, the world happily went the other way," he said. He reminded Manila's elite that the economic revival of West Germany began when former chancellor Ludwig Erhard lifted the controls imposed by U.S. high commissioner Lucius Clay, who had left for a long weekend. "This was the beginning of what the world came to call the economic miracle of West Germany." Wriston took advantage of every subsequent opportunity to rail against controls in any form. In late November he said, "The most important part of phase two" of wage and price controls was "to fix a date at which it would end."

Fed chairman Arthur Burns, meanwhile, was declaring victory. On November 1, 1971, he reported to the House Committee on Banking and Currency that "the current price and wage freeze is a major step in breaking the hold of inflation on our country." He said, "The freeze appears to have effectively halted the spiral of prices and wages" and that "we have already experienced some reduction of interest rates."

The brave—and to some, insecure—new world that Wriston and Reed were creating within Citibank paralleled the brave new world of volatile interest and exchange rates that was evolving in the marketplace. During his Far East trip, Wriston plunged into the debate over the role of the dollar. Asked by reporters if he would advise President Nixon to devalue the dollar, he replied, "I would say that is the thing for the United States to do if that's what was required to prompt other countries to revalue theirs"—a suggestion that was prominently reported in the *New York Times.*

The Nixon economic initiatives had finally brought the economic and political turmoil of the 1960s to a head. It was only a matter of time before the old fixed rate exchange system would yield to an international order in which the dollar and other currencies would float constantly against each other, their relative values dependent on the quality of each country's economic management and performance.

Since the Camp David action, some countries had attempted to use controls to preserve the old fixed rate system. A mere handful had tiptoed into the brave new world of floating rates.

Shortly after the August 1971 meeting at Camp David, Connally flew to London to meet with his European counterparts on the intensifying currency crisis. Led by French Finance Minister Valéry Giscard d'Estaing and British Chancellor of the Exchequer Anthony Barber, they pressed Connally to devalue the dollar. Connally would recall later that he was especially peeved at the Canadian finance minister. At that time the Canadian dollar was floating against the United States dollar, and never once, said Connally, did his Canadian counterpart speak up to defend the floating rate system. "And no one else did," said Connally. "I was trying to sell the floating rate in 1971, and nobody would buy."

When he returned from London, Connally met immediately with Nixon to report on his trip. Concerned that devaluing the dollar would be embarrassing for the president, he asked Nixon if it would "bother" him politically if that happened.

"Does it bother you?" Nixon asked.

"Not a bit," said Connally.

"It doesn't bother me either," Nixon told him.

Said Connally later, "He gave me carte blanche to do what we needed to do."

Meanwhile, national security adviser Henry Kissinger and Fed chairman Arthur Burns expressed to Nixon their concern that a continuation of the defiant U.S. stand toward devaluation would have damaging foreign policy and economic implications. According to one account, Nixon told Connally and Burns over lunch on November 24, 1971, that he favored settling the issue or eliminating the import surcharge.

In late November, Wriston was in Washington for a morning meeting with the president. On his way out of the White House, Connally suggested that he and Wriston adjourn to lunch at a Washington restaurant after he phoned his office. Connally was scheduled to leave for Rome that evening for a meeting of the Group of Ten, and his secretary immediately quashed their plans for a leisurely lunch. "You don't have a chance of having lunch," she said. "You have forty-two phone calls and fifteen problems. How about a ham and cheese on rye at your desk?" The two men walked briskly the few blocks to the Treasury Department.

Over sandwiches in Connally's office, they discussed the clamor among the Europeans for devaluation, and Connally aired his dilemma over how to respond to the mounting pressures caused by a clearly overvalued dollar. "At the end of the day the dollar is going to be floating," Wriston told Connally.

Wriston suggested devaluing, and he and Connally discussed the consequences of such a move, but Connally was noncommittal. Finally, Connally's secretary, besieged by impatient and important callers, stalked into the office, nodded in Wriston's direction, and said, "Out."

On his return from Italy, Connally phoned Wriston to report on his trip. "They beat up on him for twenty minutes," Wriston recalled, "saying, 'The dollar is overvalued, do something,' " lecturing him on the unfair advantage that gave the United States in world markets. Connally allowed them all to have their say, and finally it was his turn to speak.

The Europeans, apparently unaccustomed to blunt-talking government officials, were left speechless by his response. As Connally recalled, he told the assemblage, "Well, I've listened to you distinguished gentlemen, in meetings in Munich, London, and now through the meetings in Rome. The United States is prepared to devalue the dollar 10 percent." Connally said that a "hush . . . fell over the room" and lasted for forty minutes. After recovering from the shock, Britain's Anthony Barber, the first to speak up, was critical. "Oh, we can't permit that," he said. According to Connally, Barber was following the French line, out of fear that French president Georges Pompidou would veto the United Kingdom's bid for membership in the European Common Market.

"What do you mean you can't permit it?" Connally asked Barber. "You've been asking for it for months."

Barber replied that 10 percent was too much.

"Ten percent is very little," Connally replied. "What did you have in mind?"

Barber said they couldn't agree to more than 5 percent. That, said Connally, would accomplish nothing. "If that's all you're prepared to do, then there's no point in attempting to do it. . . . We might as well adjourn this meeting."

In Rome, Connally also crossed swords with Fed chairman Arthur Burns, who, in Connally's view, was struggling to preserve the prerogatives of the U.S. central bank. It was, after all, the Fed that actually handled the arrangements to swap currencies with other central banks, and Burns repeatedly beseeched Connally to allow him to work out the deals with the central bankers. "I think we can get an agreement and work this out," Burns said. According to Connally, Burns pestered him at least a half dozen times in Rome with this request, until Connally couldn't take it anymore. "I finally got a little irritated," Connally said. "God damn it, Arthur, nobody in this room has got any authority to do anything except me," Connally scolded Burns. "I'm the only one here who's got any independence." The meeting ended inconclusively, and Connally flew back to Washington without a number. Several weeks later the impasse ended with a bizarre twist after a series of meetings at the Smithsonian Institution in Washington. After the ministers from the Group of Six industrialized nations failed to agree on realignments between their own currencies, they turned to Connally in resignation, telling him that if there was to be an agreement on a revaluation of the dollar he would have to be the one to work it out. In personality and temperament, Connally was not averse to dictating terms to the Europeans and the Japanese. Taking each of them on in turn, he began by wringing commitments out of the British, the French, and the Germans. The ministers kept their cabinets up throughout the night in Europe as the agreements were hammered out. With a six-hour time difference between Washington and Bonn, Connally recalled that he struck a deal with the West German minister at about nine in the evening, and chancellor Willy Brandt called a special cabinet meeting at three in the morning to ratify it. D'Estaing woke up Pompidou, and Barber phoned Prime Minister Edward Heath. Connally was unique in that he was the only minister whose president had delegated to him the authority to transact the financial affairs of his country.

The deal with the Europeans implied a 17 percent revaluation of the Japanese yen. Late on Friday, December 17, 1971, Connally summoned the deputy finance minister of Japan to inform him that he had reached an accord with each of the other ministers and that he should notify the finance minister that Japan would have to revalue by 17 percent. Connally demanded his answer by ten o'clock the next morning, when the ministers were scheduled to ratify the agreement. He warned the functionary that if Japan didn't go along with them, he would call a press conference and "lay the blame flat on the doorsteps of the Japanese."

"Yes, sir, yes, sir," the Japanese functionary replied.

The next morning the deputy finance minister of Japan beckoned to Connally from the doorway just minutes before he was going to call the meeting to order. Connally stepped outside the room to confer with him.

"Mr. Secretary, I have talked to the finance minister and he cannot agree to the revaluation of the yen 17 percent," he said sheepishly.

Indignant, Connally replied, "Fine, thank you very much," and turned abruptly to return to the meeting.

Grabbing Connally by the coattails, the bureaucrat said, "You don't understand."

Connally cut him off. "I understand very well. I told you last night that you had to agree to 17 percent by ten this morning or we're going to adjourn the meeting and hold you solely responsible for breaking it up."

"Yes, you don't understand."

"What don't I understand?" Connally demanded impatiently.

"In 1932 the Japanese finance minister revalued the yen 17 percent, the country went into a great recession, and the finance minister committed suicide. [The current minister, therefore,] cannot agree to 17 percent. Can you give me another percentage?"

Connally told him 16.9 percent. The deal was done, and the dollar was devalued by 7.89 percent. On that day, the administration also scrapped the import surcharge.

Connally later said that Wriston's support for devaluation of the dollar "meant a great deal to me." The Smithsonian Agreements ended the speculative outflow of dollars, and some money that had left during the crisis began to return. Congress then ratified the agreements by passing the Par Value Modification Act, which was signed by President Nixon on April 3, 1972.

With the beginning of the end of the old fixed rate system, many eulogized it as having served a useful purpose in providing order to the postwar economic world and fostering world trade. Wriston debunked that idea as "polite fiction," pointing out that the world's heaviest two-way trade took place between the United States and Canada, which never set a fixed price for gold, and also permitted its exchange rate to float between September 1950 and May 1962, and again after May 1970. The exchange controls of the 1960s, he said, "were aimed not at defending the dollar but at defending the price of gold and the fixed exchange rates. Since then we have seen controls become more and more pervasive in a series of futile efforts to support inflexible rates."

Soon it would become apparent that what Wriston considered good for the world financial system was also good for Citibank.

Implicit in the goal of 15 percent earnings growth was the need to operate on a minimum of capital. The debate over capital adequacy—how little capital is too little—had been raging for years. One Fed staff member who retired in the early 1970s recalled at his farewell party that the two burning banking issues when he joined the central bank in the early 1930s were capital and banking agency consolidation. Forty years later, nothing had changed. When Wriston took command at Citibank, banks were still highly regulated institutions that operated according to their regulators' edicts. When a bank regulator ordered a client bank to get more capital, for example, the response was invariably, "When and how much?"

Not until Wriston arrived did a high-profile banker take on the issue as a personal crusade. Indeed, for Wriston leverage was not merely a concept to be applied to money and banking. It was a religion and a lifestyle and a force to be used to one's advantage in every aspect of life. Time, energy, and money were things to be levered. Wriston, fascinated with heavy equipment and the laws of physics, applied them frequently at Deer Pond Farm. Said Kathy Wriston, "His idea of a good time is sitting on a backhoe pulling up tree stumps," a pastime that soon engaged his wife as well. More than once, she said, Wriston admonished her for using muscle instead of brains. "He'd say, 'Find a lever long enough and you can move the world.'" Wriston loved tools of all kinds. On one occasion, in late winter, he was attending a business review meeting in Queens with his top managers when the heating system failed. The room felt like the Saudi desert in midsummer. After trying unsuccessfully to fix the radiator, a repairman left the room, leaving his tool kit behind. Wriston removed his jacket, sat down on the floor, took out some wrenches, and brought the thermostat down to a tolerable level.

Because of all the constraints and inhibitions caused by government regulation, the only way a banking company could produce high returns was through high leverage. "The idea," said former chief financial officer Don Howard, "was to be highly leveraged but as conservative as possible within that." Bankers like Wriston argued that for a large diversified bank the only thing that mattered was earnings, whereas the regulators insisted that capital was all that stood between solvency and failure. Wriston thought that if the world believed Citibank had enough capital, that was all the capital it needed. He could sleep well at night with virtually no capital at all. To Wriston, what counted was intellectual capital, not financial capital. High IQs, he believed, obviated the need for high capital ratios.

In contrast to industrial companies, where capital tended to be large relative to liabilities, banks typically operated with large liabilities and a small amount of capital. They were generally among the most highly leveraged business organizations, though there were periods when the industry operated with ratios ranging from 10 to 20 percent of total assets. As late as 1960, equity capital of banks averaged 9 percent of total bank assets. While there were no prescribed capital ratios at the time, regulators regarded as undercapitalized a bank with a ratio below 8 percent. But that ratio was now approaching its lowest level in American banking history; by the end of 1973, it had fallen to 6.5 percent. Citibank's was a mere 4.1 percent. In addition, First National City Corporation and other holding companies were now raising money in the debt markets and injecting those funds as capital into their bank subsidiaries—a questionable practice known as double leverage.

Until the advent of one-bank holding companies and the passage of the 1970 amendments, the Fed had virtually no power to enforce its views on national banks. In the wake of that legislation, the Fed focused more on the proper activities for bank holding companies than on how much capital they should have. Lacking well-defined views on the subject, Fed chairman Arthur Burns and his staff grappled inconclusively over capital for a few years. In those quiet corridors there were basically two competing camps: advocates of the building-block theory, which held that if each of the bank holding companies' subsidiaries was adequately capitalized, then the whole should be considered sufficiently capitalized; and supporters of the consolidated-capital theory, which asserted that if there was enough capital in the combined entity, how it was allocated among the units was unimportant. The capital question, while always a concern to the Fed, would not achieve front-burner status until at least 1973.

The Fed's undefined views on capital were reflected in the vague jawboning Wriston received in the early 1970s from Alfred Hayes, then the Fed's man in New York. Hayes was a patrician central banker whose father, like Wriston's, was a college professor. According to a former top Fed official, Hayes and Wriston seemed deferential to each other, in part, he opined, because both were faculty brats. Nonetheless, over lunch at the Fed, Hayes and his colleagues regularly reminded Wriston and his colleagues, as they did the heads of other big banks, that "you guys ought to work on your capital a little bit." According to the central banker, "Wriston would always resent that." While Wriston rarely lost his temper, his ire manifested itself in his characteristic eye twitch and sharper tone of voice. And he, in turn, would lecture Hayes on how Citibank didn't need as much capital as did small banks, which were undiversified and lacked strong management.

At the Federal Reserve Board, the functionary who served as the bearer of bad tidings was Brenton C. Leavitt. When banks got calls from Leavitt they knew they would have to raise more capital; they were said to have been "Leavitized."

There was another reason for the Fed's halfhearted interest in bank holding company capital in the early 1970s. Earlier, the Fed had become embroiled in a legal battle with a small bank over capital, a case that dragged on for years. The bank finally acceded to the Fed's demands, but the central bank paid a steep price in legal resources. "After that," said a former Fed official, "the appetite of the legal staff to take on capital issues was diminished." In the early 1970s the Fed had little evidence it could use to refute Wriston's position. That would soon change.

Wriston's ideas on capital departed sharply from the view of nearly every other Citibank chief since Moses Taylor, with the possible exception of Frank Vanderlip. On this issue, Wriston was clearly influenced by the nineteenth-century economist and journalist Walter Bagehot, author of *Lombard Street,* a seminal study of the British banking system. "He said good bankers don't need any capital, and there's not enough capital in the world to support bad bankers," Wriston said. "That's still true. Nobody asks what is the capital ratio of Westinghouse Credit, or GE Credit. . . . The most important thing is management." The old International Banking Corporation, Wriston liked to point out, "ran on practically zero capital." Proof of his thesis, he believed, could be seen in the balance sheets of history's failed banks. On the day before they went broke, Wriston asserted, their capital ratios typically exceeded the regulatory requirements. The reason that their capital ratios were high was that deposits run off rapidly as the word of problems spreads, forcing the bank to sell off assets. As it goes down the slippery slide, capital is all that remains. Wriston was convinced that no amount of capital would prevent the failure of a bank that had lost public confidence through bad lending or mismanagement. "This," he said, "led us to question whether or not the ratio in itself was an adequate measure."

Nothing riled Wriston more than hearing rival J. P. Morgan & Company, parent of the venerable Morgan Guaranty Trust, described as a rock-solid, well-capitalized institution. Wriston liked to cite Morgan as an example of a bank that did need capital because of its overdependence on purchased money and its almost total lack of stable core deposits. Moreover, as the quintessential white-shoe bank, it lacked a broad actuarial base; its clientele was limited to America's largest industrial corporations. "Walt was always a little bit cynical about J. P. Morgan," said Hans Angermueller, the Shearman & Sterling lawyer who would soon be appointed general counsel.

Wriston knew that the debate over capital would not go away, and that he would have to win it if he was going to keep his covenant with Wall Street. And he knew he would not win it by exchanging barbs with Arthur Burns in hotel hallways. It was now time, Wriston thought, to raise the discussion of things like capital and the rightful role of banking companies to a higher plane. Since taking the helm at Citibank, Wriston had attacked the status quo of the financial services industry from nearly every angle. He had locked horns with the defiant populist Wright Patman in the halls of Congress. He had deluged his new adversary, Arthur Burns, with a flood of applications seeking to expand his empire in every conceivable way. And he had used every opportunity to promulgate his free market views before receptive listeners in the business community and in the Nixon administration. It was now time, he felt, to turn the Citibank juggernaut loose in the marketplace of ideas.

He and Citibank had already discovered that they could change the world to their liking by modifying laws, inventing financial instruments, and squirming through regulatory loopholes in the United States and abroad. Now he sought to do so by challenging the intellectual underpinnings of the world in which he operated. Always enamored of think tanks, Wriston decided to transform Citibank into one. The result was an outpouring of corporate scholarship over the next couple of years that would irrevocably change the way Citibank, the banking industry, and the policymakers thought about and conducted their business for years.

The first book to emerge from the Citibank think tank was *Bank Capital Adequacy* by George Vojta, then a thirty-seven-year-old planner who had joined Citibank in 1960 and was almost immediately shipped off to Asia. The thrust of Vojta's book, which was published in February 1973, was that banks don't fail for lack of capital. They tanked, he contended, because of bad management or lack of earnings. Vojta argued that the regulators' approach to capital was based not on the notion of a going concern but on a liquidation view of the institution—the amount that might be necessary if the bank started to go down the tube. The minimal level of capital prescribed by Vojta would serve as a cushion for extraordinary losses. Moreover, the Vojta treatise proposed that capital should include subordinated debt—an idea that was anathema to Burns and the traditionalists.

"From then on at every banking forum you went to, somebody would get up and say, 'This guy Vojta's as crazy as a March hare,' but people would have to deal with it," said Wriston.

"Citi led the debate," said bank analyst David Cates. "He [Wriston] was such a charismatic leader that others followed." Henry Kaufman, a Wall Street economist who would later win fame as Wall Street's Dr. Doom, disagreed vehemently with Wriston. "If there's no need for bank capital," he said later, "then there shouldn't be private institutions, because the government is insuring the deposit side. Bank earnings can't be programmed. There's a fine line between the entrepreneurial role of bankers and the fiduciary role."

Thanks in part to Wriston's persistence, capital ratios deteriorated. "It's hard to maintain capital standards when the industry leaders aren't maintaining good capital standards," a former senior regulator said.

The capital treatise apparently reinforced the views of an already sympathetic Comptroller of the Currency. "We . . . had some reservations, but they [Citibank] did good work," said James Smith, who served as Comptroller from 1973 to 1976. "You really have to have a lot of bad things happen to eat away layers of capital," he said, adding that the treatise "probably resulted in the agency taking a more sophisticated look at capital" and examining "more closely what we were hoping to accomplish with capital and the role debt plays."

Said one former top Citibanker, "Couple that [15 percent earnings growth] with diversification and congenerics, and it really got that place going."

The only people who worried Wriston more than dumb regulators were dumb competitors. "I'll take the smart competitor any day to the dumb competitor," he used to say.

While Vojta was poring over the draft of his treatise on capital, Wriston had assigned yet another Citibank scholar the task of educating the American banking industry and the Washington regulatory establishment on how to put a price tag on money. At the time, most bankers operated under the assumption that demand deposits were free because the banks didn't pay interest on them. In the mid-1960s, Charles Kelly and John Reed had formulated the marginal cost of funds concept that Citibank used to value its inventory forever after. They discovered the hard way that the bank that prices its loans on the average cost of funds is doomed when interest rates rise. With the rise in interest rates and intensifying competition for the better corporate business, Wriston was concerned about a free-for-all in which banks that didn't understand their costs would almost literally shovel money out the door. Said one Citibank officer, "If the other guy is giving it away, you're hurt too."

Except for the august J. P. Morgan & Company, the American banking community had not gotten that message. As a primarily "wholesale" bank, or one that bought money in the money markets and lent it to corporations, Morgan understood marginal cost of funds and lamented the fact that they and Citibank were the only ones who did. Said former J. P. Morgan chairman Lewis Preston, "One of our frustrations over the years is that people didn't understand their costs. The more competitors understand their costs, the more sensible their prices." In going public with his goal of 15 percent earnings growth, Wriston was telling the world that earnings were what counted. But as long as Washington and the rest of the banking industry didn't understand how to value money, he was going to have trouble attaining that goal. It was all well and good for Citibank to understand how to use marginal costing in evaluating the economics and profitability of its loans and businesses. But that was of little use if others operated irrationally. So Kelly pounded out a seminal paper on how to put a price tag on money.

Washington in general and Wright Patman in particular were primary targets of the Kelly treatise. While Wriston did not expect Patman to read, understand, or be influenced by anything bearing the Citibank logo, he did hope that *someone* in Washington would be persuaded of the inherent unfairness in pressuring banks to keep the lid on the prime rate when banks had to pay higher market rates for large CDs to fund their loans. The irony was that Wriston was in part responsible for the problem.

To Citibank executive committee chairman Ed Palmer, Arthur Burns seemed impressed but bewildered by Citibank's work on marginal cost. In a conversation with Palmer, he indicated that he wasn't sold. "I have an account at the Riggs Bank that pays zero percent," said Burns. "Mrs. Burns has an account at four percent. So what's the real cost to Riggs Bank?" he inquired. He could easily have found the answer in the marginal cost book, which Citibank gave away for the asking. This book launched a revolution in the way banks priced their money and their loans. The concept, said Don Howard, "had a major influence in the way the organization developed. It kept you from making a lot of dumb mistakes. It affected all of your pricing."

While regulators and legislators had continued to maintain decades-old restrictive banking laws and regulations and to devise new ones, an entire industry of non-bank financial services providers had emerged to supply the same services without being subject to rate ceilings or limitations on what products and services they could offer and where. Yet another opus written by vice president Cleveland Christophe, published by Citibank, and titled *Competition in Financial Services,* pounded home for perhaps the first time the point that bankers' real competitors were former clients like Sears Roebuck, General Electric, J. C. Penney, and even Ford and General Motors. These companies were not only reducing their dependence on banks but were adding insult to injury by transforming themselves into banks. Commercial banking's share of the so-called money-related services market had declined from 57 percent in 1946 to 38 percent in 1972. Wriston hoped that the powers that be would realize that the real loser from inequitable regulation was the consumer.

Ironically, three of the most prominently mentioned non-bank competitors were firms with whom Wriston and Citibank had close personal and business ties. Wriston, of course, was on the board at J. C. Penney and at General Electric; Spencer was on the Sears board; and both Sears and J. C. Penney were represented on the First National City Corp. board. At about the time Citibank began to target Sears as bankers' enemy number one, Sears chairman Gordon Metcalf, a First National City Corporation director, conveniently retired from the board when he retired from Sears at the age of sixty-five. Meanwhile, Spencer remained on the Sears board. Some Citibankers thought that was a bit awkward.

In a 1973 speech to correspondent bankers, Wriston told his audience that "the biggest personal bank in the world today is Sears Roebuck," adding that "all you need is a shopping center and a Sears store and you then have a mutual fund, an insurance desk, accounts receivable, a credit card, and a venture capital business right next to the refrigerators."

Some say Citibank even played a role in aiding and abetting its own competition. In 1935, Citibank and Sears had worked out an arrangement that enabled Sears to boost its small merchandise financing. "At Sears," Wriston said later in a talk to senior officers, "the financial tail eventually came to wag the dog."

Sears at times had been a thorn in Citibank's side, though for reasons unrelated to financial services. In the glory days of compensating balances in the 1960s, the Big Store was always known in the banking community as a chintzy depositor. Citibank was constantly trying, usually without success, to persuade Sears to beef up its balances. On one celebrated occasion, the officer responsible for the Sears relationship, such as it was, arranged for the company treasurer to meet chairman Stillman Rockefeller. As the story goes, Rockefeller, never one for small talk, got right to the point. "Someone said we're trying to get the balances built up, but we haven't been very successful," according to an internal interview. The Sears treasurer replied, "It won't always be this way."

"No, you could drop dead," Rockefeller said to the incredulous Sears official.

"We hated Sears with a passion," said corporate secretary Carl Desch.

Sears Roebuck's involvement in financial services dated back to 1911, when the company started to lend customers money to buy merchandise. In 1931, it started Allstate Insurance. Then, in 1953, it introduced its merchandise and services credit card. When Wriston began making speeches in the early 1970s identifying Sears as the competition, Sears chairman Ed Brennan was a vice president responsible for a territory. "We were all flattered," he remarked later, and "we all read it with interest. . . . Walter Wriston probably saw that capability before we strategically decided that would be a core business of ours. . . . Wriston had a changing vision of financial services that no one else had."

The awkwardness was felt at GE as well, but apparently not enough to cause Wriston to resign from his favorite board. General Electric Credit Corporation was rapidly becoming, in effect, one of the largest commercial banks in the United States. Said Tom Paine, who supervised the TEMPO study and later returned to GE as a top officer after a stint as NASA chief, "Here was Walter Wriston sitting in, helping to guide this enormous competitor who had all kinds of freedoms he didn't have." Still, Wriston—and fellow director Lewis Preston of J. P. Morgan—always left the room when matters involving GE Credit came before the board.

Wriston was a key adviser to the conglomerate on other banking and financial matters, Paine recalled. For example, Wriston always reminded the company to make sure that a GE employee was on hand when a GE jet engine was mounted on aircraft operated by bankrupt airlines—and not to let the engine out of his sight until the check cleared.

Wriston was not a brooder, but he felt disappointed and put out. In 1972, in-house counsel Richard Stewart, a former superintendent of insurance, informed him after a brief stint that he would be joining Chubb & Son. Peeved as he was over Stewart's departure, it would represent for Wriston a unique opportunity. To date, he had shaped the banking world with instruments and ideas. While he had lobbied hard on the 1970 amendments to secure as many powers as he could for Citibank, he generally had operated within the law as he found it. Now he would work to shape the statutes to his liking. In hiring Stewart's replacement, Wriston found a man who would himself forge a reputation in the American banking industry for his uncanny ability to find loopholes in the laws that blocked Citibank's expansion across state lines and into new businesses.

Wriston and Spencer sat in Wriston's office asking each other who was the "smartest lawyer in the business who is also a good businessman." They both came up with the same name: Shearman & Sterling's Hans Angermueller. Born in Czechoslovakia in 1924, Angermueller had moved to Germany when he was six months old. Five years later, his father, an executive with I. G. Farben, the German chemical giant that would later become notorious for its role in fueling the Nazi war machine, was transferred to the United States to help the company set up operations here. Educated in New Jersey public and private schools, the stocky, broad-shouldered Angermueller was Harvard to the core. As an undergraduate, he roomed with Robert F. Kennedy and was an occasional visitor to the Kennedy family compound at Hyannis Port, where he chatted in German and French with matriarch Rose Kennedy. After a tour of duty in the military, Angermueller returned to Cambridge under the GI bill, earning a graduate degree in engineering and a law degree.

Angermueller and Wriston first crossed paths in the early 1950s, when Angermueller drew up the documentation on ship loans. More recently they had huddled over the workout of Penn Central. Wriston and Angermueller, a Renaissance man whose talents included mural painting, considered each other friends. And now, with Angermueller's appointment in December 1972 as Citibank's consigliere, the two would become allies in a David versus Goliath effort to repaint the regulatory landscape of American banking. When Angermueller arrived, Citibank was barred from opening branches in other states, engaging in securities activities, and offering bank deposit instruments at unregulated market prices. Angermueller's new mission would be to deregulate the banking industry.

Wriston gave Angermueller the hard sell. "What a salesman!" Angermueller later exclaimed, adding that Wriston had laid out the compensation package and pledged that First National City stock would never go down. Angermueller was not a seasoned lobbyist with years of experience in maneuvering in smoke-filled rooms, but he was a quick study, and his appointment ushered in a new era of activism in Citibank's approach to banking legislation and regulation. Wriston hoped that amateur night would be behind them. At the outset, he asked Angermueller to write his own job description. Angermueller stated it in one sentence: "I am here to advise you on the laws of tomorrow." Wriston was enthralled. Together, Wriston and Angermueller, soon to be referred to as the "loophole lawyer," would sally forth on a crusade to change the law to their liking.

At forty-eight, Angermueller was hardly a brash young newcomer to banking. But he, like Wriston, was somewhat naive about the way Washington worked, and he was overly optimistic about what could be accomplished there. His discovery of the entrenched power of small bankers, insurance agents, and the Securities Industry Association and their lobbying clout was an eye-opener. It soon occurred to him, he said later, that "these people held the high ground. Not the intellectual high ground but high ground in the sense of attacking." Of efforts to attack federal banking laws "broadside," Angermueller would say later, "We have learned that it doesn't work." So he embraced a state-by-state approach. In lobbying for change at the federal level, for example, Citibank had to persuade legislators from states like Montana, where the bank had no desire to operate, to vote for legislation. "The target on a state-by-state approach was smaller and more precise," he said.

Among his other duties, Angermueller was Citibank's ambassador to the Fed. At one mid-1970s gathering of bankers in New York, he railed about the restrictions placed on bank holding companies by the central bank. To roars of laughter, Fed vice chairman George Mitchell retorted, "There's one thing you can do about that. You can give up your deposit insurance." That wasn't about to happen.

Citibank didn't have many allies on Capitol Hill. One of the few was Jacob Javits, George Moore's old friend. Javits, in fact, owned shares of several banking companies, including First National City Corporation and First Chicago Corporation, according to internal Citibank documents. Shortly after Angermueller arrived, Citibank capitulated to the inevitable. If the bank was to exert any influence in Washington, it would have to set up a political action committee—a move that did not go over well at an institution which until recently was led by Stillman Rockefeller, who prided himself on never having shaken hands with his congressman. As Angermueller recalls, the reaction was, "Gee, they don't help anyway. Why should we give them money?" Others, he said, regarded it as a "form of bribe." But after a few years the PAC got up a real head of steam. When word got around that Citibank was in the campaign contribution business, outstretched hands appeared from all directions. One frequent visitor was Maurice Stans, chief money raiser for Richard Nixon in his 1968 and 1972 presidential campaigns. Angermueller said that "he used to drop by and say, 'How about $100,000?' His approaches weren't subtle."

Curiously, at about the same time Wriston mounted his frontal assault on Washington, he decided to shut down Citibank's small and mostly ineffective Washington office. In 1972, ITT, with whom Citibank had a long business relationship, became embroiled in a highly publicized scandal involving lobbyist Dita Beard. Beard was accused of working on behalf of ITT in an

unsuccessful attempt to prevent the Salvador Allende government from taking power in Chile. The Beard-ITT episode scared the bejesus out of Wriston
and pointed up the vulnerability of companies with high Washington profiles. While he did not share his predecessor's aversion to shaking hands with
congressmen, he was never keen on wining and dining them. According to
former Citibank lawyer Chris York, "Wriston saw it [Washington] as a hole
to throw money to entertain the bums in D.C.," adding that he figured his
lobbyists could do just as well taking the train or the Eastern shuttle. "He
[Wriston] was a tightwad," said York. "He would not use an extra piece of
paper if he didn't have to. He'd write a memo on my own memo."

Chase, unlike Citibank, continued to be a pussycat in its dealings with
Washington. David Rockefeller's reluctance to push the limits of regulation
stemmed at least in part from his close personal relationship with Roy C.
Haberkern, Jr., the courtly southerner who was a partner in the blue-chip law
firm of Milbank, Tweed, Hadley & McCloy. Citibank, of course, had Shearman & Sterling and its Fred Eaton. Although Eaton was regarded as somewhat more daring than Haberkern, both men were moderating influences
over their chairmen. The difference was, as Hans Angermueller recalled, that
Rockefeller listened and Wriston didn't. Rockefeller and Haberkern, said
Angermueller, "were like Tweedledum and Tweedledee. David wouldn't
walk across the street without checking with Roy."

"We tended to want to work with government and regulators to achieve
our objectives rather than to confront them," David Rockefeller said later,
noting that Milbank, Tweed's conservative view also reflected his philosophy
and that of Chase. "We were more concerned about public reactions and
government reactions and wanted to be sure what we were doing was consistent with the public interest. The two to a degree go together."

He also said that he was still comfortable with that approach, but he
added, "I can well imagine individual instances in which we would have been
more successful had we been more aggressive and less conciliatory, perhaps."

Citibank discovered that pressing its views on Capitol Hill was usually
counterproductive. It learned that being a New York bank—and an arrogant
New York bank at that—did not win many votes in Congress, and it often
allowed others to carry its water. During Wriston's reign, Citibank would be
able to count its legislative coups on one hand. Although Angermueller was
solidly in Wriston's camp on the righteousness of freedom to operate across
state lines and of what became known in the industry as a "level playing
field" with other financial industry providers, he revealed later that he privately sided with Arthur Burns and the Fed when it came to capital and earnings. Angermueller was the embodiment of intellectual capital, but he
disagreed strongly that intellectual capital was a substitute for the real thing.

If Angermueller was a reluctant soldier, he never showed it on the field
of battle. "In retrospect, 15 percent earnings growth was an ambitious target," said Angermueller later, particularly for an industry that had been quite
conservative. He knew little of the ins and outs of banking law, and when it
came to capital, he was shocked by the extent to which banks were leveraged

compared with industrial companies. "The role of capital in banks is more important than Walter believed was the case," Angermueller said—after retiring from Citibank.

Wriston received a very welcome Christmas gift in 1972. It got the Fed's blessing for its acquisition of tiny St. Louis–based Acceptance Finance Corporation, a $33 million asset consumer loan company that did business as Nationwide Finance through 85 offices in Florida, Georgia, and twelve western states. Nationwide was to be Citibank's Roman Legion. Its troops were to conquer new territory for Walter Wriston.

Despite its small size, the acquisition of Acceptance Finance was something of a gamble. Citibank paid $23 million for a company with a net worth of just $11 million and earnings in the six-figure vicinity. According to former Citibanker Jim Tozer, Bill Spencer said, "I'll do this if you can show me how this thing is going to make $10 million in five years."

The strategy for doing that called for blanketing the country with storefront "person-to-person" offices that would sell all sorts of consumer financial services and establish de facto interstate banking in the United States. In late 1974, Nationwide opened fifteen pilot "person-to-person" offices in four states to offer services such as personal credit lines, homeowner's loans, mortgages, and money management courses for consumers with incomes between $7,500 and $15,000. Since the "P-to-P's" couldn't take deposits, customers couldn't write checks, but borrowers could write payment orders. The acquisition, Wriston said at the time, "moves us closer toward the long-range goal of becoming a truly national financial services corporation." By simply changing the sign above the door, the finance offices could be converted overnight to branches of Citibank.

The plan was inspired, at least in part, by a consumer-oriented German bank known as KKB, which was acquired by Citibank at about the same time through the efforts of a bullheaded, outspoken Scottish banker named Robert F. B. Logan, a.k.a. "the Hun." Like everyone else in the Citibank empire, Logan, the SENOF in Germany, was under orders to obtain licenses and fill the gaps in the full-service concept articulated in the early 1960s by Moore and Wriston. Europe generally was and remains a weak spot, and at that time Citibank's German holdings lacked an investment banking and retail operation. Logan had become friends with the owners of troubled Trinkaus & Birkhardt, an investment bank that owned the majority stake in KKB, a funky family-run bank that catered almost exclusively to working-class Germans. While it was highly automated, its storefront branches were geared to the tastes of the local clientele. Branches in steel towns were equipped with beat-up furniture and tile floors because the steelworkers refused to patronize banks with carpeting. At a time when few other German banks were willing to lend to working people, KKB was making a bundle doing it. The bank was seen as the model for cross-selling customers on one product or service after building a relationship with them, a claim few American banks, including Citi, could make at the time.

According to Angermueller, Trinkaus & Birkhardt offered to sell Citibank its controlling interest in KKB if Citibank also bought a 15 percent stake in T&B. Characteristically, First National City Corporation agreed to buy KKB and Trinkaus even before it knew how much they would cost. Logan then went on to make what would be hailed as the best consumer acquisition ever made by Citibank—and maybe the only acquisition of *any* kind that was successful on its own merits.

The game plan for Nationwide Finance was to acquire other congenerics, including insurance companies, whose "products" could be sold through Nationwide. In late 1973, for instance, the Fed approved the acquisition of Gateway Life Insurance Company of Phoenix, a reinsurer and underwriter of credit life, accident, and health insurance. The opposition to Citibank's continued efforts to pick off pieces of the insurance business was intense. According to Citibank lawyer Chris York, the insurance lobby was so outraged that agents spat at him when he delivered a speech to the National Association of Independent Agents, which had amassed a $500,000 war chest to fight bank holding companies. Meanwhile, the nation's automobile dealers, who were up in arms over Citibank's inroads into the car leasing business, filed suit against the Comptroller of the Currency, Citibank, and other institutions in a bid to kill the plan.

Nothing argued more convincingly for the deregulation of the banking industry, particularly the elimination of Regulation Q, than the money market funds. In the short run, they were debilitating; they drained cheap, non-interest-bearing deposits out of banks, which got them back in the form of negotiable certificates of deposit paying market rates of interest. In the long run, however, Wriston couldn't have hoped for a better weapon to slay Regulation Q. Small banks, which had passionately defended Regulation Q to protect their local monopolies, soon became impassioned critics of rate ceilings.

Ironically, Henry B. R. Brown, the man who invented the money market mutual fund in 1972, had worked for Wriston in the shipping department back in the 1950s. Discouraged in their attempts to raise funds to finance business ventures in the late 1960s because of tight money, Brown and his partner had read an article that described how an increase of just one quarter of one percentage point in the permissible savings rate in California thrifts had triggered the transfer, almost overnight, of $1 billion from West Coast thrifts to East Coast thrifts. "I said if one-quarter of a percent could do that, what could we do?" Brown recalled. Brown and his partner identified states where they could set up a bank that would somehow not be subject to Regulation Q ceilings. The options were limited. While living from hand to mouth and operating out of borrowed offices, they hit on the idea of a money market mutual fund that would represent an investment in shares of a fund rather than deposits subject to bank regulation. After spending years overcoming myriad operational and SEC obstacles, the Reserve Fund was offered to the public in late 1972. It didn't take off, however, until an article on the fund appeared in the *New York Times* on January 7, 1973. Soon the phones were ringing off the hook with calls from small investors seeking a market rate for their savings. By the end of 1973, assets totaled $100 million, and other funds, including Fidelity and Dreyfus, joined the battle for the consumer dollar. The first fund consisted mainly of government securities and negotiable CDs of major banks, including Citibank. They had considered buying commercial paper, but in the aftermath of the collapse of Penn Central, that was thought to be a risky investment. With his Citibank credit training behind him, Brown scrupulously analyzed the condition of the major banks, seeking only those CDs of the most creditworthy institutions. Of Wriston's negotiable CD, Brown would later say, "We couldn't have done it without them."

Wriston later thanked his former colleague for his innovation, saying, "Henry, you did us a favor by inventing the money market fund. It started to create efficiency in the banking industry."

For some institutions, like Morgan Guaranty, which relied heavily on purchased money anyway, the money funds were a godsend. They were a major purchaser of Morgan's jumbo CDs, providing Morgan with a convenient funding mechanism. "We weren't sensitive to Regulation Q," Morgan chairman Lewis Preston said later. "The collection was done by the money market funds. We were in effect buying our money from them."

In an address to securities analysts some years later, Wriston reflected on the significance of that development. "For decades," he said, bankers have "worried about disintermediation, about money going directly from saver to user without a bank as intermediary. As usual, the blow came from the blind side. What we have today is, if I may coin a term, bi-intermediation. Instead of removing an intermediary, we've added one. At one time, banks collected deposits from families, lumped them together, and made loans. Today, a Dreyfus, an Oppenheimer, a Fidelity, collects savings from families, lumps them together, sells them to banks for CDs, and then the banks make loans. Today, instead of one intermediary between saver and user, we have two."

Suddenly bankers were forced to watch helplessly as cheap retail deposits walked out the door to the money funds and returned as largely unregulated and more expensive time deposits. The advent of the money market funds further highlighted the growing obsolescence of bank investments in brick-and-mortar branches. The money funds needed only a phone number and switchboard operators. The coming of age of money funds would also lend credence to Citibank's argument that if banks had to borrow at market rates, they should be permitted to lend at market rates as well.

The thrift industry was even more bent out of shape on money funds than Walter Wriston was. Regulated rates were intended largely to preserve the thrift industry, whose primary mission in life was to make possible the

American dream: home ownership. As the thinking went, if ceilings came off deposits, thrifts could not afford to extend mortgages, and voters could not afford to buy homes. By legislative fiat, savings and loans were able to offer cheap mortgages. In effect, savers were subsidizing home buyers. But the thrifts did not exactly stand still in the face of these new pressures. Also in 1972, the Consumer Savings Bank, a small savings bank in Worcester, Massachusetts, discovered a gaping loophole in the banking law that it believed would enable it to drive through forty-year-old rules against paying interest on checking accounts. It created the so-called negotiable order of withdrawal, or NOW account—identical in everything but name to a checking account—that paid interest while permitting customers to write checks. Within two years every New England state permitted the NOW, and two years later New York followed. By 1981 the NOW account had taken its place alongside the old passbook savings account as a permanent part of the American financial services scene.

For both banks and consumers, however, there was a downside to all this. If banks were to pay interest on checking accounts, they would have to recoup the income some other way. The NOW account accelerated the trend toward increased fees on bank services, particularly for small accounts.

Citing the NOW account, Wriston told a university audience in 1977 that "the line between commercial and savings banks is going to erode to the point where you can't see it at all."

By early 1973 it was hard for Arthur Burns and other regulators to dispute Wriston's claim that Citibank was special and deserved to be treated accordingly. On January 21, Citibank reported earnings of nearly $202 million for 1972, up 20 percent over 1971, becoming the first American banking institution to pass the $200 million mark in earnings. Not only did Citibank beat its 15 percent earnings growth target by a wide margin, but it passed rival Bank of America as the nation's most profitable banking company. In footings, Citibank remained number two, but in profits—what really mattered to Wriston—Citibank was now the bank to beat. All this was being driven by loan growth—nearly 17 percent in 1972 and a whopping 27 percent in 1973—which gave Arthur "Go Slow" Burns fits.

Although the bank's earnings were hurt by the lid Burns had placed on the prime rate, the damage was offset by the favorable impact of a devalued dollar and floating exchange rates on overseas earnings. By early 1973, Wriston could report that "now it will take 10 percent fewer marks, yen, francs, et cetera to make up one dollar of earnings abroad." Citibank would thrive on the inflationary, chaotic, free-floating financial world of the 1970s. Foreign exchange earnings would represent a sizable chunk of the company's bottom line, making stars out of intense, faceless men in shirtsleeves who lived in a world of phone consoles and ticker tapes and screamed and yelled at their counterparts in Zurich, London, and Tokyo. For years these returns would mask the difficulties Citibank experienced in corporate lending, particularly in Europe.

While visiting top monetary officials in Kuwait, Wriston savored his triumph. All of his projections and plans were on track, and then some. The cheer, however, was interrupted by a call from his old friend Aristotle Onassis. Ari's son, Alexander, had died on January 23 after injuries suffered in the crash of a private plane in Athens the day before. Two companions of the young Onassis were seriously hurt, and Alexander was brain-dead when he arrived at the hospital. After his sister, Christina, jetted in from Brazil to see him alive for the last time, doctors pulled the plug on the life-support systems.

Ari and Jackie were in New York when the tragedy struck. Seven years earlier, Onassis had consoled Wriston and Cassy when Bobby died, and Wriston was determined to return his kindness. He cut the trip to Kuwait short to be with Ari in Athens. It would be the last time Wriston would see his old friend alive.

Grieved as Onassis was over his son's death, he was also troubled by growing financial problems at Olympic Airways. The carrier's difficulties would grow worse, however. Onassis was convinced that the CIA had sabotaged his son's plane, and his public accusations to that effect progressively undermined public confidence in the airline. The pressure mounted over the next year with the quadrupling of oil prices and hence of jet fuel, and Onassis ultimately demanded, albeit unsuccessfully, a capital infusion from the Greek government.

Wriston responded to his plea for help with Olympic Airways by summoning Anne Meschino, by then one of his top transportation lenders, to Greece. The idea was to figure out a way for Onassis to hold on to the airline. After years of late-night negotiations with the Greek government, Onassis was forced to turn it back on January 15, 1975, in a settlement worth $69 million. It was not one of Onassis's better transactions. When the debts were paid off and the dust settled, Onassis was left with assets worth about $35 million, a meager return on an investment he had held for twenty years, *Fortune* concluded in October 1975. Onassis enjoyed Olympic tremendously. Said Meschino, "He hated to give it up."

Wriston by now had moved closer to his goal of creating a well-balanced institution that bobbed and weaved with the global punches, where a loss in one country or one market or business would be offset by a windfall in another according to the actuarial base. This time a drop in domestic earnings was more than offset by a 55 percent surge in overseas profits. In March 1973, Wriston announced a two-for-one stock split. Charting his own course amid the intensifying debate over bank capital, Wriston was intent on burnishing Citibank's image as an institution that was in a league of its own. Three years after Penn Central, that aura of invincibility was about to be shaken once again. This time the problem was a high-flying financial services holding company called Equity Funding.

Citibank was agent bank in a syndicate of banks that had lent $52 million to the now-shaky company. Nearly half of that amount was lent by Citibank, the rest by Wells Fargo, Franklin National, and Security National.

Before long, rumors spread through the market of trouble at Equity Funding, and the news soon burst onto the front pages of the nation's financial press. The company, it quickly emerged, had reported income from insurance policies it had fabricated out of whole cloth. Its chairman and president, Stanley Goldblum, had connived with his auditing firm, which had been taken over earlier by the firm of Seidman & Seidman, to create this fiction. For years, the opinion of an independent auditor had been considered sacrosanct. Bankers relied on auditors as if they were promises signed in blood. In fact, Equity Funding was a scam from day one. It was a massive securities fraud, pure and simple. Just like Ivar Kreuger and salad oil.

At the very moment in time when Wriston was stepping up his drive on every front to persuade Washington and Wall Street that Citibank was different from other banks—that, indeed, it was not really a bank at all but a diverse global financial institution—Equity Funding was a bombshell of an embarrassment.

Equity Funding would demonstrate once again the hazards of making loans to holding companies. Humiliation was piled on top of humiliation when it was disclosed that before the scandal broke, Equity Funding officials had conned a Citibank officer into releasing to the company $20 million worth of collateral. That security took the form of a stock certificate representing 100 percent of the stock of Northern Life Insurance Company, which was financially sound. The other banks were furious over this idiotic decision; agent banks are supposed to inform their syndicate members of any change in the status of their security. Shortly thereafter, a California insurance department official chimed in with yet another embarrassing accusation: that Citibank returned the collateral because the bank had a "very friendly relationship with the principal perpetrators of the fraud." The *Wall Street Journal* was on top of the story early on, disclosing information on the case faster than Citibank could obtain and verify its own facts. Meanwhile, as other banks concluded that they wouldn't get paid by Equity Funding, they began to demand payment from deep-pockets Citibank.

"Wriston was madder than hell," said one observer. He would drop into Angermueller's office nearly every day, show him the latest clips, and demand, "What are you going to do about this?" Citibankers were making statements to reporters that backfired, prompting the bank's press officer to order them, "If this is the best you can say, don't say anything."

According to John Ingraham, Citibank got out with all of its principal, as did all of the other banks in the group, losing only the post-bankruptcy interest. Citibank had been secured by a pledge of three insurance companies that Goldblum had acquired in 1972. When the shenanigans were uncovered, Equity Funding was about to merge Equity Funding Life of America into one of the other companies under the guise of tax savings, and was prevented from doing that when the fraud came to light. Three years later, in an unusually rapid rehabilitation, Equity Funding was revived as Equity-Orion, a new

entity built around the two insurance companies that had emerged unscathed.

For all the embarrassment, Equity Funding reinforced the lesson of
Penn Central—that Citibank was not immune from disaster. Citibank would
learn how to control its credit standards better than most. But the lessons
would prove to be inadequate and short-lived. One of those lessons was to
forbid the officers who made the mess to try to dig themselves out of it.

The Equity Funding incident was troubling, but Wriston knew that it,
too, would pass. He wasn't so sure about another thorn in his side—wage and
price controls. In January 1973, just before beginning what would turn out to
be his truncated second term, President Nixon suddenly announced that he
was terminating Phase II of the controls and replacing it with a more voluntary Phase III. Like the restraints themselves, efforts to administer them had
been marked by discord. A pay board and price commission had been established to oversee wages and prices, but most of the labor representatives had
walked off, rendering it virtually defunct. Burns supported a continuation of
controls, declaring in a December 29, 1972, speech in Toronto that if they
weren't maintained, collective bargaining agreements and the push for profits
could "generate a new wave of inflation."

Back in 1971, Wriston and Palmer had floated the prime in the hope—a
vain hope, as it turned out—that they could depoliticize the benchmark rate.
Little more than a year later, in response to harangues from Fed chairman
Arthur Burns and his Committee on Interest and Dividends, Citibank was
forced to cut the spread between the commercial paper rate and the base rate
to three-eighths of 1 percent from one half. And just a few months later, in
February 1973, Burns forced Citibank to suspend the floating base rate formula altogether. The profits of the big banks were being eroded because they
were increasingly having to pay a market rate for funds but couldn't charge a
market rate on many of their loans. In fact, the locked-in rates affected $7
billion, or 30 percent, of Wriston's $21 billion portfolio. Meanwhile, Burns
was trying to establish a "split rate" system for large businesses, which would
not be subject to CID scrutiny, and another for small businesses, whose borrowing costs were far more politically sensitive.

On April 19, Citibank announced that it was reinstating its floating rate
formula. The prime was initially set at 6¾ percent, but the formula implied a
rate three fourths of 1 percent higher. For Burns, that was like waving a red
flag before a bull. When the news hit the papers the next morning, Burns
phoned Wriston demanding an explanation and ordered his secretary to tran-
scribe the conversation for posterity. Burns insisted that Wriston "promptly"
issue a "clarifying statement."

"I don't know exactly what you would say," Wriston replied stubbornly. "The only thing I could think of to clarify would be if you put some
time frame [for a rate increase] in there."

"That might be helpful," Burns said.

"I wouldn't know how to arrive at that period," Wriston told him.
"That would be my problem."

Burns replied that Wriston's move could undermine his efforts to remove the prime from the political arena. The two men danced in circles. By the end of the conversation, Burns's anger was evident.

"Let me see what I can think up to say," Wriston said. "The problem is that issuing something may confuse it more than saying nothing and doing nothing."

"If you don't issue a clarifying statement, I'll have to take action. I don't want to take action," Burns said.

"Let me see what we can do," Wriston said.

By this time the only hope for a return to the free market was George Shultz, who had replaced John Connally as Treasury secretary in May 1972. While Wriston admired the gregarious Connally for his winning personality and formidable ability to disarm critics, he would find that he had considerably more in common with the reserved former professor whom President Nixon had chosen as Connally's replacement. Like Wriston, Shultz was the son of a scholar, a redoubtable history professor who, among other accomplishments, had founded a training institute for Wall Streeters. Having been a professor of industrial relations and dean of the University of Chicago Graduate School of Business before moving to Washington in January 1969 as President Nixon's first secretary of labor, George Shultz was a staunch monetarist and free marketeer. But unlike others in academia or government who shared Shultz's views, Wriston was a real-world practitioner. And for that reason, when Wriston spoke, Shultz did more than listen. He acted.

Wriston and Shultz had first met when Shultz moved to President Nixon's Office of Management and Budget from the Labor Department, which he had headed in the first two years of the Nixon administration. As OMB director, Shultz had been a reluctant participant in the August 1971 decision to impose wage and price controls. But when Shultz became Treasury secretary, he would become the most influential cabinet member after Henry Kissinger, and the administration's most vociferous opponent of the policy.

In late 1972, the Nixon administration recruited Harvard Dean John Dunlop to oversee the Cost of Living Council and ride herd over wages and prices. Dunlop, a labor specialist, had been shocked when Nixon announced the controls in 1971. That summer he had written a letter to the *New York Times* criticizing an editorial endorsing controls, and the week before controls were imposed, Dunlop had received a personal note from Nixon professing agreement with his letter. Dunlop and Shultz, who were old friends, formed the Labor-Management Advisory Committee in the belief that the wage and price control program couldn't function at all without the support and views of top labor leaders and businessmen. Their choices read like a Who's Who of American business and labor: for management, Steve Bechtel, Ed Carter, Heath Larry, Jim Roche, and Wriston; and for labor, I. W. Abel, George Meany, Paul Hall, Frank Fitzsimmons, and Leonard Woodcock.

But in choosing Wriston, they selected someone they knew was convinced beyond a doubt that the country couldn't function with controls. Unlike Burns, Wriston knew that controls fueled inflation rather than dampened it. Wriston's principal purpose in joining the committee was to do whatever he could to eliminate controls altogether. Predictably, this motley gathering of union chiefs and business bigwigs began on an adversarial note. They agreed that the only way they would get to first base was by avoiding issues they knew they could never agree on. But before the group's service to the Nixon administration concluded, Wriston would forge personal and philosophical bonds with some very unlikely figures, namely the late AFL-CIO chief George Meany and Paul Hall, the irreverent former head of the Seafarers International Union. The union bosses and the businessmen had barely spoken to one another before, except over the bargaining table. Each was curious about what made the other tick.

Coincidentally, Meany had squared off against Henry Wriston when he was head of President Eisenhower's Commission on National Goals. "Meany used to drive him [Henry Wriston] up the wall," said Wriston later. "He would object to everything. Dad thought he was very intractable, but at the end of the day, the commission did in fact produce a pretty good book. George went along with 90 percent of it. He represented his constituency pretty good." Describing Meany as a "friend," Wriston once said, "He can hold up a can of soup on television and destroy, with one line, an hour-long reasoned speech about why business's return on net worth is too low. What we need is somebody in the business community who is as good at the one-liners as George Meany is." Wriston certainly fit the bill.

After meeting at Treasury, the group usually adjourned to the White House for a session with Nixon. Wriston remembers those meetings as being fraught with fear over what might come out of the mouth of Paul Hall. "I was in the infantry for a while, but he had expressions no soldier could ever dream up," said Wriston, recalling Hall's habit of interspersing his otherwise eloquent statements, spoken in a resonant voice in almost Shakespearean English, with expletives from the Brooklyn docks. "We used to live in terror. We'd all sit there hanging on to our thumbs hoping that Paul would not say that in front of Nixon, and he never did." Only later, when the Watergate tapes became public, did they discover that Hall would have been right at home in the Nixon White House.

The committee deliberated over everything from whether to raise the price of bacon and the minimum wage for railway workers to whether the government should issue national identity cards, which Wriston condemned as the first step toward a police state. As free marketeers, both Shultz and Wriston agreed that the world financial system could best achieve equilibrium by freeing itself from the remaining links to the old par value foreign exchange system. In February, Nixon was forced to order yet another devaluation of the dollar, a move that sparked even greater fluctuations in its value.

Then, in March 1973, in the middle of the group's debate over wage and price controls, Shultz journeyed to Paris for a conference that would mark the end of fixed exchange rates and the beginning of a new era of floating rates. The linkage of foreign exchange rates and gold would be gone forever. The Smithsonian Agreement, Shultz said later, was "hailed by President Nixon and Secretary Connally as a great thing. I saw it as a great mistake. It got put into place much to people's relief at the time. It didn't work. At the time I became secretary of the Treasury it was clear it wasn't working."

Although the Bretton Woods system of fixed exchanges pegged to the dollar had clearly outlived its usefulness, there were those, including then undersecretary of the Treasury Paul Volcker, who were reluctant to abandon the dollar standard for the brave new world of floating rates. For reassurance that he was on the right course, Shultz turned to his New York banker friend, the only global practitioner among his advisers.

Wriston was convinced, for a variety of reasons, that the old system of parities could no longer survive. In a world where data moved around the earth in nanoseconds, the information standard, Wriston believed, had replaced the dollar standard. In effect, clinging to a fixed value for the U.S. currency was entirely inappropriate in an age when traders were able to obtain instantaneous up-to-date economic and financial data bearing on the dollar's value. Indeed, it was this recognition that led Wriston to conclude that information about money, rather than money itself, had become the foundation for the business of banking and finance. "The flow of information about a nation's fiscal, economic, military, and social policies now moves with such speed and is evaluated so quickly by so many people that it has overwhelmed any system that wasn't congruent with the marketplace. When the world grew up around the dollar standard and our relative position declined, you had to have another system," Wriston observed later.

In a November 12, 1985, Op-Ed article in the *Wall Street Journal,* Wriston cited Nixon's 1971 decision to float the dollar as a key step in the emergence of a global information standard. Shortly after the article was published, he received a handwritten note from the former president: "I often wonder whether I was right to float the dollar. . . . I just read your piece [in the *Wall Street Journal*], and I can see now I really had no alternative. Thank you for writing it, because I've been worrying about it ever since." In the early 1970s, Wriston had surprised his banking colleagues by suggesting that their competition was Sears and GE, not the bank across the street. Before long, he would add to that list his "competitors" in the information business, notably Dow Jones and Reuters.

On June 13, 1973, the Nixon administration, perhaps to demonstrate that it was dealing with matters other than Watergate, had announced a second sixty-day price freeze, over the opposition of Shultz, Dunlop, and the Labor-Management Advisory Committee. Shultz himself declared that the entire effort had been a failure. He did not say publicly at the time that the administration's decision to reimpose price controls led to his decision to quit his post, however. That decision was not made public until March 1974. Shultz was so disgusted by the June 1973 move that he relegated oversight of the entire process to Dunlop, saying, "You go do it," Dunlop said later. But probably the labor-management group's single most significant act was its unanimous insistence, beginning with a statement on July 10, 1973, and continuing for months thereafter, that Nixon scrap the program.

Wriston recalled that "one day we were sitting there and George Meany says, 'You know, Walt, this is a crazy thing, this wage-price controls.'"

"All the businessmen think it's only wage controls, and all the labor guys think it's only price controls," Wriston replied, "and as it turns out, we were both wrong."

"Well, let's get rid of the damn thing," the labor leader suggested.

"It should get a silver bullet through the head," Wriston said, prompting Meany to refer to Wriston as the "Silver Bullet" from that day forward.

"Where do we go from here?" Meany asked.

"Why don't I go out and borrow a typewriter?" Wriston said, volunteering to write a declaration of the group to the president. Wriston left the room and spent fifteen minutes pecking out a sloppily typed draft in a secretary's office.

"You're working out of your job classification," Shultz said.

"Yeah, but I'm getting the job done," Wriston replied.

After Wriston and the other members produced a document everyone agreed on, Shultz joined the meeting and asked, "This is what you fellows want?"

"Yes, sir, this is what we all want," a member of the panel replied, "except Mr. Dunlop, who wants to phase them [the controls] out."

"If they're phased out, they'll be here in the year 2000," Wriston added.

At Shultz's urging, everyone signed the document. Then, as Wriston put it, "We marched over to the White House and laid it on the president's desk," and Meany informed Nixon that there was "real political support to get rid of controls." But, as Wriston recalled with frustration, "The president didn't act on it. He acted the other way." While Dunlop oversaw the sector-by-sector phase-out of controls, the business and labor leaders continued to draft memos to the president urging him to eliminate them immediately and completely. It would be nearly a year before they would taste the fruits of their victory.

Wriston's disdain for wage and price controls was exceeded only by his antipathy toward the Eastern Bloc nations and their centralized economies. But he took the world as it was. "He wanted to find a way to interact with every system in an appropriate way," said a former top overseas officer. Although Citibank ultimately lent to Poland and Yugoslavia and helped finance Soviet trade, Wriston could never work up any enthusiasm for any Communist state other than Hungary.

Wriston was too loyal a Republican not to acquiesce to the policies of his president, however. With the warming of relations between Washington and Moscow in the early 1970s, major U.S. banks were called upon to assume a heightened role as instruments of American foreign policy. Secretary of

State Henry Kissinger was ruefully ignorant of economics and its role in global politics, and only began to appreciate its significance after the OPEC oil embargo. But according to one participant in a Pentagon meeting that preceded one of Kissinger's trips to Moscow, Kissinger spoke of the need to encourage trade and financial ties to the Soviet Union. But he also wanted to spur economic relations with the Eastern Bloc countries to wean them away from Moscow. The emphasis was to be placed, as General Alexander Haig remarked later, on those countries that "were less than dogmatic in their Marxist orientation and less supportive of the Soviet Union."

Haig said later, "I'm quite confident that credits and loans were made with a political objective in mind, and probably at the expense of more sensible financial [considerations]." He added that "on the other hand, there are times when that has to be the case."

Chase's David Rockefeller plunged wholeheartedly into forging ties to the Eastern sphere. In May 1973, Chase Manhattan opened for business at One Karl Marx Square in Moscow, becoming the first U.S. bank to operate an office there since the Bolshevik Revolution. Shortly thereafter, Bank of America also got permission to set up shop. Even as "détente" became the new buzzword in international diplomacy, Wriston remained the die-hard economic cold warrior. Unlike his less cynical counterpart at Chase, Wriston had to be dragged to Red Square. "We were probably not wholly enthusiastic about it," said international chief G. A. "Al" Costanzo, with some understatement.

Wriston's participation in the decision to open a Moscow office was one of the few instances in which he personally carried the ball on a project that ordinarily would have been delegated to the officer in charge of the territory. That, of course, was in sharp contrast to the practice of David Rockefeller and other top bankers of the era. When Wriston was approached with such proposals, he typically said, "Well, we'll have to talk to Farley," or to some other senior officer, recalled a former colleague. "Walter wanted to be sure a business was set up on a businesslike basis."

Part of the price the Soviets were trying to exact from Western bankers for the dubious privilege of operating in Moscow was the fixed rate, below-market loan, a suggestion Wriston wouldn't entertain even for his best Western customers. Victor D. Brunst, a veteran of Eastern Bloc banking, and senior international lender Victor Prall were to fly to Moscow for the final round of negotiations with the Soviets, and the Citibank backers of the Moscow office persuaded Wriston to join them there to try to break the deadlock. On their way, Brunst and Prall stopped in Hungary and Poland, visits that turned into every traveler's worst nightmare. Hungary was battling an outbreak of hoof-and-mouth disease, Prall recalled, so when they reached Poland they were removed from the plane and ordered to a decontamination chamber. Their travails continued when they reached Moscow. Because of a shortage of hotel rooms with private baths, Prall and Brunst had to share a room and a bed until Prall pulled rank and ordered Brunst to take a room without a bath. On his first visit to the public bathroom, Brunst encountered three drunken Russians standing over a single toilet and urinating all over each other.

The Wristons arrived in Moscow less than an hour after Brunst and Prall had landed. The Russians assigned them a car and driver who was built like a longshoreman and sported a butterfly tattoo on his tree-trunk-sized neck. The driver supposedly spoke no English, but after a day of riding around with him Prall was suspicious. He was certain that the man was an English-speaking KGB agent who was taking in everything they said.

"Oh, it isn't so," said Wriston.

As the car turned into Dzerzhinsky Square, where the KGB had its headquarters, Prall whispered to Wriston that he was going to say something outrageous to test his theory.

"Jeez, don't throw a bomb in the doorway!" Prall exclaimed. The driver slammed on the brakes. "I thought Walt was gonna wet his pants," Prall said later. The adventure didn't end there. At the Bolshoi, Soviets—apparently unfamiliar with Western-style sheer stockings—pinched Kathy Wriston's legs to see if they were bare or clad in panty hose. In their hotel room, for the benefit of the bugging devices, the Wristons bantered about what a wonderful time they were having; during the trip, the film in their camera turned yellow as if it had been put through an X-ray machine.

In the meetings with the Soviet officials responsible for approving the office, Wriston steadfastly refused to grant the Soviet Union the loans except on a floating-rate market basis. "They were asking for outrageous things," explained Costanzo. At a final meeting, neither party had budged and Wriston prepared to call it quits and return home. Finally, the Soviets caved in. "They realized there was no give from this guy," said Costanzo, adding that David Rockefeller had gone through the same exercise and agreed to participate in an $86 million below-market loan, said to be the first made by a U.S. bank to the Soviet Union. According to former senior officer Michael Callen, Chase did so because it was still operating on the average rather than marginal cost of funds. For Citibank, said Callen, declining to lend to the Soviet Union on the basis of an average cost of money was a "no-brainer." The Chase loan proved ill-advised for other reasons, too. It later turned out that the Soviets used the proceeds for military purposes, according to a former senior Chase officer.

To Wriston, lending to the Eastern Bloc, unlike lending to other undeveloped countries, was a political, rather than an economic, decision. No one had to remind Wriston that those czarist bonds the Soviet government had repudiated during the 1917 Revolution were still gathering dust in the vault at 399 Park. Moreover, because the Soviet Union and the Eastern Bloc nations were not members of the International Monetary Fund and the World Bank, no one had the slightest clue about their economies. "We made enough mistakes when we got information," Wriston said later. But most bothersome was the uncertainty about whether any particular dictator was going to last or whether, as Wriston put it, the Soviets "were going to come over the wall." Although Citibank lent to Yugoslavia, Hungary, and Poland's Bank Handlowy, the amounts were small relative to those of other banks, and relative to the volume of loans that Citibank later made in Latin America.

Five days in the Soviet Union was about as much as the Wristons could stand. After receiving permission to open a representative office, they gladly returned home. Their reward was an invitation to a White House state dinner, where they joined President Nixon and Soviet general secretary Leonid Brezhnev in toasting their efforts to achieve world peace. Wriston's subsequent visits to Moscow confirmed that his initial skepticism was well founded. His hotel room was bugged, and on at least one visit his luggage was broken into. Worse still, the Soviets refused to permit Citibank to screen and hire its own employees. "They were certainly KGB agents," Costanzo said later.

The Moscow office opened in the city's National Hotel in the spring of 1974, but in the six years it remained open, it never made a dime. Said Wriston, "We were under a lot of pressure to open an office. . . . As far as I know, no one ever did any business there except Pepsi."

Later, Romanian president Nicolae Ceauşescu, the tyrannical ruler of that most oppressive regime, called on the top management of the New York banks in search of one that would open an office in Bucharest. After receiving a chilly reception at Citibank, Ceauşescu strode across Park Avenue to Manny Hanny, which readily obliged him. In early 1974, at a luncheon for Ceauşescu hosted by MHT chairman Gabriel Hauge, Manufacturers announced plans to open a branch in Bucharest, the first by a Western bank in a Socialist country. One reason was that trade between the United States and Romania was the largest of any Eastern Bloc country. But later it would become clear that this trade was at the expense of the Romanian population, which was deprived of basic consumer goods in order to enable Ceauşescu to earn hard currency and tighten his grip on power. Hungary was the only Eastern Bloc nation where Citibank felt reasonably comfortable. In late 1974 it established an office there, which remains in business to this day.

Wriston clearly was more excited about his plans for a new office tower in Midtown than he was about his rep office in Moscow.

Several years earlier, a real estate developer had popped into Bill Spencer's office and asked if he'd like to buy the plot next door. Spencer replied that there was no way Citibank could ever assemble an entire city block. "I can do it," the visitor replied. The agent set up a dummy company—No Name Realty—and for several years bought up parcels in the square block area between Third and Lexington from Fifty-third to Fifty-fourth Street. Expenses were charged to earnings. Only Spencer and Wriston were aware of the plan; the bank couldn't even lend the developer any money out of concern that the effort would become public. "It was a cat-and-mouse game," said one Citibank officer. "We wanted to get the lots before the word got out and the prices went up."

According to Wriston, their agent succeeded in buying up all but two parcels, one a building reputedly occupied by individuals with Mafia ties, and another housing doctors' offices. When agents working for Wriston and Spencer visited the building allegedly used by organized crime members, they carried walkie-talkies so that colleagues outside could be sure they were safe. One of the doctors was an eye specialist whose patients included Wriston and numerous Citibankers; he resisted selling their cooperative building because of the heavy capital gains taxes they would have to pay. While reading the eye chart in the office of Dr. Walter Peretz, Wriston himself clinched the deal. He proposed a tax-free transaction in which Citibank would swap shares of its stock for shares in the co-op.

Once it owned all of the land, Citibank launched a contest, to be judged by Wriston's sister, Barbara, an expert on art and architecture, for the design of an office tower. The winner was the Cambridge, Massachusetts, architectural firm of Hugh Stubbins, Jr., who had been recommended by operations chief John Reed. In contrast to the monolithic and austere 399 Park, which contributed no public space, Citicorp Center was designed as a neighborhood mecca.

After being snookered by contractors on 111 Wall, Wriston and Spencer were determined not to repeat those mistakes. No one ever even figured out exactly what the downtown operations center really cost, because Citibank paid for cement that was never used. "This town is so crooked you have to count the bags of cement," Wriston growled later. This time the building would be built on time and on budget.

In late July, Citibank announced that the fifty-nine-story, $160 million tower would stand on a platform 112 feet, or ten stories, above the ground and would be the fifth-tallest building in Manhattan. Said director Franklin Thomas, "This building from the beginning was planned as a life force, as a center, as a source of energy and commitment back to the city and the people." In line with that goal, Citibank also agreed to build a new chapel for the congregation of Saint Peter's Lutheran Church, which had stood on the building site for seventy years. While the economics of the building may not have been daring at the time of the announcement, they would prove to be later, as the city slid inexorably into a financial abyss. By the time construction got under way, commercial rental space in the area commanded only about $7 per square foot, compared with the $14 or so a square foot Citicorp Center required to operate in the black.

In the four years since the 1969 McKinsey reorganization, the unaddressed problem of how to serve multinational customers, Citibank's traditional strength, had festered like an open sore.

There was a Mexican standoff between Citibank's domestic corporate group, which "owned" multinational clients because it happened to be headquartered in the United States, and the all-powerful SENOFs, who were responsible for dealing with the bank's overseas subsidiaries. The latter were steadfast in their refusal to relinquish control in their countries of multinationals like IBM or Du Pont. Overseas czar Al Costanzo demanded a postponement of the inevitable, and a sort of compromise was struck whereby the country heads, to protect their turf, agreed to "help out" their domestic banking colleagues. That didn't work, however, and the debate over how these customers would be served and who would serve them went on for two years, pitting corporate banking chief Reuben Richards against Costanzo. To be sure, with all of the turmoil already going on at Citibank, overhauling the International Banking Group might have caused more disruption than the bank could handle at one time. But not until Citibank fixed this problem could it truly call itself a global bank.

The McKinsey reorganization had already ignited open warfare between the country heads and leasing, one of the first so-called products to be marketed worldwide by a separate organization set up for that purpose. Said former Citibanker Michael Callen, "If I was the king of Spain and ran our Spanish operation, and some guy from a product group like leasing came in to talk to one of my customers, my attitude was, 'Nobody's allowed on my property without my approval, because I own this.' " They [product salesmen] would, according to Callen, arrive in a country without informing local officers. "Senior management's answer was 'Be mature, behave like adults.' They [senior managers] never got to the trenches to find out how much fighting and friction was going on, or the amount of ill will being generated," Callen remembered. In the early 1970s, multinational customers, relative to their size and importance to Citibank, were often treated just as shabbily as the $150-a-week waitress trying to force the Citibank back office bureaucracy to correct a $5 error on her checking account.

The evolution into the World Corporation Group began in 1971 as an attempt to gather information on the profitability of global accounts. In effect, it was a centralized information system with no account or marketing responsibility. "As we began to develop an information base," Wriston recalled, "we realized we didn't have any information that was usable. There was information, God knows. But if you said to somebody, 'What is the GM account worth?' somebody would say our New York relationship earned X dollars last year. But then you'd say, 'What about their foreign exchange business in Uruguay?' They'd reply, 'Christ, we don't know about Uruguay.' " Such problems came to Wriston's attention when the chairman of a major company called to complain. " 'Hey, with all the business we're doing with you in country Y, you're charging us an arm and a leg. Don't you want our business?' Then you'd get on the horn and call up the guys, and they'd say, 'What do we know about what someone else is doing somewhere else in the world?' " As Wriston's task force pulled together data on multinationals, they discovered that they were losing money in some countries and making it in others. They concluded that serving these customers demanded more than an information system. It called for a full-fledged marketing effort in which the entire bank would be integrated to meet the demands of this vital customer segment.

This problem surfaced with one customer after another, and with the coming of age of the multinational corporation, Wriston could continue to ignore the problem only at his peril. At stake was whether Citibank, which had relationships with 80 percent of the world's largest companies, would muddle along as a big U.S.-based bank with lots of branches and offices abroad, or become a global financial services company matching its multinational clients in worldliness and sophistication. "People in the international group, to start with, couldn't believe there was something bigger than the profit center," chief lender Reuben Richards said. "They didn't understand that it was more profitable to serve a customer as a single relationship than in the haphazard way they were doing."

Wriston unveiled the new organization in a meeting of senior officers at New York's University Club in mid-1973. Not since Citibank had set up the specialized industry group in the early 1950s had there been so much internal rancor over a reorganization, and rarely had Wriston himself been subject to more hostility from his own associates. To some, this was another example of Wriston's tendency to overhaul the bank before it had even recovered from earlier reorganizations. Wriston, however, believed the organization had to change frequently to remain competitive and reflect the marketplace, and that people who worked in a constant state of ferment were more alert than those in more stable organizations. And this, he believed, would be even more true in the deregulated world of banking that he hoped to create.

Wriston himself was only "grudgingly in favor" of a multinational unit, according to Richards. "Having run the international group, he was sort of 'from Missouri,'" Richards said. "He was worried that having a cell in each branch devoted to the World Corporation Group was going to be an irritant."

Both Wriston and Spencer were furious over the reaction of Citibank's overseas rank and file. Recalled former Citibanker Ed Hoffman, "They asked for questions and were met with a surly silence. Walt and Bill [Spencer] felt this, and were angry, and stalked out," leaving Al Costanzo to defend the plan. The reaction, acknowledged Wriston later with some understatement, "was less than enthusiastic."

In the end, Wriston, while recognizing the shortcomings of yet another bureaucracy, was forced to "jam it down everyone's throat," as one former senior officer put it. Wriston, he said, was willing "to face those kinds of issues."

Four hundred big companies, most of them domestic, were yanked out of the international and domestic corporate banking groups and handed on a silver platter to the new multinational unit. Once again, the losers had to submit to third-party binding arbitration, as if they were parties in a contested divorce suit.

The World Corporation Group was the first application of the strategic business unit concept, in which different parts of the bank were focused like a laser beam on a market segment. Appropriately, Wriston compared the SBU to the army's fields of fire. The creation of the World Corporation Group would be the ultimate test of matrix management. The challenge was to balance the need to preserve and extend Citibank's multinational relationships without totally disrupting the country organizations.

A massive paperwork infrastructure now had to be constructed that would reveal the worldwide profitability of multinational corporate accounts. And for all its logic, the WCG unleashed upon the banking world a new bureaucracy that would spend a large proportion of its time managing and coordinating and politicking and all too little time on clientele.

For many old line country officers, the World Corporation Group was a tough adjustment. "People had been developed on the theory that geography was the critical factor, and it became difficult to move from one group to another," said former personnel chief James Griffin. Like the branch officers four years earlier, they were suddenly forced either to relinquish the local business of the IBMs, Mobils, and Du Ponts or to move with them to the new group. Many officers left Citibank for local banks.

After great turmoil and many second thoughts, even by Wriston himself, the World Corporation Group was regarded by many Citibankers as one of the bank's more successful restructurings, and before long most of America's largest banks were following in Citi's footsteps. "The competition thought we had created the magic formula," said Reuben Richards. Much of the credit for that was given to Tom Theobald, who was assigned to head the new group when it was created. "He brought people together. He was a team builder," recalled one admirer. "In a short period of time you could pick up the phone and know who would be at the other end." Under the WCG, one person understood the bank's relationship with a big company around the world. Because it served the biggest and most glamorous customers, the WCG became an elite organization. "The people in the International Banking Group were insanely jealous," said one World Corporation Group officer. Even Wriston acknowledged later that "they were the pretty girl at the party." The new organization also gave Citibank clout in squeezing more business out of multinational customers. In many instances, Citibank got to know a multinational's financial needs better than the chief financial officers themselves.

The World Corporation unit did not put an end to internal competition or profit centeritis. Far from it. Customers large and small would continue to endure dealing with different units of Citibank as if they were Chase, Morgan, and the Bank of America. Despite the irritations for big customers, there were few, if any, major corporate defections. Citibank had the largest international network of any bank, and certainly Chase and Bank of America had the same problem as Citibank, if not worse. "We had such a franchise that major corporations had to do business with us," said a former Citibank officer. "We were the only game in town." They would, he said, have to sustain a lot of pain before dumping Citibank for another bank where the irritations could be even more severe.

Multinational companies not only happened to be Citibank's strongest market segment but also exemplified, as did Citibank itself, a world without barriers, boundaries, or borders. The creation of the World Corporation

Group coincided with an increasingly high, and usually negative, profile for multinationals. Big, global corporations were targeted by some cynical observers as a sinister force driven by greed and power.

The evidence for that negative view could be seen regularly in Washington, where Senator Frank Church, inspired by the ITT scandal, had embarked on a seemingly endless investigation of multinationals' overseas activities. With revelations of slush funds and payoffs, "multinational corporation" became a dirty word. Citibank was involved on the fringes of the Church committee's probe, and Latin chief George "Jack" Clark was dispatched on March 28, 1973, to Washington to assure the Church committee that Citibank—unlike ITT—had not tried to influence the Chilean elections. Clark apparently succeeded. His testimony contained the principles that were to guide Citibank's behavior abroad from that day forward.

Meanwhile, Wriston emerged as one of the leading defenders of multinationals. He saw them as a positive force for change in the developing world. "In the ancient struggle between those who believe in an open society where men, money, and ideas can move freely across national borders and those who would return to the jungle of economic nationalism," Wriston said in a speech, "the world corporation may furnish a new weight in the balance." At the same time, of course, the critics of multinationals attacked them as exploiters of developing countries for the benefit of the rich and as intermediaries in a zero-sum game where someone had to lose for someone else to gain. In contrast, Wriston viewed multinationals as machines for creating global wealth. "The reality of a global marketplace," he said at the time, "has been the driving force pushing us along the path of developing a rational world economy. Progress which has been made owes almost nothing to political imagination. It has been the managers of the multinational corporations who have seen the world whole and moved to supply mankind's needs as efficiently as politics would allow."

In his drive to create a bank that transcended state and national borders, Wriston never stopped stirring up the pot. While he was launching the controversial World Corporation Group, he was also giving his blessing to other initiatives that would earn Citibank new enemies among correspondent bank customers in the United States and around the world. Wriston knew, for example, that Citibank had to create a modern international money-transfer system before it could call itself a global bank, and every other major international bank in the world was trying to do the same thing in the early 1970s. The Europeans, at that time, were hard at work on the Society for Worldwide Interbank Financial Telecommunication (SWIFT), a cooperative venture to facilitate international payments among banks. It was introduced in 1977 and eventually handled most of the orders to make payments through the Clearing House International Payments System (CHIPS).

If Citibank could develop the premier international funds transfer system, the world's banks and multinational companies would be forced to operate through Citibank in this key function, giving it a leg up in snaring other lucrative business. Citi would become the nexus of the world's payments system. Whenever money crossed national borders, it would have to pass through Citibank. But no effort inflicted more damage on relationships with overseas correspondent banks than MARTI, an acronym for Machine Readable Telegraphic Input. MARTI was the brainchild of Reed and his lieutenants in the operating group, but Wriston gave it his blessing. Introduced in April 1973, the system was aimed largely at European multinational corporations and banks. These customers would format their transfers, which would include CHIPS, checks, and debits and credits to Citibank accounts, in a highly structured, unambiguous code that would be transmitted by telex to London and on to New York. For years, such messages were written like letters from a college student to his parents asking for more money. The sender could say, "Hi, Charley, please send $1 million," one Citibanker recalled. In contrast, MARTI's format was so rigid that money wouldn't move unless every comma was in the right place.

For all the fuss, the hardware part of MARTI was little more than an old teletype machine that punched out a paper tape of an authorized money transfer. The tape was carried by messenger to another station where it would be fed into another device that cranked out the transfer. On D day for implementation of MARTI, senior operations officer Richard Matteis reportedly ordained that henceforth Citibank would process only transfers that arrived in Citibank format. The result was utter chaos. "Every other transfer that came in was returned. The correspondent banking network [virtually] collapsed," said one observer. It was a prime example of Wriston's determination to march to his own drummer in the world banking community and his willingness to let his people experiment to their heart's content. It was also a prime example of Citibank arrogance that was unparalleled in recent banking history.

MARTI was the quintessential example of experimentation gone awry, of innovation, cost reduction, and efficiency taken to absurd extremes. Perhaps more than any other effort, it would pit the Bob White–John Reed culture of production and efficiency against the international culture of client service. Given near-complete autonomy, White and his crew of back office zealots had forgotten—or never known—how the bank really made its money. For all his technical genius, White rarely talked with customers to find out what they wanted. "The people trying to force MARTI down the correspondents' throats didn't have clients," said former international banker John Rudy.

Despite the uproar that MARTI created, and the ill will on the part of institutional customers, MARTI was a forgivable mistake in the Citibank culture. Nonetheless, according to Rudy, it was one of a series of events that would later lead to the breakup of John Reed's operating group. Many felt that Reed, White, and Matteis and their MARTI system were damaging the bank, destroying the morale of its employees, and wrecking relationships with correspondent banks and corporate customers.

White and Matteis, who lacked marketing experience, flew to Switzerland to sell the Swiss banks on MARTI. In the back office, this effort to win over the correspondents was known as "customer engineering." "I almost fell off my chair when I heard that one," said former operations secretary Maria R. Savarese. "Who did they send over to Switzerland, the charmers of Citibank, to push MARTI down the Swiss banks' throats? When I heard that, I was so hysterical I couldn't stop laughing." Added former operations officer Jeff Franklin, "Unless you wanted to take a cuckoo clock apart and talk about how it worked, White wasn't the right guy."

In one week, according to Savarese, "[Almost] every bank we had was overdrawn, and that included the Swiss banks that were never overdrawn in their lives." Debits were hitting their accounts, but credits were not. There was such pandemonium and chaos in the back offices of Citibank that when Savarese ran into White later on the street, she slapped him angrily across the face. "Do you know what you did this week?" she shouted to a shocked White. "I was like a crazy lady," she said later. Only by working around the clock over the weekend were harried workers able to restore a semblance of stability to the international payments system. Enraged bankers were calling from all over the world about the overdrafts. One sympathetic lower-level officer, on the phone for a half hour with an irate London banker, told him, "On the ladder of success at Citibank I haven't even made the first rung. Your recourse is to call Wriston."

"The banks revolted," said former operations officer Paul Rudowski, but he added that "what MARTI was trying to accomplish is in place today in every bank in the world."

Wriston would have preferred that his operations people and his international bankers work through the MARTI problem themselves, but that wasn't likely to happen. At the height of the complaints, Wriston gathered his international bankers and operating majors into a conference room at 399 Park, recalled former senior vice president Sandra Jaffee. "He in effect let them know, 'That's it. It's got to get done. Your job is to make customers happy doing this,'" she said.

New York Clearing House executive director John Lee said later, "They were proud of [MARTI] and jealously guarded it. They were trying to get market share and weren't prone to admit they were having problems." Citibank's efforts to make MARTI work caused fits for the Clearing House, which had to delay the settlement of transactions so that MARTI could catch up. Richard Matteis would later try to put the best face on the MARTI debacle. "People's resistance to MARTI made SWIFT a success," he contended.

In Wriston's view, MARTI failed because of the inability of participating institutions to agree on the format and Citibank's inability to enforce its standards. Recalling that magnetic ink encoding of checks was accomplished only because the Fed threatened the industry with financial sanctions, Wriston said, "You'd be amazed at how quickly the world responded to that."

Meanwhile, on the domestic front, Citibank in August 1973 took another swipe at the prohibitions against interstate banking. In major U.S. cities that the correspondents regarded as their turf, Citibank opened the first in what would be a network of loan production offices, or LPOs. In effect, Citibank was telling its correspondents that it wanted to get the business directly. Said corporate lending chief Reuben Richards, "People would call me and say, 'You guys, get out of our city.' I'd say, 'Hell, no. Do you tell that to Morgan?' They'd say, 'They're not here.' And I'd say, 'They will be soon.' "

For all the turmoil that Wriston was creating inside, for all the snafus and outright disasters, Citibank by the fall of 1973 was the bank to beat. Management through chaos seemed to be working. In early September its shares were approaching their all-time high of $51.50 a share, surging 9 percent in a one-week period alone. Citibank and Wriston did not know it, but they were approaching the peak of their glory, at least from the stockholders' point of view. Critics notwithstanding, *Dun's Review* selected "Walt's bank" as one of the five best-managed corporations in America. "As a result of establishing its foreign beachheads early and experimenting with every kind of financial service before diversifying at home," *Dun's* wrote in December 1973, "Citibank developed the know-how and the executives to write banking's biggest growth story." Other banks were awed by Citibank's success and sought to emulate its hard-hitting management style and rapid growth. As the world moved inexorably toward one of the most cataclysmic economic events in modern history, Citibank (a.k.a. "Fat Citi") was the most admired banking institution in the world, and Wriston the most influential banker.

13

THE ROAD TO RIO— AND RIYADH

*T*he Israeli government called it a routine patrol. On September 13, 1973, four Israeli fighter jets were cruising over the eastern Mediterranean, possibly trespassing into Syrian airspace. Syrian President Hafez al-Assad could not have found a better excuse to start a war. He ordered a contingent of MiG fighters to intercept the Israelis, who radioed for more planes. After the dogfight, which cost Syria as many as thirteen planes to Israel's one, Assad phoned Egyptian President Anwar Sadat to urge him to initiate a joint attack on Israel. Sadat obviously needed little coaxing, and that evening ordered preparations to begin.

On October 6, Egyptian and Syrian forces launched an all-out war on Israel, a deed that evoked an outpouring of official and public sympathy in the United States for the Jewish state. Responding to this show of support, the Arab states, in a meeting on October 16, pulled out a weapon far more effective than all the men and machines they were able to muster in their ill-fated Yom Kippur War. That weapon, of course, was oil, and this would represent its first major deployment since it became the world's most vital commodity. For starters, the Arab nations announced a relatively moderate 17 percent increase in the price of a barrel of crude.

Though U.S. backing of Israel provided the excuse for using the oil weapon, there was ample economic justification as well. The imposition of wage and price controls and the devaluation of the dollar had contributed to a doubling of world commodity prices. This was an economic fact of life the Arabs could no longer ignore. With U.S. and world inflation surging, the real price of oil was actually declining.

As the war ground on, each nation in turn halted oil shipments to the United States. By 1974, oil prices had risen 400 percent, and the world economic order was changed forever. If Wriston and his colleagues had somehow missed the buildup of tensions in the Mideast that preceded the September 13 dogfight, they must have been hard-pressed to ignore it then.

While the air battle raged, Citibank executive vice president G. A. Costanzo was himself approaching Beirut on the Citibank jet for a meeting with a top Saudi finance ministry official who was vacationing in the Lebanese capital. As the plane was preparing to land, the control tower ordered it out of the area. The pilots could see the air-to-air missile tracks on their radar screen and told the Beirut tower that they had no choice but to come in. "We dove into Beirut. It was kind of messy," Costanzo recalled later with some understatement. When he arrived at his seaside hotel, the Lebanese government insisted on posting an armed guard outside his room. In a Beirut press conference, Costanzo announced magnanimously that Citibank was prepared to lend or invest at least $1 billion in the Middle East. Costanzo then left for the Persian Gulf before flying on to Nairobi for the International Monetary Fund's annual conference. Soon, however, the tables would be turned, and the Middle East would be lending to Citibank.

The main item on the agenda at the private meeting in Beirut between Costanzo and Saudi Finance Minister Muhammad Al-Ali Abal Khail was the Saudi government's desire to either nationalize Citibank's Saudi operation or force it into a joint venture. That notion had been floating around the kingdom for several years. But according to Wriston, the Saudis had been encouraged to do that by an American diplomat who had forgotten what country he was being paid to serve. "We had a long argument there," said Costanzo. "I said, 'No way.' " Costanzo told him Citibank would pack up and leave before it would share control of its branches. Within a few months, as the massive shift of the world's wealth to the desert kingdom got under way, Citibank's Saudi branches would become the most profitable in the bank's empire and the envy of the world banking community. The Saudis would have even more reason to demand a piece of the action, and Citibank would have just as much reason not to give it to them.

Important as it was to Wriston to retain total control of Citibank's own Mideast gusher, that would become something of a sideshow to the main event. As billions of dollars poured into these sheikhdoms, the world's oil-consuming nations, particularly the less-developed ones, were faced with the daunting task of how to pay their skyrocketing oil import bills, the producers faced the problem of how to spend the windfall, and the world's financial chieftains confronted the dilemma of how to redress this most grievous economic imbalance since World War II. By 1974, OPEC's oil revenues were pouring in at an annual rate of more than $100 billion. The buzz phrase that was applied to this process was the "recycling of petrodollars." No one was more ready and willing to show the world how to do it than Walter B. Wriston.

Everything was now beginning to fall into place for the biggest peacetime transfer of capital—and the biggest lending spree—in world history. Regulation Q and capital controls had pushed lending to foreign borrowers offshore. The Eurocurrency market had evolved into a vast but efficient arena for syndicating multibillion-dollar credits. Citibank was well positioned to be the agent bank for large syndications. It had long ago overcome its historical antipathy toward cross-border lending and had established a beachhead in London to conduct this business. In addition, it operated a network of offices in other major money centers that, Wriston said, served as "money mobilizers" for its activities in developing nations. Citibank also had the most advanced global communications technology, including batteries of telex machines that could quickly crank out reams of loan agreements for the hundreds of institutions around the world that were clamoring to participate in these deals.

In fact, even before the embargo, Citibank was warming up to the idea of extending loans to developing countries. International lending had begun to take off in 1971. Much of the impetus for this development came from the vigorous economic growth in the developing world, most notably in Brazil and Mexico. Citibank's overseas operating earnings already amounted to well over half of the bank's total earnings. Foreign deposits at Citibank and Morgan Guaranty now exceeded domestic deposits. Historically, loan losses on foreign loans had been almost negligible. In late 1972, Citibank announced that it had made a $35 million ten-year loan to improve telecommunications in the state of Rio Grande do Sul. Billed as the largest loan ever made to Brazil, it was unique also because of its extended term. But in its eagerness for the money, Brazil also made concessions, waiving the customary 25 percent withholding tax on interest and making a deposit amounting to 25 percent of the loan.

In the early seventies even Africa appeared to glitter. On October 3, 1973, Wriston hosted a luncheon for President Mobuto Sese Seko of Zaire (the former Belgian Congo), and in his toast compared Zaire's "long and arduous struggle for independence" against colonial oppressors with America's. Over the previous several years, Wriston recounted, Citibank had made loans to Zaire totaling $84 million for things like highway construction and communications equipment. At the time, he said, Citibank was wrapping up a deal to finance a $256 million, 1,200-mile power transmission line, and was working on a proposal to finance an eleven-story office building in the nation's capital.

Zaire's economic outlook appeared to brighten further with a 1973 surge in copper prices and production. Giddy with Zaire's turn in fortunes, Mobutu commissioned a string of expensive high-profile projects, including a multimillion-dollar stadium that was inaugurated in the fall of 1974 with a music festival and a heavyweight championship fight between George Foreman and Muhammad Ali.

Ironically, just a year before the oil embargo, Citibank's own *Monthly Economic Letter* warned that many developing nations would have trouble meeting their debt payments. It noted that since 1956 nine countries (Argentina, Brazil, Chile, Peru, Ghana, India, Pakistan, Indonesia, and Turkey) had negotiated consolidations or reschedulings of more than $5 billion in outstanding debt. Among the reasons cited were the growing need for export credits and the move from aid to loans. Citibank's concerns were based on data collected in December 1970, back when Brazil owed just $3.8 billion, Mexico $3.8 billion, and the Philippines $0.8 billion, and total debts of the less developed countries (LDCs) were a piddling $66.7 billion.

Meanwhile, Citibank was losing money in its consumer business, such as it was. American banks couldn't branch outside their home states and were limited by Regulation Q in what they could pay on deposits. The traditional corporate users of bank funds now borrowed much of their capital requirements in the commercial paper market. The Fed was pressuring the big banks to curtail loan expansion and to keep the prime down on domestic business loans—while having to pay an ever higher market rate on negotiable CDs. Even before the embargo, banks were to some extent creating loan demand rather than responding to it. Chief credit officer P. Henry Mueller would later say in an internal interview that "it is clear in the pre–November 1973 era there were many instances of money being forced upon borrowers." Citibank had only one card to play, and that was international.

All that was needed was a global shock to cause these elements to coalesce into a cosmic economic explosion that would rattle the world economy. As well connected as Wriston's worldwide intelligence network was, the OPEC announcement still came as a complete surprise to him and other top bankers. "I read about it in the paper," Wriston acknowledged later. In the Western world, few had any reliable advance knowledge of the OPEC move. David Rockefeller, no stranger in Arab petroleum circles, recalled that in the early 1970s the Algerians had warned that oil prices would soon reach $24 a barrel. "I felt this was sort of a threat. I didn't believe it," Rockefeller said later. Before the hysteria over soaring oil prices ended, Rockefeller's bank would predict that the price of oil would soar to $104 a barrel.

Shortly after the announcement of the embargo, Wriston was in the office of his friend, Treasury secretary George Shultz. Shultz was not one to panic in a crisis, but his mood was grim. "This is an unmanageable situation," the secretary said, indicating that he felt there was little the government could do to mitigate the problem. Wriston reminded Shultz of the secretary's own confidence in the ability of markets to manage crises, a principle Wriston had learned at his own father's knee. Intuitively, Wriston and Shultz knew that the problem would work through the marketplace, but they also realized that they were entering a kind of economic vacuum, one of those transitional phases in world history where the only anchor to windward was a belief in the principles of economic freedom. Said Wriston, "No one in their wildest dreams thought about a group of fellows getting together and saying, 'No oil.' "

Although Wriston and his colleagues might have been surprised by the timing, this was the kind of event and opportunity they had been anticipating for a long time. Said Latin American lending head George "Jack" Clark later, "What Wriston talked about all these years finally happened, and we were set up to do it. We were ready to go. Having set up the machinery, he was pleased to see it in operation." On October 8, 1973, as OPEC was preparing the press release of the century, Wriston announced a series of top-level promotions and appointments in the international banking group. These were the men designated to lead Citibank, and thus the American banking industry, through the fallout from the oil shock that was to come. On the issue of cross-border lending, all but one were on board.

Costanzo, of course, had been running the overseas division since Wriston became president. But with his elevation to vice chairman, his prestige in the international banking fraternity rose to new heights. In the decentralized culture of Citibank, Costanzo "really owned that decision-making apparatus," as then executive vice president John Reed put it later. While Wriston and Spencer asked questions, they didn't second-guess those in whom they had already placed such confidence. Probably more than any other single individual, Costanzo embodied the optimism of American banks for the Third World and for recycling. For Costanzo, Third World lending would be a family affair; two of his four brothers were international bankers. His colleague George Vojta, who had served for nearly three years as chief planner, would now supervise the International Banking Group as well as the World Corporation Group.

Lester Garvin, a no-nonsense international banker who had spent most of his banking career in the southern cone of South America, was the lone naysayer. On that momentous day, October 8, 1973, he was elevated to chief credit officer. The grandson of U.S. missionaries in Chile, Garvin had been born there and had graduated from Dartmouth. In 1940 he went to work for Citibank. Having lived much of his life in Latin America, he had serious misgivings about the ability of countries like Brazil and Argentina to manage their own economic affairs. As a matter of principle, Garvin was opposed to commercial banks' engaging in cross-border lending. Much as Wriston prided himself on tolerating dissent, there was no room for someone in such a key position who differed so much and so strongly on such a critical issue. As Victor Prall, a former chief of Mideast operations, recalled, Garvin "yelled and hollered. He screamed and beat down the doors." But he was fighting a losing battle and nine months later he decided to take early retirement. Thanks largely to higher energy prices, the United States and the rest of the industrialized world was by year end 1973 in the grips of the worst recession since the 1930s, and domestic loan demand was rapidly evaporating.

In one of his final acts as Nixon's secretary of the Treasury, George Shultz provided yet another incentive for Third World lending. With Wriston cheering him on, Shultz in January 1974 abolished the ten-year-old controls on external lending. An end to capital controls had been expected eventually, but the announcement came as a surprise. The move was aimed at mitigating the impact of oil price hikes on oil-importing countries, which now needed to attract capital. The impact was immediate. In the first five months of 1974, foreign assets of U.S. commercial banks grew by $8.5 billion to $34 billion, exceeding the increase for all of 1973. Looking back, one leading economist saw this as a defining moment: "That gave the signal. After that, you could hardly find a banker at home."

If the naysayers were in the minority inside Citibank, the doomsdayers were out in force in the wake of the embargo, disseminating the message that the oil would run out, the global financial system would collapse, and the Arabs would take over the world. With the oil embargo emerged the phrase "fragile financial system," which reminded Wriston of Winston Churchill's answer to the French generals' warning that Hitler would wring England's neck like a chicken. "Some chicken; some neck," Churchill responded. Nonetheless, Wriston contemplated the unthinkable secondary consequences of this event for the developing countries if somehow the plug was pulled on their economic engines. Such a jolt, he mused, could trigger a leftist political upheaval that could derail the economic growth of Brazil and other Latin nations and halt their move toward the free market.

Wriston and his colleagues firmly believed that if the developing nations followed sound economic policies, they could finance their growth and current account deficits with borrowed money and adjust to the new order. "The Japanese did it, and they import 100 percent of their oil," Wriston asserted. "The Koreans did it, the Brazilians did it. The only country that didn't was the United States." His top priority was to deal with the very real crisis at hand. He sought to dispel the now widespread fear that the Arabs would either seek to own the world, on the one hand, or yank their money out of the financial system and bury it in the sand, on the other. Dollars, Wriston explained at every opportunity, could not be removed from America. If the OPEC states pulled their deposits, they would have no choice but to use them to buy goods from petroleum-importing countries, and that money would ultimately wind up back in U.S. banks. Indeed, four U.S. institutions were the principal beneficiaries: Citibank, Bank of America, Chase, and Morgan. As Victor Prall explained, "They had to put their money, if it was in dollars, with an American bank eventually. And even if they did get it to another country, another system, those banks would have to maintain money with us."

Although representatives of dozens of lesser American institutions soon fanned out through the Middle East in search of petrodollar deposits, these banks were not, for the most part, a viable alternative for Middle Eastern central bank officials. Early on, Citibank had considered assembling a special team to make sure it didn't lose deposits to aggressive regional banks in places like Philadelphia and Seattle. In a lunch with a top official of Iran's central bank, however, Prall concluded that such a unit would be superfluous. The official said, "You know damn well that if I ever got caught losing money on a bank in the United States that wasn't first class, I'd get executed."

Before long, Congress began to pressure the banks to open their books and reveal the level of petrodollar deposits from each OPEC nation. Sum-

moned in 1975 by Senator Frank Church to testify before his Foreign Relations Subcommittee on Multinational Corporations, general counsel Hans
Angermueller and Morgan counsel Boris Berkovitch artfully stonewalled the
request. They revealed little more than the fact that OPEC's surplus petrodollars in 1974 were about $60 billion, of which 8 percent to 9 percent re-
turned to the United States and four times that amount wound up in the
Euromarkets.

The flip side of American paranoia elicited by OPEC was that the
Arabs would eventually own the world, including the United States. In a De-
cember 1974 interview with the *Economist,* Wriston dismissed concerns about
Arabs buying stakes in U.S. companies and banks. Citing Dutch-owned
Lever Brothers, he said that "they have a big piece of the detergent market in
America, and what are they going to do? Are they going to say America will
be dirty from Saturday on?" Wriston was convinced that the oil cartel, like all
cartels before it, was doomed to failure. In his widely quoted and prescient
"Whale Oil, Chicken, and Energy Syndrome" speech before the august Economic Club of Detroit, later condensed in the *Reader's Digest,* he blamed the
federal bureaucracy for the energy crisis, saying that it resulted from tamper-
ing with free markets. "A scarcity of energy in the United States was assured
as long ago as 1954," Wriston declared, "when Congress empowered the
Federal Power Commission to set an artificially low wellhead price on natural gas used in interstate commerce." Wriston bore down on the doomsayers,
who he said suffered from a failure to "appreciate man's inherent ability to
adjust and innovate" and from their own inability to predict the future. Wriston dug into his treasure trove of historical anecdotes to recall the doubling in
whale oil prices, to $2.55 a gallon, that occurred when whaling was disrupted
during the Civil War. Congress, he said, responded to demands to freeze
whale oil prices or ration the commodity by doing nothing. As new alternatives, such as kerosene and electric lamps, became available, the price of
whale oil dropped, and by 1896 it was down to forty cents a gallon. "This
cycle, repeated in thousands of other instances, is one which the rulers of the
Persian Gulf might well bear in mind," Wriston remarked prophetically.

In an early 1974 edition of its *Economic Week,* Citibank likened
OPEC's action to the reparations exacted from Germany after World War I
in the Treaty of Versailles. Pointing out that the Germans responded by simply printing more marks, Citibank said that OPEC's extraction of nearly $60
billion from oil importers would be no more successful and "not much less
inflationary."

At this point, World Bank economists predicted that the aggregate
Arab trade surplus would eventually total about $1.2 trillion, according to
Costanzo. "People didn't understand there was a market process," he said,
adding that he doubted it would exceed $200 billion. It finally peaked at
about $170 billion, Costanzo said later, and continued to drop from that
level. As for the appropriate U.S. response, Citibank, in its *Economic Letter,*
recommended that the Fed expand the money supply to mitigate the impact
of the embargo. That, Citibank said, "would assist the long-run reallocation

of resources in a world in which energy prices probably will be much higher, relative to the overall price level, than in the past." Low real interest rates, resulting from easy monetary policy throughout the Western world—led by the Fed—would be an invitation to heavy borrowing. Of Wriston, former President Gerald Ford said later, "I suspect he was a calming influence on the whole situation. He wasn't as panicky as some financiers were."

In the public sector, William Simon, who replaced George Shultz as Treasury secretary in April 1974, was a cheerleader for commercial bank recycling and one of the few voices of calm. "Only Simon was saying that all cartels fall apart and that the market will take care of them," said Ford economic adviser William Seidman. "Cartels," Seidman quoted Simon as saying, "always cheat on each other." Seidman added, "He was 100 percent right." Wriston seemed to thrive on being one member of a small minority. Once he had embraced a point of view, the mere fact that five or five hundred or fifty million people happened to disagree with him would not sway him from his position and, indeed, might even bolster it. "You could fill Yankee Stadium with a massive chorus on the other side of an issue," said former Citibank executive Michael Callen, "and if it didn't make sense, if there weren't compelling new facts, he [Wriston] wouldn't budge. . . . Other people's opinions were not something Wriston sought."

To Wriston, no one embodied the Chicken Little mentality more than the bow-tied Robert Roosa, a top officer of the secretive, elitist, investment banking firm of Brown Brothers Harriman. Roosa had figured heavily at Bretton Woods and had stubbornly continued to espouse fixed exchange rates long after, in Wriston's view, they ceased to be viable. As a senior Kennedy administration Treasury official, Roosa had been largely responsible for the interest equalization tax that Wriston so despised. Ideologically and stylistically, Roosa and Brown Brothers were the antithesis of Wriston and Citibank. Brown Brothers, said a former top Citibank official, "was the prototype of the bank Citibank didn't want to be."

Wriston was often provoked by Roosa's lamentations, which included a January 1975 piece in *Foreign Affairs* on "how the Arabs would own the world," Wriston snorted. "And the only way to solve [the crisis] was to form a mutual fund, which Brown Brothers could manage." The Roosa proposal was but one of a host of schemes suggested to accomplish this task. Some proposed the creation of new government agencies while others asserted that this was a logical role for the International Monetary Fund and the World Bank.

On the face of it, the most logical official vehicles for recycling were the brother-sister team of the International Monetary Fund and the World Bank. But this was a role the IMF neither sought nor was equipped to handle. The IMF was a short-term balance-of-payments lender. It was more interested in redressing the imbalances of industrialized countries than in lending to developing nations, where its image had traditionally been one of a Dutch uncle who saddled the people with greatly resented austerity programs. The developing countries, said Jacques de Larosière, who became managing director of the IMF in 1978, "had not borrowed from the IMF because they were not ready to abide" by the agency's conditions.

The International Monetary Fund's response to the crisis was limited. In 1974, on the recommendation of managing director H. Johannes Witteveen, it set up a $3.4 billion special oil facility for hard-pressed importers that was funded by the oil-producing nations. But the principal users were Britain and Italy. Less than a year into the crisis, Witteveen warned that the private sector alone would not be able to handle recycling indefinitely. Accordingly, Simon and Secretary of State Henry Kissinger proposed in late 1974 the creation of a trust fund to be housed in the IMF and funded by OPEC and IMF gold sales.

Because the IMF was limited in its ability to lend to developing countries, its influence on their economic policies was weak. In a 1977 address, Fed chairman Arthur Burns recognized this when he said, "The leverage of the Fund in speeding the process of adjustment would clearly be enhanced if its capacity to lend were greater than it is now." Burns added that one reason "countries often are unwilling to submit to conditions imposed by the IMF is that the amount of credit available to them through the Fund's regular channels—as determined by established quotas—is in many instances small relative to their structural payments imbalances." To developing nations, the IMF's efforts to impose discipline became something of a joke. These nations could arrange bilateral loans with the governments of industrialized nations and get as much money as they needed, and more, from commercial banks. In his talk, Burns addressed that issue by warning commercial and investment bankers against "undercutting" the IMF's efforts to facilitate adjustment.

For the first several years after the oil embargo, the IMF even declined to provide commercial banks with nonpublic economic and financial data it had collected on developing countries. IMF officials wrung their hands over how much they should cooperate with commercial banks; they were concerned that their independence might be compromised if they became too cozy. Burns, for one, was in favor of the IMF supplying the banks with negative information about debtor nations, believing that it was in the Fund's interest to help banks avoid losses or even failures. By 1977, according to IMF documents, "most executive directors were inclined to agree that the Fund's cooperation with commercial banks should take the form of assisting the banks to obtain information."

As for the World Bank, its mission had largely been to finance long-term infrastructure projects—power projects, roads, and the like—extending credit over periods such as twenty years. Because its loans were theoretically repaid out of the revenues of these projects, it had developed some expertise in monitoring how and where its funds were actually spent by a government borrower—a skill that the major banks lacked. Some Citibank and World Bank officials attempted to foster co-financing, or joint lending, arrangements between the two organizations in which the commercial banks would fund the shorter maturities and the World Bank the longer-term portions of project loans.

Robert S. McNamara, the slick-haired former Ford president and defense secretary who headed the bank from 1968 to 1980, said later that he had tried unsuccessfully to enlist the cooperation of the commercial banks in co-financings. Under such an arrangement, the World Bank would have been responsible for monitoring project progress. "They [the commercial banks] thought our requirements were too onerous, too long," said McNamara later. "We wanted too much detail." But as time went on, there was less and less need for such arrangements. "The money was just being shoveled out of commercial banks," said McNamara.

But these efforts were doomed to failure from the outset, in part because of the long-term nature (sometimes twenty years) of the projects and also because of Citibank's disdain for the World Bank and its leader. Wriston dourly regarded it as a gargantuan, poorly managed bureaucracy which lent to projects that lacked any economic justification. "The World Bank lent to governments' huge socialist things. They did not really believe in the free enterprise system," said Wriston. Even in instances where World Bank lending resulted in tangible projects, Wriston questioned their underlying economics, comparing them to the Tennessee Valley Authority, the huge power project initiated by President Roosevelt during the Great Depression. "There is something tangible to show but is it really . . . good for the country, if you take the cost per kilowatt-hour?" Wriston said later. "The emphasis of the [World] Bank was in the wrong place. It should have tried to stimulate the free market economy. That's the only way to lift those people out of poverty. If that's the object of the exercise, which it is, you don't do it by building Hoover Dam."

Wriston blamed McNamara for the World Bank's approach to lending. In Wriston's view, McNamara was a bureaucrat for whom statistics, not results, were an end unto themselves. In a 1975 talk in Mexico City, Wriston warned Citibank international division officers not to fall into the trap that consumed McNamara. "Mr. McNamara got a lot of good press for his numbers just prior to building a car that could not be sold, losing a war in Asia, and building an airplane that didn't fly," Wriston said. "In my judgment his administration [at the Defense Department] has to be judged a failure, but the financial control systems which he inaugurated were not. The trouble was not with the numbers which were produced but with the too great reliance which was put on them, while at the same time blocking out or ignoring other sources of valid information. We do not plan to fall into the same trap in the Citibank. Information is not an end in itself, only a tool to aid judgment."

From 1968 to 1976, World Bank loans grew sevenfold to $6.6 billion a year, prompting widespread concern and criticism, even from insiders, about the agency's fiscal health and McNamara's leadership. While McNamara had revived the World Bank from its earlier moribund state, critics like Wriston felt that it was managed more to get the money out the door than to invest in viable projects. They contended that much of the money spent in the developing world did not wind up in the intended infrastructure projects but instead enabled the governments to waste their national savings on consumption.

At the suggestion of Treasury undersecretary Paul Volcker, the World Bank set up a unit to help recycle the OPEC surplus from oil producers to Third World oil importers. Ironically, the unit was headed by Costanzo's brother, Henry. The unit was not needed, because of the increasingly dominant role played by the major international banks. Moreover, it would have taken years for the unit to get up and running in the World Bank bureaucracy, where obtaining a capital increase sometimes took an incredible five years.

As it became clear that the multinational banks like Citi were up to the task of recycling, the IMF and the World Bank became increasingly irrelevant and debate over what they should be doing diminished in intensity. "Once the banks came up with the solution," said Mario H. Simonsen, who became Brazil's minister of finance in 1974, "everybody was relieved. There was very little support to broaden its [the IMF's] role after that." To be sure, the banks, which by then were rolling in fat syndication fees, were not pushing for IMF assistance. They were, said Simonsen, "content with the status quo." Later, Simonsen would say that, in hindsight, "the ideal solution" would have been a mix of commercial banks and international agencies. . . . To have influence, you need to have money."

Said Angel Gurria, then an obscure Mexican finance official who would years later become the country's point man in debt rescheduling negotiations, "We could put a few billion together over the phone, whereas it took a year to negotiate a few hundred million out of these guys [the IMF and World Bank]. They were no match either for our needs or for our capacity to borrow elsewhere." Besides, said Gurria, "you only need the Fund if you're in trouble, and we were doing fine." Likewise, Mexico had no use for World Bank project financing because, said Gurria, there was always "our friendly banker, who would do a medium-term bank loan and consider it an honor. And he would get promoted."

Wriston's view of the World Bank and its chief was shared by Treasury secretary William Simon. He would later recall that McNamara was constantly seeking a doubling in contributions from the Treasury. "We would refuse McNamara's request for a doubling of loan ability every time he requested it," Simon remembered. In his view, the World Bank's original role—lending for development projects, infrastructure, and building a "healthy economic system," was bastardized. "It wasn't for foreign aid, or wasn't supposed to be," he said later. In one meeting in which Simon refused McNamara's pleas for more funds, the usually icy calm World Bank chief exploded, "God damn it, Bill . . . you're trying to treat the World Bank as if it were a financial institution."

Early on, the United States attempted to persuade the OPEC nations to lend directly to the oil-importing countries, but it was rebuffed at nearly every turn. Former president Ford described the effort as "vigorous" at the outset and "tapering off" later on, apparently as the prospects for success faded. Part of the Saudi reluctance to lend was based on Moslem usury laws prohibiting the payment or receipt of interest. The Saudis went to almost absurd lengths to avoid the appearance of being in the banking business, to the point of calling their central bank the Saudi Arabian Monetary Agency (SAMA). But in the view of David Rockefeller, the big oil producers "were too greedy." He added that the "notion that the banks are the bad boys that made all the mistakes is a very simplistic view of what happened."

By not investing long term, the Saudis provided little assistance to the importing nations. According to Rockefeller, SAMA and the minister of finance refused to invest for more than five years. Early on, the Arabs reportedly considered direct investment in Brazil, whose imports from the Arab world by early 1974 were running at about five times the level of Arab imports from Brazil. But ultimately "no one could ever get them [the Arabs] to lend money to Brazil," said one international banker. "We tried with Saudi Arabia and Brazil. They said, 'You guys are crazy.' " According to Robert Hormats, then a senior National Security Council staffer, the Arabs restricted their direct Third World lending to countries fairly close to home, including the Sudan, Egypt, and Kenya. Some observers, like Citibank Latin chief Jack Clark, didn't believe direct OPEC lending was such a good idea anyway. Clark thought that a "risk-assessing, risk-taking" agency—for example, a commercial bank—was needed in between.

The Arabs weren't stupid, though. In effect, they used the Western banking system as their personal credit department. Some, like Nixon and Ford administration chief of staff Alexander Haig, felt the government should have done more. "I thought the federal government had somewhat more of an obligation to help in debt recycling, relieving the burden of Third World debt, and not just leave it up to the banks," he said later. In addition to the ill-conceived plans being hatched to recycle petrodollars, committees of all descriptions were formed to deal with the domestic consequences of the oil crisis. One committee was created to increase Americans' awareness of the need to conserve oil. That goal was to be accomplished through advertising, including billboards on highways, admonishing Americans to dim their lights and save gas. When Wriston received a letter from Senator Charles Percy inviting him to become a member of the group, he and his colleagues rolled their eyes in disbelief at the naïveté of it all. As they sat in Wriston's office chortling over the letter, one Citibanker said, "If a 400 percent increase in the price of oil isn't enough to convince the American consumer to reduce consumption, no amount of billboards is going to do it." In their panic over the prospect of running out of energy, even officials of a Republican administration somehow forgot that the American financial system is mostly a private sector operation.

In Wriston's mind, there was a principle at stake here. This was not a job for government or for quasi-government agencies. The last thing the world needed was more bureaucracy and more government interference in the world economy. Government had helped make the mess, but only the free marketplace could clean it up. Wriston acknowledged that a proper and vital role for the government—and a job that only government could handle—was to provide liquidity to the system and tax incentives to spur energy exploration, but certainly not to "micromanage" either the recycling of capital or the distribution of gasoline. The massive redistribution of capital was a job that could be handled, and should only be handled, through free market mechanisms, and the free market's principal agent, the world's commercial banking system. The fees Citibank stood to earn by facilitating the adjustment, Wriston insisted later, had nothing to do with his view that the banking system could handle the problem. "The world was at risk," he said later. And after the dust had cleared, this was not only a role the U.S. government was willing to concede to the commercial banks but one that it encouraged.

While the Nixon and Ford administrations did not exactly order U.S. banks to recycle OPEC's profits to the Third World, they clearly gave this policy their unqualified blessing. As early as 1971, according to Wriston, government guidelines for overseas lending urged U.S. financial institutions to give priority to lending to developing countries. Ford adviser William Seidman, who participated in administration discussions about the role of banks in recycling, said later, "It was seen as a beneficial thing for the world economy. The underlying argument was that we're giving them all this money and they'll be richer and more productive. The administration of which I was a part encouraged banks to recycle." While bankers themselves would later differ on the forcefulness and specificity of the government official's pleas, they generally agreed that the pressure was not overt and that they made their own decisions. But they concurred that they were definitely not discouraged by the U.S. government.

Typically, bank regulators, particularly the Fed, make their feelings known not by issuing orders but by asking questions. One former Fed official explained that a top Fed official would ask a banker, "Have your lending officers brought to your attention that you're not participating in this vital contract?"

Said Continental's Ed Bottum, "People from Treasury were calling, asking banks to recycle." And Tom Storrs, then chairman of North Carolina National Bank, said, "There were instances where there were subtle influences. Pervasive but subtle. It took the form of conversations, not as pointed as phone calls. Or would take the form of remarks at meetings, like 'If the banks knew where their interests lay . . .' "

But former Chase chairman George Champion put the blame mostly on his fellow bankers. "I don't think the government ever told them [the bankers] a damn thing. They did it. Walter Wriston started it and nobody ever questioned that. And David, as soon as he took over, couldn't wait to keep up with Walter. And John McGillicuddy, then president of Manufacturers Hanover, came in third, and went head over heels." Champion attributed the excessive lending in part on the acquiescence of bank examiners, who permitted banks to lend more than 50 percent of their capital to Brazil, most of it in the form of loans to the government or government-owned entities. Of all the nation's economic leaders, Seidman recalled, only the curmudgeonly Arthur Burns expressed deep misgivings about recycling, saying that the term itself ought to be stricken from the language. "Recycling—blah!

These are bad debts!" Burns exclaimed on at least one occasion, according to Seidman.

But whatever misgivings Burns may have expressed to colleagues in the inner sanctums of the White House, they certainly flew in the face of some of his public utterances. Indeed, Burns had supplied bankers with some good reasons to look upon the quadrupling of oil prices as a golden opportunity. In a speech at the Adam Smith Symposium in Scotland on June 5, 1973, Burns gushed over the economic progress and prospects of Brazil, which would become the largest beneficiary of the recycling process. The "highest rate of economic growth of any nation at the present time is enjoyed by Brazil, whose economic system has moved closer in recent years to the principles of Adam Smith," Burns said. "Decisions as to the direction of investment are now left largely to the business community; foreign investments are encouraged; individuals are free to choose the line of work that best suits their talents and to enjoy the rewards accorded by the market to successful performance. This system of economic organization, aided by the great natural and human resources of Brazil, is producing excellent results." He went on to say that the country's production had grown by at least 9 percent a year for the previous five years and that real output had risen in 1972 by more than 11 percent. Hours after that address, Burns flew to Paris, where he hammered home to bankers what was becoming a recurrent Burns theme: Go slow. Said Burns, "I have urged bankers in the U.S. to discipline the pace at which they are extending credit, in the interest both of our economies' present need and of sound banking practice," Burns said. "I repeat that appeal today. In doing so, I recognize that earnest efforts by commercial banks to moderate their rate of credit accommodation will not by itself be a sufficient remedy."

Burns's contradictory public statements mirrored the schizophrenia that festered within the Fed over Third World lending. On the one hand, Burns knew that the Arabs were not prepared to recycle petrodollars and that the only practical mechanism to accomplish that was the commercial banks. But on the other hand, he was concerned about runaway growth unaccompanied by proportional increases in bank capital. With the dramatic rise in overseas lending over the next several years, bank capital ratios plummeted, precipitating a stormy debate among bank regulators over whether there should be different capital guidelines for domestic and international assets. No one was more outspoken than Wriston in arguing for lower capital standards, and in particular, in asserting that because countries, unlike companies, don't "go broke" and disappear, not as much capital was required to support those assets.

One former Fed official agreed: "There was some sympathy for that."

In fact, Citibank's Al Costanzo and his IMF-trained colleagues viewed "recycling" as a misnomer, and a dangerous one at that. To many, the term suggested that money, like water, was somehow in danger of overflowing if it wasn't lent out as quickly as it came in. "It wasn't that way at all," explained Costanzo later. "It was a basic process. You had people who came to you with various projects, and if you thought they were sound projects that generated enough cash flow to pay you back you made the loan. After you made the loan, then you went out to buy the funds to fund it."

Initially, Citibank paid high rates for overnight Arab money. But it soon realized that this couldn't continue and the maturities became longer and the rates lower. At one point, Citibank placed a $3 billion cap on the volume of overnight money it took from OPEC. Citibank and other large banks discouraged short-term funds by paying unattractive rates. As Wriston told *Fortune* in March 1975, "The OPEC nations want to leave the money with us, letting the bank take the risks while they get part of the profits. We say: 'No thank you.' "

In Wriston's view, the world had no need for the IMF or the World Bank as long as it had a London-based merchant bank known as Citicorp International Bank Limited, or CIBL. Founded in 1972, CIBL (pronounced "Sybil") would soon become Citibank's principal vehicle for syndicated Eurocurrency lending and the world's largest packager of such loans. When the group was established, Citibank briefly contemplated calling it simply Citibank International Limited, or CIL. But that name was scrapped when Lord Aldington, a director, cautioned that City of London wags would inevitably dub it "Silly." Though it would certainly wind up making a lot of silly loans, its original purpose was anything but; CIBL was established to capitalize on the growing importance of the Euromarkets. Because of interest rates ceilings and reserve requirements imposed by the Fed on domestic bank deposits, it became cheaper for big syndicated deals to be assembled in funding centers such as London, Nassau, and Panama rather than in New York. That also enabled the banks to avoid New York State taxes. In the 1960s and early 1970s, Wriston and his banking colleagues in New York watched with envy as First Boston and other big investment banks collected huge fees for putting together these syndications. While the Wall Streeters supplied the brains and collected the big fees, commercial banks scraped up the crumbs by taking the risk and supplying the brawn. Though commercial banks put together syndications for countries in which they maintained branches, they did so on a so-called club basis, as a kind of courtesy to the host government.

The formation of CIBL was also a benchmark in Citibank's often ambivalent approach to investment banking. Banks had long performed activities that fell loosely under the definition of investment or merchant banking but were not outlawed by Glass-Steagall. They included loan syndicating, private placements, foreign exchange trading, government bond underwriting, and corporate finance and merger and acquisition advice. Underwriting of corporate debt and equity was prohibited.

Forty years of separation of commercial and investment banking had created two distinct cultures, the rough-and-tumble world of Wall Street, which was largely oblivious to fiduciary responsibility, and the collegial white-shoe world of commercial banking, which in this same period had suc-

ceeded in regaining the public's trust. One of the most zealous proponents of
investment banking was Citibank president Bill Spencer. As a former energy
lender, he had years of experience putting together large oil deals. "If Bill
Spencer had his druthers he would have wanted to run the investment bank
[side of Citi] more than the [commercial side]. Bill was fond of this business,"
a former colleague recalled. And he resented traditional Wall Street firms getting business he felt Citibank should have. Referring to the investment banks,
Spencer and others would say, according to Wriston crony James Farley,
"What are they doing advising the government of Brazil when we're down
there and know them?"

At about this time, Citibank woke up to the fact that it was giving away
its expertise in arranging global private placements and hired two top investment bankers to develop that business. According to former Citibank planners, a formal approach to merchant banking at Citibank had begun with
George Moore, who was invited to become a limited partner in the Wall
Street investment house of White, Weld & Company shortly after he retired.
Even in retirement, Moore was a tireless campaigner for banks in general and
for Citibank in particular to be properly compensated for their troubles. According to a former international banker at J. P. Morgan, Moore used to
"give John Meyer [then chairman of Morgan] hell for not charging the Saudis
fees for advice," a practice he felt undermined commercial banks in competing with investment banks.

Moore also prodded his former colleagues to get into the investment
banking business. With Moore acting as a go-between, White, Weld proposed to sell Citibank a 25 percent stake in the firm. There was a certain appeal to this kind of joint venture. After all, Citibank would immediately gain
access to a corps of loan salesmen without having to set up shop from
scratch. In 1971, in response to this and other proposals, Costanzo asked
Citibank's planning unit to figure out how Citibank should play the merchant banking game.

For Wriston, however, joint ventures, many of which originated with
Uncle George, created nothing but headaches. Citibank was discovering that
a 25 percent stake was fine as long as everything went well. The flip side was
that when things turned sour, the bank was on the hook for 100 percent if it
wanted to preserve its name and reputation. At least one recent instance of
this—a trouble-plagued European mutual fund distributor—was on the
minds of Citibank planners and Wriston's colleagues as they pondered the
White, Weld proposal. Accordingly, executive committee chairman Ed
Palmer and others recommended going it alone with CIBL, which was to be
separated from the commercial banking culture. CIBL would package and
syndicate large dollar-denominated loans that would typically be originated
by loan officers around the world. In addition, it would underwrite corporate
debt and other securities, activities that banks and bank holding companies
couldn't perform in the United States. In theory at least, the country officers
would originate a deal, perform the credit analysis, then call in CIBL to package and sell it. Wriston, however, had a problem with the concept underlying

CIBL. Notwithstanding his commitment to breaking down the barriers that blocked Citibank from expanding into new markets and businesses, he was nervous about investment banking. As a keen student of history, especially Citibank's, Wriston was acutely aware that the transgressions of Charlie Mitchell, who held his job some forty years earlier, had led to the Glass-Steagall Act. Recalling J. P. Morgan at the Pecora hearings, Wriston often said that he did not want the midget sitting on his knee. The bitter lessons of the Charlie Mitchell affair, including the fact that Mitchell would not have become chairman had it not been for the sexual shenanigans (and incompetence) of Jamie Stillman, were indelibly engraved in Wriston's mind.

One former top Citibank executive recalls having dinner with the Wristons when the topic of conversation turned to one of his close friends. "Behind every good man there's a woman," Kathy said.

Alluding to the Stillman affair, Wriston retorted, "Behind every man is a woman who gets him into trouble."

Wriston was a product of Main Street, not Wall Street. "If I understood the stock market I wouldn't be working," he used to say. Wriston liked the deal-oriented, risk-oriented aspect of investment banking, but he loathed the Wall Street ethic and many of the people who embraced it. Despite his elite upbringing, he was more comfortable with backhoe operators than Wall Streeters. He had to deal with the Merrill Lynches and Salomon Brothers of the world, but the Don Regans and John Gutfreunds were certainly not the kind of folks that he cared to fraternize or work with. "In the real world you spend most of your life with people you work with," he said. "Therefore, you better take a good look to see if they're the kind of people you want to spend your life with, as I think the people at the bank are. You'll have a good time. On the other hand if you go into some outfit whose value system is skewed they may pay you a million but you'll be miserable." According to former colleagues, he described more than one Wall Street investment banker as someone who would "sell his mother for a sixty-fourth." And he referred to people who showed up at the negotiating table at the last minute to claim a finder's fee for a deal as the "guys who get between the wall and the wallpaper."

Wriston had no fundamental quarrel with the separation of commercial and investment banking, and denied any interest in seeing the Glass-Steagall Act completely abolished. Citibank, he told *M.B.A.* magazine in December 1970, had no intention of patterning itself after the European merchant banks that combined the two activities. But Wriston staunchly defended the right of commercial banks to engage in activities—such as underwriting revenue bonds—that stirred debate only because they did not exist when Glass-Steagall was drafted. Wall Street, he told *Institutional Investor* in March 1977, viewed that as "the camel's-nose-under-the-tent syndrome. But the facts are that revenue bonds are a very large share of the municipal market, and at the time Mr. Glass and Mr. Steagall were signing their little bill, there wasn't any such animal." They weren't mentioned in the act, Wriston said later in a speech to fellow bankers, for the "same reason that the Post Office

Act of 1794 did not mention airmail." Another securities activity that Wriston still coveted for Citibank was the right to underwrite and distribute mutual funds, which Wriston considered akin to deposits—a battle that had been lost with the 1971 Supreme Court decision.

In reality, investment banking was already a fact of life for banks operating abroad. Citibank's planners were convinced that if Citi was to remain competitive, CIBL was essential. They developed a proposal that would be the least frightening to Wriston and the directors. As it was originally conceived, CIBL really amounted to little more than Citibank was already doing, or was empowered to do. Moreover, its goal was to originate and syndicate loans without taking much of the risk itself. At the end of an all-day Policy Committee meeting in 1972, Wriston said, "Okay, I have such sensitivities about it, I want to take it to the board," and, he added, if the board shared those concerns, the plan would be killed. But after a meeting of the full board, CIBL got the go-ahead.

Troubled as he was by the potential conflicts of interest, Wriston knew that investment banking activities were essential to operations if Citibank was to become a truly global bank and compete with the European universal banks. He also knew that traditional corporate banking was becoming less important to big companies and that it would have to become more like investment banking or disappear.

Creating CIBL "was probably the only thing I had a difficult time selling to Walt," said Costanzo. "Rightly or wrongly, we had to do it to stay in the market. It was part of the times." After receiving the imprimatur of the Bank of England, Citibank became the fifth major U.S. bank to set up a wholly owned London merchant bank. Smaller banks also set up London branches to provide their executives with an excuse to spend weekends in the British capital. Those who resisted that temptation typically did the next-best thing by setting up other "offshore" funding operations in Nassau and Panama. London now rivaled, if not surpassed, Wall Street as a global financial center.

Almost simultaneously, Citibank announced the creation of CIBL's Far East counterpart, APCO, the Asia Pacific Capital Corporation, a joint venture 15 percent of which was owned by the Fuji Bank. Its mission was to raise medium- and long-term money in the Eurodollar and Asian dollar markets to fund various development projects. Wriston, only half jokingly, referred to APCO as "Charlie Mitchell East."

Morgan's inroads into the merger and acquisition advisory business also lit a fire under Wriston, according to a report in *Business Week.* Morgan had set up a merger and acquisition unit in the 1960s, and in 1973, Morgan got Wall Street's attention when it won a mandate to arrange British American Tobacco's acquisition of Gimbel's department stores. That, the magazine said, prompted Wriston to begin beefing up his corporate finance unit by hiring top Wall Street specialists. But Wriston's generally unenthusiastic attitude toward investment banking dogged this effort for years and, some say, contributed to Citibank's relative weakness in this business into the 1990s.

No one could ever accuse George Putnam, the tall, tennis-playing Boston Brahmin who now headed up Citibank's European operations, of lacking enthusiasm, though. After the board meeting at which CIBL was approved, he emerged as the logical candidate to launch the new venture. Putnam was smooth, engaging, aggressive, and quick on his feet—"a one-man dynamo," said Farley. He had worked for years in Latin America for Bank of Boston before being recruited by Citibank in 1967. Later, as head of operations in Europe, he had succeeded in squeezing out more profits and building the network there. In a meeting in Wriston's office, Putnam recited his list of all those he felt weren't qualified for the job. "Obviously, present company is excluded," Wriston cracked.

Putnam, according to one former Citibank officer, played a key role in the decision to place CIBL under the holding company umbrella rather than under the bank. In taking that route, the founders apparently thought CIBL would enjoy vastly expanded investment banking powers. According to one expert, that decision resulted from Citibank folklore which held that corporate subsidiaries somehow had broader authority than the subsidiary of an Edge Act Corporation or a bank. In fact, there are severe constraints on a bank's ability to fund a corporate subsidiary under Federal Reserve regulation 23A. Citibank's aggressiveness in interpreting the law was severely tempered by fines of $1,000 a day for violating 23A. "We don't monkey around with 23A at Citi," a source said. In contrast, in foreign countries it is common practice for affiliates to "take care of each other." Another reason CIBL was placed under the holding company was psychological, according to a source familiar with the deliberations. Putnam, the source opined, wanted CIBL to have the status of a "sister of the bank rather than the granddaughter."

CIBL was hardly an instant hit. Pedro-Pablo Kuczynski, a former minister of energy and mines of Peru and later a top investment banker at First Boston, recalls being told by a senior Citibanker, "I don't see how you get the business. We got all these guys sitting in London, and they don't seem to be able to get it." That would soon change. As Kuczynski observed later, "Once they [the Citibankers] got CIBL cranked up, they were really in a good position." As recycling gathered momentum, CIBL grew from a tiny operation with four officers and a secretary to a juggernaut with an army of syndicators. Its London headquarters operated at an increasingly frenetic pace, and it soon became the darling of the fifteenth floor at New York headquarters. Led by CIBL, Citibank—and to a lesser extent Bank of America, Morgan, and Chase—drove the recycling machinery. Each of them was competing with the others to become the world's number one bank and achieve 15 percent earnings-per-share growth. But Citibank enjoyed a considerable edge. Measured by total deposits, Citibank was bigger and more powerful than many of the countries where it did business. "When you were dealing with Citibank," said a former Morgan officer, "you were dealing with the strongest, toughest, and most powerful."

CIBL gave rise to a generation of salesman-bankers—George Putnam being the prime example—who spent more time in the first-class cabins of

Boeing 747s than they did at home in New York and London. Nicknamed the "paperhangers," they combed the world in search of $500 million deals, funded them in Eurodollar markets such as London, Panama, and the Bahamas, and earned whopping fees by selling them to hundreds of other banks around the world, including U.S. money center and regional banks eager to play in the big time. Everywhere he went, Putnam carried with him a brown book in which he recorded, in his tiny handwriting, the terms of each transaction. "CIBL's an octopus—and George seems to be everywhere," *Institutional Investor* wrote in May 1976. One of the problems in dealing with Putnam was finding him. He was always en route from one hotel room in Rio to another in Buenos Aires. Putnam and a small fraternity of syndicate managers were the heroes of the day. Bankers throughout the world clamored for the prestige and fat fees from leading $250 million issues, but Putnam led the pack.

The appeal of syndications was intoxicating. One reason was the irresistible up-front fees. Thanks to lenient accounting rules, such fees could be counted as income immediately. By putting a $100 million loan on the books, CIBL could receive a $500,000 fee, a sum that could make the difference at the end of a quarter between making budget and not making budget. With the fees from a few such deals, a profit center manager could become a hero overnight and have his picture pinned on Wriston's "corporate property board." The absence of reserve requirements on Euromarket deposits also reduced the costs and increased the profitability of syndicated lending. Moreover, because the deals included hundreds of banks and were led by America's banking powerhouses, the thousands of smaller U.S. and foreign banks that participated figured that these deals were as risk-free as a U.S. Treasury bill. There was, they thought, safety in numbers. The small banker with a small piece of a syndication felt that because his share was so small it would be impossible for him to get into trouble. Moreover, participating bankers didn't have to do much more than sign their names.

The usual procedure for putting together a syndication was to send out an information memo to all the usual suspects, followed by a stream of telexes and a term sheet. During the heyday of Third World lending, said one Citibank officer, "You got telexes back [asking to participate] for more money than you were looking for."

Citibank had a "profound effect" in encouraging other banks to play the syndicated lending game, said Continental Bank's international chief Ed Bottum, known to his French colleagues as Monsieur Derrière. "It was a validator," he explained. "If Citibank declined to make an overseas loan, other banks would typically decline as well. On the other hand, if Citibank indicated it was prepared to make one, other banks would consider it strongly."

In the view of John McGillicuddy, former chairman of Manufacturers Hanover Trust and later of Chemical Bank, Citibank's primary influence was in appearing to other banks, mainly regionals, as a success story that could easily be emulated. "Where Citibank played an unwitting role, if you will, was that they were so successful in terms of international banking that people tended to confuse their success with the ease with which they could put on international loans of large magnitude," he said. Just getting into the game "somehow was going to transform you into an international bank the caliber of Citibank."

To the senior officer of a regional bank in America's heartland, who was used to making $3 million loans to metal fabricators in Peoria, the idea of becoming part of a syndicate and instantly putting a $50 million loan on the books was an appealing prospect. Morgan and Bankers Trust were doing it. "It was easy," said a former senior Citibank official. "You'd get to go to Santiago, ministers would have dinner with you even though you were a little bank in the Midwest. Glamour was a part of it. You had to be in this thing [the syndicate] to show you were a world-class holding company." Top regional bank officers paraded into the IMF's Washington headquarters to announce that they were setting up an international department and that they would start with Brazil and Mexico.

Third World lending, said bank analyst David Cates, "destabilized regional banks that were greedy and wanted to be swingers."

Citibank, said banking consultant Ed Furash, "induced in the marketplace a change in managerial behavior that may not have worked for the rest of the industry. The fast-track concept brought a lot of problems to banks in the United States." Citibank, he said, inspired many regional banks to recruit "hot people" and push them rapidly through the organization. Nowhere was that more true than in international lending. The list of banks that tried to replicate Citibank in domestic and international lending and got burned is a long one. It includes Chase, Seattle–First National Bank, Continental Bank, First Chicago, Bank of Boston, Manufacturers Hanover, and later, several small fry.

Some of these banks might not have been aware that the prospectuses, which were prepared by CIBL, did not always convey a complete or accurate picture of the country's prospects. "The government was never interested in letting us as managers tell the truth," Putnam said. "We couldn't tell the dark side." The governments, for example, would not permit the lead managers to describe the country's entire external debt to all its lenders. Even though CIBL often knew the true picture, it would cover itself by including in the prospectus a disclaimer: "This information has been provided to us by the borrower and we are not responsible for the content." While the more sophisticated banks were aware that the country data contained in the prospectuses were most often incomplete or hyped, others, particularly Japanese banks, participated because Citibank was in the deal. "They didn't really much bother. They'd go on our say-so," said Putnam, who even studied Japanese to enhance his ties with that country's bankers. In fact, he said, the Japanese would ask if their representatives could accompany him and other Citibank officials on their sales calls. CIBL almost always agreed, because the Japanese banks took big slugs of the deal. "They always took 30 percent of every credit as long as they could pronounce the name," said one banker. Japanese bankers operated with little idea of what they were doing or why they were doing it. And banks of all stripes set up offices in London and elsewhere mostly to be fashionable and to have an excuse to travel overseas with their wives.

To encourage its overseas branches to beat the bushes for business, Citibank, using matrix management, counted syndication fees twice. The fee for a syndication originated by a branch manager and packaged and sold by CIBL would be booked, for profit center and bonus purposes, as a fee for both units. At the end of each quarter, the double counting was eliminated for income reporting purposes. In 1973 the average spread on loans to oil-importing developing countries was 1.24 percent. But the spreads often approached 3 percentage points or more on some loans to certain countries, far more than a banker could expect on a domestic corporate loan. Bankers also were lulled into complacency because the loans were booked on a floating rate basis. The borrowers, they figured, got stuck with the interest rate risk.

There were basically five types of overseas loans. There were loans to private companies, where repayment depended on foreign exchange. On infrastructure or project loans, such as loans for nickel plants, oil refineries, or power projects, repayment was supposed to be made from the revenue stream generated by the project. Some loans to subsidiaries of U.S. companies were guaranteed by the Export-Import Bank (which helps finance sales of American goods overseas), and others were backed by the company's parent. Finally, balance-of-payments loans to governments were extended on the basis of the country's financial track record. Most of the big syndications were for governments or state-owned agencies. Large private syndications, say for mining or oil-production projects, were the exception. Citibank preferred project loans and loans to private borrowers over loans to governments.

Putnam peddled his wares like a door-to-door salesman. "If you found out what kind of perfume the international manager's secretary liked, things would start to happen," he said later. Typically he got his appointments immediately, cars met him at the airport, and he rarely suffered the indignity of arriving at a hotel to find that his room reservation had been canceled. He enjoyed a close rapport with finance ministers and dealt at the highest levels of foreign governments. An inveterate tennis player, Putnam, like Wriston, carried his racquet with him wherever he went, always managing to whip up a game with a finance minister or central banker. One of his regular partners at the IMF meetings was Philippine finance minister Cesar Virata. They would catch each other's eye across the room at receptions and shout their tennis arrangements over the heads of other partygoers.

Putnam's sidekick was a smooth-talking Citibanker named Gerard Finneran, known at Citibank as "Son of Putnam," a.k.a. "Five Shells," for his ability to move multibillion-dollar loans around the world in a flash. Finneran supervised a team of attractive women whose job it was to keep syndicate members informed about transactions. Said one former Citibanker, "Jerry managed the syndicate. He wasn't worried about the product." Finneran and Putnam "were hustlers," said Farley, underlining their ability to produce through sheer hard work. "They'd go to the IMF [meetings] and corral the ministers of finance out of their hotel rooms with their pajamas on."

Although the country officers were supposed to originate the loans and CIBL was to sell them, in practice the tail often wagged the dog. CIBL often drummed up its own deals, then called on the country folk in Latin America to take a piece of them. According to Victor Prall, "CIBL, the investment bank, would come to me after the fact. There was nothing I could do about it." To the country heads, Putnam was a godsend. "The country people loved to have George around to get deals for them," said a former Citibanker. "He was always being called to help them out. Every time countries looked more favorable Putnam would say, 'We've got to do a little more.'"

"They [CIBL] were willing to make any loan they could get through credit policy," Al Costanzo said later. "Thank God we had a good credit control mechanism"—a view many would later dispute. While CIBL couldn't make loans without the concurrence of country heads, these Citibankers were enthusiastic. "Everyone around the world was interested in increasing his profit center. And the easy way to do it was to put on a cross-border loan," according to Costanzo.

Putnam spent a lot of time fighting the Citibank bureaucracy, looking for loopholes that would allow him to sell more deals. "The bureaucracy at Citi is like a football team," Putnam used to say, as Farley recalled. "Hit the line often enough and you'll find a hole and go through."

Putnam frequently argued that if a certain deal wasn't done, Citibank would miss out on the chance to do future transactions. "The big thing was let's do the big deals," said a former colleague. "Let's put this stuff on the books and let's make money. Nobody was saying let's put a halt on things."

Putnam was constantly battling with colleagues over how much of a deal to sell and how much to keep. Wriston, Spencer, and others urged CIBL to unload as much as possible on other banks, while Putnam typically argued that Citibank had to swallow some to induce other banks to participate. "There was a lot of pressure," said Farley, on the country officers to take more of a deal, because "they had to live with" the borrowers.

"The cost of doing that [syndicated] business is retaining assets," said Palmer. That was the Good Housekeeping seal of approval. And other banks figured, said one former officer, "If it's good enough for Citi, it's good enough for us."

While Citibank often took 10 percent or so for window dressing, it also knew it could sell off most of that after the closing. Said former overseas officer Richard Valelly, "They syndicated, then washed their hands of it."

CIBL itself was not set up to hold or fund assets, so for a loan to be placed on Citibank's books, it had to be approved by a line officer in whose geographical area it would be parked. Although CIBL was a super-aggressive marketing organization, the CIBL structure was actually seen as conservative because it didn't hold any of its own assets, and—in theory, at least—it called for loans to be originated and approved by line officers.

"There was a lot of pressure to cooperate with CIBL," said Ham Meserve. "They were the fair-haired guys who could do no wrong."

The pace at which Putnam and his merry men sold their loans outstripped the ability of the bank's operations and documentation people to deal with it. Operations was in a never-ending crisis. Loans were CIBL's inventory, and to keep the fees coming in, CIBL had to have a constant supply of them. "They would say, here's a new product, new innovation, and kind of book it," said Farley, who would later oversee the operation. "They were always inventing new products, twists to things, faster than we could book it. The day CIBL was born the problem was there." Because of the logjam, earnings were sometimes overstated or understated. "I don't think CIBL ever passed inspection 100 percent," said Farley. "It always had documentation problems."

One early sore point was whether loans or bonds bought for discretionary customer accounts should be treated as securities, and how they should be priced. General counsel Hans Angermueller wanted to be sure that Citibank was never accused of stuffing customer accounts with overpriced securities. The matter was resolved with an agreement to obtain three independent market quotes from unaffiliated dealers. Angermueller was also worried that Citibank could be accused of violating Glass-Steagall prohibitions on securities underwriting. But Putnam complained that other lenders, such as the Germans, had an advantage in syndicating credit because they had wider discretion to "stuff" the managed accounts, such as correspondent banks, with syndicated paper. Executive committee chairman Ed Palmer recalls that Putnam would say, "I have one hand tied behind my back. I can't compete with Deutsche Bank. I can't stuff it." This kind of pressure from Putnam began to get on people's nerves at Citibank.

"He badgered. He sold," Palmer remembered. "Perhaps he wore out his welcome. But the guys to blame were more general [officers]. The higher authority." That would have included Wriston, Spencer, Costanzo, and of course, Palmer himself.

Like the World Corporation Group, CIBL was also plagued with turf problems. Putnam and CIBL were forever on a collision course with, for example, officers from the oil department, who would call on a major oil company to sell a term loan and find that CIBL had just sold them on a Eurodollar syndication. Still, at his peak, Putnam was one of the world's best-known international bankers. "George knew everybody," said a competing banker.

To his detractors within Citibank, Putnam seemed out of control. Said former personnel chief James Griffin, "No one ever knew what he was doing. But he was one of the best individual producers the bank ever had."

Putnam's orders were to "go get 'em, George," recalled Reuben Richards. "He did what he was told to do. That was an institutional decision. And he was getting all kinds of applause. He wasn't the cause [of the ensuing problems]."

Technically, Putnam had several bosses. As head of CIBL he reported (sort of, said Palmer later) to his mentor, executive committee chairman Palmer, who was also chairman of CIBL; to George Vojta, head of the International Banking Group; and to Al Costanzo, who supervised international operations. But for the hard-driving George Putnam, the soft-spoken Costanzo was a pushover. Angermueller later asked, "Who was his [Putnam's] boss? Sometimes I wonder."

Finneran was no easier to control. "They both pushed the envelope as far as you could in terms of the legal aspects," said Angermueller.

Other former colleagues say that Finneran was a master at playing off one profit center against another. "He would go to Brazil and say to [resident bankers] that you're not making budget," said one Citibanker. "Then he'd say to the guy in Argentina, 'Look at the loans the guys in Brazil got done.' Then to Ecuador." One of the time-honored techniques of the big bank syndicators was to put other banks on notice that if they didn't participate in the current deal they wouldn't be invited into the next one.

Finneran had his own man in Brazil with whom he would call on customers. According to former Citibanker Anthony Howkins, he also had his own dollar pool in Panama where he could temporarily store loans to Latin American countries while he looked for a permanent home for them elsewhere in the Citibank empire.

"Jerry would come in and say, 'I can make a nifty loan to so-and-so' and avoid adding to Brazil's foreign exposure by selling it or, if he couldn't sell all of it, warehouse $5 million in Panama," said a former colleague. Palmer would later say, "He may have had a little authority to hold assets," but he added, "Finneran didn't have a large secret ability to take funds."

To other observers, Wriston appeared to admire the gutsy, hard-charging style of Putnam and Finneran, and their creativity in devising angles to circumvent regulatory restrictions on what they could do and how much they could do of it. Nor was Putnam shy about taking the debate directly to Wriston for a final verdict. But according to Angermueller, Wriston unfailingly sided with the rule of law. "I can't think of an instance when I walked out and said, 'Gee, I lost and Putnam won.' " No one was more popular and sought after at a party than George Putnam and his attractive wife, Elizabeth. "Everybody loved Putnam," said Angermueller. "But we all recognized him for what he was—a very aggressive marketeer."

One legendary example of Putnam's fleetness of foot was his dealings with the leftist government of Portugal in the mid-1970s. On a Sunday morning in April 1974, Putnam and his wife were heading for a picnic on a beach in Portugal. He picked up a newspaper and saw a headline in screaming print, *"Revolução!"* Leftist revolutionaries had overthrown the country's fascist dictatorship in a bloodless purge. He dashed back to his hotel, caught a plane for Lisbon, and was the first international banker on the scene when the new government opened for business. Any new government seeks bank credit lines to show, as Putnam put it later, the rest of the world "that they're in the clover." The new Portuguese government's line of credit was a backup line for $150 million secured by the nation's gold reserves, which couldn't be sold without the syndicate's permission. Putnam got the mandate just by showing up. He quickly slapped a syndicate together and then hammered out the documentation.

Two years later, while Putnam was in London, he read in the newspaper that Portugal's socialist regime was arranging a credit with the Bank for International Settlements that involved pledging gold. Putnam knew this was a device for reneging on the loans, so he phoned the syndicate and flew to Lisbon to cancel the loan. As a courtesy, he stopped at the American embassy to notify U.S. Ambassador Frank Carlucci. "Mr. Ambassador, I don't want to take up much of your time," Putnam said respectfully. "But I wanted to tell you something you might find of interest. You remember the loan we made two years ago. We're going to pull it."

Carlucci was furious. "You can't do that," he retorted. "That's not in accordance with our attempt to have decent relations with Portugal."

"Don't shoot the messenger," Putnam pleaded. Just then Carlucci's secretary came in to the ambassador's office in an agitated state. The embassy was surrounded by Portuguese marines. Carlucci quickly lost interest in the loan and ran out to persuade the marines to leave. Meanwhile, Putnam scurried down the rear stairs and yanked the loan, infuriating the Portuguese. Despite the efforts of the Portuguese central bank's fanatical Communist lawyer to stop him, the syndicate prevailed. "Pulling such a loan was not unusual in those circumstances," said Putnam.

Now it was the investment banks that looked with jealousy at their commercial banking competitors and the access they seemed to have to unlimited amounts of cash. "The oil crisis gave him [Wriston] a license to go worldwide in such a fashion that Merrill Lynch could only look [on] like a kid with his nose up against the candy store window," said Donald Regan, then chairman of Merrill Lynch. "You're getting money pouring into you in the left hand and you've got a huge number of would-be borrowers lining up on the right, in Latin America where Citicorp had tentacles and was so well established." While Merrill wasn't necessarily hungry to make cross-border loans to developing countries, it envied Citibank's ability to tap the deposits and earn fees by acting as trustees and advisers to Kuwait and other Arab states. Regan finally gained access to the riches of the East by acquiring White, Weld, an adviser to the Saudi Arabian Monetary Agency (SAMA), that nation's central bank. "We again were at a disadvantage, but we could get in on a portion of the business. Walter saw that was a wonderful opportunity," said Regan later.

In 1975, CIBL served as a manager or co-manager for sixty-six syndicated international credits amounting to more than $6.6 billion, compared with forty deals that involved about $4.5 billion in 1974. It also handled public and private securities issues amounting to some $600 million. Since CIBL was largely a shell entity with no formal authority to supply funds or book deals on its own, its balance sheet and income statement did not begin to reflect its huge contribution to Citibank's profitability.

"The whole thing began to explode," said Costanzo. "The guys said, 'Gee, this [recycling] really works.'"

When the oil embargo hit, only one piece of the recycling apparatus was missing at Citibank. Wriston and Costanzo recognized that the bank lacked a formal system to assess the unique risks of lending to each country. As a former top official of the International Monetary Fund and World Bank, Costanzo believed that the methods and data used by that institution could also be used by a commercial bank to evaluate whether to lend to certain countries and if so, how much. Costanzo thought he knew the right man for that job: Irving Friedman, holder of a doctorate in economics, member of the IMF old boy network, and the self-described "father of IMF conditionality." Conditionality was the guiding principle for IMF lending to troubled countries in which the governments received loans in return for promises to adhere to tough economic austerity policies.

Like Costanzo, Friedman had been a participant at the Bretton Woods meeting, one of a small core of people who helped steer the battered postwar economy out of the muck of import quotas and licensing, unrealistic exchange rates, and crippled trade. There was hardly a finance minister or central banker in the world whom Friedman didn't call by his first name.

In their first meeting, Friedman asked Wriston why he wanted to hire someone who had no commercial lending experience. "I believe in stockpiling IQs," Wriston replied. In May 1974, Friedman was hired to set up and oversee a country risk unit. Costanzo's instructions to Friedman were essentially to do at Citibank what he had been doing at the International Monetary Fund and the World Bank. Just as Citibank's domestic credit staff analyzed the creditworthiness of companies, Friedman and his staff were to evaluate and monitor the creditworthiness of countries, set prudent exposure limits for them, and determine how much of Citibank's loans to various countries should be short-term or long-term, public or private.

Temperamentally, Costanzo and Friedman were polar opposites. Costanzo was mild-mannered and self-effacing, Friedman vain and egomaniacal. But the two respected each other's intellectual credentials, and they both viewed the developing world through rose-colored glasses. Friedman, in fact, was considered even more of a wide-eyed optimist than the ever-sanguine Costanzo, who described Friedman as having "a bias in wanting to be helpful to developing countries." If Wriston believed that countries wouldn't disappear, Friedman took that thinking even further. "Friedman used to say that countries can't default, that the IMF will come to the rescue," recalled a former colleague.

For what it was worth—and that later was the subject of much debate—Citibank and Friedman pioneered the formal analysis of country risk. That analysis essentially consisted of three parts. It included the study of sovereign risk, or a country's ability to meet its obligations; transfer risk, or the country's capacity to repay in dollars; and political risk, the likelihood of political disruption that could jeopardize repayment. Among the key warning signs that the Friedman unit looked for in trying to detect deterioration in a country's economic condition was its external financial position; a persistent current account deficit typically indicated that the country would eventually run out of money. Recognizing that nothing causes money to flee a country faster than an overvalued currency, they reviewed a country's exchange rate policy. Often, developing nations maintained fixed exchange rates that did not reflect the true economic condition of the country and the value of the currency.

Like Jimmy the Greek, the country risk analysts strove to be right 60 percent of the time. "Knowing what's going on is not going to do more than make you right 10 percent more [often], but that can be a crucial 10 percent," said Jack Guenther, then a top IMF Latin expert who would succeed Friedman in 1979. According to another former colleague, Friedman was astounded when he learned commercial banks lacked a mechanism to determine how much money they had collectively lent to a given country. In fact, until Friedman arrived, no one at Citibank bothered to tally up the bank's overall exposure to individual countries. While the amounts lent directly were generally known, those figures didn't always include loans made by Citibank subsidiaries and affiliates, or, say, bankers' acceptances from a Zairean shipping company registered in Panama. Among other things, Friedman devised an accounting system that kept track of cross-border exposure, and he contacted other banks in an attempt to determine what they had lent.

For all the reluctance of the IMF to lend money or share nonpublic information, the agency was nonetheless a key source of country economic and external debt statistics. But to some of those closest to the process, this was a case of the blind leading the blind. The data were often incomplete, inaccurate, and poorly organized, and its analysts far from infallible. Though IMF data on employment, inflation, and wages tended to be relatively accurate, other statistics reflected the primitive state of data-gathering in the developing world. Data on gross national product and national accounts were typically at least a year late, because most of the Third World nations didn't crunch quarterly national account statistics.

These data grossly understated total external country debt. Until it was too late, the statistics reflected only official credits, not private lending. And while Third World central banks generally knew how much *they* owed, few, if any, kept track of how much state-owned enterprises had borrowed on their own, according to Elisabeth Rabitsch, Friedman's assistant. "Governments didn't know how much they owed or had guaranteed, nor did they feel that knowledge was necessary," she said.

Ham Meserve, an officer in the country risk unit, said, "They were just beginning to understand Third World economics. We got into the idea that if the IMF blesses the country, it must be good." The IMF became the credit rating for a country. "The whole credit approval process almost by default became an IMF blessing process. I'd go down to D.C. to see who wrote the IMF report, and he'd be some twenty-seven-year-old Ph.D., or some guy from the country," Meserve remembered. Country risk analysis was, said Meserve, "a basic science that was just beginning to develop." Besides the mass of economic statistics, Friedman was interested in the monetary and economic policies being pursued by each nation's finance minister and central bank. For example, Argentina and Brazil were always characterized by stop-and-go economic policies, from price freezes to thaws, from zero inflation to 500 percent inflation.

Friedman did not believe in newfangled techniques like economic modeling. He felt that his personal contacts were more important than quantitative analysis in trying to determine if a country was getting into trouble, and in order to maintain those contacts he spent about half of his time traveling. Wriston acknowledged the subjectivity of the process when he told *The Banker* in July 1974 that "in the last analysis credit is not numbers. It's people. So in the management of a country, as in that of a company, the determinative force is the ability of a government to react to circumstances."

Initially there was little disagreement at Citibank over the need for a country risk unit or over Friedman's qualifications for running it. What irritated Citibankers no end was Friedman himself. Under Wriston, 399 Park had become a monument to individual and institutional arrogance, but Friedman turned arrogance into an art form. He was alone among the many Ph.D.'s at Citibank who insisted on being addressed as "Doctor," and he demanded as a condition of employment that his wife be permitted to travel with him on all his trips abroad—at Citibank's expense.

Friedman's ego was as fragile as some of the fledgling economies he was paid dearly to evaluate. "I loved to be treated with respect and great dignity, and have a lot of attention paid to what I said," he admitted. When he was an official at the IMF and World Bank, where his approval of a loan could prop up the regime of a Third World dictator, Friedman was given regal treatment whenever he traveled abroad. For the most part, Citibank did not lavish head-of-state treatment upon anyone except its most exalted leaders. But it was imperative for country heads to please Friedman and flatter his wife. "If you wanted to get approval for an increase in country limits and his assessment agreed with yours, it sure as hell helped," said former Brazil hand Richard Huber. But Friedman's personal idiosyncrasies and style gradually eroded his effectiveness and acceptance among his colleagues. He was a misfit in a corporate culture that generally eschewed perks and ostentation, mirroring Wriston's own Spartan personality. Friedman was shunned by many of his colleagues. His memos and phone calls went unanswered. Officers neglected to invite him to luncheons with visiting central bank governors, some of whom had grown up working under Friedman at the IMF. Wriston himself acknowledged that "folks around the world were not too pleased to see him come because he always had the biggest hotel room. That impacted on their budget." But he insisted that the process was "too complex" to be affected by plays to Friedman's ego. "Costanzo at the end of the day was the guy who called the shots," Wriston said. Still, because of the reputation of the brain trust behind the country risk unit, Citibank became a kind of Third World debt rating agency, if not for J. P. Morgan & Company, Bankers Trust, and Chase, at least for the nation's regional banks, many of whom literally couldn't locate their borrowers on a map.

Years later, after the debt crisis flared, Citibankers and others would debate whether the country risk unit was a net plus, a minus, or a neutral. Wriston was convinced that it kept Citibank from boosting its exposure in a number of countries that later made it to the basket case list. According to Wriston, the Citibank country risk model was praised and even emulated by the nation's bank regulators. "From a credit point of view, I think it was absolutely terrific," said Wriston. "So did all the regulators. But if you have a major depression, then you can say, well, it didn't hurt or help. Absent that, business as usual, I don't think there's any question but that it helped."

Wriston insisted that "the process was more restrictive than expansionist." Officially, Citibank's exposure to any one country couldn't exceed 5 percent of its total loans. But according to Costanzo, major battles were fought over country limits, as country managers complained that they were being restrained in their ability to book loans and thus to earn profits for the bank and promotions for themselves. The ceilings were reviewed periodically for each country, not just for dollar limits but also for maturities. More often than not they were adjusted upward. Individual loans within those ceilings "were approved by the regular credit process," Wriston said. Wriston defended the numbers on which these decisions were based. "You had a whole statistical base. You can say the information wasn't totally accurate. You can say the same thing about the U.S.A., and I have. But here you have it in English."

Friedman would suggest a limit, and that number would then be subject to revision and discussion. Wriston remembered that "the guys in the country always wanted to get more [credit authority], and were always bitching to Al that they didn't have enough."

Costanzo also insisted that the country risk evaluation process was often at odds with CIBL's desire to book more loans. "To them, it was a world that would never end," he said later. Yet he maintained that as heavy as Citibank's Third World exposure later turned out to be, that exposure would have been "a lot worse" without the risk analysis unit. Moreover, Costanzo regretted that the risk evaluation process wasn't established even earlier. "Without it we would have had $10 billion, not $5 billion," said Costanzo in a reference to Brazil's eventual dollar exposure. "There was nothing wrong with the system," said Costanzo, but, he added, "you could say we could have been tougher in some areas" and in the early days of the unit.

But others felt that the country risk process led Citibank, and other banks, to believe that somehow they knew what they were doing. On the strength of the country risk recommendations, Citibank intensified its activities in certain countries and expanded the list of countries to which it would lend, according to former colleagues. It was "a fraudulent concept," said a former officer, though no one intended it to be that. "We were saying, 'Don't worry about us. We have limits.' "

Said former Mideast chief Vic Prall, "I've never known anybody in Citibank who [was] turned down during my time" when he sought to exceed his sovereign limit.

Some believed that the country risk unit was in a conflict of interest from the start, because it reported to the senior officer (Costanzo) who had budget responsibility for overseas earnings, and because it was located in the same area of the bank. It was relatively easy to differentiate between the obviously risky countries and the very good ones, of course, but with "everything in between, you cannot really differentiate very much," said an international banking expert. George "Jack" Clark admitted, "We made the same mistakes as other banks but made them much more elegantly. We had four guys trained in this stuff, but our position was just as bad or worse than anybody's."

Palmer likened the country risk effort to a burglar alarm that failed to go off, and to parents establishing a diet for their children and then "letting them out of the house when the Good Humor truck went by." In the end "a lot of this is performance-driven," Palmer said candidly. "You set objectives in growth and earnings per share, and then you build a budget." In that process, he explained, it was not unheard of for exposure ceilings on certain countries, including developing nations, to be revised upward when it became apparent that growth expectations could not be met elsewhere. "That's the real world, I guess," he said.

As diligent and scientific as the country risk unit may have attempted to be in controlling Citibank's exposure, at least one variable was virtually beyond control: the appetite of other banks, including big U.S. multinationals, regionals, and foreign banks, for the kind of spreads Citibank was getting. Nor did Citibank count on the extent to which other banks would view a large Citibank syndication as a stamp of approval for that country. Citibank might determine that a country's external debt should not exceed, say, $500 million, and on that basis team up with the Morgan Bank to lead a $200 million syndication. As Byron Stinson, a former Citibank vice president, recalls, "After Citibank put its name on it, then you'd have all sorts of weird banks jumping up and doing syndications." And the debtor countries themselves gladly exploited the banks' herd instinct. As soon as Citibank took a country or company to market for the first time, earning a fat profit on a syndicated loan, banks throughout the world would rush in with more money, boosting the total exposure of the country or company well beyond the level that Citibank had determined was healthy in the first place.

In lending to the Third World, Citibank attempted to be a countercyclical lender. Citibank, of course, got into the market early. Then when other banks thought it was safe to go into the water, Citibank scrambled to get out; when other banks pulled out, Citi plunged back in. The idea was that if everybody was lending all at once and competing for business, the spreads would be so thin that no one would make any money. In theory, when spreads dropped, Citibank stopped lending. Because it understood the value of money and its profitability better than all of its competitors except for Morgan, Citibank also tended to charge higher premiums on loans than its competitors did. Correctly, Citibank charged according to its perception of a country's creditworthiness. But according to Kuczynski, the Latin debt expert, it "got confused between charging higher premiums and creditworthiness."

According to Palmer, the growth rate raised lots of questions in everybody's mind, starting with Wriston. Citibank, Palmer said, didn't just blithely lend all this money. "We agonized over it."

Cross-border lending was removed from the control of the conservative, sharp-penciled, sons of the Depression who had ridden herd on Citibank's portfolio for years. In effect, the country risk unit divorced the analysis of sovereign risk from the traditional credit process.

When it came to loans to developing countries, the views of the reigning chief credit officer did not carry nearly as much weight as did those of Clark or Costanzo. P. Henry Mueller, who replaced Garvin as credit chief in mid-1974, would later say that he protested the premise that sovereign credits were somehow different. "You either get paid or you don't," he said later. Eventually, said a former senior officer, responsibility for credit approval of overseas loans became "mushier." "If he [Mueller] had been running it [LDC lending]," said a former top Citibank international lender, "it probably would have been very conservative for all the wrong reasons."

To some Citibankers, president William Spencer seemed to feel an oilman's visceral skepticism about the international business. As the big fees started to pour in, Spencer, said Ham Meserve, "thought we were doing it with mirrors. He was highly suspicious of anything he couldn't understand." Before making a presentation to Spencer, international officers would first translate everything into language Spencer could understand and insert the necessary buzzwords. Invariably, according to Meserve, Spencer would schedule the presentations for after lunch. The real test of their effectiveness, he said, was whether Spencer stayed awake for the entire presentation.

Although the Citibank credit committee, later headed by Mueller, generally reviewed foreign as well as domestic loans, its members tended to view the foreign loans from the perspective of a traditional domestic lender. To overcome that bias, overseas staff learned to package their cross-border loans like domestic loans. Approval of a loan to a U.S. company usually called for a balance sheet and income statement with the imprimatur of a reputable auditor. This was a novel notion to many foreign companies, which, nonetheless, told their account officers that they would supply whatever they wanted.

Citibank's traditional aversion to lending longer than five years would have prevented many long-term project loans from being made. So those loans were packaged as five- to seven-year "strings" that were rolled over or taken out by other banks as the loan approached maturity. "We were making fifty-year loans to these countries and packaging them as five-year loans," said Meserve. Later it would be clear that banks erred by not restricting themselves to short-term financing and finding long-term lenders like the World Bank for the remainder.

Along with the separation of sovereign and domestic lending, other long-standing taboos went by the board and credit lessons learned in the lending school of hard knocks were forgotten in the drive for profits. One was Citibank's traditional skepticism of government or quasi-government lending. Unlike certain other institutions, such as Manufacturers Hanover, Citibank preferred lending to private companies over governments and was not as smitten with government guarantees as some other banks were.

According to Ray Kathe, government deals were essentially approved by those responsible for determining sovereign risk. "Once they approved the sovereign risk, the cross-border risk, quite often anything that came up for the government, was [also] approved."

In lending to governments, banks relinquished the control they had when they lent to private companies. In private sector lending, banks could establish tough covenants, such as restrictions on debt equity ratios, and make reasonable determinations as to whether debt would be covered by cash flow. As banks jumped onto the sovereign debt bandwagon, however, that became impossible. On loans to governments or for government-sponsored projects, it was nearly impossible to earmark the money or determine how it was to be spent. In effect, said Continental Bank lender Alberto Luzarraga, "banks financed budget deficits in spades." Theoretically, at least, Citibank declined to make balance-of-payments loans to a country without an IMF program, Costanzo insisted later. On such loans, Costanzo and Citibank didn't want to have to monitor the country and dictate its economic policies. That, said Costanzo, would have "put the banks in the position of interfering in the legitimate sovereignty of the country." Instead, the IMF set the terms, negotiated with the country, and monitored the results. "As long as the Fund put money in, we'd put money in. If the Fund held back on money, we'd hold back," said Costanzo.

The big U.S. banks took comfort in government guarantees and typically neglected to do feasibility studies on a loan to a state-owned or even private company if the government agreed to guarantee it. Said one bank lawyer, "They thought they were home free because they had a government guarantee," adding that "those government people must have been laughing all the way to the bank." The only institution for which the guarantees meant anything were those like the World Bank, which would be repaid even if the commercial banks were not.

One major difference between foreign and domestic lending is that when the foreign borrower—be it a government or a private corporation—defaults, it is next to impossible to enforce the covenants or security agreements inside the country. The lender's only recourse is to seize whatever it can outside the country. That was apparent in the case of dollar-denominated bonds issued by Germany before World War II, which defaulted when the war broke out. With no seizable assets outside Germany, public utilities conveniently reneged on their obligations, whereas shipping companies whose vessels called regularly on New York faithfully kept up their payments.

In its eagerness to originate loans, Citibank would also forget the lessons of Freeport Sulphur. Like so many of the loans made in the 1970s, this one, made in the late 1950s, was "beautifully structured," said Angermueller, with completion certificates and documentation. The nickel plant really existed and served a useful economic purpose. While Citibank eventually made a partial recovery on what came to be known as the Cuban nickel loan, the incident showed "how relatively helpless a creditor is when he tries to assert his rights in a country that had politically or economically thumbed its nose at him," said Angermueller. Unfortunately for Citibank, that experience would later be repeated many times over.

Angermueller later said he regretted not having warned Wriston forcefully enough of the consequences of defaults by foreign debtors.

Banks deceived themselves into thinking that because they had obtained so-called waivers of sovereign immunity, which in theory allowed them to sue for nonpayment in New York courts, they could collect from Brazil or Mexico if the loans went bad. According to Stephen Wallenstein, a World Bank lawyer who wrote commercial bank loan agreements in the 1970s, the banks crossed every *t* and dotted every *i* in their effort to cover themselves legally. But as things turned out, they were preoccupied with the wrong problem. "Lawyers were arguing about the number of angels on the head of a pin," he said, such as how interest would be calculated if the London Interbank Offering Rate (LIBOR) market collapsed. Ten years later they learned that what really counted was whether the nation's leadership was willing to pay.

———

As Wriston and his colleagues surveyed their empire in the months after the OPEC oil embargo, it was certainly reasonable for them to cast their gaze south of the border. In the previous five years, the economies of Brazil and other Latin American nations had grown rapidly, certainly faster than the U.S. economy. All of the social indicators, including literacy and employment, were pointing upward. Moreover, said Angermueller, "we had a kind of responsibility to help these countries in which we've been a major international bank for three quarters of a century."

To the bankers, Latin America was a godsend, particularly as compared to other parts of the Citibank overseas empire. Europe was always a tough place to do business. The Swiss, said a former international officer, "were making mincemeat of us." In France, it was difficult for an American bank to make money, since the French banks were government-owned and didn't care whether they made a profit. The German banks were inextricably interlinked with their industrial customers, reducing opportunities for foreign banks in the corporate market. Beset by soaring inflation, the U.K. by late 1974 was veering toward socialism, and Italy was a prime candidate for an IMF bailout. Bankers were more worried about Korea than they were about Brazil or Mexico or Argentina. Wriston retained his bitter taste for Canada, and was developing one for Australia. And "Japan was a tough market," said a former officer. But Citibank thought it knew Latin America as well as it did the floor plan at 399 Park. And Brazil, in particular, was now the land of opportunity, optimism, and enthusiasm. Bankers didn't need much of an excuse to lend to Brazil. Traveling to Rio with one's wife, or perhaps without her, was a whole lot more appealing than trekking to Cleveland in the dead of winter.

In lending to the Third World, Wriston took the view of the chairman of a bank that had been in business for 160 years. Since the early 1800s, Latin America had experienced one debt crisis after another. Periods of heavy borrowing had invariably been followed by default. In Wriston's mind, the lessons of the 1930s, in which the Latins again reneged on their obligations, were equally applicable to the United States and the rest of the world. The banks themselves had lost little in the defaults of the Depression era in Latin America; the bondholders were the ones who really got hurt. Wriston could honestly say that "since 1812, the Citibank has never lost a dollar on a loan guaranteed by a central bank anywhere in the world." He dismissed the 1930s defaults with the explanation that the world had changed. In choosing what history to use in making his case, Wriston recalled that the United States itself was once a developing nation. In the 1800s, Europeans invested heavily in the United States, which defaulted frequently. Indeed, back then the ancestor of Citibank itself at times hesitated to lend for development projects right in its own backyard.

Since the 1930s, U.S. commercial banks had essentially redlined Latin America. Three decades later, however, the Latins had begun to regain access to global private capital markets and to rely more heavily on them for development. But by the 1970s, memories of the 1930s had largely faded. The oil crisis presented bankers with a dream come true: liquidity and a region that was underborrowed. Confident that the central banks in Latin American countries would ultimately step up to the plate to protect their credit standing, Wriston and Costanzo overlooked the volatility of the economies of these countries. They figured that while they had often stumbled and would continue to do so, in recent years they had usually recovered by reversing bad economic policies.

In recent years, Citibank had actually been kicked out of three countries, but even those experiences had not been disasters. Citibank had gotten all of its capital out of Egypt. Although Cuba, which had seized Citibank's branches there in 1960, didn't reimburse Citibank for its losses, it was able to offset most of them. And when Allende nationalized Citibank's branches in 1971, the Chilean government agreed to repay the bank and, by 1973, had kept its promise, according to Ed Palmer. Indeed, Egypt and Chile reinforced Wriston's conviction that these misguided countries would eventually rejoin the economic mainstream. In July 1974, Egypt, which had thrown Citibank out in 1961, agreed to allow four U.S. banks, including Citibank, to set up operations there again, and later Chile did the same.

Wriston firmly believed that Third World borrowers simply had too much at stake to cut themselves off from the world financial system by defaulting on their debts. Moreover, Costanzo and Wriston both felt that if countries faltered, they would do so one at a time.

Costanzo knew that the financial basket case of one era could quickly become the economic miracle of the next. In the early 1970s, he said that the developed world was predicting the "complete economic collapse" of South Korea, which in the 1980s emerged as an economic superpower. Costanzo believed that when things got bad enough, the leadership would rise to the occasion and resolve the crisis. Above all, Wriston and his colleagues believed that because of the huge rate of return on capital in the Third World, investments in these countries would be profitable as long as policies were correct.

Wriston mustered all the bank's intellectual forces to defend and promulgate these views through speeches, interviews, and articles in leading publications, such as *Foreign Affairs.* Indeed, Citibank literally helped write the book on overseas lending. Titled *Offshore Lending by U.S. Banks,* it was published in 1975 by two bankers' organizations and included contributions by Citibank credit chiefs Henry Mueller and Lawrence Glenn. Citibank and Wriston were sometimes accused of acting in the belief that if the loans cratered, the U.S. government would step in and bail out Citibank. But Friedman said later, "I never had that view of what we were doing. I would say repeatedly, before Walter and the board, that in anything we do we're fully at risk ourselves."

The changes in the economic management of the Latin countries in recent years gave Citibank more reason for optimism. Costanzo's view of countries like Brazil, Argentina, and Mexico was shaped, too, by his work in Latin America in the 1950s, when the Latin governments were run by economic illiterates. Now the top financial authorities in many of the Latin countries were educated at the University of Chicago, Harvard, or MIT.

Citibank also had something the other banks lacked: full service branches, largely run by locals, in most Latin American countries, a region that was ill-served by local banks. Wriston had begun the internationalization of the foreign staff, but Costanzo was largely responsible for converting the overseas corps from a mostly expatriate-managed operation to one with a high percentage of foreign nationals in key positions of power and for eliminating the distinctions between American and foreign national officers. At one time, said Costanzo, nearly all of the key jobs in Argentina, for example, were held by Americans. Eventually, only a few of the top officers were American.

Citibank's long-standing presence in Latin America and its local knowledge were an inspiration to other banks eager for a piece of the pie. Citibank became the bellwether, because other banks felt that Citibank possessed an understanding of these markets that few others could claim. Citibank's very presence gave others a sense of security. On visits to Latin

American countries and other Third World nations, other bankers would always make a point of trying to discern Citibank's current opinion of the country. Said one British banker, "If Citibank took a view on an area or industry everyone else would follow." But, according to John McGillicuddy, later chairman and CEO of Manufacturers Hanover Trust and then Chemical Bank, many banks forgot that much of Citibank's success in cross-border lending resulted from being in on the ground floor with branch offices in countries like Brazil, where banks like Manufacturers Hanover operated only representative offices. And no other bank, with the possible exception of Chase and Bank of Boston, had such strong personal ties to Latin America.

The international financial community is a small one, and few knew more about it than Costanzo. As deputy director of the IMF in Latin America, he was on a first-name basis with most of the young economists who rose through the ranks to become finance ministers and central bank chiefs. Heads of state took him into their confidence. When Costanzo visited Latin American countries with other bankers and economists, it was always Costanzo whom the finance minister asked to remain behind for a private tête-à-tête. "I don't think I've ever had an ego. I think they sensed that," Costanzo concluded. His modest, open attitude encouraged trust. While the finance minister or central banker who had embarked on an outrageous economic policy would not likely have changed course as a result of a word of disapproval from Costanzo, he was clearly an influence at the margin on a number of occasions.

According to international banker Geoffrey Bell, "Citibank led the pack, and off we went to the races."

In cross-border lending, Citibank and Morgan quickly emerged as the key players in Brazil, Citibank and Bank of America in Mexico, and Morgan, Manufacturers Hanover, and Citibank in Argentina. In the Philippines, the only Asian nation whose debt became unmanageable, the principal actors were Citibank, Manny Hanny, and Bank of America.

Of all the Latin nations, Citibank reserved the warmest spot in its corporate heart for Brazil, which had been remitting earnings off and on to New York since 1915 and was one of the bank's flagship outposts. Brazil was the training ground from which Citibank exported bankers to Europe and around the world. And since 1967, Citi's feelings toward Brazil had grown even warmer as the bank participated in and profited from the country's soaring economic growth. In the late 1960s and early 1970s hardly any mention of Brazil and its economy appeared in the financial press without at least one mention of the word "miracle." Wriston was clearly impressed with the fact that Brazil was now the eighth-largest economy in the world and was blessed with vast natural and financial resources.

In the early 1970s, Brazilians were on a perpetual high. Brazilian women would wear a dress once and give it to the maid, as one former Citibanker recalled. There was, he said, no sense of a need for caution. Speculation on land and real estate was rampant. Developers bought plots of land, designed buildings, sold the apartments from floor plans, and financed the buildings as they went up. The buyers, in turn, made a killing reselling apartments they had bought with borrowed money.

The surge in oil prices intensified the long-standing love affair between Brazil and Citibank, which was willing to help Brazil finance its whopping oil bill. Although Wriston was most at home in Europe, he was clearly smitten with Brazil. Back in the 1960s he had spent "two of the best weeks of my life, and Bobby's too," he said, traveling around that country, and he regarded the Brazilians as "warm people, terrific workers. I've never met one I didn't like." Like his colleague, Anthony Howkins, he would have taken issue with Brazil's "mañana" image. Some 60 percent of the Citibank employees in Brazil attended night school, Howkins said, and arrived for work before nine and left at six. "They worked harder than we do here," he said. Though Wriston did not share their gay, laid-back temperament, he did share with them another attribute. Brazilians call it *jeito,* which means "ingenuity." Brazilians admire cleverness—the ability, as former Brazil hand Peter Greenough put it, "to finesse things." They display their *jeito* in coping with the country's oppressive bureaucracy. As a participant in one of America's most highly regulated industries, Citibank had plenty of *jeito,* as did its chairman.

Wriston viewed Brazil's recent progress as breathtaking, and greatly admired the willingness of the country's economic technocrats to make politically tough decisions, such as devaluing the currency and curbing inflation. And he was impressed with the ability of the country to attract and retain foreign capital. In a 1974 talk to Brazilian officials, Wriston praised the country for having become the largest recipient of World Bank loans, and for receiving $3.5 billion in direct foreign investment.

To bankers like Wriston and Costanzo, the creditworthiness of a country was bound up in their impressions of that country's financial managers. Citibank officials were close to Brazil's top monetary officials—so close, in fact, that an American Citibank officer married the daughter of one of them. But few finance ministers impressed Wriston more than Mario Simonsen, who was appointed finance minister when General Ernesto Geisel was inaugurated as president of Brazil in March 1974. Wriston considered Simonsen "one of the great economists of the world." Trained in math and engineering, Simonsen was a round-faced, somewhat disheveled man and amateur opera singer whom Citibank regarded as a squeaky clean intellectual. His family were bankers in Brazil and co-owned, with Lloyds Bank, the Banco Bozano Simonsen. Wriston liked Simonsen so much he recruited him for the Citicorp board in 1979.

In Brazil, the process of recycling was very real. Foreign exchange reserves that had been previously used for economic development would now be needed to pay the Saudis. Citicorp chairman John Reed recalls that the Brazilians had two choices: they could either pay the fuel tab and reduce living standards or they could borrow and spread the adjustment process out over a period of time. "We were persuaded there was legitimacy in helping countries adjust," said Reed. In 1973, Brazil was producing only 17 percent of its oil consumption, according to Simonsen. Though it had started to build hydroelectric plants, Brazil's hunger for dollars became acute after the oil crisis. Its trade deficit surged from $1 billion in 1973 to $6.2 billion in 1974.

When Geisel took office, his administration, which included Simonsen, made a critical strategic decision. In effect, they decided not to risk political discontent by allowing the rise in oil prices to get in the way of economic growth. Instead, they would support that growth with foreign borrowing. From the late 1960s until the oil shock, the Third World had become comfortable with the use of debt as their principal means of development. The Latins sharply restricted foreign investment and used borrowed money as a cheap source of capital. The Geisel plan called for spending and investment of $100 billion through the end of the decade to maintain an annual economic growth rate of 10 percent. The plan also involved developing oil and other resources so that Brazil wouldn't have to import it. Simonsen said later that if the banks hadn't recycled, Brazil would have had a 20 percent negative growth rate and suffered "a complete collapse. We would have been unable to import."

That would have meant that "we would have had something like the Great Depression in the United States," he believed. "It's hard to predict the political consequences. It would not have been smooth." Wriston, Simonsen said, "recognized the mess that would occur in the world. He knew we would have enormous disorder."

Brazil was the go-go nation of Latin America, the emerging Japan. Foreign banks responded by pouring money into the country. Brazil was willing to pay high rates for long-term loans up to fifteen years, though eight years was the norm, according to a former Citibanker. According to former Brazil central bank chief Carlos Langoni, American bank lending began largely in the form of long-term project loans. Citibank, he said, became the model that the others followed. Everyone—Wriston, Costanzo, Clark, Friedman—was bullish on the country. "I would have thought if anyone could make it, it was Brazil," said former country head George Hagerman.

Apart from those hefty up-front fees, Citibank's eleven-branch system in Brazil was yet another powerful reason to support the country's growth plan. Because of limitations on foreign bank expansion, the branch network was tiny compared with Banco Bradesco, whose one thousand–plus branches made it the largest bank in the country. But Citibank's network was surely the most profitable in Brazil. And it was the envy of every other big American bank. It was such a moneymaker, in fact, that Citibank executives tried to avoid revealing just how well they were doing, out of fear that the locals would demand to be paid on a U.S. scale, according to former officers.

Its Brazilian operations made Citibank a kind of universal bank, combining merchant banking, commercial banking, insurance, and consumer finance. But if the New York headquarters of Citibank was increasingly becoming more bureaucratic, that was not the case in Brazil, where Citibank was an entrepreneurial organization staffed with eager bankers competing with one another to make money for the bank. Said Simonsen later, "The secret of Citibank in Brazil is that it's run by Brazilians." It was also light-years ahead of the Brazilian banks, which were still labor-intensive. No Brazilian bank could compete with Citi on efficiency, training, and innovation.

Since Citibank was limited in its ability to expand in the retail banking business, it sought to concentrate on corporate lending and to capitalize on its ties to multinationals and its ability to fund itself worldwide. At the local banks, borrowing money was a highly political exercise. One's creditworthiness depended on family and social ties, wining and dining, and sometimes bribery. At Citibank, things were far more straightforward. At Citibank, said one former officer, a customer didn't have to "send five cases of whiskey four times a year. Bribes weren't necessary." Just having a Citibank checking account was prestigious and opened doors.

Citibank, said Peter Greenough, who was sent to Brazil after the first oil shock, lent to real estate developers at "horrendous spreads." Three percentage points over the London Interbank Offering Rate plus balances and flat fees of 1 to 2 percent was typical, he said, but up to seven points was not uncommon. If this seemed expensive, the Brazilian banks were frequently 5 to 20 percent more expensive, albeit in local inflated currency. Money from local banks was more expensive in part because of the lack of sophistication in the local capital markets. "Brazilians were easy to bargain with," says Greenough, because "people looked at . . . availability of capital more than anything else." Inflation was low by Latin standards, and local companies had many opportunities to make loads of money. "They weren't tremendously concerned about the cost of capital, and negotiating the fees only took a few calm moments," said Greenough. "Citibank had the spigot wide open."

Citibank's growing expertise in back office processing also enabled it to reap enormous profits. For example, banks in Brazil were paid for processing receipts and payments on government-mandated retirement funds, similar to Social Security. Unlike the Brazilian banks, which didn't like to perform this function because they processed most of their work manually, Citibank was able to automate the process and earn a fat 40-percentage-point spread. In addition, this business generated scarce local currency deposits that Citi was able to lend out.

When it came to circumventing government regulations, Citibankers in New York met their match in Rio. Brazilian banking rules changed constantly, but Brazilians quickly managed to maneuver around them by getting breaks and favors from friends and relatives in government or by devising highly creative legal interpretations or financial instruments.

Citibank assigned some of its most eager salesmen to Brazil. Richard Huber, for example, was a savvy, outspoken top officer of the Bank of Boston in Brazil when Latin chief Jack Clark recruited him to head Citibank's São Paulo branch, then the largest in the Citibank empire. He knew "who were the good guys and the crooks," he said later.

U.S. and Brazilian tax law also made local lending more enticing. Although Brazil charged foreign banks a 25 percent withholding tax on interest, U.S. banks received tax receipts from clients that they used to offset their U.S. taxes on a dollar-for-dollar basis. The bottom line in this complex system of receipts and rebates was that the American taxpayer effectively subsidized and encouraged lending by American banks to Brazil. Such tax-driven lending, said Continental Bank's Hollis Rademacher, was a "bigger factor than most people admit." Bankers would later discover that most such lending was imprudent.

There were some sore spots in the Brazilian operation. One was Banco Crefisul de Investimento, a financial services company that made dollar loans and operated a finance company, stockbrokerage and real estate firms, and engaged in activities that the Fed wouldn't have permitted in the United States. Citibank had purchased a one-third interest in Crefisul, the most it was allowed to own. In Brazil, as in Australia, restrictions on ownership caused Citibank to be less than choosy in acquiring local companies. After the closing, Citibank discovered that Crefisul had serious managerial and financial troubles. Part of the problem was Citibank's joint venture partner. Eventually Citibank forced that partner to sell and found another.

"The Americans we had there weren't savvy enough. They [the Brazilians] hoodwinked them," said Howkins. Still, Citibank became a major player in the Brazilian credit card business and also introduced electronic banking to the country. Just as it was doing in the United States, Citibank in Brazil was constantly pushing for more freedom to operate, particularly to expand its branch network. Because it was not allowed to do that, it couldn't compete head-to-head with the indigenous banks.

To a large extent, Citibank's dollar lending in Brazil was driven by its desire to obtain new licenses. Brazil used an implicit carrot-and-stick approach. On the one hand, the authorities dangled the prospect of new licenses in return for more dollar "impact loans," including agricultural and housing loans. On the other hand, they hinted that they might force Citibank to scale back its operations if it didn't extend such credits. Incidentally, the housing loans often ended up subsidizing the construction of large ranches for wealthy Brazilians rather than sheltering the homeless multitudes in the growing *favelas* of Rio and São Paulo.

Citibank's money center competitors, eager to follow in its footsteps, were also "encouraged" to make impact loans. Taking a slug of a syndicated credit would usually satisfy that requirement.

Citibank's enthusiasm for Brazil was shared even by the august Morgan Bank, spurred on by Lewis Preston, its international lending chief. One reason, Preston explained later, was that virtually all of his bank's major multinational customers had Brazilian operations. Unlike Citibank, however, Morgan was never able to establish local branches and envied Citibank's network in Brazil as a license to print money. "We were frustrated as hell," Preston said later. After the oil shock, Morgan's "lending into Brazil was aimed at trying to achieve a physical presence" in the form of "wholesale" branches.

Morgan's point man in Brazil was Colombian-born Antonio Gebauer, a high-living, Ivy League–educated banker who traveled in Brazil's speed lane with jet-setters and Rio society types. Top Brazilian central bankers and monetary officials were frequent guests at his fashionable East Side Manhattan apartment and at his weekend retreat in the Hamptons, named Samambaia—Portuguese for "fern." Gebauer became virtually a traveling chamber of commerce for Brazil and Venezuela. "It was commonly alleged if you want to get a loan from Morgan and you give a few points [of a loan] to Tony, you'd get the loan," said a former Citibanker in Brazil.

The Brazilian economy was always dominated by the heavy hand of government, and a significant—albeit indeterminable—portion of the loans made by Citibank and other U.S. banks went for corrupt and inefficient state-owned enterprises. "There was never a point in Brazil's history where the country freed itself from the shackles of government control of business," said Brazilian central banker Carlos Langoni. Since the Depression, government policy had emphasized, if not central planning, "a lot of planning, protection incentives, and subsidiaries," he said.

State borrowing, according to Langoni, was almost entirely centralized through federal and state enterprises. Private borrowing, in contrast, was in much smaller amounts. "If you had private borrowing you probably would not have had the debt crisis," said Langoni. "Private corporations are much more cautious in their borrowing."

With the first oil shock, every arm of the Brazilian government—from the national oil company to the housing and road buildings departments—had its hand out seeking to borrow as much money as possible. While Brazil, by most accounts, used the money better than Mexico did, and certainly better than Argentina, that wasn't saying much. The state-run Brazilian steel industry, for example, was among the world's most inefficient, and its legacy is an inestimable number of half-completed buildings. Every employee of any standing at Brazil's state-run companies seemed to have a Ford Galaxy and a driver at his disposal, Peter Greenough recalled. At the end of the workday, a procession of American cars lined up outside the offices of state companies. Executive offices, he said, were big enough to accommodate a badminton game. Officers traveled first class to the United States, where they stayed in the best hotels.

Much as Mario Simonsen was admired in the United States, some observers felt that he, as finance minister, was partly responsible for the growing state investments in the Brazilian economy. Paulo Sotero, a leading Brazilian journalist, said that "some people like Simonsen were talking about deregulation and privatization, but they were the [same] ones who were behind the state involvement in the economy." Brazil's economy was so driven by the public sector that it was "difficult to find entrepreneurs not hooked on state subsidies," said Sotero. In Brazil, companies don't go bankrupt. Instead, they go to the [National Economic Development Bank]." Later, after Chrysler got a federal bailout, chairman Lee Iacocca became a kind of folk hero in Brazil because he recovered with government guarantees, recalled Sotero.

Not surprisingly, a large portion of the dollars lent by Citibank and others was meant to be used for energy-related purposes. Brazil and Mexico each operated a state-owned oil company—Petrobras and Pemex, respectively—and both refused pleas by U.S. bankers to permit direct investment by U.S. oil companies. "They would have gotten tremendous direct investment if they came up with a sensible profit-sharing plan for international oil companies," said Morgan's Preston, who tried to persuade the Latins to go along with such plans. But in the end, he said, nationalism prevailed. He would later say that while the Brazilians and Mexicans endorsed the concept, they said that the notion of foreigners owning any portion of the country's mineral resources would "never fly politically."

But much of the money lent to state-owned energy companies was wasted, through corruption and mismanagement, on huge showcase projects.

One of the biggest projects begun in the post-embargo period was Brazil's Itaipu Dam, the world's largest, which was intended to supply vast amounts of electricity to Brazil and Paraguay. The entire world banking system collaborated on the financing of Itaipu, which began construction in November 1975 and whose cost by 1977 was estimated at $9.5 billion. By the mid-1980s, the project had cost more than $15 billion, according to a Bank of Boston analysis.

Additionally, foreign commercial banks—rushing in where the IMF feared to tread—even financed the oil imports of Brazil and other Third World nations with long-term loans. According to Latin debt expert Kuczynski, one of the first such loans was put together by Wells Fargo Bank in 1975. "That's very dangerous," said Kuczynski, "but it was well received."

They should have learned a lesson when, barely a month after the oil shock, Citibank led a $200 million syndication for Pertamina, the Indonesian national oil company. Before long, Pertamina had amassed $10 billion in commitments. By 1974, the company couldn't meet its obligations, and in March 1975, it essentially collapsed under its debt burden. Citibank was forced to lead one of two $425 million syndicates to rescue the company. No company suffered more from official corruption than Pertamina. According to author Karen Lissakers, the only documentation the banks received for one $25 million Pertamina loan was the "scribbled signature of General Ibnu Sutowo on the inside cover of a nightclub matchbook."

Just months after Richard Huber joined Citibank, he found himself presiding over a junk heap of retail businesses that the bank had acquired in Brazil, and over the ashes of Crefisul's modern São Paulo headquarters, which had burned to the ground on February 1, 1974, with the loss of nearly two hundred lives.

Operations chief John Reed had been in the building that week, looking into the plans of the unit to launch a nationwide marketing blitz. During his visit, Reed, according to Huber, had come to the obvious conclusion that the entire operation was out of control, and that expanding it would be a waste of money. Having finished his review just a day or so earlier, he planned to spend a day or so in Rio before heading back to the United States. Had he remained, Reed almost certainly would have been killed.

The building was such a firetrap that escape for many was impossible; people were forced to jump from windows to their death. Huber, however, managed to escape from the burning building with the computer tapes containing the company's records, enabling Citibank to piece together at least in part who owed whom money. When word of the fire reached New York, Reed was appointed acting country head for Brazil, and he returned to São Paulo over the weekend to dig the company out of the ashes. Ignoring the Brazilian central bank's instructions to shut the unit down, Reed and local staff worked around the clock to open for business on Monday in rented quarters. Over the next week, Huber observed another side of Reed, who had a reputation for ruthlessness. Reed insisted in sharing with Huber the emotional burden of representing Citibank at funerals. In addition to dealing with the human tragedy, one of the many lesser problems facing the rebuilding effort was the need for compatible computers. Coincidentally Henry Ford II happened to be visiting Brazil, and offered Citibank the use of its equipment.

Ironically, according to former personnel chief Jim Griffin, an American employee who later died in the fire had written to Citibank in New York reporting that the building was a firetrap.

The fire tragically highlighted Citibank's ineptitude in making corporate acquisitions inside or outside the United States. Citibank had performed a superficial review that revealed major discrepancies, but didn't want to offend its Brazilian partner by debating the issue. In fact, a year earlier Bank of Boston had passed on the dubious opportunity of acquiring Crefisul because it knew the company was rotten even by Brazilian standards. According to Huber, "Past-dues were ballooning, aging records were poorly kept, the whole collection process was in disarray. Citibank had bought into it but never really took control, and never really considered that the foundation was completely rotten. We had to write off millions."

In the wake of the tragedy, Citibank spent millions bringing all of its buildings around the world up to strict New York fire standards, ignoring the weaker local codes. If local standards called for one exit, Citibank would require two. And if it couldn't lease, convert, or build a suitable building, it would leave the country. Wriston and Spencer made it clear that they would not tolerate bank officers saying that Citibank was not required to meet local regulations. "They would be stone-faced if people [Citibankers] brought up the costs of complying with fire regulations because it would blow the budget," said Rudowski.

But neither the fire nor Crefisul nor other setbacks could temper the love affair between Citibank and Brazil. The country was so profitable and growing so fast that by the mid-1970s Brazil cross-border exposure was pushing beyond the rule that only about 5 percent of the bank's risk assets could be lent to a single country. According to former officers, the Citibank brass in 1975 made the critical decision to cross that Rubicon. For the next six years, Citibank loans to Brazil rose inexorably from $2 billion to $5 billion. The banks figured, said international banker Geoffrey Bell, that "if some lending is good, more must be better."

In an April 18, 1976, *New York Times* Op-Ed article, Costanzo praised Brazil's fiscal management, saying that "Brazil's balance-of-payments management in 1975 produced encouraging signs of improvement, including a $300 million surplus in the second half."

Others agreed. "Brazil looked like a great economy," said Huber, one of Brazil's biggest fans, "and the bank said 'Gee, why not? We're making a lot of money. Why not another couple of hundred million?' "

Irving Friedman was also bullish. "It's fair to say, in 1974–1975, I had a fairly favorable view of the outlook for developing countries, despite the oil crisis. I was very concerned about the way [South] Korea and Brazil would react, knowing their great dependency on imported oil, but having visited there, knowing what I did from the [International Monetary] Fund and the [World] Bank, I came back convinced they had a good strategy for dealing with the problem. I became one of those who were quite accepting of the idea that Brazil and Korea should have larger lendings from the bank."

To those who might argue that having more than 5 percent of Citibank risk assets in one country was a violation of the actuarial base theory, proponents of lending more than 5 percent to Brazil could point to the vast diversification of the projects within that very diverse nation. No one ever thought that diversification would not count for a hill of Brazilian coffee beans less than a decade later.

Despite Costanzo's optimism, he apparently was concerned that Brazil's exposure could get out of hand. He warned Anthony Howkins, who was placed in charge of the country in 1976, not to let Citibank's Brazilian outstanding loans grow faster than the bank's capital. Until the late 1960s, the Brazilian operation was making perhaps $2 million a year in profit center earnings, said Howkins. And by 1973, according to Huber, the budget for Brazil was still a mere $4 million in earnings. By 1977, however, after-tax earnings from Brazil were about $74 million, which together with earnings from cross-border lending, inspired executive committee chairman Ed Palmer to remark that "we paid our dividend out of Brazil." In a late-1970s presentation to management trainees, Wriston declared expansively that the "budget for Brazil next year exceeds the total earnings for the international banking group the day I joined it."

According to one British banker, Mario Simonsen told him of his embarrassment of riches as the lending frenzy picked up steam. "What am I going to do? All these American banks tripping down here offering me more money, lower rates, and longer terms? We're not stupid."

But somebody was.

When the first oil shock hit, banks were also enthusiastic about lending to Mexico. Although Mexico had imported some of its oil, it became self-sufficient by 1974. Later, with the discovery of huge Mexican oil reserves, the banks' enthusiasm turned into hysteria. Though Mexico's political system was considered primitive, its economy, like Brazil's, was run by sophisticated U.S.-educated technocrats who were highly regarded by their American banker friends. Mexico, said Costanzo, "is not a country used to living in [economic] chaos."

From 1953 until left-leaning President Luis Echeverría Alvarez took office in December 1970, Mexico enjoyed relative economic stability, free movement of capital, and stable exchange rates. Echeverría, however, believed in subsidies and state-owned companies, and he eschewed foreign investment. In 1973, when his finance minister reported that Mexico was out of money, he replaced him with José López Portillo, who was less shy about borrowing. Under Portillo, Mexico once again began courting overseas investors. According to Costanzo, Citibank pulled back from Mexico when Echeverría began expanding the economy. When the world began to move onto a floating exchange rate system in 1971, Mexico doggedly tried to hold on to its fixed rate, and by 1976 that policy had brought the economy to the brink of disaster. The peso was by then grossly overvalued, and Mexican capital was fleeing to safe havens in the United States. The exchange crisis sent foreign bankers fleeing for cover and forced Mexico to pay sky-high rates for money. But a 25 percent devaluation of the peso followed by a $966 million IMF stabilization program began to turn things around. After Portillo succeeded Echeverría as president in December 1976, new major oil reserves were discovered, and bankers began to descend on Mexico City in droves.

As for Argentina, it was always regarded by Citibankers who worked there as a "screwball place," as former Latin hand Howkins put it. It was self-sufficient in nearly every basic commodity, including oil. During the 1930s, it even approached the United States in grain production. At one time or another, it was one of the highest per capita consumers of wine and beef in the world. By Latin standards, Argentines were well educated. Yet since World War II, no one had been able to make the country work. Argentina,

Wriston ruefully observed, "is one of the richest countries in the world. It's had perennially bad management since I can remember." But, he said, "it doesn't take much to turn the wheel a quarter turn to turn Argentina into a cornucopia." But twelve years of Juan Perón, who was overthrown in 1955, had devastated the country's private sector and convinced Argentines that the state owed them a living.

Argentina couldn't stand the IMF and balked at its efforts to influence the country's policies. And Argentina went through finance ministers and economic policies like M&M's. These policies were erratic and undependable. "They would say we're going to limit the cost-of-living increases to 3 percent, and then the next day you'd read they'd given a 30 percent cost-of-living increase to all employees," said a former Citibanker.

Despite its flaky politics and rocky postwar financial record, however, Argentina was attractive to Citibank and to other American banks for a variety of reasons. After World War II, it was considered the most creditworthy Latin country, largely because of Perón's decision to pay off his overseas bankers. That was possible because of its gold reserves, earned in World War II by exporting vast amounts of food to Europe. Citibankers felt a certain sentimental attachment to "the Argentine," as it was known to old Latin hands. The home of Citibank's first overseas branch, Buenos Aires, exuded a European atmosphere and resembled Paris but for the signs in Spanish. Said one U.S. banker, Argentines "looked down on Brazilians," who were a motley mix of Europeans, blacks, and Indians. It offered many pleasures, at least until the early 1970s, when the country was plagued by a wave of terrorism. Citibankers enjoyed a fun-filled lifestyle in Buenos Aires that included at least two cocktail parties every night, plus tennis, polo, skiing, theater, and the biggest and cheapest steaks in the world.

Although it was constantly whipsawed by changes in bank regulations, Citibank managed to make money locally by rolling with the punches. In the early 1970s, for example, Argentina took the seemingly drastic step of confiscating deposits, but it paid Citibank a good rate to service them and raised the ceiling on the total volume of exports that a bank could finance. To show the public that they were in charge, Argentine authorities "gave and took away," said George Hagerman later. "Argentina changed so damn fast that if you were out of the country for a month, you wouldn't know what's going on."

On May 25, 1973, just months before the oil embargo, Peronism (and Perón) returned once again to Argentina, with the inauguration of Héctor Cámpora. Following Perón's instructions, Cámpora appointed Perón a general in the armed forces on June 11 and resigned from the presidency two days later. Then, on September 23, 1973, Perón was elected president. Almost immediately after taking office, Perón ordered the expropriation of seven Argentine banks controlled by U.S. institutions, one of which was Citibank. The following April, Argentina offered five of the U.S. banks $25 million for their stakes on a take-it-or-leave-it basis. To be sure, the U.S. banking establishment was not pleased about the return of Peronism to Argentina, and for good reason. By 1974, inflation was running at a rate of about 6 percent a month.

Nonetheless, in June 1974, Citibank led a syndicate of banks to make an eight-year loan of $152.5 million to the Empress Lineas Maritimas SA, an Argentine shipping concern, to build cargo ships in Germany. Guaranteed by the government-run development bank, it was the biggest Eurodollar loan ever made to Argentina. In July, as he lay on his deathbed, Perón handed over his presidential powers to his second wife, Isabel.

Not surprisingly, the public sector fed at the trough during the second Perón regime. Instead of firing superfluous workers, the military government took the easier and more popular route of cutting wages. By 1976, the economy was in ruins. So bankers were ecstatic when, in March 1976, a military junta led by General Jorgé Videla seized power and placed Isabel Perón under house arrest.

Videla appointed as his economics minister José Martínez de Hoz, who was well regarded by Citibank and the rest of the international banking community. Promising economic reforms and free market policies, he negotiated agreements with the IMF and rescheduled the country's external debt. Encouraged by de Hoz, bankers were now eager to lend the country money in a major way.

In September 1973, as Argentina was turning to the left, neighboring Chile was moving in the opposite direction. Exploiting economic chaos and social unrest, Augusto Pinochet Ugarte led a military coup that ousted Salvador Allende, who either was slain or took his own life. Shortly thereafter, Jack Clark and Wriston flew to Santiago to meet with Pinochet to discuss his policies. They were pleased with what they heard. Pinochet believed in the free market and opposed central planning. "He's a tough dictator," said Clark. "But he knew he didn't want a lot of inflation. He liked the idea of Chile being an exporting country." Chile's economic managers were free marketeers who had studied under Milton Friedman at the University of Chicago and earned the nickname "the Chicago boys." In 1975 they introduced economic measures that were regarded as revolutionary for a Third World country, including sharp reductions in tariffs and a rational tax system.

Unlike some of its neighbors, Chile did not go hog wild borrowing money in the early days of Pinochet's regime, according to Kuczynski. The loans came later. In mid-1975, Citibank and three other banks lent the Chilean government $70 million. Also by 1975, four years after its Chilean branches were expropriated, Citibank had reopened its Santiago branch, reinforcing Wriston's conviction that countries eventually seek to reestablish their credibility with the international financial community. Later, however, Citibank was accused of backing a totalitarian regime that used torture as an instrument of domestic policy.

In the early post–oil embargo period, banks tripped over each other to lend to Peru and Bolivia, two perennially troubled countries. It didn't hurt that Bolivia's minister of finance was the former head of Citibank's La Paz branch. Citibank's local Bolivian operations were immensely profitable. Here again, because of the inefficiencies of the indigenous capital markets, the bank was able to arbitrage funds at wide spreads, at one point borrowing at 7 percent and lending to the central bank at 13 percent, according to a former officer who served in the country at that time. Meanwhile, syndications to Peru, in 1973 and 1974, despite its dismal financial history, were often over-subscribed.

Asia and Eastern Europe weren't ignored either. At the IMF's annual convention in Washington in September 1974, the Korean finance minister met with Wriston, David Rockefeller, and Lewis Preston, and separately with Bank of America's Tom Clausen, and walked away from those meetings with $200 million. In March 1975, Citibank and several other banks supplied $187 million to finance a worker-owned smelter project in Yugoslavia.

One sore spot in Citibank's love affair with Latin America was the pressure for nationalization from the six signatories to the 1969 Andean Pact: Colombia, Venezuela, Peru, Chile, Bolivia, and Ecuador. At that time, Colombia and Venezuela were feeling especially flush with nationalistic pride. The Pact's Decision 24 called for foreign businesses to turn over majority control of their local operations to the host country. Although all six members were parties to Decision 24, those two enforced it most vehemently. Citibank vociferously opposed this takeover effort, threatening to quit these countries rather than comply. By forcing Citibank to share control, such policies would have limited the dividends Citibank could remit home. But they also meant that if something went wrong, Citibank would have to step up for 100 percent.

Chile, meanwhile, recognizing the benefits of foreign investment, sought unsuccessfully to amend the Andean Pact rules.

Colombia, under president Alfonso López Michelsen and finance minister Rodrigo Botero Montoya, however, was one of a few underdeveloped countries that resisted borrowing from foreign banks. Juan Sanchez, the man who had wound down Citibank's operations in Cuba, had spent years cultivating the Colombian relationship, to the point where Colombia had even issued a postage stamp commemorating Citibank's service there. But in the midst of his Colombianization drive, Michelsen and his finance minister visited the United States and met with Wriston over dinner at 399 Park to discuss the matter. According to Richard Valelly, then a Colombia-based officer, who was present at the dinner, the Colombian president drifted into a diatribe on the deterioration of American society. "The United States isn't what it used to be," Valelly recalled Michelsen saying. Then he rambled on about crime in the streets, drugs, and immorality.

Wriston's face flushed with pique. "It looks like we've imported more than coffee from your country," he fumed.

There was a stony, agonizing silence.

Thereafter, Citibank's business relationship with Colombia went from bad to worse.

But according to former officers, there was more to this enmity than just nationalistic pride. They understood that Colombia didn't appreciate

Citibank's aggressive interpretation of its banking laws. As one top bank official would acknowledge later, "We probably didn't behave ourselves [as] we should [have]. They have some regulations we thought were dumb, and we found smart ways around them, like booking loans offshore that were really to Colombian entities, and finding loopholes in the law." Some Citibankers, however, blamed former country head Edwin Hoffman—a brilliant, ambitious holder of a doctorate in molecular biology—for Colombia's hostility. Hoffman, then in his early thirties, "cut corners" there, said a former officer familiar with the episode. "It got us thrown out of Colombia." By the time that happened, Hoffman was running the Middle East for Citibank. It was an illustration, some said, of FUMU—fuck up, move up.

Wherever nationalization reared its head, Citibank fought it with a vengeance. While other banks scrounged around for local partners, Citibank typically held out to the bitter end. And in late 1976, it became the last of seven foreign banks in Colombia to surrender control when it announced that its thirty branches would become the core of the Banco Internacional de Colombia, to be 51 percent owned by Colombian nationals. As a result of this episode and others that followed, Colombia earned a place on Wriston's short list of most disliked countries. Though Colombia would be praised for its prudent fiscal management, Citibankers saw things differently. Colombia, said Valelly, was "well managed—like a whorehouse."

In Venezuela, Citibank tried to maintain a low profile, ever sensitive about its status as the only foreign bank permitted to operate there more or less freely because of its long-standing presence. Venezuelan president Carlos Andrés Pérez tried to curtail Citibank's activities under the Andean Pact. "The central bank of Venezuela," for example, considered Citibank "too aggressive" in the domestic market, according to Kuczynski. In a meeting with the president, Ed Palmer said, "Here you are trying to close down the only remaining foreign bank in your country. You should be encouraging banks to come in. This city should be the financial center of Latin America." The next day the headline in the local paper read, "Citibank Official Says Caracas Will Be the Financial Capital of Latin America," Palmer recalled.

Bankers fought among themselves to lend money to Venezuela, by then a cash-rich OPEC member. They felt, said international financier Geoffrey Bell, "if they didn't come away with a loan they'd be penalized." The competition was so stiff that countries held auctions to award the mandate to the manager who came in with the lowest fees and rate. "It was considered a great achievement to get the mandate to allow you to raise money for them," said Bell.

Citibank took an expedient view of corruption in the countries where it existed and avoided making value judgments about a country's political ideology. In assessing country risk, Irving Friedman simply attempted to determine whether official corruption in a particular country was severe enough to affect that country's creditworthiness. And in Indonesia, according to Friedman, it was definitely severe enough. Pertamina, the national oil company, "was a classic case of corruption on a large scale, and for years ruined the creditworthiness of all of Indonesia," according to Friedman.

And Citibank pulled back from a few other countries, Friedman said, because the head of state was considered corrupt. One who certainly fit that description was Anastasio Somoza Debayle, who ruled Nicaragua from 1974 to 1979. "The guy was so intimately involved in business activities, there was so much profit-making, that you doubted whether he'd run the country on the basis of what was good economic management."

Citibank, Friedman says, was also troubled about corruption in Panama, in Iran under the Shah, and "to some extent" in the Philippines, even though the bank had a long history of warm personal and business ties to that island nation. While Citibank represented less than 1 percent of the banking business in nearly all of its overseas locations, in the Philippines it enjoyed a large share of the local business. Citibank attempted to concentrate on dealings with the private sector and avoid the state-controlled entities dominated by Ferdinand Marcos's cohorts, though, as the largest foreign bank in the country, that was not always possible. "It was hard. There were pressures to lend to cronies. We said no," insisted a former country officer. Citibank's size and long-standing presence in the Philippines was a bulwark against such pressures. And in late 1975, American banks were singing the praises of the Marcos regime for its financial acumen in turning the country's economy around after a near default in 1970.

But the kickback and foreign exchange schemes perpetrated by the Marcos regime eventually contributed mightily to bankrupting the country. Philippine importers frequently struck deals with exporters from Japan and other countries in which the exporter would overinvoice orders and pay a kickback, contributing to the drain of foreign exchange and the deterioration of the peso.

But Friedman and others were prepared to tolerate a certain level of malfeasance if the leadership seemed willing and able to formulate good macroeconomic policy. "I've never taken the view that what you're looking for is a country without corruption," Friedman said. "They don't exist."

Foreign bankers essentially looked the other way at corruption in Latin America. In the 1960s, according to George Hagerman, economic management in Latin America became more political as governments increasingly preempted powers that had once belonged to central bankers. U.S. bankers, who typically dealt with the professional, U.S.-educated central bankers, generally remained oblivious to the shenanigans of political appointees in the finance ministries of developing countries. While no one was naive enough to believe that corruption in Brazil wasn't a problem, it was viewed as smaller and far less serious than the *mordida* (bribe) in Mexico and Argentina.

At least one Citibanker attributed the indigenous corruption in Latin countries to the colonial Spanish land grants, in which large tracts of land were given to a favored few, sowing the seeds, as it were, for generations of cronyism. Citibank accepted the fact that the leaders of developing countries came from families that owned major businesses, and that these officials augmented their low salaries with income from activities that in the United States would be considered a flagrant conflict of interest. "I don't stand around worrying about whether Mr. Jones has a piece of a corporation. I know his father does and his uncle does," said a former Citibanker officer. But ingrained in the Citibank code of ethics was an absolute ban on paying bribes, even a $10 bribe to get a $1 million fee. Whenever Citibank entered a new country, local officials found this policy difficult to comprehend.

"They think you're crazy," said Richard Huber. "But when it becomes known, it becomes an asset. When the little guy in the customs office in Indonesia tries to hold back some papers, [his] colleagues say, 'You can hold it until the cows come home, it's not going to get you anything. You might as well stamp it and send it on, because they just don't pay. It doesn't matter how much you screw them.' "

Citibank was also nonjudgmental in its appraisal of host government politics. To the bank, it did not matter that these countries usually fared better economically under dictators than they did as fledgling democracies. According to Wriston, Citibank avoided basing lending and credit decisions on moral judgments about the form of government in a particular country. Pointing out that most of the world's nations are saddled with authoritarian regimes, Wriston said, "I don't like 'em. I grew up in this democracy, and I believe in it. But the U.S. government has diplomatic relations with most of those governments. If we, as a private institution, let political judgments influence our lending, then we are meddling in the internal affairs of other countries. If not, we are accused of aiding and abetting societies we do not believe in. It's a very tough nut."

Notwithstanding Citibank's intensive analysis of Third World economies, its understanding of the politics of its borrowers was naive or nonexistent. That was not surprising. For years, Washington didn't talk to Wall Street and Wall Street didn't talk to Washington. Stillman Rockefeller's pride in never having met a congressman was reflected in the bank's lack of understanding of Third World politics and how that might affect creditworthiness. One key point was usually overlooked: that the political situation in a country can change overnight, altering its economic outlook and its ability and willingness to repay loans. "The biggest thing we didn't understand is the political variable," Ham Meserve admitted. "We couldn't understand why some minister in Turkey wouldn't have the political will to triple gas prices and put his economic house in order."

After that fall 1973 meeting in Beirut with Muhammad Al-Ali Abal Khail, the Saudi minister of state for finance, Costanzo flew on to Riyadh, where he found that the matter of Citibank's presence in Saudi Arabia had become something of a cause célèbre of royal family politics. In Riyadh, Costanzo was invited to a luncheon that included Abal Khail, other government officials, and several members of the royal family, including members of its Fahd faction, which was considered unscrupulous and high-handed. After lunch, someone pulled out a piece of paper, apparently including the signatures of several Saudi officials. According to Costanzo, someone passed it to Abal Khail for his signature, saying, "We think this is a good idea." Costanzo could see that this put Abal Khail into a bind. "Do you really think this is fair?" Costanzo interjected, fully expecting some minister to order him to shut up. "I think you ought to allow the minister a little more time." The Fahd faction was seeking to "Saudize" Citibank Saudi Arabia and have the shares distributed to a favored few—namely themselves.

Costanzo's remarks gave Abal Khail an opportunity to take the matter to Faisal, whom Costanzo regarded as straitlaced, and for that Abal Khail was forever grateful. That temporarily delayed the move to emasculate Citibank Saudi Arabia. "These guys were pulling a fast one," said Costanzo. "They were not [above] making money under the table. That's what I was afraid of." Abal Khail was not a royal, and the others, said Costanzo, "were using their clout as members of the royal family to put the blocks to this guy."

The pressure for nationalization was hastened by prodding from James E. Akins, the American ambassador to Saudi Arabia, whom Wriston described as an Arabist. Nationalization "wasn't a brand-new idea," said Wriston. "But I got discommoded" about the United States government getting behind it. In late 1975, Secretary of State Henry Kissinger recalled Akins, according to press reports.

In fact, Citibank had been trying to delay Saudization since 1969. At that time, even with cheap oil, Citibank Saudi was earning $1 million a year on just $1.6 million in capital. It first learned of the kingdom's desire to Saudize that year when Anwar Ali, governor of the Saudi Arabian Monetary Agency, summoned Cedric Grant, a Citibank international officer, and informed him that he wanted Citibank to cut its ownership stake to 40 percent. The good news was that, in return, Ali would award Citibank its choice of staff, licenses galore, and the chance to expand anywhere in the kingdom. If Citibank took the lead, Ali's life would be made easier because other foreign banks would soon follow. Citibank flatly rejected the deal, and for the next several years Grant, who became famous in the bank for catering in imaginative ways to wealthy Saudis, made a point of stroking Ali at every turn. Knowing Ali's passion for bridge, Grant set up games with the best players and sent him materials to help him with a book he was working on. There was no way Citibank would give up this gold mine without a fight.

In 1973, Citibank was the only American bank with branches in Saudi Arabia. Banking was never one of the Saudis' strong suits, and the indigenous banking system was woefully inadequate. Some years earlier, the Saudi Arabian Monetary Agency had been forced to bail out one of the kingdom's most prominent institutions. Since then, the nation's banking system had been dominated by foreign institutions. After the oil embargo in 1974, Citibank found itself in a commanding position in Saudi Arabia with a branch operation that was embarrassingly profitable—the most profitable in the empire, in fact. Citibank not only wound up with all those petrodollars but also raked in huge fees and commissions from the billions that flowed in and out, particularly in connection with the vast development projects now being planned or under way. Every month, Saudi Arabia received payments from its oil company partners, and a huge chunk of that money wound up at Citibank headquarters in London. Citibank also earned a tidy sum as an investment adviser to the Saudi government.

One reason the business was so profitable was that many wealthy Saudis wouldn't take interest on their deposits for religious reasons. Princes and sheikhs streamed in to open $20 million checking accounts and received services instead of interest. When a Saudi businessman visited New York, he could be sure that a Citibanker would be waiting at the airport with a limousine prepared to help him check in to a hotel. "The airport meeting was a big deal," said Ham Meserve. "Just checking in to a Western hotel for some of these guys was a trauma." Citibankers bought theater tickets for them, helped their children get into U.S. colleges, and even arranged for American medical treatment.

Citibank also made a fortune on the huge spreads earned by converting Saudi riyal deposits—which were virtually free because of Moslem usury laws forbidding interest payments—to dollars at the central bank and lending them out in the London Eurodollar market. Said Meserve, "The central bank set a band, above and below which you couldn't go. When the values were right, you converted. When we had money in Saudi Arabia it earned only 2 to 3 percent." In London, Eurodollar rates eventually soared to double-digit levels. "It was never-never land for a while." If, on the other hand, Citibank needed riyals, it would simply import dollars and use them to buy riyals from the central bank. On dollar loans, Citibank could charge a market rate of interest. In riyal lending, however, Citibank could only assess a service charge of up to 2 percent. That was fine as long as the borrower was willing to pay interest. If, however, he went belly up, Citibank had no recourse if he insisted on repaying only the principal on the grounds that paying interest was against the law.

In Saudi Arabia, as in Brazil and other developing countries, there was a certain cachet to being a Citibank customer. Citibank in Saudi Arabia had an edge because the integrity of other local banking services was as tainted as the food and water. Businessmen often paid the branch managers of local banks to tip them off about competitors' moves. As a result, businesses were reluctant to employ auditors or show their balance sheets to bankers. "One of the advantages we had was that we didn't sell information," said Meserve. "We'd have to convince them that we have a certain ethic."

The surge in oil prices was accompanied by a surge in nationalistic pride. The Saudis now wanted to gain control over the finance and banking business as they had done with the oil sector. The Saudis knew that Citibank was making a great deal of money out of their oil and their money, and they wanted to get in on the action. The same was true for many other profitable business franchises. However, Citibank was not inclined to share information about its proprietary systems—information it regarded as a state secret—so the Saudis came to believe there was not much to gain by letting Citibank continue to operate independently. But according to some Citibankers, one reason Citi was ultimately forced to sacrifice its autonomy in Saudi Arabia, as in Colombia, was its aggressive interpretation of the local laws.

"Partnership" arrangements were now anathema to Wriston, however, and he refused to sell off any Citibank branch to anyone, knowing that this would lead to a flood of such demands. As an alternative, Citibank even proposed starting another bank and operating it on a fifty-fifty basis with the Saudis. According to Michael Callen, Wriston came a hairsbreadth away from pulling out of Saudi Arabia altogether as a matter of principle, to make a statement to the world. Apparently, however, in this instance pragmatism triumphed over principle. The problem was that if Citibank gave up in Saudi Arabia, it might find itself having to do the same thing in Indonesia, Hong Kong, and other places with a nationalistic bent to them. Wriston prevailed, and through some artful foot-dragging, Citibank managed to retain its 100 percent interest in its Saudi operation for the next seven years.

Less than a decade after the oil embargo, Citibank and other U.S. banks would look like fools for the billions they had lent to the Third World, particularly Latin America. But for now they were heroes. Indeed, if the world's commercial banks had not stepped up to the plate in 1973 the disaster that was predicted for the world's financial system might well have come to pass. David Rockefeller said later, "We would have had a different and perhaps much worse world crisis. . . . There were eager lenders and eager borrowers."

"If you didn't recycle petrodollars would the world have gone down? You can't write history in the subjunctive mood, but I think it would have," Wriston said later. But as things turned out, it almost did *because* of recycling.

While Citibank did not take orders from the State Department, it had, with the quadrupling of oil prices, become in effect a private sector extension of Foggy Bottom. Both Henry and Walter Wriston had always dreamed of serving as secretary of state. Neither, of course, ever won that title, but both made an indelible impact on U.S. foreign policy—Henry in presiding over the Wristonization of the State Department in the 1950s, and Walter, twenty years later, in presiding over the largest transfer of global wealth since the Marshall Plan.

"In many ways Walter Wriston had more influence on foreign policy, over America's role in the world, than many secretaries of state," said Robert Hormats, an assistant secretary of state in the Reagan administration. Through recycling, the United States, and specifically U.S. commercial banks, became the vehicle for projecting American economic power and principles into the underdeveloped world. "If U.S. banks had not been as international as they had been in that period, then U.S. capital and trade would not have been what it was," said Hormats. "He [Wriston] probably played as large a role as anyone in extending America's financial presence around the world."

By early 1975 the fears of global chaos appeared to dissipate as the imbalances caused by the oil shock worked their way through the marketplace. Citibank was predicting a "cartel breakdown" as the OPEC surplus became a deficit. "What began in 1973–1974 as a ferocious tiger is now becoming a Cheshire cat," wrote the *Monthly Economic Letter* in June 1975. Wriston could now declare with some smugness that the naysayers and fearmongers and Chicken Littles had been thoroughly discredited. "The Euromarkets handled it," he said. "It was one of the most remarkable events of my lifetime." Morgan economist Rimmer de Vries summed up the situation: "The first recycling worked. The market was Wristonized."

14

NERVOUS MONEY

*W*riston might not have been losing any sleep over the OPEC moves, but the rest of the financial world certainly was. Americans were beginning to suffer from a malaise born out of the realization that Arabs now seemed in control of their destiny. That anxiety was reflected in the financial marketplace. With inflationary expectations growing, the Fed was forced to drive interest rates up sharply, accelerating the recession that was already under way. Soon the financial system was in the throes of a full-blown liquidity crisis, made worse by back-to-back bank failures. For sheer tumult, few periods in American financial history up to that time could match 1974. And Wriston was in the very thick of it.

One of the first industries to feel the squeeze was the real estate investments trusts, or REITs. REITs would represent the most pervasive lending disaster since the 1930s, a monument to bad credit judgment and government social engineering gone awry.

The real estate investment trusts stemmed directly from 1960s-era changes in the federal tax code aimed at accelerating the pace of housing construction. These revisions permitted the establishment of trusts that were tax-free as long as they held only real estate assets and paid out most of their earnings in taxable dividends. Banks and other lenders went haywire establishing and lending to their own REITs as well as to developers. The speculative fever taxed the banks' credit expertise to the limit. There were simply not enough competent lending officers to evaluate all the projects that were being offered.

The good news was that Citibank never created its own REIT. In 1970, Chase Manhattan earned the dubious distinction of being the first major New York bank to do so. The bad news was that Citibank went whole hog in lending to REITs and to other real estate projects as well. Wriston knew in detail the history of the bank's dismal experience in real estate lending in the 1920s, a period of furiously speculative building in the United States. Four decades later, when the bank got stuck with a portfolio of bad real estate loans in Puerto Rico, Wriston had chalked it off as a "valuable learning experience," according to former Citibank officer Richard Valelly, who said the bank eventually "worked out" those loans. By the late 1960s, bankers had learned the painful lesson that whenever developers could find willing lenders, they would "fill the world with empty buildings," as one officer put it later.

For years, credit gospel dictated that banks lend only for construction, and then only when permanent, long-term financing was lined up to "take out," or replace, the banks' money. That policy went by the board, however, with the advent of the REITs and the push for 15 percent annual earnings growth. Unlike earlier real estate financing devices, the REITs were so-called interim lenders that relied on short-term funding to finance long-term projects.

While Wriston was smart enough to prohibit the formation of a REIT, he did not anticipate the chaos that would result from lending to them. "We turned it [a Citibank REIT] down for the wrong reasons," he said later. He did so because of the conflict of interest that arose in assigning the mortgage. "Do you give the mortgage to the bank or the REIT?" he asked. To Wriston, a REIT was a financial absurdity from the outset. "You've created a company that could never build its capital structure, because you had to pay all the money out or you lost your tax deduction. It was dumb, dumb dumb. But it was somebody's idea in Congress of how to solve a problem, and the financial community grabbed on to it and built this huge deal."

At about the time Wriston was turning down a REIT, Citibank, as part of its strategic planning exercise, had identified real estate as a growth industry. As long as bankers didn't catch speculative fever, this was considered a fairly easy industry to lend to. Accordingly, Citibank in the late 1960s set up a real estate unit to beat the bushes for business. Notwithstanding Wriston's misgivings about real estate developers, he boasted to analysts in early 1973 that since 1968 Citibank's real estate loan portfolio had gone from an "almost negligible position to the point where we now rank among top real estate lenders in the United States"—a boast he would soon regret.

The sounding gun for the debacle was the December 1973 Chapter Eleven filing by Walter J. Kassuba, a real estate broker turned Palm Beach, Florida, developer. According to former chief credit officer P. Henry Mueller, Kassuba was one of the biggest apartment builders in the country, and more than a dozen REITs had lent to him. As energy prices soared and money tightened, Kassuba defaulted on his payments. He was the first to fall of a fraternity of Florida real estate tycoons.

First Wisconsin Mortgage Trust, sponsored by First Wisconsin Corporation, that state's biggest bank holding company, had lent $12 million of its $212 million in assets to Kassuba, and felt the pain almost instantly. Bankers who had not lent to the Wisconsin REIT breathed a sigh of relief and brushed the problem off as a local one. They believed that their REITs were better than that one. Soon, however, bankers to the east, west, and south felt First Wisconsin's frigid, foul wind. In just six weeks, said former Citibanker Reuben Richards, lending to REITs went from being a growth business to a severe problem. Through 1974, the real estate market went from bad to worse, and commercial paper financing for bank holding companies that had lent to REITs quickly evaporated. By midyear, America's banks were like desert wanderers who had trekked for days without water. The banking system was in the throes of a full-blown liquidity crisis.

The first banking firm to hit the skids because of imprudent real estate lending was the Beverly Hills Bancorporation in December 1973. When a borrower who owed money to the holding company couldn't repay a real estate loan, Beverly Hills couldn't find the cash to repay holders of its commercial paper. The bank was hit with an old-fashioned 1930s-style run. It was yet another prime example of the perils of lending to holding companies.

Comptroller of the Currency James Smith learned of the troubles at Beverly Hills while in California meeting with local bankers. By the time he arrived at an airport hotel to meet with the bank's creditors, an angry crowd of commercial paper holders had already gathered and were demanding their money. Citibank, it turned out, had made a loan to the holding company, and one of the first calls Smith placed was to corporate banking chief Reuben Richards. "You better get someone out here," Smith implored. The Beverly Hills bank was like an ice cream cone on a hot day: its capital was melting away by the moment. Within a few days, regulators and bankers, including Citibank, struck a deal calling for the merger of Beverly Hills National and its $98 million in deposits into San Francisco's Wells Fargo Bank. Citibank, said Smith, was instrumental in pressing the creditors to move quickly toward this solution.

Normally, the troubles at a relatively small institution like Beverly Hills would have attracted little notice in the rest of the country. Because it had been one of the first holding companies to stumble in the commercial paper market, however, it grabbed the Federal Reserve Board's undivided attention. For the Fed, Beverly Hills was the wake-up call to use the capital weapon to slow down bank holding companies, according to former officials. Then, in early January 1974, First National City Corporation stock took a pounding in New York Stock Exchange trading. Wriston told the *American Banker* of January 10 that he could think of no reason for the drop. Within six months, however, Wriston was out $1 million—on paper, at least—on his personal holdings, according to a July 22, 1974, *New York* magazine article by financial columnist Dan Dorfman.

In a talk to bank officers, Wriston hinted at some of the possible reasons for the drop in the bank's stock. Referring to the 1973 results, in which loan losses increased by 75 percent, he warned that "we should not overlook the fact that the great earnings machine that is the Citicorp covered up a multitude of sins. In the bread-and-butter transactions of making loans and getting our money back, we did not do all that well." The losses demonstrated just how big the company had gotten under his stewardship. Its 1973 pre-tax write-offs of $104 million, which included write-downs of premiums on domestic acquisitions, and operating errors, equaled the bank's entire 1966 after-tax earnings.

Besides the REIT loans, one source of the bank's growth was direct lending to developers for raw land, for which the promoters had typically paid top dollar. That land often turned out to be worth a fraction of what they had shelled out for it. Worse still, the promoters frequently reneged on promises to develop it. Some lenders were seduced by developers' claims that the developers owned a big equity stake—perhaps 50 percent—of a project themselves. In fact, the lenders should have been more concerned with whether a major tenant, such as IBM, had agreed to lease space in the building. Citibank had all sorts of rules, written and unwritten, spelling out what kinds of loans should and should not be made and to whom. It was understood, for example, that loans to casinos were a no-no, as were loans providing for a final "balloon" payment. But there was no rule against rolling the dice on raw land.

When the REITs crashed, Citibank realized that for the last several years it had served as little more than an order-taker for high-flying speculators—and sometimes even as a partner with them in their wide-eyed schemes. When the numbers were tallied, it turned out that Citibank and First Chicago had lent more to REITs than had any other banks: $750 million each. Still, Citibank's REIT loans as a percentage of shareholder equity and total loans were less than most other banks'.

The man picked to work out the problem for Citibank was thirty-six-year-old Lawrence Glenn, who had helped clean up the earlier real estate mess in Puerto Rico. As the magnitude of the real estate disaster became apparent, Glenn was summoned back to New York from Puerto Rico to fix it. "Oh, my God, did we have real estate," Glenn recalled ruefully, still amazed at what he had found.

When Glenn asked someone to draw a map showing all the properties Citibank had lent to in Atlanta, for example, his colleague drew a circle around the entire city. Citibank, he said, wound up with bowling alleys, a ski resort, a water tower in Chicago, and a beachfront condo built below the flood line in Florida. During a severe rainstorm, residents of the condo had to be rescued by boat from second-story windows, according to Glenn. To salvage what it could of its interest in that property, Citibank built a dike around it, installed massive pumps to remove the water, and somehow managed to resell it. The bank had also lent to the land company that owned Pinehurst, a North Carolina golf resort. Owned by trucking and shipping magnate Malcom McLean, the resort would later sink below the water line, and when it did, Citibank rescheduled the loan and acquired an ownership stake. "McLean was a fine gentleman and an honest man," said a former Citibanker. "He is gut fearless. He had one great idea and a couple that were not so hot."

"We ended up with a lot of wacky stuff. We grew a little too fast, with inexperienced people," Glenn said. "We thought we knew what the values were. When the market turned down, the values turned down much harder than we ever dreamed possible." Across the country, office space could hardly be given away. New York was the hardest hit. The break-even point was about $13 a square foot, but the going rate was barely $8. Cleaning up after the REITs took years, and typically called for the banks to stretch out their loans and slash their rates.

Citibank was one of the first to discover the magic of swapping out of loans in return for assets. The swaps originated with the recognition that it was better to have real estate assets on the books than loans to REITs. Just as bankers had embraced the REIT, they now grabbed on to this device as a way out of the debacle. But as everyone caught on, the price of escape rose and the opportunity to get out whole rapidly evaporated. Bad as the experience was for Citibank, the ultimate losses were not as devastating as some had predicted. In the end, write-offs amounted to less than 10 percent of the portfolio, according to Glenn—not the 25 percent some had feared. That, of course, didn't include the cost in time, energy, and opportunity.

Accepting directorships on the boards of major customers was part of the grooming process for top management. In December 1973, in a quintessential example of bad timing, up-and-coming John Reed was appointed to the board of Arlen Realty and Development Corporation, operator of the high-flying Korvettes discount department store chain, and owner and manager of real estate properties. With as much as $100 million in outstanding loans, Arlen was one of Citibank's biggest borrowers, and its chairman, Arthur Cohen, was a First National City Corporation director. After the real estate crisis broke, Cohen helped Citibank evaluate its troubled real estate portfolio. A few years later, Arlen itself was part of that portfolio.

The single most critical lesson that Citibank would take away from the REIT episode was not to lend on raw land, which Glenn described later as the principal cause of the mid-1970s losses.

As chairman, Wriston accepted some of the rap for the real estate debacle—but only some. The same decentralized culture that prevented top management from making ill-informed front-office loans also allowed real estate lending to get out of hand. Wriston prided himself on not making loans himself. He delegated lending to his loan officers and credit policy to his chief credit officer. That process clearly failed this time around.

In Wriston's view, the REITs resulted at least in part from the unhealthy influence of government policies governing taxes and other areas. "At the end of the day you have to make your own decisions," Wriston said. "You can cry that they [the government] nudged you this way or that way, and it's true they did, but it's not their responsibility either. Congress passes a lot of laws, like [anti-] redlining, and when you make loans there and they go bad, they say you're so dumb to make those loans. There are dozens of examples like that all the time. It goes with the uniform. Do the banks respond to economic policy? Yes, obviously. Are lots of things tax-driven? Of course. When the government uses tax policy or other policy like it for social engineering, you usually wind up in some kind of trouble."

Even though the federal government had encouraged REITs, "examiners went in and classified the hell out of them," said former senior deputy comptroller Paul Homan. When pressed about his bum REIT loans, Wriston reminded his interrogators that the "largest holders of bad real estate debts in the world are the U.S. Department of HUD and the U.S. Department of HEW. They own 92,000 defaulted one-family-home mortgages and are the largest holders of slum property in the world. All of those loans were made in accordance with government regulations that cover a shelf eight feet long." He said the banks went wrong "in failing to foresee that the worst recession in forty years was going to hit us. If we weren't all so polite, we'd call it a depression."

But Congress didn't tell Citibank to make bum loans to Australian real estate developers. And *that* real estate debacle, though much less publicized than the American version, would be nearly as costly. And if real estate wasn't enough, in March 1974, W. T. Grant, America's third-largest variety store chain, suffered a run on hundreds of millions of dollars of its commercial paper following the release of poor fiscal 1973 results. Had the banks not stepped up to the plate with additional funding in the spring of 1974, W. T. Grant would likely have ended then and there.

Commercial paper—the first money to burn up in a crisis—was becoming the test of a company's financial stability. Soon the firestorm would envelop the world banking system.

For several years, the Fed had been stewing over whether a holding company and its subsidiary bank should be treated together or separately for capital purposes. As a result of the problems of the Beverly Hills Bancorporation, the central bank concluded that it was impossible to distinguish between the two.

No one was more convinced of the impossibility of building fire walls between the units of a holding company than Wriston himself, a viewpoint that would prove to be a liability in the banking industry's push for expanded powers. If a holding company consumer subsidiary with the First National City Corporation name on it were to fail, Wriston knew that Citibank would be honor bound to rescue it.

Fed chairman Arthur Burns was troubled by fast growth and the manner in which it was being achieved. The banks' increased loans outstanding, he would later lament, were being supported more and more through borrowed money—negotiable CDs and holding company commercial paper rather than cheaper, more stable deposits. And, of course, he was deeply worried by the industry's declining capital cushion. Burns looked askance at the proliferation of activities under the Bank Holding Company Act amendments, but so far the Fed had turned down acquisitions by bank holding companies mostly on the grounds that an activity was anti-competitive or not closely related to banking.

In late 1973, for example, First National City Corporation suffered a major setback in its quest to offer mortgages nationwide when the Federal Reserve Board rejected its 1970 acquisition of Advance Mortgage. Charging that the "concentration of resources" outweighed the public benefits, the Fed declared that the acquisition was anti-competitive and ordered First National City to divest, though it offered the company the opportunity to reapply. But the Fed's denials only inspired more ingenuity in circumvention. Later in the year, for example, H&R Block and Citibank announced that H&R Block would set up tax units in seventy Citibank branches.

Burns had been urging banks to go slow almost from the day he became chairman of the Fed. Now he would put some teeth behind the policy. If they did not do so on their own, he would use his power over bank holding company expansion, domestically and overseas, to enforce minimum capital standards. The Fed had complete authority over foreign expansion by U.S. banks, but it had usually rubber-stamped these requests. That policy was about to change. In its lending practices, Citibank in fact had already begun to batten down the hatches. Citibankers had made themselves unpopular with competitors by their lone wolf lending tactics—greedily taking fat shares of deals and shoving other banks aside. As the recession took hold, the bank's credit policy committee ordered lenders to cut exposures and accept smaller pieces of loans. Judging from the numbers, these admonitions had little effect.

In rapid-fire succession, the Fed began summoning chiefs of bank holding companies in for jawboning sessions on capital. At that time, the Fed still had no binding capital rule for large banks, but regarded as undercapitalized an institution with a capital-to-assets ratio of less than 8 percent. No one was more resistant to the Fed's demands than Wriston. Citibank's primary regulator, the Comptroller of the Currency, was equally put out that the Fed would preempt the Comptroller's role in safety and soundness issues by calling in its clients.

Telling Wriston to go slow was akin to asking heavyweight champ Muhammad Ali to punch softly. Wriston went on the counterattack, inveighing against the obsolete U.S. banking structure and the demise of American banks. In the mid-1960s, he pointed out, sixteen out of the twenty biggest banks in the world were American and only four were foreign. That situation, he said, had reversed itself. Now, just four of the top twenty were American.

With Burns clamping down on capital and acquisitions, Wriston sounded the clarion call for nationwide banking and a wider selection of permitted financial services to cope with non-banks like Sears and Dreyfus. Incredibly, foreign banks in the United States, he pointed out, could operate banking offices in more than one state, while American institutions were limited to a single one. The response was not long in coming. At a time when *Fortune* 500 companies were starting to pack up and leave New York City for the clean streets of affluent suburbs, Connecticut's bankers were especially wary. A few days after Wriston made his pitch, the chief of the Connecticut Bankers Association declared that the prospect of incursions by New York banks "threatens to destroy small banking in the state."

Other banker pipe dreams also went by the board as the REITs debacle unfolded. If banks ever hoped to acquire thrifts, as the Hunt Commission report—the study on financial service industry reform—had recommended, those hopes were now dashed.

Feeling the squeeze from all directions, Wriston, at a policy committee meeting in February 1974, broached the topic of whether Citibank should in fact remain a bank and whether it should continue to be headquartered in the United States. "It is possible," he said, "that the race to educate the regulators to our steadily declining share of market will be lost. If it is lost and Sears and Penney inherit the market, the question can then be raised as to whether or not we should give up the banking business as it is defined in this country and become an American financial service entity with banking and related operations abroad. One might even examine the far-out option to become the first multinational financial corporation with major operations here, but [with] the preponderance of its business abroad."

By the mid-1970s, bank regulation was little changed from what it had been two decades earlier. Regulators were still attempting to micromanage their client institutions. After Comptroller of the Currency James Smith took office in 1973, for example, he discovered a low-level subordinate reviewing an application from the Bank of America to open a branch in downtown Los Angeles, and he attempted to halt such practices. "It was just insane," said Smith later.

No doubt Arthur Burns hoped for greater success in slowing down bank holding companies than he had enjoyed so far in slowing inflation with his monetary policies and wage and price controls. On February 6, 1974, Burns was forced to admit in testimony before the Senate Banking Committee that the wage and price controls he had backed were a failure. "The damage done by the controls in slowing production was significant," he conceded, "and it is very doubtful if the control program helped to moderate the average rate of inflation during 1973." His Committee on Interest and Dividends, he said, had "encountered difficulties in discharging its responsibilities." Efforts to ease the prime downward made it a "bargain rate of interest," Burns said, that caused banks to be flooded with loan requests. While pushing for wage and price controls, Burns had, in his first years on the job, maintained a loose grip on the monetary policy throttle. That began to change in 1973. "To be an effective central banker you had to risk overkill," said Wall Street economist Henry Kaufman. "Arthur Burns hesitated in the early 1970s and then did what central bankers had to do in 1973 and 1974."

Wriston and the Labor-Management Advisory Committee hammered away at what was left of the wage and price controls program every chance they got. In a statement issued on November 13, 1973, the committee declared that the "stabilization act, which is scheduled to expire April 30, 1974, should not be renewed and that no legislative authority to administer wage and price controls should be enacted for the period thereafter." By spring they were finally able to savor their hard-won victory. On June 30, 1974, after seriously damaging the economic fabric of the nation, the controls became history, and the committee self-destructed along with them.

President Gerald Ford, who took office on August 9, 1974, upon the resignation of President Nixon, despised controls, though he hadn't opposed them when they were announced in 1971. "I was shocked when Nixon in 1971 put in wage and price controls," he said later. "I was always against [them], although as a team player, I never fought them. I couldn't wait for them to get thrown out, and I suspect that Walter had a major influence on this."

Another player, Treasury secretary George Shultz, in April 1974 had actually quit the administration team because of his differences with Nixon over the controls program. Wriston regarded Shultz as a free market comrade-in-arms, one of the few senior public officials who adhered tenaciously to market principles. With Shultz's impending departure, the train passed through the station a second time for Wriston. He was Shultz's choice to succeed him at Treasury, and former executive committee chairman Ed Palmer happened to be in Wriston's office when he got the call. A paragon of bankerly discretion, Palmer started to leave so Wriston and Shultz could talk privately, but Wriston motioned for him to stay. Refusing the offer to become Treasury secretary, Wriston said flippantly, "I have a young wife. I need the capital," Palmer recalled. But Wriston really declined in 1974 for the same reason he had turned down the offer back in 1968: he wanted to hear it from "the Man"—Richard M. Nixon.

Even General Alexander Haig, the newly appointed White House chief of staff, was no substitute for the president himself. With the White House under siege, Haig was frantically struggling to keep the top posts filled and the wheels of government grinding. Wriston's refusal, said Haig, "disappointed me because he was my choice."

After declining Shultz's offer, Wriston in turn invited Shultz to join First National City Corporation, newly renamed Citicorp, as vice chairman. According to Wriston, Shultz preferred to go to work for a privately held company, and accepted a position as executive vice president of Bechtel Corporation, the international engineering giant. "The lure of the private corporation after you've been in public life . . . is very strong," said Wriston. "The more I see of private corporations, the bigger their allure. You don't fool around with the SEC and all that stuff. You do your business."

While at Bechtel, Shultz maintained his ties with conservative economists at an annual gathering over the long Washington's Birthday weekend. At the Bechtel Corporation's sprawling oceanfront retreat near Monterey, California, Shultz gathered the high priests of conservative economics and finance, including Nobel laureate Milton Friedman, empirical economist George J. Stigler (who won the Nobel Prize in 1982), and investment banker Nicholas Brady, to play golf, tennis, and debate economic policy into the early hours of the morning. At those conclaves, Kathy Wriston recalled, Milton Friedman invariably told Wriston, "Walter, you're absolutely wrong for the following three reasons." There were always three—not two or four but three. And Wriston would reply, "Can't I ever be wrong for four reasons?" Many of the participants, including Wriston, would form the core of the economic brain trust that in 1981 would introduce the nation to Reaganomics.

After leaving the government, Shultz told friends he now had to be careful what he said. "People would be apt to listen to me and act accordingly," he told one acquaintance. "That didn't happen as secretary of the Treasury." Though some saw the Treasury post as the ultimate reward for a top banker or economist, Shultz recognized that the latitude he had to shape his department to his liking was more limited than his ability to shape Bechtel, or Wriston's ability to mold Citibank.

On April 17, 1974, Nixon replaced Shultz with Wall Streeter William Simon. Philosophically, Simon and Wriston were in sync. Arthur Burns had acknowledged the failure of wage and price controls, and floating exchange rates had demonstrated their usefulness through the traumatic rise in oil prices, but government intervention and fixed exchange rates still had powerful adherents. Wriston and Citibank were determined that floating rates remain the modus operandi for the world financial markets. To be sure, Wriston and Simon were staunch allies in the fight for free markets. But Simon would never replace Shultz as a soul mate to Walter Wriston.

The recession, inflation, the quadrupling of oil prices, and an end to fixed exchange rates turned world financial markets into a floating crap game in which the chips were denominated in dollars, deutsche marks, francs, yen, cruzeiros, and a bushel basketful of other currencies. Sooner or later such volatility was bound to conspire with incompetent and corrupt management to bring down a major U.S. bank. The first public hint of trouble at New York's Franklin National Bank, then the nation's twentieth largest, was its April 18 announcement that its first-quarter earnings had plummeted to two cents a share from sixty-six cents in the same 1973 period.

Wriston was not surprised. He had for years despised Franklin and its former chairman, Arthur Roth. The ill will between Citibank and Franklin dated back at least to the late 1950s, when Roth had sued unsuccessfully to block Citibank's expansion into Long Island's prosperous Nassau County, Franklin's stronghold. About the only thing Wriston and Roth had in common was their vehement opposition to smoking on the job.

When Franklin, in 1971, sought membership in the New York Clearing House, Wriston happened to be the chairman and strenuously resisted the bid. Though still a major shareholder in Franklin, Roth by then had been replaced as chairman by glib-talking Harold Gleason.

In any event, Franklin was admitted to the Clearing House and its Clearing House Interbank Payments System (CHIPS), much to Wriston's chagrin. A year later, Franklin edged a step closer to disaster when the Italian financier Michele Sindona, later disclosed to have ties to organized crime, bought a controlling interest in Franklin New York Corporation, the bank's holding company.

Franklin was woefully ill prepared to play in Wriston's world of forex, Eurodollars, and negotiable CDs. As interest rates surged, its core deposits drained off, and Franklin was increasingly forced to fund fixed rate assets with "hot" money—specifically the paper Wriston had invented. Meanwhile, Franklin hired some foreign exchange traders of questionable repute, who soon began to roll the dice in the global forex markets.

The Fed, ironically enough, flashed a clear signal to the banking community that Franklin was in trouble. In a rare, if not unprecedented action, the central bank on May 1, 1974, rejected an application by Franklin to acquire Talcott National Corporation, a large Sindona-controlled factoring company. Under the 1970 Bank Holding Company amendments, this was certainly a permitted activity, so it was obvious to bankers that the Fed had some other good reason for its action.

On Friday, May 10, Franklin announced that it had lost money in foreign exchange trading. It suspended the dividend and asked for a halt in trading of its shares. The run on Franklin that began with that revelation was of the insidious kind. There were no lines at teller windows, no angry mobs demanding their money. Instead of rolling over their CDs, big depositors were yanking them out of Franklin and reinvesting the money elsewhere.

On the following Sunday, Franklin disclosed that trading losses and irregularities were greater than had been originally reported. In fact, Franklin was now insolvent. In Washington, the Federal Reserve Board met to figure out how to avert a depositor panic and, in a highly unusual move, announced that it would prop up Franklin at the discount window. Out of its total deposits of close to $3 billion, Franklin lost nearly $800 million in less than four days, sending it scurrying to the discount window. Never since the Depression had the United States witnessed a bank run of such magnitude.

While Franklin was unraveling, Wriston and his board were touring Brazil, cementing relationships and heaping praise on a country that would be the source of yet another liquidity crisis almost a decade later. In the wake of the Crefisul fire, the Brazilian staff could have done without a visit by the Citibank board and the constant interruptions by advance men and protocol people checking out the facilities, sampling the wine, and tasting the meals to be served to the board. While Brazil hand Richard Huber and others stood their ground against the protocol officers' attempts to arrange a black-tie stag dinner for the board, they had to, as Huber put it, "cash in a lot of chips" to persuade Brazil's movers and shakers to attend the various events.

The Citibank delegation received the red-carpet treatment in Brazil. They were briefed by the U.S. ambassador and the station chief of the Central Intelligence Agency.

On his return to New York, Wriston and his fellow bank chairmen immediately became embroiled in the Franklin crisis. Events were now moving at a breakneck pace. On Monday, May 13, 1974, Paul Luftig, the president of Franklin National, was fired, international chief Peter Shaddick, a Sindona recruit, resigned, and Gleason became president as well as chairman of Franklin National. That day, Comptroller of the Currency James Smith asked the New York banks to help him find a buyer for the deteriorating institution. On Smith's watch, the Comptroller of the Currency's supervision of Franklin National could only be described as lax, and Smith clearly was now seeking to redeem himself and his office by trying to salvage the beleaguered bank. He later blamed the Fed for part of the problem. "They let the scent of death get out too early," he contended.

In a phone conversation, Sindona told Wriston that he was placing a former Citibank foreign exchange trader named Carlo Bordoni in charge of foreign exchange trading. That was enough to set off Wriston's alarm bells. Wriston rarely forgot a name, particularly one that had caused him pain and aggravation. Indeed, through his worldwide network, he became acquainted, personally or by reputation, with most of the world's financially unsavory characters. The mention of the name Bordoni—the Milan trader Wriston had fired in the early 1960s—rekindled many memories, all of them unpleasant.

"That's interesting. He's a brilliant man, but we had a lot of control problems," Wriston said with some understatement.

"Don't worry," Sindona replied, as Wriston recalled the conversation. "We get along fine. We won't have any of those problems." In fact, Bordoni, using a Liechtenstein holding company, had helped Sindona engineer his 1972 purchase of Franklin stock, and Sindona had later appointed him to the company's board. As soon as Wriston got off the phone with Sindona, he ordered his forex traders in New York to terminate their dealings with Franklin.

He then phoned Comptroller Smith, an affable regulator popular with his constituency of nationally chartered commercial banks, to share the news with him. "Wriston advised me that Bordoni had been released by Citi because of questions about integrity," Smith recalled. A couple of days later, Smith received a call from an aide advising him that Bordoni was running Franklin National's trading room with a letter of authorization from Harold Gleason.

"Gleason said he's surveying the foreign exchange position," the aide retorted.

"He's not surveying, he's trading. I want him out," Smith demanded. Smith then called Sindona, who whined that Franklin lacked an experienced trader. Smith didn't doubt that. His concern was that Bordoni was too experienced for his own good—and too experienced for the good of Franklin and the American banking system.

For Smith and his fellow national bank regulators, foreign exchange trading was an arcane activity whose volume had exploded before the government could begin to understand or monitor it. Franklin had a forward foreign exchange position of some $2 billion, huge for a bank its size. And it appeared that losses might be as high as $40 million, according to former OCC deputy general counsel Westbrook Murphy.

If he was to gain control over Franklin, Comptroller James Smith would have to come to grips with its wildly out of control foreign exchange operations. To do that, he turned to the chairman of the national bank whose preeminence as a global trader was unchallenged. Wriston recommended that Smith bring Edwin Reichers, Citibank's former chief trader, out of retirement.

Wriston reported that Reichers, who had bailed him out of the Brussels debacle ten years earlier, had just returned to the United States after completing a consulting assignment for the central bank of the Philippines. If anyone could get his arms around Franklin's forex positions, it was the unflappable Mr. Reichers.

"I checked with Treasury to find out if Reichers was good," said Smith. "They said, 'Very good. The only trouble is he's a bullheaded s.o.b.' " That was all Smith needed to know. "That's just who we want," Smith replied. Smith tracked Reichers down on a Florida beach and recruited him. When he stormed into Franklin in mid-May, Reichers found a trader's twilight zone. "There were [foreign exchange] contracts in a bottom drawer that nobody'd ever heard about," Wriston said.

Over the next several months, Reichers slashed Franklin's huge foreign exchange exposure while the Fed continued to pump in money and Smith and his fellow regulators scrambled to find the least painful and disruptive means of disposing of this most serious challenge to the U.S. financial system in forty years. According to Smith, Fed chairman Arthur Burns urged him to call in the New York banks and force them to bail out Franklin, but Smith considered that prerogative beyond the power of his office. That was the kind of thing the head of the Bundesbank or the Bank of England would do. Smith replied, "Spoken like a true European central banker."

But Smith did travel to New York to persuade the Clearing House banks to rally around Franklin. Some, including Citibank, were reluctant to participate in a bailout. But under intense persuasion from the New York Fed and other regulators, Citibank and its Clearing House colleagues slapped together a $600 million borrowing agreement that would allow Franklin to borrow Fed funds that it couldn't obtain on the open market. That lasted all of two weeks, executive director John Lee said later. "They [Franklin National] went through $600 million like nothing. The CDs rolled off [were not replaced when they matured] so fast the $600 million was a drop in the bucket," Lee explained.

"We sought and got the cooperation of the banks," Smith said later. "Burns thought that we had more power than we did."

During the Clearing House deliberations, Wriston, who was now serving as the association's president, could barely contain his disdain for Franklin National and Gleason, according to Lee. The board and association rooms of the Clearing House are elegant settings steeped in American financial history. Hanging on the oak-paneled walls of the boardroom are oil paintings of bearded association presidents and of officials taking in notes as collateral against Clearing House scrip to squelch the Panic of 1893. Wriston didn't believe it was fitting for Gleason to sit at the big mahogany table. "He was a nice guy who was over his head," said Comptroller Smith.

In a late May 1974 interview with an Italian magazine, Sindona admitted that foreign exchange losses were now $5 million more than Franklin had reported two weeks earlier. Sindona claimed that his insurance carrier would cover the losses, but his insurer disagreed.

Meanwhile, Comptroller Smith was scrambling to find a replacement for Gleason. After being turned down by his first choice, retiring J. P. Morgan chairman John Meyer, he tapped Joseph Barr, secretary of the Treasury under Lyndon Johnson. On June 20, after just five weeks in the job, Gleason was forced out as chairman and president and replaced by Barr.

Citibank was no Franklin National, but it, too, was suffering from a liquidity squeeze. The REITs, Beverly Hills, Grant, Franklin National, and mounting loan losses had made the commercial paper markets skittish. This would not bring down the bank, but it would certainly cause Don Howard, Citibank's newly appointed chief financial officer, many sleepless nights. When he did manage to doze, his worst nightmare was running out of money. The irony was that while the Eurodollar market was awash in liquidity from the OPEC surplus, money was tight in the United States because of restrictive Fed monetary policy and interest rate ceilings. The Eurodollars couldn't be used to fund domestic loan demand. With the financial markets in turmoil, bank holding companies of all stripes were finding it increasingly difficult to raise funds.

In mid-1974, loan demand was still expanding at a rapid clip. Despite Arthur Burns's efforts to clamp down on credit, business loans surged by an unprecedented $1 billion in a single week, and by 22 percent in the second quarter. Later, Citibank announced it was jacking up its fees for standby and revolving credits to big borrowers to discourage new commitments and to curtail demand. Shortly after he appointed Howard, Wriston had a brainstorm. Citibank had been issuing floating rate paper in the Eurodollar market, and Wriston asked Howard if he could think of any reason why the bank couldn't do essentially the same thing in the United States. Interest rates on most of Citibank's assets now varied with market conditions, so it made sense for liabilities to float as well.

Back in 1961, Wriston had responded to tight money with the negotiable CD. Now he had another instrument up his sleeve: the floating rate note. This would raise enough money to overcome the liquidity crisis. Gaining acceptance for the CD, however, was a piece of cake compared with the battle he would have to wage to issue the floating rate note. Even though Congress and the Fed had for years forced American banks to live with rules that were more appropriate for a socialistic than a free market economy, they would make Wriston run the Washington gauntlet as he sought to ensure that Citibank had a reliable source of funds.

The initial offering was for $250 million in fifteen-year notes, to be issued in $1,000 units to appeal to small investors, who could buy a minimum of $5,000 and a maximum of $50,000. The proceeds would be used to finance the activities of Citi's non-bank subsidiaries such as Advance Mortgage and Nationwide Financial.

With zest for the battle, Wriston announced that "all investors, large and small, will be able to obtain for the first time a rate of interest comparable to that which was formerly available only to large individual investors and corporations." The Comptroller of the Currency gave his blessing to the plan, ruling that because the notes were offered by a bank holding company and had a long maturity, they did not violate Regulation Q. The notes were the marginal cost of funds principle in action.

Hans Angermueller didn't see the move as an end run around the rules. Rather, he said, the notes were introduced to replace shorter-term commercial paper, and could be construed as "commercial paper stapled together over time." In effect, the notes replaced the short maturities of commercial paper, which was typically issued in slugs of at least $25 million, with the relatively long maturities of the notes. "This device looked like a technique to become less dependent on what we saw as a single source of funding," Angermueller recalled.

The initiative prompted one Washington bank regulator to tell the *Washington Post* on July 28, 1974, that "Citicorp didn't say a word to the Fed about its notes. If Chase had done it, they'd have gone down there and talked about it—about its effect on the national economy, its effect on the thrift institutions and the housing industry—and might have ended up being talked out of it. Wriston does it first and asks questions later." Within days of Citibank's announcement, Chase worked up the courage to announce its own $200 million offering, and soon other financial service companies followed with variations on the Citibank theme.

Coincidentally, Citibank's announcement of the new instrument occurred the same day that the Federal Reserve turned down Citibank and Bank of America on applications to invest in foreign insurance companies— Bank of America in a joint venture with Allstate to establish a general insurance company in Switzerland, and Citibank in a partnership with Chubb to buy a stake in a Brazilian firm. If Burns and the Fed hadn't stated clearly enough their desire for banks to go slow, their rejection of these proposals made their intentions explicit. Franklin's troubles had certainly exacerbated the Fed's fears. In its statement, the Fed indicated its "general concern" with the tendency of banking companies to adopt a "policy of rapid expansion in domestic and foreign markets" that could lead to an "undue concentration of economic resources." The Fed also made it clear that since insurance underwriting by banks was prohibited in the United States, it didn't look favorably on banks doing it overseas. Heretofore, the Fed had applied capital standards only when reviewing applications for expansion into domestic businesses but had ignored foreign businesses. But just one month after blocking Citi and BOA's insurance acquisitions, the Fed turned down an application by Bankers Trust to acquire a 20 percent stake in the Manila Banking Corporation on the grounds that Bankers Trust's asset growth had outstripped liquidity and capital.

The reaction to the floating rate notes was as swift as it was sure. The fiercest opposition came from thrifts, which viewed the move as an end run around Reg Q, which of course it was. Before the week was over, thrift regulators and trade groups had fired off letters to chairman Burns and warned of the dangers the instrument contained for their client institutions. Several thrifts even filed a lawsuit to try to block the offering. Within a week, Citibank knew it had a tiger by the tail—two tigers in fact. Responding to overwhelming demand, Citicorp raised the offer to $850 million, making it at the time the largest single public debt or equity underwriting by a private company in U.S. economic history.

Wriston had just begun to dodge bullets on the floating rate note issue when another bombshell fell, this time in Germany. Its name was the Bankhaus I. D. Herstatt.

In midafternoon on Friday, June 28, 1974, Wriston and a clutch of senior-level colleagues were drinking somewhat less than vintage champagne out of paper cups, toasting to the good health of retiring chief credit officer Lester Garvin and welcoming his replacement, veteran banker P. Henry Mueller, who had started out as an office boy back in 1934. Garvin, said his colleague Victor Prall, objected so strenuously to cross-border Third World lending that his health had deteriorated. "He had to retire early or kill himself. So he retired early." With Garvin's departure, Citibank lost its most outspoken critic of cross-border lending. In an ironic twist, the global monetary crisis that erupted on the very day he retired put the fear of Third World lending in the banks for some time to come—but not long enough.

The celebration in Mueller's New York office was interrupted by a caller reporting that Chase had frozen the clearing account of Herstatt, Germany's largest private bank, which had been shut down by West German banking authorities at 4:00 P.M. on Wednesday. Coming in the midst of the Franklin crisis, not to mention America's impeachment crisis, the Herstatt failure was all the global financial system needed. On the surface, Herstatt had seemed like a responsible institution. But, like Franklin, it had speculated heavily on foreign exchange, betting incorrectly that the dollar would rise in value against the mark. Most of its $190 million in losses resulted from under-the-counter foreign exchange trading. The Germans call it *schubladengeschäft,* or business done "in the drawer," a reference to the trading slips that wound up in traders' bottom drawers. Unfortunately, no one discovered them until it was too late.

Normally the market would have been able to absorb such an event with little more than a hiccup. But the German authorities—through ignorance or selfishness or both—shut the bank down after the financial markets had closed in Germany but while they were still open in New York. When that happened, Herstatt's foreign exchange transactions were suspended in a twilight region between time zones. Moreover, the Germans had left some offices open. "They screwed it up badly," said Citibank's former chief financial officer, Don Howard. West Germany's Bundesbank had given Herstatt credit for dollar transactions, but stopped the music before dollars Herstatt owed to other banks hit their books.

Though the failure was reported on the wire services, it initially attracted relatively little attention or concern. Banks on the CHIPS network that had engaged in foreign exchange transactions with Herstatt, on their own behalf or for customers, felt the ripples right away. But in New York, at the Clearing House's small, monolithic stone headquarters on Broad Street, it was barely noticed. Thursday was notable for what didn't happen. It was an especially slow day on CHIPS, but no one imagined that this relatively obscure bank could be responsible for the sluggishness. Meanwhile, millions were pouring into the Herstatt account at Chase, but nothing was leaving. Because Chase could not expect to receive payments from Herstatt, it refused to pay out Herstatt funds to anyone else.

By Friday, it was clear there was something terribly wrong. It too was an unusually slow day for one that the Clearing House had projected to be extremely busy because it was the last business day of the first half of the year. Clearing House director John Lee was pondering this mystery when Wriston called. "You know what's going on on CHIPS?" Wriston asked.

"I know it's slow. What else is going on?" Lee asked. The Clearing House's communications network wasn't nearly as sophisticated as Citibank's. It didn't even have a Dow Jones broad tape, so Lee, despite his key position as overseer of a vast payments network, was largely out of the loop.

"It's Herstatt," Wriston replied somberly, explaining to Lee that an enormous amount of money around the globe had simply been frozen in place. Until Herstatt, banks had wired money on customers' instructions on a good-faith basis, expecting that they would shortly receive the funds from the customer. Now the world's financial institutions had lost confidence in the system, and were refusing to make payments for their customers until they themselves had received "cover" from the customer—the payments they had been promised to support their payments. CHIPS, the global network over which billions of dollars flowed every day as electronic blips, was on the verge of shutting down. If money was indeed what made the world go 'round, the world was about to come to a screeching halt.

Citibank, then the world's second-largest bank, was a kind of nexus, or pump primer, of the payments system. Because it was also the biggest clearing bank, the free flow of money through Citibank was essential to the global movement of funds. Each day more than $15 billion passed through Citibank. In the wake of the oil shock, CHIPS volume surged as petrodollar deposits and loans were moved around the world. A $100 million transaction would wind its way through five banks in one day, and by 11:00 A.M., Citibank would be running a $2 billion deficit. So when Citibank stopped moving money, the world went into overdraft.

As the mood at Garvin's party turned from gaiety to sobriety, Mueller's office was transformed from a party room to a crisis center. In the tradition of J. P. Morgan, Wriston was suddenly thrust into the role of global crisis manager. Some twenty-five or so commercial banks now were the "de facto payments mechanism of the world," as he put it later. That was a role, he said, that would make central banks nervous. "It also makes us nervous." He found himself in this unique position in part because of the importance of his institution and also because the crisis happened to explode on his watch as Clearing House president. But it also occurred because he happened to be the only chairman of a major bank on duty at the start of a summer weekend. By that time, all the rest had left Manhattan for their homes in the Westchester and Connecticut suburbs.

Wriston suggested to John Lee that the system be kept open beyond the normal late-afternoon closing in order to allow payments to continue flowing in over the weekend. That was possible because settlement wouldn't occur until Monday in any event. They were worried that Monday would be a rerun of Friday. Unless dramatic measures were taken immediately, the world banking and payments system would return to the era of the quill pen and the hand-posted ledger. Wriston scoured the bank in a futile search for John Reed or Bob White. He then phoned Richard Kane, the former chemical engineer who had helped clean up the mess in check processing several years earlier and was now running the bank's money-transfer operations. Kane was accustomed to receiving his orders from White or Reed, so a call from Wriston quickly grabbed his attention. "It was a rare event," Kane remarked wryly, looking back on that memorable day.

"I can't find Johnny or Bob. We've got a problem," Wriston said tersely. "Herstatt failed. You've got to unplug MARTI," the bank's spanking new, if flawed, international wire transfer system. Though automated, MARTI was a dumb system that wasn't programmed to check the creditworthiness of banks making transfer payments. Wriston slammed down the phone, without explaining what he meant by "unplugging" MARTI.

Kane was nervous and perplexed, stewing over what Wriston could have meant. After some frantic phone calls, he determined that Wriston meant that no money should be transferred without having already received good funds. Until now, debits were made in the morning, credits in the afternoon, and reconciliations between the two were done at the end of the day. Settlement took place the next day. By pulling the plug on MARTI, Wriston sent banks all over the world into overdraft and virtually brought the payments system to a halt.

That Friday night, Wriston moved an emergency credit unit to his operations headquarters at the foot of Wall Street, overlooking the South Street Seaport and the East River, and he and his colleagues stayed up most of the night patching together a makeshift system that would enable them to hold the world's payment network together. Meanwhile Kane and his colleagues devised a plan to track debits and credits to correspondent banks. He phoned the chief auditor in search of about thirty mathematically inclined clerks to set up account ledgers listing correspondent banks.

Wriston knew that if they were to restore confidence and get the money moving again, they would have to find a way to quickly evaluate the creditworthiness of correspondent banks. On his orders, officers scrambled to review every transaction as it came across the wire, based on the credit standing of the correspondent. As long as the total transfer orders fell under that bank's limit, the money would be allowed to move. The world's financial institutions were waiting for Citibank to pay them before they made payments to anyone else.

The mood in the operations room was tense and frenzied. For a while the task proceeded like any routine clerical operation. Within hours, however, the team realized the impact they were having on the movement of billions of dollars around the world, and the significance of their assignment finally hit home. According to one former officer present in the room, "We had all the marbles that afternoon. . . . We were saying, 'No tickee, no shirtee.' "

Wriston and his colleagues soon discovered that payments due to Citibank from Samuel Montagu & Co., the merchant banking unit of Great Britain's Midland Bank, weren't coming through because of the failure's daisy-chain effect. Someone asked, "What's the capital of Montagu?" demonstrating that he clearly didn't understand the problem for what it was.

"For crying out loud!" Wriston exclaimed in exasperation. "It's run by the Midland Bank."

"I'll check the files," the Citibanker said.

"You don't have to check the files," Wriston growled. "We're okay." On day two, said a former top official of the New York Fed, "Nobody was going to pass money until someone else passed." According to the Fed official, John Lee told Wriston that unless someone broke the logjam, the entire financial system would crash. The banks could muddle through one day, but not two. Somebody would have to step up. Somebody, said Wriston later, "would have to put the first olive back in the bottle."

That Saturday Citibank injected $10 million into the payments system to keep the money flowing. By Sunday night the system had cleared. According to the Fed official, Wriston was the first banker to release money without coverage during the liquidity crisis.

Wriston instructed Lee to call a special meeting of the chairmen of the Clearing House banks for early Monday, July 1. After a long and contentious meeting, the bankers took the unprecedented step of issuing an emergency rule in which every bank on CHIPS would have to move the money without cover, but payments (from one bank to another) would be conditional, not final. The following morning, banks that had made payments for which they hadn't received cover could withdraw them. In turn, if one bank withdrew payment, other banks down the line that had made payments expecting to receive cover could pull theirs as well. The penalty for disobedience was ejection from CHIPS.

None of the New York banks was more resistant to the arrangement than Morgan, which apparently figured that it had little to gain because it had such a blue-chip network of clients and correspondents and thus had little need for coverage. In a meeting at the bank's Broad Street headquarters with Morgan chairman John Meyer, Wriston said, "I hate to be on a different side than Morgan 'cause you guys are very smart. But tell me why we should take this risk in the system?"

"He [Meyer] sort of went around the tree backwards on a bicycle," Wriston said later, but in the end he did in fact go with the flow.

In that meeting, Wriston and Reed were stunned by their colleagues' woeful ignorance of how money really moved. Most were elitist Ivy League graduates who had come up through the credit side of their institutions and had rarely, if ever, set foot in a back office. On the way out of the meeting, Reed remarked to his boss, "Do you realize there wasn't a chairman there who knew the value date of a Euro?"

"I know that, John," Wriston replied grimly.

"He [Wriston] took charge that day at the Clearing House," said former Comptroller James Smith. "If he hadn't been there, things would have been different."

Much as the move bothered Morgan, it sent the European banks and monetary authorities—particularly the British—into cardiac arrest. Accustomed to the finality of payments, they were outraged. "We were getting all kinds of hell from central banks and banking associations around the world who thought we were trying to hedge our bets in New York and put them at risk [by making settlements conditional] while we remained solvent," Lee said. "I got telegrams. Wriston got telegrams, saying, 'You're being unfair. You have no right to do this. You're endangering the world.' "

"The European banks all screamed and yelled," said Wriston. "They said, 'Our payments are final over here.' "

"You got to be kidding," Wriston replied to at least one bellyaching European banker. Wriston flew to London to meet with Gordon Richardson, governor of the Bank of England, one of the most vigorous opponents of the American arrangement. Wriston advised the Brits to set up their own dollar clearing system, in which dollar debits and credits would be settled in London and then the Bank of England would present the Clearing House with a single debit and credit. "He never got off his chair," said Wriston later.

"That would move the credit risk to this side of the water, wouldn't it?" the British central banker said.

"Right," Wriston retorted.

"What else have you got to say, Walt?" Richardson asked.

Wriston and the Clearing House stood their ground.

Despite the complaints, Wriston's makeshift arrangement continued through the summer, and confidence slowly returned to the world banking system. It also became clear that a few institutions accounted for most of the uncovered payments and that most of them had shadowy ties to Michele Sindona.

According to former Chase Manhattan chairman Willard Butcher, it was lucky that Chase, rather than Citibank, was the clearing bank for Herstatt. Citibank's MARTI system, he said later, "was just too automated, and had they been the clearing bank for Herstatt . . . they would have been in real trouble."

Wriston would later tell Butcher, "You fellows stopped the music and correctly so."

Amazingly, the central banks of the world, including the Fed, were taken completely by surprise by Herstatt and were ill equipped to understand and deal with its fallout. For them, Herstatt was banking's wake-up call. Said former Treasury aide Robert Carswell, "It woke them up to their role as lender of last resort in a way they didn't appreciate before this," he said. The world's banking system had come closer to meltdown than at any time since the Great Depression. By dint of his imposing personality and superior knowledge of the fine points of bank operations, Wriston briefly preempted the Federal Reserve Board, shoving his jury-rigged conditional payments system down the throats of commercial and central bankers. That system held things together—this time. But it pointed up the need for a fundamental overhaul of the international payments apparatus so as to avoid future Herstatts. That fix required that settlement of international payments be accelerated from "next day" to "same day." And here too, Wriston would emerge as the central figure.

The technology and logistics of such a change were complex enough. But the real hurdle was resistance from all the institutions whose oxen would be gored. Many banks, particularly foreign ones, had a vested interest in maintaining the status quo, which guaranteed them billions in float.

To the extent that any bank enjoyed the float—the free ride—on another institution or on the Fed, it had less reason to push for a system of continuous settlement. Many foreign banks, notably the Canadians, had grown accustomed to taking advantage of Citibank and its position as the world's preeminent clearer of funds. Correspondent banks with $1 million in their accounts [with Citibank] at the beginning of the day would initiate transfers amounting to $100 million and still wind up with $1 million in their accounts at the end of the day. "They were using us not to keep funds but to do movements," said operations wizard Robert White later. The Europeans played what global bankers called the Thursday–Monday game. They made payments late on Thursday so that they wouldn't have to put up money until Monday, and in between, they arbitraged the European market against the New York market. Former Chase chairman Butcher said, "It became apparent that we bankers had to stop being salesmen and become bankers and try to put some limits on allowing the payments system to have a free ride on the capital of the New York banks."

The debate was heated. The British were especially irate. According to former Citibanker George Hagerman, the Bank of England puffed that if a bank failed, "they would handle it." Even some U.S. banks, notably Morgan, tried to derail the project, as they had attempted to do when Herstatt blew. These banks were well aware that Citibank's relationships with its correspondents left much to be desired, in part because of its unpopular MARTI system, and they felt that Wriston was pushing for same-day settlement to give Citibank a competitive edge.

Former J. P. Morgan chairman Lewis Preston acknowledged later that while his bank agreed that there were flaws in the settlement system, the bank initially opposed Wriston's proposal for same-day settlement. "We had an honest difference about whether it was necessarily in our interest when first proposed," he said later. But over time, he said, Morgan switched over to Wriston's side. Preston said one reason Morgan resisted the plan was that transaction volume at the time was relatively small, compared with what it later became.

Over a weekend, the world payments system carried an estimated $400 billion in float. Hagerman recalled that Wriston, in arguing for same-day settlement, "described a scenario where the system could unwind [under next-day settlement] and everyone would fail along the way. We might be the last, but we would fail. In same-day settlement he was tough. He said, 'That's the way it has to be.' It would have been easier to go along with everyone."

It took seven years from the Herstatt collapse before same-day settlement took effect. On October 2, 1981, the morning after it was finally implemented, Lewis Preston called the Clearing House's John Lee and said gruffly, "You know you just knocked $6 billion off our footings [assets or liabilities] last night." The good news, added Preston, was that Morgan's ratio of capital to assets rose accordingly. Overnight, the same-day settlement knocked tens of billions of float out of the world payments system, lessening significantly the threat of a systemic collapse.

Later, Citibank and other Herstatt creditors filed to declare Herstatt bankrupt under U.S. law. Citibank lodged a $10 million claim against Herstatt stemming from an overdraft, and slapped liens on the bank's German assets. When Herstatt closed, Chase was literally stuck with some $156 million it didn't know what to do with. It had received the funds when the music stopped and didn't know which claimants to give it to. "Everybody was suing everybody," said one lawyer familiar with the case. But by year end a judge had approved a deal to settle the claims.

For Citibank, there was at least one positive consequence of the Herstatt failure. In 1973 Citicorp had bought a 15 percent stake in Trinkaus & Burkhardt, a German private bank with $1 billion in assets, and a majority stake in KKB, a consumer bank owned by T&B. After Herstatt cratered, other private banks were running scared. Worried that it might be infected by the Herstatt contagion, T&B officials ran to Citibank offering to sell it 36 percent, giving it majority ownership. In September 1974, Citibank increased its stake in T&B to 51 percent. That also ensured that Citibank's original 15 percent interest would be protected. Citibank was having its own problems, to be sure, but under its protective wing, T&B sailed through the post-Herstatt world liquidity crisis and proved to be one of Citibank's few profitable acquisitions.

Another acquisition done for similar reasons didn't fare so well. Within a week, Brandts, a London merchant banking house, a unit of National &

Grindlays (jointly owned by Citibank and Lloyds Bank), acquired the British Bank of Commerce, a Glasgow-based merchant bank that was suffering a liquidity crisis in the wake of Herstatt. In 1974, National & Grindlays would lose $23.4 million after taxes—a loss that Citibank would share—thanks to bad real estate investments by Brandts.

Some in the financial community had already begun to take potshots at Citibank because of its heavy involvement overseas. "We have branches in ninety-five foreign countries," Wriston told critics, "and there is no way things are going to go down the drain tomorrow." The financial markets may not have been overly worried about Citibank, but they did not share Wriston's optimism about conditions generally. Foreign exchange markets were so spooked by these shocks that trading activity had dropped to half of its pre-failure level. Reflecting a recognition by bankers of the risks they were taking, spreads on Eurodollar loans doubled to 1 percentage point over the cost of funds from the one-half percent level immediately after the oil embargo. Banks were no longer willing to lend for twelve years; maturities fell to less than ten years. But memories would prove to be short.

For the moment, however, it appeared that the world banking system and the Eurodollar markets were on the brink of collapse. The business press wrote of financial time bombs and doomsday scenarios. That summer, even Nixon economic counselor Kenneth Rush, speaking before a national television audience, accused "greedy" banks of making "risky loans." Citibank bailed out regional bank holding companies when the market backed away from their commercial paper. Citibank had led them to the trough, then made money when the water supply dried up.

No bank was in more of a jam than Charlotte-based North Carolina National Bank. The market had suddenly stopped buying its commercial paper. Its chairman, Thomas Storrs, desperately needed a $25 million backup line. When he tracked Wriston down at a Washington hotel, Wriston explained that Citibank didn't extend lines of credit to bank holding companies. Wriston and others worried that if banks lent to each other's holding companies, the holding companies would in turn downstream the proceeds into their banking subsidiaries as capital—a kind of banker's masturbation. But Wriston easily identified a loophole in his own rules to help a friend in need. Although Citibank couldn't extend the credit line, there was nothing stopping the commercial finance subsidiary of Citibank's holding company from doing so. With that backup, NCNB could weather the storm, and Storrs was able to get his first night's sleep in weeks.

Amid the turmoil of 1974, Wriston defied those who cried that the world was coming to an end. He said that "everybody perceived that the problem was international liquidity. That wasn't the problem at all." In fact, he said, it was "really the Eurodollar that solved the liquidity problem."

After Herstatt, it was more urgent than ever for Citicorp to pull off the Great Summer Floating Rate Note Sale in order to raise some more stable money. But before that could happen, it would have to run a gauntlet consisting of Arthur Burns, Wright Patman, Congress, thrifts, the housing industry, and Wall Street, which whined that the notes would drain capital from the equity markets. For those who sought to derail the issue, the rallying cry was the *d* word: disintermediation. If Citibank was allowed to offer the notes, the reasoning went, the thrift institutions, which financed the American dream of home ownership, would lose their deposits.

"Disintermediation," Wriston often quipped, "sounds like something you should do in the bathroom." In fact, Citibank was offering the notes because Citibank itself was suffering from disintermediation caused by Regulation Q. In other words, because of statutory ceilings on rates banks could pay depositors, they were losing deposits to money market funds.

Wriston's strategy throughout the ordeal that followed was to portray himself and his institution as the defenders of the small saver, who could not get rates as high as those offered to big depositors. Borrowing a line from Stillman Rockefeller, Wriston described himself as a "simple bank clerk" and told interviewers that the notes would benefit the "little guy."

This was one of those rare occasions in which Burns and Patman saw eye to eye. Patman, of course, simply wanted to harass a big bank. Burns, however, fretted that the notes would result in the demise of the savings banks, which were allowed to pay slightly higher rates on deposits than commercial banks. Soon after Citibank filed its registration statement, the Fed wrote to the SEC, which had to pass on the prospectus, questioning whether the issue was in "the public interest."

Late on the Friday before the Fourth of July weekend, 1974, chief financial officer Don Howard received a letter from the SEC commenting on the proposed offering. An SEC comment letter typically contained several items requiring a reply; this one, said Howard, contained eighty-three. It was the longest comment letter anyone had ever seen. Wriston and Howard, however, were determined to push this issue through. That afternoon they decided to work around the clock through the weekend to address the SEC's objections, and on Monday morning Citicorp delivered to the SEC's doorstep a completely rewritten filing. "They couldn't believe we were back with a revised prospectus ready to go," said attorney Hans Angermueller, adding that the SEC gave its approval. "They wanted to stop the thing. They were hoping the Fed would stop it, and the Fed was hoping the SEC would stop it." The SEC, while never a friend of Citibank, could find no legitimate reason to reject the offering.

Coincidentally, while the SEC was deliberating over the floating rate note aimed at the little guy, it was also investigating the well-publicized Home-Stake oil scandal, which humiliated a lot of big guys, including Wriston himself.

Wriston's archnemesis, Wright Patman, tried every angle to kill the deal; ultimately he introduced a bill in the House of Representatives that would have required regulators to review every bank holding company debt issue.

On the eve of the issue, Arthur Burns called on Citibank to delay it for two weeks. Once again he spoke out of both sides of his mouth. In a letter to Senate Banking Committee chairman William Proxmire, Burns questioned whether the public interest would be well served by blocking or restricting "innovative efforts" like the floating note, but called on Proxmire to give the Fed legislative power to do so. And he also proposed help for savings institutions and the housing market. Proxmire, who also thought that the notes would be a disaster for the housing industry, promptly responded that he would introduce legislation to give the Fed the authority it wanted.

Patman, however, was forced to back down when the Treasury Department told his committee that "the Treasury is prepared to oppose even the first step toward capital controls which would thrust the government into the heart of the private decision-making process." For once, even the *New York Times* came to Citicorp's defense, with an editorial on July 18, 1974, supporting the floating note offering. "For the first time, small savers would be given access along with the wealthy to the often higher interest rates of the money market," the *Times* wrote. At the same time, the editorial suggested awarding more powers, including interest-bearing checking accounts, to the thrifts to offset the impact of the Citibank initiative.

Citicorp brought the offer to market before Congress could block it. But the bank was forced to compromise by making changes that diminished the offer's attractiveness, including a two-year delay before the notes could be redeemed at their original value. So instead of selling the $850 million originally anticipated, Citibank on July 24 unloaded $650 million of the notes.

Wriston had limited his appearances before Congress, testifying only on matters of critical importance to Citibank, such as the Bank Holding Company Act amendments. Wriston rarely referred to the inequities and hardships that a law or regulation would impose on the banking industry in general or on Citibank in particular. Instead, he spoke of the unfairness heaped upon the small saver by government control of the marketplace. On July 25, 1974, in testimony before the Senate Banking Committee, Wriston said that disintermediation among financial institutions had not been eliminated; in fact, he said, it had "become a major contributing factor toward this phenomenon." He went on to say that "those who insist upon supporting America's housing by forcing workers to accept an interest rate on their savings lower than the rate of inflation—in effect, causing small savers to lose money—are advocating having the account executive's split-level in Greenwich subsidized by the depositor in the Harlem Savings Bank. This is neither a necessary nor a just system."

Citibank won the battle to issue its notes, but lost the war, at least for the time being, to pull the teeth from Reg Q. The House and Senate approved legislation giving the Fed the power to regulate future offerings by prohibiting payment of rates above Reg Q ceilings, the very feature that made the Citibank notes attractive to begin with. While President Ford, who had just taken office upon the resignation of Richard M. Nixon, signed the bill that fall, he did so reluctantly. Describing himself as "deeply concerned" about the bill, he compared it to state usury laws, which he called "well-meaning but futile" efforts to hold down interest rates.

When the deal was done, and the proceeds of the notes began rolling in, Wriston threw a dinner for the participants and their wives on the thirty-ninth floor of 399 Park Avenue.

The floating rate issue represented yet another first, according to Wriston. It marked the end—or at least the beginning of the end—of the traditional old boy relationships between investment banks and their clients. For years, First Boston had had a lock on Citibank's underwritings. When Wriston and Howard first broached the idea of the floating rate bonds to their investment bankers, First Boston responded less than enthusiastically, saying that Citibank might be able to sell about $100 million at most. Over lunch, Salomon Brothers told Wriston that they didn't think much of the idea either. But on the third try, at Merrill Lynch, effectively a direct competitor with Citibank for the small investor's dollar, the reception was entirely different. "Merrill said, 'Great idea,'" Wriston recalled, and generated $1 billion in orders in less than a week. In the end, First Boston, Goldman, Sachs, and Merrill Lynch co-managed the issue.

But First Boston was so incensed that other investment banks were included in the underwriting that a senior executive called Wriston and asked, "What are you guys doing dealing with the enemy [Merrill Lynch]?" In the world of investment banking, this was heresy.

"Look, we asked you [what you thought about the note issue] and you told us it wasn't a very good idea," Wriston replied.

Word spread quickly among other corporate chieftains who had long felt beholden to a single Wall Street firm. One was IBM chairman Frank T. Cary. "I understand you talked to several [investment] bankers," Cary said incredulously.

"Yeah," Wriston said proudly.

Cary said his company had used the same investment banker forever. "How do I know we're getting the best deal?" the IBM chief asked.

"It's one of those wonderful things we call competition," Wriston replied. IBM, Wriston noted, then took on an additional underwriter on a subsequent offering, fracturing its long-standing investment banker relationships.

Of the floating rate notes, Wriston said later that it "not only helped solve a problem for us in the tightest money market any of us in the room can remember, it also proved there was a market out there if we have the wit and courage to find and tap it." The notes were critical in getting Citicorp through its liquidity crisis. The fever was finally broken that fall as the Fed loosened its grip on the monetary levers and interest rates started to decline.

By midsummer 1974, Wriston was juggling three medicine balls in the air at the same time. Even as he was lobbying Congress on the floating rate note issue and coping with the aftermath of the Herstatt failure, he was playing a pivotal role in resolving the future of Franklin National Bank. After Herstatt, that was imperative. "A bad day at Franklin after Herstatt could have caused everything to become unwound," said former Comptroller James Smith. It was now clear that Franklin was not going to be an unassisted rescue, however. This was shaping up as the largest bank failure in American history. On July 2, Smith wrote to FDIC chairman Frank Wille asking him to begin planning for what bank regulators euphemistically call an "assisted" merger.

At one point, Morris Schapiro, then the dean of U.S. bank analysts, proposed splitting up Franklin and selling off the pieces, possibly even to out-of-state banks such as California's Bank of America and Security Pacific. Smith was fascinated with the idea, which would have advanced the cause of interstate banking, but Fed chairman Arthur Burns rejected it out of hand. "He didn't like the politics of it," Smith explained later. Indeed, Smith said that such a move would have had to be blessed in advance by Congress. According to former secretary of the Treasury David Kennedy, a director of the Franklin National Corporation and a backer of Sindona, the New York banks weren't enamored of that idea either and also blocked Bank of America from taking over Franklin.

Three years later, Arthur Burns himself proposed legislation that would allow out-of-state acquisitions of big banks on the verge of failure. "Had an institution the size of Franklin National or U.S. National failed in certain other states, no in-state bank would have been large enough to acquire them. In such circumstances, the ability to arrange an acquisition across state boundaries would become urgent," Burns said later.

The FDIC in mid-August 1974 hauled in prospective bidders—large U.S. and foreign banks, including Chemical, Citibank, Manny Hanny, and European American—for marathon negotiations. The bank regulators wanted the government to get the best possible deal, but that wouldn't happen unless there was competitive bidding. Burns, for one, recognized that for the bidding process to appear to be serious, Citibank would have to play the shill.

Franklin was virtually worthless to Citibank. Its branch system overlapped with Citi's, and Citi clearly had no use for its loan portfolio or its London branch. But Arthur Burns obviously had lots of cards to play. Citibank had filed countless applications to buy various non-bank businesses and was pushing for interstate banking powers. Under pressure from Fed chairman Burns, Citibank knuckled under. It assigned top Shearman & Sterling lawyers to the case, ordering them to structure a bid that was certain to lose. "We were persuaded they [Citibank] were for real and that they were going to come in and buy this thing," said Comptroller of the Currency deputy general counsel Westbrook Murphy.

In midsummer, Clearing House director John Lee was summoned to the Federal Reserve and told confidentially that Franklin would fail on October 8. This was to be accomplished in a controlled way. The Fed "practically opened a vein and made me sign in blood" an agreement not to disclose this information. Franklin chairman Joe Barr, however, proceeded like a physician treating a seriously ill patient who stood a good chance of survival. He announced a strategy of retreating from overseas operations and from New York City, and returning Franklin to its Long Island roots. John Lee never informed him that the death knell on Franklin had already been sounded. Wriston and Lee were committed to removing Franklin from the Clearing House and CHIPS by D day, so as to avoid the kind of near-collapse in the international payments system that had occurred with Herstatt.

Under Clearing House rules, each bank member pledged to stand behind the others in a financial emergency. Lee was like the director of an exclusive club who had found a whore in one of the guest rooms and wanted to ease her out before the news leaked out. In a meeting with Barr, Lee was less than candid in explaining his reasons for suggesting that Franklin resign from the club. Instead of telling him the bank's obituary had already been written, he explained that resigning from the Clearing House would be one way of demonstrating his commitment to the Long Island–first strategy. When Barr agreed that resignation was a good idea, Lee asked eagerly, "When can I have your letter?"

"I wasn't all that genuine with Joe Barr," Lee confessed later. "I felt bad about keeping Joe in the dark. But if by the end of August he didn't know Franklin was failing, he was out of touch with the world."

Citibank and the regulators led everyone, including the media, to believe that Citibank was the sure bet to take over Franklin. On September 21, another vital hurdle was overcome when Sindona was forced to resign. Little by little the way was being cleared for the inevitable failure followed by the sale of Franklin National to a healthy bank.

At the root of the turmoil was rampaging inflation. Monetary and fiscal policy in the Nixon era had been a dismal failure. From 1970 to 1974, public debt grew more than $100 billion, a bigger increase than had occurred in the twenty-four years before that. Much of the blame belonged to Burns, who had backed wage and price controls of one kind or another. The economy that Gerald Ford inherited from Nixon left the new president grasping for straws when he moved into the Oval Office in August 1974.

While Wriston was prepared to give any Republican president the benefit of the doubt, he held out little hope for the success of Ford's Whip Inflation Now campaign and all the gimmickry, lapel buttons, and other hoopla that went along with it. Nonetheless, on September 28, nine months into the worst recession since the 1930s, Wriston was among the 120 business and economic leaders who participated in a Saturday afternoon summit meeting on inflation. Sitting in alphabetical order around a horseshoe-shaped table in Washington, the luminaries were given three minutes apiece to explain how inflation could be wrestled to the ground.

Wriston told the *Economist* of December 14, 1974, that there was at least one "fascinating" revelation from the summit: "an almost universal perception that our regulatory system is in a mess as far as the consumer is concerned. Now that, I think, is an astonishing step forward." Although he thought the meeting was futile, he was impressed by the discipline and control displayed by the president, who was able to "sit there listening to all this crap" just hours after his wife, Betty, had been operated on for breast cancer. As for the Whip Inflation Now program, said Wriston, "fortunately it died an unlamented death."

During the conference, Ford announced that he was, in effect, reconstituting the Labor Management Committee with the same cast of characters who had served on Nixon's labor-management panel and naming Harvard professor John Dunlop to lead it. Ford took the committee and its advice seriously, and met with it about every two months throughout the fifteen months of its existence. Under Ford, the highlight of the meetings were the confrontations between Labor leader George Meany and the president. "Meany used to beat up on him," said Wriston later. "He [Ford] used to take his pipe out of his mouth and say, 'Do I get equal time?' " Ford, of course, was deeply opposed to wage and price controls. So advising him not to enact them was easier than getting Nixon to abolish them. Nonetheless, Wriston wanted to make sure that mistake was never committed again.

———

Despite the last-ditch efforts of former Treasury secretary Joseph Barr to revive Franklin National Bank, it was clear to all by September 1974 that the patient was terminal. The only questions remaining were the details of the funeral, and who would walk away with the body.

On October 6, the Clearing House banks finally ejected Franklin National from their exclusive club. Two days later, as scheduled, Franklin was declared insolvent.

Though Citibank ultimately submitted the low offer, it spent as much money as the other banks to convince its banking colleagues that it was indeed a serious bidder. It even prepared a press release announcing the takeover in the unlikely event it hit the bid.

To Manufacturers Hanover's everlasting disappointment, it came in a close second with an offer of about $120 million. The winner was the European American Bank, a consortium of European institutions, which acquired the defunct bank for $125 million. The episode once again demonstrated that the left hand of government did not know what the right hand was doing. Shortly after the takeover, the Department of Justice's anti-trust office, while not taking issue with the acquisition of Franklin, questioned the bids of Citibank, Chemical, and Manny Hanny.

Franklin officials were later convicted of fraud in connection with the failure, and Sindona was sentenced to twenty-five years in jail. In March 1986 he died in an Italian prison. His death was deemed a suicide by Italian officials.

The events of that summer reinforced Arthur Burns's concerns and conviction that his go-slow approach was the right one. The failure of U.S. National, Franklin, and Herstatt, he said later, "transformed incipient unease into serious apprehension. Indeed, for the first time since the 1930s, major doubts began to be voiced here and there about the soundness of our nation's, and indeed the world's, banking system."

Wriston thrived on crises because he could see beyond them. And Citibank's bottom line, because of its increasingly sophisticated trading operations, in Wriston's vision, thrived on chaos in the marketplace. The greater the volatility in interest and exchange rates, the more money Citibank made. For 1974, Citibank later reported foreign exchange income of $89 million, a dramatic increase over the $54 million level the year before. Because of Citibank's financial strength, deposits flowed in during upheavals like water over Hoover Dam. Just as totalitarian governments, because of their obsession with order and stability, were abhorrent to Wriston, marketplace stability was anathema to Citibank.

Whatever lessons Franklin contained for regulators, for Wriston it only reinforced his conviction that inadequate capital had nothing to do with bank failures. Franklin turned out to be less a case of bad assets than badly priced assets. It had obviously failed to digest Citibank's treatise on the marginal cost of funds. Franklin would have collapsed even without the foreign exchange losses. In Wriston's view, the bottom line on Franklin was "bum management." As he told the *Economist* of December 14, 1974, "Whether you run a hamburger stand or a bank, if you don't have any management you go broke."

In the wake of the Franklin failure, Wriston and Burns fought their war over capital and earnings in every forum that would listen. Speaking before the Business Council days after the failure, Wriston told this exclusive cadre of *Fortune* 100 CEOs that a high rate of capital formation would not "save any nation from inflation" and that "only a free market can efficiently and equitably allocate credit and capital." And in an apparent reference to Burns's push for bank capital, he said that "various members of our government constantly talk about profits as if they were not part of our capital formation process."

Nonetheless, the volatility generated by two back-to-back bank failures clearly put the fear of God into Citibank. Perhaps more than any previous event, Franklin convinced Wriston and Don Howard that, from a funding standpoint, "it was a dangerous world out there and that we had to plan on a global basis." Now more than ever he was determined to make the bank less dependent on hot money.

If there was ever any doubt about the Fed's resolve to cut bank holding company expansion off at the knees, chairman Arthur Burns ended it at the American Bankers Association's annual meeting in Hawaii in October 1974. Though Burns addressed himself to the thousands of bankers who had flown to Honolulu, the speech sounded like a heart-to-heart talk with Walter Wriston. In the twelve months ending on June 30, 1974, Citicorp's loan portfolio had grown a whopping 33 percent—among the nation's biggest banks second only to Chase's 34 percent. But other big banks weren't far behind. After a brief and disingenuous nod to "innovative" banking, Burns lamented the decline of equity capital, heavy dependence on volatile funds, excessive loan commitments and erosion of asset quality, and heightened exposure to foreign exchange dealings and overseas operations. He made it clear that the Fed intended to impose a "breathing spell" in bank holding company expansion. Before long, Fed officials were calling for minimum capital-to-assets ratios for bank holding companies. Burns's resolve was reflected in the Fed's decision in late 1975 to reject Citibank's petition to buy several small finance companies, including the Seattle-based West Coast Corporation, a tiny, troubled consumer finance company. The pretense for the rejection was that the acquisition would be anti-competitive—a red herring, given the company's paltry $8.7 million in assets. A few months later the Fed appeared to realize the folly of its ways and reversed its ruling, concluding that the benefits to be gained from the survival of the West Coast Corporation outweighed the disadvantages.

Just as Wriston may have been on Burns's mind when he delivered his "Go slow" speech in Hawaii, Australia may have been on Wriston's mind as he pondered his rival's message. Wriston and his "partners" had divided up the globe, sorting out who should go where and when, and this was Wriston's year for Australia.

Wriston basically liked Australians. But he believed that Aussies, notably real estate developers, were inclined to "turn the corners" too fast, as he put it later. His next stop was Sydney, where he would have to "bust" a joint venture arrangement that had been causing him fits.

When the Honolulu convention ended, Wriston headed southwest to Sydney. During a refueling stopover on Majuro, a remote speck of coral in Micronesia, he met a young American who was leaning listlessly against the corrugated metal wall of a Quonset hut.

"Where are you from?" asked the young man, perplexed to see a corporate jet in this remote corner of the world.

"New York," Wriston replied. "I'm Walter Wriston, chairman of Citicorp."

The young man fell silent in stunned disbelief. He was, it turned out, the owner of a forty-foot sailboat whose Pacific cruise had been cut short not by foul wind or weather but by a disturbing telex from San Francisco. Financed with a mortgage from Citicorp, the yacht had been seized in Majuro by the bank when the owner failed to meet the payments. Citicorp's action had stranded the yacht and its crew indefinitely.

Sympathetic with the yachtsman's predicament, Wriston told him, "I'll see what I can do." On his arrival in Sydney, Wriston phoned Citicorp's San Francisco office and instructed the bank to lift the lien so the owner and his crew could sail back to the United States.

But Wriston had larger problems to deal with in Australia. Ever since George Moore cut his swimming pool deal with Walton back in 1966, the Aussies had been moving a bit too fast for the not-so-slick New York bankers. Citibank, however, was a glutton for punishment. Incredibly, five years later, while still reeling from its ill-fated love affair with Waltons, Citibank acquired a 40 percent stake in IAC (Holdings), owner of the Industrial Acceptance Corporation, an Australian company that made auto, tractor, and personal loans. It was the second-largest finance company in Australia.

IAC would prove to be an even greater headache than Waltons itself, acquired as it was on the eve of one of the deepest downturns ever in the Australian real estate market. To finance speculative office construction and the purchase of Sydney real estate, IAC issued huge volumes of high-yielding debentures bought by Australians with lump-sum retirement payments. It also financed thousands of acres of raw land in the Australian outback. To reduce its exposure, IAC sold a big slug of what proved to be bum outback loans to none other than FNCB-Waltons. A kind of loan triangle evolved among Citibank's representative office, Waltons, and IAC, in which the three units were essentially "flogging loans to each other," as a former officer put it. The whole operation lacked the kind of financial controls that might have nipped the disaster in the bud.

When a new Labor government took power in Australia in 1972, it shrank the money supply and burst the real estate bubble. Two years later, three big IAC developer-borrowers went belly up, costing IAC some $300 million, and all of a sudden the money stopped coming in.

By 1974, John Reed was traveling the world investigating the possibility of building a unified consumer business. When Reed returned from Australia, he sauntered into Wriston's office, put his finger in his mouth, blew a sharp whistle, and said, "We have a problem."

The nagging problems with Waltons, and later IAC, took up so much top management time that Citibank officers jokingly referred to Wriston as the SENOF (senior officer) of Australia. "The country was never basically successful," said one officer familiar with that business.

The IAC episode marked a turning point in Citibank's disastrous dalliance with joint ventures, which have rarely worked well in the banking industry. IAC would cause the bank to virtually swear off such arrangements—but unfortunately for Citibank, it did not swear off Australia. Citibank eventually learned that in a joint venture each partner has different goals and approaches the business differently, and that such arrangements work only when both partners understand how they're going to earn their money.

Another reason for all the trouble with joint ventures is that Citibank simply made a bad partner. It didn't work or play well with others. To the extent that Wriston "made the Citicorp team play one game, he made Citicorp very poor at playing someone else's game," said former vice chairman Tom Theobald.

By October 1974 Wriston was determined that Citibank would not be Australia's patsy. The Australian government would have to amend its policy against non-Australian control of financial institutions, or Wriston would let IAC (Holdings) fail, with all the attendant political consequences. "I had to get up and give a speech," said Wriston later, "where I took that to the edge of the cliff. I couldn't say we guaranteed it, and couldn't say we didn't." For once, Australia caved in. Citibank upped its stake from a 40 percent interest to 50.5 percent. After Wriston prevailed, an Australian newspaper opined that "I.A.C. is no doubt seen as a special case by the Government." But the price to Citibank was $150 million in hard cash. And this would by no means be the end of IAC's troubles.

Despite Wriston's warm postwar feelings toward the Australians, he was clearly put out by the stiffing Citibank had taken at their hands. In his colleagues' opinion, this colored his attitude toward the country. Some time after Wriston returned to New York, Citibank's Richard Huber mentioned to him that he was headed for Austria on a business trip. "You tell those bastards—" Wriston blurted out before Huber interrupted him. "Oh, Walt, Austria—not Australia," Huber said. "Well, you tell those people . . ." Wriston said.

15

PROBLEM BANKING

*A*fter Wriston returned from Down Under, he and Citibank had to confront another joint venture gone sour—this one was with the nearly bankrupt city of New York, which had begun to fall victim to years of profligate spending and financial gimmickry. In a struggle that would pit bankers against bureaucrats and union bosses for nearly four years, Wriston was not the official leader of the banker group, but there was little question where the real power rested. Wriston dominated the discussions, not because he talked the loudest or ran the largest bank, but because of his presence and his unique ability to cut through the confusion to identify commonsense solutions. Wriston was clearly the de facto leader of the New York financial community and the one most determined to keep the feet of the city's inept leaders to the fire.

Wriston was the quintessential New Yorker. Though his roots were rural, he viewed that vast territory west of the Hudson and north and east of Manhattan as less than fertile soil for an active mind. "All great ideas come from urban areas," he used to say. "In New York every day you meet ten people smarter than you and they're glad to tell you about it."

No major New York bank could escape, even if it wanted to, an intimate fiscal relationship with the city. The banks served as underwriters, dealers, and traders of municipal securities. They advised the city on market technicalities and bought and sold the obligations for their own accounts and those of their trust customers. Citibank's financial association with New York was a long-standing one, dating back at least to 1865, when it loaned the city $500,000 to make the payroll. When New York faced a fiscal crisis in the 1930s, Citibank was a prominent member of the committee of bankers that, as Wriston said, "put the city back together again."

Underwriting and trading in city paper was a lucrative activity. By the fall of 1974, the city owed $6 billion in short-term debt and each month had to come up with $550 million to refund notes as they came due. But the New York banks, Citibank included, performed little if any analysis of city finances, relying largely on the bond rating agencies. As Wriston would testify later, "No one outside the city could analyze the complex tax data and past

473

experience on which anticipated tax receipts were certified." The banks were afraid that if they probed too deep into the netherworld of municipal finance, they might jeopardize their relationships with the city comptroller and risk losing their share of city accounts. They had played fat, dumb, and happy while the city was living on borrowed time. So it was easy for city officials to continue their financial machinations, including an age-old practice of financing current expenses out of the capital budget. But the basic problem was that those expenses were growing faster than city revenues. Said one former state official, "The city had clearly been living beyond its means, courtesy of the willingness of lenders to lend."

New York City's financial problems had been building for years. Some even contended that they dated back to the administration of Fiorello La Guardia, widely regarded as New York's greatest mayor. But with the election of the charismatic John Lindsay as mayor in November 1965, things took a turn for the worse. Though Lindsay had promised to halt the "decline and fall" of New York, he buckled in his first crucial test. Immediately after taking office on New Year's Day 1966, he was faced with a transit strike that shut down the city's buses and subways. To get the city moving, he agreed to an overly generous wage settlement that set a dangerous precedent for future pacts. No city in the country offered more generous fringe benefits, including a provision that based a worker's pension on his final year's salary, which was typically loaded with overtime.

Between 1965 and 1975 New York's workforce expanded from 268,000 to 440,000 workers, most of it during Lindsay's two terms in office. Flimflam budgeteering became the rule, and New York City's short-term debt quintupled with ever-rising expenditures for social, medical, and educational programs and cushy union contracts. Spending for long-term capital improvements withered in the Lindsay administration, as money borrowed for such projects was diverted for operating expenses.

Meanwhile, the state, under Governor Nelson Rockefeller, was barreling along on a parallel track.

One of the fiscal gimmicks blessed by Nelson Rockefeller was the moral obligation bond. This instrument, invented by deposed attorney general John Mitchell when he was a bond lawyer, had the tacit but not the full faith and credit backing of the state. The beauty of the so-called MOB was that it allowed New York State to borrow more than the law would ordinarily permit, and the debt would never even show up on the state balance sheet. MOBs enabled Rockefeller to build his most tangible monument: a $1 billion plus boondoggle known as the Albany Mall. Rockefeller also contributed revenue anticipation notes—money borrowed in anticipation of money not yet received. RANs were joined by TANs (tax anticipation notes) and BANs (bond anticipation notes). In the end, BANs would bring down the house of cards.

By the 1970s, New York City financing was little more than a scheme in which new short-term debt was issued in ever-increasing quantities to pay off previous debts. Every month the city had to go into the market to raise hundreds of millions of dollars to pay off RANs, TANs, BANs, and other obligations.

Still, Lindsay was not without his supporters. A notable one was former union organizer Jack Bigel, who earned $750,000 a year as the adviser to the union pension funds, which would later play a key role in the crisis. Bigel and other defenders of Lindsay's largesse would later argue that in 1967, when other large American cities, including Detroit and Newark, erupted in an epidemic of race riots, looting, and burning, Lindsay helped keep New York cool. New York's financial problems, Bigel asserted, were "the price of deflecting social arson," and the city's fiscal practices would be called "innovative financing" if they were used in the private sector. In the public sector, he said, it is "robbing Peter to pay Paul." He contended that short-term debt had been used to fund general expenses since 1940. "At one time it was regarded as sound financing; a generation later it becomes fiscal gimmickry."

In identifying the time bomb in New York City finances, Chase was out in front of Citibank by a stretch. Chase economist Karen Gerard had begun to focus on the New York economy in the 1960s. During Lindsay's second term, Gerard prepared an economic analysis of New York in which she identified the underlying imbalance between revenue and spending in the budget and asserted that the problem could never be solved simply through economic growth. She didn't predict that a crisis would erupt the next day, but said she "didn't see how the city could continue to fill the gap." In the early 1970s Gerard presented the paper at a New York Clearing House meeting attended by the heads of the major banks, including Wriston and David Rockefeller. Although the bankers agreed that the paper was "interesting," they essentially ignored its findings.

In 1973 the Scott Commission, appointed by Governor Nelson Rockefeller, alerted those who would listen to the city's use of financial gimmicks and warned that the city couldn't afford all the services it offered. Lindsay retorted that the study was politically inspired.

By 1973, Wriston hadn't identified New York City as a candidate for bankruptcy, but he was becoming frustrated with what he saw as the city's move toward a welfare state and domination by special interest groups. In a talk entitled "Dissent of the Majority" to the Regional Planning Association, on April 5, 1973, Wriston warned that New York City, with its "financially ruinous" public pension plans, had come to resemble the Uruguay of the 1950s and 1960s, when "20 percent of the citizens ended up supporting 80 percent of the populace." Such generosity, he said, was driving private companies out of the city because their benefit plans could no longer compete with the city's. But he also railed at the increasing ability of a small minority of citizens to "frustrate the will of the majority, not just for days or for weeks but for years." And, he went on, "the lack of authentic power in this city certainly makes the most responsible of institutions vulnerable to the strident demands of the stubborn few."

One community activist apparently took such offense at Wriston's comments that she reportedly remarked to a friend on the way out, "I can hardly wait to get to the bank in the morning to take my money out of that man's bank."

That November 1973 city comptroller Abraham Beame, who claimed to know the city's finances like his personal checkbook, became New York's 104th mayor. One of Beame's first acts was to appoint a transition committee, which forecast a $1.3 billion deficit for the fiscal year beginning the following July, a finding that Beame disclosed publicly even before he took office.

At least one banker, retired Chase chairman George Champion, had serious misgivings about the quality of the top-level personnel Beame was selecting to oversee the city's finances. He asked to meet with Beame alone, but when he arrived, the first deputy mayor, Jim Cavanagh, was also in the office. Not one to mince words, Champion told Beame, "Abe, you're going to be the CEO of the second-largest operation in America. The CEO of every large corporation hires the best operating man he can find, puts him in charge of operations, and holds him accountable. This is what you have to do if you're going to run this operation effectively. Otherwise it's bankruptcy."

"George," Cavanagh interjected, "in business and banking it's the bottom line. In government it's jobs." A city bureaucrat for thirty years, Cavanagh was Beame's longtime crony, had been his ally in the comptroller's office, and was generally regarded as the architect of the budgetary shell game.

Later, as chairman of the Economic Development Council, Champion would oversee a report on city operations that revealed the pervasiveness of the disease that afflicted city government. The report, to Champion's regret, was never released to the press because of a deal struck at the outset with the city. "We should have publicized the crookedness we found," Champion said later. Among the more grotesque findings, said Champion, was the Board of Education's failure to monitor the inventory of school supplies, allowing widespread theft and pilferage. After overcoming stiff union resistance, the city finally was able to fire the guilty employees. "There were," said the crusty Mr. Champion, "little crooks here and little crooks there."

The city might have been able to get away with all of this in a rapidly expanding economy where federal monies were unlimited. But with the inflationary high-interest-rate onslaught that had begun in the late 1960s, New York finances were an accident waiting to happen. As if Penn Central, Lockheed, and the Arab oil shock were not enough to make investors skittish, they were followed in rapid succession by the REITs explosion, tremors in the commercial paper market, Franklin National, and Herstatt. A Congressional Budget Office study concluded that the earlier crises had exacerbated investor anxiety and uncertainty.

By the summer of 1974, the market had begun to signal that something was wrong. The city, said economist Karen Gerard, asked the banks to place their bids for underwriting in what they called the "magic box." But this time, she noted, "there were no bids in the box."

In July, New York City was forced to pay an unprecedented 7.69 percent on long bonds. In a July 26 editorial, the *Wall Street Journal* warned that the "only way" the city could get through fiscal 1975 was by borrowing against 1976. Amid disclosures of irregularities in the city's accounting practices, several banks, including Citibank, begged city officials to let them help clean up the books. The officials declined. By most accounts, Beame saw the problem as a seasonal "refunding" matter caused in part by the failure of the federal government to meet its commitments to the city fast enough, and he felt the banks were just being nasty. When Gerard reviewed the numbers in 1974, she knew that short-term debt had grown so astronomically that "none of the explanations City Hall was giving made any sense."

In the fall of 1974, rates on New York City bonds and notes began to rise much faster than interest rates in general, and the Beame administration griped that the banks were making out like bandits on what he called "usurious" rates.

Victor Gotbaum, head of the District Council 37 of the American Federation of State, City and Municipal Employees, realized the city was in trouble in October 1974 when Beame told him and a group of fellow labor leaders at City Hall that the banks no longer wanted to underwrite city paper. At that moment, Gotbaum recalled later, "I knew we were in deep shit. You can't have $13 billion in long-term debt—which was 25 percent of all local debt [in the U.S.]—and not know you're in deep shit." But Beame seemed to be living in never-never land. On October 22 he put out a press release declaring that the city's credit standing had "improved considerably" and was "solid and strong."

In a November 4 editorial, the *New York Times,* not given to hyperbole, declared the city "near bankrupt." Yet Beame and Comptroller Harrison Goldin were still trying to put the best face on things. Interviewed for a November 20 article in the trade paper *Daily Bond Buyer,* Beame said, "I'm not a rich man, but I've got a good portion of my assets in city bonds." Though Goldin acknowledged that the city had serious financial problems, he nonetheless called the city a "superb investment." To spread the risk, and broaden the market for securities, the city now planned to offer notes in $10,000 units, the first time that had happened in four years.

The city's credibility with investors was further shaken by the public squabbling between Beame and Goldin over whether the current fiscal year's deficit was $430 million, as Beame contended, or $650 million, as Goldin estimated. City records were so out of whack that the mayor's budget office and the comptroller's office showed a discrepancy of 100,000 workers on the city payroll.

In late November, Beame began to bite the bullet—sort of. He announced his intention to lay off 1,510 city employees, less than one half of 1 percent of the total, and shut down eight fire companies. This was the first time since the Depression that the city had laid off workers.

By the end of 1974 the big New York banks had begun to reduce the

level of city obligations in their trust portfolios. It was clear to Citibank officials that New York City wouldn't be able to get through fiscal 1976 without
state and federal help and higher taxes.

Even as the severity of the city's problems began to dawn on Wriston
and other bankers, it was hard for them to imagine that any future crisis
could be much worse than those they had already put behind them. Defying
the doomsayers, Wriston pronounced the U.S. banking system at year end
"in very good shape. The popular cry at the moment is to say that it's over-
strained, overlent," but "I don't see any signs on the horizon that the entire
system is seriously strained; the proof is that the system has, in fact, handled properly one of the wildest financial markets that anybody can remember. We've handled a couple of Middle East wars, shifted resources to a
new part of the world, and adapted to floating exchange rates. We've also
ridden through the failure of Herstatt [when their central bank did not pick
up the chips], the lowest stock market since 1929, and the resignation of a
president of the United States of America for the first time in history. We're
all still here."

But *New York* magazine's Dan Dorfman wasn't buying. "When you're
the boss of the First National City, the second biggest bank, you're supposed
to be cool," he wrote. Dorfman asserted that even Wriston's own troops had
their doubts and quoted an unnamed Citicorp officer: "Let Wriston sound
the trumpets of optimism. It goes with the job. But unfortunately, I have to
live in the real world."

While it would be unfair to say that Wriston was bored by New York City's
political and financial machinations, it was surely true, as another *New York*
magazine writer put it, that "Walter's heart really belongs to the world."

Through the gatherings at the Bechtel estate near Monterey, California,
with George Shultz, Milton Friedman, and their monetarist brethren, Wriston was becoming a devotee of the Laffer curve, the notion that a reduction in
the tax rate will boost consumption and capital formation and thereby total
tax revenue. He had helped convince Ford's Labor-Management Committee
[a continuation of the Nixon panel], including the AFL-CIO's George Meany
and Lane Kirkland, that there might be something to the theory. In late December 1974 the committee advised President Ford to propose to Congress a
$15 billion personal income tax cut that would be accomplished through a 5
percent tax reduction, a $70 credit per dependent, and a 12 percent increase in
the investment tax credit. The proposals were announced in a January 10
White House press conference and, according to economist John Dunlop—
now Ford's secretary of labor—helped shape the 1975 tax reduction package.

In fact, Wriston wanted to go further by throwing out the entire tax
code and replacing it with a flat percentage—with a top individual rate of 20
to 30 percent—that would be applied to all income. Presaging the tax changes
of the eighties, Wriston said, "My proposition is that you throw away the

whole damn thing and start from scratch. You put in a simple graduated income tax with a fairly low ceiling and it would raise more revenue than we raise with the Rube Goldberg contraption we've got now."

Wriston recognized that burdensome New York State and City taxes were having the same kind of destructive effect. "Some taxpayers are voting with their feet. They're leaving this town, and they're leaving this state," he said, adding that "you have to put a ceiling on tax rates and, in fact, lower them. If there is zero income tax in Connecticut and a 14 percent tax here in New York, how long will people stay here?"

Meanwhile, New York's own fiscal woes had only worsened with the deepening national recession that Wriston and his committee were trying to address with the federal tax plan. On January 7, a syndicate led by Citibank and Bankers Trust was the sole bidder on a $620 million issue of one-year tax-exempt RANs that was sold at an unprecedented 9.4 percent. For Beame, this was the last straw. He fired off a bitter news release condemning the rate, saying that he planned to take the matter up with the city's financiers to "avoid a repetition of this unfair, unwarranted, and outrageously high interest rate."

Over the next three years, Wriston, Bill Spencer, and executive committee chairman Ed Palmer were nearly interchangeable in the fiscal crisis. While Wriston was taking reporters' phone calls on his tax plan, Spencer and top bond specialist Richard Kezer got to attend the kickoff breakfast at Gracie Mansion for the most contentious financial crisis ever to beset an American city.

The entire New York banking establishment was there, including David Rockefeller and Morgan's Ellmore "Pat" Patterson. Except for Rockefeller, Beame was never close to the city's top bankers. He liked David mainly because he had always been fond of his brother Nelson. Beame would later describe his relationships with Wriston and others as "purely formal." Over breakfast, the worried mayor denied that anything was wrong and took the bankers to task for "bad-mouthing" the city. Spencer was not impressed. He was used to seeing crisp, precise budget reviews, and the presentation put on by the City Hall crowd for the moneymen was sloppy and emotional. As one attendee recalled, a mayoral aide drew a crude pie chart with crayons to show how the city's revenues were spent, and this was followed by Beame's appeal to buy the city's paper.

"I'm not sure what the objective was," one bond specialist said. "If it was to convince the Spencers and Rockefellers and Pattersons that everything was okay and that what the market was saying about city obligations was wrong, then the meeting was a total failure. If anything, it probably reinforced the fact that the people in charge were not really on top of what was going on."

Out of that meeting emerged the Financial Community Liaison Group, a blue-chip clutch of financiers that included top officials of insurance companies, savings banks, investment firms, and commercial banks. Because Morgan's Pat Patterson was now head of the New York Clearing House, an assignment that rotates among the chiefs of the member banks, he was designated head of the FCLG.

The high-profile role that would be played by those institutions was a function of their leadership, their size, and their standing as underwriters of fixed income securities. Patterson's bank boasted one of the top bond departments in the nation; its chief, Frank Smeal, was one of the country's most respected muni men. Rockefeller was Rockefeller; he was backed up by a stringy, ascetic-looking bond trader named Thomas Labrecque, who would later become Chase chairman and CEO. Wriston's top bond man was Richard Kezer, who had earned his stripes at the brokerage firm of Halsey Stuart before joining Citibank in 1966. For the next several years, these bondsmen—dubbed the New Jersey mafia because they lived within a couple of miles of each other in fashionable Jersey suburbs—would live and breathe New York City seven days a week, and often twenty-four hours a day. They would meet at each other's homes on Saturday and Sunday mornings, often to converse with bank lawyers who were virtually living out of their New York offices. As the city stumbled from crisis to crisis, grasping for ways to refinance short-term obligations as they fell due, the New Jersey mafia referred to each month's note sale as the "miracle of the month."

Soon the liaison group concluded that the city faced a shortfall of $400 million for the current year and somewhere between $1 billion and $1.5 billion for fiscal 1976.

By mid-January 1975, Beame had supposedly dismissed or forced the retirement of nearly 13,000 workers. But the city was playing the same shell game with full-time, part-time, and temporary workers that it did with the revenue and expense figures. No one could ever figure out whether the numbers were real. In early February, Beame announced that most of the layoffs had been avoided through union concessions, causing Wriston and his financial community colleagues to question the mayor's commitment to fixing the city's problems.

Tough as things were in the city of New York in January 1975, there was more pressing business for Wriston to deal with in Saudi Arabia. In the wake of the OPEC oil embargo, everyone who was anyone in American business and politics was calling on the Saudi royal family, and Wriston was no exception. The top item on the agenda for this trip was to borrow thirty-year funds, the kind of money that even Arthur Burns would bless as capital. Although preserving Citibank's fragile position in Saudi Arabia was high on the agenda of Wriston and his key aides, that was not the kind of matter a bank chairman would take up with a king. The loan would be on the table later, when Wriston and Faisal met with the finance minister and the governor of the Saudi Arabian Monetary Agency (SAMA).

Citibank's Ham Meserve learned that Wriston would be coming to

Riyadh when he received a cable from New York instructing him to redecorate several houses in the Citibank compound. At that time, when it came to shopping for home furnishings in the Mideast, Beirut was to Riyadh what Fifth Avenue was to the New York suburbs, so Mrs. Meserve and several other Citibank wives were dispatched on a shopping trip to the Lebanese capital. After weeks of waiting, the goods finally showed up in a huge van on the afternoon before the Wristons were due to arrive. Turbaned Yemeni workers were hired to unload the furniture, but suddenly stopped late in the afternoon to pray. Meserve was frantic. Nothing would budge the Yemenis from their religious duties. Only after Meserve bought and roasted a goat for them were they persuaded to complete the job in time for Wriston's arrival.

The morning after the Wristons landed in Riyadh, Mrs. Meserve went down to the kitchen at six-thirty to find Wriston in his bathrobe and slippers, preparing a breakfast tray, neatly arranging napkin and silverware and a glass of orange juice.

"What are you doing?" asked a bewildered Mrs. Meserve.

"I'm taking my wife breakfast."

"Do you do that all the time?" she asked.

To her amazement, Wriston replied that he did.

When Wriston and his colleagues, including Meserve, Costanzo, and other officials, arrived at the palace for an audience with pro-American King Faisal, they were quickly ushered into his anteroom. There Wriston encountered his erstwhile tennis partner, Illinois senator Charles Percy, who was next in line to meet his royal highness. Suddenly the Saudi protocol chief, dressed in Arab robes and kaffiyeh, appeared in the doorway to the king's chambers. As Percy stood up and started to walk in his direction, the king's aide said, "No, no," stopping him dead in his tracks. With a wave of the hand, he beckoned to the Wriston entourage, which trooped in to see the king past Percy, who appeared angry and humiliated, according to Citibankers who were there. Just as the Arab oil shock contributed mightily to inflation in the United States, it also inflated expectations of newly rich Arabs of the kinds of gifts they should receive from official visitors. On his visits to heads of state and other top government officials, Wriston enjoyed presenting them with a $1,000 Steuben glass bowl embossed with a small golden eagle. By now, however, gifts of golden Rolls Royces were commonplace. Although the king accepted Wriston's bowl with royal grace, his courtesans grimaced at the modesty of this gift from the chairman of America's second-largest bank. "Their reaction to getting this bowl was astonishing," former Citibanker Edwin Hoffman recalled. "They obviously expected some grand kind of thing."

Uppermost in Faisal's mind was the bad press the Arabs in general, and the Saudis in particular, were getting in the United States. Faisal told Wriston that he and his people had nothing against Jews, Costanzo recalled. "But he couldn't live with Zionism."

"Why don't you buy the *International Herald Tribune?*" Wriston suggested. The paper, he said, could probably be acquired for less than the value of the oil spilled on the decks of tankers on a given day. "Then you'll have your own newspaper."

At that point someone passed the coffee for the third time. Wriston had been briefed that according to Saudi custom, this was the signal for visitors to stand up and leave. Wriston dutifully rose and started to say good-bye to the king.

Faisal motioned to him to sit down. "I don't want to buy the paper," he said. "That's not my role." But he implored Wriston to return to the United States and do what he could to help promote "fairer" coverage of the Arab-Jewish issue by the American media.

Faisal was also perplexed as to why Richard Nixon was removed from power over "minor things." After all, he hadn't even tried "to assassinate anyone," the king said. About two months later the seventy-year-old king himself died at the hands of an assassin—his mentally deranged nephew.

Afterward Wriston and Costanzo and their colleagues adjourned to the desert to sip tea with Saudi princes in a large tent where guests mingled with goats and other animals. They couldn't leave the country, of course, without some discussion of the Saudization of Citibank's branches. The Saudis are not inclined to make demands, and the issue was raised almost as if it were unimportant. But the Citibankers knew that it was more than of passing interest.

Wriston failed in his primary mission—obtaining the long-term loans that would be treated as capital. The Saudis refused to lend for more than fifteen years, and they might have regarded bank holding company paper as a risky investment. In fact, in early 1975, White, Weld & Co., a SAMA adviser, counseled the agency against buying bank holding company obligations.

On his return from Riyadh, Wriston was drawn inextricably into the worsening New York City budget debacle. The demise of the Urban Development Corporation presented Hugh Carey, the newly elected New York governor, with his first crisis and gave Wriston his first opportunity—a confrontational one at that—to size up Carey. The default of the UDC would become the prologue to the fiscal crisis as well as the prototype for solving it.

A jowly former Democratic congressman from Brooklyn, Carey knew that New York's good times were history. In his first state of the state message on January 8, 1975, he conveyed that dire view of the future. "Now the times of plenty, the days of wine and roses, are over," Carey declared. He urged an austerity budget that called for reduced assistance to localities, budget cuts, and gas tax hikes, among other measures.

Right after the November election, Carey plunged into the state records, and one of the potential boondoggles that quickly surfaced was the UDC, a state agency set up by Governor Nelson Rockefeller in 1968 to build low-income housing. By early 1975, the UDC was on the verge of default. It had $1 billion in unfinished projects, owed $1 billion in bond debt, and was chalking up operating expenses at the rate of about $1 million a day.

The UDC, said Carey later, "was Rockefeller's way of saying we're going to do something. . . . It was a way of creating housing with Ponzis," where new debt is issued to pay the interest on old debt. "We had a whole bunch of Ponzis on our hands." UDC president Edward J. Logue, Carey concluded, "didn't know a bank note from a bill of exchange." The idea, of course, was to build more and more projects with a stream of debt that would never be retired. The agency was funded by so-called moral obligation bonds. A state investigative report on the UDC later concluded, "Governor Rockefeller and the UDC executives were comparable to boys playing on a beach, building sand castles with their backs to the tide."

There were signs of trouble as early as 1972. The agency was making construction commitments at a pace far ahead of its ability to fund them, and it was building housing for families who couldn't pay a market rent, the investigators found. Meanwhile, Logue wasn't supplying investment bankers with reliable financial information. According to the report, the banks in May 1973 prepared an offering prospectus for the bonds that enumerated severe problems, current and potential, at the UDC. Nonetheless, the report said, the bonds were snapped up at relatively low interest rates "by investors who appeared to react in an almost mindless manner."

In the spring of 1974, Morgan dropped out of an underwriting group. Though Citibank indicated that it would reconsider its membership in the syndicate in light of Morgan's decision, it decided to remain. In May 1974 the market sensed that the UDC would ultimately be forced to rely on the state to secure funds and the door slammed shut on UDC issues. By late 1974, the magnitude of the UDC's problems was obvious to anyone familiar with its finances. Projects that it underwrote were not generating anything near the revenues that had been expected of them. There was no way the state would ever be able to unload another UDC bond issue. The major New York banks, which had bought the UDC's paper in the past, rejected its request for a $50 million loan to get it to February 1975 when the next bond sale was scheduled.

Meanwhile, the federal government slashed some of its housing subsidies. The UDC faced default on February 25 if it couldn't come up with $105 million to pay off maturing BANs. In addition, on February 20, it would owe the banks $30 million for a bridge loan they had reluctantly made to it after Carey became governor.

Shortly after Carey took office, he appointed Richard Ravitch, a respected New York construction company executive, to try to find a way out of the UDC mess. Ravitch's findings were not encouraging. There were, Ravitch and Carey concluded, a disturbing number of people involved in the city's financial affairs, in and out of government, who had been less than forthright in their dealings. Carey knew he would have to fire Logue, who, Carey felt, was largely responsible for the mess. By early February, Logue was history. He was replaced by Ravitch, who became UDC chairman. Ironically, as Carey pointed out later, the officer in charge of the UDC account at Salomon Brothers, one of the investment banking firms that underwrote UDC debt, was William Simon, who as secretary of the Treasury would take the city to task for its financial imprudence.

This time, Carey wouldn't be able to hit up the legislature or pull money out of hats with fancy rollovers or accounting maneuvers, like understating pension funds. "Once I do that, my neck is gone," Carey told aides.

Bankers told Carey that the BANs would have to be paid before they would consider any longer-term financing. Led by Ravitch, the state took the position that it should not repay the BANs or the bridge loan unless the banks pledged long-term money. "The fact that the BANs did not technically carry the moral obligation of the state was viewed by the banks as a distinction without a difference," the report said.

As D day approached, the banks rejected various compromise refinancing proposals, and after a week of unsuccessful negotiations with the banks, Carey summoned the high and mighty of the New York banking establishment—Willard Butcher of Chase, Wriston of Citibank, Don Platten of Chemical, and John McGillicuddy of Manny Hanny—to a February 24 jawboning session in his small midtown Manhattan office. "That was where we did all our moaning and wailing and planning," Carey said later. Carey laid it on the line to the bankers, saying that the UDC "was a creature of the state but [it] is supposed to be self-funded" and [it was] badly mismanaged. The upcoming payment would be missed, but during the grace period Carey would be working on a solution.

"Walter Wriston was imperturbable," Carey recalled. "He didn't sweat an ounce. He looked like Walter Wriston always looks. He gives you the blinking stare, with the eye tic." As a congressman, Carey had had only a fleeting acquaintance with Wriston, but he knew the nation's most powerful banker was taking his measure. Carey speculated that Wriston thought he was "not a Rockefeller" but "some guy from Brooklyn on the Ways and Means Committee."

During the meeting Butcher said, "This is a serious matter; this is state paper. This has serious consequences. The state has never done this before."

"States have never been in this condition before," Carey replied.

Wriston went quickly to the guts of the matter. "I have a suggestion for you," he said tersely, as if he were lecturing a Citibank borrower who defaulted on an auto loan payment. "You pay your debts."

"These are not my debts," Carey said angrily. "I inherited this. This is a mess. But I didn't make this mess." He stood his ground, asserting, "When we're finished, some people, including some around this table, may have a lot to account for, but I won't be one of them. I would never have approved these loans."

Carey's performance apparently earned him Wriston's respect. Wriston later remarked to a friend that "he [Carey] is some piece of cheese," Wriston's oblique way of complimenting the new governor and recognizing that Carey was someone to be reckoned with.

Wriston was accustomed to seeing his adversaries jump when he barked. But "I didn't jump," Carey recalled later. "Wriston was a tough guy who graded your papers," according to Carey. "If he accepted you as a guy who had moxie, you could play on his ball team."

For Wriston, there was only one issue, and that was whether the state would stand behind its moral obligations on the bond anticipation notes (BANs), which were sold in anticipation of receiving the proceeds of bond issues. If it did not, there was no way the banks and investors would put up new money.

Ravitch said later, "I concluded that Walter Wriston was the key person" and the one he would have to win over. For a February 25 meeting with Wriston and Morgan's Patterson in Wriston's office, Ravitch brought along UDC tax lawyer Donald Schapiro. Except for his wife and general counsel Hans Angermueller, Wriston regarded lawyers as one of the necessary nuisances of a democratic capitalist society. He had absolutely no tolerance for lawyers who persisted in muddying an issue that to him was crystal clear and, worse still, doing it in a condescending manner. It did not take Schapiro long to earn Wriston's enduring ire. For hours Schapiro went around in circles with Wriston and Patterson. Wriston told him that the state must first come to the aid of its UDC stepchild and then "we'll figure out what to do."

"He [Schapiro] kept talking," said another lawyer who was present at the meeting, "and took the position that Wriston didn't understand. . . . Wriston understood everything." The lawyer added that "a lot of people were sitting around making fine distinctions. We didn't have time for that."

As Schapiro continued to go around in legal circles, Wriston suddenly slammed his empty Coca-Cola can with his fist, crushing it nearly to the thickness of an Oreo cookie. "Pay the BANs!" he demanded in a fit of anger.

"I thought there would be blood on the wall," said the lawyer.

Ravitch pleaded with the bankers to put up new money at the same time the state repaid the BANs. Ravitch was concerned that if the state paid off the banks, and the UDC later went into bankruptcy, the banks would come out ahead of other classes of creditors, such as contractors and suppliers. That, in his view, would be unfair. Wriston, however, was intractable. There was no way he would agree to put up new money until the state met its existing obligations.

The meeting broke up without a resolution. Wriston later told Carey, "The first thing you ought to do is get rid of [Schapiro]." Schapiro stayed on as the UDC's outside counsel, but apparently never showed up at another meeting where Wriston was present.

That evening Carey submitted a bill based on a Ravitch plan in which the state would set up a new Project Finance Agency to issue new debt and complete the UDC's projects. This, Ravitch said, was the same plan that had been rejected by the banks.

On February 28, the bond anticipation notes matured, and Citibank and Chase quietly set off amounts due on BANs and loans against UDC deposits and other instruments.

Wriston knew that he would be branded an s.o.b. for this move, but he had decided, particularly after his frustrating session with Schapiro, that there was no better way to get people's attention.

Ravitch also had a trick up his sleeve, however. He knew that the move would trigger a flood of claims from other creditors of the UDC seeking to get their piece of a rapidly shrinking pie. That Sunday Ravitch played his trump card. He called a meeting of the bankers at Carey's New York office. Ravitch cleverly gave each banker a copy of the UDC bankruptcy petition the state planned to file that evening. "By the end of that session the banks withdrew the setoff. We didn't make it public, but we had no choice," said Ravitch later. "We had no cash to pay employees. We had to prevent the dismemberment of assets, and [we] had to file to get the protection of the courts."

By default, as it were, Manny Hanny's president John McGillicuddy was left with the task of arranging for the financing of the new Project Finance Agency. Unlike Wriston, McGillicuddy was not wedded to ideology. Under the plan, the banks would lend the PFA $140 million, backed by half of its collateral. Citibank and Bankers Trust initially refused to participate, and state officials were pessimistic about McGillicuddy's chances of putting the deal together. To McGillicuddy, it was imperative for all of the major banks to participate, not just to complete the financing but to signal their confidence in the city's future. McGillicuddy phoned Wriston and invited him over. McGillicuddy didn't insist that Citibank take its full pro rata share but enough of a position to show a unified front. Finally Wriston relented. "You got it," he told McGillicuddy. Bankers Trust also caved in, and the bankers were able to claim that they had all participated. In the end, said Ravitch, the banks wound up doing what they had refused to do before the UDC defaulted.

The UDC problem eventually got worked out, but the damage had already been done. The state had defaulted on the BANs. There would be no turning back.

———

The real problem for Carey was not the demise of the UDC per se, but the message it was sending to individual and institutional bond investors nationwide. With the default of the UDC, anything with "New York" on it suddenly took on an unpleasant odor.

One of the little-known gimmicks that permitted the fiscal maneuvering in the city and state was the "magic window"—the three-month gap between April 1, when the state's fiscal year began, and July 1, the start of the city's fiscal year. On April 1, the state, after paying off its RANs and TANs (tax and revenue anticipation notes), would typically be in balance and would then begin borrowing again. It would then downstream the money to localities, including New York City, whose books would balance after it used the same slug of cash to pay off its own borrowings. About $4 billion swung from the state to the city through this magic window. In effect, it was like an individual using one line of credit to pay off another.

Just how fragile this system was started to become apparent to bankers and bondsmen when the UDC defaulted. In late February, the city was forced to cancel a March 6 sale of $260 million in TANs because the underwriters harbored doubts about whether the real estate tax receivables were really there.

If the default of the UDC was the prologue to the New York City budget crisis, the first chapter began when a Citicorp regional economist named Jac Friedgut rushed into Wriston's office with a dire warning. Wriston had assigned Friedgut to figure out whether the market's fears were justified. The thirty-nine-year-old South African–born Friedgut was a stellar example of Citibank's tolerance for diversity. A religious Jew, Friedgut refused to attend late-afternoon meetings on Friday. After earning a master's degree in public affairs at Princeton, he had joined Citibank in 1958 and was subsequently assigned to monitor the regional economy. While on loan to the city's finance department, he became well acquainted with its questionable budgeting practices.

In the midst of the UDC negotiations, Friedgut's memos to Wriston started to take on an increasingly gloomy and strident tone. In a March 3, 1975, memo called "The City Budget Mess," he wrote that the UDC crisis and the problems of the Metropolitan Transit Authority have "now given rise to fears that the city may be next." On March 6 there were no takers for a $537 million BAN sale. After a marathon negotiating session that lasted into the next day, an underwriting group that included Citibank lent the city the money at a whopping 8.67 percent interest. Citibank was reportedly the hardliner in pushing for 9 percent.

In their impromptu meeting, Friedgut told Wriston that the city was "going down the tubes."

"It is?" Wriston asked.

"Yes, and you're going to sit still and listen to me while I tell you why."

"You got my attention," Wriston said.

Later that day Mayor Beame told Wriston and other bankers, "It's a total lie." He summoned his deputy, Jim Cavanagh, who said, "I don't know what you folks are talking about," Wriston recalled.

Beame said he expected the banks to purchase the BANs. According to SEC documents, Wriston replied that the securities required a public market and that there was "no way [the banks] will stuff" the notes into their customers' accounts. In the opinion of his colleagues, Wriston was not a fan of Beame or Cavanagh. Said Hans Angermueller, "He got livid at the mention of those two."

On his return to 399 Park, Wriston figured this was the time to "activate the political process," as he put it later. He called New York senator Jacob Javits, his closest political ally. "Yeah, it's very interesting," Javits told him. "Right now I'm on my way to Russia to free the Soviet Jews. And then I'm going to stop in China. When I get back, I'll call."

Friedgut phoned Edward I. Koch, then a congressman representing Manhattan's Silk Stocking District, and offered to brief him and other members of New York's congressional delegation on the financial condition of the city. Despite the delegation's reluctance to attend such briefings by private interests, Koch agreed because of Friedgut's insistence that this was urgent.

While the banks were late in discovering and understanding what one fiscal expert called the "holes and mirages and Ponzi schemes" built into the city budget, they were the first to force the city to face up to its predicament.

On Saturday, March 15, 1975, the ever-worsening New York City fiscal news was punctuated by sad news from Europe: Wriston's old friend Aristotle Onassis had died in a Paris hospital. For the next several years, George Moore and Wriston would serve as financial godfathers for Christina, Ari's only direct survivor. The eulogies were barely completed when certain Scandinavian shipping interests moved to seize Onassis's assets in Greece, according to Wriston. With the help of Moore and Onassis's lawyers, the Onassis holdings were transferred in a flash to a trust in Liechtenstein. For years, until her own tragic, untimely death, Christina would look upon Moore and Wriston as her personal bankers. As a token of appreciation for Moore's frequent assistance, she gave him a fancy powerboat.

While there was little Moore and Wriston could do to help her avoid a long succession of matrimonial blunders, Wriston tried to accommodate her every request. In 1978, after marrying Sergei Kauzov, a Soviet Communist, Christina phoned Wriston to see about getting her new husband a job at Citibank's office in Paris. Wriston arranged for him to meet with the head of the shipping department in Paris, who would tutor him in ship charters. Wriston saw her alive for the last time at her suite in the Plaza Hotel in New York, where he spent the day setting up a trust to preserve her inheritance. But Kauzov "torpedoed it because he wanted the money," said Wriston.

On March 18, 1975, Friedgut traveled to Washington to brief the New York congressional delegation. Koch and the five other representatives who attended—out of a total of forty-one House members and two senators—were not prepared for what Friedgut told them: that New York was on the verge of bankruptcy.

"No one, myself included, appreciated the urgency of the message," Koch wrote later in his autobiography, *Mayor*. "It didn't seem possible. . . . It sounded alarmist and ridiculous that the City of New York had run out of money and no one would lend it any." After hearing Friedgut's presentation on the city's desperate financial condition, Koch decided to run for mayor.

"I guess Koch took it seriously," Wriston said later. "The world is fascinated by noncrises that are publicized. It's hard to get their attention on the real ones."

The next day, Friedgut staged an encore for the bank's senior officers. When he entered the Citibank auditorium, Wriston was engaged in an agitated conversation with William Spencer, who had just gotten an angry call from Beame demanding that Friedgut be canned.

After a pregnant pause, Wriston turned to Friedgut and said, "What you told the congressional delegation—was that the truth?''

Friedgut replied that it was.

"To hell with the mayor, let's get on with the meeting," Wriston said.

"If it was the truth, he [Wriston] wasn't scared of anyone," Friedgut said later.

Friedgut soon gained additional insight into the dismal state of New York City fiscal affairs at a meeting of bank staff and city, state, and federal officials. The city had announced a spate of layoffs, and Friedgut, anxious for some hard numbers, turned to James Cavanagh, the deputy mayor, and asked, "Just how many people have really been laid off? Real bodies. Not just positions." The bearlike Cavanagh reached into his back pocket and pulled out a crumpled piece of paper, straightened it out, and said that he didn't know for certain, but that one of the numbers in the total was either a five or a seven.

That was the last time Friedgut ever talked to Cavanagh. Friedgut reported the incident to Wriston, who cited it frequently to point up how little city officials understood about the financial situation.

Later, the city admitted it had laid off fewer than 2,000 of the 12,700 workers it had earlier scheduled for layoffs or forced retirements.

Beame was furious over Friedgut's pronouncements in Washington. On March 23, he called a rare Sunday press conference in an attempt to bolster confidence in the city's ability to repay its debts, and to take Citibank to task yet again. "Nobody's going to tell me how to run the city," Beame declared. Singling out Citibank for being irresponsible in its comments to the congressmen, he said that Friedgut "could at least have had the courtesy of letting us know that he was going."

"Wriston was without doubt one of the brightest bankers in the business," Beame said later. "Very sharp. But the bankers were not of any great help to the city of New York."

At the annual stockholders' meeting a couple of days later, Wriston extended the olive branch. He praised Beame's plan to cut the city's short-term borrowing, saying that "the city was fortunate to have a mayor so well equipped to read the numbers," and adding that Citibank would continue to underwrite city bonds and notes. But that same day, behind closed doors, the banks were huddled in grave discussions about the consequences of a default by the city and whether the city would pay them before it paid police and firemen and welfare recipients. They were concerned as well about their legal liabilities—whether continuing to underwrite securities could subject them to investor lawsuits. The bondsmen had to begin thinking about what would happen in April, May, and succeeding months when huge slugs of bonds would mature with no prospect of rollovers.

From December to March of 1975 the market for city paper had gotten progressively smaller. Around the end of March, three of the city's top bankers informed Governor Carey that they would no longer underwrite city paper. "That was the first time Carey was aware of the severity of the crisis," according to Richard Ravitch. "He was scared, worried." Shortly thereafter,

Ravitch and state budget director Peter Goldmark had dinner with Paul Volcker, who was about to become president of the Federal Reserve Bank of New York. The political process had finally begun to work.

Meanwhile, Carey was coming to the same assessment of Beame's fiscal expertise that the banks had. Like the bankers, Carey was hard-pressed to find out exactly what the city owed. Sitting at a table in his West Fifty-fifth Street office, he asked James Cavanagh how much the city had in RANs and TANs; Cavanagh pulled scraps of paper out of his pockets.

"Where are the books?" Carey asked.

"It would take years to look at the books," Cavanagh replied. "They're in the Municipal Building."

How much did the city owe? Carey wanted to know. He didn't get a satisfactory answer.

It was now clear to Carey that he was faced with a rerun of the UDC default. But this time the stakes were infinitely greater, and the road to a solution infinitely longer.

By now the major rating agencies were finally waking up to the city's financial condition. In a major blow, Standard & Poor's in early April suspended its single-A rating on general obligation bonds.

On April 4, 1975, Carey put the state's credit on the line when he agreed to advance the city $800 million that would otherwise not have been available to the city until the summer or fall. To make that advance possible, the bankers agreed to underwrite a special issue of state notes.

For more than three years, America's leading city would live a hand-to-mouth existence, lurching from one crisis to another. "It was sort of like reporting on the Battle of the Bulge," Wriston said later. "Things were breaking every day, every night. We dealt with it the best way we could at the time. Looking back, everybody can criticize you for doing . . . things that in the cool of the evening didn't seem too smart. But the flip side is that it all got done."

The fate of the city would largely be in the hands of three major banks—Citibank, Chase Manhattan, and Morgan Guaranty—with Bankers Trust, Chemical, and Manufacturers Hanover playing key supporting roles.

To be sure, the city's fate was sealed when the market stopped buying its paper. But no single individual did more to pull the plug than Wriston. During the depths of the budget crisis, the *Village Voice* wrote, on April 7, 1975, "Today Walter Wriston has more control over the life and death of New York City than Beame, [Comptroller Harrison] Goldin, or [City Council president Paul] O'Dwyer. And no one has ever cast a vote for Walter Wriston."

———

Halfway around the world, the war in Vietnam was also breathing its last gasp. By the end of March 1975, the American-supported government in Saigon was on a fragile footing. For Wriston it was time to pull out the handbook, written in the aftermath of Cuba, on how to close down foreign branches that were in danger of falling into unfriendly hands. For Wriston and international banking group head George Vojta in New York and their field commanders in Hong Kong, the priority was to evacuate American branch staff and, if possible, Vietnamese staff from Saigon. To the Communists, the Citicorp logo was nearly as clear a symbol of American values as the tanks, the troops, and the flag that had occupied the country for more than a decade. The consequences of an ultimate North Vietnamese victory for anyone who had worked for the Americans, civilians or military, were too terrible to contemplate.

By the first week of April, Citibank Saigon had shut down its foreign operations, including the sale of traveler's checks and foreign exchange, and only one of Citibank's three American officers remained in the country. In anticipation of a Communist takeover, the branches were made as liquid as possible, and the books were closed every night as if that night was going to be the last. An open line was hooked up between Hong Kong and Saigon, and at one point Citibank officers in the Crown Colony could hear, over the telephone, sirens wailing in Saigon. The burning of traveler's checks in an alley behind the Saigon branch had caused windows to blow out in an adjacent building, and fire trucks were rushing to the scene.

The branch was in the hands of acting manager John Riordan, a lanky, curly-haired bachelor who had served in Vietnam with the U.S. Army Medical Corps in the late 1960s. Seeking a way to return to Asia after his discharge, Riordan had stumbled upon Citibank. He loved Vietnam and, in his two years in the Saigon branch, had forged close relationships with many local staff.

As Wriston recalls, Citibank officials in Asia communicated to him that week a vague plan for spiriting the Vietnamese staff and their families out of the country by bus. Wriston said later, "I told them . . . I know some people in Washington who might be able to help." He immediately called his high-level contacts at the CIA, who advised him to scrap the bus-escape plan. For the next month, Wriston found himself on the phone each morning with the State Department and CIA, seeking to glean the latest intelligence on the situation in Saigon and looking for ways to get the Vietnamese staff out of the country. Wriston finally authorized Ed Harshfield, in Hong Kong, to charter a Pan Am 707 jet to evacuate Riordan and as many of the Vietnamese staff as possible. But Citibank officials were unable to obtain the necessary paperwork for the Vietnamese staff in time for the scheduled flight to Hong Kong, so there would be plenty of empty seats. Wriston phoned his counterparts at Chase Manhattan and Bank of America, offering their staff members seats on the plane, while Riordan was reiterating the offer in Saigon. On the evening of April 4, 1975, the Pan Am 707 took off with only twelve passengers, including just one Citibanker. The move provoked the ire of the U.S. embassy in Saigon, Saigon bankers and businessmen, and others, who called the move "premature," according to a *Wall Street Journal* report on April 7.

For more than a week after Riordan's arrival in Hong Kong, the debate raged over Citibank's obligations to its Vietnam staff, and how much effort was enough. Apparently without Wriston's knowledge, but with the consent of the State Department, Riordan got permission from his superiors to return to Saigon to try again to evacuate the branch staff. On April 13 he left Hong Kong aboard a commercial Air Vietnam flight, but he soon returned, having failed to arrange their escape. This time Vojta laid down the law. Wriston, Vojta said, was "pissed" that Riordan had returned to Saigon. "We were told that if we went back, we wouldn't go back as Citibankers," Riordan said. Vojta didn't threaten to fire his Saigon managers, but the message was clear.

Citibank officials "knew emotions were high," as Riordan put it later.

Of the three American staff members from the Saigon branch, Manager Michael McTighe was seen as the one most likely to try to mount a James Bond–style rescue operation. As a result, according to Harshfield, officials in Hong Kong ordered him to surrender his passport.

They never figured that Riordan, the quietest of the three and considered the least likely to do anything rash, would be capable of such a scheme. But on or about April 17, in defiance of orders from his superiors, Riordan boarded an Air Vietnam plane for Saigon. Over the next week he went through the formalities of adopting the thirty-six Vietnamese staff members and their sixty-eight dependents, and he arranged for them to fly to Manila or Guam on C-130 propeller-driven military transports. Only one staff member was left behind—a woman who refused to leave her aging parents, and ultimately she, too, left the country. On April 26, the same morning the airport was bombed, Riordan himself left Saigon on a military evacuation flight for the last time. He arrived in Guam about seven hours later to a hero's welcome.

The celebration was brief, however. Riordan's work was not finished. On his arrival in Guam, exhausted from the ordeal, he learned that one of the Vietnamese women had given birth en route to the Philippines, and he caught the next flight to Manila to make sure she was taken care of. At some point he phoned Harshfield in Hong Kong and said, "I understand you've been looking for me."

Harshfield delivered an unconvincing reprimand—then informed Riordan that he was to take himself on an all-expenses-paid trip around the world. Wriston later notified the relieved refugees that they would be assured of jobs with Citibank for the rest of their working lives, and he set aside $1 million for resettlement expenses. Under the circumstances, the Harvard Business School Club of New York could hardly have chosen a better time to name Wriston business statesman of the year.

Three days after Riordan's final departure from Saigon, at noon on April 29, the announcer on the U.S.-owned radio station in Vietnam said, "It is 105 degrees and rising," a message that was accompanied by Bing Crosby's recording of "White Christmas." Repeated every fifteen minutes, this was the signal to Americans still in Vietnam to flee the country. At 4:30 A.M. on April 30, a helicopter pilot entered the office of U.S. ambassador Graham Martin, the only American official still in the country, and handed him a message from President Gerald Ford that had been transmitted through the American naval fleet standing by offshore. It read, "The President of the United States directs Ambassador Martin to come out on this helicopter." Shortly thereafter, the remaining U.S. Marines lowered the embassy flag and, at 7:53 A.M., made their exit as well.

With New York City frozen out of the market, it was time, Carey concluded, to visit his old friend from his days in Congress, President Gerald R. Ford. Despite their political differences, Carey was fond of his former colleague. He would feel differently at the end of their May 14 meeting.

Hats in hand, Beame and Carey called on Ford at the White House seeking $1.5 billion to enable the city to muddle through to June 30. Ford lectured Beame as if he were a profligate child. "I'm not going to ignore you or abandon you," he told Carey. But he added that he would not lend money to a state with its own budget gap. The meeting ended as it had begun, on a sour note.

Said Ford later, "The governor and the mayor came down pleading for a total bailout, without any corrective action, involving wages, pension, cost reduction in the city. That point of view was totally unacceptable. . . . The federal government couldn't bail out a city that had acted so irresponsibly in the management of its fiscal affairs. And there had to be some hard-line pressure to force those in positions of responsibility to take the necessary corrective action."

Beame and Carey by now had little doubt where they stood. But just to make certain there was no misunderstanding, Ford formally denied their request in writing. With nowhere left to turn, it was time for the kind of fiscal invention born of fiscal necessity. The germ of a solution arose during a meeting between Carey and a small group of advisers that included state budget director Peter Goldmark and Metropolitan Life chairman Richard Shinn in the governor's Albany office.

According to Carey, Goldmark, an idealistic but practical former budget aide in the Lindsay administration, suggested tapping into the city's revenue stream and putting the state's credit behind the city. More specifically, they would divert part of the city sales tax to support the bonds, which would re-fund the city's short-term debt as it matured. To get the money back, they knew they would have to balance the city's books, and even assert state control over the city's finances—a notion that would be anathema for Beame. An independent state entity would have to be created to issue the bonds, and another unit to ensure that the city got its financial house in order. Out of this brainstorming emerged the concept that was to become known as the Municipal Assistance Corporation—Big MAC—and later its cousin, the Emergency Financial Control Board.

Meanwhile, Wriston and Citibank had become the lightning rod for the ire of the city's labor unions. As the largest and most outspoken bank in the city—the one that had blown the whistle and pulled the plug—Citibank made a convenient enemy around which union chief Victor Gotbaum could rally his troops. Union-sponsored newspaper ads singled out Citibank as New York's number one enemy and asked, "When will First National City Bank pitch in to help the city?" Charging that Citibank was leading a crusade to slash services and fire city workers, the unions called on their members to pull their money out of Citibank and to picket its 111 Wall Street offices at noon on June 4, 1975. Some ten thousand union members showed up to hear Gotbaum announce that he intended to yank $15 million in pension money out of Citibank. "Victor was a master at talking to the press," Wriston said later. "He pulled out a picket line and put it around 111 Wall and on TV, and said, 'These are the guys who took New York bust.'" Citibank tried to make the best of a tough situation. Employees were assigned to hand out balloons and ice cream. Said Wriston, "The people [picketers] who were bused in didn't know why they were there."

Morgan's Ellmore "Pat" Patterson couldn't resist the temptation to walk to 111 Wall to observe the commotion firsthand. The normally restrained banker was nearly consumed with laughter. Though Walter Wriston's bank was the focus of the protest, one of the picketers carried a hand-lettered sign that read, "Ell-E-More Patterson, you are a crummy. You won't lend us any more money." Patterson offered to buy the sign from the protester as a souvenir, but the union man declined.

Just before dawn on June 11, the New York State legislature established the Municipal Assistance Corporation and empowered it to issue $3 billion in debt on behalf of the city in three stages of $1 billion each over the next three months. In effect, $3 billion of the city's short-term obligations were to be transformed, as if by magic, into long-term MAC bonds. In meetings at the New York Clearing House, the bankers' private club on Broad Street, the bankers moved to support MAC, to prop up the city by buying $280 million in city paper for their own accounts until the MAC proceeds became available, and to peddle MAC paper to their banker colleagues from Portland, Maine, to Portland, Oregon. According to Jac Friedgut, the banks were also responsible for tacking on a provision that made MAC bonds "moral obligations" of New York State, thereby making them eligible for bank underwriting and broadening the market considerably.

But Wriston and the other bankers wanted a watchdog agency—they suggested a state budget review board—to monitor and approve New York City's budget and to slash it if necessary. By the time the state legislature passed the bill, however, Beame had managed to "defang" MAC, as Goldmark put it, by exorcising the control board powers.

On June 30, 1975, when deputy mayor Jim Cavanagh ordered nineteen thousand city workers off the payroll by midnight, it actually looked as if things were moving in the right direction. But appearances were deceiving.

The next day, thousands of city workers—including sanitation workers, police, and firemen—struck to protest the dismissals. Garbage piled up on the sidewalks, and traffic was stalled by protesting cops. Within the week,

Beame announced that new taxes would be imposed and the jobs restored. Wriston and his colleagues in the financial community were outraged, and the first MAC offering was now in jeopardy. With the bailout unraveling, Beame was forced to reinstate the firings.

For the city, MAC seemed like a painless way out of the crisis. On their face, MAC bonds were inviting. They were backed by revenues from the New York State sales tax, and the tax-free yield was higher than the rate on corporates. But in the aftermath of Beame's maneuvers, investors recognized MAC for what it was—New York City in disguise, as Wriston put it later.

Salomon and Morgan were the leaders of the first offering. Typically, a properly priced bond offering would be mostly gone in days. But by the end of the first week in July 1975, only about $200 million had been sold, with the underwriters holding the bag on the remaining $800 million. The bondsmen divided up the territory and hit the road to sell MACs. Attendance was good and investors were curious, but no one was buying. Two weeks after the issue hit the street, the underwriters met for dinner at New York's "21" Club for what was supposed to be a celebration. This was the worst-performing issue many gray-haired bondsmen had ever witnessed, and the dinner was, in the words of one participant, "the oddest closing dinner I've ever been to. It was pretty somber."

The $1 billion got sold only because the underwriters—banks, savings banks, and life insurance companies—promised to take $650 million. By July 21, 1975, underwriters had taken huge hits as the MACs lost up to one eighth of their value, sending rates soaring to 11 percent. In the wake of the disastrous first sale, Carey fired MAC chairman Thomas Flynn, replacing him with William Ellinghaus, president of New York Telephone Company. By now Beame himself was projecting a deficit for the 1976 fiscal year of $1.6 billion.

After that fiasco, it did not take a genius to figure out that the next two sales weren't likely to be barn burners. Wriston, of course, wasn't the only banker pushing for more controls over the city and its mayor. Chase's bond trader, Tom Labrecque, collaborated with his counterparts on a letter to MAC urging closer monitoring. The banks made it clear that unless the city took a sharper knife to spending, they wouldn't be buying any more MACs. They regarded Cavanagh as a big part of the problem and wanted him gone.

Things quickly went from bad to worse. The city was now faced with finding $1 billion by August 22. In August, MAC tried to float a second $1 billion issue to be led by Chase Manhattan and Merrill Lynch. This one could barely be sold at all. Citibank and Kidder Peabody were slated to underwrite the third issue in September. Out of a planned total sale of $3 billion, only $2 billion would end up sold, half of that bought by the underwriters.

Over breakfast on August 20, 1975, Citibank's Ed Palmer and Chase's Willard Butcher, along with William Ellinghaus and other bankers and MAC officials, told Carey that it was time for him to essentially take over the city. By this time, Carey recognized that the real budget gap for the 1976 fiscal year was $3.3 billion, not the $641 million Beame had claimed earlier. Still remaining to be refinanced was $2.6 billion of outstanding short-term state authority paper. But there was no way that was going to happen without the other half of MAC—the Emergency Financial Control Board. And that would require state legislative approval.

No one was more insistent than Walter Wriston that the city clean up its act before the banks bought more securities. So when Governor Carey and others wanted to impress upon the state legislators the gravity of New York City's predicament, the casting call went out to Wriston. "His role was to stare them down and talk sense," said Goldmark, adding that in one session of the legislature Wriston gave them a lesson in "Banking and Finance 101." Then, when it was time for gentleness and conciliation, it was Patterson of Morgan who got the nod.

By the end of August, Beame finally caved in to demands for a watchdog panel. Thus the way was cleared for the establishment of the Emergency Financial Control Board. In a real sense, the EFCB was a response to Wriston's recognition of the need for a group of a few "wise men" to monitor the city's finances independent of the city.

In Wriston's opinion, one of Carey's greatest feats was gathering the labor leaders in one room and persuading them to accept the idea of a control board. "It was the extraordinary leadership of Carey that saved the day. When there's real trouble he's very very good."

Despite their heavy stake in the outcome, Wriston and the other bankers didn't want to be represented on MAC or the EFCB. Wriston insisted that the city achieve a balanced budget primarily by slashing expenses rather than just by raising taxes, but he felt that for the banks to get more involved was an intrusion on the roles of elected officials. "That was one area where Wriston was clearly the leader, as to what the limits were on banks' powers," said Jac Friedgut later.

With Beame's agreement on the control board, Governor Carey, Felix Rohatyn, a top Lazard, Frères partner who played a key role in creating MAC, and the banks slapped together a $2.3 billion package that they hoped might get them to December 1 and win them enough credibility in Washington to secure the federal government's help. As part of the deal, Carey agreed to advance the city $750 million, real estate owners advanced the city property taxes, and banks and pension funds kicked in the rest. Under the bill, the city was to develop a financial plan that would result in a balanced budget by June 30, 1978. On September 9, 1975, the New York State Legislature approved the package and created the Emergency Financial Control Board. Beame and Cavanagh were now virtually stripped of their power over New York City's purse strings.

The rescue itself was modeled after International Monetary Fund austerity programs, whereby government guarantees are secured to inspire lenders to fund a country through a crisis and enable it to regain access to capital markets. In fact, the New York City fiscal crisis was a kind of dress rehearsal for the great Latin debt crisis that would follow some seven years later. In New York City and New York State, borrowers had little incentive to mend their imprudent ways as long as lenders were willing to lend. In a pattern that would later be repeated on an even grander scale, "it is not the borrower who mends his ways," as one state official put it. "It's the lender who forces it by stopping the credit process."

New York City and the State now had no choice but to pin their hopes on the federal government. Contained in the $2.3 billion package was an unwritten message to Washington that a default by the city would trigger a collapse of the state and a global financial debacle.

———

In the midst of the fight to keep New York City afloat, Wriston's lieutenants were also playing pivotal roles in the struggle to build a viable railroad system out of the remnants of Penn Central, and to prop up Zaire and foundering W. T. Grant & Co.

After being thwarted by the courts in their attempt to get out of Penn Central with a debt swap, Penn Central's creditors by 1973 were feeling a growing sense of desperation. They could see that the company's cash was being drained and its plant and equipment were deteriorating, and along with that their hopes for a reasonable recovery on their investment.

As a result of complaints from creditors and from the Interstate Commerce Commission about the erosion of the railroad's assets, Congress in 1973 passed the Regional Rail Reorganization Act, which set up a new company called Consolidated Rail Corporation, or Conrail, and ordained that the creditors would be awarded only common stock for their trouble. The plan called for the government to issue $500 million in common stock and $1.5 billion in debt, $500 million of which would be invested in plant and equipment in the Penn Central and six other bankrupt northeastern railroads. John "The Undertaker" Ingraham, Citibank's top workout artist, knew it was a pipe dream to think that the railroads could be put back on track, so to speak, with such a nominal investment. Ingraham figured that under this arrangement Conrail would run out of cash in just a few years, and he therefore opposed turning over the Penn Central rail properties to the new entity.

In a bid to block the transfer, Penn Central trustees and the banks in May 1974 sued to dismiss Penn Central from reorganization, charging that the 1973 act was unconstitutional. That move would have subjected the Penn Central to liquidation. Though the federal judge on the case agreed, ruling that Penn Central couldn't be included in the Conrail system, an appeals court overturned that decision in September. Later the Supreme Court said that the act could stand but that the creditors had to be given equitable treatment and compensation.

Wriston, Ingraham, and other bankers had concluded that the only way to get out alive was to support a long-term solution rather than a piecemeal liquidation.

In 1975, the Senate Commerce Committee held a series of hearings over a period of several months to determine the fate of the Penn Central. As spokesman for the banks, Ingraham urged that the government quickly transfer the rail assets to Conrail.

Armed with an exhaustive analysis of Penn Central's financial condition, Ingraham argued that the railroad really needed $7 billion to $10 billion over a ten-year period, not the $4.9 billion that the government was planning to invest. Ingraham felt strongly that the administration had been penny-wise and pound-foolish in refusing to invest sufficient funds in the railroad in 1973–1974, and that it continued to be unrealistic about its financial requirements. He wanted private capital markets to underwrite Conrail as quickly as possible.

Meanwhile, some bankers, notably First Chicago's curmudgeonly Robert Abboud, were still holding out hope of making a quick grab at Penn Central's collateral. In conversations with Wriston, Abboud complained, "Why can't we get our collateral and get paid?" Ingraham recalled. Abboud and Ingraham had played football together at Harvard, and Ingraham angrily took his former teammate to task for being a spoiler. Abboud would emerge that fall as a fly in New York City's ointment as well.

Despite Wriston's close ties to the Ford administration, he backed Ingraham in the face of the flak from the White House. In a September 19, 1975, *Washington Post* story, Ingraham was quoted as saying that the administration plan amounted to a confiscation of the creditors' assets and wouldn't work. He told the *Post* that the administration was "trying to rationalize the industry without money and will wind up nationalizing the whole industry." After the article appeared, Wriston got an irate call from a top Ford aide. It wasn't long before Wriston was on the phone to Ingraham.

"You know my view," Ingraham told his boss.

"Yes, I do," said Wriston. And Ingraham prevailed.

"Any other CEO could have said, 'Tone it down,' " said Ingraham later. Wriston backed his man, but suggested that creditors invite secretary of transportation William Coleman to present his views in a meeting at Citibank. Wriston would later claim with excessive understatement that his sole contribution to the Penn Central workout was to hire the hall for Coleman's visit.

"The insurance companies really let him [Coleman] have it," said Ingraham, putting him on notice that "this was not just a one-man show."

Coleman, who is black, demanded, "What makes you think you're going to get compensation? My people waited a hundred years for ours." He felt he was "set up," according to a lawyer involved in the case. Wriston, said Coleman later, "was interested in making sure the bondholders got paid something" while he was seeking to reorganize the Penn Central to "get it off the federal dole." Wriston, said Coleman, "was helping to bring that about."

When, at 12:01 A.M. on April 1, 1976, the rail assets of Penn Central and six other defunct railroads were transferred free and clear to Conrail along with a federal capital injection of $2.1 billion for new plant and equipment, the creditors' work had only just begun. The creditors wound up with what an Equitable Life executive called "not one cent in money but a bundle of paper" equivalent to the net liquidation value of the bankrupt companies. The same day, Amtrak, the National Railroad Passenger Corporation, agreed to buy the northeast rail corridor from Conrail for $87 million. Two years later, just as Ingraham had predicted, Conrail was back in the government's pocket, pleading for $1.3 billion more in federal money.

Meanwhile, Penn Central trustees and thousands of creditors—including the federal government, other railroads, banks, and insurance companies—were left holding the carcass of Penn Central, minus the rail assets. They could either compromise or battle over the assets for years. The catalyst for compromise took the form of a memo from Joseph Auerbach, special counsel for the New York, New Haven & Hartford Railroad Company, a major Penn Central creditor, to Ingraham and Equitable vice president Richard Dicker.

Citibank now realized it had two choices: either write off Penn Central or adopt the position that it would not get out until everyone else did. That meant calling a cease-fire in their battle with the bondholders, of which Equitable was the largest. Except perhaps for Abboud, the bankers knew that "we're not going to get out of this party until we are able to get everybody out. And we're not going to go hop, skip, and jump. We had tried that with the debt swap," said Ingraham.

The team of bankers and insurance men that emerged from that decision became known as the Friday Group, so named because they met on Fridays and often worked through the weekend to hammer out a reorganization plan. Although the group took the position that the government should either fund Penn Central or liquidate it in the "classic" way, they knew that liquidation was not a viable option. They were prepared to take their chances on a liquidation, "knowing full well," Ingraham said later, that "the government wasn't going to do it."

By 1978, the creditors had succeeded in reorganizing a new Penn Central around its non-rail assets. The motivation was enlightened self-interest, not statesmanship.

As part of the settlement, creditors got 90 percent of the stock. In 1980 the government and the U.S. Railway Association settled the valuation claims for the tidy sum of $2.1 billion, and a few months later the check was in the mail. In the end, Citibank recovered all of its principal and interest, according to Ingraham. Eventually, said Ingraham, the reconstituted Penn Central Corporation earned over $100 million a year—but from real estate, oil and gas, and other ventures, not from railroads.

The banks, said Brian Freeman, the lawyer who served on the Lockheed Loan Guarantee Board and was later instrumental in the bailout of Chrysler, got the government to nationalize Conrail by persuading it to pay them "on the basis of a liquidation value of the assets that never would have been achievable." Freeman contended that Uncle Sam wound up paying $2 billion more than it had to because of the way it was settled. The creditors' recovery, he said, "was much higher than otherwise because of the artful way it was passed off to the government."

In Penn Central, the banks "passed the downside to the government," and Citibank did a "super" job of manipulating the government. "The bottom line," said Freeman, "is that Walter Wriston did a super job for his constituency." Said former Citicorp vice chairman Hans Angermueller, who worked on Penn Central for two years after it failed, "From the point of view of the banks, clearly a nationalization of its debtor was to its advantage. Wriston isn't one who espouses the nationalization of industry. There was a certain degree of conflict of interest there. It helped the bank if the government paid off. Conceptually, I'm sure he was somewhat ill at ease."

Penn Central also worked out well for some former Citibankers. Former chairman George Moore's acquaintance with Penn Central and its predecessor companies dated back to the 1930s. Shortly after the bankruptcy, a Wall Street friend of Moore's who earlier had served as president of the New York Stock Exchange suggested that he buy Penn Central bonds. Everyone was buying them, the friend said. Moore was not one to pass up an investment opportunity endorsed by other members of the smart money set. He bought $500,000 worth at five cents on the dollar, for a total of $25,000, an investment he never regretted. The bonds paid off at par.

The financial crisis of W. T. Grant was also coming to a head. Grant was to retailing what Penn Central was to railroads. In October 1974 a 143-bank syndicate headed by J. P. Morgan extended Grant a $600 million line of credit to bolster and replace its existing lines of credit in the hope of getting the beleaguered retailer through the Christmas season. In early 1975 Grant reported a $175 million operating loss for 1974, the first in its nearly seventy-year history. Efforts to rehabilitate Grant were hampered by the extraordinarily large number of banks in the credit, and the fact that of the 143 banks, Grant owed $56.5 million to 116 of them. The Grant episode convinced Citibank that too many lenders made for an uncontrollable situation. In trying to negotiate extensions or a restructuring, everyone had to agree to go along.

A small bank with a small stake in a troubled company has far more leverage over large banks in restructuring a company that has not filed for bankruptcy than one that has. Out of bankruptcy, every bank, no matter how small, has one vote, regardless of whether it has $500,000 at risk or $50 million. But in bankruptcy, said Ingraham, the bank with the most money has the most to say about the outcome.

In June, Morgan, Citi, and Chase threw in the towel, saying that they would allow the 116 banks to be paid off, according to Ingraham. On October 2, Grant filed for bankruptcy, listing debts of more than $1 billion. The giant retailer owed some $640 million to twenty-seven banks, including $97 million each to Morgan, Citibank, and Chase. The bankruptcy filing prompted Citibank to write off $35 million of its exposure. It also exacerbated the REITs' difficulties, notably the Hubbard Real Estate Investments, for which Grant was the largest tenant.

According to Ingraham, Morgan asked Citibank to chair the Grant committee because Morgan had "run out of credibility with other banks in an effort to keep the company out of bankruptcy." The final straw, Ingraham said, was a trip by a top Morgan officer to Tokyo to try to persuade the Sanwa Bank to agree to an extension. A month later, Grant ran out of cash. "I sympathized with Morgan. I'd been there," Ingraham said ruefully.

Domestic loan losses, actual and potential, were Citibank's biggest headache in the fall of 1975. But problems were stirring in the Third World as well. Even as Wriston and Costanzo were patting themselves on the back for the success of recycling, Zaire was well on its way to fulfilling the skeptics' predictions. To its backers at Citibank, Zaire had seemed to have everything. They could tick off a seemingly endless list of its resources, including huge copper reserves, an outlet to the sea, and rich farmland. At Citibank, international chief George Vojta was one of Africa's leading boosters, and Zaire was a centerpiece of his push into the continent. Other banks had rushed into Zaire solely on the strength of the involvement of Citibank and other major U.S. banks. But the world's bankers, including Citibank, would soon discover that all the natural resources in the world would count for nothing if a country's leaders were corrupt and its economy badly managed. Bankers were pinning their hopes for Zaire on huge copper and cobalt mining projects; their principal argument for lending to the country was the prospect of ever-rising copper prices. But while Citibank was on the mark in predicting the demise of OPEC, it ignored similar data that would have demonstrated that copper prices, like oil prices, would ultimately plunge.

Incidentally, this wasn't the first time Citibank had gotten into trouble over copper. During the 1930s-era investigation into insider dealings, National City bailed out of shares of high-flying Anaconda, whose chairman was on the National City Company board, as the price of copper began to tumble.

The loans, according to a former Citibanker, were largely aimed at expanding existing African companies and exports. The idea was to make dollar loans to the Zairean government that were guaranteed by the central bank. Citibank tried to insist on establishing escrow accounts, which in theory would have received the payments made by copper buyers. That didn't work, the former Citibanker said, "because no sovereign country that can get money any other way" will agree to leave money with an escrow agent. Citibank and others thought that these "were good projects, so we decided to go ahead without it," he said.

One senior officer at New York's Bankers Trust recalled that he knew Zaire was in trouble when officials announced that the Muhammad Ali–George Foreman heavyweight title bout would take place there in October 1974. The elaborate and expensive preparations gave him cause for concern.

By 1975 the price of copper had fallen to 55 cents a pound from $1.74, turning a trade surplus into a $200 million deficit. Zaire had $3 billion in external debt, including about $500 million to private banks, and had fallen behind on its payments to some of them. Because it was the first country to essentially go bust, Zaire received publicity way out of proportion to the American banks' exposure. In fact, Citibank had only $110 million in loans to Zaire, of which $85 million was guaranteed by the Export-Import Bank, which had backed much of the U.S. commercial bank loans to the country. Japanese and French institutions were also large lenders to Zaire.

Zaire's financial authorities asked Citibank's Irving Friedman to get them together with the banks. For the next several years, Friedman was the Henry Kissinger of the financial world, shuttling between New York and Kinshasa and other financial capitals trying to keep Zaire afloat. From the very beginning, however, Friedman's domineering manner offended fellow bankers.

Later the bankers discovered that Zairean president Mobuto Sese Seko had diverted the loan proceeds to foreign banks and siphoned the cash flow off from projects to buy the loyalty of the country's innumerable tribes.

One Citibank officer working on the rescheduling returned from the first meeting of the Zaire steering committee in a state of shock to report in amazement that some bankers on the committee couldn't even locate the country on a map.

The Citibank-led attempt to oversee Zaire's finances had "colonialist overtones," First Boston's Latin debt expert Kuczynski later wrote. Moreover, he said, the failure of a disinterested party, such as the IMF, to participate doomed the effort.

In mid-1975, in a bizarre series of allegations, Zaire charged that the CIA was behind an alleged plot to overthrow Mobuto. The plot was never confirmed, but Mobuto kicked the U.S. ambassador out of the country and summoned his envoy home.

Some were still optimistic that the discovery of new oil and mineral sources would bring a quick end to Zaire's troubles, but that was wishful thinking.

Efforts to prop up Zaire coincided with the seemingly hopeless attempts to keep New York City from defaulting. That infuriated some of the banks' critics, who questioned how they could justify their attempt to bail out Zaire as New York careened toward bankruptcy.

In late 1975, even with the Emergency Financial Control Board in place, MAC still lacked the credibility to sell enough bonds to keep the city afloat. With a default a very real possibility, the federal government offered the only hope of salvation. Influential New Yorkers were scrambling to persuade President Ford to come to the aid of their city.

No one was antsier about the possible consequences of a default than David Rockefeller, who believed it would trigger a global financial catastrophe. Rockefeller was playing all his cards to make sure that didn't happen. In September he called his brother Nelson to arrange a meeting with Gerald Ford.

Morgan chairman Pat Patterson also thought a New York City bankruptcy would be disastrous and was using his own inside track at the White House to set up an appointment with his former college football rival.

These efforts to bypass the Treasury Department en route to the Oval Office did not sit well with Treasury secretary Simon. No one in the administration was more opposed to federal guarantees for the city than Simon was, but he was apparently even more concerned that his access to the president and his control over the New York crisis would be undermined. At least that was the feeling Wriston got when Simon phoned him that September.

"Do you know the way to the Oval Office?" Simon demanded, as Wriston recalled.

"Yeah," Wriston replied. "It runs through your front door."

"That's right," Simon replied haughtily. "Always remember that. I'm in charge of this thing."

"I know that. So what's the problem?" Wriston asked.

"David [Rockefeller] has talked to his brother."

"Well, after all, his brother's the vice president of the United States."

"He [David Rockefeller] said he's trying to set up a date with the president."

"So?" Wriston said.

"So I'm going to set it up. I'm the secretary of the Treasury."

"Fine," Wriston said, as he hung up the phone.

On September 23, Wriston, David Rockefeller, and Pat Patterson flew to Washington together for a forty-five-minute meeting with President Ford, Treasury secretary Simon, and Fed chairman Arthur Burns on "the New York financial situation."

Rockefeller pleaded for federal aid, but Wriston told the president that while life would not be pleasant, "the world would not end" if the city of New York tumbled into bankruptcy. On the other hand, Wriston added, "if the state went down then you'd have a problem. I don't recall when one of the fifty states went down, but right today, if a bond has 'New York' on it, bond buyers in Kansas City don't differentiate between the city and state." As Wriston put it later, "That was why we set up three wise [EFCB] men at the state level and why we sold state bonds. I was concerned that the state would be a large problem" if it defaulted.

But the bankers left the White House with no commitments from the president.

Ford "had a lot of pressure from [David] Rockefeller to do something," recalled William Seidman, then economic adviser to the president. He applied that pressure through his brother and other administration aides, as well as through West German chancellor Helmut Schmidt.

Rockefeller was well aware of the close personal relationship between Schmidt and Ford. In conversations with the chancellor, Rockefeller stressed that if the city went down, it would severely disrupt international financial markets, and he urged Schmidt to point up those consequences to President Ford. In October, Schmidt said publicly that he believed a New York City default would have global ramifications.

In testimony before the Joint Economic Committee of Congress the day after the bankers met with Ford, Simon set the stage for a city in bankruptcy, saying that the administration would propose changes in the federal bankruptcy laws to enable local governments to apply them more easily. Other bills had already been introduced with this objective. Simon, said Hugh Carey, "was saying things like 'Bankruptcy is a cathartic experience. It's not bad at all.' " Simon estimated that the federal government couldn't advance the city more than $200 million.

As default loomed, bank regulators convened in Washington to assess the likely damage on the U.S. banking system from a default. Undersecretary of the Treasury Ed Yeo summoned Comptroller James Smith and FDIC chairman Frank Wille. Smith had ordered a survey of how much New York paper was held by national banks and had informed Yeo that three or four smaller banks would fail or get into trouble if the city went into default. And the FDIC's analysis concluded that one hundred banks with big portfolios of New York City securities would be in difficulty if the city defaulted. Yeo posed the next obvious question: What if New York State went down, too? The answer: Three or four more banks would be in trouble. And, asked Yeo, what if the city and state's default causes a general cataclysm? Smith replied that there would be nothing they could do. "If that happens," he said, "we'll be up with the Congress on what to do about that." Simon would later write that the major bank regulators—including Burns and Wille—concluded that "a default by New York City was controllable within the national economic system, and most of the bankers with whom I dealt privately understood this to be the case."

Burns testified later that some suggested that the Fed extend emergency funds, but indicated that no formal application was ever made, and that if it had been made, it would likely have been rejected. Burns also said that a New York City default could require write-offs that might "seriously" cut the reserves of some banks and could lead to "serious strains" in financial markets. But, he concluded, the harm would "probably be short-lived." Nonetheless, Burns wasn't taking any chances. Through September and October 1975 the Fed, along with other major central banks, intervened in foreign exchange markets to prop up the dollar when it appeared New York City would go down. The Fed also promised to lend to banks threatened with insolvency by a New York default and agreed to allow banks to value their New York City paper at pre-default levels.

By October 1975 pension funds, banks, and other financial institutions were balking at purchasing their allotments of MAC bonds, as called for in the state's bailout plan.

In the three years that New York City staggered from one funding crisis to another, at no time did it come closer to bankruptcy than on October 17, when it escaped going down in flames by less than two hours. On October 16, Richard Ravitch and other Carey aides flew to Washington to give members of the Senate Banking and Currency Committee a private presentation on the city's finances. When they landed back in New York, one of them phoned Carey's office and got an earful of disconcerting news. United Federation of Teachers chief Albert Shanker had called to report that the union pension fund trustees had voted against buying $150 million in MAC paper. That meant that the city now had to come up with about $450 million to pay its workers the next day. At ten-thirty that night Ravitch was summoned to Carey's office. He dressed quickly and hailed a cab to the governor's office, where Carey instructed him to hurry to Shanker's apartment. Through the night, until five in the morning, Ravitch argued, cajoled, and pleaded with Shanker to put up the money.

At two o'clock in the morning, Ford economic counselor William Seidman received a phone call from New York reporting that "we just issued checks, and they're going to bounce. The city's going to go broke tomorrow. You've got to wake up the president."

"I'm not going to wake up the president," Seidman replied. "If you're going to bounce checks, go ahead and bounce them."

That morning, the headlines in the New York newspapers declared that the city was going broke. This time Shanker called Carey's office, asking for a private meeting with Ravitch and Carey. Finally, at two in the afternoon, Shanker relented. That left one more hurdle to be overcome. The banks were due to close in less than an hour. To be sure debt holders got paid, the banks had to be kept open beyond their normal hours. Ravitch tried in vain to reach Morgan chairman Patterson, who as head of the Clearing House would issue the order to keep the banks open. Patterson's secretary, apparently unaware of who Ravitch was, kept insisting, "You don't understand. The city is in serious trouble. Mr. Patterson can't come to the phone." Ravitch finally managed to persuade the secretary that Patterson should take his call. Patterson then phoned the Comptroller of the Currency and the New York State banking superintendent, who authorized the banks to remain open. Nothing quite like this had ever taken place, even during the Depression.

On October 18, in an unprecedented Saturday afternoon hearing, Patterson, Rockefeller, and Wriston testified before the Senate Banking Committee on the city's condition. Wriston found himself between a Rockefeller and a hard place on federal guarantees for the city.

The banks were paddling up the creek in unison, but they differed on the consequences of default and on just how far they could go in averting it. The problem couldn't be solved without participation by the banks, but the banks couldn't afford to eat a lot of illiquid paper.

They attempted to find a middle ground between their visceral aversion to federal meddling in the city's affairs and the recognition that a federal bail-out of the city—and in effect the banks—was the only way to avoid default. They sought to couch their appeal for a rescue by pressing for financial reforms. Although Wriston and Rockefeller had signed off on the joint statement read by Patterson, Wriston's heart wasn't in it. He felt that the city should be forced to solve its own problems. But as the head of the city's largest bank, he could not be seen doing anything that would jeopardize the city's recovery. "I was passive," Wriston said later. "I lay in the weeds . . . because philosophically I couldn't support it. But I didn't go down and rattle the cans and say you shouldn't do it." And he said: "That didn't mean that I didn't work like the devil to try to keep the city solvent, and did in fact do that."

Breaking ranks with his colleagues, Wriston told the panel that he believed a default would be "containable, with some trauma." He said he joined in the statement out of his concern about the social consequences of a default—"no policemen, no firemen, no welfare checks." The "social trauma," he opined, could not be contained. "So the question of the financial ripple is moot, in my opinion." The unspoken concern was whether mobs of rioters would prevent the banks from even opening for business if the city defaulted. According to Ed Palmer, Citibank prepared no doomsday report, and its only "war room" was a mental one. But among the contingencies being talked about were whether city workers would have to be paid in scrip and whether there would be enough police to protect employees and bank property.

For the next three years Wriston was torn between his mandate to protect Citibank, his long-standing philosophical aversion to bailouts, and his determination to push the city and state toward a solution. He feared the heavy hand of Washington and knew that once such interference began, there would be no stopping it. One city would mean 40,000 cities.

"I suspect he found a way to rationalize Fed guarantees in the case of the city," Morgan's Lew Preston said later. "He was comfortable staying quiet in that kind of situation."

And Felix Rohatyn said dryly, "He's a very intelligent man. It's clear that for the head of one of New York's biggest banks to take a public position for bankruptcy for the city would have been impossible to do."

Rockefeller was the pragmatist. He would later say that in the case of Lockheed, New York City, and later Chrysler, "the public didn't lose anything by virtue of having an underpinning [government aid] at a critical moment in time.

"I still feel it was absolutely critical that the federal government provide support for the city" and that the federal government "got a very good return on the money they put up," Rockefeller said later.

Bank of America was a major player in the municipal and government bond markets and a major holder of New York City and State debentures. It did not share the glee of some other non–New York banks at the city's possible default. The Senate Banking Committee wanted to hear from someone outside the center of the storm who had a stake in New York's finances, so Bank of America's Tom Clausen got the call.

During a break in the testimony, Wriston whispered to Clausen, "We'll give you Beame and we'll take Alioto"—Joseph L. Alioto, San Francisco's well-regarded mayor.

While Wriston judiciously chose to remain mum in his opposition to federal guarantees, other bankers, notably Robert Abboud, the pesky chairman of the First National Bank of Chicago, journeyed to Washington to join Bill Simon in rubbing New York City's nose in the dirt. Abboud infuriated his New York rivals with a proposal for a new form of bankruptcy filing for municipalities, namely New York.

According to Carey, Abboud told Chicago Mayor Richard Daley that a New York collapse "would be good for Chicago, and Dick Daley was listening." Illinois senator Adlai E. Stevenson III, said Carey, was another major stumbling block in New York's efforts to obtain assistance. "I couldn't find out why," Carey said. The New York governor later concluded that Abboud was also pressuring Stevenson to block federal guarantees, so Carey flew to Chicago to press his point to Daley personally. "We go down, you go down too," Carey said, as one Irish politician to another. "Abboud was a bad act," he added.

"I wasn't pleased with those folks when we were struggling to save it [the city]," said Wriston. He was annoyed as well by the constant prodding of the *Wall Street Journal* editorial page to "throw it [the city] into Title Eleven," as Wriston put it later.

Simon was also critical of the banks, believing that they should have seen the problem coming. Of the bankers, Simon wrote later that "with rare exceptions their cowardice in this situation was calamitous. These gentlemen were frightened out of their wits." By now the big New York banks held about $2 billion in city obligations. Chase was the most exposed, with $400 million, then Citibank, with $340 million.

Three years later Palmer would testify before the Senate Committee on Banking, Housing and Urban Affairs that Citibank, on a single issue of MAC bonds, lost more in a month than "we had ever made in our lifetime on profits on selling New York securities."

Wrote Simon, "It was one of the saddest days of my life when financial giants like Pat Patterson of Morgan Guaranty and Walter Wriston, who had been steadfast for so long, caved in and finally joined the others in asking Washington for federal aid." Wriston, he wrote, "sacrificed his principles and went along with a bailout."

While Wriston called Ford's position "highly responsible," Simon said that many "gutless" financiers encouraged him in private, saying, "God damn it, Bill, you're on the right track . . . hang in there . . . don't give them a thing," but they declined to testify in favor of his position. The bankers responded, said Simon, "Well . . . let me call you back." They concluded, he said, that it was "wiser to 'keep a low profile.' " And he praised First Chicago's Robert Abboud for supporting him.

Simon clearly had nothing but contempt for the unions, and their hottempered leader, Victor Gotbaum. "New York's unions clung tenaciously to the concept that the banks were responsible for these developments that so outraged them, as if the banks had been responsible for their own devouring of the city's budget," he wrote later. "Gotbaum went on television, snarling, 'you can tell Simon, up yours!' " Simon wrote.

"Bill was very hard on the city," Wriston recalled. "On the other hand, if you look at the numbers and what had happened, it would be hard to fault him philosophically on what he said. We did have all the problems he described. The flip side of that is that those of us who were working to save the city didn't enjoy having the mistakes pointed out on television."

Richard Reeves, writing in *New York* magazine, called Beame, Rockefeller, and Wriston "three most unpersuasive citizens." He said they were "simply not making a convincing case in their pleading for federal help to stay out of the modern governmental equivalent of debtor's prison," adding that they "came on like three whining horsemen of the apocalypse, heavy on tears, dire predictions and a special kind of arrogance, and light on facts, figures and arguments."

Wisconsin senator William Proxmire, chairman of the Senate Banking Committee, had asked the bankers if the banks could take 20 percent of the deficit if the government took 80 percent. Reeves quoted Senator Edward Brooke as saying that when "when Proxmire said 20 percent, David Rockefeller just cringed. His hands were shaking. When I mentioned 50 percent he almost fell off his chair."

In the Senate, Proxmire emerged as New York's leading supporter. Having worked in New York for J. P. Morgan & Co. early in his career, he was more sympathetic to the plight of the city than most other legislators.

At this point, Chase had more to lose than Citibank. Said Hugh Carey, "Chase had a lot of state paper and was becoming a weaker bank." He added, "I didn't look upon Citibank as being very much on the hook." According to bankers involved in the negotiations, Chemical Bank, for one, encountered severe funding pressures as a result of its holdings.

"The banks were vociferous in wanting to get bailed out," Bill Seidman said. "They didn't want to make any new loans when the old loans were in jeopardy. They were all interested in the city secondarily."

Some said later that the federal government would never have espoused bankruptcy if it had understood the magic window, the machinations made possible by the gap between the city and state fiscal years, and how it linked city, state, and state authority paper. While the Federal Reserve came to understand this system, some charged that the Treasury Department was slow to grasp it. That, they said, caused Simon and others at Treasury to believe until late in the game that the city could go bankrupt without causing a domino effect. "There was a feeling at Treasury that banks could be defaulted on and there would be enough money to run the city," said one source. But if the city had gone down, the state would not have been able to finance itself the following spring and meet its obligations on welfare, payroll, and allotments to localities.

By the fall of 1975 virtually every major business or agency that did business with the city was attempting to determine how a default would affect them and how they would respond to it. For example, Consolidated Edison, New York's electric utility, had to face up to the possibility of what would happen if New York couldn't pay its light bill. Con Ed would then be unable to pay its state and local taxes. There was no way the city problem could be contained without spreading to the state.

Up to their eyeballs in New York City paper, bankers and bondsmen also sat in their Park Avenue and Wall Street offices contemplating doomsday. Among the possibilities they feared were a plunge in the U.S. dollar and the stock market, and the collapse of banks like Continental Illinois, First Chicago, and the Bank of Boston. Some envisioned a domino effect that would end with a worldwide depression.

But even the severe financial shocks of 1973 and 1974 had not brought the world to an end. Calling the consequences of a default "exaggerated," Citibank's *Monthly Economic Letter* wrote in November 1975, "No one can guarantee that a default would not generate major cumulative disruptions. But the probability of a chain reaction leading to collapse seems small, and certainly much smaller than in the summer of 1974, when financial markets were drum tight and the recession was about to deepen." The idea of a chain reaction of disasters—the domino effect—is a "distraction," the letter said. "It's the wrong thing to worry about." The thing to worry about, as Wriston had testified before the Senate Banking Committee, was what the newsletter euphemistically called "severe local problems"—rioting and looting.

At the White House, Ford and his advisers were playing a high-stakes poker game with the future of the city of New York—and the president's reelection prospects—hanging in the balance. According to Ford economic adviser William Seidman, the strategy was to keep the pressure on the city, while recognizing that ultimately the federal government would have to toss in the final nickel. Ford was attempting to show the rest of the country that, as Seidman put it, he was a "tough budget-balancing conservative" while recognizing that the nation's biggest and most important city was failing. According to Seidman, who served as liaison between the White House and the Treasury, he and Simon "had agreed we had to hang tough, and we weren't going to give them [New York City] anything until the unions caved in, the banks caved in, and everybody put something into the pot." He added, "Ford never veered off course at all. He knew exactly where he was going from the beginning. It was a tough poker game, and he wasn't going to win unless he stayed [on course]."

Ford got into trouble in trying to communicate his position, however. He was scheduled to deliver a speech dealing with the city crisis to the National Press Club, and two rival White House factions were feuding bitterly over just how hard nosed the address should be. The fight focused on just a few lines in the prepared speech, Seidman recalled. He and Simon, contrary to popular belief, were in favor of remaining tough without appearing to rule out the possibility of federal assistance. The politicos, led by chief of staff Donald Rumsfeld, saw the speech as a heaven-sent opportunity to make political hay in Middle America by exploiting the popular image of New York as a modern-day Sodom and Gomorrah.

On October 29, 1975, a day that was to live in infamy in New York City, Ford rejected the city's request for federal aid. "I can tell you—and tell you now—that I am prepared to veto any bill that has as its purpose a federal bailout of New York City to prevent default," he declared. He proposed that Congress enact legislation that would allow the city to operate in bankruptcy, a plan that included the issuance of debt certificates. He called the discussion of a world financial collapse "scare talk."

The next day, October 30, the headline in the New York *Daily News* screamed, "Ford to New York: Drop Dead." The headline itself made news throughout the country. Ford never said that in so many words. But as Morgan's Pat Patterson said later, that was the "net result."

After the speech, "everybody blamed everybody else, since it turned out to be a disaster," Seidman said. That would have never happened, Seidman said, if he could have deleted a couple of sentences. Ford's speechwriter took the fall, but the real blame, Seidman said, belonged on the "political side"—with Rumsfeld, who was responsible for the final language, which was intended in part to "deal with the conservative challenge to the Ford presidency." Rumsfeld, said Hugh Carey later, "had Jerry on the wrong kick."

Ford would later contend that the *News* headline cost him the election, and he has held a grudge against the paper ever since. In an interview in the midst of the tabloid's own struggle for survival years later, Ford said, "That paper may go broke. I won't be sad. I'm sure that headline prevented us from winning New York . . . and if we [had] won New York, we would have won the election. It was a very erroneous, inaccurate, unfair headline."

Carey himself later defended Ford. He never said "Drop dead" or anything resembling it, Carey said. "He gave me time. He had to say no. If he had said yes that day we'd have been dead."

Incredibly, just a few days before the "Drop Dead" headline appeared, the Ford administration had asked the Senate Foreign Aid Subcommittee for emergency assistance for Zaire. *New York Times* columnist William Safire had reported on October 27 that Minnesota senator Hubert Humphrey responded to the request by bellowing, "Not one damn dime . . . Come back with a package dealing with New York City. Otherwise it's no go."

By November, with no federal guarantees in sight, New York City was facing its biggest, and possibly its final, battle for solvency. The deadline was now November 21, 1975. Some $1 billion in city notes were coming due on that date, and New York State controller Arthur Levitt didn't have the money or the time to find it. The commercial and savings banks and the union pension funds had been pushed to the wall. In a November 7 meeting with Levitt, Goldmark, and MAC board members Felix Rohatyn and Simon Rifkind, "we racked our brains for a solution," Carey recalled. "Goldmark had run out of ideas. Felix was hanging his head in a corner. Levitt, who had turned us down, was munching pastrami and talking about Al Smith [the legendary

1920s-era New York governor], and what a great guy he was, and about Franklin Roosevelt and how he closed the banks."

And out of Levitt's musings about long-departed Democrats came the brainstorm. "If Roosevelt could declare a moratorium," Levitt said, "why couldn't you?"

"That would be challenged legally," Carey replied. Then, sensing Levitt was onto something, he asked, "How long would that [the legal challenge] take?"

"Sixty years or a year," Rifkind replied.

But now they needed time as well as money, and they figured that by the time the legal process was played out, they would have bought themselves another year.

Carey and his advisers concluded that the only way to obtain federal seasonal loans and stave off bankruptcy was to declare a moratorium on the repayment of the city's short-term debt. They agreed that before they took such a fateful step, the city's bankers might want to be informed. Staring glumly across the table at Carey, the Big Three of the New York banking establishment—Wriston, Rockefeller, and Patterson—later told him that such a move would wreck New York State's credit.

"We know it's a terrible idea," Rohatyn said. "On the other hand we think bankruptcy is a worse idea. If you have a better idea, tell us. If you don't have a better idea we'd like your support."

The bankers were hard-pressed to come up with an answer. Finally, as Rohatyn recalls, Wriston said, "We can't think of anything better. We hate the idea. You hate the idea. But we'll support you."

"Several of the big banks at times were not happy with positions we took at MAC," Rohatyn later recalled. "On the other hand, looking back, they would realize we not only helped save the city but saved the banks billions of dollars."

The upshot of these meetings was that on November 15, 1975, the New York State Legislature passed the Emergency Moratorium Act, which imposed a three-year freeze on principal payments on $1.6 billion of short-term paper. The gambit was brilliant. But in effect the city defaulted on its notes.

With the moratorium in place, Carey by the end of November succeeded in putting together a two-and-a-half-year $6.8 billion financing package that included pension fund purchases of $2.53 billion in bonds (a union concession Wriston had insisted on), loans from the state, and new taxes. (In his tax package, Carey took revenge on the bankers for refusing to endorse a federal solution until the state closed its own budget gap. The bill he signed on December 20 included nuisance taxes on the banks.) MAC and the city persuaded the banks and union pension funds to roll over their $850 million in city notes until the moratorium was lifted and to accept a cut in rates to 6 percent from as much as 9.5 percent and extension of maturities on an additional $1.6 billion in MAC bonds they had bought earlier. The recovery plan was aimed at balancing the city budget by June 30, 1978, and eliminating the budget deficit. Now the city would need only $2.3 billion in short-term sea-sonal loans. "So we did it. It did save us," said Rohatyn later.

As a bonus, Carey and the bankers succeeded in forcing the resignation of the first deputy mayor, Jim Cavanagh, who represented, at least for the banks, the personification of everything that was wrong with the city's man-agement. And it took a while for Beame to realize that he was no longer truly in charge of his own destiny. Beame learned of the moratorium in the same way that almost everyone else did: he read about it in the papers. He rightly viewed the freeze as a circumvention of his own efforts with the Washington establishment. "Unbeknownst to me, Rohatyn and the governor sort of went around me. They went to Washington. I had been dealing with Washington a good deal," he said. Beame had opposed such a move because, as he put it later, "New York City bonds are a good investment. They are a first lien on all revenues, state aid, everything. They come first."

Suddenly all things now seemed possible. MAC and the Emergency Financial Control Board had been established. New taxes had been enacted and the state budget gap closed. Now that the state had stepped up, Carey could make a credible pitch to Congress and the administration for guarantees.

"Okay, get your bill through," Ford told Carey in a mid-November White House meeting. Ford admitted that he still didn't have the votes in Congress for guarantees and suggested Carey begin his quest for congressio-nal support with House Republican leader John Rhodes. On November 15, Carey and Rhodes agreed on compromise legislation. Rhodes told Carey that a lot of congressmen who wouldn't vote for a bailout *would* vote for bank-ruptcy, but if both bills were introduced at the same time, a member could inform his constituents that he really voted for bankruptcy "because the bail-out's not going to work and the bankruptcy bill is going to take over."

On November 26, Ford officially backed off from his earlier stance and agreed to support the city's request for seasonal loans. Then Congress passed a bill supplying the city with $2.3 billion in short-term financing, which Presi-dent Ford signed on December 9. Congress gave the city some breathing room and imposed at the same time some discipline. Carey explained that "the remedy had to be tough to swallow to prevent others from going the same route."

"What Ford did quite skillfully was to pressure the city to reform it-self," Wriston said. "And at the end of the day it also got the guarantee."

Ultimately it was fear of the unknown that kept New York City out of bankruptcy. No one was certain just what would happen if the city went down, and "you don't want to do something where you can't see the end of it," said one lawyer involved in the negotiations.

When Ford finally came on board, he made it clear that he wished to deal only with Carey, not with Beame or anyone else in the city bureaucracy. Carey's name was on the $2.3 billion of seasonal borrowing, and his state was the guarantor of city payments. Ford didn't want to see Beame in the Oval Office again, according to Carey.

Likewise, Wriston wanted little to do with Beame and others who he felt had created the mess. But, said Hugh Carey later, "if you were contributing to a solution, [Wriston] was reasonable and listened. Sometimes you'd see him sitting in a corner of a room listening, and seeing if something made sense. If it didn't, you could detect it on his face."

Wriston knew that while the city had received a stay of execution, much damage had already been done. For one thing, the nation's municipal markets had suffered a severe blow. "Nobody in his right mind is going to believe that you have a first lien on the taxes of a municipality when the crunch is on," Wriston said in a January 1976 speech to correspondent bankers. "They are going to pay the cops, and they're going to pay the firemen, and then they're going to pay the bonds," he said.

While Wriston was a persistent advocate of financial controls, he was also troubled by the fact that for all practical purposes the city's elected officials were no longer in charge. "The city of New York is now being run by nonelected officials, which in the long term is very bad," he said. "It's being run by the Financial Control Board and the secretary of the Treasury of the United States, who every day receives a New York City cash flow report on his desk."

Wriston believed that if the city was to achieve long-term health, it would have to create a climate that was pro-business or, at worst, neutral. In that connection he was frustrated by Carey's seeming inability to address long-term issues while dealing with the crisis at hand. Wriston persisted in pressing Carey on matters such as the state's usury ceiling, which at the time limited what banks could charge on mortgages and consumer loans. "He [Wriston] had other quarrels with New York State," said Carey. "He was not happy with the way the state was handling business, and was carrying on a crusade to change the ways of the state and city toward business. I can't say he was wrong. He was right, but I couldn't achieve all those things while trying to carry a sick patient around."

The passage of the seasonal financing bill was a momentary high, but the problems of the city and state were far from over. In just a few months another crisis would bring the city to the precipice once again.

The flak that Wriston was taking over Citibank's role in the city crisis was less bothersome than the public flogging Citi and other banks were taking over the shaky condition of their domestic loan portfolios. For over a year, the business press had been castigating the big banks for their bum REITs and other real estate loans. In February 1975, even *Playboy,* not known for its financial reporting, chimed in with what Wriston called a "scare" article.

One fact was not commonly known: Citibank had blown its real estate portfolio not just in the United States, but in virtually every developed country where it was engaged in real estate lending. The real estate loans were taking their toll on Citicorp stock. After bearish bank analyst George Salem of Drexel Burnham predicted in October 1975 that the banks would have to write off as much as 25 percent of the $7.2 billion of loans to REITs, bank stocks plunged to new lows. In December, Citicorp shares tumbled again when First Boston analyst William Weiant, citing Citicorp's problem loans in a December 12 *Wall Street Journal* "Heard on the Street" column, advised investors not to buy Citicorp common shares until its 1975 results were in.

And if the REITs weren't enough, there were the losses at Penn Central, W. T. Grant, Industrial Acceptance Corporation, and Grindlays Bank Limited. By early 1976, holding companies and non-banks appeared to be something less than the prizes they had once seemed to be.

The 1975 results were indeed disappointing. Early in 1976, in a policy meeting on John's Island, South Carolina, Wriston lamented 1975 as the first year in which Citicorp failed to attain its 15 percent earnings goal. It was the kind of year that prompted Wriston to say, "Ted Williams hit .407 the best year he ever lived, which means that he was out more than he was on base. We do a little better than that."

Nonetheless, in early January, it seemed to Wriston that he had picked the right time to be in the Caribbean. On January 11, 1976, as snow, sleet, and driving rain assaulted New York City, it was a picture postcard day in Jamaica, where Wriston was meeting with Citibank auditors from around the world. Before returning to New York, he had hoped to get in another set of tennis. Those plans were dashed when he received a phone call alerting him to an article that had appeared that morning in the *Washington Post* under the headline "Citibank, Chase Manhattan on U.S. 'Problem List.' " Citing a Comptroller of the Currency bank examination report completed a year earlier, the article asserted that Citibank and Chase Manhattan were on the regulator's list of troubled banks. According to the article, the examiner's report rated Citibank's management as "good" and its overall condition "fair," while describing Chase's management and overall condition as "poor." Bad real estate loans, including the REITs, were cited as a major culprit. The story didn't come as a total surprise. Both Wriston and Rockefeller had been called by the *Post* and given the opportunity to rebut the exam findings. Wriston said, "All I'm saying is the condition of this bank is excellent. Period. Full stop." Nonetheless, Wriston packed his bags immediately and flew back to New York to oversee a team of more than twenty bankers, lawyers, and flacks in preparing a rebuttal.

Meanwhile, Comptroller of the Currency Jim Smith rushed to his office after reading the article. The article, he concluded, was based on a 1974 exam. His office had indeed criticized the two big banks, but as Smith would assert then and later, they suffered from "no fundamental infirmities" and either had resolved or were in the process of resolving the problems that had sparked the criticisms. Smith phoned Wriston and Rockefeller to coordinate their remarks to the press and then called his boss, secretary of the Treasury Bill Simon, to deliberate over whether Smith should stick to his plans to fly to Europe for meetings with his counterparts there. He and Simon decided that it was more important than ever for him to stick to his travel plans. The European central bankers were edgy. "There was," said Smith later, "genuine concern [in Europe] whether the second- and third-largest banks in the United States were on the brink of insolvency." In the aftermath of its prize-winning coverage of Watergate, the *Washington Post* enjoyed enormous credibility in the mid-1970s, while the government's had sunk to an all-time low.

Through the ice-slicked streets of Manhattan, messengers carried out Wriston's reply to newspapers and wire services. In a rare display of harmony, Chase and Citibank teamed up to blast the article. The *Post* report, they said, "was misleading, irresponsible and at variance with the facts." In fact, the *Post* wrote high up in the story that "there is no indication that either of the giant banks, which hold $1 of every $10 on deposit in U.S. banks, faces any immediate financial difficulties." Citing the respect that both banks commanded, the examiners rated Citibank's future prospects as "excellent" barring a worldwide catastrophe, and Chase's as "fair."

For the regulators, auditing Citibank was a nightmare. Citicorp's global auditing staff equaled or exceeded the 3,300 on the Comptroller's payroll. An on-site exam of Citibank took six months, and the report wasn't completed for another nine. During that time, Citibank would have grown by $15 billion, or more than a third. "Walt had no time for examiners," said a former senior Citibanker. "He held them at bay."

Smith and other bank regulators stumbled all over each other in trying to reassure the public and protect their client banks. Smith announced that day that "these two banks continue to be among the soundest banking institutions in the world." John Heimann, the New York State banking superintendent at that time, accused the *Post* story of "striking at the public confidence without contributing sufficiently to the public understanding."

In the wake of the *Post* story, even Arthur Burns deemed it wise to announce that in the past three short months the industry had become "more stable." Just a month earlier, on December 14, he had spoken in dire tones about the many bankrupt businesses and about individuals who had lost their nest eggs through imprudent investments, pointing out that "not a few of our nation's commercial banks face the possibility of large losses on dubious loans."

While Citibank's domestic units avoided a major run, its Hong Kong operations weren't so lucky. The Chinese move their money at the first sign of trouble. So when the January 11 *Post* story hit the wire in the British Crown Colony, depositors panicked. "It was a run like you wouldn't believe," said executive vice president Charles Long later. Citibank rushed in currency by helicopter and speedboat in an attempt to meet the demand, but the cash at its branches there flowed out like a surging ebb tide. By the end of the week, however, it had all returned.

Ten days later, on January 22, 1976, the *New York Times* went to press with its own exclusive "problem bank" story. This one listed the thirty-five bank holding companies on the Fed's problem list. Chase, but not Citicorp, had the misfortune of showing up on this list.

While he never spilled his bank's darkest secrets, Wriston had been

ahead of the pack in his willingness to reveal more about Citibank's operations and about how and where it earned its money.

In fact, according to one former top Fed official, Wriston was the first
to disclose publicly his bank's discount-window borrowings—the banking
equivalent of a parishioner announcing at a church supper that he has a vene-
real disease. Market watchers had traditionally looked at discount-window
borrowing as a sure sign that a bank was in trouble, but by casually disclosing
this activity Wriston neutralized its potentially harmful effects.

Nonetheless, Wriston drew a line between what he saw as the justifiable
needs of the marketplace for information and demands that would destroy
the industry's propensity for risk-taking. For him the issue had implications
that went well beyond the banking industry. Total disclosure would shrink
the supply of credit to American enterprise and could trigger or hasten the
collapse of businesses suffering temporary difficulties, or "the W. T. Grant
syndrome—no inventories without cash," as Wriston put it later. "The current journalistic buzzword, 'classified loan,' has been floated about as if it
were some kind of Typhoid Mary," he said at the time. "What front-page
sensationalism forgets is that one man's classified loan [a loan not paying interest or principal or both] is another man's hope for the future."

Shortly after the *Post* story appeared, Wriston phoned Lane Kirkland,
then the second-in-command to George Meany at the AFL-CIO. He had
become friends with both men through the Labor-Management Advisory
Committee. "Look, what we're talking about is jobs," Wriston told the labor
leader. Describing the Grant syndrome, Wriston warned Kirkland, "You're
going to have a couple of hundred thousand unemployed, and they're all
going to be your constituents. . . . Will you help us?"

According to Wriston, Kirkland answered with a terse and unequivocal yes.

Wriston also feared that excessive disclosure would render the bank
exam useless as a management tool, which he knew had happened in the insurance industry. After the *Post* story appeared, Wriston phoned a friend, a
former insurance commissioner, to pick his brain about insurance company
exams. The friend informed him that the results of those exams were made
public after being reviewed by the company and the examiner.

"Then I assume [they say] nothing," Wriston said. "That's correct," the
friend replied. In contrast to confidential bank exam reports, which Wriston
regarded as useful "diagnostic" management tools, insurance exam reports
were mere historical documents that said little about loans. "If we move
down this disclosure road," Wriston told a gathering of bankers, "we will
disclose more and more about less and less, until we will get to the point of
the insurance business, which I personally think is a pretty bad way to go."

The Senate Banking Committee immediately announced that it was
launching an investigation of the Comptroller for his handling of "problem
banks."

Meanwhile, officials of the Office of the Comptroller of the Currency managed to persuade the House Government Operations subcommittee to delay a subpoena of seven years' worth of Citibank and Chase exam reports, and to settle for a summary version of the material. And Wriston politely declined an invitation to testify before the committee.

On February 5, 1976, Comptroller James Smith appeared before the Senate Banking Committee to defend his record, and his banks.

The fallout from the *Washington Post* article consumed the last several months of Smith's tenure. He had been trying to implement major changes in examination procedure that stemmed from the Franklin failure, but was constantly distracted by congressional criticism of his agency's supervisory policies. Those procedures emphasized the inspection of internal systems and de-emphasized the examination of individual assets.

According to Smith, the *Post* article stemmed from and precipitated high-level intrigue involving the bank regulatory agencies and Senator William Proxmire's Senate Banking Committee. At the time, Proxmire was mulling over possible legislation to consolidate the bank regulatory agencies, which the Comptroller vehemently opposed. Smith initially suspected that the leaks came from someone in his own agency who was opposed to the exam changes. But he soon concluded from telltale information in the *Post* story that the reports were leaked by a top Federal Reserve Board staff member seeking to humiliate the Comptroller and to give Proxmire more ammunition in his fight for unification.

Wriston, like Smith, was opposed to the consolidation of the regulatory agencies. Under such an arrangement, the Federal Reserve, not the Comptroller, would wind up as the surviving entity. Centralized power, in all its forms, was anathema to Wriston. But the notion of an even more powerful Fed was his worst possible nightmare. In a meeting in late January 1976 with Citibank's correspondent bankers, Wriston said, "The not-so-invisible political hand is building a life-support system for the idea of a single monolithic bank regulatory agency even though, in my view, the present system ain't broke." Wriston always worried about creeping government control over private enterprise, about what he perceived as the growing move toward "national chartering" of all U.S. corporations and toward placing regulators on bank boards of directors. Quoting Irving Kristol, one of his favorite right-wing columnists, he said at the time that if American capitalism succumbed to government control, he would do all he could to make sure the tombstone did not read "nolo contendere."

Although the Comptroller of the Currency survived and the drive for consolidation was placed on the back burner by its proponents, the man who held the office did not survive. Beset by marital and financial problems, the beleaguered James Smith resigned in June 1976. But in an indication of the close ties between the Comptroller's Office and its national bank clients, Wriston, on July 11, 1977, dashed off a letter to the Woodrow Wilson School of Public and International Affairs at Princeton recommending Smith for a Rockefeller Public Service Award. He praised Smith for not breaching "customer privacy" and not taking "panic measures" on troubled banks. There were limits to Wriston's powers of persuasion, however, and Smith did not get the award.

For all his complaints about an unfriendly press, Wriston was a natural with the media and a master of the snappy quote and sound bite. He enjoyed the give-and-take with reporters, and with a few exceptions, his stewardship at Citibank was marked by mostly favorable coverage. Asked by a colleague for advice in dealing with the media, he once said, "Never answer the question and don't give up the mike." Wriston would later explain that he operated according to the Javits Method, a reference to the late New York senator who made an art form of saying what he wanted to say regardless of the question that was asked. "They'd ask him what he thought of some left-handed Irishman, and Javits would say, 'I'm very happy you asked about that because of their views on the Palestinian uprising.' " Then, Wriston said, Javits would proceed to give his own views on the uprising.

But with the publication of the infamous "problem bank" story, Wriston would look upon the fourth estate with a heightened cynicism. Wriston hit the lecture and luncheon circuit, decrying, with characteristic wit and sarcasm, the publicity and the "hue and cry" in the media about "go-go bankers." In his session with the correspondent bankers, Wriston quipped, "The rumor that the picture of me in *Time* magazine shows me looking through the crosshairs of my telescope at a reporter from the *Washington Post* is simply not true." The reporter who wrote the story "didn't even know that debits were next to the window and credits were next to the wall. He didn't know anything, except that he was going to kill us." He accused the press of being too hostile to the American capitalistic system by "incessantly accenting the negative that erodes optimism, one of the cornerstones of democracy." One specific nemesis, and the object of numerous "Wristonisms," was the *New York Times,* which he and other corporate titans viewed as anti-business. "The *Times* can say that there are no calories in a Clark bar and get away with it," Wriston complained.

Wriston obviously didn't like loan losses, and recognized that the level of charge-offs would at times be disappointing. But he also recognized that if the bank never lost money on a bum loan, it was not assuming any risk. And the important thing to him was not the losses but whether the risks were kept within the bank's "risk-taking capability" and whether they indicated mismanagement. "The difference between a skinflint banker and a reckless lender is a recession," said Wriston.

"If you tell politicians that if we took no risk there would be no loans to consumers or small businesses, and that fair-weather banks are absolutely no help in a time of trouble, and that losses inseparable from risk-taking are not a headline but rather the cost of doing business, the politician will be surprised to learn this," Wriston told correspondent bankers at the January meeting. Citibank, he said, "has never been a fair-weather bank." Wriston also told the bankers that he had just met with the top editors, including the banking editors, of a national business news magazine. He said that "they didn't have the faintest, foggiest notion of loan losses." Nor, Wriston said, did many bureaucrats in the federal regulatory agencies understand that loan losses were built into the fees and rates that banks charged on loans. In making consumer loans, Wriston pointed out, Citibank wrote off a portion of each one from the moment it was made.

Bad as the real estate portfolio looked at the time, very few loans turned out to be total losses. There was always some value to be salvaged. Mired as he was in the REIT quagmire, real estate workout man Larry Glenn was convinced that the underwater land in Florida and the other turkeys in the bank's portfolio would be a complete loss. Without knowing the specifics of the portfolio, Wriston assured him that Citibank would recover 30 percent. "No, Walt, we'll never get any of this back. This is a write-off," Glenn insisted. But in the end, Citibank recovered close to what Wriston had predicted.

The same would be true of W. T. Grant, which was about to be hit with the wrecker's ball. In early 1976, Citibank workout man John Ingraham returned from a meeting on the final stages of Equity Funding. Ingraham was feeling optimistic about his ability to revive failed companies, but as he looked at Grant, the problem appeared to be unsolvable. "How in hell could we bring this rat's nest alive?" he remarked to a colleague. "The numbers looked awful." He told Wriston he could expect to get back 35 to 40 cents on the dollar in the next year and a total of 50 cents on the dollar in perhaps three to four years.

According to a former top Fed official, the Fed, in its oblique way, pressured the banks to keep lending to W. T. Grant in its final days, and that "bought them a few weeks of life." Then finally, in February 1976, the banks pulled the plug on Grant, which became the biggest failure in retailing history up to that time. The bankers had concluded that the retail chain's operations were so poorly managed that it would be "speculative" to sink $200 million into its rehabilitation. In the marketplace, Grant was damaged goods. In the five months since the bankruptcy filing, vendors had declined to ship merchandise except on a cash basis, and Grant had lost $173 million.

For Ingraham, the liquidation was a major disappointment. He had been trying to accomplish for Grant what he felt he was about to achieve for Penn Central and what he had already accomplished for Equity Funding, which later reemerged as Orion Capital. By 1977, Citibank had recovered the $28 million it had lent to Equity Funding, and a year later the bank recovered $24 million on its $97 million in loans to Grant. In the end, the creditors grossly underestimated Grant's receivables, and the banks eventually recovered 95 cents on the dollar. Said George Moore, "We probably dumped W. T. Grant a little too fast. If we had played along with that a little longer, we probably would have recovered."

To be sure, bad loans weren't Wriston's favorite topic. Asked in 1977 whether the credit losses were behind Citibank, Wriston quipped, "That's an administrative matter. I only handle policy."

But even as Citibank continued to whittle down its REIT loans, from $741 million at the end of 1975 to $564 million by the end of 1976, other mini-debacles, notably loans to manufacturers of citizens band radios and ship-owners, loomed on the horizon, along with a parade of de facto Third World defaults, including Zaire, Peru, Turkey, and Nicaragua.

Wriston knew these episodes would pass, but he was troubled about the basic flaws that they pointed up. For all of Citibank's putative prowess in lending money and getting it back, these events revealed troubling deficiencies in the process by which loans were made and monitored. Loan growth and matrix management had gotten ahead of financial and credit controls.

While Citibank's procedures for credit analysis and extension were historically tighter than those of most other banks, the process for monitoring its billions in loans already on the books was not much more sophisticated than that of a country bank. Citibank lenders had reacted too slowly to red flags at some large borrowers. "The administrative controls were vastly over-extended by the number of clients served," said one former officer. Loan standards and documentation, and auditing of loans on the books, had not kept pace with the frenetic growth of Citibank under Wriston. In the generally rising markets that had prevailed for the last sixteen years, Citibank had deceived itself into thinking that its controls were foolproof. When the real estate and stock market crashed, the inadequacies were visible for all to see. Loan auditors traveled the world reviewing the portfolio. But there was no formal system for managing lending or for auditing the mechanism by which the loans were made, documented, and monitored.

The idea was to develop a way to formalize lending and portfolio management to make sure that a loan that was healthy when it was made didn't get into trouble along the way. The system addressed the loan-making process from approval through review, including how to identify the customers the bank should be dealing with. The process would be handled not out of the credit policy unit but out of the comptroller's office. For the most part, the comptroller's procedures would keep Citibank out of trouble for a decade.

The losses over the past two years also reinforced Wriston's skepticism about holding companies. In the United States, the non-bank subsidiaries of Citicorp earned a mere $13.9 million in 1975. Chase's subsidiaries did even worse, losing nearly as much as Citicorp made.

Overseas, Citibank had stumbled into one minefield after another. Citing Crefisul and IAC as examples of the failure of the joint venture effort, Citicorp embarked on a drive to acquire total control of these holdings or sell them off completely, as it had done with Grindlays. With some understatement, Wriston said, "Our worldwide acquisition record has not been that good, while our de novo expansion has been successful."

He seemed to envy the anonymity with which other holding companies managed their operations. "Except for our lending officers, very few people are aware of the fact that GM is a holding company—maybe we can learn something from them," he said.

Indeed, the flaws of bank holding companies were showing up all over. In February 1976, Chattanooga's Hamilton National Bank tanked after buying bad real estate loans from the mortgage unit of parent Hamilton Bancshares, which had $1.1 billion in assets. At the time, it was the third-largest bank failure in U.S. history. The failure ensnared a number of other large banks, including Citibank, because of close financial ties between these institutions.

While Citibank didn't make the Fed's problem bank list, it was virtually married to a bank that did. It had made a large loan to a borrower who put up his shares of Data Lease Financial Corporation, the parent of Florida's Miami National Bank, as collateral. When the bank and the loan went bad, Wriston attempted to recover the investment by appointing Joseph Stefan, an old pal from his poker-playing days in Stuyvesant Town, to run Miami National. Stefan had been an operations man, not a lender. He had left Citibank in the wake of a personal spat with a superior and had never distinguished himself in the banking business. Nonetheless, Citibank set Stefan up with a Mercedes and a luxury apartment at the Jockey Club. But Stefan went wild making loans on condos and restaurants, vastly exceeding the bank's legal lending limit. In 1981, he and other bank officials were indicted on racketeering charges stemming from loans they allegedly made to the Outriggers Club condo, which became one of Miami's biggest real estate disasters. The loans, investigators charged, wound up in the pockets of the bankers and their friends. The Spanish bank that had acquired Miami National about a year earlier was stunned. But no one was more shocked and dismayed than Wriston, who was dragged into the endless litigation. "I was astonished," Wriston said later. In the end, Stefan got off with five years' probation and 1,000 hours of community service, according to court documents.

Troubled by the vulnerability of the holding company, particularly to liquidity crises, Wriston was more determined than ever to make Citibank less dependent on volatile purchased money. A speech he delivered to officers on July 21, 1976, indicated that he had apparently also gotten some religion on capital. Citicorp and Citibank "must be managed and capitalized in such a way as to remain the strongest financial institution in the world," he said. Still, Wriston was able to boast at the spring 1976 annual meeting that Citicorp was one of just four companies listed on the New York Stock Exchange that had paid dividends every year since 1813.

If the *Washington Post* was Wriston's number one enemy, then the Securities and Exchange Commission was a close second. While the *Post* was blasting Citibank and Chase, the SEC was feeding the flames by proposing to make public the banks' classified loans. The commission was also proposing various accounting changes that, in Wriston's view, would have altered dramatically the way banks lent money in the United States.

Wriston considered himself the world's foremost amateur accountant and lawyer. Kathy Wriston also had a passionate professional and intellectual interest in accounting, and on their Friday evening drives from Manhattan to Deer Pond Farm, she and Wriston often argued heatedly about arcane accounting rules.

Nothing unleashed Wriston's fury more than his confrontations with the SEC over rules governing accounting for bum loans. In Wriston's view, the SEC, in the name of chief accountant John "Sandy" Burton, and a faction of the accounting community sought to promulgate rules that would overnight cause banks to return to the days of the short-term self-liquidating loan and thereby stifle long-term investment. For more than a decade, no one did more to nip this effort in the bud than Wriston.

Wriston was also troubled by the constant changes in accounting rules that made year-to-year consistency in the bank's balance sheet and income statement impossible. "My dream," said Wriston, "was to keep the books of the bank the same way two years in a row."

Wriston's face-off with the SEC began with a call from Sandy Burton, who accused Wriston of "managing earnings" by taking an excessively large loan loss reserve. Implicit in this accusation was the suggestion that Wriston would be able to conveniently unleash those earnings at some later date when he needed them to dress up his income statement. Burton lured Wriston to Washington to discuss the matter, a meeting Wriston expected to be small and intimate. When Wriston walked into a conference room with Hans Angermueller and chief financial officer Don Howard, he found himself, to his shock and dismay, face to face with all of the commissioners, who proceeded to interrogate him about the reserve. "You have no loans to credit against it [the reserve]," the commission declared.

Barely able to contain his temper, Wriston snapped, "That's right. We don't allocate against it. We write off our bad debts."

"Well, then," the stone-faced commissioners interjected, "you're managing earnings."

"We're going into a recession," Wriston told them. "It's common prudence to take a bigger loan loss reserve." Ironically, while Arthur Burns was pressing Wriston to boost his capital cushion, Burton was taking him to task for effectively doing just that.

"They [the SEC] just about accused us of jimmying our books," Wriston said later. Angermueller sensed that his boss was at the flash point and might wind up saying something he would regret later. "You'd be a great help in settling this if you got out of here and went home," he whispered in Wriston's ear. By this time the irascible Don Howard was also straining to contain his anger, so Angermueller gently coaxed both men out into the corridor and suggested they take the next shuttle back to New York. Wriston did go home, and the matter was then settled, with Citibank retaining its reserve. As a result of that debate, the captains of industry later decided that they didn't want to be pushed around by the SEC. "The business community got together and said, 'Why don't we hire a bunch of guys to lay out accounting rules so we know what's going on?' '' Wriston said, and the SEC supported that. The result was the creation in 1973 of the Financial Accounting Standards Board (FASB), which Wriston hoped would offset the power of Burton and the SEC in rule making. But sometimes FASB itself came back to haunt him.

Before long, Burton, the SEC, and the Financial Accounting Standards Board were on the attack. This time the issue was current value accounting, which holds that all bank assets should be assigned fair market values so far as is possible. As loans are restructured or renegotiated, for example, any losses should be charged against earnings. Ironically, according to Wriston, the push to apply this principle to bank assets arose out of the New York City budget crisis, in which the Municipal Assistance Corporation asked the banks to stretch the maturities on city obligations, a restructuring that the SEC would contend called for a write-down of the assets on the banks' books. If there was ever a case of damned if you do, damned if you don't, in the history of American banking, this certainly was it.

To Wriston, there was no greater threat to the American banking modus operandi than current value accounting. He viewed it as a full-employment program for CPAs, who would bill many extra hours for time spent marking up or marking down. Wriston believed in marking assets such as securities to market, because in fact there *was* a market. But the SEC was pushing for rules that would require loans to be valued regularly—a herculean task, because no market existed for these instruments. Wriston appeared anywhere and everywhere to rail against this proposal, and he didn't concern himself with flattering his audience. Flattery, at any rate, was not one of his strong suits.

On June 21, 1976, he traveled to the Miami convention of the National Association of Accountants to attack the problem at the source. He cautioned his audience that if bankers were required to mark their long-term loans and other assets to market on a regular basis, and charge any losses to earnings, they would end up buying only short-term securities that were "relatively unaffected" by interest rate fluctuations. "The advocates of current value accounting score intellectual points with each other without thoroughly taking into account the side effects on society of their laboratory experiments," he said. "Just as war has been said to be too important to be left to the generals, so with great respect I am suggesting that accounting rules are too important to be left only to the accountants." Wriston argued that the move would cut loan expansion, boost unemployment, and stall the nation's recovery from the recession. What he did not say was that it would also bite into Citicorp's thin capital cushion and make it exceedingly difficult to achieve 15 percent earnings growth.

On June 24, a few days after Wriston's Miami speech, *American Banker* editorialized, "Bankers see the issue of present value accounting looming up before them like King Kong, and they are huddling together to defend against the monster." The editorial pointed out that in the space of one week six banking groups had created an "Inter-Association Committee on Bank Accounting" to wage war on the proposed rules.

Even Fed chairman Arthur Burns, who locked horns with Wriston more often than he embraced him, rushed to the banks' defense with a letter protesting the proposed rules, realizing perhaps that it was a bit much to expect the banks to recycle petrodollars, bail out New York City, bolster capital levels, and mark to market at the same time. "If the banks that held the city's obligations had been required to record an immediate write-down of, say, 25 percent of principal as a result of the restructuring, that restructuring just might not have happened," Burns said.

The only way to defang the SEC, Wriston concluded, was to remove the principal antagonist. Banks, of course, don't take out contracts on their enemies. But Wriston was not above political horse-trading. In a bold exercise of raw banking power, Wriston helped orchestrate a career change for Sandy Burton: that fall, Burton left Washington and the SEC for a new job as New York City's deputy mayor for finance. And by the end of 1976 the Financial Accounting Standards Board had scaled down its original proposal into a mere shadow of its former self.

It was not easy to be numero uno at the nation's most important bank. Citibank's size and Wriston's combativeness had made the bank an easy and logical target for critics of all kinds, from Ralph Nader to the *Washington Post* and the SEC. However troublesome and annoying Wriston found these critics and the problems they identified, they were mere nuisances compared with the real sores that festered within Citibank out of the public view. Some of them were of Wriston's own making.

For the first 160 or so years of its existence, Citibank was a gentlemen's bank. After Wriston took the helm, that quickly began to change. By the mid-1970s, the changes that Wriston had wrought within Citibank—McKinseyization, the back office revolution, the 15 percent earnings growth target, the leadership role in recycling petrodollars, and matrix management—were pulling apart the old Citibank just as they were lighting a fire under the American banking industry. They were pitting profit center against profit center, international against domestic, the back office operative against the customer man, officers wedded to geography against those charged with serving global customers, old-time relationship bankers against a new breed of transaction bankers. Citicorp was expanding so rapidly that it was losing touch with its constituencies—its correspondent banks, corporate customers, and retail customers. Organizational and technological changes occurred too fast, and those who couldn't take the heat knew their only option was to get out of the kitchen. To be sure, Citibank was America's premier banking institution, but it had paid a stiff price for that status. The old culture was being devastated.

Wriston almost preferred that his new hires had little or no interest in banking and no academic preparation for it. What counted was IQ. "Citi would hire violin majors and throw them into the computer room," said one former officer. "When they did the job well they did it 120 percent better. When they failed, they would do it only 85 percent as well." These people adapted quickly to the rogue culture Wriston had begun to establish. Citibankers regarded their competitors with contempt and treated them accordingly. Genteel rules of behavior, social niceties, and men in gray flannel suits had no place in Wriston's Citibank. "Citibank was a club-breaker, a rule-breaker," said former Citibanker Peter Greenough. "Citibank played so that there was nothing left for anyone else."

As a result of these attitudes and tactics, Citibank became so disliked by its banking peers that its officers sometimes found themselves socially ostracized. "You'd go to a cocktail party," said Greenough, and "say you were from Citibank, and within three minutes there would be almost nobody standing around you." Some felt that the cowboy mentality often caused Citibank to shoot itself in the foot. "Sometimes," said Greenough, "driving the soft bargain is the thing to do."

The competition between Citibank's own profit centers was just as intense as the rivalry between banks. On at least one occasion those rivalries even led to fistfights on the corporate playground. According to former Citibanker Kamal Mustafa, they exploded in the parking lot of Barrett, Haentjens & Company, a Hazelton, Pennsylvania, pump maker. As the company's executives watched in astonishment from their office windows, one Citibank officer savagely pummeled his colleague over the hood of a car in retaliation for arguing with him in the company's boardroom. "He just beat the shit out of him," recalled Mustafa.

According to a Chase real estate officer, Citibank officers who joined Chase said they'd had to lock their papers up in their desks at night for fear that their co-workers would steal them in a quest for client leads. The competitive pressure, said Harvard Business School professor Charles Williams, "went a little far. You want pressure to accomplish," he said, but sometimes people spend more time thinking about where they stand "than about getting the job done."

Customer service was also a casualty of rapid change. Back office errors were still rampant, and responses to complaints were agonizingly slow. In a speech to his troops, Wriston acknowledged this problem: "With all of the things we did well in 1976, we still did not achieve the quality of customer service that we are all capable of delivering."

Ironically, while Wriston's time horizon was long-term, the organizational structures and incentives he had created encouraged corporate myopia. He seemed to acknowledge that when he said, "Some say that our international measurement systems put more emphasis on short-term profit than on long-term good service." The push to look good in a given quarter produced bad business decisions by the zillions. Managers known for "making budget" sometimes lost millions of dollars in the effort to do so. Citibanker Cedric Grant cited the example of a senior manager in London who sold a cheap long-term lease on the bank's Berkeley Square branch, a move that looked good in the short run but awful in the long term.

Nor had the generation-old conflicts between the specialist and the generalist and between the territory and the product gone away. Indeed, they had intensified with the advent of the World Corporation Group and matrix management, the concept that broke up the old geographic organization. Wriston was not one to dismiss lightly the notion of understanding the territory. With the benefit of hindsight, he conceded that the bank "lost something when it lost an area perspective. We no longer have our man in Chicago. Perhaps we should." Overseas, he added, "it is crucial that we do not lose this particular perspective. Area knowledge or area know-how has to be maintained." Wriston acknowledged that matrix management was not perfect and that "lack of clarity" concerning the matrix was leading to "confusion about accountability and responsibility." He added, "There are no tracks in the snow for us to follow: there are no other organizations that we should emulate; but hopefully we can take the best from many."

Wriston was trying to create a truly global organization, not merely a U.S. company with overseas operations. To the extent that he clung to the remnants of a geographic structure, that goal would remain elusive. But while the matrix organization seemed necessary, there was little doubt that it was creating strains. For one thing, in the international arena it was not always clear who was in charge. The lines between the International Banking Group, CIBL, and top Citibank officials were both dotted and solid. George Vojta, Tom Theobald, Al Costanzo, George Putnam, Ed Palmer, and George Clark all had a piece of the international pie, but it was not always clear what piece.

In an attempt to gain more control over foreign activities and to further clarify the lines of communication between the country chiefs in Vojta's international banking group and other units, Citibank created yet another layer of bureaucracy—the area corporate officer. Wriston acknowledged the intensified divisions between international, which now provided most of Citicorp's earnings, and domestic, where the loan losses of recent years had dissipated earnings. A common complaint among international officers was "We make all the money, and you guys in New York piss it away."

In investing in research and development and trying to achieve control, Wriston lamented later, "we put those people with special skills in a special building. It effectively divorced them from the rest of the organization. We had a communication breakdown." He said the bank developed a "them and us syndrome," and added that "we concentrated appropriately on control, technology, and developing new management skills, but neglected the need to maintain the communications links."

Another change in the culture that was not universally well received was the emergence of a cult of the manager. With McKinseyization and profit centers, managers rather than bankers became the Citibank elite. Managerial skills were more highly prized than banking skills, and those who were more interested in being good bankers were often left in the dust when the titles and salaries were handed out. Officers who remained in the same position too long, even if their customers appreciated the stability, worried that their chances for promotion would be jeopardized. According to Professor Williams, Tom Theobald tried to stretch the average length of an assignment from three years to five years because customers complained—though perhaps not to the right person, Williams said—about turnover among account officers. Williams personally knew of one customer who went through seven account officers in three years.

Finally, in the mid-1970s, Wriston realized that something had to be done to demonstrate that top bankers remained a useful commodity in the nation's largest bank. The embodiment of this conflict between banking and management was Fred Bradley, widely recognized as one of the nation's leading experts in aircraft finance. "I made it clear to people in the bank what my preference was if there was a choice between doing something administrative and doing something for the customer," Bradley said later. "There were people who got frustrated about that, but the bank came to the realization at that point that they had to have both—the manager and the lender." In 1975, Citibank gave up trying to transform Bradley from a banker to a manager and named him one of its first "senior bankers."

"We are not yet in danger of losing our most important attraction: being an exciting, innovative, worthwhile, and enjoyable place to work," Wriston said, "but there are warning flags flying."

"Wriston just lost his way in allowing the whole culture to be torn up," complained a former officer.

In the midst of all this tumult, Wriston asked his friend and director, "Mil" Batten, who had retired as chairman of J. C. Penney in October 1974, to travel around the world and report on what was troubling the Citicorp family. Batten was to study the "fears, conflicts, angers" of people on the line, said one former officer, and, as Wriston said, open the "lines of communication." Batten apparently did the job too well. The accusations leveled in the Nader report were child's play compared with Batten's findings. The "Batten Report" was unrelenting in its frankness, even including suggestions of personal misconduct of certain top Citicorp officials on overseas trips.

Wriston was stunned. He kept the report under lock and key and limited its distribution to a handful of close associates. "It was very thorough," a former senior Citicorp official said of the report, who speculated that Wriston didn't release it for fear of the impact on "top-level morale."

Given the folksy, paternalistic culture of J. C. Penney, it was almost inevitable that Batten's report on the dog-eat-dog, Young Turk mentality at Citibank would be highly critical. Said Ed Palmer, "Walt had a kind of love-hate with Batten and J. C. Penney. Wriston thought Penney was a bunch of farmers and dry goods salesmen."

Shortly before Batten finished his report, a senior Citibank official asked him if he thought his friendship with Wriston would survive it. Batten supposedly was unsure. But when he was named chairman of the New York Stock Exchange in May 1976, he retained all of his corporate directorships except Citicorp, which he said he gave up because "potential conflicts of interest" could arise in connection with efforts of commercial banks to get into the investment banking business. Years later, Batten denied that his resignation from Citicorp was related to his report and still refused to discuss its contents. It was done for Wriston's eyes only, Batten said. Wriston's reaction was one of "careful listening" and no comments, Batten said, adding that Wriston acted on some of his recommendations.

But in internal talks to employees and officers, Wriston spoke in general terms about some of the troubling conclusions Batten had reached. The report, Wriston said, suggested that competitive pressures and high goals had caused some employees to fudge results to indicate that goals had been met when they had not and that some employees had taken shortcuts that compromised Citibank's ethical standards and obligations to customers.

"No branch, no country, or no group is an island," Wriston said in remarks to officers. "Competition between what we once described as a confederation of entrepreneurs is healthy so long as we clearly recognize that we all wear the same sweater that bears only the names of Citicorp and Citibank, not that of any individual group." And he acknowledged the strains caused by the technological revolution when he said, "We can all long for the good old days of simple organization charts and hand-posted ledgers, but they are gone and we must learn to adjust to modern technology."

With the approach of the U.S. bicentennial celebration, there was little to cheer about at City Hall or in Albany in the spring of 1976. Because of the close financial link between the city and state through the "magic window," the state's creditworthiness was now severely tarnished. State agencies that had been financed by moral obligation bonds no longer had any credibility in the marketplace. And the state was on the hook to the city for $800 million. In the upcoming annual spring refinancing, the state would have to raise some $4 billion, mostly for advances to cities, including New York, for the second quarter. Failure of the state to balance its budget through a successful refinancing would mean that there would be no money for New York City and other localities. Another $4 billion would have to be raised through bond sales over the rest of the year. In the past, this fiscal rite of spring had been a routine event kicked off by a brief visit by state controller Arthur Levitt to New York City to pat the the bankers on the back for performing their civic duty. This year it would not be so easy. Early in the year, Wriston calculated the odds of pulling off the sale at about fifty-fifty.

It was imperative that the state be seen as capable of running the show. The old methods for unloading state paper would no longer work.

Led by Pat Patterson, Walter Wriston, and David Rockefeller, the eleven New York Clearing House banks agreed to buy $1 billion in state obligations if the state could find the remainder elsewhere by April 15. Until this time, the state pension funds had not contributed to the bailout of the city or to the financing of the state. Levitt would be forced to put in state pension fund money on a first-in, last-out basis. To make the budget, everyone else would have to be paid out before the pension funds. A trio of top central bankers was assembled to back up Levitt. Said one former Citibanker, "This was desperation time."

Few banking conclaves are more prestigious than the meetings of the Association of Reserve City Bankers, which convenes every spring at a Florida resort hotel. Vital to the success of the state financing was the participation of non–New York banks, many of which were about as sympathetic to the plight of the nation's largest city as a coyote would be to a calf. Bankers from Peoria and San Francisco and Little Rock tended to regard Citibank and Morgan and Chase with the same disdain as many residents of the heartland regarded New Yorkers generally—as arrogant, abrupt, and rude. New York and its bankers were finally getting the comeuppance they had long deserved. According to then state budget director Peter Goldmark, one out-of-state banker remarked at the time, "Hey, you guys went down the road with this crazy city. You guys invented this. Now you want us to come to the rescue?"

The New York triumvirate stood up in front of their fellow bankers at the hotel and told them that they had to continue to support New York State because the consequences of not doing so were "unimaginable."

"Walt showed up and told these people they were crazy if they thought that if the ship sank they wouldn't be on it," said Joseph Doyle, a Shearman & Sterling partner.

Wriston split up the list of out-of-town bankers with his New York colleagues, and each corralled enough of them in hotel suites to complete the deal. "Walter was one of the few guys capable of pulling that kind of thing off," Chemical Bank chairman John McGillicuddy said later. Wriston told his banking colleagues that a disruption at this time would have an impact on their communities, their cost of borrowing.

The trio escorted their "country cousins" down a hotel corridor and past the open door of a suite where Federal Reserve Board chairman Arthur Burns could be seen holding court. Burns had decreed that the New York State notes were an acceptable bank investment so long as the state balanced its budget and bailed out the state agencies. Few bankers, with the possible exception of Wriston himself, wanted to get on the wrong side of the chairman of the Federal Reserve Board.

In the weeks leading up to the spring financing, at least one out-of-town banker said, according to Goldmark, "I'm going to be with you but I'm going to make those guys sweat another week. That's the deal. You got it. We'll tell you what you can say when."

Bank of America, vital to the success of the financing, demanded, as a condition of its investment, that the Comptroller set aside enough money to ensure that note holders would get paid.

Wriston later recalled that he made his last sale of the evening to a top officer of Pittsburgh's Mellon Bank at a hotel bar.

In the end, however, greed as much as moral suasion won the day. As one regulator put it, "the coupons that got put on that stuff [the bonds] were irresistible."

"If we hadn't had that meeting . . . and sold those bonds, the state would have gone down. It's that simple," Wriston said later. It was entirely a case of enlightened self-interest. For their efforts, the New York bankers received no direct compensation, because they were helping the state in making a direct sale.

With that sale a success, the state and city and the banks breathed another collective sigh of relief. And once again it was a brief one.

16
___
WHERE THE MONEY IS

*W*hen Walter Wriston was asked why he'd decided to make a major investment in consumer banking, he responded, "Because that's where the money is." In a mid-1970s interview he added, "I see that $1.2 trillion out there, and I don't see any number that looks like it anywhere else." More than six years would pass—years in which Wriston and his youthful protégé, John Reed, endured bitter criticism from colleagues, the press, Wall Street, and fellow bankers—before Wriston could claim that there was any money, much less real growth potential, in consumer banking. In reality, Citibank had recognized the importance of the individual borrower and saver since the 1920s, when it set up the original compound interest and personal loan departments. In the decades since then, Citibank had peddled services such as loans, checking accounts, and savings accounts. But never in all those years had consumer banking been run as a truly unified business.

In addition to the more or less successful tradition of personal lending at Citibank, another factor weighed heavily in favor of the new thrust: Wriston's own attitude toward personal credit. His were not the typical views of someone raised in thrift-conscious, Depression-era Appleton. Rather, they were the views of a World War II veteran who felt he had postponed the good life long enough.

Prodded by the TEMPO study, Wriston and Citibank started taking the consumers more seriously in the late 1960s. By the mid-1970s they had arrived at the novel conclusion that the real future lay with those consumers, not with *Fortune* 500 companies, the bank's traditional strong suit. By then there were many good reasons for reaching such a conclusion. Concerned that its own use of the CD and commercial paper market had reached what Wriston called "the high end of prudent market share," Citibank was desperately seeking a more reliable source of funds. Wriston had played enough of a role in the Franklin and Herstatt crises to appreciate the whimsical nature of the purchased-money market he had helped create. "You shouldn't put all your eggs in one basket," he said later. "So you looked around for another basket." Then, too, accelerated foreign bank expansion in the

United States was chipping away at the commercial lending business.

Citibank was not even sure it was making money on the hodgepodge of services, including branch banking and credit cards, that fell under the banner of retail banking. Most commercial banks, particularly the big New York money centers, did not view retail banking as a desirable business in the mid-1970s. Costs were steep in New York, and competition from thrift institutions was stiffening. "The bookkeeping [in retail banking] wasn't rigorous," Wriston explained. "I was told we were [making money], but on a fully loaded basis we were not." By 1975, overseas earnings constituted 70 percent of Citibank's total, up from 60 percent in 1973, and Wriston knew intuitively that the party overseas wasn't going to last forever. In examining flow-of-funds tables, Wriston, Reed, et al. saw very little besides cross-border lending that looked as attractive as retail banking. Moreover, the financial services industry was so fragmented that no single bank's overall market share exceeded a single digit.

Reed had concluded from reviewing those tables that a consumer bank could eventually rake in $1 billion after taxes. "John had a flair for marshaling numbers," said former trader Paul De Rosa. "He took the total consumer debt and ascribed a market share to Citibank and took a spread on the market share."

Director Lawrence Fouraker added, "The view emerged that households were the last large untapped source of capital, and no one was going after the household as a source of capital on a nationwide basis or on a coordinated, managed basis."

Bill Spencer was an insomniac, and Reed a workaholic. So both men arrived at the office hours before Wriston and typically spent the early morning brainstorming like a couple of college fraternity brothers preparing for the big final exam. To Reed, who had helped devise the early congeneric strategy, the businesses that Citibank had since acquired around the world were like the bone fragments of some prehistoric creature. Until they were assembled by the paleontologist, they formed no unified whole. In one session with his mentor, Reed observed that Citibank should "get its arms around" this loose confederation of consumer companies in the United States and overseas. "It struck me that we didn't know what we were doing," he said bluntly. "It didn't have a common business purpose. They were a collection of activities with no career path."

The New York branches were the flagship of sorts. The branch system's traditional reason for being was to supply the fodder—"cheap" demand deposits—to the rest of the bank; branch profits typically rose or fell along with interest rates. That rationale inspired the opening of scores of new locations. The operation was so fragmented that auto loans, checking, credit cards, and mortgages were all compartmentalized in separate fiefdoms. In the mid-1970s, consumer lending was not a big source of branch earnings.

The New York banking division had historically taken a myopic view of its business. According to former Citibanker Richard Kovacevich, the branch system believed its business was to sell checking accounts and personal loans. "We used to pride ourselves that we had a 33 percent market share. We were losing our ass and had 33 percent market share." But these figures included just commercial banks. Many customers maintained small checking account balances at Citibank and large savings accounts or certificates of deposit at savings banks. In fact, in the early 1970s, the average account balance of individual Citibank customers was a paltry $317.

In the early 1970s, the branch system had begun to toy with new marketing ideas, with mixed success. In 1973, for example, Citibank introduced an Everything account, modeled after the defunct Everything Card, becoming the first New York bank to offer customers a combination of services for a fixed monthly fee. This deal included discounts on auto and personal loans. That same year, in a push to boost its personal lending business, it opened two experimental Money Shops, patterned after those in Great Britain, to originate personal loan applications. Decorated with Early American–style furniture, these shops stayed open longer than the ordinary branches, but were later shut down because they didn't make any money.

The branch system was also the distribution outlet for the Master Charge card, the bank's primary credit card. At the time, the bank card industry consisted largely of Master Charge and BankAmericard, but individual banks received no brand-name recognition as card issuers; most consumers didn't even know what bank had issued them. Cards were seen as an adjunct to the branch network and were marketed by banks to their branch customers in their territory. Citibank's earlier experiments with travel and entertainment cards had been a failure. Neither the Carte Blanche nor the Diners Club card ever achieved the critical mass needed for a cost-efficient operation.

In upstate New York, Citibank had been buying tiny banks since 1971 with a view toward merging them into a branch network after January 1, 1976, the trigger date of the new state law. If there ever was an example of banking regulation favoring existing institutions over the interests of the consumer, the New York State banking law was it. Citibank was limited in the number and size of banks it could acquire, and it suffered through a four-year waiting period while local banks snapped up the best locations and dug in against the inevitable onslaught of big-city banks. Still, upstate bankers were furious about Citibank's move. One prominent Rochester banker accused the big banks of "strip-mining" the region's financial resources and deploying them elsewhere. Citibank's experience in upstate New York also pointed up the inequities in federal regulation that enabled foreign banks, but not domestic institutions, to buy other large U.S. banks. By 1977, the problems upstate had gotten so bad that some were recommending to Wriston that the bank shut down much of that operation. According to Frank Partel, a former Citibanker who worked on upstate expansion, Citibank postponed expenditures for minor repairs on the branch offices there—even for leaky roofs— until Wriston made a decision; he was reluctant to give up, since upstate expansion was seen as the vanguard of interstate banking. Also, there was no way Citibank could close half of its branch system while it was lobbying regulators and Congress for permission to expand nationwide, Wriston told Partel. Meanwhile, Citibank was taking grief from the national bank examiners over the upstate banks' weak financial condition. "When are you going to start making some money?" they nagged.

If nothing else, Citibank's snowbelt experience provided Wriston with a compelling argument for the power to cross state lines. The essence of the argument was that if Citibank bombed in Buffalo, it should be permitted the opportunity to fail in California, Texas, and Florida as well. In later testimony, Wriston told the Senate Banking Committee that when Citibank moved upstate the local banks "handed us our head. We went up there to compete and we found what you have long known, that small banks in a small town had built relationships with family and friends and the community and a political apparatus that are so strong that it would be very, very difficult indeed to dislodge those." He added that "it took us six to nine years to break even."

Outside of New York State, Citibank's principal consumer banking operation was its Nationwide Financial Services unit, which by 1977 boasted 184 offices in twenty-one states and $378 million in receivables, up from the original 85 offices in fifteen states and $29 million in receivables. But future acquisitions were in jeopardy because of the Fed's go-slow policy.

Despite Wriston's enthusiasm for interstate banking, he wasn't convinced in the mid-1970s that a nationwide branch network would even be profitable. He cited the example of one Australian bank with more than a thousand branches whose total profits were less than those of one Citibank division. "We already have de facto interstate banking through Edge Act offices and account relationships we maintain with customers across the nation," he said. But there was little doubt that given the chance to set up branch networks in choice out-of-state markets, he would have seized the moment.

In late 1973, Citibank suffered a severe setback in its desire to offer mortgages nationwide when the Federal Reserve Board rejected its 1970 acquisition of Advance Mortgage. While protesting that decision, Citi held on to the unit until 1979.

Overseas, where retail expansion paralleled the push in the United States, the consumer units were a mixed bag at best, but all told, there were many more misses than hits in the dozens upon dozens of consumer units scattered around the United States and the globe. In the United Kingdom, Citibank's Money Shops, which featured Mod-style mini-skirted British "Citigirls" in their advertising, were a "big mess that never came close to meeting their objectives," said consumer banker Richard Braddock. Describing the Money Shops as a "flippant concept," Braddock said they were established on the theory that selling money was like selling shirts. Among other problems, Citibank found itself locked out of the best London locations and had to compete with the big British clearing banks, which could branch nationwide. "A lot of things . . . went wrong," said Braddock. "It seemed like a good idea at the time." Before long, however, the Money Shops became a minor footnote in British financial history. Citibank and other U.S.-based international banks were closing down some of their conventional branches in the United Kingdom and on the Continent as well. One reason was that changes in British tax laws now made it difficult for American expatriates to escape onerous U.K. income taxes using the U.S. banks' London branches.

Reed had spent more than five years trying to gain control of the back office and apply technology to serving the consumer. Now he saw how consumer banking could be a good business in its own right. Having grown up in Argentina, he loved to travel overseas, and took several extended trips abroad each year to visit Citibank facilities. Traveling abroad was a way of keeping himself out of a mental rut and enabling him to think on a global scale. He was delighted with the chance to jet around the world to study the retail banking operations of Citibank and its competitors.

In his global travels, Reed was often shocked by what he found. He returned from Australia, for example, to report to Wriston that Waltons, a perennial headache since the mid-1960s, was a "natural disaster." And in Brazil, of course, Reed was nearly burned by what he found. One of the few operations, if not the only one, that was making real money was KKB, the German consumer bank that became the model for customer service and relationship-building. Its chief, the flamboyant Stefan Kaminsky, was an articulate proponent of full-service banking and of the notion that everyone is a potential borrower or depositor or both. Kaminsky, according to former Citibankers, struck up a close personal relationship with Reed, who drew heavily from the KKB model in making his case for an integrated consumer business with himself as the head of it. According to former Citibanker Victor Prall, Kaminsky "outlined the whole ball of wax and where we ought to go." Reed, he said, simply "lifted from the presentation by Kaminsky. He just created a dog and pony show."

Ordinarily Wriston and Spencer placed no constraints on Reed's mission and burdened him with no responsibility other than to file expense reports. "It would have been possible for me to come back and say, 'Hey, Walt, there's nothing there,' " Reed said later. He was not asked to produce a formal eighty-page or eighty-pound report, as other banks might have demanded; Reed's conclusions could be set down in just a few pages. He determined, as he said later in a newspaper interview, that banks were not serving customers "as well as they should be." He went on to say, for example, that it was "difficult for customers to use checks outside of paying bills by mail from home," and that "bankers have to get on our horses and provide a mechanism for customers to consummate transactions outside."

Reed's plan called for an entirely new approach to serving consumers. As he put it later in an interview, the idea was to "start with the customer and the four types of needs the customer has—for borrowing, saving, transaction accounts, and advice—and then produce a marketing umbrella, offering a set of products through a delivery system designed to satisfy these fundamental needs and get a reasonable rate of return." One of his challenges would be to budge old-time branch personnel away from the notion that their mission in life was to "run branches or to issue cards or to finance automobiles." Those things, he said, were merely different kinds of products to offer customers. Citibank, he believed, should organize itself not according to the products that it sold but according to the households with which it sought a relationship. To Reed the future of consumer banking was the plastic card and the telephone. Together they would enable Citibank to expand nationwide. Although Reed considered Wriston's 15 percent earnings growth target an "unnatural" rate, he would acknowledge later that it was the spark that caused him to mull over different approaches to the consumer business. The upshot of Reed's travels was that in August 1974 Reed was handed responsibility for all of Citibank's domestic and worldwide consumer-related businesses. The move to consolidate and make sense of the diverse consumer businesses represented the second application of the so-called strategic business unit concept first used in setting up the World Corporation Group.

Led by Citibank, the nation's banks and financial institutions would now fire the opening salvos in the financial services revolution. They would embark on a massive and hotly competitive scramble to soak up the deposits of American consumers and to stuff their customers' wallets with pieces of plastic. A banner headline in *Newsweek* later said it all: "Bank Warfare." This warfare broke out in the midst of the severe recession of the mid-1970s. To some, this seemed akin to launching a ship in the middle of a hurricane, but Reed was undeterred. He felt that this was as good a time as any to build a market position because other banks were vulnerable. Former overseas officer Jim Tozer recalls that Reed declared, "To hell with the economy. We'll drive right through it."

In mid-1975 the wisdom of Reed's decision was endorsed by Citibank's economics department. The June 1975 issue of the *Monthly Economic Letter* concluded that "once incomes are on an upward track and expectations begin to improve, consumers should respond with a dramatic shift in their preference for tangible assets. And the result should be strong demand for consumer durable goods—and thus for credit."

As part of yet another massive overhaul that accompanied Reed's new assignment, Jim Farley, head of the branch banking operation, was tapped to head up a new consolidated merchant banking group. One of the unwritten rules of management at Citibank was that Farley would never work directly for Reed, whom he had known as a kid in Argentina. That situation would have been awkward at best, and furthermore, no two men could have been more different in style and temperament. Farley had blocked Reed's efforts to install the Citicard I automatic teller machine into his branches and couldn't stomach the price of making a go of consumer banking. Farley, Reed said later, would never advance the money for a venture as speculative and long-term as cash machines. He used to say that ATMs were "too expensive, too prone to vandalism, and too impersonal." And yet, Farley was not yet prepared to be kicked upstairs as a vice chairman and to spend the rest of his career doing nothing but taking customers on golf outings—much as he loved golf outings.

Everything came together at a September 1975 meeting at a Princeton, New Jersey, hotel, where scores of managers from around the world had gathered to kick off Reed's plan. They came from Australia and Europe and Asia, but Reed's reputation for ruthlessness had preceded him. They were less interested in the future of consumer banking in America than in whether there was any future for them at all under this banking wunderkind. Bill Spencer's job was to explain the future to them. One attendee recalls Spencer exhorting the troops, "We got one hundred people in the room. If everyone contributed a million dollars, we'd be satisfied," he said.

The original goal was for the consumers to generate 25 percent of total earnings. Once that goal was set, the bets that would flow from it would be big bets with big payoffs—or big losses. Big bets were part of the Citibank machismo; neither Reed nor Wriston had the time or the patience to build a business up over many years in small, cautious increments.

Beneath the veneer of civility among the bankers at the Princeton meeting, there were hostile undercurrents. To the beleaguered SENOF, who had just been stripped of his multinational clients, this was another victory for that god-awful matrix management. He would soon be sharing authority on his turf, in his country, with lowly retail bankers. Following the conference, according to former Citibanker Ed Harshfield, matrix management was extended to the consumer business in ten countries. In bringing Wriston and Spencer to Princeton, Reed had aimed to seal the plan, to shut down resistance. "It was a power battle. Everyone had different agendas," said one former top official. The upshot was the creation of a new division, divided into four units: the New York branches, credit cards, domestic consumer finance, and international consumer finance. The moves in consumer and in merchant banking reflected Wriston's conclusion that, after years of buying businesses helter-skelter, it was time for consolidation.

Despite, or perhaps because of, his background as an engineer whose primary experience had been in management information systems and operations, Reed decided early on that his new venture would be run not by bankers but by marketeers who had sold coffee, beer, and cigarettes. He still tended to look at business problems with cold, clinical logic, and marketing remained a mystery to him. In 1973, he had begun to learn something about retail marketing when he joined the board of Arlen Realty, which owned Korvettes, then a successful chain of discount stores. But his real immersion began in 1975 when the chairman of Philip Morris invited him to join that company's board. No company had more influence on the bold adventure that was to come than Philip Morris, Reed said later. "I frankly don't believe I could have started the consumer business at Citibank if I wasn't on the Philip Morris board," Reed said. That experience, he said, "taught me what a consumer marketing–oriented company looks like, feels like, and acts like." It gave him the confidence to approach the consumer banking business with the mind-set and skills of a marketeer, not a technocrat.

To date, Citibank had had only a few real marketing types. But Reed's experience, brief thus far, as a Philip Morris director convinced him that the consumer banking unit would have to be led by executives with marketing backgrounds, and he combed the nation's leading consumer products firms— and at least one tropical island beach—to find them. Bringing in mid-career executives and placing them in top positions was itself a revolutionary idea in banking. One imported executive who would play a key role in consumer banking was Richard Kovacevich, a tall, loquacious Pacific northwesterner with Hollywood-style good looks, who had founded a toy company and joined General Mills after it bought his company. Reed met Kovacevich on a Virgin Islands beach, where Kovacevich was vacationing after deciding, as Wriston put it, that "the job wasn't much fun and he didn't fit into Betty Crocker's life." Within a few months after being hired by Reed in October 1975 as head of domestic consumer finance, Kovacevich was one of the top sixty people in the corporation. "That was unheard of in the industry," he said later.

Incidentally, Reed's decision to join the Philip Morris board created a minor furor in the corridors of 399 Park. Cigarette packs had long included the surgeon general's warning of the dangers of smoking, which Wriston had for years regarded as a sign of inferior intelligence. Like high school freshmen trying to catch a few drags without getting caught by the principal, top Citi- bank officers who smoked, including international banking chief George Vojta, sneaked off to the executive washroom to avoid being spotted by chairman Wriston. Reed himself is a nonsmoker whose father, a smoker, died of lung cancer. But Reed often behaved like a naughty child who seemed to delight in shocking his colleagues and superiors. Some speculated that Reed accepted the directorship at Philip Morris at least in part to tweak Walter Bigelow.

Wriston's hawklike brows were raised higher still when, the following year, Reed joined the board of the Sloan Kettering Cancer Institute, where his father had been treated in the early 1960s. Wriston told Reed, "I don't understand how you can be on the Memorial Sloan Kettering Board and the Philip Morris board. I just don't understand that." One reason, Reed later admitted, was that he loved to savor the aroma of uncut tobacco at the Philip Morris warehouses in Richmond, Virginia.

Meanwhile, Rick Braddock, Citibank's original marketeer, did not hit it off with Reed. After a stint as head of marketing for the New York branch banking unit, Braddock was offered to Reed as his chief of staff. Reed had little use for staff people and had a reputation for making poor use of them. Said Braddock later, "He'd have meetings with line people and forget to in- vite staff." Braddock arrived in Reed's consumer group with other built-in disadvantages: he hadn't joined Reed at the outset of the long march; he had not been hired by Reed; he had never ridden with him in the car from Green- wich; and he hadn't struggled with him late into the night as he sought to contain the blowups in check processing or stock transfer. Moreover, Brad- dock, according to former colleagues, resisted many of Reed's moves, so Reed sent him packing for more than three years to London, where he ran the consumer business in the United Kingdom and then Europe. To most people,

London would be a desirable destination. But in the Reed culture, it was purgatory.

Wriston's early vision of the value of the consumer business to Citibank differed sharply from his own, Reed explained later. Wriston had worked years before as an inspector in Citibank's branch system, but since then he had rarely come face to face with the lowly individual depositor or borrower. He was by now the quintessential international corporate banker, and despite his concern about the waning opportunities for lending to America's top corporations, he viewed consumers largely as a source of cheap deposits that would make that arm of the business more profitable, according to Reed.

But Reed, unlike Wriston, now viewed consumer banking as a self-sustaining business in its own right. He was plainly irritated at his boss's view of his fledgling business as little more than a source of liquidity—like humans raised to supply blood to a monster in some Grade B horror flick. Wriston considered the consumer business attractive as a net source of funds, but Reed disagreed. "That's not really why it was attractive. That was a very bankerish view of the consumer business," he said later. Finally Reed went to Wriston and said, "You know, Walt, I really wish you'd quit saying that. . . . All you're doing is communicating to my people that you're out of touch with our vision of why the business makes sense." In Reed's view, consumers were "perfectly legitimate demanders of financial services" who would, as the U.S. economy grew and prospered, rank with corporations as the banks' "core customers."

From then on, said Reed, Wriston no longer expressed that view publicly, even if he continued to believe it. Reed, said a former colleague, was "pro-retail and anti-everything else. He had a pejorative term—'transactors'—for people who actually went out and made loans." He "ridiculed rich people, fancy people," said a colleague, including some of Citibank's preppy Ivy League corporate banker types. Ironically Reed himself was later featured in magazine ads, along with family and dog, as "the kind of man who reads *Scientific American.*" The image that Reed projected, while relaxed and even intellectual, was that of an elite preppy corporate comer.

In a March 1976 memo titled "From the Beach," which Reed wrote while vacationing in the Caribbean, he spelled out to his key managers his vision of the business and his philosophy of management. For Reed's disciples, the "From the Beach" memo would become a kind of gospel that would determine how they carried out their mission and how they related to their leader for the next half decade. "It should be pretty clear that we are creating something new," he wrote, reminding his managers that their objective was not simply to be in the "loan business or the deposit business," but to be in the business of serving people's financial needs. The picture he painted of the condition of retail banking at Citibank was a dismal one. As a means of serving Citibank's individual customers, the branches, he asserted, were "overdesigned"—too big, inefficient, and expensive—and as a device for serving corporate customers, they were totally unnecessary. The card business was vulnerable to inflation, the domestic businesses suffered from their "birth" as "congenerics," and the "overseas consumer effort—even more than in New York—has taken a back seat to the explosive growth of the IBG [International Banking Group]."

The notion that control should precede profitability and that profitability should precede growth was a management dictum that the bank had learned on the Brazilian campus of the school of hard knocks. Citibank had had a terrible experience in Brazil with Crefisul, the consumer finance company one-third owned by Citibank, which sold what Reed described later as a "crazy" consumer loan product called Crefipop. Robert Mylod, who ran Advance Mortgage, recalled that "if you walked into the room and talked about expansion before controls, it was not a very good idea."

Just as Reed was peeved at Wriston's failure early on to share his vision of the consumer business, Wriston was miffed at the resistance he received from Reed and others when he tried to make one of his dreams come true. First National City Corporation had already been changed to Citicorp, but Wriston had always yearned to change the name of First National City Bank to a variation of the original short and sweet name it had been given back in 1812—City Bank. As easy as that seemed, Wriston realized it was a logistical and legal nightmare that would call for changing the signs on every branch, revising thousands of forms, and dealing with a myriad of other details. And while the chairman could dream on, the idea wasn't universally embraced by the people on the line who would have to implement it. The resistance Wriston encountered reminded him of a remark attributed to President Kennedy during the Cuban missile crisis. When Kennedy learned that a U.S. fighter plane had violated Soviet airspace, Kennedy fumed, "There is always some so-and-so who doesn't get the word."

Three weeks after the plan to change the bank's official name to Citibank had been submitted to the board, and after a design firm had been hired to create a new logo, Wriston was stunned by a visit from senior branch executives who delivered a presentation on why the company couldn't be called Citibank. "I listened to these guys and couldn't believe it," Wriston said later. "I said, 'Can you *hear,* fellows? We've done it.' " According to former Reed aide Paul Rudowski, Reed himself thought Wriston was wrong to change the name. "He [Reed] said it would cost a lot of money and, most important, confuse customers." In February 1976, the chairman got his wish, and on March 1 First National City officially became Citibank.

Citibank's decision to go full bore on consumer banking was made in the nick of time. It would soon be joined in a major way by the big brokerage and investment banking houses, which were already accumulating in their money market accounts funds that had once belonged to banks and thrifts. On May 1, 1975, in part as a result of efforts by New York's Merrill Lynch, the long-standing fixed commission rate on brokerage accounts was finally broken, unleashing a free-for-all among investment houses for the consumer dollar. Donald Regan, then chairman of Merrill Lynch, would later observe that May Day was a "prelude" to Merrill's invention in 1977 of its cash management account, essentially an integrated package of services that linked a credit card with a Merrill Lynch money market fund and check-writing privileges.

When it was introduced, the CMA called for a $20,000 minimum balance in cash, securities, or both and a $28 annual fee. Even though the new account paid 12.5 percent interest when the banks could only offer 5.5 percent, the public was slow to embrace the CMA. At the end of the first year, only 4,000 customers had signed up. By 1982, however, some 533,000 customers had CMAs, with $32 billion in assets. Over dinner Wriston once remarked to Regan that his CMA was the most innovative device to appear in the financial services industry since he (Wriston) had invented the negotiable CD.

Reed regarded "bricks-and-mortar branches" as corporate dinosaurs that guzzled too much of the bank's money. Many branches, like the ones at the Pan Am and Mobil buildings in New York, were established to pull in big corporate accounts. They included elegant dining rooms with chefs and waiters, and they became so well known for their cuisine that some bankers dined each day in a different location.

But "branch managers didn't have clue one about the consumer," Reed concluded. In his view, banking was now national in scope. Consumers were looking far beyond the branches for many products once sold there. Those who would not walk more than two blocks to a branch for a checking account would shop for mortgages within a thirty-mile radius and would buy insurance from companies located anywhere in the country. According to Richard Kovacevich, Reed longed for the day when the branch system would earn a mere $35 million—less than 6 percent of 1975 operating profits—in its own right. And some of Reed's early strategic and organizational decisions would almost ensure such a modest outcome.

By reorganizing the branch banking group into six geographical units, Reed took decentralization and the strategic business unit concept to their absurd conclusion. The result was total confusion in the minds of many retail customers. Managers in Queens and Manhattan ran newspapers and radio ads that reached customers throughout the metropolitan area. As a result, customers in Westchester were drawn into a local branch to inquire about an auto loan they'd heard about on the radio, but were told the loan wasn't available there.

Reed was so bent on focusing branch managers on the individual consumer that he ordered them to ignore small businesses—known at Citibank as B&Ps, for business and professionals—many of which had been the mainstay of branch profits. By making it clear that small businesses were not his top priority, he caused Citibank to fall even further behind than it was already in that key segment of the New York banking market.

Wriston shared Reed's view that branches were no longer a viable way of catering to consumers and acknowledged that the branches were doing a poor job in serving individuals. "We know one of the most valuable things that a man or woman has is his lunch hour, and we succeed in eating up most of that lunch hour by making our customers stand in line," Wriston told correspondent bankers. "This delay causes an enormous pressure for change in the banking system," he said. "We believe that an effective electronic funds transfer system may be the only way out of the room if we are to continue to supply the services consumers want." Reed and Wriston doubted that the future of consumer banking lay with the branches. But without automated teller machines (ATMs) or customer activated terminals (CATs), the branches had no future whatsoever. Reed was determined to deploy ATMs in all of Citibank's 271 New York–area branches. Citibank couldn't take credit for being the first to install cash machines, but it would be the first to do so on a massive scale. ATMs were also seen as a way of mitigating inflation-driven increases in the operational and real estate expenses of bricks and mortar branches. The inroads made by the money market funds supplied further impetus for the development of teller machines.

The Citicard, of course, was the foundation for the ATMs. By 1974, Citibank had extended the Citicard machine well beyond its initial use in approving checks. Customers could now check balances, clearings, credit availability, and other account data on an up-to-the-minute basis in all Citibank branches. Shortly thereafter, the bank took the concept a step further, enabling customers to use their cards to authorize check-cashing and Master Charge purchases without having to present identification. The Citicard I was the infrastructure on which the ATMs network would later be built and the "training wheels" that got Citibank customers used to them. The only difference between the old network and the new one was that the old one simply provided information, whereas the new one also dispensed cash.

Originally, according to former technology chief Paul Glaser, Citibank did not intend to install ATMs branch-wide, largely because they were deemed to be too unreliable and expensive. The idea was to install the Citicard check-authorization system in New York–area supermarkets and retail businesses, followed by ATMs that would merely dispense cash. "We hoped to cover the world," said Glaser. "We had a vision of putting everybody out of business. We had this great thing where you couldn't deal with the retailer unless you were a Citibank customer." But the reception at the supermarkets was negative; for one thing, the owners wanted to get paid for cooperating; they did not want to have the machines installed in their stores as a convenience for shoppers. And they certainly weren't about to do anything that would incur the wrath of shoppers who were not Citibank customers. In August 1974, the Fed, on questionable grounds, threw a roadblock into Citibank's path by asserting that the plan would violate the Bank Holding Company Act. But the Fed finally acquiesced, and Citibank installed thousands of "Citibank Shopping" terminals in the New York area to guarantee the checks of both Citibank and non-Citibank customers. The longer-term dream was to create a nationwide network that would enable merchants throughout the country to use Citibank to debit a customer's account instantaneously.

Citibank's creation of the Citicard network was beginning to instill fear in the hearts of other New York banks. Four of its major rivals responded with a plan for a joint venture point-of-sale network that would enable any customer to get approval to cash checks and make credit-card purchases. Soon Citibank announced that it planned to franchise the Citicard to correspondent banks. Other U.S. banks, including Chicago's Continental Illinois and San Francisco's Wells Fargo, quickly followed Citibank's lead with similar networks. Crocker Bank in San Francisco, Tommy Wilcox's new home, followed a year later. In building his consumer business, Reed tried everything, much of which didn't work. The supermarket debit card, for example, bombed at the checkout counter. In that case, and in many others, Citibank was simply ahead of its time.

By early spring 1975, Citibank had installed six cash machines in Manhattan as a test of freestanding ATMs. Although the Bank of America had decided that installing cash machines in every branch would be a dismal failure, Reed concluded from his experiment that the only way to determine whether they would be successful was to install them full bore, two in each branch. Having decided that a gradual, cautious approach was not the right one, Citibank knew that big bucks would be required for widespread implementation. Everything—hardware, software, telecommunications lines—would have to be put in place and on-line at the same time. The decision to go with ATMs was not a major one, Glaser recalls, but the fall 1975 decision to proceed full bore and spend more than $100 million on the installation of ATMs certainly was. The final price tag, Wriston said later, was more like $160 million, but the bankers figured they could earn back the whole investment by picking up another 1 to 2 percent of the market. Reed liked to take long-shot bets. But Wriston and Spencer made the decision with little hesitation. As Reed tested the ATMs for deployment in the New York market, in the back of his mind was his plan to export them to other states and countries.

Wriston didn't require detailed technical knowledge of ATMs or computers to write the check for one of the largest capital expenditures in Citibank history. Indeed, some of those close to the project swore that he was computer illiterate. He did, however, possess a broad vision of the consumer business and what it could mean in the long term for the bank. In the end, that was all that mattered.

Once Wriston gave the go-ahead, money was the last thing the implementers had to worry about. "We never had to go beg for money," said Glaser.

The prospect of losses and heavy R&D expenses for years to come nearly affected the skyline of New York City, according to Wriston. In looking for ways to cut costs, Citibank executives determined that by altering the plans to eliminate the angled roof of the new building, they could slice as much as $700,000 off the bank's expense line. Wriston agreed to consider that plan, but said he would have to consult first with the architect, Hugh Stubbins. Stubbins was furious that Wriston would even think about eliminating the building's most distinctive design feature, one that was unique in American architecture. After a long debate, Wriston and Spencer decided that compared with the total cost of $160 million, $700,000 would get lost in the rounding. It was certainly not worth the price of upsetting the renowned architect. "This guy is the architect, and he thinks [the slanted roof is] the greatest thing," Wriston explained to his colleagues. "So let's do it." Citicorp's symbol would remain in the shape of the number 1.

After the original plans for Citicorp Center were completed, a study was undertaken to determine if the slanted roof of the building could be used to catch the sun's rays to produce solar energy. The slope of the roof in the design was altered to face south instead of north. But plans for a solar generator were dropped after an MIT study showed it would not be cost-effective. New York, it seemed, was not quite sunny enough, either literally or financially.

It did not take a rocket scientist to appreciate the possibilities of electronic funds transfer and how it dovetailed neatly into Wriston's expansionist aims. To Wriston, the notion that electronic blips don't respect political boundaries was a law of nature. As always, Wriston believed technology would outpace regulation and legislation.

As Reed's ATMs began to loom as something more than a novelty, their potential as an agent of expansion across geographic boundaries began to dawn on the American banking industry and its regulators. When Citibank installed its Citibank Shopping network, more than forty of the three thousand locations were across the Hudson River in New Jersey. That drove New Jersey bankers wild. They petitioned the legislature to stop Citibank with a bill deeming that ATMs were branches, not merely Formica-and-steel receptacles for dispensing cash and taking deposits. Reed predicted that electronic banking would mean "five to ten years of turmoil in consumer banking."

Bankers were already deluging their regulators with mail asking if they had to file an application for a branch when they set up a freestanding ATM. The Comptroller, unlike the Fed, tended to take a permissive view.

The Comptroller's counsel, Westbrook Murphy, promptly drafted a ruling stating that ATMs weren't branches and that the Comptroller wouldn't regulate them, a move that stirred up a furor among the nation's independent bankers. The Comptroller lost the battle in court, but to some extent won the war in the states. After losing in both the district court and the appeals court, a number of states borrowed language from Murphy's ruling in writing statutes that permitted all or some of what the Comptroller had intended. "We were front and center" on ATMs, said Comptroller James

Smith later. "We felt that technological advancement shouldn't be hog-tied by old branch restrictions." Other powers weren't of like mind, however; in a decision that "set branching back five years," according to Murphy, the Supreme Court in October 1976 refused to review a lower-court ruling that ATMs were indeed branches and therefore could not be installed where branches themselves were illegal.

In seeking to advance the cause of bank deregulation, the Comptroller's office was often ahead of the industry it was charged with regulating, so much so that at least one newly designated Comptroller had to be oriented to his agency's permissive style. In a meeting with his senior staff shortly after his appointment as Comptroller by President Jimmy Carter, John Heimann, previously the New York State superintendent of banking, remarked with some amazement that "the banks seem to think they can call here and get an idea whether an application would be successful. I think they ought to just file the application and take their chances." It was left to Murphy to enlighten this newcomer on the agency's modus operandi. "I think you're missing something," he told Heimann. "Many times the way the system works is we dream up some idea to move the industry along and then go out and beat the bushes for a bank crazy enough to try it." Often, the logical candidate was Wriston's Citibank.

By the mid to late 1970s, Wriston had resigned himself to the reality that nationwide expansion would not resemble the Oklahoma land rush, where in one glorious moment banks would be permitted to open branches or acquire other banks in other states. Rather, it would happen slowly, through agreements between states to permit each other's banking institutions to operate on their turf. The buzzword for this process was "reciprocity."

Despite Wriston's enthusiasm for electronic funds transfer system (EFTS) technology, he knew instinctively that it had its limits. Convenient as it might be, the debit card, in contrast to the credit card or the check, had one key built-in disadvantage: it meant that in the battle of the "float"—the availability of funds—the bank, not the consumer, was the winner. Using a debit card on an EFTS network meant that the funds would be deducted instantly from the customer's account. "I don't know anybody . . . who has any interest whatsoever in having their account instantly debited to pay Bloomingdale's," Wriston told Columbia Business School alumni. He recalled that after he went to work for Citibank in New York, he continued to maintain a checking account at a Washington, D.C., bank that was not a member of the Fed, so, he said, "I could cash a check on Wednesday with the certain knowledge that it wasn't going to hit for eleven days." As to whether the debit card would ever be embraced by consumers, "I'm still sort of from Missouri," Wriston admitted. He believed that EFTS would have more of an impact on companies than on individual consumers. Early attempts at electronic bill paying would meet with only mild success.

At a Citibank conclave on Shelter Island, a fashionably unfashionable bucolic setting sandwiched between Long Island's North and South Forks, John Reed defiantly told his troops that he would go full bore with the installation. He had little in the way of studies to prove that the effort would succeed; he had only his own belief that the future lay in electronics. Indeed, there were any number of reasons for hesitating, the least of which was cost. During the meeting, while a steady rain fell throughout the day and into the evening, Reed "gave them the vision," as he put it later. "Guys," he said, "we've got to change the branches. We're going to electronify the teller positions, [and install] cash machines and customer service terminals."

Besides cost and reliability, there was a host of other concerns. Some doubted whether people would really use the ATMs. Everyone worried about security. Wriston pointed out that London had cash machines even before New York and that people used to adjourn from the neighborhood pub, mugs in hand, and pour bitters into the machines, literally gumming up the works. Wriston wanted to know if there was a way to prevent that.

Citibank decided to build its ATMs from scratch rather than buy them off the shelf because the commercially available machines lacked "good human factors," according to chief technology officer Paul Glaser. Machines then available couldn't be hooked up to the central network that was already in place at Citibank, and software couldn't be installed from a central location. Citibank also felt that consumers wanted a receipt for their transactions, a phone to contact a customer service representative, and a video screen rather than just buttons. It was difficult to persuade other vendors to custom-design and manufacture such a machine, said Glaser, "so we decided to do it ourselves."

Nearly every physical need was reflected in the design of the ATMs. President Bill Spencer, for example, wore bifocals, and demanded that the screen be easily readable by people like him. One early option was to build the machines into walls, which would have been cheaper and easier than placing them so that the screens were horizontal. In part to accommodate customers like Spencer, the machines were installed with horizontal screens.

For much of 1976, Reed and his colleagues refereed a running battle between the long-haired California wunderkinds at Transaction Technology, Inc., and the marketeers in New York over who would be held responsible for missing the deadline for implementation. The marketing and branch people were convinced that there was no way the technical types could make good on their promise to complete the machines by the end of the year.

And Reed's vision of full and rapid deployment of ATMs was not universally shared within the ranks at Citibank, either. Reed and branch banking chief Jim Tozer, who previously was in charge of Citibank's fledgling merchant bank, argued incessantly over nearly every aspect of the game plan, notably the cost and pace of the installation and who should head it up. Tozer resisted Reed's plan to put two ATMs in every branch, though Tozer later asserted that he, not Reed, wanted twenty-four-hour availability.

Tozer also favored layoffs to offset installation costs, and articles appeared in the local media indicating that this would happen. As a result, branch employees initially resisted the conversion. To calm those fears, Reed decreed that there would be no staff cuts. On the contrary, he told employees that he expected the ATMs would attract more customers to the point where they would have to hire more staff. In the back office, the goal was to cut costs, which meant laying off people. But to build a viable consumer business, Reed knew he couldn't fire tellers every time the business ran into trouble. Later it appeared that even Reed himself might get the ax, but at no time, Reed said later, did he cut staff.

In early 1977, Citibank announced that it was launching the largest ATM network in the nation.

Meanwhile, Tozer and Citibank parted company because Tozer didn't share Reed's faith. Tozer, said Reed, "wouldn't embrace the concept, and gave eighty-seven reasons why it couldn't be done. I just knew I was right, but I couldn't tell you why."

In the wake of that confrontation, Richard Kovacevich, the toy company founder, took over the New York branches and the ATM implementation in mid-1977. "He was the agent who said, 'Yes, we can do that and will do that,'" said Reed. "He merchandised it, and we were greatly successful with cash machines." Kovacevich quickly brought the branch folk around. Gathering them in groups in the Citibank auditorium, he presented a film that used cartoon characters to describe the installation process and prepare them for the dirt and disruption that was to come.

But even Kovacevich would later confess to having reservations about Citibank's compulsion to be the first and the fastest; he was convinced that there was more money to be made by being a "quick" number two, like IBM, which achieved its success not so much through innovation as through implementation and sales. Kovacevich strongly took issue with Reed—who insisted on developing proprietary leading-edge computer hardware—believing that Citibank could buy mainframes and system hardware off the shelf and differentiate itself in the marketplace through its software. Spurning the advice of his associates, Reed wasted tens of millions manufacturing his own hardware and the chips that went into it, and building the software into the hardware in a fashion that made it difficult to change and update the software. "I didn't feel we could afford to keep up with all the changes in technology," Kovacevich said. "I think we tried to do too much." While Kovacevich agreed that Citibank should assemble its own ATMs from components—the key to ATMs is the software, which wasn't being designed effectively at the time by other vendors—he objected to spending hundreds of millions on hardware and basic research on operating systems. "John was giving speeches about having leading-edge technology," Kovacevich said later. "I couldn't give a damn about leading-edge technology. I care about leading-edge marketing. Technology is a means to an end. Citibank never wanted anyone else to lead the way in financial services." And he added: "I would have much more cautiously installed them [the ATMs]." On that issue, he admitted later, "I was wrong." He later realized that Citibank couldn't claim that "The Citi Never Sleeps" if it didn't put ATMs in every branch. In any event, the race to electronic banking was on; two weeks after Citibank announced it would install twenty-four-hour ATMs throughout its branch network, Chase could respond only with a plan to establish "savings centers" with financial counselors to set up new accounts.

Reed didn't go out of his way to hide the price tag of the effort. To some colleagues, it was clear he wanted to send a message to competitors and would-be competitors: If you want to play ball with us you've got to write big checks. Reed was trying to scare others out of the retail banking business. In 1978, Bankers Trust announced it was dumping its retail business, and officers confirm that one reason was the high cost of continuing to be a significant player in it. Internally, said Tozer, Wriston talked only in terms of the project's *variable* costs, but outside the bank he referred to the much higher fixed *and* variable expenses.

The laborious and disruptive process of renovating the branches accomplished more than simply changing their physical appearance. As Reed would recall later, ripping out the interior of every branch in New York and redesigning the teller counters sent an unmistakable message to employees as well as to customers that the old ways of doing business and serving customers were gone forever. "The biggest effect of putting in cash machines," Reed said, "was . . . the fact that we communicated to nine thousand people that things were going to be different." The new design was intended to be customer-friendly. New teller counters without steel bars were designed to enhance contact with customers and enable tellers to deal with them at eye level rather than looking down at them. According to Reed, the idea was to communicate through design that Citibank would be open and straightforward. At the time, he said, the bank was paying below-market rates on passbook savings, a fact that was not apparent to all customers. Along with the installation, those rates were raised one-quarter percent to competitive levels. Other changes accompanied the installation of the ATMs. In early 1977, Citibank dropped its decades-old passbook savings account, informing customers that they could now get the same information from their Citicards and monthly statements. Meanwhile, other banks smugly declared that they would not follow in Citi's footsteps.

On ATMs, Kovacevich disagreed with Reed mostly on the pace and extent of installation. On the future role of the branches, however, they were worlds apart. Reed essentially believed the branches had no future. Kovacevich thought they did if they took some lessons from savings banks, which commercial bankers then saw as their biggest competitor for the consumer dollar. When Reed took over retail banking, commercial banks in general and Citibank in particular were not major players in mortgage lending, for example. That was the traditional mandate of thrift institutions. Kovacevich would change that. "Our strategy," Kovacevich told Reed, should be to "look and smell like a savings bank."

"Mortgages?" Reed asked skeptically when Kovacevich suggested that the consumer business should include making home mortgages in a major way. In late 1977, Citibank announced that it would make $10 million available for low down payment mortgages in Brooklyn, and offered co-op loans with no principal payment for the first five years. "Bankers thought we were off the wall," said Kovacevich later. Citibank eventually became one of the biggest mortgage lenders in the country.

Reed believed that the future of consumer banking was the credit card; the foundation of Reed's nationwide electronic funds transfer strategy was made of plastic. Plastic could be used to do everything from selling hospital insurance, which it was already doing, to collecting deposits, which it would attempt to do later. "I thought he was wrong in believing the branch system would go away," Kovacevich recalled.

Unlike Kovacevich, who had to battle decades of stubborn tradition to convince his colleagues in the branches that they were in the consumer banking business, David Phillips was in the enviable position of being able to create a business culture virtually from scratch. Tall, athletic, and mustachioed, Phillips joined Citibank as a manager in Reed's operating group in 1970 from Polaroid, where he was comptroller of the new products group. Like many other executives recruited by Reed, Phillips was reluctant to become a banker or work for bankers. Reed thought that instinct was the right one.

Credit cards, said Phillips, "started with a clean slate. The other guys had to change people's minds." In the Citibank status hierarchy, where branch bankers ranked just a notch above operations folk, the credit-card people, operating out of a lone outpost on Long Island, hadn't even received a ranking. Over the next five years, Phillips would preside over the building of a business that would ultimately represent the largest source of earnings for the company, and would contribute in no small way to the emergence of the credit-card society. Along the way, Citibank would suffer losses that to that point were the highest in its history.

Meanwhile, Reed asked Richard Kane, the former chemical engineer who had helped clean up check processing, to take charge of Citibank's floundering Master Charge operation.

In February 1976, Kane discovered one reason Master Charge never made money as a stand-alone product: the merchant operation was literally being run out of shoe boxes. When he arrived at Master Charge's Huntington, Long Island, offices for the first time, clerks brought him merchant charge slips that had been stuffed in boxes for over two months. He learned that Citibank had paid the merchants but had not yet billed the issuing banks! Unwittingly, Citibank was offering a "buy now pay *much* later" plan for its banking friends and their customers in Chicago, Los Angeles, and Seattle. Operating according to Reed's rules, Kane set out to get this horror under control. He worked through the backlog until by year end, charge tickets didn't sit around for more than a day, Kane said later.

Kane's early attempt to satisfy Reed's second commandment— profitability—would prove more controversial, however. At the time, cardholders who paid up every month, never maintaining a balance, were essentially getting a free ride, courtesy of Citibank. Because Citibank paid its

merchants weeks before it received payment for a purchase from its cardholders, Citibank was in effect making an interest-free short-term loan to cardholders who never accumulated a balance on which interest could be charged.
Citibank would break even on these accounts from the 1 percent interchange
fee paid by other banks only if those customers racked up annual charges of
$10,000 a year. The losses on customers who paid up every month clearly
could not be made up on volume. In searching for a way to put this business
in the black, Kane discovered that there was no legal reason these customers
couldn't be charged for the privilege of using Citibank's plastic. State law, in
fact, permitted a seventy-cent monthly minimum fee for such customers.
Kane approached Phillips with the idea of slapping them with a fifty-cent
monthly charge. But Phillips deferred to Reed, who felt that the monthly fee
would be a mistake. "These are people who pay up," Reed said. "We want
those people."

"But you said make [this business] profitable," Kane replied. The
monthly fee is "the only way I can see to make those holders profitable."

Reed felt the fee was a "crazy" idea, but preventing Kane from doing it
would mean undercutting the principle of decentralization that Citibank held
dear. "You're the business manager," Reed said. "Go do it."

Kane then moved quickly. In early 1976 notices were mailed to cardholders announcing that the fee would be imposed in April 1976. Soon there
were headlines announcing the unprecedented Citibank move, provoking a
brouhaha that would dog Citibank for years.

Earlier, Citibank had raised finance charges for overdue cardholders
and had begun charging interest on average daily balances from the date of
purchase if there was any balance due from one month to the next, prompting
consumer advocate Betty Furness to say that the new procedure was "a
beauty—for Citibank, not the consumer." But that criticism was nothing
compared with the firestorm ignited by the fifty-cent levy. Other banks called
from all over the country to congratulate Citibank for its bold stroke, said
Kane, but none had the audacity to follow suit. Cardholders wrote to complain that by imposing the fee Citibank was labeling them borrowers when
they had never been in debt before. Angry cardholders stormed into branches
and threw their cards in tellers' faces, forcing Citibank to take special security
measures.

The Citi Master Charge "charge of the fee brigade" ignited "one of the
biggest firefights" we ever had, said executive vice president Charles Long. It
was also a politician's dream: a chance to score points with constituents by
bashing the big banks. Lawmakers in Albany introduced a bill that would
have banned fees for paid-up cardholders, and U.S. Representatives Frank
Annunzio and Walter Fauntroy announced that they would ask the Congress
to pass legislation to block the fee, saying the Citibank move discriminated
against cash buyers. It was the kind of opportunity that Wright Patman
would have relished. With Patman's ouster as head of the full banking committee in 1975 and his death in March 1976, Annunzio had inherited the gavel
of the Citibank-bashing populist. Earlier, Congress had sided with banks and

credit-card issuers by defeating a proposal that would have let merchants tack a 5 percent charge on credit-card purchases. Surprisingly, Citibank's archenemy, Ralph Nader, and his Public Interest Research Group didn't oppose the fee. As one of Nader's Raiders told *American Banker,* "If they [the cardholders] don't like it, they can go to another bank." Reed had never consulted with Spencer or Wriston on the move, and like everyone else, they read about it in the newspapers.

While Wriston was certainly sympathetic with the ultimate aim of the move—to reverse the losses of the fledgling credit-card effort—he took his subordinates to the woodshed for failing to think it through. To the public, it appeared Citibank was punishing people who paid their bills on time. "Did you talk to anybody about this?" Wriston demanded. "Did you talk to any government relations or consumer affairs people?"

"We talked to each other," his embarrassed subordinates replied.

In defending a policy or a point of view, or advocating a change in policy, Wriston always attempted to discuss the issue in terms of its impact on customers rather than its impact on Citibank. He knew, of course, that few outsiders would cry for Citibank. After the dust settled, Citibank lost fewer than 2 percent of its accounts as a result of the new monthly fee, and it increased its revenue.

Incredibly, in June 1978, a New York State Supreme Court judge invalidated the Master Charge fee, calling it "unfairly discriminatory to assess a service charge against one who promptly pays." Representative Frank Annunzio declared his pleasure over the ruling, saying that he was disappointed that Citibank, "one of the country's largest banks, should have to be told by a court to do what it morally should have done six months ago." Finally, in August 1979, an appeals court dismissed the bank's appeal on the lower court's order to make $3 million in payments to hundreds of thousands of cardholders.

According to executive vice president Charles Long, the public relations debacle caused by the monthly fee resulted in the introduction of a "canary system"—so called for the use of a canary by miners to test for methane gas—before new consumer products were launched by Citibank. Wriston assembled a group of three people from public affairs, consumer affairs, and advertising to review all new products. Ironically, by the 1980s, nearly every credit-card issuer in America charged a basic annual fee, often many times the six dollars a year Citibank had attempted to levy.

Fortunately, other banking traditions died more quietly than the no-fee credit card. One of those was the link between the branches and the cards. It was Phillips, said Reed later, who first broached the novel idea that there was no law requiring credit cards to be connected with the branch system. Once Citibank discarded that baggage and recognized that the relationship between a bank and its credit-card customers could be carried on by mail or telephone, the entire country emerged as fertile ground for selling plastic.

For years, the bankers who had run Citibank's lackluster credit-card operations had respected each other's turf. When Citibank Master Charge customers informed the bank that they were moving out of the region, Citibank sent them the names of other MasterCard issuers near their new home. Then it dawned on one of Phillips's men that there was no good reason to give away a customer. Citibank was ready to go national and remove another prohibition against interstate banking. Reed was intrigued by the branch mind-set that had confined the credit-card business to geographical areas. In later remarks, he said that this restriction was "self-imposed and unrelated to economics. . . . Statistically we have the worst credit problems in New York." Even if Citibank solicited customers "blindly," he said, it "would wind up with a better portfolio than we have learned to live with in New York City."

Citibank's opening appeared in early 1976, when the BankAmericard decided to permit banks that issued Master Charge cards to also distribute BankAmericards. While Citibank was opposed to "duality," it knew it had to join BankAmericard to guard its merchant customer business from inroads by other banks. To remain competitive, it had to be able to process payments for merchant customers who accepted both cards. Duality was accompanied by another move that further blurred the distinctions between financial services providers. Master Charge and BankAmericard amended their rules to allow S&Ls, savings banks, and credit unions to issue their cards.

Citibank originally had figured on expanding its credit-card operation in a fashion that was modest by the bank's traditional standards. Planners had been awarded $1 million to launch an advertising campaign. That move in part stemmed from the recognition that, as Wriston put it, credit cards are a "chicken-and-egg business." What he meant was that in starting up this business, card issuers must persuade merchants to accept the card before they have signed up cardholders, and must promote it to prospective customers before they have signed up many merchants.

Citibank decided to move into the credit-card business big-time after it heard rumors that BankAmericard planned a big mid-1977 advertising campaign to herald the change of its name to Visa. "Somebody said this smells like an opportunity," said Kane. The plan was to exploit the confusion surrounding the name change through mass mailings of Visa cards that would earn Citibank brand-name recognition as the leading issuer of credit cards. The marketeers went back to Wriston for another $4 million and targeted twenty-five states, most of them in the East, in which to blitz prospective customers with cards. All the customer had to do was sign the card and return the form.

Citibank bought up lists of prospective cardholders and took them to credit bureaus. But because these agencies were not completely automated at the time, a lot of information fell through the cracks. Incredibly, senior branch officials objected to mailings to branch customers, fearing that the credit card would eat into their revolving credit business. For a bank that prided itself on its technical sophistication, Citibank's early approach to expansion was decidedly naive. It conducted a test mailing, but only on the response to its mailing, not on the quality of the prospective customers.

Richard Kovacevich, an advocate of the go-slow approach, was ap-

palled by the thought of deluging the nation with ten million credit cards.
"Those of us in packaged goods were saying, 'Have you ever heard of test
markets?' You only have to bat .300 to lead the league," he explained later.
"Going slow helps you learn things." But going slow wasn't the Wriston
style, or the Reed style or the Phillips style or the Citibank style. Citibank
believed in taking big bets, as long as it believed it could weather the worst
possible outcome. If it was worth doing, it was worth doing in a big way. In a
mid-1977 promotional maneuver unprecedented in the credit-card business,
Citibank mailed out more than 20 million letters and received 4 million acceptances. The good news was that the ploy succeeded beyond Citibank's
wildest dreams. As expected, customers of other banks thought that responding to Citibank advertisements was the way to apply for their new card with
the new name. One small bank ran a newspaper ad saying that it was the only
bank its customers needed. Oddly, the ad included the Citibank letter and
coupon. Readers even clipped that coupon and sent it to Citibank for a card.

Citibank's credit-card honchos knew little about national marketing
or direct mail. They later learned various gimmicks for raising the response
rate even more. A red stamp saying "preferred customer, process immediately" on the return envelope added one-half percent more responses.
Using "Office of the President" in the return address generated another
one-quarter percent. They found that first-class mail produced a better response than bulk rate.

The bad news was that Citi's cards were being counterfeited. Also, the
bank soon discovered that it had "bought a lot of deadbeats"—new cardholders whom it "didn't know how to manage," Wriston said. By casting a
wide net, it had hauled in convicts and even dogs and cats. One card was
issued to a cat named Charley A. Thompson, according to former Citibanker
Ed Harshfield. That would have been amusing if it had not been punishingly
expensive.

The mass mailing was not well received by traditional credit men, either. They had no experience with statistical credit analysis. Early in the campaign, Kane received a phone call from credit chief P. Henry Mueller, a
veteran credit man whom Reed and others referred to with mild sarcasm as
"P. Henry." Mueller dourly informed him that his father had received a pre-
approved application. Kane thought that was terrific until he heard the rest
of the story. "My father's been dead for twenty years," Mueller said grimly.

"Oh, God," Kane thought. Kane had bought mailing lists from the
phone company, and Mueller's mother had never changed her listing. When
the list was submitted to the credit bureau, it reported that Mr. Mueller had
not had a credit problem in at least twenty years.

Nor did the blitz play well in areas far from Citibank's home turf.
Banks were outraged at Citibank's aggressive, insolent drive into what they
regarded as their territory. Nowhere was the anger more virulent than in St.
Louis, where bankers condemned Citibank for their audacity in charging into
"their market." To Wriston, this was as if Ford tried to block GM from
opening a "showroom in St. Louis because Ford was already there," Wriston

commented years later. "That kind of mind-set blows my mind." But he accepted the flak as the price of entrepreneurship. "Once you turn a team of talented people loose and say, 'Go build a business,' you're liable to get a lot of elbows." Phillips felt the pain in other anatomic areas: "What we did was build a wagon train to the West Coast. We got calluses on the ass, arrows in the back."

To avoid New York City taxes and to gain the benefit of country bank reserve requirements, Citibank shifted its credit-card portfolio to a Buffalo-based subsidiary. The business was growing so fast that the treasurer's department often missed its daily forecast of assets by $100 million. According to former Citibanker Frank Partel, the bank's treasury unit was hard-pressed to keep up with the credit card's capital demands. "All of a sudden," said Partel, "another hundred million" would show up out of nowhere.

Wriston and Reed knew that there would be a trade-off between credit cards, where Citibank aspired to be the preeminent issuer, and correspondent bank services, where it had always been a mediocre performer. By improving the quality of its correspondent services, Citibank hoped to overcome the hostility generated by the credit-card campaign.

The decision to become a national player would call for mailings of credit cards that would cost Citibank upward of $25 million a year, not to mention staggering credit losses. Six years would pass before the business crept into the black.

In the mid-1970s, customer service was a disaster. In his "From the Beach" memo, Reed acknowledged the depth and breadth of the problem. "The relationship with customers has been characterized by . . . poor service, poor products, bad pricing, and other negatives." Reed lamented the fact that the bank had not devoted adequate resources to the problem or adequately organized for it. "More importantly, we do not have a service attitude," he wrote, but "there is a potential capacity to deliver service, to smile, to take that one extra step which we do not deliver."

Nor was Wriston oblivious to the frustration experienced by the man on the street in trying to get action from his institution. He found out about one instance of poor service from his first wife's sister, Geraldine Emmerts, who had spent months trying to get her name changed from Gerald on her MasterCard. Finally she turned the card over to Wriston, who quickly returned the corrected card with a letter signed "Love, Waltrine," which quickly became his new nickname.

For consumers with a problem but without a friend at the bank, life wasn't so easy. In previous years, banks had gladly accepted consumers' deposits while treating them like poor relations. That began to change with the advent of pro-consumer government regulations, the growing recognition that providing banking services for the consumer was good business, and even Ralph Nader's biased Citibank study. The new solicitude was made manifest in 1973 with the appointment of former Miss America Bess Myerson as consumer affairs adviser to Citibank. The bank then began to implement innovations even Nader would have admired. A Citibank survey revealed that women had more difficulty obtaining credit cards than men did. Later, Citibank published a forty-page book titled "Borrowing Basics for Women," explaining how women could build a credit history, avoid discrimination, and foil difficult male officers.

In early 1975, the bank brought plain English to the world of arcane loan agreements when it introduced a simplified loan form that used only one-third as many words as the old one. It also jettisoned a number of punitive clauses, including a so-called cross default provision, wherein a borrower would be placed in default on a personal loan if he or she reneged on other loans. And in an apparent direct response to one of Nader's criticisms, Citibank permitted delinquent customers sued by the bank to reply by mail instead of having to appear in court.

But those efforts didn't end the horror stories. In one instance, a female lawyer who had $5,000 in a Citibank private banking account suddenly learned that her checks were bouncing all over Manhattan, and shortly thereafter got a call from an account officer informing her that she had no money in the account. The customer was livid. She insisted that she had more than enough money in her account to cover the checks. She called a bank officer and demanded to know what had happened to the money. "It'll turn up," the banker replied. "This happens from time to time." Incredibly, the officer told the customer there was nothing the bank could do until the money showed up. When it *did* reappear in the account, the customer stormed into the branch, withdrew the funds in cash, and took her money to a nearby branch of Morgan Guaranty.

Customer service had always been a kind of afterthought in American banking. The banks' advertisements of superior customer service were a variation on one of America's big lies: "The check is in the mail." Often that check was lost, incorrectly debited or credited, mailed to the wrong customer, or never sent out at all. Poor service stemmed in part from the Wristonian view of consumers as mere sources of funds, an attitude that gave rise to the proliferation of credit unions and other boutique financial services providers. Like greengrocers with an oversupply of cantaloupes, bankers, in periods of excessive liquidity, went on the air to promote mortgages or automobile loans, abandoning such offers three months later when their liquidity positions shrank. The consumer's "friend at Chase Manhattan" or elsewhere might be a very good friend in periods of low corporate loan demand and a fiend when demand rose. "People had been numbed into a [low] level of expectation of service from banks," said Reed lieutenant Charles Long, but "they all felt comfortable with the fact that banks lied. The consumer had an expectation that he couldn't trust banks, but he had no alternative because [all banks] behaved the same way."

The marketing types who had joined the bank since the early 1970s convinced Reed that the lack of a service attitude and the absence of retail banking technology made it impossible for Citibank to make good on promises of superior service. The marketing experts further insisted that the worst thing the bank could do was to advertise something it couldn't deliver. Reed decided that business managers responsible for consumer products could not use the word "service" in their advertising until they could actually provide satisfactory customer service.

Citibank's dismal customer service reputation intruded in Wriston's private life at the most awkward moments. On one occasion, the Wristons and four other couples, including the chairmen of three *Fortune* 500 companies, arrived for dinner at Lutèce, an expensive four-star French restaurant on Manhattan's East Side. Wriston's secretary had made reservations, but when he and his party arrived, there was no record of them, and no table waiting. Wriston was fuming and, with his embarrassed friends looking on, dressed down the maître d' for this unpardonable error. He let the maître d' know that he was the chairman of Citibank. The harried maître d' summoned the owner, who was not impressed. "I've spent fifteen minutes waiting on your teller lines," the owner sniffed.

"Yeah," Wriston replied angrily. "But you didn't have a reservation." Wriston and his friends left Lutèce and went to one of his exclusive clubs. There, they sat at an unoccupied table and were told that it was reserved. Meanwhile, Lutèce was on the phone to report that a table had become available. "Forget it," Wriston said, resigning himself to waiting for a table at his club, just like an ordinary depositor on a lunch-hour teller line.

Citibank officials later referred to these as the "bad old days" in its customer service history. In addition to its back office snafus, Citibank drove its customers to rage and frustration when they tried to correct bank foul-ups. According to Dinah Nemeroff, a senior officer for customer relations, one customer contacted the bank twenty times and received no response, while another customer called once and got forty-four responses. Things were so disorganized that at one time ten different units investigated a single customer complaint.

Wriston was so concerned about the service problem that he read virtually every complaint letter addressed to his office, colleagues said, and could even identify a branch from the number and type of complaints it was receiving.

Over the next five years, in John Reed's high-stakes gamble to establish Citibank as America's leading consumer bank, he and his colleagues piddled away untold millions trying out various consumer offerings that simply never flew. Those blunders arguably were the normal miscalculations that go with building a business, with entrepreneurship. But Reed's decision to embrace the long-term pool rate would prove to be an even more expensive matter. This decision, which was entirely avoidable, ultimately cost Citibank upward of half a billion dollars, and almost cost Reed his job. In effect, Reed bet the entire bank on a concept that was a repudiation of the very scripture that Reed himself had written and preached for more than a decade.

Stripped to its basics, Reed's long-term pool argument went this way: because Reed was developing a business for the long term, the price at which he borrowed money from the Citibank pool to fund his business—mortgages, credit cards, personal loans, and the like—should likewise be a long-term rate, effectively in the neighborhood of 8.25 percent, calculated as the average of the marginal cost of funds over an extended period of time. This was, said Wriston, "the swami's best guess" about long-term rates. The long-term pool rate was adjusted infrequently and in small increments. The main idea was that builders of a business shouldn't have to react to every rise and fall in the cost of funds. According to Richard Kane, Reed ordered his staff not to read the *Wall Street Journal,* at least the page that reports money rates.

At this time virtually every other profit center in the Citibank empire figured its cost of money on a marginal, or ninety-day, basis. The long-term pool would have been fine as long as interest rates remained reasonably steady, but this was the volatile 1970s, and such optimism would prove unjustified. The long-term pool rate was an internal measuring stick—a warped one, as things turned out.

Reed did not have control over, or responsibility for, funding his own operation during this period. That was the province of chief financial officer Don Howard, who regarded Reed and his colleagues as amateurs when it came to funding. In this complex world of profit centers, matrix management, marginal cost of funds, and long-term pools, Reed's consumer business was living in a dreamworld where his money over the long haul was supposedly costing a mere 8.25 percent; theoretically he would make money by lending it out at 12 percent. The long-term pool rate was perpetuated by money traders who made money for their profit center as long as they could buy short-term money in the marketplace cheaper than they could sell it into the long-term pool to Reed. In a kind of financial masturbation, a trader could buy money at 7¾ percent and sell it to Reed at 8 percent; he earned one-quarter percent for his profit center. The flaw in this system was that Reed's consumer group did not learn how to buy and sell its own funds.

The conservative approach would have been to acquire bona fide long-term money of from one to five years. As time went on, Citibank did begin to issue more and more long-term debt and match it against long-term assets. In the meantime, the long-term pool rate remained a largely theoretical one that did not reflect marketplace reality. One consequence of obtaining artificially cheap money was that Reed's men underpriced their services. They pushed aggressively into businesses where the slim margins would have been obvious if Reed had been buying his own money at a realistic market rate.

The long-term pool, said former Citibank president Rick Braddock, "allowed some rather simplistic thinking about interest rates, which . . . precluded the individual bank from building an impressive treasury capability until well after we should have. It exposed us to some real financial chaos, particularly in the card business when rates took off and we were not properly funded to deal with it." Former senior officer Mike Callen added that "they [Reed and his team] were living in a fairyland. The treasury guys were taking no responsibility because they were making money on these transactions." But Wriston bought the concept, apparently believing that a chief financial officer of the caliber of Don Howard would "step in and blow the whistle," as Callen put it later. But, in reality, Howard had little control over Reed's operation.

Reed was also pushing to impose the long-term pool concept on the overseas consumer business, a move that officers in the field vehemently resisted. Those who managed Citibank's operations in volatile economies, where interest rates sometimes fluctuated as much as 10 percent in a three-month period, regarded the concept as incredibly naive. In those countries, longer-term loans—say, for example, a ten-year mortgage in Colombia— were typically funded with ten-year money, on what bankers called a "matched book." While the bank assumed the credit risk that the borrower might prove to be a deadbeat, it took essentially no interest rate risk. In meetings with Reed and his colleagues, according to one former international officer, "they'd talk about how they fund long-term mortgages with short-term money, because the United States is different, because it hasn't had inflation since World War II." He added that the "guys in the field thought the guys in New York were nuts on this issue. . . . We'd say, 'You guys are out to lunch. You can't apply this to these economies. You'll bankrupt the company. Furthermore, you ought to watch out applying it to the U.S. economy.' "

In one presentation to senior officers on an overseas trip that included president Bill Spencer, a top Reed aide sought to sell his overseas counterparts on the long-term pool concept. In that meeting it became clear that he didn't even know what a yield curve was, according to former Citibanker Ed Hoffman. "We essentially almost stoned him out of there," said Hoffman.

Spencer was furious. On leaving Singapore, Spencer told the officer, "If this ever happens to me again where I'm humiliated, you're gone."

Reed was already persona non grata overseas, and the long-term pool rate debate didn't add to his standing. By his own admission, Reed was often treated "shabbily" when he traveled abroad. "I've been left on street corners," he said later, referring to the time he drove from Belgium to meet another officer at an intersection in Düsseldorf. Not wanting his driver to have to wait for him, he got out of the car and told him to return to Brussels. Reed, who didn't speak German and had no German currency, waited on the corner for more than an hour with two suitcases for a country officer who never showed up.

"Intellectually," Kovacevich said, Reed was correct about the pool rate. But it was "the worst decision ever made. We fought a hundred times on the long-term pool. Walt was with John on that."

For the next seven years, John Reed's consumer business taxed the patience and the earnings of Citibank. Year after year, in meeting after meeting, Reed would apologize to the board and his colleagues for unkept promises and unmet budgets. By the end of the decade, the flaws in the long-term pool rate were apparent to everyone.

When Reed was given the mandate to create a consumer business, his long-time lieutenant, Bob White, inherited the operating group. When Reed had that job, he had argued vigorously for the right to perform the back office functions for every Citibank front office department. Once he took charge of the consumer effort, however, he insisted on running his own operations, asserting that he wanted to be in total control of his expenses as well as his revenues.

This transition coincided with another turning point in American technological history: the coming of age of the minicomputer. By now American businesses had grown accustomed to the big mainframes that performed processing functions for many different departments. Managers vied for access to the computer, which was jealously guarded by the pale men who made up the mysterious data processing priesthood.

Wriston recognized that the manager who failed to adapt to change was doomed. But change was often wrenching—and expensive—especially in technology. During the 1960s and early 1970s, Wriston and Citibank had subscribed to the conventional wisdom that the world would continue to be run by mainframes. Accordingly, the bank bought real estate, including the Westchester Country Club and a polo field on Long Island, in which to house the big boxes of the future. But the vision of a mainframe-dominated future was shattered in an early-1970s meeting when, Wriston recalled, "Bob White came around one day and says, 'The world's not going that way. The world is going to PCs made possible by these little chips and distributive networks, and we ain't going to have any big boxes.' . . . We sold the polo field, we sold Arrowwood [a resort and conference center]. We were all 100 percent wrong." And by the late 1980s, Citibank had only a handful of the big boxes remaining in its arsenal.

White's philosophy of management was to try to create small organizations out of large ones and to reduce big problems to small ones. Now, with the advent of the minicomputer, he could embark on the next phase of the overhaul, wherein the work of the back office would be cut and diced even further. The aim of this stage, known as Project Paradise, was to use minicomputers to break the work of the back office down into segments that would serve the customers for whom it was being performed. So, for example, all letters of credit would be divided by geographic region, instead of being dumped into one huge pile. In theory, front office account officers would get acquainted with the workers responsible for processing the paperwork for their customers, and the back office workers would develop an understanding of and a devotion to a relatively small group of customers. White and his operation would become one of the first and largest users of the new minicomputers in American business. Project Paradise was really all about improving customer service and facilitating communication between the back office, the front office, and the customer.

In 1970, systems were designed and installed over a weekend. In implementing Project Paradise, Citibank demonstrated that it had learned at least one lesson: someone should talk to the customer. In the letter-of-credit operation, Citibank was proud that it could finally process a letter in twenty-four hours—that is, until Richard Kane talked to an executive at Continental Grain, who said, "Son, do you have any idea what the demurrage [charges caused by delays] is on a ship sitting with a cargo of grain for twenty-four hours?" A cargo of grain couldn't be unloaded until the company had assurance that the buyer could pay. It needed the letter of credit not in twenty-four hours, but in twenty minutes.

One of White's aides, Richard Matteis, created the White Room, a sterile, windowless all-white area at operations headquarters in which an attractive young woman, dressed entirely in white, would process the transactions while observers took notes on everything she did. The White Room was set up to find ways to make operations more efficient, but it was named to please Bob White himself.

There was little doubt that Project Paradise was the way to go. But like the initial effort to bring banking up to speed, the road to paradise was filled with craters. Once again, the earlier upheavals would be repeated in the mid-1970s, with all of the earlier pain and suffering.

One pitfall of decentralization was that managers, in the new age of minicomputer hardware, had so much freedom that they could choose their hardware and software without regard to what the manager in another department was using, even if those departments had to deal with each other. One channel might use DEC and specialized software, and another IBM, and later find out the two were incompatible. Often managers didn't care about compatibility as long as they could show results by the end of the year and receive their bonuses and promotions. This was the flip side of the pile-of-shit theory of management. "If you met the goal at the end of the year, you'd be promoted and given a channel that was bigger or more complicated, and the guy who came in after you [replaced you] was going to have the easiest job in the world," said one former manager. "Bullshit, he was the guy who had to dig everybody out after the shit hit the fan. . . . The first guys were the ones who got the cushy jobs and bonuses, not the second guys." In fact, managers often timed implementation to occur *after* they left and moved on to a more important job.

Project Paradise was anything but paradise in the stock transfer unit, where the snafus dated back to 1969, when Citibank had begun to automate its records. Now, in converting from mainframe processing, the same problems were appearing again in the summer of 1976 for different reasons. Things were so bad that other banks had to come to Citibank's rescue over the Labor Day weekend to set the records straight. Even the Comptroller of the Currency and the Securities and Exchange Commission got into the act by launching investigations into the delays.

The drive to "make the numbers" also forced the stock transfer unit to cut its budget, so it had no supplies for months. Workers launched guerrilla raids to steal staplers and pencils from other departments. They responded to phone complaints by simply taking receivers off the hook. Even after laboring around the clock for weeks, those working on the stock transfer automation project knew the work couldn't be done by the fall deadline. But, explained former operations officer Jeffrey Franklin, "they had committed to it. If they didn't convert and reduce the head count . . . they wouldn't come in on budget and wouldn't get promoted." When the conversion began, "all hell broke loose," Franklin recalled. "The credits were being made, but the debits were not. Dividends were being paid in significantly larger amounts than they should have been, and the bank had to eat the loss." Innumerable accounts were out of whack by hundreds of thousands of dollars. Heads rolled, and a new team, under Larry Small, came in and over a period of a year finally whittled the discrepancies down to manageable size.

Said Franklin, "Paradise was a noble adventure. The ultimate goal was to enhance client service. It didn't work that way because not enough time was given to it. But it was definitely the way to go."

The same phenomenon that had convinced Wriston that consumer banking was the wave of the future also led him, albeit nervously, to conclude that Citibank would have to become more like Wall Street. Commercial banking was slowly suffocating from that insidious disease known as disintermediation, inflicted on it in part by the securities industry. The investment banks underwrote the commercial paper for large corporations that was replacing bank borrowings, and sold the money market mutual funds that were draining consumer deposits from bank coffers. Relationship banking was going the way of the drugstore soda fountain, and banks would either have to find a way to compete with investment banks or watch their corporate banking business wither and die. After fixed brokerage commissions were eliminated, Wall Streeters had to fight for every crumb. If there had ever been any collegiality between commercial and investment bankers, it was about to end.

Then, in the mid-1970s, the commercial banks began to launch the first serious salvos against the Glass-Steagall Act since its passage some forty years earlier.

One clear indication of the growing breach between commercial and investment bankers occurred in early 1973, when the two-year-old Securities Industry Association, whose membership included banks as well as brokerage firms, came out against bank underwriting of revenue bonds. Citibank, North Carolina National Bank, and Atlanta's Citizens and Southern recognized somewhat belatedly where their bread was buttered and quit the lobbying group, never to rejoin.

Before long, banks were getting under the brokers' skin with plans for new or expanded activities that the brokers felt invaded their turf; the securities industry also attacked the bank's right to engage in private placements, which involved serving as a middleman for parties seeking to invest large amounts of money or for borrowers in need of non-bank funds. But Wriston's nervousness about investment banking, as well as his aversion to hiring people whose sole aim in life was to make money, would for years prevent Citibank's investment banking operation from becoming a real force to reckon with on Wall Street. His goals for merchant, or investment, banking at Citibank were modest at best.

Wriston saw clearly the logic of pulling various so-called merchant banking functions together into one unit, much as he was doing in the consumer business. Accordingly, in late 1974, Citibank created its merchant banking group. "Merchant banking is not new to us," said Wriston in a talk to international banking officers. "What is new is our search for synergy by putting all these vehicles together under one roof and giving them a sense of managerial focus and direction." Wriston's support of the merchant bank did not require a giant ideological leap of faith, since Citibank was already engaged in these activities. But proposals to set up the merchant bank as a freestanding, quasi-autonomous entity scared the bejesus out of Wriston, who insisted that it grow up within the Citibank culture, not outside of it. And at the time, he refused to allow the merchant banking group to incorporate the term "investment bank" into its name. With the exception of syndicated lending, most of the merchant banking activities were performing poorly, according to former Citibankers. Citibank, claimed former trader Paul De Rosa, had "never done any mergers and acquisitions, and the Euro-bond business was a loser."

Wriston made it abundantly clear that he had no interest in going into the brokerage business or in underwriting corporate securities in the United States, and said so in letters to the SEC. He told the commission that Citibank couldn't figure out how to make any money in the brokerage business and recognized the potential conflict. The SEC, however, was skeptical about Citibank's lack of interest.

But Wriston vigorously defended, against rising protests from the securities industry lobby, his right to continue to perform activities that were not specifically prohibited by the Glass-Steagall Act, including revenue bond underwriting and private placements. To Wriston, the original intent of the act—preventing speculation with bank deposits—had been bastardized into a form of protection for the securities industry. "One of the wonderful things about the Glass-Steagall Act," Wriston told Columbia Business School alumni in 1977, "is that almost no one who talks about it has read it, so you have rather wide latitude in discussing it." Wriston, of course, carefully read every law and regulation that related in any way to banking. Glass-Steagall, he said, was "intended to protect depositors, not bank competitors." He told fellow bankers that if the act was enforced as its drafters intended, it could "promote both efficiency and our most advanced aspirations."

Referring to private placements, Wriston pointed out in the session with the Columbia alumni that "we've been doing this for twenty years." To uproarious laughter, Wriston added, "The only problem was that we didn't have the meter running on our desk, so we decided to begin to sell what we used to give away, as the lady said."

To his fellow bankers Wriston once said, "The SIA [Securities Industry Association] contends that this activity is forbidden by the Glass-Steagall Act, which raises an interesting question. If it is illegal, at what point did it become illegal? When you charged a fee? When you talked to the insurance companies to introduce the corporation? When you suggested to the corporation where to look for the money? Or did you take your first step into crime when you gave your customer some advice?"

Official support for rethinking Glass-Steagall was weak at best. And Wriston's ambivalent attitude toward Glass-Steagall—and the concerns he expressed about the transparent relationship between securities affiliates and the banks—went a long way toward undermining the banking industry's efforts to break down this barrier and earned him the wrath of colleagues trying to do so. One of the key issues in the debate over the safety of commercial banks engaging in debt and equity underwriting was whether the bank and the securities activities could be separated—legally and in the eyes of the public. Wriston doubted that they could and said so on several occasions, claiming that "if your name is on the door," then the parent would be compelled to rescue any subsidiary or affiliate. Wriston's statement, which he made in at least one Capitol Hill appearance, came back to haunt him; it was frequently invoked by opponents of bank participation in investment banking. Said former comptroller James Smith, "I think Walter regretted saying that." In fact, Smith said, there was only one instance in recent times—the 1976 failure of Hamilton National—where the troubled affiliate brought down the bank.

Reed took an even more jaundiced view of Wall Street and its practitioners than Wriston did. While Wriston, at least in public, was mostly respectful of the establishment, Reed never seemed comfortable with it. Though he lived in the corporate executives' haven of Greenwich, Connecticut, he showed his maverick nature by driving to the train station in a yellow Volkswagen with a flower on the antenna. According to a former colleague, "John isn't the kind of person who joins clubs, though he likes prestigious golf clubs. He's egalitarian, but likes helicopters. He likes to be 'of the people.' " But when it came to Wall Street, concern about too many shady transactions, said former Citibanker Frank Partel, was "one of the reasons Reed doesn't like brokerages" and investment bankers.

Though the Volkswagen eventually metamorphosed into a Mercedes and he acquired vacation homes in Vermont and the Caribbean, Reed fit to a tee the Wriston ideal of the Citibank philosopher-prince who disdained personal wealth. "We have always felt that people should be more interested in the business of the company and in the customers of the company [than] in how much money they take home," said Reed. That was a "fundamental value issue."

His staff were supposed to be driven by the thrill of being on the cutting edge of technology and building the world's premier consumer bank, and were expected to be satisfied with comfortable—but not excessive—incomes during their career. Financially, the big payoff would come at the end of their service to Mother Bank, after they had built up a treasure trove of equity and cash as a result of 12 to 15 percent appreciation in book value stock. Reed told them he would pay them what they needed, and if they needed more, they should come to see him. Trader Paul De Rosa said that "he figured if you were going to be working twenty hours a day for the bank, you didn't need the money, and you wouldn't have a big house and a socialite wife who would get in the way of running the bank."

According to one former Citibank investment banker, Bill Spencer believed in paying competitive salaries to Citibankers who engaged in Wall Street activities, and in the early 1970s he pushed through a bonus plan for certain specialists. In the ongoing compensation battle between uptown and downtown, no one personified the uptown view more than Tom Theobald, who vigorously opposed paying Wall Street–scale salaries to anybody. Reed claimed that Citibank's refusal to compete with Wall Street on compensation had less to do with concern about inflated salaries than with the bank's interest in attracting to the bank people cast in the Wriston mold.

Some, like De Rosa, did not share these values, and chafed at the notion that there was a higher purpose than making money. "In business," he said, "people are supposed to make money and enjoy making money. [The] Reed and Wriston style was to get you to believe there was some purpose of business that transcended making money. That was something I couldn't buy." The Wriston style, in or out of the office, was always in marked contrast to that of his Wall Street counterparts. Said De Rosa, "When you spent a weekend with Tom Strauss of Salomon Brothers you knew you're going to get a helicopter to pick you up. With Wriston, you were going to drive yourself to his small house in Connecticut where he'd greet you in Bermuda shorts and you'd talk about books. . . . We thought Citibank would be one of the best investment banks, but we wanted to be paid."

Another barrier to investment banking realizing its full potential was the constant turnover in the leadership, beginning with Jim Tozer and then Jim Farley, and their commercial banking mind-set. Farley, for all his back-slapping conviviality and small-business instincts, had earned his stripes in the branch system and was more of a bureaucrat than a deal-maker. Said one former officer, "To compete with Salomon you've got to be in the business for years."

One who did have the investment banker temperament was Mark Kessenich, who in 1977 took over Citibank's money market unit, which traded government securities. Prior to his arrival, operations had hardly been satisfactory. "Mark thought serious money could be made if done in a systematic way," De Rosa said.

Although few questioned the rationale for placing all of these related activities together under one management, there was little doubt that this development would represent yet another dagger in the heart of relationship banking at Citibank, and yet another source of the internal strife that was already rampant.

Citibank's investment bank "was treading on the toes of a lot of old-time corporate lending officers who had relationships with Du Pont and Exxon," said a former officer. All of a sudden merchant bankers also wanted access to these same customers, often to offer them alternatives to the traditional kind of financing provided by white-shoe corporate lenders. The creation of the merchant bank, however, came at a time when large corporations like Du Pont and Exxon were demanding fewer of the services historically provided by corporate lenders. They could now issue debt in the public markets, often commanding lower rates than the banks themselves. "The customer was saying, 'I don't need a ninety-day loan. Give me something else or I can't do business with you,'" said Jim Farley.

There was a time when a major company would automatically call his relationship banker when he needed a line of credit. In some instances, the links between top company officers and their bankers were like those of a close-knit family. For example, the ties between Citibank and Caltex, a joint venture between Standard Oil of California and Texaco, went back decades. Every year, top officers of Caltex met their counterparts at Citibank for a tournament they called the Caltex Cup. Into the 1970s, there was never any question that Citibank would be called upon to assemble a credit line for its golf partners when one was required. But even that relationship later took on a less sentimental tone. On one golf outing, Farley asked a senior Caltex officer what the relationship meant to the company. "It means you'll get a call if you're out of line," one Caltex official replied. "If you don't have a relationship, you won't get a call at all."

The merchant bank—especially its Citibank International Bank Limited, or CIBL unit—assumed a higher public profile than the traditional commercial bank. CIBL was becoming a force to be reckoned with. New activities were being added at a rapid pace: bond trading, underwriting, and corporate finance. CIBL appeared prominently in the tombstone ads that ran in the *Wall Street Journal,* and merchant bankers were frequently mentioned in glowing terms in the business press. The commercial bankers at Citi resented CIBL's success and notoriety.

But Citibank was not destined to become a major force in the aspect of merchant banking where the amateurs are truly separated from the pros: advising companies, for a fee, on things like capital structure and merger and acquisition transactions. To be sure, part of the problem was regulatory. But most of it, Citibankers would acknowledge later, stemmed from Citibank's own organizational and cultural biases and from its view that commercial and investment banking were in fact separate, distinct, and even competing activities.

While the distinctions were clear internally, the big multinational customers they hoped to serve couldn't have cared less how Citibank was organized. "You couldn't go in and say, 'We're just here as commercial bankers to lend you money,'" Michael Callen asserted. "Nobody wanted you to lend them money, especially large companies. They wanted you to solve problems."

17

THE TURKEYS COME HOME TO ROOST

*W*ithin three years after OPEC shocked the world by jacking up oil prices, the evidence was mounting that recycling wasn't going so smoothly. Wall Street analysts and congressional committees now questioned international lending in general and the Wriston lending machine in particular.

And so once again Wriston and his merry band of optimists hit the speakers' circuit to assure the world that everything would work out. By most accounts, Wriston's gift for allaying fears about international lending was considerable, but there was good reason to ask questions. By the end of 1977, according to IMF documents, the external debt of Third World countries had soared to $244 billion from $91 billion at the end of 1972. They now owed U.S. commercial banks more than $50 billion. Although these loans by 1977 made up only 8 percent of the total assets of the nation's nine largest banks, the banks were, on average, deriving at least half of their net earnings from such lending.

In effect, by financing Third World deficits, Citibank and its brethren were helping to finance wasteful social and economic development programs that enabled the leaders of these countries to stay in power. With all the borrowed money pouring into Latin America, the money supply, and consequently inflation, in those countries rose sharply. In many cases, U.S. banks, said former Citibanker Byron Stinson, were extending short- and medium-term loans for projects that really required long-term financing. By mid-1976, Zaire had defaulted, and Peru and Turkey were waiting in the wings. Of its $3 billion in external debt, Zaire owed $162 million to the twenty-one largest U.S. banks, and Peru, also with external debts of about $3 billion, owed them $1 billion. Mexico was suffering from a currency crisis and Argentina, as usual, was on the skids.

By this time, even Britain and Italy were nearly in the tank, and they were more of a worry in international financial circles than less developed countries like Brazil. Citibank, for one, cut back on its lending to the United Kingdom. In 1977 major U.S. banks, including Citi, Manny Hanny, Chase, and Bank of America, declined to participate in a $1.5 billion loan to the

Bank of England, no less, because the spread was too thin.

Still, the world's multinational banks, led by Citibank, had demonstrated that they were the only feasible mechanism for recycling petrodollars. Official international financial institutions, notably the International Monetary Fund, had shown that they were both unwilling and unprepared to play that role on the scale required.

Meanwhile, Fed chairman Arthur Burns agonized as foreign loans zoomed way out of proportion to bank capital. Low capital levels during the Wriston years enabled Citicorp to rack up high returns in shareholders' equity, including the 16.1 percent it achieved in 1976. Thin as Citi's capital cushion was, Citicorp made it even thinner by embarking on a stock buyback program in 1977 that had the effect of bolstering earnings per share. The regulators and analysts were not pleased and didn't hesitate to say so.

On Wall Street, one of the biggest bears was analyst George Salem, later of Prudential Securities. Other analysts, he said, continued to write bullish reports about Citicorp because the company "is one of the biggest investment banking clients." Salem said later, "All I'm good at is saying the emperor wears no clothes, the books are cooked, and accounting lags reality."

When Zaire halted principal and interest payments in June 1975 on its more than $700 million in commercial bank debt, American bankers learned that the guerrilla warfare skills required for a Third World leader to gain independence for his country were different from those he needed to balance a budget.

According to former Africa hand Hamilton Meserve, International Banking Group chief George Vojta believed that by expanding into Africa Citibank could duplicate the success it had enjoyed in the Middle East. But Africa differed from the Middle East in a fundamental way: in Africa there was no cash. The effort to bring Zaire into the community of debt-honoring nations was a fruitless one. In mid-1976, the so-called Paris Club, representing the industrialized creditor nations, renegotiated $800 million owed by Zaire, and just one month later Zaire failed to pay again.

In what would prove to be a forerunner of many reschedulings to come, country risk expert Irving Friedman would pioneer the restructuring process with Zaire as the guinea pig. Zaire was unable to come to terms with the IMF, so the peripatetic Friedman put on his IMF hat to attempt to work out a program. Officially, Friedman and Citibank, as the leader of the bank group, refused to reschedule, saying they didn't want to set a bad precedent. But by the end of 1976, the banks agreed to renegotiate $375 million and to raise $250 million in new money on a "best efforts" basis, if Zaire would sign an agreement with the IMF and pay its overdue interest. The $250 million was exactly the amount Zaire owed through 1978. By early 1977, however, internal discord in Zaire's copper-mining regions had derailed negotiations and threatened to further undermine the country's ability to repay. The IMF agreed to a loan of $90 million but canceled it in late 1977 after making only one disbursement. At the end of 1977, Zaire still owed commercial banks

$130 million in principal for 1976 and 1977, and Friedman was still scouring the globe in search of $250 million to repay old loans. One rescheduling simply led the country headlong into the next one. A cartoon in a major financial magazine depicted Friedman jetting back and forth between Zaire and the United States. He became known as the "Dr. Kissinger of the financial world."

Citibank knew it had a problem when an eighteen-month grace period expired and Zaire couldn't pay up. Bankers flew to Zaire and discovered that ground hadn't even been broken for an airport for which loans had been extended. The money, Meserve said, had "gone to [President] Mobutu's account and [been used] to buy off tribes." Mobutu himself was said by international bankers to have squirreled away $4 billion in Switzerland. "We didn't understand the policies of the country," Meserve said. "Citibank had no idea about the cultures it was lending to." Eventually, most banks wrote off their Zaire loans, but they learned one valuable lesson from this episode: countries with the money to pay their debts are more of a problem than those that don't.

No one extrapolated from Zaire—and, for that matter, Peru and Turkey—to other LDCs. Zaire was seen as "one guy ripping off the country—a special case of copper prices collapsing, a special case susceptible to management," one bank economist said. Isolated case though it was, Zaire served as a dress rehearsal for the workouts that would come later. Shortly after Zaire began to topple, Sudan followed in its footsteps. "We decided that these people didn't understand what a debt was. They thought this was just a polite way to make a gift to them," said one Citibanker. After that, Citibank pulled in its horns on Sudan.

Peru, also suffering from falling copper prices, followed quickly on the heels of Zaire. With its economy collapsing, Peru in 1976 approached the private banks for about $400 million to repay principal and interest on its foreign debt. The Peruvian government had already hit the fund up for $200 million and would now be subject to draconian austerity measures. But Friedman said the bank program would be even more stringent. Led by Friedman and Citibank, a bankers' committee put together a $386 million loan package modeled after the IMF programs. Other bankers said they went along with it only because of Citibank's immense clout. As a condition for receiving the first half of the money, Peru, under orders from the banks, devalued its currency, slashed the budget, fired leftist officials, and removed price controls, prompting criticism of the banks for interfering in the internal affairs of foreign countries. The IMF also expressed strong disapproval of the banks for preempting its traditional role.

But Peru's rehabilitation didn't last long. By the end of 1976, it was pleading with the banks for more money. Peruvian president Francisco Morales Bermúdez confirmed on December 30, 1976, that his administration, ostensibly fearing a Chilean invasion, was purchasing thirty-six fighter jets from the Soviet Union for $250 million. As the extent of Peru's problems became evident, Citibank quietly wound down its exposure, according to former Citibank Latin hand George Hagerman, by foisting the loans off on other banks. Peruvian government officials were livid when they discovered this. They wanted answers, and Hagerman didn't want to confront them alone. "They're just going to beat me up," he told colleagues. Though Citibankers avoided Irving Friedman during his overseas junkets, he was handy to have around to beard a finance minister or central banker. For all his idiosyncrasies, Friedman could be tough, and often lectured finance ministers as if they were schoolboys. As Hagerman sat with his jaw agape, Friedman scolded the Peruvian finance minister on his profligate fiscal practices. "You want more money from us and you bought thirty-six MiGs?" Friedman bellowed indignantly. Hagerman expected them to be led off to a firing squad, but the Peruvians accepted their browbeating without protest. Before long, other banks were beating up on Peru as well. At least some of Citibank's zeal in lending in dollars to countries like Peru stemmed from its concern that the authorities would curtail its profitable local currency operations or even force it to shut down its branches. "They have the ability to turn off your water," said former executive committee chairman Ed Palmer. "Twenty years of goodwill may ride on one transaction."

Friedman later reported to a congressional panel that he had told Peruvian officials that they wouldn't get any more money from private banks until they humbled themselves before the IMF. In the fall of 1977, Peru bowed to the inevitable and signed an agreement with the IMF committing itself to an austerity program. As usual, the knife cut deepest among the poor, and they rioted in the streets. But after receiving $100 million from the IMF, Peru, which was found to have cooked its books, was declared in violation of its IMF agreement and in 1978 came back to the banks for more money.

The multinational banks would soon be confronted with a de facto default in Turkey as well. More than two hundred banks had made loans disguised as $2.1 billion in deposits in Turkish banks, which they then converted to local currency for local loans. According to bankers involved in these negotiations, Citibank delayed the resolution for more than a year by insisting that 100 percent of the banks participate. "Citibank's attitude was that the last $6 million would hold it [the completion of the deal] up," said a former international lending officer who was familiar with the transaction. Ultimately the banks rescheduled $2.5 billion and some extended a new loan of $500 million.

Of all of Citibank's developing country clients in Asia, the only one that suffered from the Latin disease was in many ways more Latin than Asian: the Philippines. Though Citibank was the largest foreign bank in the country and gladly led or participated in the many Eurosyndicated loans completed after the oil shock, New York's Manufacturers Hanover Trust took the lead in rescheduling its debt in 1976, the same year that the Philippines played host to some five thousand international financiers at the annual conference of the International Monetary Fund and World Bank, an event for which the spendthrift regime of Imelda and Ferdinand Marcos built thirteen new hotels.

No project would epitomize the indigenous corruption in the Philippines more than the Westinghouse nuclear plant, a 620-megawatt reactor that was to be the nation's first such facility. The total cost was initially estimated at $1.1 billion, to be financed by a mix of financing from the Export-Import Bank and other sources, including a $257 million syndicated loan led by Citibank's investment banking unit.

By 1978, two years after construction began, news of how the contracts and financing had been awarded began to leak out. According to a January 1978 report in the *New York Times*, Westinghouse acknowledged it had paid commissions to Herminio T. Disini, a golfing partner of Marcos and husband of a first cousin of his wife, to get the contract—commissions estimated at between $4 million and $35 million. According to the *Times*, Disini had also helped Citibank share the role of lead agent on the financing. In 1978, Citibank was forced to ease the terms of the loan. But the final chapter in the saga of the nuclear plant would not be written for nearly two decades.

It was clear that lending more money to the Philippines was a bad idea. The country's economic fundamentals were deteriorating, and Marcos appeared to be losing his grip on power. In 1977, the World Bank, the United States, and Japan advised the Philippines to slash its 1978 borrowing plans by half.

Ray Kathe, Citibank's Mr. Asia, also took credit for Citibank's decision to slow down in the Philippines and to resist the temptation to go overboard in lending to other Asian countries. "We could have had . . . trouble in Asia if . . . I had not resisted these fellows who wanted to lend a lot more money to some of the countries," Kathe said. "The Philippines got a lot of their money elsewhere. Once you get deeply involved, whether it's a company or a government, it's not so easy to say, 'Today everything must be paid back.' "

Some Third World countries consciously avoided the debt buildup. Colombia, Malaysia, and Indonesia, for example, were generally models of good debt management. But Third World egos were not insignificant contributors to the eventual demise of many of these countries. For the leaders of many developing nations, building certain key industries, such as steel, was a sign of economic maturity, whether those industries were economically viable for their countries or not. And Third World borrowers were often as gullible as their bankers. As in any other situation where money flows freely, this lending spree was a boon for scam artists posing as deal makers and money lenders. They traveled the world armed with business cards identifying themselves as representatives of everything from fictitious Saudi institutions to the White House, and they offered jumbo loans at below-market rates. The catch was that the would-be borrower would have to pay an "advance fee." Said international financier Geoffrey Bell, who compiled what he called a "Christmas list" of con men, "It was endemic. I used to spend a lot of time telling them [Third World borrowers] this money didn't exist."

Even while loans to Third World countries were under scrutiny by bureaucrats, analysts, and politicians, Wriston and his partners rebuked the doomsayers and declared victory over oil shock number one. In speech after speech, article after article, Wriston ridiculed the critics for worrying about crises that never came. With the worst of the New York City budget crisis over, he was able to point to that episode as evidence that people's worst fears are seldom justified. "Armageddon never arrives," he said. "People with their intellectual capital invested in the end of the world are not getting a good return. But they're still waiting."

In a speech to the United Nations ambassadors, Wriston reminded his audience that "it was only yesterday when our government was urging the private sector to lend to and invest in the developing world." Wriston and Costanzo chafed at the inclination of some in Washington and the press to throw all less developed countries (LDCs) into the same basket with the likes of Peru and Zaire.

"LDC," said Wriston, "is a name given to . . . a great diversity of nations. It is a definition that tries to lump together India, with its six hundred million people, and Singapore, with fewer than three million; or Tanzania, where nine of ten people live in the country, and Argentina, where eight of ten live in the cities." Some countries, he said, "are able to handle large amounts of debt, and some are not." Wriston and others would discover, to their dismay, that all these countries had more in common than he would have liked to believe.

For Wriston, the actuarial base was a religion, and his faith in it was absolute. In an April 1977 talk to the Wharton School, executive committee chairman Ed Palmer pointed out that no country accounted for more than 7 percent of loans except the United States, and only the U.S., Brazil, and the United Kingdom generated as much as 5 percent of earnings. Wriston insisted that Citibank generally had a 1 percent to 2 percent market share in its overseas markets, though some were larger. "The upside potential is enormous, and the downside risk is monitored with great care," he told *Euromoney* in July 1978. "We never know where trouble will come from, so we never have too much exposure anywhere, but we have some chips in every game in town." He said loans and LDCs were grouped according to high-, middle-, and low-income countries and, within each country, according to whether they were local currency, foreign currency, or guaranteed loans.

The Middle East, said Palmer, was the upside. For twenty years, he said, "we maintained branches in several lonely sandy countries that suddenly one day turned into a major world financial center called OPEC." In Zaire—the downside—Citibank's exposure was "heavily weighted" toward local currency, guaranteed loans, and short-term self-liquidating loans. "In the worst-case scenario for default, which we do not expect to occur, the effect on our financial condition would be barely perceptible."

"When some commodity prices were down," Wriston said in July 1976, "the OPEC countries were thriving. When the OPEC nations developed deficits, the industrial nations recovered from their slump and commodity prices rebounded." Wriston emphasized that the difficulties that had cropped up so far in overseas lending should be addressed "with a rifle and not a shotgun."

Some legislators at this point had begun to charge that by lending overseas instead of to domestic borrowers, banks were slowing the domestic economic recovery.

"Nonsense," Wriston responded. "Industry is running over with liquidity." He and his colleagues insisted that the problem in the domestic economy was lack of demand, not lack of supply. In fact, because Third World borrowers were growing much more rapidly than the United States, they had a greater appetite for loans than did U.S. borrowers.

The improvement in the condition of countries like Mexico and Korea reconfirmed Wriston and Costanzo's conviction that Third World economies could be turned around quickly by manipulating the levers and pressing the right buttons. Two years before, in 1975, they were fretting over South Korea, said Wriston. Now, in March 1977, "their gold and dollar reserves are the highest in their history. Their ratio of debt service to exports is the lowest."

Costanzo predicted that payments would not be stretched out in "more than two or three" countries. Such renegotiations, he pointed out, were "nothing new" in international banking, having occurred with some frequency in Latin American back in the 1950s. "But," he said, "in every case the new debt schedule was met. In fact, during the whole postwar period not one cent was written off for balance-of-payments reasons."

George Moore later contended that until the day he retired, Citibank had a limit of 10 percent of capital and surplus that could be lent to one country. Germany, the United Kingdom, and Japan were the three exceptions; there Citibank would go to 20 percent. Not included in the limit, he said, were loans guaranteed by the Export-Import Bank, subsidiaries of companies like IBM and GM, and short-term self-liquidating transactions. Moore claimed that when he was in charge, "every [loan] ticket had to say it was within the sovereign limit." And he blamed Costanzo for leading Wriston into the abyss of LDC lending.

Even Spencer, the no-nonsense Coloradan who, colleagues said, regarded Third World loans as smoke-and-mirrors lending, was at least publicly toeing the Wriston-Costanzo line. In an internal publication, he said that the bank's record on Third World loans was "superb—a lot better than it is on domestic loans."

Irving Friedman also remained sanguine. As a champion of recycling, he out-Wristoned Wriston in his frequent speeches and pronouncements. In congressional testimony, Friedman continued to express his confidence—unfounded, it would turn out—that the commercial banks would not reschedule their Zaire debt. "Zaire," he said, would have "to pay back all its past debt in order to become eligible for new funds." While putting in a plug for his latest book, Friedman urged increases in quotas for the IMF—to more than double the current level—to raise the fund to $100 billion.

In response to the questions raised about Third World lending, most regulators supported the commercial banks. William Simon, as Treasury secretary under Nixon and then Ford, "made banks heroes for participating," said financier Geoffrey Bell, who blames central bankers, including the Fed, the Bank of England, and the Bundesbank, for much of what later happened. "A supervisor's job when you got 200 percent of capital in these loans is to say, 'Don't you think you chaps have overdone it?' "

In his comments on the foreign lending problems, Fed chairman Arthur Burns once again spoke out of both sides of his mouth. On the one hand, Burns bemoaned the "thinning of the capital cushion" and the fueling of asset growth using short-term borrowed money, as he told the Senate Banking Committee in March. But if he urged caution, as all central bankers tend to do, he pronounced the banking system "improving" from the problems of the previous several years and praised the banks for their role in recycling. Indebtedness of non-oil-producing LDCs, he said, was "less worrisome" when compared with the LDCs' industrial production and exports. Moreover, he pointed out that losses on foreign loans were "relatively smaller" than those on domestic loans. A month later, he was even more effusive in his praise of the banks' role in recycling: "Had the banks not done so, the recent recession would have been more severe than it was, since there was no official mechanism in place that could have coped with recycling of funds on the vast scale that become necessary in 1974."

Even Fed governor Henry C. Wallich, the highly regarded former Yale economist whom some would remember as the leading doubting Thomas, was reassuring. Asked by a Senate banking subcommittee in August 1977 if he thought banks were overextended, he said, "In my honest opinion, no, not that I know of." When asked by Senator H. John Heinz III what would happen to Citibank if Turkey repudiated its debts, Wallich even echoed the words that Wriston would be pilloried for a few years later. If Turkey was "in such straits," he said, it would conclude that its future rested on its credit standing. "No country can duck below the waves or disappear from the surface of the earth, unlike a corporation, which goes out of business."

Wriston would have appreciated Wallich's response to Senator William Proxmire. Wallich cited Cuba as an extreme situation, in which the banks lost all of their assets but also declined to assume responsibility for their liabilities. Echoing Wriston, he said, "You would have to think of the utterly unlikely event of a whole range of countries doing something similar before you reach a real problem." And, he added, "the outstanding loans will, of course, in the normal course of events all be paid, but that does not mean that the country is getting out of debt." Because these are growing, capital-importing countries, he said, new loans are being added while others are being paid off.

But Proxmire would prove to be the most prophetic economist of them all when he asked, "Isn't it more likely that you're going to have a coincidence of recession or prosperity in most countries?"

While acknowledging that this could occur, Wallich emphasized the "substantial differences" among the borrowing countries in their adjustment to higher oil prices.

In fact, in at least one instance the U.S. government discouraged the World Bank from extending loans so that commercial banks could make them instead. In the mid-1970s, one source said, the Secretary of the Treasury told former World Bank president Robert S. McNamara that the U.S. government did not want the World Bank, as the lender of last resort, lending to Colombia. That, the cabinet officer said, was the job of the commercial banks. Colombian finance minister Rodrigo Botero was one of the few Latin finance officials who resisted the temptation to borrow large amounts of short-term high-cost money for domestic consumption and white elephant–type projects. Botero wanted to initiate long-term development projects with long-term World Bank–type money. "I think you're wrong, and Rodrigo is right," McNamara told the Treasury secretary. "And, number two, you don't run this bank. This is subject to the board." The United States had 20 percent of the votes on the World Bank board.

"We're not going to allow it," the Treasury secretary shot back.

"You get your votes and I'll get mine," McNamara replied. McNamara is said to have prevailed.

Wriston was far more concerned about his domestic portfolio and his ventures in the United Kingdom and Australia than he was about Zaire or Peru.

Citibank's total problem loans had risen in 1976 to a tad over $2 billion, up 15 percent in that year. Outside the United States, troubled loans nearly doubled, to $691 million. Take, for example, real estate. From practically nothing in 1970, Citi's commercial real estate loans had skyrocketed to $3 billion in 1975. By the end of 1976, nonperforming U.S. real estate assets amounted to $1.1 billion, more than half of Citicorp's total nonperforming loans, according to internal company documents.

As the glut in the tanker market took hold, Citibank also suffered sharp losses in shipbuilding, but other banks lost their entire portfolios. At the peak of the concern over shipping losses, Citibank initially declined to disclose the extent of the problem. Consequently, the story threatened to erupt far out of proportion to the size of the write-offs. Amid a barrage of media calls, a bank flack tracked Wriston down at an indoor tennis court in Queens, where he was playing with his friend Mike Wallace. Called off the court, Wriston ordered, "Give them the numbers." The problem quickly went away.

Meanwhile, the market in loans to citizens band radio makers was tanking. "When we decided everyone wanted a CB radio, we overestimated . . . how fast manufacturers and suppliers would grow," recalled former Citibanker George Davis.

Overseas, the troubles with the Industrial Acceptance Corporation continued to fester. Citicorp would have to ante up about $29 million after tax to control that problem. Citibank's efforts to prop up FNCB-Waltons pitted Wriston against his nemesis Arthur Burns, as always obsessed with micromanaging the nation's banking system. When an Australian co-lender wrote some bad real estate loans, Citibank was forced to infuse its share—$3.5 million (Australian)—into Waltons. Although Citibank officials scurried to Washington to inform the Fed, central bank documents show that Fed officials were upset by Citibank's handling of the incident. Apparently, the Fed thought Citibank was trying to circumvent its approval process over the injection of the $3.5 million, and Wriston had to fly to Phoenix to confer with Burns over the incident.

In London, Grindlays was still a mess. Besides owning a pile of troubled real estate, its Oxford-educated merchant bankers wouldn't have anything to do with the Grindlays commercial bankers, most of whom were Scots with only a high school education. Victor Prall, among others, was assigned to work on the problem. One of his first acts was to consolidate everyone into the same building. "They would not sit down at the same table with each other. I had to knock some heads together," he said later. He used clever tactics to get out of some of the bad loans. Since Brandts had lent money to an Argentine department store, Prall was able to work out a swap with the central bank. Brandts had also lent to a holding company for a nearly defunct Brazilian bank. The Brazilian central bank said it would bail out any Brazilian bank, but not a bank holding company. By this time Brazil was beginning to experience some trouble borrowing. In return for a loan to Brazil, Prall persuaded the central bank to assume the guarantee of the bank for the loan to the holding company.

By now *Business Week,* in its November 7, 1977, issue, was proclaiming that "the glory days" were over at Citicorp. As Wriston's Citicorp was gearing up to prepare a new ten-year plan, Wriston could boast that his 1971 goal of 15 percent compound earnings growth had been met—sometimes. Since 1974, Wriston had failed to meet his covenant with Wall Street. And in 1977, Citicorp suffered its first earnings decline—6.5 percent—since 1961.

Wriston took solace in the assertion by Peter Drucker that "even the most competent management bats around .300, at best, in dealing with innovation and planning for the future."

Meanwhile, the IMF—the one official agency that was empowered to make balance-of-payments loans—was still perfectly content to let Walter Wriston do the heavy lifting, and Wriston was delighted to oblige.

In Moore's view, the IMF and World Bank had weak leadership. "They . . . said, 'If Walter Wriston is ready to do it, why should we?' "

To get the IMF's help and attention, said Robert Hormats, a former deputy assistant secretary of state for economic and business affairs, "You had to be in intensive care." During the mid to late 1970s, the IMF was in part diverted by the problems of Italy and the United Kingdom, but by 1977 many bankers were calling for the IMF to do more.

Burns was troubled by the minor role the IMF had played in the adjust-ment process, and by the stinginess of OPEC in helping the LDCs. He took the Arabs to task for their greed. In 1977, a number of Arab states created an Arab Monetary Fund to help other Arab countries suffering from balance-of-payments difficulties, but it was not until 1981 that the Arab banks even participated in loan syndications to other borrowers.

At an April 1977 meeting in Washington, the Interim Committee of IMF Board of Governors voted 14 billion in special drawing rights (SDRs), or $16.2 billion, for the Witteveen facility, a special line of credit named for the former IMF chief and earmarked for hard-pressed non-oil-producing LDCs. Major contributions were to come from the oil-exporting nations, in particular Saudi Arabia, and from major industrial nations, including the United States and West Germany. The *Wall Street Journal* on September 26, 1977, blasted the facility as a "bailout plan for the big banks." But State and Treasury wanted Congress to approve the facility so that the commercial banks would keep the money flowing to these borrowers. Other than the oil facility, there was no serious attempt to get international institutions in-volved on a major scale.

Even though IMF and World Bank delegations traveled to these Third World countries every year and produced voluminous reports, the data on which the entire world financial system was hanging were still paltry indeed. Nor did the IMF enforce its own rules concerning the timeliness of reporting national statistics, according to former deputy secretary of the Treasury Rob-ert Carswell, a former Shearman & Sterling attorney. But he said the real mistake was "lending without an adequate notion of where the funds were going to be used and what the country's programs were." Former Citicorp chairman George Moore said the central banks published false figures and, in the case of the Philippines, issued them eight months late. All this prompted the Fed and other central banks, led by the Bank for International Settle-ments, to organize an effort to gather additional data on credit volume and debt maturities on a country-by-country basis and to share that information with private lenders.

Jacques de Larosière would later say that not long after he took over as managing director of the IMF in 1978, "I was somewhat disturbed by figures of mounting indebtedness." He recalled that in 1979 he asked his executive committee, "Isn't this whole situation getting out of hand?" and suggested a paper on LDC debt. The resulting paper said essentially, "Don't worry—growth is very good." The argument was that interest rates, while high, were still negative relative to inflation and to the prices of exported commodities. "We should have been perhaps more wary on the dangers of the accumula-tion [of debt]," de Larosière said later. Although the International Monetary Fund urged more adjustment, "maybe we didn't do it forcefully enough," he admitted. "It was difficult because the world was absolutely awash with money." And even if the IMF *had* been more forceful, said de Larosière, "I don't think it would have made much difference." That view was reflected in the sign that was displayed at one IMF meeting. It read: "Who's listening?" But de Larosière didn't believe that the IMF should play a larger lending role. "We were not a long-term lending institution," he said. "I think it was right to keep the focus on the short- to medium-term balance-of-payments problems of the country. That's basically what we did."

One reason that American banks felt comfortable about lending to developing countries was certainly the kid gloves treatment these loans had always gotten from the regulators. And one reason they received this treatment was the influence and intervention of Wriston and Citibank. Unlike questionable domestic loans, which were classified "other asset especially mentioned" (OAEM), substandard, doubtful, or loss, depending on the likelihood of recovery, country loans, at least until the late 1970s, generally escaped being treated in a way that would force a bank to acknowledge a loss on them.

In fact, as the banks were shoveling their money out the door, a fierce debate was raging among bank regulators on whether such special treatment was really appropriate and whether banks should be required to set aside reserves based on their exposure to such countries—just as if they were W. T. Grant or Penn Central. Had the debate been settled earlier, and in favor of tough rather than lenient treatment, the course of world financial history would have been markedly different.

According to Paul Homan, then a top official at the Office of the Comptroller of the Currency, the debate over country classification had its origins at the California regional office of the Comptroller's office in the late 1960s, well before the 1973 oil shock and the first wave of massive U.S. bank lending to developing countries. At that time, the California office, which was run by a tough-minded regional administrator, began tagging a few countries, notably Argentina, with the "other assets especially mentioned" or "substandard" labels. Said Homan, "Argentina was always a problem or potential problem," but never so serious at that early stage as to force the issue of placing it in the "doubtful" or "loss" category, which would have called for the banks to write down 50 to 100 percent of their Argentine loans. Meanwhile, the nationally chartered New York and Chicago banks got off scot free on the same loans because the officials of the Comptroller's office were opposed to country classification.

Eventually the conflict was resolved in favor of classification. But then national banks cried foul, because the Comptroller's standards were tougher than those imposed on state-chartered banks, which are regulated by state banking departments and the Federal Reserve Board or the Federal Deposit Insurance Corporation, depending on whether they are members of the Fed system. According to former deputy Comptroller William Martin, the Comptroller's office tended to be "hard-line," the Fed "moderate," and the FDIC "confused."

On this issue, the Fed was also betwixt and between. The regulators knew that as soon as a particular country's debt became classified, that country would be less inclined to pay it off.

In 1976 the Comptroller of the Currency and the Fed set up separate rating systems for foreign loans that assigned different labels to the same countries. The OCC concluded that loans to several countries should be classified "substandard," while the Fed assigned that label to just one country. This prompted the General Accounting Office to suggest a single system for classification for all the bank agencies.

"OAEM" and "substandard" weren't terribly controversial—the "substandard" label would be a call to stop new lending—but the "doubtful" label certainly was.

The national bank examiners felt insecure about their ability to evaluate countries. Though they viewed countries like Zaire as clear cut, the examiners approached others, like Brazil, with a feeling of inadequacy. Martin and others at the OCC and the Fed were nervous about debt-laden Brazil, where inflation was running at a double-digit clip. "We sort of said, 'This doesn't look so good. It couldn't go on forever,' " Martin said later. "It was still a really glamorous country at that time. We were afraid to say anything [for fear that] people would laugh at us."

Countries applied diplomatic pressure to force the banking agencies to rescind classification decisions. Whenever the OCC classified a country, Martin said, "the bankers would tell the countries. They'd tell their ambassadors. The ambassadors would tell [former secretary of state Henry] Kissinger, and Kissinger would call the OCC." A battle royal raged over classifying Mexico. "The first big foreign exchange crisis in Mexico was very sobering," said one former regulator. At one point, according to a former top Fed official, the Mexican ambassador called on Kissinger to run interference with the bank regulators. Meanwhile, the official said, Citibank also threatened to call the State Department. At about this time, Mexico found a big oil field. "We were looking at them pretty closely; then came the oil discovery," Martin recalled. "That was going to save Mexico."

Argentina, meanwhile, alternated back and forth between OAEM (other asset especially mentioned) and substandard, prompting on at least one occasion a visit to Comptroller Smith from the Argentine ambassador.

Citibank, of course, was vehemently opposed to country classification, and lobbied the issue heavily in Washington. "Wriston did scream his head off," Martin recalled. Citibank argued, he said, that if a country "can never be a loss, how can it be substandard?"

Wriston and Kissinger became friends while Kissinger was secretary of state under Nixon and Ford. After Kissinger left government in 1976, that relationship deepened, aided by the proximity of their country homes in northwestern Connecticut and their apartments on Manhattan's East Side. Kissinger later acknowledged that he would have been receptive to such arguments.

What really brought the country classification issue to public attention was the move by the Comptroller of the Currency to classify Italy, then in the midst of an economic crisis. That made it the first industrial country to be classified, affecting all credit, public and private. While that didn't require a write-down by the banks, it did deter banks from making any additional loans to the country. Opponents of classifying industrialized countries argued that it should not be done because those countries could generate foreign exchange.

This confusion was resolved, at least for the time being, in the late 1970s with the creation of an obscure but influential bank agency called the Interagency Country Exposure Review Committee. This agency was an attempt to bring uniformity and fairness to the classification process. Made up of nine members, three from each major agency, this review committee met about four times a year. It wasn't empowered to act on its own but made recommendations to the heads of the agencies.

When regulators began collecting data on bank country exposure, they were often stunned by what they found. On one occasion, FDIC official Christie Sciacca was startled to receive a report from a $2 billion institution reporting $40 million in loans to troubled Jamaica. Sciacca immediately phoned the bank's executive vice president, demanding to know why he had that much exposure in Jamaica. "The guy was perplexed," said Sciacca later, and denied that his bank had any loans there. As it turned out, the bank had $40 million in Eurodollar deposits in the Cayman Islands, an offshore banking center most often used by big banks to book deposits and make international loans. The bank couldn't find the Caymans on the regulators' list, "so we looked on a map and Jamaica was closest," the banker said. "We figured it was close enough for government work."

The regulators set up a matrix showing bank loan concentrations for countries in three categories: major industrial nations, a mid-level group of industrial countries, and less developed countries. A large concentration in a strong country was more acceptable than a smaller concentration in a weak country. As a rule of thumb, Sciacca said, regulators figured that a bank should have not more than 5 percent of capital tied up in loans to a weak country.

In seeking an appropriate number to reserve for country debt, the banks assembled what in effect were baskets of basket-case countries against which they would take general reserves. That avoided the problem of pointing a finger at a specific country and requiring the bank to take a loan loss provision.

The process for evaluating foreign exposure, former Fed chairman Paul Volcker said later, was a "very intelligent system. Did it work? No. It tried to give cautionary signals where human beings were either looking for a green or red signal. It said we want to give you various degrees of amber. It was intended to moderate [foreign lending] without killing it. It fell short of moderating, and sure didn't kill it."

Inside as well as outside Citibank, Wriston's view that countries don't disappear clearly dominated the discussion. Adding to Wriston's confidence was his faith in the bank's country risk unit as an early warning system. If Citibank officials who were not involved in international lending had any misgivings about LDC exposure, they apparently didn't express them to their colleagues. In Citibank's permissive, chaotic culture, managers of different businesses avoided interfering in their colleagues' activities. "People let other people run their own things," said John Reed. During the controversy on foreign debt, "I was as quiet as a field mouse," he added. "I was trying to keep from drowning in the red ink in my business."

One top Citibank manager who did have second thoughts about overseas lending was Tom Theobald, then head of the World Corporation Group. By the late 1970s, Theobald was becoming increasingly alarmed, according to former associates, about the surge in cross-border lending. His caution was suspect, however, because, as head of the multinational group, Theobald was seen as a rival of George Vojta, then chief of the International Banking Group. "At the time," said former Citibanker Byron Stinson, "it appeared that Theobald was being overshadowed by this thing called government lending. . . . We weren't listening to him because of the theory that LDCs can't get into trouble."

Directors occasionally asked Wriston whether Citibank was overexposed in the Third World, but as former director and Du Pont chairman Irving Shapiro recalled, "The response was always the same: 'Governments never go broke.' " Referring to Wriston's 15 percent earnings growth goal, Shapiro said, "In a sense you did what you had to do to get that."

At board meetings, Wriston assured directors that Citibank was protected by its early warning system, the country risk unit, which Citibank had invented. But many had serious doubts about the effectiveness of that unit. "Look at Peru," Wriston said later. "We picked that one up early and cranked it down very rapidly. Our exposure in Peru would have been very much higher without [the country risk unit]." Citibank also got out of Bolivia early by persuading other banks to assume its dollar loans. But one international lending expert at Citibank recalled, "You didn't get a whole lot of thanks for that. You make money by putting loans on," she said, not cutting exposure levels.

"Latin America for Wriston was a blind spot, but he was the best banker in the country," former senior deputy Comptroller of the Currency Paul Homan said later. "Citibank always followed the laws of large numbers. They could be slowed down but never badly hurt," he said. Citibank would later wish that were true.

18

DISNEYLAND ON THE POTOMAC

*W*riston's 1971 decision to court Wall Street meant that he would have to break bread with the financial press as well. He later inaugurated a tradition in which reporters would dine leisurely with him and his colleagues, then end the evening with fine cigars and cordials. The highlight of the occasion was the "Fearless Forecast," in which journalists would attempt to predict the gross national product, consumer price index, and other key economic indicators for the next twelve months. One evening in early 1976, the last question was "Who would be the winner of the Democratic primaries and the general election?"

Those who knew Wriston best did not regard political savvy as his forte. But Andrew Tobias later wrote in the June 1976 issue of *Esquire* that Wriston said his "money was on Carter," while Tobias picked Hubert Humphrey as the Democratic nominee and Ford as the winner.

If Wriston had any inside information about Carter's prospects, it would most likely have come from Du Pont chairman and chief executive Irving Shapiro, the resident Democrat on the Citicorp board and one of America's most influential businessmen.

When Jimmy Carter blew into Washington in January 1977, few leading businessmen had even met the Georgia governor, much less forged a friendship with him. Shapiro and General Electric chairman Reginald Jones were the closest links the business community had to Carter.

As Wriston got to know the President, he became less and less impressed with his policies. Wriston admired Carter's keen intellect and graciousness, however. Wriston, Shapiro, Reg Jones, and a small cadre of top business leaders would occasionally gather in the family dining room of the White House, where Carter would grill them on everything from the economy to the Clearing House Interbank Payments System (CHIPS), which Wriston had helped set up. Despite their party differences, Wriston and Carter were soul mates on some issues dear to Wriston's heart. Carter had come to Washington as a believer in deregulation, and he did in fact substantially decontrol the airline and trucking industries. And Carter shared with

Wriston an aversion to government red tape and paperwork.

Nonetheless, to Wriston, Carter's Washington was "Disneyland on the Potomac." Despite his attempts to appear friendly to big business, Carter alienated Wriston and others in the business community in a variety of ways, and Wriston came to regard Carter's performance in economic policy as among the worst of any American president. Carter signaled his economic views early in the race. "I'd put my emphasis on employment and take my chances on inflation," he said, making clear his preference for expansionist policies to further his social goals.

While businessmen did talk to the Carter White House, they were troubled that the administration had no coherent plan for the economy. "Stu [Eisenstadt] talks to us," Wriston told *Fortune* magazine in January 1978. "So does Juanita [Kreps], Mike [Blumenthal] and Charlie [Schultze]. So they wonder, 'Why don't you love me when we invite you to the dance every day?' " Wriston then explained why: "We—and the markets—want a logical consistent strategy. Not conversations about pieces of a plan. So the dialogue has broken down. They believe they've told us what we want to hear. But the markets say not."

In contrast to Carter and his economic advisers, Arthur Burns was opposed to overstimulation of the economy. In a statement before the House Budget Committee weeks after Carter took office, he said, "It seems doubtful to me, as I have previously indicated, that any special efforts to stimulate growth—at least any of a conventional character—are now needed to ensure broad economic expansion this year and on into 1978. I realize that a majority of this committee, as well as the able members of President Carter's economic team, feel differently." Unfortunately for the economy, Burns was probably not as opposed as he should have been to overstimulation.

At about the time Carter was launching his deregulation drive, Wriston and Citibank were shifting theirs into high gear.

Led by Angermueller, Citibank in 1978 formalized its attack on regulation. The new approach was incorporated into the acronym TARGS, which stood for tax, activities, Regulation Q, geography, and supervision. One of the hot buttons was reserve requirements, which called for banks to maintain a portion of their deposits as reserves with the Fed. Citibank regarded this as a non-interest-bearing form of taxation. Glass-Steagall and insurance were federal issues, whereas geographic expansion was largely a state matter. The idea was to challenge each in a way that was most suitable for the "laws you're trying to attack," Hans Angermueller said later. "Walter Wriston didn't come in and say, 'Here are all the targets. Pick up your shields and charge.' It was an evolutionary thing to think we could influence our own environment."

Wriston even appealed to his shareholders at annual meetings to pressure legislators to end rules that discriminated against banks. While some writers viewed banks as a powerful lobby, that was not how Wriston and Citibank saw things. Though they sometimes managed to kill or modify legislation that they considered ridiculous, they were not especially effective on Capitol Hill in advancing the cause of competitive equality. Part of the problem was Citibank's arrogance.

Still, Wriston pressed his case every chance he got. In January 1977 he succeeded Morgan chairman Pat Patterson on the Federal Reserve Advisory Council, a panel of high-powered bankers that served as a kind of sounding board for the chairman and the board. Ken Guenther, a former Fed staff member, claimed that the "twelve fat-cat bankers" enjoyed "access to the board that no one [else] in the world [has]. It's undemocratic as hell."

Wriston was bored by much of the agenda, notably the economic briefings, and was absent from many of the meetings, according to council minutes. When he did attend, however, he never hesitated to needle the Fed chairman. Under Burns, members of the advisory council had to suffer through an obligatory briefing that was considerably less sophisticated than what the bankers would have received from their own staff economists. "I told Burns that [we could have gotten] the economic briefing . . . from Mike Jensen [an NBC economics correspondent] on channel [4]. We said, 'You know, we read the *New York Times.* We don't need economic briefings. They don't add anything to our knowledge. We live in the marketplace. What we want to do is talk about the issues.' He was very upset about that."

High on Wriston's wish list was eliminating reserves on deposits. The Fed, he said in a 1977 speech to the Columbia Business School Club, is "the most profitable corporation in the world." The previous year it had earned $6 billion. "You could make it too if you didn't pay anything for your inventory. Citibank's got $1.2 billion every day over in the stone palace [the Federal Reserve building] on which we get zero." Wriston figured that belonging to the Fed cost Citibank $100 million in 1976. Thanks to reserve requirements, banks that had a choice were canceling their membership in the central bank at a rapid clip. Wriston was pushing for an alternative package deal in which the banks could pay depositors interest on checking accounts while the Fed would pay interest on bank reserves.

What especially galled Wriston and other U.S. bankers was that foreign banks operating in the United States were getting off scot-free. That meant they could lend money more cheaply than U.S. banks. As a result, in just over five years, the number of foreign banks and facilities approximately doubled, and by 1978, foreign banks accounted for about 25 percent of the outstanding commercial and industrial loans. But as Wriston told *Institutional Investor,* "I'm the last guy you'll ever hear cry about competition. What I'd like to do is, instead of trying to put handcuffs on foreign banks, take the handcuffs off us."

The Fed concurred—to a point. It was not about to take the shackles off U.S. banks, but it agreed with Wriston and others that the playing field had to be leveled, to recall the overused metaphor of the era. Not surprisingly, the Fed emerged as the leader in the push for a bill to make foreign banks pay for deposit insurance and keep reserves with it.

Wriston also lashed out at the regulators over paperwork and legal burdens, declaring in an August 1977 speech before the American College of Trial Lawyers, "Not only do we not know what the law is, we cannot afford to find out. The rich may be able to hire enough lawyers to read at least some of the laws and regulations that pour out of government at all levels, but the poor find out only by being accosted in the street." In one day, Wriston said, "no less than 242 committees and subcommittees were in session for a legislative purpose. No wonder they produce such an indigestible mass of legislation."

Egged on by their litigious chairman, Citicorp lawyers fought other battles in the courts like legal gladiators. When Citicorp moved into the data processing business, selling computer time to other companies, it trampled the toes of the time-sharing industry. ADAPSO, the computer trade group, sued Citibank on the grounds that it represented "illegal" competition at "ruinously low prices." That case would smolder for years.

Citibank contributed to at least one legislative success on the fringes of banking. No institution had been more involved in the major bankruptcy cases of the era than Citibank. So it was fitting that workout man John Ingraham should have a hand in helping to reform the bankruptcy code to emphasize rehabilitation rather than liquidation.

Another way Wriston hoped to level the field—for banks as well as for the United States—was through an international banking center, or banking free trade zone, in New York that would make it competitive with Singapore, London, Nassau, and other offshore funding centers. The idea was to enable U.S. banks to take deposits and make foreign loans without being subject to state or local taxes or reserve requirements. Citibank figured that fifty thousand jobs would be created in New York if this came to pass. Several years earlier the Fed had rejected a similar proposal on the grounds that it would undermine Fed control of domestic money and credit as funds were shifted to such branches. In a July 15, 1977, letter to Burns, Wriston resurrected the idea, he wrote, to help New York "regain its position as the financial center of the world." In a memo written ten days later, Fed staff pooh-poohed the proposal, saying the center would likely replace lending and deposit business "already occurring at domestic banking offices."

The bill authorizing international banking free trade zones passed the New York State legislature in 1978 with flying colors. In part, that reflected Citibank's slick new approach to dealing with legislators. The bank had managed to win over New York State speaker Stanley Steingut, a die-hard New Deal Democrat and an unlikely bankers' ally. Rumor had it, according to Bill Spencer, that "Citibank had Stanley by the throat. Like many rumors, this one had a grain of truth to it." At a luncheon at Citibank—probably the first time a Democrat from Brooklyn had ever dined there—Steingut soiled his tie and asked if someone could get him another one. "The inimitable [corporate secretary] Carl Desch went away and got one, only this one was a Citibank tie and when Steingut left that afternoon, he was a walking advertisement." Steingut wound up becoming the bill's sponsor. It took another three years to sell the Fed on the idea, and in December 1981 the first IBF finally opened.

But in the end, a former Fed official said, "I don't think [the IBFs] mattered much."

Jimmy Carter also swept into office believing that the U.S. government should be a force to push for an end to human rights abuses around the world. During the campaign, he had singled out Brazil for special attention as a violator of human rights, and in early 1977 First Lady Rosalynn Carter, during a visit to Brazil, met with American missionaries who had been abused by officials there. That meeting didn't help the already strained Brazilian-U.S. relations. In an independent study early in the Carter administration, researchers concluded that six major banks, including Citibank, also helped prop up Chile's repressive Pinochet regime and effectively sabotaged Carter's human rights policy. Argentina, another major borrower, also had a dismal human rights record. But Citibank had a long-standing policy of ignoring morality and politics in choosing where to operate and lend money. The bank opted not to do business in such a country only if the nation's policies jeopardized its creditworthiness.

In the case of Brazil, with $27 billion in foreign loans, including $10 billion from private commercial banks, the international banks had replaced the U.S. Treasury as the source of the country's foreign aid. As the *Washington Post* wrote on March 30, 1977, Brazil could now thumb its nose at State Department accusations of human rights violations. But while Wriston and his bank may have made Carter's human rights policy more difficult to execute, he was instrumental in resolving a related issue—the Arab boycott of Israel—that was dear to Carter's heart. The boycott had been in effect since the creation of Israel after World War II, but the issue had intensified with the quadrupling of oil prices and the resulting surge in trade between the United States and the Mideast—to the point where it had emerged as an emotional issue in the 1976 presidential campaign, when Carter backed tough anti-boycott legislation while Ford opposed it.

It became virtually impossible for commercial transactions to get done without dealing with the boycott, and given the huge volume of business being done in the Middle East, the issue had significant economic consequences. Without doubt, the boycott had cost the United States in terms of lost exports. In a very practical sense, the big commercial banks were in the thick of the issue and couldn't avoid leaving a paper trail implicating them for tacitly bowing to the boycott. As the world's preeminent international bank, Citibank probably was more deeply involved in facilitating trade, notably as an issuer of commercial letters of credit, in the Middle East than any other financial institution. (Letters of credit authorize a bank to pay an exporter as soon as the conditions set by the buyer and seller are met.)

The banks became the target of demands for information from government panels, both federal and New York State, which were seeking to find ways to break the boycott. Citibank general counsel Hans Angermueller was summoned to testify as to Citibank's role in the boycott before a New York State legislative committee considering a state anti-boycott law. Angermueller testified that this was a federal matter and that it would be silly for states to pass a host of slightly varying laws. Ironically, for most banks, letters of credit were more trouble than they were worth. Banks issued them largely as an accommodation for customers; the profits they generated were relatively small, particularly when measured against the mass of litigation that they gave rise to.

Incidentally, the Jewish groups might have been even more incensed if they knew of certain other transactions that had nothing to do with the boycott. According to a senior Citibank officer, Citibank in the early 1970s received an order to establish a letter of credit for Lebanon to purchase machine gun bullets from a U.S. munitions maker. The request triggered a series of frantic closed-door meetings. Officers wrung their hands over what would happen if Jewish employees in Citibank's back offices discovered the documents. There would, they feared, be pickets out in front of Citibank headquarters. According to the Citibank officer, the executive in charge of that unit was known for creative solutions. He ordered the paperwork processed through the Houston Edge Act office, where the bank employed few, if any, Jews.

In late 1976, as the pressure grew for anti-boycott legislation, tension mounted between business groups, which didn't want to be saddled with yet another set of well-intentioned but unworkable rules, and Jewish groups, which wanted the toughest law they could get without precipitating an anti-Semitic backlash. Meanwhile, the Saudis had apparently gotten the message that they had better soften their line or they would face punishing legislation. One of the first indications of Saudi Arabia's change of attitude came shortly after the November election in a phone call to Wriston from Frank Jungers, chairman and chief executive of the Arabian-American Oil Company (Aramco), in which Jungers indicated that the Saudis would like to find ways to improve relations with the United States.

Wriston's links with the incoming Carter regime were, of course, tangential at best. The one man he knew he could count on to deliver Jungers's message to the White House was veteran State Department adviser Max Kampelman. In a phone conversation several weeks after the election, Wriston told Kampelman of his discussions with Aramco, and invited him to meet with him and Angermueller in New York to discuss how the Saudis might proceed. Shortly thereafter, Wriston introduced Kampelman to Jungers. Kampelman felt that the place to begin was with Zbigniew Brzezinski, who was expected to become Carter's national security adviser. Kampelman quickly arranged the meeting with Brzezinski.

Citicorp director Irving Shapiro had also gotten into the loop. Besides being the closest link between the Carter administration and the business community, Shapiro was also Jewish and savvy in the ways of Washington. Jewish organizations also agreed that the participation of Anti-Defamation League national chairman Burton Joseph, a grain company executive, was vital.

Influential Democrats didn't want the Carter administration to become bogged down at the outset in a nasty fight over the Arab boycott of Israel. Shortly after the inauguration, Shapiro convened a group of CEOs that included the heavies of American business. Besides Wriston, the group included Exxon chairman Clifton C. Garvin, Jr.; Thomas Murphy, chairman of General Motors; Reginald Jones, head of General Electric; H. Brewster Atwater, president of General Mills; David Rockefeller of Chase, and George Shultz, then chairman of Bechtel. On January 28, 1977, at a meeting hosted by Seagram chairman Edgar Bronfman, a leading supporter of Israel and backer of Jewish causes, at his company's Midtown Manhattan headquarters, the mostly WASP senior statesmen of American business faced off against top officials of the Anti-Defamation League. In a meeting that lasted nearly all day, the conferees discussed such things as the arcane legal aspects of letters of credit. But it was, at times, an emotional gathering, with the leaders of the Jewish community arguing passionately against the boycott and for close ties between the United States and Israel. The result was the formation of a working group, to be led by Hans Angermueller, representing U.S. business, and Kampelman, leading the effort on behalf of the Jewish community, to forge a compromise between the two groups that would produce a joint set of principles.

Angermueller, in turn, recruited international lawyer John Hoffman of Shearman & Sterling, to work on the problem on a day-to-day basis. In contrast to cool and calm Angermueller, the wiry John Hoffman was a scrappy, rough-and-tumble litigator. Out of often stormy negotiations with lawyers for the Jewish groups, Hoffman and his counterparts from the outside law firms for GE and Du Pont hammered out a two-page statement of principles that became the blueprint for legislation.

Inevitably, word leaked out about the meeting at Seagram. As John Hoffman recalls, both the Carter administration and Congress were delighted that the representatives of the two groups with the greatest stake in the issue were thrashing it out. Politically, the boycott was a prickly issue for Congress and the White House. Congress, said Hoffman later, was perfectly content to avoid a heated confrontation on the floor on such a no-win matter. Carter assigned Stu Eisenstadt, his domestic policy adviser, who was close to Kampelman, to be point man for the effort.

The Saudis, meanwhile, were seeking to calm the waters without appearing to lose face. "The Saudis had their own [information] pipeline," Shapiro said later. "They knew what the game was and who was playing it." If the business leaders were to make some headway with the Jewish groups, Shapiro knew they would have to get the Saudis to halt some of the most infuriating Arab practices. Through Aramco, Shapiro passed that message on to the Saudis, and a few days later received an oblique reply indicating that the Arabs had decided on their own to stop their most offensive activities.

By the end of February the committee had hammered out the principles, accomplished, as one author put it, in a "self-congratulatory" atmosphere. Once the draft statement of principles was agreed upon, Wriston, Garvin, Jones, and Shapiro led the way in enlisting the backing of the Business Roundtable's policy committee, while their counterparts in the Jewish organizations lined up support among their constituents.

When the vote was taken, only three CEOs, notably Mobil chairman Raleigh Warner and Lee L. Morgan, chairman of Caterpillar Tractor Company, voted against adopting the legislation, according to Shapiro. Warner, said Shapiro, was on the Caterpillar board, and "delivered that CEO." Warner was playing up to the Arabs. "It was very naive," Shapiro said later.

The fragility of the agreement between the Jewish leaders and the businessmen began to emerge in congressional hearings to consider amendments to the Export Administration Act. Jack Yingling, Citicorp's lobbyist in Washington, was following the proceedings closely. The Business Roundtable and the Jewish leadership had told Senator Adlai Stevenson III that they had reached a compromise, and Stevenson was going along with it.

As the anti-boycott amendments went into markup sessions in late March, it appeared that the pact would fall through because "the Jewish leadership had not carried out their commitment," Yingling said. Shapiro later told the *Washington Post* of April 1 that the ADL–Business Roundtable negotiations were "a romance that has outlived its usefulness." By early April, as Congress was getting ready to leave for the Easter recess, the pact was "going to hell in a handbasket," Shapiro said.

The statement of principles contained prohibitions against several kinds of pro-boycott offenses: discriminating against American citizens on the basis of race, religion, sex, ethnic or national origins; providing information about an American citizen's background or presence or absence on a blacklist; and complying with secondary or tertiary boycotts. Significantly, the principles didn't forbid American citizens from complying with the laws of a country that barred imports from certain other countries. But the exporter who buckled under orders by importing countries not to export to a third country could be subject to criminal prosecution.

Even Shapiro was prompted to declare that the Jewish groups were reneging on a deal. Then, in an ironic twist, a New York lawyer with a name that couldn't have been more Germanic—Hans Angermueller—got a call from the head of the American Jewish Congress informing him that the Jewish Congress no longer trusted Shapiro. "You mean Hans Angermueller is going to be working on this and Irv Shapiro is not?" Angermueller asked incredulously.

"That *is* pretty ludicrous," the Jewish leader admitted.

Said Shapiro, "The interesting sidelight is that here was this very German guy dealing with this subject in a very sensitive way."

Wriston, meanwhile, was in Phoenix, and at two o'clock in the morning he received a call from another CEO involved in pushing the legislation. "This thing is off the track," the CEO reported, and implored Wriston to attend a meeting eight hours later in Management & Budget director Bert Lance's office in Washington. Wriston prepared to leave for Washington immediately.

In Bert Lance, Wriston and his business colleagues found a sympathetic ear. "This is crazy," Lance said. "You guys are completely right."

"He put on his hat, figuratively speaking, and walked out the door into the Oval Office" to convince Carter that he should proceed with plans to sign the bill, Wriston said later.

Lance "put the car back on track," Angermueller recalled, and everything came together in the White House situation room several weeks later.

On April 8, the Jewish organizations issued a joint statement criticizing the Carter administration for not backing tougher anti-boycott legislation. Seeking to keep the Jewish and business groups at arm's length, the White House rejected Shapiro's request for a meeting between the president, Wriston, Garvin, Shultz, and Shapiro himself, according to one published account. But about ten days later the Jewish leaders and business leaders reconvened and struck a new compromise. At the end of the month, Shapiro, Garvin, Shultz, and Wriston fired off cables to the Business Roundtable.

In June, Congress passed the anti-boycott amendments to the Export Administration Act with little opposition, and on June 22 President Carter signed them.

The pats on the back at the bill-signing ceremony in the White House Rose Garden didn't end the debate. The Jewish groups, to Shapiro's dismay, continued to seek to incorporate their tough stance in the regulations, which were to be written by the Commerce Department. "You had some people in the Jewish agencies who were wild" and couldn't be dealt with on any rational basis at all, Shapiro recalled.

"It was terribly emotional. People call you anti-Semitic," said Angermueller. Shapiro later defended the banks against accusations that they actually went along with the boycott, asserting that only a handful complied deliberately.

On January 18, 1978, the anti-boycott rules took effect. Shapiro himself was later called upon to explain to the Department of Commerce an apparent Du Pont violation of the very regulations he had helped draft. Citibank continued to be sensitive to the issue. In 1979 it pulled out of a $33 million syndication to Algeria when it heard that Banque Rothschild of Paris was being excluded from the group because of its Jewish origins.

If the Arab boycott episode left any doubt about the impact of big banks on the affairs of nations, it was ultimately dispelled by the role that U.S. banks played in forcing the hand of the South African government on the issue of apartheid. Unlike the boycott, which essentially left Wriston's radar screen after the passage of the anti-boycott legislation, South Africa was a lingering headache that he bequeathed to his successor in 1984.

For senior bank officials in South Africa, where Citibank operated branches, race was a major concern. One former officer who served there recalled that he spent 40 percent of his time on race-related matters. The bank attempted to make its operations in South Africa more like those of an American bank, while the South African government generally turned a blind eye to the anti-apartheid practices of Citibank and other American companies. In 1976, Citibank employed 215 people in South Africa, a fifth of them non-white. Former International executive George Vojta said in a 1976 article that starting salaries for blacks more than quadrupled from 1960 to 1974, while the pay of whites doubled. According to Wriston, Citibank was the first foreign organization in the country to establish a pension plan for blacks and was among the first banks to appoint black officers. It desegregated the bathrooms, teller lines, lobbies, and cafeterias.

A key force behind Citicorp's decision to remain in South Africa as long as it did was Citicorp director and Ford Foundation president Franklin Thomas, a black man who had conducted important studies of apartheid and had made many trips to South Africa. Thomas felt that Citicorp could be a greater force for change by staying than by leaving. That view was confirmed when Thomas, Bill and Kay Spencer, and Urban League head Vernon Jordan, a close friend of Wriston, traveled to South Africa in mid-1976 in the wake of anti-apartheid riots in the black townships. For Jordan and Thomas, the trip was an emotional experience. On a visit to a Xerox plant, for example, Jordan presented certificates to five black youths who had completed a training course, a ceremony replete with hugs and black power handshakes. "I decided I didn't have the right to come back to New York and vote those kids out of work to facilitate my own moral orgasm. If those kids had said we want you to pull out, I might have come to a different conclusion. But no one was telling me that," Jordan said later.

Accordingly, Wriston recalled, Thomas, Jordan, and Spencer advised Citibank to "keep doing what we had been doing all along—that is, press against the outer limits of the law." Still, he defended Citibank's right to lend money without regard to the value system of the country that received it. "The positive side of [South Africa's] credit position," he conceded, "is that diamonds and gold are relatively good exports. If we were to base our lending decisions on the purity of political systems, I'm not sure we could justify every loan we make to New York City."

Jordan said later that "Citibank took Frank's advice on disinvestment and on making loans to South Africa. Xerox took my advice about staying in South Africa and [doing] something beyond just training people—involving itself in the community."

Jordan and Thomas concluded that blacks would be hurt the most by the bank's departure. "If you're going to have a post-apartheid South Africa you need a black middle class. The presence of American companies is one guarantee of it," Jordan said.

The apartheid issue was not clearly understood by the religious and civil rights activists who urged institutional holders of Citicorp stock to divest their shares unless Citicorp left South Africa. The church groups opposing

Citibank's presence in South Africa irritated Wriston. "It was a dialogue of the deaf," Wriston said. "To accuse us of supporting [apartheid] when we had [employees from] every race known to man was ludicrous," he said later. "Our attitude was," one former bank officer said, "We're not going to let third parties tell us where we can do business." Still, the church groups created a kind of bargaining chip for Citibank in pressuring the South African government.

In early 1977, at about the same time Citibank was helping to draft the anti-boycott principles, it became one of the the early signers of the Sullivan Principles, named for the Reverend Leon Sullivan of Philadelphia's Zion Baptist Church. The intention was to promote fair employment practices and to end apartheid in South Africa. By early 1978, forty-nine other companies had signed up.

And in March 1978, Citibank upped the stakes by halting new lending to the government of South Africa and to companies controlled by the government. It said, however, that it would continue lending to private companies because they created jobs for all South Africans.

Indeed, big multinational banks like Citibank were always in a bind when it came to lending to any government, whether it was Brazil, Chile, Argentina, the Philippines, South Africa—or New York City.

The months of apparent fiscal tranquillity that followed New York State's spring refinancing ended on November 19, 1976, when the State Court of Appeals declared the moratorium unconstitutional under state law. "It was a great moratorium while it lasted," the *Daily News* headline read on November 22, 1976. "We stole that year," as New York governor Hugh Carey put it later. But now the city would have to repay all its notes in full. The court order gave the Municipal Assistance Corporation and the city ninety days to raise more than $1.8 billion, including $1 billion in short-term notes covered by the moratorium. Now, however, the city had a more sympathetic ear in the White House. "Bankruptcy is not a viable alternative for New York City," President-elect Carter told Carey at the time, "and we have eliminated that as a possibility."

When the court ruling was handed up, Mayor Abe Beame was touring Israel as head of a mayoral delegation. According to custom, Beame left a note at the Wailing Wall. The message was simple: "Help." On returning to his hotel, Beame received a frantic call from New York informing him of the court decision and he flew home on the next available flight.

He and MAC officials immediately went back to the table to try to persuade the banks and unions to buy more MAC bonds to refinance the $1 billion in short-term notes. Led by Wriston, the banks balked at the plan. They wanted to know the city's plans for closing its $500 million budget deficit. This was the time, they figured, to put pressure on the city to clean up its fiscal act now and forever. They demanded that the powers of MAC and the

Emergency Financial Control Board (which was due to expire June 30, 1978) be replaced with an even tougher Budget Review Board. They wanted tight controls on short-term debt, a debt service fund, and a contingency fund to make up for underestimated shortfalls. In mid-January 1977 the banks insisted on a five-year extension of the seasonal loans. There was plenty of justification for such demands. The city was run so poorly that it had a backlog of millions of dollars of unpaid parking tickets. "The banks put their collective foot down," said Beame later.

The battle lines were drawn when Beame, the unions, and MAC chairman Felix Rohatyn flatly rejected the banks' demands. "I won't stand for that," Beame said. "New York is not a child. . . . We're not going to be led by the hand all the time." The unions were furious at the proposal. They hated the EFCB because it hog-tied them in their contract negotiations. Like Beame, they wanted to get rid of it as soon as possible.

Union adviser Jack Bigel threatened that the pension funds would stop buying bonds until the banks clarified their position.

"We thought the banks were going too far," Rohatyn said later. He told the *New York Times,* "The banks are looking at the city as if it were an alcoholic coming out of an eight-month drying-out period. They're saying that, when the city takes its next step into the neighborhood bar, somebody better be around holding its hand." *Village Voice* columnist Jack Newfield denounced the banks' move in a January 31 story headlined "The Bankers' Plot: Taking Over New York for Good."

The city had to come up with $983 million, and the retirement system and the banks had to figure out a way to find $819 million. "It was a Mexican standoff," said Bigel. One of the problems in forging a consensus in New York, opined former Chase economist Karen Gerard, was the lack of a central power structure; the city had a different power elite for each sector: real estate, banking, retailing. But now these two key power centers—the banks and the unions—that had had little to do with each other before, were forced to sit down across the table from each other.

Their first face-to-face meeting, in late January 1977 at Gracie Mansion, the mayor's residence, was a motley gathering. On one side of the table were the WASPs of the nation's banking establishment: Wriston, Rockefeller, Pat Patterson of Morgan Guaranty, the official leader of the bank group, and Bankers Trust's Alfred Brittain III, a stiff, icy man whom Bigel referred to as "the Third" and who was "the most uptight," according to Victor Gotbaum. Patterson, he felt, was the "warmest of the bunch." On the other side were the union leaders, who were mostly Jews, Italians, and other "ethnics," as Gotbaum called them. Of the bankers, only Wriston had had much contact with union chieftains, but the city's labor leaders had no previous exposure to the blue-blood bankers. Gotbaum later recalled that he hadn't known the world of banking and finance at all before 1975 and resented having to meet with the bankers. "My first reaction was, 'Who are these bastards?' " he said. "We were all uptight with each other. It was a completely different world for both of us."

Then, in late February, things exploded in the Blue Room at City Hall. After the bankers and union leaders had met for several hours, Gotbaum recalls, a banker remarked that a proposal made by the unions "seems reasonable." In the kinds of negotiations in which Gotbaum had earned his spurs, such a statement by a city official would have established a point of no return, virtually locking the city into that position. But it soon became clear that this was not the bankers' intent. "This is awful," Beame whispered to Gotbaum, referring to the bankers' apparent about-face. In fact, the bankers hadn't budged from their initial position.

Gotbaum was not one to hide his emotions. Bolting from his chair, he shouted, "Shove it up your ass!" at the horrified bankers and stalked out of the room with Bigel in tow. The next day, March 1, 1977, the *Times* reported that Beame had accused the banks of dragging their feet and holding "a gun at our heads."

That evening at home, Gotbaum fumed to his wife Betsy about the moneymen. "This guy Wriston, he doesn't play from the top of the deck," he complained.

From his wife, a tennis pro and later New York City parks commissioner, Gotbaum got a lesson in noblesse oblige. "Victor, you're not so bright," she said. "They [the bankers] weren't misleading you. These are my people. They were just being polite. They're not like you. They don't get contentious when they disagree. They don't bang on the table."

"She was right," Gotbaum said later. For perhaps the first time, Gotbaum realized that perhaps some of the miscommunication between the bankers and the union men was his own fault.

But Wriston was unmoved by the union leaders' hostility to the bankers' proposal. Quoting Charles Sanford of Bankers Trust, he told securities analysts in early March, "As some fellow put it, the mayor can burn the book, but he can't kill the idea." Wriston said he expected the proposal to "rise Phoenix-like from the ashes sometime after the mayoral primaries." Wriston would later acknowledge that the bankers' demands were off base and politically naive.

The city was facing certain default in March 1977 if an agreement couldn't be reached. With no help from the banks and little from the unions, the city managed to overcome this crisis by speeding up the sale of mortgages on city properties and scraping up cash from other sources. But the city was still not out of the woods.

In the wake of that contentious meeting, union consultant Jack Bigel recognized that the city couldn't survive if the banks and the unions couldn't sit across the table from each other. "We may have won the rhetorical battle," he said, "but the war is still going on."

Although Pat Patterson was the official head of the bank delegation, Bigel decided to call Wriston, whom he viewed as the de facto leader of the bankers.

Bigel's secretary bet her boss that the nation's top banker wouldn't bother to return his phone call, but Wriston figured, as he said later, that "if

Sadat can talk to Begin, Bigel can talk to me." Wriston did return Bigel's call, inviting him to lunch at Citibank.

Bigel was impressed that Wriston didn't ask him what the agenda would be before extending the invitation. "I just said I had an idea," Bigel recalled. There were, however, a few conditions. Wriston asked Bigel to stop calling him a fascist. While denying that he ever uttered such a statement, Bigel told Wriston that he didn't take issue with Wriston's description of him as an "unregenerate socialist."

Bigel actually seemed to lead a dual life. His political preferences were clearly left-leaning, yet he had made a fortune advising union pension funds, and he lived in a luxury Fifth Avenue apartment. Hugh Carey later described Bigel as a "dyed-in-the-wool Marxian socialist" who became a capitalist. "If he were a capitalist full-time he'd make a lot of money."

For Bigel, his first one-on-one with Wriston was a revelation. "I'm a New Yorker too," Wriston told him. "I wasn't born with a silver spoon in my mouth." He reminded Bigel that his first job with Citibank had paid $3,000 a year. Bigel said later that bankers like Wriston, Rockefeller, and Patterson showed infinitely more genuine concern about the city's plight than did certain investment bankers—namely Peter G. Peterson, the co-CEO of Lehman Brothers who had been secretary of commerce in the Nixon administration. In one meeting, Peterson told Bigel that the " 'trial and tribulation would be good for the city,' and he didn't think he should play a role. I never forgot that," Bigel said later.

Out of Wriston and Bigel's meeting emerged the concept of an informal group of labor leaders and bankers that would meet regularly to discuss ways to end the crisis. Once the group was organized, Wriston said, "we all sat down together and decided you don't resolve problems by throwing stones at each other." The Labor-Management Committee was the model for the Municipal Union–Financial Leaders Group, or MUFLG—pronounced "Muffle." From its first meeting in April 1977, Muffle, at Wriston's suggestion, didn't include on its agenda items on which the members couldn't possibly agree. "There are some subjects we could just forget," said Wriston. "But after you put those aside there [was still] a whole range of issues that could be helped."

When bankers and union men walked into a Citibank conference room for their inaugural meeting, the tension was so thick it could have been cut with a knife. It was measurably reduced by the time they walked out, said Citibank economist George Roniger. "There were probably a lot of people thinking, 'Where's the curveball?' My reaction after the first meeting was that we didn't save the city, but we did walk out of the room with an understanding that we were not going to snipe at each other." For the union chiefs, the exercise would often prove awkward. They had staked out intractable positions with their members based on often erroneous data. No one knew how many employees there were, or the level of the deficit or debt.

One of the rules established at the outset was that Muffle was not to become a forum to enable one side to gain an edge over the other; there were

to be no reporters at the meetings, no press statements, and no press conferences. At one point, a top *New York Times* reporter stumbled on a story
based on one meeting that, if published, could have sabotaged Muffle. Wriston told the reporter, "You've got the ability to blow us out of the water. You
can kill it." The story never ran.

One matter that both sides could easily agree on was the debilitating
effects of welfare costs. The group even lobbied Congress for the interests of
New York City on such issues as taxation and welfare reform.

No one had any problem with a proposal on welfare. But for the
unions, taxes were the source of wage and payroll increases and, ultimately,
of power. The idea that lower taxes could produce more revenue and help
avoid destroying jobs was alien to them. George Roniger later recalled that
teachers union chief Albert Shanker expressed surprise that New York City
corporate and real estate taxes were so far out of line with those of the rest of
the country.

Incredibly, the heads of five unions signed a report saying that New
York's taxes were excessive. That report concluded, "Further cuts in taxes
are needed in coming years as part of a full, well thought out plan necessary
to hold, attract and create the jobs that are the very foundation of the city's
economic base." In a joint letter to Governor Carey, they urged that personal
and corporate income taxes be reduced, and in January 1978, Carey proposed and received a $1 billion tax cut.

"Why are you doing all these things?" Roniger once asked his boss.

"Because I live here," Wriston snapped.

While Muffle produced numerous papers and proposals, its most significant contributions occurred outside the meetings. Wriston and his staff
soon found themselves entertaining labor leaders and their wives at home.
Even the Gotbaums and the Wristons, the oddest of allies, eventually became friends of a sort. Their relationship had not yet reached that point,
though, when Wriston asked Betsy Gotbaum if she would join him for a
doubles match.

"I'm not going to play tennis with *you,*" Mrs. Gotbaum replied. Wriston "wasn't used to being turned down," she said later.

Wriston had a knack for reducing tension with humor. Gotbaum's un-
kempt hair had become something of a personal trademark, giving the union
leader the appearance of having spent the entire night in marathon negotiations. Whenever Gotbaum arrived at a meeting, Wriston made a teasing remark about his hair. Gotbaum later said that as time went on, he discovered
that Wriston "had a wry sense of humor and was bright as hell. Then I began
to feel more comfortable with him. But to this day I don't think [the bankers]
made enough of a sacrifice."

That fall, at Wriston's suggestion, he and Gotbaum filmed a television
commercial imploring New Yorkers to vote in the upcoming mayoral election. Wriston said, "Victor and I may disagree on some things, but we do
agree that everyone . . . should vote."

In 1978, after a number of cops had been shot to death, Betsy Gotbaum asked New York–area businesses to donate money for bulletproof vests for the city's sixteen thousand patrolmen, which the city couldn't afford to buy because of budget cutbacks. Citibank stepped up with a $100,000 contribution.

But Wriston's newfound friendships didn't stop the accusations of Citibank's complicity in triggering the fiscal crisis. On August 26, 1977, less than two weeks before the mayoral primary, the SEC released an exhaustive study accusing the banks of deceiving investors about the city's condition and "dumping" up to $2.5 billion in New York City securities from fall 1974 to spring 1975 on the basis of inside information. A state legislative committee had made the dumping charges in an earlier report based on the records of one bank. As early as January 1974, it said, "bank advisers were warning about the impending fiscal crisis in New York City." Noting that in October 1974 a $200 million New York City bond issue was "substantially" unsold, the report accused the banks of ringing the alarm only when they were unable to sell securities from their own portfolios.

The SEC charged the banks with keeping the "market going for the sole purpose of buying time to dispose of their own holdings of city notes" as the crisis deepened in early 1975. Citing a survey of individual investors, which supposedly found that 90 percent of them were unaware of the risks they incurred in buying city notes, the SEC charged that "naive investors were deliberately misled by unscrupulous underwriters."

Wriston was the point man in refuting the accusations. That October, in testimony before the New York State Assembly Banking Committee, Democratic politicians tried to bait him into blowing his cool. But his performance was vintage Wriston. He apparently impressed a reporter for the *New York Times,* who watched the repartee between him and a liberal Queens Democrat. "Mr. Wriston, you must know from your years in the city that all mayors are liars," the legislator said.

Wriston, the *Times* reported, "leaned into the microphone and said, 'no comment,' staying cool as a batter who lets a fat pitch go by because he knows his main job is to bunt."

When the assemblyman pressed Wriston on why he didn't say, "Look, I'm not going to let you have another damn dollar," Wriston responded, "There isn't any sudden moment in history when a light goes on. . . . We knew no more than the city government offered in press release after press release."

The assemblyman asked if banks employed "information-gathering experts."

None who can "penetrate the political process," Wriston replied. The small investor, Wriston asserted, "would have had to be deaf, dumb, and living in a closet" not to be aware of the budgetary machinations. "I suppose in theory it is possible to imagine a person at that time who had at least $10,000 to invest, who never read a newspaper, who never saw a fiscal crisis headline, who never heard a high-decibel debate on radio or television, and who invested without the least inkling that there might be a worm in the apple. It is possible to imagine one [such person]. Two is extremely doubtful. And 90 percent is ridiculous on the face of it. There is a more believable explanation: New York City had a credibility problem in reverse. Rather than too little investment credibility, it had too much," he claimed.

"Some guys said, 'You bought those city bonds because you were greedy and you were making a high-interest return and didn't give a damn about whether the numbers were good,' " Wriston said. "Then the contrary view came up: 'You didn't buy enough bonds and therefore you let the city get into trouble.' Everybody puts their own spin on what happened. [But] spin . . . didn't enter into the calculation. Sometimes it does. But very often it doesn't."

The banks knew about "some of the gimmicks . . . such as charging current expenses to capital budgets," Wriston testified, but he admitted that "we should have known earlier. We did not, but . . . the whole system was designed to prevent anybody from finding out. That is true of the rating services. It is true of the state and it was true of ourselves." The mayor and the city comptroller, Wriston charged, had certified that the budget was balanced.

In an hour of sparring, Wriston showed himself to be a master of verbal self-defense. "The panel of politicians hardly wrung a 'confession' from the banker," the *Times* wrote. Indeed, Wriston was able to get in the last word, speaking of the "considerable pride" he felt for helping to rescue the city. Even though the city's figures had long been suspect, it would have been difficult for the banks to resist the enormous political and public pressure to lend to the city. On the dumping charges, investment banker Felix Rohatyn said later, "There's no reason to believe that. I never looked into it." To the extent that the banks sold city bonds, "they're entitled to do it," according to Rohatyn. "I don't believe if they did it that they did it with deliberation or illegal use of information or any political purpose."

"Banks are in a difficult position in lending to governments, here or in Latin America," Rohatyn explained. "If they don't lend enough, they come under great criticism that by withholding credit, they are interfering with social policies and inflicting hardship on people. And if they lend too much, . . . they don't get their money back and are still held responsible for what comes afterward. It's a very delicate line to draw."

Said Rohatyn, "It was only [when] they were incapable of lending more, because the amounts were too big for their capital, that this situation came to a head. If lending had continued for two or three more years, I don't think we would have ever been able to bring the situation under control."

Ultimately the banks never took any significant losses. Citibank was most successful in reducing its New York City bond holdings, according to former Chase economist Karen Gerard. Citibank considered itself fortunate to have wound up with a minimum of city paper.

The SEC report also came down hard on the city comptroller, Harrison J. Goldin, and Mayor Beame, accusing them of using "deceptive practices masking the city's true and disastrous financial condition." Though Beame tried to deflect the criticism to the banks, the report would prove to be the coup de grâce to his political career. Governor Hugh Carey, meanwhile, had no use for Beame and supported the mayoral bid of a little-known politician named Mario Cuomo.

After losing the mayoral primary to U.S. Representative Edward I. Koch, Beame said that the city now faced "years of rebuilding based on the solid foundation we have carefully laid," and took credit for saving the city. But Beame forecast a $249 million deficit in the fiscal 1979 budget, some $163 million more than he had predicted in the spring.

Shortly after Ed Koch was elected, Wriston and the Muffle men decided it would be sound politics to brief the new mayor on the new group's mission, and let him know that Muffle wanted to work with him, not against him. In a meeting in Wriston's conference room, Koch showed no enthusiasm for the group then or later. He referred to Muffle as "Sniffle." As Wriston recalled, he would say, "They're sniveling all the time." Nor did Koch care much for Wriston personally. Wriston, said Koch, was a "very tough guy. Cynical." Their relationship, he added, was "never a hostile one. But never a warm one. We were never friends."

Koch regarded Muffle as a challenge to his mayoral authority and typically dismissed the group's proposals and recommendations. In one of its monthly meetings, attended by Koch and chaired by Wriston and Bigel, Chase economist Karen Gerard presented what some called a seminal paper on the future of the city's economy. Koch "was obviously kind of bored with economic data; there was very little mention of his name," Bigel said later.

On the elevator after the meeting, Koch cracked to Bigel, "Are all your meetings this exciting?"

"Ed," Bigel replied, "you may not have known it but this was one of the most important papers dealing with the city anybody ever put together." Bigel said later, "I knew why he was bored. He was not the central figure. It was not a one-act play we were doing. He is assiduous in everything he does, including [taking credit.]"

It was a "terrific" paper, said Wriston. "Koch came in and brushed the whole thing under the rug."

To some, Muffle looked like a convenient forum to enable Bigel to bash Koch. Said one bank source, "There was a fair amount of criticism of him and his policies." Sometimes Koch read about it the next day in the *New York Times.*

Koch felt that the union men were much smarter and shrewder than the bankers and used Muffle to con them. "They [the union leaders] spend all their time on the issue of how can they get more salaries, more pensions, more fringe benefits out of the city and how can they use organizations as pressure points to effectuate what it is they want. And that's their job," Koch said later. "And I believe that the bankers loved to be able to say, 'Meet my friend Victor Gotbaum.' I don't think Gotbaum gives a damn about saying, 'Oh, meet my friend Walter Wriston.' "

"It's a straw man," said Wriston of Koch's criticism. "What we do is about as sinister as a Girl Scout cookie sale, and if we did it on a national level, they'd call it patriotism."

By 1977, the city had begun to introduce managerial improvements, including techniques like a management information system to forecast cash flow. But it still faced formidable financial hurdles. In early February 1978, the Senate Banking Committee decided not to extend federal guarantees past June 30 and urged local financial institutions to contribute more. Federal guarantees for a $2.25 billion long-term loan were not needed, the committee said. But in early March, the Carter administration came out in favor of fifteen-year federal guarantees for $2 billion worth of bonds. Two months later Carter pledged his support to the legislation and in mid-May eleven banks agreed to purchase $500 million in MAC bonds as part of the $4.5 billion deal.

Treasury secretary Michael Blumenthal threatened that unless the financing plan assembled by the city was viable, the Congress would back off. He lectured the bankers in the Fed boardroom, telling them in effect that if they "don't get their act together they're not going to get the guarantees," said one participant. And with the June 30 deadline just days away, the hardnosed Senator Proxmire was still pressing the city and the banks to the wall.

Rohatyn called on Citibank's Ed Palmer to recruit bankers for the witness table at the Senate hearings on the guarantees. According to Palmer, "Felix came to me and said, 'We've got to get the people from New York [to testify]. Do you think you can get Walter?' " Though Wriston knew the guarantees were essential, he was never comfortable pleading for government bailouts of any kind. He begged off, saying he was busy, Palmer recalled. Palmer was designated to take the beating from Congress. Said Palmer later, "I think he'd say he was not all that unhappy to have me do it to try to preserve his record." Unlike Wriston, the ideologue, Palmer was a pragmatist. Getting the guarantees, said Palmer, "was in Citibank's best interest."

In the hearings, Proxmire chastised the banks, the unions, and the state for not sacrificing enough. Lecturing Palmer and his fellow bankers as if they were schoolboys, the senator said he favored the seasonal loans, but felt things were now "quite different." Palmer could not take issue with Proxmire's logic. "I do not argue with your skeptical approach. I applaud it," Palmer said. Seeking to disassociate himself from a plan that included government guarantees, Palmer said that the guarantees weren't the banks' plan, but "it's the only plan we've got and we think it's workable." He protested that Citibank had increased its city and MAC investments to $445 million from $320 million in 1975 and planned to add more. The guarantees, he said, were needed not for the banks but because the city couldn't otherwise market its obligations.

Proxmire wasn't about to let Palmer off without chastising him for lending more to defunct Third World countries than to his own hometown: "If you can loan $75 billion abroad, I can't understand why you can't dig up a couple of billion for your own city." In defending Citibank's Third World lending record, Palmer set himself up for more punishment. Referring to

Zaire, Palmer explained that most of Citibank's loans to that country were guaranteed by the Export-Import Bank. "That," Proxmire replied, "is one of the best arguments I have heard for being skeptical of federal guarantees."

In late July the banks, MAC, the state, and the federal government conditionally agreed to lend New York City $2.55 billion. With that in hand, the Senate passed the guarantee legislation, awarding the city $1.65 billion in four-year guarantees—possibly to be extended later for up to fifteen years—and taking over where the three-year seasonal loan program left off. It was the first time Congress had ever authorized such guarantees for an American city.

About this time, three of the principal warhorses of the budget crisis— Wriston, Bigel, and Rohatyn—met in a dining room at Citibank headquarters to cut the deal that would dispose of the $819 million in remaining New York City notes still held by the banks. Writing on cocktail napkins bearing the Citibank logo, they agreed that the banks would receive MAC bonds structured in such a way that they would wind up with investment-grade bonds. "We were down to negotiating the last half of 1 percent on the interest rate, writing on the cocktail napkins," said Rohatyn later. Wriston was demanding 8 percent, and the city 7 percent. The rate was agreed upon at 7½ percent when, Rohatyn said, "Wriston finally cut the salami in two and we made the deal." That, he said, "really wound everything up and ended the major bankruptcy crisis."

On August 8, 1978, President Carter traveled to New York to sign the bill on the the steps of City Hall before an exuberant crowd of five thousand while a band played "Happy Days Are Here Again." A year later all was forgiven. The SEC decided not to press criminal charges against the banks for allegedly conning investors into buying city bonds while they were unloading the bonds themselves.

But John "Sandy" Burton, the former SEC chief accountant and deputy mayor, declined to exonerate the banks. "Where you stand depends on where you sit," he said. "It's reasonable to say that the banks, along with the rest of the capital markets, didn't require information soon enough. The fact that the city showed a balanced budget while borrowing heavily should have been a red flag."

Through Muffle, the banks and unions struck the compromise over the future role of the Emergency Financial Control Board, and the conditions under which it would become a passive player. Martin Shefter wrote that Muffle's principal contribution "lies in what it has prevented its members from doing—namely, advancing or defending their interests in ways that the city's other creditors would not tolerate. This, in turn, has contributed to the survival of the arrangements that saved the city from bankrutpcy in 1975."

Now, with the guarantees in place, the key players in the crisis had time to argue over who had saved the city. Rivalries and feuds abounded. There was Koch versus Beame, Carey versus Rohatyn, and the more subtle Rohatyn versus Wriston.

Though he arrived late on the scene, Koch wasn't shy about taking the credit. Those who had fought the early battles considered the mayor's self-congratulations misplaced. No one chafed more than Governor Carey at Koch's patting himself on the back for things he didn't do. By the time Koch was elected, Carey pointed out, the Financial Control Board virtually ran New York and transferred to the state the costs of the City University, welfare, and transit. "He [Koch] got the easiest job of any mayor in history, with more money and less to do," Carey said.

While Lindsay and Beame had used funds intended for capital improvement on short-term expenses, Koch wound up placing more emphasis on balancing the budget, which he succeeded in doing, but he virtually ignored capital improvements to infrastructure, including bridges and roads. "It's to Koch's credit that, even though he was handed the city in better shape, he followed through. He didn't allow backsliding," said former Citibank economist Jac Friedgut. In 1977, Koch was the "right person at the right time."

For years, Koch and Beame traded insults publicly over who had helped or hurt the city most. Beame accused Koch of repeating the same mistakes that had led to the first budget crisis by putting money intended for capital improvements into the expense budget.

Referring to Wriston and his fellow bankers, Koch said later in an interview, "They had no confidence in Abe Beame to change things. They liked Abe Beame because he was no threat to them—to either the banks or the unions. He was a very pliable guy. He was the guy who put us on the edge of bankruptcy. And then he said, 'Oh, I did everything. I, Abe Beame, I did this, I did that. I did everything. I'm the one. I, Abe Beame, brought the city back from its problems.' " Koch added that Beame was seeking to borrow money right up until the banks closed the window. The city's capital budget was being used for operational expenses, and "Abe Beame had to know it."

As the drama ground on, Rohatyn—dubbed "Felix the Fixer" by the media—got most of the bouquets as the city's savior, though some say Rohatyn was overly concerned about getting adequate credit for his role. Rohatyn disputed charges of a rivalry between himself and Wriston. "There were very few people at my wedding," he said, "and Walter Wriston was one of them." And Rohatyn told an interviewer that "no banker understands the problems of black unemployment better than Wriston. He may be further to the right than other bankers, but he has more empathy."

Asked later by *The New Yorker* to name his greatest failure, Wriston said, "Maybe we should have . . . realized sooner that New York City was in trouble."

Even as New York's politicians were seeking to pillory Wriston on the witness stand in October 1977, he and his new slanted-roof skyscraper were being toasted as the saviors of an East Side neighborhood. Wriston had put his own institution on the line in a big way in building Citicorp Center. It was, said Hugh Carey, "a sign of confidence in the city."

Citicorp Center was built by a construction company headed by Richard Ravitch, the point man for Governor Carey in the Urban Development Corporation crisis. Ravitch now faced a crisis of a different sort: Citicorp

Center was virtually complete when an engineer discovered that the building would not be able to withstand once-in-a-century wind loads. The steel structure would have to be reinforced, no mean undertaking in a nearly finished building.

Ravitch was the builder, not the designer. But he was summoned, tail between his legs, to Wriston's office. In Ravitch's presence, Wriston quickly made a series of decisions intended to protect Citibank from culpability and the public from possible harm. According to one former top Citibank officer, the American Red Cross stepped in with a contingency plan, including plans for ambulances and medical teams, in case the newly completed building collapsed. Working around the clock for a month, workers tore down walls and installed heavy steel plates in the building's core column, eliminating the danger.

While Citicorp Center was not conceived as a symbol of the bank, it quickly became one. The completion of the building coincided with the financial resurrection of the city. As the debate over the guarantees was nearing a climax, Citibank took out full-page ads showing a photo looking up from beneath pillars of the building. The caption read, "Why is Citibank staying in New York? We grew up here."

From his offices at 399 Park, Wriston had gazed upon deteriorating four-story tenements whose commercial tenants included garish peep shows and massage parlors. Proud of his new showpiece, Wriston was now determined to rid the area of sleaze. According to one colleague, Wriston ordered his aides, "I want those gone." As a result of a series of transactions, the area surrounding Citicorp Center was eventually stripped of sex shops. And cleaning up the neighborhood proved to be immensely profitable. According to Citibank venture capitalist William Comfort, Citibank netted $60 million in the course of buying and reselling the buildings housing the sex shops.

Citibank also had to deal with the more pedestrian problem of what to do about large, potentially lethal hunks of snow that slid off the slanted roof of the new building onto the sidewalk. As Citibank officials wrung their hands over this problem, Al Costanzo remarked in exasperation, "Why do we always have to be on the cutting edge of everything?"

From the Arab boycott episode, Wriston had gathered that Management & Budget director Bert Lance was a man of action and common sense. Many regarded him as the most sensible Carter administration official, but his tenure was short. Just months into the new administration, Lance was besieged by accusations of insider dealings while he was president of the National Bank of Georgia. Documents surfaced showing that Lance had received a $2.4 million loan from New York's Manufacturers Hanovers Trust in 1975 to buy stock in his bank, even though Citibank was then the Georgia bank's New York correspondent. In a memo, a Manufacturers officer wrote that by extending the loan, it would likely get more business from Lance's bank.

As Citicorp executive committee chairman Ed Palmer, attorney Hans Angermueller, and public relations men huddled to prepare Palmer to testify before the congressional kangaroo court that accompanied Lance's resignation, they struggled to find a way to explain why they didn't lend to Bert. In the end, Palmer sanctimoniously dismissed Lance's practices as unworthy of Citicorp.

Pen in hand, Henry Wriston, now eighty-eight years old but sharp as ever, rode to Bert Lance's defense, a debt Lance would later acknowledge in his memoirs. In a stinging *New York Times* Op-Ed article on September 30, 1977, the elder Wriston called the Senate committee's behavior "scandalous" and urged that its chairman, Senator Abraham Ribicoff, be censured or dismissed. The senators, he wrote, were determined to "make every past peccadillo into a manifestation of gross misbehavior."

Just months later, Walter Wriston lost his foremost ally and confidant. Until a week before his death on March 8, 1978, after a long illness, Henry Wriston was still reading his son's speeches and correcting his deficiencies in grammar and logic, Wriston later recalled in a *New Yorker* interview.

On his deathbed at New York Hospital, Kathy Wriston recalled, Henry kept mumbling the name of Walter's dog, Black Robin.

Wriston must have been thinking of his father when he responded to an interviewer who asked how he got his best ideas. "Great books are great, but there's nothing as great as the talk of a great man," he said.

In the wake of the Bert Lance "mess," as bankers called it, Congress enacted the Financial Institutions Regulatory Act, which, among other things, imposed restrictions on loans banks could make to their officers, directors, and stockholders. Citibank officers would now have to borrow from the U.S. Trust Company of New York.

The Bert Lance affair inspired Citicorp to put together what Wriston claimed was the world's first corporate policy manual. To avoid the sort of real or apparent conflicts of interest that had brought Bert down, the manual required every officer to sign a statement that would be sent for inspection to Citibank's accounting firm. If questions arose, the matter would be referred to a Committee on Good Corporate Practice, which would have the final say.

Early in his career, Wriston was sensitive, perhaps excessively so, to possible conflicts of interest. But while he came down hard on clear conflicts of interest, his earlier rigidity was gradually tempered with a recognition that values changed with time and place.

Citibank, in fact, had been established by New York merchants who had served as directors and in effect made loans to themselves. More than a century later, insider dealings were neither uncommon nor unacceptable. Wriston recalled that not long after joining Citibank, he had visited a Citibank vice president, Daniel A. Freeman Jr., at his palatial residence in New York's Westchester County. Wriston was stunned that a vice president could have amassed enough money to purchase such a magnificent home. Never inhibited, Wriston asked Freeman how he'd made all his money. "Well, my boy," Freeman began, "Citibank bought Farmers' Loan and Trust."

"Yeah, I know they did," Wriston replied snippily. Freeman went on to explain how when he learned of the plan to buy Farmers', he bought the stock of the bank on margin, doubling his investment every day until the deal was complete. At that time, in 1929, Freeman said, "that was the normal accepted thing to do. Today, when somebody sends you a TV set for Christmas you have to send it back."

"It is remarkable," Wriston observed later, "that in my lifetime we've gone from that to worrying what to do if somebody gives you a bottle of Scotch or something." The issue had reached the point where "to make a loan to a director you have to . . . have separate committees."

In 1977, even as Wriston and company were congratulating themselves for having avoided catching the brunt of the Lance mess, they became embroiled in their own in-house version of Lancegate. Once again, the bane of Wriston's existence was one of those damn traders—this one a young Paris-based Citibank foreign exchange trader named David Edwards, who accused Citibank of shorting the U.S. dollar and using illegal techniques to avoid paying local taxes on foreign exchange transactions.

This affair dragged on for more than six years. Before it was over, the name of Walter Wriston had been sullied in the headlines of the nation's major newspapers and his institution had been compared with the Mafia by a United States congressman. The SEC, the Justice Department, congressional committees, and foreign monetary authorities launched investigations. And Citibank spent millions in executive, legal, and public relations time in damage control.

Citibank by then was indisputably the world's most important, and arguably its best, foreign exchange dealer, with nearly 10 percent of the world market by early 1979. The bank was uniquely positioned to capitalize on the volatility that had occurred since the collapse of the Bretton Woods agreement. And when the dollar began its precipitous slide in the 1970s, Citibank made out like a bandit. In 1978, its pre-tax foreign exchange earnings soared to $104 million, or nearly 13 percent of income before securities gains, from $13 million the year before. In fact, Citibank's rich exchange trading profits covered up a multitude of problems, particularly in Europe, where constant turnover among account officers prevented Citibank from developing strong long-term relationships with local companies.

David Edwards, a Texan, was typical of the smart young crowd Wriston had attracted to Citibank. In late 1974 he had been posted to the forex trading floor at the Paris branch. He later told *Fortune* that he got a call from a trader at the Bourse informing him that the dollar was plunging. "Aw, shit," Edwards replied, hanging up the phone so hard that the receiver broke in his hand. Seconds later, the phone rang again. The same trader was on the line again, reporting that he had bought dollars.

"You did *what?*" Edwards demanded. The trader replied that Edwards had told him, *"Achète,"* which means "buy" in French. That evening Edwards walked into his boss's office and said, "I've got a funny story to tell you, but it's going to cost you a quarter of a million dollars to hear it."

And Edwards would learn that being a whistle-blower at Citibank did not do much for one's career.

In October 1975, Edwards informed his boss, Chuck Young, that a Citibank foreign exchange trader named Jean Pierre De Laet, a Belgian, was taking kickbacks. According to Citibank, Edwards's charges were promptly investigated and found to be without foundation.

In July 1976, as the matter continued to fester, Edwards's close friend Bill Clinton, then Arkansas attorney general–elect, persuaded him to return to the United States to help out in Carter's presidential campaign.

Young, according to *Fortune,* later testified to the SEC that De Laet, who left the bank in 1978, violated Citibank's conflict-of-interest rules. French authorities reportedly discovered that De Laet had handled twenty-four "phony" foreign exchange transactions. For his part, De Laet told *Fortune* that Edwards "had no proof at all" of such wrongdoing.

But the more far-reaching of Edwards's allegations was that Citibank loans that were booked in one location were moved to other locations, such as Nassau, to dress up a profit center for Citibank's internal management reporting and to reduce taxes. In later hearings, Representative John Dingell described Citibank's Nassau branch as "little more than a fellow in a bathing suit on the beach accompanied by his telex machine."

After returning to Paris in early 1977, Edwards discussed his concerns with Citibank veteran and trusted overseas hand Freeman Huntington, who ordered him to park himself in Texas. Edwards later met with international chief George Vojta, who was about to turn over the reins of the international unit to Tom Theobald and begin working on Citibank's next ten-year plan. According to the *Fortune* account, Vojta instructed his traders to stop parking profits in Nassau.

For his trouble, Edwards was treated like a pariah. According to Citibank, Edwards was reassigned to government lending in New York in 1977, but he considered the post "unacceptable" and stated that he planned to stay in the treasury unit until his charges were resolved. Shortly thereafter, Edwards's lawyer notified the bank in writing that Edwards would quit by October 1978 if certain demands were met. These included a Citibank grant for a research project on how to boost American exports, help in finding another job, and a continuation of his subsidized apartment.

After Theobald replaced Vojta in August 1977, Edwards began putting together a "blue book" documenting his allegations that Citibank was illegally "parking" foreign exchange transactions in low-tax jurisdictions.

On February 9, 1978, according to later testimony by Hans Anger-mueller, Citibank notified Edwards that he was dismissed. Four days later, he sent Citicorp directors and top officers copies of his 106-page report citing examples of these illegal practices. According to Wriston, "I immediately urged that the charges be investigated by the examining committee of the bank and the audit committee of Citicorp, two bodies, all of whose members are outside directors."

In July 1978 Edwards sued Citibank, charging wrongful dismissal, and demanded $14 million in compensation. About a year later, a New York State Supreme Court judge dismissed the suit, ruling that it was without legal grounds.

Edwards claimed in court documents that Citibank and other major U.S. banks intentionally drove down the dollar to boost their profits. In a fictionalized article set in a London trading room, Edwards described how this maneuver worked. When the supervisors learn the Swiss are going to sell dollars, he explained, "the trader tells his lieutenants, 'We're going to hit the dollar again today. Henry, you take the lead. Dump $20 million against the mark, $10 [million] against Swiss francs, and $20 [million] against sterling. Don, let Henry kick the hell out of the dollar.' " Edwards's charges, plus the article, which appeared in *MBA* magazine, unleashed a storm of debate over the power of a banking institution to manipulate the dollar and triggered central bank investigations into Citibank's foreign exchange dealings.

In replying to the charges, Theobald described them as "good entertainment" but said they had "no particularly immediate relation to reality." Wriston referred to accusations that banks were responsible for the plunge in the dollar as "flights of fancy."

Wriston and Angermueller decided that the only way to put the affair behind them was to conduct an intensive investigation. That decision, as well as the choice of Shearman & Sterling to carry it out, was greeted with incredulity inside and outside Citibank. Wriston later asked Harvard Business School dean Lawrence Fouraker, head of the directors' audit committee, to have the committee undertake its own investigation. There was little precedent at the time for corporations investigating themselves, and many Citibankers feared that this would create a paper trail that would be an open invitation to massive lawsuits.

The man picked to conduct the investigation of the Edwards affair was tough, wiry John Hoffman, who had worked on the anti-boycott legislation and earned his foreign exchange stripes during the Herstatt crisis.

Hoffman and several colleagues made a grand tour of Citibank facilities in Europe, interrogating outside auditors, traders, and lawyers on local laws and practices. Hoffman later insisted that Wriston never interfered with the inquiry. He said he talked to Wriston from time to time about the schedule for completion, and only on the evening before the presentation to the board informed him "in general terms how it was coming out."

According to Hoffman, the practices that constituted violations of rules alleged by Edwards had "long since been abandoned." Some insiders, however, doubted whether the lawyers really were experienced enough to get to the root of the problem. Said one former Citibanker, "The scuttlebutt was that it was a good thing for the bank that those guys didn't know where to look."

Giving the assignment to Citibank's outside counsel left the bank wide open to criticism. And *American Lawyer* claimed that Shearman & Sterling insiders said, in effect, that the firm's report distorted the facts. Throughout it all, Citibank maintained that Edwards was a troublemaker and that any infractions were few and minor, the result of the difficulties in interpreting the myriad regulations that govern foreign exchange and tax transactions in the dozens of countries where Citibank operated.

In early 1979, Citibank was forced to admit that David Edwards's allegations were being investigated by the SEC, which was still probing allegations that the banks had dumped New York City securities. The SEC, said a former Citibanker, "had a hard-on for Citibank." The feeling was mutual. Wriston summed up his feelings about the agency in a speech that October in which he said that it "created a response to a felt need to protect the investor against fraud. It was a worthy objective, but little by little its role has expanded until now it's attempting to dictate everything from how a board of directors should govern a company to how lawyers should exercise their professional judgment."

Wriston had done a masterful job in discrediting the Nader report. But, as Citibank officials acknowledged years later, he failed abysmally in his handling of Edwards. According to sources familiar with the episode, Edwards early on did not appear to be out to get Citibank and did attempt to work within the system. Citibank's fatal error was in telling Edwards, in essence, that it didn't care to bother with him. And once Edwards "left the reservation," said one source, "he became a zealot." The affair went downhill from there. In the end Edwards's charges prompted institution-wide soul-searching about the bank's policy of following the letter, but perhaps not the spirit, of the laws under which it was supposed to operate.

In Wriston's view, the controls broke down at the Paris desk of Freeman Huntington. Unbeknownst to his colleagues, Huntington was suffering from terminal cancer. While struggling to prolong his days on the job, he apparently ignored various memos and documents, including some related to Edwards. Only after he died in September 1977 did Citibank discover that the source of the most serious crisis to face Walter Wriston since he became chairman had been stashed in Huntington's desk drawer. "I think if he had been healthy it never would have happened, because he was a superb guy," Wriston said later.

The seeds of the Edwards episode had been planted in 1968 during the McKinsey reorganization. Until then tax planning had always been centralized at the head office. In decentralizing global business units, someone had recommended that profit center managers be empowered to manage not only their revenue and expenses but their tax positions as well. In effect, mid-level managers under orders to boost bottom-line earnings by 15 percent a year were given another means to make that happen. Country heads huddled with local lawyers on how they could file their tax returns to put expenses in high-tax districts and revenues in low-tax districts. While Edwards felt that Citibank was evading taxes, Citibank felt it was merely "managing its tax position," said former senior officer Michael Callen. "Very few people manage it up; you manage it down. As long as you don't break the laws in doing that, you can be considered a good citizen."

Citibank's world, then, was viewed as a series of rooms with varying tax rates, and according to Angermueller, if "this room charges a tax rate of 70 percent and that room charges a 10 percent rate, you'll try to see how close you can get to getting the benefit of the 10 percent rate rather than the penalty of the 70 percent rate." The controls, he added, "were not adequate to overcome the motivation. People began to play games."

Said former Citibanker Anthony Howkins, "There were a lot of conflicting pressures, a push for profits. Stock options. Constant turnover. People were making bad decisions and leaving someone else to pick up the chips."

Citibank was always regarded as extraordinarily imaginative in avoiding taxes. Said one former Morgan banker, "Morgan used to wait for [Citibank's] annual report to come out to figure out how they did it this time. They [the Morgan bankers] were convinced that Citibank never paid any taxes." One Morgan bean counter, the banker said, referred to Citibank's annual report as "fascinating reading—the most creative accounting."

Wriston disdained borders of any kind. As it expanded worldwide, Citibank tried to remake the rules to its liking. In many countries, it operated in a gray zone where the rules were complex and unclear. So Citibank filled the void with its own interpretations. While there is no evidence that Wriston instructed anyone to do anything that would break the law in any country, he had clearly created a hard-driving entrepreneurial culture that encouraged pushing the edge of the envelope.

Nowhere was that more true than in foreign exchange dealings. The bank did not venture into the realm of out-and-out criminality, perhaps, but it went far enough to earn the disdain of the governments of Switzerland and Italy.

Citicorp's written policy on its behavior in foreign countries emerged out of 1973 testimony given by senior international officer George "Jack" Clark to the Senate Foreign Relations Subcommittee on multinational corporations, which was investigating the role played by ITT in the Chilean elections. The philosophy, said Angermueller, who had prepared Clark's testimony, was that in a foreign country "we're a guest and have to obey the laws and rules." But that philosophy, he said, "came back to haunt us" in the Edwards case. "There's an inherent conflict between trying to minimize an institution's taxes and compliance with local law. In trying to move the center of gravity of taxable income from a high-tax country to a low-tax country, we found that hard to reconcile with [the policy] that you obey the laws and regulations of a host country."

J. P. Morgan & Company, also a major foreign exchange dealer, managed to avoid any Edwards affairs of its own. "We had a very strict rule," said chairman Lew Preston. "Earnings in a country are taxed in that country."

Even before the Edwards affair became public, Wriston's bank was accused of using its offshore facilities, notably Nassau in the Bahamas, as tax havens. The *Times* asserted that by booking loans there, Citibank avoided paying New York State and City taxes, because the island government levied no taxes on profits.

Wriston, as usual, was ready with a reply. In response to a question posed at a Columbia University forum, he said, "We borrow money in one foreign country and we lend it to another. We do not lend any money to an American-based company in the United States from anywhere except the city of New York, period. So that the idea that you should borrow Eurodollars in London and lend them to Brazil by way of New York is about like saying if you manufacture an automobile in Tokyo for sale in Singapore, you ought to ship it to New York." He explained that Citibank lent out of Nassau because there were no reserve requirements on Eurodollars, resulting in lower funding costs. Wriston pointed out that by booking business in Nassau, Citibank actually increased its tax bill because when the bank didn't pay foreign taxes, the federal rate of 48 percent applied. But, of course, Citibank had other ways to cut that rate down to size.

The Bahamian operation was used to avoid New York State taxes, and for good reason. "We didn't think we should pay taxes for a loan to a German company in Patagonia," said former Latin hand Anthony Howkins.

In the case of David Edwards, instead of addressing the problem, Citibank attacked Edwards's character and ability, describing him in one article as "totally incompetent." According to Wriston, what Edwards really wanted out of the episode was a $1 million payoff. "He came in and said, 'For $1 million I'll go away,'" Wriston said later. "It was a whole blackmail deal."

Angermueller would later take issue with Wriston on Edwards's alleged $1 million extortion attempt. "I don't know anything about $1 million. I know he did propose that rather than be discharged, he be given an office and an opportunity to write his ideas on international trade for a period of six months. That's as far as it got to any kind of threat in my judgment."

The Edwards affair was a seminal event in the life of Wriston and Citicorp. In the opinion of some familiar with the episode, Citicorp paid a steep price in top management time and energy. Not only did the episode humiliate the bank, but it depressed and upset Wriston as much as anything in his career. Said Angermueller, "It was a constant irritant to the organization—not only an irritant but personal pain, anguish to Walt."

Wriston would later contend that as soon as he heard about the charges, he dashed off a memo asking his top aides to "please look into this." Those instructions, he said, were later twisted to suggest that he wanted it "overlooked" rather than looked at. "You were dealing with something so arcane [that] almost no one understood it," Wriston said later. It was a mess, a god-awful mess, and like all messes it got misinterpreted.

The Edwards episode, Wriston acknowledged later, "affected me deeply because it impugns the integrity of the organization," not to mention his own.

Angermueller denied that the Edwards affair slowed Citibank's expansion efforts. But, he said, it "clearly distracted resources from being more effectively used."

Neither Angermueller nor Hoffman had ever met Edwards. But Angermueller would acknowledge later that the matter should have been handled much differently. "I would have gotten in touch with Mr. Edwards earlier, but I was advised that he was a kook, a nut, and that I shouldn't do that. My inclination was to have sat down with him and say, 'tell me what did you find that is wrong,' " said Angermueller. "There was a feeling here that he was misguided. I don't think anyone gave him a full opportunity to explain what he had in mind."

For Citibank, the David Edwards episode was the wake-up call—or, more accurately, the bomb blast—that signaled that the bank's growth had far outpaced its financial controls. Regulators compared Citibank to a car barreling through traffic at 120 miles per hour while other vehicles crashed into each other trying to keep up.

More than any other single event, the episode forced Wriston to recognize that decentralization had to be accompanied by adequate centralized controls over things like foreign exchange and tax planning. It also demonstrated that decentralization worked only so long as the people were capable and trustworthy. One result of the Edwards affair was that tax policy was centralized, relieving the local country head of "having to diddle with taxes," as former Citibanker Howkins put it.

The episode also weakened the power some senior officers had enjoyed. "It reminded us that no man is an island," Michael Callen said. "You have people whom you have a lot of confidence in and who do a great job, and they tend to become entities unto themselves. Like foreign exchange traders." Callen cited as an example his own service as treasurer for the Mideast region: "If an auditor came along and said, 'We think what you're doing is questionable, given the laws of the country,' and I said, 'Shut up. You don't know what you're talking about,' I probably would have had more power than the auditor. That's not good." Big moneymakers, said Callen, can quickly wind up "outside your normal control mechanism." Citibank's auditors, he pointed out, should have "said what it took Edwards to say. You've got to be careful in a corporation about building a personality cult." Under Wriston, Callen suggested, such cults developed because of the faith Wriston had in his people, particularly his top managers.

Harvard professor Charles Williams had a low opinion of Edwards and felt that the bank made mistakes as well. "I don't think anybody comes out too well in that," he said. But Williams was sympathetic with the frustration faced by a global bank in having to deal with local rules that the locals themselves often violated. "They're certainly an international bank that wants to treat the world as their oyster, and [they] inevitably run into some conflict with the local regulations, particularly local regulations that are artificial and don't make economic sense."

It would be nearly impossible to measure in dollar terms the impact of the Edwards episode on Citibank's relations with its host governments, or on its efforts to expand its operations in these countries. "If you were one of the countries involved in the thing, you had to wonder whether Citibank was a useful citizen," said one source.

In early 1979, the Justice Department got into the act, launching a probe to determine whether Citibank and other banks had manipulated the value of the dollar. But Citibank's foreign exchange positions, in and of themselves, didn't give it the muscle to cause the dollar to reverse course, any more than a canoe paddle could alter the direction of a supertanker. "If you take a position ideologically that you're going to short the dollar, you'll get clobbered," said former top officer Edwin Hoffman. "It is true that Citibank made a fortune shorting the dollar on the way down in the late 1970s by catching the trend," Hoffman admitted. A trader, he said, "has to be amoral. He has to go with the market."

Indeed, Citibank exerted an influence well beyond its transaction volume. According to one former senior government official, an institution like Citibank can have a market impact that is "at least" as important as that of the central bank, because of the ability of the bank and its customers to trade on margin. As a result, he said, "they can mobilize resources that are certainly a match for anything the U.S. Treasury is willing to put in." What Citibank had, he said, was "not control but influence over amounts of money in those markets that had to have made them a real factor." But he added that "they're not in it for policy reasons. They're in it to make money."

Later, in the early 1980s, when the dollar was on the rise, Citibank and other major currency dealers did the same thing in reverse. "These guys got no soul," one regulator said. "They don't give a shit which direction things are going." Under chairman G. William Miller, the Federal Reserve Board intervened in world currency markets to try to prop up the dollar. Miller, who had replaced Arthur Burns in 1978, said that "traders in that era [the late 1970s] tried to get on one side of the market. I don't know if Citibank was any different than the others." Because the market was thin, he said, "we had to have the major central banks in there as buyers or sellers to create another side of the transaction. We decided that if something is going on where everybody gets on one side of the market, we'll make it expensive for them." In late 1978, the Fed, instead of entering into currency swaps with other central banks, began borrowing foreign-denominated securities, allowing it to intervene without expanding the money supply of the foreign country. Looking back, Miller said he was pleased with the results. "I think the intervention worked."

It was clear to Wriston that he would have to achieve his own victories, because they certainly weren't going to be created for him in Washington, or anywhere else, for that matter. In early 1978, he got some help from an unlikely source—Mother Nature. John Reed and his consumer group had completed the installation of automated teller machines (ATMs) in more than half of its 277 branches when a mid-January storm dumped more than a foot of snow on New York City, bringing the Big Apple to a virtual standstill.

Citibank would have been hard-pressed to plan a better media campaign to introduce New Yorkers, long accustomed to the inconveniences of nine-to-three banking, to the advantages of cash machines. But only a marketing man like Richard Kovacevich would have the imagination to identify the opportunity, and the energy to run with it. As the ferocity of the storm began to dawn on him, Kovacevich asked his marketing chief, half in jest, "Why don't we make a commercial?"

Within seventy-two hours, the commercial—showing New Yorkers of every description trudging through slush and sleet, throughout the day and night, into Citibank ATM installations—was shot, edited, processed, and on the air with its new campaign slogan: "The Citi Never Sleeps."

Citibank was so decentralized that Wriston didn't even know about the commercial until he saw it on television like everyone else. Delighted and amazed, he picked up the phone and called Kovacevich. "How did you guys do that? Who thought of that?" he asked.

As Kovacevich later recalled, "That's when Walt began to appreciate us marketing types."

According to Citibank, customers' use of the machines surged 20 percent during the storm.

The members of John Reed's inner circle were mystified by their competitors' failure to gather intelligence on consumer response to the ATMs. The other banks, in fact, belittled Citi's effort and congratulated themselves for not having made such a risky investment. The skeptics, Wriston recalled, said that "old people couldn't use them, women didn't like them, everybody would get mugged, and security was no good."

In the end, the other banks, which had poured money into brick-and-mortar branches, found themselves caught off guard by Citibank's massive deployment of ATMS.

Shortly after Citibank's grand opening, Manny Hanny president John McGillicuddy, in comments to bank analysts, conceded that Citibank had raised its retail market share with the ATMs, but the increases were "far from what they said they wanted to get." The ATMs, he said, weren't boosting dollar volume, but Citibank was attracting younger customers. And, he said, "I'd hate to be the [Citibank] guy swinging on the rope waiting for [the payoff] to come."

To Reed and his colleagues, McGillicuddy's comments were fighting words. Even though McGillicuddy later called to apologize, insisting that the quote was taken out of context, Citibank saw the remark as drawing the battle line in the consumer banking wars that would soon follow. McGillicuddy's view of ATMs was shared on the West Coast at Tom Clausen's Bank of America as well. Among other managerial shortcomings, Clausen failed to understand that technology was a different discipline altogether from banking. Karen Shaw, a Washington, D.C., banking consultant, said that Clausen would "take some vice president who crapped out as a regional manager and [make him an operations manager]. The only professionals Clausen recognized were bankers. He assigned [to the operations department] people who didn't know a slipped disk from a floppy disk." In contrast to Citibank's retail team, Bank of America's was led by a man with a high school education who reported to Clausen that Bank of America's ATMs frequently broke down and that customers didn't like them. In one late-1970s meeting, when Citibank was still hemorrhaging from its investment in ATMs, Clausen reportedly remarked, "At least we're not wasting $200 million on ATMS." With 1,100 branches and billions in savings deposits earning no more than the 5.5 percent Reg Q ceiling, Bank of America was like a big savings bank, lulled into complacency by all those seemingly stable core deposits. Before long, however, it would experience a rude awakening.

In 1977, while Citibank was spending heavily on the ATM installation, Bank of America earned $395 million, $14 million more than rival Citibank, whose profits had been weakened by the cost of installation. *Forbes,* apparently oblivious to the economics of consumer banking, lauded Clausen as a banking statesman for having passed Citicorp by a nose in earnings. "Tom Clausen isn't given to gloating," one journalist wrote naively, "but in his quiet way he says, 'We have regained our rightful position as the world's most profitable bank.' "

Within a year, Citibank would edge ahead in the asset race, to $91.5 billion compared with Bank of America's $91.3 billion, and before long would surpass it in profits as well.

Chase also bought the conventional wisdom. At a banking conference in April 1979, Chase retail banking chief Fred Hammer said higher credit lines, not new services like ATMs, differentiated one bank from another and yielded increases in market share. By the late 1970s, Chase had managed to install just 120 ATMs in 60 branches.

When the other banks finally awakened to the potential of ATMs, it was almost too late. By the end of the year, Citibank boasted the largest ATM network in the nation, with more than four hundred machines. Citibank's decision to develop its own proprietary technology would have profound effects on the entire U.S. banking industry. The other banks had to play catch-up, and spent years developing shared teller networks. But not until the early 1980s could they begin to replicate the Citibank network.

By the early 1990s, according to former chief technologist Paul Glaser, Citibank had the highest usage of ATMs of any bank in the world, with the possible exception of Japanese banks. Like a proud father, Wriston bragged about his electronic machines: "People love them. The machines are polite, bilingual in English and Spanish, and are available twenty-four hours a day, without coffee breaks." Unlike human tellers, they took abuse without complaining. In fact, one customer of another bank in Brooklyn pulled out a gun and shot a malfunctioning ATM.

In the long run, the ATMs dramatically lowered the transaction cost of serving individual customers, and Citibank's competitors were forced to match it in both services and price.

McGillicuddy later observed that "it's great to admire [Citibank], it's great to learn from them, but don't let them lure you into the cave because they'll bash your brains out. They're a big organization, and you can't go toe to toe with them everywhere on every issue." While conceding Citibank's success with ATMs, McGillicuddy said, "Not everything worked. They buried a lot of elephants over there."

Early on, the ATMs weren't without their headaches. Wriston would have done well, for example, to hire bank robber Willie Sutton as a consultant on how to crime-proof the devices. The mass introduction of ATMs to the New York market was followed by a spate of high-tech rip-offs of Citibank customers. For example, until Citibank reprogrammed the machines to require insertion of the plastic Citicard prior to each transaction, some customers who neglected to sign off the machines after executing a transaction were ripped off by the next user, who simply reentered the cycle and asked for cash. "For everything you design there's someone staying up nights figuring out how to rip it off," said Wriston. Newspaper stories about the thefts quickly led to legislation to limit the consumer's liability for unauthorized withdrawals, or "remote mugging," as one consumer advocate called it.

Reed by now had convinced Wriston that the future also lay in plastic. A big part of the credit card marketing plan included deluging lower- and middle-income consumers around the nation with Visa cards emblazoned with the Citicorp logo. Soon other banks were scrambling to get on the national credit card bandwagon with aggressive solicitations for Visa and Master Charge.

Robert H. Grant, then senior vice president of First National State Bank of New Jersey, told a journalist that in early 1978 the Citibank program "scared the hell out of me." Nonetheless, he said, bankers were still "dumbfounded" at the huge amounts of money Citibank was spending trying to "achieve nationwide penetration."

The program was also scaring the hell out of Citibank. Its early estimates of credit losses—about $60 million—proved to be far short of the mark. And Reed and credit-card executive David Phillips were unprepared for the invisible monster that they would later call "the wave."

From the wounds inflicted by its early mailings of credit cards, Reed and Phillips determined that there was a pattern to the credit-card business cycle that could be used to predict very accurately the timing and amount of revenues and losses beginning in the initial months of a mailing. The mailing generated customer responses, typically about 2 percent, followed by the mailing of the actual card and its use by the consumer. What they didn't count on in that cycle was a "wave" of credit losses that would last some twenty-two months. Since Citibank did not then charge an annual fee, many months would pass before it began receiving revenues from the cards that were not offset by high credit losses.

"When you put a piece of plastic in someone's hand, you can't control it," said Ed Harshfield, a key member of Reed's team. "It takes about nine to twelve months to realize what's happened and its impact on profit and loss.

You could see delinquency numbers, but it's six months before you take the first write-off. But since it's a three-month mailing cycle it takes nine months to know what hit you."

Moreover, said Richard Kane, another top consumer banking officer, Citibank also discovered that the "good guys" used up to 60 percent of their credit limit over a period of time. "They start slowly. The bad guys will run it up in a month," he said. Eventually, however, they found that the good guys would "overcome" the bad ones. In 1978, they could only hope that delinquencies would level off, which didn't happen for another year.

Said Reed later, "We were smarter at deciding what we wanted to do than in executing." Eventually, he and his colleagues came to regard "the wave" almost as an object of beauty for its elegant predictability. Based on the "seasoning" of the portfolio, "you can predict delinquencies," said Harshfield. Added Reed, "We can say, 'Hey, it's month seventeen; this is where we should be.' " Only later did the bank discover credit scoring, a technique for evaluating a prospective customer's creditworthiness from information gleaned from its existing credit-card customers.

Citibank didn't use credit scoring for its initial mailings, other than that based on demographic information about customers. Later it found that there was little logic to creditworthiness. People who had lived in an apartment less than six months or more than three years were good bets; those in between were not so good. Early on, wealthy people without jobs were turned down. Eventually, Citibank sought to expand its potential customers to include people such as college students, who didn't fit the mold.

Meanwhile, Citibank was trying to replicate overseas what it was doing at home, often with equally disastrous results. In Asia for example, it initiated a six-year plan for consumer banking. There, its target markets—the Philippines, Australia, and Hong Kong—were called the "two dogs and a rabbit." The rabbit was Hong Kong, the only one of the three markets that was making money. Installing and maintaining ATMs in Hong Kong wasn't easy, Harshfield recalled. It was tough to find spare parts, the electrical current was different, and "you couldn't just call Docutel [the ATM maker] and get service."

Reed sought to expand the portfolio in every possible way. In 1977 he bought for something over $2 million the NAC Credit Corporation, the floundering credit-card subsidiary of Korvettes department stores, a unit of Arlen Realty & Development Corporation. Korvettes had not promoted its card vigorously, and only 17,000 of 700,000 cards were then active. Citibank thought it could use the NAC operation to break into the Baltimore-Washington area. But the NAC opportunity became a problem in mid-1978. Highly leveraged Arlen by then was headed for the corporate graveyard. Citibank had well over $60 million, and perhaps as much as $100 million, in loans outstanding to the company. Arlen was forced to sell Korvettes to a French firm, some of whose owners had been convicted of stock fraud and manipulation in France in connection with an earlier transaction. The episode was a major embarrassment for Citicorp, and people close to the company questioned whether Reed, as a director, had fallen asleep at the switch. The NAC cards turned out to be among the worst in the portfolio.

Under pressure, Arlen chairman Arthur Cohen left the Citicorp board in early 1979 and Reed was told in no uncertain terms to sever his ties to Arlen. "I had Angermueller walk in the room and read me my rights," said Reed later, only partly in jest. But Reed obstinately refused to quit the Arlen board until the problem was disposed of. Cohen lost his shirt on his investment in Korvettes but Arlen was restructured as a maker of building materials and steering wheels. On October 16, 1989, *Forbes* reported that Cohen was alive and well and that the company had a market value of $8 million.

Mysteriously, Citibank was now so enamored of credit cards that in 1978 it reacquired Carte Blanche from Avco, which had bought it from Citicorp a decade earlier. Citicorp had yet to learn that it almost always did better building a business from scratch than acquiring someone else's.

The ATM and credit-card programs had greatly intensified the competition for the consumers' loan and deposit business. Banks, savings institutions, and brokerages vied ferociously for the consumer dollar. With the introduction of NOW (negotiable order of withdrawal) accounts, Citibank fought back and pursued savings bank customers with a vengeance, trying to entice them to transfer their money to interest-bearing checking accounts. Citi and its competitors sought to capture all of a consumer's business with accounts that encouraged them to keep all their money—checking and savings and CDs—with them. By keeping total deposits of $3,000, a Citicard account customer could avoid service fees on checking accounts, in contrast with the fees of 75 cents monthly plus 15 cents per check or ATM withdrawal on regular checking accounts.

Citibank lit a fire under other banks that had forgotten the meaning of the word "competition." In Florida, for example, Barnett Bank reacted to the Yankee aggression by doing a mailing of its own to more than than 350,000 Visa customers. What had begun as a defensive move actually hauled in new business for Barnett. Citibank's mailing, according to a top Barnett official, got "us out of bed" and forced the bank to recognize that "there's a hell of a lot of service in a Visa account that we didn't push." That campaign, which included stuffers that read "Don't take Visa cards from strangers," gained Barnett 25,000 new customers.

Over the next several years, with the outlays for such things as branch renovations and new computers, Citibank's expenses surged while losses from bad credit-card debts mounted. "We have red ink all over the place here, and we're going to lose some more money for a little while," Reed said in late 1978.

In his finest hour as a banking executive, Wriston continued to write the checks, convinced in his gut that eventually the business would pay off. "I'd go in and talk to my partner, Billy [Spencer], and he'd say, 'Do you realize that this is the biggest goddamn risk we've ever taken?'" Wriston said later.

In the late 1970s, with consumer banking losing millions and the prospects for profitable lending to American corporations dimming, the only bright spot in the Citibank galaxy was international banking, including local operations in Latin America and international loan syndications. In a very real way, the fat fees from the nine-figure loan syndications were footing the bill for John Reed's operation. Walter Wriston's tolerance for pain seemed unlimited. But without those earnings, even Wriston would have had to say enough is enough. While there may never have been direct orders from Wriston to open the international earnings valve completely to compensate for the absence of earnings from other sectors, former top executives acknowledge that there was implicit pressure on the income-producing businesses to help Citibank meet its earnings growth targets. Said credit guru P. Henry Mueller, "All the money being made [in international] made it possible for John Reed to lose a lot of money."

In the three years after Herstatt, the banks had largely dictated terms to foreign borrowers. But by early 1978, the fears over Herstatt and the previous year's congressional hearings were all but forgotten and terms had turned in favor of borrowers. In fact, with a drop in rates, many less developed countries moved to prepay floating rate loans made at fat spreads in the wake of the oil shock, and to refinance them at thinner spreads and fixed rates. In these instances the borrower's gain was the bank's loss. The banks had failed to insert prepayment penalities in loan agreements and had no choice but to go along with borrowers' demands. Only Brazil among the major LDC borrowers opted to continue borrowing at higher rates, in the hope of locking up long-term money and ingratiating itself with lenders. Though Brazil was an oil importer, Citibank's Latin experts felt it had weathered the first oil shock. And they were eager to lend more money at robust spreads.

In general, in a world flush with liquidity, the banks were once again beating the bushes for loans. Driven by tough profit goals, loan-starved Citibank domestic officers crossed turf lines to grab pieces of seemingly lucrative international business. In the mid-1970s, according to confidential Citibank documents, the head of the national banking group boasted at meetings about the steady rise in asset growth and profits of his Houston operation— the result, he said, of loan targets he'd given to his local manager. "The next year," said former top Citibank officer Ed Hoffman in a confidential presentation years later, the "Houston, Texas, business was a credit disaster. His business manager had been sneaking over the border to make loans to non-target Mexican clients as well as smaller entrepreneurial Texas clients. Those of us who have been losing money on . . . target Mexican clients can tell you how bad the non-target clients must have been."

There were many reasons for LDCs to borrow and not very many not to. At the time, interest rates in real terms were negative. The dollar was weak. Commodity prices were rising faster than inflation. Nearly every expert was predicting rising oil prices.

By the late 1970s, Citibank had made about one eighth of all foreign loans by U.S. banks and one third of all local currency loans. More than 80 percent of its earnings were now generated overseas, and Brazil alone accounted for most of that. The international unit had become the bank's elite. "Around here it's Djakarta that pays the check," Wriston used to say.

But the enthusiasm for overseas lending masked some serious problems. A lot of the money Brazil and Mexico were now borrowing was being used to repay interest. According to one top bank regulator, country risk officers told lenders that there was no way many of their Third World borrowers could ever repay their loans. When asked why they had made the loans, the answer, he said, was "competition." Big U.S. commercial banks made loans to Pakistan on the assumption that the U.S. government would come to Pakistan's aid because of fears that it would otherwise fall into the Soviet orbit. "An awful lot was taken on by banks," he said, on "the explicit assumption that the public sector would backstop it."

Mexico's newfound status as a major oil power was behind the rush by thousands of banks to lend there. Petroleum, President López Portillo figured, was the key to economic prosperity. Although Mexico still suffered from severe unemployment and poverty, that was offset by twenty billion barrels of proven crude oil and natural gas reserves and possible reserves of about 200 billion barrels by the fall of 1978. Mexico had kept its deal with the IMF, and inflation had dropped sharply.

In the four years since the beginning of the oil embargo, Brazil's debt had doubled to about $30 billion, more than that of any other developing country. And although economic growth had declined from the days of the economic "miracle," bankers—increasingly European and Japanese—were eager to get in on the action. By 1978, Brazil was flush with borrowed funds. Syndications were oversubscribed, which created demand for the next deal. Brazil was apparently oblivious to the fact that its large floating rate debt created a huge interest rate risk.

Citibankers heaped praise on Brazil's economic management. As Brazil chief Richard Huber told *Business Week:* "What gives us confidence in Brazil is the way the country is managed. You don't make loans with the idea of recovering all the capital—not in this century anyway. Instead you look to see how the money is being used. Are they buying caviar and Cadillacs for the generals' sons? No. The loans are going into productive projects—the right kind of thing to help make the economy stronger."

But Robert Logan, who had spent the early years of his banking career in Brazil, was skeptical. "Costanzo defended Brazil," he said. "I can remember when people were talking about all the debt Brazil had. Al had all the numbers. He said they could take on more credit. I always used to worry about them paying the bills. After living in Brazil and seeing all the graft and corruption [I knew] it was always mañana."

Wriston, in a September 1978 speech in São Paolo, chimed in with a ringing endorsement of non-oil-producing LDCs in general and of Brazil in particular. Declaring victory over the oil shock and the naysayers, he said, "While the oil problem is still very much with us, the doomsday prognosticators have moved on to new and more promising topics." Wriston's optimism apparently was contagious. The chief Latin economist for a big New York bank later told *Business Week* that he had warned his chairman that the bank was overexposed in Brazil, but the bank head had dismissed his concerns after Wriston's São Paolo speech. The bank, *Business Week* said, continued to lend large sums to Brazil.

If there was an example of an area where earnings could be managed (fudged), said one former officer, it was Brazil. "People [Citibank managers] were tucking things away so they had reserves if they needed them. Do we report the fee this year or next? There were things we could do to impact the level of profits."

By now, as Wriston told shareholders at the annual meeting in April 1978, Brazil was the largest single source of earnings for the company. According to former personnel chief Robert Feagles, George Vojta, during his tenure as second-in-command to Al Costanzo, favored shooting for a long-term goal of $1 billion in annual earnings from Brazil. Though Wriston and Costanzo were not entirely comfortable with the kind of exposure that would produce those kinds of earnings, they let Vojta ignore the limits and roll the dice in Brazil at a time when earnings were weak elsewhere.

Wriston even heaped praise on Argentina, the black sheep of the international financial community.

Citibank was the foreign banks' role model. Citibank charged foreign bankers $5,000—not including room and board—for three-week courses on money management. Many of the students were the offspring of leading foreign businessmen and government officials. Wriston personally approved of sherry at lunch, but after hours nearly everything was allowed. Though the "gamblers" used fake money, the party scene—including roulette wheels, crap tables, and booze—at Citicorp's conference center was a metaphor for the LDC lending binge itself. At the end of the course, each graduate had his picture taken receiving his diploma from Wriston.

The intense competition soon drove the margins to razor-thin levels. One writer called it "spread madness," but that, Wriston joked, "sounds like [the title of] a pornographic movie."

Spreads on syndicated loans to Brazil, which was always ready to pay up for its money, plummeted to about 1.63 percent in the first quarter of 1978, down from about 2.08 percent in the final quarter of 1977. The squeeze on margins became even tighter as European and Japanese banks, which had looser capital requirements, rushed in to play the Eurosyndication game. That also reduced the U.S. banks' share of this market.

Trouble was, the banks as well as the regulators confused low spreads with low risk.

Although Citibank tried to hold the line on spreads, one barrier crumbled after another. The 1.25 percent that had prevailed at the time of the first oil shock "was gone within six months," said international financier Geoffrey Bell. "I remember Citibank saying they'd never cut the margin below 1.25 percent," he said. "If they had all kept one and a quarter"—which many then considered the "proper margin"—"they would be in better shape. The world was just too liquid."

In 1977, Citibank declared that it planned to hold the line at 1 percent over the London Interbank Offering Rate.

At one early-morning meeting of Citibank's asset liability committee, Costanzo turned to loan salesman George Putnam and asked how long it would take to put an Iranian deal on the books if Citibank let the 1 percent floor collapse. They were shocked when Putnam replied, "Give me until lunchtime." Before long the norm had fallen to 0.75 percent, and soon that floor gave way as well.

Later, however, when interest rates surged to 15 percent and beyond, an eighth of a point was not going to make one iota of difference.

Spread madness in the international market reflected what was already going on in domestic lending. In 1975, domestic loan demand was so weak that banks had to create it themselves. They started to drop their insistence on compensating balances, and as *Institutional Investor* pointed out, Citibank and Morgan couldn't enforce their demands for the traditional facility fee in a major transaction because of soft loan demand.

Wriston would later tell Reuters that Citicorp began to turn down Eurosyndicated loans in early 1978 when it decided that spreads were too thin. Then, in a mid-1978 interview with *Institutional Investor,* Wriston predicted that the thin spreads wouldn't endure, that "somebody will get hurt, and spreads will widen again. It's popular right now to say they never will."

Still, the huge volume of earnings from overseas, and in particular from Brazil, did by 1978 give Wriston pause. Said country risk chief Irving Friedman, "Word came down when we got to 80 percent of earnings overseas, that we [had] to cut that back. That's wisdom."

Sometime in 1978, top IMF Latin official Jack Guenther was strolling with Citibank's George Clark along a beach near Rio. Though Clark was a veteran Latin hand, he was forever bemused by the fun-loving, devil-may-care Brazilian temperament. As he watched these bronzed, nearly naked Latins flirt and frolic on the beach on what was supposed to be a workday, he turned to Guenther and said, "You know, we've got $3 billion in this place!"

19

SHOCK TREATMENT

hile Arthur Burns didn't let up in his campaign to get banks to boost their capital ratios, in late 1977 it seemed that Wriston's arguments about earnings had begun to hit home with the Fed chairman. Upon returning from a fall visit to Paris, Wriston found on his desk a copy of a speech by Burns in which he said that corporate earnings "are at an unsatisfactory level." Pleasantly surprised, Wriston fired off a complimentary note.

Wriston had always had a grudging respect for Burns's brain, even though he regarded his handling of monetary policy as ineffective and his views on bank regulation and capital as misguided. It didn't take him long to come to a far less favorable assessment of Burns's successor, G. William Miller, the former chairman of Textron, the Providence, Rhode Island–based conglomerate.

Late in the afternoon of December 28, 1977, a few months after he was forced to resign from the Carter administration, Bert Lance personally notified Wriston and Manny Hanny of the president's choice of Miller to succeed Burns—before it was officially announced. That, incidentally, raised the eyebrows of *New York Times* columnist William Safire and prompted the *Village Voice* to refer to the episode as the final scandal in the Lance saga, suggesting that Wriston could have traded on the information before the markets closed.

While he was generally well regarded for his management of Textron, Miller lacked the economic policy credentials needed for the Fed post. He was not a central banker and, according to one former Fed colleague, "didn't like banks."

Whatever their differences, Wriston and Burns did agree that inflation, now the worst in the nation's history, was an insidious disease. In early 1978, it was running at double-digit annual rates and, on some products and services, at triple-digit levels. Although the Fed had been applying the brakes to the money supply since the fall, Burns was forced to acknowledge in his parting remarks to reporters on January 30, 1978, that there was "no progress" toward less inflation the year before, and he blamed inflation on "fundamental mistakes of government policy made in the mid-1960s."

Wriston certainly was no inflationist. But if inflation was America's silent thief, as he put it, it was also Citibank's silent partner in its push to achieve 15 percent earnings growth. Inflation-driven market volatility produced huge trading profits. In the first quarter of 1978, after two periods of decline, Citicorp's net surged 15.5 percent to $106.3 million, while Chase Manhattan's soared nearly 50 percent.

Still, Citibank's economics establishment was alarmed over the Carter stimulus program. Wriston knew inflation-driven profits couldn't be sustained over the long haul and was bitterly critical of Carter administration policies that emphasized cutting unemployment rather than inflation. Almost from the moment Carter was inaugurated, Wriston and Citibank campaigned vigorously for an anti-inflation policy and criticized the Fed and the administration for overstimulating the economy.

In testimony before the Joint Economic Committee of Congress in February 1978, Wriston urged a "less expansionary policy" and the reduction of the federal deficit. Advocating tough measures to halt inflation, he said, "We must stop pretending that it is possible to fine-tune our economy."

While Citibank was accused of shorting the dollar, Wriston in fact regarded a soft greenback as a contributor to inflation. Expectations of a declining dollar, he said, "cause great uncertainty for decision-makers, but it intensifies inflation pressures in the United States, not only by raising the prices of imports but [also by] weakening the competition that confronts domestic producers."

Indeed, Wriston found little redeeming value in any of the Carter economic programs. In the January 1978 *Monthly Economic Letter,* he lambasted the president's energy program, saying that by keeping U.S. oil prices below world levels, price controls only encourage higher energy consumption.

Fed chairman Miller started off by saying all the right things. In appearances before the banking committees, he called inflation the nation's "number one" problem. But by midyear he began to show his true colors. In a key meeting of the Fed's Board of Governors, Miller voted against his colleagues when they moved to raise the benchmark discount rate a quarter of a point to 7.25 percent, becoming the first Fed chairman to be overruled by his board on a discount rate increase. By year end, most economists saw a 1979 recession as almost inevitable. As loan demand and interest rates headed north, economists, including Citibank's chief economist, Leif Olsen, were becoming increasingly worried about a credit crunch.

The jury was in on G. William Miller. It was clear that Miller was Carter's puppet and that the central bank's priority was to cut unemployment, not reduce inflation. Calling Miller a "fainthearted inflation fighter," *Fortune* wrote on December 31, 1978, that he "talked a good line but his monetary policy betrays his tough talk." In the first few months of his tenure, *Fortune* said, Miller had been viewed as "infallible"—"the next best thing to a Swiss gnome." The discount rate vote was the first sign that this was a misperception.

Wriston by now was so disgusted with the government's economic policy that he took the unusual step of devoting six full pages in Citibank's 1978 annual report to an essay titled "Is Inflation Inevitable?" It was a barely disguised call for a change in administration. "Can the situation be turned around?" Citibank wondered. "That depends on the desires—expressed through votes—of the people who lose more than they gain from government policies that nurture inflation. That group is getting larger, for the consequences of inflation have been widespread." It went on to say that "making the situation even worse have been government attempts to mask the effects of inflation and direct the public's attention away from its true cause. As one result, price controls, income policies and other forms of direct market intervention—all of which aggravate the effects of inflation—are now viewed by many as a welcome solution."

Miller would later cite as evidence of his own anti-inflation stance his raising of the discount rate on several occasions. But according to monetary experts, he confused raising rates with tightening the money supply. Wriston and friends regarded Miller as an incompetent, the worst of the postwar Fed chairmen. Wriston later said politely that Miller's "intellectual base was more commercial than public policy."

Miller, however, blamed the problem on the excessive "liberal" monetary policy of the 1972 period. "If I had any regrets I probably would have been even a little more aggressive in tightening money a little earlier," he acknowledged, adding that the administration already thought the Fed was "too tight." He later claimed that the departure of many banks from the Federal Reserve reduced the assets in the system and "made it more difficult to exercise monetary policy." Though he was also regarded by many as a half-hearted deregulator, Miller later defended his accomplishments in that arena as well. At the time, he said, policymakers had to decide whether to allow non-bank institutions to offer the same kinds of instruments as banks and whether to let banks expand their offerings.

Miller took credit for pushing through a six-month $10,000 certificate of deposit paying a market rate of interest that took effect on June 1, 1978. The idea, he said, was to "give banks and S&Ls some hope of competing without destroying their low-cost deposits, which if you suddenly made them pay a market rate of interest would all go bankrupt." Miller also claimed credit for passage of the International Banking Act of 1978, saying in an interview that "if it were not for me the [act] wouldn't have been passed." It was, he said, "practically dead" when he appeared before Congress to urge Senator Adlai Stevenson to "get moving with it." Though it did not take effect for a couple of years, it did provide relief for American banks, though not enough for some.

Although Miller had barely taken office, the Fed, on his watch, also ordered Citibank to finally divest itself of Advance Mortgage, a major blow to its goal of being a nationwide mortgage banker. Compared with the more reasonable anti-trust criteria that came along later, the grounds for the order were absurd: Citibank was the nation's biggest bank, and Detroit-based Advance Mortgage the second-largest mortgage lender. Advance Mortgage's market share was "infinitesimal," Angermueller said later, but it was saddled with the "second largest" label. "It was like the second-largest mouse." But Angermueller would later cite the loss of Advance Mortgage as an example of how Citibank's—and Wriston's—confrontational style was counterproductive. Citibank "might have gotten better treatment," he said, if it had "listened to the other guy"—the Fed—"instead of hurling epithets in the air." Wriston insisted on taking the battle to the courts, despite the fact that the court challenge, as Angermueller put it later, "was not my style." The case went all the way to the Supreme Court, which, in June 1979, declined to hear it.

Meanwhile, Citibankers were pressing to level the field outside of the United States as well. Canadian banks, for example, enjoyed infinitely more powers in the United States than U.S. banks did there. But since the mid-1970s the $1 billion Citicorp Limited, under the controversial yet influential Greek-born Anthony Mantzavinos, had been conducting a media campaign to persuade the Canadians to ease their banking laws. Not coincidentally, Citibank in mid-1978 headed up a ninety-bank syndicate to put together a $3 billion revolving credit to prop up the Canadian dollar, which in mid-April had plunged to a forty-five-year low of 86.92 cents against the greenback. Canada was proposing revisions in its Bank Act that would allow U.S. banks to operate under a federal charter. U.S. officials, including New York State superintendent of banking Muriel Siebert, put the screws to the Canadians. One Canadian official described a letter from Siebert as a "discreet reminder that our Canadian banks are hostages in the United States to our treatment of American banks here." The 1980 Bank Act made it easier for foreign banks to get charters, but slapped restrictions on growth. Later, Canada liberalized its foreign bank rules somewhat—but never enough for Citicorp.

It was bad enough, in Wriston's view, that the Carter administration and the new Fed chief were unwilling or unable to combat inflation. It was even worse that they placed nonsensical hurdles in the way of others seeking to help them find ways to fight it. For example, after delivering a major speech on inflation, Carter, according to former labor secretary and Labor-Management Committee chairman John Dunlop, called on the committee—one of Wriston's favorite extracurricular activities—to advise him on ways to cut inflation. At the committee meetings, Wriston focused attention on the issue of rising health care costs by pointing out that "there is more health care than steel in an automobile."

Though Carter didn't attend the committee meetings, the White House arranged for several cabinet members, led by Treasury secretary Michael Blumenthal, to participate. The committee, which one Carter administration official called "just about the most important" labor-management panel "ever to sit in this country," and the administration set up a joint staff and produced tomes on inflation. In late 1978, however, the committee received a bolt from the blue: a letter from the attorney general, Griffin Bell, informing the panel, as Dunlop recalled, that it was in fact a government advisory committee and therefore had to open its meetings to the public. Unless that happened, Blumenthal, for one, would no longer be permitted to attend. Bell put the group on notice that they could not meet even by themselves. That didn't sit well with either business or labor. It was, said Dunlop, "the most outrageous thing in all my years of dealing with the government." As a result, the members took the group private and hired their own staff to run it.

All considered, Citibank and the other big banks and their Third World borrowers had weathered the first oil shock well. Recycling, Part I, was a real success. Recycling, Part II, was another matter altogether.

On November 5, 1978, years of bottled-up fury toward the regime of the Shah finally turned into riots in the streets of Teheran. Mobs of enraged Muslim Fundamentalists tossed pictures of the Shah onto bonfires while the Iranian Army watched idly. Soon that army would seize control of the government.

Wriston's State Department contacts and Fletcher network notwithstanding, the revolution caught Citibank, Chase, and everyone else by surprise. Barely a year earlier, in a speech that could have been titled "Famous Last Words," Bill Spencer had uncharacteristically heaped unctuous praise on the Shah at a gathering promoting investment in Iran. "Since 1954," Spencer had said, "through the vision and enlightened policies advanced by his imperial majesty, the Shah, an accelerated industrial revolution has been transforming Iran. Unlike some revolutions, however, Iran's economic surge has been characterized by political stability, a more equitable distribution of income, a rising standard of living, and improved levels of education."

Indeed, the December 1978 issue of *Euromoney* carried a tombstone ad dated October 20 for a $60 million medium-term loan, arranged by Chase, Citibank's CIBL, and several other banks. Luckily for Citibank, about six months earlier it managed to slash its stake in the Iranians' Bank, which it had acquired in 1969, to 5 percent from 35 percent. The official explanation was that it sold down because of its policy against overseas joint ventures in which Citibank didn't have control. That policy resulted from its experience with Waltons and Grindlays, among other episodes. But according to G. A. Costanzo, Citibank sold out in Iran because its original partner had sold his stake to "some people we didn't trust, who we thought were crooked." It was "just lucky," he said. "None of us had any inkling as to what would happen."

But in 1978, Costanzo did get a tip that another OPEC price boost was in the offing. Sheikh Ahmed Zaki al-Yamani, the Saudi oil minister, invited Costanzo and a couple of other top U.S. executives to meet with him in London. There, he told them that OPEC would have to boost the price of oil further because the United States had failed to take adequate conservation measures. In mid-December, OPEC announced a schedule of price hikes in quarterly installments starting on New Year's Day, to total 14.5 percent by October 1. "It's better to have the increases in doses," the sheikh said. OPEC rationalized the increases by saying that the OPEC surplus of the previous two years had already vanished. But that was before Iran called a halt to oil exports.

Coincidentally, as the bonfires were burning in Teheran, Walter and Kathy Wriston were in Hong Kong, preparing for a one-week visit to mainland China, where they would discuss reestablishing Citibank's relationship with the country that had confiscated its branches some thirty years before. One evening at the Grill Room of Hong Kong's Mandarin Oriental Hotel, Wriston, a lover of elitist gossip, regaled colleagues with tales about other CEOs, including the head of a giant consumer products company who had once made a pass at his wife.

Kathy Wriston had not been enthusiastic about this trip. Iran Air was the only carrier flying out of China, and it was then on strike, she recalled, in protest against the Shah. She said, "I'll do anything for Mother Bank, but I don't want to go into China with no way out." Wriston put his foot down. "We want the Chinese business," he said.

In his public statements leading up to the announcement of an agreement with China, Wriston downplayed his interest. After all, he pointed out, it was illegal to lend to a country that was in default on its obligations. In a February 1979 interview, he said, "Maybe I'm not as excited about the potential for the market as I should be." But by early 1979, Citibank had forged new ties to the Bank of China, linking the country up with ten U.S. banks. And China had agreed to pay Citibank 41 cents on the dollar for the seized assets.

As the banks were kissing and making up with China, they were wringing their hands over how to disengage from Iran. Banks with loans outstanding to Iran were contemplating declaring their loans in default.

But in the months following the Shah's downfall, the Iranians kept paying on their loans. By April 1979, the Shah's pal David Rockefeller was able to declare that the new government was behaving responsibly and honoring its obligations. In June, however, Iran seized private banks, and a month later Citibank was ordered to curtail its local operations.

Meanwhile, despite the flurry of concern that had been raised about Third World lending when Zaire, Turkey, and Sudan bit the dust, the long gas lines and the surge in oil prices that accompanied the Iranian revolution had once again silenced the critics. As the conventional logic went, the LDC loans had been basically sound so far, so new loans, made in even greater amounts, would continue to remain sound. Accordingly the official agencies, the U.S. Treasury, and the other industrialized nations were more than willing to let the American banks lend more money to the Third World. And Wriston had the biggest lending machine around.

Once again there was no shortage of forecasters to predict that oil had nowhere to go but to the stratosphere. At one closed-door meeting at the New York Fed that included Fed president Paul Volcker and David Rockefeller, regulators and bankers sat around a table "wringing their hands" over what to do in the face of a price of $18 per barrel of oil, according to one participant. "So many government figures were so relieved that our whole economy didn't come to a screeching halt from dollars being kept under mattresses. What was perceived as a fundamental threat was resolved by the American banking system getting those dollars back. You had to do *something* with them," he said.

According to Morgan economist Rimmer de Vries, the success the banks had following the first oil shock in 1973 "gave the banks a degree of confidence" after the second one in 1979. Though in absolute terms it was not as severe as the first, its effects would prove much worse. The first oil shock, said one Citibanker, "scared everybody," but the borrowers "fundamentally adjusted out of that. For lenders to LDCs, the key issue was whether non-oil LDCs would be able to adjust from this oil shock as well as they had the first." In fact, as Angermueller later pointed out, by 1978 the current accounts of the industrial and developing nations had returned to pre-1973 levels.

The lending frenzy began anew and 1979 would turn out to be what *Euromoney* called the "Year of the Gunslinger." Bankers tripped over one another to lend to the developing countries, particularly oil-rich Mexico. Foreign banks, notably the Japanese and European institutions, made loans at the skinniest of spreads.

As bank exposure to developing nations burgeoned, examiners began questioning how to interpret regulations that generally prohibited banks from lending more than 10 percent of their capital to any single borrower. In Latin America, where government-owned steel companies and electric companies were the rule rather than the exception, it was often unclear where the public sector ended and the private sector began. This posed a very real problem: should a loan to Brazil's government-owned steel company be included in the 10 percent limit on loans to the government of Brazil? Citibank, among others, said no; the loans should not be consolidated, or aggregated, to use the regulatory jargon of the day. To aggregate would mean that Third World lending would, if not screech to a halt, shift from the fast lane into the slow lane. The race would be over just as it was getting started. Everyone—the examiners, Treasury, the banks, even the State Department—had a vital interest in the outcome. At the time, no one anticipated that once these countries got into trouble, it would make little difference what was public and what was private.

Out of that debate emerged the so-called means and purpose test. Under this guideline, loans to a state-owned entity would be treated separately if, according to Westbrook Murphy, former deputy general counsel to the Comptroller of the Currency, "the purpose was to finance that entity and the entity had the means to pay back." First proposed in early 1978, this guideline took effect in 1979, just after OPEC raised oil prices. Although one top official of the Comptroller of the Currency said at the time that he didn't expect it to have a significant impact on lending, that was not the view years later.

The man on whose shoulders this little-publicized but ultimately momentous decision fell was Comptroller of the Currency John Heimann, an affable, boyish man who had served as New York State's banking superintendent. "It hit me after I first got there," said Heimann later. "There was pressure to make a decision." All of the big banks lobbied heavily for the separate limit rule. According to former Fed chairman Paul Volcker, banking authorities were "ambivalent" about the rule and in the end decided in favor of relaxation, thereby permitting Brazil and Mexico to take on much more debt.

By the spring of 1979 the question was not whether there would be a recession but how severe it would be and how long it would last. Asked by *Women's Wear Daily* of May 29 when the recession would hit, Wriston replied, "We're in it right now." Citibank had concluded that a "soft landing" was unlikely but that this recession wouldn't be as harmful to the United States or to developing nations as the one in 1974–1975.

Ever the optimist, Costanzo could speak with even greater confidence and authority than he had the first time around. In a July 8, 1979, letter to the *New York Times,* he dismissed fears that higher oil prices represented a "fatal threat to importing nations." Since 1974, he said, the world has learned that "straight line projections of the OPEC oil surplus are invalid." Predictions of a $650 billion OPEC surplus by 1980 proved unfounded, he wrote. The LDCs would survive, he said, because their export earnings had more than doubled from 1973 to 1978, from $67 billion to $151 billion. In a speech in São Paulo, he gushed, "the actual performance by the world's developing economies has been nothing less than spectacular." And he flattered his hosts by noting that "Brazil's performance has been the most spectacular" in Latin America.

Still, Costanzo didn't give his lenders a blank check in Brazil. In April 1979, when Jack Guenther, a Harvard-trained IMF official cut in the George Clark–Al Costanzo mold, joined the country risk unit, Costanzo told him he had assured the board that the rate of growth for the Brazilian portfolio wouldn't exceed the rate for the bank's total portfolio. Said Guenther, "It was not like we had people out there doing anything they wanted." Maybe not anything. But almost anything.

In the wake of the second oil shock the banks' love affair with Mexico intensified. In a September 1979 speech commemorating Citibank's fiftieth anniversary there, Ed Palmer said that "prosperity increases rather than reduces Mexico's needs." Lending to Mexico was largely for oil production, and specifically to Pemex, the state-owned oil company. In the opinion of the American banks, no Mexican borrower was more creditworthy than Pemex. Even though Pemex was government-owned, a lot of "moral authority" loans were made to the company without government guarantees. No one, sources said, ever even asked for confirmation of Pemex's reserve reports. In early 1978, Citibank International Bank Limited, or CIBL, was one of the leaders on a $1 billion term credit to the company.

At first the banks took comfort in the notion that much of their exposure was supposedly self-liquidating, but in the end these loans would prove to be more or less permanent. "We thought it was the best kind of loan you could make to a developing country," said former Morgan chairman Lewis Preston. But the banks might not have fully appreciated just how corrupt Pemex was. For example, one of López Portillo's cabinet ministers, Jorge Diaz Serrano, who had been head of Pemex, was later convicted in a $34 million fraud.

Pemex tapped into the dollar market to fund local costs. One of the many questionable Pemex loans was a $300 million syndication to construct a new headquarters building in Mexico City. Costanzo explained that López Portillo "counted on oil too much," figuring that "if we get into trouble we'll open the spigot."

Despite its oil riches, Venezuela also borrowed huge amounts of money it didn't need. As one top international banker recalled, Mexico and Venezuela "said they saw a unique opportunity to grow in a short period of time." And buoyed up by the surge in the prices of commodities like silver and copper, even Peru looked as if it had turned the corner—again. In fact, in early 1979, it rescheduled debts of $800 million with nearly three hundred banks.

And if Citibank had slowed down its activities in the Philippines, one couldn't tell it from the tombstone ads in the banking magazines. In mid-1979, in what was described as a reversal in policy, the Philippines, like Brazil, decided to borrow from foreign banks rather than institute austerity measures. CIBL was most often the leader of big syndications to the Philippines—to the electric company, for instance, and in early 1980 a $200 million ten-year loan to the Central Bank of the Philippines.

To an inveterate optimist, the LDC debt situation in 1979 seemed to support Wriston's view that countries don't go out of existence or repudiate their debts. When, for example, the Sandinistas seized power from the dictatorial right-wing regime of Anastasio Somoza in Nicaragua, the revolutionary leaders initially told bankers to collect their money from the ousted dictator. They soon reconsidered, however. Led by Latin hand William Rhodes, the banks rescheduled $600 million in bank debt, including $56 million belonging to Citibank, on easier terms.

Indeed, there was hardly an LDC that Citibank didn't like. One exception, ironically enough, was Colombia, one of the few Latin countries that resisted overborrowing. Ever since the country had nationalized part of Citibank's local operation, Colombia had not been high on Wriston's list of favorites. And the Colombian coffee scandal, in which Citibank's collateral essentially evaporated, didn't help matters. In this deal, which was reminiscent of the long-ago salad oil scam, one of Citibank's New York lending units hooked up with a Colombian exporter that local banks had long refused to touch. Anyone who had ever worked in the international unit knew that in lending on commodities it paid to visit the warehouse to make sure the goods really existed. The New York bankers, however, flew into Colombia and extended about $45 million in loans to finance coffee exports without tasting, or even smelling, the coffee. When Citibank discovered it had been duped, apparently by its own officers as well as by the Colombians, it dispatched lawyers to Colombian courthouses to search for documents proving that the debt really existed. But the documentation, it turned out, had been stolen from the courts, and an armored car containing other documents was later hijacked.

According to one former Citibanker familiar with the situation, a bank officer had issued an "inordinate" number of letters of credit in favor of the Colombian coffee exporters. It turned out that the officer was siphoning off commissions. Most of the loans, the source said, were written off. Coming on top of nationalization, the coffee scandal, said veteran Latin hand Juan Sanchez, "soured Wriston on Colombia."

Lawrence Small, the former operations chief who ran the New York unit that had made the loans, tried to put the best face on things in his comments to the media, describing the episode to the *Wall Street Journal* as a "record-keeping snarl." It was that, and more. According to the late Ed Hoffman, a former country head of Colombia, Small was "shouting that the Colombians are terrible people," that the "courts didn't work, and we shouldn't do business with them."

Small, to his credit, was one of the few top Citibankers, former colleagues said, who seemed uncomfortable lending to Latin nations. Historically, he felt, the strength and stability of Latin institutions had "never been anywhere near" that of American institutions. And he would say later, "I'm skeptical of the behavior of some of the Latin governments because it's very clear that they have a track record of making promises that they were going to do certain things, and then simply breaking the promises."

Citibank's Tom Theobald also continued to question aggressive lending at thin spreads. He circulated a memo at about this time that raised red flags about Citibank's "piling on all this debt," as one former associate put it.

Still, Theobald never apparently put himself on the line by demanding that the game come to a stop. Said John Reed later, "If Tom had said—and he never did—'I think this is a mistake and I simply am not going to do it unless you order me to,' we wouldn't have made those loans. Tom clearly was never go-go," but, said Reed, Theobald had the responsibility for running the International Banking Group for several years. Publicly, Theobald toed the Citibank line, telling the *Wall Street Journal* that critics of Third World lending were xenophobic. "I don't think the risk is any greater there than here," he said.

Other bankers were nervous too. Once again, David Rockefeller was worried, but this time for good reason. He warned in June that this time around "some developing nations may have already reached their borrowing capacity and some commercial banks may be confronted with the limits of country exposure." This time, he said, more cooperation from official agencies was "imperative" in recycling.

But the reminders that less developed countries could get into trouble were still relatively small and inconsequential. Turkey was now the biggest headache. Things were so bad there that the country had run out of Turkish coffee, and Turks were faced with blackouts, endless gas lines, and a $10 billion external debt. In late August of 1979 it renegotiated $2.2 billion of its debt to 250 banks.

While Costanzo was downplaying concern about a buildup of LDC debt, others at Citibank were pooh-poohing the latest hand-wringing over the "overextended consumer." Citibank was now at the vortex of what *Time* later called "the most significant change in the way people handle money since Marco Polo discovered the Chinese using paper currency in the twelfth century."

Citibank clearly had a lot at stake in its bet on the consumer. The push for the consumer dollar—loans and deposits—was the new financial battleground. Banks and non-banks alike were slugging it out for a piece of the action. Since the banks were still laboring under Reg Q, the rise in interest rates brought on by higher oil prices and inflation exacerbated their competitive disadvantage.

While Citibank introduced new services such as telephone bill paying, Chase finally got around to launching its New York ATM program, saying it would install 120 machines in 60 branches. Meanwhile, Manufacturers Hanover, in a takeoff on Citibank's retail banking slogan, charged in newspaper ads that "We caught the Citi napping" in paying three-quarters of 1 percent less than Manny Hanny did on passbook savings. But as *American Banker* pointed out, the Manufacturers ads neglected to mention that Citibank's "statement" savings accounts actually yielded more than its accounts did. Citibank claimed that depositors could get a better return on their savings accounts than they could on those offered by savings banks, even though the savings banks could pay one-quarter percent more. When the savings banks cried foul, the Comptroller leaned on Citibank to drop the promotions.

Banks and non-banks were fighting it out over credit cards and traveler's checks as well. In May 1978, after Citibank moved to reacquire Carte Blanche, American Express sued the U.S. attorney general, contending that it was deprived of vital information on the Justice Department decision; the deal went through anyway. With the price of money escalating, the traveler's check business was especially attractive. Traveler's check issuers did not make their money on the nominal commissions they charged customers but on the so-called float. That was because the checks spent days, weeks, or months in the customer's wallet or in transit, allowing issuers to invest the money in various instruments in the meantime. So in 1980, when Interbank, the issuer of MasterCard, moved to sell its own brand-name Master Charge traveler's checks through some eight thousand member banks, Citibank filed an anti-trust suit accusing Interbank of conspiring to dominate the business. Citibank dropped the suit in May 1980.

Then, when American Express launched a television advertising campaign depicting a traveler who had lost his checks in a foreign city being told he couldn't be helped because they weren't American Express checks, Citibank hit the ceiling, and the airwaves, to accuse its competitor of running deceptive ads. Citibank also retaliated with full-page ads in the *Wall Street Journal* and other publications. In a July 23, 1979, letter to the national networks, Citi threatened to haul American Express into court. American Express finally added a tag line to its commercials noting that other traveler's checks made refunds too.

But one leading industry observer, Professor Paul Horvitz, took Citibank—the self-appointed defender of free competition—to task for making such a fuss. "Citicorp accuses American Express of contributing to consumer fears, and they are right," he editorialized in the September 5 issue of *American Banker,* "but much advertising seeks to encourage fear—fear of bad breath or fear of ring around the collar or fear of irritation from rough bathroom tissue." Citibank, he said, should not "expect some government agency or the courts to interfere with their competitors' advertising."

While these battles for the consumer dollar were deadly serious, some of the skirmishes were lighthearted. The next time actor Karl Malden was in L.A. to film an American Express commercial, he decided at the end of a long day of shooting to have some fun at the expense of his old pal. Staring directly into the camera, he said, "Walt, I just want you to know, I read that ad in the *Wall Street Journal.* Now, why did you do it, Walt?" After waxing nostalgic about their strolls together in Peter Cooper Village, Malden went on, "After all, Walt, you're a big shot with Citibank, and I'm still trying to make a living. What are you trying to do?" He arranged for the tape to be shipped to Wriston.

But corporate feuds were forgotten in the face of humanitarian concerns. When the wife of American Express chairman and CEO James Robinson became seriously ill at a Business Council meeting in Hot Springs, Virginia, the American Express jet had already taken off. So when Robinson asked Wriston if he could borrow his GulfStream to fly her back to New York for treatment, Wriston didn't hesitate to say yes.

If there was one issue the big banks agreed on, it was the need to get rid of Reg Q. Wriston had been railing against Reg Q for years, of course. But with the surging interest rates in 1979, the inequity was there for all to see. Even the most unsophisticated consumers who had never heard of Reg Q knew they were now behind the eight ball. If they didn't have $10,000 for a six-month certificate of deposit, they were losing to inflation. Indeed, at about this time depositors were subsidizing borrowers to the tune of about $50 billion annually.

Wriston went public with an ad campaign depicting the little saver leaving a trail of dollars behind him as he tried to catch up to the fat cat with a $10,000 CD. The message read, "The law keeps interest rates so low that savers are losing to inflation."

"If you want more interest on your money," one ad implored, fire off letters to your senators and congressmen. Bank of America also climbed on the bandwagon with ads of its own.

In May, less than a week after the first Citibank ads ran, President Jimmy Carter came out in favor of ending controls, overhauling bank and thrift regulation, and allowing all federally insured banks to offer NOW accounts. In attacking Reg Q, Wriston demonstrated philosophical and ideological consistency, his hallmark. In 1979 it was his turn to lead the U.S. savings bond drive in New York. He found this particularly distasteful because rates available on money funds had surged past savings bond yields. Manny Hanny chairman Gabriel Hauge, a formal, scholarly man, had led the campaign the year before, and in his pep talk at the kickoff cocktail party he had roused savings bond workers to action with patriotic platitudes. Wriston, as Clearing House director Lee recalls, couldn't bring himself to do more than lend his name to the effort. "I think he suspected [the bonds] were sort of a fraud on the public," Lee said later. When it was time to exhort his fellow bankers to action, Wriston said, "And now I want to turn this meeting over to Gabe Hauge, who can tell you with great eloquence why you should be working hard on this." Hauge, having had no warning, proceeded to deliver the same speech he had given the previous year.

After President Jimmy Carter demanded the resignations of his cabinet in July 1979, one of those he gladly accepted was that of Treasury secretary W. Michael Blumenthal, who felt that Carter had done too little too late in fighting inflation. Under Fed chairman G. William Miller, the money supply surged at 9 percent annually, while the inflation rate climbed from 8 percent to 14 percent. At the time, Wriston complained that "since 1967 the government has caused the money supply to grow nearly three times as fast as the goods and services that can be bought with it." Inflation was so severe that in mid-1979 the price of an ounce of gold passed the $300 mark for the first time ever. Put in more human terms, hard-pressed grandmothers were melting down their jewelry for cash.

But Blumenthal, said a former administration official, "did the unpardonable." He expressed his displeasure with Carter's policies to others. "That got back to the president and then their relationship deteriorated." Carter now had to search for a new Treasury secretary willing to serve in a floundering Democratic administration. Even Du Pont chairman Irving Shapiro, one of the few top businessmen who was still a Carter loyalist, declined the invitation.

"They asked a whole bunch of people, and everybody's looking out the window," Wriston recalled. "We were sitting around one day and said, 'Look, the way to get a secretary of the Treasury is to get a guy who's already there.'" Attention quickly focused on Miller. Wriston, among others, felt that Miller's most significant contribution at the Fed was to post No Smoking signs at its headquarters. Said Wriston with some understatement, "His standing with other central bankers of the world could probably be improved [if he were to become Treasury secretary]. They thought it had been amateur night before. He was a fine industrialist. Everything he did at Textron was terrific." But at the Fed, Wriston said, "he was a fish out of water." Shapiro called Carter, who thought that was a great idea. "Now who do I get for the Fed?" Carter asked.

According to one published account, Treasury undersecretary Anthony Solomon was lounging at poolside on a Saturday afternoon when Carter phoned. Carter asked him to continue in his position and to recommend a new Fed chief. Carter reportedly replied to Solomon's recommendation by saying, "Who's Paul Volcker?" Asked why not David Rockefeller, Solomon replied that Rockefeller didn't have a "technical understanding" of the Fed's operations. Carter reportedly didn't understand why that was necessary, despite the fact that it had become apparent that this was one of the major deficiencies of the chairman who was about to be replaced.

Although the president and Wriston were at opposite ends of the political spectrum, Carter knew the next Fed chairman would have to command the respect of top bankers like Wriston. When Carter phoned, Wriston told him, "You have to get someone who foreign central bankers don't say, 'Who dat?' The guy whose name they know is Paul Volcker."

At six foot seven, Volcker was one of the few people Wriston had to look up to. Wriston, of course, had no use for central bankers, but if the country had to have one, he felt that Volcker was the right bureaucrat for the job. Wriston regarded him as a man of "massive intellect and absolute integrity." Except for a brief stint as a Chase economist, every job Volcker had held for the previous thirty years appeared to be yet another rung on the career ladder that would take him to the top job at the Fed. But Volcker scared the bejesus out of others, who considered him ultraconservative, even right wing, and worried that once appointed, he would not play on the Carter team. Volcker had long criticized Arthur Burns's gradualistic approach to fighting inflation, particularly after the first oil shock. Burns was worried, said a senior Fed official, that if he came down too hard Congress would revolt and turn the central bank into a branch of the Treasury Department. As New York Fed president, Volcker had regarded Miller's monetary policy as too easy, and sometimes voted against him. According to William Greider's *Secrets of the Temple,* Bert Lance told Gerald Rafshoon, a White House aide, "I don't know who the President is thinking of for the Fed chairman, but I want you to tell him something for me. He should not appoint Paul Volcker. If he appoints Volcker, he will be mortgaging his reelection to the Federal Reserve."

The cigar-smoking, dry-humored Volcker arrived in Washington with a huge pewter ashtray inscribed, "When you've left New York, you ain't going nowhere." In his case, nothing would have been further from the truth. "I was as responsible as anybody for getting him the job," Wriston said later. It was a contribution Wriston would live to regret.

Just days after being appointed, Volcker instructed Stephen Axilrod, the slightly built financial technician who operated the valves that controlled the flow of money into the nation's economy, to secretly begin working out a plan that would represent a 180-degree shift in the way the Fed conducted monetary policy and waged war against inflation. In its impact on the economy, that move ranked among the most significant events of the postwar period: the Bretton Woods agreement, Nixon's move to float exchange rates, the 1973 oil shock.

Axilrod believed that the Fed had been too cautious in the pre-Volcker period. The surge in oil prices and its aftermath were seminal events that, in hindsight, had called for bold Fed measures to counteract them. These were "big changes," Axilrod said. "You shouldn't move in small ways against them." During that period, he said, the Fed was also faced with the problem of evaluating the impact of consumer shifts out of demand deposits and into other instruments such as money market funds and NOW accounts. Axilrod later blamed half of the double-digit late-1970s inflation rate on oil prices, and half on the Fed.

Although Volcker did not immediately announce his anti-inflation strategy, he quickly made it clear that the Fed would no longer conduct business as usual. In early testimony before Congress, he said he would pursue a tight monetary policy.

Wriston and his colleagues at Citibank had seen this movie before. In Wriston's view, Burns and Miller had also talked a good line about inflation but had done little about it. Citibank regarded monetary policy formulation as a kind of joke. Wriston had never believed that the numbers such as M1 (currency and demand deposits) that the Fed relied on for making monetary policy were of any value, and he'd been telling that to the central bank for years. "The facts are that when they [Fed officials] began to look at it they found [the numbers] weren't any good," said Wriston. "There was an attempt to recast the statistics in a more meaningful way. The minutes would show in those days they [the Fed] were trying to get a better handle on the numbers." But failing to take Volcker seriously was a fundamental miscalculation that Citicorp and Wriston, among others, would live to regret. It soon became apparent that the world was not big enough for two egos as big as Wriston's and Volcker's.

According to John Reed, he and other top Citicorp officials, in a meeting shortly after Volcker's congressional testimony, expressed doubt about his chances of success. "Volcker was testifying he was going to bring the world to a halt, and everybody laughed," Reed said later. Although Volcker was respected by the banking community, he was still seen as "just another head of the Federal Reserve from New York." And Carter was not perceived as decisive enough to take strong action to halt inflation.

Moreover, Citicorp's policy board, and particularly North American corporate banking chief Lawrence Small, believed inflation had become so deeply ingrained in America that no one could end it. Small, said Reed bluntly, was a persuasive voice that there was a "tremendous bias in society for inflation. Everybody loves it. They're never going to stop it. We're going to learn to live with it and like it just like the Brazilians." The policymakers at Citibank believed that 6, 8, or even 10 percent inflation was something that the United States could not only learn to live with but enjoy. The view was, said Reed, that the "business community loves inflation. It solves all their problems. It allows earnings to go up each year, and lets them increase prices all the time." And no business thrived on inflation more than Citibank.

"Politicians loved [inflation] because they had money to play with," Reed said. "Unions love it because they have wage increases. The only people who don't like inflation are people who live on fixed incomes, and who ever heard of them? . . . We were very cynical politically about the willingness of society to give it up. So when Volcker testified we didn't believe it. If we had, it wouldn't have taken a great genius to have figured out what came next."

Aided by inflation, the 1970s were prosperous years for the developing world. Exports grew rapidly, at about the same rate as countries' debts. "Citibank took a reasonably rosy view of the inflationary setting of the 1970s in terms of what it would do for countries' creditworthiness," said Latin debt expert Pedro-Pablo Kuczynski.

Less than two months after he was sworn in, Volcker flew to Belgrade to attend the annual meeting of the IMF and World Bank. One key member of the Volcker team who was not part of the Fed entourage was Stephen Axilrod. Volcker had told him, "You've got to stay home and save the dollar." In fact, Axilrod was drafting a plan even as Volcker prepared to leave for Europe to implement his revolutionary new approach to monetary policy, and was patched through to Volcker's plane to consult with his boss on their plans as he flew over the Atlantic. At Belgrade, Volcker's fellow central bankers continued to hound him about the havoc that the falling dollar was wreaking on the world economy, and the need for the United States to put its economic house in order. As Costanzo recalls, Treasury secretary William Miller was assuring European bankers that "everything was going to work out all right." But the Europeans told Costanzo that Miller didn't make any sense. Meanwhile, the price of gold shot above $400 an ounce, persuading Volcker that he could accomplish more in Washington than in Belgrade, so he cut short his stay and returned home.

Shortly after he returned, Volcker appeared at the American Bankers Association's annual convention in New Orleans to announce an overhaul in the Fed's approach to monetary policy that would instantly turn the world economic order upside down with staggering increases in interest rates. The Volcker move was one of the most revolutionary in the annals of central banking. Volcker announced that the Fed would now conduct monetary policy by seeking to control the *supply* of money rather than the *cost* of money, as reflected in the discount and Fed funds rates. As Volcker told the conventioneers, "Those measures were not designed to make your life as bankers easier."

"He gave the world fair notice," said Axilrod later. "He gave speeches saying he was going to stick to it, but it took a long time for people to believe it."

Wriston remembered that "suddenly you knew the ball game was going to be over. He couched [his plan] in very strange central bank language."

Wriston and Citibank were highly supportive of Volcker's move, both publicly and privately. Several weeks later, on October 30, 1979, in remarks to senior officers, Wriston described Volcker's action as "painful but therapeutic." And chief economist Leif Olsen, in testimony before the Senate Banking Committee, said of Volcker's earlier testimony on the Fed policy that "in the many years that I have followed Federal Reserve monetary policy, I have never before heard a chairman of the Federal Reserve say so many sensible things at one time as chairman Volcker said this morning."

Six months later, on April 28, 1980, Wriston was still a believer. In a talk to bank senior officers, Wriston said that despite the volatility caused by the Fed action—in four weeks in the first quarter, rates had surged a breathtaking five percentage points—"these actions by the Federal Reserve were required, and in time they will moderate our inflation, but getting there will create difficulties. Since, as a nation, we permitted inflation to rage out of control for years, measures to contain it must be increasingly strong." And he added that if the Fed "continues this policy steadfastly, inflation must start downward. Indeed, the economy is already starting to slow, and interest rates should decline further as a result."

After the Fed announcement, short-term interest rates headed for the stratosphere. By early November, Citibank's prime rate formula implied an imminent increase to 15½ from 15¼. Congress tried to jawbone Wriston to hold the lid on it. Fellow Wisconsinite Henry S. Reuss, chairman of the House Banking Committee, fired off a telegram to Wriston trying to persuade him not to boost the prime. Wriston replied that Citibank would proceed cautiously but would hike the rate anyway. "The world is carefully watching to see whether or not political pressure on interest rates will force the Fed to abort its program of using the monetary aggregates as the primary tool of monetary policy and thus weaken our credibility in fighting inflation," he said. In this instance, however, Citibank let Chase lead the uptick to 15½ percent.

The result of the Volcker initiative was the deepest recession since the 1930s. Nearly every sector of the economy was knocked on its ear by the unprecedented combination of 20 percent–plus rates and sluggish growth. Home building was particularly hard hit. According to one former Fed official, "Home builders came in and said, 'We're dying. High interest rates are murderous for our business, but keep it because it's the right thing for the country.'" But, the official said, the developers added that they couldn't make statements like that in public.

Soon, Third World debtors that had been borrowing at rates equal to inflation and repaying in ever-cheaper dollars would have to pay real interest rates in real dollars. With the world moving into recession, commodity prices plummeted, and along with that, the borrowers' ability to earn dollars from exports to repay their debt. Frederick H. Schultz, vice chairman of the Fed, said, "We were pretty clearly faced with a choice between economic slowdown and hyperinflation and flight from the dollar. As we sat there and watched the economic situation deteriorate, it became quite clear we had a dangerous situation on our hands. We decided we had to take draconian measures to get inflation under control."

Before, during, and after the Volcker initiative, the banks, in assessing country risk and setting country limits, continued to focus on individual countries. It would take three more years for the banking world to appreciate the significance of the Volcker move. "We had set limits, long- and short-term, on each country," said Lewis Preston of Morgan. "We didn't look at the whole. That clearly was a mistake."

Wriston's faith in the actuarial base would now collide head-on with his equally strong belief in a global economy. On the one hand, he was convinced that by diversifying globally he would build a business in which one negative event might affect one or two countries but not all of them. On the other hand, he waxed eloquent about a global economy in which nations would be inextricably linked. Unfortunately for Wriston and Citibank, this global linkage occurred sooner than he would have liked. He discovered that if Third World countries overborrowed and interest rates went through the roof, the actuarial base would be rendered meaningless. "We said two things and we got confused," said former Citibanker William Heron. Citibank had never imagined that high interest rates and low commodity prices would combine to hit so many countries at the same time.

Wriston didn't criticize Volcker, however, until the impact of Volcker's action became known. The question, said Angermueller, was "whether it [monetary tightening] should have been done in a more gradual fashion rather than slamming on the brakes and letting the passengers go through the windshield." But at the time, no one at Citibank seemed to grasp the longer-range implications of the Volcker initiative. Costanzo, for one, remained the wide-eyed optimist. On November 7, 1979, just weeks after the Fed move, he told Citibank customers in Monterrey, Mexico, "There is no doubt that private financial markets have come through a most difficult phase in their development. But they have emerged stronger and more resilient than ever. Having overcome the awesome challenges of the 1970s, the financial markets of the world are today more resourceful, more confident, and more capable of dealing with the financial needs of an expanding global economy in the 1980s."

As George "Jack" Clark recalled, after the anti-inflation program got under way, "we should have said, 'Oh, boy, the world has changed. Inflation is going to be high. We better stop lending, because dollar lending is going to be in trouble.' We didn't do that. There wasn't a word of discussion. Not by Clark or Costanzo."

In focusing more on Brazil than on Washington and the Fed, Citibank was watching the wrong country, observed John Reed later. The bank's overseas intelligence system was better than the one it used at home, Reed went on, and Citibank took comfort in its long experience in South America and the feeling that it knew the people and economy.

"We knew the guys overseas. We knew our credits. We'd been in business for fifty years. What we all missed," said Wriston, was that after Volcker returned from Belgrade, "there was no creation of money for six months."

But the evidence suggests that Citibank should have been paying closer attention to Brazil as well. In October 1978, Brazil's electoral college rubber-stamped outgoing president Ernesto Geisel's choice of a successor—João Baptista de Oliveira Figueiredo, who would breeze into office promising to liberalize authoritarian rule and eventually to install a democratic government.

By late 1978 the business press headlines were announcing, "Brazil's 'Economic Miracle' Has Lost Its Luster." That year, according to one account, Brazil had borrowed $12.25 billion, 60 percent of which was loaned to the private sector. About that time, finance minister Mario Simonsen, in a bid to slow inflation, put out the word that Brazil would halt borrowing by government agencies and state-owned companies in 1979. When Figueiredo took power in March 1979, Simonsen moved up to planning minister with responsibility for agriculture, finance, and the central bank, and the administration announced new rules that would curtail the ability of the private companies to borrow overseas. Figueiredo promised to ratchet up the battle against inflation and balance the country's international accounts. If that had happened, it would have been a radical departure from Brazil's pattern to date, which had been characterized by heavy public and private spending with little regard to the financial consequences. But Figueiredo's words were one thing and his deeds another.

Indeed, President Figueiredo had little aptitude for or interest in economic matters, according to Citibank senior officers. That became clear when Wriston visited him not long after he took office. Latin hand Anthony Howkins recalled that the agenda was to have included a serious discussion on the economy and a plea for more banking licenses. Instead, Figueiredo spent almost entire time babbling about his grandchildren, even though "we had some serious things to talk to him about," said Howkins, who was embarrassed by the incident.

Former Citibank Brazil hand Peter Greenough recalled that Wriston's visit to Brazil in 1979 was "like visiting royalty, a symbol of the rightful recognition of Brazil. There was a feeling that it was the beginning of a golden age for Brazil."

But as one author put it, 1979 would prove to be the "high point" of the Brazilian miracle. Manufacturing now made up 28 percent of gross domestic product, up from 26 percent two decades earlier, significantly higher than that of most developing nations. Things went downhill from there. Though 1979 exports amounted to $15 billion, imports increased because of higher oil prices. Two thirds of Brazil's export earnings were now needed to service external debt. Lenders were becoming nervous about the country's economic policies, but because of strong exports and economic growth, commercial bankers were still willing to lend to the country. In looking at Brazil, Citibank saw only a nation that was one of the world's largest steel and auto producers, and a generator of a lot of internal savings. Lost in the shuffle were the millions of Indians who streamed out of the Amazon jungle in a usually futile search for the good life.

Simonsen's track record was far from perfect. Money supply and inflation had surged at an alarming rate. But almost at the same time Volcker was on his way in, Simonsen was on his way out—involuntarily. In his place, Figueiredo appointed agricultural minister Antonio Delfim Netto, a pudgy, self-assured economist with a passion for oysters and nightlife. Delfim Netto was one of the original architects of the Brazilian miracle and had served as ambassador to France under Geisel. Ernane Galveas, a Delfim crony, was appointed finance minister. After Delfim Netto bumped Simonsen, any hope of controlling inflation went out the window. Instead, Brazil, as it had done after the first oil shock, stepped on the gas, accelerating monetary expansion and public investment. "This country will only confront inflation by growing more. Reducing production is not the way out," Delfim Netto said at the time.

Simonsen countered that it was a "growth policy that was no longer sustainable." At year end, Netto devalued the cruzeiro against the dollar by 30 percent, a move that took its toll on the profits of big multinational corporations.

If by the end of 1979 anyone had any inkling that in two and one half years the world would face the worst financial crisis since the Great Depression, it was already too late to do much about it, in the view of many economists. The die was already cast. By this time, according to Simonsen, who had been appointed to the Citibank board, Brazil was piling on new debt largely to refinance the interest payments on the old debt. From 1964 to 1979, Simonsen claimed, Brazil was, "according to international reports, a well-managed country." From 1979 to 1982 it entered the "doubtful category."

At the end of 1979, even as Brazil's fortunes were taking a turn for the worse, Brazil negotiated, with considerable difficulty, the last of the billion-plus megaloans. That $1.2 billion doozy, ostensibly for a gasohol program, was "hard to subscribe," said Simonsen. Brazil got the money, but by now many banks were clearly getting nervous. The terms were less generous than they had been. Eventually, said Simonsen, this became a "general purpose" loan. And by 1980, it was no longer a question of whether Brazil would have to reschedule its massive debt, but when. Both Citibank and Morgan had misjudged Brazil big-time.

Part of the problem the banks ran into with all of the LDCs was that after bank exposure mounted, banks gradually lost any influence they might have had over the countries' economic policies. Bankers were relieved that something was being done about inflation, but they were getting nervous about the increased LDC borrowing triggered by Volcker's anti-inflation initiatives. Eurobankers were getting more finicky about the kinds of deals they participated in, and less generous about terms.

By early 1980, a number of bank watchers were sounding alarms. Still, Costanzo told the _Wall Street Journal_ of February 20, 1980, that the developing countries "have a little more elbow room" because the value of their gold stock had surged and because in 1979 they "borrowed more than they really needed." Recycling, he said, is "still a very manageable picture overall." Publicly, at least, even Volcker was reasonably sanguine. In an appearance before the National Press Club, he said that rising energy prices could lead to "some rescheduling" of developing country obligations, but that the problem was "manageable."

For all the hand-wringing, *Euromoney* in February 1980 called Citicorp's 1979 international lending performance—it led the pack in international loans and loan volume—a "triumph."

———————

Citibank had been caught off guard by Paul Volcker. But it was not about to be caught off guard by the Ayatollah Khomeini.

Wriston and Citibank, unlike Rockefeller and Chase, were not close to the Shah and the Iranians. Although Wriston, at one time or another, had met the head of state of nearly every country his institution did business in, he had never shaken hands with the Shah. Of the dozen or so U.S. banks with Iranian deposits, according to Shearman & Sterling lawyer John Hoffman, Bank of America had the most cash, and Chase managed most of the syndications. Citibank's Iranian business mainly involved oil shipments and letter of credit business on behalf of U.S. oil companies, said Hoffman.

But just as Wriston kept himself plugged into his ubiquitous "Fletcher network," other top Citicorp officials around the world sought to build their own Rolodex files of officials, and even former and would-be officials, in the governments of the countries they supervised. Among the Iranians Edwin Hoffman had met in his capacity as head of Mideast operations for Citibank was Abolhassan Bani-Sadr, an Iranian economist who had been living in exile in Paris for about fifteen years.

Hoffman had concluded that Bani-Sadr was a dangerous man, "a nut," as he put it later. Bani-Sadr had told him in so many words that Iran was overborrowed because of pressure from Western banks and should not pay off the loans. "I felt if he ever came to power our loans would be expropriated," Hoffman said later. Bani-Sadr's message would later remind him that, as in the case of Hitler's *Mein Kampf,* a good starting point in anticipating the policies of a country is simply to read or listen to what its leaders, or leaders-in-waiting, have to say.

When Hoffman learned that Bani-Sadr had returned to Iran to play a key role in the Ayatollah's Revolutionary Council, he immediately phoned Hans Angermueller to tell him how "dangerous" Bani-Sadr was. Angermueller recalls that Hoffman told him, "I have a feeling things are going to get worse and we ought to be prepared to move very quickly" to reduce Citibank's exposure to the country.

From the time the Shah was ousted from power, Citibank had known that its loans to that country were in jeopardy. According to Hoffman, Citibank had cut its exposure over the previous nine months to about $200 million from more than $400 million. That, he said years later in an internal memo, "may have been accomplished at the expense of some client relationships, although I do not think that we really want a particularly good rapport with Khomeini's central bank today unless we were working for Oliver North and the U.S. National Security Council."

Meanwhile, Iran's deposits with Citibank in New York had begun to dwindle as Iran shifted money from the United States to London, according to Angermueller.

Ed Hoffman's worst fears were realized on November 4, 1979, when screaming Iranian fanatics stormed the American embassy in Teheran and took about sixty Americans hostage. Incredibly, the Iranians neglected to pull their deposits from U.S. banks before taking the hostages. "After the revolution they had trouble getting their act together on who was in charge of the bureaucracy," lawyer John Hoffman explained, and Iran had $2.6 billion in loans outstanding to U.S. banks, including the Export-Import Bank of the United States.

After the embassy seizure, Edwin Hoffman phoned Angermueller at home to schedule an emergency meeting. At that conference, held November 6, they were joined by attorney John Hoffman, no relation to Ed, but a close friend and associate of Angermueller.

"I need a reason for offsetting," Ed Hoffman said.

John Hoffman's reply was unequivocal: "There's no way you can do it." Normally, a bank can't seize a customer's deposits unless the customer has defaulted on his loans.

"You got a week to find one," Ed Hoffman snapped back.

Poring through the law books, John Hoffman soon found the requisite legal foundation, if not the rationale: an obscure New York State law that could be construed to permit Citibank to offset its loans against Iranian assets throughout the world. "We then set in motion all the tools which would have allowed us [to offset the loans]," recalled Ed Hoffman. "Our problem was that from a political standpoint we expected the State Department not to support it." Hoffman knew that Foggy Bottom didn't want to upset further its already tenuous relationship with the new Iranian regime.

On November 12, the United States slapped a prohibition on oil imports from Iran. Then, early on the morning of November 14, 1979, Iran announced it would pull $12 billion in deposits from U.S. banks and shift them to European institutions that didn't participate in the boycott. At about that time, Angermueller received a call at his New Jersey home from Ed Hoffman, and Hoffman then called Wriston at his apartment in Manhattan to inform them that the government now intended to freeze all of Iran's assets held by U.S. banks.

Angermueller dressed quickly and caught an early train to Manhattan. Shortly after his arrival, he was joined by John Hoffman. When word came from deputy Treasury secretary Robert Carswell that President Carter had signed the freeze order, Citibank was ready to move. It now possessed both the law and the excuse for using it. The telexes had already been drafted. Carswell asked his former colleagues to request that the bank's European branches take a reading on the impact of the order on international financial markets and report back to him.

As a result of these events John Hoffman soon became a key player in the hostage drama that preoccupied the United States for more than a year.

Citibank now set out to cast the widest possible legal net to haul in the largest cache of Iranian assets against which Iran's loans could be set off. John Hoffman was confident he had found the most efficient method, which became known as the Big Mullah theory, from a phrase coined by Shearman & Sterling partner G. Alfred "Moby" Mudge. One of the requirements of the so-called set off laws is that there be what lawyers call "mutuality"—the same folks have to be on both sides of the transaction. Iranian deposits couldn't be set off against Saudi loans, for example. And here, according to John Hoffman, the Iranians unwittingly played into Citibank's hands. In the wake of the Iranian revolution, everything from industrial conglomerates to a shoe company that previously had been in the private sector was merged into the public sector. As John Hoffman saw things, the law could be interpreted to mean that Citibank could set off Iran's obligations against all of Iran's assets around the world, no matter whose name the assets were in and regardless of whether the obligations had matured or not. Under the Big Mullah theory, if it looked Iranian, smelled Iranian, and had an Iranian name, it was, Angermueller said, "all part of one Big Mullah." Hoffman and Angermueller described the maneuver to Wriston, whom Angermueller considered the world's leading amateur lawyer.

Wriston smiled wryly. "This is imaginative," he said admiringly. "I guess you're applying the golden rule: If you've got the gold, you make the rules."

Before implementing the plan, Wriston phoned superstar trader Ernst Brutsche to solicit his view on the likely impact of the freeze and the set off plan on the foreign exchange and money markets. Brutsche didn't think it would even cause a ripple. Costanzo, who was out of town, echoed Brutsche's opinion. "Do it!" Wriston commanded.

The order went out from the fifteenth floor to Citibank locations around the world to execute the setoff. According to Ed Hoffman, Citibank offset $200 million in loans against $700 million in deposits, leaving $500 million to spare. Angermueller and John Hoffman called their pal Carswell at Treasury and told him what they had done. There was a long pause.

"There are some around here who think you can't do that," Carswell said.

"We think we can," Angermueller and Hoffman replied.

Treasury Secretary G. William Miller told a reporter that "banks cannot set off deposits unless there is a default." Other banks also questioned Citibank's "right of offset," saying that the Iranian assets now belonged to the U.S. government, not to Citibank.

Shortly after the news of the Citibank move got out, Angermueller got a call from top Chase executive Bob Douglass, a longtime aide and confidant of the Rockefeller family, and Milbank Tweed's Francis D. Logan, Chase's top outside counsel. Douglass was perplexed at the legal basis for the Citibank action. "How'd ya do that?" he asked.

"It's the old section 151 trick," Angermueller gloated.

"The what?" Douglass asked. "Boy, do you guys have some balls." A few hours later Douglass called Angermueller again. "We had a fit of courage," Douglass reported. "We did the same thing." That move was especially beneficial to Chase, which had led a syndicated $500 million loan to the Shah that the Iranian legislature had never signed off on, as Iran's constitution required.

When asked about the offset in an interview, published in the *Milwaukee Journal* on January 18, 1981, Wriston replied, "I personally take the view that no country that kidnapped American diplomats deserves the protection of international law. And besides, I would rather have the Ayatollah Khomeini suing me for his money in an American court than me suing him for my money in Teheran."

The frozen funds covered the amounts owed by Iran by a wide margin, but some were perplexed about why the Iranians had let themselves wind up with more attachable deposits than loans. Debtor countries would rarely, if ever, again make the mistake of leaving behind attachable funds.

Despite the assurances from Brutsche and others that the world would not come to an end as a result of the freeze and the offset, that view was not universally shared at Citibank, in Washington, or among the media. "Everybody was thinking about Paul Erdman's book [*The Crash of 1979*]," John Hoffman recalled. Carswell, Angermueller, and Hoffman agreed that the situation was potentially explosive and that someone with credibility ought to say publicly that "the world isn't coming to an end because of this," that "it's not the crash of 1979," said John Hoffman. Angermueller broached the idea to Wriston that morning, and later Wriston and Carswell, in a phone conversation, agreed that Wriston should go on the air. After Carswell left Shearman & Sterling for Treasury, he and Wriston, in order to avoid any appearance of a conflict of interest, had rarely talked with each other about anything. Iran, however, was an exception.

To Wriston, the whole episode seemed like a rerun of the first oil shock in October 1973. Then the hysteria had revolved around whether the lights would go out; this time, the issue was whether the Arabs would pull their money. "In the second one," said Wriston later, "we were talking about real money." As reporters and television cameras streamed into Citibank's fifteenth-floor boardroom for a press conference, a nervous Angermueller asked Wriston, "What the hell are you going to say?"

Angermueller blanched at Wriston's reply: "I don't know." Said Wriston later, "It was one time when I saw palpable terror on the faces of my colleagues." Angermueller, said Wriston, was "scared to death I was going to put my foot in my mouth."

As Wriston's colleagues watched nervously from the back of the boardroom packed with television cameras and reporters, Wriston delivered an extemporaneous address from notes on a scrap of paper on how the Euromarkets worked. To palliate any fear that the freeze would prompt overseas depositors to pull their money out of their Eurodollar accounts, he pointed out that the dollars were actually in the United States and could be taken out only in a suitcase. Referring to the simple "T" accounts used by accountants to balance debits and credits, Wriston tried to assure the panic-stricken that the dollars wouldn't somehow disappear into the sands of Saudi Arabia. "Oddly enough," he said later, "this was a brand-new idea."

Said Larry Small, "The easiest way is the Wriston way of doing things." When confronted with complex transactions, he always said, Small recalled, "Let's go back to the "T" account."

Wriston explained that the only entity that could create dollars was the Federal Reserve and that those dollars couldn't be transferred overseas. In a Eurotransaction, for example, whereby Barclays Bank transferred $10 million in Eurodollars to an Arab bank, all that would happen is Citibank would receive a cable from Barclays ordering it to debit Barclays and credit the Arab bank, but the Citibank balance sheet would remain unchanged. The dollars that back up Eurodollars don't leave the United States.

After that press conference, if there were any lingering doubts about the legality of offsetting, they were dispelled on November 23, when Bani-Sadr announced that foreign debts incurred by the Shah wouldn't be repaid—a statement the banks interpreted as a repudiation. Five days later, Iran's Bank Markazi demanded payment on its foreign accounts. U.S. banks ignored the demand. As a result, Bank Markazi sued five U.S. banks in the United Kingdom—and later in France—and the banks responded with countersuits demanding repayment of outstanding loans to Iran. They also slapped one attachment after another on Iranian assets in the United States.

Wriston's bank was leery of loans to princes, largely because they are nearly impossible to collect if things go wrong. In Iran, however, it made at least one exception—a dollar loan to an aluminum company made with the guarantee of the Princess Ashraf, the Shah's twin sister. With the Shah out of power and the princess living on a palatial Los Angeles estate, the aluminum company had defaulted on its obligation, so Citibank set out to collect its money. Ed Hoffman was forced to negotiate with the law firm that represented the Shah's interests in the United States. To serve the papers, Citibank now had to penetrate the gates of the princess's mansion. According to Hoffman, Citibank's man in Los Angeles sat patiently for hours in his Volkswagen Beetle outside the estate waiting for an opportune moment. As the gates swung open to admit a Rolls Royce sedan, the Citibanker hit the accelerator, rode in on the Rolls's tail, jumped out of his car, and served the papers on a man believed to be the princess's husband, who arrived at the door to greet his guests.

Citibank thought it had settled the matter when it agreed to forgive part of the interest. It turned out, recalled Hoffman, that the aluminum company intended to repay the rest of the loan with Iranian bonds issued during the

Shah's regime, calculated at their face value. "No way," said Citi. After striking an agreement with the company to accept the bonds at their market value, a Citibank officer in Paris was ordered to pick up the actual bonds, drive through the night to Amsterdam, where the market for these instruments was located, and unload them for cash. In the meantime, for reasons no one completely understood, the new Iranian government agreed to pay off the bonds at face value, and Citibank ultimately got repaid on the loan with interest.

In its drive to make the numbers, Citibank was not a place for the faint of heart. Richard Valelly, as a top officer in Iran, claims to have resisted pressure to make certain politically sensitive loans, including one to the Shah's sister. Valelly had been approached by an emissary of the princess and, like any good banker, had asked to speak with her about the purpose of the loan. She declined. "I wouldn't make a loan to someone who wouldn't talk to me," Valelly said years later. "They transferred me because I wasn't aggressive enough." But later, when the Shah fell, loans to the Shah and his family became public, including the loan, later made by Citibank, that Valelly had turned down. "I got blamed for making loans I didn't make," Valelly said.

While Wriston and his pals from Shearman & Sterling were spinning a legal web around the Ayatollah Khomeini, Lee Iacocca and the Chrysler Corporation were reeling from the effects of the doubling of gas prices triggered by the Iranian revolution. Bailing out the nation's third-largest automaker would call for the most complex financial transaction in American history. In his bid to save the company, Iacocca would come to regard Wriston with nearly as much disdain as he undoubtedly felt toward the fanatical Iranian ruler.

After being fired from his post at Ford Motor Company by Henry Ford II, Iacocca had signed on as president of the troubled Chrysler Corporation on November 2, 1978, on the eve of the second oil shock. Though the Ayatollah had certainly made a contribution, bad management was at the root of Chrysler's problems. Even in the aftermath of the first oil shock, Chrysler had continued to concentrate on making big cars. Now Chrysler was whining that the Japanese compacts were crushing it.

In the second quarter of 1979, Chrysler lost $207 million, on top of more than $204 million in 1978. Chrysler had been scraping by through the sale of receivables due on loans made to dealers by Chrysler Financial, which had borrowed about 75 percent of the $1.63 billion Chrysler Corporation owed to its banks. With about $40 million in outstanding loans, Manny Hanny was Chrysler's lead bank, while Citibank was owed $29 million. In mid-1979, chairman John J. Riccardo was forced to plead, unsuccessfully, with the federal government for $1 billion in tax credits. In effect, Chrysler declared itself bankrupt. It teetered on the edge until June 1980, when it received its first check under the Chrysler Loan Guarantee Act.

In early August 1979, the day after G. William Miller was sworn in as Treasury secretary, he met with President Carter to inform him that the administration was likely to be pressured into going along with legislation to bail out Chrysler—a prospect he regarded as a "disaster." Iacocca later wrote in his autobiography that Miller's move to Treasury was critical for Chrysler. At the Fed, he wrote, Miller had opposed a bailout, but he changed his mind when he arrived at Treasury, to which Carter had delegated the problem.

"We either better shoot it down or take control," Miller said he told Carter. Carter instructed him, he said, to take control and do what he thought was right. Miller was determined not to let Chrysler become another Penn Central. In that case, none of the various constituencies had made any sacrifices. The government, Miller said, came to the rescue by deciding to "pump in money to take care of everything." The Treasury calculated that Chrysler really needed $3 billion, not $1 billion, to survive. In the end, the government agreed to guarantee half, as long as the other half came out of the hides of suppliers, banks, unions, and state governments. Miller was convinced that Chapter Eleven was not a viable alternative for a maker of big-ticket durable items like automobiles. He figured that the Treasury would lose more than $3 billion in revenues annually if Chrysler failed.

Citibank, however, made it clear early on that it wasn't going to be an easy touch. For one thing, it chafed at the move by some three hundred small banks to cut and run and leave their big bank brethren holding the bag. Exactly one week after the Iranian asset freeze, Wriston was in Washington adding his influential voice to the chorus of business leaders now in favor of allowing Chrysler to go down the tube. One key politician who shared that sentiment was Senate Banking Committee chairman William Proxmire, who was counting on Wriston, in his testimony, to deliver a compelling and quotable argument against a rescue. He would not be disappointed.

Working in Chrysler's favor was the fact that 1980 was a presidential election year, and there were jobs at stake. "If we had closed down Chrysler I doubt if we would have lost 5 percent of the jobs Chrysler had," Proxmire contended. He believed Ford, GM, and other companies would absorb the other 95 percent.

On November 21, 1979, in hearings before the Senate Banking Committee, Wriston lashed out at the plan. Citing Justice Hugo Black on free competition, he argued that unfettered competition would yield the lowest prices, the highest quality, and the best use of economic resources. "We seem to be moving more and more in the direction of dealing, not with broad national problems, but with the affairs of specific corporations, and in ever greater detail." And once again, he didn't miss the opportunity to slam Regulation Q and other regulatory injustices that limited small savers' interest to 6 percent or less while allowing savers with more than $10,000 to earn 12 percent or more.

Seated next to Wriston at the hearing table was John McGillicuddy, then president of Manufacturers Hanover, who was credited with bringing the Chrysler account to his bank and with helping to rescue Chrysler from financial ruin earlier in the decade. Thanks to McGillicuddy's close relationship with Iacocca and Chrysler, Manny Hanny was now out on a limb. Failure to secure loan guarantees for Chrysler would mean a huge hit and a loss of face for Manufacturers. Manny Hanny was constantly at odds with Citibank. As Chrysler saw things, Citibank was angry at Manny Hanny because Manny Hanny was Chrysler's lead bank, and Chrysler had deteriorated so quickly right under Manny Hanny's nose. Said one observer, "You do expect your senior bank in the credit to let you know when something's going on."

McGillicuddy didn't hold out much hope for Chrysler either and refused to commit himself to more loans. But he was convinced that the $1.2 billion Chrysler needed couldn't be raised as a debtor-in-possession. "I thought bankruptcy was the kiss of death in the ability to sell cars," he said later. "I understood where he [Wriston] was coming from, and he understood where I was coming from. There was no personal bitterness involved," he insisted. Angry as he was at Wriston at the time, he did his best to contain his temper. After Wriston delivered his testimony, McGillicuddy turned to him and said, "Well, at least you're consistent." As McGillicuddy recalled, "We both walked in with a smile and came out with a smile."

David Rockefeller also favored federal guarantees for Chrysler. He later pointed out that Lockheed, New York City, and Chrysler were instances in which "the public didn't lose anything by virtue of having an underpinning at a critical moment in time."

For once, however, Ralph Nader and Walter Wriston were on the same side. And, not surprisingly, Ford and GM also opposed the Loan Guarantee Act, as did the Business Roundtable, prompting Chrysler to resign from that group.

The comments of Wriston and other bankers, Proxmire concluded, provided "devastating evidence that Congress should not approve a federal loan guarantee for Chrysler."

Wriston was baffled that the U.S. government would consider bailing out Chrysler even while it was trying to break up IBM. A year earlier, Wriston had told *Time,* "So the government is suing to dismember IBM. The question is, what is the public good of knocking IBM off? The ultimate conclusion to all this nonsense is that people cry, 'Let's break up the Yankees— because they are so successful.' " Yet as things turned out, breaking up IBM probably wouldn't have done it any harm.

What grated on Iacocca and his colleagues most was Citibank's view that Chrysler would be just like any other bankruptcy. Chrysler and other supporters of a federal bailout believed that Chrysler's long-term survival, like that of a bank, depended on the confidence of suppliers and customers. They also argued that the company's failure would sink many well-run vendor companies as well. Opponents contended that other car makers would absorb Chrysler's manufacturing capacity and that the economy as a whole would not lose much if Chrysler went under. Chrysler chief financial officer Robert S. "Steve" Miller, however, argued that GM and Ford had excess big car capacity, and that Ford, for one, "couldn't use our capacity for three years down the road."

In its studies, said Steve Miller—dubbed "Big Miller" to distinguish him from the much shorter G. William Miller, known as "Little Miller"—the government had concluded that Chrysler could make it. Citibank, on the other hand, had done studies, which Miller said Chrysler never had the opportunity to review, that convinced the big bank that the company would not survive even with guarantees and that the banks would be better off trying to get 20 cents on the dollar in bankruptcy court. The Citibankers, said Steve Miller later, "thought they had the logic on this case and [that] no one could see things as clearly as they could."

Ironically, even after Wriston testified against a bailout, one of his top customer men, Reuben Richards, a senior Citicorp lender responsible for the Chrysler relationship, was battling to hold Chrysler's lending group together and lobbying Treasury secretary William Miller for a government rescue. Such seeming incongruities didn't bother Wriston. "If he felt strongly on something he'd do his own thing," said Richards later. He had no problem "if I acted differently." But there were 500,000 American jobs at stake, and if they were lost, the government would pay more in unemployment and welfare benefits than guarantees would cost.

Ultimately, Congress approved the $1.5 billion Loan Guarantee Act, which called for the U.S. government to take Chrysler as collateral. The act also required lenders, unions, and suppliers to make concessions.

At least one senior government official involved in the bailout, Brian Freeman, opined that Wriston's testimony reflected the higher level of political sophistication the banks had achieved since Penn Central, Lockheed, and the New York City budget crisis. Conveniently, New York City's seasonal borrowing arrangement became the model for Chrysler. There, he said, the banks were able to pass the downside on to the government, get paid interest, and receive no upside. In Lockheed, they had received a guarantee and fees. And now, in the case of Chrysler, they would be forced to make concessions, but in return would receive warrants entitling them to a share of future profits. Said Freeman, "It took the banks five years to figure out how to play the process in Washington," but now there was "less flailing around, more focus, more artfulness." According to Freeman, the banks made out better from Congress because they were a "reluctant bride." Wriston was the leader in creating the perception that "he would just as soon [see] the thing get liquidated," said Freeman, a position he felt was more strategic than philosophical.

Wriston continued to lament the bailout legislation even after its passage. In a January 1980 speech, he declared that private ownership had "become so subverted that the employees, including the professional managers, have in effect become wards of the state."

Indeed, Chrysler's troubles with Citibank didn't end with Wriston's testimony. In the legislation, Congress had laid out what the banks' contribution would have to be. Chrysler would now have to persuade the banks as a group to get on board and then to thrash out how much each category of bank should kick in. And of course Chrysler would have to get the big New York banks to sign on before it could take on the rest of the banking world.

Whatever effect Wriston's testimony had on the final outcome, Citibank's strategy of keeping Chrysler's feet to the fire most certainly prolonged the company's agony. By playing the spoiler, Citibank complicated the negotiations and certainly delayed the completion of an agreement with the big banks—by up to four months, according to Steve Miller.

The man assigned to keep the pressure on Chrysler was lanky, pipe-smoking Peter Fitts, then a young and aggressive Citibank workout specialist. "Fitts is a strong personality, a tough guy, somewhat intimidating," said Miller. But, he conceded, Fitts was also cool and professional.

In early 1980, shortly after the passage of the legislation, it became clear to Miller that Citibank would be his major problem. At that time, Miller figured Chrysler might make it through another sixty days before going broke. He found one Citibanker's attitude cavalier. "They were saying, 'There's no hurry here.' "

"Wait a minute," Miller replied. "We're going to run out of cash."

"You can always stiff your suppliers," the Citibanker said. "This thing may take till September."

For Miller, September seemed like the end of the world, but in fact, the Citibanker's remarks proved prophetic.

The pivotal problem was that some four hundred banks had made loans to Chrysler, and their financial interests differed widely. While all of the negotiations were aimed at the factory operations, any changes in the terms of the loans to the manufacturing arm, said Steve Miller, would tend to improve the "quality and viability of the loans to the finance company." For Citibank's credit men, the Chrysler episode demonstrated that parent companies' obligations couldn't be separated from those of their finance units.

Complicating things further were the conflicts and biases brought to the negotiating table by the banks. Nothing was more frustrating for Chrysler than being caught up in the bankers' petty animosities over who had shafted whom on previous deals. The European banks were still seething over the reluctance of U.S. banks to pitch in on a troubled West German company, while the Japanese banks simply wanted out because they viewed Chrysler as an American problem. Meanwhile, the Canadian banks were relatively sanguine about how they would emerge from a Chrysler bankruptcy, because Canadian bankruptcy laws were more protective of banks there. "The Americans would jump up and down and scream," said one observer. "The Canadians would treat them like dirt." The U.S. bankers, he said, would cool their heels in a Toronto office, only to discover at the end of the day that their Canadian counterparts had already left. The small-town banks, of course, despised Citibank and the other big New York banks. Citibank was invading their turf with its mass mailings of credit cards and threats to expand across state lines. "It was an impossible puzzle," said Steve Miller later.

As the negotiations wore on, the banks and Chrysler were constantly at each other's throats over the accuracy and credibility of the automaker's cash forecasts. Steve Miller explained: "When a company is in the black, no one particularly cares whether six-month cash forecasts are off by half a billion dollars. But a one half or three quarters of 1 percent miss back then [1980]—that was everything."

Citibank had regarded the creation of its workout department as a quantum leap forward in handling troubled credits. Steve Miller, however, saw things differently. By now, most banks had what Miller called this "terrible" department, which he regarded as an inflexible device dominated by lawyers who kept score according to "how much meat they can scrape off a dead carcass. Their only measurement is cash out in a short period of time."

To Miller, Peter Fitts was the personification of Citibank haughtiness. "Some people come to negotiations intending to get a deal done and get on with it," said Miller. "And some seem to come wanting to score points, to demonstrate their negotiating skills, get a few extra things. I don't think being hard to deal with gets you a better deal in the long run. . . . We would have life-and-death fights" over whether the banks would get two cents or three cents more on the dollar when "they could have gotten double."

In his autobiography, Iacocca would later say of Peter Fitts and a like-minded workout man from the Irving Trust Company: "Their general attitude was that we at Chrysler were dummies who didn't know what we were doing. These guys didn't care about jobs or investments. The only thing that mattered was the return on their money." After acknowledging Wriston's status as the nation's most influential banker, Iacocca described Wriston as "our albatross." He wrote that "Citibank was sure we were going bankrupt, and they couldn't wait to get their fifteen cents on the dollar—which is what we had proposed as a settlement. Citibank seems to enjoy its reputation as a hard-nosed outfit. Anytime they could set up a roadblock in our way they did."

"Lee Iacocca hates Walt for that to this day," says one Citicorp insider.

Negotiating with the banks was a debilitating experience for Chrysler and its dealers, employees, and suppliers. "The process was very costly," said Steve Miller. "I'm sure we could have bled less, lost less muscle, been a little stronger, more stable, had we been able to contract that period." Nonetheless, he acknowledged that "it forced us to do things that made us lean and mean."

When Chrysler ran out of money in June, it drew on the first $400 million in funds under the congressional act. For three weeks it had survived only by cutting off payments to suppliers. But by mid-1980, most of the banks had signed on. And once Chrysler had succeeded in obtaining agreement with the big banks, Citibank, as Steve Miller recalls, "got on the team and did a lot of work to beat the bushes to get the little guys."

Ironically, Iacocca later wrote, "To be honest, when I was president of Ford, I don't think I would have listened to those arguments either. I probably would have said to Chrysler, "Leave the government out of this. I believe in the survival of the fittest. Let the marginal guy go broke."

In the end, Chrysler served as a dress rehearsal for the rescue of the big banks from the LDC crisis.

To some bankers, Citibank's tough stand on Chrysler appeared to be part of a broader push by the bank in the late 1970s to sharply curtail lending to rust-belt America. "They moved out of the rust belt in a narrow time frame in a broad way," said Hollis Rademacher, then a senior officer at Chicago's Continental Bank. "Their assessment was that the world was changing, and U.S. industries are not competitive." The signs of this shift, says Rademacher, were apparent in a number of ways. More and more, he said, Citibank began to insist on restrictive covenants in loan agreements, and it declined to participate in loan syndicates unless it was the lead bank. To some extent, other large banks followed the Citibank example.

According to Lewis Preston, former chairman of J. P. Morgan & Company, Citibank tightened up on the rust belt by shifting from balance-sheet lending to secured lending [lending on the basis of asset values]. Citibank's move to secure its position in loans forced other banks to do the same. Said Preston, "Another bank, to protect its position, is not going to have Citibank in a favored position."

20

CITISTAKES

*W*hen Wriston and his associates assumed the leadership of Citibank in the late 1960s, they did so knowing that they were in many ways woefully ill-prepared to run a big bank. "My partners and I were very conscious that we got a lot of on-the-job training as, prior to our appointment, we had been given no experience in a good many facets of the business," Wriston said later.

Stillman Rockefeller had made decisions like a battlefield commander, rarely taking colleagues into his confidence. Wriston was determined that this would not happen again. Next time around, he wanted an orderly transition that would allow the board to scrutinize the performance of several candidates over a number of years. This new approach would give rise to one of the most highly publicized horse races in American business history—and, some would say, one of the most destructive.

The lineup of potential successors consisted of Thomas Theobald, age forty-two, who had successfully gotten the World Corporation Group off the ground and had later run international, and who would now be responsible for all institutional, corporate, and government business; John Reed, forty years old, whose consumer business was still deep in the red and who would now head all of the bank's business for individuals; and Hans Angermueller, age fifty-five, Wriston's trusted friend and consigliere, who would run legal and external affairs. With an increasing number of bureaucratic layers, Citibank was running out of titles. So all three members of the triumvirate were promoted to senior executive vice president.

The plan that gave rise to the horse race was the brainchild of strategic thinker George Vojta, matrix management engineer and creator of the World Corporation Group. After several years as international chief, he donned that hat once again in 1978 to spend over a year devising the new ten-year plan. Vojta's ivory-towerish demeanor was reflected in the report, which started with a dissertation on the relationship between ancient nomadic tribes and disintermediation.

Called Project Merlin, the plan sought to address the growing pains Citicorp had endured during Wriston's first full decade as CEO. Citibank, in those years, had become unwieldy and bureaucratic. That bureaucracy had dampened the entrepreneurial spirit that had prevailed in his days as head of international and then as president. He wanted to return the bank to those glory days of yesteryear. Citibank was learning that business initiatives that fell clearly into a single bailiwick got executed reasonably well. Those that crossed organizational lines often turned out miserably. Wriston anticipated that in the 1980s Citicorp would become a $250 billion company, and he was determined to prepare for that. That preparation, he told his colleagues, demanded further decentralization, more individual decision-making, and closer ties to the marketplace.

Vojta's ten-year plan in many ways reflected what Wriston and his colleagues already knew. Citibank's business mix was out of whack; 80 percent of its earnings were coming from overseas activities. More emphasis had to be placed on the domestic market. But everyone knew that Citibank's prospects for doing more business with *Fortune* 500 companies were dwindling, as they were in New York State generally. Citibank's future lay in serving consumers and middle-market companies. In remarks to top officers, Wriston said he expected the consumer business to generate as much as 30 percent of the bank's earnings by the mid-1980s. In fact, said credit officer Larry Glenn, "the problem wasn't too much international earnings. The problem was we had a lousy business in the United States." The ten-year plan also sought to figure out what to do about investment banking, a growing bone of contention within Citicorp. At the end of the rainbow was a pot containing $1 billion in earnings.

Decentralization and rapid growth had created a need for vastly improved financial controls. "Matrix management, tax issues—those changes had gotten ahead of controls. We needed a discipline more prevalent in industry than [in] banking," said top Citibanker Paul J. Collins.

In fact, managers who joined Citibank from non-banking concerns were appalled at how lax the financial controls were. "The finance and control function of industry is far superior to that of banks," said one former officer. Checks and balances between the controller and other managers were lacking. "They [Citibank] didn't know profits by product line or service," he said. He was horrified that it took nearly three weeks to determine how much the bank had earned in any given month. Errors were rampant, and there were often big discrepancies between the numbers used in internal reporting and those filed publicly.

Though some say the David Edwards affair prompted Citibank to focus on the need for improved controls, others say the real trigger was the $1 billion that fell through the cracks. According to former top Citibanker Michael Callen, Citibank understated its assets and deposits in its financial statements in the late 1970s when it eliminated a large offshore account in reconciling intercompany transactions. "That upset a lot of people," said Callen, though it was later uncovered in an audit. To beef up weak controls, Wriston hired Thomas E. Jones, a pale, cheery Englishman who had been one of ITT's top bean counters.

Theobald emerged from the reorganization as the front-runner. He was a capable manager and the quintessential corporate banker, but he lacked the imagination and vision of John Reed.

Reed was seen as a junior version of Walter Wriston, a futurist who shared Wriston's entrepreneurial, risk-taking ethic. But Reed later told an interviewer that "there are times when I wish I had gray hair, and less of it, and was sort of quiet and distinguished."

Although some of Angermueller's colleagues took potshots at him for his alleged lack of managerial ability, this reputation apparently did not stem from any failed attempt to run a business. In its June 8, 1981, issue, *American Banker* quoted a Citibank "insider" as saying that "Hans does not yet understand money." Still, Angermueller laughed all the way to the bank; he was Citi's fifth-highest-paid officer. In point of fact, one means of building a reputation as a manager was to build an empire to be managed. That could be achieved by exploiting a market. But it could also be done by persuading top managers that certain business units should be included under one's umbrella. "You saw Tom building up, John building up. Frankly, I don't know what I was supposed to build up," Angermueller said later. "The general counsel's office was never more than three guys and a dog. . . . I didn't run any business. I never had the opportunity or the inclination." At an institution known for its arrogance, Angermueller was a good-natured, engaging exception. In a telling remark to the *Wall Street Journal* on December 18, 1980, he said, "It's in the interest of the institution to moderate that arrogance. Sure we're at the cutting edge, but that doesn't mean we should look down our nose at everyone else. . . . I don't know why I got caught up in this tripartite race. I didn't regard myself as a contender. The fact that the newspapers chose to build a horse race was more of their making than mine." Recalling the often unpleasant rivalry between Walter Wriston and Tom Wilcox, Angermueller figured that he might have been thrown into the race for "dilutive effect," to reduce tensions between Theobald and Reed.

That might have been Angermueller's view, but Wriston denied later that this was his intention. Wriston felt a genuine personal affection for his loophole lawyer and was fascinated by his ability, and that of his legal disciples, to design clever ways through and around rules and regulations. In one instance, recalled Ed Hoffman, Angermueller's men helped structure a deal for Exxon to take its Reliance Electric Company unit private. Citibank, he said, ended up owning all of it, lawfully circumventing rules barring banks from owning industrial companies.

Meanwhile, George Vojta felt justified in drawing a box on the chart where his name would go. Vojta, whose name in Finnish means "rising sun," at first considered himself a contender for Wriston's job and was stunned when he learned that this was not what Wriston had in mind. Wriston called Vojta the "finest conceptual thinker I've ever known," but in the inner sanctums of Citibank this was translated to mean that Wriston did not regard him as a good manager. Wriston felt his most important responsibility was to put the right people in the right jobs. Doing that, of course, entailed assuaging the egos of people whose view of their skills exceeded or differed from that of the chairman. Vojta's talent lay in "thinking about tomorrow," as Wriston put it, not in administration.

"George wanted a job he wasn't going to get," Wriston said later. Wriston loathed bureaucratic doublespeak, and fumed when he learned that Vojta had, in an elliptical way, made implied promises to several subordinates that they would be given the same top job in London. "George would say, 'We will manage toward a situation in which opportunities in London will present themselves that might be congruent with your talents.' The result was that you have five guys go home and tell their wives that they would be going to London," Wriston said. The sun had set on Vojta's Citibank career.

As early as 1979, Wriston, Al Costanzo, Ed Palmer, and Bill Spencer began to turn the bank over to the new generation. Citibanker Rick Roesch remembers that they accompanied the policy committee to the bank's conference center in Westchester, where Wriston told the group that he and his partners were leaving and would return in a week. "We're going to leave you guys to decide what the strategic plan should be," Wriston told them. That week, said Roesch, "cemented the future of the consumer business."

As part of their grooming, Wriston later delegated to the three contenders certain duties traditionally exercised by the CEO. They were assigned to head up new committees covering functions that transcended their current roles. Reed was never a people person. In a bid to remedy that, he was appointed head of a personnel committee. In that capacity, he "had to rise above being head of consumer," Roesch observed. Angermueller was put in charge of the acquisitions and divestitures committee, and Theobald chaired a finance committee that was created later in the wake of funds management debacles.

The three-way competition filtered down through layer after layer of the Citibank organizational chart, pitting friend against friend in a corporate civil war. At every level, disciples of the three contenders duked it out on the battlefield. To many, this was the last stand for the old Citibank culture, politicizing the institution like no event before it. Citibankers, said former officer Peter Greenough, conspired to sabotage others' efforts instead of cooperating for the good of the bank. For example, they withheld information that might have helped others generate business, and they undermined colleagues who were traveling or on vacation.

Of this "open competition," Harvard professor Charles Williams remarked in un-Harvard-like fashion, "I think it stinks." He felt it pressured people on lower rungs of the ladder to "declare their allegiances and preferences." That means, he says, that "people spend a fair amount of time and energy on the horse race when they ought to be thinking about other things. Also, it means you've got a clear loser. If you let the parties get identified, it's very hard for the losers to stay in the organization and be happy. If they're good men, why have them lost?"

One casualty of the new organization was the World Corporation Group (WCG), the centerpiece of Citibank's experiment with matrix management. By most accounts, that unit really worked. At a time when business was becoming more and more global, it made sense to treat a multinational company as a global relationship, rather than have the heads of each country serve the company as if it operated only in their territory. If anything, the unit seemed to many to make even more sense in 1979 than it had in 1973. But the WCG had also made Citibank more bureaucratic by creating more layers of staff and management to control, coordinate, and communicate. The matrix just got to the point where it grated on people," said one former officer.

Former merchant banking chief Robert Logan stated, "The matrix screwed up Citibank. It superimposed a huge cost structure."

Wriston and others felt that the organization had been in place long enough so that the culture of global relationship banking had been created and the organization, and its bureaucracy, could be disbanded. Then, as the thinking went, the former officers of the WCG could be "seeded" throughout the Citibank empire, and informal networking would replace paperwork. Instead of remaining a line organization, the WCG became an "informational thing," Wriston said later, "which is the way it started. It came full circle."

Reuben Richards commented that "the competition was shocked when we broke [the WCG] up. They thought we had created the magic formula." Indeed, for many banks, both U.S. and foreign, the group had become the banking industry's template for serving global corporations.

Just as the other big banks had followed Citibank's lead in creating units like the World Corporation Group, they followed once again in disbanding them. At Citibank, said chief accounting officer Tom Jones, the idea was that Tom Theobald, who was taking over all of commercial banking, would now extend the success of the WCG to the entire commercial banking operation.

But former officers say that the real reason the unit was broken up was political. It was done, they say, largely to appease Theobald and Lawrence Small, the newly appointed head of institutional banking for North America. Neither of them wanted to share responsibility for major corporations headquartered in the United States. Small, according to former colleagues, felt that the WCG had become "too elitist." As part of the restructuring, he essentially integrated the unit into his organization.

Former senior officer Michael Callen saw the dissolution of the WCG as one of Citibank's "dumber" decisions. "It [the WCG] was successful. Everybody loved it, and we dissolved it." This move, Callen contended, meant that instead of providing a global company with Citibank's global resources, the bank would once again provide them only with the best person or resources available in the country where it was based. Meanwhile, he said, competitors were increasingly dealing with global companies in a global manner.

"There were things Goldman, Sachs was doing for these clients [that] we weren't doing, and they took away very large amounts of business, and still do, that there is no particular reason we couldn't have ourselves."

The Citibank reorganization and the disbanding of the World Corporation Group represented a turning point not only in the history of Citicorp but in the annals of American banking as well. In a real way, it marked the end of the era of relationship banking and the old "interest differential" bank and ushered in the new age of transactional banking and swaps, futures, and leveraged buyouts. Products and deals now came into their own. Asset-based financing, leasing, receivables financing—these were now products to be sold. Each product line had its own sales force that competed with the old line account officer for the attention of corporate treasurers. Companies no longer relied on a single bank or a handful of banks to supply all of their financial needs but instead began to buy products from the lowest bidder. And more and more, Citibank's earnings were now derived from supplying services to companies for a fee.

The appointment of Lawrence Small, the former back office aide-de-camp to Reed, as head of institutional banking for North America not only reflected this trend but strongly reinforced it. This was a style of banking with which Small, as a "process manager," in Citibank lingo, was entirely comfortable.

Small's appointment was classic Wriston. Though Small had little experience as a corporate banker, Wriston regarded him as someone with long-term potential. No one knew anything about his inclination for risk-taking, but according to a former officer, Wriston said, "He never let us down."

That move brought the same kind of culture shock to corporate banking as Small, Reed, and White had brought to operations. Into this genteel white-shoe world, Small introduced aggressive sales objectives, management information systems, forecasts, and targets. If Small's appointment didn't trigger the move away from the rust belt, it certainly accelerated it.

Under Small, Citibank became a national corporate banking powerhouse. He further decentralized corporate banking, uprooting corporate lenders from New York and dispatching them to the countryside. Previous efforts to station bankers around the country—in Edge Act and loan production offices—had not been very successful. The Fed had concluded that Edge Act units intensified competition and were good for regional economies, but they were never big moneymakers. And as for the loan production offices, "we got the leftovers, companies no one else wanted," said George Davis, one of Small's deputies. "We used to count sales calls [in the loan production offices]," said Davis. "If you didn't meet a quota terrible things happened."

This practice was in stark contrast to that of the old school as embodied in Reuben Richards, one of Citibank's quintessential relationship bankers, and ten years Small's senior, who was dispatched to Europe. "The bankers were horrified, apoplectic, red-faced," said George Davis. In the opinion of many observers, the old-style relationship bankers didn't agree with Small's approach to doing things, so they left the bank.

Richards recalled that "all of a sudden 'me' turned into a very important part of the equation. You couple that with profit centers and products, and you could see what would happen."

Small, an accomplished guitarist, spent hours on the corporate jet shuttling from one company to another. To relax, he hooked his electric guitar up to his Sony Walkman so as not to distract the pilots. As a musician, he understood Leonard Bernstein's distinction between the good musician who could hit all the right notes and the great one who could play between the notes. This distinction is what Small called "the edge." Similarly, in his appraisals of colleagues, he differentiated between good managers and great ones.

In his new job, Small introduced the notion of syndicating domestic loans. At one point he "called us up to get $1 billion off the books," said a former officer. When account officers explained that borrowers didn't want their loans sold into the secondary market, Small told them if they didn't do it, he would pull them off the account.

As he and Reed had done in operations, Small took an ax to expenses. He "ripped away the support staff—secretaries, staff people, management information system [MIS] people—and placed them in a common resource pool," said Davis.

Citibank's move greatly intensified competition in American corporate banking. In contrast, Morgan did not suffer from the dilemma of transactional banking versus relationship banking. Intoned former chairman Lewis Preston, "We always stayed more toward a relationship orientation."

Meanwhile, Citibank recognized that as long as it was opening loan production offices and mailing credit-card applications on the home turf of out-of-state banks, it would never compete in correspondent banking by playing Mr. Nice Guy. So it instructed Bob White, the soft-spoken but hard-nosed back office whiz, to sell back office automated technology, automated teller systems, and technical advice to correspondents. White spent millions developing systems for other banks, but he could never sign up enough to make any money.

Just as Wriston and Spencer had allowed Reed almost total freedom to succeed or fail with the operations overhaul, Reed was equally permissive with trusted subordinates like White. Later, in part to be closer to his home, White moved his Financial Institutions Services Group to Stamford, Connecticut, without notifying the bank's top management. Much as Spencer admired White, he was furious over this move. "I chewed him out for half an hour," Spencer recalled.

Closely related to Citibank's decision to dissolve the World Corporation Group was Wriston's pivotal decision not to integrate its investment banking activities into a single investment bank that could compete head to head with traditional Wall Street firms. In 1980 there were those who believed Citibank missed a critical opportunity, and lost considerable ground to J. P. Morgan and Bankers Trust, when Wriston opted not to bring investment banking together under one roof.

By the late 1970s, the commercial banking business that Wriston had inherited in 1970 had changed dramatically. The biggest companies—General Motors, IBM, and the rest of the *Fortune* 500—no longer needed big commercial banks to meet their routine funding needs. They could raise money in the commercial paper markets more cheaply than they could borrow it from the banks. Rust-belt companies like Chrysler needed banks, but banks had begun to shy away from them. Citibank's elitist culture had never encouraged the development of middle-market corporate businesses—companies with revenues of $5 million to $100 million. Corporations now needed highly skilled people who could give them good financial advice. The distinctions between commercial banking and investment banking were becoming less important than their similarities. Eventually, all commercial bankers would have to become investment bankers.

Overseas, Citibank could do almost anything it wanted in investment banking. To be sure, Citibank's ability to perform certain investment banking functions in the United States was curtailed by the Glass-Steagall Act. Its standing as a merger and acquisition adviser was undercut in part because it couldn't underwrite and deal in equity securities. Perhaps more than anything, investment banking at Citibank suffered from constant management turnover, a problem that beset other operations as well. In contrast, the heads of Goldman, Sachs, the investment banking firm that Citibank most admired, ran the firm until they retired or died.

Citibank's obsession with the cult of the manager—the notion that good managers are interchangeable—also applied to investment banking. Would-be investment bankers at Citibank felt like wallflowers at the party. "We were always the odd man out," said a former Citibanker. "Heading investment banking at Citibank was not looked on as a good career," said another former Citibanker. He believed that under the right management investment banking could have achieved Goldman's success, but at Citibank, he said, "every year you get a new incentive plan," and there were "way too many staffies."

Citibank's investment banking–related business at the turn of the decade was a mixed bag. One of its most promising businesses, however, was risk management. The volatility in the financial markets the last several years had spawned a new industry within an industry—financial futures, derivatives, and various other risk-management devices. They had evolved directly from commodity futures, which farmers and others had used for years as a hedge against the risks associated with weather and the vagaries of the markets ranging from wheat to pork bellies. Futures markets were developed for ninety-day commercial paper, Treasury bonds, and mortgage securities, enabling companies and institutions to protect themselves or to profit from rate changes. Futures were developed for interest rates, stock indexes, and currencies. In 1979 the trade in financial futures accounted for a relatively tiny portion of total futures trading. A few years later, however, it accounted for most of it.

The centerpiece of the new product culture, and of investment banking at Citibank, was the currency swap, an instrument that was simple in name and principle but arcane and complex in execution. This was a device tailor-made to be sold by an institution with thousands of customers worldwide, and its invention by a brilliant young black lawyer represented a landmark in the globalization of Walter Wriston's Citibank. Indeed, it ranked in importance with the negotiable CD, the Eurocurrency CD, and the World Corporation Group. Ironically, profit centeritis came perilously close to destroying a unique market for Citibank that would generate over the years hundreds of millions in bottom-line income.

The man most responsible for inventing and introducing the swap to Citibank was Peter Eccles, a Harvard Law graduate. After stints with a top law firm and with Goldman, Sachs, Eccles joined a small merchant banking firm seeking to get into the pockets of big U.S. multinationals. There Eccles made the discovery that global companies often had local currency reserves in certain countries that were blocked by exchange controls in the same way that Citibank's own profits in some countries were blocked at one time or another. A big elevator company, for example, with operations in Brazil and Argentina might have $5 million in blocked Brazilian cruzeiros and no way to put it to use locally. At the same time, that company might lack pesos in Argentina, where it would like to construct a plant. To solve the problem of this elevator company, Eccles would seek out another big company, say a construction equipment manufacturer, with exactly the opposite problem: no Brazilian cruzeiros but lots of Argentine pesos. He would then negotiate a currency swap between the elevator company and the equipment company.

In fact, Eccles's first currency swap involved buyers and sellers on opposite sides of a deal done in U.S. dollars and Australian dollars, which were then subject to exchange controls.

The basis for the currency swap was the fact that multinational companies enter into long-term foreign exchange obligations around the globe that leave them with large assets and liabilities denominated in foreign currencies. These assets and liabilities pose serious earnings risks from currency fluctuations when there is no long-term forex market. An American company, for instance, might incur $20 million in ten-year fixed rate debt, denominated in (80 million) French francs, in order to buy a ship from a French yard. But the company does not want to owe $30 million ten years later because of foreign exchange fluctuations. To guard against that, the American company could obtain a commitment from a counterparty—say, a French company issuing $20 million in ten-year debt in the U.S. capital markets—to pay it 80 million in French francs ten years later. The American company would receive the francs, the French company the dollars, and the bank a fee for arranging the transaction. In effect, the intent of a swap is to make sure that each party comes out whole. In foreign exchange markets that operate free of exchange controls, short-term transactions, such as the purchase and sale of grain, oil, and other commodities, these risks can be hedged with forward contracts in currency bought at a stated rate good for a certain period. The swap market, however, emerged because there was no way to hedge long-term foreign exchange risks or to hedge in currencies subject to controls. "Where we were operating is where the foreign exchange market had no activity," said Eccles.

Chief financial officers threw out the welcome mat for Eccles and his swap men. Trouble was, his small firm could execute such transactions by acting as an intermediary only with the world's largest and most creditworthy companies, because each one would have to approve the other's credit. Another factor that made the deals difficult was that the different parties in such transactions were typically represented by different investment banking firms. "Every deal was extremely tough. We could only do it when it was the only way a company could solve its problem," Eccles said. He concluded that the one institution in the world that could bring together both parties was Citibank. "First Boston had its clients, and Goldman its clients," he said, but Citibank had relationships with all of their clients. And here was another good reason for Citibank to be in the investment banking business: it could act as the intermediary between the two parties, without either of them having to know the other's identity or credit standing. For a fee, Citibank could assess the credit risks and "guarantee" that both parties would keep their part of the bargain.

For Eccles, however, arriving at Citibank was like taking a cold shower. Whereas Goldman was driven by an obsession with closing deals, Citibank was bogged down in bureaucracy and profit centeritis. The first transaction, a sterling dollar swap for less than $20 million between Corning Glass and a British firm, took nearly eight months to complete. Eccles couldn't understand why the transaction couldn't be closed quickly. He thought it was because the Citibank International Bank Limited in London didn't have investment banking experience. He later learned the real reason: London thought he was trying to steal their profits on the transaction. Eccles's proposed solution shocked the folks in London. "You can have all the profits," he informed his dumbfounded colleagues. "Just let me close."

Shortly after that swap, Eccles closed on a $100 million swap between two top-rated companies, earning for Citibank a cool $2 million fee and a personal visit by Wriston. The swap, Wriston told Eccles, reminded him of the negotiable CD. Like the CD, the swap demonstrated once again that "thinking big makes big things happen," Wriston said. To Wriston, global utopia is a world without borders or barriers, where information and goods flow freely from one nation to another. The very existence of different currencies for different countries is an impediment to trade and, as Eccles put it later, "an anachronism in a global world. In a sense we were curing the anachronism."

Citibank set up a swaps group to sell this product to multinationals. While the event was not marked by pomp and ceremony, it was a milestone in Citibank's evolution from a New York bank with overseas branches to a truly global institution. With the creation of the World Corporation Group, Citibank had begun to deal with its multinational customers on a global basis. With swaps, it brought to the marketplace a natural competitive advantage that it had not yet made use of. It was a victory over profit centeritis, the institutional disease that continually ravaged Citibank, preventing it from capitalizing on its unique advantage as the nation's only truly worldwide financial institution. "Once you had created this way of working together globally, you tended to think about the business on those terms," said Eccles. Next to syndications, swaps became the single most profitable part of investment banking at Citibank.

Besides creating a new profit wellspring, the swap made clear the need for a coordinated approach to dealing with corporate customers. It also underscored the growing importance of financial technology over credit. While young and often inexperienced credit officers from the traditional corporate banking unit were seeking to sell money to customers, swaps specialists were combing the world for counter-parties. Account officers, said Eccles, tended to approach customers to sell them money, not to find out how they could solve a problem. Citibank swaps specialists soon devised a variation on the theme: the interest rate swap. Just as big corporations might have too little of one currency and too much of another, they also might wish they had more floating rate debt and less fixed rate, or vice versa. The extreme volatility in interest rates compounded the predicament for many companies, contributing to the usefulness of interest rate swaps.

Early on, Citibank dominated the interest rate swaps business, handling perhaps 80 percent of the activity, according to one former officer. In 1982 the market amounted to about $3 billion in nominal terms. By the mid-1980s, Citibank's share amounted to some $17.5 billion.

For a while, Citibank managed to keep its new technology mostly to itself. Swaps were being done by investment banks, but they couldn't compete with Citibank, which had access to all of the counter-parties. According to Eccles, "It wasn't clear to others what we were doing, and we weren't making it clear, either." Customers knew and cared only that Citibank could do a ten-year forward contract, say, on the pound sterling. Said Eccles, "All they knew was that Citibank could solve the problem, not how it was done." By the early 1980s, swaps specialists were among the hottest tickets on Wall Street, with twenty-six-year-olds often commanding upward of $500,000 a year.

But the success of "products" like swaps may have helped convince Citibankers that selling products was an end in itself, rather than a method of helping the customer solve a problem. And swaps soon became an internal battleground. Three groups within Citibank competed to sell swaps to the same customers. As Michael Callen explained later, a company might have been better off issuing long-term debt rather than a swap to hedge against higher interest rates, but if there were three Citibankers "in the room, all of whom sold swaps," the customer would invariably wind up buying a swap.

By the late 1970s, another new buzz phrase—"leveraged buyout"—

crept into the corporate finance lexicon. This occurred just as venture capital financing, a business that had seemed so attractive just a decade earlier, began to fade. Leveraged buyouts became the centerpiece of investment banking in the 1970s. Ten years later they would loom large as a partial cause of Citibank's near destruction.

The leveraged buyout, or LBO, trend got started because many of the mergers and acquisitions slapped together during the acquisition boom of the 1960s were really ill conceived. In an LBO, bankers, lending on the assets rather than cash flow, were able, in their own minds at least, to lend more money. The loan amount could be expanded by lending on the supposedly liquid value of the assets. In 1980, Citibank announced it would boost its LBO fund by $100 million, adding that it had lately made investments of over $20 million in five companies. Leveraged buyouts made Wriston nervous, however. "In 1980," said a top Citibank dealmaker, "Wriston was saying LBOs were the next disaster."

In the view of Russ Carson, a former head of Citibank's venture capital unit, the end of the venture capital era and the beginning of the LBO era occurred around 1978 and stemmed largely from the preference of investment banker William Comfort for big, complex transactions that produced a quick buck, rather than small, simple ones where the returns took longer. Eventually, the volume of LBOs dwarfed venture capital deals. In 1978 all but one of the professionals in the venture capital unit quit, mostly to strike out on their own. Former Citibank venture capital specialists and the firms they founded came to represent a critical source of start-up financing in the United States, but their departure left Citibank a much smaller player in the business.

The notion that a good manager could manage anything certainly did not apply in Citibank's investment management unit, where a long succession of fast-track managers produced mostly dismal returns for institutional investors—returns that would have gotten them fired from a Wall Street firm. Citibank had jumped into the growth stock market in the late 1960s and had ridden it down in the mid-1970s bear market. Moreover, Wriston's pronouncements about long-term thinking somehow didn't apply to investment management. "They were in a fairly shortsighted, short-term-result mode," said one former Citibanker. The people running the investment management unit didn't seem to realize that in order to compete with Wall Street, and with successful asset managers, they would have to put together a cadre of veteran investment professionals.

By 1977 investment management had become a major embarrassment to the bank. Pension funds were moving their money out of Citibank by the billions. At one point, Ford Motor Company read the riot act to Citibank for its dismal performance. Finally, in 1977, Wriston hired a professional investment manager, Peter Vermilye. Under Vermilye, Citibank's performance improved, but former officers claim that Citibank, and Wriston, resisted Vermilye's attempt to build a global investment management powerhouse by hiring top M.B.A.'s who would sell a variety of funds to clients around the world. Citibank's annual growth imperative was still very much in force, and in this area at least, "they wanted to see results right away," said one source.

George Vojta and merchant banking chief Robert Logan knew that if a big commercial bank like Citibank was to compete for the business of the world's top companies, all of the pieces of investment banking would have to be pulled together and commercial bankers would have to become more and more like investment bankers. In the opinion of some Citibankers, Logan was the closest thing to a real investment banker that Citibank ever had. "He had drive, spark, enthusiasm," said one former colleague.

According to former Citibankers, Logan and Vojta teamed up to pitch the idea of merging investment management and merchant banking into a real worldwide investment banking group that they would run. Under this plan, the investment bank would share equal billing with the other I's in the Citibank empire—the individual and the institutional bank.

The cornerstone of the Vojta plan was his recommendation that the bank's treasury functions, then part of Citibank's worldwide commercial banking and institutional banking operations, be pulled out of those operations and integrated with the merchant banking unit. This proposal, however, was laden with political and financial implications. Income from the treasury profit center, which included trading activities, was a huge contributor to the worldwide income of the institutional bank, and whoever got the treasury units would receive credit for hundreds of millions in profits.

By most accounts, Wriston and Spencer were initially receptive to the proposal. But the heirs apparent weren't buying. The most vociferous opponent was Tom Theobald, the traditional commercial banker. Theobald's main objection centered on compensation. He felt it would be destructive to have loan officers earning $50,000 a year working the same roof with investment bankers making more than ten times that amount. Wriston, said Reed, opposed "formula-driven compensation" and discouraged the investment bankers' grab for big bucks. According to Citibanker Rick Roesch, "Wriston slowed down inflationary compensation." Reed also opposed incentive compensation linked to short-term results. Nonetheless, he said, incentive compensation "crept" into investment banking–related businesses such as venture capital, bond trading, and foreign exchange.

Citibankers also debated the trade-offs between serving as the premier money-raiser for large deals and earning the huge advisory fees associated with mergers and acquisitions, à la Goldman, Sachs and Morgan Stanley. Those in favor of sticking to the former argued that many firms called themselves advisers, whereas Citibank was one of a very few banks capable of raising billions in short order.

Vojta had a completely different vision of the bank and of the future of banking than did Reed and Theobald. Paul De Rosa, a top bond trader, said that Vojta "was a strong spokesman for the strategy of serving the principal corporations of the world." Wriston made the final decision to reject the Vojta-Logan proposal, and some regarded this decision as a critical strategic mistake that would affect Citibank's ability to compete in investment banking for years to come. Until the treasury functions were put under investment banking in 1985, said Paul Collins, "it didn't have the right focus. It slowed us down." Collins himself had been among those who advised Wriston that it would be "disruptive" to move the treasury operations.

Wriston's decision may have been due in part to Logan's irascible manner. "He's probably one of the best bankers in the world," said Wriston later. "He can do it all—set up the books, make the loans; he does it well. He can play every instrument in the band." But, he said, "his problem is his inability to work in a big organization where you have to get along with colleagues, listen to what other people have to say, and sometimes make accommodations. That's not his schtick."

Logan later said that "Wriston didn't disagree with the recommendations" to consolidate key investment banking functions, but doing so "would have meant a massive reorganization." Meanwhile, J. P. Morgan and Bankers Trust were reaching an entirely different decision about the future importance of investment banking based on the same set of facts.

If Citibank had adopted the Logan-Vojta plan, Angermueller said, "we might have avoided some of the credit problems that were later encountered," because merchant bankers lay off risk rather than assume it themselves.

Nowhere was the discomfort with the investment banking culture more apparent than with Trinkaus & Burkhardt, the West German subsidiary Citicorp had picked up in 1973 along with KKB, the retail bank. Now Citibank was moving to sell Trinkaus, in part to acquire more of KKB, according to former corporate secretary Carl Desch. Although Citibank didn't report publicly on the profitability of individual units such as Trinkaus, it had by all accounts been one of Citibank's few truly successful acquisitions. According to Desch, KKB at one point earned more than $35 million a year, but, he said, Trinkaus & Burkhardt "can make that in a week."

Logan, who had acquired T & B in the first place, got the message that since he understood it best, he would have to sell it. When the British partners arrived, Logan sensed that the deal was going to get done. And a deal was the last thing Logan wanted. He was determined to make one last attempt to dissuade Wriston from selling. While the prospective buyers from the Midland Bank cooled their heels in Logan's fourteenth-floor office, he ascended the spiral staircase to Wriston's. "It's a strategic mistake to sell [Trinkaus]," he told Wriston.

"You really believe strongly about this?" Wriston inquired, and he immediately summoned Reed, Spencer, Theobald, and Angermueller. "It's stupid to sell this," Logan exhorted in his melodic Scottish burr. Reed seemed apathetic, caught up as he was in running his troubled retail business. Angermueller, of course, liked Germany and seemed to favor holding on to the subsidiary, but he nonetheless remained on the fence, in Logan's view.

Theobald, however, insisted on selling. Logan and Theobald had been constantly at each other's throats, and in Logan's view, Theobald wanted to clip his rival's wings. "I think on Trinkaus Walter knew I was right," Logan said, but "if he had said he disagreed [with the decision to sell it], he would have destroyed Tom's credibility." In 1980, Citibank unloaded Trinkaus at a tidy profit.

Before long, however, it became clear that the purchaser was the real winner. By nearly all accounts, unloading Trinkaus was a major strategic blunder. It could have enabled Citibank to become a significant force in the German banking market, where Citibank was floundering. Indeed, Citibank had never been a force to reckon with in Europe.

As for Robert Logan, the advocate of integrated investment banking, he had by 1981 lost much of his power. Government securities, municipals, and money markets were peeled off from the merchant banking unit and combined with foreign currency into a unit under finance chief Don Howard. Logan was left with mergers and acquisitions, CIBL, and corporate finance. "Bob Logan was kneecapped overnight," said a colleague. "Nothing but an anorexic skeleton was left." In March 1981, Logan quit.

Once Wriston signed off on the concept of a unified investment banking unit in 1982, he handed it to Paul Collins, the quintessential Citibank manager, whose forte was numbers and planning. By then, as the Roaring Eighties were gathering steam, Citibank had already lost much of its momentum.

21

HOME ON THE RANGE

ith the turn of the decade, three huge "rocks"—Citispeak for problems—sat on John Reed's desk: huge credit-card losses; problems in the Person-to-Person mortgage portfolio; and a severely mismatched book of loans and deposits.

John Reed's bet on credit cards, and indeed his entire consumer business, was now in deep trouble. In the wake of Paul Volcker's Saturday Night Special, short-term rates headed steadily northward, and by December 1979 the yield on the three-month Treasury bill stood at 12 percent. New York State had imposed usury ceilings that restricted banks from charging more than 12 percent on the first $500 of credit-card loans and 18 percent on amounts above that. That translated into an average gross return of about 14 percent. Like the thrifts, Citi had booked low-yield, fixed-rate mortgages at low fixed rates that were now under water. Reed's problems would inflict considerable damage on Wriston's cherished bottom line, causing 1980 return on equity to plummet to 13.5 percent from 16.1 percent in 1979 and return on assets to fall to an anemic .47 percent from .58 percent. By now Wriston had been forced to modify his 1971 goal of 15 percent annual earnings per share growth to a range of 12 percent to 18 percent.

Though some pieces of the Reed empire were profitable, the consumer business as a whole was deep in the red.

It was one thing to pass out credit cards like party favors in a vibrant and forgiving low interest rate economy; it was quite another to conduct such an experiment in mass merchandising with the country mired in recession and suffering under double-digit interest rates. While Wriston made light of the predicament—"We lend money at 8 percent, borrow it at 18 percent, and make it up on volume"—the situation was dead serious and becoming more so with each passing day. Partly as a result of the credit-card losses, net income in the first quarter of 1980 plunged 33 percent from the same period the year before to $77 million.

To his detractors, Reed seemed to be moving helter-skelter without a plan or a strategy, without any real sense of what could or would work. There were Visa cards, ATMs, half-baked acquisitions. Recalled one colleague,

"John said, 'This is one big research and development thing. We've got to try everything, and the market will tell us what the right answer is.' " The sharks of corporate banking were chomping for John Reed's head. At least one of Reed's senior colleagues had the temerity to tell Wriston that Reed should be fired and he should take over the business. Reed admitted that "if you [had taken] a vote among the senior people, probably most would have said, 'This is an effort that doesn't make sense, and we shouldn't support it.' "

In the early days, said Reed, consumer banking was viewed by the corporate bankers with "certain misgivings." Corporate lenders believed that Citibank should emulate the House of Morgan, not Sears Roebuck. But when annual bonuses plummeted from 6 percent of salary to nothing, that incited a palace revolt. Said Richard Kovacevich, "When people weren't getting their bonuses there weren't 10 percent of Citibank employees who believed we ought to have a consumer business." By Christmas 1980, NCB, the initials for the old National City Bank, came to stand for "No Christmas Bonuses." The white-shoe crowd gave Reed's men dirty looks in the officers' dining room. Said Wriston, "They beat up on John and me."

Gingerly, the bank's directors asked Wriston whether he was really comfortable with the losses. "There was a feeling that maybe this wasn't the best idea we ever had," Wriston said. As one director put it, "Some directors had a very dim view of John Reed because he was losing all that money. People did go to Wriston and say, 'You're making a big mistake.' " Another director concluded that he could never support Reed for the bank's top job.

On at least one occasion, when top officers gave updates on their businesses to their colleagues, Wriston—not Reed—delivered the presentation on the consumer business, former officers recalled. "Wriston took all the flak. If Reed had gotten up, there could have been open hostility," said Kovacevich. "He [Wriston] fought the battle for us."

For all his zaniness, Reed was known to his friends as someone who would not walk away from trouble. This was seen, too, in his personal life, as he sought to cope with problems at home. Nor did Reed try to put the best face on things. In presentations to Wriston on his various initiatives, Reed typically emphasized the worst possible outcome, recalled former Citibanker William Heron.

Things were tough all over. Even the chairman, who by this time was earning $700,000 annually, still found himself severely strapped. Wriston had borrowed heavily to buy Citicorp stock, and when the prime rate shot through 20 percent, dividend payments no longer covered interest expense. Kathy Wriston was a shrewd money manager, but even she couldn't close the gap between interest and dividends.

Wriston saw as one of his principal duties maintaining the morale of those in the vanguard of Citibank's big gamble, including that of Reed himself. But while Spencer and Wriston supported their young protégé, they were clearly jittery. Intermittently, Reed said, they called to remind him that he was "really losing a lot of money" and that he should "reduce the size of the operation and sell off bits and pieces—the classic business reaction when you're losing money." Reed refused. "I'd say, 'I'm sorry, I don't want to do that.'" And they never forced Reed to take those measures. "They had to probe," said Reed. If they hadn't, "they'd [have been] stark raving mad."

Though Reed never doubted the correctness of the consumer drive or of his strategy, he had begun to prepare himself for the possibility that Wriston and Spencer might soon call an end to it all. Wriston could easily have killed Reed's initiative, and profits would have shot up in a flash. This was at a time when critics of American business were blasting its short-term orientation; Wriston was a long-haul man.

Both he and Spencer found solace in the belief that they were the financial service industry's Christopher Columbus. "Our compass wasn't any better than [Columbus's]. We started out east by sailing west," said Wriston.

Moreover, they were convinced that the consumer banking effort, like international lending, met Wriston's acid test for a viable new business venture. In late 1979 he told a gathering that "the society which promises no risk and whose leaders use the word 'risk' only as a pejorative may be able to protect life, but there will be no liberty and very little pursuit of happiness. . . . 'Be nice, feel guilty, and play safe.' If there was ever a prescription for producing a dismal future, that has to be it."

Out of this experience and others that followed, Reed concluded that it took seven to ten years to build a business, Wriston said in later years. Despite the severe losses and rock-bottom morale, Wriston never set a deadline for achieving success in the consumer business—or, for that matter, in any of the many other new businesses Citibank started from scratch. Still, the question of whether to continue in the consumer business "was a day-to-day thing," Wriston confessed. "I also had a lot of confidence in the folks operating it [the consumer business]. They made some horrendous mistakes. On the other hand the intellectual concept is correct."

The losses in the consumer initiative were all the scarier because of the storm clouds gathering over the international and domestic economies. Changes in accounting rules, mainly in Brazil, forced Citibank to take a $100 million pre-tax loss. In the past, Brazil's fat spreads had easily covered such losses, but now Wriston fretted that that might no longer be the case.

In a January 17, 1980, talk to top officers, Wriston gave the international unit plenty of reason to speed up rather than slow down. Scanning his list of business units, Wriston browbeat the international group for doing the "worst job" and failing to meet its budget by almost $55 million after tax. In terms of expectations, that was an even worse performance than that of the consumer group, he said. On the other hand, he complimented his national banking group—"the star performer"—for exceeding the plan by about $47 million after tax. All the other units, Wriston said, surpassed expectations, and the World Corporation Group posted the "largest year-to-year increase among banking groups." As its reward, it was disbanded.

With the heavy losses in the consumer business, the last thing Citibank needed was a showcase office in the heart of "the evil empire" that had produced virtually no business since it was opened in 1974. Wriston had been unenthusiastic about opening an office in the Soviet Union in the first place, but he had succumbed to pressure from the Nixon administration to contribute to the spirit of détente. But during the evening news on Christmas Day 1979, Wriston felt nothing but revulsion at the sight of Soviet tanks rumbling into Afghanistan. There was no longer any political reason, and certainly no financial reason, for Citibank to remain in Moscow. Early in 1980, Wriston strolled into the office of one of his overseas executives and asked, "Why do we have this office in Moscow?" Nobody had a good answer. "Close it down," Wriston ordered. Afghanistan "gave him a convenient excuse to undo something he thought was a mistake to start with," said Jack Clark.

Amid the gloom and doom there were some flickers of light and hope. Despite the early losses from deadbeat credit-card holders, the marketeers had begun to fathom the statistical phenomenon that they had dubbed "the wave." Understanding the wave was the key to the profitability of the credit-card business. Now they could predict delinquency trends with great accuracy. They had begun to apply sophisticated credit-scoring techniques in evaluating applications for credit cards, in an effort to weed out the con artists and convicts. Thanks in part to the cash machines, Citibank's share of the New York market was rising dramatically. According to Kovacevich, even in the dark days of 1980, Citibank's New York banking division earned about $120 million pre-tax, more than three times the amount Reed had once dreamed about.

Hard hit as Citibank was by credit-card problems, Citicorp's funding squeeze was responsible for most of the losses. This resulted from external economic and regulatory forces and from mismanagement, notably John Reed's insistence on the delusionary long-term pool rate. By 1980 it was clear that an 8¼ percent long-term rate was not merely theoretical—it was pure fiction. With funds now costing 18 percent and credit cards yielding an average of 14 percent, the credit-card business was staggering under a negative spread of 4 percent. In a world of banking make-believe, the credit-card portfolio might still be earning the difference between the pool rate and 14 percent, or a gross spread of 5¾ percent. But in the real world where money was bought and sold, Reed was losing his shirt. Wriston often remarked that borrowing short and lending long was the role for a banker. But in operating off the long-term pool, the bank lost $500 million after taxes over a three-year period, according to former Citibanker Ed Hoffman. "With an appropriate treasury strategy," Hoffman contended, "we could have bought 8 percent money in 1977 and 1978. But no one did. . . . There's a difference between taking risks and putting your footprint in the snow—and just plain stupidity."

Reed was hypersensitive about the long-term pool issue. He admonished his critics: "You're supposed to be in the consumer business. We're marketeers. You're coming at this from a balance sheet management approach." According to former consumer executive Frank Partel, another reason Reed embraced the long-term pool was that he believed banks had a social obligation to assume interest rate risk for consumers. Institutions that proved their social value would be long-term survivors, he believed.

While acknowledging that the strategy ultimately *was* flawed, Reed persisted in defending it, saying "any concept we had of what interest rates were likely to be was blown off the face of the earth by the monetary policy of Mr. Paul Volcker [then chairman of the Fed] and his brethren."

In large part, Citibank was being kept on life support by other financial innovations that were more viable, such as its negotiable certificates of deposit and commercial paper. As Wriston put it in his state of the corporation address in early 1980, the CD "gave money center banks a way to continue to fund themselves at least for a few years." Even in nominal terms, demand deposits at the New York banks hadn't risen in five years. Citibank was grasping for every possible way to raise cheap deposits. It also contemplated paying interest on traveler's checks.

One seemingly innocuous method—Citibank called it "pots and pans"—enjoyed surprising success. In early 1980, Wriston boasted that gifts of toasters, appliances, and other items had helped rake in $1 billion in new deposits the year before. Along with commercial paper, Wriston gave the program a large share of the credit for funding domestic loans, in the same way that Eurodollars had financed the overseas portfolio. Though such programs had long been a mainstay of thrifts, Citicorp was probably the first big commercial bank to "go the pots and pans route," as one officer told a reporter. Unfortunately, the way Citibank executed the giveaway promotion also happened to be illegal, and perhaps more than any single incident, it damaged Wriston's relationship with the new Fed chairman for the rest of his days at Citibank. Ironically, Wriston got it right when he told analysts that Citicorp was "giving away pots and pans with reckless abandon."

As the nation plunged toward a recession and rates shot skyward, Citibank in March 1980 launched its "Grand Slam Gift Giveaway" of toasters and other appliances to attract new depositors. These were no chintzy seconds. Even the most unsophisticated shopper could see that these premiums had cost Citibank much more than the $10 and $50 limits the Fed had placed on the value of "gifts" banks could offer in return for deposits of $5,000 and $10,000.

Wriston's problems began as a result of a complaint by a Citibank competitor, prompting a warning by the Comptroller of the Currency and later a Fed investigation. The Fed reportedly discovered that Citibank was keeping two sets of books—one for itself and one for the regulators—to disguise the true value of the gifts. Citi attempted to justify the program by citing invoices purportedly showing that expenditures for these items were considerably below what Citibank had actually paid for them. The Fed, to its regret, permitted Citibank to hire its own investigators to get to the bottom of the matter. And somehow the perpetrators of this heinous crime, and the brains behind it, were never publicly identified. Though the Fed appreciated how the rule could be violated in the first instance, it lost its patience when Citibank continued the practice even after the Fed had issued a cease-and-desist order. On top of that, Citibank officials were later accused of lying about the transaction. These repeat violations convinced the Fed that Citicorp and Wriston believed that rules were meant for other people and other institutions.

In contrast, the Fed responded to the more publicized David Edwards affair with a big yawn. If Citicorp had committed violations, they were merely violations of foreign rules. Even the prim and proper central bank understood that keeping up with ever-changing tax codes of the nearly one hundred countries where Citicorp operated was a formidable task. The central bank also tolerated Wriston's attacks on Mother Fed as a bureaucratic proponent of archaic laws, and even brushed off reports that Citibank had shorted the dollar and thereby contributed to its decline.

But breaking the banking laws of the United States—the laws the Fed was charged with upholding—was another matter entirely. In the case of the pots-and-pans giveaway, the law was Reg Q, the centerpiece of Federal Reserve regulation. Volcker was incensed at Wriston's attempts to circumvent the pots-and-pans rules. He felt obligated to uphold the law whether he agreed with it or not. The Fed seriously considered levying a $1 million penalty in the first-ever use of its fining authority, but in July 1981 it settled on $350,000, the largest fine ever imposed by a banking agency, according to *American Banker.* But to the Fed's dismay, $350,000 wasn't enough to grab much media attention. Though Citibank claimed that its growth in New York market share was due to its new ATMs, one rival banker snickered later that the gains during this period were "due to illegal promotions, not ATMs."

Reed accepted the rap for the pots-and-pans debacle. Describing the incident as a "considerable embarrassment" in a later interview with *Retail Banker International,* he said, "It was a violation of law and we are not very pleased about that kind of thing.

"We got in all kinds of trouble because the guys would sail too close to the regulations," Wriston said later. But Wriston blamed the incident on "price control, which screws up markets." Reed, according to Wriston, "jumped" on the problem and discovered "all kinds of crap." Two employees, he said, were stuffing phony invoices into their bottom drawer. "The whole regulation [Reg Q] was stupid, but that wasn't the issue. You watch the Knicks play the Bulls and they [the Knicks] get five fouls in the first quarter because the coach tells them to play an aggressive game. The Bulls [also] played an aggressive game and didn't get five fouls. That's a bum rap."

But even the normally sympathetic Comptroller of the Currency was hard-pressed not to acknowledge that Citibank had broken the law. While declining to discuss exactly what he told Wriston after the incident, Comptroller John Heimann said later, "Let's put it this way. It was part of my job to have heart-to-heart conversations."

As Charles Partee, head of the Fed committee on bank supervision, told author William Greider, "You don't get him [Wriston] to do anything by persuasion and argument, that's for sure." Governor Partee said that because of Citibank's political and financial influence, the nation's top fifty big banks "talk back to you."

In Washington, Citicorp counted on Hans Angermueller to take the hard edge off Citicorp's image. Describing him as a "real charmer," Kenneth Guenther, executive director of the Independent Bankers Association, said "Hans is very good at keeping the windows and doors open."

Citibank suffered in other ways, too. Since the regulators knew that Citibank would attempt to make an end run around every regulation they wrote, they tried to anticipate any loophole it might discover. The result, therefore, was more tangled regulations. This was neither the first nor the last instance in which Citibank pushed its interpretation of the banking law to the very edge of the envelope.

Monetary policy, not bank regulation, was the Fed's primary focus. And Wriston clearly had a higher regard for chairman Paul Volcker's prowess as a manager of monetary policy than as a bank regulator, a role Volcker actually regarded as his strongest suit. For the next four years, and even after Wriston had retired from Citibank and Volcker from the Fed, the two men were at each other's throats over virtually every bank supervisory issue, from rate regulation to bank powers and capital adequacy. And more than anyone before him, Volcker succeeded in frustrating Wriston's efforts to expand the business of his institution. But more significantly, Volcker's battle to lick inflation inflicted serious damage on Wriston's own empire and on his standing as an international banker.

Volcker wasn't in his post long before he began to butt heads with Wriston over capital adequacy. "Wriston and his people would troop to the Fed to argue that banks in general and Citibank in particular didn't have to hold "any significant capital," Volcker said later. "That made an impression on me, and what made an even greater impression on me was that he could make it sound so persuasive. I had some reservations, to say the least. What it all came down to was that you didn't need any capital if you were going to increase earnings every year. That didn't allow for the possibility that you wouldn't make your earnings every year and might have some bad loans." Volcker considered Wriston's opinions not merely misguided but dangerous as well, given his standing in the industry. "It's hard to maintain capital standards when the industry leaders themselves aren't sensitive to maintaining good capital standards," he said. "No doubt Citibank was the bandleader in the new approach toward banking." In fact, according to former Citibank lawyer Robert Dinerstein, the Fed told Citicorp it had two standards for regulating bank holding companies—one for Citi and a second for all others. "They felt they couldn't permit us to get too far ahead of the pack for fear that others would try to emulate us and not be able to do so," he said.

To deal with the threat of higher capital standards, Wriston dusted off Citicorp's treatise on capital adequacy and published an updated version, which again opposed fixed capital ratios and asserted that liquidity and earnings as well as capital should be considered in assessing a banking company's financial strength. "Where I come apart with [Volcker] is I believe in markets," Wriston said later. "We have a philosophical difference over whether Papa knows best or the markets know best, and I think we probably always will." Volcker, he said, "has a fundamental belief in the Volcker standard. I believe in deregulation and I think it's fair to say Paul did not." When asked later by a reporter what he thought of Volcker, Wriston replied, "I'll answer that if you tell me what you think of your editor."

Wriston and his men ate lesser regulators for breakfast. Few bureaucrats relished the prospect of going head to head with him. William Martin, a former deputy Comptroller of the Currency, attended a meeting of Citibank's Audit and Examining Committees at about the time the regulators were contemplating installing examiners at Citicorp full time. "They [Wriston and his officers] were tough," he said. "I was a lowly little government clerk. They were just eating me up. There were bears to the left of me, bears to the right of me. There was blood all over the place, and it was all mine."

Finally, in an act of mercy, Wriston raised his head at the meeting and said, "I think I see where regulators are coming from. They have their job to do."

From that excruciating experience, Martin learned never to attend a meeting unless he could control it. Indeed, controlling Citicorp was becoming an increasingly difficult task for bank examiners. Said former Treasury secretary David Kennedy, "I'm not sure any examiner could examine them and know what their status was."

For months, Citibank had been lobbying the New York State Legislature and Governor Hugh Carey seeking relief from the usury ceiling, to no avail. While Wriston got a sympathetic hearing from Carey, the Democrat-controlled legislature, particularly the New York City delegation, was anti-bank, and with an election on the horizon, the legislators saw no advantage in doing anything that could be perceived as hurting consumers while helping banks. For populist legislators, the usury issue was ensnared in the politically sensitive issue of redlining, in which the banks allegedly refused to lend money for mortgages and other purposes in depressed neighborhoods. The real reason for their refusal was that they couldn't make any money at it. In late 1978, thanks in part to Wriston's romance with the unions, the state legislature raised the ceiling for mortgages, but it was still below the market rate. Fixed rate mortgages made at low rates with short-term money were under water. At year end, the New York State ceiling on mortgage loans was suspended, but the suspension was due to expire on March 31.

Richard Kovacevich, the gung-ho cheerleader of the New York banking division, moved to take advantage of this opening. Citibank, he believed, should be a giant savings bank. He thought the centerpiece should be mortgages, which would cement borrowers to the bank and make them amenable to a whole host of other financial services and products. With the savings banks pulling back from new mortgage lending because surging rates were further jeopardizing their already troubled portfolios, mortgage money was drying up faster than a puddle in the Mojave Desert. Now was the time, Kovacevich urged, to build relationships with consumers. Despite his contempt for white shoe commercial bankers, he did agree with them on one thing: making mortgages that lost money was nuts. Kovacevich had promised New York State legislative leaders to commit a large chunk of mortgage money to New York if they removed the 10 percent mortgage ceiling.

At Wriston's Citibank, bold moves were frequently made with little discussion, few if any memos, and no exhaustive studies. "John [Reed] didn't look at three pounds of marketing studies," Kovacevich said later. After a brief conversation, Reed and Kovacevich agreed to hold a press conference announcing that they would earmark $1 billion for mortgages for single-family homes and co-ops in the New York City area. But neither Reed nor Kovacevich thought to inform the bank's policy committee, and Reed forgot to tell Wriston. The next day, February 5, 1980, Wriston, along with the other readers of the *New York Times,* learned about the plan for the first time. "Commercial banks didn't understand. They thought we were stark raving mad," Kovacevich said later. Reed "took the heat" for not informing the policy committee first. Now Citibank actually had a chance to earn a positive spread on the mortgage portfolio. Equally important, the initiative would go a long way toward capturing the market traditionally dominated by thrift institutions. Not long after being forced to sell Advance Mortgage, Citicorp was back in business as Citicorp Homeowners and began snapping up mortgage portfolios.

The funding squeeze was even more pronounced in consumer lending, including credit-card lending. Nationally chartered banks like Citibank got some relief from a loophole that enabled them to charge one percentage point more than the state usury ceiling for some consumer loans. But that wasn't nearly enough. And the legislature could not have cared less. They felt Citibank was permanently anchored to New York and couldn't possibly leave.

Looking back, Governor Hugh Carey felt that the legislators' stand "was a way of showing a rebellious attitude, of putting them on the side of the consumer. The redlining issue was a principal way of getting votes." In the wake of the Urban Development Corporation episode, said Carey, the banks "weren't going to put depositors' money [somewhere] with no hope of return. They'd been scorched." And there was no convincing a Harlem assemblyman that his constituents would be better off if banks could charge them 19.8 percent on their Visa-card balances. But if Citibank was unable to raise credit-card rates in New York, and couldn't find a more hospitable state, its only alternative would be to, as Angermueller put it in a later speech, "dismantle the credit-card business or take our losses and pray." Meanwhile Citibank was taking it on the chin from New York's populist attorney general, Robert Abrams, who had sued the bank to rescind retroactive rate increases on revolving credit lines.

The solution that Citibank chanced upon in January 1980 occurred serendipitously at a corporate retreat of top executives in Pennsylvania's Pocono Mountains. At the time, no one could foresee that Citibank would be able to implement the solution, or that it would ultimately seal the chairmanship for John Reed. Or even more significantly, that it would dramatically reshape American banking by blasting a gaping hole in the wall that for years had stopped bank holding companies from establishing banks outside their home states.

A slide that credit-card czar Dave Phillips flashed on the screen at the conference vividly illustrated the dilemma: in bankers' lingo, Citibank had a pricing problem. Losses and operating expenses chewed up 100 percent of the credit-card revenue as it flowed through the front door. Phillips commented that if Citibank could price as it pleased, unconstrained by the usury limits, it might even make money in the credit-card business. In California, which didn't have a usury ceiling, Bank of America was making a fortune on credit cards.

As Charles Long, now executive vice president, remembers it, a bank lawyer remarked offhandedly that if only Citi could use the so-called Marquette decision—a December 1978 Supreme Court ruling that permitted banks to charge a rate based on the location of either the bank or the customer, at the bank's option—the business would work. Wriston had recognized that the Marquette decision offered hope to Citicorp. But it apparently wasn't until the powwow in the Poconos that Citibank swung into action.

The Marquette ruling, Angermueller concluded, would allow a national bank to "export" the rate prevailing in the home state to other states. If Citibank could persuade one of those states to open its doors, Citibank would be home free. Pursuing the notion over coffee, Long and his colleagues assigned several staff members to scour the country for states where usury ceilings were either nonexistent or high enough to permit Citibank to make money. Besides California, they turned up five: Hawaii, Rhode Island, Nevada, Missouri, and South Dakota, all of which had usury ceilings in the neighborhood of 22 percent or higher. Hawaii was eliminated because of distance and communications problems, and Rhode Island and Nevada were scratched because their legislatures weren't in session. Rhode Island wasn't attractive anyway because it was the home of Representative Fernand St Germain, who had inherited Wright Patman's mantle as the nemesis of big banks. Under federal banking laws, a banking institution could not operate a bank in another state unless that state extended an invitation. Because it didn't track banking legislation on a state-by-state basis at that time, Citibank was unaware that a bill to raise South Dakota's usury ceiling was in the works, according to Long. Soon, however, Citibank wised up and retained law firms in every state to follow banking legislation there.

Some senior Citibank officials who had lived through earlier fishing expeditions rolled their eyeballs at the entire exercise. "It had an unreal feel," said Ed Hoffman. "We were back trying to find a magic wand."

Having lived for many years in Kansas City, Missouri, Long instinctively favored the "show me" state for its large labor pool and good communications. Reaching the right people there was no problem. But mighty Citicorp enjoyed closer ties with most heads of state than it did with the leadership of South Dakota, and the word went out to Citicorp executives seeking someone who knew someone with a connection—any connection—to the office of South Dakota governor William "Wild Bill" Janklow.

The product of a Jewish father and Norwegian mother, Janklow is a self-described "Jewegian" from Flandreau, South Dakota, who dropped out of high school in 1956 to join the marines. He managed to sneak into the University of South Dakota without a high school diploma, and displayed the same kind of gall in law school, where he riled officials by making a practice of parking in the dean's reserved space. After graduation from law school, Janklow became a legal aid lawyer on the Rosebud Indian reservation. In six years he defended suspects in thirty murder cases, and in 1968 he was named the Outstanding Legal Aid Lawyer in America. Five years later, however, he found himself prosecuting those he had once represented. After an Indian was murdered, Indians rioted at Custer, South Dakota. Janklow was appointed prosecutor and succeeded in obtaining a one- to five-year sentence against the mother of the slain Indian, who had participated in the protest against the state for failing to prosecute the murderer. During his successful 1974 campaign for state attorney general, Janklow was dogged by seven-year-old charges by an Indian girl that he had raped her when he and his wife were serving as her unofficial foster parents. Several federal investigations, according to local reports, determined that the accusations were groundless. Those charges and Janklow's role as prosecutor were later discussed in Peter Matthiessen's book, *In the Spirit of Crazy Horse,* which described him as a "self-proclaimed 'Indian fighter' in the tradition of George Armstrong Custer"—except, as one Indian put it, "at least 'Longhair' had style."

After being elected governor in 1978, Janklow did demonstrate flair and style. He prided himself on getting his personal philosophy out of *Parade* magazine and only half jokingly claimed legendary pols Huey Long and Chicago mayor Richard J. Daley as his role models.

As governor, Janklow thrived on controversy, shunned the trappings of office, and favored quick, pragmatic solutions to problems. When he took office, the railway that hauled the grain of South Dakota's farmers to market was on the verge of bankruptcy. Janklow saved the farmers by levying a sales tax that enabled the state to buy abandoned track and lease it to another railroad.

Janklow balanced the state's budget by slashing it across the board. He banned the use of legal-size notebooks in government offices because they required more costly legal-size folders and file cabinets. He later determined that the state had too many colleges and not enough prisons. So he built a fence around a state college and converted it into a minimum-security prison.

Politically, Janklow was riding high. But South Dakota wasn't. Though it had its distinctions, prosperity wasn't one of them. Janklow liked to point out that South Dakota, with some 150 Minuteman missile silos, was the world's third-leading nuclear power and one of just a few locations that couldn't be hit by a missile launched from a Soviet sub. Corporate and personal income taxes were nonexistent, and property taxes were low. But in the years before Janklow took office, per capita income had dropped from twenty-first in the United States to thirty-fifth, he claimed. South Dakota's 700,000 residents had suffered from the impact of Jimmy Carter's Soviet grain embargo, just as Citibank was suffering from his economic policy. Several years of drought had added to the misery for farmers and bankers. Janklow was frustrated that South Dakota was merely educating children and exporting them to other states. South Dakota was as desperate for jobs as Citibank was for an opening in the usury ceiling.

Citibank was grasping at every straw. Charles Long had a friend with some tie to Governor Janklow's office. Someone else knew of a customer in Minneapolis who knew Janklow. And someone else knew someone in Sioux Falls whose brother had gone to law school with the governor. In one day, Janklow recalls, he received four calls—a grand slam, as he put it—from people phoning on behalf of Citibank.

The day before Long was scheduled to leave on a business trip to Panama, he received a call from Janklow's office inviting him to come to Pierre the next day, February 14, Saint Valentine's Day. That meeting was the beginning of a long love affair between Citicorp and South Dakota. The bank couldn't have chosen a better emissary to deal with the earthy but temperamental governor than affable, easygoing Charlie Long, of whom one friend said, "Every time you talk to Charlie it's like going to confession."

That first meeting with Janklow was awkward and confusing, Long recalled, for reasons neither of them understood until later. Janklow thought that Long had flown to Pierre to talk with him about the pending usury elimination bill. "It wasn't until a second meeting that he understood that even if that bill didn't pass—and it did—we would have gone [to South Dakota] anyway" because the old rate ceiling was still high enough for Citibank to make money, Long said. Although many observers, including the local media, concluded that Citibank had lobbied for the end to the usury law, a South Dakota Bankers Association official insisted that the repeal was South Dakota's idea and that it was under way before Citibank arrived. South Dakota effectively eliminated the ceiling on February 19, five days after Citibank arrived on the scene.

Citibank had really come to persuade Janklow to enact legislation enabling an out-of-state bank to set up shop in South Dakota. In that meeting, Long gave Janklow a quickie course on U.S. banking law—the bank holding company act, McFadden, and the recent Marquette decision. Janklow was a prosecutor, not a bank lawyer. This was Greek to him. While Long was somewhat encouraged by his reception in South Dakota, he was still privately hoping that the deal would go to his home state, Missouri. "TWA and Ford had just laid off a whole bunch of people. Kansas City was the economic center of gravity for communications. I knew the labor market, which was one of [Citibank's] biggest concerns," Long explained later. At the outset, Long told

Janklow that if Missouri came through, Citicorp would move there. But if South Dakota passed the bill, Citibank would reward the state with some kind of facility.

Citicorp lobbied hard in Missouri, throwing breakfasts and luncheons for business and political leaders, but no state was more xenophobic than Missouri. Although its governor, unlike Janklow, declined to deal with the Citibankers personally, Citibank's promise of some two thousand jobs won it the backing of the business community and a sympathetic ear from the state legislature. In Missouri, Citibank's enemies were other bankers. Despite Long's assurances that Citibank wouldn't compete with them, they wanted no part of the New York Goliath. At one dinner meeting, several top St. Louis bankers told Long of their "outrage" that Citibank was asking Missouri for favors after "polluting the market" with mass mailings of credit cards. "You've created such a bad image of the product and are in trouble now because of your irresponsible behavior and credit losses," the bankers railed. "And you want us to bail you out?"

The local bankers were greatly amused by a story recounted at the dinner about a janitor at a local bank who had borrowed up to his eyeballs. The bank's maintenance manager had discussed the janitor's plight with a loan officer, who showed him how the janitor could consolidate all his loans into one payment. About two weeks later the janitor informed the banker cheerfully that everything was okay because he had obtained a cash advance on a new credit card that he used to pay off the loan to the bank, and then he had used up the rest of the credit line. Citibank had issued the new card to the worker with virtually no questions asked. Because the Missouri bankers objected so strongly to Citibank's proposal, the politicians washed their hands of the issue, Long recalled.

Citibank also faced skeptics in South Dakota. Janklow told the Citibankers that the selling job would be up to them. "You're coming out here with a Brooklyn accent," Janklow told Long. "We don't like slick guys from Wall Street out here. We've all seen *The Music Man* many times, and we're not buying trombones from strangers. You've got a job to do."

But Janklow did arrange a meeting for Long with every group that had a stake in any legislation aimed at attracting Citicorp to the state. Like a rancher on a roundup, Janklow herded bankers and business and political leaders into Pierre's Holiday Inn to hear Long's presentation of Citicorp's plans for South Dakota. As usual, the opposition, what there was of it, consisted of local bankers. Of the hundred-plus banks in the state, about forty were owned by Minnesota banks under laws that had grandfathered their out-of-state ownership. Later in this meeting, while Long cooled his heels in a hallway, Janklow told the bankers that no matter what happened elsewhere, Citibank would move an operation to South Dakota and bring in four hundred jobs. If they picked the state for the entire operation, that would mean nearly three thousand jobs.

He then invited the bankers to grill Long about Citicorp's plans. After the question-and-answer session, Long once again left the room, and Janklow invited the bankers to thrash out among themselves their objections to Citicorp's proposal. "If you guys don't want to do it we won't do it," Janklow told them, "but you've got to share the problem with me. "After caucusing, the bankers passed a resolution inviting Citibank to the state.

Janklow loved a fight and had come to the meeting armed with a list of arguments with which to do battle. He was disappointed in the lack of enemy fire, and he felt defeated when the president of the bankers' association, an elderly small-town banker, told him, "I don't think we should pass up an opportunity like this." Long then moved to win over the state's legislators. Some were clearly nervous about the bank's offer. Incredibly, said Janklow, one key legislator, a hardware store owner in tiny, isolated Kadoka—"It's not the end of the world," said Janklow, "but you can see the end of the world from Kadoka"—was "deeply concerned" that Citibank would compete for customers by offering toasters and other small appliances as promotional gifts to South Dakotans.

To placate the bankers and their legislators, Citibank agreed in effect not to compete with South Dakota institutions. Its facility would be inconveniently located for retail customers. Rates on deposits would be lower than those offered by the local banks and lower than those it offered to out-of-state customers. And it promised that no one in South Dakota with a Citibank credit card would receive promotional "stuffers."

While Long lobbied in South Dakota, Wriston made another appeal to Governor Carey to eliminate the New York usury ceiling. In late February, Citibank publicly threatened to pull its credit-card operation out of New York if the ceilings weren't raised. Though more than two thousand jobs were at stake, the governor responded with little more than tea and sympathy. Meanwhile, South Dakota bankers debated the capitalization requirements for Citibank. Local bankers wanted the capital level high enough to discourage an influx of small banks, but not high enough to discourage big banks with lots of jobs. According to one bankers' association executive, South Dakota bankers chortled at the thought that they were holding up the city slickers by requiring $25 million. Later on, they were stunned when Citibank injected $250 million.

Negotiations on the bill went right down to the wire in the forty-day legislative session on details like pots-and-pans giveaways. On March 12, 1980, just two days before recessing, the legislators took two hours to pass, in a landslide vote, a bill extending an official invitation to Citibank, which wasted no time applying for a state bank charter.

That same day, Long phoned his colleague Richard D. McCrossen, a former top operations officer. "Dick," he blurted out, "you're going to love South Dakota," and then promptly hung up the phone.

In a thank-you letter, Wriston praised Janklow effusively for his "strong faith" in free enterprise and for South Dakota's "willingness to let free market forces work." He might have added his heartfelt thanks for saving Citibank.

Two days after the governor of South Dakota signed the bill that would bail out Citicorp, President Jimmy Carter invoked a never-used act that would put the nation's economy into the tank. Of all the gyrations that the Carter administration and the Fed took the economy through from 1979 to 1982, the most volatile swings resulted from credit controls. Ironically, Carter used powers given the president under the Credit Control Act of 1969, which was signed into law by Richard Nixon. Wriston spluttered in frustration that "these standby powers had never been invoked until now, but it appears that the government now intends to punish us for its own sins." The measures included cutbacks in various kinds of commercial and consumer lending. Volcker himself was opposed to wage, price, and credit controls. He had told the Senate Banking Committee in late February that credit controls were not effective in dealing with the root causes of inflation. He pointed out later that they delayed by some nine months the economic recovery. A Federal Reserve Board with backbone could legally have voted to reject the Carter proposals. But as Stephen Axilrod, the Fed official who operated the levers of monetary policy, said later, "When the president of the United States says, 'Let's do this,' it's hard not to," particularly if the Fed can't supply a good reason not to go along.

When Fed officials met in Washington on Saint Patrick's Day 1980 to discuss the measures, they agreed that credit restraints were overkill, given everything else they were doing to fight inflation. Since the controls were relatively mild, few expected them to have much of an effect. But officials underestimated the American consumer's willingness to stop borrowing. Citibank bought big newspaper ads, and Wriston took to the airwaves and Op-Ed pages to condemn credit and rate controls. He regarded controls as an "infringement on personal liberty," as he said later, and a threat to his consumer business and to the national economy.

Meanwhile, Citibank turned off the spigot on credit cards, consumer loans, and mortgages. It stopped accepting new applications for credit-card and installment loans and approved applications from existing customers selectively. And it slashed overdraft privileges to $500 from a maximum level of $15,000. Citibank was chaotic enough without credit controls. But the Carter initiative created absolute confusion in Citibank branches. Customers, who now cared less about the rate on a loan than they did about whether they could obtain one at all, weren't able to get the same answer twice about whether they qualified for a loan.

Fed vice chairman Frederick H. Schultz was designated credit-control czar. He was a reluctant dictator, regarding controls as anathema and his assignment as totally distasteful. Wriston and Schultz commiserated on several occasions about the program, and Schultz recalled that Wriston helped him "crystallize his thinking" about it.

Amid the turmoil, there were moments of high comedy. When Wriston and his troops arrived in the elegant boardroom of the Federal Reserve Bank of New York for a meeting, they got an icy reception from one top official who had received a form letter from Citibank advising him that his checking credit line was to be cut in half to $2,500. Twenty years earlier, when he began his Fed career as a mere law clerk, he had received a credit line of $500, and as he rose in salary and rank, that had grown to $5,000.

"Not you. My God," said an embarrassed Wriston. If Wriston had planned on a confrontational meeting with the supervisors, that expectation was dashed in an instant.

"From then on, the meeting was one of great cooperation," the official said later.

In fact, according to a former Fed official, Wriston was not altogether dismayed by the credit restraint program. In effect, it gave him an excuse not to make unprofitable loans. On the surface, it appeared that higher interest rates would generate more profits for the banks, but the diminished credit quality implied by such rates offset any possible advantage. By spring, it was obvious to Wriston that the economy would soon go over the edge of the cliff. Consumers had taken credit controls seriously, even to the point of cutting up their cards. "They stopped that plastic spending in a dramatic way," said Fed vice chairman Schultz. The result, of course, was the longest and most severe recession since World War II. In awe and horror, Wriston and his economists watched the wild gyrations in interest rates. From 1933 through 1971, the prime rate had changed just 48 times, an average of just over once a year. Over the next nine years, to 1981, it was adjusted 261 times, and in 1980 it was changed 39 times. By following Carter's orders, the Fed, as a former top official put it, had been "party to a sharp break in the economy." At its peak, the prime hit 21.5 percent.

The good news, for Wriston, was that high interest rates would mean the beginning of the end of Reg Q. In the spring of 1980, the campaign took on the appearance of a populist crusade. Citibank plastered its branch lobbies with posters attacking Washington for its inability to pay depositors competitive rates. Led by Angermueller and Citibank's Washington lobbyists, the bank recruited some unlikely bedfellows, including Ralph Nader, the labor unions, the Gray Panthers, and the American Association of Retired Persons. "They were a pretty effective ally," said one former officer. Citibank had given the Panthers advice on how senior citizens could hold on to their homes, and in return, Angermueller said later, they made a substantial low-interest deposit with the bank.

Richard Kovacevich, for one, buttonholed banking regulators in their offices and at cocktail parties, to the point where Volcker later asked a top Citicorp officer, "Who was that guy with the funny name who backed me into the shrimp bowl?" at a Washington reception. But Citicorp's contribution was less its deft handling of Washington legislators than its accomplishments over a period of two decades in making interest rate regulation almost irrelevant and in pointing out to savers how they were subsidizing borrowers.

On March 13, 1980, the day before the controls took effect, Wriston, in an Op-Ed piece in the *Washington Post*, wrote that "people are pretty smart. They had no trouble figuring out that if they earn 3 percent on their savings when inflation is in double digits, then the system is stealing them blind. They also perceive that if they borrow at 9 percent or 12 percent when inflation is 18 percent then they're beating the system. Under these pressures, consumers show unimpeachable logic and common sense by saving less and borrowing more. That experts find this behavior to be 'atypical' is astonishing." He urged the federal government to strike two powerful blows against inflation by preempting state usury ceilings and by eliminating Regulation Q.

Just weeks after he announced the imposition of credit controls, President Carter signed the Depository Institutions Deregulation and Monetary Decontrol Act, considered the most important banking bill since the 1930s. Besides calling for a six-year phase-out of Reg Q, the legislation lowered bank reserve requirements by scrapping the system of graduated reserves. By now, Wriston figured, it cost Citibank $65 million after tax to belong to the Fed. Because the legislation eliminated almost $14.5 billion in reserve requirements, some viewed it as a tax cut for banks. Small community banks escaped the reserve requirements altogether. The idea, of course, was not to give the banks a gift but to stem the exodus of banks from the system, which made it more difficult for the Fed to conduct monetary policy. Significantly, the act also raised the deposit insurance ceiling to $100,000 from $40,000.

For his efforts, Wriston received a commemorative pen and a letter from Carter lauding him for playing a key role in "creating the climate which made the bill possible. . . . For years," Carter wrote, "you have been a leading spokesman for the need to provide a fair return to the small saver, achieve competitive equity and reform our financial system."

Deregulating the liability side of banks' balance sheets without deregulating the asset side was later cited as one of the root causes of the savings and loan crisis. As always, the solution to one problem created a new set of problems. Thrift institutions, protected for years from market forces, now had to do more than buy money at a fixed regulated price and sell it at another fixed regulated price. Most thrifts were not up to that task. Advocates of a higher deposit insurance ceiling later regarded the hike in the ceiling as a major mistake, made because they feared that with the end of Reg Q, the thrifts would come under intense earnings pressures. Deregulation, said former deputy Treasury secretary Robert Carswell, set the stage for the high-flying S&L players "to take the money and really run with it." Wriston, looking back at the hike in the insurance ceiling, concluded that "when Fernand St Germain kicked up [deposit insurance coverage] to $100,000 one Friday night, he put a blanket over deposits that don't deserve" such protection.

Lifting Reg Q, incidentally, did not cause the mortgage market to dry up, as some expected. In fact, it led to the development of the secondary market in which mortgages were packaged and sold as securities.

What Walter Wriston giveth he also taketh away. While depositors now received market rates, many also paid higher fees. New accounts were introduced that rewarded a customer for banking with a single institution. Typically, the fees were waived for a customer who maintained a large total balance, and jacked up for the customer with a small account. Even as Wriston was being taken to the woodshed over pots and pans, his loophole lawyers were trying to find other schemes to circumvent Reg Q. But like the pots-and-pans giveaways, these new strategies thrust Wriston into more head-to-head battles with Volcker and the Fed.

One of Wriston's schemes was so unwieldy that Wriston himself dubbed it the "the hulk." Under a complicated arrangement with a small bank in Maine, a customer could buy a $10,000 certificate of deposit by putting up $3,000, the bank would lend the difference, and the customer would receive a rate above Reg Q. This transaction was so bizarre that Citibankers could never figure out how it worked, much less explain it to customers. "The hulk" was so fraught with controversy that Citibank didn't want to risk jeopardizing the bank's South Dakota operation by introducing it then.

Out of the short dalliance with "the hulk" emerged the idea of a national credit card that would pay interest on credit balances in excess of the Reg Q ceiling. The theory was that such balances weren't deposits, so Reg Q didn't apply. One writer described this tactic as a "mini-mail-order bank." The plan was to use the credit-card unit the bank had bought from Arlen Realty, call it the Choice card, and offer it to 150,000 households in the Washington-Baltimore vicinity. In early 1980, Citibank said it was notified by the SEC that the plan was acceptable as long as it was not offered as a "deposit-generating device." Without bothering to inform the Fed, Citibank introduced the program in September 1980, announcing it would pay 8.45 percent on credit balances. Four days later the Fed called Angermueller and ordered Citibank to stop the promotion dead in its tracks. This maneuver was a flagrant assault on the central bank that the Fed wouldn't tolerate. Fed officials fumed at Citibank's attempt to circumvent the payments system, interest rate ceilings, and reserve requirements in one giant leap.

The new market instruments, such as the negotiable CD and the NOW account, devised by Citibank and other innovative institutions, did not necessarily undermine monetary policy, but, as Volcker said later, they "sure changed the way it worked." Wriston was defiant, however. He wanted to haul the Fed into court, but that went against Hans Angermueller's better legal judgment. "Every time we go to court we get our rear end handed to us," he said later. Wriston was furious. He called Angermueller and demanded to know who made the decision not to litigate. "He gave me holy hell," said Angermueller. Wriston, Angermuller said, had a faith that the judicial system would decide correctly, a view that was not shared by Citibank's legal advisers. Angermueller was opposed to going to the mat on every initiative. "It was a little bit of a smart-ass thing to pay interest on credit balances," he said. "It was not exactly what I'd like to go into the highest court in the land with and say this is certainly a perfectly normal commercial transaction unrelated to Reg Q."

Even as Reg Q was clobbering the banks, Congress and the Fed took aim at the Eurodollar market, which they had unwittingly created. As Wriston observed, the Fed had been trying unsuccessfully to regulate this market for twenty years. He believed that if the free market was allowed to operate, rates would eventually drop. The Fed was worried, said former financial technician Stephen Axilrod, about whether a money supply was being created "outside the United States outside of monetary control." But the real reason had more to do with the Fed's inclination to try to regulate any economic system in which a dollar changes hands.

The Fed's Capitol Hill ally on the bill was Jim Leach, Iowa's otherwise financially sophisticated congressman, who introduced the Eurocurrency Market Control Act in mid-1979. Wriston was determined to nip this new regulation in the bud. "Just as the high seas are free to carry the world's commerce—stateless waters, as it were—so the Euromarkets are stateless markets that clear the world's financial transactions with a speed and efficiency unmatched in history," Wriston wrote in the *American Banker* of September 28, 1979. In the congressional hearings, Morgan vice chairman Dennis Weatherstone carried the water for the banks. Dismissing such controls as a bad idea, he declared that the way to "fix the alleged problem" was to end such domestic controls as Reg Q, non-interest-bearing reserves, and prohibitions on paying interest on short-term bank deposits. Eventually the Fed threw in the towel and the bill died an unlamented death.

Citibank's Charles Long was now convinced that South Dakota was the promised land, but not all of his senior colleagues shared his enthusiasm. Many policy board members were quite amused by the notion of worldly-wise Citicorp clod-hopping in South Dakota, and asked Long what he had been smoking. But one by one, board members rose in defense of the sparsely populated prairie state. One said that his wife had grown up near Dell Rapids. "If she ever hears you talking like that, you guys are in trouble," he chided.

Other South Dakota connections appeared out of left field. Said Governor Janklow, "It really took the South Dakota connections on the policy committee to stop the hee-hawing."

There were those, however, who stood to lose, and lose big, if Citicorp moved to South Dakota. Several large companies in the state, notorious for paying their workers poorly, were worried that Citicorp would boost wage levels. They bad-mouthed Sioux Falls—which Citibank was now mulling as a site for a facility—to bank officials, according to Janklow. "You'd never find workers here. The turnover's huge. They're undependable and hard to train," they warned Citicorp.

Much as Wriston admired the mind of John Reed, he shuddered whenever his youthful protégé felt compelled to speak it in public. Reed loved to gab with reporters, eagerly telling them everything that they wanted to know about Citibank's plans—and then some. Reed's loose lips prompted Wriston to admonish his flacks, "Whatever you do, keep little Johnny away from reporters." Reed justified Wriston's apprehensions on March 25, 1980, when Citibank held its annual full-court press luncheon for analysts and financial writers, all of whom had been beating up on Wriston and Citibank for the faltering consumer business. Citibank had made no secret of its interest in moving into Sioux Falls, but had not yet disclosed a timetable or applied to regulators for permission to operate its proposed new bank. Responding to a question about the consumer business, Reed stunned the guests and his colleagues by blurting out, "We would like very much to celebrate the Fourth of July in Sioux Falls, South Dakota."

Bank regulators do not like to learn about their banks' plans in the newspapers. "The Fed," said Ed Hoffman later, "went bonkers."

That luncheon was obviously still fresh in Wriston's mind about a month later when the policy committee gathered to hear a presentation on plans to change the name of the company's traveler's checks from First National City Bank to Citicorp. Hoffman and Reed had been debating this switch for years. Reed wanted to stick with First National City. Comparing Citicorp with General Motors, he argued that GM, in advertising its cars, touted Oldsmobiles and Pontiacs, not its corporate name. Hoffman contended that there wasn't enough money in the budget to market several names, including First National City, which had gone out with the green eyeshade. Reed had finally agreed to go with Citicorp, and Hoffman appeared at the meeting with a sample of the new check, made counterfeit-proof by shooting a virtually irreproducible photograph through the bottom of a Coke bottle. The plan, Hoffman said, called for Reed to host a press conference to announce the name change. Wriston quickly interjected. "Does John need to do another press conference?" Just then Angermueller arrived late for the meeting, obviously unaware of the issue then on the table, and Wriston said to him, "Hans, we don't need John to do a press conference on traveler's checks, do we?"

"No, no, I don't think we do," Angermueller replied, somewhat nonplussed.

"We just wanted to keep John out of the press, period," said one Citibank official later.

In November 1980, when the Comptroller of the Currency approved Citibank's petition to charter a new bank in Sioux Falls, the Fed couldn't object. After all, other banks, including Bank of America, were already the beneficiaries of more enlightened state regulation. Looking at the application with a jaundiced eye because it seemed to violate prohibitions on interstate banking, the Fed found no violation of law and no threat to the safety and soundness of Citicorp.

Wriston now had to get Albany to put up or shut up. He told New York State legislators that if they didn't act, Citibank would be forced to move its entire credit-card operations to South Dakota. Once again Wriston was told to wait until after Election Day.

In a bid to eliminate whatever skepticism remained in the minds of his top-level colleagues about South Dakota, Charles Long invited Janklow to address the policy committee. For most of Citibank's ruling elite, this was the first opportunity to meet the governor, a western legend in his own right. At least one top executive was not prepared for the sight of a nearly middle-aged man with massive steel braces on his teeth that resembled those worn by Jaws, the hulking agent of evil in the James Bond movies.

"That's a bit vain, the guy is forty-one years old," the Citibanker muttered derisively. "I guess as a politician he has to take care of cosmetics."

But he felt like slinking under his chair when he heard Long's solemn explanation: "Those braces hold his jaw and his skull together." Janklow was fitted with them after suffering head injuries in a plane crash—whose cause was never determined—that occurred while he was serving as South Dakota's attorney general.

Janklow's first appearance before Citicorp's board was high-level evidence that what goes around comes around. Well before most people in South Dakota had ever heard of Citibank, and before most Citibankers ever heard of South Dakota, director Don Seibert, chairman of J. C. Penney, had passed through Pierre, the state capital, on a brief inspection tour. With the shopping opportunities limited in that tiny outpost of 10,000 people, Janklow's wife complained incessantly to her husband about the slim pickings at the local Penney outlet. When Seibert dropped by the governor's office on a courtesy call, Janklow took him to task for his "crummy" store. That was not an episode Seibert could easily forget. So when Janklow was introduced around the boardroom to the leaders of corporate America, the response from Seibert was anything but warm. "The governor and I have already met," the stone-faced Seibert said curtly.

Janklow's tongue was even sharper than Wriston's. Before visiting Bill Spencer in his trophy-filled office, Janklow had been briefed on his African bongo, an animal so elusive that hunters claim they consider themselves successful if they find its droppings. When Janklow asked Spencer where he found "that muley deer," Spencer's face turned ashen and he stared at Janklow in total contempt.

Meanwhile, the New York State Legislature still hadn't gotten the message that deregulation was the wave of the future, nor had it taken seriously Citibank's threat to move its credit-card operation to South Dakota. Carey leaned on state legislative leaders, bringing in top Fed officials to explain the issue, distributing lists of institutions that planned to leave, and plying them with steak and beer in the residential quarters of the governor's mansion. This got the runner to first base. But after the state senate passed a bill raising the usury ceiling, it couldn't forge a compromise with the assembly. Herman "Denny" Farrell, chairman of the Assembly Banking Committee, opposed raising the ceiling, and the legislature ended its session with no action being taken. Farrell would later acknowledge that "most people, including myself, didn't fully understand the ramifications of Marquette." If he had pushed to raise the ceiling that spring, Farrell said, "I would have gotten myself lynched." And he acknowledged that "I can lose my seat for voting for an increase. It's not something I'm prepared to do."

Citibank was talking about 2,500 jobs and assuring Janklow that it would set up the credit-card facility in South Dakota even if New York State changed the law. "Never in my wildest dreams I thought I'd end up with 2,500 positions in South Dakota," Janklow said later. New York would have to acquire 200,000 new jobs to have the same impact as 2,500 jobs would have on Sioux Falls, population 90,000, he figured.

But on at least one occasion Citicorp's best-laid plans nearly came unglued because of a communications breakdown. Months after Citibank and South Dakota had popped the first bottle of champagne to celebrate their engagement, top Citibank operations executives were dispatched to Sioux Falls to begin the humdrum tasks of site selection and manpower planning. One officer clearly was out of the loop. At a dinner meeting with the governor and other South Dakota officials, he suggested that the facility should first be set up as a regional processing center with a view toward transferring the entire credit-card operation there later. Furious, Janklow jumped on a table and raged about Citibank reneging on its agreement.

At around midnight Charlie Long, who had returned to managing the international consumer business, got a panicky call from a colleague who was phoning from outside the banquet hall where the governor was railing.

"I've got a problem," the banker said. "The governor is irrational, he won't talk to me. He said that commitments have been made by Citi and I'm backing down."

"Tell Bill I'm on the phone," Long ordered.

Janklow grabbed the phone away from the Citibank executive. "All the fears that South Dakotans had have come true," he said angrily.

"What are you talking about?" Long replied.

"These fucking New York bankers are now reneging. I'm going to become the Panamanian registry for a banking activity that will just be a booking center, and I won't have the jobs. You don't understand that as a politician there are two things I have to keep in mind: one is Democrats, the other is votes. And I will not let you do this. I will derail the whole operation."

Barely pausing to catch his breath, Janklow told Long that "these guys don't understand the commitment. They keep referring to a planning document that said you were going to start off slow."

The so-called planning document turned out to be a newsletter that Janklow had sent to constituents in which he described the Citibank deal. "You are the author," Long reminded him. "I shared that with Walter Wriston, and whatever is in that document we are committed to do." Janklow had forgotten about the newsletter. The next morning, Long phoned Wriston, then flew to Sioux Falls to further smooth Janklow's ruffled feathers. "You should know that Walter Wriston said, 'Our marker's out, and our marker's good.' If you want to call him, you can call him."

One of the privileges Janklow earned by bailing out the nation's largest banking company was induction into the inner circle of Citicorp's ruling elite, something akin to membership in an Ivy League secret society. Later known as director emeritus of Citicorp, Janklow discovered that one of the rituals used by this high-powered clique to relieve the stress of seventy-hour work weeks was to poke fun at one another over dinner. One recipient of their barbs was Hans Angermueller. Janklow recalled one dinner vividly. "All these guys are sitting around a table, all stacking the shit on Hans. They called him a shoe clerk, said he couldn't speak the language and had a funny accent. They just heaped shit on him all night."

Finally, late in the evening, Angermueller said, "Governor, let me tell you something. You see all these people. They heap shit on me, but there is one thing they all know. Outside of you, I can fire every son of a bitch in this room." According to Janklow, no one laughed.

Janklow, meanwhile, hit the road seeking to turn South Dakota into the plastic capital of the country, and the capital of whatever other kind of service industry it could possibly attract. Now that Citibank had paved the way to Sioux Falls, other banks, including Chase and Chemical, began moving there as well. By May 1981, South Dakota officials said that more than twenty big U.S. banks had requested information on the state. Tongue in cheek, Janklow sent engraved invitations to his "exception" to virtually every U.S. bank. The invitation read: "The State of South Dakota cordially invites you to a Douglas Amendment exception to the Bank Holding Company Act of 1956." Janklow became a regular at banking conventions, where he debated what he called the "Janklow theory of interstate banking" with all comers. Other governors were horrified that he was letting "those predators" come to his state. "Governor after governor didn't believe we were doing it," Janklow recalled with a big grin. "I used to call people and ask what laws we had to change to get them out here," he acknowledged later. But he blew his top when an executive of Shearson Lehman Brothers, which had underwritten its fair share of the state's bond offerings, referred to South Dakota in congressional testimony as "rent-a-state." "They never did another fucking deal in this state," Janklow said. At the end of the decade he announced proudly that at least seven credit-card issuers employing nearly four thousand people had set up shop in South Dakota.

Like Custer, Citicorp made its last stand in South Dakota. But unlike the general, Citicorp emerged from the exercise alive and well. In the process, Citicorp learned at least two lessons: that state-by-state expansion was definitely the way to go, and that jobs—an asset that didn't show up on the balance sheet—were the key to entry. Gaining entrée meant, said Long later, that "your business is not hostage to geography. . . . The feeling that there was no way out—those days were over." Nationwide banking was under way even though interstate banking legislation had at the federal level gone nowhere.

Haunted by visions of being gobbled up by Citibank, regional and community banks from coast to coast fought with a vengeance its attempts to expand outside its borders. Citibank was a "convenient devil," said Kenneth Guenther, the former Burns aide who was now executive director of the Independent Bankers Association. In a slide presentation to small bank chiefs by bank consultant Alex Sheshunoff, Citibank was portrayed as a crocodile "working alone and biting off chunks wherever it could." But, Guenther conceded, Citicorp was "as responsible as anybody for breaking down interstate banking at the national level." Guenther credited Wriston with this predatory image. "He's a very, very arrogant man," Guenther said. "Someone who's easy to dislike on first, second, or third glance."

Wriston tried to allay the bankers' fears. In an early-1981 talk to securities analysts, he said, "Why would we buy anything? We have the offices. We have the people. All we do is change the name over the front door and do business." There were other good reasons not to gobble up small banks. "The small bank in the small community does a super job, and we can't compete with it."

While Fed chairman Paul Volcker didn't feel that geographic limitations made sense, he was concerned about a small number of banks becoming too big if they were allowed to expand freely across state borders. He later pointed out that he was "never a defender" of regulations against interstate branching. "I was trying to work up some sympathy for interstate banking," Volcker explained. The limitation he proposed—having in mind the possibility of turf-hungry Citibank acquiring Bank of America—was that no one bank would acquire more than 4 percent of the nation's deposits. He did so, he said, not so much out of his own fear of bigness but to offer a practical, politically salable proposal. The obstacle was not the Fed, he said, but divisiveness and squabbling among the bankers themselves.

Shortly after its archrival's coup in South Dakota, Chase Manhattan dispatched representatives to Delaware to promote legislation that would open that state to outside banks. The local bankers association "shot Chase down in flames," according to Citicorp director Irving Shapiro. "I mobilized the troops," he said, and phoned Delaware governor Pierre S. du Pont IV. Pointing out what Citibank had accomplished in South Dakota, Shapiro said that Delaware was a much more natural place for banks than South Dakota. "We ought to step up to this thing," Shapiro urged. Meanwhile, Morgan Guaranty of New York had arrived in Delaware and Chase had promised to bring jobs to the state in return for more liberal banking laws. Shapiro told the governor that Citibank had been welcomed with open arms in South Dakota, where it would become the largest single employer.

In January 1981 Delaware enacted banking laws that ultimately brought more than twenty banks to the state and radically altered the skyline of Wilmington. In August 1981, Citibank itself petitioned to open a Delaware unit to supply cash management and other corporate banking services.

Meanwhile Citicorp was expanding with its P-to-P's, or the Person-to-Person units, though Reed didn't envision, as some speculated, ever converting the finance offices to branches. Describing Person-to-Person as "McDonald's when McDonald's was only a hamburger," he said, "We've got to get breakfasts and french fries and Cokes and stuff into it."

In the wake of their success in playing the South Dakota card, Wriston and his loophole lawyers began pondering still other moves to free themselves from the shackles of constrictive regulation. In an interview published in the *New York Times* on May 31, 1981, Wriston acknowledged that Citicorp was thinking about dropping its bank charter, spinning off Citibank, acquiring a securities firm and an insurance company, and setting up non-bank consumer banks in every state. One of the acknowledged disadvantages of the plan was that Citibank would forfeit billions in interest-free checking deposits in its branch system.

Surprising as that revelation was, it was one of the less radical ideas Wriston and his colleagues were mulling over at the time. In contrast to some other banks, Citicorp did not shoot its managers for proposing offbeat ideas, and the search for the ultimate loophole gave rise to lots of them. According to corporate secretary Carl Desch, Citibank discussed rechartering the company in another country, such as Luxembourg, and "becoming a Merrill Lynch. Our aim was to get rid of all the boundaries in the world." Incredibly, Citibank and Wriston even contemplated *buying* a country, possibly an island in the Caribbean, where the giant institution could operate autonomously. There was, however, at least one other small problem with all of these proposals. Citicorp would forfeit access to the Fed discount window, not to mention that vast safety net that the American regulatory apparatus throws under troubled banks and their depositors. "That [idea] was from smoking too much of the stuff from Acapulco," Angermueller quipped later. "You very quickly come to the point where [these proposals are] all very nice from a pure legal point of view, but the bank runs on money. You've got to attract money to the liability side. And the only way to attract that is to make sure if you ever run into a liquidity problem there's a central bank to which you have access." Besides, he said, "nobody would buy your stocks, bonds, and [certificates of] deposits."

Five years later, Chase Manhattan announced with much fanfare that it, too, was thinking about giving up its banking charter. After reportedly spending some $2 million reinventing the wheel that Citibank had already discarded, Chase also scrapped the idea.

"There were," Wriston quipped to a colleague, "lots of dead cats in the air," Wristonese for the malaise and foreboding caused by tight money, sky-high interest rates, and talk of a prolonged recession. With the turn of the decade, two of the first dead cats to drop out of the air onto Wriston's doorstep were the Hunt brothers and First Pennsylvania Bank.

Silver was for years an obsession with Nelson Bunker and William Herbert Hunt, two sons by the first marriage of H. L. Hunt, the eccentric and fabulously rich Texas oilman. Later, Lamar, another son by H.L.'s first wife, caught the bug. With help from rich Arabs, the Hunt boys in 1979 set out to corner the world silver market by buying up silver futures. From $9 an ounce in August, the price surged to more than $50 an ounce in January. But when the Chicago Board of Trade ruled that silver could be traded only to liquidate positions, the price plummeted, falling to $10 an ounce by March. On March 26, 1980, a day after putting in a $135 million margin call to the Hunts, Bache Halsey Stuart Shields, their broker, notified the Commodity Futures Trading Commission that it was in deep trouble. Certain commercial banks, including First Chicago, were also in jeopardy. According to former deputy Treasury secretary Robert Carswell, "There was a real risk that a couple of New York Stock Exchange firms would go under and that their customers would go under. Trades would have gotten stopped, and once that happens it's hard to stop." The stock exchange firms appointed an emergency committee, but refused to put up any money. At the time, the government had no power to force them to bail out the endangered institutions. Paul Volcker tapped the Morgan bank, the institution he regarded as the private sector's central bank, to head the $1 billion rescue.

Citibank first learned of the Hunts' predicament when president William Spencer received an early-morning phone call from a Wall Street friend. The caller suggested that Spencer try to convene a meeting of key Hunt bankers in Boca Raton, Florida, where top bankers, including Ed Palmer and Walter Wriston, were attending the spring meeting of the elite Reserve City Bankers Association. Spencer immediately found out who would be attending and flew to Boca. Meanwhile, Palmer returned to New York to monitor Citibank's liquidity position. Well into the night, frantic commodity dealers phoned their bankers seeking information on the deliberations.

Late that Sunday night, Fed vice chairman Frederick Schultz received an urgent phone call from Paul Volcker, who was in Boca Raton, instructing him to tell the rest of the board that they should gather around the big table at eight o'clock the next morning. Volcker was concerned that if the crisis wasn't resolved by then, the board might have to move quickly to avert a financial panic before the markets opened. "The worry was that the silver market was going to crash the next morning," said Spencer. As the bankers worked through the night, Volcker, clad in pajamas and slippers, checked on the progress of the discussions several times. By morning, the bankers had assembled a loan to prop up the market. Volcker called off the Red Alert.

Don Regan, chairman of Merrill Lynch, whose exposure to the Hunts was rumored to have put it under water, was scheduled to debate Wriston on Monday on financial industry regulation. He had flown down to Florida on Sunday and closeted himself in his suite immediately after checking into the hotel. What he did not know was that the hotel desk clerk had misspelled his name. He learned only the next morning the havoc that had caused for the American banking establishment. As Regan slept soundly, Volcker, Wriston, John McGillicuddy of Manufacturers Hanover, and the chief executives of other major banks and investment banks scoured the country for the missing Mr. Regan. When Regan phoned his office that morning, he discovered that everyone who was anyone in American banking was asking, "Where the hell is Regan?" McGillicuddy had alerted Regan's office that he wanted to meet him for an early breakfast, and it was from McGillicuddy that Regan first learned of the crisis. At that meeting, McGillicuddy sat next to Bank of America's Tom Clausen, who asked if he had any direct exposure to the Hunts. Neither bank did, according to McGillicuddy. "So why are we here?" Clausen asked.

"I suspect we're here because we're the deep pockets and this is a big problem," McGillicuddy replied.

Amid the confusion, Wriston and Regan realized that the show planned for that day would have to go on, in part to avoid contributing to any panic. "The two of us had to leave this meeting, where literally [Wriston's] bank and my firm [Merrill Lynch] were facing losses of hundreds of millions, and go down to debate," Regan recalled. "We kidded each other, how this was becoming quite a thing with us, and whether we should wear straw hats and canes and go out and do a soft-shoe routine." In his talk, Wriston described the "bank of the future," which would accept deposits, pay a market rate of interest, extend loans, and underwrite stock. Once Wriston picked up a catchy line he would use it and reuse it until it got intolerably stale. "The bank of the future that I have described already exists. Don Regan runs it, and it's called Merrill Lynch Pierce Fenner & Smith. I for one applaud him for it."

"Fine, Walter," Regan retorted, "if you want to run Merrill Lynch come on over. I'd love to run your bank for a while and get a share of those profits you're making, vis-à-vis what we can eke out at Merrill Lynch."

To which Wriston replied, "I just wish I had the right to get into your business the way you're getting into mine with the CMA."

Regan offered to open a cash management account for him anytime he wanted. Countered Wriston: "Don't call me for a loan if you need one, or want one." The repartee brought down the house, and the two financiers received a standing ovation. But as Regan recalled later, "Anyone who listened to that debate would never have realized the problems the two of us were facing upstairs in that very hotel, and what had been going on all night."

Everyone may have enjoyed the performance, but not everyone was a fan of Wriston and Citibank. Especially Missouri bankers. During the presentation, one of them stood up and shouted, "Your damn bank sent my wife a credit card with a $1,000 line. What do you know about her credit? And besides that, you're in my market. Stay out of my market!"

The Hunt bailout plan was struck in broad terms the next morning and called for the banks to make loans based on the Hunts' oil reserves. In that discussion, according to McGillicuddy, Spencer's contribution was vital, since he was intimately familiar with the Hunt oil fields. For Spencer, the Hunt silver crisis only added to the frustration he was feeling over the credit-card fiasco. Because of the crisis, Spencer arrived late for a meeting of Citibank consumer executives to discuss that faltering effort. Spencer asked his colleagues how things were going. Their answers were noncommittal. "This is bullshit," said Reed aide Ed Harshfield. "People are feeling very bad."

Harshfield later recalled he was the only one at the meeting who didn't receive a good-bye from the boss at the elevator.

Later, a colleague told him, "Spencer's not going to fire you. He's going to kill you."

By the end of May, thirteen banks, led by Morgan and First National Bank of Dallas, signed a deal to stretch out the Hunt loans over ten years and to extend a $1.1 billion loan to their Placid Oil Company, which in turn lent the money to the Hunts. John McGillicuddy summed up the situation: "We got repaid by being sued and spent a hell of a lot of money defending ourselves against our unconscionable acts."

When the Hunts collapsed, Wriston wanted to be sure that chief financial officer Don Howard had a lot of extra liquidity on hand. Ninety-nine times out of a hundred, Howard would say that he already had taken care of that. The Hunt crisis, said a former senior officer, caused Citibank to be forever conscious of the need for liquidity. The *Washington Post,* on March 30, 1980, saw a silver lining in the Hunts' troubles. "The collapse of the silver market may give a much needed psychological boost to the Federal Reserve's effort to cut back on consumer credit," the *Post* wrote. "There is nothing like the spectacle of the rich guys getting their comeuppance to make us feel a little less put-upon when the cashier announces regretfully that Visa says we have exceeded our credit limit."

Meanwhile, First Pennsylvania Bank was also about to face its day of reckoning. Philadelphia-based First Pennsy was the nation's oldest banking institution. It had survived every financial crisis in the nation's history. But it was now in its death throes because its former chairman and CEO, John R. Bunting, Jr., had bet the bank on declining interest rates by using short-term purchased money to finance a huge portfolio of long-term bonds.

Citibank was the largest bank lender to the First Pennsylvania Corporation, the holding company. So it was natural that Citibank should take the lead in trying to salvage the venerable institution. It was also awkward. Brash, arrogant Citibank was not universally loved by its banking peers, and no one wanted to participate in what could be construed as a bailout of Citibank. "Nobody was anxious to pull our chestnuts out of the fire," said executive committee chairman Ed Palmer, who got the call for help from George A. Butler, Bunting's successor.

A dozen or so of First Pennsy's bankers gathered in New York in search of a solution in mid-April 1980. Palmer was reluctant even to show up at the meeting, to avoid reminding the other banks there that Citibank had the most to lose from a default and the most to gain from a bailout. The bankers were not happy. They growled that they had been lured to New York without knowing just how bad things really were. While Morgan Stanley investment banker Ted Dunn, who was chairing the gathering, attempted to calm the other bankers, Palmer arrived and took a chair against a wall behind the investment bankers. Dunn, as Palmer recalls, was losing control of the meeting. Morgan Stanley president Bob Baldwin whispered to Palmer, "You've got to say something." Palmer had come with the intent of listening, not speaking. As Palmer looked around the table, he saw Texans and Californians, whose animus for New York banks in general, and for Citibank in particular, was well known.

Finally, Palmer drew a breath and stood before the gathering. "I'm going to say something that might not seem relevant," he began. He then told the other bankers that he and his wife had watched a TV program the night before dealing with the 1930s bank runs, which emphasized the importance of public confidence in the banking system. Back then Morgan and Citibank had passed up an opportunity to save the Bank of United States, whose failure on December 11, 1930, triggered bank runs throughout the country. Eventually, he said, depositors of the bank, which had no connection to the federal government, got most of their money back. "Morgan and Citibank let them go and they shouldn't have," he said. The bankers had been on the verge of walking out of the meeting, which would have left the problem entirely in the hands of the government. Instead, they remained and subscribed to a rescue deal that called for the FDIC and twenty-five banks to lend First Pennsy $500 million and to extend a credit line of more than $1 billion. Palmer had urged the banks not to strip First Pennsy of any incentive to repair itself by taking a lot of warrants [rights to purchase stock] up front. "We should be concerned about getting paid back but not [about] making a profit out of it," Palmer said. But in the end, greed prevailed. If the banks were going to save First Pennsy, they would also take their pound of flesh.

For Wriston, the First Pennsy crisis pointed up the absurdities in U.S. banking regulation: a foreign bank—Hong Kong & Shanghai Banking Corporation—was allowed to buy troubled Marine Midland while Pittsburgh's Mellon Bank, which wanted to buy First Pennsy, was prohibited from doing so. Wriston bluntly warned fellow bankers that "it's definitely time to take another look at the whole regulatory process and do a little cost-benefit analysis."

Making big bets on commodity prices and interest rates in a volatile economy was disastrous for the Hunts and First Pennsy. But it was also very costly for Citibank. Until Paul Volcker's arrival on the monetary scene, Wriston and his chief economist, Leif Olsen, believed they were smart enough to forecast interest rates with great accuracy and take positions based on those projections. Although chief financial officer Don Howard had been trained as a banker, he possessed a trader's temperament. Like Olsen, he believed interest rate models could accurately predict interest rate trends. Unlike Olsen, however, he was in a position to place bets on his view on interest rates. Big bets. While a foreign exchange trader who exceeded his limits and cost the bank $40 million would almost invariably be fired, a CFO who bet on interest rates and lost $100 million was not considered deserving of capital punishment.

With rates at an all-time high and the recession deepening, long-term government securities seemed like a safe and profitable haven for spare cash. In March, Don Howard asked Tom Theobald and Ed Palmer for permission to buy $5 billion in long-term government securities. Howard thought the rate increase earlier that year was an overcorrection. Citibankers were not averse to big bets, but this request far exceeded their risk-taking appetite, and they refused to let Howard buy any securities. By midyear 1980, however, the credit controls had taken hold, and interest rates tumbled. Howard looked like a genius. The $5 billion investment he wanted to make would have earned the bank $1 billion.

Now Howard was convinced of the infallibility of his forecasting skills, and he predicted that with the recession deepening, interest rates would continue to plunge. Around Labor Day, while Palmer was away, Howard approached Bill Spencer for permission to buy more than $1 billion in government securities. This time Howard's request was approved. But this time the market turned against him. Rates shot up instead of down, and the bank lost a quick and cool $100 million. Howard was no big fan of decision-making by committee, and that included the Asset Liability Committee. According to Ed Hoffman, Howard bought the bonds without consulting with the committee. Theobald was furious and, according to former Citibank officers told Wriston this was bad management at its worst. This did not, former officers said, endear Theobald to Wriston.

That summer, Howard was apparently so absorbed in his big bet that he once showed up on the tennis court for a match wearing wing tips instead of sneakers.

Wriston himself was convinced that interest rates would fall. "Remember Brussels. Hang on longer," Wriston said, recalling the incident in which the trader could have made back his money if he maintained his position a few days longer.

At the time, according to a former senior officer, certain young funds managers favored a conservative strategy of matching loans and deposits of similar maturities over a riskier approach that left an interest rate "gap." Wriston would say later that he had nothing do with matching and gapping. Citibank's gap—the difference between long-term assets and liabilities subject to changes in rates—was as much as $5.5 billion in the 1980–1981 period, a gap big enough to sail an aircraft carrier through. Wriston believed that the role of bankers was to borrow short and lend long, and that if they did it right, they could make lots of money. The more conservative approach is to match up assets and liabilities of the same maturities and make a profit on the rate difference. "Walt resisted that," said a former colleague, but "finally threw in the towel."

"We're too big to ever be perfectly positioned," Ed Palmer said several months later in a meeting with securities analysts. "We guessed wrong, and by the time our crystal ball cleared, we had missed the market." The gapping problem was not limited to New York. Citibank also had mile-wide gaps in its funding centers in London and Nassau, the home of its largest treasury units.

This was the last time that Citi ever bet the bank on an interest rate outlook. Citibank had already begun to realize, as Reed said later, that its stockholders were not buying Citicorp shares so it could invest in government bonds, and it reduced its holdings of government securities substantially. In a talk to analysts in New York on October 21, 1982, Wriston said that Citibank had established a "more conservative funding policy, and we no longer run sizable negative long-term gaps, nor do we try to base funding policy on our ability to predict the course of rates in the short term." This was the era of the risk managers, whose job would now be to match maturities and hedge open positions.

As a result of the funding problems, Citibank set up a finance committee under Theobold made up of the heads of its key business units. Don Howard later was forced to relinquish his responsibility for short-term money market operations, though he retained control over such activities as long-term funding and capital planning.

Making the wrong interest rate forecast eventually contributed to the demise of Citibank's huge economics department, which was bigger than the economics faculties of most large universities. One of the first steps in that direction occurred in mid-1981 when Citibank ceased publication of its venerable *Monthly Economic Letter*. Chief economist Leif Olsen tried to put the best face on that decision when he told a reporter that the reason was the abundance of similar free publications. "What was once a lonely tree on a barren plan has now become part of a forest," he wrote in a final issue.

Of Olsen, Wriston would say later, "His forecasts were pretty well on the money for years. Then, like all the other economists, he missed the wild upsurge."

Reed would later describe the funding debacle as a "Howard-Wriston deal which I knew nothing of—only heard gossip about." But the episode left an indelible mark on Citicorp's modus operandi. "We were so burned by that," Reed explained later, "that some of my colleagues, not including myself, made a fetish about knowing nothing about interest rates. That was a stupid thing to have done. . . . You have to have a point of view. You should be humble, and shouldn't make any mistake that your point of view is going to be all that accurate. But to fail to think about it at all is to sign up for purposeful ignorance."

While fighting turf wars with Merrill Lynch and Missouri bankers, Wriston was also preoccupied with his own turf war in Sherman, Connecticut. Not surprisingly, when Wriston or Citibank needed Shearman & Sterling's toughest and most tenacious litigator, they usually called on John Hoffman, a veteran of the Herstatt and Edwards affairs. And now, for his most important client, Hoffman set out to fight the Great Range War, a.k.a. the Battle of Norma's Pond.

The Wristons had a dispute with a neighbor over the joint purchase of a plot of land with a pond adjoining their property, a landscape that seemed to be a scene out of a Norman Rockwell painting. While Wriston was usually able to contain his temper, even in front of congressional demagogues, Deer

Pond Farm was another matter altogether. Wriston brought all the legal might of Citicorp and one of the nation's preeminent law firms down on his hapless neighbor. Hoffman slapped the neighbor with a lawsuit, tying up the disputed property in legal bondage and forcing the neighbor to stick to his original agreement with Wriston, Wriston said.

In early May 1980, about the time he was resolving the crisis in the rolling hills of western Connecticut, he received a phone call from a lawyer in Stuttgart, West Germany, concerning another crisis of somewhat more global significance. The lawyer was handling Citibank's Iranian litigation in Germany. In the wake of the asset freeze brought on by the Iranian revolution and the taking of American hostages in 1979, John Hoffman was representing Citibank against the Iranians in several countries, including the United Kingdom, where about $3 billion in Iranian deposits was frozen. In West Germany, Citibank was suing the Iranians for default on loans and attaching shares they held in Krupp and the engineering firm of Deutsche Babcock, investments made during the Shah's reign.

Hans Angermueller and John Hoffman were all too familiar with the long and dreary history of litigation stemming from Citibank's ties to Russia, China, and Cuba. The two lawyers thought that the Iran episode was shaping up as a lifetime annuity for attorneys, and they feared that the financial entanglements were so complex it was unlikely they could get the hostages out. At any rate, Hoffman knew that ultimately any settlement would have a financial angle to it. Hoffman phoned officials at Treasury and the State Department to offer some suggestions on how banks might help end the standoff. In earlier conversations, Hoffman, Angermueller, deputy Treasury secretary Robert Carswell, and other Treasury and State Department officials had formulated two plans (A and B) in which the U.S. government would unfreeze Iranian assets, Iran's cross-border debt to the United States would be paid out of frozen deposits, and the hostages would be set free. The trouble was, there were no Iranians, or even their representatives, to talk to. Sooner or later, Hoffman and Angermueller figured, somebody would have to call.

The call came on May 2 from Citibank's German lawyer, Peter Mailander, who reported that his partner had just been approached by the Iranians' counsel, a Peter Heinemann, suggesting that the Iranians might consider an "economic solution" to the hostage standoff. Heinemann, a former Shearman & Sterling trainee, proposed a deal whereby Citibank would release Iran's shares of Krupp and Citibank would receive a portion of its loans. The Iranians, Mailander told Hoffman, had established two ground rules for discussions: they demanded absolute secrecy, and they wouldn't put up any more money. The Iranians claimed that their initiative had been authorized by three top Iranian officials, including president Abolhassan Bani-Sadr. Hoffman investigated further and concluded that the proposal was on the level. Hoffman later learned that the Iranians' German lawyers had approached Bank of America and Morgan Guaranty Trust Company, neither of which apparently showed any interest in negotiating an agreement.

Hoffman immediately reported the conversation with Mailander to Angermueller, who summoned him to 399 Park to huddle with Wriston on this dramatic, back channel overture. It was the kind of event that sent Wriston's adrenaline rushing. He had never achieved his dream of being appointed Secretary of State, but the chairmanship of the world's largest bank did sometimes offer an opportunity to practice statecraft. This was one such occasion.

Tempting as it might have been to cut a side deal that benefited Citicorp exclusively, Wriston said the State Department would have to be informed and Citicorp's reply to the Iranians would have to reflect the interests of the United States and the hostages. Sitting at the round table in his office, Wriston lectured Hoffman and Angermueller on an obscure, rarely applied law that prohibits private citizens from conducting diplomacy for the United States. "I'm not going to go to jail for violating the Logan Act," Wriston said sternly. Hoffman nodded solemnly, trying to appear familiar with the law when in fact he'd never heard of it before. After the meeting he rushed back to his office to look up the law and discovered that it had been applied only once, and in that case the alleged violator had been acquitted. Coincidentally, that case also involved Iran.

"I'll phone Washington," Angermueller volunteered.

"No, you won't," Wriston replied tersely, and instructed him to get on the shuttle to discuss the Iranian proposal in person. "The Russians have a microwave that can pick up phone conversations," Wriston explained.

Angermueller couldn't believe what he was hearing. "You've been reading too many spy novels," Angermueller said, chuckling. Wriston, Angermueller revealed later, was convinced that the Russians were "in on every telephone conversation"—with some justification; the Russians intercepted non-wire phone conversations in the same fashion as did America's National Security Agency.

On May 6, Angermueller and Hoffman met with Carswell in Washington. When Angermueller returned, he sheepishly admitted to Wriston, "You were right"—the Russians were listening. Shortly thereafter, on May 13, Carswell gave Hoffman the green light to conduct his private channel diplomacy.

It could have been a scene in a John Le Carré novel, a place that Angermueller thought was the perfect spot for a first meeting, on May 15, 1980, between Hoffman and Iran's German go-betweens. The Schloss Kronberg was an old castle near Frankfurt that had been home of the kaiser's mother as well as a temporary lodging for General Eisenhower. Not being in the center of Frankfurt, with its many banks, the castle, which had been converted into a hotel, appeared to offer the kind of privacy that was needed for such a sensitive mission. Angermueller assured Hoffman that there was little chance he would run into anyone he knew. But when Hoffman entered the lobby, the first person he spotted was former Treasury secretary Michael Blumenthal. Hoffman made a point of avoiding him. At Citibank, only Angermueller and Wriston knew anything about the mission. Even Hoffman's client, Citibank's Middle Eastern group, was not told, but served merely as the cover for his secret travels. "I'd been spending months flying back and forth, so I'd just pick up and go and nobody thought anything about that."

At the meeting, Hoffman told the Iranian representatives that the U.S. government would have to be constantly informed, that there could be no Citibank side deal, and that the entire transaction hinged on the release of the hostages. Out of these early discussions emerged Plan C, which called for Iran to release the hostages and for the United States to transmit to a "neutral bank" Iranian funds over and above the amounts owed to creditors, to unfreeze other accounts, and to place some of the frozen assets in a special fund to be used to settle remaining claims. Over the next six months, Hoffman held secret meetings to discuss this plan at his home in Chappaqua, New York, as well as in Europe and Bermuda. That the role played by Hoffman and the banks was becoming vital to the eventual solution of the hostage crisis became clear on September 12, 1980, when the Ayatollah Khomeini announced four conditions for the hostage release, three of which were financial.

Ultimately, Hoffman and Angermueller began to feel that another bank with a stake in the outcome should at least be informed of the discussions. Despite the public institutional rivalry that had long been waged between Citibank and Chase, there were long-standing close personal ties between their lawyers and law firms and between top officials at both banks. Hoffman felt most comfortable with his old and trusted friend, Milbank Tweed's Francis D. Logan, with whom he had worked in sorting out the wreckage from earlier crises, including Herstatt. Bringing Chase into the loop involved certain risks. To the Iranians, Chase was David Rockefeller and Rockefeller was the Shah. With some understatement, Hoffman said later, "If the Iranians had found out Chase was involved, they would have been very upset." Logan's involvement had to be a state secret. He would work with Hoffman but be isolated from Chase. Hoffman would have to be able to deny categorically that Chase was a party to the discussions. The arrangement became known as "Logan in a Box." Hoffman otherwise attempted to convey a sense of normalcy, relieving stress by training for the New York marathon, held every fall. At about the time Hoffman was approaching the finish line in Central Park, Hoffman's plan C for the release of the hostages was about to breathe its last gasp.

Wriston's keen interest in Hoffman's mission was almost literally interrupted by gunshots. On May 29, 1980, National Urban League president Vernon Jordan, Wriston's friend and fellow J. C. Penney director, was shot and critically wounded in Fort Wayne, Indiana. While Jordan was lying in an Indiana hospital, it became clear that he would not survive without more sophisticated treatment. Wriston immediately arranged for him to be moved to New York Hospital, where Wriston served as a trustee. Every morning thereafter, Wriston stopped by Jordan's room, maintaining a brief and often silent vigil until Jordan was discharged. Said Jordan, "He clearly made the hospital understand that there was nothing I should not have. He made it clear the hospital was to be at my disposal." Added Ford Foundation president Franklin Thomas, "I think Vernon would say, 'When I think of a half dozen people in the world that I would be comfortable with in the biggest battle of my life . . . Walter Wriston would be on that very short list.' "

In late October, former Ku Klux Klan member Joseph Paul Franklin was arrested in Florida on suspicion of shooting Jordan. He was also charged with the murder of two blacks in Salt Lake City and was a suspect in eight other killings.

After Jordan recovered, Wriston tapped him to become a director of New York Hospital. "That wasn't difficult to do," Jordan said later, "because in part I owe my life to that hospital."

Because of the gyrations in Citibank's bond portfolio, Wriston in 1980 felt his biggest risk was the interest rate gap, not loans to less developed countries. As for the LDCs, he said, "Our sovereign risk procedure has served us well, but we must keep a careful watch over our exposure." And he indicated that American foreign policy was a bigger threat to the overseas portfolio than was U.S. economic policy. But by now Citibank and other big international banks were in effect financing the balance-of-payments deficits of Brazil, Mexico, and the rest. The banks, in other words, were the prisoners of their Third World borrowers. Though Citibank had tried to slow loan growth, it had already lent so much money that it couldn't stop now even if it wanted to. With corporate banking virtually dead and the consumer banking effort suffering huge losses, Citibank's dependence on syndication fees was like a drug user's addiction to cocaine.

For those who were concerned about Third World debt, Brazil, as an oil importer, was the major worry. The *Wall Street Journal* of February 4, 1980, predicted a gloomy year for Brazil. Even veteran loan syndicator Jerry Finneran acknowledged later that it was absurd that Brazil could get a fifteen-year loan in 1981 at a mere five eighths over the London Interbank Offering Rate. "Everybody thought this was the thing to do." It was certainly right for some: according to one former international lender, Brazilian officials extracted 2 to 3 percent of the syndicated loans as kickbacks.

Even as a $1.8 billion jumbo loan to Venezuela—Euromoney's deal of the year—was being hammered out, a $450 million loan to the Instituto de Puertos (the ports department), for which Citibank served as agent, stumbled into default. To be sure, Citibank was trying to cut its cross-border lending and expand its local-currency activities, including consumer and investment banking. In Brazil, for example, Citibank sought to emphasize lending in cruzeiros and being repaid in cruzeiros rather than dollars. "Unfortunately, we may have gone too far before that strategy was able to be executed," Richard Kovacevich said.

Still, no one wanted to pull the plug on cross-border lending. Latin America was making $250 million a year, and the newly initiated consumer effort was losing millions. Said Wriston confidant James Farley, who in 1980 was placed in charge of the bank's Latin American business, "I certainly didn't want to be the one to call it quits to the earnings machine we had."

John Reed would later contend that "it's easy to criticize cross-border lending now and say, 'Gee whiz, humbug,' but the reality is if we [hadn't had] the growth in earnings, it would have been very hard to be as brave. It paid a lot of the bills. . . . In a sense the LDC loans were funding the retail bank's losses." But, he added, "I don't think people consciously said, 'Let's go out and make more LDC loans to fund John Reed.' If anything, the inclination would have been to say, 'Let's stop making LDC loans and let John Reed go down the tubes.' "

By 1980, Citibank had forfeited the opportunity to lead the way in putting the brakes on lending to Brazil and other Third World countries. This was the last chance for the banks to say, "no new money." If the lending could have been sharply curtailed in 1979 and 1980, experts claimed later, there probably would not have been a debt crisis. "It [Citibank] could not slow down in a way that was healthy even for Brazil," said former central bank chief Carlos Langoni.

According to international czar G. A. Costanzo, Citibank in the late 1970s and early 1980s turned cautious. While the cross-border exposure of other banks—notably regionals and European institutions—was still growing at nearly a 30 percent annual rate, Citibank was restricting growth to about 5 percent annually. "We already had more than we should have," Costanzo acknowledged later. That may have been true for some slice of the portfolio, but not for the LDC portfolio as a whole. An internal analysis by former Citibanker Ed Hoffman indicated that the slowdown was inconsistent at best. In 1980, Citi's cross-border exposure to five key LDCs—Brazil, Argentina, Mexico, the Philippines, and Venezuela—surged to nearly $10.7 billion from about $7.8 billion at year end 1979.

As concerns about Brazil and other LDCs mounted, Wriston once again disparaged the critics. "When OPEC raised the energy ante, [critics predicted that] the impossible attempt to recycle petrodollars was going to break the banks. It didn't even bend them," Wriston told securities analysts on March 25, 1980. "Then [the doomsayers thought that] the LDCs were going to go broke and drag the banks down with them. We have yet to lose a dollar on an LDC loan."

Wriston dispatched his economists to Washington to pour oil on troubled waters. In testimony before a subcommittee of the House Banking Committee in early 1980, former Citibanker Harold van Buren Cleveland, while urging quota increases for the IMF, said that the impact of the second oil shock of 1979 in slowing economic growth was "much milder" than the first one. He concluded that "there are reasonable grounds for expecting the debt burden of developing countries that do most of the borrowing to remain manageable."

According to one top international officer, Citibank may have been lulled into excessive optimism by watching, or by relying on, the wrong numbers. In some countries, for example, the current account balance, which reflects, among other things, the difference between exports and imports, gave no cause for panic. In one meeting of the Federal Advisory Council, before Third World debt had become a serious problem, Fed vice chairman Frederick Schultz mentioned that Paul Volcker had expressed concern about the large volume of loans banks had been making to these countries. "I don't agree," Wriston responded. "They're the best loans I have. Sovereign nations don't go bankrupt."

Privately, however, some top Citibankers were getting nervous. A number of LDC watchers by this time were saying that "this thing isn't adjusting out right," one top Citibanker recalled. "You could see the charts. The developing countries weren't coming back." Debt levels were increasing. Economic adjustment was being financed with more borrowing. Internally there were debates over whether Citibank should continue lending. Some were saying, "We better stop here because [Third World economies are not] behaving" the way they did after the first oil shock. The worriers "got a tremendous clobbering over the head from Costanzo and Wriston," the former official said. They expressed confidence that these countries had been able to adjust before and would do so again. They said that no fundamental change in policy was called for. Wriston and Citicorp recognized the need to hold the line on overseas loan growth. But the revival of some countries once deemed basket cases lent credibility to Wriston and Costanzo's argument that countries don't go bankrupt.

In an interview in the July 1980 issue of *Euromoney,* country risk chief Irving Friedman said that Peru and Gabon "have turned it around" and that Turkey "seems to be in the process of turning around." And indeed, rather than taking a hit when a borrowing country got into trouble, Citibank was sometimes rewarded for helping to steer the country out of it. Nowhere was that more true than in Turkey, which encountered a severe economic crisis in the late 1970s marked by civil strife, plummeting industrial output, and a scarcity of vital supplies like heating oil. With Citibank's help, Turkey's economic minister Turgut Özal, an alumnus of the World Bank and a close friend of Al Costanzo, restructured the country's debt. Inflation dropped from 130 percent in early 1980 to 30 percent two years later, to the point where in 1982 Turkey was able to syndicate about $300 million in international loans. After the military kicked out Premier Süleyman Demirel in September 1980, Özal became deputy premier and later president. "Özal came in and put in a free market economy, and they're current and nobody even remembers [the earlier crisis]," Wriston asserted. Turkey's central bank had maintained an account with Citibank since 1946, and Citibank had operated a liaison office in Istanbul since 1975. But Citicorp had been trying to break into Turkey in a more significant way for decades. On several occasions, it thought it had a deal to establish branches and even placed prospective country heads on standby in case an agreement materialized. Finally, in May 1980, Turkey rewarded Citicorp for its help by issuing a decree allowing it to open the first branch of a foreign bank in the country.

That new branch nearly proved fatal for some of Citibank's top international specialists, including George "Jack" Clark. In May 1981 four terrorists hijacked a Turkish jet with 110 passengers aboard, including five Citibankers, and ordered the pilot to fly to Bulgaria. The hijackers, described as leftist extremists, singled out the bankers and threatened to kill them. Back in New York, Wriston was awakened by a call from the State Department and immediately got on the phone to bankers' wives all over the world. He found that the Citibank support network had already swung into action on behalf of one Athens-based officer who was aboard the hijacked plane. That officer's wife told Wriston that 30 people were in her living room and that they had run out of beer. After the plane landed in Bulgaria, authorities there coaxed two hijackers off the plane and arrested them. As the passengers overpowered one of the remaining terrorists, another started shooting. But the Citibankers and the other passengers escaped unharmed. When it was over, Wriston traveled to Washington to present the State Department duty officer with a Steuben eagle for his efforts.

Closer to home, Wriston took every opportunity to assure Latin borrowers that Citibank would stick by them. In a speech on September 9 to Mexico City's Bankers Club, Wriston celebrated the close historical ties between Citibank and Mexico. "We are confident and optimistic about our future together," he said. But many wealthy Mexicans clearly didn't share Wriston's confidence. In May 1980, Mexico City mayor Carlos Hank Gonzalez plopped down $875,000 in cold cash for a twenty-room Tudor-style mansion on six acres in fashionable New Canaan, Connecticut, not far, in fact, from Costanzo's home. The purchase, and the mayor's habit of arriving at his home on weekends by helicopter, subsequently provoked a scandal of sorts in Mexico. But two years passed before the significance of Gonzalez's lifestyle became evident to American bankers: the smart money was leaving Mexico.

Even as the big banks were preparing to recycle petrodollars again, they were expanding their operations on Miami's exclusive Brickell Avenue to catch the residue from recycling. Miami was becoming the banking center for Latin America and the receptacle for its fugitive capital. In effect, cross-border loans "round-tripped" from offshore funding centers to Latin America, winding up in private banking offices as well as real estate, in Miami, south Texas, and Vail, Colorado, to name a few favored locations. According to financier Geoffrey Bell, well-heeled Latins enjoyed a tax benefit by borrowing in local currency, offsetting the interest against local taxes, then converting the money to dollars on which the income was not taxed. In the private banking business, Citibank, Bell marveled, was "particularly skillful." Its international private banking unit chased a "global elite" group of some five thousand individuals worth more than $100 million. According to a consultant cited by author Karin Lissakers, Citibank held $26 billion in deposits from this group, half from Latin America. American Express even offered a "black card" carrying a $500,000-plus credit line and a private plane and bodyguard service.

The money flowing into Miami, of course, was not entirely innocent. According to Citibankers, financial officials of countries such as Venezuela used insider information about planned changes in economic policies for their own benefit, often flying from Caracas to Miami to deposit dollars in U.S. banks, including Citibank. A huge, though inestimable, chunk of it was drug money.

By December 1980 it was clear at the Morgan that Citicorp's earlier rose-colored view of the situation was not warranted. In the December 1980 issue of *World Financial Markets,* it wrote that the second oil shock was "hitting the developing countries harder than the rest" and that "financing their balance-of-payments deficits will be more difficult this time and is going to require innovative institutional thinking and initiative." The market was also trying to tell Wriston something. Citicorp was still outperforming its money center brethren, yet its shares were trading for a mere five times earnings, compared with twelve times just a few years before. But, asked former Citibanker George Davis, "who has the perspective to take the punch bowl away at the right moment?"

22

WRISTONOMICS

*I*n early 1980, as the presidential campaign of John Connally (whom Wriston had supported financially and philosophically) was going down in flames, Citibank's chief economist Leif Olsen received a call from a fellow member of a conservative West Coast think tank composed largely of aides to former California governor and presidential candidate Ronald Reagan. Reagan was en route to New York, and Olsen's friend thought it would be nice if Reagan and Wriston, who hadn't met before, got acquainted. So a visit to Citibank was arranged for Reagan. No one even recognized the future president when Olsen led him up to the private dining room at 399 Park for a lunch with a few Republican faithfuls.

"Everybody went after him on economic and monetary policy," said Wriston. "He walked out with everybody's vote. That's when I realized he was a very smart guy who conned people into thinking he was just a dope." For Wriston, the emergence of Ronald Reagan represented the culmination of years of belief in the so-called Chicago school of monetarist thought. All those collegial debates at the Bechtel estate with Milton Friedman and Bechtel president George Shultz would soon reach intellectual and political fruition. As the Reagan bandwagon gathered steam, Reagan tapped Shultz to assemble a team of economic policy advisers, so he naturally called on the crowd that had gathered at Monterey, California. Shultz's high opinion of Reagan was good enough for Wriston. Said Kathy Wriston later, "If Shultz tells you the guy is good you have to vote for him." Wriston soon became part of the Reagan inner circle of economic advisers who made up the Economic Policy Coordinating Committee, and the only one who could claim to have day-to-day practical experience operating in the global financial markets. These twelve men, as Reagan economic adviser Martin Anderson put it later, were the "board of directors for the development of Reaganomics." Unlike many of them, Wriston was not an old friend of Reagan's. But because he had real-world experience, his views carried a special weight. In constructing Reagan economic policy, Wriston, said Anderson, "was one of the senior carpenters."

No presidential candidate in recent times had held a set of economic views closer to his own and to those of his idol, Adam Smith, than Reagan. He, too, believed that markets were smarter than bureaucrats and that government intervention in the marketplace should be eliminated. Reagan's views on economics were simple and well defined. He didn't need a staff of ideologues to create economic policy from whole cloth. What he did need was help in presenting it to the American public. And as president, he would look to Wriston and this circle of conservative economists for reinforcement as he conveyed his views to voters and, later, promulgated and defended them in Washington.

On August 29, 1980, Reagan convened the believers at Wexford, a rented estate in Virginia's fox-hunting country that was built by President Kennedy, to draft a blueprint for Reaganomics. That agenda was to be spelled out in a speech in Chicago on September 9. The Who's Who of Reaganomics were there, including George Shultz, economist Alan Greenspan, and Representative Jack Kemp, who regarded Wriston as "one of America's sharpest and most creative minds." Wriston and other participants remembered the gathering as much for its historic significance as for the fact that from early morning until late afternoon, as they slaved over what Wriston called a "terrible" first draft of the policy address, no one offered them so much as a glass of water. Economics aside, perhaps one of the most notable "enhancements" to the speech was the contribution of Reagan confidant Lyn Nofziger, according to fellow Reagan insider Charls Walker. Reagan would later be forced to apologize for stating in that speech that Carter kicked off his campaign in the same Alabama town that gave birth to the Ku Klux Klan. In fact, the Klan got its start in Tennessee.

For years, Wriston, like Shultz, had worshiped at the shrine of University of Chicago economist Milton Friedman. As a signatory to orthodox Reaganomics, Wriston also reaffirmed his faith in the teachings of economist Arthur Laffer, inventor of the "Laffer curve," which held that tax revenues would rise if tax rates dropped—the underpinning of the seminal 1981 tax-cutting legislation. In fact, Wriston contended, Alexander Hamilton had actually articulated the theory behind the Laffer curve two hundred years earlier in the Federalist papers, in which he said that if customs duties were raised to an intolerable level, smuggling would rise and revenues would decline.

"For a time he was really hooked on it," said a colleague. "He really thought Laffer was a genius." But in embracing Reaganomics, Wriston also gave up, at least publicly, some long-held views. For years he had professed that the growing budget deficit was a cause of the nation's economic decline. Later, however, as the deficit burgeoned under the new president, Wriston changed his tune, insisting that the old enemy was both inconsequential and irrelevant. Still, according to his inner circle of colleagues, Wriston seemed to have his doubts. "Walt kind of went along with that and, I guess, felt kind of committed," said Al Costanzo, but "he never was sure about that." Costanzo told Wriston he felt that large budget deficits were dangerous and that "it was fine if they could be reduced by cutting expenditures, but if they couldn't, higher taxes were preferable to huge deficits." Even Wriston's pal Leif Olsen, then Citibank's chief economist, would later say that supply side economics "hasn't demonstrated that it's all that successful."

After Reagan's landslide victory, the economic team convened again, this time in Los Angeles, to transform theory into action. In a fourteen-page typewritten report, signed by Shultz, Wriston, and eleven other members of the Coordinating Committee on Economic Policy, the group urged the president-elect to move immediately after his inauguration to cut spending and taxes, eliminate oil price controls, halt the flow of burdensome new regulations, and prevail on the Fed to moderate the gyrations in money supply. So, once again, Reagan assured Americans that he would reduce taxes and spending.

The Reagan revolution had begun. Even the defiant Democrats in the New York State Legislature began to get the message that the world had changed. Recognizing that the national tide had now turned in favor of deregulation, the legislature in November finally got around to lifting the state usury ceiling. But that move was too little too late. Citibank had already made its pledge to South Dakota. In a storm of indignant protest, legislators screamed accusations of betrayal. When Citibank confirmed it would transfer its credit-card operations to South Dakota despite the passage of the New York State law, the *Village Voice* of December 24, 1980, placed Wriston on its list of "Greediest Cases." As Hans Angermueller said later in a speech in South Dakota, "We can contend with enemies like the *Village Voice* as long as we have friends like you, the people of South Dakota."

South Dakota governor William J. Janklow was always nervous that Citibank was using his state merely as a bargaining chip to save itself from high interest rates and that it would return to its roots as soon as New York eliminated the usury ceiling. Once again Wriston had to reassure the temperamental governor that his marker was good. Citicorp would move to South Dakota no matter what. In early 1981, the Fed and the Comptroller of the Currency gave their final blessings to Citibank's application, and the bank wasted no time in setting up its South Dakota office. The New York State Legislature had blown it. Assemblyman Denny Farrell and his hapless colleagues now experienced the full impact of Citibank's strategy. Farrell's administrative aide had been badgering him for months—including a four-hour marathon debate in a car—to support a boost in the usury ceiling. Until the Reagan victory, Farrell resisted, but he later acknowledged that "suddenly I became in favor of deregulation. I got into the flow." Farrell later revealed his personal and political agony as he grappled with usury as the new black chairman of the assembly banking committee: "In retrospect, it was a hard time for me. The hard part from my perspective is you must show leadership but you can't be overridden."

Now the state legislators were reduced to making lame jokes in their conversations with Citibankers about having to put cowcatchers on the nosewheels of airplanes in order to land in Sioux Falls. But Citibank had the last laugh. While gearing up for the move west, Citibank mailed out millions of letters announcing a new credit-card rate of 19.8%, thereby saving the day for John Reed.

After the election, Wriston discovered that the train sometimes did pass through the same station twice, and for the third time, he would miss it.

The final vote count was barely in before speculation on Reagan's cabinet choices got under way. Political columnist Joseph Kraft wrote that Wriston was an "obvious" candidate for Treasury secretary, along with Alan Greenspan and former Treasury secretary John Connally. Though the *New York Times* reported on November 21, 1980, that former Treasury secretary William Simon was the leading contender for that post, it added that Wriston was a "strong outside possibility." Wriston had all he could do to evade reporters. But according to colleagues, he seemed to savor every minute of the attention. Arriving to deliver a speech at New York's Americana Hotel, he had to sneak out through the kitchen.

"I always thought Walter Wriston would be Ronald Reagan's secretary of the Treasury," said Don Regan, the man who ultimately got the nod. But right after the election, a friend and campaign insider called Regan to say that "there's a small number of names and you're still on it."

"Those guys are still ahead of me. There's no way it could happen," Regan remembered telling the caller.

Regan was eager for the job and wasn't shy about saying so. And he was fortunate in having as his patron saint the powerful adviser to President-elect Reagan, William Casey, who had been the top outside lawyer for Merrill Lynch.

According to E. Pendleton James, a member of Reagan's so-called kitchen cabinet and a Wriston fan, the decision to focus on Regan was made at the President-elect's home in Pacific Palisades shortly after the election. James was an executive recruiter whose long friendship with Reagan put him on the inside track for the top personnel job. During the transition, James would take candidates for cabinet and sub-cabinet jobs to lunch at Washington's University Club, then make his recommendations to adviser Ed Meese, who would meet them over lunch before proposing them to the president-elect.

At Pacific Palisades were the president's longtime supporters and the men who would form his inner circle of advisers in the White House: George Bush, Michael Deaver, Jim Baker, William Casey, Pendleton James, and Justin Dart. According to Reagan aide Jack Svahn, Justin Dart was a major promoter of Simon. "We were all being buffeted about on the idea of Simon getting the post," James remembered. Simon was number one on the short list, followed by Wriston, Regan, and politically conservative drugstore-chain executive Lewis E. Lehrman.

Simon, coincidentally, had been elected to the Citicorp board after Gerald Ford was voted out of office. It was not a choice Wriston initiated, but he didn't object to it at the time. "I thought it was a great idea. If you can get the secretary of the Treasury, I can't think of better preparation [for serving as a director]." Wriston later had second thoughts about William Simon.

The transition team had been trying to reach Simon in Saudi Arabia to discuss the job. The phone rang, and it was Simon calling on a scratchy connection. Reagan picked up the phone in another room. When, as James recalled, Reagan emerged, he announced that "Bill Simon doesn't want to be in the administration." Most of those present disguised their relief with expressions of false dismay, according to James. Simon's conditions were totally unacceptable to the new president. In effect, he insisted on becoming the economic czar of the Reagan administration with total authority over the Office of Management and Budget, the Council of Economic Advisers, and the Treasury Department—conditions no president could possibly accept.

"He also wanted . . . to have the sole relationship with the Federal Reserve," said Regan. "Simon definitely wanted monetary policy."

Another drawback to Simon, according to Washington insiders, was his unpopularity on Capitol Hill. When Senator Robert Dole discovered Simon was a candidate, "he exploded," according to one high-level Republican. "He didn't want any more Bill Simon."

Simon later denied these accounts and any desire to ride herd over Budget and the Council of Economic Advisers. He told acquaintances at the time that he had lost money while at Treasury and didn't want to uproot his family again. "I was going to be Treasury secretary. There was no doubt about that," said Simon later. "I turned the job down. I made the call. That's a fait accompli. It's never been an issue."

The *New York Times* predicted on December 3 that Wriston would be Reagan's pick for Treasury, Alexander Haig for State, Caspar Weinberger for Defense, and William French Smith for attorney general. The *Times* got it right for everyone but Wriston. Within days, the leakers were putting out the word that Wriston was reluctant to go into government. That may have been true earlier, but it wasn't the case now. In any event, with Simon out of contention, the names of Lew Lehrman and Don Regan also rose to the surface. According to Pendleton James, Lehrman favored a return to the gold standard, a view that by this time was not highly regarded by serious economists. Lehrman apparently didn't make it past one lunch with James.

Simon claimed later that he introduced Casey to Reagan, and recommended him as Reagan's campaign chairman. Reagan, he added, "didn't know Bill Casey from the man in the moon."

Regan's appointment was nearly sealed when he met Ed Meese for the obligatory University Club lunch. Meese, who didn't know Regan well, said later, "I was tremendously impressed that Regan had answers I thought were totally in accord with what the president thought on economic and fiscal matters. I recommended him strongly, but this was not in competition with Wriston or anybody else." With that kind of backing, Wriston's chances dropped to practically nil.

On December 9, Wriston attended a dinner party for Reagan at the New York home of philanthropist Brooke Astor, but left not knowing that two days later the president-elect would name Regan and seven others to cabinet posts. Regan's appointment to the Treasury post "always mystified me," Bill Simon said later. "I thought Walt would get it."

"Casey," said Reagan economic adviser Martin Anderson, "was a very powerful voice. . . . [If] Bill Casey says, 'I want X,' that's what counts."

Wriston and Casey were not friends. "Walt didn't have a high regard for Casey, for good reason," said one Wriston acquaintance. The reason was Multiponics, an obscure southern agricultural concern that had filed for bankruptcy in 1971. The company had planned to grow vegetables in nutrient solutions instead of soil. Earlier that year Wriston was informed of possible grounds for a lawsuit against the Multiponics board, which had included Casey, who at the time the problems came to Wriston's attention was chairman of the Securities and Exchange Commission. Citibank was the trustee for Multiponics's subordinated debt holders, and Shearman & Sterling and others had turned up evidence of shady dealings at the company. After running the company into the ground, the insiders were now walking away with the company's assets, leaving debt holders and others holding the bag. The prospect of a suit against the company provoked considerable commotion; the Citibanker responsible for the account apparently had doubts about the wisdom of suing a powerful figure like Casey. The case wound up in the hands of Robert Dineen, Wriston's brother-in-law, who was asked to write a memo explaining Casey's involvement for Wriston and the Citicorp board.

After working late into one night, Dineen got a call from his brother-in-law the next day instructing him to pursue the case. Dineen was not surprised by Wriston's decision. "Let the chips fall where they may," he ordered. Wriston would never regret that decision, but some say it came back to haunt him a decade later. As founder, board member, and general counsel of the southern firm, Casey and other Multiponics directors were accused by shareholders in a 1973 federal lawsuit of gross mismanagement and self-dealing in connection with the company's demise.

Beginning with his nomination as SEC chairman in 1971, Casey was dogged by allegations of business impropriety as he moved from one high-level government post to another in a succession of Republican administrations. Multiponics loomed as an issue again in 1973 when Nixon appointed him undersecretary of state for economic affairs, and yet again seven years later after President Reagan named him to the top job at the Central Intelligence Agency. In July 1981, a federal judge ruled that Casey was aware of securities misrepresentations in the Multiponics suit, but four months later that judge rescinded his earlier ruling.

Citibank sued Multiponics on the grounds that "the stock had been watered and there wasn't any business there. It was a dead cinch case, we were told," Wriston recalled years after the uproar. "It was really a bad-news deal, and Casey was really involved," he said. "And suddenly . . . a good old boy judge appeared, and the opinion was reversed, and Bill walked away from that train wreck."

While there was no question in Wriston's mind that the Multiponics case represented an egregious lack of integrity, Wriston was pragmatic enough to recognize that he would have to deal with Casey as long as he was chairman of Citicorp and Casey was director of the CIA. "You have lunch every day with people who are suing you," Wriston remarked. Indeed, Wriston would later say that he admired Casey's performance at the CIA and talked to him frequently while he served there.

With the opening of the Reagan era, it seemed that Wriston's moment of destiny had arrived, and this time Wriston was ready. Wriston would no doubt have accepted the Treasury job if he had been asked by the president or perhaps an acceptable representative. Wriston was now sixty-one years old, less than four years away from retirement. Citibank was in reasonably good shape, and a succession plan had been implemented. But in Kathy Wriston's opinion, a cabinet post would not have been an easy role for him. Looking back, she said, "I don't think he would have been too good at carrying out policies he didn't like."

While Wriston seemed to relish all the attention, he did nothing to promote himself for the job. He still expected that if the president wanted him, he would pick up the phone and call. During the period of speculation, he told a colleague, "No one has asked. . . . My grandmother always told me, 'If the president of the United States asks you to do something you do it.' "

But former presidential aide Jack Svahn contended that "most of the people who wound up in those positions ran hot and heavy campaigns. [But as] for the guy who really would like the job but says, 'Well, gee, if I'm asked, I'll serve,' he just wasn't in the running. . . . There were a lot of people who felt that way, and most stayed in the private sector. That's fairly normal, because that's the way they're used to doing business. [But] some of the initial appointees were the ones who were running around saying, 'No, I'm not interested,' and at the same time [they were calling] every friend they ever knew to get their support."

According to former Treasury aide Tom Dawson, "there was a lot of grumbling about Walter Wriston . . . because he was considered to be too much of a New York banker, and conservative Californians were skeptical of that." Among the other non-reasons that were bandied about, said Hans Angermueller, was the possibility that conflicts of interest might arise from Citibank's status as a major U.S. government bond dealer. But, he noted, "here was [Don Regan of] Merrill, one of the major bond dealers in the U.S., and suddenly the conflict didn't appear."

Wriston didn't hide his bitterness over the way the episode was handled. During a mid-January visit to Lawrence University to speak to students, one of the locals told him, "We folks from the boonies are very disappointed that you won't be serving in Mr. Reagan's cabinet."

"You're very nice," Wriston replied, according to local press reports, "but no one ever asked me." He added later at a press conference, "All I know is what I read in the newspaper. I don't consider [that] the best way to communicate."

To be sure, Wriston wasn't the only one who felt he was misled in the intrigue swirling around cabinet appointments. Alexander Haig admitted, "I knew I wasn't the first choice" for secretary of state, adding that he learned later the Reagans wanted George Shultz and that Shultz coveted the job. Shultz's appointment was quashed, at least for the moment, Haig said, by conservative members of the Reagan kitchen cabinet, like Justin Dart, who considered Shultz soft on communism. Then, Haig said, Ronald Reagan, in his "duplicitous tricky way," called him and said Shultz had turned the job down.

While Wriston was ducking questions from reporters, Shearman & Sterling lawyer John Hoffman was quietly moving into the final phase of his back-channel diplomacy with the Iranians. A plan had been on the table for the last several months—Plan C—calling for the banks to get repaid in full with interest. In late fall, however, the Iranians suddenly changed their position. Apparently seeking to maintain ties with Western banks, they were now proposing a deal—Plan D—in which the banks wouldn't initially get all their money back. Under this arrangement, matured claims would be set off, an escrow account would be created for debt payments, and Iran's central bank would guarantee unpaid obligations. On returning from an overseas trip in mid-November, Hoffman immediately briefed deputy Secretary of the Treasury Robert Carswell, who doubted the plan would work because it was so complex, Hoffman later admitted. To date, Chase was the only other bank, and Frank Logan the only other non-Citicorp bank lawyer, in the loop. Now, however, the chairmen of the other big banks would have to be let in on the secret. Surprisingly, instead of being annoyed that they were left out, they readily offered to help. Angermueller recalled that Manny Hanny's John McGillicuddy, for one, asked, "Whom do you want and when do you want them?"

Now, in the final phase of the negotiations, Hoffman would come face to face with his adversaries for the first time. He had begun to prep himself on Iranian history and Islam, immersing himself in the Koran and books on militant Islam. His reading gave him a deeper appreciation of the Iranians as a people with a long history of being trampled on and who were therefore distrustful of outsiders. He got a taste of that lack of trust in his first meeting with Mehdi Navab, Iran's ambassador to West Germany, at Iran's embassy in Bonn in December 1980. The building was guarded by what appeared to be a German armored personnel carrier. Accompanied by two German colleagues, Hoffman presented himself at an embassy security post that resembled a drive-in teller window and was buzzed in by a muscular, bearded Iranian security guard who looked the part of a Hezbollah commando. Hoffman and his associates found themselves alone in a reception room staring at a larger-than-life portrait of the Ayatollah Khomeini.

Sitting in a conference room fingering his prayer beads, the Iranian ambassador alternated between serious discussions of the crisis and diatribes on the "imperialist banks that had their feet on the necks of the oppressed." Hoffman knew boilerplate when he heard it and assumed that this was intended for some hidden microphone. The diplomat finally turned to Hoffman and asked, "Are you trying to trick us?"

"No," Hoffman replied. "That wouldn't do me any good. I'm just trying to work out a deal."

As Hoffman left, Navab gave him a Christmas card with greetings in English, German, and Farsi.

On December 21, the optimism of that auspicious meeting was dispelled when the Iranians demanded $24 billion for the release of the hostages. But in another meeting with Navab in Germany that week, Hoffman got his first inkling that things might turn out all right. In a Bonn hotel on New Year's Eve, Navab said that he would support a settlement and that he was leaving for Teheran the next day to present the deal to the hostage committee. He then excused himself, but shortly thereafter returned with his two daughters, whom he introduced to Hoffman. That, Hoffman concluded, was the real signal that the deal was a go. The ambassador had introduced his children to the Great Satan.

As the negotiations proceeded into January 1981, one of the sticking points was the interest rate to be paid on Iranians' deposits. There was no rule manual to help them decide this matter. Hoffman was concerned that the banks as a group wouldn't be able to agree on a single rate; that might prompt some Washington bureaucrat to object to the deal on anti-trust grounds. By this time, the bankers, their lawyers, and the Iranians were negotiating in New York on the details. To end the standoff, someone proposed that the Iranians be given twenty minutes to extract what they could from each bank. The office used for that purpose became known as the "dentist's chair." It turned out that $90 million of the $130 million in dispute was at Bank of America, which, according to one banker, had accrued the Iranians' interest at a below-market rate. When that rate was revised, the San Francisco institution had to readjust its reported earnings.

Once again, on Sunday, January 11, 1981, negotiators were frustrated when an Iranian official announced that Plan D was unacceptable, and demanded the banks' "last and best offer." Then, on January 15, the bankers and lawyers were hustled to Washington to discuss a new proposal from the Iranians via the Algerians. In a reversion to Plan C, the Iranians were now proposing to repay $3.6 billion in bank loans upon the release of the hostages and to place in escrow the disputed $5.1 billion. But they were now claiming interest that exceeded the earlier claims, leaving the banks to fight over how to handle the shortfall.

By January 17, the transaction had taken shape, but the bankers and lawyers were hung up on the details. Sitting around a table in the office of the secretary of the Treasury, William Miller, were the banking industry's top legal minds. The Treasury offices were filled with exhausted, unshaven lawyers and bankers and buckets of half-eaten Kentucky fried chicken. The lawyers and bankers were trying to hammer out a draft of a telex of the payment order that would move the money and free the hostages.

"Jesus, this is never going to work," Hoffman later remembered saying to himself. "They're going to be drafting for the next thirty-six weeks." Hoffman grabbed Angermueller in a hallway and voiced his fears: "I can't begin to understand what these guys are writing. I could never explain this to the Iranians. We have to stop [trying to] design the perfect wheel and go with the wheel that will go."

Angermueller and Hoffman announced to an unreceptive audience that what they were doing wasn't going to work. "That went over poorly," Hoffman recalled, so the two adjourned to another office. Writing on his ubiquitous yellow pad, Angermueller, in less than an hour, composed a concise two-part telex, one part for the bank and the other for the Fed, with blank spaces where the numbers would go. The rest of the bank legal team immediately accepted the simplified Angermueller version, which was then wired to Algiers. "If [Angermueller] hadn't done that, we'd still be sitting there drafting," Hoffman said later.

On Sunday, January 18, Treasury tested the telex code words, which are used for security, and switched on its computers. The official message was to go out on January 19, but the plan hit a snag. Even though the Iranians had representatives in London who could have sent the payment order, they for some reason insisted on retyping it and issuing it from Teheran. After all the fuss about language, the lawyers and bankers and diplomats gathered at Treasury didn't know whether or not they would get anything at all.

Just after midnight on January 20, Teheran warned of dire consequences if the money wasn't moved into the Iranian accounts. According to a later published account, Carswell paced the floors, saying, "We're dead in the water." By early morning, the small window of time in which the hostages could fly out of Iran was closing. The plane would have to take off before nightfall in Iran, because the Iranians didn't want to turn on the airport lights and create a target for the Iraqis. And Carter had signed an order that would expire at noon when Reagan was sworn into office. As Hoffman recalls, someone shouted that the telex machine light had flashed on. Something was about to come across the wire. It was a wrong number from Germany.

Shortly thereafter, the telex light flashed again. The machine pecked out the names of Bankers Trust and Bank of America. Bankers and lawyers who were asleep on the floor awoke, cheering and yelling. The cheering stopped when the message halted. The test code was wrong—the Iranians had misread the code book. The machine started up and the message continued. The numbers were garbled, and the message was gobbledygook. Hoffman got on the phone to London with the Iranians' lawyer. Meanwhile, Treasury secretary Miller, he recalled later, ordered the banks to make the payments despite the scrambled, four-foot-long telex. "Ten of the twelve bankers who were sitting there instantly [agreed to pay]," said Miller, including Citibank. Two of them, however, said they couldn't pay just on Miller's say-so. Miller gritted his teeth and said, "Fine. Let's get your senior people on the phone."

The holdouts quickly changed their tune. "As we think about it," one of them admitted sheepishly, "we could do it also."

Finally, another message came over the wire, and this time it was letter perfect: "You have been instructed to move the money." It reminded the bankers that the fate of the hostages was in their hands. Shortly after 4:00 A.M., the American banks moved $5.53 billion from accounts in London and Paris to the New York Fed. A little over two hours later an escrow agreement was signed in Algiers, and a half hour after that an escrow account was set up in London. At 6:45 A.M., $7.977 billion, in the form of electronic impulses, moved from the Fed account to dollar account number one at the Bank of England. At noon Reagan was sworn in as fortieth president of the United States. Wriston did not attend the ceremony; he was in New York conducting a Citicorp board meeting.

At 12:25 P.M., eastern standard time, on January 20, the planes carrying the hostages left Teheran and soon cleared Iranian airspace. And $3.667 billion had moved across the Atlantic from the Bank of England to the New York Fed, repaying the syndicated loans. By this time virtually all of the Carter people had vacated their offices, leaving only Carswell pacing the halls on behalf of the outgoing administration.

Citibank, of course, picked up the tab for Hoffman's legal bill. When the opportunity later arose for other banks to chip in, it was "met with limited enthusiasm," Hoffman recalled. In the end, only Chase volunteered.

As the Iranian hostage crisis was coming to an end, another hostage drama was beginning to unfold in Washington, this one involving the beleaguered Chrysler Corporation. On the last day of the Carter administration, the Chrysler Loan Guarantee Board approved the drawdown of the last $400 million of the loans. The catch was that Chrysler was given one month to get the bankers to sign on. Once again Citibank would hold Chrysler's feet to the fire. According to the *American Banker* of February 11, 1981, Citibank was convinced that Chrysler would run out of cash soon after it received the government funds and that it wouldn't even get fifteen cents on the dollar on its loans.

Shortly after Reagan's inauguration, newly installed Treasury secretary Don Regan made it clear that he had little personal commitment to the Chrysler bailout. According to chief financial officer Steve Miller, Regan informed Chrysler that he would go along with the disbursement if all the banks signed on, only because the bailout "was Jimmy Carter's last act." But, Miller added, Regan made it clear that if the banks were not on board he would not reopen negotiations and would simply let the company go into bankruptcy. Times were tough all around. Wildly fluctuating interest rates had taken their toll at Citibank, and the consumer business was still in the red. The bank's workout man, Peter Fitts, was determined to squeeze another two or three cents on the dollar out of Chrysler in dividend or interest payments. Many other banks had the same idea.

On the Sunday after the inauguration, Steve Miller traveled to Washington to meet with Reagan administration officials. When he arrived, a Treasury aide handed him a press release stating that because of the failure of the banks to sign on, authorization for the drawdown was to be withdrawn and Chrysler placed into liquidation. Signed by Secretary Regan, the release was to hit the wires at noon. In what was to be one of the first of many showdowns between Fed Chairman Paul Volcker and Citibank, Volcker opposed releasing more government funds that would wind up in the banks' till. According to Miller, Volcker insisted that the money be used directly to rebuild the company.

That morning, Miller envisioned all his work since the fall of 1979 being undone in hours. He phoned Volcker, pleading that "if you don't bend and let a little more cash go out the door to these banks, it's all over." He then put in a call to Fitts at Citibank, begging him to "be a little bit reasonable about this." In the end, he managed to persuade Volcker and Fitts to budge ever so slightly. At five minutes before noon, Miller was back in the Treasury aide's office. After confirming Miller's account with both Volcker and Fitts, the official ripped up the press release. Nonetheless, Citibank's demands for more cash pressed Chrysler against the wall over the next twelve months. During that period, Chrysler at times had less than $10 million in its checking accounts. Citibank "really screwed us down tighter," said Miller. He might not have appreciated then just how precarious his position was with the Loan Guarantee Board, but he certainly did later. In fact, he said that the board had concluded that there was plenty of excess auto industry capacity and that if Chrysler requested more money, it would let Chrysler go belly up. Said Miller, "If I had known that, I would have gotten less sleep."

As distasteful as the prospect of Wriston as Treasury secretary might have been for Lee Iacocca, it is hard to imagine two highly placed people with more ill feeling for each other than Don Regan and Iacocca. The relationship started badly and never got better. Early in the Reagan administration, a photo appeared in a newspaper showing Iacocca with New York Yankee owner George Steinbrenner in the dugout during spring training. According to Steve Miller, Regan "flipped out." He said, "Here I am working in Washington trying to save this great company and the chairman is in Florida, having flown in the company jet, living the high life." In fact, says Miller, Iacocca had moved his seriously ill wife to Florida and visited her on weekends; she died in 1983. "Regan never lifted a finger to help [Chrysler]," said Miller. "He said, 'Carter wrote this loan agreement, and if you meet the terms you're okay.' It was a Wall Street document to him."

Later, Chrysler locked horns with Regan once again. In a display of chutzpah unprecedented in American business, Iacocca told the government that since the company was emerging from its troubles seven years ahead of schedule the government shouldn't make a profit on the warrants. Regan disagreed. According to Steve Miller, Regan said, "They're up for sale to the highest bidder." And that, Miller recalled, was a "very sore point between us and Regan."

William Miller, the former Treasury secretary, was sore at Chrysler about it as well. "I blew my top," he recalled. "I didn't do the deal because if we lose it's not worth anything and if we win we don't get anything." Miller fired off a letter to every member of every congressional committee that had anything to do with the bailout and insisted that Chrysler keep its part of the bargain. At that point, Iacocca backed off.

The U.S. government ultimately realized a profit on Chrysler, raking in $327 million on the warrants, in addition to fees. And, in the aftermath of the Chrysler bailout, Lee Iacocca resigned from the Business Roundtable and never returned.

Wriston's opposition to federal guarantees in the hearing room didn't stop him from supporting Chrysler in the showroom. When the company rolled out its new K-car line, Wriston bought a red station wagon to use at his country home. But the animus between Chrysler and Citibank continued long after Chrysler left the intensive care unit, and even after Wriston retired from Citibank in 1984. For all of the sparks that flew during the long siege of 1980 and 1981, Steve Miller was angriest about an incident that occurred in 1983 when Chrysler was trying to get off the public dole and back into the private capital markets. To accomplish that, it needed some twenty banks to waive a loan covenant. According to Miller, Citibank declined to show up at the negotiating table, but gave the impression that it would go along with any agreement. By holding out, Citibank, according to Miller, forced him to cut a side deal in which Citibank would get a $100,000 consulting fee to go along with the closing. That, said Miller, "was trivial," nothing more than Citibank playing one-upmanship, and "that is the only thing that bothers me. Everything else was a matter of business philosophy, business judgment, hard bargaining."

Miller admitted later that "we never said anything [about that side deal]. We would have pissed off every other bank." Later, Miller said he felt bad about agreeing to that concession and was upset at Citibank for twisting his arm to do so. "I didn't believe Citibank would stoop to that," he said. Somewhat later Citibank was one of a few banks in a credit agreement with Gulfstream. When Chrysler bought Gulfstream in 1985, Citibank dropped out of the credit. "There was no good reason to do that except there was still the shadow of Walter Wriston walking the halls," Miller said cynically.

Wriston had lost his last shot at serving as a cabinet officer, but his status as a business statesman got a booster shot with the change in administration. Although Citicorp put coal, not bonuses, in its officers' Christmas stockings, Citicorp by the end of 1980 had bypassed Bank of America as the nation's largest banking company, with $115 billion in assets. Bank of America was more profitable, but it had not made any investment in the future. In January 1981, Wriston was appointed chairman of the Business Council, succeeding GE chairman Reginald Jones. There, Wriston took the statesmanlike approach in dealing with the sad case of former Fed chairman and Treasury secretary William Miller. Traditionally, former Treasury secretaries, regardless of party, continued to be honored guests at the Business Council. But Miller's reputation was so sullied because of his poor handling of monetary and economic policy that members talked of disinviting him. Tough and cynical as he was toward people who were able to fight back, Wriston characteristically showed mercy to the discredited and the down-and-out. He put a swift end to the "Ban Miller" movement. Said one former Carter administration official, "He didn't think you should treat people that way."

Wriston's booby prize for his yeoman campaign service was a charter membership on the President's Economic Policy Advisory Board, the brainchild of top domestic policy adviser Martin Anderson. Philosophically the group's membership ranged from Arthur Burns to Art Laffer, a believer in the gold standard. Nobel laureate Milton Friedman was one of its purists, arguing like an economic Don Quixote as if political realities didn't exist. The monetarists, recalled Reagan aide Jack Svahn, actually believed that airplanes fly because of monetary policy. Ronald Reagan, of course, loved to remind the assemblage that he had received a bachelor's degree in economics from Eureka College.

Then there was Bill Simon. According to Wriston, "He was sitting around waiting for the great American depression." Wriston gritted his teeth at what he said was Simon's habit of sniping at Reagan policy in public. When Wriston could stomach it no longer, he chastised Simon for his remarks. "You have the opportunity to tell [the president] that," Wriston fumed. When Simon did show up to criticize Reagan to his face, Reagan listened politely and said, "That's an interesting view." Then, said Wriston, "Bill departed and never came back again."

In the first critical year of the Reagan administration, when economic policy was emphasized above all else, the group met about a half dozen times in the Roosevelt Room at the White House. After meeting for two hours in the morning, they were joined by the president, at which time chairman George Shultz would summarize the morning's proceedings and moderate the discussion. It was a "table full of egos," as one Reagan administration official put it. By all accounts, the group, particularly in its early years, served the purpose for which it was intended: acting as a high-powered cheerleading squad for Reaganomics in the face of intense criticism from reporters, academics, and politicians and making sure that the program laid out in the campaign was carried out intact. With others constantly pressuring Reagan to be more flexible on taxes and defense spending, the advisory board was there to help him ward off the demons. Jack Svahn remembered that the board "was more confirmation than change. He [Reagan] always said, 'We've got to get the deficit down,' and they always said the deficit was the number one issue. When he said tax reform, they said tax reform." Opposing Reagan on taxes was heresy. No issue was more central to the Reagan program than cutting taxes, and there Wriston may have exerted his greatest influence. Differences on tax policy splintered the unity of the administration's fiscal policy advisers, notably budget director David Stockman and Treasury secretary Donald Regan. Stockman was the quintessential public policy wonk, and Regan, Wriston said, "was convinced that Stockman was trying to talk the president into raising taxes."

Wriston told a journalist that "one of these days Don Regan is going to eat Dave Stockman for breakfast." Regan alternately tried to play down the rivalry and openly acknowledged it. Referring to Stockman, he said, "The press has tried to drive a wedge between us. . . . It's not as though we're jumping for a basket and I try to give him the elbow." But he added: In a few months "you should look to see who is the economic spokesman. . . . I will be."

Indeed, by the end of 1981, Don Regan had elbowed Stockman aside. As reported in *U.S. News & World Report,* Regan was the primary spokesman on economic policy, with Council of Economic Advisers chairman Murray Weidenbaum a "distant second." Then there were four key outsiders: Alan Greenspan, George Shultz, Paul McCracken, and Walter Wriston. At one meeting of the President's Economic Policy Advisory Board, a sub-cabinet-level official quickly learned the perils of even mentioning new or higher taxes when he suggested imposing a value-added tax. "There was silence in the room," the former official recalled. Later, a senior Treasury aide took him aside, to say, "You don't even discuss taxes with Reagan." The chastened official said, "I saw my career capping before my eyes."

Wriston felt that big business—as personified by lobbyist Charls Walker—was, ironically, resistant to lower taxes. "The business community was not in favor of cutting marginal tax rates," Wriston said later. "They had all these [things] they love—the investment tax credit, flow-through, and accelerated depreciation. And Charlie Walker's whole panoply of 'capital building enterprises.' I took the reverse view. What I like to know in running a business is whether it's successful, and I don't need a tax attorney to tell me." Sources said Reagan aide James Baker later kicked Walker off the advisory board because of disagreements over tax policy.

According to one former member, Reagan sometimes repeated verbatim a thought that was first voiced by a participant at an advisory board meeting: "Corporate taxes are dumb taxes. We ought to get rid of them." Early on, when media pundits and others cried for tax increases, Reagan solicited the views of his economic policy board. Said Anderson, "They would simply, without him asking, reinforce that he was on the right track, that the strategy was working." White House staff—the Beltway crowd—and Treasury secretary Regan weren't exactly thrilled with the board. Regan wanted the advisory board to report to him and to control its operating budget, suggestions that the board's White House backers rejected out of hand.

Reagan clearly enjoyed the interaction with Wriston and the economists and often stayed with the group for more than an hour, while his staff "would fidget and fidget and fidget," Wriston recalled, but the president would say, "Look, I enjoy talking to these people." According to Wriston, "They [the White House staff] were very nervous about him talking directly to people without being filtered by the bureaucracy," but "it brought the fresh wind of the marketplace through the cabinet room."

Meanwhile, over at the Fed, Paul Volcker and his colleagues, including vice chairman Fred Schultz, were greatly dismayed by the new arrivals. "We were frankly disturbed by many of the Reagan economic appointees who we felt were ideologues who had a particular theoretical view of the world and not much practical experience and who were pushing the administration in directions that would cause a lot of problems in the future," Schultz said later. These "disturbing" appointees included Donald Regan—"A person who holds very strong views and also is not greatly burdened with humility," Schultz said—and economist Paul Craig Roberts—"He absolutely believes he is right and his view of the world is the only correct one"—and Milton Friedman. "People like that are willing to use the nation as an economic research lab and try things out without regard to what may be very serious consequences," Schultz said.

Traditionally, the Treasury secretary and the Fed chairman ate breakfast with each other every Thursday. But after his first breakfast with Regan, Volcker returned to his office "much disturbed," Schultz recalled.

"We're going to have a lot of trouble," Volcker told Schultz.

According to *Secrets of the Temple,* Regan told a colleague that he and Ronald Reagan had discussed "abolishing the Fed."

Schultz credited David Stockman with eventually seeing the light. At his first breakfast with Stockman, Schultz recalled that the budget director didn't ask him a single question. A year later, just before Stockman resigned, he did a "remarkable turnaround," Schultz said. "He was one of few who, after getting into office and trying to deal with the practical problems of running the economy of the country, came to conclusion that some of these extreme ideas were dangerous."

But taxes and monetary policy were not the only items on the agenda of the President's Economic Policy Advisory Board. Wriston quashed debates over the merits of fixed exchange rates and the gold standard by reminding his colleagues that the world in fact was on the "information standard," Laffer recalled. The board also became another forum for Wriston's long-standing angst over Japan's refusal to practice free trade. Laffer said, "He got very strong on it," pointing out that Japan had refused to allow U.S. banks to operate in Japan with anything approaching the freedom the Japanese institutions enjoyed in the United States. "He was an extraordinarily important member of that group."

President Reagan, of course, didn't always follow the board members' recommendations. When Laffer and a few others advocated a return to the gold standard, Wriston recalled that Reagan blew the group away by giving them a lecture on gold. "He listened to all this stuff, and then said, 'Let me tell you about gold,' and gave us a capsule history of the use of gold in trade," adding his reasons for opposing a return to the gold standard.

The advisory board also opposed voluntary quotas on automobile imports, according to Milton Friedman, but the administration implemented them because they were backed by Commerce secretary Malcolm Baldrige. Wriston, said Friedman, was an "effective voice in pressing for what I regarded as the right policy, strongly resisting pressures for higher taxes and government spending and pressing for deregulation." Wriston believed that government would spend all the money it took in. He frequently pointed out that New York City suffered from the highest marginal tax rates in the country and, he said, "almost went broke."

"Did it [the economic board] change the . . . planet?" Laffer asked. "It changed it by being the Rock of Gibraltar for what he [Reagan] believed in."

Indeed, President Reagan began to do just as he had promised. In one of his first acts, he eliminated controls on oil prices, setting the stage for the era of deregulation. Very quickly, as if taking its cue from the new market-oriented administration, the financial services industry began to fulfill some of Wriston's early prophecies. In March 1981, the Prudential Insurance Company announced that it would merge with the securities firm of Bache Halsey Stuart Shields, and a month later American Express said it would combine with Shearson Loeb Rhoades. That fall, Sears began to take the shape Wriston had anticipated. In the space of a week, Sears announced plans to acquire Coldwell, Banker & Company, the real estate firm, and the Dean Witter Reynolds Organization. The *Wall Street Journal* declared on October 12, 1981, that "bankers and savings and loan associations will face a new Goliath." It quoted Wriston as saying that ten years before, he had warned that banks' primary competitor in the 1980s would be Sears, not other banks. "Nobody listened," Wriston told the *Journal.* Later, however, Sears would discover what a big mistake it had made by diversifying into financial services.

Coincidentally, Citibank had just published its *Old Bank Robbers to Where the New Money Is,* which compared Sears to Ma Barker and Willie Sutton. "In Ma Barker's day," Citibank wrote, "Sears was where America Shops. Today Sears is where America Banks." Though the *Journal* quoted sources who questioned Sears's strategy, it said that if the obstacles blocking non-banks from getting into the banking business were dismantled, "Sears almost overnight could set up tellers in its 2,300 selling outlets." But Sears wasn't the only non-bank that was sticking up banks. There was J. C. Penney, too, and even Baldwin Piano.

Wriston's battle for equality with the new financial services giants challenged the imagination of Citibank's wordsmiths. Wriston spent an evening at the small Greenwich Village apartment of one of his writers creating captions for a forthcoming presentation they called "Hooray for Hollywood." In a November 11, 1981, talk in Los Angeles, Wriston compared Tinseltown to bank regulation: "Hollywood and today's banking regulation, after all, spring from the same genus: the world of fantasy." He joked that the Glass-Steagall Act was devised by Groucho and Chico, and showed a slide of a gun-toting W. C. Fields as a "stern regulator of banking." And the caption on a slide of Frankenstein's monster and his bride read, "Legislators determined that a marriage of banking and industry would simply be too fearsome."

One-stop shopping had arrived, or so it seemed. It happened that Sears's bold moves nearly coincided with Wriston's testimony, on October 29, before the Senate Banking Committee on the proposed Financial Institutions Restructuring and Services Act of 1981. Wriston drew chuckles from the legislators when he joked that Sears "had hoped to be with us today but could not, because it is in the process of buying a securities firm and a real estate company." He went on to say that Merrill's money market fund exceeded Citibank's domestic deposits by $2 billion. "We've been at it since 1812 and they've been at it almost twenty-four months."

Wriston knew that 36 million U.S. households—almost half the total—had some kind of business relationship with Sears, through its credit card, Allstate Insurance, or its catalog. It was a given, as one author put it, that Sears "presents the most formidable single challenge to banks in the evolving financial services industry."

Yet at this hearing, Wriston helped pull the rug out from under the banks' efforts to get into the corporate securities underwriting business for years to come when he declared that "it is inconceivable that any major bank would walk away from any subsidiary of its holding company. If your name's on the door, all of your capital funds are going to be behind it in the real world. Lawyers can say you have separation, but the marketplace is persuasive, and it would not see it that way."

Just a day before American Express shareholders approved its merger with Shearson Loeb Rhoades, Wriston bemoaned the fact that his rival could complete the huge deal in weeks, when it took Citibank more than two years to open a single "lonely" consumer finance office in Connecticut with just a few employees. Alluding to fellow Appletonian Harry Houdini, he told a public affairs conference that "it's no wonder that we often feel like we are not only chained and handcuffed, but are competing from inside a locked trunk which has just been dumped into the middle of the ocean." Wriston was convinced banks were an endangered species. He predicted, only half in jest, that one day people would talk of banks in the past tense, just as his grandparents had recounted tales to him about traveling west in covered wagons and making their own candles and clothes.

In Congress and in the statehouses, however, Wriston was learning how to play the legislative game. In May 1981, Citibank even managed to get its reciprocal banking bill through an assembly committee in Illinois, but the bill died later in the legislative pipeline. Despite the setback, Citibank was pleased that it had gotten that far. One reason was a trip that Bill Spencer had taken to Chicago to cozy up to Chicago mayor Jane Byrne. Afterward, Spencer said later, things began to change in the legislature. As a spin-off, Citibank wound up extending a loan to the city, a first for Citibank.

Wriston was infuriated that Japanese banks, but not New York banks, could acquire California institutions. In 1979, the California legislature killed a Citicorp-sponsored bill that would have allowed out-of-state banks to branch there. During a mid-February 1981 lobbying expedition to California, Wriston tried to persuade the state's powerful and charismatic speaker, Willy Brown, that "banks don't pollute, and they create jobs. I hope," Wriston told him, that "someday an American passport will be as good in California as a Japanese one." As he said later, "The idea that Fuji Bank could buy a bank that Citibank couldn't I thought was highly discriminatory."

When Wriston arrived at the office of California's New Age governor, Edmund G. "Jerry" Brown, Jr., and saw a table in his reception room set up with diet Coke, cheese, crackers, and yogurt, Wriston assumed there was going to be a reception that day, but after a brief conversation, Brown invited Wriston to join him for lunch. "Help yourself," Brown said. "I'm going to have a dish of apple yogurt."

It was not the hearty meat-and-potatoes fare Wriston was accustomed to outside of La La Land. "It was very California," Wriston said later. "I must say I was somewhat startled."

Wriston now knew that an institution that wanted a bill passed had to serve up more than yogurt. Citibank contributed heavily to the campaigns of Governor Brown, Los Angeles mayor Tom Bradley, and key California state legislators and even flew some of them and their aides and wives on all-expense-paid trips to New York, ostensibly for "discussions" with bank officials. Besides talk, the package included suites at the Waldorf and tickets to Broadway plays. From 1979 to early 1982, according to an April 9, 1982, report in the *Wall Street Journal,* Citibank spent almost $300,000 to influence California banking legislation . The aim was to induce California to pass so-called reciprocal legislation to allow New York banks to enter California if New York did the same. Not surprisingly, California bankers vigorously opposed the effort and formed an Ad Hoc Citicorp Task Force to fight the legislation. But Citicorp's efforts did eventually pay off.

Wriston's love affair with Ronald Reagan did not make his drive to level the financial playing field any easier. Early in the administration, a task force was set up under vice president George Bush to study bank regulation, but it wound up accomplishing nothing. Congressional hearings on financial industry reform, however, brought Wriston head to head with the "Big Nanny," Paul Volcker. While Wriston, backed by the Reagan administration, pleaded for powers to enable banks to compete with non-banks, Volcker opposed even permitting banks to offer money funds. Wriston's request, however, became politically intertwined with the thrift industry's demand for commercial bank powers, which Volcker also opposed. Volcker didn't want Sears encroaching on Citibank's turf and didn't want Citibank in the retail clothing business. But, to Wriston, competition from non-banks like Sears was already a fact of life.

He was already anticipating a new wave of competition: information providers. These included Dow Jones and Reuters. Reuters, he said, "was among the first to grasp clearly the relationship between communications and finance." It had created what Wriston called a global electronic trading marketplace with video screens in four thousand banks and foreign exchange locations. Traders no longer needed banks and other financial institutions to buy and sell financial instruments. Reuters was the embodiment of the information standard, which had now replaced the dollar and gold standard and every other standard. As he told a group of correspondent bankers, the irresponsible actions of any government "will move with the speed of light to the trading rooms of the world and be reflected in the rate on their currency in seconds." To Wriston, Citibank itself was a vast cable machine, much like Foggy Bottom. "Citibank is the greatest nexus of information flow in the world," he often said. He acknowledged that Citibank wasn't necessarily smart enough to use all the data that flowed into it, but the information was there for the asking. Besides the usual public data, Wriston could phone his credit-card chief for a reading on consumer spending as reflected in volume of credit-card transactions.

In his view, computers, satellites, electronic funds transfer technology, and trading screens had begun to render obsolete the distinctions between banks as places to make deposits and get loans, brokerage firms as places to buy and sell securities, and thrifts as places to save money and obtain mortgages. "You can't tell the players without a scorecard," Wriston asserted in an early 1981 speech. Technology, he said, "was eliminating the constraints of time, geography, and volume in financial transactions. A man in Texas could withdraw his money from a savings and loan, phone a toll-free telephone number in Arizona, and wire his money to a money market fund in Boston or anywhere else on earth. "The financial marketplace today is everywhere anytime." That, he claimed, was the real world. "But in the Alice in Wonderland world of Glass-Steagall, McFadden, the Douglas Amendment, Reg Q, and protected special interests, we still need ten messenger boys to get the money across the street—one messenger boy for mortgages, another for stocks, another for installments, and so on."

Just as American politicians generally limited banks to their home states, international politics blocked the flow of data across national boundaries. Wriston attempted to enlist the press in his campaign to eliminate artificial barriers to the free flow of information. Speaking to reporters at the National Press Club in Washington on September 17, he said that the "streams of electrons which carry our financial data and your news dispatches are identical. In fact, they usually travel mixed together. The same satellite which may carry the general ledger of Citibank from country to country also carries the latest AP dispatches and the front page of the *Wall Street Journal.* They are all riding, so to speak, in the same stagecoach." Wriston warned the reporters that "you might find it worthwhile to start keeping track of how governments and lawmakers propose to check our bank ledgers without simultaneously monitoring your news dispatches."

If there was a unique Wriston contribution to the Reagan administration, Reagan adviser Martin Anderson pointed out, it was in introducing the president to the significance of information technology.

———

As Wriston, the candidate for Treasury secretary, was being hung out to dry by Bill Casey, Ed Palmer was on a whirlwind tour of Eastern Europe picking up what might have been the first inkling that Poland was in desperate straits and wasn't going to be able to pay its debts. Citicorp, unlike David Rockefeller's Chase Manhattan, wasn't keen on lending to Communist countries. In a meeting with Polish officials, Palmer said later, "they started to walk around the situation, talking about a medium-term credit for the importation of raw materials and foodstuffs." A freeze had damaged the potato crop, forcing the country to boost imports. Coal production was down. Solidarity leader Lech Walesa was leading strikes at the shipyards. For bankers, it is a no-no to lend money for five years to buy goods like coffee that would be consumed immediately. Lecturing the Poles, Palmer said, "This coffee is pretty good, but you know when you get around to paying for it five years from now you've forgotten how it tasted."

Now Citibank faced the dilemma of how to cut its exposure without making matters in Poland worse and jeopardizing its remaining investments.

Poland's mounting debt problems were inextricably intertwined with the growing anger of the nation's workers. There was no way that worker demands could be met as long as 70 percent of the country's hard currency income was earmarked for principal and interest payments. Obviously Poland wasn't merely the bankers' problem. The State Department was concerned that the debt burden and shortages of food and other commodities would derail democratic reforms. The challenge was to find a way to enable Poland to meet its obligations without jeopardizing that process.

Until now the financial problems had been limited to small countries with relatively little debt. But with the virtual bankruptcy of Poland, which by 1981 was laboring under $24 billion in external debt, the stakes were increased considerably. For 1981, Poland owed almost $12 billion in interest and principal, and couldn't come close to paying even a tiny portion of that.

The crisis escalated in January 1981 when Western bankers refused the pleas of deputy president Jan Woloszyn of Poland's Bank Handlowy for $1 billion in loans and yanked their short-term lines. Two months later, in London, Woloszyn delivered more bad news to some five hundred banks: Poland had run out of money. Bankers had always thought that the Soviet Union would bail out another Council for Mutual Economic Assistance (Comecon) country. They were wrong.

Because the U.S. banks' exposure in Poland was small compared with that of the Europeans, the Americans could play hardball. They considered Polish debt largely a European—and in particular, a German—problem. The Americans ruled out a rescheduling or new loans until the Poles came clean on their financial condition. Said one international banker, "The divisions between the Europeans and Americans were clearly more pronounced in the Polish situation. There was severe resentment on the part of the Europeans that the Americans were running the show." Soon the situation would be reversed.

Poland, incidentally, was one of the first major countries in which banks would later be forced to write off a portion of their debts. According to William Martin, former deputy Comptroller of the Currency for multinational banking, banks charged off 10 to 20 percent of their loans. Though the banks had charged off countries like Zaire and Bolivia, "the one that shook people up was Poland," Martin recalled.

Once again, Wriston, Costanzo, and their colleagues were forced to mount a defense against an onslaught of doomsayers, a task that was becoming increasingly difficult. By early 1981, evidence of a global recession was there for all to see. It was one thing to dismiss countries like Zaire, Bolivia, and Sudan as insignificant and irrelevant. But now Poland had bitten the dust. On January 28, the *Wall Street Journal* laid out the situation when it referred to the $500 billion owed by developing countries as a "new mountain on the planet" and questioned whether the "debt mountain is also a volcano." Costanzo felt compelled to refute the *Journal*'s story point by point, noting that the $500 billion included $46 billion loaned to six OPEC nations and $117 billion in undisbursed lines, and that all except $2.5 billion of the $45 billion increase in the twelve-month period through mid-year 1980 was in the form of short-term credits. "In the last decade these countries have demonstrated their ability to take corrective economic policy measures to adjust their balance of payments to changing world economic forces," Costanzo said in a talk. "Are these countries about to go down the drain and default on their external obligations? Quite the contrary."

Wriston heaped scorn on the Chicken Littles at every opportunity. Speaking before the World Affairs Council on March 6, he invoked author Barbara Tuchman, who wrote that doomsayers "take a trend and extend it, forgetting that the doom factor sooner or later generates a coping mechanism." When the sky falls, Wriston told reporters at his annual dinner meeting with the financial press, "it seems to fall more commonly on folks like Penn Central, Grant's, and Itel than abroad, while governments—even Nicaragua, Iran, and New York—pay their debts."

Citibank's senior international advisers were hauled out in March to reassure securities analysts that all was well in international lending. Titled "Risks and Rewards of Overseas Banking," that presentation years later would be held up to ridicule by top Citibankers. "I do not see any generalized crisis building up or any inevitable problem that cannot be handled by good management," one speaker said. Top Citibanker Ed Hoffman subsequently remarked wryly in a talk on problem loans, "It got worse as the discussion proceeded. I'm told it is out of print."

Though planner George Vojta's talents were considerable, he got it wrong this time. While conceding that Citibank was troubled by low Euromarket spreads, he downplayed the problem, saying that Citibank was aware of the risks and was managing them. He told the analysts that Citibank viewed Africa as one of four emerging business opportunities. After all of Citibank's debacles in Africa, it was difficult to comprehend how that continent could be perceived as a major business opportunity. "We were very niggardly on Africa, thank God," says Costanzo. The area officers "felt we didn't see the future there."

In March 1981, Vojta was named deputy to Costanzo, who was now months away from retirement. Disappointed at having been left out of the running for Wriston's job, he quit three months later. After working briefly at two other jobs that didn't pan out, Vojta got a call from Wriston, who offered to put in a word for him. One morning, the *New York Times* ran a story announcing that Vojta had been appointed chief financial officer at Phibro Corporation. That day, Wriston received irate phone calls from the heads of two companies to which he had recommended Vojta, both of whom had apparently understood from Vojta that he would be reporting to work for them that morning, Wriston recalled. "They ate me up one side and down another," he said. Vojta, according to a friend, continued to hold a grudge against Wriston for not appointing him to one of Citibank's top posts. "He will not show up when Wriston is in a room, and will get up to leave when he comes." Vojta declined to comment on this incident or on his relationship with Wriston.

At the May 1981 meeting of the International Monetary Conference in Lausanne, Switzerland, Wriston told fellow senior bankers that people who thought Third World defaults would trigger a global monetary crisis had been shown to be wrong, "and those of us who believe the market would work proved correct." Paul Volcker, who was sitting in the back of the room, recalled that Wriston said, "Lending to the LDCs is like lending on U.S. Treasury bills." Wriston emphasized that the U.S. government itself managed to repay its debts by issuing more Treasuries. Listening to Wriston's assurance, Volcker pondered whether he should take Wriston on in public, but decided that it would not be seemly for the Fed chairman to debate the CEO of Citicorp from the floor of a banking conference. Only one lone voice rose in dissent. His name was Henry Wallich, one of a handful of government officials who asked tough questions about commercial bank LDC lending. Wallich "suggested there might be some differences between Guatemala and the United States," Volcker recalled dryly. According to the June 5 *American Banker,* Wallich retorted that a man driving a car 150 mph for an hour without an accident could not be certain that he would not have an accident later.

If there was a single indicator that the good times were over at Citibank, it was seen in the August 1981 departure of loan supersalesman George Putnam for Crocker National Bank in San Francisco, run by former Wriston rival Tommy Wilcox. According to Robert F. B. Logan, loan syndication at Citi was scaled back in the early 1980s, and Putnam complained this was hurting his profit-and-loss statement.

But in the real world Wriston had good reason to be more worried about his loans in the OPEC countries than about those to the non-oil LDCs.

Saudi Arabia was not your typical LDC, but loans were already going into the tank there. After years of stalling, Citibank in early 1980 was finally forced to "Saudize" its operations there by selling a majority stake to the Saudis and forming a joint venture with them called the Saudi American Bank (SAMBA). This was the first time that Citibank had relinquished control over a foreign operation while remaining a minority holder. Having lost control, Citibank—the unpleasant memory of past joint ventures still fresh—took its name off the door.

The good news was that it now would be able to branch beyond its two offices in Riyadh and Jidda. In the years following the first oil shock, Citibank had profited handily by collecting the deposits of rich Saudis. By the late 1970s it had concluded that it should be making loans as well. Shortly after Citibanker Michael Callen took over as CEO of the newly Saudized entity, he flew home to report on the new affiliate. With SAMBA growing at a mind-boggling 200 percent annual rate, it was statistically the world's most profitable bank. Callen regarded this as a unique opportunity to score points with the boss. "I was so full of myself," Callen recalled later, as he described to Wriston how fast the bank was growing and how much money it was making. He concluded his presentation by saying, "Isn't that something?"

"Yep," Wriston said bluntly. "It smells."

"Excuse me?" Callen asked nervously.

"Anything that grows that fast smells," Wriston said. "It isn't the real world. Just worry about how much you've got to give back."

According to internal documents, the Saudi portfolio peaked at $312 million in 1981. Much of the money was used by princes and princesses to speculate on real estate. Until this time, the portfolio had been essentially loss-free, but within five years nearly half would have been written off or placed on nonaccrual, according to the documents. And just as Citibank discovered that making loans to princes and princesses or Saudi government officials could be financially hazardous, it also learned that collecting on such loans in the Saudi court system was nearly impossible. Like real estate values nearly everywhere else, property values there plunged with the onset of the 1981–1982 recession. Furthermore, the Saudi courts refused to hear cases in which members of the royal family were defendants. Citibank's Ed Hoffman later established a rule forbidding loans to the royal family.

Meanwhile, next door in Kuwait, financial authorities were seething at Citibank over leaks to the press by a Jewish employee involving the management of billions in Kuwaiti investments. Then a Citibank account officer, in internal conversations, called his Kuwaiti counterpart incompetent, according to Costanzo, and his remarks were leaked to a financial reporter by another employee who had lived in Israel. "She [the employee responsible for the leak] was a little disgruntled on the job," Costanzo said. "I think she thought she was doing something for Israel." The result was that Kuwait moved some $7 billion in funds out of Citibank, including $4 billion to the Wall Street firm of Morgan Stanley. Costanzo immediately got on the plane to Kuwait and sought out Sheikh Al-Ateeqi, a member of the royal family, at his desert home to explain the gaffe and beg for forgiveness—and the money. He may have been forgiven, but he didn't get the money.

For Wriston, it was pleasant to have good friends in the White House and in the statehouse in Pierre, South Dakota. The tide seemed to be turning for the country and for Citicorp. Indeed, Wriston, to borrow a line from a former GM chief, felt that what was good for Citicorp was good for the country.

Having done battle with nearly every politician he had ever met, Wriston was incredulous at the reception he received in June from "Wild Bill" Janklow when the Citibank Gulfstream landed at Sioux Falls's tiny airport. "I couldn't get over it," Wriston said. "He drove his own car, and they said, 'Hey, we like to have you here. You're creating jobs, you don't pollute. Thanks for coming'—instead of getting your head handed to you every morning in Albany. It was one of the great experiences of my life." South Dakota, said Wriston, "was the breakthrough that permitted us to go from breathing through a straw under water to making some money."

In his remarks opening the South Dakota credit-card facility, a sprawling $7.5 million beige-colored building near the end of a runway, Wriston waxed eloquent about his non–New York roots and those of other top Citibankers, including Rick Roesch from Aberdeen, South Dakota, Spencer from Colorado, and Costanzo from Alabama. "At the time it seemed as if it might be easier to carve the heads of the other thirty-five presidents in the tops of mountains than it would have been to open a bank in another state," Wriston said. And indeed, an article in *Forbes* magazine of November 21, 1983, included a sketch depicting Wriston's head chiseled into Mount Rushmore next to the original occupants. After cutting a ribbon made of oversized Citibank credit cards, Wriston took off for Washington, leaving his colleagues behind to bask in South Dakota hospitality.

To cement the bond with his newfound friends, Janklow activated a local National Guard helicopter squadron with great regularity. The governor's guided tour typically began at the Rapid City airport, where the helicopters fetched the Citibankers and flew them to Custer State Park. "I'd have the park people tell us where the buffalo were, and then we'd swoop down on the herd, the largest in the world, and get them stampeding across the prairie, a sight that quickened the pulse of even the most hard-nosed big-city banker. Then we'd do Rushmore," said Janklow, and wind up back in Rapid City. At day's end, an obviously moved Hans Angermueller put his arm around Janklow and told him, "Governor, you'll never know as long as you live how, for one short period of time, you made a very old man feel like a very young boy."

Tom Theobald joined Janklow and his fellow Citibankers for the governor's annual pheasant hunt. Before setting out in small teams, the hunters were warned that state law permitted the shooting of roosters but not hens. "We explain the difference between a male and female, saying that if you shoot a hen you'll get a chicken and a hundred-dollar fine," Janklow said later. At a time when all of the candidates for the chairmanship were trying to avoid transgressions of any kind, Theobald, of all people, killed a hen. "He was heartsick," recalled Janklow. A year later Janklow sent Theobald an official governor's pardon—and a stuffed pheasant. For his part, Janklow said in jest, "I don't even hunt. I don't like shooting animals. I believe in shooting people."

Hokey as it sounds, the relationship between Citibank and South Dakota would become something of a model in business-government relations. Besides low taxes, few unions, and little violent crime, there were other benefits of doing business in South Dakota. With no tall buildings, Citibank enjoyed better satellite transmission than in New York. It could send a letter half a day faster from Long Island to Sioux Falls than to New York City. And Citibankers could drive from the airport to downtown in less than five minutes because, as Janklow used to say, "main street ends where the runway begins." Moreover, Citibank's telephone operators, said Janklow, speak virtually accentless American English. And Citibank, as it turned out, needed fewer employees because South Dakotans, it turned out, worked harder than New Yorkers. These were happy days; Citibank tripped over itself to be Mr. Nice Guy. According to Janklow, it virtually guaranteed every computer major in the state a job, and made a point of hiring deaf people and blind switchboard operators. In an effort to be a good corporate citizen, Citibank in 1983 rejuvenated the South Dakota symphony with a $32,000 contribution, nearly half of what it gave that year to New York's Lincoln Center. The joke was, the *American Banker* of August 21, 1984, reported, that Citibank "bought itself an orchestra." According to one former official, Citibank also led a fund drive that raised $1 million for the local boys' club—$300,000 more than was expected. Moreover, said Janklow, Citicorp's donations to local charities forced other less generous companies to dig deeper into their pockets: "Citicorp set the standard that others now have to emulate."

But most important, perhaps thanks to Citibank, the recession that hammered nearly every other region in the country virtually bypassed South Dakota. In Sioux Falls, unemployment was a mere 3.7 percent, just behind Stamford, Connecticut's, 3.5 percent, according to the *New York Times*. In 1994, Sioux Falls boasted the lowest unemployment rate of any city in the nation.

And for John Reed, South Dakota and all the good news came along in the nick of time. The New York State Legislature finally scrapped the usury ceiling after South Dakota's implications set in. That, Wriston told a conference in June, would boost credit-card revenues by $100 million in 1981. And in the first quarter of 1981, just a couple of years after Citibank got slapped for charging fees to cardholders who paid right away, the bank raised $14 million by imposing card fees for the first time. In the credit-card business, Citibank now was so far out in front of other banks that some institutions, such as Bank of New York and European American, were forced to offer "no fee" cards in a desperate bid to catch up. Also, it was now clear for all to see that the ATM installation was also a brilliant stroke. Thanks largely to the ATMs, Citibank's New York deposits skyrocketed 26 percent in 1981, compared with 5 percent throughout the metropolitan area market, and its share of New York deposits had doubled to 9.2 percent since 1977. By now Citicorp's customer service had improved to the point where Citibank could feel reasonably comfortable boasting in its advertising about customer service, as reflected in such measures as waiting times on ATM and teller lines. In other ways, though, Citibank didn't seem to learn from its painful experiences. When it refused to compensate customers who were victims of alleged ATM con artists, New York State attorney general Robert Abrams hauled Citibank into court and forced the bank to reimburse them.

While much of the improvement in Reed's prospects in 1981 resulted from the repricing of the credit cards, a goodly portion also stemmed from intermediate-term debt, raised at relatively low rates, that Citicorp allocated solely to the individual bank. Said chief financial officer Don Howard, "John's improvement in 1980–1981 was 90 percent because we changed the pool rate, not because the business was that much better." That decision, said Howard, "made a hero out of John."

Despite its teething troubles, Citibank continued to bet new money on consumer banking innovations and on acquisitions of questionable value. In late 1980 it introduced a banking-by-phone service, and in mid-1981, it established Home Base, a home banking service. Then, when credit-card czar Dave Phillips proposed buying Diners Club, John Reed, who loved to buy things, was intrigued, even though the nation's second-largest card operation was poorly managed and had been spilling red ink for years. After eight months of negotiations, Citibank bought Diners Club in mid-1981 from Continental Corporation, which obviously knew nothing about running a credit-card operation. And in 1981, Citibank offered a Visa "preferred card" to go head to head with American Express's gold card. Then, further expanding its mortgage business, Citibank offered an adjustable rate mortgage to first-time home purchasers and in 1983 introduced a home equity loan, the first one in the New York area that enabled the customer to write checks on the credit line and dictate the terms of his loan.

Wriston and Reed's willingness to bet huge sums of money on the future was not diminished even in the face of the huge losses the bank was suffering in its consumer business. In 1981, Wriston announced that the bank had invested $500 million in technology and planned to lay out another $100 million in 1982. Reed and his colleagues had concluded when they first launched the consumer business that its future lay in creating many links with the consumer—what bankers call relationship banking. With characteristic hubris, Reed launched an ambitious effort to create a technological foundation for these relationships. By the time it was abandoned four years later, this consumer banking system piddled away another $100 million of shareholders' money. The idea, as chief technology officer Paul Glaser explained later, was to pull all consumer relationships together into one integrated database. A customer with, say, a trust or brokerage account would be able to make inquiries about his account from a single terminal, and Citibank in turn would be able to sell the customer on new services with full knowledge of those he already had. All transactions would be posted to the account immediately, instead of at the end of the day. And once a customer opened one account with Citibank, he would not have to fill out stacks of forms to set up additional accounts. It was to be the banking system of the future. By 1984, however, Citibank had given up on the project. "It was too large; we took on too much at one time," according to Glaser. "It was probably a little ahead of its time."

Reed's drive into consumer banking exacted a human toll as well as a financial cost. Indeed, Reed himself was one of the victims. Said a colleague, "He spent less and less time on his marriage and more time on the bank." His associate David Phillips, after the credit-card troubles, was assigned to Latin America. On a skiing trip in Chile, Phillips's daughter was asphyxiated by a gas heater. That was one of the few times Reed's colleagues saw their boss let go. "It was an emotional time," said Reed later. "I can see how people would say, 'That really got to John.'" Phillips, who felt he had been a driving force in Citibank's consumer business, quit in the fall of 1981 after Reed appointed Rick Braddock chief of U.S. consumer banking. "Dave got screwed," said Frank Partel, a former colleague. "Phillips expanded the credit-card business, blew it up, and fixed it, but there was a lag effect." Wriston, meanwhile, took care of other casualties of the battle for Citicorp's top jobs. When consumer executive and former Paris hand John Fogarty failed to make the cut for a loftier post, Wriston found him a job as head of the U.S. Lawn Tennis Association.

Ultimately, however, the consumer business succeeded beyond anyone's wildest expectations. It was so successful, in fact, that it did not become the source of cheap funding that Wriston had originally envisioned. While the growth of consumer deposits added stability to Citibank's funding, the business itself later became a net user rather than a net provider of funds to the bank as a whole. As consumer banking turned profitable, Reed began to face some of the same compensation pressures felt elsewhere in the bank. Reed's people were now upset that they weren't earning nearly as much as their counterparts at rival American Express.

Putting modesty aside, Reed later puffed that deluging the country with credit cards was "one of the most brilliant things we did."

Within weeks of the ribbon-cutting in Sioux Falls that would take the wraps off Citibank's profits, there was a bill-signing in Washington that would, Wriston believed, unleash the nation's economy. As a member of the President's Economic Policy Advisory Board, Wriston was in the thick of the deliberations over the Economic Recovery Tax Act of 1981, the centerpiece of Reaganomics and the most sweeping revision of the IRS code in more than a quarter century.

In the trade-offs over the marginal tax rate and capital gains, Wriston began to appreciate Reagan's deal-making acumen. Some purists favored eliminating the capital gains tax, which was then 28 percent, and cutting the marginal rate below the 50 percent level Reagan felt comfortable with. Reagan knew intuitively that this would never fly politically. So, according to Murray Weidenbaum, then chairman of the Council of Economic Advisers, Reagan stuck with the 50 percent maximum tax rate even though certain advisers were convinced more revenue would be generated at a lower rate. Reagan also refused to give in to pressure from some hard-core supply-siders to do away with capital gains entirely, Wriston said. "We've got to have a salable political package," Reagan said, as Wriston recalled. "I'll give that one up to get the better deal on marginal rates." When Milton Friedman persisted in arguing the point, Reagan glared at him and declared with finality, "I've already decided that one."

Reagan actually believed that the Democrats would take the initiative in lowering the capital gains tax themselves because he felt they realized that cutting the tax was a good idea. "I'll let them twist my arm," Reagan quipped slyly.

As the pitched battle over the tax bill was reaching its peak in Congress, Wriston was returning from the U.K. on a commercial flight. The pilot came back from the cockpit to speak with him. Leaning over Wriston's seat, he said, "You're not going to believe this, but the president is on the phone."

"I'm not going to believe that," Wriston replied. Then he went into the cockpit to take the call.

"Hey, Walt," Reagan opened with his sly chuckle before telling Wriston that a Democratic congressman had actually proposed cutting the capital gains rate even more than Reagan had. "I just want you to know that I have reluctantly agreed to go along with it." And then he laughed and hung up, according to Wriston.

In a historic vote, both houses of Congress in late July voted for cuts that would reduce taxes by nearly $40 billion starting October 1, 1981, the beginning of the 1982 fiscal year. As part of the package, the capital gains rate was slashed to 20 percent.

Subsequently, however, Wriston may have influenced policy in a direction opposite to the one he intended. The occasion was a dinner later that summer at Washington's Kennedy Center for the Performing Arts, where the Wristons were seated with Fed vice chairman Frederick Schultz and Senator Robert Dole, chairman of the Senate Finance Committee. Wriston and Schultz got into a heated debate over the tax cut, with Schultz arguing that "this was going to cause a lot of problems." Wriston, of course, disagreed. The debate, while stormy, was not angry. "You're foolish to get into an angry debate with Walter Wriston," Schultz said later. "He's very bright and handles the language extremely well. Walter and I were as forceful as we could be in outlining and defending our positions." Schultz emphasized that while he favored a tax cut, he believed it was essential to cut spending as well. If that didn't happen, the country would be left with a huge deficit that would lead to higher interest rates.

That, of course, triggered Wriston's canned supply-side speech. "Oh, no," Schultz recalls Wriston saying. Echoing Art Laffer, Wriston said, "That [spending] will cause the economy to be stimulated so strongly that we won't have any deficit, and even with lower tax rates, government revenue will be just as high."

Schultz told him, "We have a dangerous situation on our hands" and added that with the economy just emerging from years of rampant inflation, the Fed was compelled to continue reining in the money supply. The debate concluded without a resolution.

Dole had listened carefully but declined to commit himself to one view or another. A week later, however, Dole bumped into Schultz in the elevator at the Watergate Apartments, where they both lived. "I think you won that argument," Dole told Schultz. Dole later sponsored measures to rescind some of the more extreme cuts that had been approved in the earlier legislation. These were incorporated in the Tax Equity and Fiscal Responsibility Act of 1982.

Over dinner and on the airwaves, Wriston defended the Reagan program and pushed the Fed to tighten further. In Japan and Germany he found support for the notion that the deficit didn't matter. On *Meet the Press* on June 28, 1981, he observed that Japan's deficit was three times that of the United States relative to gross national product, while the inflation rate in Japan was one-third that of the United States. In GNP terms, West Germany's budget deficit was 50 percent higher than America's, while the rate of inflation was half.

"I thought the most important thing we had to do was to continue to have a steady, predictable monetary policy, and I think that the change that the Fed announced in October of 1979 was a very important one in that regard," Wriston remarked later.

At a White House meeting in early November, Wriston, Frederick Schultz, Alan Greenspan, and Paul McCracken—the "four wise men"—urged the president to stay the course, according to the *New York Times*. Cutting taxes and federal spending, they claimed, was the best way to cut the budget deficit. Moreover, they argued that the president should not raise taxes even if that decision meant a deficit in 1984. Wriston was riding high. Adam Smith was alive and well and living in the White House. *U.S. News* voted the chairman of Citibank one of the thirty most influential Americans and *the* single most influential person in finance. Another business publication named him the best chief executive officer of a money center bank. And Citibank's consumer business was turning around. In 1981, with three more years left at Citibank before his retirement, it looked as if Wriston would retire a hero.

Less optimistic observers, however, took note of some unsettling straws in the wind. Though few picked up on it in mid-1981, deregulation was al-

ready starting to undermine oil prices. Ironically, just as oil prices were starting to fall, some of the nation's largest companies—namely Du Pont, Mobil,
and Seagram—backed by their banks, launched a feeding frenzy for Conoco,
the big oil company. While Chase was leading a $3 billion, thirty-bank credit
for Du Pont, Citibank was out raising money for rival Mobil. This did not sit
well with Citibank director Irving Shapiro, who had just retired as chairman
of Du Pont. In conversations with Shapiro, Wriston justified Citibank's role
by citing the "fungibility of money." According to Shapiro, "That didn't
wash [with companies like his own] who had relationships with Citibank.
They didn't take kindly to Citibank being on the other side." Added Shapiro
later: "It was a snappy line but it doesn't do much for business relationships . . . Walt is simply wrong." That, he contended, is the difference between being intellectually bright and having wisdom. "Wisdom says you
can't do that to good customers. You don't have to be a genius to figure that
out." In the end, Du Pont prevailed, however.

At this point, in August 1981, Inferential Focus, an intelligence-
gathering service for big companies, reflected on the battle for Conoco in a
letter to clients, saying that Conoco might not be the "bargain" people
claimed it was. "Since it has taken eight years for the oil merger feeding
frenzy to begin, it is quite likely that we are witnessing a phenomenon seen so
often before—where confidence was at its highest point just before a fundamental change." Indeed, the weakening of oil prices would bring about a
drastic change in the ability of other Citibank borrowers—notably Mexico—
to repay their debts. And that would cause many of the former faithful to
have grave doubts about the Wriston credo that countries don't go bankrupt.

23

THE EDGE OF THE ABYSS

*I*t was not, in itself, a remarkable event. But the timing was certainly uncanny.

On November 16, 1981, Al Costanzo, Citibank's international czar, turned sixty-five, and Citibank's top management, as was the custom, celebrated that event by giving him a roast. If Wriston now believed that his faith in Costanzo and the recycling of petrodollars was misplaced, he gave no hint of it in his farewell remarks to this gentle optimist from Alabama. "Al's place in the history of the bank is assured," Wriston said prophetically, noting that from a boyhood "peddling cabbage" in Edgewater, Alabama, he went on to doing the same for Citibank overseas. It was, said the chairman, a classic Horatio Alger story: "From a rural southern boyhood, skinny-dipping in the swimming hole—probably the last time in his career that Al left himself overexposed—to his current eminence as our chief negotiator with everyone from eastern potentates to airplane hijackers," a reference to the May 1981 terrorist incident. "I understand Al promised them [the hijackers] a higher rate of return from Citibank CDs than they could expect from a life of crime."

Citibank's parting gift to Costanzo recognized his abiding interest in Japanese culture and language, and represented as well a metaphoric gibe at critics of Third World lending. It was a seventeenth-century scroll inscribed with the words of a poet speaking to a kitchen helper: "Although he has read many books, nobody asks for his knowledge." To this the kitchen worker replies: "Although he has swept the way clean, the dust returns again."

"It kind of epitomizes," Wriston concluded, "the way Al and I have felt after we've explained for the umpteenth time why we lend money to LDCs—then, the next day, the press throws the same old dust in people's eyes." The only thing Wriston omitted from his tribute was Costanzo's exquisite timing. Whether Wriston cared to acknowledge it or not, the downhill slide in Third World lending was already under way, and Costanzo was getting out just in the nick of time. It would soon be all too apparent that LDC lending was *not* one of those snafus one director might have been thinking of when he remarked, "Citibank seems to make a lot of mistakes, but they are the right kind of mistakes." Citibank had blundered into a massive buildup of Third World debt in an effort, as Wriston put it, "to build a new earnings stream for tomorrow," but the mighty stream was drying up in the harsh desert of reality.

In the wake of the first oil shock, the current account deficits of developing countries were financed in three roughly equal portions by grants and equity investment, official loans, and commercial bank loans. But now the commercial bank portion was approaching an ominous one-half of the total. Still, when Costanzo headed for retirement in Florida, the relatively small exposure in Poland looked like the banks' biggest overseas worry. After months of arm wrestling with their European counterparts, U.S. banks in September 1981 forced the Poles to agree to bring interest payments current by December 10. When they failed to meet that deadline, default became a real possibility and Western bankers put more pressure on the Poles. In mid-December, in the face of massive strikes and civil strife, the Communist regime declared martial law. Concern mounted that the Soviet Union might invade Poland to put down the rebellion.

In the midst of the crisis, some bankers suggested that it wouldn't be so bad if the generals took control. Tom Theobald, a contender for the Citibank throne, was asked by an interviewer about his views on a military takeover. "Who knows which political system works?" he replied. "The only test we care about is, can they pay their bills?" Some Citicorp wags thought Theobald jeopardized his chances for the top job with his seemingly callous and offhand response. That episode may have prompted Theobald, not to mention Reed and Angermueller, to maintain a low profile, fearing that they might blurt out something that would ruffle Wriston's feathers. Later, as reported by the July 1983 *Institutional Investor,* Theobald quoted a Chinese aphorism: "The nail that stands up gets hammered down."

While he was never enthusiastic about lending to Communist bloc countries, Wriston sympathized with the Polish people. In a speech to the nation two days before Christmas, President Reagan called on Americans to light candles to demonstrate their solidarity with the Poles. On the day before Christmas, an idea flashed into Wriston's mind: he would turn Citicorp Center into one giant candle, at least on paper. He phoned a marketing officer and ordered him to produce a full-page newspaper ad showing the building as a lighted candle, with the message, "Let the light of millions of candles in American homes give notice that the light of freedom is not going to be extinguished." On Christmas Eve, the executive rushed to Washington, got Ronald Reagan's signature as an endorsement of the message, and rushed the ad into print.

Some Reagan administration officials and influential private citizens, including financier Felix Rohatyn, had become obsessed by the notion that by pushing Poland into default on its $26 billion in debt they could stick it to the Soviets, who they thought would have to pick up the tab. In effect, they wanted to use sovereign debt as an instrument of U.S. foreign policy. According to bankers and former government officials, Wriston played a key role in persuading the Reagan administration that this was a bad idea. In a January 24 appearance on *Face the Nation,* Wriston said such a move would "illustrate very clearly to the Poles that they have only one friend: Russia. And it doesn't seem to me too productive." Taking a potshot at Rohatyn and the New York City fiscal follies, Wriston said, "He suddenly believes that bankruptcy is good for some other place, which is somewhat of a switch." Forcing Poland into default would have activated rules that would in turn have curtailed balance-of-payments lending to the country by the IMF and triggered Poland's economic collapse. Wriston "spent a lot of time on the phone with Treasury and State," according to then assistant secretary of state Robert Hormats, who said that the State Department shared Wriston's view.

The issue came to a head in an auspicious White House meeting with President Reagan and other top government officials, in which Wriston and others, according to participants, succeeded in killing the idea of a declaration of default. They argued that if this weapon were used against the Poles it could later backfire and hurt the United States and its banks in Latin America.

In March 1982, Poland paid more than $290 million to its banks, and in early April the banks agreed to reschedule the country's 1981 debt. In effect, the debt was postponed in a generous deal that called for a four-year grace period with repayment over eight years starting in 1986. The ink was barely dry when the Poles and the banks began squabbling over 1982 payments. To settle that argument, the banks paid themselves half of the Poles' $1.1 billion in 1982 interest with a three-year trade financing. Even though no principal payments were made, this hat trick allowed the banks to book the interest and avoid write-offs for the time being. By now it was clear that the Soviets wouldn't provide a safety net, and Poland's difficulties began to spread to other Eastern bloc countries. These nations, including Yugoslavia, owed the West about $100 billion. Banks began to pull back from other Communist countries such as Romania, which soon came begging for a rescheduling. Bulgaria and Hungary were also on the brink.

One of the most blatant examples of government jawboning of the banks was the April 1982 effort by undersecretary of state Lawrence Eagleburger to persuade them to continue lending to Yugoslavia, where he had once served as ambassador and which enjoyed special status at Foggy Bottom. With a third of that country's estimated $10.5 billion in debt coming due over the next year, banks were loath to throw good money after bad there and elsewhere in Eastern Europe. In the face of all this, however, after Yugoslavia imposed tough austerity measures in October 1982, a Citibank-led syndicate lent the country $200 million.

For Wriston and the American banks, Poland was troublesome but not life-threatening. Though they didn't appreciate it at the time, the real problem was the time bomb ticking in Latin America. Argentina was now expending huge sums on military equipment, for reasons that would soon become clear. And Mexico, giddy over its oil reserves, had failed to diversify its economy. In 1981 alone, Mexico's external debt surged nearly 50 percent to $80 billion. Meanwhile, Brazil, beset by hyperinflation and forced to borrow vast amounts to pay its oil bill, had amassed more than $90 billion in debts. Citibank now had a whopping $4.6 billion, or 83 percent of its capital, in dollar exposure to Brazil. In the ratios that count to bankers, Citibank's exposure relative to its capital, and relative to that of other banks, was large only in Brazil. Elsewhere—in Mexico, for example—Citibank was in the middle of the pack. One policy flaw that plagued virtually all of the Latin economies was fixed, overvalued exchange rates. Even Chile, which was considered well managed, and Venezuela, a major oil exporter, labored under this burden.

Though Costanzo and others contended that Citibank's LDC loan growth was slower than that of other banks in the early 1980s, others were more self-critical. In an internal presentation, Hoffman called Mexico the bank's "worst failure." There, exposure rose rapidly until just a few months before Mexico ran out of money in August 1982. The bank's only success in the Third World was the reduction from 1980 to 1983 of exposure in sub-Saharan Africa, but that was an easy call. In contrast, the Philippines was a classic case of a bank being sucked into lending too much. Citibank wound up with exposure of $1.6 billion, more than 5 percent of the country's gross domestic product. To its dismay, Citibank would later learn that it had been betrayed by the country in which it had put so much faith: the Philippines had cooked the books.

By 1981, Third World countries were borrowing more and more short-term money. The bankers thought they were minimizing their risk by lending short-term. But they were wrong.

If there was a point at which a keen observer might have first detected that the gravy train no longer made stops in Mexico, it was June 1, 1981. On that day, Jorge Diaz Serrano, the corrupt chief of Pemex, the national oil company, was forced to lower the price for top-grade crude. Mexico's growth, as well as the borrowing that supported it, was based largely on the belief that oil prices would always rise. By the end of 1981, Pemex had amassed borrowings of $20 billion, including $10 million raised in 1981 alone. Meanwhile, as spending and borrowing rose, exports declined.

About a month after Mexico cut oil prices, Citibank country risk expert Jack Guenther flew to Mexico, where he was told by Leopoldo Solis, a senior economic adviser to President José López Portillo, that he and other advisers had convinced López Portillo that Mexico should take measures to adjust to lower oil prices. Solis added that Guenther would hear some good news to that effect in the president's September 1, 1981, state of the union speech. Even though September 1 came and went without good news, few believed Mexico was in trouble. But Solis, said Guenther, viewed his presence in Mexico as a sign that the New York banks were worried. Mexico's former finance minister, Jesús Silva Herzog, asserted later in an interview that the "Mexican government made a very serious mistake" in interpreting the drop in price as a "temporary decline" requiring no adjustment in economic policy. But López Portillo thought that if he got into trouble he could simply open the oil spigot. In July and August, Silva Herzog pointed out, $9 billion fled the country, a gap Mexico attempted to fill by borrowing lots of short-term money. "That meant by early 1982 we had the problem of paying back short-term borrowings and finding growing resistance on the part of commercial banks," he said.

Banks that foresaw trouble and wanted to cut their exposure in Mexico could do so only by refusing to roll over short-term loans. The problem was, in doing that they would only make a "serious situation worse," as one banker put it.

According to former deputy Treasury secretary R. T. "Tim" McNamar, a Treasury department aide at the U.S. embassy in Mexico City was raising warning flags on the country's financial condition in the fall of 1981, prior to President Reagan's late-October meeting in Cancún with López Portillo. The Treasury aide reported in his cables that Mexico was in "real trouble" and asserted that the Mexicans were "fudging" reserve and other figures.

In Cancún, Treasury secretary Donald Regan raised these questions with Mexican financial authorities and asked for updated financial statistics. "No problem. No problem," was the Mexicans' stock reply to such requests. By now, Treasury *knew* it had a serious problem. But it adopted a low-key policy and apparently did not voice its concerns to bankers, or to anyone else outside a small circle within Treasury and the Fed. "It didn't make sense to go around saying, 'Guess what? We think there is a big problem in Mexico. The country is going to be insolvent.' A lot of people [later] criticized us for not doing that," McNamar admitted. According to Leopoldo Solis, he and other advisers were warning López Portillo to stop borrowing money, but Pemex was "telling him we have to think optimistically."

But, as Angel Gurria, a top Mexican finance official, told an American colleague, halting the borrowing binge was tough to do when the banks were still pushing money on Mexico at thin spreads over the London Interbank Offering Rate (LIBOR).

If Treasury officials had the inside track on Mexico, they apparently didn't share it with their stepchild agency, the Comptroller of the Currency. Said former senior deputy Comptroller Paul Homan, "We thought Mexico was going to be just fine. We thought oil would save everything. Treasury never told us a thing. . . . We didn't know about Mexico until it was upon us. We blew that one."

Despite mounting evidence of capital flight and other problems, the State Department and the CIA, according to Robert Hormats, were also "sanguine" about Mexico, which—like other Third World borrowers—was an eager believer in the gospel that countries don't go bankrupt.

Even as Mexico was running out of money, Angel Gurria said, the banks were offering Mexico "a year more and an eighth less," figuring, he said, they'd compensate for the longer maturities and lower rates by charging stiffer fees. Citibankers, he said, were still tripping over each other in the finance ministry offices trying to sell Mexico on one loan instrument or another. "There was a lot of competition and backstabbing. Everybody was putting out a new product. One day we'd have one Citibank guy come visit, the next day another. One didn't know about the other, and they were actually competing." Some, he said, were trying to lend, others to do a bond issue, syndication, straight loan, or revolving line of credit. In 1981, Gurria recalled, López Portillo, Gurria, and other top aides embarked on a whirlwind five-country road show to raise money, slapping together a half dozen or so deals in a week. Gurria explained long after the crisis was over that he had been too tired from jet lag to lose any sleep over all the money Mexico was borrowing. But, he admitted, "borrowing $20 billion for the future of Mexico in a year is something I still cannot fully grasp."

On February 5, 1982, López Portillo declared that he would "defend the peso like a dog," but about two weeks later he was forced to recognize the impossibility of keeping that promise. The peso was devalued and quickly plummeted more than 40 percent against the dollar. As a result, Portillo fired his finance minister and central bank chief and replaced them with Jesús Silva Herzog, a.k.a. Chucho, and Miguel Mancera. The next month he gave Mexican workers a huge pay hike, exacerbating the nation's financial woes. Even as Mexico was hurtling into a financial abyss, President López Portillo was tapping public funds to build himself a multimillion-dollar compound on a hill near Mexico City. It was called Dog Hill, a takeoff on his comment on how he would defend the peso.

Despite the surge in Brazil's borrowing, bankers found solace in its vast economy and its strong exports. "In spite of the chaos," Al Costanzo said later, Brazil "had the good sense to maintain realistic foreign exchange rates so exports continued to grow." Ever the optimist, Costanzo still believed that with the right policies Brazil could turn things around. Out of sight of their bankers, the Brazilian financial authorities themselves were getting jittery. In 1981, recalled former Brazil central bank chief Carlos Langoni, "we saw the market becoming tougher. Brazil was paying higher spreads." In contrast to Mexico, Brazil was always willing to pay fat spreads for longer terms, but that was getting more and more difficult. Practically speaking, said Langoni, Brazil in 1981 had to go to market every week to borrow $1 billion. "We knew the process was coming to an end, but everyone was hoping for a soft landing," he said.

However, former Citibank Latin American expert Anthony Howkins said, "I was concerned about the political risk, not that debt would escalate from $42 billion to $95 billion."

Bankers would later comfort themselves with the thought that Brazil used its money better than Mexico and infinitely better than Argentina. At least Brazil had a private sector, something lacking in Argentina. Once again, that perennially troubled country was getting ready to snatch defeat from the jaws of victory. All told, from 1974 through 1982, Argentina borrowed $32 billion, more than triple its $10 billion current account deficit. Part of the reason, said John Reed later, was the popularity among bankers of José Martinez de Hoz, who had become economic minister when a junta headed by General Jorge Videla took power back in March 1976. "Banks lent too much money to Argentina when Martinez was minister," said Reed, "because he was well known and everybody liked him."

"Argentina is a great place," said one former officer who served there. "You just have to replace the Argentines."

As the clock began to strike midnight for Third World lending, it started to dawn on Citibank that billions of dollars from their loans were turning up in other banks and in Citibank's own private banking division as deposits of wealthy Latins, Filipinos, and other nationals. That should not have come as a shock to Wriston and other students of economic history: capital flight is as old as national borders, and history is replete with examples of nervous citizens of troubled countries moving their money and other valuables elsewhere. Frenchmen profited from the 1720 Mississippi Bubble by moving their gains elsewhere, and German Jews rushed to spirit their gold to Switzerland and other safe havens before World War II. Wherever there are bad economic policies, money will come in the front door and go out the back as flight capital. Although the banks blamed the Latins for capital flight, nearly every large U.S. bank operated a private banking division that scoured the world for just such deposits.

In October 1981, in the wake of an IMF mission to Mexico, country risk expert Jack Guenther met with an IMF official who was crunching Mexico's numbers. Like Guenther, the official had concluded that Mexico's current account deficit would be about $12 billion. Moreover, the "errors and omissions" line—the difference between estimated and actual reserves—is usually viewed as a rough proxy for flight capital. That number was over $5 billion. "Any reasonable Mexican would try to diversify his risk," said Guenther. "The problem comes when everybody is trying to get his money out."

For all its other deficiencies, Brazil managed to keep capital flight under control. And, said a British banker, "there was enough opportunity in Brazil to keep it there." Venezuela, on the other hand, had the highest rate of capital flight per capita of any Latin nation, according to international financier Geoffrey Bell. Most of its $35 billion in public and private debt wound up overseas, he said.

Wriston, of course, regarded Citibank as a vast cable machine in which money was information and the bank's overseas branches were sensors that monitored the economic pulse of the countries in which they operated. But for all of Citibank's sophistication, no one systematically tracked the ebb and flow of funds in a way that would reveal much about a country's economic prospects or about whether Citibank should continue lending there. According to John Reed, Citibank knew these movements of funds were taking place "but didn't put it together. The reason was they lacked the systemic framework. No one was looking at it [funds flows] as a global system." Reed compared this to someone who obliges a friend by regularly forwarding his mail and discovers after four years that he has been a pawn in a massive drug scam. "You knew the specifics," said Reed, "but you didn't put them together."

Because the big banks were competing with one another for the same money, there was little incentive for them to share their information. And "nobody," said a former Citibank official, "could see the whole picture by looking at his own."

For his part, Wriston said that he didn't collect data on capital flight. Yet he knew from his colleagues from the old overseas division the significance of capital flows as a harbinger of trouble. In the 1960s, such an oversight could have been excused, because few banks or institutions back then fully appreciated the financial links among nations. But with the breakdown of the Bretton Woods system, it became abundantly clear that the world economy was interconnected. As late as 1982, Reed observed, the Hong Kong Shanghai Bank was the only major international financial institution that realized that local savings were being replaced by bank loans. Reed explained that "the local guys were taking money out and putting it in Switzerland, and we were lending them the money to replace it. We were fully aware that deposits would end up in Switzerland," he said. By 1990, Citibank had more deposits from Latin America than loans. "God knows what the Swiss have. They must have eight hundred times," he said.

Although Citicorp lacked a system for watching funds flows, Citicorp officers informally watched individual accounts for clues to economic trends. According to one former senior executive, Citibank in London carefully monitored the flow of funds in and out of the London account of a top Saudi official for tip-offs that the Saudi currency would be devalued. Inevitably, the former official said, an increase in the flow of funds into the account would be followed by devaluation. Transactions executed by one influential Mexican customer, Costanzo said, were often a precursor to trouble. In the 1970s, in anticipation of moves by President Echeverría that would lead to devaluation of the peso, Costanzo recalled, the customer would move money into Citibank. Citibank could also monitor capital flight through the sale of traveler's checks.

Richard Kovacevich, who became head of Citibank's international consumer business in 1982, was not an international lender. But he started having doubts about LDC lending when he saw anecdotal evidence of Latins, including the mayor of Mexico City, shifting money to the United States. Wealthy Latins were purchasing expensive condominiums at Olympic Towers, a Fifth Avenue luxury building, with loans from Citibank. No one, said Morgan economist Rimmer de Vries, focused on capital flight until 1983.

Even as Citibankers were asserting publicly that there was no problem, internally some were already maneuvering to cover their behinds from the debacle they sensed was about to begin. At a January 1982 policy meeting, top executives were treated to presentations on cross-border risk, according to internal Citibank documents. In one, Jack Guenther and George "Jack" Clark said there would not be "generalized" cross-border risk problems and that troubled countries would simply have to pay higher spreads for money. But as former Citibanker Ed Hoffman said several years later in an internal presentation, "it was quite clear rather quickly that the object of the session, from the point of view of the line managers on the panel, was to demonstrate that final authority in cross-border management had rested in the New York staff during the period of explosive cross-border growth, not the line." And Hoffman went on to state that "for many of us that approach was . . . wrong and downright insulting to our management efforts. We knew who was responsible. To blame Jack Clark, Jack Guenther, or Al Costanzo was a real cop-out." Following that meeting, Hoffman said, the accountability of line management in the institutional division was "reemphasized."

By now the rating agencies were beginning to get nervous about Citibank, but more because of its domestic loans than its LDC loans. Indeed, it was a sad day at Citicorp when Standard & Poor's, in late 1981, stripped Citicorp of its treasured triple-A debt rating. This was followed four months later by a similar move by Moody's. Citicorp thus earned the dubious distinction of being the first top-tier bank holding company in recent memory to lose that triple-A status.

High unemployment and interest rates and the recession didn't help much. Now that the consequences were obvious, Wriston took mild exception with Paul Volcker's monetary policy. Granting that it had, on balance, been "current and right, and had cut the inflation rate to 9 percent from about 13 percent," Wriston told *Face the Nation* on January 24, 1982, that the "amplitudes of the swings were too high." Asked if Volcker was a poor manager, Wriston said, "I don't think necessarily that is so. There is a lot of difference between policy and execution when you are selling and buying funds in the marketplace." While complaining that unemployment was now excessive, Wriston said he wouldn't change his economic prescription from the one he had offered on *Face the Nation* two years earlier: reduced government spending and tight money.

Still, Wriston and Citibank were convinced that rates were too high and would begin falling by midyear. When Wriston reiterated that forecast at the May meeting of the Business Council, Exxon chairman and CEO Clifton Garvin zinged him: "I think my friend Walter is right. But I am not sure *when* he is right. That's the problem." Among bank economists, the ability to predict interest rates was one measure of competence and a source of pride or embarrassment, as the case might be. In 1980 and 1981 they experienced nothing but embarrassment.

The bank economists' nemesis was Salomon Brothers' Dr. Henry Kaufman, a.k.a. Dr. Doom, whom they sniped at in public and in private. At one

Business Council meeting, according to Wriston colleagues, Wriston said that Kaufman was right on interest rates about one time out of six. While Citibank was forecasting a decline in rates, Kaufman was predicting a continuation of record long-term rates. But no one seemed to pay much attention to Citibank. When Dr. Doom spoke, the markets listened—a fact that caused great angst at 399 Park. "There was a lot of competitive jealousy," admitted former Citibank economist Harold van Buren Cleveland, for the attention he got and what he was said to be earning. And though Wriston believed in tight money, he, unlike Kaufman, did not seem troubled by the run-up in personal debt that his institution was encouraging.

For some time, until March 1982, Citibank used a clever and remarkably accurate system for anticipating the crucial money supply numbers released by the Fed each Thursday. Thus the bank got a jump on short-term interest rates. Paul De Rosa, a vice president in Citibank's money market division, polled about ten big banks to obtain the data they intended to report that week, and from those figures he calculated an overall forecast for cash and checking deposits. De Rosa's forecast was known as the "Citibank survey," and the results were shared with the other banks. In early March, for example, Citibank forecast a $3 billion increase in cash and checking accounts; the actual increase turned out to be $3.4 billion before adjustments. Trouble was, this system could be construed as using insider information. Sally Heinemann, a savvy *Journal of Commerce* reporter, got wind of the scheme and wrote about it in a March 22, 1982, article in which she reported that the Fed was unaware of the survey. "We have a feeling that the Fed is not too crazy about this," one banker was quoted as saying. Asked about the uncanny $3 billion forecast, De Rosa told Heinemann it was a "lucky week." After the article ran, Wriston, who generally had no problem with dancing circles around the Fed, called a halt to the survey. "While we were not doing anything wrong," he wrote in an article, "the chances of somebody trying to find something wrong are high."

The mega-bankers, including Wriston, had never looked upon their Third World borrowers as anything but individual countries with unique risk profiles. In the spring of 1982, the notion that they would all wind up as economic basket cases within months of each other was a worst-case scenario that was never even contemplated. But by late March 1982, the events that would trigger the Latin American debt crisis were unfolding in Buenos Aires and London. In March the Argentine military government fixed April 2 as the date to redress an old grievance with the United Kingdom. It would dispatch a naval force to retake the Falklands, a bleak and sparsely settled island group off the coast of Argentina, most of whose residents were sheep.

On the day of the attack, Argentina was among the most indebted of Third World borrowers, with total external borrowings of about $40 billion, including nearly $9 billion in loans from U.S. banks. In addition to New

York's Manufacturers Hanover Trust, Citibank, and Morgan Guaranty, major lenders included Britain's National Westminster Bank and Lloyds. News that the Argentine navy had attacked a British possession was all that the bankers, particularly the Brits, needed to hear. Although the British government froze some $1 billion in Argentine assets held in the U.K., Argentina scrupulously avoided defaulting on its debt. But that would not impress the world financial community.

Overnight Argentina became a pariah. By lending the country so much money with no strings attached, the world's commercial banks had actually helped to finance the military action. For two more months, Argentina persisted in its folly in the South Atlantic, until it was overwhelmed by superior British forces. Although Argentina's record at financial management had historically been among the worst of the Latin American nations, it had, said Citibank's William Rhodes, "always made an effort to repay its external obligations." Nonetheless, when the first shot was fired, it rattled nerves in the boardrooms from Park Avenue to the City in London. Argentina was financially doomed.

On the other side of Park Avenue, Bankers Trust's David Sias called his colleagues into his office for an emergency meeting, according to a bank officer who was there. Argentina had recently completed a transaction involving Bankers Trust. Sias's colleagues were silent as they contemplated the enormity of the Argentine madness, and awaited their bosses' assessment of what the Falklands attack meant for them and their institution. Sias then spoke. "I don't know about the rest of you guys, but I'm rooting for Argentina," he joked. But Argentina's military regime ignored back-channel efforts by other Latin countries to persuade them to call off the war.

Argentina continued to repay its foreign debt to all but its British creditors. Trouble was, loan syndication agreements stipulated that if a borrower refused to pay one country, all of the member banks would share the repayments. European banks as a group quickly stopped lending to Argentina, and the country's ability to tap global debt markets screeched to a halt.

For perhaps the first time, Argentina's reputation as a bad credit risk began to rub off on other Latin debtors. "The Falklands thing was influential," Wriston said, because "Argentina went broke financing the war. They spent like sailors." At least one Wriston pal took issue with that analysis. Alexander Haig, who as secretary of state tried to mediate the dispute, later exclaimed, "What triggered the panic on Third World debt was Third World debt!"

For troubled Mexico, the Falklands War was like a match thrown into a tank of high-octane gasoline. Weeks after Mexico devalued the peso, newly appointed finance minister Jesús Silva Herzog, in a mid-May 1982 press conference, boldly declared that because of the austerity measures triggered by the devaluation, economic growth for the year was likely to be zero, not the 6 percent the politicians were counting on. That statement, he said later, "was not favorably received by the president or the political system in Mexico." Meanwhile, after months of rumors, one of Mexico's largest private companies, Grupo Alfa, suffered staggering losses and suspended payments on $2.3 billion of loans, including $100 million from Citibank, which had thought its loans were secured. Alfa's U.S. bankers soon discovered what happened when a private company defaulted in a country with a corrupt court system. More than any single event, Alfa's collapse signaled that Mexico's private sector was also in trouble.

One of the secrets of Citibank's success in Latin America was its ability to make money in times of turmoil. With Mexico's economy in chaos, a top Citibank official flew to Mexico City in search of moneymaking opportunities. "We knew they were having a hard time in foreign exchange, the exchange rate was bad, and there was a lot of capital flight," the official said. "We saw an opportunity in distress to make a $300 million swap with the Bank of Mexico. It was a wise-ass sort of thing." In that transaction, Citibank wound up with pesos that its Mexico City office could lend at a high return.

Meanwhile, the sparring between the Mexicans and Treasury continued well into the spring when a get-acquainted meeting was scheduled with newly appointed finance minister Silva Herzog. On that occasion, Treasury officials asked again for current economic data, and Silva Herzog reportedly replied, "I'm having trouble getting it myself." Silva Herzog was making frequent undercover trips to Washington, where he advised Volcker and others that little could be done to change Mexican economic policy until after the elections. To disguise his visits, Silva Herzog flew out of Mexico City on a government plane late on Thursday afternoons, arriving in Washington after midnight for appointments the next morning. He would return to Mexico City in time for Friday evening social events, so that no one would suspect that he'd been out of the country. For a while, he kept the window open. In late April 1982, the Fed secretly lent Mexico $600 million, the first of several short-term bridge loans known as currency swaps. Volcker, meanwhile, urged Mexico to seek help from the IMF—a step that was anathema to Third World countries because the Fund typically imposed severe austerity measures—but President López Portillo kept procrastinating.

If Citibank's top management had any knowledge of what was to come, it was not reflected in president William Spencer's May 19 dinner speech to customers in Mexico City. Recalling that in 1929 Citibank became the first U.S. bank to open a branch in Mexico, Spencer reminded his audience that during the Depression Citibank had taken some "unorthodox risks to help out hard-pressed customers." Just a month before, Spencer said, Citibank had reaffirmed its "commitment to Mexico's future" by leading a $2 billion, 128-bank syndicated loan to Pemex.

By May and June, there were other portents of doom and gloom concerning Mexico that would have been apparent to the alert observer. The Mexicans were trying to find money wherever in the world they could. This time no one even pretended that this was not a shell game in which new loans were made to pay interest on the old. In Mexico's greatest hour of need, officials gave their old friends at the Bank of America the honor of leading a $2.5

billion jumbo syndication. From the outset, that transaction did not go well. According to one international lender, each of the big banks was asked to kick in at least $100 million, with the assurance that it would be able to sell down to perhaps $40 million. That proved to be optimistic, and few if any of the participants were able to unload much. According to one banker, "Anybody with a brain looked at it and said, 'That's it. This is the last thing that can be done.' Finally, some folks started looking at the numbers, which had been cooked to some extent by the Mexicans." Bankers finally began to wonder how long this could go on. According to international bankers, top executives of Bank of America spent hours on the phone leading their colleagues into the loading chute for the slaughter. In the end, according to Silva Herzog, the loan was oversubscribed. At the signing ceremony, he said, bankers expressed confidence that Mexico would be able to overcome its "temporary problems."

Investment bankers at Merrill Lynch were also pulling out all the stops to slap together a $100 million Mexican bond issue. It required an unprecedented 18.5 percent coupon to persuade investors to take the bait. "You looked at that," one banker said, "and said it's all over. If they're prepared to spend 18.5 percent for ten-year money, clearly the situation has reached the point where they are completely desperate."

As the era of LDC lending was reaching a climax, the old guard at Citicorp was getting out in the nick of time. Coincident with the retirements of Spencer and Palmer, Wriston kept the three-way succession race alive by not naming a president to replace Spencer. Instead, he appointed Reed, Theobald, and Angermueller to vice chairmen and director. Rank-and-file executives were currying favor with all three members of what they called the "vice squad"—just in case.

While Theobald and Angermueller gladly accepted their appointments, Wriston had to drag Reed into the boardroom like a naughty child. "I was totally consumed with the consumer business," Reed said later. "All this crap of board meetings and running the company was a rip-roaring pain in the ass. . . . I figured if I had to do it, I'd do it with good grace. But it was a waste of time. What was I doing sitting on the fifteenth floor when I should have been on the third floor with my people?"

Wriston empathized with the growing pains Reed experienced in this rite of passage to the pinnacle of American business. Wriston, of course, had been there himself.

Less noticed, but at least as significant as the departure of Palmer and Spencer, was the retirement of old school chief credit officer P. Henry Mueller. At his retirement dinner, Wriston presented the forty-eight-year veteran with a leather-bound edition of his *Credit Endpapers* and noted that what the book "illustrates is that Hank has that rare quality—wisdom." Mueller was also the last of the Citibank chief credit men who had taken the job expecting to retire from it. According to colleagues, Lawrence Glenn, his forty-four-year-old replacement, was more ambitious. And as events would later prove, he indeed lacked that rare quality Wriston had attributed to Mueller. Spencer and Palmer reluctantly moved in near each other in what Wriston called "Heritage Village," the suite of offices for retired senior officers.

In the spring of 1982 there was good reason for Reed not to waste his time in board meetings. His most serious crisis was a public relations fiasco in the New York branch system. With the consumer business barely profitable, Reed's managers were struggling to shave costs and pick up revenue at every opportunity. One manager in the New York branch banking division thought he had found a way when he hit on the idea of charging small depositors for using human tellers instead of ATMs. He tested the idea in a remote enclave of Long Island, and the results looked promising. But what played on Long Island bombed at Broadway and Seventy-second Street. When the story hit the press, Citibank was attacked by customers, consumer advocates, and legislators. It was a scene reminiscent of the attempt to impose the fifty-cent fee back in 1976. The Citicorp "canary system," created back then for testing potential time bombs, had failed. The canary had apparently died or flown the coop. Credit-card customers by now had accepted annual card charges without balking. But the freedom to use a teller was regarded as a constitutional right. Citibanker William Heron, who had suggested charging customers for using tellers, believed that his career was over when he was summoned to a board meeting to explain the move. For all his apparent ruthlessness, Reed invariably closed ranks with subordinates when they were taken to the woodshed. To Heron's amazement, Reed took the heat, explaining to the board that he had been aware of the plan beforehand. "I don't think he had any knowledge of it," Heron said later.

Citibank was equally opportunistic in its effort to cross state borders to pick up cheap deposits. Wriston had been trying to get into California for years, even though it meant suffering through yogurt lunches with Governor Jerry Brown. In 1982, New York State passed legislation that would permit California banks to set up shop in New York if New York banks could do the same. California banks then had little interest in reciprocating. But in early 1982 Citicorp got a lucky break.

One casualty of the interest rate deregulation urged by Wriston himself was the Fidelity Financial Corporation, parent of Fidelity Savings & Loan Association, a troubled $2.9 billion Oakland-based thrift. The Federal Savings & Loan Insurance Corporation had been looking for a California buyer for months, but couldn't find one interested in taking over Fidelity without government aid. Finally, on April 14, FSLIC was forced to seize the defunct thrift. When Citi learned Fidelity was on the block, it lunged at the opportunity. Like most of Citibank's business moves, the bid for Fidelity was ad hoc and did not result from some secret plan to acquire dying thrifts.

The California banks and thrifts were terrified by Citibank's first step onto their turf.

When the Federal Savings and Loan Insurance Corporation informed Citibank that the prize was theirs, California's thrifts flexed their political muscle and persuaded their congressional delegation to force the agency to renege on the deal and give them another chance to bid, even though FSLIC's stated policy had been to award the bank to the highest bidder. Period. And FSLIC director Brent Beesley had told the bidders to make their best bid the first time. Meanwhile, the state's youthful savings and loan commissioner, Linda Tsao Yang, who wanted state banks to take care of their own, accused FSLIC of "stacking the deck" in favor of Citibank. Now, in late June, Beesley was forced to bring the bad news to Wriston: FSLIC would have to hold a second round of bidding. In a fit of temper, Wriston expressed his disappointment at being betrayed by his own government.

In late July 1982, Citibank dispatched Charles Long, fresh from his success in South Dakota, to convince California of its good intentions. In a San Francisco press conference, Long accused the California Bankers Association of trying to deny Citibank the right to compete in the state. Meanwhile, he said, "the welcome mat is out" for California banks in Midtown Manhattan. He promised that Citibank would keep all the Fidelity branches open and not fire any employees—indeed Citi would hire more. To get Fidelity, Citibank then had to submit a bid that would cost FSLIC $143 million less than the next-highest bid, and $302 million less than FSLIC would lay out if it had to run the institution itself. And, for starters, it had to inject $80 million in new capital into the thrift. Still, many analysts said at the time that Citicorp got a bargain. Kenneth Guenther, executive director of the Independent Bankers Association, said the move "blows the structure of banking in this country apart." That, of course, was exactly what Wriston had in mind.

Still, the Californians weren't giving up. Another bidder charged that its offer should have won, and Commissioner Yang stubbornly continued to protest the acquisition even after Governor Brown suspended her for eight days and ordered her not to talk to the press. She later disobeyed a direct order not to testify at Federal Reserve Board hearings in San Francisco. Finally, in late September 1982, the Fed approved the acquisition, and Citicorp became the first U.S. bank holding company to acquire an S&L across state lines. The Fed, however, attached stringent conditions on Citicorp Savings. For example, it prohibited Citibank from linking Fidelity to other Citibank units in California that would give the thrift a competitive advantage, though it lifted those constraints less than a year later.

Wriston hustled out to San Francisco to give his new employees a history lesson and indoctrinate them into the Citicorp culture. He told officers and managers that when the 1906 earthquake hit, Citibank had sent one of its vice presidents to San Francisco on the Union Pacific Railroad, which it had financed. The officer had carried with him a suitcase full of money to help Bay Area banks "restore confidence." Seventy-six years later Wriston assured Fidelity employees that no branches would be closed and no employees laid off. Citicorp, he said, "believes in a meritocracy: providing opportunities and rewarding effort."

Even with the Fed's approval, however, Citibank's travails weren't over. Ruling on a lawsuit opposing the takeover, a federal judge described the federal seizure as a "CIA-like operation" and reversed the move. That ruling was overturned by an appeals court, and the Supreme Court in May 1983 let the appeals court decision stand. In June 1983, Citibank announced that it was merging Citicorp Savings with its California Person-to-Person offices, which made consumer and mortgage loans. As part of the deal, however, Citicorp could continue to sell credit life, accident insurance, and other insurance only in the old Person-to-Person offices. The move to San Francisco earned Wriston a spot on the cover of the November 29 issue of *Fortune,* where he was pictured in a cowboy hat next to the headline "Citicorp Goes West."

Partly because of his philosophy and partly out of institutional self-interest, Wriston had always opposed federal bailouts of thrift institutions; but he was prepared to perform that job for the government if he could keep the thrift. Of the opposition to Citibank acquiring Fidelity, he told Minneapolis business leaders that the thrifts are "lying in the intensive care ward of the hospital and worrying about the color of the blood donors who want to save them. It doesn't make any sense."

In South Dakota and Delaware, Citibank had discovered that waging a state-by-state battle for legislative change was the most effective way of leaping across geographic boundaries. Now, serendipitously, it had discovered yet another: failed thrifts. The supply of same would become abundant. Thus Citibank eliminated another prohibition against interstate banking. Indeed, Citicorp was no more astute in its appraisal of thrifts than it had been in analyzing prospective acquisitions in Africa, Iran, and Brazil. It repeated some of the same mistakes it had made in the 1970s when it acquired the pisswinkle banks in upstate New York: buying institutions with a trivial market share. Repairing the defunct thrifts and eking out a meager profit took more money and manpower than Wriston and Reed had bargained for. "We paid a lot of money for those things and didn't understand as much as we could," former Citibanker Jack Heilshorn admitted later.

The real money, however, was not made on taking in deposits and making consumer loans. One of the hidden assets of savings and loan institutions was that they alone could own the preferred stock of the quasi-government corporations that bought mortgages and other loans and converted them to securities, before the preferred stock was converted to common shares. In the early 1970s, Bill Spencer had helped set up Sallie Mae, the Student Loan Marketing Association, and arranged for Citicorp's venture capital unit to buy a stake in the new entity. Later, when chief financial officer Don Howard replaced Spencer on the Sallie Mae board, he concluded that the agency's accounting was so conservative that ultimately the shares would prove to be a good investment. At that time, only universities and financial institutions active in the student loan business could own Sallie Mae's stock. So Howard bought up shares of other institutions that were trying to get rid of them, ultimately becoming Sallie Mae's largest holder. Although Howard lost $100 million on low-yielding bonds, he turned a $300 million profit on Sallie Mae stock. To Howard, Freddie Mac (Federal Home Loan Mortgage Corporation) was the spitting image of Sallie Mae. Every S&L could own up to 25,000 shares, and when Citibank was about to take over Fidelity, its owners approached Citi to buy the relatively illiquid Freddie Mac shares in its portfolio. Convinced that Freddie Mac, like Sallie Mae, would ultimately have to go public, Howard jumped at the opportunity and arranged to purchase the maximum allowable stake. With S&Ls getting into trouble at an alarming rate, Howard knew that the federal government would have to unlock any hidden S&L assets it could find. One way to do that was to take Freddie Mac public. So every time Citibank acquired an S&L, Howard quietly scooped up as many Freddie Mac shares as he could. In 1989, the agency did go public as a hybrid public-private sector entity. Said Howard, "It was a gold mine."

As late as mid-June of 1982, Federal Reserve Board chairman Paul Volcker let the world know, in Fedspeak, that he had no intention of easing the fiercely restrictive monetary policy that had driven short-term interest rates as high as 21 percent, unleashing unprecedented hardship on every sector of the economy. A couple of weeks later, however, Volcker began to change his mind. In the first week of July, Volcker and the board became aware of a problem with a small Oklahoma bank that began to drive home the fragility of the economy and the financial system. Penn Square was a shopping center bank in Oklahoma City that had made billions of oil and gas loans, most of them to flaky operators, and then sold them to several of the nation's largest and most prestigious banking institutions, including Continental Illinois, Chase Manhattan, and Seattle-First. Its oil and gas lending czar, Bill Patterson, was notorious for making loans on cocktail napkins and for drinking beer out of cowboy boots. After Penn Square was shut down on July 5 by the Comptroller of the Currency, those big sophisticated banks were forced to post horrendous losses. Just weeks before, the Fed had ordered Chase to make good on millions in obligations it incurred through its ill-fated ties to Drysdale Government Securities. And the central bank was also having premonitions of trouble in Mexico. By then, said Don Regan, "Volcker had seen the error of his ways and realized the recovery wasn't coming about."

"Penn Square did have a great deal of influence [on monetary policy]," Regan asserted. "The Fed knew that, because of the reverberations, they had to make money easier. That helped bring the recovery about sooner and faster."

Incidentally, at about this time, the Treasury department initiated a study on the possible impact on banks of a ten-dollar drop in the price of a barrel of oil. "We laughed at the thought that prices could fall by ten dollars," said former deputy Comptroller of the Currency William Martin. "We ran the exercise but thought it was silly." Another reason for the study, Martin said, was that the U.S. government was exploring ways to undermine the Soviet Union's ability to generate foreign exchange through oil and gas production, and thereby destabilize it economically. But they concluded that such a development "would be a disaster for everybody," not just for the Soviet Union.

Wriston and his board were delighted by Chase's misfortune in getting sandbagged in two major debacles in two months—episodes that would take their toll on Chase for years to come. With Chase suffering from an institutional identity crisis, Citibank was able to gallop even farther ahead of its longtime rival. But Citibank, too, got its comeuppance. Though it narrowly managed to avoid doing business with Bill Patterson and Penn Square, it didn't escape the energy debacle altogether. When oil prices tanked, Canada's giant Dome Petroleum nearly failed because of an ambitious acquisition program financed by a Citibank-led syndicate. Citibank would also write off some $250 million of its $2 billion second mortgage and mobile home loans, mostly to blue-collar workers in the booming Sunbelt. Clouds would soon obscure the sun that had shone so kindly on those states.

———

The Treasury Department had fretted over Mexico for a year, and those concerns had intensified in the spring when Treasury secretary Donald Regan met with Jesús Silva Herzog, the finance minister, at a conference. According to Regan, Silva Herzog made comments that prompted Regan to ask him to give "some warning" if there was going to be trouble.

"Don't worry, Don. We'll give you plenty of warning," Silva Herzog replied, with his characteristic twinkle.

According to finance official Angel Gurria, he and Silva Herzog traveled to Washington in mid-1982 to inform Regan that "there was going to be a big problem. The money's getting out of the country, and the banks aren't rolling. They didn't want to listen. Don Regan had an obvious case of cognitive dissonance. You don't want to hear what they're telling you because you don't like it, so you block it out."

U.S. Treasury officials made the same complaint about the Mexicans. "Treasury and others had been preaching to the Mexicans: get your act in order—your economy is going to go down the tube," said a Regan aide. "There was a sense at Treasury and the Fed that these countries were following policies of folly and, particularly in the case of Mexico, that they weren't listening."

Still, the Treasury was unprepared for the debacle that was about to erupt. Between August 1982 and December 1984, about $20 billion in loans to Mexico were due to mature, and for the three months or so beginning August 23, Mexico was supposed to repay more than $8 billion. But the Fed had just executed a $700 million swap with Mexico—enough, so everyone thought, to keep Mexico afloat until September. For Donald Regan, the Latin American debt crisis began with a phone call from Jesús Silva Herzog on Thursday, August 12, just as Regan was about to leave Washington for the weekend. Silva Herzog asked him if he remembered their earlier conversation. Sensing that he was about to hear some very bad news, Regan replied, "Yeah, I remember it."

"Well, the time is here. I need money," Silva Herzog announced. In effect, Silva Herzog was informing Regan that Mexico was broke.

"How much do you need?" Regan asked.

"About a billion."

Payments of about $300 million, a sum that exceeded the country's liquid reserves, were coming due the following Monday. Though Mexico had tried to keep up interest payments, there was no way it could pay principal. Regan lit into Chucho as if Mexico's finance minister were a teenager who had squandered his allowance. "I told him I wanted to see him at Treasury in twelve hours." Silva Herzog was in no position to argue. Late that afternoon, he and his colleagues left for Washington. Right after hanging up the phone, Regan phoned Volcker. "Do you know what's going on?" Regan asked. Volcker did. While Silva Herzog was on the phone with Regan, the head of Mexico's central bank had called his counterpart in Washington. Over the following weekend, Volcker phoned the heads of the world's major central banks.

In the days before they left for Washington, Silva Herzog and Mexico's central bank chief had asked their colleagues to think about how they should break the bad news to their bankers. Day and night, they stewed over their dilemma, and whether they should bring in lawyers to draft a telegram. One morning Angel Gurria, the finance ministry aide, gave them a list of those who should be involved. It was not a list of bank chairmen, for the Mexicans had concluded this was not simply a banking problem. Instead, the list read: Ronald Reagan, Margaret Thatcher, Japanese prime minister Zenko Suzuki, and the heads of other major industrialized nations. Silva Herzog had reached the same conclusion—that this was a systemic problem, not merely a bank problem. After arriving in Washington, the Mexican officials made the rounds of the Treasury and the Fed, where they reviewed their maturing loans line by line.

Then it was the banks' turn to hear the bad news. It wasn't easy to reach the heads of the nation's top banks on a weekend in the dog days of August. Nearly all of them were playing golf, fishing, or relaxing at their summer residences. Wriston was on vacation in Sherman, Connecticut, and Tom Theobald was running the bank. Most of the bankers, Silva Herzog said later, "were taken by surprise." But Silva Herzog remembered that when he reached Wriston, he "didn't get a negative reaction. He understood the seriousness of the problem," and the two men began deliberating over how to "play it."

Regan recalled later that Wriston phoned him to emphasize "how really bad this thing is," and that "there are a lot of banks in deep trouble if we [don't] handle it correctly."

One of the reasons Wriston got "so deeply involved in the crisis was not just because Citi was at risk, but it was at my urging," Regan claimed years later.

Over the next several days, Don Regan, deputy Treasury secretary Tim McNamar, and the heads of the world's central banks put together a $4 billion rescue package that included a $1 billion U.S. advance payment on Mexican oil, central bank credit lines of $1.5 billion, and a $1 billion U.S. credit line for food imports.

The oil deal didn't endear Donald Regan to the Mexicans. In effect, by purchasing oil at a substantial discount off the world price, the United States had made a loan at a rate of more than 30 percent. To avoid a special appropriation, the transaction was done through the Defense Department, which accumulates oil for strategic purposes. The transaction, however, called for Mexico to sign an agreement with the IMF to get its economic house in order. Gurria was furious with Regan over the oil deal. "He said he wanted to deliver to American taxpayers the same [returns] he delivered to Merrill Lynch shareholders," Gurria said. "I don't know who he screwed at Merrill, but in this case he screwed Mexico at a time of its worst need."

Meanwhile, a committee headed by Morgan started working on ways to raise new money. They proposed a scheme, according to a participant, in which various utilities and the U.S. government would build pipelines under the Gulf of Mexico to transport Mexican natural gas to Louisiana and Texas. "Pricing policies would be changed, Congress would get involved. It would take five years," one international lender recalled. "Morgan had it all worked out." And the banks would simply make a syndicated loan secured by all the gas that was to come. That deal never got to first base.

Soon it would be clear that the problem could not be solved with public monies and complex schemes like the one Morgan had devised. The private commercial banks would have to cough up new money. And Mexico's debt, unlike Poland's, couldn't simply be swept under the rug. Volcker tapped Bank of America and Citibank to become co-heads of a fourteen-member advisory committee.

Wriston searched the top ranks of Citibank's international unit for someone to chair the Mexico advisory committee, but the likely candidates ran for cover. Careers at Citicorp were made by booking loans and earning fees, not by cleaning up messes. The man on whose shoulders the Third World debt crisis would ultimately fall was William R. Rhodes, a cigar-smoking forty-seven-year-old international banker who had been shipped off to Venezuela shortly after joining Citibank in 1957. Rhodes's credentials included passable Spanish and good relations with Gurria and Silva Herzog. A few years earlier he had worked with them on the Nicaragua negotiations, in which the Mexicans had acted as advisers to Nicaragua.

Rhodes, who was on vacation in Quebec, was summoned back to New York for a meeting with the Mexicans and their bankers. The man from Bank of America mistook Rhodes for a low-level assistant. But Bill Rhodes not only wound up at the head of the Mexico committee but, over the next decade, became the U.S. commercial bank point man on Third World debt. Rhodes was no intellectual, but he was a tireless and capable manager. "No one at any of the other banks came close," said one former Treasury official.

Nonetheless, Rhodes himself was responsible for putting on the books his fair share of the loans that he would be charged with removing. Although Citibank was somewhat more conservative than the other banks, said Latin expert Pedro-Pablo Kuczynski, the bank and Rhodes "were still pushing loans till the very end." According to Kuczynski, Rhodes visited Kuczynski, then a Peruvian cabinet minister, in Peru in late 1981 to offer him a $200 million loan, which he awarded to Manny Hanny. "He was very disappointed," said Kuczynski later. But Rhodes, more than any other single banker, was also responsible for extricating the commercial banks from their morass. As Silva Herzog remembers it, "nobody would say or do anything without talking to Wriston" or to his surrogate, William Rhodes. When Silva Herzog or Don Regan or Jacques de Larosière spoke to Rhodes, they knew they were, in effect, dealing with Wriston himself.

The Mexicans arrived in New York with no plan for dealing with their problem. They tried to assure their bankers that they had done everything they could and that they would go to the IMF. "Some people stood up and pledged money," Silva Herzog recalled, and said, " 'We trust you. We think you're going to be okay. We actually have authority to get you over this.' They thought it was a liquidity problem. It was very moving." Citibank, according to former officers, asked Silva Herzog if he had a list of all creditors. There was none. Mexico—and most of the other LDCs—didn't even know how much they owed, said Elisabeth Rabitsch, formerly of Citibank's country risk unit. Squads of technicians were hastily assembled to try to figure out how much Mexico owed and to whom. Mexico did not make matters any easier for the IMF and the banks because it was months late in supplying the IMF with its economic numbers.

When Treasury aide Tim McNamar phoned the Japanese vice minister of finance and informed him that Mexico owed Japan's banks about $24 billion, for example, the Japanese official insisted that the amount was just $10 billion, a portion of which was trade credit. "I've lost $14 billion somewhere," McNamar replied. Less than an hour later the Japanese minister called back to inform him the U.S. numbers were correct. The Japanese had omitted long-term debt with maturities over one year.

Finally, on August 20, the United States government itemized the package it hoped would ease the worst financial crisis in half a century. Besides the central bank loans, the oil prepayment, and the food import credit line, the deal called for the IMF to extend $4.5 billion and for the commercial banks to make up to $1 billion in new loans and defer $10 billion in repayments. The task now was to bring Mexico's lenders on board.

The euphemism Mexico used for the bailout was "rollover." According to Silva Herzog, Mexico came within a hairsbreadth of taking the drastic step of formally declaring a moratorium, but backed off as the frightening legal and financial implications of such a measure became clear. A formal moratorium, Silva Herzog said, would have triggered the cancellation of a $1 billion line of credit from the Commodity Credit Corporation, which Mexico relied upon to buy American corn. That in turn would have resulted in an acute shortage of cornmeal for tortillas, the staple food of the Mexican peasantry. And that would likely have incited a popular revolution that the López Portillo government would have been hard-pressed to contain.

After meeting with the bankers at the Federal Reserve Bank of New York, Silva Herzog flew home, arriving in smog-enveloped Mexico City early in the morning. He was filled with conflicting emotions. He felt, on the one hand, abject horror at having to preside over a nation that was flat broke and, on the other, a "high sense of responsibility" that he was participating in momentous decisions that would have profound implications for his own country and the rest of the world. He briefed Mexican president López Portillo on the meeting and then drove to his weekend retreat south of the city. On his arrival, he donned his peasant garb and took a seat on a bench in the zocalo—the village square—where, in the company of simple people leading simple lives, he contemplated the complex events of the last twenty-four hours.

Many bankers and financial authorities were convinced that the global banking system would go down. However Wriston and Volcker felt about each other, they now knew they had to stand firm with other financial leaders to demonstrate that this wouldn't happen. "The object of the exercise was to keep the banking system viable," Wriston said later. "You do what it takes to do that." Wriston and his colleagues had seen so many countries tank and recover that they believed they could straighten Mexico out, too. They found solace, for example, in newly rehabilitated Turkey. "One of the troubles in 1982 was that we said, 'Oh, yeah, we handled that problem in 1979 in Turkey. Now we'll do [the same] in Mexico," said senior international officer George "Jack" Clark.

Now that the world was mired in a recession and the Mexicans couldn't pay, Wriston hypocritically blamed Volcker for the debacle. From the moment in October 1979 when Volcker announced his new approach to monetary policy, Wriston had offered words of encouragement. If anything, Wriston had complained that Volcker was not fighting inflation vigorously enough and never suggested, publicly at least, that the Fed change course. Only late in the game did he hint that perhaps the Fed had come down too hard. Shortly before the Mexican crisis broke, in response to a question about whether he agreed with the Fed's critics, he told a journalist that it was "easy to criticize from the outside when you don't have the responsibility. Sure, the board could make some technical changes that I think would improve its control of the money supply. But the important point is that it should stick to its current policy of managing a slow growth in the money supply.

"What nobody knew was that Volcker was going to lock the wheels of the world," Wriston said later. "And when he threw the United States into the deepest recession since 1933, it spread to the whole world, and that's what started the, quote, 'international debt crisis.' " Moreover, Wriston said, Volcker's policy "did in fact offset the salubrious effect of tax reductions and started the myth that reducing tax rates creates a deficit." Wriston later admitted that he had "misjudged" in thinking that Volcker would reduce the "money supply increases over time, crank it down a couple of percent a year," as monetarist Milton Friedman had recommended. "Instead he just stopped it. I don't know if he could have stopped runaway inflation any other way. I happen to believe he [could have]." Wriston was more than sympathetic to Milton Friedman's neat idea of getting rid of the Fed and simply allowing the money supply to rise 3 percent per year. "Yes, I supported him [Volcker]," Wriston said, "and, yes, I supported getting rid of horrendous inflation. But I didn't understand that they could just lock up the wheels of the world. The result was that all of the export ratios that we all monitored and dissected that were in good shape on day one became lousy on day four because the exports of those countries that had come into the United States suddenly ceased."

Others saw things differently. Many of those whose economic views Wriston respected most did not share Wriston's antipathy for Volcker or his view that the problems of the Latin borrowers stemmed from U.S. policies. One former Fed officer threw the problem back in Wriston's court, saying that the crisis was triggered by the banks' refusal to continue lending fresh money. Hans Angermueller, among others at Citibank, agreed that his boss wasn't critical of Volcker until the crisis erupted. "Wriston's attitude had a tendency to change at that point in time," recalled former Fed vice chairman Fred Schultz. "He turned around and said in effect, 'These were good loans until the Fed messed it up.' "

Costanzo was one of many who believed that Volcker had saved the economy, contending that the Mexican crisis occurred because the Mexicans themselves "let their financial situation get out of control." If any American policymaker was to blame, he argued, it was William Miller, who he said pushed inflationary policies at the Fed and then at Treasury. "Miller's the bad guy, not Volcker," said Costanzo.

Still, for all the accolades that Volcker received for his role in this crisis and others, some Citibankers privately felt that Volcker regarded the world financial system as more fragile than it really was and thus was more inclined to panic than he should have been. They felt that his rush to find a solution in the early days of the Mexican crisis prevented needed reforms from being made. "He felt the world would fall apart on the weekend," said one senior Citibanker.

In the wake of the pots-and-pans episode and other attempts to circumvent banking regulations, Citibank's standing with Volcker and his colleagues had plunged so low that top-level Citicorp executives could barely get in the front door of the Fed when they showed up on official business. So Robert Carswell, the Shearman & Sterling partner who had served as a Treasury official in the Carter administration, was tapped by Citibank to introduce Bill Rhodes to Washington policymakers who would be involved in the Mexican debt negotiations. Treasury and the Fed tried to avoid dealing with Wriston, whom they regarded as stubborn and abrasive. Wriston was so argumentative, in fact, that Volcker was often forced to communicate with him through Morgan chairman Lewis Preston, who regarded Citibank as a selfish institution. Volcker, however, made light of the friction: "Where we were at cross-purposes was on the regulatory side. When the international debt crisis erupted, we had to work together. He took a responsible role. Our views coincided much more than they didn't."

The initial diagnosis of the problem by virtually all of the participants, including Silva Herzog and Wriston, proved to be seriously flawed. Wriston, said Silva Herzog, agreed with him that Mexico had a "short-term liquidity" problem, but "we were all wrong. . . . I'm pretty sure that if the diagnosis had been . . . a structural problem, the recipe [for solving it] would have been different." In contrast to Wriston, who appeared cool and collected, Hans Angermueller was shaken by the crisis, according to his colleagues. He ordered the public relations staff to distance themselves from the press.

If the news that Mexico was broke was the financial equivalent of a hurricane, then López Portillo's September 1 nationalization of Mexican private banks was an earthquake. Portillo disclosed that plan in his long-winded state of the union speech just as bankers around the world were boarding their planes for what would be a tumultuous IMF annual conference in Toronto. Citibankers in New York heard about the nationalization before their colleagues in Mexico, because advance copies of the speech were distributed to the American press. One top Citibanker phoned the bank's Mexico country head, who was watching the speech on television, to discuss the move. The man in Mexico reacted incredulously; Portillo hadn't gotten to that part yet.

Nationalization, said Bill Rhodes, really shocked the bankers. As a result, the well-regarded Mexican central bank chief, Miguel Mancera, abruptly resigned and was replaced by an economic radical. López Portillo had told Silva Herzog about his plans just the day before. When Chucho replied that he would have to resign, López Portillo persuaded him to stay. Nationalizing the banks, Silva Herzog said later, was like cutting off the left arm of someone with tuberculosis: "It didn't have anything to do with the sickness. It didn't help solve the crisis but only complicated it further, [delaying by several years the eventual solution.] The problem wasn't the ownership of banks but the wrong economic policies."

The bankers were alarmed by the radical ideas of the new central bank chief. "If Chucho [Silva Herzog] and Mancera had been in charge, we would not have had the crisis of 1982," said Jack Clark, who added that "maybe Portillo was off his rocker by then." But some bankers, notably Americans, welcomed nationalization, figuring—incorrectly—that their loans to these institutions would be safer now that they were controlled by the government. When Rhodes heard the news, he phoned Silva Herzog to tell him that it would be difficult for Citicorp to chair the Mexican committee if Citi was subject to the order. In 1938, when Mexico nationalized the oil companies,

Citibank had been the only foreign bank that stayed put. Said Silva Herzog, "We always respected that attitude toward Mexico." So Citicorp was the exception.

All of the doomsday fears now being felt in world money centers rippled into the meeting rooms of Toronto hotel rooms as thousands of central and commercial bankers, their faces drawn and subdued, spilled into the city for the IMF conference. With the financial system in a tailspin, the conviviality that had typified earlier IMF meetings was totally absent now. This was crisis management time, time to pay for all the excesses of the past decade. "You could smell the distress," said one participant. "These were not happy campers."

The bankers were bailing frantically while trying to plug up the holes in their battered financial boats. They wondered if they could keep them afloat long enough to determine the extent of the problem, including each bank's exposure, how many countries were affected, and which would be the next to fall. During the meeting, a visibly nervous Paul Volcker hauled Wriston out of the shower to discuss the mounting crisis. At Toronto, Wriston recalled, "we had 150-odd finance ministers, 50-odd central bankers, 1,000 journalists, 1,000 commercial bankers, a large supply of whiskey, and a reasonably small city, [all of which] produced an enormous head of steam driving the engine called 'the end of the world is coming.' It was the *Titanic*. We were just rearranging the deck chairs."

Meanwhile, the banks, particularly the small ones, were trying to figure out how to foist their exposure off on others. "As soon as the first trouble began, eight hundred banks flew the coup, and all that was left was a few of the largest banks," Costanzo remembered. One top officer of a major British bank was approached by his counterpart at a small European institution, who said, "I'm just in for thirty days. I presume I'm not in." The Brit replied tersely: "Oh, yes, you are." When the music stopped, it didn't matter whether a bank's exposure was short- or long-term. It was now in for the duration.

Others blamed the U.S. government. Said former Treasury official McNamar, "One of the shibboleths is that government got us into it, the government's got to get us out. That's plain bullshit."

Brazilophiles dismissed suggestions that the crisis that had enveloped Argentina and Mexico would spill over to Brazil. Brazilian minister Delfim Netto behaved as if things were hunky-dory back home, bankers said later. Antonio Gebauer, Morgan's head honcho in Latin America, passed the time at a bar in Toronto with his Latin finance friends, "moaning and groaning," as one former colleague put it. "But they thought it was a temporary problem." Colleagues said that Gebauer and his Citibank sidekick, Jerry Finneran, just couldn't believe that the game was over, that the days of flying on the Concorde to London for lunch were gone forever.

Initially, according to former Morgan chairman Lewis Preston, the IMF reacted to the Mexican crisis just as it had to the economic crises of the United Kingdom and Italy in the mid-1970s. Like the commercial banks, it viewed the crisis as a mere cash squeeze. But then, after years of maintaining its distance from the LDCs, the IMF, in the person of Jacques de Larosière, finally stepped into the fray. From now on it would be impossible for the Frenchman they called the M.D. (managing director) to stick rigidly to the IMF's charter, even if he was inclined to. From August onward, the IMF served as an intermediary, hammering out adjustment programs with the debtor nations to prepare for negotiations between the countries and the banks. As de Larosière saw it, "It was clear to me that the banks wouldn't agree to rescheduling new money agreements if they were not satisfied that the economic problems of debtors were significantly improved so that eventually there would be light at the end of the tunnel." Before the Mexican crisis, the borrowers and bankers, including Wriston, had little use for the IMF, or for de Larosière, and Wriston did not know him well. But that changed in August 1982.

In the past, said de Larosière, the LDCs had not borrowed from the IMF, in part because "they weren't ready to abide by the . . . conditions" it established. "I quickly understood that it would be impossible to treat the problem without very close collaboration between the IMF and commercial bankers."

After Mexico blew up, said one senior Citibanker, "the people at the IMF would tell you they [had been] warning the banks for years."

In Toronto, the IMF negotiated with Jesús Silva Herzog on a plan that would be tolerable to López Portillo. The IMF's proposal for Mexico to cut its deficit in half did not fit that criterion. According to Jack Guenther, Silva Herzog asked the IMF to redraft its memo to say that Mexico would cut inflation in half, which amounted to the same thing but was a more acceptable prescription. "They were afraid that Portillo would react strongly," Guenther remembered.

Meanwhile, Treasury secretary Donald Regan wanted the banks and the official agencies to solve the problem. Regan objected to proposals to boost the IMF's funding to deal with the crisis. From August through December, U.S. Treasury officials treated their neighbors to the south like spendthrift offspring, dispensing funds to Mexico on a daily basis. The United States simply didn't trust the Mexicans. They wanted to be sure the money they shipped south was used for essential imports and not simply to pay back monies owed to the banks. That, they clearly feared, would make the Mexican rescue look like a taxpayer bailout of imprudent big banks. In the words of former Chemical Bank chairman John McGillicuddy, "The U.S. government went up there [Toronto] with the message that there was no need to increase funding on the part of the IMF and World Bank. The problem was a temporary one that could be worked out in a reasonable period of time." In Toronto, bankers crossed their fingers that the system would survive until Miguel de la Madrid Hurtado, who had been elected president on July 4, replaced Portillo in December 1982. The idea was to keep the ball rolling until de la Madrid took office, when the bankers figured they could patch up the problem. Their worst fear was that Portillo might stage a coup and remain in power. Country risk expert Irving Friedman had left Citibank before Mexico neared a meltdown, but he was dismayed by the spectacle he was now witnessing from afar. "I had never really faced up to the idea that a Mexican president . . . would be as . . . negligent of the interests of his country as Portillo."

Even before the IMF conference in Toronto, Wriston had been seeking a way to pour some oil on the troubled financial waters. Working with Will Sparks, a former speechwriter for President Johnson, he drafted an Op-Ed column for the *New York Times* and ran it past his top international aides in Toronto. Several were nervous. They felt it would stir up the waters rather than calm them. They were right. In writing the piece, which ran on September 14, 1982, under the headline "Banking Against Disaster," Wriston had no idea this article would engrave in stone, as it were, the phrase that, more than any other, would be forever linked with his name: "Countries don't go bankrupt." Wriston wrote that "if a country undertakes policies that contain a formula for solving its balance-of-payments problems over time, it will find that financing for its investment projects and for any temporary balance-of-payments gap is almost always available; however, if the adjustment policies show no foreseeable long-term solution, financing will not be forthcoming, but the country does not go bankrupt."

While Wriston chafed at the reaction to the column, which he felt was based on an oversimplification of his statement and a perversion of the intent of the article, others—even within Citicorp—felt that "Countries don't go bankrupt" was a reasonable sound bite. But the pundits and wits of the international banking circuit had a field day at Wriston's expense. "Countries don't go bankrupt, but banks that lend to them do," they chortled.

One, Lord Lever, later called Wriston the "tooth fairy of world banking." And even Lee Iacocca got his revenge. In his autobiography, published several years later, he wrote that he didn't "see anybody getting tough with them for making bad loans. I'd sure like to be the workout guy who asks Citicorp to start skipping dividends and its officers to take pay cuts." That would come later.

The day after Wriston's Op-Ed piece appeared, the *Times* ran an article by *Times* economics columnist Leonard Silk. Silk quoted Wriston's nemesis, Robert Roosa, who described Wriston's article as "soporific" and "just plain cotton candy."

Some of Wriston's banking colleagues may have agreed with him, but at least one, Chase chairman Willard Butcher, said "I wish to hell they [countries] did go bankrupt." Then, he said, there would be a court of law where banks could attach a country's assets. About this time, the Fed had determined that the banks' prospects for collecting their overseas debts through legal maneuvering were virtually nil. Indeed, the notion of collecting debts or attaching collateral fell by the wayside in the scramble to keep the interest coming in and postpone indefinitely the question of collection.

Even some of Wriston's right-wing admirers were not impressed by his Op-Ed article. On September 28, his friends on the editorial page of the *Wall Street Journal* paraphrased his argument: "Sovereign nations never die, they just roll over."

"I'm truly sorry he has this LDC thing," George Moore said later. "He never talked to me about it. He knows how I felt," and "they [Citibank] knew they violated Moore's rules."

While Wriston's successor would later gripe to colleagues about having to travel to Latin America to "collect some of Walt's loans," John Reed defended his mentor's effort to put an idea into the marketplace. "He was saying to the banking community, 'Hey, you're not dealing here with a fragile entity that can disappear. These are countries of governments and people and citizens. Keep the faith. . . . There will be a mechanism that, in conjunction with the IMF, will stabilize the situation and bring them back to life.' "

Alexander Haig, the former secretary of state, said that "first the federal government encouraged recycling loans to developing countries. Then, when things got tough, the U.S. government told the banking world, 'These jerks made all the bad loans; now you carry the burden of dealing with it.' I thought that was a sad irony."

The U.S. Department of the Treasury, according to Tim McNamar, was delighted that Wriston had stated what the Treasury itself could not say publicly. "We weren't about to do anything to undermine the Wriston view that countries don't go bankrupt. It wasn't in our interest to have that debate in public. If he wanted to say that, and [if] a lot of people wanted to believe that, that meant we didn't have to say that. He was, I think, correct."

Wriston apparently had a calming effect on his fellow chairmen, including the stuffy Alfred Brittain III of Bankers Trust. Despite expressions of concern by his officers, Brittain often said that he had "talked with Walter, and he said it's okay. It's under control," according to a former Brittain colleague.

Although Wriston was unprepared for the public flogging he received in the aftermath of the *Times* Op-Ed piece, he was philosophical about it. "By beating up on me, [they] defused the atmosphere. People said I was stupid instead of saying the world would stop," he said, adding that "there was the danger of a systemic failure if the atmosphere became irrational." Even as the economies of Latin America fell apart, Wriston continued to maintain that the more serious threat to global economic stability was a Herstatt-type crisis stemming from the billions of dollars in "daylight overdrafts" that the Fed moved around the world each day.

As if the critics of Latin debt weren't enough of a headache, Wriston took more pounding in congressional hearings on the David Edwards foreign exchange affair, which couldn't have been more poorly timed. Professor Abraham Briloff of the Bernard Baruch Graduate School of Business issued a "seven-point indictment" of the Securities and Exchange Commission, charging that most of Citicorp's 9 percent increase in 1981 income before securities transactions, or about $41 million, was the product of "tenuous" accounting. Some six weeks later, on October 25, 1982, Wriston appeared before securities analysts to predict that Citicorp would achieve a 20 percent return on equity and would increase earnings at between 12 percent and 18 percent through the rest of the decade, triggering a surge in the price of Citicorp stock.

Wriston certainly got more respect in the West Wing of the White House than he did in the press, Congress, or academia. In September 1982, George Shultz replaced Haig as secretary of state and, in a White House meeting, turned over the chairmanship of the President's Economic Policy Advisory Board to his friend Walter. While Wriston never made it to Washington in a high-level official capacity, he experienced political power vicariously through his close friendship with the likes of Henry Kissinger and Shultz. According to one former Reagan administration official who was present at that board meeting, Wriston "was a little nervous" leading the group for the first time. "It was the only time I'd seen him so careful."

Wriston, according to advisory board members, used the forum to reassure Reagan on Latin debt. In several meetings, Wriston advised the president that the problem was "serious but manageable" and cautioned him against overreacting. "The system is going to survive," he assured Reagan. "Somebody's going to get hurt, but it's not the end of the world." Wriston told everyone who would listen, as he said later, that "no bank will fail because of this, but a lot will fail on good American real estate." According to former Reagan adviser Martin Anderson, Wriston's role as the biggest Third World lender actually increased rather than diminished his influence.

Even as Wriston was seeking to calm the waters, however, his cherished beliefs about banking and global economics were being buffeted by the storm. One was the actuarial base theory. In 1982 and 1983, said Hans Angermueller, that theory "essentially didn't work." Another endangered notion was the belief that lending to the private sector was safer than lending to governments. In lending to Latin America, Citibank had always encouraged loans to top private companies. According to an officer at a competing New York bank, "My impression was that they'd decide who were the best private sector names [companies] and do business with them. Chase or Bank of America would get what was left over." Angermueller later boasted that only a small fraction of Citicorp's more than $50 billion in cross-border loans had been made to sovereign governments; the vast majority had gone to public and private borrowers involved in commercial activities, including more than a third to bona fide private sector borrowers such as foreign subsidiaries of U.S. multinationals. In contrast, European and Japanese banks, and certain American banks, such as Manny Hanny, took comfort in the belief that they would be protected by lending to governments and receiving guarantees. But now all those nice distinctions made little difference. Every bank, whether its loans were to corrupt state-owned companies or to private firms, were thrown together into the same pot.

Mexico, Brazil, and Argentina, with nearly $200 billion in debt among them, were now known as the "MBA problem." If these three countries had been one giant corporation whose debt was bad, Citicorp and the rest of the U.S. banking system would have been under water. After growing at a rate of about 16 percent in 1980 and 1981, Brazilian exports sank in 1982 by 9 percent. Since the end of 1981, its short-term debt had nearly doubled to $14 billion, and it needed $3.6 billion in fresh funds to close its balance-of-payments deficit by December 1982. In the meantime it was exhausting its reserves in trying to stay afloat. By the time Brazil's central bank woke up and attempted to exert control over the country's borrowers, it was already too late. Nonetheless, Brazil maintained that it had enough money to meet its obligations. But according to published reports, U.S. ambassador to Brazil Langhorne Motley cabled the State Department on September 21 that "Japanese banks are out of the market, European banks are scared, regional U.S. banks don't want to hear about Brazil, and major U.S. banks are proceeding with extreme caution." In beating a retreat, U.S. and other Western commercial banks began yanking their trade and other short-term credits to Latin America. Traders refused to sell the debtor countries any money. One of the victims was the Banco do Brasil. Part commercial, part central bank, Banco do Brasil was the most profitable bank in the country, largely because it held the reserves of the banking system, including Citibank's cruzeiro reserves.

Regulators were worried that Mexico, Brazil, and Argentina might declare default at the same time, forcing all their loans to be classified as nonperforming. That would cause a mad rush by investors out of short-term CDs into Treasuries. "Having that happen to a dozen major international banks simultaneously would have produced an implosion of credit that would have resulted in a severe recession, and conceivably a global depression," said Tim McNamar. Treasury, however, was not especially concerned about the failure of a single big bank, even if it was Citibank. "Citibank could fail and it would spoil part of a weekend for a lot of people," McNamar said. "No big deal." And to add insult to insolvency, the Latin finance ministers weren't shy about threatening the United States with default, even if they knew it was economic suicide.

Treasury wanted to deal with the three big debtor countries one at a time. Though some bankers were saying that Mexico was the only problem, Volcker knew better. Regan knew better. And Wriston knew better.

Sitting in the Citibank dining room on an Indian summer day, the bankers were sweating from the insufficient air-conditioning as well as from an uneasy feeling that Mexico wouldn't be a quick and easy fix. "We've come to the conclusion that the standard syndicated loan may not solve the problem," Rhodes said, as one banker recalled. Overnight, reality had caught up with the bankers. Under pressure from Paul Volcker and Jacques de Larosière, Mexico announced on November 10, 1982, that it had struck an agreement with the IMF to cut its deficit and external borrowing. The enforced plans for austerity in the country was the only good news. At a November 16 meeting at the New York Fed, de Larosière stunned the bankers with the bad news. Before the IMF would contribute, the banks would have to cough up $5 billion in new money, or 7 percent of their existing exposure. And they would need the money by December 15. As part of the $8.3 billion package, the banks would roll over $1.3 billion and the U.S. and other governments would kick in $2 billion. And Volcker promised the U.S. banks that the new loans wouldn't be classified. In effect, the banks would once again extend new loans to pay interest on the old ones. Jacques de Larosière made it clear that unless the banks participated, they might end up with nothing. Volcker, who later described de Larosière as his "companion in arms," helped with the arm-twisting.

Of Mexico's five hundred or so commercial bank lenders, including 170 U.S. banks, Citicorp, with $3.27 billion outstanding, had to fork over the biggest chunk after the agreement was signed. Citibank knew it had to go along and that it had to persuade the other banks to do so as well. This, however, was no charitable exercise. Citibank would put up new money, but it insisted on stiffer rescheduling fees and rates for Mexico in return.

During that meeting at the Fed, the new activism of the IMF became clear. In a radical departure from his usual manner, de Larosière acted first and explained things later. He made it known that he would not get involved in the minutiae of negotiations between the banks and the debtors and that the IMF would not contribute until the "bulk" of the financing was assured. "That language," he stated firmly, "was extremely well understood by Mr. Wriston, in particular."

Mexico challenged the International Monetary Fund's traditional archaic modus operandi. There was nothing controversial about sending IMF missions to deadbeat countries to assess their economic condition. It was another thing, said de Larosière, to link a decision on an IMF program with refinancing by the commercial banks. Moreover, he unloaded his plan without even running it by the IMF board. "It just sort of came," de Larosière said later. "I felt if I had systematically explained the procedures . . . it would have delayed action." Country executive directors would have asked their governments for instructions and the plan would have been debated to death. "You couldn't afford that," according to de Larosière. "The world was about to crumble financially. If we hadn't patched the whole thing up very quickly"—and Wriston, he said, was a key player in that—"I don't think we would have made it."

Wriston now became a pitchman for Mexico and for cooperation. The New York City budget crisis, he felt, was just the model for solving the debt crisis. New York, he said, solved its problem through "simple Benjamin Franklin economics. It balanced its budget."

Bankers asked de Larosière during the meeting at the Fed how many banks would have to participate. "One hundred percent," he replied. But this had never been done before, the bankers complained, and it couldn't be done by December. "We're going to do it this time," the managing director said, though he later relented and agreed to 95 percent.

The Japanese, in particular, didn't exactly rush to advance their share. "They had to be prodded," said Regan aide Thomas Dawson. "We called the right person in Tokyo, and they did come up with the money."

Down the line, troubled Michigan National lost a bid to force Citicorp to refund its share of a Pemex loan. Said Dawson, "I often had a sneaking suspicion that the Fed may have rubber-hosed Michigan National on occasion" to get them to pay their share. Chemical and Manny Hanny were "scared to death," said one international banker. They were willing to give borrowers "anything they wanted." Others—like Bankers Trust, Bank of Montreal, and Citibank—took a tougher stance. The complex array of credit lines extended by U.S. banks to Mexican borrowers gave rise to gamesmanship by various banks in trying to reduce their base exposure.

The negotiations were occasionally stormy, but each side recognized that it needed the other. If a borrower became confrontational, the banks could cut their trade credits. But if the banks got their backs up, they might not get paid. With the collapse of Mexico, and with Brazil and Argentina on the brink, it was clear that the IMF was severely underfunded: it would soon be down to a paltry $26 billion in lendable funds. De Larosière determined that the IMF would need an increase of at least 50 percent—and probably 100 percent—in its quota, but he didn't get much sympathy from the secretary of the Treasury. Donald Regan, said a former top official of a multilateral institution, fought de Larosière "tooth and nail," hampering the IMF's ability to "deal effectively with the debt crisis." Regan "grudgingly" said he'd favor just 15 percent, the official recalled. "De Larosière literally put his job on the line."

The wild card that could have brought down the entire banking system was Pemex, Mexico's corrupt state-owned oil company. Bank of America had managed a $4 billion bankers' acceptance facility to the company. But no one seemed to know how much money Pemex had. What the insiders knew but didn't want anyone else to discover was that Pemex had pledged its oil as collateral many times over. That was why they held their breath when a small southern bank posed a simple question: "May we see the documents?"

According to a senior international banker who was familiar with the problem, "None of the banks in the acceptance facility were lied to, but they were never told the full extent of what was going on. That would have brought the whole thing down," including Mexico and the Bank of America. A "conscious decision" was made by those responsible to cover it all up, he said. In effect, the bankers decided simply to wait until the security arrangements expired.

Though Pemex borrowed a humongous amount of money, it didn't by itself bring down Mexico, said one Mexican finance official. There were "very many inefficiencies, corruption. It [Pemex] needed a lot of improvement," he said. The problem, however, "was macroeconomic policies." Early in the Mexican crisis, according to Jesús Silva Herzog, the finance minister, the banks wanted to guarantee the repayment of the restructured debt by tapping directly into Pemex's kitty. "I said, 'Get the hell out of here,' " Silva Herzog recalled. "They accepted that [such a move] was inconceivable."

Mexico, then, became the prototype of the rescue packages for Brazil and Argentina. The message went out to other troubled borrowers that to get a deal like Mexico's, one had to behave like Mexico. The trouble was that concessions given to one country were invariably demanded by the next one.

Though Brazil supposedly had a better idea than Mexico how much debt it had, according to international bankers, its short-term funding problems were far more threatening. When the financial crisis hit, Brazil's lenders demanded a tough IMF program. But Brazil signed and then violated countless letters of intent with the IMF, a practice that embarrassed the country for years afterward. In October 1982, central bank chief Carlos Langoni turned to his old friend Al Costanzo, now retired, to help play Dialing for Dollars. The idea was to keep Brazil afloat until December, when a comprehensive package, including IMF loans, could be signed, sealed, and delivered. The Brazilians, said a former Citibanker, didn't want to go to the IMF until after their November elections. Costanzo recalled that he phoned about ten of the world's major banks to help raise about $900 million in interim finance lines.

When Brazilian financial authorities visited New York, one of their first appointments was lunch with Morgan chairman Lewis Preston. It was then that the awful truth about Brazil's financial condition started to dawn on the bankers. At this critical meeting the Brazilians disclosed that large portions of their reserves were actually "due froms," or IOUs, from Poland and Iraq, to which they had been supplying military equipment. Morgan had thought that Brazil's reserves amounted to more than $8 billion, but the total turned out to be much less. Said Preston grimly, "We were stunned that they were headed down the Mexican path." Morgan urged the Brazilians to share this information with the other banks. "Obviously they hadn't done so," Preston said later. Citibank also believed the reserves were greater than they turned out to be. When the Citibankers finally got to see the statement of reserves, one shrieked in horror, "Oh, my God! We've got a humongous problem."

In fact, said Thomas Dawson, who visited Brazil's central bank, "the Brazilians were out of money, period." Dawson's aide actually inspected the vault and learned that Brazil had gotten rid of its gold, purportedly with the help of a New York bank. In November 1982, Brazil finally faced reality and requested a moratorium on principal payments owed to commercial banks. Still, it persisted in trying to give the impression that all Brazil needed was a one-year refinancing.

Behind the scenes, the Treasury Department and the Fed were patching together an emergency loan package consisting of a low-interest $1.2 billion in the form of a Treasury swap with Brazil's central bank, plus $600 million from U.S. banks. Curiously, President Reagan announced the package at a press briefing during his early-December visit to Brazil, taking his own cabinet by surprise. Treasury secretary Regan and secretary of state Shultz were suddenly prevailed on to call their own press briefing to explain what had happened. But the emergency loans did little if anything to mitigate the world financial system's concerns about Brazil.

The task of working out a plan to bail out Brazil fell on Brazilophiles Jerry Finneran of Citibank and Antonio Gebauer of Morgan. The choice of these two loan salesmen for such an important and delicate task proved to be a fiasco. Finneran and Gebauer, former colleagues said, didn't believe Brazil had a debt crisis and treated the episode as just another splendid opportunity to make a fortune on fees. "All they needed to do was supply some liquidity," said a former Treasury official. The deal Gebauer and Finneran pasted together included no IMF conditions. Finneran was regarded as bright and engaging and a good paperhanger. "He can do one thing at a time very well," said former Citibanker Richard Huber. "But handling a multifaceted task like restructuring the debt of Brazil was not Jerry's long suit." And Gebauer was regarded as arrogant and domineering. At an IMF briefing on Mexico, one banker recalled, an IMF official predicted expansively that Mexico's public sector deficit would be eliminated, even after devaluing the currency by half. When a banker asked how that was possible, Gebauer interrupted and "declared that this wasn't a relevant issue," the banker recalled. Later, it became clear that Gebauer was crooked as well as cocky.

Finneran and Gebauer cooked up a four-point plan that they intended to shove down the throats of their banking colleagues. Jacques de Larosière had promised that if the banks came up with $4.4 billion in new money, or 7 percent of their existing exposure, he would ask the IMF to pony up another $5.5 billion. In addition, the plan called for rolling over $4 billion in loans coming due in 1983 and maintaining $8.8 billion in trade lines and $9 billion in interbank deposits.

Unlike the Mexican rescue plan, Brazil's called for different banks to oversee different pieces. Morgan would find the new money, Citibank would work on rescheduling the existing $4 billion, Chase would handle the trade lines, and Bankers Trust would take care of the interbank lines. That, wrote Latin debt expert Pedro-Pablo Kuczynski, was one reason the plan was doomed to failure.

Finneran and Gebauer decided to concentrate on the banks with the biggest exposure. The European bankers were leery of the Morgan-Citibank alliance from the outset and demanded that every bank mired in Brazil contribute its share. Lloyds Bank in particular was afraid that Morgan and Citibank would formulate a deal for the New York bankers and impose it on the Europeans. Lloyds, for one, rejected Brazil's appeal for emergency loans unless the IMF participated and imposed tough measures. Finneran and Gebauer regarded Lloyds as a banking museum piece staffed by colonialist stuffed shirts who were more Victorian than Queen Victoria. "They [Finneran and Gebauer] were smarter than anyone else and were going to run the whole thing," said former Citibanker Richard Huber. Paraphrasing Abraham Lincoln, he said, "Sometimes you can piss off some of the people all of the time [or] all of the people some of the time, but they managed to piss off all the people all the time." Morgan and Citi sat at the pinnacle of American banking, and "no two institutions were more prepared to kick anybody in the nuts," said a senior officer at another large bank.

Even as Brazil was falling apart, Citibank's line organization in Brazil, according to former Citibankers, was still urging more lending. The Brazilian banks' cash crunch nearly caused CHIPS, the Clearing House Interbank Payments System, which Wriston had helped establish, to crash. It was the worst threat to the stability of the world's payment system since the Herstatt crisis. At one point the commercial banks, fearing that all payments in the world would stop, à la Herstatt, asked the Fed to kick Banco do Brasil out of the network. Then, on December 13, the *New York Times* reported that Banco do Brasil could repay only $175 million in obligations due the week before and had to be bailed out by the New York banks.

Battles occurred almost daily among the big banks over whether to keep the Banco do Brasil open or to shut it down for good. At one dinner party, Jerry Finneran tried to persuade Wriston crony Jim Farley to roll over Banco do Brasil once again; this time Farley refused. Finneran set out in search of Wriston and persuaded him to reverse Farley's decision. The patient was to be kept alive at least one more night. Downtown at the New York Fed, the wire transfer system had been kept open while awaiting the bankers' verdict.

Some banks had to have their arms twisted. On one occasion the Canadian Imperial Bank of Commerce refused to put up $25 million, and Morgan's Dennis Weatherstone had to be called to bring the Canadians along, according to one participant. Brazil's Carlos Langoni remembered that "the banks weren't prepared to face a situation like the debt crisis. That was clear from the way they behaved after the Mexican default." While they were preparing to lend new money, they were cutting the short-term interbank and trade lines, Langoni recalled, and Brazil—with the help of Paul Volcker— had to put heavy pressure on the banks not to back away. Meanwhile, in Brazil, said Langoni, "the natural reaction of the people was 'Why pay those banks?' "

The Fed assigned two top officials to sit in on the bank meetings. One Fed observer "was shocked at what was happening," a commercial banker recalled. "Gee, I didn't know it was that bad," the central bank official blurted out.

Even as CHIPS was coming apart, Wriston said on *Face the Nation* on December 5, 1982, that the odds that the financial system would disintegrate because of the LDC problem were "close to zero." Almost everyone else involved in the crisis would likely have placed the odds higher than that.

Jack Guenther later asserted that without its country risk apparatus Citibank would have had $8 billion in Brazil instead of the $4 billion plus it wound up with in 1982.

Each side accused the other of shortsightedness—of mistakenly viewing the problem as a short-term liquidity crisis. "Wriston wasn't fully aware of the dimensions of the crisis," in Langoni's opinion. "The Reagan administration was a disaster in dealing with the debt crisis. Regan had no vision. The United States lost the chance [to speed up] the process. They had the erroneous view," he contended, "that with some IMF assistance and bank refinancing, the problem could be resolved." But, he conceded, "you can't blame any one person for the debt crisis. We have our share of responsibility. We kept rolling over imbalances." And, he added, "you can also blame the IMF and World Bank," which, he said, visited the country every year. "They could have pointed out the trends," but on the contrary, "the IMF was very pleased that the private banks took over responsibility."

Fortunately, as the LDC crisis was going through one of its most frightening phases, things were looking brighter for other commercial banking activities, including the consumer business. With the passage in 1982 of the Garn–St Germain bill, Congress delivered rate relief to commercial banks, allowing them to compete head to head with the money funds for the first time. By December 1, money fund assets had reached $232 billion, of which about $50 billion belonged to Merrill Lynch alone. The price the nation paid, however, was a steep one: giving commercial banking powers to thrift institutions contributed to their collapse a few years later.

Wriston might not have been pleased about the new powers given to the thrifts or about the ban on insurance underwriting by bank holding companies, but gaining the authority to offer money market funds was a significant victory for big banks. For small banks and thrifts, which had generally benefited from cheap money, the legislation was bittersweet. Citibank and others had been trying for years to figure out ways around Reg Q ceilings. Citi, for example, in early September 1982, had come up with an "insured money market rate" account based on a 3½-year $5,000 minimum CD that used overdraft privileges, or "bookkeeping loans," to give holders a market rate. Under pressure from the Fed, Citibank withdrew the offering after about five weeks. In the end, the new accounts, as approved by the Depository Institutions Deregulation Committee, called for minimum balances of $2,500 and restricted depositors to six transactions a month.

In Wriston's opinion, no bank was as well managed as his own. He was worried that other banks would offer excessive rates on deposits, just as they underpriced their loans. "The critical question is how banks will price their services," he told a journalist. "Will we go the airline route, charging $99 and giving a steak dinner to fly across the country?" He said he expected banks to pay more than they should for deposits, then lower their rates after they realized they were losing money. And now with the power to offer a new money market rate account, Citibank could take on Merrill Lynch's cash management account. In the spring it announced its "Focus account," which called for a minimum balance of $10,000 and offered a preferred Visa card, discount brokerage, and other services—all for a $144 annual fee. In later hearings, Wriston praised Senator Jake Garn for the bill, which he said "finally got banks out of the 1930s and into the late 1970s."

While his colleagues at the bank worked around the clock to prop up the Banco do Brasil, Wriston took time out on Monday, December 13, to attend a benefit for New York Hospital, his favorite charity. As a trustee, Wriston used his persuasive powers to make the star-studded event one of the most successful social and fund-raising events of the season. Ann Azzara, his protocol officer, asked Wriston how much he wanted to raise.

"Half a million," Wriston replied.

"So we raise $1 million?" she asked.

"You got it."

And it worked. After being relieved of $50,000, one contributor left Wriston's office shaking his head. "That was the most I ever paid for a rubber chicken dinner," he sighed. The event brought together one of the most diverse assortments of the rich and famous ever assembled in New York. While Henry Kissinger, Happy Rockefeller, Douglas Fairbanks Jr., and William S. Paley of CBS chatted at one table, Wriston and dinner partner Raquel Welch discussed economics and politics at another. The net result was the most money that had ever been raised in one night for New York Hospital.

Several months later, Wriston's long-standing ban on front office loans was put to its toughest test when Raquel Welch phoned Wriston to say she'd like to come up and see him sometime. "Terrific," Wriston replied. At the appointed time Ms. Welch appeared at Citibank dressed in an Argentine gaucho outfit, leather boots, and colorful scarves, as if she were auditioning for a part in the Latin American financial soap opera then being played out on the fifteenth floor. "What can I do for you?" Wriston inquired. When she explained that she needed a loan to buy an apartment, the chairman surprised her with the news that the head of the bank didn't make loans. Wriston buzzed his secretary, Gerry Stover, and asked her to phone one of his real estate lenders. "He came up and saw Raquel sitting there," Wriston later recalled, and his jaw literally dropped. Wriston told his star-struck subordinate to escort the actress to an office to discuss her request.

"You go on with Raquel," Wriston instructed after advising the actress that his real estate man would make the decision. "I have nothing to do with it," he told her.

The New York Hospital soiree was probably a welcome respite for Wriston from the rigors of keeping less developed countries afloat. But only a few blocks away at the Plaza Hotel, Jerry Finneran and Antonio Gebauer were doing a song-and-dance routine with the Brazilians. Central bank chief Carlos Langoni presented the four-part plan devised by Finneran and

Gebauer. There was no way, Langoni told the gathering of bankers, that Brazil could meet its obligations for 1983, and urged that they approve the plan by December 31 to avoid actual default.

Most of the audience for this vaudeville act found the Brazilians' routine less than entertaining. Though Finneran and Gebauer constantly bickered over the details of their Brazil rescue plan, one banker said that they agreed on at least one thing: "They [Finneran and Gebauer] wanted to create a creditors committee and keep the power to themselves." That meant excluding foreign banks, among others. When someone suggested including Lloyds, which had a large exposure to Brazil, Gebauer replied, "No, they're assholes."

Well, then, how about the Japanese?

"No, they're terrible people. You can't work with them," Gebauer said.

Of those left out of the discussions, the Europeans, in particular, were furious. One international banker claimed that Finneran and Gebauer "made veiled threats" that the Fed would take to the woodshed any bank that resisted their plan. The regional U.S. banks weren't too happy, either. They had first learned about the details of the deal in the newspapers, and they refused to go along. Some of the top bankers at regional institutions were apparently unaware that they had any exposure at all to Brazil. For the smaller banks, rolling over debt wasn't so bad, but new money was. This, they felt, was nothing more than a bailout of Walter Wriston and Citibank, as one press report put it. "The U.S. banking system never coughed up its fair share of the [rescheduling]," complained a top British banker, "because the small banks refused to participate."

The Brazilian officials involved in cooking the books knew they needed to buy time. According to one banker, Morgan would have liked to write off its Latin exposure and be done with it, but it was afraid that would force Manny Hanny and Chemical to follow suit. Write-offs were postponed, said the banker, "to keep Manny Hanny and Chemical from going bust." So, not surprisingly, other banks, particularly U.S. regionals and smaller European institutions, wanted to wash their hands of the whole mess. Many of them were prepared to unload their LDC loans even at a steep discount. That later led to the emergence of a trading market for LDC debt. This development created a major dilemma, and considerable trepidation, for Wriston's Citibank and for some even more vulnerable institutions. The consequences were potentially disastrous. Wriston's long-standing belief in the free market function performed by the world's traders now collided head-on with his determined opposition to Citibank's allocating reserves and writing down troubled loans for specific countries. If the value of the loans to Brazil, Mexico, or Bolivia was now to be adjusted daily by traders, the banks would be hard-pressed to maintain the fiction that these loans should continue to be kept on the books at face value. When Citibank started trading LDC debt at a discount, some top executives tried to shut down the operation, according to traders. According to Pedro-Pablo Kuczynski, LDC loans of about $20 billion were bought and sold between 1983 and 1986. The financial collapse of Latin America would once again raise that decade-old issue of country classification. Now banks and regulators would be faced with a Hobson's choice. While logic dictated that these loans should be written down, that seemed unfair if banks were to be asked to put in new money. (Unlike the big U.S. banks, the regionals and Europeans were setting aside reserves for these loans.) This was one rare instance in which Citibank and the Fed were on the same side. Both Citibank and the Fed put pressure on the Interagency Country Exposure Review Committee, saying, in effect, "You've got to be nice to those unfortunate countries." One former top official of the Office of the Comptroller of the Currency admitted that "we realized we couldn't tell banks to reserve for Argentina, but we wanted a general increase in the level of reserves. We couldn't get away with it on a country-by-country basis." Once again the debate between the hard-liners and the soft-liners at the Comptroller's office intensified, with each faction aligning itself with its counterparts at the other bank agencies.

In mid-December, Citibank's hundreds of telex machines worked overtime cranking out term sheets on the Brazil deal and the $5 billion Mexican new money deal. With two thirty-page telexes going out to some five hundred banks, Western Union was tied up for days, according to Shearman & Sterling lawyer Robert Dineen, Wriston's brother-in-law. Whether the other banks liked it or not, Citibank had to run the show. Not only did it have the largest loan exposure on its books, but it also owned the telex machines. Just days before Christmas 1982, the banks had raised $4.3 billion for Mexico. Moreover, Citibank monopolized the microphone as the deals were put together. Though Citibank, as the agent bank, was supposed to carry out the collective decisions of the syndicate, it stood at the head of the class. Citibank may not have cheated its fellow syndicate members, but other bankers say that it scripted the negotiations in such a way that it rarely, if ever, came out behind them. In the Mexican restructuring, for example, according to one senior international banker who was involved, lease payments were excluded from the loan totals. It was no coincidence that Citibank operated the largest leasing operation in Latin America. Loans made initially to the government and then to the private sector—another big chunk of Morgan and Citibank outstandings—were also excluded, and these loans were subsequently repaid. "Where it mattered [Citibank] made damn sure their position got covered," the banker said. "There was very little you could do. You walk into the room. Their guys are holding the chalk, and you can't write on the board. They will negotiate first for Citi, then for [other] banks. If your interest coincides [with theirs], fine. If it doesn't, sorry about that."

Because of its operations in the debtor nations, Citibank had different interests in the restructuring negotiations than did other banks, particularly the regionals. Even if Citibank's cross-border business was disintegrating, its operations in Brazil remained viable. Still, said former Citibanker Peter Eccles, who ran a Citibank unit in Brazil in the early 1980s, the debt problems prompted Brazil to block Citibank from opening additional branches. And Citibank shelved plans to set up a shared Citi–Banco do Brasil ATM network.

Later, Citibank pushed the idea of including a provision for debt equity swaps in rescheduling agreements. In a debt equity swap, a bank would sell its debt at a discount in return for an equity stake in a government-owned entity or in some other local enterprise. Banks liked this device not because it gave them an investment but because it provided an exit mechanism. As more countries moved to privatize state-owned companies, debt equity swaps grew in popularity. But for a regional bank, observed a former top U.S. government official, "the last thing on your mind" was getting an equity stake in an Argentine company.

According to Silva Herzog, Citibank's position in Mexico and its status as the most important member of the advisory committee gave it an advantage in executing debt equity swaps. Later, after Wriston retired, said Silva Herzog, Citibank attempted to link the expansion of its Mexican business with the terms of the restructuring agreements. On several occasions, Silva Herzog said, Citibank officials asked the Mexicans why they "didn't give Citibank in Mexico a greater role. Those suggestions were never accepted, basically because we didn't want to negotiate that link to any exercise of restructuring or new money."

At Bankers Trust, for one, lenders close to the negotiations felt that Citibank was wheeling and dealing for its own benefit. But chairman Al Brittain's faith in Wriston was unshakable. "Walter has done more for our industry than anybody," Brittain said, according to a former colleague.

If Citibank had any problems in Latin America, one would never have known it from the 1982 year-end results; Citibank reported a 35 percent surge in earnings, the steepest of any major bank holding company. And the Third World debt crisis did little or nothing to hurt Wriston's clout, his salary, or his standing among his peers. In a Gallup poll, top businessmen rated him the most admired of all business leaders. And, in 1982, he became the first commercial banker to earn more than $1 million a year, with $1.16 million in salary and bonuses.

By early 1983, six months of haranguing had brought Angel Gurria and Bill Rhodes, Mexico, and virtually all of the world's major banks close to a finale on Mexico's first big new money deal. This was to be a historic first in the frustrating eight years of Latin debt rescheduling. The only major holdouts were the leading German banks, which balked at throwing good money after bad. Deutsche Bank, then West Germany's largest, and Dresdner Bank, in particular, were playing hardball. With nearly all of the $5 billion committed, the deal was not in danger of collapsing, but German participation was nonetheless vital to the full success of the bailout. Sitting in Rhodes's office in February 1983, Gurria and Rhodes were pulling out all the stops in an attempt to bring them around. When Wriston strolled in, Gurria was on the line to Werner Blessing, then head of Deutsche Bank's international unit, whose father had once headed the powerful Bundesbank. According to Gurria, Blessing was stonewalling, insisting that Mexico was really an American problem. In the Polish negotiations, of course, the situation was reversed: the American banks claimed at the time that Poland was mostly West Germany's problem. Among other things, Blessing was concerned about being hit up for more money later on, if the rescue didn't work. Frustrated, Gurria handed the receiver to Wriston. Appealing to long-standing banking ties and friendships, including the one he had enjoyed with Blessing's own father, Wriston implored the German banker to play ball. "I just can't believe that the Deutsche Bank is going to balk. We're almost there."

"He [Wriston] really gave Blessing a big talk, almost like a father figure, about the need for a cooperative effort," said Gurria. Wriston then handed the phone back to Gurria, saying that Blessing wanted to talk with him.

"Well, Angel, I think we would be in a position to consider it [the rescheduling plan] favorably," Blessing said humbly. "Of course, it would have to go to the board." He then sought assurance that Deutsche Bank wouldn't be pressed to put up more than its fair share if the other German banks refused to participate. Gurria wasn't authorized to make such a promise, but he did so nonetheless. "It was kind of a face-saving thing to say yes but not to concede that [Blessing's] honor had been twisted or that he had been sweet-talked by Walter Wriston," Gurria said. "He never really expected that I had such a powerful weapon by my side."

With Deutsche Bank on board, only Dresdner still needed to be brought around. Gurria could reach only one of Dresdner's relatively junior officials. Once again the rightly fearful German banker recited a litany of reasons for staying out of the deal, and once again Wriston got on the line. This time he scolded the young officer like an angry parent. "Are you telling me that I can now go out in the halls of the world and announce that we have put together the largest package of bank financing ever to get out of the debt crisis through cooperative effort, and the only bank in the world that is not cooperating is Dresdner? I'm about to say that in five minutes. I have the press out there, and that's precisely what I'm going to say."

The German banker did an about-face. "Wait, wait, wait," he pleaded.

Someone else picked up the phone. "We're in," the other German banker said.

With that, Wriston, Gurria, and Rhodes embraced each other. "You can call your [finance] minister and tell him you got a deal," Wriston told Gurria triumphantly.

By March 23, 1983, Mexico had the entire $5 billion in new money that it had asked for. Still to be signed was the deal to reschedule $20 billion in old debt. But with President Miguel de la Madrid Hurtado in office and the program in place, things were looking up for Mexico. "There was a dramatic turnaround in the first year of de la Madrid. The exchange rate went way up, and the balance of payments came around better than almost anybody would have thought," said Jack Guenther. "There was very little political reaction."

But at least one banker felt that the banks gave away the store, failing to pressure Mexico into adopting tough reforms. "You had the Mexicans by the nuts in 1983. They would do anything you wanted," he said. "That opportunity was lost when we signed the agreement."

Though the Mexican negotiations were sometimes stormy, they were not nearly as acrimonious as the effort to work out a deal for Brazil. Here too the German banks were a thorn in the side of the Americans. Even as the bankers, Brazil, and the IMF were preparing to sign the bailout package slapped together by Finneran and Gebauer, it was obvious that Brazil was teetering on the edge, and so was the deal. The cruzeiro was so inflated that on February 21, Brazil was forced to announce a 30 percent devaluation. Led by Citibank and Morgan, the big New York banks were still running a daily nip-and-tuck race to prop up the Banco do Brasil by rolling over its overnight lines. In February, Brazil's central bank chief, Carlos Langoni, personally spent three weeks at the bank's money market desk closing its books every night with the big banks.

Wriston was now running out of patience. He knew that in supporting the Banco do Brasil, the American banks were in effect paying off the short-term paper lines of the European institutions, notably the Germans. The showdown over Brazil took place at the Manhattan apartment of New York Federal Reserve Bank president Anthony Solomon. Volcker flew in from Washington on the shuttle and was joined by the chairmen of Brazil's Big Four banks: Citibank, Chase, Bankers, and Morgan. Wriston was determined to pull Citibank's short-term lines to the Banco do Brasil. Brazil, Wriston said, was paying off the German banks while the Germans were "making speeches about how imprudent we were." Wriston boldly announced that he planned to wind down Citibank's $500 million exposure by $100 million a day and be out completely in five days. Chase chairman Bill Butcher, always ready to follow the Citibank lead, announced that he backed Wriston and would follow suit. Volcker was horrified. In so many words he declared that the "world would stop," according to Wriston. "That's too bad," Wriston replied.

Morgan's taciturn chairman, Lewis Preston, as usual had little to say. "We never did know what they were going to do," said Wriston of Preston and Morgan. "Paul [Volcker] got on the late shuttle and went back [to Washington]," Wriston recalled. "We did it, and the world didn't stop. Nobody even noticed."

Just before the Brazil restructuring agreement was signed, Wriston called to his office a Citibank officer who had worked around the clock on Banco do Brasil. She feared the worst—that Brazil had declared a moratorium. Instead, when she arrived, Wriston handed her a $20,000 bonus check. That, she said later, was "why people were ready to do battle for Walt Wriston."

The deal was on shaky ground even before it was signed. Nonetheless, the Brazilians, on February 24, used some of the proceeds to throw a dinner for their bankers at the Waldorf-Astoria. The dinner was a memorable one, to put it mildly. Incredibly, even as the Brazilians were toasting their lenders, they put them on notice that they would have to postpone repayment of the loans.

Gebauer was in a foul mood. After the signing, he held a party in a suite in the Waldorf-Astoria, where he lobbed insults in Portuguese at a senior Brazilian central bank official. In full view of top bankers, the two men pushed and shoved each other. Fists flew. According to a former Morgan officer, Lew Preston was told of the incident the next morning, but laughed it off. "Everyone thought [Gebauer] would be fired," the banker said. "But Preston loved Tony. They told Gebauer to take some time off." At the same party, Farley browbeat Finneran to the point of tears.

Nonetheless, on February 25, the day after the key meeting of minds, hundreds of bankers affixed their signatures to the loan agreement drafted by Morgan and Citibank. Then, on February 28, the IMF signed off on $5 billion in loans to Brazil, launching the biggest bailout ever of a Third World country. Bankers were so preoccupied with Mexico, Brazil, and Argentina that smaller trouble spots such as Bolivia "could have been in default for a month and nobody would have known," observed former Treasury aide Thomas Dawson.

Venezuela, however, did manage to get the bankers' attention. An oil-producing country that should never have quaffed at the bankers' trough and gotten into trouble, Venezuela was now seeking to reschedule $9 billion in debt. Its economic policy skills were among the worst, and its currency, the bolivar, was grossly overvalued. The country also subsidized imports, to the point where a bottle of the best Scotch cost just two dollars. Citibank had lent about $750 million to Venezuela's private sector, and its losses there would soon throw more cold water on the already discredited notion that private sector lending was safer than lending to governments. Said former Brazil finance minister Mario Simonsen, "Venezuela should never be a debtor country because it always had a surplus."

Finally, on February 18, 1983, known as Black Friday, the country shut down its foreign exchange markets. When they reopened two weeks later, the country had devalued its currency and instituted a four-tier market. The move left many of Citibank's local customers bankrupt and also triggered huge losses for multinational customers. In a bid to enable these companies to cope with the shortfall, the country instituted a subsidy program pegged to the new rate. Instead of aggressively trying to collect from its customers, Citibank decided to play along with the system, charging off only those loans that couldn't possibly be repaid, according to internal Citibank documents. About $600 million of the exposure, not guaranteed or cash-collateralized outside the country, was subject to the system. All along, Citibank was optimistic that the portfolio would not crater entirely because of the political clout they felt the country's private sector enjoyed. Venezuela's difficulties got less publicity than those of other Latin American countries, but in percentage terms the portfolio was one of Citibank's most troubled. Beginning in January 1983, Citibank wrote down nearly half of it. But perhaps the biggest letdown in Venezuela was the stiffing Citicorp took at the hands of, incredibly, General Electric, a dramatic illustration of the fact that some of Citi's bum LDC loans were actually credits to subsidiaries of U.S. multinationals. Citibank had made a loan to a wholly owned GE unit there. Because GE had neglected to hedge its liability, it owed Citibank more dollars after devaluation. Even though Wriston was on the board of GE, the giant manufacturer declined to repay Citibank. Two top bank officers had to be dispatched to GE's Fairfield, Connecticut, headquarters to thrash out the problem. "It was awkward for Walt," one former top officer dryly remarked.

Citibank had lent in dollars to the Latin subsidiaries of companies like GE and GM without reaching a complete understanding with those companies on the parent's responsibility to repay. The parents wanted to avoid guarantees because they clouded their balance sheets. In some cases, instead of a guarantee from the U.S. parent, Citibank got only a comfort letter saying, Hans Angermueller recalled, "This is our subsidiary. We don't let subs go bankrupt. But it wasn't quite a guarantee." Angermueller derived little "comfort" from such letters. This was yet another example, Angermueller said, of the helplessness of creditors in countries that decide that they're not going to pay, or even allow local companies to pay.

By spring 1983 the impact of the debt crisis was visible in the streets of Latin American cities. In Brazil, the IMF austerity plan wasn't going over well at all. Millions of Brazilians were unemployed, sick, and destitute. In April, São Paulo workers rioted in the streets and soon the disorder spread to Rio. Back in the United States, meanwhile, many speculated that continued high interest rates resulted directly from bad loans to Latin America. Treasury secretary Donald Regan accused the banks of propping up rates, adding that "banks, faced with a lot of problem loans, both domestic and international, are doing their utmost to keep their earnings by keeping their interest rates up."

Though Wriston expected abuse from the media and from Washington over the debt crisis, he wasn't accustomed to it from his own board. He tolerated dissent, but only to a point. Seven months after Wriston had published his "Countries can't go bankrupt" Op-Ed piece in the *Times,* William Simon, still a member of the Citicorp board, issued a rejoinder that left Wriston and his directors apoplectic. In the midst of the debate on the so-called IMF bailout bill, the man whom Wriston derisively referred to as "that bond trader" published his own Op-Ed piece in the *Wall Street Journal* on April 6, 1983, under the headline "Cut Off the International Loan Lushes." Condemning the plan to increase the IMF quota of the United States, Simon wrote, "We are witnessing the tragic spectacle of the deficit-ridden rescuing the bankrupt with an outpouring of more American red ink—and the taxpayer is left holding the bag."

Just three years after raising his voice against a Chrysler bailout, Wriston was now calling for passage of the IMF quota bill, which was effectively a bailout of big banks like his. Under the plan, the IMF lending authority would be raised to $100 billion from $66 billion, including an $8.4 billion U.S. contribution. When the Reagan administration requested the increase, liberals and conservatives reacted with equal fury, calling it a big bank rescue. A typical reaction was that of Senator Charles Mathias, quoted in the *Washington Post* on February 8: "Why should I vote $10 billion to bail out Citicorp or the Chase Manhattan Bank?"

Some critics even went so far as to accuse the big banks of making the loans *knowing* the government would never permit a big bank to fail. "It's a non sequitur," Wriston said, "to say we are reckless because we expect that they will bail us out. Human motivations are basically to excel and do the best you can, not to do poorly in the hope that someone will rescue you."

After the *Washington Post* published an editorial backing the bill, Wriston's old nemesis, Nader's Public Interest Research Group, launched a counterstrike. In a letter to the *Post,* one of Nader's key people charged that new IMF loans to LDCs would be used to pay interest on loans to commercial banks, "not to develop their economies or expand their imports [U.S. exports]."

Prophetically, Bill Simon in his *Wall Street Journal* piece cited the recommendation made by former Chase chairman George Champion that banks write down their nonperforming loans and set up larger reserves against their foreign credits. Wriston and the other directors were already fuming over Simon's poor attendance record at board meetings. "He was quite an absentee, as he is on a lot of things," said Wriston later. But the *Journal* piece was the last straw. Shortly after the article appeared, Walter's naughty director was ushered out of the Citicorp boardroom.

On Third World lending, Wriston asserted that Bill Simon had "been sitting there for five years approving it all. The question arose, 'How can you out of the clear blue sky without talking to me or another director take a totally contrary view in the public press?' It didn't sell too well around the [boardroom] table," Wriston said later. Simon had quite a different view of what had happened and why, contending that he was overwhelmed with directorships and had decided to resign from all of his boards except Xerox. "Wriston was greatly disappointed to see me resign," Simon claimed in later years.

———

By spring 1983 it was obvious that the first Brazil deal was a disaster. Brazil had failed to cut its spending and had not complied with other provisions of the IMF agreement. In a matter of months much of the money had evaporated, prompting the banks to stop paying out on the line of credit. Brazil soon needed another $6.5 billion from the banks. "It became very clear that this was not the right approach," said a former Treasury official. It was also clear that the agreement was a failure largely because of Gebauer and Finneran, who loved Brazil not wisely but too well. Finneran and Gebauer had excluded foreign banks, regionals, and even Manny Hanny and Chemical from their workout meetings, causing the chairmen of the latter two institutions to complain to Volcker about their high-handed tactics. In public, Finneran and Gebauer feuded with each other; theirs was, in the words of one international banker, a "love-hate relationship."

Once again, at the end of May, top American bankers were summoned to Tony Solomon's apartment. Wriston and Preston were there, as was Chemical Bank chairman Donald Platten. Some regarded Platten as a softy on the Latins because he is said to have complained bitterly to his colleagues that the rates they were charging the Brazilians were too greedy. According to bankers familiar with the discussions at Solomon's apartment, Volcker was "brutal." He ordered the New York banks to get new leadership and cut in the foreigners. Gebauer and Finneran were off the case. Bill Rhodes was assigned to take over Brazil. By now Rhodes was becoming the autonomous global debt negotiator. Said Angel Gurria, "His advantage was he could smell very clearly the limits to a deal and what could get done. Then he'd push it. He'd push his chairman, his bank, other chairmen, and the Fed, anyone who stood in the way, because he thought that was the thing to do. I've seen him courteously contradict Wriston."

Wriston, in an October 1983 *Euromoney* interview, later tried to put the best face on things. He denied that the meeting with Volcker concerned the firing of Finneran and Gebauer. Preston, however, was more candid. Looking back at it all, he felt that "it was clear that their [Finneran and Gebauer's] handling of the original Brazil refinancing had left thick scars on the relationships with other lending institutions. Tony Gebauer had to be moved. We were calling various banks trying to get them to take a reasonable pro rata share," said Preston. "But we clearly hadn't realized how rough he [Gebauer] had been in getting them into the new money package." Kicking out Finneran and Gebauer, however, did nothing to change the outlook for Brazil. Its government and bankers were making no progress in forging an agreement with the IMF that would get new money flowing into the country again.

By now Brazil's central bank chief, Carlos Langoni, had concluded that new money to repay interest was not enough. He proposed that instead of a $6.5 billion "new money facility," Brazil be allowed to recapitalize interest. That would mean that interest due would simply be added to the principal rather than repaid. That, Langoni felt, would shift financial decision-making from the banks back to Brazil. That suggestion was anathema to the bankers, at least the Americans. According to Langoni, when he dropped this idea on the advisory committee, Rhodes said that he didn't "want Brazil to become a Nicaragua."

The only good Latin debt news was a Supreme Court ruling, twenty-three years after the fact, that Citicorp could refuse to pay on a letter of credit to a Cuban bank in order to recover the losses it sustained when Castro seized its branches.

By 1983, when Fed chairman Paul Volcker was up for reappointment, the good feelings Wriston had felt for him in the summer of 1979 had not merely cooled; they had evaporated entirely. Two years away from retirement, Wriston had seen his legacy stained by Third World debt. And the man he blamed for putting the Third World and their loans in the tank was Paul Volcker.

In Washington, a city notorious for unholy alliances, Don Regan and Wriston commiserated often about their disdain for Volcker and their desire to block his reappointment to the second most powerful job in America. Wriston and Regan didn't go on picnics together, but they were soul mates on the subjects of deregulation and Paul Volcker. Ironically, this was the same Donald Regan who viewed Wriston's Economic Policy Advisory Board as a challenge to his own power. Wriston, Regan said, bolstered his resolve in dealing with Volcker. Volcker chafed at Regan's role as head of the DIDC board, the panel set up to phase out interest-rate ceilings. "I'm a free market man. I wanted almost immediate deregulation. Again I would play that off Wriston," Regan said. Wriston's own free market views, he said, "supplemented or strengthened my own position with more confidence that I was on the right track."

Regan, of course, owed Volcker nothing. But in a massive show of support for Volcker and his policies, the U.S. financial community, with the notable exception of Wriston, lobbied White House chief of staff James Baker for his (Volcker's) reappointment. "They had convinced Jim Baker that if he didn't reappoint him [Volcker], Wall Street would collapse, and the recovery that was under way would be aborted," Regan asserted. Meanwhile, said Regan, Volcker and his allies were working Capitol Hill, telling members of Congress that it would be "bad politics" to force Volcker out. It would, said Regan, "look like the president was trying to manufacture the money supply by turning out Volcker and getting some patsy in there." In the minds of the powerful in Washington and on Wall Street, Volcker had become irreplaceable.

Wriston, Regan recalled, did not publicly and overtly campaign against Volcker, but he made his views known when asked if Volcker was irreplaceable. "No one is irreplaceable," Wriston would say.

"He [Wriston] didn't think Wall Street or Midtown Manhattan would collapse if Volcker wasn't reappointed. He thought it would be a two- or three-day thing," according to Regan.

One of those whom Regan recommended as a replacement for Volcker was, in fact, Walter Wriston, who, Regan said, would have made a "brilliant" Fed chairman. Moreover, said Regan, President Reagan "always did like Walter." Despite Third World debt, Wriston, according to one survey, ranked as the number one leader in finance—ahead of Volcker. But Regan added that he was forced to tell President Reagan that Wriston had "baggage" in the form of LDC loans. They concluded, he said, that Congress would view a Wriston appointment as akin to "letting the fox into the hen coop" and that he would encounter "rough going" in confirmation hearings. Wriston appeared to have taken himself out of the running in March when he told a financial group that because the Fed's job is to regulate U.S. banks, it wouldn't be appropriate to appoint a commercial banker to the chairmanship. "All my life I've been on the other side of the fence," he told a questioner, suggesting that any replacement for Volcker should be a regulator. Meanwhile, the *New York Times* reported on May 25, 1983, that Wriston had recommended Costanzo, of all people, to succeed Volcker!

Of the talk about Wriston replacing him as Fed chairman, Volcker later said, "I don't think I took it seriously. Proxmire would have had him on the stand for eight months." In fact, according to a former Reagan administration Treasury official, some wanted the president to appoint Don Regan, just to get him out of the administration. In the end, President Reagan grudgingly reappointed Volcker. "In 1983, we were still looking at the trees," said Don Regan. "We didn't see the woods. We didn't know we were well out of trouble. . . . The mystique of Volcker had really more to do with it [his reappointment] than anything else."

Not the least of Wriston's gripes was that the bank regulators, led by Volcker, were demanding that seventeen of the nation's largest banks meet a capital-to-assets ratio of no less than 5 percent. Though Citibank and several other big banks met the requirement, Wriston objected to such rigid standards. This, among other things, was the quid pro quo for the so-called IMF bailout legislation, which gave Congress a powerful lever to influence how loans would be made in the United States. It was time once again for Wriston to update his speeches on capital adequacy. At the same time that Wriston was filling up his portfolio with Third World debt, he was arguing that his bank didn't need capital. Bad LDC loans and little capital, said a former colleague dryly, made for "an unfortunate combination."

Capital was a more sensitive issue for American banks than it was for the Japanese or Germans. "The Germans managed their earnings and reserved the hell out of stuff," said Thomas Dawson.

Congress also wanted banks to keep reserves against LDC loans. Wriston responded to that suggestion in March in his usual acerbic style: "We've got more amateur loan officers down there than I've ever known." Then Congress sidestepped the issue of mandating reserves against specific countries by demanding that banks boost their capital. So while Wriston may once again have deflected the pressure for country classification, he didn't get off scot-free. The IMF funding bill gave rise to a system, to be implemented several years later, of capital requirements based on the riskiness of bank assets. For example, loans to blue-chip industrial nations would be viewed on a par with Treasury securities. As one top Citibanker put it, the legislation, passed in November 1983, led to the "hardening" of the Interagency Country Exposure Review Committee into a unit that mandated reserves rather than allowing the banks to determine for themselves what the reserves should be.

Later, when asked by *Euromoney* if he was pleased that Volcker was reappointed, Wriston disingenuously replied, "He's made an enormous contribution at a very difficult time."

Had Wriston become Fed chairman, the appointment would have come at an awkward moment. The prolonged agony of the David Edwards affair, which had grated on Wriston for six years, was now heading for a climax. Wriston and his colleagues might have thought they had put the episode largely behind them in December 1981, when they persuaded the SEC to discard a stinging report that asserted, among other things, that between 1973 and 1978 Citibank had shifted about $46 million in trading profits from high-tax to low-tax jurisdictions. Contending that the amounts were too small and the charges inadequately proven, the SEC decided not to prosecute. "I certainly couldn't take exception to that," Wriston said, insisting that "there wasn't a case." The Comptroller of the Currency also decided against any action. Some would hint later, however, that this was one of Wriston's rewards for being a Reagan administration insider.

The SEC's staff report implied that Wriston had told traders that Citibank's management understood there were legal risks in foreign exchange trading. Hans Angermueller asserted that the report "intentionally misrepresents" Wriston's actions, that Wriston was referring to economic risks, not legal risks. The report was also critical of Shearman & Sterling's internal investigation, calling it "incomplete, false, and misleading." Citibank's strategy was to question the competence and standing of the SEC staff investigators. "The staff guy made it his agenda," said lawyer John Hoffman. "A fellow down there [at the SEC] wrote a wild story about it," Wriston said.

After the SEC decided not to act on its own report, one staff member turned it over to Representative John Dingell's House Commerce Committee, well known for leaking documents to reporters. Nothing got under Wriston's skin more than press coverage of the David Edwards affair. He and his colleagues thought they had taken their publicity hits for Edwards years ago and that the matter had become yesterday's news. But that was not to be. On February 18, 1982, the story erupted once again in the *New York Times*. The article, by investigative reporter Jeff Gerth, carried Wriston's picture with a caption stating that SEC staff had charged that he authorized "disguised foreign exchange transactions." Angermueller read the article on the train that morning. Not surprisingly, both he and Wriston homed in on the same paragraph.

"The *Times* wrote on the front page that I was a crook," Wriston said later. Wriston's public relations advisers had assured him that Gerth, who had a reputation as hell on wheels, wasn't really all that bad. They advised Wriston to meet with him. Angermueller, however, had counseled against it. Wriston shoved the *New York Times* at one of his flacks. "Nice guy," he growled. His counterattack was an angry letter to the *Times*. In it he wrote that "Joseph McCarthy in his 'best days' could not improve on your caption," which, he said, "quoted some unnamed source," and he condemned the *Times* for implying that he had approved illegal transactions. In fact, the caption cited SEC staff. Then, in a March 7, 1982, editorial, the *Washington Post* joined in the fight, sharply criticizing SEC chairman John Shad, who, it said, "has some strange ideas about protecting investors. His words and actions so far suggest he's more interested in protecting corporate officers." Although Wriston had enjoyed Citibank's annual press dinner in years past, what with the cigars, drinks, easy banter and ribbing, he was becoming ever more cynical about the media.

Fortune, meanwhile, was seeking to get its licks in, too. According to a former Citibanker, it approached the bank about doing a piece on how top management responds to crises. In its wisdom, Citibank decided it shouldn't preempt Congressman Dingell, and told the magazine it would cooperate after the hearings. *Fortune* went ahead and wrote the story without Wriston's cooperation. *Fortune,* Wriston charged, paid Edwards's way to France, first class, "took pictures of him, and wrote this nonsensical story." After the article appeared on January 10, 1983, Wriston severed all ties to *Fortune.* He ordered all Citibank advertising canceled and for years refused to have anything to do with the magazine's editorial staff.

Dingell's committee had raked Citicorp—minus Wriston—over the coals at the September 1982 congressional hearings. Now, on June 28, 1983, it was time for the heavy hitters—Wriston, Citibank director Darwin Smith, Angermueller, and Hoffman—to face the bright lights. To advise them, Citibank hired the top guns, including veteran Washington lawyer and erstwhile presidential adviser Lloyd Cutler. In the hearings, Dingell said that Citicorp's Nassau office "has been described by observers as little more than a fellow in a bathing suit on the beach accompanied by his telex machine." Wriston was indignant. The Bahamian operation was, in fact, a 250-employee branch office with its own four-story building. And he flatly denied reports that Citicorp had "parked" $46 million in foreign exchange profits in low-tax countries during the 1970s. While insisting that Citicorp's own systems picked up the few "questionable" foreign exchange transactions, Wriston downplayed even those incidents by pointing out that foreign exchange regulations and rates during that period "were more volatile than at any time since World War II." Only twenty-six out of millions of transactions from 1973 to 1978 "were the basis for fines or penalties," Wriston said.

Citibank disclosed that, after all the investigations and furor, Citibank had agreed to fines totaling just $1.2 million in two countries, France and Switzerland, to settle alleged violations of local forex or tax regulations and had entered into tax settlements amounting to about $10 million in four countries, said to include Germany, concerning forex transactions. Wriston said that the Swiss National Bank, in a January 3, 1980, letter, informed Citibank that it (the Swiss Bank) had "terminated its investigations."

Wriston was usually very controlled and difficult to provoke. But that changed when Congressman John Markey stated, "I have heard this matter referred to as if it sends a very distinct message to the Citicorp employees, that the message is the message of the Mafia, and that the message which applies here is the code of silence: shut up or you are out." Wriston was furious and didn't hesitate to show it. "I resent that you used the word Mafia in connection with Citicorp. In the first place, as I said to you to begin with, this person [David Edwards] said that his boss was a crook; he [the boss] was investigated and no charges were ever sustained to this day." Dingell, appropriately, figured this was a good time to declare a time-out.

All considered, the Citibankers felt that they had emerged from the gauntlet in reasonably good condition. While they had taken some licks from Congressman Al Gore, among others, John Dingell, to their surprise, had conducted a reasonably sedate hearing. At the end, Wriston approached Dingell to shake hands and thank him for the "orderly way" he had run the meeting, as Angermueller recalled.

After the hearing, Wriston called his daughter Cassy at home in Darien, Connecticut. His son-in-law picked up the phone. "So, Walter," he chortled, "are you calling from jail?"

On the return flight to New York, Wriston was in an upbeat mood. The hearings had given him a chance to set the record straight, he felt, and the six-year Edwards nightmare was finally over—more or less. In fact, during the hearings, the participants had felt a not unpleasant surge of adrenaline and, as John Hoffman admitted later, "we were sort of sorry it was over."

Later, Wriston threw a dinner for thirty-five officers and employees who had helped prepare for the hearings. There, Wriston handed out the accolades, describing the contribution each one had made to the effort. "We might have done it better, but at the end of the day I don't know of any corporate investigation that was done more thoroughly, that had every single regulatory body in the world sign off," Wriston asserted.

By the fall of 1983, Wriston was already declaring victory over the Mexican crisis. In an elaborate ceremony at Lincoln Center's New York State Theater, the banks and Mexico signed the agreement to reschedule $20 billion in old debt. Later, in an October 1983 interview with *Euromoney,* Wriston claimed that, in Mexico, "we did it right." The country's balance of payments, he noted, was in surplus and Mexico was pumping 2.8 million barrels of oil a day. But that country's troubles and the Third World debt crisis in general were far from over, the naive pronouncements of Wriston and *Fortune* magazine notwithstanding. All Citicorp could hope for was to find a way to overcome each crisis as it erupted, while buying time to bolster reserves and fight its way out of the quagmire. Even as toasts were being exchanged with the Mexicans, Argentina and Brazil were demonstrating just how shaky and unreliable they would be for years to come.

In mid-August, Argentina received a pledge of a third $300 million installment on a $1.1 billion loan from the IMF and shortly thereafter signed a five-year $1.5 billion loan agreement with some three hundred banks. Less than a month later, Argentina was pleading for a delay on the repayment of

$300 million in short-term loans that banks had extended earlier that year.

But Brazil was now the sick man of the world financial community. There, angry, hungry mobs looted supermarkets. Workers struck in protest of IMF austerity measures. Brazilians were losing all hope that their lives would ever improve and were talking seriously about debt repudiation. The country was now more than two months behind in its interest payments, and with the end of the quarter approaching, national banks, including Citibank, feared that they would have to classify their loans as "nonperforming." By June 30, Citicorp's nonperforming overseas loans had soared to $1.7 billion from $704 million the year before. In August, Bill Rhodes and other top bankers journeyed to Brazil to warn monetary officials to get their house in order.

Even central bank chief Carlos Langoni was disgusted, and in September 1983 handed in his resignation. Years later he would say only that he resigned because the government was "not able to commit itself to a serious program of adjustment." At least one other observer, however, contended that Langoni really quit because he opposed the IMF's austerity measures.

By the time the moneymen were due to gather in Washington for the annual IMF meeting, it was clear that the Brazilian package wasn't going to fly even if the banks kicked in $6.5 billion. Things came to a head in the twelfth-floor boardroom of the IMF where managing director Jacques de Larosière had convened Wriston and other top bankers. There, Volcker and de Larosière, comrades-in-arms, made it clear once again that the banks would have to pony up. The bankers, said de Larosière, thought the amounts were too large and that Brazil's balance-of-payments needs had not been well assessed. De Larosière shrugged it off later, saying, "The usual thing."

Standing at the lectern, de Larosière told the bankers, as Wriston recalled later, "It's your problem."

Wriston was the first to speak up: "Let us discuss this among ourselves."

With that, de Larosière, Volcker, and other officials left the room, allowing the bankers to caucus. For a brief moment, de Larosière's departure left a physical and spiritual void in the chairman's seat. It was up to Wriston to fill it. "I sat in the chair because nobody else was going to sit there. We had to have some leadership," Wriston recalled.

"What are we going to do about this?" Wriston asked his colleagues. Answering his own question, he said, "We're going to have to raise the money." By this time, bankers viewed Brazil and its Latin neighbors as a financial black hole. They had thought they were making the supreme sacrifice in agreeing to the earlier figure, and now they were being shaken down for even more. Manny Hanny's John McGillicuddy, whose institution was the most vulnerable to the troubles of the Latin countries, helped Wriston break the deadlock. "We've got to do it," he said regretfully.

Manny Hanny was in. One by one, the remaining bankers declared reluctantly that they were in as well. Forty minutes after John McGillicuddy stepped up, the syndicate was in place for the biggest bank loan in history, exceeding some expectations by about $1 billion. It was part of an $11.8 billion package that also included export credits and deferral of Brazil's debt to other governments. About an hour later, de Larosière and Volcker were invited back. They couldn't have been more pleased. Though some five hundred other banks would have to be persuaded to cough up their share, the logjam was broken—for the moment. In November the IMF approved the agreement.

While Wriston would never admit that cross-border lending was a flawed concept, Hans Angermueller was more contrite. He pointed out that less than a year after Mexico blew, one-third of the company's assets were in cross-border loans. In Angermueller's words, "There is no question that in our drive for the 'reward' end of the spectrum we may have lost sight of the 'risk' end."

Wriston, however, refused to bend. "The media has been watching the wrong rathole" in its concern about the possible impact of Third World lending on the banking industry, he argued at the time. Argentina, he claimed, "isn't the real problem. It's people who speak English. They live in Texas and are in the oil business."

And as Wriston's successor later discovered, they also lived in New York and were in the real estate business.

24

SUCCESSION, SUCCESSION

*F*or a CEO, no decision is more critical than the choice of a successor. And few corporate succession dramas attracted more attention and caused more speculation than the one at Citicorp, where three very different personalities vied for the most coveted job in American banking.

Hans Angermueller, the brilliant Harvard-educated lawyer and master strategist, seemed the wisest of the three, a man with "an anchor to windward," as director Frank Thomas put it. Angermueller, however, viewed himself as a stalking-horse for the two "serious" candidates, and said later that he never wanted the job. He never asked Wriston to count him out, though, because that "didn't seem the smart, diplomatic thing to do."

While there was clearly a John Reed camp and a Tom Theobald camp, the Angermueller faction was not so visible. Politically speaking, he was something of a third party candidate. Still, a lot of people, including several board members, thought Angermueller would make a good compromise, a low-risk alternative who would not get Citicorp into trouble. And if he became chairman, Citicorp would likely hold on to Reed and Theobald, who could gain more exposure to different areas of the bank by swapping jobs. Upon Angermueller's retirement in 1989, one of the two could then inherit his job.

Tom Theobald's backers, meanwhile, pointed out correctly that John Reed had never made a loan in his life. "People did object to John on the basis that he has never been a banker and never made a loan," according to one board member.

Reed knew computers and assembly lines, whereas Theobald understood money and markets. In the opinion of his detractors, Reed's grasp of financial markets was meager for a man who would head up an institution that was one of the world's major market players. As consumer czar, Reed had virtually stayed out of the money markets, as reflected in the fact that the consumer business didn't even have its own treasury operation. In building a business over the long term, Reed was a big-time gambler. But his critics felt that he had no stomach for investment banking or trading. And his human relations skills left much to be desired.

Reed's supporters, on the other hand, asserted that Theobald had never spent any time in consumer banking, which by 1983 accounted for an increasing portion of the bank's profits. While Theobald was regarded as very bright, his mind, in the opinion of one colleague, had "a pedestrian quality to it."

Theobald, said former tech whiz Robert White, was not a risk-taker. "He was an investor. . . . It would have been a repudiation of the whole Wriston period if he had put Tom in in place of John. Tom is a good corporate banker but doesn't have imagination or flair. It wasn't like he had two fantastic choices and it didn't make a lot of difference. He had two very good choices and it made an entire difference."

Midway through the race, Wriston recalled, a "very famous" former government official dropped in to visit. After referring to the destructive 1970s succession contest at First Chicago, the visitor predicted that the same thing would occur at Citicorp. He told Wriston that "the only way to solve this problem is to bring in somebody from the outside—like me."

"Well, thank you very much," Wriston replied, but "these folks all work together pretty well. [Citicorp is] a big outfit, and we think it may just work."

"You're making a terrible mistake," the would-be chairman said. "The whole bank will self-destruct." Ironically, time would prove him close to the mark.

Even some of Wriston's fellow CEOs were critical of Wriston's handling of his succession. Edmund T. Pratt Jr., chairman of Pfizer Inc., which would later elect Wriston to its board, said that "I wouldn't do it [the way Wriston did], but ultimately they got a good leader."

Above all, "it pitted friend against friend," lamented one former Citibanker.

Earlier in the year, at the annual meeting, corporate gadfly Evelyn Y. Davis stood up and proclaimed that she had identified Wriston's successor from the seating arrangement. Angermueller, she noted, was seated nearest to Wriston and directly behind the Citicorp logo. "That would be a leap of logic, even for you," Wriston replied.

In 1983, Wriston began preparing his directors for the succession exercise. He had talked with them about the strengths and weaknesses of each candidate and had provided other backup information. His intent was to create a consensus so that by the time he formally indicated his choice everyone would be in harmony. If Wriston's choice was not totally obvious to the directors by September 1983, it certainly was by the time they journeyed to California for a round of meetings, dinners, and ceremonies, including the groundbreaking for Citicorp Center, a forty-two-story tower in downtown Los Angeles. Wriston loved these occasions, in part because he could show off his skill at operating heavy equipment. Perched atop a bulldozer, Wriston crowed that "me and Dar [Darwin E. Smith, chairman and CEO of Kimberly-Clark Corporation] are the only guys who know how to run a bulldozer."

Then it was on to San Francisco to the Napa Valley wine country, where Wriston had decided to announce his preference to his board. Meeting with three or four directors at a time, from early in the morning until late at night over a two-day period, Wriston told each group in turn, "Now that the old crock is leaving, we've got to get in the new guy. We're lucky that we've got five or six people who could run the institution very well, and now we're going to have a discussion about who it should be." Wriston listened patiently to the directors' views, and they were by no means unanimous. Though the personnel committee backed John Reed, who was Wriston's choice, Angermueller and Theobald had their supporters as well. And, according to director Robert Hatfield, some directors felt Wriston should be persuaded to remain as chairman for another couple of years.

Wriston's goal by the time the decision had to be announced was for the board to be unanimously behind it. But while directors may harbor their own opinions and their own doubts, it is a rare board that will, in the end, attempt to deny the chief executive his choice. Director J. Peter Grace probably voiced the prevailing view. When he met with Wriston he quoted Will Rogers: "Everybody's stupid except on different subjects. On this subject, I'm stupid as hell. Whatever you want, you get."

There was no question in the mind of Walt Wriston that John Reed, by virtue of his youth, vision, and proven record of building a business, was the one best equipped to lead Citibank into the next millennium.

Some Citibankers were convinced that Reed had made such an impression immediately after his arrival at Citibank in 1965 that Wriston had him pegged then and there as his successor. Nonsense, said Wriston. "The world doesn't work that way. The world works incrementally. It's one piece of evidence pasted on another."

Anyone who understood Wriston knew that for him to have selected anyone but Reed would have been a repudiation of everything he believed in. Neither Hans Angermueller, the loyal counselor, nor Tom Theobald, the consummate customer man, had ever built a business from scratch or put his job on the line. For years Wriston had been singing the praises of entrepreneurs and pioneers. Wriston and Reed were spiritual and intellectual soul mates. Said former corporate secretary, Carl Desch, Reed "was cast a little like Walter because of his risk-taking ability." Or, as another former Citibanker put it, "Walt saw Reed as . . . someone who would perpetuate the values he believed in."

Much of what Citicorp did could be predicted, or anticipated, by watching what GE did, and GE, with Wriston's wholehearted support, had just picked fortyish Jack Welch as chairman. In fact, former GE chairman Reginald Jones later admitted that the choice of Welch was not a foregone conclusion and that many board members had opposed it. Wriston, he said, was a leader in shoring up support for Jones's successor.

Fortunately for Reed, his consumer business had begun to show signs of life by 1982, less because the business was being managed better than because the gross yield on credit-card balances was now 19.8 percent and most other interest rates had dropped dramatically. After the phenomenal losses caused by deadbeat customers and the long-term pool, *any* improvement would have been very noticeable. "Everybody saw it as incredibly good timing" for Reed, said a former Citibanker. To some cynics it appeared that Wriston delayed his decision until the consumer bank had turned around so that he could justify choosing the man he wanted in the first place.

In an earlier speech, Wriston had said that the individual bank completed the "profit turnaround" in 1983. And he predicted that consumer would be the "swing factor" in the expected earnings increase that year. It did not matter to Wriston that by the time he had to make his recommendation the consumer business was not an overwhelming moneymaker. After all, Wriston had been head of the overseas division for more than seven years when he was anointed, and the real bottom-line profits were minuscule. But what counted most to Wriston, as it did to Stillman Rockefeller, was that the man they would tap had succeeded in building an organization, if not profits. The profits, it was hoped, would soon follow. "It is fair to say that if the consumer business hadn't been looking up at the point where I had to make a recommendation, things might have been different," Wriston said later. "You can't write history in the subjunctive; it did look up. Obviously, if the thing had been a natural disaster you would have had a different set of facts and therefore a different conclusion, but it turned out it did work."

Having cast the die, Wriston wanted to be sure that it remained a secret until he was ready to retire. "One reason it did," Wriston quipped, "is that we didn't have any investment bankers on the board." *That* potential problem had been avoided when Bill Simon was prevailed upon to leave.

Wriston kept the news from even his closest friends, although he chatted with them about the pros and cons of one over the other. Occasionally, in the company of Wriston's extended family, Kathy would blurt out something she liked or disliked about one or another, prompting Wriston to scowl at her from across the table. Said Wriston's friend Barrett Emmerts, "It was a taboo subject."

Ironically, in some respects the succession race fostered a paralyzing caution in the contenders that was at odds with the risk-taking culture Wriston had tried to create. Over the next several months, as the contest moved down to the wire, Reed, for one, made sure he didn't stray too far from the ranch, for fear of finding himself out of the fifteenth-floor information loop. When Reed toured the branches, his secretary, like the mother of a teenager on curfew, made it clear to his subordinates that they had to get him back to his office by three o'clock.

The Reed camp was also worried, Citibankers said later, that a scandal involving certain troubled loans made by his private banking unit would derail his chances. According to the *Wall Street Journal*, Federal Aviation Administration chief J. Lynn Helms and a business partner had borrowed nearly

$30 million, including $21.5 million from Citicorp, to engage in some questionable dealings. After Helms's activities were revealed in the *Journal,* Helms was forced to resign his post and subsequently filed for bankruptcy. The loan losses may have cost Reed some sleep, but they were not enough to cost him the top job in American banking.

Though he now had less than a year to go before handing the keys to the vault to Reed, Wriston was not going to be a lame-duck chairman. While trying to keep the lid on the Third World debt crisis, Wriston stirred up the other pots as much in these final months as he had since he became chairman. Chaotically, serendipitously, Citibank added an array of new businesses and expanded its geographic reach and powers. Few banking companies were more adept at packaging a concept into something that grabbed people's attention. Before the year was out, Wriston's vision of Citicorp coalesced into what he called his "Five *I*" strategy, which he unveiled in his March 1984 swan song to analysts. To Citibank's three existing *I*'s—the individual bank, the institutional bank, and the investment bank—he now added two more: insurance and information. Wriston expected this Five *I*'s strategy to become an enduring legacy. But that was not to be.

Besides leaving Citibank with a visionary successor and a new strategy, Wriston had hoped to get Citicorp's stock up to fifty dollars a share before he left, and he wanted to turn in $1 billion in earnings for his final year, colleagues said later. As 1984 approached, Wriston loyalists were determined to "get one for the Gipper," as former Citibank lawyer Chris York put it. "Walt didn't push, but the troops did," he said. In 1984, "we turned over every rock to [deliver] $1 billion." They fell $110 million short.

In the talk to analysts the following March, Wriston alluded to that goal when he said, "We envisage a world of 35 million Citicorp customers producing earnings of thirty dollars per customer," adding that "we can now see a time in which it will become a billion-dollar business." As it turned out, the only barrier blocking that goal was Wriston's handpicked successor. Since Wriston had chosen the man who built the individual bank to succeed him, it was no surprise that this *I* was his top priority. He wanted to make Citibank a national consumer bank any way he could. If Citibank had had its druthers, Angermueller later recalled, it would have liked to acquire First Interstate Bancorp, a Los Angeles–based bank holding company that, through quirks in the banking law, was "grandfathered" to operate in a number of western states. One attraction of those states, Angermueller said, was that they were rapidly growing and populated with elderly people, who tend to maintain low-interest deposits with banks. But Citicorp was not that lucky.

The next-best thing was to acquire a large regional bank in a fast-growing state. But by now the regional banks had discovered a new legal weapon to protect themselves from big bad Citicorp. In crossing state lines, Citicorp was forced to take a multipronged approach, not unlike the strategy Wriston had employed in the overseas division to place pins on the map. While trying to bust through federal and state barriers, Citicorp was poised to grab every opportunity that came its way. And where it couldn't get into a new, attractive market with bricks and mortar, it tried to do so with cash machines or plastic. Angermueller's job was to figure out how to get in, while consumer executive Rick Braddock's assignment was to pick the targets.

By the fall of 1983, Citibank was on a roll, leaping over state borders in a single bound. To its own amazement, Citibank had ensconced itself in South Dakota, Delaware, and California and had announced plans to set up a full-service bank in Maine, the first state to roll out the welcome mat completely to out-of-state banks. "If five years ago I'd told you that we would own a $3 billion savings and loan in California, have a bank in Delaware and Maine and South Dakota, own Diners Club and Carte Blanche, and have offices in forty states, you would have said, 'I don't know what he's smoking,' " Wriston told a journalist at the time.

The arrangement in Maine was ideal. In early 1983, Citibank announced that it would open a bank to conduct full-service banking in Maine, which, like New York, had a reciprocal interstate banking law on the books. Trouble was, with a small population, there wasn't all that much business to conduct. "I profoundly hope that 'as Maine goes, so goes the nation,' " Hans Angermueller told the *New York Times.* But Wriston's aggressive interstate strategy earned him enemies in virtually every state. When a Paragould, Arkansas, banker, Marlin Jackson, chairman of Security Bank, spotted an ad in his local paper offering high yields on deposits at Citicorp's South Dakota bank, he fired off a letter to Wriston inviting him to "choose his weapons and meet me under the oaks at dawn." To combat Citicorp and its brethren, Jackson formed the Coalition for Regional Banking, whose only known member was Jackson himself.

Wriston may have chuckled at the antics of the country banker, but he had no interest in opening branches in Arkansas. He was not, however, amused by Jackson's counterparts in more desirable spots like Massachusetts, Connecticut, and Florida. Now, more than ever, the debate over how interstate banking should proceed sharply divided the American banking industry. The regional banks wanted time to grow so they wouldn't be gobbled up by money centers. Stockholders of Florida institutions might have been delighted with top dollar offers from New York institutions, but senior managers were not about to lie down and be replaced by friends and colleagues of Walter Wriston. Their key to job security was a device called the regional compact. Under this arrangement, only banks inside these regions could acquire each other. For example, under the New England compact, banks in Massachusetts and Rhode Island could purchase banks in Connecticut, but New York or New Jersey banks couldn't buy banks in any of those states.

In the wake of a series of New England mergers under the compact, Wriston decided to try to correct this perceived inequity. Wriston had never shied away from litigation. "He got exercised at the idea that a group of states got together and said everybody inside is equal but anybody outside is unequal. Those are the kinds of things he gets excited about," said Anger-mueller.

Citicorp's legal eagles realized that the only way to stop regional compacts was to challenge them as unconstitutional. Charging that the laws fostered "divisive regionalism," Citicorp in December filed suit to block them. But Citicorp lost at the district court and appeals court levels. For once, the nation's largest and smallest banks were on the same team. Citicorp archenemy Kenneth Guenther, executive director of the Independent Bankers Association, said that the court decisions create "a quasi-monopolistic situation for larger regional banks by protecting them from money center banks." New York State and Chase joined with Citi to take the case to the next and final step, the Supreme Court. The justices' decision, which was handed down after Wriston retired, would shape the banking industry for years.

Florida, of course, was another natural destination. Here too the regional compact movement had caught on. Citibank was pushing for legislation that would allow it to establish de novo full-service banking facilities, on the theory that this approach would be less threatening to big Florida banking companies. This move, however, prompted Florida bankers to work with officials in neighboring states, including Georgia and North Carolina, to establish a southeast regional compact.

Paul Volcker was philosophically sympathetic to interstate banking and was backing Citibank in its fight over regional compacts, but he feared concentrations of banking power. In congressional testimony, he said he was opposed to big banks merging if they held 2 to 3 percent of banking assets. And therein lay the rub. If Citibank got too big by expanding across state borders, someone would have to draw the line. So Volcker proposed a regional plan as a stepping-stone to full national banking.

The debate over this issue was acrimonious, to say the least. In edgy discussions at the Fed, recalled banking lawyer Rodgin Cohen, the "Fed tried to wind its way without offending anybody." At one point, representatives of the regional banks stalked out of the room, said Cohen. In Volcker's view, the banking industry couldn't get its act together. Even after Citibank lost its regional compact case at the appeals court level, it was so convinced, one lobbyist said, that it would win in the Supreme Court that it helped kill a compromise banking law that would have affirmed the compacts while providing a "trigger" that would have effectively permitted national banking three years later.

Still, Wriston's efforts, according to the lobbyist, "brought the debate [over interstate versus regional expansion] into focus."

While waiting for full interstate banking, Citibank had to seize its opportunities as they came. It didn't have to wait long. The thrift industry's losses continued to be Citibank's gain. Soon, Citibank would unlock the back door to Illinois and Florida as it had done in California. And, as it had done with

Fidelity, it would have to slug its way in, burdened by its reputation as a voracious New York bank that would decimate the local competition. Even as Citibank was announcing its plans to open up in Maine, much farther down the coast the Federal Home Loan Bank Board was getting ready to seize another failing thrift: Biscayne Federal Savings & Loan in south Florida. In May, the fire sale attracted some fifty bidders, including Citibank. Meanwhile, the bank board put on the block Chicago's second-largest thrift, First Federal Savings & Loan, which it had taken over in April 1982. Like a circling hawk, Citicorp was ready and waiting to snatch its prey. Among its rival bidders was Sears Roebuck, which Wriston had long ago singled out as his primary competitor.

Citibank was already a major commercial lender in Florida, engaged in nearly every activity that local banks performed except deposit-taking. Florida, unlike California, appeared to have some prominent bankers who were willing to acknowledge that Citibank was a worthy and fair competitor. Steve Klein, executive vice president of Flagship Bank of Miami, told a reporter that Citibank was a capable, aggressive rival that didn't pull the rug out from under the market by offering bargain-basement rates. Other Florida bankers, citing a *New York* magazine survey which concluded that Citibank's customer service record was worse than that of any other New York bank, felt they had nothing to fear.

Given the Fed's concerns about capital, Citicorp probably should have considered itself lucky to be able to buy the thrifts at all. One condition of the sale was that Citicorp would have to raise $350 million in new reserves to back up the additional $7 billion in thrift deposits. Despite this obstacle, Citibank would be able to celebrate Christmas 1983 in two new states. In just two days, the Federal Home Loan Bank Board approved Citicorp's bid to acquire First Federal, a $4 billion-asset thrift with sixty-one offices in Chicago and central Illinois, at an initial cost to Citicorp of about $118 million, and then Biscayne Federal in Florida. The acquisitions were made by Citicorp Person-to-Person, its St. Louis–based consumer finance and industrial banking unit. But to be sure it would get them, Citicorp had to submit bids that were substantially above the next-highest offers.

Citicorp was not yet home free in Illinois, however. Continental Illinois and the First National Bank of Chicago were dead set against allowing Citibank to gain an important toehold on their turf. They had reportedly agreed to lend $250 million to one of the competing bidders. Everyone from local bankers to the state banking commissioner and populist Congressman Frank Annunzio lambasted the decision to award the thrift to Citicorp. "I'm very disappointed that an outsider is coming in," Annunzio told a reporter. Even as Florida bankers were protesting Citicorp's acquisition there, the Illinois attorney general, acting at the behest of the state's bankers, was preparing to file a lawsuit to block the deal. Illinois bankers fired off letters protesting the acquisition. One, published in *American Banker* on January 9, 1984, was especially prescient. "We are extremely troubled that Citicorp, with its serious capital adequacy problems and questionable foreign loans, was found to be the best solution for First Federal," wrote David W. Combs, president of the Independent Community Banks of Illinois.

One group, however, the National Center for the Prevention of Sudden Infant Death Syndrome, rallied to Citicorp's defense, citing its contributions of money and managerial expertise. Citicorp's status as the largest student loan bank in the United States, with $1.2 billion outstanding to 430,000 students, including 10,000 in Illinois, gave it another arrow in its quiver as it sought, like Cupid, to win the hearts of legislators in Illinois and other states.

Prior to the Fed hearings on the proposed acquisition, Wriston phoned Senator Charles Percy to solicit his support. Wriston had known the Illinois senator since Percy's days as chairman and CEO of Bell & Howell, and the two occasionally played tennis together. Wriston recalled later that he boasted to Percy about how Citibank, as it expanded outside of New York, had created nonpolluting jobs, and, borrowing GE's advertising slogan, told him about "all the good things we bring to life."

"Yes, yes, I understand," Wriston remembers Percy saying. "I'm not going to raise any real ruckus. I may put in a statement because, you know, I'm running for reelection."

Later, Wriston flew to Phoenix to play in the Senators Cup tennis tournament, an event in which Percy usually participated. Before Percy arrived, Wriston received a call from New York reporting that Percy had strongly objected to Citibank's deal in the Fed hearings. He recommended that the Fed postpone its decision to "provide a greater opportunity to explore possible solutions. I am hopeful that [state officials] will be given every opportunity to air their case."

Wriston was outraged. When Percy arrived for the tournament, Wriston took him to task: "That was a terrible thing to go and testify against us."

"It's going to be a close election," Percy explained, according to Wriston. "I need all the help I can get." In the November 1984 election, however, Percy's Senate career came to a close. But Wriston was convinced that the betrayal by Percy resulted from a back room deal with the "Big Nanny," Paul Volcker.

While not standing in the way of Citibank's acquisition of Fidelity Savings and other failed thrifts, Volcker and the Fed, as was their practice, imposed a restriction that would make the acquisitions less desirable. These so-called tandem restrictions prevented Citibank from using the acquired thrift to cross-sell its services and vice versa. Citibank could operate the thrifts as stand-alone entities but could not in any meaningful way integrate them into its banking operations. It couldn't even sell its own traveler's checks in the newly acquired thrifts. "The philosophical basis for [that restriction] escapes me," Wriston said later. "It was like telling the American Express Fireman's Fund it can't sell American Express traveler's checks."

The Fed viewed the tandem restrictions as a kind of Rubicon in the separation of powers between thrifts, banks, and other financial services providers. It was concerned that if banks like Citibank could cross-sell their services with those of a thrift, then every provider would jump in and the barriers between thrifts and banks would break down. The tandem restriction, according to regulators, was a kind of holding action intended to prevent the barriers from breaking down helter-skelter.

"Chuck Percy, to protect his constituency, made a trade with Paul [Volcker]," Wriston charged. Wriston figured that the alleged deal called for Percy to oppose Citibank's entry into Illinois to give Volcker the excuse to impose the tandem restrictions. Wriston said, "Paul's a nice practical politician. He made that trade. I have no proof, but I'd bet eight to five that's what happened. That's the way Washington works." Replied Volcker: "There was never any deal with Percy."

"I basically was in favor of banks buying thrifts," said Volcker later. "There was one hell of a lot of opposition to that in Washington. In my view, I did what was feasible by finding a politically acceptable way for Citibank to buy these things. If we had done what they wanted us to do we would have gotten our ears pinned back and they would have gotten nothing. They freely accepted tandem restrictions as a way to get access and six months later, they said, 'Aren't these things awful.' "

In advance of the hearings, Citicorp managed to finagle a puff piece in *American Banker* on January 3, 1984, on how Betty Sue Peabody, president of Citicorp Savings in California, had "quickly" turned the thrift into a "moneymaker."

Some Citibankers doubted that Citicorp Savings had turned the corner so fast. Said former Citibank corporate secretary Paul Kolterjahn, "The savings banks were a drain on manpower. We had to change management twice in Florida. We pretty much took them as they were. There were tremendous bad loans."

To be sure, Citicorp Savings had nowhere to go but up.

Before the year was out, Citicorp had also launched efforts to open pipsqueak "industrial banks" in several new states and to open a national bank in Maryland to offer a nationwide credit card. Industrial banks—essentially finance companies that also took deposits—were turn-of-the-century regulatory antiques. Having begun in the late 1970s to establish them from scratch or buy them, by mid-1984, Citibank had twenty-two in seven states.

Meanwhile, Citibank was lobbying New Mexico's state legislature for changes in its banking laws that would permit a credit-card facility there too. For the time being, Citibank was already as big as it wanted to be in South Dakota. But, because it was concerned that a power failure or some other calamity could jeopardize its entire credit-card operation, Citibank wanted to open additional credit-card facilities elsewhere. Holding out the promise of a thousand new jobs, Citicorp was pushing for legislative changes that would allow it to acquire federally and state-chartered banks; the federally chartered institution would issue credit cards, and the state bank would engage in securities underwriting.

When New Mexico governor Tony Anaya forced his director of financial institutions and the state securities chief from office, it appeared that things would swing in Citicorp's favor. The governor subsequently said he would introduce a bill that would allow out-of-state banks to acquire or set up new banks in the state. But in early February 1984, New Mexico lawmakers, egged on by local bankers, turned thumbs down on the legislation.

When Nevada governor Richard Bryan heard about Citicorp's rough sledding in New Mexico, he placed a call to Wriston. "Do you speak to Democrats?" the governor asked.

"I certainly do," Wriston replied.

Bryan then asked Wriston a question he wasn't used to hearing. "I'd like to talk with you about inducing Citibank to come to Nevada." Wriston was prepared to be induced and invited the governor to lunch two days later.

The governor appeared with a clutch of bankers, businessmen, and staff and got right to the point. Aware of the jobs that the credit-card operation had created in South Dakota, Bryan told Wriston bluntly, "I'd like some of that." Wriston was pleased to accommodate him. The two men talked about power capacity, the local job market, and whether a post office could be built to handle tens of millions of letters a year.

Now that the bank had South Dakota under its belt, Nevada needed Citibank more than Citibank needed Nevada, and Wriston, ever the straight arrow, was chary of Nevada's reputation as a mecca for gambling and organized crime. Las Vegas, as one of the state's two major labor markets, was a natural choice for another credit-card facility, if Citibank opted to build one in Nevada at all. But Wriston chafed at the notion of customers mailing their payments to a Las Vegas address. "I believed it would be a dumb thing to do. I could see a lot of wags chortling about it in local bars."

In a meeting with Bryan and other state officials in New York, Wriston asked if Citibank could have its own post office and zip code if it set up shop in Nevada.

"You can have whatever you want," the governor replied. "You can come to Nevada and let your customers go double or nothing on their credit-card bills. What do you need to do it?"

"A law that permits a limited-purpose national bank," Wriston replied. Wriston's own in-house legislators, Angermueller and a colleague, spared the governor the time and expense by whipping up a draft bill similar to South Dakota's. Citicorp persuaded the Nevada legislature to convene in special session and, according to local bankers, even offered to fly the lawmakers from their hometowns to Carson City, the state capital, to pass the so-called Citicorp bill, but in the end, Nevada taxpayers picked up the tab. The law was passed, and Citicorp built a huge credit-card processing center employing hundreds of workers.

Similarly, Citicorp sought to endear itself to Marylanders by pointing up the lack of competition there for student loans and offering to forfeit the usual state subsidy of $40 per application if given the chance to make loans there. The Maryland legislature passed a bill enabling out-of-state banks to open one office to the public and another that wouldn't steal customers from local banks and thrifts. In May 1984 the Fed signed off on a limited-service bank that permitted Citibank to market its Choice card throughout the country.

At a 1983 meeting in New York between top representatives of major New York banks and the leaders of the California assembly, Hans Angermueller, on the back of an envelope, penned a draft of the reciprocal banking bill that would later be enacted in largely unaltered form. "That was the icebreaker," he said. But by the time it took effect, neither Citicorp nor the other big banks would have enough money to buy California banks.

Where it couldn't gain territory with bricks and mortar, Citibank tried to do so with plastic, reflecting Reed's view that that mode of delivering financial services was more efficient anyway. In early 1984 it rolled out a financial account—called "Bank in a Card"—through its South Dakota operation. This account included a credit card, a checking account paying 7 percent on balances greater than $2,500, a money market account, and a credit line of as much as $25,000. Introduced in Atlanta, Tampa, and Minneapolis, the account was aptly dubbed the "carpetbagger account" by consumer columnist Jane Bryant Quinn, who noted that consumers receiving 11 percent on a one-year CD could earn 12.25 percent from Citibank South Dakota. Several months later, Citibank announced that the response had exceeded expectations. It declined to specify how many accounts it had picked up, but added that by 1985 it planned to expand the account to twenty cities.

In Nebraska, Citibank outraged local bankers by setting up two "sales offices" that supplied customers with self-addressed stamped envelopes to mail their checks to Citibank.

Elsewhere, Citibank also bought stakeout investments in banks that it dreamed of acquiring once the barriers fell. Other institutions, including Marine Midland, Chemical, and Chase, started buying non-voting equity interests to gain a foothold.

Citicorp also wanted to be a player in Texas, whose banks were still among the nation's most powerful. But Texans had no interest in seeing Citibank invade their state. Much as Citibank would have preferred to operate its own branch network, it had begun to recognize that it was more important to penetrate an important market and give its customers access to funds than to insist on exclusivity. So it linked up with an ATM network in Dallas that enabled its customers to use hundreds of machines in Texas and adjacent states. The real estate and energy lending debacles soon devastated Texas banks, prompting one Citibanker to remark, "Thank God for interstate banking barriers. They kept us from getting into that."

Whatever reservations Wriston had about the securities business, he and his colleagues certainly lusted after the fees earned by full-fledged investment bankers. In a speech on May 21, 1984, before senior overseas bankers, Angermueller reported on a luncheon he'd had with his counterpart at Morgan, who dazzled him with the latest compensation figures in the "fat-cat securities business." The seventy partners at one investment banking firm, Angermueller reported, had earned more than $2 million each in 1983, and four hundred associates made over $200,000 each. "Those are truly monopoly rewards," he griped.

Nonetheless, when it came to the third *I*—investment banking—Wriston was still nervous and ambivalent. As the investment banking boom of the 1980s was gathering momentum, Citibank, on paper at least, seemed to have it all. It performed many investment banking–related functions, notably foreign exchange trading and swaps, which generated huge revenues. And it was one of the three leading dealers in U.S. government securities. It played a key role in finding ways around rules barring certain investment banking activities, and created some of the most important financial innovations of the 1980s, such as securities backed by loans. But Wriston and his bank were still hung up on the notion that any good Citibank manager could run an investment bank and be content without a seven-figure Wall Street salary. As a result, Citibank trailed far behind traditional Wall Street firms in obscenely profitable activities like underwriting and giving merger and acquisition advice—services that separated powerhouses like Goldman, Sachs from the wanna-bes. Though Citibank boasted that it was the first bank to rank among the top twenty merger and acquisition specialists, that really wasn't saying much. For his part, Wriston felt that Citibank's future in investment banking lay overseas, in performing "merger, barter, and arbitrage" in countries "many people might never consider prime markets." Now in the twilight of his career, Wriston had other priorities.

In 1982, Citibank finally got around to consolidating more of its investment banking activities into a single investment banking group, nearly as Robert Logan and George Vojta had proposed it in 1979—but without Logan and Vojta. Instead, it was set up under Paul Collins, the personification of Citibank's managerial cult. The deal had been done in the serenity of Wriston's Deer Pond Farm, where Wriston led the executives who would head the reorganized unit on a tour of his William Simon and George Shultz Forests. Left unresolved was the nagging compensation issue. Citicorp was late out of the starting gate in investment banking, and this move was not bold enough to enable it to realize the potential it seemed to have as Wriston was preparing to make his exit.

Angermueller felt that it would be futile to take on the powerful securities industry frontally, a political fact of life that would remain true for years to come. The Securities Industry Association, he said, "had money coming out of the kazoo to fund lobbyists . . . and others they kept in business in D.C." He believed that Goldman, Sachs, First Boston, Morgan Stanley, and Salomon Brothers were committed to keeping Glass-Steagall on the books and that retail houses like Merrill Lynch would be among the first to "see the light." Moreover, Wriston himself was queasy about banks underwriting corporate securities, particularly equities, and said so publicly. One reason he objected to it publicly was tactical, he said later. "I said that at a point in time when I didn't want to give people a counterargument" that would get in the way of the main goal. "My colleagues wished I'd never said that. They keep . . . beating me over the head with it. I still think it's not too bad an argument. If we can get everything else I've argued for over the years, I'm not going to worry about that." Even Lincoln, he observed, said that if he could have saved the Union without freeing the slaves he would have done so.

Wriston's words would come back to haunt him even after he retired. In Senate debate in September 1984 over a restructuring bill, Senator John Heinz dredged up Wriston's October 1981 testimony. Wriston, he said, "shares my skepticism" that securities activities can be walled off from the rest of the bank.

Paul Volcker often told Hans Angermueller that he was "playing [his] boss's remarks back," but Angermueller was convinced that fire walls could protect the bank, and he did not believe that equity was necessarily more risky than debt. "I don't know whether a share of AT&T is more risky than a [Michael] Milken-invented junk bond of Revco [a discount drug chain that went bankrupt in 1988 but has since recovered]," Angermueller said years later. "I don't draw that clear distinction that all equity is dangerous and all debt is good." Ever the admirer of things Germanic, Angermueller still preferred the German universal bank model where all activities are contained within the bank, or the British example, where the bank operates and funds subsidiaries that are free to deal with the bank in any way they see fit. But, he said, "it's unrealistic to think that we could persuade Congress to go for a universal banking system at this time."

By now, less than a year before Wriston was to step down, the world of banking was markedly different from the one Wriston had entered thirty-eight years earlier. In 1946, Citibank was a bond house. But when it made commercial loans, it kept them on the books and required corporate borrowers to maintain compensating balances. Though Citibank had long viewed commercial lending as a "commodity" business with thin spreads, that was even truer now. The idea now was to make loans that could be sold off. Asset growth was no longer the be-all and end-all. Noting in his remarks to financial analysts on March 7, 1984, that in 1983 Citibank's investment bank had sold off more than $2 billion in loans generated by the institutional bank, Wriston said, "We are stretching our imagination to take assets off our books, not put them on." That number, he predicted, would likely double in 1984 and would "easily" reach the $20 billion mark over the next five years. Another benefit was that asset sales relieved pressure to boost capital.

One way Citibank later accomplished this was by setting up a unit called Chatsworth Funding, which sold commercial paper to buy pools of Citibank loans. In turn, Chatsworth paper was backed by Travelers Indemnity Company. This development gave rise to a transaction called asset securitization, in which loans were packaged and sold as securities to investors. That allowed banks to create liquidity when they needed it. For Citibank, this new financial "technology" arrived just in time.

The legal means to engage in asset securitization and related activities began with Mark F. Kessenich, a man with the instincts of an investment banker for whom working at a commercial bank was less than satisfying. Then head of Citibank's money market division, Kessenich fumed about his inability to engage in securities underwriting. In early 1983, shortly after being appointed general counsel for the division, Robert Dinerstein approached Kessenich with a legal angle that he thought could be their way out of the box. Section 20 of the Glass-Steagall Act contained a provision that allowed a bank affiliate to engage in certain securities activities that were off limits to the bank itself, as long as those activities were not the institution's primary revenue producers. The provision hadn't been entirely overlooked by bank lawyers, but they had either viewed it as a constraint on bank activities or believed that trying to exploit it was a lost cause.

A year earlier, Citibank had received Federal Reserve Board approval to set up a government securities unit, and Dinerstein, Angermueller, and others concluded that, compared with the volume of already permissible activities that would be conducted in the new subsidiary, the volume of the proposed activities they would like to conduct would be relatively small. On that basis, they could argue that they would comply with the "not principally engaged" provision of Section 20. These activities were the underwriting of commercial paper, municipal revenue bonds, mortgage-backed securities, corporate debt, and other securities.

Dinerstein took the idea to Angermueller's acquisition committee, which thought it was worth pursuing. But this time, Wriston—much as he admired legal ingenuity—was skeptical, according to Dinerstein. Given all the initiatives already in the hopper and Citibank's poor standing in the eyes of Paul Volcker, it seemed to Wriston a futile exercise. Still, Dinerstein was given the chance to make his pitch at a meeting of the elite policy committee. Coincidentally, when he arrived at his office that morning, he found on his desk a U.S. Appeals Court decision on the acquisition by Bank of America of Charles Schwab, the discount brokerage. The court upheld the deal as consistent with Glass-Steagall, largely on the basis of Section 20. Bank holding companies, the decision stated, could underwrite securities that banks could not.

A year after Dinerstein first broached the idea, Wriston finally became persuaded that it might work. The result was the first major fracture of Glass-Steagall since the legislation was enacted in the 1930s. "I had the impression this was not [Wriston's] highest priority," Dinerstein said later. "It wasn't as important to him as retail or insurance."

The first application, which included a request to underwrite corporate debt, did not sit well with Volcker and his staff at the Fed. According to Hans Angermueller, Volcker demanded in early 1985 that Citibank withdraw its petition, threatening that if it didn't he'd make sure that "you never get rid of Glass-Steagall." When the application was refiled, corporate debt was dropped. The final application consisted of mortgage-backed securities, commercial paper, municipal revenue bonds, and consumer receivables.

"Only Citibank had the gumption to try it," said top banking lawyer Rodgin Cohen. "Other banks . . . weren't willing to spend the time and money," despite Cohen's contention that the idea wouldn't necessarily be received antagonistically by the Fed. According to Cohen, the officers of at least one major New York bank said they were perfectly content to be second. Citibank, however, believed that "if the system benefits, I benefit," said Cohen. "If Citibank hadn't done it, nothing would ever have happened."

Like CDs and credit cards and all the other Citicorp probes into deep financial space, it was déjà vu all over again, as Yogi Berra is reported to have said.

Citibank embraced Section 20, but it refused to push ahead on other fronts that Dinerstein, for one, believed would have left Citibank better positioned. Dinerstein also proposed setting up a private-label mutual fund that would be sold to correspondent banks and individual customers. Under this plan, Citibank would have been the adviser and processor, and an outside mutual fund would have been the seller, thereby avoiding any Glass-Steagall problems. Citibank went so far as to discuss the idea with Fidelity Investments, but in the end "turned it down flat," said Dinerstein. "They [Citibank] didn't know what it meant. They made some splendid decisions and made some not so splendid decisions." Later, hundreds of banks, including Citibank, offered private-label mutual funds, but on this front Citibank lost the opportunity to take the lead. It did, however, push into mutual funds in a modest way, becoming the first big bank to offer a mutual fund alternative to the Keogh plan and the Individual Retirement Account.

For all its frustrations, being a Citicorp lawyer, said Dinerstein, was like being "a pig in shit." Working there was like "walking into a meeting of anarchists," he went on. Decisions "never were made. People just did things until they were told they [couldn't]." There was a constant tug-of-war between the corporate bureaucracy and the business units and, of course, among business units. Wriston, he said, was the "sun" that kept these "planets" in his solar system. "If he wasn't there, centrifugal force would pull the place apart."

Even though Citicorp had devised the legal argument for penetrating Glass-Steagall and applied to the Fed well before other major banks, its top priority was interstate banking. Washington regulators could cope with only so many Citicorp initiatives at one time. In deciding which powers should be pushed for the hardest, Wriston and Angermueller acted as the traffic cops. The regional compact issue, said Dinerstein, "was something that couldn't be compromised." Section 20, said Dinerstein, took second place until that matter got resolved.

Meanwhile, Citibank made another chink in the armor of Wall Street when it secured Fed approval to start up a discount brokerage to be called Citicorp Financial Services. Though the move was challenged in court, the Supreme Court upheld the ruling in mid-1984, and that fall the brokerage unit celebrated the opening of its first branch office. Soon the Fed approved Citibank as a market maker in the financial futures business as well.

But in general, Citicorp allowed Bankers Trust and J. P. Morgan to carry the water on Glass-Steagall. In 1984, reflecting its deep interest in that issue, Morgan published an influential treatise titled "Rethinking Glass-Steagall." Morgan seriously considered giving up its bank charter and dropping deposit insurance in order to enjoy full investment banking powers. But according to its chief, Lewis Preston, it concluded that access to the Fed discount window—the ultimate safety net—outweighed those advantages. According to Angermueller, Preston attempted unsuccessfully to persuade Citicorp to join Morgan in giving the demolition of Glass-Steagall its undivided attention. Preston could never fathom Citibank's lust for the insurance business or for interstate banking. "Lew Preston kept saying, 'Why do you want to get into that business? Let's get down to just Glass-Steagall.' [Although] we were with him on Glass-Steagall, it was not our sole preoccupation," Angermueller said.

Though Lew Preston and Paul Volcker were close friends, Preston shared Citicorp's frustration with Volcker's tendency to waffle on securities powers. And Preston later decided that Volcker was probably comfortable with Morgan being in the securities business but less so with other less experienced institutions.

———

Overseas, Citibank prepared for the so-called Big Bang, the deregulation of the London financial markets, including the elimination of fixed commissions, which was to come in 1986. U.S. firms would then be able to join the London Stock Exchange instead of having to deal through London brokers. Even though Citibank had a long, sad history of screwing up acquisitions, in 1983 it paid $30 million for nearly 30 percent of Vickers da Costa, a mid-sized brokerage with offices in Tokyo, Singapore, Hong Kong, and New York, which specialized in Asian securities. Citibank's main goal was to gain a foothold in the securities markets of Japan, which had always been hostile to American financial institutions as well as American goods. Coincidentally, President Reagan, during his November 1983 trip to Japan, had urged officials to remove the barriers that blocked non-Japanese financial institutions from operating in Japanese markets.

To complement the Vickers acquisition, Citibank soon acquired a stake in Scrimgeour Kemp-Gee, a London stock brokerage. Said former Citibanker Anthony Howkins, who negotiated the purchase of Vickers, the "theory was to buy an underwriter, broker, gilt dealer, and have the whole package." But Vickers and Scrimgeour would turn out to be a questionable combination. Vickers was a "gentleman's club" that made huge commissions, Howkins said. He recalled that one key Vickers official failed to appear at a negotiating session because he was fox hunting. The Scrimgeour staff was somewhat more serious, and the effort to integrate the two firms was disastrous, according to former Citibanker Peter Greenough. "The Scrimgeour people pissed all over" the Vickers bankers, he said. "They would sit right next to each other and not talk to each other." Because of these cultural clashes, the combination never realized in practice the potential that it appeared to have on paper.

Of course, this was not the first time that culture clashes in Britain had undermined a Citibank acquisition. Citibank never seemed to learn that trying to marry the Citibank culture with that of British financial institutions was like trying to mate a mongoose and a cobra. Even as Citibank was congratulating itself on its acquisition of Vickers and Scrimgeour, it was finally selling Grindlays, the stodgy British bank that had caused it so much grief for years, to the Australia and New Zealand Banking Group. Wriston sidestepped the real problem when he said that "what was once a sound strategy was approaching the position where our fellows and theirs might be sitting in the same room for the same customer." That, in fact, was what Citibankers— in the spirit of unfriendly competition—were doing everywhere.

Indeed, the biggest obstacle facing Citibank's effort to be a player in investment banking was Citibank itself. Citibankers battled incessantly over compensation and turf. Money market division staff, for example, fought with the merchant bankers over who should peddle money market products. In the mid-1980s, said one former senior investment banking officer, "we were very close to being very good at government trading, foreign exchange swaps, and were beginning to develop in other areas." Five years later, however, he admitted that "our efforts are largely irrelevant now."

Wriston had high hopes for his two new I's. He had long recognized that he was really in the information business and, to some extent, the insurance business, though not to the degree he wanted. Citibank figured that the average household spent an average of $2,100 a year on financial services, and that the bank was barred from earning about $1,500 of that amount, much of it in potential insurance sales. Wriston believed that insurance and banking were similar and related activities. He also believed that Citibank could sell homeowner, auto, and term life insurance for much smaller commissions than those charged by traditional brokers.

Breaking into insurance overseas was relatively easy, but penetrating the U.S. market in a meaningful way was another matter altogether. Independent insurance agents weren't about to hand their business over to Wriston without a fight. One of Wriston's biggest regrets was being thwarted by the Department of Justice in his 1969 bid to buy the Chubb Corporation, the insurer. "That would have given us a wonderful base for the insurance business," he mused in an interview. Citibank did, however, manage to grab bits and pieces of the U.S. insurance business, in part through its role as a mortgage lender, and by mid-1984 it underwrote about $1.5 billion in credit-related insurance. It had started to sell life insurance in two branches, in space leased to the American International Life Assurance Company. Meanwhile it was expanding its insurance activities overseas. For example, in 1984 it received the go-ahead to underwrite life insurance in the United Kingdom, a major extension of powers for holding companies abroad. It also acquired a small U.K. commercial insurance broker.

But Wriston had all but given up hope that the U.S. government would ever make a gift to bank holding companies of insurance powers. "We may not wake up one day with a law enacted that gives us the green light for our insurance activities, but bit by bit the pieces will fall," he predicted in a March 7, 1984, talk to bank analysts. So when South Dakota governor Bill Janklow, high from his success in bringing jobs to South Dakota, asked Citibank what his state and Citibank could do next, insurance was the obvious answer.

By the 1980s Citibank operated a sophisticated and well-oiled lobbying and lawyering machine in virtually every state where it yearned to do business. Citibank's recognition of the importance of influence peddling was reflected in comments Hans Angermueller made in November 1981 to the board's public issues committee. "It might also be useful," he said, "for Citibankers to frequent the local symphony hall or the town hall. Who can tell where our friends will come from? If we had had the foresight to cultivate Mormon insurance brokers years ago, what a friend we might have had in Jake Garn," the Utah Republican who in 1981 became chairman of the Senate Banking Committee. So much for Stillman Rockefeller's disdain for politicians.

Getting the South Dakota banking legislation passed was a piece of cake compared with the struggle to enact an insurance bill. Said executive vice president Charles Long, "With the bankers, you could put them all in one room. You couldn't do that with the insurance agents." South Dakota's independent banks and insurance agents were apoplectic. Backed by the big national insurance companies, they mobilized a massive campaign to undermine Citicorp's effort, suing to kill the bill. According to former Citibank South Dakota president Fred Winkler, the giant insurers "preached doom and gloom while canceling agent relationships." They had the "agents whipped into such an emotional frenzy they weren't watching what was happening with the big insurance companies."

But Citibank was no longer shy when it came to wining and dining legislators. It unleashed its lobbying machine at full force, spreading the wealth around liberally in lobbying state legislators. One banker later told a journalist that South Dakota "may become a subsidiary of Citibank." Janklow's so-called jobs bill allowed out-of-state banks to acquire or establish a state-chartered bank to own an insurance company. But the legislation was restrictive, limiting sales to customers outside the state. It seized on the fact that the 1970 amendments to the Bank Holding Company Act limited bank holding companies but not banks. Shortly after the passage of the South Dakota legislation, Citibank said it would acquire a $15.5 million-deposit bank, American State Bank of Rapid City, and get into "all facets" of insurance through South Dakota. Passing the legislation, said Citicorp executive Charles Long later, was "like waving a red flag" before federal banking regulators.

Besides their differences over capital, Wriston had any number of other reasons for wanting to see Paul Volcker spend all of his time fly-fishing, his favorite leisure time activity. One of them was Volcker's skeptical view of the South Dakota bill. While Volcker did not protest Citibank's move to South Dakota in search of freedom from usury ceilings, he fumed at its attempt to use the state to do an end run around the Bank Holding Company Act by trying to engage nationally in a business that was not closely related to banking. It was "smart-ass" banking at its worst. "That certainly should be a matter for a national decision, and not a South Dakota decision," Volcker huffed.

Citibank's bid to establish a limited bank in South Dakota with the power to offer insurance nationally came amid a raging debate over whether commercial firms should be allowed to acquire so-called "non-bank banks." Citibank, of course, was not the only financial services company skilled at discovering loopholes. In 1980, Gulf & Western acquired a California bank and peeled off its commercial loan portfolio, thereby escaping from the constraints of the Bank Holding Company Act, which defined a bank as an institution that accepted insured deposits *and* made commercial loans. Gulf & Western overcame another barrier separating commerce and banking. The non-bank bank created another opening for the likes of Sears and American Express to add banklike services to their offerings. Non-bank banks soon became the rage.

Volcker, for one, was adamantly opposed to commercial firms muscling their way into banking through the back door. At one point the Comptroller of the Currency, with the Fed's blessing, slapped a temporary moratorium on the creation of national banks by non-banking concerns. The ban was now becoming a catalyst not only for legislation to fill the non-bank bank loophole but also to rethink the entire U.S. financial services structure. In opposing the moratorium, Wriston was an unlikely ally of the chairmen of American Express, Bank of America, Merrill Lynch, and even Sears.

On June 27, 1983, in hearings before the Senate Banking Committee, Wriston, as he had done in the battle against Reg Q, took up the cause of the hapless consumer. Responding to a question from Senator John Heinz, who asked if the public was endangered by a moratorium, Wriston replied, "Yes, those who want to get financial services but have been blocked will be prohibited from getting them. The consumer is the one who is voting for deregulation." Even as the hearings were taking place in Washington, D.C. J.C. Penney was signing a deal to acquire a tiny national bank and sell off its commercial loans in order to offer other financial services.

Defending the South Dakota legislation, Wriston argued that the "insurance business has no federal policy," and that it is regulated entirely by the states. Wriston relished the chance to beard the enemy on its own turf. On November 16, 1983, in the midst of Citicorp's campaign to get permission to offer life insurance nationwide through South Dakota, he appeared at the convention of the American Council of Life Insurance, where he compared his visit to Sadat's first journey to Israel. Pulling no punches, he reminded the insurers that before 1980, just 4 percent of insurance holding companies, in terms of assets, were involved in banking, compared with 17 percent in 1983. He asserted that the move toward one-stop shopping was as logical as the evolution of the supermarket. And he chastised the insurers for seeking to block the creation of a national policy on insurance while pushing for a federal moratorium "on what states can permit banks to do." Quoting from *Alice in Wonderland,* he said, "It is 'curiouser and curiouser.' "

A year after Wriston retired, he lost that battle. On August 1, 1985, the Fed announced that it had rejected Citicorp's bid to buy the American State Bank of Rapid City, South Dakota. It would take another five years to win the war.

Besides insurance, the other new business Wriston wanted to launch before he retired was information. Walter, like his father, Henry, had a long-time interest in information technology. "I meet guys on the street. That's my information system. It's not very precise," Wriston said. The real point was that "information about money has become almost as important as money itself." And Citibank, as a massive global cable network, had probably more information about money than any other organization—more, perhaps, than even the U.S. Treasury Department. In an early-1980s lunch with Fernand St Germain, Angermueller recalled that the congressman asked Wriston a question: given the opportunity to acquire a single financial institution, which one would it be. Without hesitating a moment, Wriston named Reuters. In early 1984, Citibank joined forces with the global news service to distribute Citibank's economic forecasts. And in May of that year Wriston joined the Reuters board.

Information, and in particular its geopolitical ramifications, was Wriston's favorite hobbyhorse. He believed that information technology was making national borders irrelevant, in effect altering long-held definitions of national sovereignty. When George Shultz became secretary of state in 1982, he appointed Wriston his special adviser on telecommunications policy.

Citibank had a very real stake in all of this. In 1982, it became a satellite landlord. It paid $24 million for two transponders on the Westar V, a communications satellite launched in June into a 22,000-mile-high orbit. Thus Citibank became the first financial institution with its own satellite. The bank's primary goal was to cut its $80 million annual bill for transmitting and receiving computerized information, phone calls, and teleconferencing. The transponders were capable of transmitting data within the United States and overseas. Overseas, however, the flow of data and information was limited not by technology but by regulation and bureaucracy. One of Wriston's missions in life was now to persuade foreign governments that "everybody has more to gain from the free flow of data and information" than anyone stood to gain from restrictions. Wriston was in the thick of State Department–led negotiations to forge agreements on access to airwaves. "There's a tendency for people in a field like that to be fascinated by technology," Shultz said later. "People get wrapped up in the details of negotiations. It's hard to get people to get up above the important ins and outs of what they're doing and to think broadly and grandly. Walt does that; he's good at it. . . . He saw the information revolution probably before any other leaders in the industry."

Citibank already was engaged in various activities in which information was the product, but these activities were never linked together as a business. Citibank had numerous information networks. By now it had set up terminals in the headquarters of 7,000 corporate customers and expected to have them at 12,000 locations ten years later. So it was inevitable that Citicorp would fight a lengthy court battle with the data processors for the right to sell electronic data processing services to its customers. The data processors fretted that Citicorp would use its might to underprice their services. Finally, in the wake of an administrative law ruling that data processing services were closely related to banking, the Fed approved the plan. Now Citicorp could sell services for electronic funds transfer, home banking, and other information delivery and transmission applications.

In theory, at least, the potential of the information business was unlimited. The credit-card database, for example, was a mother lode of potentially marketable information on holders' product preferences. On a macro level, data on regional buying patterns could be gathered and sold to other marketing companies. A maker of food processors, for example, might be interested in the household income of its customers, or whether buyers of those machines would also be likely to buy juicers. On an individual level, a holder who bought baby clothes might be a likely candidate for a new insurance policy. Wriston believed that by the mid-1990s, the fifth *I*—information services linking electronic publishing, telecommunications, and banking—could rake in revenues of $6 billion.

That was a terrific idea. The only problem was in the execution.

In pushing for new powers, Volcker felt that Citicorp would have been more successful if it had gotten in bed with the Fed. But Citicorp's poor relationship with Volcker and the Fed was not the only obstacle standing in the way of new powers. The international debt crisis was the other. For one thing, Citibank and its peers had less money to spend because they were forced to increase reserves. Equally important, when they appeared on Capitol Hill, they got no respect, to borrow a line from comedian Rodney Dangerfield. "When we came in with shiny faces and said we want more powers," Angermueller remembered, "the usual answer was 'What—to cause more catastrophes?'" No sooner had one Latin brushfire been put out than another erupted somewhere else, providing continual reminders of the banks' shortcomings. On December 8, 1983, fifteen months after it essentially defaulted, Mexico was asking for more money. At a Mexico City news conference that followed a meeting between Wriston and Mexican President Miguel de la Madrid Hurtado, Wriston appeared with Silva Herzog as the finance minister announced that Mexico would seek as much as $4 billion in new loans from international banks the following year. Even as Mexico was pleading for more money, restructuring expert Bill Rhodes was predicting at a *Financial Times* conference in London that Mexico would lead the LDCs back to the voluntary markets. Mexico had weathered the storm, he said, adding that he hoped that would soon be true for Brazil and other borrowers.

Argentina, however, was years away from rehabilitation. But as part of the ongoing effort to buy time and perpetuate the fiction that countries like Argentina were viable, Wriston and other bankers kept up the make-believe. In October 1983, Raúl Alfonsín, in democratic elections, was elected president of Argentina, replacing the military regime that had blundered into the disastrous Falklands War. Given Argentina's always precarious economic and political condition, its bank creditors, including Citibank, wanted to ensure the success of the new administration and not further jeopardize their chances of recovering the billions already at risk there. In order for the country to appear current on its external debt to commercial banks when the new government took office in December, the banks agreed to allow it to draw down on a credit line extended the previous spring. In this shell game of making one loan to pay off the interest on earlier loans, the funds were to come in and go out almost simultaneously on December 2, 1983. Normally, the CHIPS system, the electronic payment mechanism over which tens of billions are transferred every working day, closes at 5:00 P.M.; keeping it open later requires the concurrence of a majority of its members. Wriston always liked to be in the thick of the action, and on that Friday, the action was in Citibank's telex room, where a clutch of bankers, lawyers, and Argentine monetary officials had gathered to watch the bucks flow in and out of Citibank. Just as the bankers began congratulating one another for constructing yet another bridge to nowhere, the final telex arrived. It was hopelessly garbled.

Someone shoved the telex at Wriston and asked him, "Is it good enough?" He turned to Robert Dineen, his brother-in-law and the lawyer who headed Shearman & Sterling's Argentina legal team, and repeated the question. Dineen scanned the message and pronounced it legally valid. Wriston then grabbed the telex, and said, "Then it's good enough for me," and the transaction was complete.

Right after Argentina got its loan, its minister of the economy, in mid-December, hit the foreign banks up for another postponement on its debt payments.

By the spring of 1984, with his Citicorp career close to an end, Wriston had managed to help sweep the problems of Mexico and Brazil under the carpet. Now he set out to declare victory over the LDC crisis. He could tell reporters that the Latin debt problem, while serious, was "much improved from this time a year ago." Argentina, of course, was a glaring exception. Before this time, the Latin American nations had basically wanted to pay but had been unable to do so because they didn't have the foreign exchange. Now, however, both Argentina and Venezuela had the foreign exchange but were refusing to pay. Argentina, which was $45 billion in debt and $2 billion behind on its payments, was by far the bigger problem. It was time for a replay of an old and familiar script: extending another so-called bridge loan to

Argentina. In March 1984, when monetary officials and bankers met in Uruguay, the bridge loan that the banks had made to Argentina in December 1983 was already eighty-five days past due. Five more days and the banks would have to place the loan, and Argentina, on their list of nonperforming credits. For close to two years the world financial community had played rollover with this dismally managed country. If a new source of financing wasn't found quickly, Argentina's hopes for recovery from its economic quagmire would be dim indeed. And it would become the first of the Latin nations to officially default on its debt, with all the unthinkable financial and economic consequences that such an event creates.

On this occasion, the U.S. Treasury and the Federal Reserve Board teamed up to propose yet another bridge loan to be funded, in a bizarre twist, by other Latin debtors and a $100 million contribution from four big U.S. banks. Wriston phoned Bill Rhodes in Argentina to get his opinion on the proposal. Rhodes insisted that the bank group should include non-U.S. banks as well and should be secured with whatever collateral could be attached outside of Argentina. Argentina's guarantee was now, of course, totally worthless. All the parties agreed to the proposal, and it seemed like a done deal. The Fed phoned Dineen and Rhodes, informing them that the deal would have to be done overnight. Then, at 3:00 A.M., Dineen received another call from the Fed notifying him that it had been overruled by the Treasury Department: the loan would have to be made on an unsecured basis. "I'm sorry," Dineen responded, "our instructions are to do it secured." When he heard that the Treasury had backed off, he congratulated himself on his prowess as a negotiator. He would later learn that Washington had contacted Wriston, who characteristically had stood his ground. The transaction simply could not be done the way the government wanted to do it, because the banks would not participate. The loan was made as originally agreed, on a secured basis. The March 1984 skirmish over the Argentine bridge loan was noteworthy for yet another reason. It marked the entry into the debt restructuring follies of David Mulford, assistant secretary of the Treasury for international affairs, a man who would become the nemesis of U.S. banks for his pro-debtor leanings. For the next seven years, Mulford, according to top bankers, actually supported the Latin debtors to the detriment of the banks, encouraging them to demand a reduction in their principal. At the very least, he did not discourage them from defaulting.

If there was ever a time when a country should have been classified, this was it and Argentina was the one. But once again, Argentina got a stay of execution. Some banks, however, voluntarily wrote down their Argentine loans, and the marketplace dealt harshly with those deemed to be overexposed.

Notwithstanding the ongoing LDC problems, Citicorp shareholders continued to heap praise on Wriston as he presided over his last annual meeting. On April 8, *New York Times* reporter Robert Bennett wrote that "despite his fairly dry presentation there was a sense through the audience that this meeting was out of the ordinary. That sense materialized when the audience burst into applause." Wriston was not one to be sentimental to the point of getting teary-eyed, but he was clearly surprised and pleased. The audience applauded again, Bennett reported, when one longtime stockholder stood up and said, "We want to thank you."

As usual, Wriston delivered his report on quarterly earnings, which had declined 2.2 percent from the year-earlier period. While he gave it, all eyes were focused on the three men—Reed, Theobald, and Angermueller—sitting to Wriston's right. But on the question of who would succeed him, Wriston's lips remained sealed.

As the inevitable showdown date neared, the rivalry between the Reed and Theobald camps turned increasingly testy. Former consumer executive Ed Harshfield recalls that John Reed was scheduled to visit Tokyo in April 1984, so Harshfield, who was convinced that Reed would get the nod, told the top Citibank executive in Tokyo to treat Reed as if he were the chairman-designate. That meant that Reed should meet with the finance minister, not his deputies. Citibank's chief in Tokyo was a Theobald man, and was equally convinced the nod would go to him. He was furious, recalled Harshfield, and protested that the finance minister was not available. "Make sure Reed gets to see the number one," Harshfield ordered.

Even Wriston's grandson was applying the pressure. During a meeting in Puerto Rico, Wriston's secretary, Gerry Stover, arranged for young Christopher, whom Wriston called "the hope of the world," to get on the speakerphone and say, "Grandpa, when are you going to pick a new chairman?" Meanwhile, guitar-playing Larry Small and friends belted out a parody of the song "Tradition" from *Fiddler on the Roof,* aptly retitled "Succession."

Though Wriston's actuarial base theory had by now been discredited, his belief in an interdependent financial system got plenty of support in the spring of 1984.

By early 1984, it was becoming apparent that the problems at Continental Illinois went well beyond those of the rogue Penn Square Bank of Oklahoma City. Continental's reputation as the preeminent oil and gas lender had disintegrated on the evening of July 5, 1982, and its credibility as a corporate lender in general went downhill from there. Continental was a financial time bomb ready to explode. After a Japanese wire service report ignited a global run, the conflagration spread to Manufacturers Hanover, which was then very much in the news because it had the highest level of exposure as a percentage of capital to Argentina of all the big U.S. banks.

As the U.S. government was groping for ways to keep Continental afloat, Citibank was exploring a private sector solution. Wriston was always shopping for expansion opportunities, but Citibank's appetite in Illinois was not what it had been a couple of years before. Citibank had already succeeded in breaking into Illinois with the acquisition of the failed thrifts, and the prospect of acquiring a failing commercial bank whose customers to a large degree overlapped with its own was not terribly enticing. Citibank in fact hated Continental because of the low rates it charged on loans, and Continental despised Citibank for invading its turf. Nevertheless, Citi dispatched an army of one hundred workout specialists to Chicago with instructions to dig through the bank's books, page by excruciating page.

The Citibank solution called for a venture capitalist, perhaps the Bass brothers of Texas, to set up a corporation that would buy all of the bad loans. Citibank's workout team—which "fortunately at that moment wasn't too overburdened," said Wriston—would try to salvage the loans. Citibank would be compensated on a sliding scale according to how much of the original loan value it was able to recover. "It was all an accepted deal, but the Fed didn't want any part of it," said Wriston later. In late May 1984, according to the *American Banker* of May 29, Wriston stated that he doubted that Citibank or anyone else would buy Continental: "I know of no one in the world who can take on $35 billion in short-term paper every morning. It's an unconventional problem that has to be solved in an unconventional way." Meanwhile, First Chicago and Chemical also walked away from the opportunity.

Wriston, however, wanted no part of the so-called safety net that the Fed and Paul Volcker were putting together for the foundering bank. Regulators demanded that the big banks extend credit lines to Continental Illinois and buy $500 million in notes. The FDIC would put up the remainder of a $2 billion capital infusion.

Representing Citibank at the negotiating table was Tom Theobald, still an apparent contender to succeed Wriston. In a secret meeting with the Comptroller of the Currency and Federal Reserve Board at a Morgan Guaranty branch in Midtown Manhattan, Morgan chairman Lew Preston, Volcker's link to the big banks, asked bankers to phone their colleagues around the country for contributions. One top regulator recalled Theobald's response: "When my house is on fire I call the fire department and my insurance company, not my neighbor." Theobald demanded that the government guarantee Citibank's share.

As the pressure from the Fed and other banks mounted, Theobald told Wriston, who was in California, "Volcker is cramming this down our throats, and I don't like any part of it." Although Volcker and Wriston scrupulously avoided all but the most essential business contact with each other, even to the point of ignoring each other while sitting at adjoining tables at restaurants, it was clear that Volcker would have to pressure Wriston to save Continental. As Wriston recalls, the central banker chose an "unseemly hour" to make the phone call. Following a minimal exchange of pleasantries, Volcker complained that Theobald was being "unreasonable" in his resistance to the Fed package.

"Well, he's probably trying to protect the shareholders of Citicorp, which is what we pay him for," Wriston replied sourly.

Volcker's response contained none of the usual oblique Fedspeak. It was blunt and to the point: "This is bigger than both of us, and you've got to come along." There was no way even Wriston could refuse an outright order from the commander. But Wriston claimed later that by holding out, Citibank got better terms than it would have if it had caved in immediately to the Fed's demands. Morgan led the sixteen-bank group that ultimately extended a $4.5 billion line to Continental. Within days, that became a $5.5 billion line and the bank group grew to twenty-eight. With $2 billion from the government, the total tab came to $7.5 billion.

Wriston didn't believe that the government should have rescued Continental or its bondholders, but he knew that this was not the issue to exploit at this time as part of his ideological war with Paul Volcker. Continental bondholders got bailed out along with big depositors. "My instinct," said Wriston later, "is that bondholders are not entitled to protection, neither are equity owners, and neither are depositors with more than $100,000. The perception has grown up that everybody's entitled."

Preston, unlike Wriston, was worried that scores of midwestern banks had sold Fed funds to Continental amounting to three times their capital. Preston agreed with Wriston in theory, but not in practice, that Continental should be allowed to fail.

In a devilish way, Wriston took some satisfaction in the demise, around this time, of another big bank. In 1981, in a bid to gain a foothold in the U.S. market, London-based Midland Bank bought Crocker Bank of San Francisco, which chairman Tommy Wilcox liked to call "Citibank West." Midland might not have realized at the time that Atomic Tommy had an obsession with showing up Wriston and that he had loaded up the books with real estate and condo loans to boost the size of his bank. A year after Midland took over, Wilcox retired with a fat consulting fee. Though it wasn't apparent at the time, Wilcox left Crocker holding a portfolio that was about to fall off a cliff. Before long, Wilcox's incompetence and vanity became obvious for all to see.

It seemed inevitable that the collapse of Continental Illinois would slow the march of deregulation. But Wriston dismissed that talk. As he told one journalist, "I don't think this has any impact other than some hearings." And he added, "When you consider what we have coped with—the debt crisis, the recycling of OPEC money, Continental Illinois—we should be optimistic." But behind the scenes, Continental's failure put the fear of God into Citibank in that it reinforced once again Citibank's concern about its heavy reliance on purchased funds. Continental was another good reason to grab cheap deposits across state lines.

With the approach of the second anniversary of the debt crisis, there was yet another Rubicon to be crossed. The venue this time was the elite International Monetary Conference, a gathering of the world's top bankers, which this year was scheduled for Philadelphia. In early May 1984, New York Fed president Anthony Solomon had proposed placing a ceiling on interest rates on new and renegotiated loans to the Third World, and Volcker joined Solomon in pressuring the banks to cut rates to Mexico. Meanwhile, the Germans, speaking from a position of relative strength, were pushing the idea of capitalizing interest on the loans—in other words, converting interest to principal. To do this would have been tantamount to throwing in the towel.

Wriston opposed such concessions. According to the *New York Times* of June 5, he said that loan spreads were linked to the country's economic and financial performance. He had shed no tears for Continental, nor was he about to cry for Argentina, Brazil, or Mexico. He recognized the need to buy time, but he was not about to give away the store.

Ever since the onset of the debt crisis, each year's debt had been dealt with as it appeared. But by now it was clear that the fire-fighting approach to the debt crisis that had been used for nearly two years could not go on forever. A more comprehensive approach was needed. The answer was multi-year rescheduling, wherein the world's banking institutions would not merely reschedule debt from one year to the next but would instead stretch it out over a period of several years.

Paul Volcker and Jacques de Larosière were the major backers of this strategy, but Wriston considered it preferable to debt concessions and capitalizing interest. The latter was, in effect, an admission that the effort to get the LDCs back into the marketplace was a futile one. The Germans balked at lending new money. Wriston, on the other hand, agreed with Volcker and de Larosière that the commercial banks would have to cooperate with the IMF and extend new loans. It would now be up to Wriston and William Rhodes to make that happen.

The conference would precipitate a showdown with German bankers and others over this new phase in the debt crisis. Compared with the U.S. institutions, the European banks had huge exposure in Eastern Europe and relatively less in Latin America, but the Europeans, and in particular the Germans, had shored up their reserves faster than American banks. They were also helped along by the devaluation of the dollar against the mark. Since they had made the loans in dollars, their exposure in marks relative to their capital diminished. Because of their hidden reserves, European banks could afford to make concessions to their borrowers.

So when Deutsche Bank managing director Alfred Herrhausen took the floor at one of the closed-door sessions to expound on the vast superiority of German banks over American institutions, his argument sounded to Wriston like a rerun of what he had heard more than forty years earlier. Wriston and Preston, who had butted heads just days before over Continental, now gnashed their teeth in unison as they listened to the German; it was one of those rare occasions when Wriston and his rival were in total accord. For the Germans to "imply that they were more prudent irritated the hell out of Wriston," Preston said later. At the time, Preston whispered to Wriston, "We'll reply to that tomorrow."

Accounting was, of course, one of Wriston's preoccupations, and he had more than a passing acquaintance with German accounting and bank regulation, which permitted institutions to own commercial enterprises to beef up their balance sheets with huge hidden reserves in the form of stock in those companies. These relationships made it almost impossible for American banks to compete for corporate business against German banks, and these other holdings made German bankers less concerned than Americans about return on assets and equity. Wriston spent much of that evening on the phone with his accounting chief, Tom Jones, working on a reply to Herrhausen.

The next day, Wriston informed the gathering that comparing German and American bank balance sheets was like comparing apples and oranges. American banks were just as sound as their German counterparts, if not more so. He pointed out that German banks didn't even consolidate their operations in Luxembourg, where their Euro loans were then located.

Finally Volcker took the floor to cast the final vote on the relative strengths of German versus American banks. "I agree with Walt," Volcker pronounced, Wriston recalled. "I have had occasion to look at the balance sheets of all the banks, including U.S. banks, and what [Wriston] said about accounting is true. They do their accounting very differently over there. . . . Whether you capitalize all further interest or only that portion which exceeds a 'reasonable rate,' whatever that might be, you do not cure the problem. You only hide it. The global marketplace will not be fooled."

Wriston, said Mexico's Angel Gurria, played a "pivotal role" in moving to multiyear rescheduling. Mexico had been pushing for this since 1983, in the face of stiff opposition from the entire global banking fraternity. "In 1983," according to Gurria, "we said, 'Let's go multiyear,' and they said, 'Go to hell.' " Silva Herzog and Gurria did not attend the International Monetary Conference, but they were prepared to fly to Philadelphia to plead with the bankers in case the efforts of de Larosière, Volcker, and Wriston failed.

In the end "Walt's view prevailed, and I think it was the correct view," John Reed said after it was all over. The first such multiyear accord was negotiated with Mexico later that year.

At Philadelphia, Wriston was "clearly the dominant presence," said a senior U.S. banker who attended the conference. When he got there, it was like "God had just arrived. Everybody deferred to him."

Wriston once again made his pitch about countries being different from companies. "Unlike a business corporation," he told the gathering, "a country has almost unlimited assets in its people, its government, its natural resources, its infrastructure, and its national political will." But that political will was showing signs of weakening. At a June 1984 meeting of Latin debtors at Cartagena, Colombia, convened by President Belisario Betancur Cuartas, the borrowers formed the Cartagena Group and rattled their sabers about a debtors' cartel. Worried bankers moved to find ways to attach those countries' assets. But because two big debtors—Mexico and Brazil—had misgivings about the cartel, it never succeeded in wielding any real clout. Nonetheless, the threat alone was enough to send shares of money center banks plunging.

After he returned from Philadelphia, with barely three months left before he would enter what he called "statutory senility," Wriston decided it was time to inform the winner of the horse race that had preoccupied Citibankers and the financial press for nearly four years. He pulled Reed aside one evening and told him, "I'm recommending you to run the place."

While Reed hadn't known for sure, he had suspected for some time he was Wriston's choice and sensed that the decision had really been made much earlier. But, he said, "I didn't spend a hell of a lot of time worrying about it." Wriston and Reed discussed the idea of appointing a president, but agreed that such a move would be premature. According to Reed, they even discussed, however briefly, naming Theobald chairman, to serve in an outside role, and designating Reed president and presumably chief executive officer, to be the "hands-on, inside guy," the same kind of relationship that Moore and Wriston had from 1967 to 1970. "I had no idea whether Tom would stay or not stay," said Reed later. "It obviously was not something I could talk to him about." While there were no quid pro quos, Wriston soon made it clear that he wanted a few people close to him to end their careers at Citibank with dignity. Foremost among them was Jim Farley.

With only Wriston, Reed, and the outside directors in on the big secret, Citicorp's top managers and directors flew to the United Kingdom, a junket that would include a train trip from Scotland to London in a luxuriously outfitted railroad car. That trip presented more than a few awkward moments for Reed. On the train, Reed and Theobald talked briefly about the succession, and on a visit to the Bank of England, Wriston scrupulously avoided sending any signals to Angermueller or Theobald or the governor of the Bank of England. Wriston introduced his successor in an almost offhand manner, saying, "Reed over here runs the consumer business."

Since Wriston had made his first overseas board trip to Great Britain many years before, it seemed fitting that the board's final tribute should take place there. Wriston's orders to his staff were to "make it like it was then but nicer." The trip was planned with all the pomp and ceremony of a state visit, and included three speaking appearances before the U.K.'s business and political elite. Wriston's protocol officer, Ann Azzara, who had a knack for moving mountains, had heard that the board had traveled on the old Orient Express from Gleneagles to London back in 1969. The Orient Express, however, was no longer operated by British Rail, but by a company headed by James B. Sherwood, president of Sea Containers Limited. The train, Azzara was told, couldn't be routed on the London-to-Scotland run and was already booked for another trip. Azzara recalled the connection between Sea-Land Service Inc. founder Malcom McLean and Sherwood. Since Wriston was in part responsible for McLean's success, and McLean for Sherwood's, the Orient Express was made available for Citicorp. Because terrorist attacks by the IRA on London targets had become too frequent for comfort, the tracks over which the special train would travel were inspected beforehand, and a helicopter carrying security agents flew over the train for the entire journey.

For the first time, Wriston's close associates sensed in their colleague a hint of nostalgia and perhaps a tinge of sadness. The trip was a homecoming of sorts. In one of his final speeches as chairman, to customers at Merchant Taylors Hall in London, he celebrated the life and work of his "patron saint," Adam Smith, while dismissing the dire predictions made for 1984 in the George Orwell novel. And a few days later he collected the president's medal from the Royal Society of Medicine Foundation for his contributions to health, having served for four years as chairman of the Business Roundtable's health care task force.

At the top of Wriston's agenda on his return to New York was the announcement of his successor. On June 19, just hours before the announcement at Citicorp was to cross the Dow Jones tape, Wriston called Tom Theobald into his office to give him the bad news. Theobald was stunned, not so much because he had lost the race but because of Wriston's timing. The news would soon be announced on radio and television and in the afternoon newspapers. Theobald barely had time to notify his family before they heard about it elsewhere. "It was unnecessarily engineered," he said later. "He had apparently made up his mind months if not years before. It's a bit tough on somebody when it's going to end up on the front pages. I would like to have told my wife."

Nonetheless, Theobald decided to remain at Citibank, at least for now. His $700,000-a-year job was not one for slouches: if the institutional bank had been a stand-alone institution, its $87 billion in assets would still have placed it ahead of third-ranked Chase.

Wriston then summoned Angermueller. "Guess what?" Wriston said, as Angermueller recalls. "John won the lottery." An audible sigh of relief escaped Angermueller's lips.

Wriston remarked about Reed's exuberance, youth, and innovativeness. Angermueller agreed. "I hope you stick around to help him," said Wriston.

"I'll have him if he'll have me," Angermueller replied.

For nearly four years, Angermueller had had to put up with being asked at cocktail parties how the succession race was going. Angermueller recalled that when people offered their support, he "sort of said thank you and let it go at that. Most people did it because they thought it was the nice thing to do." Reed's tactful gift to Angermueller was Wriston's office. Angermueller couldn't have been happier.

About this time, Wriston in a speech came as close as he ever would to saying publicly why Reed got the job and Theobald didn't. "Real leadership requires vision. And vision, by definition, is a view of the future that cannot be proved at the moment of utterance. That makes it no less important."

Shortly after the announcement, George Moore visited Tom Theobald to urge him to remain with Citibank, and then offered Reed his congratulations. Theobald reminded Moore of a conversation they'd had years earlier in which Moore had told him that no one should remain in a job for more than ten years. "You start making mistakes, know all the answers, and stop listening," Moore had told him at the time. "Take over the investment bank,"

Moore now counseled Theobald. "We're in third place on that. If you want to borrow $2 billion you don't go to Citibank. You go to Deutsche Bank. We haven't got the placing power that they've got." Moore was convinced that Citibank would never really become the world's premier financial institution until it exceeded Deutsche Bank's ability to distribute debt securities.

Moore then presented his case to Reed, and one year later Reed announced that Theobald would take over investment banking operations. But the real reason Theobald stayed, he acknowledged later, was that his wife asked for a divorce, and he didn't want to change jobs and possibly uproot his children while dealing with that trauma.

In his conversation with Reed, Moore recalled, Reed confessed his ignorance about Third World lending and reminded Moore that he had been toiling in the back office when those loans were made. "What do I do about it [LDC debt]?" Reed asked.

"You've got one way out," Moore replied. "You're not going to lose any money, but you're playing Russian roulette, and the bank can't stand that. Raise capital." Moore was convinced that, despite the debt crisis, Brazil would grow twice as fast as Japan and the United States over the next generation. He assured Reed that the problem would eventually go away through a combination of inflation, growth, conversion of debt into equity, and IMF and World Bank intervention.

Wriston had always tried to create a sense of family inside Citibank, but that effort was sometimes strained by the immense pressures that he put on the organization. After the succession announcement, he was aided by his wife, Kathy, who briefed Sally Reed on the fine points of being the first lady of Citibank.

The choice of Reed, of course, was as clear a statement as Wriston could have made that he no longer considered it necessary for the top man at Citibank to be a lender. Wriston himself had not made a loan in more than twenty years. The notion that the chairman should be a manager and not necessarily a lender was, however, a novel one in American banking in 1984.

As the Wriston era drew to a close, at least one other top banker recognized that Wriston's approach to choosing a successor was probably the correct one. Manufacturers Hanover had suffered a close brush with death in the wake of the run on Continental Illinois. For the next seven years, until its historic 1991 announcement that it would merge with Chemical, Manny Hanny was treated like the weak sister of American banking, largely because of its heavy Latin American exposure. John McGillicuddy, who had become president of Manufacturers the same year Wriston became chairman of Citibank, later recalled that as he and Wriston "became closer . . . he'd always talk about himself as not being a lender any longer. I found that hard to understand. But I understand it fully now. You get to the point where that's not what you're there for." Pointing out that he had come of age in an era of traditional bank chairmen who considered themselves bankers first, McGillicuddy said, "Walter seemed to appreciate sooner than others in the industry that [banking is] not that different from an industrial company where you're the manager. And as the manager you've got to step apart from the process and take a broader view and delegate more day-to-day responsibility. [Wriston] was ahead of the curve from a managerial point of view, style and otherwise."

Though Reed might have been ignorant of Third World debt at first, he was soon forced to assume that burden, which would occupy much of his time for nearly a decade. During the summer of 1984, Argentina's economic minister, Bernardo Grinspun, threatened to retaliate against the advisory committee for demanding that it meet its obligations. Because it operated branches in Argentina, Citibank had the most to lose. Still, Wriston, Rhodes, and Reed agreed that the U.S. banks should stick to their guns and treat the challenge as just a threat. Argentina's ill-tempered economic minister soon joined that not-so-exclusive club of former Argentine economic ministers.

Though a successor had been announced, at least one top Citibanker found out the hard way that Wriston was still calling the shots. During the summer of 1984, Wriston, Donald Regan, and others expected that interest rates would move lower by the end of the year. Regan, of course, had been lambasting the banks for keeping rates high. Ronald Reagan's supporters didn't like the idea of rates rising as the presidential election approached.

Shortly after Reed was named chairman, the news flashed across Mike Callen's Reuters screen that First Chicago had boosted its prime rate one half point to 13 percent, the highest level since October 1982. With Wriston now serving as chairman of the President's Economic Policy Advisory Board, Citibank was not anxious to be the pacesetter in increasing the prime. But within seconds after the First Chicago move, Callen, then a top treasury officer, gave the order to follow suit. Wriston had never specifically told him to hold the line on the prime, but Callen's action did not sit well with Wriston. Citibank had in the early 1970s pioneered in the creation of a floating prime rate that would move up and down according to a formula. The bank thereby avoided political charges that it was manipulating rates. But as time went on, it became clear that judgment couldn't be eliminated entirely from the rate-setting process, even as the prime itself became a less important measure of what major corporate borrowers actually paid for money.

Wriston was quickly on the line to Callen. "That was a marginal call at best," Wriston seethed. "What the hell do you guys think about, or don't you think at all?"

There was silence at Callen's end of the line. The obvious answer was that hiking the prime at a time when there was upward pressure on rates would represent a big kick to interest revenues. Citibank typically earned more money when rates fell, but if it hesitated to raise the prime when rates rose it would forfeit interest revenues. That, however, was not the statesman-like explanation. Even though Wriston was just weeks from retirement, none of Callen's colleagues volunteered to take the heat with him and absorb some of Wriston's ire. "He apparently had told the White House there would be some restraint in terms of moving interest rates up, going into the election," Callen speculated. Speaking of Wriston's reaction, Callen said later, "If you represent [to Washington] that you will practice restraint and not make economic problems worse, and [if you try] to serve as something of a shock absorber, and [then] some turkey makes your word look rather foolish, I can understand how you can get upset."

Indeed, the White House was not pleased with the banks' move. In a speech before an agricultural group, President Reagan said higher interest rates resulted from fears of renewed inflation—and called those worries baseless: "There is no excuse for interest rates being at the level they are right now, other than fear of the future." In October, as the economy slowed down and the Fed eased its grip on the money supply, however, banks started cutting rates once again. In a series of three cuts, the prime dropped from 13 percent to 12 percent—just in time for the election.

As Wriston got closer to his final day, the flow of honors and directorships accelerated. Wriston was elected to the board of Pfizer and a few days later collected an honorary law doctorate from Wesleyan for his "quiet success in working with labor, business and political leaders." And *Working Woman* magazine, in August 1984, acknowledged his contributions to the advancement of women in business. In an editor's note, the magazine wrote, "Happy birthday, Walter Wriston. WW ♡ WW." Among the more bankerly honors that Citicorp bestowed on its departing chairman was a $750,000 donation to the Fletcher School, to be earmarked for Citicorp Wriston Scholars. Fletcher had always been one of Wriston's favorite causes, and according to school officials, he signed the letter to captains of industry appealing for contributions.

When Ed Palmer and Bill Spencer had retired, Wriston threw a dinner that featured a videotaped roast of the two men and their careers. When it was his turn, however, Wriston put out the word that he didn't want an elaborate affair. That didn't sit well with longtime director Peter Grace, who orchestrated a full-blown soiree, complete with a takeoff by actor Karl Malden on the "Don't leave home without it" commercials of archrival American Express.

One of the tributes Wriston received was a letter from President Reagan. In fact, it was the White House's second try at writing a testimonial letter: Peter Grace didn't like the first one and returned it to Reagan for a rewrite!

For his retirement dinner, staffers designed a program that resembled a needlepoint pillow. Titled "Needlepoints: A Walter Wriston Sampler," and complete with a needle with a hank of red yarn, it contained some of the barbs Wriston had delivered over the years.

Besides the top echelon of Citicorp, America's business elite turned up at "21" for the crabmeat and endive, crepes with chicken hash, and roast saddle of veal. John Reed's gift to his mentor was a rare, leather-bound edition of Adam Smith's *Inquiry into the Nature and Causes of the Wealth of Nations,* and he gave Kathy a pair of pruning shears and a hammock. And an irreverent artist friend presented Wriston with a painting depicting Wriston as Jesus Christ, with members of his policy board as the disciples, at the Last Supper. In the matter of gifts, Wriston eschewed sentimentality in favor of practicality. When Paul Kolterjahn, the corporate secretary, asked him what he wanted from the policy committee for a retirement present, he didn't hesitate: a stump cutter—a heavy device consisting of a huge wheel studded with tungsten teeth that can cut off a stump below ground level. Wriston was unaware of the lengths to which Kolterjahn would have to go to purchase the tool and arrange for it to be shipped to the bank and presented to him. Kolterjahn scoured the Northeast for stump cutter distributors, arranged for the machine to be unloaded at a building entrance used by armored cars, and then handed out hard hats to members of the policy committee for the formal presentation. The hard part, however, was transporting it from mid-Manhattan to Sherman, Connecticut.

Much as Wriston loved his stump cutter, one other retirement gift that he must have been proud of was an October 20, 1984, survey by *American Banker.* By 1984, the study concluded, two-thirds of the public viewed banks more as businesses than as utilities. While no such poll measured the attitudes of the banking public in 1946 when Wriston skipped up the marble steps at 55 Wall Street for the first time, it is likely that more people would have regarded banks as quasi-governmental institutions than as businesses.

Comparing Wriston to J. P. Morgan and Bank of America founder A. P. Giannini, the *Wall Street Journal*'s Charles Stabler wrote on August 30 that the risk-free world of banking in 1967 when Wriston became president was transformed to a risky, aggressive, innovative, and exciting enterprise. Although high interest rates, technology, high energy costs, and the collapse of the Bretton Woods monetary system had a lot to do with this, Stabler said that "the adaptation of banks to this revolution, and even the encouragement of it, is Walt Wriston's doing."

One former Citicorp executive told the *Wall Street Journal* that when you walk into Citicorp headquarters "you realize that you are at one of the vortexes of power in the world. It's like an aircraft carrier revving up to thirty knots. The place shakes."

That was in stark contrast to the atmosphere at rival Bank of America. As Wriston was preparing to depart, several older, middle-level Bank of America officers gathered for dinner in San Francisco. These men had joined the bank when it was run like a civil service bureaucracy in which an employee was virtually assured of promotions and raises as long as he showed up on time. Later, B of A attempted to emulate Wriston's meritocracy, and many of these people were frozen in place. At the dinner, one of them proposed an "anti-toast" to Wriston for his role in disrupting their careers, according to a former Citibank officer.

When Wriston retired, Citibank was, among other superlatives, the biggest aircraft and shipping lender, the most important foreign exchange trader and cash management bank, the top banker to multinationals, and the loan syndicator and swaps dealer extraordinaire. During Wriston's nearly seventeen-year reign, Citibank had overtaken Chase and Bank of America to become America's largest banking institution and its premier corporate lender. But these were becoming somewhat dubious distinctions.

Citibank was becoming, by default, the only truly global bank. It would never pull back from business overseas. But because of the LDC crisis, many of the other institutions, which Citibank had led into the international arena, had already begun to withdraw. In 1983, the last full year before Wriston retired, Citicorp earned an impressive 16 percent return on equity, making it the year's most profitable money center banking company.

But for all the honors, Wriston was leaving his institution on shaky ground and, some would say, in shaky hands. For one thing, he would bequeath to his successor a company that was insufficiently capitalized to withstand the knocks it would take over the next eight years at the hands of the Latin nations and other deadbeat borrowers. In the view of Peter Rona, a former executive at IBJ Schroder Bank and Trust Company, Wriston left Citicorp so badly cushioned that even a middling Japanese institution could take it over if it were so inclined.

To be sure, many bankers differed sharply with Wriston over the purpose and goals of a bank. Rona, for example, said that one Wriston "heresy" was his conviction that bank managers work for the shareholders. Wrong, contended Rona. They work for the depositors. Accordingly, the penalty for making bad credit decisions should be "severe and immediate," he said.

Question: "The death penalty?"

"Yes," he said.

Said Jack Clark years later, "The press on Walt has always been that he's the leading American banker. Yet the bank that he left suffers from two fundamental problems that grew out of his watch. You can't square the two. The fact is that we were left with this portfolio and [later] had to take $4 billion out of equity, and may not see the light at the end of the tunnel yet. How come you're such a great banker if this is what happened?"

The Latin debt crisis would take its toll on the bankers who made the loans and tried to negotiate their way out of them. According to one international banker's calculation, the careers of at least fifty top international bankers were destroyed by the debacle, not to mention the heart attacks, nervous breakdowns, and broken marriages that resulted from the crisis.

In his remarks at the International Monetary Conference in Philadelphia in June 1984, Wriston came as close as he would ever come to admitting that he'd made a fundamental error. "The technical lending problem that surfaced in many less developed countries was the lack of equity," he said.

"Too much was financed by debt and too little by equity. In many countries this state of affairs was as much a political decision as an economic one, brought on by national policies that tended to equate foreign capital with exploitation. With the blinding clarity of hindsight, we bankers, along with many others, made a mistake in not recognizing the seriousness of this structural defect, which would become readily apparent at the advent of a worldwide recession."

But by now many were convinced that Wriston's choice of a successor—by his own account the most important decision a sitting CEO can make—would prove to be Wriston's biggest mistake. Even the taciturn Stillman Rockefeller said, "It takes a banker to run a bank."

Big-company CEOs handle succession differently. Some signal their choice years before they retire and spend those years training their successors. Other corporate chiefs may pick them later and stay around—either on the board or down the hall—to offer advice. Wriston, however, tapped John Reed three months before he retired. Reed was exposed to the duties of a CEO, but he never served in that capacity until the day after Wriston left.

Wriston was staunchly opposed to retired chairmen remaining on the board or near the boardroom. One thing was certain: he would no longer be formally involved in Citicorp's business. "There's nothing worse than having the last guy looking over your shoulder," he said. After you retire, "you get out of touch with incredible rapidity." And he said, "We have a plan for the 1990s, the people to make it happen, and I am going to love watching from the sidelines when that plan comes together."

As it turned out, Wriston would watch from the sidelines as his bank almost came apart.

25

THE LEGACY

*T*hough Wriston joked to friends about going from "who's who to who's that?" he did not look forward to retirement at all, according to intimates. Some said that even in retirement, he continued to compete with his father, who wielded influence in American life for years after he left Brown.

On the most superficial level, Wriston, like other captains of finance and industry, hated to give up that most coveted perquisite of American business: the corporate jet. Perhaps more than any other symbol of corporate power, the jet separates the players from the also-rans, providing those able to commandeer them with global freedom of movement nearly on a par with that enjoyed by the president of the United States. "I don't sit around thinking, 'Don't I wish I was chairman of Citibank?'," Wriston said later. But he admitted wistfully, "It would be nice to have an airplane now and then."

Even more than he regretted being deprived on August 31, 1984 of his cherished Gulfstream, Wriston dreaded the prospect of losing his place in the American power structure and the information loop. He was, said a friend, terribly "frightened" of giving up his seat at the big table with the likes of Henry Kissinger and George Shultz, and he feared that the phone calls, much less the dinner invitations, from the Oval Office would become much fewer and farther between.

Wriston enjoyed nothing more than the occasional gatherings of the President's Economic Policy Advisory Board (PEPAB). Important as this economic cheerleading squad was in Reagan's first term, by his second term it had largely outlived its original purpose. Reaganomics was already woven into the fabric of the public sector and the focus of the Reagan administration had largely shifted to foreign policy. The Board was now meeting only once or twice a year, addressing the economic crises of the moment. In the view of many panel members, the advisory board enabled Wriston to influence policy on the Third World debt crisis. Said former White House domestic policy adviser Jack Svahn, "A lot of times there was a concern that we had to do something." But Wriston put a stop to such talk, "Your banker knows when debts are bad. Wait until your banker tells you they're bad."

In the fall of 1985, PEPAB suffered a major blow when Donald Regan became President Reagan's chief of staff. In his new and powerful role, Regan seized the opportunity to get rid of the advisory board, which members felt he regarded as a threat, or at least a nuisance. In late October, Wriston learned that Regan had in effect dissolved the board and unceremoniously "fired" him as chairman a few weeks earlier. The presidential order creating PEPAB, it turned out, had expired on October 1, and Regan, Svahn said, "refused to renew it." Only after intense lobbying by its members was PEPAB subsequently reinstated, along with Wriston as chairman, for a two-year term, and two years later given another two-year lease on life. But it was all over by September 30, 1989.

Even as it became clear that the supply-side formula had not worked—lower taxes, instead of generating more revenue, led to a widening of the deficit—Wriston served as a lightning rod for the administration by insisting on the lecture circuit that budget deficits don't matter. Fed policy, not supply-side economics, Wriston asserted, crippled the economy and caused the sharp decline in tax revenues. The deficit, he declared in an October 1988 Business Council speech, was a fiction caused by a governmental accounting system that inappropriately treated long-term capital outlays such as roads, as cash expenditures. There is little evidence that the deficit hurts the economy, he said, or crowds out capital. Even after he and Paul Volcker retired, they remained ideological rivals. Arriving at the Homestead in Hot Springs, Virginia, for that 1988 Business Council meeting, Wriston was greeted by Volcker, who zinged him by asking, "Couldn't they get anyone qualified to talk about the deficit?"

Wriston had his last shot at a cabinet post in 1980, but he turned down other government posts after he retired. His friend, Secretary of State George Shultz, offered him ambassadorships. "They were good ones," Wriston said coyly, while declining to name the countries. One, said a friend, was Japan. He wouldn't have taken that one if his life depended on it, the friend said. Wriston refused these offers because in an age of advanced telecommunications and jet travel, the "latitude of the ambassador to make a constructive contribution is extremely narrow," he said. If, for example, there's a problem in Germany, an undersecretary—not the ambassador—flies over in Air Force 3. CNN has virtually replaced the ambassador's reporting function. "The primary job of an ambassador is to make friends with the natives."

Instead of rolling out the red carpet for Shultz as the Secretary's man in Tokyo or some other foreign capital, Wriston and two friends in 1985 threw a sixty-fifth birthday bash for him and 150 guests at San Francisco's Bohemian Club, giving the affair all the attention to detail a mother would lavish on a party for her five-year-old child. Concerned that even the decorations befit the man and the occasion, Wriston personally scoured the country for miniature ceramic eagle place settings. It was "just a family-type party," Wriston said at the time.

He continued to lobby for liberalization in banking laws that would permit the expansion of banks like his. By 1987, largely because of the strength in the yen against the dollar, Japanese banks had surged ahead of U.S. banks in size and power. But in his June 18, 1987 testimony before the Senate Banking Committee, Wriston, arguing for legislative changes that would permit the growth of "superbanks," contended that a major reason was that deregulation had not proceeded fast enough. As he had done for fifteen years, he complained of the "one-way street" in the laws separating banking and commerce. And in 1988 Wriston was in the vanguard of the push to "reinvent" government as a member of Reagan's Commission on Privatization, which recommended more private-sector involvement in many government activities and outright divestiture of others.

In part because of his concern about lawsuits brought against directors, Wriston turned down many more directorships than he accepted. But at those companies where he served on the board, he often played the role of kingmaker.

At Chubb Corp., Wriston influenced the succession in 1988 in a oblique way. He had always regarded anyone who smoked as an ignoramus and would never support a CEO candidate who did. So when Wriston and other directors of the insurance concern were deliberating the elevation of president Dean O'Hare, a heavy smoker, to the top post, he blurted out that "anyone who wasn't smart enough not to destroy himself with cigarettes isn't smart enough to run a company." Wriston's comment quickly reached O'Hare's ears, and became the news of the week around every water cooler at Chubb headquarters. O'Hare went cold turkey and kicked the habit completely a couple of years later. "He did stop smoking and he did become chairman," Wriston said slyly.

Against the advice of friends, Wriston in 1985 joined the board of perennially troubled Pan Am. Besides his fascination with airplanes, one reason he became a director was to return a favor—in fact, lots of favors. Citibank's expansion around the globe had in some respects paralleled Pan Am's, and Citibank eventually established a beachhead in most Pan Am destinations, and vice versa. Whenever children of overseas employees needed emergency medicines or equipment, Wriston asked his pilot friends to run mercy missions, delivering these supplies to remote Citibank outposts. In many countries, Pan Am was a kind of extension of the U.S. government. Pilots delivered pouches between U.S. embassies and Washington. Wriston called Pan Am a "national treasure. Not to have a world-class player with the American flag on it is crazy." But clearly another attraction was the free lifetime World Pass given to each director.

To be sure, Pan Am's demise was caused in part by government regulation. But mismanagement probably had more to do with it. Among its more disastrous moves was its 1979 acquisition of National Airlines, which was saddled with a high cost structure. When Wriston joined the board, he was shocked at what he found. Like the Citibank of old, Pan Am had no idea what parts of its business were profitable or not. He was frustrated by the lack of credible information. Top management gave him numbers and made representations he knew to be wrong. "He knew what he was being told was nonsense," said Thomas Plaskett, who later became Pan Am's chairman. There was no way, Plaskett said, they could achieve the results they were promising. "Yet when he would ask questions and probe he wouldn't get any answers. With Walter Wriston you only do that once. He's the kind of boss who if you ever lied to him you not only lose your credibility but support," said Plaskett.

In early 1986, Citibank, at Wriston's behest, tried unsuccessfully to find a possible merger candidate and helped Pan Am analyze its route structure to identify operating inefficiencies. In 1987, airline financier Fred Bradley collaborated with Wriston to arrange a $150 million Citicorp-led financing. By 1987, acrimony between labor groups and management had intensified; labor costs were out of control and Pan Am continued to hemorrhage. Wriston knew something had to give. Management—chairman C. Edward Acker and vice chairman Martin R. Shugrue Jr.—had recommended a settlement, director William Coleman said later, that Wriston, Coleman, and other directors concluded was a poor one. The board rejected management's recommendation for the contract.

The board's discontent with Acker and Shugrue was growing. The final straw came when they implied that the problem had been solved. Wriston and Coleman knew it hadn't. And, in 1987, Pan Am posted losses of $265.3 million.

Wriston employed various techniques to get his message across. They ranged from the circuitous, when he wanted to offer unsolicited advice to his successor at Citi or to the president of Chubb Corp., to the blunt. To avoid any possible lawsuits resulting from misunderstandings as to who said what to whom, Wriston and Coleman together marched into Acker's and Shugrue's offices in January 1988 and demanded that both men resign. Following this management restructuring, Pan Am got $180 million in givebacks from the unions.

For two weeks, Pan Am was without a CEO and flew on autopilot as Coleman and Wriston pitched in to manage the airline. Wriston tried to make sure there was cash on hand to pay the bills. He also asked an associate to contact Thomas Plaskett, whom he had known when Plaskett was chief financial officer in the 1970s at American Airlines. Citibank had played a key financial role in American's expansion. After Plaskett came aboard as CEO of Pan Am in 1988, Wriston helped him find a new chief financial officer, Richard Francis.

In 1988, Pan Am continued selling assets by unloading Pan Am World Services, the contract services unit, to Johnson Controls. These asset sales were painful. On this one Wriston said, as Plaskett recalled, "One of these days we've got to stop cutting off the tail to feed the dog."

But the mortal blow to Pan Am came four days before Christmas 1988, when a terrorist bomb brought down Pan Am flight 103, en route from London to New York, over Lockerbee, Scotland, killing all 258 passengers and crew.

After the bombing, Plaskett was besieged with frantic phone calls from directors. Virtually all of them wanted to know more about the bombing and the impact it was having on the company. Wriston, according to Plaskett, was the only director who phoned repeatedly out of concern about him personally. Wriston called, said Plaskett, to say "he knew what I was going through and how difficult it was. He wanted me to know he was there. It was more than just a call from an interested and concerned director."

For airline executives, plane crashes are a grim but inevitable part of operations. Wriston and Plaskett took this one as an unusually personal loss. It turned out that Charles T. Fisher III, chairman of the National Bank of Detroit, had a son, a Citibank officer in London, who was a passenger on the plane. Plaskett had worked for American and GM, where Fisher served as a director.

In the wake of the tragedy, directors debated how much information should be disclosed to the public. There were always some who said, "This information may not be a hundred percent certain. Hold it for another two weeks." Wriston, said Coleman, "was certainly one of the directors who said, consistent with national security considerations, we should disclose everything that happened . . . as soon as we got it, and not try to cover it up." Then, in June 1989, Pan Am's chances of survival grew slimmer when it made an unsuccessful $3.3 billion bid for Northwest Airlines.

Just as the impact of Lockerbee was starting to wear off, the prospect and the reality of the 1991 Gulf War sent the price of jet fuel through the roof. That, Wriston said, was the coup de grace.

Plaskett felt that Pan Am's problems ultimately "flowed from the government and government actions." Pan Am couldn't get the internal routes it needed to grow domestically and feed passengers into its international flights yet the government even hacked away at its international franchise by awarding those routes to other carriers. Wriston tried to advance Pan Am's cause in Washington. When it came to Pan Am, Wriston left ideology on the survival of the fittest and government intervention at home, tempering principles with pragmatism. "He is not a zealot," Plaskett said. "He's always been willing to pick up the phone to call Secretary Brady to give us an opportunity to tell our story."

But the dismemberment continued. In negotiations with UAL Corp., parent of United Airlines, to sell its Latin American and other routes, Pan Am brought a lot of emotional and historical baggage to the table. There were, gut-wrenching concerns about separating Pan Am from Heathrow Airport, where it had operated for half a century. Plaskett recalled that Wriston expressed the sentiment of the board that "we had to have more than an asset sale. We had to have a strong and substantive marketing agreement with UAL." In the end, however, that hardly mattered. Sadly, in September 1991 Wriston and his fellow directors presided over the sale of the Pan Am shuttle and most of the trans-Atlantic routes to Delta Airlines. Finally, that December Pan Am shut down its operations completely, and UAL Corp. later bought its Latin routes out of bankruptcy court for $135 million.

As a Pfizer Inc. director, Wriston brought his strongly held views about the role of the retired chairman to his new boards. There he vehemently opposed the idea of a retired chairman staying on as an elder statesman. Chairman Edmund Pratt argued that his predecessor remained on the board for ten years. "It was wonderful, helpful," he said. "That's our culture." But Pratt joked to his board, "We have at least one director who feels very strongly the other way. Fortunately, he's retiring before I am."

At General Electric, Wriston had played a key role in supporting former chairman Reginald Jones's desire to appoint Jack Welch as his successor. In 1981, that was not a foregone conclusion, Jones said later. Other candidates had their own supporters on the GE board. And after Welch became chairman Wriston backed him in his sensitive decision to unload an Australian coal company Jones had bought a few years earlier. More important, Walt and Kathy Wriston had introduced the divorced executive to his new wife, a Shearman & Sterling lawyer.

Unfortunately for Welch, he ignored Wriston's advice on Kidder, Peabody. Wriston usually excused himself when matters involving GE's financial services activities came before the board. But, said Welch, he "made us mad as hell giving speeches about it." According to Welch, Wriston warned him that "in this game you're only buying people. He kept saying you don't know those people well enough." As the deal was about to be completed, Wriston told him, "I hope you know what you're getting yourself into."

Understandably, Welch at the time didn't regard the Kidder deal as a "break the bank" issue. After all, the price tag for Kidder represented just about 3 percent of the $20 billion GE spent on acquisitions in the 1980s.

Wriston's advice came back to haunt Welch when Martin Siegel, cohead of mergers and acquisitions at Drexel Burnham, was charged with insider trading in connection with transactions when he worked at Kidder. In an interview, Welch acknowledged that "we might have been smarter if we had never purchased Kidder. There was a guy in there who was a bad apple." In April 1994, Welch discovered to his horror that there was more than one bad apple. He learned that $350 million in bond-trading profits the firm had reported for 1993 simply didn't exist; they were, auditors charged, fabricated by a bond trader named Joseph Jett. After months of embarrassing disclosures, GE finally sold the firm to Paine Webber for $670 million in stock.

Though Wriston might have been sliding slowly out of the Washington loop, he remained on the leading edge of technology by accepting membership on the boards of companies like Tandem Computers Inc., a California maker of transaction-processing systems, which he joined in July 1986. When Shultz left the State Department in 1989, Wriston persuaded him to join the Tandem board. The chaos and informality of an entrepreneurial, high-tech company was a bit much for an ex–cabinet officer accustomed to fat briefing books. According to Wriston, Shultz nearly quit after the first meeting. "Somebody would ask a question and they [Tandem executives] would yell down the hall, and some kid would come in and answer it."

"We calmed George down," he said. "We said, 'These entrepreneurs. They don't have staff and briefing books. They want to do business.' "

It was clear to Wriston that Shultz was in sync after his first annual meeting. When a shareholder got into an argument with a company executive over Tandem's failure to pay a dividend, Shultz turned to Wriston and asked, "You're not going to muzzle me, are you?"

"Go right ahead," Wriston said.

Shultz proceeded to describe how he invested his own money after he left government, placing some of it in income-producing assets and others in growth stocks. That, he said, "is what you've got here." Sensing she was outgunned, the woman clammed up.

"George," Wriston said, "is now having a tremendous time, like I do."

Between board meetings Wriston produced occasional Op-Ed articles and two books, *Risk and Other Four Letter Words,* a synthesis of his speeches, and the *Twilight of Sovereignty,* a primer on the information revolution. He continued to advance his conservative views through the Manhattan Institute, which he helped found. And to fund his Keogh, he said, he gave speeches at about $15,000 a pop.

"My shelf life is remarkable," said Wriston. "I never walk the streets of New York without seeing somebody I knew or who knew me. The moral of that story is always be with your own wife."

The one activity Wriston did not engage in was meddling—at least directly—in the affairs of Citicorp. If there was one accomplishment that Wriston prided himself on most, it was "building a team with a very deep bench," as he commented to the Citicorp newspaper upon his retirement. Consequently, he figured, meddling would not be necessary. Wriston rarely visited 399 Park except on social occasions, such as retirement parties for close friends, and never offered gratuitous advice or asked for favors from his successor. Reed, Wriston said, called him about once a year, if that. "I don't resent that in the slightest. What do I know about it [Citibank] anymore? You're out of that bank in a week and the world changes." Before Citi's woes deepened, he said, "I read what they send me, hold on to my stock, and stand in the bleachers and cheer what they're doing."

Reed, in fact, made a point of not visiting him. "I thought he really wanted to get away from the bank and not be a part of it," Reed said later. But Wriston did have ways to make his feelings known to Reed, especially when he became upset about the forced departure of a favored colleague. "He tends to moan and groan publicly," said Reed later. "He's very disciplined in what he talks to me about. Sometimes he gets so carried away in what he says to others that he knows will [talk] to me. Then he knows I know, and I know he knows I know."

By the early 1990s, Wriston had good reason to moan and groan loudly and clearly. Besides having inherited an inadequately capitalized institution saddled with Third World debt, Reed was woefully ill-prepared by his experience as consumer chief to run the nation's largest bank. Reed regarded himself as more competent than Wriston, who, he told friends, was really a shy, insecure man who lived in the shadow of his father. But Reed's competence certainly wasn't in corporate banking, still the guts of Citibank.

In many ways, however, the Citibank culture now reflected Reed's way of doing things as much as or more than it did Wriston's. Citibank was now far more concerned with procedures and processes than when Wriston had taken over, to the point where it resembled the same bureaucratic government agencies Wriston abhorred.

It was also Reed's misfortune to become Citicorp chairman in a much more difficult economic climate than the one in which Wriston was chairman. Though the U.S. economy was well on the road to recovery from the deepest economic downturn since the Depression, it was no longer the world's most vigorous. The Japanese economic steamroller was barreling ahead of America's. In the mid-1980s, Citicorp was still the largest banking company in the world, but Japanese financial institutions were overtaking America's in global financial power and influence; four of the ten largest banks in the world were Japanese. A decade later Citicorp, though still the largest bank in the United States, ranked 29th in the world. As one former Citibanker observed, an expanding, dominant economy, like the one enjoyed by Wriston, "allows you to do things you can't do when it's no longer dominant, or when the U.S. banking system is no longer number one."

Reed would later say that the Japanese banks' ranking "doesn't bother me at all." He regarded this as an insignificant statistic that resulted from a strengthening yen. "They're not our fiercest competition in the world." Still, by the time Reed took over, U.S. commercial banks in general, and Citibank in particular, had lost much of their value as an intermediary for the nation's largest and most creditworthy companies.

In the early days, Reed seemed to fit into his role at Citibank as if fate had, for once, done a perfect job. Shortly after he took over, his public relations staff got the word that they were to destroy what one admirer called "all those old nerdy pictures" of Reed. And he also worked hard to heal the wounds of the succession with rivals Tom Theobald and Hans Angermueller; despite Theobald's earlier sniping at the consumer business, Reed did not show him the door.

That October 1984, he presided confidently at his coming-out party as the new leader of the American banking industry. It was a lavish Citicorp Center reception for 3,000 fellow bankers attending the American Bankers Association's annual convention.

One of the first signs of John Reed's efforts to put his imprint on the bank was a program, launched in mid-1984, that was dubbed Project Delta— Delta, of course being the mathematical symbol for change. It was ostensibly a cost-cutting exercise aimed at reducing expenses by 40 percent by year end, but in fact, said insiders, it was really intended to relegate staff to what Reed regarded as their rightful position. To Reed, the only people who contributed materially to a business's success were line people. Reed did add one staff member, a brain truster who spent much of his time reading books for his boss.

One of Wriston's long-standing dreams was for Citibank to reach $1 billion in annual earnings around the time he retired. But by the end of 1985, as it appeared that Citibank's earnings would come within a hairsbreadth of that milestone, Reed was faced with the public relations problem of whether results should be massaged or reported just as they came off the calculator tape. Financial managers at an institution the size of Citibank have considerable leeway in dressing up the year-end balance sheet and income statement. So when Citibank reported earnings of $998 million for 1985, some Citi watchers snickered that Reed was tweaking Wriston by denying him the satisfaction of seeing Citi pass the $1 billion mark soon after he retired. Not so, said Reed later. "Obviously we could have made it $1.03 billion." But Reed was concerned that the market would conclude that Citibank had cooked the books, and that the real number was more like $995 million. Instead, Reed asked his chief number cruncher, Tom Jones, if somehow earnings couldn't be pushed to $1.066 billion, which Reed, as a history buff, regarded as a "nice" number. Jones came back with the disappointing news that this would be stretching it. "To hell with it," Reed told Jones. "I'm glad I did. I don't want to become one of those Geneens [Harold Geneen, creator of the ITT conglomerate] who get driven by the symbols of success rather than success itself." . . . Reflecting his self-image as a "plain vanilla," straightforward person, Reed ordered that the covers of future annual reports be white.

The differences in style between Wriston and Reed were glaring. Indeed, Reed's early moves were more stylistic than substantive.

Wriston never forgot that he was chairman, but Reed sometimes seemed so chaotic and unassertive that his associates had to remind him that he was the boss. "Stand up, identify yourself, take charge!" one senior colleague sometimes admonished him.

Unlike Wriston, Reed didn't seem to like to press the flesh, and many who worked at 399 Park for years had never seen him in person. Some said they felt Reed was embarrassed by his inability to remember the names of colleagues.

Yet in his private life, Reed considered himself a man of the people, someone with a modest ego, smaller certainly than those of others who had jobs like his. He describes himself as a "blue jeans kind of guy" who likes to listen to his hi-fi and considers his driver, J.C., a native of Britain who is a crack mechanic and carpenter, as one of his best friends. But according to a former colleague, Reed was once asked what he missed about being chairman. His answer: "Friends." Former personnel chief Jim Griffin quoted Reed as saying, "I have one friend in the bank, but I can't remember his name and I don't know where he works."

On his overseas trips as chairman, he resented the insensitive treatment he said he received at the hands of his own organization. "I'm not a human being as far as Citicorp's concerned. I'm a thing. I get moved around from

place to place." Though he told his schedulers that he wanted an hour between his last business meeting and dinner on his overseas trips to change his
clothes, "inevitably they give you fifteen minutes."

Two years after he became chairman, he isolated himself even more.
Supposedly to improve communication among his top managers, he consolidated them in new glass-enclosed offices, complete with Japanese garden
and private elevator, on the second floor of Citibank headquarters. The move
may have improved communication on the upper levels, but it cut them off
from close, day-to-day contact with their own people. Reportedly built at a
cost of more than $20 million the suite included a library for Reed that he
called his "temple." Once completed, an insider said, Citibank spent upward
of $1,000 a week just on flowers for the "temple."

Though Reed essentially shared Wriston's vision of a global bank, he regarded Wriston's "Five I's" [the Individual, Institutional, and Investment
banks, plus Information and Insurance] as gimmickry, according to colleagues. To Reed, none of the "I's" was as important as his Individual Bank.
His commitment to the others varied in intensity, but in virtually every instance that commitment was decidedly less than Wriston's.

Reed's ambition was to create a global and national consumer bank.
He had thought he could do this largely through ATMs, the telephone, credit
cards, and the U.S. mail. But the failure of the "financial account" convinced
him that he needed to cover the U.S. with branches, perhaps a couple of thousand by the end of the century. As consumer executive Rick Braddock told
the *American Banker* on March 27, 1987, the bank then realized it also
needed "some physical presence." One of Reed's barometers of success in retail banking was 5,000 customers per branch, and $70 earnings from each
customer.

Reed also wanted to integrate the card and branch businesses, to some
extent returning to the old arrangement. But instead of the branches driving
the card business, the cards would drive the branches. Reed figured that the
credit-card business was his most profitable activity, and in October 1988 determined that he could sell it for as much as $7 billion, "which is damn near
the value of Citibank," he said. Another key goal was to link up Citibank's
worldwide ATM network, so that customers could use their Citicards to access their accounts anywhere in the world.

In 1985, Reed expanded Citibank's reach by acquiring, or agreeing to
acquire, banks or thrifts in Arizona, Utah, and Nevada, and commercial and
investment banks in a dozen foreign countries.

A year later, Citi broke into the District of Columbia with the acquisition of a troubled thrift, but not without getting some egg on its face. In response to questions from the *Washington Post,* Citi revealed that two
registered lobbyists had paid more than $60,000 to a friend and adviser of a

member of Washington's City Council, which was involved in approving the acquisition. The payments, the *Post* reported on January 30, 1987, were made by the now-defunct law firm of Finley Kumble and charged to Citibank as legal fees.

Citibank also coveted Bank of America and First Interstate. When Bank of America ran into trouble in the mid-1980s, chief financial officer Don Howard felt that the market had undervalued B of A's California franchise, so Citibank acquired a $150 million stakeout investment. First Interstate, on the other hand, was attractive because it was "grandfathered" to operate in thirteen western states. By 1986, Bank of America was rumored to be close to insolvency. Citibank could acquire B of A only if it collapsed, but it had no interest in convincing the world that B of A was failing. Ironically, when First Interstate made a run at acquiring its big competitor, B of A, Citibank owned stakes in both the would-be buyer and the target.

In 1986, Howard tried to persuade Reed to merge with the Chemical Bank, a deal that could have been consummated by exchanging one share of Citi for one of Chemical. That would have gained Citibank a lock on New York's middle market, which it was never able to obtain on its own. Reed declined.

Reed had little or no interest or background in corporate or investment banking. He and his colleagues who built the consumer business were, in Citibank parlance, "process managers," not deal-makers. The consumer business, observed one top Citibanker, is more of a statistical exercise than corporate banking. Very few people were stars at both. Reed had installed good controls in the individual bank. But he did not, said former consumer executive Richard Kane, do that in the institutional bank.

In the view of colleagues, he regarded people who hadn't grown up with him in the retail business as his stepchildren, and he was perfectly happy to delegate the nonretail businesses entirely to them. That was fine as long as a veteran lender like Tom Theobald was in charge of corporate banking.

A year after his accession, however, Reed was ready to redraw the Wriston organization chart in a major way. The realignment was a fateful one. Reed ended years of speculation on who would head up retail banking by appointing Richard Braddock, Citibank's original marketeer, to that position.

One of Reed's miscalculations concerned Richard Kovacevich, the marketing whiz who ramrodded the ATMs into the branches. Kovacevich had made no secret of the fact that he felt he deserved the job that Braddock got, but Reed believed that Kovacevich would recover and remain at Citibank. For his part, Reed later claimed that he never felt insecure during transition periods when he collected a paycheck but lacked a specific assignment, and grossly miscalculated the anxiety other executives feel when they are forced to operate without such a structure.

At the press conference announcing the changes, Reed was asked, "What's going to happen to Kovacevich?" Reporters' jaws dropped at

Reed's response, which seemed intended to send a message to Kovacevich. "We're scrounging around the bank for something for him to do," Reed said, as PR man John Maloney blanched.

Reed would later explain that "out of ignorance, it never really crossed my mind that he was going to be uptight about putting Braddock in the job he had wanted," adding that "there was no question in my mind that he [Kovacevich] was going to be a major player."

"I thought he knew that," Reed went on. "I failed to understand that people can't tolerate being seen publicly not being in a cubbyhole. People need a lot more structure than I realized." Despite Reed's attempts to persuade him to stay, Kovacevich soon accepted an offer to become president of Norwest Bank in Minneapolis, where he was very successful.

"Dick was one of the guys I really liked. I was really unhappy about that," Reed admitted with some obvious sadness.

There were apparently no hard feelings between Braddock and Kovacevich: Kovacevich's daughter Lori later married Braddock's son, Durk.

Significantly, Reed appointed his old ally, Larry Small, the flamenco guitar player who had begun the long march with him in the back office and suffered with him through the dark days of the consumer business, to head up the institutional bank. Meanwhile Theobald, the staunch opponent of paying investment banking salaries at Citibank, was named head of investment banking. And after years of hand-wringing over how to organize investment banking, the highly profitable treasury operation was finally consolidated into the investment bank.

Small—a.k.a. "the German"—was regarded as autocratic and risk-averse. He had rebuilt Citibank's North American corporate business less by building revenues than by slashing costs. In fact, Reed's biggest fear about appointing Small to the new post was that he would "be so risk-averse that he wouldn't build the business." Unfortunately, Reed was afraid of the wrong thing. He may have unwittingly set up a horse race for the presidency of Citicorp between Small and Braddock.

With Small and Theobald in place, Reed felt he could simply delegate corporate banking. In fact, he virtually washed his hands of it. Said one former colleague, "John never showed any desire to meet or call on customers or work with account officers." He would much rather read a good book on Taoism and Confucianism, or attend meetings on global markets at the Santa Fe Institute, one of his favorite think tanks.

Wriston, in the view of colleagues, was careful about how he managed his time and spent much of it overseeing the general management of the bank. "Wriston might not have been on top of every business day by day, but he certainly was week by week," said former Citibanker Richard Huber. In contrast, Reed as a manager was "very hands off," Huber said. In his view, Reed felt he had inherited the mantle of world banking statesman once held by David Rockefeller. It seemed like more fun to fly around the world and have lunch with popes and potentates than to get down there in the trenches, and find out how many government [bond] traders we really needed, and should we be in the municipal bond business," he said.

In the mid-1980s, the traditional institutional lending business was in the doldrums, but the merger, buyout, and junk bond boom was gathering steam. And it appeared that there was no limit to how high commercial and residential real estate could go. It was a heady time for deal-makers and traders. At a Christmas Party in 1985, Citibank traders gathered at the Palladium, a Manhattan club & disco. According to an eyewitness, one top trader stripped naked and started dancing. When the bouncers ran after him, a senior manager pursued the bouncers, all the while yelling at them not to hurt his best trader.

Small, according to former Citibankers, sneered at humdrum businesses that didn't do large volumes of transactions and rake in huge front-end fees. The commercial real estate and LBO fees were irresistible. Citibank's bias, said one investment banker, was in favor of taking hog shares of real estate and LBO loans and selling off the rest to others.

While Wriston said that size was never important to him, Citibank now paid bonuses for putting assets on the books. "There was a perversion of the credit apparatus because of incentive compensation," said a former senior executive. Volume-based bonus pools, "ever so slightly twisted perspectives." Sales and credit became one and the same. For Citicorp to have an aggressive business strategy but not a conservative capital strategy, said another executive, was a prescription for disaster.

Small was proud of the relationships he had cultivated with Robert Campeau, the high-flying Canadian real estate tycoon; Donald Trump; and Toronto's secretive Reichmann brothers, operators of Olympia & York, to name a few. These were the "new people who are significant players in the world of finance," he said later.

In Small's view, they were the 1980s equivalents of Aristotle Onassis and Stavros Niarchos. And just as Wriston had earned his stripes as a deal-maker by cultivating the Greek shipowners, Small would earn his by doing deals for flamboyant LBO artists and real estate moguls. Said Small, "You get the call because they know you and can count on you and feel that you have a team that has the skills to put it together."

Still, in the view of colleagues, Small's tough, authoritarian style and low tolerance for dissent or mistakes discouraged prudent risk-taking. "Larry's approach is cut, cut, cut," said one Citibank officer. Under Small, the institutional bank was overcontrolled to the point that officers on the front lines were afraid to back seemingly prudent deals. "You fail a credit inspection, you're fired, you make a bum loan, you're fired." That, the Citibanker said, caused people to spend their time perfecting credit files rather than looking for good deals. In the end, those credit files were very far from perfect.

One of Small's early moves was to take an ax to the European operation. He assigned two aides to take charge of Europe, and according to Citibank officers, instructed them to slash costs and close branches that weren't generating acceptable profits. Earlier, the European operation had begun to push into lending to middle market companies. Now it pulled back. Small's disciples went on a firing binge, then on a hiring binge. Demoralized by the mayhem, some of Citibank's best European hands quit in disgust.

One of Small's disciples was Michael Callen, who got Small's old job when Small moved up. Callen's view, said a former senior colleague, was that more is better. "If you're going to do $300 million, why not $500 million, or if $500 million why not $1 billion. Mike said, 'Why not do subordinated debt? You make more money on it.' He didn't seem to understand that more money involved more risk." According to one former senior officer, evidence that Small and Callen lacked the stature of the Wriston team was seen in the fact that neither of them was ever elected to a blue-chip corporate board. Callen and Braddock competed for a prestigious slot on the Eastman Kodak board, and Braddock won out.

Citibank backed virtually all the LBO kings. Citi was there when the high-living Robert Campeau acquired Allied Stores, [whose holdings included Brooks Brothers and Bonwit Teller] in 1986 for $3.6 billion, and later when he needed $6.6 billion for Federated, parent of Bloomingdale's and Abraham & Straus, among others. Small developed a close personal relationship with Campeau, and flew in his plane to the 1988 Winter Olympics in Calgary. Campeau, according to *Fortune* of June 18, 1990, had been treated for mental breakdowns and had a wife and a mistress, and children by both women. "I was appalled," said Wriston.

Relationship banking went by the board. Hungry for fees, Citibank backed takeover artist Ronald Perelman in his unsuccessful 1987 hostile bid for the Gillette Company, despite the fact that the razor manufacturer was an old customer. Small was the transactional banker through and through. "Larry believed customers would screw the banks if there was money to be made, so [Citi] should go for it." And as one veteran banker complained, "The transaction guys get paid a lot more money than relationship guys." Even Reed himself later confessed that Citibankers became "deal junkies" in the 1980s. "It was a deal a day," said one former officer in the LBO unit. "There was a feeling"—albeit one that was not really articulated—said one former senior officer, that Citibank had to "work out of the LDC [problem] by boosting earnings on domestic businesses."

Besides these big deals with the household names of the LBO business, Citi underwrote countless other transactions with people who achieved notoriety only after they went bust. It bankrolled a $14 million leveraged buyout of a California mushroom farm that later failed, and lent tens of millions to thirty-two-year-old William Stoecker, a would-be takeover artist from Chicago who was forced into bankruptcy in early 1989. When the dust finally settled on that debacle, $250 million was simply unaccounted for. According to one officer familiar with the Stoecker episode, Stoecker's entré was a Citibank private banking officer who wrote a "to whom it may concern letter" praising him.

In 1986, Australia handed out banking licenses to foreign financial institutions, including Citibank, that enabled them to offer a wide array of services. But once again, the Aussies got the better end of the deal. As it had done in the early 1970s, Citibank went hog wild lending to Australian wheeler-dealers. That enthusiasm would come back to haunt it.

Although Wriston, colleagues said, regarded leveraged buyouts as a time bomb while he was chairman, he changed his tune after he retired, and made piles of money like all his fellow lucky stockholders when one company in which he invested was bought out—supplementing the 40 percent returns he earned as a member of an exclusive group of CEOs that invests in the American European Association, a fund headed by former Goldman, Sachs senior partner John Whitehead.

Junk bond king Mike Milken and Wriston were soul mates of sorts. Milken, friends say, admired Wriston's penchant for risk taking. And Wriston viewed junk bonds as a device that, much like his own negotiable CD, enabled capital-starved companies to tap the markets. Milken, Wriston said, did a lot "to change the financial structure of the country. Whether he went too far in implementing his dreams . . . I don't know." Though Wriston said Milken got the most of the media's attention for junk bond–financed takeovers, what he also did was "liquefy the balance sheets of midsized corporations that were the prisoners of regional banks." For these companies to be able to borrow for ten years instead of ninety days, was a "net plus for the capital markets of the world." As for takeovers, or the use of junk to finance them, Wriston was more ambivalent. On that subject, "you can start a fight in a bar room . . . there are excellent arguments on both sides. At the end of the day, the threat of a takeover helps drive American management to become more competitive in the world," he said. But Kathy Wriston had quite a different view. She hated hostile takeovers. Unlike Wriston, she had lived through them, as a director of Federated. "She's seen the human carnage, which is substantial," said Wriston.

One fateful Citibank decision was to focus on about fifteen or so top real estate operators, and to back them in a major way. It seemed that because they were engaged in many projects throughout the country that they had diversified their risk. A former Chase real estate lender said, "Citibank wanted to corner the New York commercial real estate market. They succeeded." About the same time, Reed fired his economics department. For all its shortcomings in predicting interest rates, it had, one former senior executive pointed out, established a close relationship with the credit policy department, advising it on trends such as home building. Apparently unnoticed by the Citibank real estate department was the Tax Reform Act of 1986, which would soon wipe out the benefits of tax-sheltered real estate investments such as limited partnerships.

In the 1970s, Citibank learned that lending on undeveloped land was like rolling the dice. Citibank didn't make exactly the same mistakes. It varied them slightly in the 1980s. Citibank and others violated a basic principle of real estate lending that called for short-term construction loans to be extended only after long-term takeout financing had been arranged. Now commercial banks did their own takeouts.

In April 1990, just before Citibank's real estate portfolio exploded, chief credit officer Lawrence Glenn said, "Today we don't finance undeveloped land, only income-producing properties. . . . Today we deal with only the best, most experienced operators."

One of Citi's favorites was "Donnie" Trump, as he was known to friends. One of his most visible achievements was using his own resources to totally gut and rebuild the old Commodore Hotel at Grand Central Station, and turning it into ultramodern Grand Hyatt. Said one rival banker, "Citi used to fawn all over him." Though Manny Hanny usually led the way on Donnie's deals, such as his Trump's Castle casino, Citibank rarely, if ever, remained on the sidelines.

Another Citibank client was the Canadian-based Reichmann family.

The family-controlled Olympia & York made an audacious commitment to create Canary Wharf, a $7 billion project built along deteriorating Thames waterfront that was intended as a third London business district. That deal, said one former officer, was a prime example of a bad decision that resulted from vague lines of responsibility. "Who the hell was responsible for real estate in London? Everyone was," he said. And in 1987, Citibank underwrote the construction of two office towers in midtown Manhattan that would soon become notorious white elephants—750 Seventh Avenue and 1540 Broadway.

Because real estate loans were growing so rapidly, Reed spent one entire, long day reviewing the real estate portfolio in 1987 and asked lenders if the deals really made sense. Barely concealing his anger, he said later, "It was typical of this place. The response was, 'Oh, everything's fine.' "

"We missed an opportunity," Reed said. "The reason, frankly, is the sociology of this place. When you ask a question like this, the presenter, instead of taking the question and considering it seriously, basically tries to get you to go away and quit bugging him. It's Vietnam all over again." While Reed wasn't intimidated by corporate bankers, he was reluctant, he said, to "sort of say, 'Hey, I know more than you do.' " Former officer George Hagerman recalls that the level of real estate exposure "was never questioned in policy committee meetings." In a late 1980s presentation to analysts, Citibank boasted that it was the "largest real estate bank in the U.S."

Commercial real estate lending was not the only segment of the real estate business in which the bank let down its guard. Citibank, according to former thrift regulators, virtually invented the business of making so called "low doc [documentation] loans"—and even "no doc loans"—for single-family homes, condos, and co-ops. These loans were extended for 80 percent and more of the purchase price with little paperwork and financial checks. The Citibank example, as always, inspired other institutions, including the S & Ls, to enter the fray. The results were disastrous. "Citibank," said the regulator, "forced others to take more risk in 'low doc' loans." Citibank's 1980s lending practices were ironically if not intentionally exemplified by the decor in one Chicago branch of Citicorp Savings, where the walls were plastered with fake five dollar bills and signs saying, "Another day, another $5 million to lend."

The old credit policies were routinely violated under the new regime, according to former officers. Credit skills declined "precipitously" after Wriston left, said a former senior officer.

Lawrence Glenn, then credit policy chief, would later say that the thing that separates Citibank from Morgan and Chase is that "we have a very clear notion of the need to develop specific credit processes in each business, for shipping, or a real estate company." That may have been true. But a year later it would be clear that what really separated Citibank from Morgan was loan losses.

Glenn boasted about Citibank's decentralized approach to credit control. "We don't have a department that pores over how much we have to chemical companies." And he added, "The miracle of the Citibank system is that information flows in very quickly. It's rare that the person in the credit policy chair doesn't know what's going on."

The "fundamental control system," said Glenn, calls for three signatures to be accountable for each loan. "I believe in that system. It still works." Wriston, Glenn said, observed that "lending is the last of the great crafts where the craftsman signs his work."

But by the end of the decade, few Citibankers would have disagreed with the observation of one former Citibanker that there was an entire layer of management that "doesn't understand banking."

Meanwhile, the investment bank did not prosper under Tom Theobald. "Investment banking was never anything at Citibank. Citi did it halfheartedly," said former corporate secretary Carl Desch. And Theobald didn't have his heart in it at all, in the view of colleagues.

As salaries and bonuses for rate swap experts and other specialists soared in the 1980s, Theobald declined to meet the competition, promoting many top specialists to jump ship for other Wall Street firms. Critics complained that Theobald tried to recycle commercial lenders into investment bankers, instead of hiring experienced Wall Streeters. Theobald was afraid of being stuck with a high-cost operation when the boom screeched to a halt, as he was convinced it would. To be sure, the investment bank made money on activities, such as trading, that were previously housed in the commercial bank. But it fell behind J. P. Morgan and Bankers Trust, which were beginning to make strides in activities once dominated by Wall Street firms, such as advising buyers and targets on acquisitions. Citibank had concluded, former officers say, that it could make more money on loan charges than on advisory fees. It believed it could tap its global network of corporate clients for potential advisory clients. But because Citi hired third-string personnel instead of top Wall Street mergers-and-acquisitions specialists to head this operation, Citibank never became a leader in giving advice.

One bright spot continued to be the venture capital operation headed by William Comfort, reputedly one of Citibank's highest-paid executives, who had a knack for picking the right LBO and venture capital deals for Citi-bank to invest in. "The secret," said former trader Paul De Rosa, is "co-investing."

But questionable personnel changes elsewhere decimated morale. John C. Botts, the well-regarded head of CIBL in London, quit to set up his own firm when another officer was appointed to share authority with him.

According to one published account, Reed made an inspection tour of the London operations, including Scrimgeour Vickers, in late 1985, telling one executive, "This is one hell of a fine company you guys have bought. Just be sure you don't go and fuck it up." That's exactly what would happen.

Given Citibank's own lackluster record of making acquisitions, it was not surprising that it lacked credibility to advise others. Citibank executives contemplating acquisitions didn't even consult the bank's own M & A specialists, and acquisitions continued to be a haphazard process.

In no case was that more apparent than in Citibank's $680 million acquisition in 1986 of Quotron, the centerpiece of its ill-fated effort to launch the information business. It may have been true, as Wriston said later in one of his numerous speeches on the information society, that the "basis for wealth had evolved from land to labor to information." But it didn't take long for Citibank to discover that the Quotron deal was a turning point in the erosion of Citicorp's wealth.

Reed may have had reason to believe that he knew the people behind Quotron. What he didn't realize was that Quotron was rapidly becoming an obsolete system, soon to be relegated to the high-tech trash heap by a former Salomon Brothers trader named Michael Bloomberg. Bloomberg was launching a global financial information network with custom-designed, user-friendly terminals. By 1995, the Bloomberg system was the system of choice, with more than 50,000 screens worldwide.

Wriston may have been the intellectual father of the information business, but he was not to blame, he insisted later, for Reed's decision to acquire Quotron.

By the late 1980s, it was already clear that the information business was not going to produce positive results anytime soon. "It's still a business of the mid to late 1990s. It's proving to be a tough business," conceded vice chairman Paul Collins.

For more than two years, John Reed stayed out of the limelight, working behind the scenes to understand Citibank and, some say, avoiding changes that would make it appear that he differed sharply with Wriston on how to run the company. But he did.

Although Wriston chose a successor who shared both his vision of the future and his feisty temperament, he also picked one who strongly disagreed with him on how to deal with the albatross Wriston had bequeathed to Citicorp and the American system.

As Citibank's consumer banking czar, Reed, in his own words, was too busy selling credit cards to worry much over Third World debt, much less challenge it. Reed later said that before he became chairman "I read about it [Third World debt] in the newspaper, but I didn't pay much attention."

As a manager, Reed lived by his lists: lists of problems, lists of priorities, lists of things to do. When he became chairman, the item at the top of all of them was sovereign debt. Reed's goal now was to put it behind Citicorp.

Reed's view of Latin Americans was not shaded by political correctness. Whenever the Latins—in contrast to the Asians—encountered hard times, they figured, said Reed, that "someone will bail us out of this. Not to worry." Reed even compared his own children to Third World borrowers. "They assume if they go broke they won't go broke. There's a debilitative quality. You have to let them go broke."

When Reed assumed the mantle of leadership of the nation's banking industry, said former director Irving Shapiro, he also knew he would eventually have to take write-downs. According to Shapiro, one major reason he did not do this immediately was that Peat Marwick Mitchell & Co. had just signed off on Citicorp's financial statements. "So he had to wait a reasonable time to take the action he wanted to take."

In the meantime, he embarked on his own custom-designed education program that included tutorials by leading economists, briefings by Shearman & Sterling on the legal background of debt moratoriums, and a long chat with Paul Volcker on IMF conditionality. "I wanted to know whether it was real or fiction," Reed said, and "how burdensome it was for countries."

"I had studied economics at school, so I wasn't illiterate," Reed said, "but I hadn't focused on this issue." Reed not only focused on the issue, he took it over from those, like Bill Rhodes, to whom Wriston had delegated it. George Moore had thought he was an expert on Latin America because he was married to a Spanish woman. Likewise, Reed thought he could take charge of Latin debt because he had grown up in Argentina. Noting Reed's fluency in Spanish, a former colleague said, "He had a unique perch, as head of the largest bank, to try to help the system, but he didn't have the place set up to work the other macro issues." During his first six years as chairman, Reed estimated that he spent upward of half his time on cross-border debt.

Soon after taking over, Reed traveled to Washington with a peace offering for the Fed. In his conversations with Volcker, he acknowledged the past tensions between the real and would-be central banks, and agreed to notify the Fed before dashing through loopholes in the law.

In those early meetings, Reed indicated to Volcker that he'd like to set aside a sizable reserve for Third World debt. Volcker was in favor of gradual reserving, not one big hit.

Early on, Reed said he intended to keep earnings flat and take the normal growth into reserves. Reed would often say that he had unlimited tolerance for pain. But Citicorp did not. It had been built on the premise of 15 percent annual compound earnings growth. "This is not an organization that feels good with no growth in earnings. The organization was creaking and groaning," Reed said. "I was perfectly willing to have no growth in earnings for ten years. It didn't bother me any, but it was bothering everyone else." By now analysts were complaining that Reed didn't have the "right stuff."

In working the debt crisis, Reed liked traveling overseas and schmoozing with heads of state. Reed was not as sophisticated in his understanding of world affairs as Wriston, and according to colleagues, was inclined to get "pumped up" by his tête-à-têtes with foreign leaders, even if they were deadbeats. But Reed denied that he did this to feed his ego. In fact, he said, he turned down opportunities to meet with the heads of G-7 countries. "I don't have anything to talk to them about, and I don't think they have anything they want to talk to me about." But he wanted to be able to pick up the phone and call the leader of a nation that owed him money. "When I see the president of Brazil I'm talking to the principal manager of Brazil's debt problem. What Collor [Fernando Collor de Mello who became president of Brazil in 1990] says he intends to do [relates] directly to the $3.4 billion he owes me."

The debt crisis was increasingly becoming an American problem, and in particular an American money center bank problem. The regional and foreign banks wanted to dump the whole mess in the hands of the New York banks. By 1985 the players in the debt crisis were suffering from battle fatigue. The first phase of the crisis, said former Brazil finance minister and Citicorp director Mario Simonsen, was dominated by the view that countries were motivated to repay their debts so that they could regain access to the international credit markets.

But in 1985 few banks had any appetite for LDC lending. The year before, as Hans Angermueller explained in a speech, only about $18 billion, less than 1% of global savings, flowed into the non-oil LDCs, and much of that was in connection with "forced lending" plans.

Treasury secretary James Baker agreed with Volcker that the three-year effort to keep the banks interested in propping up the LDCs had run out of steam and that the banks were extricating themselves too easily. The dilemma they faced was how to keep the banks involved, while at the same time requiring that they take reserves for some portion of their existing loans.

The so-called Baker plan, drafted largely by Volcker on an early-October 1985 flight to Seoul for the annual meeting of the IMF, was an attempt to reinvigorate the debt negotiations by placing the emphasis on LDC economic growth, bringing in the World Bank, and establishing long-term targets for new money to accomplish that.

The Baker plan urged the injection of $20 billion in new commercial bank loans by 1989 to fifteen LDCs. Wriston came out in favor of the idea. "It's an absolutely superb objective," he said several weeks after the announcement.

Even as the banks were being pushed to lend new money, the Comptroller of the Currency, as Morgan's *World Financial Markets* pointed out in February 1986, was telling banks they would have to treat new loans as problem credits. Meanwhile, a bill was being introduced to eliminate banks' ability to deduct loan loss provisions on their tax returns. Citibank endorsed the plan. In a speech in December, Angermueller described it as "the right message at the right time." But he, for one, said there were a few other things the debtors need to do to attract bank financing that Baker neglected to mention. He thought it would also be nice if the developing countries also promised to make "regular" principal and interest payments on their outstanding debt.

Trouble was, said Wriston's brother-in-law Robert Dineen, the plan did not force the LDCs to change their economic policies. "Countries would agree to IMF programs and there would be another election and that would (go by the boards)," he said. The LDCs' cavalier attitude toward paying their debts was evident at a gala 1985 dinner celebrating Ecuador's rescheduling agreement. On that occasion, recalled a top British banker, the Ecuadorians "were already talking about rescheduling again."

Besides trying to patch things up with Volcker, Reed tried his best to be deferential to older bank chairmen. "I went out of my way when I became chairman to try to be respectful and considerate of the Lew Prestons of the world, and others who would find having a forty-five-year-old kid at Citicorp as a minor social irritant." The era of good feelings did not last long.

For Mexico, everything that could go wrong had gone wrong. In September 1985, the country had suffered a devastating earthquake and in early 1986 oil prices had collapsed. In 1986, Mexico needed more money and was again making veiled threats about halting interest payments. After negotiating an agreement with Mexico that Reed and other bankers felt had some teeth in it, Volcker and the IMF, according to Reed, cut a deal with Mexico that called for the Mexicans to make some changes in economic policies but also required the banks to make what Reed called a "straight loan" to the Mexican government. According to Citibank debt negotiator Bill Rhodes, the U.S. government feared that if Mexico's unstable economy blew up completely, illegal immigration across the Rio Grande would surge. So the United States leaned heavily on the banks to go along with the deal. Volcker insisted that the banks lend $7.7 billion in new money to Mexico. He felt that rates on the loans to the LDCs were too high and wanted the banks to make interest rate concessions to boot.

Reed was apoplectic. In his view, Mexico didn't need all this money. It would delay, rather than accelerate, Mexico's return to the capital markets. Reed warned that at the end of three years Mexico would simply be back for another three years, and it would become a permanent concession.

The proposed transaction did not, said Reed, include provisions for debt-equity swaps and other benefits that would make it attractive to Citibank. Reed wanted the Mexican deal to include a menu of options—including debt-equity swaps—which was opposed by the Mexicans.

Volcker and the IMF also opposed these options, said Reed. "They felt we should just shut up and lend money to the government and quit screwing around. I just felt that I had my own stockholders. I don't work for the U.S. government."

"I think Paul felt that the private sector should act more like a government entity in supporting the developing countries," Reed said later. Reed was angry that "for all practical purposes the banks were pawns of Mr. Volcker and the IMF," which he said was working out agreements with the countries and dictating to the banks how much they would have to contribute. "What in hell were we funding?" Reed asked. "I wanted to know if there was any reason to believe it would produce results."

Reed's desire to dominate the debt negotiations led to some strained moments between him and Bill Rhodes, to whom Wriston had virtually delegated the matter, allowing Rhodes to bask in whatever glory came his way. "Walt delegated but didn't abdicate," said a colleague of both men. Reed, on the other hand, "likes to run things." Sometimes Rhodes was even forced to defend Volcker, the nemesis of Citibank, and as one source recalls, "he'd get his head chopped off" when he did. Moreover, Reed made public statements and called meetings of CEOs that, in the view of colleagues, undermined Rhodes's influence and prestige as a negotiator. Said one British banker, "Reed thinks he knows it all. Reed would say, 'Don't tell me about Brazil, I lived there.'"

Now the banks were forced to choose up sides. Morgan's Lewis Preston allied with his friend, Paul Volcker. "There was a suspicion," Preston recalled, "on the part of other banks that packages might have advantages for Citibank that they might not have for others." So Morgan Bank for one, in sometimes acrimonious discussions with Citibank, pushed to get the deal done and chastised Citibank for holding up the works by demanding options skewed in its favor.

Reed might have assumed that as chairman of Citicorp he was automatically the dean of American banking. But other banks, and certainly Fed chairman Paul Volcker, didn't quite see things that way. While Volcker might have enjoyed an easier personal relationship with Reed than he did with his predecessor, he often found Reed's approach to the debt problem unnerving. In one meeting in Washington with Volcker, Reed fought over an eighth of a percentage point. Usually, compromises over rates would be resolved by adjusting maturities. Rates had never been sliced thinner than one eighth. So for the first time the salami was cut into sixteenths.

The new restructuring affected almost $44 billion in debt, and reduced rates on $8.6 billion on new loans agreed to in 1983 and 1984. Mexico wound up with a $6 billion twelve-year loan at $\frac{13}{16}$ of a percentage point over LIBOR, including a $1 billion World Bank co-financing arrangement. In the view of one Salomon Brothers Latin debt trader, the banks in 1986 extended new money for "political reasons," but swapped out of it right away. After those contentious Mexican negotiations, Reed was determined to wrest control of the debt problem away from Volcker, the IMF, and the Latins. Soon he would get his chance.

By early 1987, Reed was feeling fairly pleased with himself. His pride and joy, the Individual Bank, had cranked out $462 million in earnings in 1986, up 41 percent over the year before. Citicorp Savings, he told analysts in January 1987, had turned around. The investment bank, he boasted, had in 1986 developed a capacity to trade and distribute securities around the world.

The sovereign debt portfolio was his biggest concern. He had been adding millions in reserves, including $460 million in 1986 alone. As he told the *Wall Street Journal* of February 4, 1987, "It's a crummy world out there."

In March, his concern deepened when Brazil did the unthinkable: Believing it could gain some leverage over the banks, it declared a moratorium on $121 billion of its debt.

For a while, it had looked as if things were moving in the right direction in Brazil. In 1985, Brazil watchers applauded the election of the first non-military government in more than two decades. In February 1986, Brazil announced a new stabilization policy called the Cruzado Plan and a month later hammered out a new rescheduling agreement with its commercial bank lenders. But the Cruzado Plan was filled with loopholes and failed even as it was just getting started.

By the mid-1980s, according to Mario Simonsen, Brazil conveniently convinced itself that it was the victim of the unilateral decision of the United States to raise interest rates and that it "should not pay the whole thing now even if we can. It was a common view."

The Brazilians were incited by economists such as Harvard professor Jeffrey Sachs, Senator Bill Bradley and others who were pushing the notion of debt forgiveness.

The debt crisis had taken another major turn. So far, the debtors had maintained that they were willing to repay if only they could. In 1982, Mexico had threatened such a measure, and others had threatened to do so since. But each time reason carried the day. Now the politics of nationalism in Brazil, which had the capacity to repay its debt, had won out over good economics. Brazil had lost the will to pay.

In Congressional hearings on April 23, 1987, international financial advisor Dr. Paul Sacks declared that the real watershed was not the moratorium but the "Americanization" of the debt problem—a North and South American problem rather than a global problem. "A central component of the Americanization is the loss of competitiveness suffered by U.S. money center banks to their Japanese, European, and U.S. regional bank counterparts," he said. "While these other banks exit in search of greater opportunities elsewhere, U.S. money center banks are left shouldering the burden of Third World debt." European, Japanese, and U.S. regional banks were writing down their loans and heading for the exit, leaving the problem to the weakened money centers. One reason was that the decline in the value of the dollar had reduced the exposure of the European and Japanese banks.

In declaring the moratorium, however, Brazil forgot the bitter lessons of other countries—such as Peru—that had defaulted on their debt.

If Reed harbored any doubts about the need to send a dramatic message to the marketplace, those doubts were now evaporating. He believed that the financial markets had been "spooked" into believing that the banks would forever remain prisoners of Third World debt, and he wanted to unshackle Citibank from it in one fell swoop.

"I felt we had to do something that would communicate to the market that we could handle this problem, put it behind us, and buy ourselves some flexibility, in terms of how we managed our position."

And he added: "I recognized it could be unsettling."

Reed assigned a three-man task force consisting of Edwin Hoffman, chief accountant Tom Jones, and Latin hand Richard Huber to study the reserve issue. According to one participant, there was "general coalescence" around $3 billion, though some felt the number should be higher. That was deemed the largest amount Citibank could set aside without being seriously wounded. In any case, that figure represented the total of the bank's earnings for the last four years of Wriston's watch.

In the banking equivalent of the D day invasion, Reed in May instructed his senior staff in Latin America to fly to Miami for a secret briefing on the plan, so that they would be prepared to explain it to central bankers and leaders of Citibank's host countries.

And in an un-Wriston-like display of humility, Reed journeyed to Washington early in the week of May 11 to explain to Paul Volcker the rationale and the accounting, in all its arcane complexity. While Volcker didn't try to dissuade him, Reed concluded that the world's most powerful central banker thought he was wrong. But Reed had trapped Volcker. "It's hard for the chairman of the Fed to say to the chairman of the largest bank in the country that you shouldn't take reserves."

"I think he felt that that action would make it impossible to put together new loan deals for borrowing countries," and if that happened the banks would quit lending and the whole process would unravel. Reed didn't believe that would happen. If his "little debtor countries," as he often called them, deserved new money, they would get it.

Although Reed was always respectful of Volcker's intellect, he was equally intrigued with his apparent inability to fathom the accounting behind the proposed action. "It was the first time I realized that running the Fed and being an economist doesn't force you to live with the craziness that's called financial accounting."

Later that week, Reed breakfasted with New York Federal Reserve Bank chief Gerald Corrigan. At the top of the agenda was liquidity. Without telling the traders what Citibank was up to, the order went out: Get liquid. Reed flew to Washington again to brief Comptroller of the Currency Robert Clarke and Treasury Secretary James Baker. While Volcker was what Reed described as "cautiously supportive," Baker "thought it was a good idea and was very supportive and immediately supported it in the press." On Friday, Reed sent briefing papers by courier to directors.

By Sunday evening, the magnitude of what Reed would announce on

Tuesday had started to hit home. For a brief period, the cocksure technocrat wallowed in indecision.

"I thought to myself, 'Jesus, what if the market responds poorly? What if there's a liquidity run on the bank?' " Despite all of the precautions, Reed for a few fleeting moments felt a hollowness in the pit of his stomach and contemplated scrapping the plan. "For all of the precautions, you had to say to yourself, 'Kid, maybe you're wrong.'

"Then my normal practicality came back and I thought it through step by step, and said that it is the right thing to do." In the days leading up to the announcement, according to former Citibanker Frank Partel, Reed and his colleagues were chortling over how Walter Bigelow Wriston would take the news.

Reed had reserved for Monday, May 18, one of the duties he looked forward to the least: informing the man who had given him his job. Until then, it was the only business decision he made as chairman that he ever talked to Wriston about beforehand. He was going to meet with Wriston not to consult with him on it, but to tell him what he was going to do.

Reed knew that as soon as the announcement was made, the press calls would pour into Wriston's office, and many journalists would view it as a major shift in strategy. Reed knew this was a message he had to deliver in person. "I was expecting him to be pissed off," said Reed. "It obviously was a hard thing for me to do to go over there and say, 'Hey, Walt, I'm gonna take $3 billion and create the biggest loss the corporation ever had in its history.' "

But Reed, said former director Irving Shapiro, "is not the kind of guy to be deterred by hurting anybody's feelings."

When Reed told Wriston what he was going to propose to the directors at the board meeting the next day, Wriston "was visibly surprised," he said. Reed was fully prepared for Wriston to regard his successor's decision as a total rejection of his view of LDC lending, but if that was how Wriston felt, he didn't show it, said Reed. "He didn't know it was coming. Yet I think he very quickly saw why it might make sense under those circumstances. You could hear him putting it into context. Walt's the original change man. He knew the posture he left the bank in wasn't necessarily going to be the posture for the bank at a later time. He didn't say, 'God, how could you change this thing that I left you with.' He said, 'Yeah, I could see how the world's moving this way.' "

Reed sensed that Wriston was delivering a speech, in effect rehearsing for the inevitable interviews the next day.

In hindsight, as Reed saw it, Wriston's reaction was totally consistent with his tendency to believe first and doubt later. "If I walked up to Walt and said, 'Hey, I went to the moon yesterday and it's made of blue cheese,' his initial reaction would be, 'Gee, John's been to the moon and it's made of blue cheese.' Then he'd start backing off and say, 'Maybe John's had too much to drink.' His first instinct is to believe, then he'll run through his various tests to make sure he's not being naive."

When Reed returned to his home in Greenwich, Connecticut, there was a message waiting for him that caused him to think he would go into cardiac arrest. Volcker was calling from a party of Fed officials, and left word for Reed to return the call to his home later. Reed was now worried that Volcker had changed his mind about Reed's plan. By this time, there was no turning back, and Citibank was already watching the Australian markets—the first to open on the business day—and then Tokyo, for signs of unusual activity.

"I was scared Paul would say something to me that would require serious modification of what we were doing," said Reed. When Reed finally reached him, it was clear Volcker was resigned to the inevitable. "John," he asked, "you're going to do this thing tomorrow, aren't you?" As it turned out, Volcker had called to solicit Reed's opinion on whether the Fed should prepare a press release responding to the Citibank move, one that would assure other banks that this was Citibank's decision alone, and that they weren't necessarily expected to play follow the leader. "We were trying very hard not to make everybody do the same thing," said Reed.

When the Citicorp directors gathered in the boardroom Tuesday morning, Reed traced the history of the debt crisis and, as expected, received their endorsement. Citibank officials were poised to alert the media at exactly 4:00 P.M., when the markets closed in New York, that there would be a press conference and major announcement a half hour later. That left four hours between the end of the board meeting and the closing bell on the New York Stock Exchange for Reed to contemplate what he was about to do.

Reed and his inner circle had gone to great lengths to inform others of the decision only on a need-to-know basis, and didn't want to unwittingly leak the news. "I didn't want to go around the bank gossiping," Reed said. "There was this crazy moment between what I knew would be two very adrenaline-producing things."

So shortly after the board meeting he set out on a solitary stroll through midtown Manhattan. If any of the hundreds of pedestrians recognized him, they were certainly unaware that this anonymous average citizen would in a few hours make an announcement that would reverberate like a thunderclap through the financial markets of the world. He grabbed a sandwich, bought a pair of shoes, and browsed in bookstores. Reed rarely left the bank during the day, and certainly not for fun. "I can remember feeling sort of nuts walking down Fifth Avenue in the middle of the afternoon."

On returning to the bank, Reed got on the phone to Lew Preston at Morgan, John McGillicuddy at Manny Hanny, and Tom Clausen at Bank America, the latter two institutions being among the weakest major banks in America, and therefore the most threatened by the Citicorp initiative.

Incredibly, the news never leaked. At 4:30 P.M. Reed startled a roomful of newspaper and television reporters with an announcement that put his stamp on Citicorp and American banking, a stamp that would endure for years to come.

Asked at the news conference if he had called the chairmen of the other big banks personally, and if so, which ones, Reed gloated that he personally spoke to McGillicuddy and Clausen, earning for himself their enduring fury.

Some would roundly criticize Reed for keeping his secret from the rest of his banking peers until the very last minute. "I didn't think that in the management of a private institution which is competitive in the marketplace you should go down and talk with your buddies. It's inside information."

As expected, the phone soon began ringing in Wriston's office, and at a dinner speech that evening he was besieged by reporters. "John's absolutely right. It was the right thing to do," Wriston told a reporter, prompting Reed to say later that "there are very few guys who could honestly mouth those words for their successor."

"It was a brilliant thing for John to do," Wriston insisted later. "People think you take a position based on yesterday and you maintain it tomorrow and tomorrow is different than yesterday. I've never done that in my life. I don't plan to start now," he said.

In effect, though, it was just an accounting maneuver. No real money was really lost by Citibank. But Citibankers, including retirees, who had received book value stock as part of their compensation plans, watched in horror as the value of their holdings plummeted. And they were mad as hell.

One writer described Reed's provision as a declaration of independence from the "paternal guidance of the Fed."

Before the decision was announced, Brazil and Mexican debt was selling for about 75 to 80 cents on the dollar. Afterward, however, debt prices plummeted and Citicorp stock surged. Shares of strong banks like J. P. Morgan and Bankers Trust edged up slightly, whereas share prices of weaker banks, notably Manny Hanny and Bank of America, dropped. Most analysts had underestimated the negative impact on debt prices and the positive impact on Citicorp shares.

Huber, who was responsible for Citibank's debt-trading operation, knew the move would cost Citi in its debt-trading position, but couldn't sell down the position for fear of tipping Citibank's hand. As a result, the LDC trading desk lost $5 million.

The move would produce a deficit for the quarter of $2.5 billion, more than double the amount suffered by Continental Illinois when it was bailed out by regulators in the second quarter of 1984. Citi pulled rabbits out of the hat to offset the deficit. Even after selling condominium shares in Citicorp Center and 399 Park to the Dai-ichi Mutual Life Insurance Company for $670 million, among other maneuvers, Citicorp still ended the year with a $1.182 billion loss.

Though a Fed spokesman declared that the action was taken "entirely at Citicorp's initiative" and that the central bank didn't view it as a precedent for other banks, Reed's decision forced other banks to follow suit, and resulted in a $10 billion loss in the quarter for the banking industry. That was the worst quarter, and 1987 was the worst year, in American banking history.

Reed's initiative also sent a strong signal to Latin America. It now meant that the banks would be willing to accept less than 100 cents on the dollar for their loans. "I don't think an accounting charge, transferring capital to reserves, strengthens the balance sheet of a bank one bit, but it changed the perception in Latin America," said one top banker.

The move also had favorable long-term tax benefits. In the view of rival bankers, this was yet another example of Citibank operating in its own best interest, to bolster its own tax position. The action promoted discord among all the banks that had lent to the LDCs, notably between Citibank and Morgan. Lewis Preston was furious that Reed had acted unilaterally and forced the hands of his competitors. Two years later, Morgan would get its revenge.

After the write-down, Don Howard approached Reed with the idea of selling a $1 billion stock issue. First Boston had come up with the idea, but Merrill's proposal to sell the stock through its retail distribution network won the day. Reed urged that the issue be unloaded in September, before the World Bank–IMF meeting. He felt that that meeting would bring only bad news. He was right.

For Reed, this was certainly the season for bold initiatives. Right on the heels of taking the reserve, he resolved another of Citibank's most wrenching issues. In June 1987, Citicorp finally decided to call it quits in South Africa. It was an issue not clearly understood by the activists who urged institutional holders of Citicorp stock to divest their shares unless Citicorp left South Africa. "We broke the law in South Africa. We had integrated banking platforms, and hired black managers," Wriston said months after Reed announced the decision. "But when fifteen pension funds are selling your stock, what can you do?"

In fact, a key force behind Citicorp's decision to remain in South Africa as long as it did was Citicorp director and Ford Foundation president Franklin Thomas, a black man who had overseen major studies of apartheid and had made many trips there himself. For years, Thomas felt that Citicorp, which operated several branches in South Africa, could be a greater force for change by remaining than by leaving. In August 1985 Chase, whose stake in South Africa was substantially less than Citibank's, concluded it could make a more profound statement by bailing out. The Chase announcement triggered a massive financial run on the country, prompting the government to suspend payments on loans to international banks. Thomas had for long urged against disinvestment, and had been pilloried for his views. "If you're no longer there," he argued, "it tends to go off the agenda."

Finally, as the crisis intensified, Franklin Thomas and Vernon Jordan, who served with Wriston on the board of J. C. Penney, journeyed to the strife-torn country to assess the situation for themselves and their respective corporate boards. Said Wriston later, "They came back and said, 'It's time to leave.' " Thomas explains the decision: "The role of business in South Africa had become a hurdle. It became a roadblock to talking about the problem." At Citicorp, he said, a growing portion of senior management's time was taken up debating the matter. Meanwhile, efforts by groups favoring disinvestment were gathering momentum. "That raised questions of fiduciary duties," Thomas said. On top of that, the government of South Africa was becoming even more resistant to change. "Any prominent U.S. company operating there during this swing to the right had to spend an inordinate amount of time rationalizing its presence."

Citibank's exit at this critical juncture furthered isolated the South African regime and drove another nail into the coffin of apartheid.

After the 1986 Mexican deal, Reed may have wanted Volcker out of the Fed even more than Wriston did. With Volcker's reappointment coming up for renewal again in 1987, Hans Angermueller began to lobby aggressively against a third term for the Fed chairman.

Volcker was a guest at one PEPAB meeting in early 1987, shortly before Reagan had to decide on Volcker's future. Watching from across the Roosevelt room as Reagan whispered to Volcker, Wriston said to economist Art Laffer, "From God's mouth to my ear."

According to Kenneth Guenther, Independent Bankers Association executive director, "Citibank played a role behind the scenes in making sure Volcker was not reappointed." Indeed, Volcker turned out to be replaceable. The U.S. banking system and financial markets nearly came apart during the early days of the tenure of his successor, Alan Greenspan, but things would not likely have played out much differently had Volcker remained on the job.

For Citicorp, the departures of Thomas Theobald and Donald Howard may have been more significant. Though Theobald did not do much to make Citibank an investment banking powerhouse, he represented the last of the senior-level traditional bankers and students of the old Citibank credit culture.

In 1987, as had long been rumored, Theobald accepted the top job at beleaguered Continental Illinois. He quickly improved morale and refocused the renamed Continental Bank into a reasonably reliable corporate institution, albeit one that never became a major player again. Seven years later, he sold Continental to Bank of America for $1.9 billion, and left a very wealthy man.

Theobald was the one top Citibank executive who knew the customers. He was replaced with Michael Callen, an aloof former Mideast hand who was unpopular with his subordinates.

The investment bank did not fare well under Callen. One visible manifestation of the troubles the bank was experiencing in Europe occurred in Dublin, where a bond trader at Scrimgeour's unit there lost over $20 million by exceeding his authority. Finally, in 1989, Citi closed Scrimgeour Vickers, taking a $65 million write-down. So much for the Big Bang.

To many Wall Streeters, it looked as though J. P. Morgan and Bankers Trust had taken the right path. In 1989, Morgan gained Fed approval to underwrite and deal in corporate debt through a securities affiliate, becoming the first bank to be empowered to do so. Meanwhile, the Securities Industry

Association, which had long campaigned against bank efforts to intrude on what it regarded as the turf of securities firms, now appeared to be relaxing its opposition.

Some Citibankers also felt the departure of Don Howard, Reed's decades-old rival, was a fateful one. When he left, one colleague opined that no one was appointed to allocate the bank's capital to different businesses in a disciplined way, in accordance with the risks of those businesses.

If Reed's reserve bombshell was a turning point in Citibank's exit from the Latin debt crisis, so the October 19, 1987, stock market crash was a watershed in its entry into the commercial real estate and leveraged-buyout lending crisis—though few appreciated that at the time. In fact, colleagues congratulated Reed on his superb market timing. He had got the big stock deal and the building sales done just in the nick of time.

At the urging of Federal Reserve Bank of New York president Gerald Corrigan, Citibank, among other banks, lent a "hell of a lot of money to the brokerage community" to support the "whole structure," said Reed. As for Wriston, nothing got his adrenaline surging more than a megacrisis in the financial markets. When the market collapsed, Wriston's concern, as always, was not whether the market, if left to its own devices, would self-correct— that was a foregone conclusion. His real worry was that government officials, economic pundits, the media, and other "experts" would tamper with free market mechanisms and make matters even worse. More specifically, he was concerned that they would "fool around" with the New York Stock Exchange by failing to recognize that in an era of global markets the Big Board "was just one node on the network." Wriston said later that he was sure there would be additional volatility until world markets adjusted to the "new equilibrium. But if you're going to tell me some government agency should say a share of stock should sell at twelve times expected earnings, I don't think that's the answer either."

That evening, Secretary of State George Shultz phoned Wriston for his analysis of the day's tumultuous events. Wriston assured him that he didn't believe the crash would have a significant effect on the economy, adding that he planned to write the president a letter urging him to stick to his economic policies despite the momentary disruption and pressures to do otherwise. Shultz assured him he would deliver the letter to Reagan personally.

In his letter of October 27, 1987, Wriston reminded Reagan that the world operates on the information standard, pointing out that within two minutes after the president of the United States makes a statement, "more than 200,000 screens light up in hundreds of trading rooms, in dozens of countries, and traders buy or sell our currency and our stocks and bonds based on their evaluation of what you said."

"No matter what action we take," he went on, "the screens will continue to light up, judgments will be made, and for the first time in history there is no place on the planet to hide from economic policy mistakes." Wriston pointed out that the "ill-advised" closing of the Hong Kong stock exchange was followed immediately by declining prices in the Hong Kong,

Tokyo, and New York markets, and the suggestion by a U.S. official (SEC chairman David Ruder) that he was considering shutting down the New York Stock Exchange caused world markets to fall even further.

Commending the Federal Reserve's move to pump liquidity into the system, Wriston urged Reagan to resist calls for protectionism and higher taxes and to concentrate instead on cutting government spending. Reagan later quoted the Wriston letter in a White House staff meeting on the crisis, and its recommendations were incorporated into the report on the crash by Nicholas Brady, later Treasury secretary under President George Bush.

Reed and his bank seemed to have emerged from the crash and his write-down relatively unscathed. Indeed, colleagues said his bold stroke on Latin debt had left him cockier than ever. When asked by a reporter at the October 1988 meeting of the Business Council if he was going to be around that evening, Reed replied, "Am I going to be around? I'm going to be the center of attention."

That same month, he took ten top aides on a brainstorming trip to Cape Cod, Massachusetts, to deliberate on, among other things, whether they should buy or build a middle market business, or buy a large European or American bank. The floundering information business and Quotron were also high on the agenda.

On paper at least, 1988 looked like a banner year for Citibank, with reported earnings of $1.875 billion. Reed's compensation had rocketed 114 percent in 1988 to $1.8 million, and he had borrowed to buy 100,000 shares of Citicorp stock. At the time, Reed told the *U.S. Banker* of May 1989 that investing his own money gave him the feeling that he was working for himself. "I'm getting some of the psychic pleasure that businessmen get when they run their own company," he said, adding that his goal was to acquire a total of 500,000 shares.

Wriston pointed to 1988 results as evidence that even after LDC debt Citibank remained the world's leading financial institution. "Is the institution you left still around? And did it earn $1.875 billion after tax last year? And is it arguably the greatest financial institution in the world? And the answer to all that is yes. Did we fall down fifteen times getting there? Of course."

Wriston crowed that for all the fuss over Third World debt, Citibank was still alive and well, whereas Texas banks that had lent for real estate and oil and gas had either failed or been taken over. "Americans are still reasonably parochial," he said. "They'd rather make a bad loan in Texas than a good loan in Brazil." And he added, "My friend Ben Love [former chairman and CEO of Texas Commerce Bancshares, which was acquired by Chemical Banking Corp. in 1987] used to say that Texas Commerce is the soundest, best bank in the world, and you crazy guys in New York are lending money to those folks who speak a funny language. It occurs to me those boys across the street are still around and Texas Commerce isn't. It occurs to me one of those crazy New York banks took it over."

The 1988 results also reflected Brazil's decision to pay its banks $3.76 billion, representing two years' worth of late interest. Once again, $2 billion was from a so-called "interim financing" facility from those banks. That added $436 million to Citicorp's bottom line. But it wasn't long before the Brazilians were behind again.

Larry Small was appalled by the Latin's failure to keep their promises. "It's very clear," he said, "that they have a track record of making promises that they were going to do certain things, and then simply breaking the promises." To Small, the financial "comportment" of the Brazilians compared unfavorably with that of the Australians. Even though Australia was running a balance-of-payments deficit and had a foreign debt the size of Mexico's, Australia kept its promises. That may have been true of the government, but not of its real estate operators, to whom Small's institutional bank had lent millions—loans that would soon go bad.

But some harbored serious doubts whether 1988 earnings were for real. The 1988 provision for loan losses of $1.33 billion, $500 million less than the 1986 level, was artificially low, according to one knowledgeable Citibank source. And, he added, the fees on loans and other transactions were artificially high, given that many of the underlying deals ultimately went sour.

In fact, in the first quarter of 1989, earnings rose 48 percent but nonperforming loans surged by more than $1 billion. James McDermott, then chief of research at Keefe, Bruyette & Woods, told the *American Banker* of April 19, 1989, that those nonperformers were "one disturbing aspect" of the first-quarter results. Things would get even more disturbing as the months wore on.

Still, Reed didn't seem especially worried. In early 1989, after returning tanned and relaxed from his vacation on the beach in Jamaica, he sauntered into the office of Hans Angermueller and teased a visitor, "You look awfully pale. You really need to get some sun."

"Well, John, you certainly have been getting some sun," the visitor said. "But who the hell has been running the bank?"

"Oh, the bank runs by itself. It doesn't need me," Reed replied.

By 1989, it was evident to the incoming Bush administration that the Baker Plan, now more than three years old, hadn't accomplished much except to buy time. Although LDC debt no longer threatened to bring down the banking system, officials felt a new approach was needed to accelerate the end of the debt problem and stimulate growth in the developing countries by reducing their $1.3 trillion debt burden. The upshot was the so-called Brady Plan, authored by Treasury undersecretary David Mulford and named for Treasury secretary Nicholas Brady. As originally conceived, the plan called only for debt reduction. But after intense lobbying by Citibank, among others, the proposal provided for a reduction of about 20 percent in the LDC's debts to the commercial banks. While the Baker Plan had stressed new lending and voluntary debt reduction, the Brady Plan reversed that emphasis. One dollar of principal reduction, it was estimated, would reduce interest payments by

10 cents a year. And Mexico, first out of the gate in the debt crisis, was to be the guinea pig.

Citibank wasn't thrilled with the idea. But Rhodes and Reed plunged into the fray, seeking to work out a deal that incorporated the administration plan with an arrangement Reed could live with. Reed, as usual, was impatient with the pace of the discussions. New money was the major sticking point; because Reed intended to remain in Latin America, he favored the new money approach. Finally, as one former colleague put it, Reed decided that "if he got enough important people together he would get them to agree on terms." He gathered the elite of the world banking establishment, including Preston of Morgan, Butcher of Chase, and Clausen of the Bank of America, at 399 Park, and sequestered them until 3:00 A.M. one morning arguing over new-money, and how much Mexico should be charged for it. "John felt he had a program and the banks ought to agree to put up fresh money. Their directors had told these banks, no new money. They might have wanted to participate but they had their marching orders," said a colleague. Reed, according to an account in the *New York Times* of July 31, 1989, kept the discussions alive by agreeing to drop a proposal whereby the banks could charge Mexico more interest in the future, while retaining a clause that would allow the banks to "recapture" additional interest if Mexico enjoyed a windfall in oil revenues.

Nonetheless, in an agreement reached July 23, 1989, between the Mexicans and the bank advisory group, the banks wound up with the menu of options that Citibank had been pushing for. They could either exchange existing loans for 30-year bonds, discounted at 35 percent and paying LIBOR plus $\frac{13}{16}$; swap the loans for bonds at the same face value by paying a fixed rate of 6.25 percent; or make new 15-year loans amounting to a quarter of their existing outstandings.

Some were pushing not merely for reduction but for forgiveness. There, Reed drew the line. "Debt forgiveness is a word you'll never hear in this bank," Reed said at a later annual meeting.

It was bad enough, said former Chase chairman David Rockefeller, that Bush administration officials blamed the debt crisis on the banks and demanded that they take the full brunt of debt reduction. Worse still, he said, those officials, notably David Mulford, actually advised Latin finance officials to abrogate their contractual obligations and insist on further bank write-downs.

Pointing out that in the early 1990s Brazil's trade surplus was the world's third largest, Chase's Willard Butcher said, "It's not an economic problem. . . . They don't care to repay and the U.S. government told them they don't have to." Similarly, he said, Mexico's non-oil exports had grown more than sixfold since the crisis began to more than $18 billion. "Then I'm told they can't pay their debts. That's obviously lunacy. Of course they can pay. They don't choose too."

And Wriston said at the time, "If the government would get out of the way we could finish this issue."

By 1989, Morgan, unlike Citibank, could afford to write off 100 percent of its loans. Lewis Preston was not pleased with Citibank for its May 1987 surprise. Citibank's move, said Preston later, "certainly encouraged us to consider it. It took a while to absorb the significance of [Citibank's action]. We decided we were going to follow our own destiny." So now Morgan forced Citicorp to add another $1 billion to its LDC reserve account.

After Preston retired, Reed sent him a note expressing regret that they couldn't agree on Reed's reserve decision. Preston replied that he understood why Reed did it, and that it was the right decision for Citibank. "After all, you're paid by Citibank," Preston wrote.

That September, Citibank rented Washington's restored Union Station to fete international financiers attending the IMF annual meeting. The entertainment consisted of circus acts, including jugglers and tightrope walkers, that were veritable metaphors for the debt crisis itself. There, country risk official George "Jack" Clark, now months away from retirement, goodnaturedly told William Rhodes's daughter that her father was "trying to collect all the bum loans I made."

In an elaborate ceremony on February 4, 1990, in Mexico City, attended by Mexican president Carlos Salinas de Gortari, Treasury secretary Brady, Reed, and other top bankers and officials, the bankers signed the accord, which covered some $48 million in bank debt, thereby slashing Mexico's external debt by $14.57 billion. Against a background of a Mexican flag made of flowers in the Patio de Palacio Nationale, President Salinas promised to "double" Mexico's fiscal discipline. As Salinas spoke, Reed joked and chatted with others at the big table. And Brady said that "Mexico is on the move again. . . . A new dawn is rising. Mexico stands as a beacon of hope for other debtor nations."

After the deal was signed, Mexico did look as though it was on the move. In 1990, Angel Gurria, undersecretary in the Finance Ministry pointed to all the signs of improvement: growth, reduced inflation and interest rates, less dependence on oil and privatization of state enterprises, and a surge in foreign direct investment. Only complacency, protectionism, or a dramatic rise in interest rates could derail the recovery, he said.

As for the chances of a return to the negotiating table two years from February 1990, Gurria said it would happen only in the event of a major crisis, such as oil dropping to a dollar a barrel, or a "Martian invasion." In fact, exactly five years later the Mexicans were back at the table, without an invasion from Mars. Led by the Harvard-educated Salinas, Mexico moved to open its stock market to foreign investors, privatize state-owned companies, and reprivatize the banking system, which had been nationalized eight years earlier. In December 1990, Mexico announced it would sell its controlling stake in Telefonos de Mexico to a group of private Mexican and foreign investors, and raised $2.3 billion in the sale.

Many of these privatization efforts stumbled. But by 1991 Mexico was enjoying a spectacular investment boom. And in August 1992, the United States announced a a free-trade agreement that would abolish customs duties on thousands of goods, open up Mexican financial markets, and block European and Asian companies from avoiding U.S. tariffs by shipping through Mexico. A decade after it crashed in August 1982, Mexico had become the darling of foreign investors. Even Grupo Alfa, Mexico's largest bankrupt company, eventually repaid Citibank much of what it owed, said Wriston, proving that there *was* a difference between lending to private enterprises and lending to the government.

Though the other Latin debtors stalled and stumbled in repaying their loans, they finally began to embrace democracy and free markets. In 1989, Argentina was mired in an inflationary spiral in which consumer prices rose nearly 800 percent, leading to the election of Peronist Carlos Menem. Banks had received no interest since 1988, forcing regulators in June 1989 to order banks with Argentine loans to write them down by 20 percent. Worst hit was Manny Hanny, which was later forced to merge with Chemical Bank. Ignoring worker protests, Menem soon launched Argentina's privatization program, beginning with ENtel, the dinosaurlike phone company. In a deal that included a debt-equity swap, Citibank and a Spanish phone company wound up buying the southern operations of the company. Even the Buenos Aires zoo was placed in private hands. In November 1991, in a sweeping decree, Menem ordered the deregulation of the nation's economy. With economic policy seemingly on the right track, investors still appeared willing to overlook official corruption. Menem himself was forced to relinquish a Ferrari he had received from an Italian businessman.

Menem ordered privatization of major government-owned businesses to be completed by 1992. In August of that year, the U.S. banks, led by Citicorp, reached an agreement to forgive more than a third of Argentina's $23 billion in bank debt in return for repayment of overdue interest and resumption of debt payments. "With this agreement," said Rhodes, "we are looking at the end of the debt crisis."

Even Brazil seemed like a country with a future once again when forty-year-old Fernando Collor de Mello took office as president in March 1990, after a hard-fought campaign in which debt repayment was a key issue. Espousing free markets, privatization, and fiscal discipline, he launched a draconian anti-inflation program, freezing the currency and replacing the cruzado with the cruzeiro. As a result, he brought the country to a screeching halt. At the Citicorp annual meeting in April 1990, Reed sighed, "Anybody who believes that somebody who lends money has leverage need only look at Brazil." And like so many other Latin administrations, Collor's was soon in ruins, amid charges by his own brother of corruption in the administration. In July 1992, the banks reached a debt-reduction accord with Brazil on $44 billion in medium- and long-term debt, and a second agreement on certain overdue interest. But that agreement was threatened by the prospect of Collor's impeachment, and wasn't consummated until 1994.

With Argentina and Brazil still behind in their interest payments, regulators, realizing that the banks could now take their hits without failing, ordered write-offs on loans to those countries.

The most exciting success story of Latin America was Chile, which transformed itself into an export powerhouse by embracing free market economics. There Citicorp, through debt-equity swaps, wound up as part owner of a $460 million pulp plant. Chile pioneered privatizations in Latin America even before Mexico. Chile and Uruguay would emerge from the morass as strong as or stronger than ever.

The *Wall Street Journal* reported on September 20, 1991, that "the First World is rediscovering the Third World." Suddenly, the MBAs [Mexico, Brazil, and Argentina] of 1982 and newly privatized telephone, food processing, transportation, and other companies were the hot new investments.

But the Latin debt crisis had taken the wind out of the sails of most U.S. banks that operated overseas. They had lost their competitive edge in Asia, Europe, and elsewhere and were shutting down their offices and returning home.

As Reed said in a September 1989 speech to the Washington Economic Club, "The United States is in some important ways withdrawing from the world, and there is no question that the American banks are withdrawing from international banking. There are probably only four or five American banks that have a serious interest internationally, if that. This reflects our own economic situation as a net borrower, and it reflects the reaction of the American government to the Latin American debt crisis, which was basically to punish the banks for having been so stupid." And he added, "This means that American companies around the world aren't going to have American banks, and I think that is a potential problem for this country."

By 1995, Reed figured, as he told shareholders in April, that the LDC debt episode would ultimately cost Citibank "less than half" of the total of $4 billion in reserves it had set aside in the 1980s,

For Citibank, LDC lending was an expensive lesson that he compared to knocking out his front tooth as a kid. "You never get the tooth back." But who knows, he mused, that "might have kept me from sticking my head in a vise."

Forbes on October 29, 1991, declared the debt crisis over and wrote that "Wriston maybe was right after all."

Most bankers and economists agreed that some good had come of the debt episode. These countries rejected the closed economic model and privatized state-owned enterprises, and joined GATT, the General Agreement on Tariffs and Trade.

"I don't have any question that the socialist model has failed, and the only people who don't know it are the Argentines and the City of New York. Even Gorbachev knows it," Wriston said before the Russian leader was swept from power in the former Soviet Union.

The debt issue, Reed declared, "is behind us because the Latins realize no one's going to help them."

But just as Citibank had begun to put the Third World debt crisis behind it, it slammed headlong into the next one. Wriston called it good old American real estate. In the 1990s, Citibank, like other financial institutions, would have to pay the price for the 1980s, just as they did in the 1980s for the 1970s. Prophetically, Michael Callen told analysts in the late 1980s that "the only thing that can stop us is ourselves." And that is exactly who would stop Citibank.

26

TO HELL AND BACK

ith the Mexican debt agreement in his pocket, Reed was looking like a banker statesman. He was spending more time in the big think department, meeting and greeting foreign leaders, and in Capitol Hill corridors. In July 13, 1989 testimony before the Senate Banking Committee, for example, he called for an overhaul of the U.S. financial system, including discarding boundaries between commercial and investment banking, eliminating geographic barriers to expansion, and integrating the savings and loan and insurance industries with commercial banking.

But Reed was nervous. He couldn't quite put his finger on it, but that summer he began to have nagging doubts about what he called "Small's world," the institutional and corporate business run by Lawrence Small. This was a goodly chunk of Citicorp, and it included the bank's surging commercial real estate portfolio.

"I had sensed that something wasn't right," Reed said later. While traveling in Venezuela—Reed typically traveled in Latin America in August because, he said, no work gets done that month in North America—he found himself trading nasty "CitiMail" messages with Small.

The economy had slowed down, but, said Reed, "the business was not performing the way people said it was. I didn't sense that they properly understood what was happening or could work it." And he was becoming concerned, somewhat belatedly, that Citi, as he told *U.S. Banker* of May 1989, was "getting unduly transaction oriented."

Besides the numbers cranked out by the accounting department, Citibank's faltering performance was becoming obvious in the marketplace—to the point where it even disrupted the markets. Just how inept Citibank was in the merger and acquisition game became clear in October 1989, when Citibank and Chase failed to make good on a promise to assemble $3 billion for a buyout of UAL Corp., parent of United Airlines. When the staggering $300-per-share bid fell through, UAL shares plummeted by almost $57 a share, closing at $222.875 a share. Citicorp shares dropped $5.50, triggering a 190-point dive in the Dow. Some Wall Streeters believed that the collapsed deal resulted from the troubles Campeau's faltering Federated and Allied Department stores were having making their junk bond payments. Just six months earlier, Citibank celebrated its dubious success in getting back a loan to Campeau won by Security Pacific in 1987, a refinancing of Citibank's and Manny Hanny's original 1986 loan. Takeover stocks and junk bonds were dealt a body blow from which they wouldn't recover for years. Fred Bradley, Citibank's own top airline lender, wasn't involved in the deal. He and Wriston were opposed to leveraged buyouts of airlines. "I felt there were problems. It was a blessing that UAL didn't work," Bradley said.

Over Christmas, Reed took his budgets and printouts to his Jamaican hideaway. Reed's visits there caused considerable consternation among his colleagues. To get to his home from the airport, he had to travel through one of the island's worst slums. After putting up much resistance, Reed finally accepted a security contingency plan that would take effect if civil strife erupted while he was in residence. But now he was more worried about his numbers. As he worked ten hours a day on them, he wasn't happy with what he was seeing. Small, meanwhile, had flown to Australia to meet with customers.

By year end, the writing was on the wall. For 1989, Citibank would earn a mere $498 million, or $1.16 a share, roughly a fourth of the previous year's earnings. Bad as things were, Reed could thank heaven and Governor Bill Janklow for the consumer business, which was responsible for $800 million, or 43 percent, of operating earnings.

Over lunch on their return, Reed told Small bluntly, "I want to pull you out of your job." Reed appointed consumer executive Richard Braddock president and demoted Small, who had run an empire of 38,000, to vice chairman and chairman of the executive committee, with one secretary reporting to him. Outwardly, Small took the move in stride. As one former colleague put it, "Larry is the consummate actor. He said, 'This is terrific. It frees me up to focus on customers.'"

Wriston was one of many who criticized Reed for not firing Small. "Hey, Walt, I take your criticism," Reed told him. "You're correct. But let me tell you something. I wasn't born knowing how to manage. I learned a lot of it at Citibank. I learned it watching you, Bill [Spencer], and others." He felt Wriston didn't give him credit for removing Small from his job early. But as it turned out, it was not early enough. Reed would say that what he hadn't realized was that Small "never looked at the business. He only looked at the process. He said, 'If you fail the credit audit I'm going to fire you.' But he never looked at the credits."

Citicorp's emerging real estate and LBO troubles drove home to Reed the dangers of confusing style with results. Small, of course, was the quintessential well-organized "process manager." "Just because guys have neat desks, lots of reviews and numbers, doesn't mean they will necessarily do a good job," Reed said. Citibank's last real banker, Reed now realized, was his mentor, Bill Spencer.

Of Small, he said that "it wasn't that he saw [a risk] and took the risk.

He didn't see it." Years later Reed said, "All of us would say Larry is risk-averse, yet he produced a lot of risks."

Demoting Small was hard, Reed said, "because Larry is a friend of mine. I've lost that friendship." Reed would say that he admired a lot of Small's qualities, "but from a professional point of view he turns out to be flawed. I hate to say it, but it's true."

"I assumed," Reed said, "when we're paying guys $1 million a year you assume they know what the fuck [they're] doing."

Small would later say that one of the intellectual attributes he admired most in Moore and Wriston was their skill in "pattern recognition." Moore once said that one of the most important skills is to "recognize the same girl with different clothes." Unfortunately, Small, at least in Reed's view, did not share that ability. About a year later, Small left to become president and chief operating officer of the Federal National Mortgage Association (Fannie Mae), the quasi-government agency that buys mortgages and resells them as securities.

In late 1989, as Reed was stewing over his numbers in Jamaica, the real estate market took another blow. The "Massachusetts miracle" was going the way of the "Brazilian miracle." Regulators stormed into the Bank of New England, which had gone hog wild making real estate loans. Days before Christmas, its aggressive chairman, Walter Connolly, was forced to resign, and the bank later posted a staggering $1.2 billion quarterly loss. Unloading every asset it could, it sold its credit-card operation to Citicorp for $828 million. Under the gun for their belated handling of BNE, regulators came down like gangbusters on institutions throughout the country, virtually cutting off bank credit for real estate transactions. "That just killed the market," said Reed. "From then on you couldn't sell buildings for love or money." If the credit crunch and the recession that it triggered needed a starting date, the 1989 examination of Bank of New England was it. Reed would later describe the downturn as a "regulatory recession." When the government finally seized BNE and two banking affiliates a year later in a $2.3 billion rescue, BNE was so far gone that the "rescue" was merely an afterthought.

Ironically, in a rambling speech to financial leaders at the New York Economic Club on January 30, 1990, Reed said he believed that one of the roles of banks in society was to absorb shocks. Citibank would now begin to absorb them to the point of fracture. In a matter of weeks, Citicorp's perception of its real estate portfolio swung 180 degrees, according to insiders. In February 1990, one top real estate lender delivered a presentation to the board that pointed up some problems. "It was not as good as we would like it, but not as bad as it could be," said a former officer. Ten days later, he said, write-offs of $100 million seemed to show up out of nowhere. The auditors and review process had missed the problem. "John was not thrilled," the officer said. The lack of a real-time portfolio information system was now obvious for all to see. Incredibly, said the officer, "nobody was interested in the fact that real estate outstandings were $13 billion." The idea, he said, "was to put on everything you can to make good money and it will sort itself out."

That was just the beginning. In the first quarter of 1990, the U.S. real estate market plunged. Nearly overnight, the impact of the 1986 tax changes and overbuilding, in part triggered by overlending by now-defunct thrift institutions, came home to roost. The Japanese, who had helped hype the market in the first place, now retreated en masse. The Japanese banks, however, would soon have their own problems. They merely disguised their losses with an accounting system that made New York City's lucid in comparison. "After the comptroller said what he said, forget it," Reed said in a 1991 interview. "Liquidity evaporated and hasn't come back since." For Reed, the early years of the decade of the 1990s were to be a black hole.

Citi's problems were heavily concentrated: domestic real estate, Australia, Brazil, and highly leveraged transactions. The biggest chunk of the leveraged deals—16 percent—were in media and entertainment. By 1991, Citibank had made more than $13 billion in commercial real estate loans, more than a third in the western United States. Nearly 43 percent of them were now nonperforming. Citibank had lent up to 80 percent or more of the value of the properties, putting Citibank's investment underwater when values plunged 40 percent or more. Residential mortgages were turning sour too.

In early 1990, Citicorp debt was downgraded by the major rating agencies, and by 1991 some of it had been reduced to junk bond status. Ratings are not as important in consumer banking as they are in corporate banking. Individual depositors generally don't know a bank's credit rating, and don't care. But the rating downgrades cost Citibank dearly. Not only did they increase the cost of purchased money, but they also hurt its ability to execute certain capital markets transactions, such as swaps.

In the first quarter of 1990, earnings fell 56 percent and the loan loss provision surged 80 percent.

At the April 1990 annual meeting, Reed declared the real estate market "frozen," noting that "typically the down cycle in real estate lasts three years." Things were getting tight all over. Arizona, where Citi had bought a bank in 1986, was a "black hole," Reed conceded.

At a later annual meeting, one testy shareholder asked Reed how he had lent so much on real estate. "We made a mistake," Reed said. "If you make two mistakes they send you back a grade," the shareholder scowled.

As late as 1989, Citibank was still lending heavily to real estate developers. For example, in Atlanta it underwrote One Peachtree Center, developed by builder John Portman. But by midyear 1990, Donald Trump was on the skids. Trump had started out as a good customer. But in the opinion of former Citibank officers, he, like other developers, got carried away. "We did one deal too many with people who were okay," shrugged a former officer. With $2 billion in bank debt, Trump's lenders moved to restructure his empire, including his new Taj Mahal casino in Atlantic City, which had opened in April 1990 with great fanfare, but which quickly proved disappointing. Bankers had bought Trump's pitch that the "magic" of his name would enhance the value of his properties, so that they could dispense with the traditional credit analysis. The Donald, one banker told the *Wall Street Journal,* "will have to trim the fat: get rid of the boat, the mansions, the helicopter." But Trump got over this hump by persuading the banks to extend a new loan to pay interest, enabling him to hold on to all his assets.

Trump's problems paled alongside those of his Canadian counterparts, the Reichmann brothers. Through vast, ambitious projects in the United States and the United Kingdom, their Olympia & York had amassed debts of nearly $20 billion. It was the largest commercial landlord in the United States; the restructuring, akin in complexity to that of a Third World country, was the largest of any private company in history. Citibank alone was owed close to $500 million. By the spring of 1992, the Canadian parent had filed for bankruptcy, and later Canary Wharf entered the more draconian British equivalent.

Australia once again was a disaster, proof positive that Citibank had no institutional memory. Over a two-year period, Citibank racked up about $1.2 billion in loans to high-flying real estate developers and other promoters, most of which would ultimately have to be written off. "In Australia, if there's a fool, it's us," said former Citibanker William Heron. Highly leveraged transactions, which included LBOs, also suffered, though at the end of the day they were a pimple compared with the real estate cancer. In January 1990, Campeau's Allied and Federated units, which owed Citibank $288 million, filed for bankruptcy. Incredibly, Citi had backed Campeau up to nine months before everything unraveled.

If there was any consolation, Citi—thanks to Wriston's intervention—avoided major involvement in the troubles of corpulent British media magnate Robert Maxwell. Wriston had a passing acquaintance with Maxwell as a director of Reuters. When Wriston came aboard, Reuters had two classes of stock, one of which was owned by the British press association, which had designated Maxwell a director. Wriston didn't like the idea that a company chairman couldn't fully control who got elected to his board. So he urged Reuters to buy out the press association's shares. At one point, Maxwell was censured by the Reuters board and the London Stock Exchange for illegal trading.

Before heading home from a trip to London, Wriston stopped by Citibank's main branch in London to warn it about Maxwell. "Be very careful. Don't do anything," he told branch officials. In early 1991, Maxwell was looking for financing to buy the stumbling *New York Daily News,* which he agreed to do in March. Recalling Wriston's earlier visit, the branch phoned him to get his view on the deal. "I told them some other things and they stayed away from it," Wriston said. In November 1991, as Maxwell's empire was being exposed as a shell game, he was found drowned in the Mediterranean near his yacht, an apparent suicide.

Unlike Wriston, Reed never really developed that kind of external or internal intelligence network. Few people were daring enough to bring him bad news and, colleagues said, he never took it very well. The only ones who came close to giving it, they said, were Farley, the Wriston holdover, and

Paul Collins. But Reed had dispatched Farley to the West Coast, and Collins to London.

In September 1990 it was Chase's turn to shock Citi. When Chase announced that it would add $650 million to its reserve for loan losses, mostly for bad real estate loans, the market went wild. That put more pressure on Reed to raise more capital. "The Chase announcement took us totally by surprise," he said.

Reed insisted that Citibank's portfolio was really no better or worse than anybody else's. But Citibank was not supposed to be like anybody else. It was supposed to be special. Now the only bank that could be considered solid gold was J. P. Morgan, which had made few real estate loans at all.

"The safeguards were overridden," one former officer said. "People didn't sound warnings. In the old days, we had a lot of people watching the patient, but the people and the equipment disappeared."

"The credit process we had was not perfect, but it worked," Wriston said. "Somehow it broke down. I don't know why. There was no George Scott around," Wriston remembered. Credit policy chief Lawrence Glenn had enjoyed a reputation for being pretty tough. "I thought so," Wriston said. Before Citibank dropped like a rock, Wriston said, "I have nothing but admiration for Johnny. He does a lot of things differently than I do, and that, after all, is why the hell you change managers. . . . This fellow has a remarkable brain and he's growing every day. It is really wonderful to watch. . . . I can't stand these guys who sit around and say my successor is screwing up."

But bad loans weren't Reed's only problem.

That was apparent to him late one afternoon in December 1990, when he and president Rick Braddock were meeting in the sanctity of Reed's private library. As they talked, a steady stream of black Lincoln Town Cars pulled up to the curb or double-parked in front of the building. In the heyday of the 1980s, such a motorcade usually signaled an important meeting of bankers and lawyers over a billion-dollar leveraged buyout.

"Guess we're doing some business," Reed remarked hopefully. Braddock knew better. "Bet we're not," he replied. The two men glared at each other, and Reed quickly got the message. Without putting on a coat, he went outside to ask each driver who had ordered the cars. Each driver confirmed Braddock's suspicion. Citicorp employees, from officers to secretaries, were routinely ordering the limousines, intended only for those who worked late into the evening, to chauffeur them home in the late afternoon and early evening. Citi had grown fat and dumb. And now it was not so happy.

Even as Citibank's difficulties worsened, Reed was confident that as long as the economy grew at all Citi would be able to earn its way out of them. But if, as some predicted, the recession deepened to a negative 3 percent growth, Citibank would be in dire straits. If that happened, Reed would be forced to consider selling his crown jewels—even the credit-card business.

He was not pleased with the Bush administration's economic policy. The problem was that there was none. At one point, as the recession took a turn for the worse, Reed spent a weekend on the phone talking to Treasury secretary Brady and other Washington officials. "Let me tell you, they heard the riot act," he said. "I haven't gone down and yelled and screamed," he said at the time. "Maybe I should."

By 1991, Wriston was also fed up with the Bush administration and its economic non-policy—and not just because Bush didn't play tennis with him anymore. "What is frightening to me is I don't think the current incumbent [Bush] appears to have any fixed values other than loving his grandchildren. I don't see any direction in economic policy," he said in 1992.

But Citi and the banks did have a friend at the Fed. As the economy screeched to a halt, interest rates, with a push from the central bank, plummeted to their lowest levels in decades. And because the cost of money plunged faster than loan rates, bank loan spreads grew fatter.

No one in Washington was as disliked at 399 Park as Representative John Dingell, who had flogged Citi over the Edwards affair. In mid-1991, he delivered the unkindest and most dangerous cut of all. He declared at hearings that Citibank was "technically insolvent" and "struggling to survive." When Dingell made his comment, Reed and his colleagues "went bananas," said a former senior officer. FDIC chairman L. William Seidman rode to Citi's defense. Of Dingell, Reed said, "I assume he's trying to assert an interest in legislation, and the best way to do it was to . . . make an outrageous statement that can attract attention."

A year later without mentioning Citi by name, erstwhile presidential candidate Ross Perot, in an interview with ABC's Peter Jennings, described the bank as insolvent. It turned out, as reported in the *New York Times,* that Perot had been shorting Citi stock [selling borrowed shares on the expectation that the price would fall]. As if the charges of insolvency by a loose-lipped Representative Dingell weren't enough, Reed also had to contend with charges of infidelity in the gossip columns. Sally Reed had filed for a divorce in late 1990 and Reed moved out of their home in Greenwich shortly thereafter. Then, on June 12, 1991, *Daily News* gossip columnist Richard Johnson reported that Reed was having an affair with Cynthia McCarthy, a married stewardess on the Citicorp jet. Wriston was horror-stricken. On the day the article appeared, Wriston told a friend, "This is a terrible day for Citibank."

"He's your boy," the friend said.

Wriston replied, "He's not my boy anymore."

Wriston, in a tough admission, told friends he "goofed" in picking Reed.

It didn't take long for Wall Street traders to start the humor mill turning. In one wisecrack that quickly made the rounds, the captain comes on the loudspeaker and says, "Would the stewardess please return to an upright position before landing."

After the *Daily News* article appeared, Reed told colleagues at a meeting that he planned to cut down on his foreign travel. Reed had made the statement with a straight face. But everyone else bit his lip.

At a board meeting following publication of the article, Reed started to explain his personal circumstances to the board. "They stopped me," he said, "and said, 'forget it.' " He said he assumed that Wriston had explained his domestic situation to the board before they elected him chairman.

Reed acknowledged that his marital problems "consumed a lot of my energy. It didn't make it impossible to do my job. But it was a distraction." Worse still, it hurt his relationship with his children, he said.

By now, many were speculating that the board would demand his resignation, if not for his personal indiscretions, then for his performance as chairman. Hardly a week went by without more bad news and fresh rumors that Reed's days were numbered. Some began to question whether Citibank was simply too big for one person to run, and whether it should be split up. Directors confided to friends that one of the problems they faced as they pondered John Reed's future was that there were few alternatives to Reed left inside the bank. Those who were responsible for the damage had been fired. Others had left on their own. And there were few non-Citibankers in the United States who might be able to wrap their arms around Citicorp fast enough to save it. Reed himself wisecracked, according to one executive, that he kept his job because the board "prefers the devil you know to the devil you don't." Another thing working in Reed's favor was that by now more than half of the outside directors had been elected on his recommendation.

Asked at the 1992 annual meeting if he would consider resigning, Reed said, "If there was a period of time when I couldn't get the job done I suspect the board will look for new management. This management is firmly determined to get the job done in 1992." Reed managed to convince a nervous board that he would turn things around.

Some even speculated that Paul Volcker would be installed as chairman, or that Wriston would be hauled out of retirement. That wasn't about to happen, but Wriston was no longer keeping his nose out of Citicorp's affairs entirely. As Reed said at the time, "I see more of him [Wriston] recently because he really is worried about what we're going through."

Stillman Rockefeller, who at eighty-eight still rode the train in from Greenwich to his office several times a week, summed the situation up tersely in a brief sidewalk interview. Rockefeller blamed Wriston for picking Reed. "He [Wriston] sure made a mess of things."

Yet even as Citibank was suffering from its problems, it did not relinquish its role as a source of liquidity for other troubled firms. One was Salomon Brothers, whose CFO was Donald Howard, late of Citicorp. "Howard," said Reed at the time, "must be running around making sure those who lend continue to lend." That included his former employer. "We keep everybody afloat. It's part of the process," Reed said.

Reed sometimes exacerbated his own problems with his bluntness. In a speech to Chicago business executives that was reported in the *Wall Street Journal* of September 23, 1991, he declared that real estate write-offs would continue longer than he had expected. He added that values would plummet 30 percent before they stabilized. That statement by the nation's largest real estate lender, experts said later, itself caused values to decline. Reed felt one of his major weaknesses was his inability to present himself to the outside world in a sophisticated way, for which he was widely criticized inside the bank. His speech in Chicago may have been one such example.

When the bad news rained, it poured. In the third quarter of 1991, Citicorp disclosed a loss of $885 million. After having already slashed the dividend—Citicorp's sacred cash cow—Reed was now forced to take the drastic step of eliminating it entirely. Citi could no longer boast that it had paid dividends without interruption since 1813. Reed now owned 500,000 shares himself, and was using the dividends to pay off the loans he took out to buy them. So these measures squeezed Reed personally. "I'm sensitive to that. I'm embarrassed by that," he told analysts. Half of the deficit resulted from a write-down of the ill-fated Quotron acquisition. By now, the Wall Street firms were ripping out their Quotron machines and replacing them with the box of choice, the Bloomberg terminal. By 1992, just a handful of firms still used the Quotron.

In November 1991, Reed canned senior executives of a credit-card unit for inflating revenues. And in December, more unfounded rumors about new Citicorp troubles and Reed's impending resignation sent Citi stock plummeting to $8.63 a share, the lowest level since the 1960s. That month, the cover of *Institutional Investor* depicted Citibank's treasured "Credit Doctrine for Lending Officers" wrapped around a fish.

Citibank may not have been insolvent, but its condition was clearly a cause for alarm. In August 1992, it was forced to disclose that regulators had demanded that it sign a "memo of understanding"—an "MOU" in regulators' shorthand—admitting that its difficulties were critical enough to require intensive regulatory supervision. Examiners, one Citibank officer said, regularly took over the boardroom to go through the loan portfolio piece by piece. In fact, Reed admitted later, Citi came "very close" to the abyss in December 1991, when the comptroller of "the Currency declined to sign off on Citi's reserve levels. But Citi was deemed "too big to fail."

In the thick of the S & L crisis, Wriston was dumbfounded at how Lincoln Savings, one of the costliest thrift failures of them all, was able to corral five U.S. senators to pressure regulators not to take action against it. "I don't think the commercial banking business could marshal one U.S. senator to talk to any one of the regulators."

One humiliation was heaped on top of another. Regulators ordered Citi to lower second-quarter 1992 earnings by $28 million, saying it exaggerated the value of its mortgage-servicing business. Chastising Citi for its sloppy lending practices, the regulators asserted that nearly 13 percent of its residential mortgage loans were delinquent. As Citi had done sixteen years before in the problem bank episode, it contested the regulators' findings, saying they were filled with errors. The number was only 5 percent, Citi insisted. Whatever it was, Braddock, though well-regarded as a manager, was ultimately responsible, and took the fall, adding to Reed's reputation as Citicorp's resident "serial killer." In Reed's view, the mortgage debacle was the "most dangerous" point for Citi. "It was a question of their [the regulators'] feeling that we had serious control problems."

If there was one silver lining, it was that the memo of understanding essentially blocked Citicorp from making more bad acquisitions even if it had wanted to.

Reed seemed to take the heat well, though he complained that "people talk about Citicorp as if we were the only people in America with a troubled real estate portfolio. No one is writing articles that [Tom] Labrecque is going to get fired from Chase, [Walter] Shipley from Chemical, [John] McGillicuddy from Manufacturers, or [Robert] Smith from Security Pacific." To be sure, much of the U.S. banking industry was in the same sinking boat.

Amid the criticism, Reed at least was aided by the knowledge that "never in my career did anybody think I was doing anything right." When he ran operations, "everybody said, 'God, he's tearing up the operating group. When I was running the consumer business, it was [considered] a big mistake."

Reed said the stress level he felt during Citicorp's crisis was "about comparable" to what he had endured during the dark days of the consumer business. Then, he said, "I was less in charge of things. Now at least I'm very much in charge. . . . Being in charge is better in terms of stress. You can sort of look in the mirror and say, 'Hey Reed, do what you think is right.' The only person I look to is myself."

And he added, "Despite the fact that the whole world thinks I'm an idiot . . . my collapsing under pressure is not likely."

There were few bright spots in this gloomy landscape. One of them was the consumer business in general and credit cards in particular.

For all its other woes, Citibank was now the only global consumer bank and was making solid profits there. The beauty of the international consumer business is that it could generate local currency deposits, which could be lent to local customers instead of dollars. Said one former top Citibanker, "Wriston understood that. . . . One of the reasons he wanted to build the international consumer business was so we wouldn't have to make cross-border loans to do business with customers in these countries."

"The difference between Citibank and the others," said Wriston, "is we have this huge branch network in Latin America that makes money year in, year out. No other financial institution has that network. We've been remitting profits from Brazil every year through this whole mess. That's what everybody who beats us up over cross-border doesn't realize, and we're not about to put it on the broad tape either."

Citibank's goal was to introduce its "Citi-One" account, with local variations, at branches throughout the world and to link up its ATMs all over the world. That would enable a New York customer to obtain cash and information on his account in Munich or Athens or Hong Kong just as he did at home.

Citi's consumer banks in Germany and Spain were big successes. In

Spain, Citi had rehabilitated a failing bank it bought from the Spanish government and renamed it Citibank España. Following in the tradition established by Wriston and George Moore, it revolutionized consumer banking in Spain by providing conveniences customers had never known before, such as granting car loans in forty-eight hours instead of two months. In early 1991, Reed said the California savings unit was profitable and declared that Citicorp Savings in Chicago was "getting respectable." Another saving grace for Citicorp was its global infrastructure. Bad as its loan portfolio was, virtually every multinational corporation had to deal with Citicorp. It was the market maker in foreign exchange, which covered up a multitude of losses. In 1992, foreign exchange trading revenues of more than $1 billion represented over 100 percent of earnings.

One treasury officer of a multinational company recalled that even as his company was prudently keeping its balances at Citibank during its crisis to a minimum, it dropped Manufacturers Hanover and Chemical Bank as paying agents, saving $50,000 a year, because of Citibank's ability to quickly disburse and clear checks in any currency, virtually anywhere in the world. Overseas, Citibank officers get "immediate access," he said, to senior company officials.

———

By now, there was plenty of blame to go around. While Reed assumed most of it himself, others didn't get off easily either.

Reed would later blame his institution's decline on the "quest for profitability." No, he insisted, it was not the LDC problem that caused his corporate bankers to stretch, but rather the success of the consumer business. "I think the people in the corporate business felt that to be credible internally they had to be as important to the company as the consumer business. When the consumer business said they were going to make $1 billion a year, the corporate guys felt they had to [as well]."

"It was a crazy era," Reed said. "If you had any assets and they weren't fully leveraged, you weren't doing your job as a manager."

"We've had this underlying variable imposed on us called taking reserves for cross-border loans." But Reed admitted that the problems of Citicorp were not Wriston's. "I can't lay the blame on a guy who retired seven years ago," Reed said in mid-1991. By the mid-1990s, cross border, real estate, and LBO's had cost Citicorp upward of $9 billion in write-offs alone, enough, in theory at least, to have bought Chase Manhattan, with Wells Fargo thrown in for good measure (based on year-end 1992 valuations). Though Reed took the blame for the real estate and LBO disasters, he did point out that some of those who oversaw them were discovered and appointed to their jobs by his predecessor. Chief credit officer Lawrence Glenn, for example, was named to that post by Wriston.

Reed now regretted not having wider banking experience and getting more involved in the corporate business, but added that delegation was the Citibank tradition.

"I assumed the people running it knew what they were doing, but it turned out I was wrong, for which I will never forgive myself. There was a whole set of folks who let themselves, the institution, me down. [It was] just incompetence in every sense of the word." Meanwhile, "the corporate guys are feeling bad about themselves, so they run around saying Reed doesn't love them." Not so, said Reed. His problem with them was that they brought home a bad report card.

Just as it had done in lending to the LDCs, Citibank ignored what Reed called the "macro-externalities" that led to the collapse of the real estate market. Still, he had no regrets about disbanding the economics department. "Line management was persuasive in saying, 'Hey, we know what we're doing.' The economics department wouldn't have stopped that."

Reed concluded that the problem with the loan portfolio was not the structure of individual deals but the portfolio concentrations. "We never have had a focus on portfolio management," Reed said. "We should have."

Still, the LDC debt crisis was clearly a distraction. "I was busy with cross-border," Reed said, "where there were obvious indications of need. I had a hell of a lot of learning to do, but I must say it took an awful lot of my time. To good end."

Countering charges that he got too involved in the LDC crisis, Reed insisted that his personal involvement was essential, because only he could phone Volcker or Mexican president Salinas. "Putting together the Mexican deal certainly required personal intervention at the chairman level of all the major lending banks."

Wriston, Reed said, would feel that he had done a "crappy job" in terms of public leadership. "He's correct. Walt was very good at positioning himself and the company." Added Reed, "I'm going to have to add that to my collection of tricks."

Humbled by his troubles, Reed acknowledged that, twenty years after he earned his reputation as a brash young technocrat, "I'm not quite so brash. I don't think of the world as simply as I did then."

When a banker's world starts caving in, the first reaction is to slash, sell, and fire. Reed, said a former Citibank officer, "gave everybody a dull hatchet and said go out and hack." To save their own jobs, they eliminated those of thousands of others. In 1990, Reed began by firing 3,600 employees. That wave was followed in December 1990 by another 4,400. Reed wasn't kidding when he told U.S. Banker of May 1989 that "I'm a talker." He casually mentioned to one multinational customer over dinner at the Four Seasons that 20,000 people would be let go before the bloodletting ended, not the 9,000 or so already announced, according to one former senior officer.

Citibankers had always been assertive and sure of themselves. Now they were plagued by self-doubt and uncertainty about the survival of their institution. Morale sank to an all-time low. Citibank's internal competition may have worked when business was growing. As Citibank faltered and jobs were eliminated, the backstabbing turned vicious. People who were once friends scrambled to save their jobs. Said one observer, "It was like people trying to get out of a building in a fire."

"The covenant of trust is gone," one officer said at the time. Citicorp was paralyzed, and the atmosphere of gloom and doom wasn't lost on corporate customers. "CFOs called asking what's going on. Customers have really been battered around on this one," said a former officer.

By 1991, Reed had concluded he had to cut a staggering $1.5 billion of expenses out of Citicorp. As he told analysts in January 1991, "All large companies get sloppy, and we are no exception." Watching the town cars from his library window "crystallized" Reed's thinking about expenses, he said later.

In addition to limos, every expense item was now subject to scrutiny. One night, Reed noticed that all the lights were still on at Citicorp's new highrise operations center across the river in Queens. When he called to ask why, he was told they were needed for the cleaning people.

But Reed needed to do much more than turn the lights out. After years of opposing (for the most part successfully) Fed chairman Arthur Burns's efforts to force banks like his to raise more capital, Wriston took special satisfaction from an unusual admission Burns made a couple of years after Wriston retired. Over dinner at a financial conference in Cannes, France, where they were on a panel together, Burns said, "You know, Walter, you sure turned out to be right. You really have to earn money to sell equity."

Wriston was startled and pleased. When he recovered, he said, "This is a historic occasion. I wish I could immortalize it with something," Wriston said. But Burns's admission would be of little consolation a few years later to John Reed. Reed would learn that while you have to earn money to sell equity, you also need equity to stay alive.

Thanks to the debt crisis, bank regulators now had the ammunition they needed to require global bank capital standards. The regulators in the eighties devised—and in mid-1988 the Fed approved—a set of capital ratios tied to the risks of assets on banks' books; under this so-called Basle Accord, riskless assets such as Treasuries would not require capital, whereas assets such as commercial real estate loans would call for banks to allocate a certain percentage of capital against them. By the time this effort began in earnest, Wriston no longer had his perch as Citicorp chairman to speak out against them. And just a year before these rules were to go into effect at the end of 1992, Citicorp failed to meet them. Reed now needed to boost capital by $4 billion to $5 billion.

Reed, unlike Wriston, did believe that banks needed capital. Turning his back on the Wriston era, he declared that "the departure for us is embracing the notion of being strongly capitalized. We had felt we could run with thin capital. For years, the strength of the company was its diversification of earnings. That's clearly not enough," he said.

But Citibank was troubled by the new global capital standards. Under these rules, preferred stock that didn't carry a fixed dividend rate would no longer be accepted as equity. Citibank thought that was ridiculous, and lobbied the regulators to include it—to no avail, according to former chief financial officer Don Howard. With the stroke of a pen, Citibank was deprived of billions of life-sustaining equity capital.

In a February 7, 1992, *Wall Street Journal* Op-Ed article, Wriston complained that the regulators constantly changed the capital rules, to the point where capital adequacy "has become a race with no finish line." While "defining away" the preferred stock, Wriston wrote, regulators redefined assets, assigning a riskless label to government securities. That allowed the government, he wrote, to finance its huge debt by selling the securities to the banks, which would not have to allocate capital to them.

So Citicorp scrounged the world for capital. Someone asked Reed if he planned to sell the rest of its interest in Citicorp Center. "Are you kidding?" Reed replied. "You can't give it away."

Perhaps the most reliable treasure trove was the venture capital unit headed by Oklahoman Bill Comfort, who reputedly drew a bigger paycheck than Reed for the success of his operation. Inside Citi, Comfort was untouchable. He often wore golfing garb to work and relaxed in his spacious office by practicing his putting. From 1985 until 1992, his unit had posted real gains of about $900 million and unrealized gains of about $600 million, Citicorp sources said. Whenever Reed got in a jam, one of the people he turned to for some nonrecurring earnings was Bill Comfort.

One eagerly welcomed investor emerged from Saudi Arabia, proof positive of Wriston's argument that OPEC surpluses didn't disappear into the desert sands. Prince al-Waleed bin Talal, now thirty-five, had good feelings about Citibank, having received a loan from Citi in 1979. He had a long-standing relationship with the Swiss private banking office of Citibank, and for three years had been contemplating an investment. The deal gave him an 11 percent dividend on convertible preferred stock and the right to convert those shares to common equity once the price per share hit $16. That would give him a 4.9 percent stake and make him Citicorp's single largest holder.

Shortly after meeting the prince for the first time, Reed said, "He, like all investors, is interested in making money. I just wanted to make sure he understood what the game plan is and how we're going to manage the place. He's going to make a lot of money. I wish I had $590 million earning 11 percent while I watch the price of the stock."

In 1992, Citicorp gave its preferred shareholders the opportunity to exchange their shares for common at a higher price. And it later offered common shareholders the chance to acquire more stock at a 2.5 percent discount from the market price.

Another device that helped save Citicorp, and which Citicorp helped pioneer, was asset securitization. Like mortgage securitization, this new technique involved packaging assets, such as credit-card receivables, and selling them as securities to investors instead of keeping them on the books. Without securitization, Citi could never have expanded its consumer business. In March 1990, for example, Citibank sold $1.4 billion of consumer receivables packaged as securities, the largest such transaction in the three years since the market started.

Compounding Reed's problems was a regulatory push for banks to use mark-to-market accounting, the issue Wriston so successfully deflected during his entire chairmanship. Commercial real estate loans—Citi's Achille's heel—now had to be written down as values dropped. "It's a crazy concept for a bank. We all benefit from the fact that time is a great healer," Reed said. In Reed's view, mark-to-market was just one example of the fact that Wriston ran the bank in a less hostile world, one that was more amenable to being shaped to his liking. The only area in the external world where Reed felt his influence had been felt was in the cross-border debt negotiations.

Wriston continued to try to pin the troubles of the banks on regulation. In a November 12, 1990, *Wall Street Journal* survey on how troubled banks might recover, he said, "There are structural problems that have to be fixed." Banks needed to be able to expand nationwide. And laws needed to be changed to allow industrial companies to buy more than 9.9 percent of a commercial bank. Wriston proposed allowing cash-rich industrial companies, like drug companies, to buy 49 percent stakes in troubled banks— though he did not name his own. After it recovered, the bank would buy the shares back, enabling the companies to earn a 20 percent return.

When the bank's problems began to snowball, Reed confessed that he was "overwhelmed by the burden of it. I was dragging my tail." In his business or personal life, Reed admitted that he was sometimes less than decisive. He had, for example, spent four years deliberating over what kind of hi-fi to buy until one of his children demanded, "Stop talking about it and buy it." Reed considered himself a builder, not a "runner." And so far he had not done a very good job of "running."

Around March 1991, he said, he realized that, as unpleasant as it would be, he would have to pull himself together and bite the bullet to rebuild the bank—not just dart from one crisis to the other.

"I went from being an embattled executive to being a person driven to make some very fundamental transformations in the company." Reed set out to fix the broken Citicorp credit culture, the destructive internal competitiveness, and spendthrift attitudes. He was now determined that by 1993, Citibank would be stronger, better capitalized, and more focused.

When John sees a problem, a former colleague said admiringly, "He says, 'I'll fix it.'"

As he had done with the LDC crisis, Reed in mid-1991 announced that he was taking personal charge of real estate lending and corporate banking in Australia, removing those activities from the control of Michael Callen. With real estate values down an estimated 30 percent from their highs, in October 1991 Reed tapped Robert A. McCormack, a veteran of the Third World reschedulings, to be the Bill Rhodes of the real estate debacle. Instead of taking a fire sale approach that would cause more losses, McCormack was to take a long-term view of the market. And Reed later set up a dozen task forces to work on such problems as bad assets and heavy expenses. Then in early 1992, to add some luster to Citicorp's tarnished reputation, he named director Onno Ruding, a highly respected former Netherlands finance minister, to vice chairman for corporate banking.

First and foremost, Reed had to repair the damage to the bank's risk-management systems, including its credit culture and methods for monitoring loans. As the portfolio grew, Citibank had not felt it needed a system for monitoring loans and establishing exposure limits by industry and location. Now, humbly, it set up a system to do just that. Reed was determined to give credit policy officers a more "independent" check-and-balance role than they had enjoyed in the past, and to focus on market risk as well as credit risk.

Reed now recognized that decentralization à la Wriston had its drawbacks. Reed aimed his scalpel at layers of bureaucratic flab built up since the McKinsey reorganization, and at the bank's overemphasis on process over substance. In early 1991, Reed said that he planned to reduce senior management to twenty-one from thirty-four. The management structure would be thinned down, "starting with me," he said. Administrators, auditors, controllers, human resources specialists, and especially lawyers would be let go or their functions consolidated, while people who dealt with customers would remain. By cutting five executive vice presidents with geographic responsibility in different parts of the world, Reed said, he eliminated 600 staff members associated with each of them. "I can find no difference in our ability to run the business internationally. I have one guy in New York with international responsibility and he has nine guys in the field." Of the approximately 17,000 people Reed had put on the street by mid-1991, most of them, he said, were "fat."

Bank officers had gotten to the point where they couldn't write a letter to a customer without checking it with a Shearman & Sterling or in-house attorney. Reed revealed that the chairman's letter for the annual report, normally read by six people, including lawyers, would now be written by him and reviewed by just one other person. "It might not be as smooth," he quipped. But it would surely cost a lot less.

Reed also eliminated monthly budget meetings, saying that they had become "show and tell as opposed to substantive discussions."

No one believed in leverage more than Wriston, but Citicorp had failed to use its size to its full advantage. It had always allowed each business manager to exert near-total control over every activity, including purchasing. At long last, purchasing was centralized so that Citibank could get better deals on everything from phone calls to travel and entertainment. Citibank also stopped offering business managers what one analyst called "hardware and software à la carte."

Stunned by his setbacks, Reed set out to change the sociology and attitudes of Citibank and Citibankers. He reevaluated, for example, the criteria he used for choosing top people. In a videotaped presentation, Reed lamented the lack of wisdom among managers and cited Theobald as one manager who possessed it. Now, Reed ordered, managers would be evaluated for how they treated their people as well as their bottom-line performance.

In mid-1991, Reed boasted, "I now figure I can run the whole fucking place. I have to and I will. I'm just as good a corporate banker as any of those corporate bankers, not because I know anything about banking but because I know enough about business."

As Citibank's problems took hold, Reed looked to 1993 as the year when he and his institution would begin to come out of the woods. He was right.

"It's now coming back," Wriston glowed as the patient showed signs of recovery. "It's the greatest franchise in the world. Probably no one could have withstood what they've gone through."

Reed was finally assembling a team that was relatively untainted by the credit debacle. An important new addition was Christopher Steffan, a tough cost-cutter who traded his job as chief financial officer at floundering Eastman Kodak for the same post at Citi.

Reed had worked like the devil to save Citicorp. But he couldn't have succeeded if Fed chairman Alan Greenspan had not been working the monetary levers on behalf of Citi and other beleaguered banks.

By 1993, as bank profits improved and regulators, realizing they had come down too hard on the banks to begin with, started to remove regulatory impediments to bank lending, the credit crunch began to ease.

One of the biggest winners was Prince al-Waleed bin Talal of Saudi Arabia. In mid-1993, he sold 3.457 million shares of Citicorp for $95.5 million, or $27.625 per share, more than doubling his money on that transaction in some two and a half years.

But the Citibank that came back from the dead was a much different Citibank than the one Wriston had retired from or envisioned.

Decentralizing, experimenting, taking big risks, and battling regulators had worked in the optimistic, high-growth era in which Wriston served as chairman. But with Citibank on the defensive, these strategies were luxuries it could no longer afford. Indeed, the Citibank of 1995, some officers say, more closely resembles the conservative bank of Stillman Rockefeller rather than the aggressive one of Walter Wriston. "We're going back to fundamentals," said John Ingraham, the veteran workout man. Accordingly, Reed concluded that Citibank would have to become a more focused place. By 1995, Wriston's five I's" had been cut to just two or three. "Information is a disaster, and insurance never went anywhere," said Ingraham.

Citibank also threw in the towel on middle market lending and investment banking. "Major expansion in the U.S. middle market or into broadbased investment banking is not our objective," Reed wrote in his 1994 letter to shareholders. If there remains a Wriston legacy, it is that two-thirds of Citibank's earnings were now coming from consumers.

Wriston had, in Reed's opinion, nearly realized Citicorp as a global institution. The global consumer business got its start under Wriston, but became more interconnected under Reed, notably by flipping the ATM switch to allow retail customers to use their Citicards anywhere. Though Reed was convinced that most of Citicorp's future profits would be derived from the consumer, he felt that corporate banking would always be the intellectual cornerstone of the company. "There are no exciting consumer financial institutions that I know of," he said.

Reed wanted to strengthen Citicorp's traditionally weak corporate business in Europe and Japan. He wanted to get technology "baked into the place," in the form of on-line interactive systems where bank "products" could be delivered to the customer through computers. In the corporate arena, Citibank's increased globalization was reflected in its financing of the construction of a tower in Germany, the tallest building in Europe, by placing the paper in Japan.

Ironically, in John Reed's newly refocused Citicorp, Wriston's fifth "I"—insurance—was relegated to a minor role just as Citibank won a major battle for insurance powers. In early 1992, the Supreme Court let stand an appeals court ruling that allowed the bank to circumvent prohibitions against bank underwriting of insurance by doing it through a Delaware banking unit. Now Citibank could sell its own insurance through New York branches, along with mutual funds and annuities.

With fewer "I's" to focus on, he could finally focus on himself. On September 2, 1994, in a small, private Chicago ceremony, he married Cynthia McCarthy.

EPILOGUE

Whenever Citicorp ran into trouble and critics beat up on Wriston for his blunders, Wriston implicitly compared himself and Citibank with baseball greats like Ted Williams and Joe DiMaggio. People can zero in on his mistakes and those of his institution, he said in later years, "or they can focus on our batting average. One of the things that fascinates me is that if you hit .400 in baseball you're in the Hall of Fame." He evidently thought his batting average was a pretty good one.

But a batting average, even though Wriston was prepared to use it to quantify his own performance, is a trite and one-dimensional measure of his life and career. A more meaningful metaphor is the Olympic scoring system, which judges artistic as well as technical merit.

In the banking Olympics, Wriston would probably qualify for a bronze medal on technical merit alone. Judged according to the returns he delivered to shareholders, his performance was better than average for his big-bank peers, but not spectacularly so. Wriston was a good banker, but not the best.

On August 31, 1984, Wriston's last day on the job, Citicorp shares closed at $17.31, compared with $6.75 when he became CEO seventeen years earlier, an increase of 156.5 percent, slightly better than the average 148 percent appreciation for large banks, according to an index compiled by Keefe, Bruyette & Woods, a bank securities firm.*

And by naming a non-banker to take charge of an undercapitalized bank, Wriston set the stage for billions of dollars in losses to shareholders on his successor's watch.

In the artistic merit category—intellectual and industry leadership and innovation, the figure eights and somersaults—Wriston deserves higher marks.

---

*If the Wriston era is assumed to have really ended on May 20, 1987, the day after Reed announced his special LDC reserve, the appreciation would be 293.5 percent, slightly below the Keefe big bank average. Measured on annual total return, which includes dividends, Wriston's performance through 1984 and 1987 was 10 percent and 11 percent, respectively.

While A. P. Giannini and J. P. Morgan are deservedly in a league of their own for having started great banking institutions from scratch, no banker and institution did more to free the financial services industry and the U.S. economy from the regulatory gridlock of the 1930s than Wriston and Citibank did. In the last half of the twentieth century, Wriston was surely the mold-breaker.

By inventing new instruments, such as the negotiable CD, introducing new ideas in the marketplace, and devising new loopholes, he chipped away at archaic pricing, product, and geographic barriers, and freed banks to compete with each other—and with non-bank competitive financial service organizations not subject to the banking industry's rules. And though Wriston's Citibank was chaotic and internally competitive, it provided the climate for risk-taking and creativity that allowed others to devise instruments—such as the currency swap—that broke down barriers to the free and efficient flow of capital.

By 1994, a number of items on the Wriston wish list had begun to come true. He finally got his wish on interstate banking, when Congress passed a law dropping these barriers. And though Wriston never pressed as hard to eliminate Glass-Steagall as he did to get rid of prohibitions against interstate banking and interest rate ceilings, he welcomed moves, now regarded as imminent, to do away with the barriers between investment and commercial banking and banking and commerce.

Ironically, as that was happening, the non-bank financial supermarkets that Wriston regarded as banking's stiffest potential competition fifteen years earlier were shadows of their former selves. Sears had given up on the concept, spun off Allstate insurance, and returned to its retailing roots. Likewise, the American Express/Shearson Lehman Brothers marriage had proved to be a fiasco. None of the synergies that American Express Chairman James Robinson and Shearson chairman Sandy Weill had envisioned back in 1981 had come to pass, and American Express by 1994 had gotten rid of Shearson Lehman and refocused on its credit card. Prudential Insurance would now have to shell out more than $1 billion to investors in soured limited partnership investments sold to them in the 1980s by its Prudential Securities unit. Apart from Merrill Lynch, Citibank was the closest thing to a financial supermarket still standing.

Wriston waffled on his commitment to investment banking. For a while, it appeared that his would-be successor, George Vojta, had led Bankers Trust to the promised land by transforming it into a trading house. But Bankers Trust forgot its customers along the way. In the wake of derivatives losses, the Procter and Gamble Company and Gibson Greetings Inc. sued BT in 1994, claiming the bank had misrepresented these products to them. Reed's task looked easy in contrast to that of BT chairman Charles Sanford. Reed had plenty of bum loans to dispose of, but Bankers Trust was faced with the task of restoring a lost reputation.

If there was a flaw in Wriston's intellectual leadership of the banking industry, it was his insistence that highly aggressive banks don't need capital as long as they are diversified and well-managed. Citicorp and other institutions that bought this line were ill-prepared to absorb the losses from their bad LDC, real estate, and LBO loans. In steering Citibank and the banking industry into the decade-long LDC debacle, Wriston relied on an inappropriate historical analogy. Even so, the crisis achieved what no army could: It pushed the Third World, particularly in Latin America, into the arms of Adam Smith. And by December 1994, when Mexico and other emerging markets blew up as they had more than twelve years earlier, investors, not banks, were left holding the bag.

But Wriston also guided the banking industry through many of the major financial crises of the postwar era, including Penn Central, Herstatt, Franklin National, and New York City's near brush with bankruptcy. In 1995, as Wriston was fading from the world stage, he left a vacuum in American economic and financial leadership that few were willing or able to fill. Indeed, as New York City ran into financial trouble again in the 1990s, there were no bankers with the wherewithal or interest to help patch it up again.

In an era when it was difficult to find a public figure untainted with personal scandal or financial malfeasance, Wriston stood above the pack for personal integrity. While he became a wealthy man as Citicorp chairman, there is absolutely no evidence that his business judgments, though sometimes off the mark, were ever skewed by personal greed.

Wriston's time horizon transcended Citibank's decade-long troubles. He prided himself on building an institution "that would survive in the new world and be pre-eminent over time. It will go up and down and have problems." But he said, it has an "infrastructure that no one else has duplicated and I don't think they're about to." That was true even as Citicorp was losing its ranking as the largest U.S. banking company to a combined Chase Manhattan and Chemical Bank, which in August 1995 announced plans to merge and retain the more prestigious Chase name. But Reed's bank is also narrower in focus, less ambitious, less of a player than it was under Wriston. It has largely abdicated the role it served in the Wriston era as an industry and intellectual leader and proponent of change. One reason surely was that John Reed lacks Wriston's commanding presence and prestige. Another, of course, was that the world itself had changed. In 1995, with the Latin debt and real estate crises behind him, Reed could concentrate on minding the store, expanding the global retail network, fine-tuning Citibank's operations and technology, selling telephone banking to customers, eliminating consumer transaction fees, and, with Citicorp stock trading at more than $60 a share, counting the paper gains on his stock options. Moreover, in the deregulated economy that Wriston had helped create, there were fewer external battles for John Reed to fight, even if he had the inclination to fight them.

Still, if one was to define Wriston's true legacy, it was Citicorp's emergence as the world's only international bank, one that has, at long last, even rewarded shareholders by making money. In light of the pain and suffering Mother Bank had just endured, that's about all that Walter B. Wriston could have wished for.

NOTES AND SOURCES

AUTHOR'S NOTE

Because of the hundreds of interviews conducted for this book, the notes and sources are primarily references to material from periodicals, documents, books, and other publications. In general, quotations attributed to individuals are from the author's interviews. Complete titles of books and publishing data for works cited will be found in the bibliography.

PROLOGUE

2   Questions about Citicorp's solvency: Quint, Michael, "Dingell's Sweeping Claims About Citicorp's Solvency," *New York Times,* Aug. 1, 1991, and Bloomberg Business News, "We're Solvent, Citicorp Says," *New York Times,* July 8, 1992.
2   Affair with stewardess: Johnson, Richard, "Citicorp Chief Banking on New Love," *Daily News* (New York), June 12, 1991.

CHAPTER 1

5   Wriston family history: Interviews with Walter Wriston and Barbara Wriston; *A Pioneer's Odyssey,* privately published memoir of Jennie Atcheson Wriston; *Essays and Talks,* unpublished papers of Dr. Henry Wriston.
7   Details of Henry Wriston's activities at Wesleyan from Wesleyan yearbook, *Olla Podrida,* 1912; *Humanist As Educator: The Public Life of Henry Merritt Wriston;* unpublished interview, Wesleyan University archives.
8   *Executive Agents in American Foreign Relations,* 1929.
8   "The cable and the wireless": *Essays and Talks,* speech by Henry Wriston before Society of Colonial Wars, Connecticut, Dec. 10, 1924.
9   Details of Henry Wriston's Lawrence College presidency: Interviews with Richard Warch, Charles Breunig and Ted Cloak; Lawrence College archives; *Academic Procession.*
10 "Must have some grasp": *Essays and Talks,* commencement address to Lawrence College seniors, 1926.
10 "When I inquired": *Academic Procession,* p. 189.
10 "I simply haunted": Unpublished Wesleyan interview, Wesleyan U. archives, p. 18.
10 "I never had any of those": *Academic Procession,* p. 152.
11 "When something unusual": Ibid., p. 112.
11 "I was urged": Ibid., p. 216.
11 "Should make clear": Ibid.
12 "When I became a president": Ibid., p. 99.
14 "Flawed concept": *Essays and Talks.*
14 "Armies of bureaucrats": *Essays and Talks,* speech to executive committee and board of governors of American Paper and Pulp Association, Appleton, Wisconsin, June 5, 1936.

15   "The railroad financier": Ibid.

16   Some of the details of Walter Wriston's high school activities: *Clarion*, the Appleton High School yearbook, 1937.

18   "It seems to me": "Wriston Wins Parker Contest With Speech on Defeatism of Youth," *Wesleyan Argus*, May 4, 1939.

20   Neumann, Sigmund, *The Permanent Revolution.*

20   "The necessity of breaking down": *Wesleyan University Alumnus*, Nov. 1956, p. 13.

21   Details of Bobby Wriston's college activities: Connecticut College archives.

22   "Freedom of speech": "Propaganda and Freedom . . . ," *Wesleyan Argus*, April 22, 1940.

22   Letter from Wendell Willkie to Wriston: Ibid., Oct. 10, 1940.

22   "Henry challenged": Address delivered over radio station WEAN, Oct. 21, 1940, Lawrence University archives.

23   "This June": *Olla Podrida*, 1941.

23   Honors thesis: Wesleyan University archives.

24   Debate with Smith: Radio Forum Broadcast, Dec. 7, 1941.

24   References to the *Op Ten Noort:* State Department documents, including letter from Netherlands ambassador to Cordell Hull, July 3, 1942, National Archives.

CHAPTER 2

Early history of Citibank: *Citibank 1812–1970; The Business Career of Moses Taylor; First Billion; From Farm Boy to Financier; Congress Investigates: A Documented History; Wall Street under Oath;* Moody, John, and Turner, George Kibbe, "Masters of Capital in America," *McClure's* Magazine, May, June, and July 1911, and Citibank archives.

29   Letter from Henry Wriston to Randolph Burgess, Feb. 18, 1937: Brown University archives.

29   "Stone-cold dead": Brooks, John, "The Money Machine," *New Yorker*, Jan. 5, 1981.

30   "Personal control, silence": *Business Career of Moses Taylor*, p. 273.

31   "Keep silent": *From Farm Boy to Financier*, p. 112.

32   " 'Twasn't the money": *First Billion*, p. 48.

33   "Avoided reporters": *Farm Boy*, p. 116.

33   "Into an adventure": Ibid., p. 155.

34   "Ridiculously strong and liquid": *Citibank 1812–1970*, p. 52.

35   "Had made investments": *First Billion*, p. 204.

35   "Government supervision and control": *Triumph of Conservatism*, p. 189.

36   "Has gone about far enough": *Congress Investigates: A Documented History*, vol. 3, p. 2267.

36   "I stand charged": "Wall Street Defended to Owen and Glass," *New York Times*, Nov. 11, 1913.

38   "We evidently have": *Citibank 1812–1970*, p. 80.

38   "It was a rude": Ibid., p. 101.

38   "Kerensky fell": *They told Barron: Conversations and Revelations of an American Pepys in Wall Street*, p. 30.

38   "Accept the presidency of the bank": *First Billion*, p. 13.

38   "With the mourners": Ibid., p. 7.
39   Account of Jamie Stillman's domestic troubles: Ibid., p. 263.
39   "An astonishing capacity": *Farm Boy,* p. 287.
39   "Considered himself": James Stillman Rockefeller, unpublished internal interview, Citibank archives.
40   "I hardly think": *Wall Street under Oath,* p. 123.
40   "If I go into": Wriston, speech to correspondent bankers, Jan. 29, 1977.
41   Details of Citibank's relationship with Ivar Kreuger: *Kreuger: Genius and Swindler* p. 77, 202; and "Ask Court to Oust Kreuger Trustee," *New York Times,* Sept. 14, 1932.
41   "Careless in the fulfillment": Ibid., p. 100.
41   "Inspired confidence": *Farm Boy,* p. 155.
42   "The industrial condition": *The Great Crash 1929,* p. 94.
42   "Purely technical": Ibid., p. 105.
42   "Greatest bank": *Foreign Expansion of American Banks,* p. 142.
43   "Undesirable or worthless": *Congress Investigates,* vol. 4, p. 2,555.
43   "All wrong": *Wall Street under Oath,* p. 85.
44   "Looms up": Ibid., p. 154.
44   "I've got a grandson": *Congress Investigates,* p. 2,569.
46   Balance sheet data for 1945, 1949: Citibank annual reports.
47   "The country was settled": Brown, Stanley H., "The Man Who Beat the Rockefeller Bank," *New York* magazine, Oct. 9, 1972.
48   Balance sheet data on Chase and Citibank: Citibank annual reports; *The Chase,* pp. 18–19.
50   "Persuaded people": Brooks, John, "The Money Machine," *New Yorker,* Jan. 5, 1981.
52   Henry Wriston wedding announcement: "Dean Woodworth to Marry President of Brown," *Oberlin Alumni Magazine,* Brown University archives.
53   General Marshall's speech at Brown: "Commencement Jottings," *Brown Alumni Monthly,* July–Aug. 1947.
55   "If we had a committee": Lewis B. Cuyler, unpublished memoirs, Citibank archives.
57   Details about Moore: *A Banker's Life,* interviews with Moore and Wriston.
58   The "way to manage": Ibid., p. 19.

CHAPTER 3

Some of the details on Aristotle Onassis's life and business activities contained in *Ari: the Life and Times of Aristotle Onassis* by Peter Evans, and *Aristotle Onassis.*

64   "Went gung-ho flat out": Wriston, unpublished internal interview, May 1977, Citibank archives.
70   "If you're going to jump": George Moore, unpublished internal interview, Citibank archives.
70   "He's a funny guy": Wriston, unpublished internal interview, Citibank archives.
70   "I have no use": Wriston, unpublished internal interview, Citibank archives.
71   "Word filtered down": Wriston, speech at policy meeting, March 3, 1976.
75   "Come over here": Wriston, unpublished internal interview, July 14, 1978, Citibank archives.

76   "Appeared on Capitol Hill": Wriston, transcript of testimony on ship financing in hearings before the House Committee on Merchant Marine and Fisheries, Apr. 27, 1954, p. 64.

81   "McLean is pioneering": "I.C.C. Aide Urges Waterman Sale," *New York Times,* Nov. 28, 1956.

83   Balance sheet data from 1951 and 1955: Citibank annual reports. Some of Wriston's comments on the creation of the special industries group from speech to staff at offshore conference, March 4, 1976.

CHAPTER 4

Details on branch locations from Citibank annual reports and Citibank archives.

86   "You're too old": Wriston, unpublished internal interview, July 14, 1978, Citibank archives.

89   Reference to $15 million in loans to Argentina: "Two New York Banks Grant $15 Million Credits to Argentina," *Wall Street Journal,* Jan. 23, 1956.

91   "It's fun to build": Wriston, unpublished internal interview, July 14, 1978, Citibank archives.

96   "Stands in need of repair": Waggoner, Walter H., "Dulles Adopting New Staff Policy," *New York Times,* June 16, 1954.

97   "The search for first class": *Academic Procession,* p. 105.

101   "The morale in": Wriston, unpublished internal interview, July 14, 1978, Citibank archives.

106   "You're wrong": Moore, unpublished internal interview, Citibank archives.

108   "Advances were never completely liquidated": George C. Scott, unpublished internal interview, Citibank archives.

109   "I came into the business": Wriston, unpublished internal interview, July 14, 1978, Citibank archives.

110   "What is this balance of payments?": Ibid.

110   "Who are all these people?": Ibid.

111   "I'd better hire this guy": Moore, unpublished internal interview, May 12, 1978 and May 15, 1978, Citibank archives.

111   Balance sheet data from 1949 and 1959: Citibank annual reports.

112   Details of banks' increase in savings rate: from *The Chase,* p. 82.

113   "I want to put some money": Wriston, unpublished internal interview, May 1977, Citibank archives.

113   "We need deposits": John Exter memo to Citibank senior management, September 1959, Exter personal files.

CHAPTER 5

117   "I don't care": Wriston, unpublished internal interview, July 14, 1978, Citibank archives.

117   "Politics in the head": Stillman Rockefeller, unpublished internal interview, Oct. 21, 1980, Citibank archives.

121   "He was the kind": Edward Palmer, unpublished internal interview, Citibank archives.

122   "Was the worst": Wriston, unpublished internal interview, July 14, 1978, Citibank archives.

123   "Prudent pioneering": "Wriston Encourages CB's 'Prudent Pioneering' over-
       seas," *Citibank* magazine, March–April 1966.
124   "Advancement for women": *Citibank* magazine, August 1967, p. 5.
135   " 'Nationalize' or 'socialize' ": *Political, Economic and Social Thought of
       Fidel Castro,* p. 153.

CHAPTER 6

141   "I had something to do with the CD": Hambelton, James R., "Wriston, No
       Respecter of Sacred Cows, Maintains Competitive Spirit at FNCB," *Ameri-
       can Banker,* July 5, 1967.
141   Announcement of introduction of negotiable CD: Kraus, Albert L., "Interest
       on Time Deposits Paid by the First National City Bank," *New York Times,*
       Feb. 21, 1961.
141   By 1967, outstanding CDs: Speech by George S. Moore at American Bankers
       Association Monetary Conference, Pebble Beach, California, Mar. 16, 1967.
143   The rate of growth: Henry Kaufman, speech to New York World Financial
       Center Conference, Apr. 30, 1976.
143   The U.S. banking system would be smaller: Rose, Sanford, "Three Cheers for
       Commercial Paper," *American Banker,* Aug. 21, 1979.
144   Correspondence and documents pertaining to June 30, 1961, White House
       meeting, including guest list and June 30, 1961, letter from Wriston to Presi-
       dent Kennedy: Kennedy Library, Boston.
145   "The goal was to spur": Metz, Robert, "Kennedy Proposes Tax Credit of
       30% for Latin Investors," *New York Times,* Apr. 8, 1963.
146   The minority memo: "Dissent Is Denied in Latin-Aid Plan," *New York
       Times,* Apr. 9, 1963; "A Reappraisal of the Alliance for Progress," by Emilio
       G. Collado, David Rockefeller, Walter B. Wriston, Wriston files.
146   "Hated Latin Americans": Wriston, unpublished internal interview, July 14,
       1978, Citibank archives.
147   "Made 10,000 enemies overnight": Sheehan, Robert, "What's Rocking
       Those Rocks, The Banks," *Fortune,* October 1963.
147   On December 19: "Comptroller Bars First National City Merger Proposal,"
       Wall Street Journal, Dec. 20, 1961.
152   "La Banca Sexy": Gunn, John Oliver, "Walter B. Wriston, Banker of the
       Year," *Finance,* Oct. 1970.
154   Reference to Swiss deposits: Cowan, Edward, "Citibank Plans Swiss Branch:
       Will Conform to Secrecy Rules," *New York Times,* May 24, 1963.
160   Details on the salad oil scandal: "First National City Has $3.8 Million In-
       volved in the Salad Oil Case," *Wall Street Journal,* Jan. 22, 1964; Wright,
       Robert A., "Food-Oil Scandal Nears New Phase," *New York Times,* Jan. 27,
       1964; "The Great Salad Oil Scandal"; Wise, T.A., "The Bank with the Board-
       inghouse Reach," *Fortune,* September 1965.
160   A year later: "Estimate of Collectible Haupt Loans Is Raised by First Na-
       tional City," *Wall Street Journal,* Jan. 20, 1965.
161   Moore pledged: Details on World's Fair loans in *Power Broker,* p. 1105;
       Wise, T.A., "The Bank with the Boardinghouse Reach," *Fortune,* Sept. 1965;
       Alden, Robert, "Moses Criticizes Banker; Defends Finances of Fair" *New
       York Times,* Jan. 21, 1965.
161   The alliance was hampered: *A Thousand Days,* p. 791.

169   "Our lives have been shaped": Wriston, speech to National Association of Manufacturers, New York, Dec. 3, 1964.

171   "Before attacking the root cause": Transcript of hearings before the Subcommittee on National Security and International Operations of Committee on Government Operation, May 13, 1965, part 1, p. 23.

CHAPTER 7

181   "There was total chaos": Wriston, unpublished internal interview, July 14, 1978, Citibank archives,

190   "Fateful policies of 1965": Speech by Arthur Burns to American Bankers Association, Annual Monetary Conference, Hot Springs, Virginia, May 18, 1970.

195   Justice Department challenged: "Saxon Scores Agency's Suit to Block Bank's Carte Blanche Purchase," *Wall Street Journal,* Jan. 3, 1966.

203   Some of the details on the Home Stake oil swindle from *Stealing from the Rich.*

206   Some of the details of the Mercantile acquisition from *The Mercantile Affair;* and internal Citibank publications.

207   "Our Curb on U.S. Bank": *Mercantile Affair,* p. 1.

207   "Rallied to Citibank's defense": Ibid., p. 87.

207   "As a matter of ordinary courtesy": "U.S. Bank Says It Was Unaware that Canada Opposed Acquisition," *Wall Street Journal,* Jan. 25, 1967.

207   "Bank clerk": *Mercantile Affair,* p. 100.

CHAPTER 8

211   Report of Citibank announcement of appointments: Allan, John H., "First National City Names New Chiefs," *New York Times* and "First National City Bank Names Moore, 62, as Chairman and Wriston, 47, as President," *Wall Street Journal,* June 7, 1967.

212   "The king is dead": "Moore and Wriston of First National City," *Fortune,* July 1967.

212   "Been cooler to me": Stillman Rockefeller, unpublished internal interview, Citibank archives.

213   "Make George feel bad": Wriston, unpublished internal interview, July 14, 1978, Citibank archives.

214   "My mother had the baby": Hambelton, James R., "Wriston, No Respecter of Sacred Cows, Maintains Competitive Spirit at FNCB," *American Banker,* July 5, 1967.

217   "The business of banking": "The One-Bank Holding Company: Threat or Threshold?" *Fortune,* November 1968.

217   Details of mutual fund litigation: "N.A.S.D. Loses Round to Banks on Funds," *Wall Street Journal,* Nov. 22, 1967, "First National City to Resume Accepting Investors in Pool Fought by Mutual Funds," Nov. 21, 1969.

223   "Siamese twins": *Farm Boy,* p. 152.

225   "Foreign exchange controls in peacetime": Wriston, speech to business and government leaders, Milan, Jan. 1968.

225   "Rates are going up": "The Dollar Feels a Growing Crunch," *Newsweek,* June 3, 1968.

227   "We went the holding company route": Wriston, speech to International Banking Group, Mexico City, July 21, 1975.

227   Losses on securities transactions: Citibank annual reports.

228   "We were running wide open": Wriston, speech to Services Management Group, May 10, 1977.

228   "Passive administration": Wriston, speech to bank officers, 1975.

229   "The hardest part": *Citinews,* April 12, 1972.

231   "Our job is to help": "Why Citibank Is More Than a Bank," *Business Week,* Nov. 16, 1968.

231   "Any banker who marries": Irving Shapiro, quoted in *Needlepoints,* souvenir program, Wriston retirement dinner.

236   "Virtually unlimited": Zimmerman, William, "One-Bank Holding Company Listing on NY Stock Exchange," July 3, 1968.

236   "Commercial banks, long the butt": "Banks Start Banking on Diversity," *Business Week,* July 13, 1968.

236   "The most important day": Brooks, John, "The Money Machine," *New Yorker,* Jan. 5, 1981.

237   "The word 'loophole' ": Wriston, speech to correspondent bank forum, Feb. 7, 1970.

237   "A cartelized economy": "The One-Bank Holding Company: Threat or Threshold?" *Fortune,* Nov. 1968.

238   "permissiveness"; "repetition of serious errors": "Banks Head for Crisis of Identity," *Business Week,* Oct. 5, 1968.

240   Reference to David Rockefeller's candidacy for Treasury secretary: *The Chase,* p. 327.

240   Letter referring to similarity in appearance of Wriston and Joe DiMaggio: "Not Casey Stengel, either," *Business Week,* Dec. 7, 1968.

241   "The men who distrust freedom": Wriston, speech to National Foreign Trade Council, Nov. 20, 1968.

CHAPTER 9

242   "He sat there": Wriston, unpublished internal interview, May 1977, Citibank archives.

242   "In an open society": Wriston, speech to staff, July 27, 1976.

244   "I don't know whether": Wriston, unpublished internal interview, July 14, 1978, Citibank Archives.

245   "The days when": "Internal Reorganization Planned Before Jan. 1 by First National City," *Wall Street Journal,* Nov. 15, 1968.

246   "New supervisors": Wriston, speech to correspondent bankers, Feb. 1969.

250   "So we started": Brown, Stanley H., "The Man Who Beat the Rockefeller Bank," *New York* magazine, Oct. 9, 1972.

256   "The ability to make": Meyer, Sheldon, "FNCB HC Seeks Big Insurance Company to Maximize Efforts in Financial Sector," *American Banker,* Jan. 21, 1969.

256   "Dominated by some fifty": Rose, Sanford, "The Case for the One-Bank Holding Company," *Fortune,* May 15, 1969.

257   "Not as dangerous": Ibid.

258   Details of Senate bill: *Congressional Record,* Senate, Mar. 24, 1969.

259   "Investigative letter": Strachan, Stanley, "Justice Investigating Proposed Affiliation of FNC Corp.," *American Banker,* March 12, 1969.
259   "Concern for concentrations": Ibid.
260   "Think small": Strachan, Stanley, " 'Think Small' Is Justice Anti-Trust Message on Bank-Insurance Ties," *American Banker,* June 20, 1969.
261   "Significant market power": "McLaren Says Loan Power Key to FNC-Chubb Challenge," *American Banker,* June 27, 1969.
266   "To service our clients": William I. Spencer, speech to Harvard Business School Club, April 4, 1972.
267   "Result, not the cause": *Citibank News,* June 26, 1969.
267   "Although the banks": William I. Spencer, speech to Harvard Business School Club, April 4, 1972.
268   "The CD funded the world": Field, Peter, and Adam, Nigel, "Champion of the Citi," *Euromoney,* Oct. 1983.
268   Details on holding company legislation: *Congressional Record,* Feb. 17, 1969–Dec. 31, 1970, and Bank Holding Company Amendments of 1970: Report of the Committee on Banking and Currency, U.S. Senate, Aug. 10, 1970.
270   "Serious reservations": Dale, Edwin L., Jr., "Reluctant Nixon Signs Bill That Lets Him Curb Credit," *New York Times,* Dec. 25, 1969.
270   "We bankers were all successful": Wriston, speech to correspondent bank forum, Feb. 7, 1970.
271   "Success in outstripping": Bennett, Robert A., "FNCB's Jump into Second Place over Chase Represents Trend, Not a Statistical Fluke," *American Banker,* Feb. 3, 1970.
273   "The Man Who Beat": Brown, Stanley H., "The Man Who Beat the Rockefeller Bank," *New York* magazine, Oct. 9, 1972.

CHAPTER 10

Some of the details of Citibank's back office problems are contained in Harvard Business School case studies 474-165, 475-061, 474-166, and 475-062; speech by Robert B. White to the National Operations and Automation Conference of the American Bankers Association, Chicago, June 4, 1973; Newman, Barry, "In the Back Office of a Bank, 'Blipping' Is Not Appreciated," *Wall Street Journal,* June 6, 1975.

291   "Significant breakthrough": Tyson, David O., "Citibank Introduces Check Card Different from Others, Claimed to Be More Fraud Proof," *American Banker,* Oct. 25, 1973.
291   "At the moment": Wriston, speech, February 22, 1974.
293   Scantlin's contest and American Bankers Association criteria: Interviews with present and former Citibank officers; Brooke, Phillip, "Citicorp Says Students Find Cheap, Easy Ways to Defraud Magnetic Stripe Cards," *American Banker,* April 9, 1973.

CHAPTER 11

304   "Could pass for a small-town druggist": Pierson, John, "White House Power," *Wall Street Journal,* May 20, 1969.
306   Arthur Burns, statement before the Senate Committee on Banking and Currency, May 14, 1970.

307   Hunt Commission recommendations: "Report of the President's Commission on Financial Structure & Regulation."

308   "A dill pickle": Quoted in *Needlepoints,* souvenir program, Wriston retirement dinner, 1984.

311   Wriston's testimony before the Senate Committee on Banking, Housing and Urban Affairs, May 26, 1970, p. 779.

312   Citibank survey on "financial supermarkets": "FNCO Survey Finds Consumers, Executives Want Banks to Be Financial Supermarkets," *American Banker,* June 25, 1970.

312   "U.S. has some of the best": Wallich, Henry C., "Banks Need More Freedom to Compete," *Fortune,* Mar. 1970.

313   Some of the details on Citibank's involvement with the Penn Central contained in "The Wreck of the Penn Central," Loving, Rush, Jr., "The Penn Central," *Fortune,* Aug. 1970.

315   Announcement of $17.2 million loss: "Penn Central Suffers Deficit of $17.2 Million," *Wall Street Journal,* Apr. 23, 1970.

316   "There's no way": Reich, Cary, Wriston interview in "The Way It Was," *Institutional Investor,* June 1987.

318   "We're in a tank": Ibid.

318   Some of the details of the commercial paper market following the Penn Central collapse: "Fed Cracks Q Ceiling to Help the Banks," *Business Week,* June 27, 1970; Heinemann, Erich, "How Banks Rallied on a Loan for Chrysler," *New York Times,* July 7, 1970.

320   "Citibank's Jude": "The Workout Man," *Forbes,* July 1, 1975.

320   Details of proposed swap agreement: Bedingfield, Robert E., "Penn Central and Banks Reach Loan Pact," *New York Times,* May 25, 1971.

321   Some of the details of the Lockheed bailout: "The Case for Helping Lockheed," *Business Week,* May 15, 1971. "Lockheed Digs Itself Out of a Hole," *Business Week,* Jan. 29, 1972. Heinemann, H. Erich, "24 Banks Agree on Plan for Lockheed Financing," *New York Times,* July 22, 1970. Jones, William H., "New Financial Plan for Lockheed Readied," *Washington Post,* May 5, 1976. Jones, William H., "Lockheed, Banks Agree to Remove Federal Guarantees from Loans," *Washington Post,* Sept. 29, 1977. Carley, William M., "Lockheed's Lenders, Who Forced Shakeup, Feud Over Its Future," *Wall Street Journal,* Apr. 8, 1976.

326   Supreme Court decision on mutual funds: Kohlmeier, Louis M., "High Court Bars Commercial Banks from Invading Mutual Fund Area," *Wall Street Journal,* Apr. 6, 1971.

330   "European Common Market": Wriston, speech to the American Club, Paris, Feb. 22, 1971.

330   "Multi-faceted incomes policy": Arthur Burns, statement before the Senate Banking Committee, Subcommittee on Financial Institutions, Mar. 31, 1971, Federal Reserve Board Library, Washington.

330   "When Reichers left": Wriston, unpublished internal interview, May 1977, Citibank archives.

332   "Preferential treatment": "Nader Unit to Study National City Bank," *New York Times,* June 16, 1970.

333   Citibank's losses on Penn Central: Heinemann, Erich, "City Bank Assays its 1970 Results," *New York Times,* June 21, 1971.

333   Nader report: Ibid.

333   "You're born with a conflict": Cerra, Frances, "Citibank Answers Nader's Raiders," *Newsday,* Aug. 10, 1971.

334   "Of the banks in New York": Stabler, Charles N., "Citibank Grows at Expense of Consumers, Nader Group Says: Bank Alleges Cynicism," *Wall Street Journal,* June 21, 1971.

334   Citibank rebuttal to Nader report: *Citibank, Nader and the Facts,* 1974.

334   "Were very bright": Cerra, Frances, "Citibank Answers Nader's Raiders," *Newsday,* Aug. 10, 1971.

334   "Worst National Piggybank": Olson, Gail, "Women's Lib Group Boycotts FNCB Office," *American Banker,* Aug. 27, 1971.

335   "Principal weakness": Wriston, speech to senior officers, Apr. 22, 1974.

335   "We don't think we can justify": "Wriston Denies Nader Bid for New Quiz of Investments," *Citibank News,* Oct. 14, 1971.

335   "Basically a retread": Allan, John H., "Citibank Book Spurs New Clash," *New York Times,* Jan. 17, 1974.

336   Some of the details on the deliberations over wage and price controls in *The International Monetary System 1945–1976.*

336   "Consider . . . open mind": *International Monetary System 1945–1976,* p. 184.

337   "Inflation doesn't grow on trees": *If You Ask Me,* unpublished excerpts of articles and speeches, p. 22, Citibank archives.

338   "Englishmen visiting my office": Wriston, speech to insurance forum, Nov. 2, 1972.

339   Reference to Pan Am 747: "First National City Bankmanship," *Investor's Reader,* Oct. 7, 1970.

339   Garvin negotiations with Chilean government: Lester Garvin, unpublished memoir Citibank archives.

CHAPTER 12

340   "While our numbers": Metz, Robert, "Market Place: A Big Bank Tells What Its Goal Is," *New York Times,* Oct. 27, 1971.

344   "Later, however, it turned out": Thomas Theobald, unpublished internal interview, Citibank archives.

346   "We are hopeful": Spencer, speech to Harvard Business School Club, Apr. 4, 1972.

346   "Substantial removal": Kaufman, speech to World Financial Center conference, Apr. 30, 1976.

348   "Despite the volume": "Stumbling off a Ruinous Course," *American Banker,* Nov. 9, 1971.

348   "The most important part": "Wriston Says FNCB HC Expects to Attain Goal," *American Banker,* Nov. 22, 1971.

348   "The current price": Burns testimony before the House Committee on Banking and Currency, November 1, 1971.

348   "I would say that": Halloran, Richard, "City Bank's Head Favors Devalued Dollar, if Needed," *New York Times,* Oct. 26, 1971.

349   Details on Connally meetings on devaluation: Interviews with Connally and Wriston.

349   Account of lunch with Nixon: *The International Monetary System 1945–1976*, p. 201.

352   "Polite fiction": Wriston, Speech to Bankers' Association for Foreign Trade, May 9, 1972.

357   "The biggest personal bank": Wriston, speech to Correspondent Bank Forum, Dec. 7, 1973.

358   "The financial tail": Wriston, speech to senior officers, July 31, 1979.

358   "Someone said we're trying": Stillman Rockefeller, unpublished internal interview, Citibank archives.

362   "Moves us closer": Wriston, remarks to securities analysts, Feb. 22, 1973.

364   "Worried about disintermediation": Wriston, speech to securities analysts, Mar. 25, 1980.

365   "Now it will take": Weberman, Ben, "15% Growth Plan Aided by Devaluation, Says Wriston of Citibank," *American Banker*, Feb. 23, 1973.

367   Some of the details of Equity Funding scandal: *The Great Wall Street Scandal;* Blundell, William, "Equity Funding Collateral Was Returned by Citibank Just Before Scandal, Filing Says," *Wall Street Journal*, Apr. 23, 1973. "Citibank Didn't Warn Other Lenders of Action in Equity Funding Loan," *Wall Street Journal*, Apr. 24, 1973. Foldessy, Edward P., "Citibank Partners in Equity Funding Loan Seek to Avoid Loss Due to Collateral Shift," *Wall Street Journal*, Apr. 26, 1973. Foldessy, Edward P., "Citibank Said Tricked into Giving Collateral Back to Equity Funding," *Wall Street Journal*, Apr. 30, 1973.

367   "Very friendly relationship": Weinstein, Henry, "Role of Citibank at Equity Scored by Insurance Aide," *New York Times*, May 2, 1973.

368   "Generate a new wave of inflation": *Reflections of an Economic Policy Maker*, p. 143.

368   Citibank announcement on floating rate formula: "Citibank Adopts Floating Prime; Irving Trust Joins," Oct. 22, 1971.

368   "Burns insisted": Transcript of Apr. 20, 1973, telephone conversation between Wriston and Burns, Gerald Ford Library.

375   Ceauşescu lunch at Manufacturers Hanover: *Topics* (Manufacturers Hanover employee newspaper), Jan. 1974.

380   "The world corporation may furnish": Wriston, speech to Conference Board, Sept. 18, 1973.

CHAPTER 13

384   Details on prelude to 1973 war: *Kissinger*, p. 453.

385   "In a Beirut press conference": "Citicorp Will Invest, Lend Up to $1 Billion in the Arab Countries," *Wall Street Journal*, Sept. 17, 1973.

386   Data on Citibank operating earnings and Citibank and Morgan foreign deposits: Citibank 1973 annual report; Weberman, Ben, "Foreign Deposits Top Domestic at Citibank, Morgan Guaranty," *American Banker*, Aug. 7, 1973.

386   "Just a year before": "Debt Weighs Heavily on Developing Nations," *Monthly Economic Letter*, Oct. 1972.

387   "It is clear": Henry Mueller, unpublished memoirs, Citibank archives.

388   Data on foreign assets of U.S. commercial banks; Conover, Lynn, "Brimmer Says Banks Have Been a Big Source of Capital Outflows Since Controls Ended," *American Banker,* July 18, 1974.

390   "Artfully stonewalled": Hans Angermueller, testimony before Senate Foreign Relations Subcommittee on Multinational Corporations, July 16, 1975.

390   "They have a big piece": "Americans Talk Cool," *Economist,* Dec. 14, 1974.

390   "A scarcity of energy": Wriston, speech to Economic Club of Detroit, Feb. 26, 1974; "The Trouble with Government Regulation," *Reader's Digest,* July 1974.

390   "Not much less inflationary": Quoted in *American Banker,* Jan. 25, 1974.

391   "Wriston was often provoked": Farmanfarmaian, Khodadad; Cutowski, Armin; Okita, Saburo; Roosa, Robert V.; and Wilson, Carroll L., "How Can the World Afford OPEC Oil?" *Foreign Affairs,* Jan. 1975.

392   "The leverage of the Fund": Burns, speech to Columbia Graduate School of Business, Apr. 12, 1977.

393   "Mr. McNamara got a lot of good press": Wriston, speech to international officers, Mexico City, July 21, 1975.

393   Data on World Bank loans: Levine, Richard J., "Growth of World Bank Under McNamara Rule Generates Controversy," *Wall Street Journal,* Oct. 5, 1976.

397   "Burns gushed over": *Reflections of an Economic Policy Maker,* p. 23.

397   "I have urged": *Reflections of an Economic Policy Maker,* p. 155.

400   "Same reason that the Post Office Act": Wriston, speech to Reserve City Bankers Association, Jan. 31, 1977.

405   Data on loan spreads: *Debt and Crisis in Latin America,* p. 109.

409   Data on CIBL results: Edward Palmer, remarks to CIBL board, Jan. 30, 1976.

426   Data on Itaipu Dam cost: Bank of Boston report, São Paulo, Nov. 19, 1984.

426   Data on Pertamina loans: "Citibank Leads Loan to Indonesia Concern," *American Banker,* Nov. 8, 1973.

426   "Scribbled signature": *Banks, Borrowers and the Establishment,* p. 180.

427   Account of Crefisul fire: "At Least 222 Die in São Paulo Fire; Worst Tragedy in Citibank's History," *Citibank News,* Feb. 15, 1974.

428   "Budget for Brazil next year": Wriston, speech to management trainees, class of 1973.

431   Citibank loan to Empress Lineas Maritimas: "Bank Syndicate Makes Loan," *American Banker,* June 12, 1974.

431   Loans to Chilean government in 1975: "Chile Will Get Credits of $70 Million from 4 US Banks," *American Banker,* July 31, 1975.

431   "Citibank was accused": Groshko, John M., "Several U.S. Banks Accused of Undercutting Policy on Chile," *Washington Post,* April 12, 1978.

432   "Korean finance minister met": Pearlstine, Norman and Lipsky, Seth, "Fund Drive; South Korea Learns It's Getting Harder to Borrow Nowadays," *Wall Street Journal,* Feb. 14, 1975.

433   Announcement of conversion of Colombian operations: Kutler, Jeffrey, "Citibank to Act on Colombia 51% Rule," *American Banker,* Nov. 24, 1976.

435   "I don't like 'em": *If You Ask Me,* unpublished excerpts of speeches and articles, p. 105, Citibank archives.

CHAPTER 14

441   "Almost negligible position": Wriston, remarks to securities analysts, Feb. 23, 1973.

441   Account of bankruptcy of Walter Kassuba: "Walter J. Kassuba, A Big Builder Files Under Chap. 11," *Wall Street Journal,* Dec. 27, 1973.

442   Financial problems of Beverly Hills Bancorporation: "Beverly Hills Bancorp Has Liquidity Woes," *Wall Street Journal,* Dec. 31, 1973.

442   "We should not overlook": Wriston, speech to Citibank officers, Feb. 22, 1974.

443   Citibank REIT loans: "The Damage REITS Have Done to Bank Lending," *Business Week,* Mar. 31, 1975.

443   Citibank loans to Pinehurst: "Citibank Group to Get the Pinehurst Resort," *New York Times,* Mar. 4, 1982.

446   "Concentration of resources": Dowling, Robert, "Fed Turns Down Citicorp Mortgage Company Acquisition: Would Consider New Application," *American Banker,* Dec. 28, 1973.

447   "Threatens to destroy": Jordan, Patricia, "Conn. Bankers Warned of Inroads from New York," *American Banker,* June 10, 1974.

447   "Stabilization act": *Dispute Resolution,* p. 253.

449   Some of the details on collapse of Franklin: *Failure of the Franklin National Bank;* speech by FDIC chairman Frank Wille to Savings Bank Association of New York State, Nov. 23, 1974; and Rose, Sanford, "What Really Went Wrong at Franklin National," *Fortune,* Oct. 1974.

449   Announcement of plunge in Franklin's earnings: "Franklin New York Shows Profit Drop to 2 Cents per Share," *New York Times,* Apr. 19, 1974.

453   Sindona interview with Italian magazine: Allan, John H., "Added Loss by Franklin National of $5 Million Cited by Sindona," *New York Times,* May 25, 1974.

454   "All investors, large and small": Quint, Michael, "Citicorp Plans Innovative Note Financing, Will Top Savings; Other BHCS May Follow," *American Banker,* June 20, 1974.

455   Details of Herstatt failure: "West Germany Tells Major Bank to Be Liquidated," *Wall Street Journal,* June 27, 1974, and Janssen, Richard F., "Fears About Stability of the Banking System in West Are Spreading," July 26, 1974; "What Went Wrong at Herstatt," *Business Week,* Aug. 3, 1974.

462   Reference to bad real estate loans by Brandts: "Natl & Grindlays Had $23.4 Million 1974 Loss," *American Banker,* Apr. 23, 1975.

462   "We have branches": Dorfman, Dan, "Keeping Cool with Wriston," *New York,* July 22, 1974.

463   "Disintermediation . . . sounds like": "Banking at the Crossroads," *Forbes,* June 15, 1968.

463   "The public interest": "Reserve Opposes Citicorp's Notes," *New York Times,* July 3, 1974.

464   "Innovative efforts": Arthur Burns, letter of July 9, 1974, to Senator William Proxmire, contained in transcript of hearings before the Senate Banking Committee, July 24, 1974.

465   "Not only helped solve": Wriston, remarks at offshore conference, 1975.

466   "Had an institution the size of Franklin National": Arthur Burns, testimony before Senate Committee on Banking Housing and Urban Affairs, March 10, 1977.

468   "Shortly after the takeover": "Justice Questioned Three Proposals to Acquire Franklin," *American Banker,* Nov. 8, 1974.

469   Foreign exchange earnings in 1974: Citibank annual report.

469   "Save any nation": Wriston, speech to Business Council, Oct. 12, 1974.

470   Report of effort to acquire West Coast Corporation: "Citicorp's Plan to Buy 3 Firms Rejected by Fed," *Wall Street Journal,* Nov. 11, 1975, and "Citicorp May Fight Fed's Bar on Buying 3 Finance Concerns," Nov. 12, 1975.

471   IAC losses: "Citicorp's Australian Salvage Operation," *Business Week,* May 2, 1977.

CHAPTER 15

473   Figures on New York City debt in fall 1974: Program Planners, a New York pension consulting firm.

473   "No one outside the city": Wriston, statement before New York State Assembly Banking Committee, Oct. 11, 1974.

474   Statistics on city work force: "An Interesting Statistic," *Daily News* (New York), Dec. 2, 1974.

475   Scott Commission: Lambert, Bruce, "Stuart Nash Scott Dead at 85, Studied New York City's Finances," *New York Times,* Mar. 2, 1992.

478   "In very good shape": Survey—World Finance, *The Economist,* Dec. 14, 1974.

478   "Walter's heart": Pileggi, Nicholas, "The 36 Who Run New York," *New York* magazine, Jan. 9, 1978.

478   "My proposition": *If You Ask Me,* unpublished excerpts of speeches and articles, p. 19, Citibank archives.

482   "Now the times of plenty": Clines, Francis X., "Carey Urges Less Localities Aid, Budget Cut, 10¢ Gasoline Tax Rise," quoted in the *New York Times,* Jan. 9, 1975.

483   Report to the governor by the New York State Moreland Act Commission on the Urban Development Corporation and other state financing agencies, Mar. 31, 1976.

487   "The City Budget Mess": Friedgut memo contained in Securities and Exchange Commission staff report, Aug. 1977, p. 122.

487   "No way [the banks] will stuff": Ibid., p. 140.

487   "Yeah, it's very interesting": Reich, Cary, "The Way It Was," *Institutional Investor,* June 1987.

488   "No one, myself included": *Mayor,* p. 13.

489   "The city was fortunate": Allan, John H., "Mayor's Plan to Cut Borrowing Cited," *New York Times,* Mar. 26, 1975.

493   "The President of the United States directs": *Vietnam,* p. 471.

495   "Carey fired MAC chairman Thomas Flynn": Poster, Thomas, and Sherman, William, "Carey Ousts Flynn as Big Mac Chief," *Daily News,* July 23, 1975.

500   W. T. Grant financial crisis: "Citibank Says It Wrote Off Part of Loan to Grant," *Wall Street Journal,* Oct. 7, 1975; "How Grant Lost $175 Million Last Year," *Business Week,* Feb. 24, 1975.

500   "It also exacerbated": "W.T. Grant: Ripples from a Collapsing Giant," *Business Week,* Oct. 20, 1975.

503   "The New York financial situation": Lieberman, Mark, "Simon Sees Bad Example If US Bails Out City," *Daily News,* Sept. 24, 1975.

504   "Schmidt said publicly": Farnsworth, Clyde, "Some Europeans Fearful of Effects of City Defaults," *New York Times,* Oct. 7, 1975.

504   "Administration would propose changes": William Simon, testimony before the Joint Economic Committee of Congress, Sept. 24, 1975.

504   "Some suggested that the Fed": *Reflections of an Economic Policy Maker,* p. 300.

505   "Wriston found himself": Wriston, transcript of testimony before the Senate Committee on Banking, Housing, and Urban Affairs, Oct. 18, 1975.

507   "It was one of the saddest days": *Time for Truth,* p. 159.

507   "Simon clearly had nothing": Ibid., p. 157.

508   "Three most unpersuasive": Reeves, Richard, "Will Congress Save New York? Don't Bet on It," *New York* magazine, Nov. 3, 1975.

509   "I can tell you": Tolchin, Martin, "Ford, Castigating City, Asserts He'd Veto Fund Guarantees, Offers Bankruptcy Bill," *New York Times,* Oct. 30, 1975.

513   "Nobody in his right mind": Wriston, speech to correspondent bankers, Jan. 31, 1976.

514   "Ted Williams hit": Wriston speech at offshore policy committee meeting, John's Island, South Carolina, Mar. 4, 1976.

515   "Was misleading, irresponsible": "Citibank Corrects 'Misleading, Irresponsible' Stories," *Citibank News,* Jan. 22, 1976.

515   "These two banks continue": "Statement by Comptroller and Banks," *New York Times,* Jan. 12, 1976.

515   "More stable": Hutnyan, Joseph D., "Burns Sees Banking More Stable Since His '74 Loan Warning," *American Banker,* Jan. 21, 1976.

515   "Not a few of our nation's": *Reflections of an Economic Policy Maker,* p. 227.

516   "The current journalistic buzzword": Wriston, remarks to unspecified audience, Jan. 27, 1976.

516   "Then I assume": Wriston, speech to correspondent bank forum, Jan. 31, 1976.

517   "The not-so-invisible": Ibid.

517   "Quoting Irving Kristol": Wriston, remarks to correspondent bankers, Nov. 8, 1976.

517   "Beset by marital and financial": "Currency Comptroller Smith Resigns After Criticism; Personal Reasons Cited," *Wall Street Journal,* June 22, 1976.

517   Letter of recommendation for James Smith: Citibank archives.

518   "If you tell politicians": Wriston speech to correspondent bankers, Jan. 31, 1976.

520   "Our worldwide acquisition": Wriston, speech at policy committee meeting, Mar. 4, 1976.

521   Details of Joseph Stefan's activities: Russell, James, "Miami National Rated 'Problem,' Claims Recovery," *Miami Herald,* Jan. 23, 1976; Rosenblatt, Andy, "U.S. Probing Bank's Loans to Outrigger," Apr. 6, 1980; Rosenblatt, Andy, "Bankers Indicted in Building-Loan Fraud," Mar. 27, 1982; Klement, Alice, "Six Indicted for Bilking Bank, Condo," Oct. 7, 1981.

524   "If the banks that held": Wriston, remarks to Financial Accounting Standards Board at public hearing, July 27, 1976.

525 "With all of the things": Wriston, remarks to staff, Jan. 19, 1977.
526 "Lost something when it lost": Wriston, speech at policy committee meeting, Mar. 4, 1976.
526 "We put those people": Wriston, remarks to Services Management Group, May 10, 1977.
527 "We are not yet in danger": Wriston, speech at policy committee meeting, Mar. 4, 1976.
528 "No branch, no country": Wriston, speech to staff, Jan. 19, 1977.

CHAPTER 16

531 "Because that's where the money is": Loomis, Carol J., "Citicorp's Rocky Affair with the Consumer," *Fortune,* Mar. 24, 1980.
531 "I see that $1.2 trillion": Ibid.
533 "Strip-mining": "Upstate Operations of NYC Banks Attacked as 'Strip-Mining' of Economic Resources," *American Banker,* Apr. 10, 1975.
534 "Handed us our head": Wriston, testimony before the Senate Banking Committee, June 27, 1983.
535 "He determined": Bishopric, Carol A., "Reed of Citibank Urges Improved Consumer Service, Points to New Payments Mechanism," *American Banker,* Nov. 1, 1974.
535 "Start with the customer": "The Fourth Need," *American Banker,* Feb. 14, 1979.
539 "From the Beach": Memo, Mar. 9, 1976, Citicorp files.
540 "There is always some": *To Move a Nation,* p. 221.
542 "We know one of the most": Wriston, speech to correspondent bankers, Nov. 8, 1976.
544 "Five to ten years of turmoil": "Bank Cards Take Over the Country," *Business Week,* Aug. 4, 1975.
545 "I don't know anybody": Wriston, remarks to Columbia Business School Club of New York, Mar. 24, 1977.
551 "Unfairly discriminatory": "Citibank to Appeal Card Fee Ruling," *American Banker,* June 15, 1978.
554 "The relationship with customers": Memo, Mar. 9, 1976.
562 "Merchant banking is not new to us": Wriston speech to international banking group, July 1975.
562 "One of the wonderful things": Wriston, remarks to Columbia Business School Club of New York, Mar. 24, 1977.
563 "If your name is on the door": Wriston, transcript of testimony before the Committee on Banking, Housing, and Urban Affairs, U.S. Senate, Oct. 29, 1981.

CHAPTER 17

567 Data on Zaire debt: Belliveau, Nancy, "Heading off Zaire's Default," *Institutional Investor,* Mar. 1977.
568 "But by the end of 1976": Ibid.
568 "Zaire still owed": Crittenden, Ann, "Citibank's Bid to Get $250 Million For Zaire Is Still Unsuccessful," *New York Times,* Dec. 17, 1977.
569 Data on Peru debt: "Why the Banks Bailed Out Peru," *Business Week,* Mar. 21, 1977.

571   Westinghouse payments: Butterfield, Fox, "Marcos, Facing criticism, May End $1 Billion Westinghouse Contract," *New York Times,* Jan. 14, 1978; Kramer, Barry, "In the Philippines, It's Whom You Know That Can Really Count," *Wall Street Journal,* Jan. 12, 1978, and Kramer, Barry, "Marcos Sets Review of Philippine Award for Nuclear Plant Westinghouse Builds," Jan. 16, 1978.

572   "Armageddon never arrives": *If You Ask Me,* op. cit., p. 83.

572   "No country accounted": Edward Palmer, speech to Wharton Graduate School of Business, April 14, 1977.

573   "Nonsense": Wiegold, C. Frederic, "Wriston Says US Banks' Overseas Loan Problems Need Specific, Not General Target," *American Banker,* Mar. 9, 1977.

573   "Their gold and dollar reserves": Wriston, remarks to Columbia Business School Club of New York, Mar. 24, 1977.

573   "Costanzo predicted": Costanzo, speech to *Financial Times* conference, Apr. 29, 1976.

573   "Even Spencer": "Dialog Between Spencer, Staff Members," *Citinews,* Dec. 15, 1977.

573   "Zaire . . . would have to": Irving Friedman, transcript of testimony before Senate Banking Committee Subcommittee on International Finance, Aug. 29–30, 1977.

574   "Thinning of the capital cushion": *Reflection of an Economic Policy Maker,* p. 399.

574   "Had the banks not done so": Ibid., p. 455.

574   "In my honest opinion": Henry Wallich, transcript of testimony before Senate Banking Committee, Subcommittee on International Finance, Aug. 29–30, 1977.

575   Data on nonperforming real estate loans: "2 Billion of Problems," *Economist,* Mar. 12, 1977.

576   "Citibank's efforts to prop up": Wriston letter to Arthur Burns, Apr. 6, 1977, Gerald Ford Library.

CHAPTER 18

583   "I'd put my emphasis": Silk, Leonard, "Carter's Economics," *New York Times,* July 14, 1976.

583   "It seems doubtful to me": *Reflections of an Economic Policy Maker,* p. 311.

584   "The most profitable corporation": Wriston speech to Columbia Business School Club of New York, Mar. 24, 1977.

585   "Regain its position": Wriston, letter to Burns, July 15, 1977, in Gerald R. Ford Library.

585   "Citibank had Stanley": Spencer, speech to New York State Legislative Council, Dec. 10, 1981.

586   Study on bank lending to Pinochet regime: Groshko, John M., "Several U.S. Banks Accused of Undercutting Policy on Chile," *Washington Post,* Apr. 12, 1978.

589   "self-congratulatory": *Congress, the Executive Branch, and Special Interests,* p. 180.

589   "Going to hell": Ibid., p. 201.

590   Rejection of Shapiro's request for meeting with Carter: Ibid., p. 208.

591   "Starting salaries for blacks": "How to Resist Apartheid," *American Banker,*
       Oct. 5, 1976.

594   "As some fellow put it": Silk, Leonard, "Banks Seek to Avoid Public Rows
       with the City in Fiscal Discussions," *New York Times,* Mar. 9, 1977.

595   "Wriston asked Bigel": *Union Power,* p. 413.

596   "Further cuts in taxes": "Taxes in New York City," "Municipal Union/
       Financial Leaders Group," July 21, 1977.

596   "Victor and I may disagree": Mattera, Anthony F., "Wriston, Union Chief
       Join Hands in NYC Vote Plea," *American Banker,* Oct. 21, 1977.

597   " 'Dumping' up to $2.5 billion": Securities and Exchange Commission Staff
       Report on Transactions in Securities of the City of New York.

597   "Bank advisers were warning": Haddad, William F., et al, "The Banks and
       the Municipal Crisis: Public Responsibility and Private Profit," p. 6.

597   "That October, in testimony": Clines, Francis X., "About New York," *New
       York Times,* Oct. 15, 1977.

599   "Years of rebuilding": "Beame Says He Is Giving Koch a City in Condition
       to Be Rebuilt," *New York Times,* Dec. 30, 1977.

600   "If you can loan": Edward Palmer, transcript of testimony before the Senate
       Banking Committee, June 12, 1978.

601   "Lies in what it has prevented": Shefter, *Political Crisis/Fiscal Crisis,* pp.
       189–90.

602   "No banker understands": Egan, Jack, "The Money Men: New York's Top
       Bankers," *New York* magazine, Dec. 1, 1980.

602   "Maybe we should have": Brooks, John, "The Money Machine," *New
       Yorker,* Jan. 5, 1981.

605   Some details of the Edwards affairs: *Off the Books;* Rowan, Roy, "The Mav-
       erick Who Yelled Fool at Citibank," *Fortune,* Jan. 10, 1983.

605   "Aw, shit": *Fortune,* Jan. 10, 1983.

606   "Citibank notified Edwards": Angermueller, transcript of testimony on Ed-
       wards affair before the House Committee on Energy and Commerce, June 28,
       1983.

607   "The trader tells his lieutenants": Edwards, David, "The Trading Room,"
       M.B.A. magazine, June–July 1978.

607   "Insiders said, in effect": Brill, Steven, "What Price Loyalty?" *American Law-
       yer,* Aug. 1982.

609   "Wriston's bank was accused": Crittenden, Ann, "Growing Bahamian Loan
       Activity by U.S. Banks Causes Concern," *New York Times,* Mar. 3, 1977.

610   "We borrow money": Wriston, remarks to Columbia Business School Club
       of New York, Mar. 24, 1977.

612   "The Justice Department got into the act": *American Banker,* Apr. 10, 1979.

613   "Far from what they said": Gross, Laura, "McGillicuddy Sees Citi ATM Shy
       of Goal," *American Banker,* June 16, 1978.

614   "Tom Clausen isn't given": Sturm, Paul, "How BankAmerica Passed Citi-
       corp," *Forbes,* Mar. 6, 1978.

615   "Scared the hell out of me": Rubenstein, James, " 'Coming to Grips' with
       Citibank's Card Challenge," *American Banker,* May 16, 1978.

617   "Got us out of bed": "Barnett Bank's Reaction to Citibank Visa Mailing
       Strikes Paydirt," *Bank Letter,* Feb. 22, 1978.

617   "We have red ink": "You Deserve a Break Today, or the McDonald's Ap-
       proach to Banking," *Payment Systems Action Report,* Nov. 6, 1978.

618 "The next year": "Myths and Realities of Credit at Citicorp," Edwin Hoffman, internal presentation to bank officers, Feb. 19, 1987.

619 "Around here it's Djakarta": Rose, Sanford, "Why They Call It Fat City," *Fortune,* Mar. 1975.

619 "What gives us confidence": "The Brazilian Gamble," *Business Week,* Dec. 5, 1977.

620 "Chief Latin economist": "Citibank's Pervasive Influence on International Lending; The Greatest Exposure in the Third World, But Its Profits are Up," *Business Week*, May 16, 1983.

620 "Spread madness": Kaplan, Gilbert, "Walter Wriston on the Issues—and on Himself," *Institutional Investor,* Sept. 1978.

CHAPTER 19

622 "Are at an unsatisfactory level": *Reflections of an Economic Policy Maker,* p. 41.

622 Appointment of Miller: *New York Times,* Feb. 12, 1978; *Village Voice,* Feb. 16, 1978.

622 "No progress": *Reflections of an Economic Policy Maker,* p. 255.

623 "Citicorp's net": Milletti, Mario A., "Citicorp Reports Operating Earnings," *New York Times,* Apr. 19, 1978.

623 "Less expansionary policy": Wriston, testimony before Joint Economic Committee of Congress, Feb. 22, 1978.

624 "Is Inflation Inevitable?": Citibank annual report, 1978.

625 Letter from Bell: Papers of John T. Dunlop, Kennedy Library, Boston.

626 "Since 1954": Spencer, speech to investment conference, Sept. 16, 1977.

627 "Maybe I'm not as excited": *If You Ask Me,* op. cit., p. 46.

627 "By April": "Iran Seen Responsible on Debt," *American Banker,* Apr. 5, 1979.

628 "The lending frenzy": "Year of the Gunslinger," *Euromoney,* May 1980.

630 Conviction of Jorge Diaz Serrano: *The Mexicans,* p. 175.

630 Some details of the coffee fraud: Foldessy, Edward P., "Citibank Is Untangling Records in Loans of $45 Million to Coffee Exporting Group," *Wall Street Journal,* Apr. 19, 1979.

632 "The Citibank ads": Brouillette, Geoff, "B of A, Citibank Drive on Req Q," *American Banker,* May 18, 1979, and Gross, Laura, "MHT Heats Savings Dollar Fight," July 20, 1979.

635 "Solomon was lounging at poolside": *Volcker: Portrait of the Money Man,* p. 1.

635 "When you've left New York": *The Money Bazaars,* p. 11.

636 Volcker testimony: "Fed Chief Pledges Tight Money Policy Will Continue; Warns Against a Tax Cut," *Wall Street Journal,* Sept. 9, 1979.

638 "The world is carefully watching": Berry, John M., "Citibank Implies Further Rate Hike," *Washington Post,* Nov. 2, 1979.

640 "High point": *Brazil,* p. 170.

641 "This country will only confront": Conine, Ernest, "Brazil Tries Its Miracle on Inflation," *Los Angeles Times,* Sept. 13, 1979.

642 "Some rescheduling": "Volcker Says Any Drop in Interest Rates Doesn't Signal an Easier Monetary Policy," *Wall Street Journal,* Jan. 3, 1980.

644   "Banks cannot set off": Wiegold, C. Frederic, "Carter Freezes Iran Assets in U.S.; Citibank Pays Off Teheran Loans," *American Banker*, Nov. 15, 1979.

645   Details of Wriston press conference: Bennett, Robert A., "Concern Is Expressed by U.S. Bankers," *New York Times*, Nov. 15, 1979.

647   Details on the Chrysler bailout: Interviews with Wriston, John F. McGillicuddy, Steve Miller, and G. William Miller; *Iacocca: An Autobiography; Going for Broke;* hearings before the Senate Banking Committee, Nov. 21, 1979; articles in the *American Banker, Wall Street Journal, New York Times.*

647   Chrysler's second-quarter results: "Chrysler Posts a 2nd Quarter Deficit of $207.1 Million, "*Wall Street Journal*, Aug. 1, 1979.

652   "Their general attitude": *Iacocca*, p. 239.

CHAPTER 20

656   "There are times": Reich, Cary, "Walt's Triumphant Farewell," *Institutional Investor*, July 1983.

CHAPTER 21

669   "We lend money at 8 percent": *Needlepoints*, souvenir program, Wriston retirement dinner.

673   "Go the pots and pans route": Lohr, Steve, "Banks Pushing Gifts to Draw Deposits," *New York Times*, Apr. 9, 1980.

674   "The largest fine ever imposed": Battey, Phil, and Gross, Laura, "Fed Fines Citibank $350,000," *American Banker*, July 23, 1981.

674   "Considerable embarrassment": Lafferty, Michael, "Citibank Undertakes Big Retail Reorganization," *Retail Banker International*, Oct. 5, 1981.

674   "You don't get him": *Secrets of the Temple*, p. 439.

676   "I'll answer that": Schumer, Fran R., "Banking on the Future," *Barron's*, Apr. 12, 1982.

678   "Marquette decision": "Top Court Rules on Interest Rates for Bank Cards," *Wall Street Journal*, Dec. 19, 1978.

679   Some details on Janklow and South Dakota: Mickelson, Monty, "William J. Janklow," *Commercial West Magazine*, Jan. 28, 1984; Murphy, Todd, "Janklow Ends 8 Controversial Years," *Sioux Falls Argus Leader*, Jan. 11, 1987.

679   "Charges by an Indian girl": *In the Spirit of Crazy Horse*, p. 108.

682   "Thank-you letter": Wriston to Janklow, Mar. 14, 1980, Citicorp files.

683   "These standby powers": Wriston, remarks at Thomas Storrs testimonial, May 7, 1980.

685   "Creating the climate": President Carter letter to Wriston, April 29, 1980, Carter Library, Atlanta.

688   "We would very much": "Citicorp Transfer of Credit Card Center to South Dakota Has July Target Date," *Wall Street Journal*, Mar. 26, 1980.

695   "Bank of the future": Wriston, speech to Reserve City Bankers, Boca Raton, Florida, Mar. 31, 1980.

697   Details on bet on interest rates: Interviews with Wriston, Donald Howard, Edward Palmer; Citibank financial statements, speeches, articles, and other documents; change of responsibility for Donald Howard discussed in Mul-

cahy, Laura, "Citibank's Downgrading of Howard May Herald Big Change in Strategy," *American Banker,* Sept. 17, 1981.

698   "We're too big": Janssen Richard F., "Citicorp Vows to Act on 'Costly Lesson' It Learned Last Year." *Wall Street Journal,* Mar. 25, 1981.

699   "What was once": Forde, John P., "Citibank's Letter Dies at 77," *American Banker,* Aug. 19, 1981.

703   "Our sovereign risk": Wriston, presentation to board of directors, May 20, 1980.

704   Cross-border exposure of five key LDCs: "Myths and Realities of Credit at Citicorp," internal presentation by Edwin Hoffman, Feb. 19, 1987.

704   "Much milder": Transcript of testimony before House Banking Subcommittee on International Trade, Investment, and Monetary Policy, Feb. 4, 1980, p. 268.

706   Hijacking of Turkish jet: Howe, Marvine, "Turkish Jet Hijacked to Bulgaria; 5 American Bankers Threatened," *New York Times,* May 25, 1981.

706   Description of New Canaan home: "Latin America: The Other Side of Debt," *Economist,* June 23, 1984.

706   "Black card": *Banks, Borrowers, and the Establishment,* p. 155.

CHAPTER 22

709   "Reagan would later be forced": Smith, Terence, "Carter Assails Reagan Remark About the Klan as an Insult to the South," *New York Times,* Sept. 3, 1980.

710   "A fourteen-page report": "Economic Strategy for the Reagan Administration," Nov. 16, 1980, Wriston files.

713   "Dinner party for Reagan": Purnick, Joyce, "Who's Invited to the Party Mrs. Astor's Giving Reagan," *New York Times,* Dec. 6, 1980.

713   Details on the Multiponics case: Penn, Stanley, "SEC Head to Be Sued for Role as a Director of Small Firm in 68–70," *Wall Street Journal,* Jan. 15, 1973; "SEC Chief, 16 Accused In $2.1 Million Action by Bankruptcy Trustee," Jan. 18, 1973; "CIA Head Casey Knew That Securities Leaflet Misled, Judge Rules," July 15, 1981; "CIA Chief Casey to Face Senate Inquiry on Multiponics Role, Agency Procedure," July 20, 1981; and "Judge Rescinds Ruling That CIA Head Casey Violated Securities Laws," Nov. 11, 1981.

714   "We folks from the boonies": Curley, Anne, "Local Boy Makes Good," *Milwaukee Journal,* Jan. 18, 1981.

715   Details of Iranian negotiations: *American Hostages in Iran;* interviews with Wriston, Hans Angermueller, Robert Carswell, and John Hoffman.

722   "One of these days": Welles, Chris, "The Making of a Treasury Secretary," *Institutional Investor,* Mar., 1981.

722   "The press has tried": Ibid.

727   "Was eliminating the constraints": Wriston, speech to Securities Industry Association, Jan. 21, 1981.

729   "In the last decade": Costanzo, speech on LDC debt to unspecified audience, 1981.

729   "It got worse": "The Myths and Realities of Credit at Citicorp," internal presentation by Edwin Hoffman, Feb. 19, 1987.

730   "Lending to the LDCs": Wriston, speech to the International Monetary Conference, June 4, 1981.

731   "The Saudi portfolio peaked": Hoffman, "Myths and Realities."

734   Wriston's disclosures of technology investment: Remarks to securities analysts, New York, Mar. 23, 1982.

736   Account of dinner at Kennedy Center: Interview with Frederick Schultz; *Secrets of the Temple*, p. 424.

CHAPTER 23

739   "Al's place in the history": Wriston, speech to Citicorp officers, Nov. 18, 1981.

740   "Who knows which": Salamon, Julie, "To Some Bankers with Loans to Poland, Military Crackdown Isn't All Bad News," *Wall Street Journal*, Dec. 21, 1981.

740   Reagan speech and Citibank ads: Dougherty, Philip H., "Citicorp Lights Candle in Response to Reagan," *New York Times*, Dec. 29, 1981.

741   "Illustrate very clearly": Transcript of "Face the Nation," Jan. 24, 1982.

741   Data on Poland's loan payments: *Debt Shock*, p. 78

742   Data on Mexico's external debt: *The Mexican Rescue*, p. 35.

742   Data on Citicorp's Brazilian exposure: Citicorp annual reports.

742   "Worst failure": Hoffman, "Myths and Realities."

744   "Defend the peso": *The Mexicans*, p. 174.

744   Data on Argentina's loans: *Banks, Borrowers and the Establishment*, p. 149.

747   " 'generalized' cross-border": Hoffman, "Myths and Realities."

747   "I think my friend": Fuerbriger, Jonathan, "No Clear Remedies for those High Interest Rates," *New York Times*, May 16, 1982.

749   Herzog May 1982 press conference: "Zero Mexican Growth Seen," *New York Times*, May 19, 1982.

750   Problems of Grupo Alfa: Rout, Lawrence, "Alfa of Mexico Stops Paying Debt, Principal," *Wall Street Journal*, Apr. 28, 1982.

751   Merrill Lynch syndication: *The Mexican Rescue*, p. 37.

753   "Stacking the deck": Brouillette, Geoff, "Calif. S&L Commissioner Accuses FSLIC of Handling Bids Unfairly," *American Banker*, July 19, 1982.

754   "Lying in the intensive care": *Minneapolis Tribune*, July 10, 1982.

760   "Easy to criticize": *U.S. News & World Report*, May 31, 1982.

763   "We had 150-odd": *Mexican Rescue*, p. 40.

765   "See anybody getting tough": *Iacocca*, p. 243.

766   "Seven-point indictment": McCormick, Linda, "Regulators and Accountants Hit in Citicorp Quiz," *American Banker*, Sept. 20, 1982.

769   "Simple Benjamin Franklin economics": Delamaide, Darrell, "LDC Debts: European Banks vs. U.S. Banks," *Institutional Investor*, Sept. 1984.

772   Kuczynski's comment on Brazil package: *Latin American Debt*, p. 93.

774   "The critical question": Bennett, Robert, "Wide Effects of Bank Changes," *New York Times*, Dec. 8, 1982.

775   "A benefit for the New York Hospital": *New York Times*, Dec. 15, 1983.

776   "LDC loans": *Latin American Debt*, p. 167.

785   "Ranked as the number one leader": "Who Runs America," *U.S. News & World Report*, May 23, 1983.

787   "Intentionally misrepresents": Angermueller, statement before the House Committee on Energy and Commerce, June 28, 1983.

787   "Incomplete, false and misleading": Gerth, Jeff, "S.E.C. Overruled Staff on Finding That Citicorp Hid Foreign Profits," *New York Times,* Feb. 18, 1982.

787   "An angry letter to the *Times*": "Offending Captions," *New York Times,* Feb. 23, 1982.

788   "Were more volatile": Wriston, transcript of testimony before the House Energy and Commerce Committee, June 28, 1983.

789   Details on Argentine loan: "Argentina Signs $1.5 Billion Loan," *Journal of Commerce,* Aug. 17, 1983.

790   Data on Citicorp nonperforming overseas loans: "Citicorp's Overdue Loans Abroad Rose 142% in Year," *Wall Street Journal,* Sept. 8, 1983.

790   Details on IMF meeting on Brazil: Interviews with Wriston, John McGillicuddy, Jacques de Larosière, and Paul Volcker; Kilborn, Peter, "Brazil's Debts Cast a Shadow," *New York Times,* Sept. 30, 1983.

791   "There is no question": Hans Angermueller, speech to sovereign risk seminar, June 21, 1983.

791   "The media has been watching": Gross, Laura, "Wriston Argues for Banks Selling Insurance; Citicorp Chief Tells Life Group that Protected Markets No Longer Exist," *American Banker,* Nov. 17, 1983.

CHAPTER 24

793   "That would be a leap": Reich, Cary, "Walt's Triumphant Farewell," *Institutional Investor,* July 1983.

795   "A scandal involving": Kwitny, Jonathan, "Some Private Ventures of FAA Chief Show a Pattern of Failure," *Wall Street Journal,* Oct. 7, 1983; and "Helms, Ex-Head of FAA, Takes the Fifth on Questions of Private Business Dealings," *Wall Street Journal,* Apr. 30, 1984.

796   " 'Five *I*' strategy": Wriston, speech to securities analysts, New York, Mar. 7, 1984.

797   "If five years ago": *If You Ask Me,* unpublished excerpts of articles and speeches, Citibank archives.

797   "I profoundly hope": Bennett, Robert A., "Citicorp Plans Bank in Maine," *New York Times,* Mar. 28, 1983.

797   "Choose his weapons": "State Bank Regulator Forms Group to Promote Regional Bank Compacts," *Bureau of National Affairs,* Mar. 2, 1984.

798   "A quasi-monopolistic": Fraust, Bart, "Court Lifts Cloud Over Regional Interstate Laws," *American Banker,* Aug. 3, 1984.

799   "Capable, aggressive": Rubin, Emily F., "Citicorp Aggressive in State, but It Lacks a 'Front Door,' " *Miami Herald,* May 10, 1983.

799   "I'm very disappointed": Gruber, William, and Barnhart, Bill, "Citicorp to Buy First Federal," *Chicago Tribune,* Dec. 16, 1983.

803   "Carpetbagger account": Quinn, Jane Bryant, "The New Carpetbaggers," *Newsweek,* Nov. 12, 1984.

804   "Merger, barter, and arbitrage": Wriston, speech to financial analysts, Mar. 7, 1984.

805   "Shares my skepticism": Noble, Kenneth B., "Wriston View of Banking Bill," *New York Times,* Sept. 18, 1984.

810   "May become a subsidiary": "South Dakota's New Love Affair with Big Banks," *U.S. News & World Report,* Jan. 30, 1984.

814   "Bill Rhodes was predicting": *Latin American Debt,* p. 134.

814   "Much improved": Rowe, James L., Jr., "Still Serious but 'Much Improved';
       Wriston Says Latin Debt Better," *Washington Post,* Apr. 18, 1984.
816   Account of Wriston's role in Continental bailout: Interviews with Wriston,
       Thomas Theobald, Lewis Preston, and Paul Volcker; *Belly Up: The Collapse
       of the Penn Square Bank.*
818   "I don't think this": "The New Shape of Banking," *Business Week,* June 18,
       1984.
820   "Unlike a business corporation": Wriston, speech to International Monetary
       Conference, Philadelphia, June 4, 1984.
826   "You realize": Hertzberg, Daniel, "Citibank Leads the Banking Field in Size,
       Power, and Arrogance," *Wall Street Journal,* May 11, 1984.
827   Citicorp 1983 results: Annual report, 1983.
828   "We have a plan": Wriston, speech to analysts, Mar. 7, 1984.

CHAPTER 25

851   " 'Americanization' of the debt problem": Dr. Paul Sacks, testimony before
       the Committee on Banking, Finance, and Urban Affairs, House of Repre-
       sentatives, April 23, 1987, p. 16.

BIBLIOGRAPHY

BOOKS AND PAMPHLETS

Anderson, Martin. *The Power of Ideas in the Making of Economic Policy*. Palo Alto: Hoover Institution, Stanford University, 1987.

———. *Revolution*. San Diego and New York: Harcourt Brace Jovanovich, 1988.

Auletta, Ken. *The Streets Were Paved With Gold*. New York: Random House, 1975.

Bagehot, Walter. *Lombard Street*. New York: Scribner Armstrong & Co., 1873.

Bellush, Jewel, and Bernard Bellush. *Union Power and New York: Victor Gotbaum and District Council 37*. New York: Praeger, 1984.

Boettcher, Thomas D. *Vietnam—The Valor and the Sorrow*. Boston: Little Brown, 1985.

Bogdanowicz-Bindert, Christine A. *Solving the Global Debt Crisis*. Institutional Investor Series in Finance. New York: Institutional Investor, 1990.

Burns, Arthur F. *Reflections of an Economic Policy Maker: Speeches and Congressional Statements, 1969–1978*. Washington, D.C.: American Enterprise Institute for Public Policy Research, 1978.

Caro, Robert A. *The Power Broker: Robert Moses and the fall of New York*. New York: Knopf, 1974.

Castro, Fidel. *Political, Economic and Social Thought of Fidel Castro*. Havana: Editorial Lex, 1959.

Chacel, Julian M., Pamela S. Falk, and David V. Fleischer (editors). *Brazil's Economic and Political Future*. Boulder, Colorado: Westview Press, 1988.

Chernow, Ron. *The House of Morgan: An American Banking Dynasty and the Rise of Modern Finance*. New York: Atlantic Monthly Press, 1990.

Chill, Dan S. *The Arab Boycott of Israel—Economic Aggression and World Reaction*. New York: Praeger Publishers, 1976.

Christopher, Warren, et al. *American Hostages in Iran: The Conduct of a Crisis*. [A Council on Foreign Relations Book.] New Haven: Yale University Press, 1985.

Cleveland, Harold van B., and Thomas F. Huertas. *Citibank, 1812–1970*. Harvard Studies in Business History, 37. Cambridge: Harvard University Press, 1985.

Clyde, William Phelps. *Foreign Expansion of American Banks*. New York: Arno Press, 1976.

Compton, Eric N. *The New World of Commercial Banking*. Lexington, Massachusetts: Lexington Books, 1987.

Current, Richard Nelson. *Wisconsin*. New York: W. W. Norton, 1977.

Daughen, Joseph R., and Peter Binzen. *The Wreck of the Penn Central*. Boston: Little, Brown, 1971.

Davis, L. J. *Onassis, Aristotle and Christina*. New York: St. Martin's Press, 1986.

Delamaide, Darrell. *Debt Shock: The Full Story of the World Credit Crisis*. Updated edition. New York: Anchor Books, 1985.

Devlin, Robert. *Debt and Crisis in Latin America: The Supply Side of the Story*. Princeton: Princeton University Press, 1989.

Dirks, Raymond L., and Leonard Gross. *The Great Wall Street Scandal*. New York: McGraw-Hill, 1974.

Drucker, Peter F. *Management: Tasks, Responsibilities, Practices.* New York: Harper and Row, 1974.

Dunlop, John T. *Dispute Resolution: Negotiation and Consensus Building.* Dover, Massachusetts: Auburn House Publishing Company, 1984.

Evans, Peter. *Ari: The Life and Times of Aristotle Onassis.* New York: Summit Books, 1986.

Fay, Stephen. *Beyond Greed.* New York: Viking Press, 1982.

Fayerweather, John. *The Mercantile Bank Affair: A Case Study of Canadian Nationalism and a Multinational Firm.* New York: New York University Press, 1974.

Ferretti, Fred. *The Year the Big Apple Went Bust.* New York: Putnam, 1976.

Fraser, Nicholas, et al. *Aristotle Onassis.* Philadelphia and New York: J.B. Lippincott, 1977.

Friars, Eileen M., and Robert N. Gogel (editors). *The Financial Services Handbook: Executive Insights and Solutions.* New York: John Wiley and Sons, 1987.

Friedman, Irving S. *The World Debt Dilemma: Managing Country Risk.* Washington, D.C.: Council for International Banking Studies; Philadelphia: Robert Morris Associates, 1983.

————. *Toward World Prosperity: Reshaping the Global Money System.* Lexington, Massachusetts: Lexington Books, 1987.

Galbraith, John Kenneth. *The Great Crash 1929.* 50th Anniversary Edition. Boston: Houghton Mifflin, 1979.

George, Susan. *A Fate Worse than Debt.* Revised edition. New York: Grove Weidenfeld, 1990.

Golembe, Carter H., and David S. Holland. *Federal Regulation of Banking 1983–84.* Washington, D.C.: Golembe Associates, Inc., 1975.

Greider, William. *Secrets of the Temple: How the Federal Reserve Runs the Country.* New York: Simon & Schuster, 1987.

Hamilton, Adrian. *The Financial Revolution.* New York: The Free Press, 1986.

Hastings, Max, and Simon Jenkins. *Battle for the Falklands.* New York: Norton & Co., 1983.

Hector, Gary. *Breaking the Bank: The Decline of BankAmerica.* Boston: Little, Brown, 1988.

Hilsman, Roger, *To Move a Nation: The Politics of Foreign Policy in the Administration of John F. Kennedy."* New York: Dell Publishing Co., 1967.

Hodas, Daniel. *The Business Career of Moses Taylor.* New York: New York University Press, 1976.

Hutchison, Robert A. *Off the Books: Citibank and the World's Biggest Money Game.* New York: William Morrow and Company, 1986.

Iaccoca, Lee, with Sonny Kleinfield. *Talking Straight.* New York: Bantam Books, 1988.

————, with William Novak. *Iacocca: An Autobiography.* New York: Bantam Books, 1984.

Johnston, Moira. *Roller Coaster: The Bank of America and the Future of American Banking.* New York: Ticknor and Fields, 1990.

Kalb, Marvin, and Bernard Kalb. *Kissinger.* Boston: Little, Brown, 1974.

Koch, Edward I., with William Rauch. *Mayor.* New York: Simon & Schuster, 1984.

Kolko, Gabriel. *Triumph of Conservatism.* New York: Free Press, 1963.

Kraft, Joseph. *The Mexican Rescue.* New York: The Group of Thirty, 1984.

Kuczynski, Pedro-Pablo. *Latin American Debt.* Baltimore: Johns Hopkins University Press, 1988.

Lampert, Hope. *Behind Closed Doors: Wheeling and Dealing in the Banking World.* New York: Atheneum, 1986.

Lance, Bert, with Bill Gilbert. *The Truth of the Matter.* New York: Summit Books, 1991.

Leinsdorf, David, and Donald Etra. *Citibank: Ralph Nader's Study Group Report on First National City Bank.* Foreword by Ralph Nader. New York: Grossman, 1973.

Lessard, Donald. R, and John Williamson (editors). *Capital Flight and Third World Debt.* Washington, D.C.: Institute for International Economics, 1987.

Levinson, Jerome, and Juan de Onis. *The Alliance That Lost Its Way. A Twentieth Century Fund Study.* Chicago: Quadrangle Books, 1970.

Lissakers, Karin. *Banks, Borrowers, and the Establishment: A Revisionist Account of the International Debt Crisis.* New York: Basic Books, 1991.

Makin, John H. *The Global Debt Crisis: America's Growing Involvement.* New York: Basic Books, 1984.

Mathis, F. John (editor). *Offshore Lending by U.S. Commercial Banks.* First edition. Washington, D.C.: Bankers' Association for Foreign Trade & Robert Morris Associates, 1976.

Matthiessen, Peter. *In the Spirit of Crazy Horse.* New York: Penguin, 1992.

Mayer, Martin. *The Diplomats.* Garden City, N.Y.: Doubleday & Co., 1983.

———. *The Money Bazaars: Understanding the Banking Revolution Around Us.* New York: E. P. Dutton, 1984.

McClintick, David. *Stealing from the Rich: The Home-Stake Oil Swindle.* New York: M. Evans, 1977.

Miller, Norman C. *The Great Salad Oil Scandal.* New York: Coward-McCann, 1965.

Moore, George. "Term Loans and Interim Financing," in *Business Loans of American Commercial Banks.* Benjamin H. Beckhart (editor). New York: Ronald Press, 1959.

Moore, George S. *The Banker's Life.* New York: W. W. Norton, 1987.

Moritz, Michael, and Barrett Seaman. *Going for Broke: The Chrysler Story.* New York: Doubleday, 1981.

Neikirk, William R. *Volcker: Portrait of the Money Man.* New York: Congdon and Weed, 1987.

Neumann, Sigmund. *The Permanent Revolution.* New York: Harper, 1942.

Newhouse, John. *The Sporty Game.* New York: Alfred A. Knopf, 1982.

Oster, Patrick. *The Mexicans: A Personal Portrait of a People.* New York: William Morrow and Company, 1989.

Pecora, Ferdinand. *Wall Street Under Oath.* New York: Simon & Schuster, 1939.

Persico, Joseph E. *Casey: The Lives and Secrets of William J. Casey: From the OSS to the CIA.* New York: Viking Press, 1990.

Robertson, Ross M. *The Comptroller and Bank Supervision.* Washington: The Office of the Comptroller of the Currency, 1968.

Roett, Riordan. *Brazil Politics in a Patrimonial Society.* Third edition. New York: Praeger, 1984.

Schlesinger, Arthur M., Jr. *A Thousand Days: John F. Kennedy in the White House.* Boston: Houghton Mifflin, 1965.

Schlesinger, Arthur M. Jr., and Roger Bruns (editors). *Congress Investigates: A Documented History 1792–1974.* Vols. III & IV. New York: Chelsea House Publishers, 1975.

Shefter, Martin. *Political Crisis/Fiscal Crisis: The Collapse and Revival of New York City.* Introduction to Paperback Edition, 1987. New York: Basic Books, 1985.

Shultz, George. *Public Policy Behind the Headlines.* New York: W. W. Norton, 1977.

Simon, William E. *A Time for Truth.* New York: Reader's Digest Press, McGraw-Hill, 1978.

Solomon, Robert. *The International Monetary System, 1945–1976: An Insider's View.* New York: Harper and Row, 1977.

———. *An Overview of the International Debt Crisis* (Brookings Discussion Papers in International Economics). Washington: Brookings Institution, July 1989.

Spero, Joan Edelman. *The Failure of Franklin National Bank.* New York: Columbia U. Press, 1980.

Teslik, Kennan Lee. *Congress, the Executive Branch, and Special Interests: The American Response to the Arab Boycott of Israel.* Contributions in Political Science, no. 80. Westport, Connecticut: Greenwood Press, n.d.

Theberge, James D., and Roger W. Fontaine. *Latin America: Struggle for Progress. Critical Choices for Americans.* Vol. XIV. Lexington, Massachusetts: Lexington Books, 1977.

Vanderlip, Frank A., in collaboration with Boyden Sparkes. *From Farm Boy to Financier.* New York and London: D. Appleton-Century, 1935.

Van Horn, Harold E. *Humanist as Educator: The Public Life of Henry Merritt Wriston* (doctoral dissertation). University of Denver, December 1968.

Volcker, Paul, and Toyoo Gyohten. *Changing Fortunes.* New York: Times Books, 1992.

Wilson, John Donald. *The Chase: The Chase Manhattan Bank, N.A., 1945–1985.* Boston: Harvard Business School Press, 1986.

Winkler, John K. *The First Billion: The Stillmans and the National City Bank.* New York: Vanguard Press, 1934.

Wriston, Henry. *Executive Agents in American Foreign Relations.* Baltimore: Johns Hopkins Press, 1929.

Wriston, Henry M. *Academic Procession: Reflections of a College President.* New York: Columbia University, 1959.

Wriston, Jennie Atcheson. *A Pioneer's Odyssey.* Privately published. 1943.

Wriston, Walter B. *The Embargo as an Instrument of Foreign Policy.* (honors thesis). Wesleyan University Archives, 1941.

———. *Risk & Other Four-Letter Words.* New York: Harper and Row, 1986.

———. *Twilight of Sovereignty: How the Information Revolution Is Transforming Our World.* New York: Scribner, 1992.

Zweig, Phillip L., *Belly-Up: The Collapse of the Penn Square Bank,* New York: Crown Publishers, 1985.

GOVERNMENT DOCUMENTS

"Analysis of Federal Reserve Policies as They Affect Interest Rates and Credit Markets." Hearing before the Subcommittee on Domestic Monetary Policy of the Committee on Banking, Finance and Urban Affairs, House of Representatives, 97th Congress, First Session. July 28, 1981. p. 27.

"The Argentine Debt." Hearing before the Subcommittee on International Finance and Monetary Policy of the Committee on Banking, Housing and Urban Affairs, U.S. Senate, 98th Congress, Second Session. May 3, 1984.

"Arab Boycott." Hearings before the Subcommittee on International Finance, Committee on Banking, Housing and Urban Affairs, U.S. Senate, 95th Congress, First Session. February 21, 22, and 28; March 15, 1977. p. 465.

"Bank Holding Company Act Amendments of 1970." Report of the Committee on Banking and Currency, United States Senate, to accompany H. R. 6778, together with Supplementary and Individual Views. Report No. 91-1084. 91st Congress, Second Session. Aug. 10, 1970.

"Bank Holding Companies." Report together with Prevailing Views, Additional Views, and Individual Views, Report No. 91-387. 91st Congress, First Session. July 23, 1969.

"Brazilian Debt Crisis." Hearing before the Subcommittee on International Finance, Trade and Monetary Policy of the Committee on Banking, Finance and Urban Affairs, House of Representatives, 100th Congress, First Session. April 23, 1987.

"Candidates for Assistant Secretary for Latin American Affairs," May 24, 1961, Kennedy Library.

"Chrysler Corporation Loan Guarantee Act of 1979." Hearings before the Committee on Banking, Housing and Urban Affairs, U.S. Senate, 96th Congress, First Session. Nov. 21, 1979.

"Conduct of National Security Policy." Hearings before the Subcommittee on National Security and International Operations of the Committee on Government Operations, U.S. Senate, 89th Congress, First Session. May 13, 1965. p. 19.

Corrigan, E. Gerald. *Financial Market Structure: A Longer View.* New York: Federal Reserve Board, Jan. 1987.

Economic Strategy for the Reagan Administration, A Report to President-Elect Ronald Reagan from his Coordinating Committee on Economic Policy, Nov. 16, 1980.

"The Eurocurrency Market Control Act of 1979." Hearings before the Subcommittee on Domestic Monetary Policy and the Subcommittee on International Trade, Investment and Monetary Policy of the Committee on Banking, Finance and Urban Affairs, House of Representatives, 96th Congress, First Session. June 26, 1979.

"Federal Reserve Policy Actions." Hearings before the Committee on Banking, Housing and Urban Affairs, U.S. Senate, 96th Congress, First Session. October 15, 1979. p. 88.

"Financial Institutions Restructuring and Services Act of 1981." Hearings before the Committee on Banking Housing and Urban Affairs, U.S. Senate, 97th Congress, First Session. October 29, 1981, p. 559.

"Financial Services Industry Oversight." Hearings before the Committee on Banking and Currency, U.S. Senate, 98th Congress, First Session. June 27, 1983, p. 1029.

Haddad, William F., et al., The Banks and the Municipal Crisis: Public Responsibility and Private Profit, Special Report to Honorable Stanley Steingut, Nov. 15, 1976.

"International Banking Operations." Hearings before the Subcommittee on Financial Institutions, Supervision, Regulation and Insurance, Committee on Banking, Housing and Urban Affairs, House of Representatives, 95th Congress, First Session. March 24 and April 6, 1977.

"International Debt." Hearings before the Subcommittee on International Finance, Committee on Banking, Housing and Urban Affairs, U.S. Senate, 95th Congress, First Session. August 29–30, 1977.

"Invitation List." Presidential Luncheon, June 30, 1961, Kennedy Library.

"Latin American Development and Western Hemisphere Trade." Hearings before the Subcommittee on Inter-American Economic Relationships of the Joint Economic Committee Congress of the United States, 89th Congress, First Session. September 8, 9, and 10, 1965.

"Memorandum on hospital ships." Department of State, July 9, 10, 11, 25 and September 14, 1942; Letter from Henry L. Stinson, Secretary of War to Secretary of State Cordell Hull, Aug. 8, 1942; Letter from Navy Secretary Frank Knox to Secretary of State Cordell Hull, Aug. 3, 1942; Letter from H. N. Boon, Secretary of Netherlands Embassy, to Walter B. Wriston, Department of State, Sept. 15, 1942; and other miscellaneous letters, memos, and telegrams concerning Op ten Noort.

"Minutes." Board of Governors of the Federal Reserve System, Conference with the Federal Advisory Council," Feb. 4, May 6, Sept. 9, Nov. 4, 1977; Feb. 3, May 5, Sept. 8, Nov. 3, 1978.

"Multinational Corporations and United States foreign policy," Hearings before the Committee on Foreign Relations subcommittee on Multinational Corporations, 94th Congress, First Session. July 16, 1975.

"New York City Financial Aid." Hearings before the Committee on Banking, Housing and Urban Affairs, U.S. Senate, 95th Congress, Second Session. June 12, 1978.

"New York City Loan Guarantee Act." Hearings before the Committee on Banking, Housing and Urban Affairs, U.S. Senate, 96th Congress, Second Session. Jan. 28, 1980.

"New York City's Fiscal Problem: Its Origins, Potential Repercussions, and Some Alternative Policy Responses," Congress of the U.S., Congressional Budget Office. Oct. 10, 1975.

"New York City Fiscal Problems and Remedial Options." Hearings before the Committee on Banking, Housing and Urban Affairs, U.S. Senate, 94th Congress, First Session. Oct. 18, 1975.

"The 1978 Economic Report of the President." Hearings before the Joint Economic Committee, U.S. Congress, 95th Congress, Second Session. February 22, 1978. p. 569.

"One-Bank Holding Company Legislation of 1970." Hearings before the Committee on Banking and Currency, U.S. Senate, 91st Congress, Second Session. May 26, 1970. p. 779.

"Overdrafts and Correspondent Banking Practices." Hearings before the Committee on Banking, Housing and Urban Affairs, U.S. Senate, 95th Congress, First Session. September 26, 27, and 28, 1977. p. 360.

"Oversight on the New York City Seasonal Financing Act." Hearings before the Committee on Banking, Housing and Urban Affairs, U.S. Senate, 95th Congress, First Session. May 16, 1977.

"President's 1967 Tax Proposals." Hearings before the Committee on Ways and Means, House of Representatives, September 13, 1967, 90th Congress, First Session. p. 660.

"Private Financing of New Ship Construction." Hearings before a Subcommittee of the Committee on Interstate and Foreign Commerce, U.S. Senate, 83rd Congress, Second Session. Apr. 8, 1954.

Privatization. Report of the President's Commission on Privatization, David F. Linowes, chairman. March 1988.

"Railroads—1975." Hearings before the Subcommittee on Surface Transportation of the Committee on Commerce, U.S. Senate, 94th Congress, First Session. Parts 1–4.

Reed, John S. Statement before the Committee on Banking, Housing and Urban Affairs, U.S. Senate. July 13, 1989.

The Report of the President's Commission on Financial Structure & Regulation. Washington: U.S. Government Printing Office, 1971.

Restoring Credit and Confidence—A Reform Program for New York State and its Public Authorities. Report to the Governor by the New York State Morehead Act Commission on the Urban Development Commission and other State Financing Agencies, March 31, 1976.

"SEC and Citicorp." Hearings before the Subcommittee on Oversight and Investigations of the Committee on Energy and Commerce, House of Representatives, 97th Congress, Second Session. September 13 and 17, 1982.

Securities and Exchange Commission Staff Report on Transactions in Securities of the City of New York—Subcommittee on Economic Stabilization of the Committee on Banking, Finance and Urban Affairs, House of Representatives, 95th Congress, First Session. Aug. 1977.

Statement of William R. Rhodes before the Committee on Banking, Finance and Urban Affairs, U.S. House of Representatives, Washington, Jan. 4, 1989.

"Study of Trade-Out and Build Activities of Onassis Companies." Hearings before the Special Subcommittee of the Committee on Merchant Marine and Fisheries, 85th Congress, Second Session. June 19, 1958. p. 165.

"To Amend the Bretton Woods Agreements Act to Authorize Consent to an Increase in the United States Quota in the International Monetary Fund." Hearings before the Subcommittee on International Trade, Investment and Monetary Policy of the Committee on Banking, Finance and Urban Affairs, House of Representatives, 96th Congress, Second Session. 1980. p. 268.

"To Facilitate Private Financing of New Ship Construction." Hearings before the Committee on Merchant Marine and Fisheries," House of Representatives, 83rd Congress, Second Session. April 27, 1954.

"United States Balance of Payments." Hearings before the Joint Economic Committee Congress of the United States. Part 2. Outlook for the United States Balance of Payments, 88th Congress, First Session. July 29 and 30, 1963.

"Variable Rate Securities and Disintermediation." Hearings before the Committee on Banking, Housing and Urban Affairs, Subcommittee on Financial Institutions. U.S. Senate, 93rd Congress, Second Session. July 25, 1974. p. 89.

The Witteveen Facility and the OPEC Financial Surpluses, Hearing before the Subcommittee on Foreign Economic Policy of the Committee on Foreign Relations, U.S. Senate, 95th Congress, First Session. September 21, 1977. p. 145.

Wriston, Testimony before the New York State Assembly Committee on Banking, Oct. 11, 1977.

OTHER DOCUMENTS AND PUBLICATIONS

"A Reappraisal of the Alliance for Progress." Joint memorandum by Emilio G. Collado, David Rockefeller, and Walter B. Wriston. Undated.

Christophe, Cleveland. *Competition in Financial Services.* New York: First National City Corp. 1974.

Citibank, Nader and the Facts. New York: First National City Bank, 1974.

"Connecticut College Student Record Card, Barbara Brengle." Connecticut College Archives.

Discussion Text, "Wake up, America!" Radio Forum Broadcast, December 7, 1941. "Can there be a substantial reduction in non-defense expenditures of the Federal Government?" Discussion by Henry M. Wriston and Hon. T. V. Smith, former

Congressman-at-large from Illinois. Moderator Fred G. Clark. Sponsored and released by The American Economic Foundation, Cleveland, Ohio.

Enke, Stephen, et al. Transportation Technology Forecast. Prepared for First National City Bank New York. Santa Barbara, California: Tempo, General Electric Center for Advanced Studies, 1967.

Ethical Standards and Conflict of Interest Policy. Citicorp. June 1976.

"From the Beach." Memorandum from John S. Reed to staff, March 9, 1976.

First National City Bank New York. FNCB Futures: Summary Report. Santa Barbara, California: Tempo, General Electric Center for Advanced Studies, 1967.

Hoffman, Edwin. *The Myths and Realities of Credit at Citicorp.* Internal Presentation. 1987.

Johnson, Norris O. *Eurodollars in the New International Money Market.* First National City Bank, 1964.

Kelly, Charles W. *Valuing Your Money Inventory: The Marginal Cost Approach.* Citicorp, 1974.

Kelly, Charles W. "Organization Unit Profitability," Bank Management Seminar, December 14–15, 1970.

Letter from Dr. Henry Wriston to Dr. W. Randolph Burgess, Sept. 25, 1936; Letter from W. Randolph Burgess to Dr. Henry Wriston, Feb. 18, 1937.

"Minutes." Municipal Union/Financial Leaders Group, Apr. 7, 1977–Sept. 23, 1986.

Mueller, P. Henry. *Credit Doctrine for Lending Officers.* New York: Citicorp, 2nd Edition, 1981.

Sanchez, Juan. Memo on Cuba. Juan Sanchez files. June 1959.

"Taxes in New York City." Municipal Union/Financial Leaders Group, July 21, 1977.

Vojta, George. Bank Capital Adequacy, First National City Corp, New York, 1970.

Wriston, Walter B. *If You Ask Me.* Unpublished quotations. Citibank archives. Undated.

PERIODICALS

"Clarion." Appleton (Wis.) High School Yearbook, 1936–7.

"Henry Merritt Wriston, 1889–1978." *Brown Alumni Monthly,* Vol. 78, (April 1978), pp. 8–9.

"IBC: Fiftieth Anniversary of Citibank's Giant Step." *Citibank* magazine, Oct. 1965.

Matteis, Richard J. "The New Back Office Focuses on Customer Service." *Harvard Business Review,* Mar.–Apr. 1979.

McIntyre, John K. "Life with Henry," *Brown Alumni Monthly,* Vol. LXV No. 8, May 1965, p. 20.

"The Transportation Department," *Number 8* (Citibank internal publication), June 1959.

Olla Podrida, Wesleyan University Yearbook, 1912. Wesleyan U. Archives.

Wesleyan University Bulletin (Catalogue), 1938–9; 1939–40; 1940–41; 1941–42. Wesleyan University Archives.

Wriston, Walter B. "Technology and Sovereignty." *Foreign Affairs* (Winter 1988–1989).

LIST OF ON-THE-RECORD SOURCES

Note: Titles indicated are the most recent ones relevant to Wriston's life and career.

Al Ambs, former Citibank officer
Martin Anderson, former Reagan economic adviser
Hans H. Angermueller, former vice chairman, Citicorp
Stephen Axilrod, former Federal Reserve Board official
Ann Azzara, Citicorp protocol officer
William "Mil" Batten, former chairman & CEO, J. C. Penney Co.
Abraham Beame, former mayor, New York City
Geoffrey Bell, international financial adviser
Robert Bevan, American Bankers Association lobbyist
Jack Bigel, union pension consultant
Ed Bottum, Continental Bank officer
Richard S. Braddock, former president, Citicorp
Frederick W. Bradley, Jr., former Citibank officer
Richard Brengle, former Wriston brother-in-law
Edward Brennan, chairman & CEO, Sears Roebuck & Co.
Charles Breunig, professor emeritus, Lawrence University
Henry B. R. Brown, former Citibank officer; co-founder, Reserve Fund
John "Sandy" Burton, former chief accountant, Securities and Exchange Commission and deputy mayor, New York City
Willard Butcher, former chairman & CEO, Chase Manhattan Corp.
Michael A. Callen, former Citibank officer
Hugh Carey, former Governor, State of New York
Russell Carson, former Citibank officer
Robert Carswell, former deputy secretary of the Treasury
David Cates, bank analyst
George Champion, former co-CEO, Chase Manhattan Corp.
George "Jack" Clark, former Citibank officer
A. W. "Tom" Clausen, former chairman, Bank Americorp
Ted Cloak, professor emeritus, Lawrence University
H. Lansing "Nick" Clute, former Citibank officer
Rodgin Cohen, partner, Sullivan & Cromwell
William Coleman, former Transportation secretary
Paul J. Collins, vice chairman, Citicorp
John Connally, former secretary of the Treasury
G. A. Costanzo, former vice chairman, Citicorp
Thomas Creamer, former Citibank officer
George S. Davis, former Citibank officer
Thomas Dawson, former Treasury official
Jacques de Larosiere, former managing director, International Monetary Fund
Paul De Rosa, former Citibank officer
Rimmer de Vries, international economist, J. P. Morgan & Co.
Carl Desch, former corporate secretary, Citicorp
Robert Dineen, Wriston's brother-in-law, partner Shearman & Sterling
Robert Dinerstein, former Citibank lawyer

Joseph Doyle, partner, Shearman & Sterling
John Dunlop, former Secretary of Labor
Peter Drucker, management professor
Betty Brown Ducklow, childhood acquaintance
Peter Eccles, former Citibank officer
Barrett Emmerts, Wriston friend
John Exter, former Citibank officer
Stephen Eyre, former corporate secretary, Citicorp
Jack Faison, Wesleyan fraternity brother
James D. Farley, former vice chairman, Citicorp
Herman "Denny" Farrell, Jr., New York State assemblyman
Robert W. Feagles, former personnel chief, Citicorp
Gerard Finneran, former Citibank officer
John Fisher, former officer, Bank One
John Fogarty, former Citibank officer
Gerald R. Ford, former president of the United States
Lawrence E. Fouraker, former director, Citicorp
Brian Freeman, former executive director, Chrysler Loan Guarantee Board
Jac Friedgut, former economist, Citibank
Irving S. Friedman, former country risk head, Citibank
Milton Friedman, Nobel laureate in economics
Jeffrey M. Franklin, former Citibank officer
Edward Furash, banking consultant
Karen Gerard, former Chase economist
Paul F. Glaser, former chief technology officer, Citicorp
Lawrence R. Glenn, Citibank officer
Peter Goldmark, former New York State budget director
Carter Golembe, bank regulatory consultant
Betsy Gotbaum, wife of Victor
Victor Gotbaum, union leader
J. Peter Grace, former chairman & CEO, W. R. Grace & Co.
Cedric Grant, Citibank officer
Peter Greenough, former Citibank officer
James Griffin, former personnel chief, Citicorp
Jack Guenther, Citibank country risk officer
Kenneth Guenther, executive director, Independent Bankers Association of America
Angel Gurria, Mexican finance ministry official
George E. Hagerman, Jr., former Citibank officer
Alexander Haig, former Secretary of State
Henry Harfield, partner, Shearman & Sterling
Edward G. Harshfield, former Citibank officer
John W. Heilshorn, former Citibank officer
John Heimann, former Comptroller of the Currency
Rose Heinritz, mother of childhood girlfriend
Dale J. Hekhuis, former project leader, TEMPO
William J. Heron, Jr., former Citibank officer
Robert L. Hoguet, Jr., former Citibank officer
Edwin P. Hoffman, former Citibank officer
John Hoffman, former partner, Shearman & Sterling
David Holland, Federal Deposit Insurance Corp. analyst

Paul M. Homan, former senior deputy Comptroller of the Currency
Robert D. Hormats, former assistant Secretary of State
Donald S. Howard, former chief financial officer, Citicorp
Anthony Howkins, former Citibank officer
Richard L. Huber, former Citibank officer
John Ingraham, Citibank officer
Thomas Ivanyi, former Citibank officer
E. Pendleton James, Reagan personnel adviser
William J. Janklow, governor of South Dakota
George P. Jenkins, former director, Citicorp; former chairman, Metropolitan Life
Reginald Jones, former chairman & CEO, General Electric Co.
Vernon E. Jordan, Jr., former president, National Urban League
Max Kampelman, State Department adviser
Richard Kane, former Citibank officer
Raymond Kathe, former Citibank officer
Henry Kaufman, economist
Charles Kelly, former Citibank officer
David Kennedy, former secretary of the Treasury
Lane Kirkland, president, AFL-CIO
Henry A. Kissinger, former Secretary of State
Edward I. Koch, former mayor, New York City
Paul Kolterjahn, former corporate secretary, Citicorp
Richard Kovacevich, former Citibank officer
Pedro-Pablo Kuczynski, former chairman, First Boston International
Arthur Laffer, economist; member of President's Economic Policy Board
Carlos Langoni, former head, Brazilian central bank
John Lee, former executive director, New York Clearing House
David Leinsdorf, former Nader's raider
Thomas Lincoln, former Onassis lawyer
Robert F. B. Logan, former Citibank officer
Charles E. Long, executive vice president, Citicorp
Kenneth MacWilliams, investment banker
Karl Malden, actor
William E. Martin, former deputy Comptroller of the Currency
Richard Matteis, former Citibank officer
John F. McGillicuddy, former chairman, Chemical Banking Corp.
Malcom McLean, founder, Sea-Land Service
R. T. "Tim" McNamar, former deputy secretary of the Treasury
Robert S. McNamara, former president, World Bank
Edwin Meese, former U.S. attorney general
Anne Meschino, former Citibank officer
Hamilton Meserve, former Citibank officer
Robert Meyjes, former Citibank officer
G. William Miller, former chairman, Federal Reserve Board; former Secretary of the
    Treasury.
Robert S. (Steve) Miller, former chief financial officer, Chrysler Corp.
George Mitchell, former vice chairman, Federal Reserve Board
George S. Moore, former chairman, First National City Corp.
P. Henry Mueller, former chief credit officer, Citicorp
Westbrook Murphy, former deputy general counsel, Comptroller of the Currency

Kamal Mustafa, former Citibank officer
Robert Mylod, former Citibank officer
Paul Nadler, banking professor, Rutgers University
Leif Olsen, former chief economist, Citibank
Thomas O. Paine, former director, TEMPO
Edward Palmer, former executive committee chairman, Citicorp
Frank Partel, former Citibank officer
Ellmore "Pat" Patterson, former chairman & CEO, J. P. Morgan & Co.
Richard Perkins, former executive committee chairman, First National City Corp.
David Phillips, former Citibank officer
Thomas G. Plaskett, former chairman & CEO, Pan Am Corp.
David Potts, former scholar-in-residence, Wesleyan University
Victor Prall, former Citibank officer
Edmund T. Pratt, Jr., former chairman & CEO, Pfizer Inc.
Lewis Preston, former chairman & CEO, J. P. Morgan & Co.
John R. Price, government relations director, Chemical Banking Corp.
William Proxmire, former U.S. senator from Wisconsin
George Putnam, former Citibank officer
Catherine "Cassy" Quintal, Wriston's daughter
Richard Quintal, Wriston's son-in-law
Elisabeth Rabitsch, former Citibank country risk analyst
Hollis Rademacher, former Continental Bank officer
Richard Ravitch, former chairman, Urban Development Corp.
Donald T. Regan, former secretary of the Treasury
John S. Reed, chairman & CEO, Citicorp
John Reeve, Wriston childhood acquaintance
Edwin Reichers, former Citibank officer
William R. Rhodes, vice chairman, Citicorp
Reuben Richards, former Citibank officer
John Riordan, former Citibank officer
David Rockefeller, former chairman & CEO, Chase Manhattan Corp.
Felix Rohatyn, senior partner, Lazard Freres
Peter Rona, former IBJ Schroder Bank and Trust Co. officer
George Roniger, former Citibank economist
James Stillman Rockefeller, former chairman & CEO, First National City Corp.
Frederick A. Roesch, Citibank officer
Paul Rudowski, former Citibank officer
John Rudy, former Citibank officer
George Salem, bank analyst
Juan Sanchez, former Citibank officer
Walter Saunders, former officer, Metropolitan Life Insurance Co.
Maria Savarese, former secretary, Citibank
Frederick H. Schultz, former vice chairman, Federal Reserve Board
Christie Sciacca, former FDIC official
George C. Scott, former vice chairman, First National City Corp.
Charles Seibert, former Citibank officer
L. William Seidman, Ford economic adviser
Irving S. Shapiro, former chairman, E. I. du Pont de Nemours & Co.; former director,
    Citicorp
Richard Shinn, former chairman, Metropolitan Life

George P. Shultz, former Secretary of State
Jesus Silva Herzog, former Mexican finance minister
William E. Simon, former secretary of the Treasury
Mario H. Simonsen, former Brazil finance minister
Lawrence M. Small, former vice chairman, Citicorp
James Smith, former Comptroller of the Currency
William I. Spencer, former president, Citicorp
Byron Stinson, former Citibank officer
Thomas Storrs, former chairman & CEO, North Carolina National Bank
Jack Svahn, former Reagan adviser
Thomas C. Theobald, former vice chairman, Citicorp
Franklin A. Thomas, president, Ford Foundation
James Tozer, former Citibank officer
Nancy Valelly, wife of Richard
Richard Valelly, former Citibank officer
Paul A. Volcker, former chairman, Federal Reserve Board
Charls Walker, former deputy Treasury secretary
Richard Warch, president, Lawrence University
Murray Weidenbaum, former chairman, Council of Economic Advisers
Richard Wheeler, former Citibank officer
Robert B. White, former Citibank officer
Thomas R. Wilcox, former vice chairman, First National City Corp.
Charles Williams, professor emeritus, Harvard University
Fred Winkler, former president, Citibank South Dakota
Gordon Wolfe, former Citibank officer
Barbara Wriston, Wriston's sister
Kathryn D. Wriston, Wriston's wife
Walter B. Wriston, former chairman & CEO, Citicorp
Jack Yingling, former bank lobbyist
Christopher York, former Citicorp lawyer

ACKNOWLEDGMENTS

What I originally intended as a short biography of Walter Wriston that was to take no more than two years to complete evolved into a history of the post–World War II financial services industry that took seven calendar years to write. Along the way I had help from hundreds of present and former Citibankers, including some who requested anonymity. To all of them I am deeply grateful.

This book became a family affair. No one contributed more than my wife, Josie, who spent weeks in the New York Public Library helping with the research. She later brought her superb editing skills to a review of the manuscript, from rough draft to page proofs. And most of all, she provided comfort and encouragement when the task of sorting through a mass of often conflicting material seemed insurmountable. My mother, Myrillyn March Zweig, spent days in the University of North Carolina library in Chapel Hill searching for articles and other material. My sister, Margaret Lee, helped out by transcribing tapes of interviews.

I also owe a great debt to Chris Welles, my editor at *Business Week* and one of the all-stars of American business journalism, for reviewing the manuscript and making many valuable suggestions for shaping and organizing material. Additionally, he demonstrated extraordinary patience as I struggled in the last two years of this project to juggle its demands with my duties at *Business Week* in the course of fourteen-hour days. My two previous editors, Matt Winkler of Bloomberg Business News and Aloysius Ehrbar, former publisher of *Corporate Finance* magazine, were also helpful and supportive. Bill Zimmerman, my former editor at *American Banker,* generously gave me access to the newspaper's library and photocopier.

Dr. William Ford, Weatherford professor of banking and finance at Middle Tennessee State University, gave unselfishly of his time in reviewing the manuscript for technical accuracy and making many important suggestions that I incorporated into the text. James O'Shea Wade, my editor at Crown, brought his sharp scalpel and skill at phrase turning to the 2,000-plus-page draft. Meanwhile, his assistant, Paul Boccardi, diligently and efficiently kept the wheels of production turning. And Donna Ryan, who copy-edited the manuscript, is surely among the best practitioners of her craft anywhere.

Dr. Joan Silverman, former Citibank archivist and researcher, brought her own keen understanding of Citibank to her reading of the manuscript. And Rebecca Morris, a former Citibank speechwriter, provided many useful insights and helped me locate valuable archival material. Foundation Center librarian Maré Valgemae, a woman with a photographic memory, encyclopedic mind, and generous spirit, also eased the research burden. John Maloney, former head of corporate communications at Citibank, graciously opened the right doors for me at Citibank and made me feel welcome.

I am grateful also to Betty Brown Ducklow, a contemporary of Wriston's in Appleton, Wisconsin, who held a wonderful reception for me at her home, where she introduced me to many of my subject's high school friends and classmates. Their recollections were an invaluable contribution to my understanding of the youthful Wriston. President Richard Warch of Lawrence University made the school's archives available to me and introduced me to some of Dr. Henry Wriston's colleagues. Margaret Mitchell and Elizabeth Swaim, archivists at Brown University and Wesleyan University respectively, cheerfully searched their files to meet my frequent and often frantic requests for documents. Jamie Russell, librarian at *Business Week,* also helped with some of the research. The many dedicated staff librarians in the New York Public Library's economics department, for years my second home, earned my sincere thanks and admiration.

This book might have taken even longer if it were not for Darius Stafford, now an executive with Computerland New York, who patiently walked me through bewildering software programs to save months of work on disks I thought had been lost. After spending more than an hour on the phone assisting a total stranger, he refused any compensation. But he won a customer for life.

Finally, to the hundreds of people who gave a nugget of advice or an hour of their time, but whose names I may have neglected to include, my thanks and apologies.

INDEX

Abal Khail, Muhammad Al-Ali, 385,
435–36
Abboud, Robert, 498–99, 507
Abrams, Robert, 677, 734
Academic Procession (H. M. Wriston), 10,
97
Acceptance Finance Corporation, 362–63
accounting:
and budget deficit, 830
current value, 523–24
in foreign countries, 185, 819–20, 869
and liquidity, 855
mark-to-market, 880
Acheson, Dean, 25
acquisitions, 123, 324–25, 362–63, 846, 875
congenerics, 153, 199–202, 258–61, 363
of entry vehicles, 328–29
and joint ventures, 153, 200, 399–400
swimming pool deals for, 200–202, 262,
471
see also specific targets
actuarial base theory, 138–39, 153, 572, 639,
767, 816
Adams, Sherman, 182
ADAPSO, 585
Advance Mortgage, 258, 260, 446, 454, 534,
624–25, 677
AFL-CIO, 76, 173, 516
Africa, 90, 170, 386, 501, 568, 730, 742
Akins, James E., 436
Aldington, Lord Toby, 261–62
Aldrich, Nelson, 34–35, 36
Alexander Proudfoot Company, 172–73,
276
Ali, Anwar, 436
Allende Gossens, Salvador, 339, 418, 431
Alliance for Progress, 145–46, 161
Allstate Insurance, 358, 454, 725, 885
Ambs, Al, 72, 76, 313
American Banker, 143, 182, 826
American Bankers Association, 149, 238,
275, 292–93, 323, 470
American Council of Life Insurance,
811–12
American European Association, 843
American Express Company, 128, 160–61,
195, 216, 632–33, 724, 725, 811, 885
American International Life Assurance
Company, 809–10

American State Bank of Rapid City, 810,
812
Amtrak, 499
Anaya, Tony, 802
Anderson, Martin, 708, 713, 721, 728, 767
Angermueller, Hans, 257, 354, 390, 487,
522, 710, 767, 857
and Arab boycott of Israel, 587–90
and deregulation, 359–62, 583, 625, 639,
684, 686
and Edwards case, 606, 607, 609–11,
787–89
and expansion, 675, 678, 796–98, 802–3,
807, 813
and floating rate notes, 454, 463
and investment banking, 667, 804–8
and overseas banking, 138, 407–8, 417,
628, 642–45, 700–702, 715, 717, 761,
762, 782, 791, 848–49
and Penn Central, 320, 359, 500
and ship financing, 65, 359
and succession, 654, 656, 657, 751,
792–94, 816, 821–22, 836
Annunzio, Frank, 550, 799
APCO (Asia Pacific Company), 264, 401
Appleton, Wisconsin, Wriston family in,
8–14
Arabs, *see* Middle East
Aramco (Arabian-American Oil Company),
587, 588
Arbuckle, Ernest, 311
Argentina, 62, 220, 578, 586, 620
and debt crisis, 770–71, 777, 781, 789–91,
814–15, 816, 824, 863
and Falklands, 748–49
IMF in, 164, 431
overseas banking in, 37, 41, 86, 87,
88–89, 108, 114, 188, 221, 386, 420,
429–32, 434, 567, 704, 741–42, 744–45,
768
Reed in, 186, 187
Arlen Realty and Development
Corporation, 444, 616–17
Asia:
leasing in, 327
military bases in, 87, 167–68
overseas banking in, 115, 166–68, 263–66,
432, 570–71
postwar strategy in, 89–90

926